CONTENTS

THE NATIONWIDE
FOOTBALL ANNUAL
2015–2016

Published by SportsBooks Limited, 9 St Aubyns Place, York, YO24 1EQ
First published in 1887

A CIP catalogue record for this book is available from the British Library.

Editorial compilation by Stuart Barnes

ISBN-13 9781907524486

Front cover photograph of manager Eddie Howe and chairman Jeff Mostyn celebrating Bournemouth's promotion to the Premier League. Back cover: Chelsea's Didier Drogba and Cesc Fabregas holding aloft the Premier League Trophy.

Printed and bound in the UK by CPI Group (UK) Ltd, Croydon CR0 4YY

COMMENT

By Stuart Barnes

Just when it seemed the summer was bringing much-needed respite from the managerial madness engulfing English football, Leicester City announced the dismissal of Nigel Pearson. Little more than a month after supporters were celebrating Premier League survival, the club cited 'fundamental differences' for a decision which many in the game rightly regarded as 'unfair and illogical.' Pearson, by his own admission, can be a stubborn and spiky character, who became involved in some controversial incidents last season. But when it mattered most, he was the leading figure in preserving top-grade football against all the odds and that surely should have been the overriding consideration. Regrettably, he was only the latest victim of some bizarre decisions at board level. Slavisa Jokanovic, who as Watford's fourth manager of the campaign not only steadied the ship but took the club back to the Premier League, departed after declining the terms offered to stay on. At Brentford, Mark Warburton was told that even if he gained promotion he would become a victim of the owner's management 'remodelling.' A measure of Warburton's standing came when Rangers decided he was the man to regain their place in the Scottish Premiership. Amazingly, 52 of the 92 league clubs changed manager at least once during, or at the end of, the season.' Of those, 18 were in the Championship, described by Ipswich's Mick McCarthy – one of the six survivors – as a 'bonkers division.' In some cases, the length of tenure was just days. Many others lasted a few months. Sir Alex Ferguson and Arsene Wenger must be looking on aghast.

$$* * *$$

On the positive side, the achievements of Eddie Howe and Ronald Koeman merit special mention. Howe took Bournemouth into the Premier League and was a worthy recipient of the LMA's Manager of the Year award. Do we have a future England manager in the making, some leading figures are asking? Koeman inherited a Southampton side in the process of losing five of their best players to Liverpool, Arsenal and Manchester United. Many predicted a relegation struggle. Instead, he led his new team into Europe after plugging the gaps by shrewd work in the transfer market. In other seasons, Koeman would have walked away with one of the managerial awards. It is also worth admiring the conduct of the respective managers as Southend and Wycombe entered a tense penalty shoot-out in the League Two Play-off Final. Phil Brown and Gareth Ainsworth shared their emotions together on the touchline and after Southend's victory Brown applauded the dignity shown by his rival in defeat. A nice touch, gentlemen.

$$* * *$$

Who would have thought that another failure in the European Under-21 Championship would be quickly forgotten as England reached the semi-finals of the Women's World Cup? Manager Mark Sampson's tactical acumen brought the best out of his players, whose organised and enterprising football deserved better than a semi-final defeat inflicted by Laura Bassett's stoppage-time own goal against Japan. What a pity that Great Britain will not field a team in the 2016 Olympics because of opposition from the other home nations, worried about their independence at international level. The consolation comes with the knowledge that England's performances, and eventual third place, are likely to bring about a surge in interest – and participation – in the women's game.

$$* * *$$

At some point in the new season, one of the most enduring records in the game will almost certainly be broken. Wayne Rooney is now one behind Sir Bobby Charlton's tally of 49 England goals. With the final four Euro 2016 qualifiers in September and October, the record could be his sooner rather than later, fitness permitting. Sir Bobby, who retired from international football after the 1970 World Cup, is sure to be among the first to shake Rooney's hand – and there seems every chance that in the next two or three years Peter Shilton will be preparing his congratulations as the 105-cap Manchester United closes in on his record of 125.

EURO 2016 BECKONS FOR WALES AND NORTHERN IRELAND

An increase in teams for the 2016 European Championship in France met strong opposition in some quarters when it was first mooted. England and Germany were among those insisting that having 24 countries, instead of the usual 16, would devalue the tournament. But the proposal, originally put forward by Scotland and the Republic of Ireland, was carried by a large majority and UEFA president Michel Platini expressed confidence that standards would not fall. For Wales and Northern Ireland, the changed format offered the opportunity of making a long overdue impact in a major championship and it is one both have seized impressively. In fact, performances so far in qualifying suggest they have a real chance of topping their respective groups and not needing the new cushion of a runners-up place to guarantee reaching the finals.

Wales, in particular, are in a powerful position after Gareth Bale's goal brought victory over Belgium in front of a sell-out crowd at the Cardiff City Stadium. They have a three-point lead and such is the momentum Bale has helped Chris Coleman's team generate that it seems nothing can stop them breaking through for the first time since the 1958 World Cup. Northern Ireland, under Michael O'Neill, set the pace in their group with away wins over Hungary and Greece. Kyle Lafferty continued to score important goals and victory in the return leg against Hungary should be enough to deliver a top-two place alongside Romania. It would be their first appearance on the big stage since the 1986 World Cup. Two highly-charged matches between Scotland and the Republic of Ireland brought Gordon Strachan's team four points and Hampden will be buzzing again for games against Poland and Germany. They stand two points ahead of the Republic, who also play return legs against the top two and may need something from one of them to claim a play-off place.

For England, there was the luxury of going into the summer break boasting maximum points after a sixth straight win in Slovenia, where Wayne Rooney's 48th international goal took him to within one of Sir Bobby Charlton's all-time record and Jack Wilshere opened his account with two spectacular strikes in his 28th international. Maintaining that run should keep confidence bubbling ahead of a tournament in which England badly need to do well, with a miserable World Cup in Brazil having extended a long run of failure at the highest level since a semi-final place was achieved in Euro 96. Play-off dates are November 12-14 for first legs and November 15-15 for return matches. The draw for the finals is on December 12, with the first match on June 10, 2016 and the final on July 10. The ten venues and provisional capacities are: Bordeaux (43,000), Lens (35,000), Lille (50,000), Lyon (58,000), Marseille (67,000), Nice (35,000), Parc de Princes, Paris (48,000), Stade de France, St Denis (80,000), St Etienne (41,000), Toulouse (33,000).

QUALIFYING TABLES

(Group winners, runners-up and the best of the third-placed teams qualify for the finals. The other sides finishing third play-off for four more four places. France qualify as the hosts

GROUP A

	P	W	D	L	F	A	Pts
Iceland	6	5	0	1	14	3	15
Czech Rep	6	4	1	1	12	8	13
Holland	6	3	1	2	13	6	10
Turkey	6	2	2	2	7	8	8
Latvia	6	0	3	3	2	13	3
Kazakhstan	6	0	1	5	4	14	1

Results: Kazakhstan 0 Latvia 0, Czech Rep 2 Holland 1, Iceland 3 Turkey 0, Latvia 0 Iceland 3, Holland 3 Kazakhstan 1, Turkey 1 Czech Rep 2, Kazakhstan 2 Czech Rep 4, Iceland 2 Holland 0, Latvia 1 Turkey 1, Holland 6 Latvia 0, Czech Rep 2 Iceland 1, Turkey

3, Kazakhstan 1, Kazakhstan 0 Iceland 3, Czech Rep 1 Latvia 1, Holland 1 Turkey 1, Kazakhstan 0 Turkey 1, Iceland 2 Czech Rep 1, Latvia 0 Holland 2

To play – Sep 3: Czech Rep v Kazakhstan, Holland v Iceland, Turkey v Latvia; Sep 6: Latvia v Czech Rep, Turkey v Holland, Iceland v Kazakhstan; Oct 10: Iceland v Latvia, Kazakhstan v Holland, Czech Rep v Turkey; Oct 13: Latvia v Kazakhstan, Holland v Czech Rep, Turkey v Iceland

GROUP B

	P	W	D	L	F	A	Pts
Wales	6	4	2	0	8	2	14
Belgium	6	3	2	1	13	2	11
Israel	6	3	0	3	10	9	9
Cyprus	6	3	0	3	12	11	9
Bosnia-Herz	6	2	2	2	8	7	8
Andorra	6	0	0	6	3	23	0

Results: Andorra 1 Wales 2, Bosnia-Herz 1 Cyprus 2, Belgium 6 Andorra 0, Cyprus 1 Israel 2, Wales 0 Bosnia-Herz 0, Andorra 1 Israel 4, Bosnia-Herz 1 Belgium 1, Wales 2 Cyprus 1, Belgium 0 Wales 0, Cyprus 5 Andorra 0, Israel 3 Bosnia-Herz 0, Israel 0 Belgium 1, Israel 0 Wales 3, Andorra 0 Bosnia-Herz 3, Belgium 5 Cyprus 0, Andorra 1 Cyprus 3, Bosnia-Herz 3 Israel 1, Wales 1 Belgium 0

To play – Sep 3: Belgium v Bosnia-Herz, Cyprus v Wales, Israel v Andorra; Sep 6: Wales v Israel, Bosnia-Herz v Andorra, Cyprus v Belgium; Oct 10: Andorra v Belgium, Bosnia-Herz v Wales, Israel v Cyprus; Oct 13: Belgium v Israel, Cyprus v Bosnia-Herz, Wales v Andorra

GROUP C

	P	W	D	L	F	A	Pts
Slovakia	6	6	0	0	13	3	18
Spain	6	5	0	1	15	3	15
Ukraine	6	4	0	2	9	2	12
Belarus	6	1	1	4	4	11	4
Macedonia	6	1	0	5	6	14	3
Luxembourg	6	0	1	5	3	17	1

Results: Luxembourg 1 Belarus 1, Spain 5 Macedonia 1, Ukraine 0 Slovakia 1, Belarus 0 Ukraine 2, Macedonia 3 Luxembourg 2, Slovakia 2 Spain 1, Ukraine 1 Macedonia 0, Belarus 1 Slovakia 3, Luxembourg 0 Spain 4, Luxembourg 0 Ukraine 3, Macedonia 0 Slovakia 2, Spain 3 Belarus 0, Macedonia 1 Belarus 2, Slovakia 3 Luxembourg 0, Spain 1 Ukraine 0, Belarus 0 Spain 1, Ukraine 3 Luxembourg 0, Slovakia 2 Macedonia 1

To play – Sep 5: Luxembourg v Macedonia, Ukraine v Belarus, Spain v Slovakia; Sep 8: Belarus v Luxembourg, Macedonia v Spain, Slovakia v Ukraine; Oct 9: Macedonia v Ukraine, Slovakia v Belarus, Spain v Luxembourg; Oct 12: Belarus v Macedonia, Luxembourg v Slovakia, Ukraine v Spain

GROUP D

	P	W	D	L	F	A	Pts
Poland	6	4	2	0	20	3	14
Germany	6	4	1	1	16	4	13
Scotland	6	3	2	1	12	6	11
Rep of Ireland	6	2	3	1	12	5	9
Georgia	6	1	0	5	4	13	3
Gibraltar	6	0	0	6	1	34	0

Results: Georgia 1 Rep of Ireland 2, Germany 2 Scotland 1, Gibraltar 0 Poland 7, Rep of Ireland 7 Gibraltar 0, Scotland 1 Georgia 0, Poland 2 Germany 0, Germany 1 Rep of Ireland

1, Gibraltar 0 Georgia 3, Poland 2 Scotland 2, Georgia 0 Poland 4, Germany 4 Gibraltar 0, Scotland 1 Rep of Ireland 0, Georgia 0 Germany 2, Scotland 6 Gibraltar 1, Rep of Ireland 1 Poland 1, Poland 4 Georgia 0, Rep of Ireland 1 Scotland 1, Gibraltar 0 Germany 7
To play – Sep 4: Georgia v Scotland, Germany v Poland, Gibraltar v Rep of Ireland; Sep 7: Poland v Gibraltar, Rep of Ireland v Georgia, Scotland v Germany; Oct 8: Georgia v Gibraltar, Rep of Ireland v Germany, Scotland v Poland; Oct 11: Germany v Georgia, Gibraltar v Scotland, Poland v Rep of Ireland

GROUP E

	P	W	D	L	F	A	Pts
England	6	6	0	0	18	3	18
Switzerland	6	4	0	2	13	4	12
Slovenia	6	3	0	3	12	7	9
Estonia	6	2	1	3	3	5	7
Lithuania	6	2	0	4	4	12	6
San Marino	6	0	1	5	0	19	1

Results: Estonia 1 Slovenia 0, San Marino 0 Lithuania 2, Switzerland 0 England 2, Lithuania 1 Estonia 0, England 5 San Marino 0, Slovenia 1 Switzerland 0, Estonia 0 England 1, Lithuania 0 Slovenia 2, San Marino 0 Switzerland 4, England 3 Slovenia 1, San Marino 0 Estonia 0, Switzerland 4 Lithuania 0, England 4 Lithuania 0, Slovenia 6 San Marino 0, Switzerland 3 Estonia 0, Estonia 2 San Marino 0, Slovenia 2 England 3, Lithuania 1 Switzerland 2
To play – Sep 5: Estonia v Lithuania, San Marino v England, Switzerland v Slovenia; Sept 8: England v Switzerland, Lithuania v San Marino, Slovenia v Estonia; Oct 9: England v Estonia, Slovenia v Lithuania, Switzerland v San Marino; Oct 12: Estonia v Switzerland, Lithuania v England, San Marino v Slovenia

GROUP F

	P	W	D	L	F	A	Pts
Romania	6	4	2	0	7	1	14
N Ireland	6	4	1	1	8	4	13
Hungary	6	3	2	1	5	3	11
Faroe Is	6	2	0	4	4	8	6
Finland	6	1	1	4	5	8	4
Greece	6	0	2	4	2	7	2

Results: Hungary 1 N Ireland 2, Faroe Is 1 Finland 3, Greece 0 Romania 1, Romania 1 Hungary 1, Finland 1 Greece 1, N Ireland 2 Faroe Is 0, Faroe Is 0 Hungary 1, Finland 0 Romania 2, Greece 0 N Ireland 2, Greece 0 Faroe Is 1, Hungary 1 Finland 0, Romania 2 N Ireland 0, Romania 1 Faroe Is 0, N Ireland 2 Finland 1, Hungary 0 Greece 0, Finland 0 Hungary 1, Faroe Is 2 Greece 1, N Ireland 0 Romania 0
To play – Sep 4: Faroe Is v N Ireland, Greece v Finland, Hungary v Romania; Sep 7: Finland v Faroe Is, N Ireland v Hungary, Romania v Greece; Oct 8: Hungary v Faroe Is, N Ireland v Greece, Romania v Finland; Oct 11: Faroe Is v Romania, Finland v N Ireland, Greece v Hungary

GROUP G

	P	W	D	L	F	A	Pts
Austria	6	5	1	0	11	2	16
Sweden	6	3	3	0	10	4	12
Russia	6	2	2	2	9	4	8
Montenegro	6	1	2	3	4	8	5
Liechtenstein	6	1	2	3	2	12	5
Moldova	6	0	2	4	3	9	2

Results: Russia 4 Liechtenstein 0, Austria 1 Sweden 1, Montenegro 2 Moldova 0, Liechtenstein 0 Montenegro 0, Moldova 1 Austria 2, Sweden 1 Russia 1, Austria 1 Montenegro 0, Russia 1 Moldova 1, Sweden 2 Liechtenstein 0, Austria 1 Russia 0, Moldova 0 Liechtenstein 1, Montenegro 1 Sweden 1, Liechtenstein 0 Austria 5, Moldova 0 Sweden 2, Montenegro 0 Russia 3 (walkover, original match abandoned – crowd disturbances), Liechtenstein 1 Moldova 1, Russia 0 Austria 1, Sweden 3 Montenegro 1
To play – Sep 5: Russia v Sweden, Austria v Moldova, Montenegro v Liechtenstein; Sep 8: Moldova v Montenegro, Liechtenstein v Russia, Sweden v Austria; Oct 9 Liechtenstein v Sweden, Moldova v Russia, Montenegro v Austria; Oct 12: Austria v Liechtenstein, Russia v Montenegro, Sweden v Moldova

GROUP H

	P	W	D	L	F	A	Pts
Croatia	6	4	2	0	16	3	14
Italy	6	3	3	0	9	5	12
Norway	6	3	1	2	7	8	10
Bulgaria	6	2	2	2	7	7	8
Azerbaijan	6	1	1	4	4	11	4
Malta	6	0	1	5	1	10	1

Results: Azerbaijan 1 Bulgaria 2, Croatia 2 Malta 0, Norway 0 Italy 2, Bulgaria 0 Croatia 1, Italy 2 Azerbaijan 1, Malta 0 Norway 3, Croatia 6 Azerbaijan 0, Malta 0 Italy 1, Norway 2 Bulgaria 1, Azerbaijan 0 Norway 1, Bulgaria 1 Malta 1, Italy 1 Croatia 1, Azerbaijan 2 Malta 0, Croatia 5 Norway 1, Bulgaria 2 Italy 2, Croatia 1 Italy 1, Malta 0 Bulgaria 1, Norway 0 Azerbaijan 0
To play – Sep 3: Azerbaijan v Croatia, Bulgaria v Norway, Italy v Malta; Sep 6: Malta v Azerbaijan, Norway v Croatia, Italy v Bulgaria; Oct 10: Azerbaijan v Italy, Norway v Malta, Croatia v Bulgaria; Oct 13: Bulgaria v Azerbaijan, Italy v Norway, Malta v Croatia

GROUP I

	P	W	D	L	F	A	Pts
Portugal	5	4	0	1	7	4	12
Denmark	5	3	1	1	8	4	10
Albania	4	2	1	1	4	5	7
Serbia*	5	1	1	3	6	8	1
Armenia	5	0	1	4	5	9	1

*3 pts deducted for crowd disturbances

Results: Denmark 2 Armenia 1, Portugal 0 Albania 1, Armenia 1 Serbia 1, Albania 1 Denmark 1, Denmark 0 Portugal 1, Serbia 3 Albania 0 (walkover, original match abandoned – crowd disturbances), Serbia 1 Denmark 1, Portugal 1 Armenia 0, Albania 2 Armenia 1, Portugal 2 Serbia 1, Armenia 2 Portugal 3, Denmark 2 Serbia 0
To play – Sep 4: Denmark v Albania, Serbia v Armenia; Sep 7: Armenia v Denmark, Albania v Portugal; Oct 8: Albania v Serbia, Portugal v Denmark; Oct 11: Armenia v Albania, Serbia v Portugal

TEARS – BUT A SENSE OF PRIDE
FOR ENGLAND WOMEN

They arrived as underdogs for a tournament carrying little significance for much of the sporting public. They came home having lit up the summer by reaching the semi-finals of the World Cup and going close to a place in the final. England captured the nation's attention with their performances in Canada which could now transform the profile of women's football in this country. Defeat by France in the opening group fixture seemed to match the pre-tournament rating and stirred nothing more here than a passing interest in their fortunes. But they went on to beat Mexico and Colombia to go through as runners-up, then overcame Norway in the first knock-out round, with Lucy Bronze firing a spectacular 25-yard winner. When Mark Sampson's squad then defeated the hosts by the same 2-1 margin in front of a 54,000 crowd for the quarter-final in Vancouver, the complexion had changed totally.

Perhaps the most significant tribute to the achievement came with the contrast made to the repeated failings of the England men in international competition. It had been 25 years since they made it to the last four of the World Cup in Italy, where Paul Gascoigne's tears accompanied a penalty shoot-out defeat by West Germany. This time, the tears were shed by Notts County defender Laura Bassett after she unwittingly diverted a cross into her own net in the second minute of stoppage-time to give defending champions Japan a 2-1 win in Edmonton. It was a cruel climax, not just for how it came about but because Toni Duggan and Claire Rafferty both hit the crossbar, while Ellen White and Jill Scott also went close during a strong second-half showing. Much of the credit went to Sampson and his staff, who planned meticulously, made changes when they thought necessary and spent hours refining tactics. As one of the three best Europeans, England reached the standard needed for a Great Britain side to compete in the Olympics in Rio de Janeiro next year, as they did in London four years ago. But that is unlikely to happen – for a men's team as well. The Scottish, Welsh and Northern Irish FAs insist 2012 was a one-off and will not risk their independence in the international game with a repeat. The British Olympic Association will now campaign to be represented in Tokyo in 2020.

England – and Bassett – put the defeat behind them to beat Germany for the first time in 21 attempts in the third-place decider. A third penalty of the tournament by their most-capped player, Liverpool midfielder Fara Williams on her 147th appearance, gave them a 1-0 victory in extra-time. It was the best performance by an England team since Bobby Moore lifted the World Cup in 1966, the men having finished fourth in 1990. The USA won the final for a record third time, scoring four times in the first 16 minutes to overcome defending champions Japan by a record 5-2. Three of them were scored by captain Carli Lloyd, including one from the half-way line. It matched the highest scoring men's final – Brazil 5 Sweden 2 in 1958.

GROUP A

	P	W	D	L	F	A	Pts
Canada Q	3	1	2	0	2	1	5
China Q	3	1	1	1	3	3	4
Holland Q	3	1	1	1	2	2	4
New Zealand	3	0	2	1	2	3	2

Results: Canada 1 China 0, New Zealand 0 Holland 1, China 1 Holland 0, Canada 0 New Zealand 0, China 2 New Zealand 2, Holland 1 Canada 1

GROUP B

	P	W	D	L	F	A	Pts
Germany Q	3	2	1	0	15	1	7
Norway Q	3	2	1	0	8	2	7
Thailand	3	1	0	2	3	10	3
Ivory Coast	3	0	0	3	3	16	0

Results: Norway 4, Thailand 0, Germany 10 Ivory Coast 0, Germany 1, Norway 1, Ivory Coast 2 Thailand 3, Ivory Coast 1 Norway 3, Thailand 0 Germany 4

GROUP C

	P	W	D	L	F	A	Pts
Japan Q	3	3	0	0	4	1	9
Cameroon Q	3	2	0	1	9	3	6
Switzerland Q	3	1	0	2	11	4	3
Ecuador	3	0	0	3	1	17	0

Results: Cameroon 6 Ecuador 0, Japan 1 Switzerland 0, Switzerland 10 Ecuador 1, Japan 2 Cameroon 1, Ecuador 0 Japan 1, Switzerland 1 Cameroon 2

GROUP D

	P	W	D	L	F	A	Pts
USA Q	3	2	1	0	4	1	7
Australia Q	3	1	1	1	4	4	4
Sweden Q	3	0	3	0	4	4	3
Nigeria	3	0	1	2	3	6	1

Results: Sweden 3 Nigeria 3, USA 3 Australia 1, Australia 2 Nigeria 0, USA 0 Sweden 0, Australia 1 Sweden 1, Nigeria 0 USA 1

GROUP E

	P	W	D	L	F	A	Pts
Brazil Q	3	3	0	0	4	0	9
South Korea Q	3	1	1	1	4	5	4
Costa Rica	3	0	2	1	3	4	2
Spain	3	0	1	2	2	4	1

Results: Spain 1 Costa Rica 1, Brazil 2 South Korea 0, Brazil 1 Spain 0, South Korea 2 Costa Rica 2, South Korea 2 Spain 1, Costa Rica 0 Brazil 1

GROUP F

	P	W	D	L	F	A	Pts
France Q	3	2	0	1	6	2	6
England Q	3	2	0	1	4	3	6
Colombia Q	3	1	1	1	4	3	4
Mexico	3	0	1	2	2	8	1

Match-day 1

France 1 (Le Sommer 29) **England** 0. Att: 11,686 (Moncton)
England (4-4-1-1): Bardsley, A Scott (Kirby 68), Houghton, Bassett, Rafferty, Williams, White (Duggan 60), J Scott, Chapman (Moore 76), Bronze, Aluko. **Booked:** Chapman
Other result: Colombia 1 Mexico 1

Match-day 2

England 2 (Kirby 70, Carney 82) **Mexico** 1 (Ibarra 90). Att: 13,138 (Moncton)
England (4-3-3): Bardsley, Bronze (A Scott 85), Houghton, Bassett, Rafferty (Greenwood 53), J Scott (Carney 66), Williams, Moore, Kirby, Aluko, Duggan. **Booked:** Carney
Other result: France 0 Colombia 2

Match-day 3

England 2 (Carney 15, Williams 38 pen) **Colombia** 1 (Andrade 90). Att: 13,862 (Montreal)
England (4-3-3): Bardsley, A Scott, Houghton, Stoney, Greenwood, Nobbs, Williams, Moore, Carney (Sanderson 56), Duggan (Taylor 81), Kirby (Potter 66). **Booked:** A Scott
Other result: Mexico 0 France 5

ROUND OF 16

Norway 1 (Gulbrandsen 54) **England** 2 (Houghton 61, Bronze 76). Att: 19,829 (Ottawa)
England (4-2-3-1): Bardsley, Bronze, Houghton, Bassett, Rafferty, Moore, Williams, Carney, Chapman, Kirkby (J Scott 54), Duggan (Taylor 63)
Other results: Brazil 0 Australia 1, Canada 1 Switzerland 0, China 1 Cameroon 0, France 3 South Korea 0, Germany 4 Sweden 1, Japan 2 Holland 1, USA 2 Colombia 0

QUARTER-FINALS

England 2 (Taylor 11, Bronze 44) **Canada** 1 (Sinclair 42). Att: 54,057 (Vancouver)
England (4-2-3-1): Bardsley (Chamberlain 52), Bronze, Houghton, Bassett, Rafferty, Moore, Williams (White 79), J Scott, Chapman, Carney (Stoney 90), Taylor. **Booked**: Moore
Other results: Australia 0 Japan 1. Att: 19,814 (Edmonton). China 0 USA 1. Att: 24,141 (Ottawa). Germany 1 France 1 (aet, Germany won 5-4 on pens). Att: 24,859 (Montreal)

SEMI-FINALS

Japan 2 (Miyama 32 pen, Bassett 90 og) **England** 1 (Williams 40 pen). Att: 31,467 (Edmonton)
England (4-3-3): Bardsley, Bronze (A Scott 75), Houghton, Bassett, Rafferty, Moore, Williams (Carney 85), Chapman, J Scott, Taylor (White 60), Duggan. **Booked**: Rafferty.
Other result: USA 2 (Lloyd 69 pen, O'Hara 84) Germany 0. Att: 51,176 (Montreal)

THIRD PLACE PLAY-OFF

Germany 0 **England** 1 (Williams 108 pen) – aet. Att: 28,120 (Edmonton)
England (3-5-2): Bardsley, Houghton, Bassett, Potter, Bronze, J Scott, Williams (Stoney 112), Chapman (Sanderson 80), Greenwood, White (Aluko 61), Carney. **Booked**: Chapman, Bardsley, Bassett.

FINAL

USA 5 (Lloyd 3, 5, 16, Holiday 14, Heath 54) **Japan** 2 (Ogimi 27, Johnston 52 og). Att: 53,341 (Vancouver).

England's squad: Bardsley (Manchester City), Chamberlain (Arsenal), Telford (Notts Co); Bassett (Notts Co), Bronze (Manchester City), Greenwood (Notts Co), Houghton (Manchester City), Rafferty (Chelsea), A Scott (Arsenal), Stoney (Arsenal), Carney (Birmingham), Chapman (Chelsea), Moore (Birmingham), Nobbs (Arsenal), Potter (Birmingham), J Scott (Manchester City), Williams (Liverpool); Aluko (Chelsea), Duggan (Manchester City), Kirby (Reading), Sanderson (Arsenal), Taylor (Portland), White (Notts Co)

THE THINGS THEY SAY ...

'It really is heartbreaking – a tough way to go out. The players have inspired a nation and deserve to go home as heroes. They will have special memories for the rest of their lives. It's a horrible moment for Laura, but without her we could not have reached the semi-final. She was outstanding over the tournament. That is how she will be remembered' – **Mark Sampson**, England manager.

'I know how much Laura wears her heart on her sleeve. She has been our rock and is a great example for any player. I know she will bounce back from it' – **Toni Duggan**, England striker.

'Football can be cruel at times. It just wasn't to be. But I am so proud of the girls. They gave everything for the jersey' – **Steph Houghton**, England captain.

"It feels like the nation has fallen in love with the Lionesses' – **Kelly Simmons**, FA director of women's football.

SAME AGAIN AS ENGLAND BOW OUT EARLY

The sense of *déjà vu* lingered as England came home beaten and bowed from the European Under-21 Championship. It was a third straight flop in the tournament, another case of failing to qualify for their group and resulted in another inquest at the FA into how things went wrong. The manner of defeat also had echoes of the two previous finals under Stuart Pearce. In 2011, England paid the price for lapses of concentration when conceding two goals in quick succession to the Czech Republic in their third, decisive match. In 2013, there had been high hopes after a successful build-up – nine straight victories. This time, under Gareth Southgate, they had won 15 out of 17 games, been undefeated in qualifying and beaten Germany and Portugal in friendlies. But after losing to Portugal when it mattered, then overcoming Sweden, they conceded two goals in three minutes midway through the first-half against Italy, went down 3-1 and finished bottom of the section. There were some mitigating circumstances. Saido Berahino, who arrived in the Czech Republic having scored 20 goals during the season for West Bromwich Albion, sustained a knee injury in training on the eve of the tournament and took no part in it. John Stones, the Everton defender, had to miss the first two matches with concussion, while Tottenham's Alex Pritchard limped out of the win over Sweden with an ankle injury. The key area for discussion, however, was the composition of the squad. Players like Raheem Sterling, Phil Jones, Alex Oxlade-Chamberlain and Ross Barkley were eligible to play. But the decision was taken by Southgate – who expressed a wish to continue in the job – and the FA director of elite development, Dan Ashworth, to stick with the players who had been regular members of the squad. The problem with England at this level, historically, is that too many are not established in club sides and lack the experience of big matches. The debate will continue as England prepare for the start of qualifying for the 2017 finals against Norway in September. Their other group opponents are Switzerland, Bosnia-Herzegovia and Kazakhstan. A new format will have 12 finalists, instead of eight, with the nine group winners going through, alongside two of the best four runners-up after play-offs, and hosts Poland. Sweden won the title for the first time. They beat favourites Portugal on penalties in the final, with Patrik Carlgren saving the decisive spot-kick from William Carvalho, one of the outstanding players of the tournament.

GROUP A
(All matches in Prague)

Match-day 1
Czech Republic 1 (Kaderabek 35) **Denmark** 2 (Vestergaard 56, Sisto 84). Att: 15,987. **Germany** 1 (Emre Can 17) **Serbia** 1 (Djuricic 8). Att: 5,490.

Match-day 2
Czech Republic 4 (Kliment 8, 21, 56, Frydek 59) **Serbia** 0. Att: 16,253. **Germany** 3 (Volland 32, 48, Ginter 53) **Denmark** 0. Att: 13,268.

Match-day 3
Czech Republic 1 (Krejci 66) **Germany** 1 (Schulz 55). Att: 18,068. **Denmark** 2 (Jensen 21, Fischer 47) **Serbia** 0. Att: 4,297.

	P	W	D	L	F	A	Pts
Denmark Q	3	2	0	1	4	4	6
Germany Q	3	1	2	0	5	2	5
Czech Rep	3	1	1	1	6	3	4
Serbia	3	0	1	2	1	7	1

GROUP B

Match-day 1
England 0 **Portugal** 1 (Joao Mario 57). Att: 7,167 (Uherske Hradiste)
England (4-2-3-1): Butland, Jenkinson, Moore, Gibson, Garbutt, Ward-Prowse (Hughes 54),

Chalobah, Redmond, Carroll (Pritchard 79), Lingard (Ings 71), Kane. **Booked**: Gibson, Jenkinson
Italy 1 (Berardi 29 pen) **Sweden** 2 (Guidetti 56, Kiese Thelin 86 pen). Att: 6,719 (Olomouc)

Match-day 2
Sweden 0 **England** 1 (Lingard 85). Att: 11,257 (Olomouc)
England (4-2-3-1): Butland, Jenkinson, Moore, Gibson, Garbutt, Hughes (Ings 46), Chalobah,
Redmond, Carroll (Loftus-Cheek 73), Pritchard (Lingard 62), Kane
Italy 0 **Portugal** 0. Att: 7,085 (Uherske Hradiste)

Match-day 3
England 1 (Redmond 90) **Italy** 3 (Belotti 25, Benassi 27, 72). Att: 11,563 (Olomouc)
England (4-2-3-1): Butland, Jenkinson, Stones, Gibson, Garbutt, Forster-Caskey (Loftus-Cheek
63), Chalobah, Redmond, Ings, Lingard, Kane. **Booked**: Loftus-Cheek
Portugal 1 (Paciencia 82) **Sweden** 1 (Tibbling 89). Att: 7,263 (Uherske Hradiste)

	P	W	D	L	F	A	Pts
Portugal Q	3	1	2	0	2	1	5
Sweden Q	3	1	1	1	3	3	4
Italy	3	1	1	1	4	3	4
England	3	1	0	2	2	4	3

SEMI-FINALS

Denmark 1 (Bech 63) **Sweden** 4 (Guidetti 23 pen, Tibbling 26, Quaison 83, Hiljemark 90). Att:
9,834 (Prague)

Portugal 5 (Silva 25, Ricardo 33, Joao Mario 45, Cavaleiro 45, Horta 71) **Germany** 0. Att: 9,876
(Olomouc)

FINAL

Sweden 0 **Portugal** 0 (aet, Sweden won 4-3 on pens. Att: 18,867 (Prague, June 30, 2015)

England squad: Bettinelli (Fulham), Bond (Watford), Butland (Stoke); Chambers (Arsenal),
Garbutt (Everton), Gibson (Middlesbrough), Jenkinson Arsenal), Keane (Burnley), Moore
(Leicester), Stones (Everton), Targett (Southampton); Carroll (Tottenham), Chalobah (Chelsea),
Hughes (Derby), Forster-Caskey (Brighton), Lingard (Manchester Utd), Loftus-Cheek (Chelsea),
Pritchard (Tottenham), Redmond (Norwich), Ward-Prowse (Southampton); Berahino (WBA)
replaced by Afobe (Wolves), Ings (Liverpool), Kane (Tottenham)

THE THINGS THEY SAY...

● 'Youth teams are there to help develop players and give them experience to get into the seniors.
The players who hadn't competed in the two-year cycle and lead-up to the Championship were
not considered. The debate will be reopened now, but we stand by the decision Gareth and I
made. You never know when you drop players into a new group whether it will be the right thing
to do' – **Dan Ashworth**, FA director of elite development.

● 'I think what we have done is raise the profile of the team and the style with which we've
played. People will look at that, I'm sure, when making their decision. It was a cruel defeat
(against Italy), but that's the nature of football' – **Gareth Southgate**, England coach.

● 'There are fine margins in these tournaments and we conceded two sloppy goals and they have
cost us. You have to be ruthless at both ends of the pitch and were weren't' – **Jack Butland**,
England's goalkeeper.

● 'We never learn. What a wasted opportunity to gather invaluable international experience.
Exasperatingly amateurish approach' – **Gary Lineker**, former England striker, insisting that the
best available squad should have been selected.

DAY BY DAY DIARY 2014–15

JULY 2014

18 A joint takeover of Doncaster Rovers by Louis Tomlinson, Doncaster-born singer with One Direction, and former club chairman John Ryan falls through.

19 Philipp Lahm, Germany's World Cup-winning captain, retires from international football after winning 113 caps.

21 Steven Gerrard, the England captain, calls time on his international career after winning 114 caps.

22 James Rodriguez, Colombia's Golden Boot winner at the World Cup, joins Real Madrid from Monaco for £60m.

23 Leicester break their club record with the £8m signing of Leonardo Ulloa from Brighton.

25 Didier Drogba, the player voted Chelsea's best-ever by fans, returns to the club on a one-year contract after spells in China and Turkey.

27 Dejan Lovren becomes the third Southampton player to move to Liverpool, joining Adam Lallana and Rickie Lambert at Anfield for £20m.

28 Calum Chambers continues the exodus from St Mary's, signing for Arsenal for a fee rising to £16m.

29 Ross Barkley, regarded as England's great new hope, signs a new four-year contract with Everton.

30 The Premier League announce the introduction of the vanishing spray used to mark defensive walls during the World Cup. The Football League will trial it in the Johnstone's Paint Trophy.

31 Everton pay a club record £28m for Chelsea's Romelu Lukaku after the Belgium World Cup striker's successful season on loan at Goodison Park. Danny Rose signs a five-year contract with Tottenham after establishing himself in the team last season.

AUGUST 2014

2 A crowd of 109,318 at the University of Michigan Stadium – the biggest for a soccer game in America – see Manchester United defeat Real Madrid 3-1 to win a pre-season tournament.

3 Former Chelsea stalwart Frank Lampard makes an immediate return to the Premier League, joining Manchester City on a six-month loan ahead of his debut season for New York City.

4 The Premier League unveil a new European cup competition involving English under-21 teams and Continental sides.

5 Howard Webb, widely regarded as the best referee of his generation, retires after a 25-year career to take up a technical role with the governing body for officials.

6 Celtic lose 6-1 on aggregate to Legia Warsaw in the third qualifying round of the Champions League. Britt Assombalonga, Peterborough's top scorer, joins Nottingham Forest for £5.5m – a record fee for both clubs.

7 John Stones, on the stand-by list for England's World Cup squad, signs a new five-year contract with Everton.

8 Celtic are reinstated to the Champions League after UEFA expel Legia Warsaw for fielding an ineligible player against the Scottish champions.

9 Mark Robins becomes the first managerial casualty of the new season, following Huddersfield's 4-0 home defeat by Bournemouth on the opening day of the new Football League campaign. Cambridge United and Luton both make a winning return to the league with 1-0 successes over Plymouth and Carlisle respectively.

10 Arsenal defeat Manchester City 3-0 in the Community Shield at Wembley.

11 Manchester City pay £31.9m for Porto's Eliaquim Mangala, a British record fee for a defender. Former FA chief executive and Tranmere player Mark Palios, along with his lawyer wife Nicola, take over the Birkenhead club from Peter Johnson.

12 Two goals by Cristiano Ronaldo give Real Madrid a 2-0 win over Sevilla in the European Super Cup in front of a crowd of 30,854 – a record for Cardiff City Stadium and for the annual match between the Champions League winners and the Europa League champions.

13 Former England manager Glenn Hoddle joins the coaching staff at Queens Park Rangers after an eight-year absence from the domestic game. David Silva signs a new five-year contract with Manchester City.

14 Captain Vincent Kompany and Sergio Aguero sign new five-year contracts with Manchester City. Arsenal's Per Mertesacker announces his retirement from international football, the third member of Germany's World Cup-winning team to do so after captain Philipp Lahm and Miroslav Klose.

15 Tony Pulis, the Premier League's Manager of the Year for leading Crystal Palace away from the threat of relegation, leaves the club on the eve of the new season over a disagreement with chairman Steve Parish on transfer policy. The Court of Arbitration for Sport reject an appeal by Luis Suarez against his four-month ban for biting Italy's Giorgio Chiellini at the World Cup, but allow the player to train with his new club, Barcelona. UEFA turn down Legia Warsaw's appeal against their expulsion.

16 Manchester United are beaten at home by Swansea in new manager Louis van Gaal's first game in the Premier League.

17 Manchester City open their defence of the title by winning at Newcastle.

18 Crystal Palace are fined an undisclosed sum by the Premier League for breaching a 'good faith' rule by obtaining information about Cardiff's line-up ahead of the teams' match in April, 2014. Norwich defender Martin Olsson is banned for three games and fined £3,000 by the FA for placing his hand on referee Simon Hooper before being sent off against Wolves.

19 Coventry agree a deal with the owners of the Ricoh Arena to return to the stadium after playing home games at Northampton since the start of the 2013–14 season because of a long-running dispute over rent.

20 Manchester United sign Argentina World Cup defender Marcos Rojo from Sporting Lisbon for £16m. Edin Dzeko signs a new four-year contract with Manchester City.

21 Former Cardiff manager Malky Mackay is ruled out of contention for the vacant Crystal Palace job over claims of misconduct.

22 Cardiff are reported to have sent a dossier to the FA alleging exchanges of 'racist, sexist and homophobic' texts and e-mail messages between Malky Mackay and Iain Moody, his former head of recruitment. Mackay apologises and Moody resigns as Palace's sporting director.

23 Barry Davies makes a one-off return to the BBC Match of the Day commentary box to cover Crystal Palace v West Ham for the 50th anniversary edition of the programme.

25 Liverpool sign former Manchester City striker Mario Balotelli from AC Milan for £16m, taking their summer spending to almost £120m.

26 Manchester United break the British transfer record by paying £59.7m for Angel di Maria, Real Madrid's Argentina World Cup midfield player. Hours later, United's 'shadow' team, including seven internationals, are humbled 4-0 by MK Dons in round two of the Capital One Cup in front of a record crowd of nearly 27,000 for the League One club. Frank Lampard announces his retirement from international football after winning 106 England caps. Celtic fail to take advantage of their Champions League reprieve, losing 2-1 on aggregate to Maribor in the play-off round. Ross County sack manager Derek Adams and his father George, the club's director of football, after losing their first four Scottish Premiership games of the season.

27 Arsenal reach the group stage for the 17th successive season by beating Besiktas 1-0 on aggregate. Neil Warnock returns as Crystal Palace manager, having previously been in charge from 2007–10.

28 Wayne Rooney is named England's new captain. Dave Hockaday is sacked after 70 days and six games as Leeds manager. Hull's first European campaign ends with defeat by Lokeren on the away goals rule in the Europa League play-offs. Tottenham reach the group stage by defeating AEL Limassol 5-1 on aggregate.

29 Chelsea's Fernando Torres, a £50m buy in January 2011, joins AC Milan on a two-year loan.

31 Giuseppe Sannino resigns as Watford manager with his side lying second in the Championship.

SEPTEMBER 2014

1   The summer transfer window closes with Premier League clubs having spent a record £835m – £205m more than the previous highest in 2013. Manchester United, the biggest spenders, take their outlay to £149 by signing Daley Blind from Ajax for £13.8m and Radamel Falcao on loan from Monaco with a view to a future permanent deal. Another major deal takes United's Danny Welbeck to Arsenal for £16m. Two clubs break their transfer records – Hull paying £10m for Abel Hernandez from Palerrmo and Crystal Palace buying James McArthur from Wigan for £7m. Two managers lose their jobs after poor starts to the season – Carlisle's Graham Kavanagh and Colchester's Joe Dunne, who is replaced immediately by the club's head of youth, Tony Humes.

2   Former Brighton manager Oscar Garcia takes over at Watford. Chelsea's Cesar Azpilicueta signs a new five-year contract.

3   Wayne Rooney marks his first match as captain with the only goal, from the penalty spot, of a friendly against Norway, watched by the lowest crowd for an England match at the new Wembley – 40,181. Former Charlton manager Chris Powell takes charge at Huddersfield.

4   Peter Reid, former Manchester City and Sunderland manager, is appointed coach to Indian Super League club Mumbai.

5   Coventry's return to the Ricoh Arena draws a crowd of more than 27,000 for the victory over Gillingham.

7   Aiden McGeady's 90th minute goal, his second of the game, gives the Republic of Ireland a 2-1 victory over Georgia in their opening European Championship qualifier. Northern Ireland also win away by that scoreline, thanks to Kyle Lafferty's strike in the 88th minute against Hungary. Scotland push World Cup winners Germany all the way in Dortmund before losing 2-1 to two Thomas Muller goals.

8   Two by Danny Welbeck get England off to a successful start – 2-0 in Switzerland against their main rivals for the top spot in Group E.

9   Gareth Bale is another two-goal marksman as Wales come from behind to win 2-1 in Andorra. Jim McIntyre leaves Queen of the South to become Ross County's new manager.

10 Gabriel Agbonlahor agrees a new four-year contract with Aston Villa.

11 Thibaut Courtois signs a new five-year deal after ousting Petr Cech as Chelsea's No 1 goalkeeper.

12 Accrington manager James Beattie leaves the League Two club by mutual agreement.

13 Tottenham deny claims by an American investment firm, Cain Hoy, that discussions are taking place about a takeover of the club.

15 Newcastle manager Alan Pardew, under pressure after a poor start to the season, is given a vote of confidence by owner Mike Ashley.

16 Alan Hutton signs a new three-year contract with Aston Villa, having previously been told he had no future at the club.

17 Felix Magath is sacked after seven months as Fulham manager with his relegated side bottom of the Championship. Aston Villa's Paul Lambert signs a contract extension through to June, 2018. John Coleman returns to Accrington for a second spell as manager.

18 There are two more managerial casualties. Ole Gunnar Solskjaer is fired after nine months in charge at Cardiff with his relegated team eighth from bottom. Port Vale's Micky Adams resigns in the wake of six successive defeats.

19 Wembley is chosen for the semi-finals and final of Euro 2020 to be staged across 13 cities. Hampden Park and the Aviva Stadium in Dublin will also host matches. Keith Curle, former Notts County manager, takes over at Carlisle.

20 Tottenham's Benoit Assou-Ekotto is banned for three matches and fined £50,000 by the FA for publicly backing Nicolas Anelka's controversial 'quenelle' gesture last season.

21 FIFA are accused of a cover-up after insisting their report into alleged corruption in the bidding process for the 2018 and 2022 World Cups will not be published.

23 Leeds appoint former Slovenia international Darko Milanic as their new manager. In a record-equalling penalty shoot-out for English professional football, Liverpool beat Middlesbrough 14-13 to reach the fourth round of the Capital One Cup.

24 Russell Slade, League One's longest-serving manager with four years at Leyton Orient, resigns after the club reject an approach for his services from Cardiff.

25 Fulham are fined £5,000 by the FA for misconduct by players during the match against Nottingham Forest.

27 FIFA agree to set up a working group to implement a ban on third-party ownership of players.

28 Craig Dawson signs a new three-year contract with West Bromwich Albion after scoring his first goal for the club against Burnley.

29 Oscar Garcia, in charge at Watford for 27 days, steps down for health reasons and is replaced by new coach Billy McKinlay. Portsmouth announce they are debt free, less than 18 months after the Supporters' Trust takeover with the club facing liquidation.

30 Francesco Totti, 38, overtakes Ryan Giggs as the oldest Champions League scorer with his goal in Roma's group match against Manchester City at the Etihad.

OCTOBER 2014

1 Danny Welbeck scores the first hat-trick of his career in Arsenal's 4-1 victory over Galatasaray.

2 Daniel Sturridge signs a new five-year contract with Liverpool.

3 Manager Dougie Freedman parts company by mutual consent with Bolton with his side second from bottom after ten matches.

4 Colin Cooper resigns as Hartlepool manager after a 3-0 home defeat by fellow-strugglers Carlisle keeps them bottom of League Two.

5 Cardiff's pursuit of Russell Slade is successful when he is confirmed as their new manager.

6 Roy Keane hits back at Sir Alex Ferguson after being criticised in his former Manchester United manager's own autobiography.

7 Billy McKinlay is dismissed after two matches with Watford and replaced by former Chelsea midfielder Slavisa Jokanovic, who becomes the club's fourth manager in 37 days.

8 Russ Wilcox, who led Scunthorpe to promotion with a league record 28 unbeaten matches for a new manager, is sacked with his side second from bottom of League One.

9 England defeat San Marino 5-0 in their second European Championship qualifying match.

10 Wales share a goalless draw with Bosnia-Herzegovina. Huddersfield's Mark Robins, the season's first managerial casualty, takes over at Scunthorpe.

11 Robbie Keane scores a hat-trick in the first 18 minutes as the Republic of Ireland defeat Gibraltar 7-0, taking his goals tally in European Championship qualifiers to 21 – a record for any player. Northern Ireland maintain their successful start with a 2-0 victory over the Faroe Islands.

12 England are 1-0 winners away to Estonia, who play for most of the second half with ten men after captain Ragnar Klavan is sent off for a second yellow card. Former Celtic manager Neil Lennon is named Bolton's replacement for Dougie Freedman. Liverpool retain the FA Women's Super League title on goal difference from Chelsea on the final day of the season.

13 Wales overcome the loss of Simon Church with a shoulder injury after 70 seconds and a straight red card for Andy Ball two minutes into the second half to beat Cyprus 2-1. Two more managers depart. Rob Edwards is sacked by bottom-of-the-table Tranmere after five months in the job. Nigel Worthington resigns at York with his team third from the foot of the table.

14 John O'Shea marks his 100th Republic of Ireland appearance with a stoppage-time goal for a 1-1 draw away to Germany. Northern Ireland make it three opening qualifying wins for the first time in their history with a 2-0 success in Greece, Kyle Lafferty having scored in each game. Scotland also do well on their travels, holding Poland to a 2-2 draw. English referee Martin Atkinson abandons a group game in Belgrade shortly before half-time when Serbia and Albania players clash after a remote-controlled drone flies over the pitch carrying a pro-Albania banner. England reach the European Under-21 Championship finals by beating Croatia 4-2 on aggregate in a play-off.

15 Russ Wilcox makes a rapid return to management when taking over at York.

16 John O'Shea is given a new two-year contract by Sunderland. Former Port Vale manager Micky Adams takes over at Tranmere.

17 Manchester City move into a new £200m training ground opposite the Eithad Stadium. Swindon and Leyton Orient are fined £5,500 and £4,000 respectively for a stoppage-time fracas involving players from both teams.

18 John O'Shea's successful week turns sour when Sunderland are crushed 8-0 by Southampton in the Premier League.

20 Lee Clark becomes the ninth managerial casualty of the season in the Championship when sacked by Birmingham after two wins in the first 12 matches. Tony Fernandes, the Queens Park Rangers owner, orders Harry Redknapp and Adel Taarabt to end their 'embarrassing' public spat after the midfield player denies his manager's accusation that he is three stones overweight.

21 Chelsea, 6-0 winners over Maribor, contribute to a record-breaking Champions League programme of 40 goals in eight group games. Bayern Munich and Shakhtar Donetsk both score seven, with the Ukrainian side's Luiz Adriano on the mark five times to equal Lionel Messi's tally for Barcelona in 2012. The FA announce that general secretary Alex Horne will leave in January after 11 years with the governing body.

22 Liverpool's Mario Balotelli is reprimanded by manager Brendan Rodgers for swopping shirts with defender Pepe at half-time of the 3-0 Champions League home defeat by Real Madrid. Paul Murray, youth team coach at Oldham is appointed Hartlepool's new manager.

23 Erik Lamela scores a wonder goal in Tottenham's 5-1 Europa League win over Asteras Tripolis, wrapping his left foot behind his right to curl the ball into the net from the edge of the penalty box.

25 Leeds owner Massimo Cellino sacks his second manager of the season after six games in charge, Darko Milanic having lasted 32 days at Elland Road. With the season less than three months old, Milanic is the 20th managerial casualty in the four divisions.

27 Mauro Milanese, Leyton Orient's sporting director and a former Queens Park Rangers defender, is appointed manager.

28 Jose Riga is dismissed as manager of bottom-of-the-table Blackpool after five months in the job. Burton's Gary Rowett takes over at Birmingham.

29 Rio Ferdinand is banned for three Queens Park Rangers games, fined £25,000 and ordered to attend an education programme by the FA for an abusive comment on *Twitter*. Former Fulham defender Kit Symons is appointed manager of the club after gaining 13 points in seven games as caretaker. Coach Robert Page, who played alongside Symons for Wales, becomes Port Vale's new manager after his spell as caretaker.

30 The managerial merry-go-round continues with Lee Clark taking over at Blackpool. Aleksandar Tonev, on loan at Celtic from Aston Villa, is banned for seven matches by the Scottish FA for racially abusing Aberdeen's Shay Logan.

31 Everton post a record annual profit of £28.2m. Northampton manager Chris Wilder is given a two-match touchline ban and fined £500 by the FA for remarks to referee Keith Hill during the match against Cheltenham. Mark Yates, Cheltenham manager, is fined £500 for his behaviour towards Cambridge manager Richard Money.

NOVEMBER 2014

1 Neil Redfearn, the Leeds caretaker between Dave Hockaday's departure and Darko Milanic's appointment, is given the job on a permanent basis.

2 Motherwell's Stuart McCall, appointed in December 2010 and the second longest-serving manager in Scottish football, resigns after a fifth successive defeat.

4 Liverpool manager Brendan Rodgers rejects accusations of 'throwing in the towel' by fielding a weakened team in the Champions League return match with Real Madrid which they lose 1-0.

5 Manchester City have Fernandinho and Yaya Toure sent off in the home defeat by CSKA Moscow. Crystal Palace manager Neil Warnock is fined £9,000 by the FA for claiming referee Craig Pawson was 'influenced' by Chelsea during his side's home defeat by the Premier League leaders. Southampton open a new £40m training complex.

6   England manager Roy Hodgson expresses concern that American football games at Wembley are damaging the pitch. A tied vote by club chairmen – 34 in favour, 34 against – results in no approval for artificial pitches for League One and League Two clubs in the 2015–16 season.

7   England are drawn in a group with Italy, Portugal and Sweden for the 2015 European Under-21 Championship.

8   Stirling Albion win a record penalty shoot-out for Scottish football by 13-12 after 28 spot-kicks in a Scottish Cup third round replay against Hurlford.

9   Worcester, from the Conference North, spring the biggest surprise of the FA Cup first round, beating Coventry 2-1 at the Ricoh Arena.

10 Oscar signs a new five-year contract with Chelsea. Blackpool are fined £30,000, with half the sum suspended, for fielding an ineligible player, Donervon Daniels, in the defeat by Millwall.

11 David Moyes returns to football, seven months after his dismissal by Manchester United, as head coach of Real Sociedad. Tottenham and Aston Villa are both fined £20,000 by the FA for a players' scuffle. Sir Stanley Matthews' 1953 FA Cup winner's medal is sold at auction for a record £220,000.

12 Uwe Rosler is sacked as Wigan manager after a single win in 12 games leaves his side third from bottom. Burton appoint former Chelsea striker Jimmy Floyd Hasselbaink as their new manager.

13 England are accused in a FIFA report of flouting rules when bidding for the 2018 World Cup. It clears Qatar of allegations of corruption in winning the vote for the 2022 tournament. The FA claim the report is a whitewash and contradicts the findings of its chief investigator. Blackburn coach Craig Short and Millwall assistant manager Marc Bircham are fined £2,000 and £1,000 respectively by the FA for a touchline altercation.

14 Scotland defeat the Republic of Ireland 1-0 with a goal by Shaun Maloney in their European Championship qualifier. Northern Ireland drop points for the first time when losing 2-0 in Romania. Livingston are deducted five Scottish Championship points and fined £10,000 for breaching SPFL rules relating to non-payment of tax. Peterhead are fined £10,000, part of which is suspended, and ordered to replay their League One game against Ayr for fielding defender Reece Donaldson while suspended.

15 Wayne Rooney marks his 100th England appearance with a penalty in the 3-1 victory over Slovenia.

16 Wales keep their early momentum going by holding group favourites Belgium to a goalless draw away from home.

17 Queens Park Rangers and Sunderland are both fined £20,000 by the FA for players confronting referees Mike Dean and Lee Mason during matches against Manchester City and Everton respectively.

18 Two more goals by Wayne Rooney in a 3-1 victory over Scotland at Celtic Park take him to within three of Sir Bobby Charlton's all-time England record tally of 49. Andrew Robertson nets his first for Scotland. Robbie Brady is on the mark twice as the Republic of Ireland defeat the USA 4-1 in another friendly, while Anthony Pilkington scores his first for the team.

19 Former Cardiff manager Malky Mackay takes over at Wigan. Swansea's Wilfried Bony signs an extension to his contract, keeping him at the club until 2018.

20 Sheffield United bow to pressure from supporters, the general public and sponsors by withdrawing an offer to former striker Ched Evans to train with the club following his release from prison.

21 Paul Cox steps down as Mansfield manager by mutual consent after nine matches without a victory.

23 A record crowd of 45,619 for an England women's international see captain Karen Carney win her 100th cap in a 3-0 defeat by European champions Germany at Wembley.

24 Mark Yates, English football's third longest-serving manager behind Arsenal's Arsene Wenger and Exeter's Paul Tisdale, is sacked after nearly five years at Cheltenham in the wake of four successive league defeats.

25 Sergio Aguero keeps alive Manchester City's chances of reaching the knock-out stage of the Champions League with a hat-trick in the 3-2 victory over Bayern Munich. Chelsea go through by beating Schalke 5-0 away from home in their penultimate game. Barcelona's Lionel Messi takes his tally in the competition to a record 74, overtaking Real Madrid's Raul.

26 Arsenal go through from their group for the 15th successive season with a 2-0 success against Borussia Dortmund. Paul Buckle, former Torquay, Bristol Rovers and Luton manager, takes over at Cheltenham. Peterborough rename their London Road ground the Abax Stadium as part of a £500,000 sponsorship deal with a Norwegian company.

27 Everton, Tottenham and Celtic qualify for the knock-out stage of the Europa League.

28 Roy Keane leaves Aston Villa after five months as assistant manager, citing the difficulty in combining the job with his position as Martin O'Neill's No 2 with the Republic of Ireland. Everton and West Ham are both fined £20,000 by the FA for misbehavior by players.

29 Premier League clubs are shown to have paid a record £115.3m to agents in the 12 months to September, 2014, with Chelsea (£16.8m), Liverpool (£14.3m) and Manchester City (£12.8m) the biggest spenders.

DECEMBER 2014

1 The Football League ban Leeds owner Massimo Cellino from running the club until his conviction in an Italian court for tax evasion is spent in March, 2015

4 The FA fine Stoke chairman Peter Coates £5,000 for accusing referees of showing bias against his club.

5 Paul Murray is sacked after 45 days as Hartlepool manager with his side bottom of the table and beaten at home by Blyth in the FA Cup. Mansfield captain Adam Murray, 33, becomes the youngest manager in the four divisions after a spell as caretaker.

6 Clubs observe a minute's silence to commemorate the 100th anniversary of the First World War's Christmas truce when troops played impromptu football games.

8 After 43 days as Leyton Orient manager, Mauro Milanese is replaced by former Genoa coach Fabio Liverani. Milanese, winner of two of his eight games, returns to the role of sporting director.

9 Liverpool are held 1-1 by Basle at Anfield in their final Champions League group game and fail to reach the knock-out stage. With his side second from bottom of the Scottish Premiership, Tommy Craig is sacked as St Mirren manager after 19 games in charge.

10 Manchester City overcome the absence of leading scorer Sergio Aguero and captain Vincent Kompany to beat Roma 2-0 away to go through to the last 16.

11 Middlesbrough manager Aitor Karanka is given a one-match touchline ban and fined £2,000 by the FA after being sent to the stands in stoppage-time of the match against Blackburn.

12 Ian Baraclough, former Scunthorpe manager, takes charge of Motherwell.

14 Ally McCoist resigns after four years as Rangers manager, triggering a 12-month notice period.

15 Reading manager Nigel Adkins is sacked in the wake of a 6-1 defeat by Birmingham – the club's biggest in the league in 15 years. Blackburn, Leeds and Nottingham Forest have a transfer ban imposed for the January 2015 window for breaching the Football League's financial fair play rules. Chesterfield are ordered to replay the FA Cup second round tie against MK Dons after fielding an ineligible player, on-loan Georg Margreitter, in their 1-0 victory.

16 Thierry Henry announces his retirement after a glittering 20-year career in club and international football. Former West Bromwich Albion manager Steve Clarke succeeds Nigel Adkins. Ronnie Moore, formerly in charge of Oldham, Rotherham and Tranmere, is appointed Hartlepool manager.

17 In the longest penalty shoot-out in the history of the FA Cup competition proper, Scunthorpe beat Worcester 14-13 after 32 spot-kicks in a second round replay.

18 Liverpool's Mario Balotelli is banned for one match and fined £25,000 by the FA for making racist and anti-semitic comments on social media.

19 Manchester City's Joe Hart signs a new contract through to 2019. Leicester manager Nigel

Pearson receives a one-match touchline ban and £10,000 fine from the FA for using insulting language towards a spectator. Six months after being demoted from the Conference into the Southern League for failing to pay football creditors, Hereford are wound up in the High Court.

20 Barnsley's Danny Wilson marks his 1,000th game as a manager with a 2-0 victory over Leyton Orient, having previously been in charge of Sheffield Wednesday, Bristol City, MK Dons, Hartlepool, Swindon and Sheffield United. Real Madrid beat the South American champions San Lorenzo, from Argentina, 2-0 with goals by Sergio Ramos and Gareth Bale in the World Club Cup Final in Morocco.

21 Ally McCoist is placed on 'gardening leave' by Rangers, leaves the club and is replaced on an interim basis until the end of the season by his assistant, Kenny McDowall.

22 Sami Hyypia, manager of Brighton for six months, resigns with his side third from bottom after a single win in 18 league games.

23 Wolves chairman Steve Morgan is fined £2,500 by the FA for confronting referee Mike Jones on the touchline after his club's defeat by Bournemouth.

24 The Scottish FA refuse permission for Newcastle owner Mike Ashley to increase his shareholding at Rangers.

26 Fifteen players are sent off in the Boxing Day Football League programme of matches.

27 Neil Warnock, in charge for four months, becomes the season's first Premier League manager to be sacked, with Crystal Palace third from bottom after a single win in 12 games. Crawley manager John Gregory steps down to undergo open heart surgery and is replaced on an interim basis by Dean Saunders, formerly at Doncaster and Wolves.

28 Alan Pardew, appointed by Newcastle in December, 2010 and the second longest-serving Premier League manager to Arsene Wenger, resigns with six years of his contract remaining, the club having agreed a compensation package for him to join Crystal Palace.

29 Alan Irvine is dismissed after six months in charge of West Bromwich Albion with his side having lost seven of nine matches to drop to within a point of the relegation zone.

30 Papiss Cisse is banned for three matches by the FA after being caught on camera elbowing Seamus Coleman in Newcastle's game with Everton. Aston Villa are fined £30,000 for their players' protests at the red card – later rescinded – shown to Gabriel Agbonlahor against Manchester United. Sheffield United receive a £4,000 fine for the behaviour of their bench during a Capital One Cup tie with Southampton.

31 Wigan owner Dave Whelan is banned from football-related activities for six weeks and fined £50,000 by the FA for offensive comments about Jewish and Chinese people, made following the appointment of Malky Mackay as manager. Chris Hughton, former Newcastle, Birmingham and Norwich manager, is appointed by Brighton. Gillingham, two points away from the bottom four, sack their manager Peter Taylor. Swansea's Jonjo Shelvey, caught on camera elbowing Liverpool's Emre Can, is banned for four fixtures by the FA, having been sent off earlier in the season against Everton.

JANUARY 2015

1 Steven Gerrard announces he will end his 26-year association with Liverpool at the end of the season to seek 'a new challenge.' Tony Pulis returns to Premier League management with West Bromwich Albion. Brendon Batson, former West Bromwich Albion defender and one of the pioneers for black footballers, receives an OBE in the New Year's Honours. So does Northern Ireland's Jim Boyce, a vice-president of FIFA. Former Portsmouth stalwart and charity worker Linvoy Primus is awarded an MBE.

2 Alan Pardew is confirmed as the new manager of Crystal Palace, one of his former clubs as a player.

3 League Two Exeter secure a club record £1.75m fee from the sale of midfielder Matt Grimes to Swansea.

4 Sheffield United take pride of place in the FA Cup third round, beating Queens Park Rangers 3-0 at Loftus Road.

5 Neil Adams, manager of Norwich for nine months, resigns following an FA Cup defeat by Preston.

6 Steven Gerrard agrees to join Major League Soccer team LA Galaxy in the summer, having turned down other offers from clubs in the Premier League, Europe and the Middle East.

7 Oldham abandon talks to sign Ched Evans after threats made to directors and employees of the League One club and pressure from sponsors.

8 Alex Neil, 33-year-old manager of Scottish Premiership club Hamilton, is appointed the new Norwich manager.

9 Cardiff return to their traditional blue kit after owner Vincent Tan bows to pressure from supporters unhappy about the team playing in red.

11 Bob Peeters, in charge of Charlton for eight months, is dismissed after a single victory in 12 league matches.

12 Cristiano Ronaldo is crowned the world's best player for the second successive year, again beating Lionel Messi into second place, with Manuel Neuer third in the FIFA voting.

13 Guy Luzon, former coach to Standard Liege, succeeds Bob Peeters at The Valley.

14 Manchester City sign Wilfried Bony, Swansea's leading scorer, for £28m, a record fee for the Welsh club.

15 The Crown Prosecution Service drop the case against 13 footballers over alleged match-fixing because of insufficient evidence. Gareth Southgate signs a 12-month extension to his contract as head coach of the England Under-21 team.

16 Leicester pay a club record £9m for Croatia striker Andrej Kramaric from Rijeka. The club are fined £20,000 by the FA for their players' involvement in a brawl during the game against Aston Villa.

17 Scunthorpe lose both goalkeepers, Sam Slocombe and his replacement Jamie Severn, with broken arms during the home defeat by Bristol City.

19 Kenny McDowall, caretaker manager of Rangers, hands in his notice and begins a 12-month notice period.

20 All 20 Premier League clubs from the 2013–14 season are included in the richest 40 in the world, according to figures from accountants Deloitte.

22 Aston Villa are fined £60,000 by the FA for the players' brawl in the match with Leicester. Karl Robinson, the MK Dons manager, is given a four-match touchline ban and £3,000 fine by the FA for insulting language towards a Bradford player. Peterborough manager Darren Ferguson receives a two-game ban and £1,000 fine for misconduct at half-time of the game with Colchester.

23 Phil Parkinson, the Bradford manager, and his assistant Steve Parkin are both fined £1,000 by the FA after being sent to the stands during the match against Millwall. Martin Canning is appointed player-manager of Hamilton.

24 Bradford deliver one of the biggest giant-killing performances in the history of the FA Cup when turning a 2-0 deficit into a 4-2 victory over Chelsea in a fourth round tie at Stamford Bridge.

25 Fabian Delph signs a new four-and-a-half-year contract with Aston Villa.

26 John Carver, Newcastle's caretaker manager, is given the job until the end of the season.

27 An extra-time header by Branislav Ivanovic gives Chelsea a 2-1 aggregate victory over Liverpool and a place in the Capital One Cup Final. Rangers agree a £10m loan from Newcastle owner Mike Ashley's Sports Direct company to ease the club's 'perilous' financial position.

28 Christian Eriksen's 88th minute goal gives Tottenham a 3-2 aggregate win over Sheffield United in the second semi-final. The FA fine Chelsea manager Jose Mourinho £25,000 for claiming there is a 'campaign' to influence referees' decisions against his team.

29 Sheffield Wednesday owner Milan Mandaric sells the club to Thai businessman Dejphon Chansiri for a reported £30m. The BBC pay £204m to retain Match of the Day highlights of Premier League matches for a further three years from 2016–17.

30 Diego Costa is banned for three games by the FA after being caught on camera stamping on Emre Can in Chelsea's win over Liverpool. Watford's Gabriele Angella is sent off for bringing down Callum Wilson after 28 seconds at Bournemouth. James Ward-Prowse signs a five-and-a-half-year contract with Southampton. Stoke's Robert Huth is banned for two matches and fined £15,000 by the FA for improper comments on social media.

31 On the 100th anniversary of the birth of the club's most famous player, Sir Stanley Matthews, Jon Walters scores a hat-trick in Stoke's 3-1 win over Queens Park Rangers.

FEBRUARY 2015

1 Nottingham Forest manager Stuart Pearce is sacked after a single victory in 11 league and cup games. Pearce, appointed in April 2014, is replaced by former Crystal Palace and Bolton manager Dougie Freedman. In the first 'Old Firm' derby for nearly three years – following the demise of Rangers – Celtic defeat their rivals 2-0 to set up a Scottish League Cup Final against Dundee United.

2 Chelsea are involved in the biggest deals on deadline-day for winter transfers – paying £23.3m for Fiorentina's Colombia winger Juan Cuadrado and selling Andre Schurrle to Wolfsburg for £22m. MK Dons receive a club record £5m for 18-year-old Dele Alli, who is loaned back by Tottenham for the remainder of the season. Spending by Premier League clubs totals £130m, matching the figure of 2014. Harry Kane signs a new five-and-a-half-year contract with Tottenham after scoring 20 goals in all competitions this season.

3 Harry Redknapp resigns as Queens Park Rangers manager after being told he needs surgery on both knees. Philippe Coutinho signs a new contract keeping him at Liverpool until 2020.

4 West Ham are fined £71,000 by FIFA for fielding Diafra Sakho in an FA Cup fourth round tie against Bristol City after telling the Senegal FA he was unfit to join their squad for the Africa Cup of Nations. Yeovil manager Gary Johnson is sacked with his side bottom of League One. The FA fine Millwall £6,000 and Bradford £3,000 for a players' melee during their FA Cup replay.

5 Kilmarnock manager Allan Johnston announces he will leave at the end of the season, following the club's decision to sell Robbie Muirhead to Dundee United, but goes immediately.

7 Gillingham appoint Newport's Justin Edinburgh as their new manager after agreeing compensation with the Welsh club.

8 Manchester City's Yaya Toure captains Ivory Coast to victory in the Africa Cup of Nations Final – a 9-8 penalty shoot-out after a goalless draw with Ghana.

9 The FA remind Leicester manager Nigel Pearson of his responsibilities, but take no disciplinary action over an incident in which he appeared to grab the throat of Crystal Palace midfielder James McArthur after being knocked over on the touchline. Leicester deny reports of Pearson's sacking and reinstatement.

10 The Premier League sell live TV rights for 2016–19 for £5.13bn – an increase of 71 per cent on the current deal. Sky pay £4.17bn for five of the seven packages and BT £960m for the two others. West Ham's James Tomkins signs a new contract through to 2020.

11 The Football Supporters' Federation call for top flight clubs to reduce ticket prices. Former Minister for Sport Richard Caborn urges club owners to commit more to grass-roots initiatives. Aston Villa manager Paul Lambert is sacked after his side fall into the relegation zone in the wake of ten games without a win and just two goals scored.

12 Danny Wilson is sacked by Barnsley, less than two months after his 1,000th game as a manager. Eden Hazard signs a new five-and-a-half-year contract with Chelsea worth a reported £200,000 a week. Branislav Ivanovic escapes FA action over a confrontation with James McCarthy in Chelsea's win over Everton.

13 Academy manager Chris Ramsey takes charge at Queens Park Rangers until the end of the season. Cheltenham dismiss Paul Buckle after 79 days and a single victory in his 13 matches as their manager.

14 Former Tottenham manager Tim Sherwood takes over at Villa Park.

15 Sunderland become Bradford's latest FA Cup victims, beaten 2-0 at Valley Parade in round five.

17 Brentford announce that manager Mark Warburton will leave at the end of the season – despite taking the club up from League One and challenging for a play-off place in the Championship.

18 Manchester United manager Louis van Gaal is warned about his future conduct by the FA over criticism of referee Chris Foy after the FA Cup tie at Cambridge.

19 Football League clubs receive a double financial boost – an extension of the broadcasting deal with Sky and a new agreement for a proportion of Premier League television money.

20 West Ham are fined £30,000 by the FA for misconduct by their players following the dismissal of goalkeeper Adrian against Southampton – a red card overturned on appeal. Sunderland manager Gus Poyet writes an open letter to supporters urging them to stay united as their team battles to avoid relegation.

21 Darren Ferguson is sacked for the second time as Peterborough manager, after his side fall into the bottom half of the table.

22 Coventry dismiss their manager, Steven Pressley, five months into a four-year contract, with his team in the relegation zone after failing to win in seven games.

23 The FA take no action against Burnley's Ashley Barnes for a tackle on Nemanja Matic which Chelsea manager Jose Mourinho calls 'criminal.'

24 A FIFA task force recommend that the 2022 World Cup in Qatar be moved from the summer to the winter for safety reasons. The Premier League warn of major disruption to domestic football. Nemanja Matic has his red card ban for retaliating reduced from three matches to two. Caretaker Jimmy Dack is appointed Newport manager until the end of the season.

25 Brighton are fined £90,000 for breaches of FA rules on agents relating to the purchase of Dale Stephens from Charlton. Agents Alex Levack, Matthew Kleinman and Ali Rahnama are suspended from transfer activities for various periods. UEFA fine Celtic £7,300 for crowd disturbances during their Europa League game against Dinamo Zagreb. Lee Johnson leaves Oldham to become Barnsley's new manager.

26 Everton are the only British side to reach the last 16 of the Europa League, defeating Young Boys 7-2 on aggregate, with Romelu Lukaku scoring five of their goals over the two legs. Liverpool lose on penalties to Besiktas, Tottenham are beaten 3-1 by Fiorentina and Celtic go down 4-3 to Inter Milan. Chelsea sign a five-year shirt sponsorship, worth £38m a year, with a Japanese company which manufactures tyres. Mark Noble signs a new contract with West Ham through to 2021.

27 UEFA fine Hull £145,000 for breaching Financial Fair Play rules. Liverpool are cleared.

28 The rule-making International FA Board, meeting in Belfast, put back a decision on introducing video technology to help referees for further consideration.

MARCH 2015

1 Jose Mourinho wins the first trophy of his second spell as Chelsea manager – a 2-0 victory over Tottenham in the Capital One Cup Final, with John Terry opening the scoring and Kyle Walker conceding an own goal.

2 Wes Brown wins an appeal against his sending-off by referee Roger East in Sunderland's game against Manchester United after TV replays show team-mate John O'Shea fouling Radamel Falcao. Chelsea and Everton are both fined £30,000 by the FA for misbehaviour by their players at Stamford Bridge. Francis Coquelin is rewarded for establishing a place in Arsenal's midfield with a new four-and-a-half-year contract.

3 Tony Mowbray, former Middlesbrough, Celtic and West Bromwich Albion manager, takes over at Coventry. Wigan owner Dave Whelan steps down as club chairman and hands the role to his 23-year-old grandson, David Sharpe. Crystal Palace captain Mile Jedinak is banned for four matches by the FA after being caught on camera elbowing West Ham's Diafra Sakho. Newcastle owner Mike Ashley is fined £7,500 by the Scottish FA for breaching 'dual ownership' rules with his involvement in Rangers.

4 Swansea's Bafetimbi Gomis collapses during the match against Tottenham at White Hart Lane – an echo of Fabrice Muamba's cardiac arrest there in 2012. The French striker is later given the all-clear in hospital.

5 Roy Hodgson is reported to have told the FA he wants to stay on as England manager after Euro 2016 and have another crack at the World Cup.

6 Papiss Cisse is banned for seven matches by the FA after admitting spitting at Jonny Evans

in Newcastle's game against Manchester United. A consortium headed by South Africa-based businessman Dave King takes control of Rangers.

7 Jonny Evans, who denies spitting at the Newcastle player, is banned for six games.

8 The FA begin an inquiry into pitch invasions, intimidation of players and seats ripped out at the FA Cup sixth round tie between Aston Villa and West Bromwich Albion.

9 Millwall manager Ian Holloway is sacked with his team second from bottom, eight points from safety. Coach Neil Harris takes over until the end of the season.

10 Hull manager Steve Bruce agrees a new three-year contract with the club.

11 Chelsea lose on away goals to ten-man Paris St-Germain in the last 16 of the Champions League.

12 Paul Paton, sent off in Dundee United's Scottish Cup tie against Celtic, has the red card quashed by the Scottish FA on the grounds of mistaken identity. Celtic's Virgil van Dijk also has his dismissal overturned, freeing both players to play in the teams' League Cup Final. West Ham's Carlton Cole is fined £20,000 by the FA for sending abusive comments to a Tottenham supporter on *Twitter*. Bournemouth's Harry Arter is banned for one game and fined £2,000 for misconduct after the game against Brentford.

13 Former Motherwell manager Stuart McCall takes over at Rangers until the end of the season, replacing caretaker Kenny McDowall.

15 Ronny Deila wins his first trophy as Celtic manager, his side beating Dundee United 2-0 in the League Cup Final with goals from Kris Commons and substitute James Forrest. Dundee have captain Sean Dillon sent off.

16 Gus Poyet is sacked following a 4-0 home defeat by Aston Villa which leaves Sunderland a point off the relegation zone. Former Holland manager Dick Advocaat is appointed until the end of the season.

17 Arsenal go out of the Champions League at the last-16 stage for the fifth successive season. They beat Monaco 2-0, but lose on away goals after a 3-1 defeat in the first leg at the Emirates. West Bromwich Albion's Chris Brunt is banned for one match and fined £8,000 by the FA for abusing a match official after the FA Cup defeat by Aston Villa.

18 Manchester City lose 3-1 on aggregate to Barcelona, leaving the Premier League without a team in the quarter-finals for the second time in three seasons.

19 Everton are beaten 6-4 on aggregate by Dynamo Kiev in the Europa League, leaving England without a side in a European quarter-final for the first time since the 1992–93 season. Louis van Gaal, manager of Manchester United, reveals the job will be his last in football.

20 FIFA's executive committee confirm a winter World Cup in Qatar in 2022, with the final taking place on Sunday, December 18 after a shortened tournament of 28 days.

21 There are two more cases of mistaken identity, West Bromwich Albion's Gareth McAuley is sent off by Neil Swarbrick after team-mate Craig Dawson fouls Manchester City's Wilfried Bony. Richard Clark dismisses Fulham's Cauley Woodrow for handball against Huddersfield, then changes his mind after protests and orders off Shaun Hutchinson.

22 Referees' chief Mike Riley calls for video technology to be trialled to help officials. Steven Gerrard is sent off 38 seconds after coming off the bench in his last game for Liverpool against arch-rivals Manchester United. Bristol City become the first club to win the Football League Trophy three times when beating Walsall 2-0 in front of a 72,000 crowd at Wembley. Hearts win the Scottish Championship title with seven matches still to play.

23 The FA transfer Gareth's McAuley red card to Craig Dawson. Notts County manager Shaun Derry is sacked with his side one place above the relegation zone.

24 FA chairman Greg Dyke's campaign for more home-grown players in the Premier League is backed by the president of UEFA, Michel Platini. Manchester United director David Gill is elected Britain's FIFA vice-president to succeed Northern Ireland's Jim Boyce.

25 Martin Skrtel is banned for three matches by the FA, on the basis of video evidence, for stamping on goalkeeper David de Gea in Liverpool's match against Manchester United.

26 Les Ferdinand, director of football at Queens Park Rangers, is fined £12,000 and banned from the touchline for one match by the FA for his behaviour towards a match official after the home defeat by Tottenham. Chelsea captain John Terry signs a new 12-month contract.

27 Tottenham's Harry Kane makes a dream debut for England, scoring with a header 79 seconds after coming off the bench in the European Championship qualifier against Lithuania. England win 4-0, with Raheem Sterling also on the mark for the first time for his country. Stoke manager Mark Hughes signs a new four-year-contract. The FA fine Hull £30,000 for failing to control their players against Leicester. Fulham are fined £20,000 for the same offence, against Leeds.

28 Gareth Bale scores twice and provides an assist for Aaron Ramsey as Wales go top of their group with a 3-0 away win over Israel.

29 Steven Fletcher nets Scotland's first hat-trick since Colin Stein's feat against Cyprus in 1969. His side win 6-1 against Gilbraltar, whose consolation is their first-ever competitive goal. Kyle Lafferty's brace gives Northern Ireland a 2-1 victory over Finland, while Shane Long earns the Republic of Ireland a 1-1 draw against Poland with a stoppage-time equaliser. North Ferriby, a village club on the banks of the Humber, retrieve a 2-0 deficit to hold FA Trophy Final favourites Wrexham to a 3-3 draw after extra-time, then win a penalty shoot-out 5-4.

30 Wrexham sack manager Kevin Wilkin following their defeat at Wembley, blaming a failure to challenge for promotion from the Conference. Gary Johnson, dismissed by League One's bottom club Yeovil, is appointed manager of Cheltenham, bottom of League Two, until the end of the season. Reading are given a suspended £30,000 fine for breaching Football League rules by borrowing from a company with an interest in three other clubs.

31 A spectacular strike by substitute Andros Townsend earns England a 1-1 draw in a friendly international in Turin. Newcastle post a record annual profit of £18.7m.

APRIL 2015

1 Liverpool's Raheem Sterling upsets his club with a TV interview in which says he is not ready to sign a new contract.

2 Brendan Rodgers, the Liverpool manager, says Sterling has two-and-a-half-years left on his present contract and insists he will not be joining another club in the summer.

3 Gary Locke is given the Kilmarnock manager's job on a permanent basis after two months as caretaker.

4 Stoke's Charlie Adam scores with a shot from inside his own half – measured at 66 yards – against Chelsea.

6 Malky Mackay is sacked after four-and-a-half-months as Wigan manager with his side on the brink of being relegated. Blackpool become the first Football League side to go down, with six Championship matches still to play. The Football Conference is renamed the National League.

7 Wigan appoint club captain Gary Caldwell to replace Malky Mackay. After initially turning down the job for family reasons, former Tottenham coach Ricardo Moniz agrees to become Notts County's new manager.

8 Blackburn and Liverpool finally settle their FA Cup replay after having to wait a month because of the international break and UEFA's insistence on Champions League games taking priority. The Premier League side win 1-0 to reach the semi-finals.

9 Four days after joining Torquay as an advisor, Paul Sturrock leaves to become manager of relegation-bound Yeovil – his eighth club.

10 Swindon's Raphael Branco is banned for three games by the FA after being caught on video elbowing Bristol City's former Swindon player Aden Flint.

11 Paul Sturrock's new team are relegated from League One with four fixtures remaining.

12 Saido Berahino is reprimanded by West Bromwich Albion after being shown on video inhaling nitrous oxide – laughing gas.

13 Andy Awford, who led Portsmouth away from the threat of relegation to the Conference in 2014, is sacked after failing to deliver a promotion challenge this season.

14 Bristol City are the first team to be promoted, following a 6-0 away win over Bradford in League One.

15 Dagenham midfielder Joss Labadie is banned for six months by the FA for biting Stevenage's

Ronnie Henry – 13 months after a ten-match ban for the same offence while playing for Torquay against Chesterfield. Joel Ward signs a contract extension with Crystal Palace through to the summer of 2018.

16 Six players are shortlisted for the PFA Player of the Year award – Diego Costa, Philippe Coutinho, David de Gea, Eden Hazard, Harry Kane and Alexis Sanchez. Liverpool's Raheem Sterling is reminded by the club of his professional responsibilities after being shown inhaling nitrous oxide.

17 Holders Arsenal beat Reading 2-1 in extra-time to reach FA Cup Final for a record 19th time. Falkirk defeat Hibernian 1-0 in the first Scottish Cup semi-final.

18 Liverpool lose 2-1 to Aston Villa in the second FA Cup semi-final, ending Steven Gerrard's hopes of a dream finale to his career at Anfield. Celtic's bid for the treble is dashed by a 3-2 extra-time defeat by Inverness after goalkeeper Craig Gordon is sent off early in the second-half. Bristol City win the League One title.

19 With Tranmere on the brink of dropping into the Conference, manager Micky Adams leaves the club by mutual consent.

20 Chris Smalling signs a new contract keeping him at Manchester United until 2019. Jon Moss is chosen to referee the FA Cup Final.

21 West Ham announce plans to cut season-ticket prices when moving to the Olympic Stadium in 2016.

22 Jordan Henderson signs a new five-year contract with Liverpool.

23 Aston Villa's Jack Grealish becomes another player to be spoken to by his club after being pictured inhaling nitrous oxide.

24 Rotherham, battling against relegation, are deducted three points and fined £30,000 – half which is suspended – by the Football League for fielding an ineligible player, Farren Rawson, in their win over Brighton.

25 A minute's silence is observed at all games to mark the 30th anniversary of the Bradford fire disaster in which 56 supporters died. Watford are promoted to the Premier League. Tranmere and Cheltenham are relegated from the Football League. Barnet return as Conference champions.

26 Chelsea's Eden Hazard is voted the PFA Player of the Year. Tottenham's Harry Kane wins the Young Player of the Year award.

27 Bournemouth, a club on the brink of folding in 2008, win promotion to the Premier League.

29 Caretaker Neil Harris is appointed Millwall's permanent manager, a day after the club are relegated.

30 Terry Butcher, former England captain and Hibernian manager, is appointed Newport's new manager.

MAY 2015

2 John Carver, Newcastle's interim manager, accuses Mike Williamson of deliberately getting himself sent off during the 3-0 defeat at Leicester – an allegation the player denies. Celtic are crowned Scottish champions for the fourth successive season. Bournemouth win the Championship title. Burton finish top of League Two. Blackpool's home game against Huddersfield is abandoned early in the second after a pitch invasion by supporters protesting against the club's owners.

3 Chelsea clinch the Premier League title with three matches remaining. Celtic's Stefan Johansen is named Scottish PFA Player of the Year. John Hughes (Inverness) is named Scotland's Manager of the Year.

4 Oldham appoint Sunderland coach Darren Kelly as their new manager.

5 Newcastle captain Fabricio Coloccini writes an open letter to supporters apologising for the failings of his relegation-threatened team. Relegated Tranmere name Gary Brabin, formerly in charge of Luton and Cambridge, as their new manager.

6 Graham Taylor denies claims in a new book that he was ordered by the FA to limit the number of black players he picked while England manager

7 Manchester United set up the summer's first major transfer – PSV Eindhoven's Holland winger Memphis Depay for £25m.

8 Lee Clark resigns as manager of relegated Blackpool. John Gregory steps down at Crawley after six months recuperating from heart surgery. St Mirren are relegated from the Scottish Premiership

9 Burnley are relegated after one season in the Premier League.

10 Paul Cook leaves Chesterfield to become Portsmouth's new manager. Jay Rodriguez signs a new contract through to 2019 with Southampton.

11 In the highest scoring match in the history of the play-offs, Swindon and Sheffield United draw 5-5. Swindon reach the final with a record aggregate score for the two legs of 7-6.

12 The Football Writers' Association choose Chelsea's Eden Hazard as their Footballer of the Year. The Scottish Professional Football League sign a £4m, two-year title sponsorship deal across all four divisions with betting company Ladbrokes.

13 Chesterfield appoint Dean Saunders, interim manager at Crawley last season, to succeed Paul Cook.

14 Aston Villa are fined £200,000 by the FA for a pitch invasion by supporters after their FA Cup quarter-final win over West Bromwich Albion. The Football League declare the abandoned Blackpool-Huddersfield game a goalless draw. Brad Friedel, 43, announces his retirement after a 21-year goalkeeping career with Liverpool, Blackburn, Aston Villa and Tottenham.

15 Jake Livermore, Hull's £8m midfield player, is suspended by the club after testing positive for cocaine.

16 Sadio Mane, Southampton's Senegalese winger, scores the fastest-ever Premier League hat-trick – in two minutes 56 seconds – against Aston Villa. Two other players are suspended for failing drug tests – Sheffield United midfielder Jose Baxter and Wolves goalkeeper Aaron McCarey.

17 Bristol Rovers return to the Football League at the first attempt, beating Grimsby 5-3 on penalties after the teams finish 1-1 in the Conference Play-off Final.

18 Chris Ramsey, Queens Park Rangers caretaker since Harry Redknapp's resignation, is given the job on a permanent basis.

19 Former Cheltenham manager Mark Yates takes charge at Crawley.

20 Former Brentford and Wigan manager Uwe Rosler replaces Neil Redfearn at Leeds. Celtic goalkeeper Craig Gordon is chosen Player of the Year by the Scottish football writers.

21 Former England striker Teddy Sheringham takes up his first manager's job, replacing Graham Westley at Stevenage. Jordon Ibe and Jon Flanagan sign contract extensions at Liverpool.

22 Dave Robertson is appointed Peterborough manager after three months as caretaker.

23 Southend beat Wycombe 7-6 on penalties after the League Two Play-off Final ends 1-1.

24 Hull are relegated from the Premier League. West Ham decide not to renew the contract of manager Sam Allardyce. Jermaine Beckford scores a hat-trick as Preston defeat Swindon 4-0 in the League One Play-off Final.

25 Norwich return to the Premier League at the first attempt, beating Middlesbrough 2-0 in the Championship Play-off Final. Steve McClaren is sacked by Derby, the 17th Championship club to have at least one change of manager during the season. Sheffield United's Nigel Clough is also dismissed for failing to win promotion.

26 The Football League announce that Capital One will withdraw sponsorship of the League Cup after the 2015–16 season.

27 Eddie Howe is named the League Managers' Association Manager of the Year for taking Bournemouth into the Premier League. Dick Advocaat declines an offer to stay on after leading Sunderland away from the threat of relegation. Sevilla beat the Ukraine side Dnipro 3-2 in the Europa League Final for a record fourth win in the competition.

28 Prime Minister David Cameron, UEFA president Michel Platini and FA chairman Greg Dyke call for the resignation of FIFA president Sepp Blatter after seven officials of the world governing body are among 14 people arrested on suspicion of bribery and corruption. Abel Hernandez is suspended by the FA for the first three matches of the new season after being caught on camera punching Phil Jones in Hull's match against Manchester United. Plymouth manager John Sheridan leaves the club by mutual consent after expressing a wish to return to the north of England. West Ham coach Ian Hendon is named Leyton Orient's new manager.

29 Sepp Blatter is re-elected at the FIFA congress and claims a 'hate' campaign against his organisation. Former Manchester United and England captain Rio Ferdinand retires after being released by Queens Park Rangers.

30 Arsenal win the FA Cup for a record 12th time, beating Aston Villa 4-0. The FA announce the competitions's first title sponsorship – a reported £30m, three-year deal with the Emirates airline. Inverness win the Scottish Cup for the first time, defeating Falkirk 2-1. David Gill refuses to take his place on FIFA's executive committee while Sepp Blatter remains president.

31 Former Real Madrid assistant coach Paul Clement succeeds Steve McClaren at Derby. Motherwell beat Rangers 6-1 on aggregate in the Scottish Premiership Play-off Final. Aaron Hughes becomes Northern Ireland's most capped outfield player when winning his 96th cap in a 1-1 draw with Qatar in a friendly international at Crewe. Stuart Dallas scores his first international goal for the Irish.

JUNE 2015

1 Marinus Dijkhuizen, coach of Dutch club Excelsior, is named Brentford's new manager. Gary Teale leaves relegated St Mirren by mutual consent.

2 Sepp Blatter bows to widespread pressure and resigns. Neil McDonald, former West Ham assistant, becomes Blackpool's new manager.

3 Dick Advocaat has a change of heart and decides to stay on and try to turn Sunderland into top-ten club.

4 FIFA are revealed to have paid the FA of Ireland more than £3m not to proceed with legal action over the infamous handball by France striker Thierry Henry which cost the Republic the chance of place in the 2010 World Cup Finals.

5 Slavisa Jokanovic, who led Watford into the Premier League, is unable to agree new terms with the club and is replaced by former Valencia and Atletico Madrid coach Quique Sanchez Flores. The Football League, at their summer meeting, agree to open up more opportunities for black, Asian or ethnic managers. Ipswich midfield player Teddy Bishop is fined £3,000 by the FA for breaching betting regulations.

6 Barcelona beat Juventus 3-1 in the Champions League Final in Berlin to complete a hat-trick of honours for the season, having won the La Liga title and the Spanish Cup.

7 England and the Republic of Ireland draw 0-0 in a friendly international in Dublin – the teams' first meeting there since 1995 when rioting fans forced the game to be abandoned.

8 Slaven Bilic, former Besiktas and Croatia coach, is appointed the new manager of West Ham, the club he played for between 1996-97.

9 Newcastle sack caretaker-manager John Carver and appoint Steve McClaren on a permanent basis. England lose 1-0 to France in their opening game of the Women's World Cup in Canada.

10 Blackpool chairman Karl Oyston is banned from all football activity for six weeks and fined £40,000 by the FA for replying to abuse with offensive text messages to a supporter. Former Ross County manager Derek Adams takes charge at Plymouth

11 Sheffield Wednesday sack manager Stuart Gray after his team's 13th place finish in the Championship.

12 A goal by Gareth Bale takes Wales closer to a place in Euro 2016. They beat Belgium 1-0 to go top of their group. Frank Lampard, winner of 106 England caps, and Swansea chairman Huw Jenkins are awarded an OBE in the Queen's Birthday Honours. Former England women's captain Casey Stoney gets an MBE. Jim Montgomery, famous for his double save for Sunderland in the 1973 FA Cup Final win over Leeds, receives a British Empire Medal.

13 An own goal by John O'Shea gives Scotland a 1-1 draw with the Republic of Ireland in Dublin. Northern Ireland share a goalless draw with Romania. England women beat Mexico 2-1 in their second match of the tournament with goals by Fran Kirby and Karen Carney.

14 Jack Wilshere scores two spectacular goals, his first for his country, as England maintain their 100 per cent qualifying record with a 3-2 away win over Slovenia. Wayne Rooney's 86th minute winner takes him to within one of Sir Bobby Charlton's all-time record of 49

15 Former Brentford manager Mark Warburton takes over at Rangers after Stuart McCall's short-term contract is not renewed. Chelsea announce plans for a new stadium at Stamford Bridge with a capacity of more than 60,000.

16 Manager Alex Neil signs an improved contract, the terms of which are not disclosed, after taking Norwich back into the Premier League. Fulham's Ryan Tunnicliffe is banned for the first two matches of the new season and fined £5,000 by the FA for posting a derogatory comment about the Championship Player of the Year, Patrick Bamford, on *Twitter*.

17 Jack Wilshere is fined £40,000 by the FA for singing offensive songs about Tottenham on Arsenal's open-top bus parade following their FA Cup victory. England women reach the last 16 by defeating Colombia 2-1 with goals from Karen Carney and Fara Williams from the penalty spot.

18 England lose 1-0 to Portugal in their opening match in the European Under-21 Championship Finals in the Czech Republic. Bilel Mohsni, banned for four games for kicking and punching Lee Erwin at the end of Rangers' Premiership play-off defeat by Motherwell, is given an extra three matches by the Scottish FA for 'excessive misconduct'.

19 Everton's Phil Jagielka signs a contract extension through to 2018. Stoke's Charlie Adam agrees a new one-year deal.

21 An 85th minute goal by Jesse Lingard gives England Under-21s a 1-0 victory over Sweden in their second match of the tournament.

22 England women reach the quarter-finals for the first time, coming from behind to defeat Sweden 2-1 with goals by Steph Houghton and Lucy Bronze. Recruitment group JPNG announce their takeover of League Two Hartlepool.

23 Liverpool sign Brazil striker Roberto Firmino from the German club Hoffenheim for £28m.

24 England lose 3-1 to Italy and go out of the Under-21 tournament, failing to reach the knock-out stage for the third successive time.

25 Promoted Bournemouth break their transfer record by paying £8m for Ipswich defender Tyrone Mings. Ray Wilkins returns to football as Tim Sherwood's assistant at Aston Villa.

28 Goals by Jodie Taylor and Lucy Bronze put England's women into the semi-finals with a 2-1 victory over hosts Canada in front of a 54,000 crowd in Vancouver.

29 Petr Cech joins Arsenal for £10m after 11 seasons and more than 400 appearances for Chelsea. Four players sign long-term contract extensions – Phil Jones (Manchester United) and Jeff Schlupp (Leicester) to 2019 and Aaron Cresswell (West Ham) and Luke Garbutt (Everton) to 2020.

30 Nigel Pearson, who led Leicester away from the threat of relegation against all the odds, is sacked, the club citing 'fundamental differences' with the manager. Carlos Carvalhal, former Sporting Lisbon and Besiktas coach, takes over at Sheffield Wednesday. Cardiff's Millennium Stadium is chosen for the 2017 Champions League Final. Swansea's James Demetriou is fined £700 by the FA for breaching betting rules.

JULY 2015

1 Lee Cattermole signs a new five-year contract with Sunderland.

2 England lose their World Cup semi-final in heartbreaking fashion, an own goal by Laura Bassett in the second minute of stoppage-time giving Japan a 2-1 victory.

3 Derby sign Hull's Tom Ince for a club record £4.75m. Manchester City have restrictions on their transfer spending and Champions League squad size lifted by UEFA. Radamel Falcao joins Chelsea from Monaco on loan after failing to gain a permanent move to Manchester United. Troy Deeney signs a new five-year contract with Watford.

4 An extra-time penalty by Fara Williams gives England their first victory in 21 meetings with Germany. A 1-0 win in the third-place play-off delivers the best performance by an England team since Bobby Moore lifted the World Cup in 1966.

5 Phil Neville, former Manchester United and Everton defender, becomes assistant manager of Valencia. Tottenham's Nabil Bentaleb signs a new five-year contract.

6 Watford break their transfer record with the £6m signing of Etienne Capoue from Tottenham.

7 James McArthur signs a new three-year contract with Crystal Palace.

ENGLISH TABLES 2014–2015

BARCLAYS PREMIER LEAGUE

		P	Home					Away					Gd	Pts
			W	D	L	F	A	W	D	L	F	A		
1	Chelsea	38	15	4	0	36	9	11	5	3	37	23	41	87
2	Manchester City	38	14	3	2	44	14	10	4	5	39	24	45	79
3	Arsenal	38	12	5	2	41	14	10	4	5	30	22	35	75
4	Manchester Utd	38	14	2	3	41	15	6	8	5	21	22	25	70
5	Tottenham	38	10	3	6	31	24	9	4	6	27	29	5	64
6	Liverpool	38	10	5	4	30	20	8	3	8	22	28	4	62
7	Southampton	38	11	4	4	37	13	7	2	10	17	20	21	60
8	Swansea	38	9	5	5	27	22	7	3	9	19	27	-3	56
9	Stoke	38	10	3	6	32	22	5	6	8	16	23	3	54
10	Crystal Palace	38	6	3	10	21	27	7	6	6	26	24	-4	48
11	Everton	38	7	7	5	27	21	5	4	10	21	29	-2	47
12	West Ham	38	9	4	6	25	18	3	7	9	19	29	-3	47
13	WBA	38	7	4	8	24	26	4	7	8	14	25	-13	44
14	Leicester	38	7	5	7	28	22	4	3	12	18	33	-9	41
15	Newcastle	38	7	5	7	26	27	3	4	12	14	36	-23	39
16	Sunderland	38	4	8	7	16	27	3	9	7	15	26	-22	38
17	Aston Villa	38	5	6	8	18	25	5	2	12	13	32	-26	38
18	Hull	38	5	5	9	19	24	3	6	10	14	27	-18	35
19	Burnley	38	4	7	8	14	21	3	5	11	14	32	-25	33
20	QPR	38	6	5	8	23	24	2	1	16	19	49	-31	30

Chelsea, Manchester City and Arsenal go into Champions League group stage; Manchester Utd into play-off round. Tottenham and Liverpool into Europa League group stage; Southampton into third qualifying round; West Ham into first qualifying round

Prize-money (league position): 1 £98.9m, 2 £98.5m, 3 £96.5m, 4 £96.7m, 5 £88.7m, 6 £92.7m, 7 £82.5m, 8 £80.5m, 9 £77.8m, 10 £77.3m, 11 £80.5m, 12 £76.3m, 13 £72.8m, 14 £71.6m, 15 £77.8m, 16 £69.8m, 17 £68.6m, 18 66.6m, 19 £65.3m, 20 £64.8m

Biggest win: Southampton 8 Sunderland 0

Highest aggregate score: Everton 3 Chelsea 6

Highest attendance: 75,454 (Manchester Utd v WBA)

Lowest attendance: 16,163 (QPR v Stoke)

Player of Year: Eden Hazard (Chelsea)

Manager of Year: Jose Mourinho (Chelseas)

Golden Boot: 26 Sergio Aguero (Manchester City)

Golden Glove: 14 clean sheets Joe Hart (Manchester City)

PFA Team of Year: De Gea (Manchester Utd), Ivanovic (Chelsea), Terry (Chelsea), Cahill (Chelsea), Bertrand (Southampton), Sanchez (Arsenal), Kane (Tottenham), Diego Costa (Chelsea)

Leading scorers (all competitions): 32 Aguero (Manchester City); 31 Kane (Tottenham); 25 Sanchez (Arsenal); 20 Berahino (WBA), Diego Costa (Chelsea), Lukaku (Everton); 19 Giroud (Arsenal), Hazard (Chelsea); 18 Austin (QPR); 16 Pelle (Southampton); 15 Benteke (Aston Villa); 14 Rooney (Manchester Utd); 13 Gerrard (Liverpool), Ulloa (Leicester); 12 Biram Diouf (Stoke), Sakho (West Ham), Silva (Manchester City); 11 Cisse (Newcastle), Mirallas (Everton), Sterling (Liverpool), Toure (Manchester City)

Also: 11 Bony (Manchester City – 9 for Swansea)

SKY BET CHAMPIONSHIP

		Home					Away						
	P	W	D	L	F	A	W	D	L	F	A	Gd	Pts
1 Bournemouth	46	13	7	3	48	25	13	5	5	50	20	53	90
2 Watford	46	14	4	5	48	22	13	4	6	43	28	41	89
3 Norwich	46	12	6	5	50	24	13	5	5	38	24	40	86
4 Middlesbrough	46	15	5	3	42	12	10	5	8	26	25	31	85
5 Brentford	46	12	6	5	46	28	11	3	9	32	31	19	78
6 Ipswich	46	15	5	3	40	18	7	7	9	32	36	18	78
7 Wolves	46	13	6	4	42	23	9	6	8	28	33	14	78
8 Derby	46	12	7	4	48	24	9	7	7	37	32	29	77
9 Blackburn	46	11	6	6	37	28	6	10	7	29	31	7	67
10 Birmingham	46	10	7	6	29	31	6	8	9	25	33	-10	63
11 Cardiff	46	10	5	8	31	30	6	9	8	26	31	-4	62
12 Charlton	46	9	9	5	32	27	5	9	9	22	33	-6	60
13 Sheffield Wed	46	5	11	7	16	20	9	7	7	27	29	-6	60
14 Nottm Forest	46	9	5	9	37	32	6	9	8	34	37	2	59
15 Leeds	46	8	6	9	22	24	7	5	11	28	37	-11	56
16 Huddersfield	46	8	8	7	34	34	5	8	10	24	41	-17	55
17 Fulham	46	9	5	9	36	38	5	5	13	26	45	-21	52
18 Bolton	46	9	8	6	35	27	4	4	15	19	40	-13	51
19 Reading	46	8	5	10	24	25	5	6	12	24	44	-21	50
20 Brighton	46	6	8	9	26	29	4	9	10	18	25	-10	47
21 Rotherham*	46	8	7	8	31	34	3	9	11	15	33	-21	46
22 Millwall	46	5	7	11	25	40	4	7	12	17	36	-34	41
23 Wigan	46	3	8	12	18	29	6	4	13	21	35	-25	39
24 Blackpool	46	4	7	12	18	35	0	7	16	18	56	-55	26

*3 pts deducted for ineligible player

Biggest win: Birmingham 0 Bournemouth 8
Highest aggregate score: Watford 7 Blackpool 2
Highest attendance: 33,381 (Middlesbrough v Brighton)
Lowest attendance: 8,317 (Millwall v Reading)
Player of Year: Patrick Bamford (Middlesbrough)
Manager of Year: Eddie Howe (Bournemouth)
Top league scorer: 27 Daryl Murphy (Ipswich)
PFA Team of Year: Westwood (Sheffield Wed), Francis (Bournemouth), Martin (Norwich), Keogh (Derby), Friend (Middlesbrough), Pritchard (Brentford), Sako (Wolves), Leadbitter (Middlesbrough), Ritchie (Bournemouth), Deeney (Watford), Murphy (Ipswich)
Leading scorers (all competitions): 27 Murphy (Ipswich); 23 Wilson (Bournemouth); 22 Gestede (Blackburn); 21 Deeney (Watford), Jerome (Norwich), Martin (Derby), Rhodes (Blackburn); 20 Ighalo (Watford); 19 Bamford (Middlesbrough), McCormack (Fulham); 17 Gray (Brentford), Kermorgant (Bournemouth); 16 Vydra (Watford); 15 Antonio (Nottm Forest), Assombalonga (Nottm Forest), Dicko (Wolves), Donaldson (Birmingham), Johnson (Norwich), Ritchie (Bournemouth), Sako (Wolves); 14 Pitman (Bournemouth), Wells (Huddersfield); 13 Leadbitter (Middlesbrough)
Also: 32 Afobe (Wolves – 19 for MK Dons); 30 Doyle (Cardiff – 25 for Chesterfield); 23 Sears (Ipswich – 14 for Colchester); 14 Jones (Cardiff – 1 for Bournemouth), Bent (Derby – 2 for Brighton)

SKY BET LEAGUE ONE

		P	W	D	L	F	A	W	D	L	F	A	Gd	Pts
				Home						Away				
1	Bristol City	46	16	5	2	48	17	13	7	3	48	21	58	99
2	MK Dons	46	16	3	4	60	19	11	7	5	41	25	57	91
3	Preston	46	13	9	1	43	21	12	5	6	36	19	39	89
4	Swindon	46	12	5	6	38	28	11	5	7	38	29	19	79
5	Sheffield Utd	46	10	7	6	35	24	9	7	7	31	29	13	71
6	Chesterfield	46	12	4	7	42	26	7	8	8	26	29	13	69
7	Bradford	46	8	6	9	26	33	9	8	6	29	22	0	65
8	Rochdale	46	11	3	9	36	29	8	3	12	36	37	6	63
9	Peterborough	46	10	5	8	27	26	8	4	11	26	30	-3	63
10	Fleetwood	46	8	9	6	28	27	9	3	11	21	25	-3	63
11	Barnsley	46	11	5	7	41	29	6	6	11	21	32	1	62
12	Gillingham	46	11	6	6	37	29	5	8	10	28	37	-1	62
13	Doncaster	46	7	6	10	24	29	9	7	7	34	33	-4	61
14	Walsall	46	8	8	7	28	24	9	8	7	22	30	-4	59
15	Oldham	46	8	8	7	32	34	6	7	10	22	33	-13	57
16	Scunthorpe	46	9	6	8	27	28	5	8	10	35	47	-13	56
17	Coventry	46	6	9	8	25	33	7	7	9	24	27	-11	55
18	Port Vale	46	8	5	10	31	31	7	4	12	24	34	-10	54
19	Colchester	46	7	4	12	30	36	7	6	10	28	41	-19	52
20	Crewe	46	8	7	8	21	28	6	3	14	22	47	-32	52
21	Notts Co	46	5	6	12	24	33	7	8	8	21	30	-18	50
22	Crawley	46	9	6	8	30	33	4	5	14	23	46	-26	50
23	Leyton Orient	46	5	6	12	30	34	7	7	9	29	35	-10	49
24	Yeovil	46	5	7	11	17	33	5	3	15	19	42	-39	40

Biggest win: MK Dons 7 Oldham 0
Highest aggregate score: Bristol City 8 Walsall 2
Highest attendance: 27,306 (Coventry v Gillingham)
Lowest attendance: 1,905 (Crawley v Fleetwood)
Player of Year: Joe Garner (Preston)
Manager of Year: Steve Cotterill (Bristol City)
Top league scorer: 25 Joe Garner (Preston)
PFA Team of Year: Fielding (Bristol City), Byrne (Swindon), Flint (Bristol City), Clarke (Preston), Bryan (Bristol City), Smith (Bristol City), Luongo (Swindon), Freeman (Bristol City), Alli (MK Dons), Doyle (Chesterfield), Garner (Preston).
Leading scorers (all competitions): 27 Garner (Preston); 22 Grigg (MK Dons), Henderson (Rochdale), Williams (Swindon); 21 McLeod (Crawley), Wilbraham (Bristol City); 20 Bradshaw (Walsall); 18 McDonald (Gillingham), Smith (Swindon); 17 Madden (Scunthorpe); 16 Alli (MK Dons), Vincenti (Rochdale); 15 Forte (Oldham); 14 Agard (Bristol City), Clarke (Bradford), Hourihane (Barnsley), Tyson (Doncaster); 13 Baxter (Sheffield Utd), Dagnall (Leyton Orient), Gallagher (Preston), Washington (Peterborough), Winnall (Barnsley)
Also: 22 Done (Sheffield Utd – 14 for Rochdale); 20 Beckford (Preston – 2 for Bolton)

SKY BET LEAGUE TWO

				Home				Away					
		P	W	D	L	F	A	W	D	L	F	A	Gd	Pts
1	Burton	46	16	4	3	34	13	12	6	5	35	26	30	94
2	Shrewsbury	46	17	4	2	43	11	10	4	9	24	20	36	89
3	Bury	46	14	3	6	33	20	12	4	7	27	20	20	85
4	Wycombe	46	10	7	6	30	25	13	8	2	37	20	22	84
5	Southend	46	12	8	3	25	9	12	4	7	29	29	16	84
6	Stevenage	46	15	3	5	37	23	5	9	9	25	31	8	72
7	Plymouth	46	13	6	4	34	14	7	5	11	21	23	18	71
8	Luton	46	13	4	6	37	19	6	7	10	17	25	10	68
9	Newport	46	9	7	7	30	25	9	4	10	21	29	-3	65
10	Exeter	46	8	8	7	30	29	9	5	9	31	36	-4	64
11	Morecambe	46	8	6	9	26	28	9	6	8	27	24	1	63
12	Northampton	46	13	2	8	39	27	5	5	13	28	35	5	61
13	Oxford	46	7	9	7	27	24	8	7	8	23	25	1	61
14	Dag & Red	46	9	3	11	30	26	8	5	10	28	33	-1	59
15	AFC Wimbledon	46	10	8	5	34	25	4	8	11	20	35	-6	58
16	Portsmouth	46	11	6	6	34	23	3	9	11	18	31	-2	57
17	Accrington	46	10	6	7	33	32	5	5	13	25	45	-19	56
18	York	46	5	10	8	16	21	6	9	8	30	30	-5	52
19	Cambridge	46	5	5	11	34	33	6	7	10	27	33	-5	51
20	Carlisle	46	9	5	9	35	37	5	3	15	21	37	-18	50
21	Mansfield	46	10	5	8	24	24	3	4	16	14	38	-24	48
22	Hartlepool	46	8	5	10	22	30	4	4	15	17	40	-31	45
23	Cheltenham	46	5	8	10	22	30	4	6	13	18	37	-27	41
24	Tranmere	46	5	7	11	26	34	4	5	14	19	33	-22	39

Biggest win: Cambridge 5 Carlisle 0, Shrewsbury 5 Bury 0
Highest aggregate score: Northampton 4 Accrington 5
Highest attendance: 17,558 (Portsmouth v Wimbledon)
Lowest attendance: 919 (Accrington v Burton)
Player of Year: Danny Mayor (Bury)
Manager of Year: Gareth Ainsworth (Wycombe)
Top league scorer: 19 Jamie Cureton (Dagenham)
PFA Team of Year: Bentley (Southend), Edwards (Burton), Goldson (Shrewsbury), McNulty (Luton), Coker (Southend), Mayor (Bury), Wallace (Portsmouth), Grimes (Exeter), Woods (Shrewsbury), Reid (Plymouth), Tubbs (Portsmouth)
Leading scorers (all competitions): 20 Cureton (Dagenham), Reid (Plymouth); 18 Richards (Northampton); 17 Collins (Shrewsbury), Wallace (Portsmouth); 16 Corr (Southend), Hylton (Oxford); 15 Akinfenwa (Wimbledon), Hayes (Wycombe); 14 Cullen (Luton), Nardiello (Bury); 13 Alessandra (Plymouth), Power (Tranmere); 12 Redshaw (Morecambe); 11 Dempsey (Carlisle), Ellison (Morecambe), O'Connor (Newport)
Also: 24 Tubbs (Portsmouth – 15 for Wimbledon)

BARCLAYS PREMIER LEAGUE RESULTS 2014–2015

	Arsenal	Aston Villa	Burnley	Chelsea	Crystal Palace	Everton	Hull	Leicester	Liverpool	Manchester City	Manchester Utd	Newcastle	QPR	Southampton	Stoke	Sunderland	Swansea	Tottenham	WBA	West Ham
Arsenal	–	5-0	3-0	0-0	2-1	2-0	2-2	2-1	4-1	2-2	1-2	4-1	2-1	1-0	3-0	0-0	0-1	1-1	4-1	3-0
Aston Villa	0-3	–	0-1	1-2	0-0	3-2	2-1	2-1	0-2	0-2	1-1	0-0	3-3	1-0	1-2	0-0	0-1	1-2	2-1	1-0
Burnley	0-1	1-1	–	1-3	2-3	1-3	1-0	0-1	0-1	1-0	0-0	1-1	2-1	1-0	0-0	0-0	0-1	0-0	2-2	1-3
Chelsea	2-0	3-0	1-3	–	1-0	1-0	2-0	2-0	1-1	1-1	1-0	2-0	2-1	1-3	2-1	3-1	4-2	3-0	2-0	2-0
Crystal Palace	1-2	0-1	2-3	1-2	–	0-1	0-2	2-0	3-1	2-1	1-2	1-1	3-1	1-3	1-1	1-3	1-0	2-1	0-2	1-3
Everton	2-2	3-0	1-0	3-6	2-3	–	1-1	2-2	0-0	1-1	3-0	3-0	3-1	1-0	0-1	0-2	0-0	0-1	0-0	2-1
Hull	1-3	1-0	2-2	2-3	0-1	2-0	–	0-1	1-0	2-4	0-0	0-3	5-1	1-0	0-1	1-1	0-1	1-2	0-0	2-2
Leicester	1-1	1-0	2-0	1-3	1-3	2-2	0-1	–	1-3	0-0	5-3	3-0	0-0	2-1	0-1	0-0	2-0	1-2	2-1	2-1
Liverpool	2-2	0-1	2-0	1-2	3-0	1-1	3-1	2-2	–	2-1	1-2	2-0	2-1	2-1	1-0	0-0	4-1	3-2	2-1	2-0
Manchester City	0-2	3-2	2-2	1-1	1-0	3-0	1-1	2-0	3-1	–	1-0	5-0	6-0	2-0	0-1	3-2	2-1	4-1	3-0	2-1
Manchester Utd	1-1	3-1	3-1	1-1	3-3	2-1	0-0	3-1	3-0	1-0	–	3-1	4-0	2-1	2-1	2-0	1-2	3-0	0-1	2-0
Newcastle	1-2	1-0	3-3	2-1	0-0	3-2	3-0	1-0	1-0	0-2	0-1	–	2-1	1-2	1-1	0-1	2-3	1-3	1-1	2-1
QPR	1-2	2-0	2-0	0-1	1-0	1-2	2-2	3-2	2-3	2-2	0-2	2-1	–	1-0	2-2	1-0	1-1	1-2	3-2	2-0
Southampton	2-0	6-1	0-1	1-2	1-2	3-0	0-1	2-0	0-2	0-3	1-2	4-0	2-1	–	1-0	8-0	0-1	2-2	0-0	1-3
Stoke	3-2	0-1	1-2	0-2	2-1	2-0	2-0	0-1	6-1	1-4	3-1	1-0	3-1	2-1	–	1-1	2-1	3-0	2-0	1-0
Sunderland	0-2	0-4	2-0	0-5	1-4	1-1	1-0	0-0	0-1	1-4	1-0	1-0	0-2	2-1	3-1	–	0-0	2-2	0-0	1-0
Swansea	2-1	1-0	1-0	5-3	1-1	1-1	3-1	2-0	0-1	2-4	1-0	2-2	4-0	0-1	2-0	1-1	–	3-2	3-0	2-0
Tottenham	2-1	1-0	2-1	3-0	2-1	2-1	2-0	4-3	0-3	0-1	2-2	0-2	1-4	1-0	1-2	2-1	3-2	–	0-1	2-2
WBA	0-1	1-0	4-0	3-0	2-2	0-2	1-0	2-3	0-0	1-3	0-0	1-2	1-2	1-0	1-1	2-2	2-0	0-3	–	1-1
West Ham	1-2	0-0	1-0	0-1	1-3	1-2	3-0	2-0	3-1	2-1	1-1	2-0	0-0	1-3	1-1	1-0	3-1	0-1	1-1	–

SKY BET CHAMPIONSHIP RESULTS 2014–2015

Home \ Away	Birmingham	Blackburn	Blackpool	Bolton	Bournemouth	Brentford	Brighton	Cardiff	Charlton	Derby	Fulham	Huddersfield	Ipswich	Leeds	Middlesbrough	Millwall	Norwich	Nottm Forest	Reading	Rotherham	Sheffield Wed	Watford	Wigan	Wolves
Birmingham	–	2-2	1-0	0-1	4-2	1-1	4-3	2-0	1-1	2-2	0-1	4-2	1-1	1-1	1-3	2-2	1-3	1-3	0-0	0-1	0-0	4-0	0-0	0-0
Blackburn	1-0	–	1-1	1-0	3-2	3-1	0-1	1-1	2-0	2-3	0-1	0-0	3-2	0-3	0-0	2-0	1-2	3-3	1-2	1-0	1-2	1-0	2-1	0-1
Blackpool	1-0	1-2	–	1-1	1-6	1-2	0-1	3-2	0-3	2-0	0-1	0-0	0-0	1-1	0-1	1-0	1-3	4-4	1-3	1-1	0-1	1-3	1-3	0-0
Bolton	0-1	1-1	1-1	–	1-2	3-1	1-0	1-1	0-3	0-2	3-1	1-0	0-0	1-1	1-2	2-2	1-3	4-4	1-2	3-0	0-1	3-4	3-1	2-2
Bournemouth	4-2	0-0	4-0	3-0	–	1-0	3-2	5-3	1-0	2-2	2-0	1-1	2-2	1-3	0-0	2-2	2-3	1-2	3-0	1-1	2-2	2-0	2-0	2-1
Brentford	1-1	3-1	0-1	2-2	3-1	–	3-2	1-2	1-1	2-0	2-1	4-1	2-4	2-0	1-5	3-0	0-1	2-2	1-2	1-0	2-2	0-2	3-0	4-0
Brighton	4-3	0-0	3-2	0-3	3-1	0-0	–	1-1	1-2	2-0	1-2	3-1	3-2	2-0	0-1	6-1	0-1	2-3	0-1	1-0	0-1	1-2	3-0	1-1
Cardiff	2-0	1-1	2-3	2-1	1-1	3-0	0-0	–	1-2	0-2	1-0	3-0	3-2	3-1	2-1	0-0	2-4	2-1	4-0	0-0	2-1	2-4	1-0	0-1
Charlton	1-1	1-3	3-0	4-1	2-0	1-1	0-1	1-1	–	3-2	1-1	0-2	0-1	0-2	0-3	3-2	2-3	1-2	2-1	3-0	2-1	2-4	1-0	1-1
Derby	2-2	0-1	1-1	2-0	1-5	1-1	0-1	1-1	3-2	–	5-1	4-1	1-2	2-0	4-3	0-1	2-3	1-2	2-1	1-1	3-2	0-5	2-2	5-0
Fulham	0-1	2-2	2-2	4-0	0-4	1-4	3-0	2-1	2-0	3-2	–	2-2	2-1	0-3	4-3	0-1	1-0	3-2	0-1	0-1	4-0	3-1	0-0	1-4
Huddersfield	4-2	2-2	4-2	1-5	1-0	1-1	1-1	0-0	1-1	0-1	5-1	–	2-1	0-3	1-2	2-1	0-1	3-2	0-0	0-0	4-0	1-0	0-2	2-1
Ipswich	1-1	1-0	3-1	1-0	1-0	1-1	2-0	2-1	3-0	2-4	1-1	2-2	–	4-1	1-2	1-0	0-1	2-1	1-2	2-1	1-1	1-0	0-2	1-1
Leeds	1-3	0-3	3-1	1-0	0-0	1-0	0-0	2-1	2-1	1-2	0-1	3-0	4-1	–	0-1	3-0	1-1	0-0	2-1	2-0	2-3	0-3	1-0	4-3
Middlesbrough	1-3	2-2	2-1	1-0	0-2	2-3	0-1	0-0	2-1	3-3	0-2	1-3	0-1	2-0	–	3-0	1-4	0-0	1-1	0-3	2-3	0-1	2-0	3-3
Millwall	2-2	3-1	4-0	2-1	2-3	1-2	3-3	2-1	0-1	3-3	4-2	5-0	2-0	1-1	1-5	–	1-1	3-1	3-2	2-1	0-2	1-1	1-2	2-0
Norwich	3-1	1-3	3-0	4-1	2-0	3-1	1-2	3-1	2-0	1-1	3-0	5-0	2-0	0-2	1-0	6-1	–	3-1	2-0	2-0	0-2	0-1	3-0	2-0
Nottm Forest	1-3	0-0	3-0	3-0	0-1	0-2	1-1	1-1	0-3	0-3	1-2	2-2	1-2	0-2	0-0	3-2	2-1	–	2-1	3-0	0-2	1-3	3-0	1-2
Reading	0-1	2-0	0-0	4-2	0-2	0-2	1-0	1-1	1-1	0-0	0-3	1-1	1-1	0-2	0-3	3-2	2-1	0-3	–	3-0	2-0	0-1	0-1	3-3
Rotherham	0-1	2-0	1-1	0-1	1-1	0-2	2-1	1-0	1-1	0-0	1-1	2-2	2-1	1-1	0-3	2-1	2-0	0-0	2-1	–	1-0	2-4	1-2	1-0
Sheffield Wed	0-0	1-0	1-0	1-2	0-2	0-1	1-1	5-0	1-1	0-0	0-1	1-1	0-1	4-1	2-0	1-0	0-3	0-1	2-1	3-0	–	2-3	1-1	1-0
Watford	0-0	1-0	7-2	3-0	1-1	2-1	1-1	0-1	1-1	2-0	1-0	4-2	0-1	4-1	2-0	3-1	1-2	2-2	4-1	3-0	1-1	–	2-1	0-1
Wigan	4-0	1-1	1-0	1-0	1-3	0-0	2-1	0-1	0-3	0-2	3-3	0-1	1-2	1-1	1-1	0-1	0-1	0-0	2-2	1-2	0-1	0-2	–	2-2
Wolves	0-0	3-1	2-0	1-2	1-2	3-0	1-1	0-1	1-1	2-0	3-0	1-3	1-1	4-3	2-0	4-2	2-0	0-3	1-0	5-0	3-0	2-2	2-2	–

SKY BET LEAGUE ONE RESULTS 2014–2015

	Barnsley	Bradford	Bristol City	Chesterfield	Colchester	Coventry	Crawley	Crewe	Doncaster	Fleetwood	Gillingham	Leyton Orient	MK Dons	Notts Co	Oldham	Peterborough	Port Vale	Preston	Rochdale	Scunthorpe	Sheffield	Swindon	Walsall	Yeovil
Barnsley	–	3-1	2-2	1-1	3-2	1-0	0-1	2-0	1-1	1-2	4-1	2-0	3-5	2-3	1-0	1-1	2-1	1-1	5-0	1-2	0-2	0-3	3-0	2-0
Bradford	1-0	–	0-6	0-1	1-1	3-2	1-0	2-0	1-2	2-2	1-0	3-1	2-1	2-1	2-0	0-1	2-1	0-3	1-2	2-1	0-2	1-2	3-0	1-3
Bristol City	2-2	2-2	–	0-1	0-0	0-0	3-0	3-0	3-0	2-2	2-0	0-0	2-1	4-0	1-0	0-1	3-1	0-1	1-2	2-0	1-3	8-2	2-0	2-1
Chesterfield	2-1	0-1	0-2	–	6-0	2-3	3-0	1-0	2-2	3-0	3-0	2-3	0-1	1-1	1-1	3-2	3-0	2-1	2-1	4-1	3-2	0-3	1-0	0-0
Colchester	3-1	0-0	3-2	2-1	–	0-1	2-3	2-3	0-1	2-1	1-2	2-0	0-1	0-1	2-2	1-3	1-2	1-0	1-4	2-2	2-3	1-1	0-2	2-0
Coventry	2-2	1-3	1-3	1-1	0-1	–	2-2	2-3	1-3	2-1	1-2	0-1	0-1	0-1	1-1	1-3	2-3	1-3	2-2	1-1	1-0	0-3	0-0	2-0
Crawley	5-1	1-3	1-2	1-1	0-0	1-2	–	2-2	0-5	1-0	1-2	0-1	2-2	2-0	2-0	0-2	2-1	0-4	0-4	1-2	1-1	1-1	0-0	2-0
Crewe	1-2	0-1	1-0	1-1	0-0	1-2	1-1	–	1-1	2-0	3-1	1-0	0-5	0-3	2-0	1-4	2-1	2-1	2-5	2-0	2-2	0-0	1-1	1-0
Doncaster	1-0	0-3	1-3	3-2	1-0	1-3	2-1	2-1	–	1-2	2-1	0-2	0-0	0-0	0-2	0-2	1-3	0-4	2-2	5-2	0-1	0-2	0-2	3-0
Fleetwood	0-0	3-3	3-3	1-2	2-2	0-0	3-1	0-0	3-1	–	1-0	1-1	0-3	0-0	0-2	1-1	0-0	1-3	1-0	0-3	2-2	2-2	0-0	4-0
Gillingham	0-1	1-0	1-3	0-1	1-1	1-0	1-1	2-0	3-1	0-1	–	3-2	4-2	3-1	3-2	2-1	2-2	0-2	1-0	1-4	2-0	2-2	0-0	2-0
Leyton Orient	0-0	0-2	1-3	2-3	2-2	1-3	4-1	4-1	1-1	0-1	3-3	–	0-0	4-1	3-0	0-2	0-1	0-2	2-3	1-4	2-1	1-2	0-3	0-2
MK Dons	2-0	1-2	1-2	6-0	6-0	5-3	2-0	6-1	3-0	4-2	4-2	6-1	–	4-1	3-0	3-0	3-1	1-3	2-2	2-0	2-2	2-1	0-3	5-1
Notts Co	2-3	1-1	1-2	0-1	0-0	0-0	1-1	1-1	1-1	1-1	1-2	6-1	0-1	–	7-0	0-0	1-1	1-3	1-0	2-2	1-2	0-3	0-1	1-1
Oldham	1-0	2-0	1-0	1-1	2-2	1-1	2-0	2-0	0-1	0-2	2-1	3-0	0-0	0-0	–	3-0	1-1	1-1	2-3	2-2	2-1	0-0	1-0	3-0
Peterborough	2-1	0-3	1-0	1-0	1-2	1-0	4-3	3-0	3-0	1-2	0-0	3-0	3-2	0-0	0-2	–	3-1	0-1	2-1	1-2	2-1	1-2	0-3	1-0
Port Vale	2-1	1-2	0-3	1-2	0-2	2-3	2-3	0-5	0-1	2-2	2-2	0-0	0-2	0-2	2-1	0-1	–	0-1	1-0	2-0	2-1	1-1	1-1	4-0
Preston	1-0	1-2	3-3	1-2	4-2	1-1	2-0	2-1	2-2	0-2	2-0	1-1	1-1	1-1	1-0	2-0	3-0	–	1-0	2-0	1-1	3-0	1-1	3-0
Rochdale	1-3	1-1	1-1	3-3	1-0	2-0	2-1	2-1	1-0	3-0	3-0	2-0	2-3	1-1	1-0	2-0	1-0	3-0	–	3-1	4-0	2-4	0-1	2-1
Scunthorpe	0-1	0-2	0-2	1-0	2-1	0-1	4-1	4-0	1-3	2-0	2-1	1-0	2-3	2-2	1-1	2-0	1-0	3-0	3-1	–	3-1	3-1	1-0	2-1
Sheffield	0-1	1-1	1-2	2-0	2-0	1-1	2-1	2-1	3-2	0-2	2-1	1-2	1-2	1-1	1-1	2-0	1-1	0-4	2-1	4-0	–	2-0	1-1	1-1
Swindon	2-0	2-1	1-0	3-1	1-1	2-1	1-2	2-0	0-1	0-3	0-3	2-2	0-3	3-0	2-2	0-0	1-0	1-0	2-3	0-3	5-2	–	3-3	2-0
Walsall	3-1	0-0	1-1	0-0	0-1	1-1	5-0	0-1	3-0	1-0	3-1	3-1	1-4	2-2	2-0	0-2	3-1	0-2	3-2	1-4	1-1	1-4	–	1-2
Yeovil	1-1	2-3	0-3	2-3	2-0	0-0	1-1	1-0	0-3	0-1	2-2	0-2	2-1	2-1	2-1	2-1	0-2	0-1	0-3	1-1	1-1	1-1	0-1	–

SKY BET LEAGUE TWO RESULTS 2014-2015

	AFC Wimbledon	Accrington	Burton	Bury	Cambridge	Carlisle	Cheltenham	Dag & Red	Exeter	Hartlepool	Luton	Mansfield	Morecambe	Newport	Northampton	Oxford	Plymouth	Portsmouth	Shrewsbury	Southend	Stevenage	Tranmere	Wycombe	York
AFC Wimbledon	–	2-1	3-0	3-2	1-2	1-3	1-1	1-0	4-1	1-2	3-2	0-1	1-1	2-0	2-2	0-0	1-1	0-2	2-2	0-0	2-3	2-2	0-0	2-1
Accrington	1-0	–	1-0	0-1	0-1	3-1	1-1	1-2	2-3	3-1	2-2	2-1	2-1	0-2	1-5	1-0	1-1	2-3	1-2	0-1	2-1	3-2	1-1	2-2
Burton	0-0	3-0	–	3-1	1-3	1-1	0-1	1-2	1-0	4-0	1-0	2-1	0-2	0-2	3-1	1-0	1-0	1-1	1-0	0-1	1-1	0-0	1-1	2-0
Bury	2-0	2-1	3-1	–	2-0	2-1	0-1	0-2	1-0	0-1	1-0	2-0	0-2	1-3	2-1	0-1	2-1	3-0	0-0	0-1	2-1	1-0	1-1	2-2
Cambridge	0-0	2-2	2-3	0-2	–	5-0	1-2	1-1	1-2	2-1	1-0	3-1	1-2	4-0	2-1	5-1	1-0	2-6	0-0	1-1	1-1	1-2	2-3	0-3
Carlisle	4-4	1-0	3-4	0-3	5-0	–	0-0	1-1	1-3	3-3	0-1	3-1	1-1	2-3	2-1	1-1	0-3	2-2	1-2	1-1	3-0	1-2	1-4	0-3
Cheltenham	1-1	2-0	1-3	1-0	2-1	0-0	–	3-1	1-3	4-0	1-2	1-1	1-1	2-3	3-2	1-1	2-0	2-2	1-2	1-1	3-0	2-0	2-3	0-3
Dag & Red	4-0	4-0	1-3	1-0	2-3	4-2	3-1	–	1-2	2-0	0-0	1-1	0-3	2-3	0-2	0-0	2-0	2-1	3-2	1-3	0-1	0-1	1-4	0-1
Exeter	3-2	1-2	1-1	2-1	2-2	2-0	1-0	–	–	1-2	1-1	1-2	1-0	2-2	0-2	1-1	3-2	1-0	3-2	0-1	0-1	1-2	0-1	2-0
Hartlepool	1-0	2-0	0-1	1-1	0-3	0-3	1-0	0-2	2-1	–	1-2	1-1	1-0	2-2	0-2	3-0	1-3	0-1	1-2	0-1	0-0	0-0	1-4	0-1
Luton	0-1	1-0	2-0	0-1	1-0	1-0	1-0	–	2-1	3-0	–	3-0	0-2	2-2	1-0	0-0	1-3	2-0	0-0	0-1	1-3	1-0	1-3	2-0
Mansfield	2-1	0-1	1-2	0-1	3-2	0-1	1-2	0-2	2-3	1-1	1-0	–	1-0	3-0	0-2	2-0	1-0	1-2	0-1	1-2	2-0	1-0	0-3	1-4
Morecambe	1-1	1-1	1-2	1-0	0-2	0-1	0-2	0-1	0-1	3-0	3-0	2-1	–	3-2	0-1	2-1	0-0	3-1	1-4	3-1	2-0	0-0	0-3	1-1
Newport	2-0	4-1	1-1	2-3	0-2	2-1	1-0	1-0	2-3	1-1	2-1	0-1	0-1	–	3-2	0-1	2-0	2-0	1-1	1-1	2-0	0-1	0-2	3-1
Northampton	2-0	4-5	1-2	2-0	0-2	0-2	1-0	4-0	1-0	5-1	2-1	3-0	3-0	1-0	–	1-3	2-3	0-1	1-1	1-1	2-0	1-1	2-3	3-0
Oxford	0-0	3-1	0-1	2-1	2-0	0-1	1-2	3-0	2-2	0-2	1-1	1-1	1-1	1-0	1-0	–	0-0	0-0	0-2	2-3	0-0	2-0	1-2	0-0
Plymouth	1-1	1-1	1-1	0-2	3-0	3-0	3-0	1-0	3-0	2-0	0-1	2-1	3-0	1-0	0-0	1-2	–	0-3	0-2	2-1	3-0	2-0	1-2	1-1
Portsmouth	0-2	2-3	1-1	1-0	2-1	3-0	2-2	3-0	1-0	1-1	0-1	1-1	3-0	0-1	2-0	0-0	3-1	–	0-2	1-2	3-2	3-2	2-3	1-1
Shrewsbury	2-0	4-0	1-0	5-0	1-1	1-1	3-1	2-0	4-0	3-0	2-0	2-0	2-1	0-0	2-0	2-0	2-0	2-1	–	1-1	3-2	2-1	0-0	1-0
Southend	0-1	1-2	0-0	1-1	0-0	1-0	2-0	2-0	1-1	3-0	1-2	2-0	0-1	2-1	2-0	1-1	0-0	2-0	1-1	–	2-0	1-0	1-0	2-3
Stevenage	2-1	2-1	1-0	0-0	3-2	1-0	2-3	2-3	0-2	1-0	1-2	2-1	2-1	2-1	2-1	0-1	1-0	1-0	1-0	4-2	–	0-0	2-3	2-0
Tranmere	1-1	3-0	1-4	0-0	1-0	0-2	2-3	1-1	2-1	1-1	3-1	0-0	2-1	0-0	2-1	0-3	0-1	3-1	2-1	1-2	–	–	1-2	1-1
Wycombe	2-0	2-2	1-3	0-0	1-0	2-3	1-0	0-2	0-1	1-4	1-0	2-1	0-1	1-2	1-1	2-3	0-2	0-2	1-0	4-1	2-2	0-2	–	1-0
York	2-3	1-0	1-1	0-1	2-2	0-0	1-0	0-1	2-0	0-1	0-0	1-1	2-1	1-1	1-1	0-1	0-0	0-0	0-1	2-3	0-2	2-0	0-0	–

HOWE STRIKES GOLD AT THE GOLDSANDS

Rags-to-riches stories are rare in football, but the rise of Bournemouth certainly belongs in that category. Seven years ago, their very existence was under threat, not only through a deduction of 17 points imposed by the Football League, but with the bailiffs at the door. Their League status was preserved with victory in the season's last three matches; the club were saved from extinction by bucket collections at the ground and by Jeff Mostyn writing a cheque for £100,000. Two years later, Russia billionaire Maxim Demin, whose petrochenicals business is based in Surrey, bought into the club – and the rise up the football pyramid began.

As a boy of ten, Eddie Howe cheered on the team from the Dean Court terraces. He went on to play for them and in January 2009 became the League's youngest manager at 31. In January 2011, Burnley paid £300,000 compensation to engage him and it cost Bournemouth £1.4m to get him back in October 2012 when they stood 21st in League One. Six months later, they won promotion. On April 27 this year, a 3-0 home win over Bolton completed the rise from rock bottom to the Premier League with its £120m jackpot and with Mostyn a proud chairman. Another 3-0 victory five days later at Charlton confirmed promotion as champions.

Under Howe, it was a third promotion in six seasons – 2010, 2013, 2015. In the darkest days of 2008, when players and staff went unpaid and the club were so close to being wound up, nobody could have imagined that seven years later the likes of Chelsea, Arsenal, Manchester United and Liverpool would have a place in their fixture list. They are the smallest club the Premier League has known. The name changed from Bournemouth & Boscombe Athletic to AFC Bournemouth in 1972 and the prefix puts them alphabetically top of the Premier League membership, displacing Arsenal. Dean Court has been home since 1910. Now the restructured Goldsands Stadium, its capacity is 12,000 all-seated, compared with the all-time attendance record of 28,799 for an FA Cup sixth round tie against Manchester United in March, 1957. It is largely a 'family club' with most of the backroom staff former Bournemouth players. Howe, who thoroughly deserved the accolade of League Managers' Association Manager of the Year, insists the passing game that has taken his side to the top division of English football is practised at all levels from juniors upwards. While he has been busy through the close season preparing for life among the elite, there has been plenty of activity in the camp, with undersoil heating installed to comply with Premier League rules and the press box moved and expanded. Jamie Redknapp, who began his career at the club in seasons 1989–91, believes Howe could achieve a lot more in the game. 'He is responsible for a dynamic team full of hungry players and I wonder if we are seeing an England manager in the making.' – **Albert Sewell**

EDDIE HOWE – FACT FILE

Born: 29.11.77
Birthplace: Amersham; **Height:** 5ft 11
Playing position: Defender
1995: Made his senior debut for Bournemouth against Hull
1998: Selected for England's under-21 squad for the Toulon Tournament
2002: Signed by Harry Redknapp for Portsmouth for £400,000
2004: Loaned to Swindon and back to Bournemouth. Rejoined Bournemouth permanently
2006: Promoted to player-coach by manager Kevin Bond
2007: Forced to retire from playing with a knee injury
2008: Lost his job when Bond was sacked. Returned as youth coach under Jimmy Quinn
2009: Appointed manager after Quinn's dismissal and preserved Bournemouth's Football League status – despite a deduction of 17 points
2010: Won promotion from League Two as runners-up to Notts County
2011: Appointed manager of Burnley
2012: Left Burnley citing 'personal reasons' and returned in charge of Bournemouth
2013: Won promotion to the Championship as runners-up to Doncaster
2015: Won promotion to the Premier League as champions and named League Managers' Association Manager of the Year

HIGHLIGHTS OF THE PREMIER LEAGUE SEASON 2014–15

AUGUST 2014

16 Manchester United, under new manager Louis van Gaal and with Wayne Rooney as their new captain, lose at home on the opening day of a Premier League season for the first time. They go down 2-1 to Swansea, for whom Ki Sung-yueng scores his first goal for the club after a season on loan on at Sunderland and Gylfi Sigurdsson marks his return after two years at Tottenham with the winner. Two other debut managers enjoy better fortunes. Mauricio Pochettino's new Spurs signing, Eric Dier, nets the only goal at Upton Park in stoppage-time. His side lose Kyle Naughton to a straight red card for conceding a penalty, which Mark Noble misses, and West Ham also go down to ten men when James Collins is shown a second yellow. Alan Irvine, at West Bromwich Albion, opens with a 2-2 draw against Sunderland, courtesy of two goals from Saido Berahino, one from the spot. Leicester's record signing, Leonardo Ulloa, is on the mark in a 2-2 draw with Everton, who have Aiden McGeady on the scoresheet for the first time. Another promoted side, Queens Park Rangers, pay the price for Charlie Austin's penalty being saved by Allan McGregor, losing at home to the only goal from Hull's James Chester. Brede Hangeland makes a scoring debut for Crystal Palace, who have coach Keith Millen in charge following the departure of Tony Pulis 48 hours earlier. But they lose Jason Puncheon to a second booking and fall 2-1 to Aaron Ramsey's strike in added time for Arsenal.

17 Manchester City open their title defence with a 2-0 success at Newcastle, rounded off by substitute Sergio Aguero in time added on, while runners-up Liverpool overcome Southampton 2-1 with a 79th minute winner from Daniel Sturridge.

18 Chelsea come from behind to win 3-1 away to the third promoted side, Burnley, helped by a debut goal from Diego Costa.

23 Arsenal pass another test of their powers of recovery at Everton, where Aaron Ramsey (83) and substitute Olivier Giroud (90) transform a 2-0 deficit into a point gained. Mauro Zarate marks his West Ham debut in style with a fine volleyed goal in a 3-1 success away to Crystal Palace, while Nathan Dyer celebrates his 100th Premier League appearance for Swansea with the only goal against Burnley. Newcastle's Mike Williamson is sent off for a second booking in the goalless draw at Villa Park.

24 Harry Redknapp's return to White Hart Lane is an unhappy one as Queens Park Rangers lose 4-0 to Tottenham, with the second of Nacer Chadli's goals involving a build-up of 48 passes. Jack Rodwell opens his account for Sunderland in a 1-1 draw against Manchester United, while Hull and Stoke share the same scoreline. The home side resist strongly after James Chester receives a straight red card and are unlucky when Ryan Shawcross's equaliser in the 83rd minute stems from a throw-in wrongly given against them.

25 In the first 'heavyweight' match of the season, a brace by Stevan Jovetic and a strike by Sergio Aguero 23 seconds after coming off the bench deliver Manchester City's 3-1 victory over Liverpool.

30 Diego Costa launches an early contender for match of the season with a goal after 35 seconds at Goodison Park, then rounds off Chelsea's 6-3 win over Everton with a second in the 90th minute. In between, there are five goals in the space of 11 second-half minutes, including one by substitute Samuel Eto'o with his first touch on his debut for the home side. Neil Warnock's first match of a second spell as Crystal Palace manager delivers another feast of goals after Dwight Gayle's opener for his team with just 29 seconds gone at St James' Park. Daryl Janmaat, 18-year-old Rolando Aarons and Mike Williamson are on the mark for the first time for Newcastle. But Wilfried Zaha, back at Palace on loan, has the final say in the fifth minute of stoppage-time to secure a 3-3 scoreline. Mame Biram Diouf also opens his account to give Stoke a notable 1-0 win over Manchester City, finishing off an 80-yard run to end his new club's run of 12 successive away defeats by the two Manchester sides. Morgan Schneiderlin matches his tally for the whole of the 2013-14 season with a brace in Southampton's 3-1 success at West Ham, while Nathan Dyer nets twice as Swansea defeat West Bromwich Albion 3-0.

31 Steven Gerrard overtakes Jan Molby's record of 42 successful penalties and Alberto Moreno scores a fine, individual first goal for the club as Liverpool win 3-0 at Tottenham. Chelsea and Swansea boast the only 100 per cent records after the opening three matches.

SEPTEMBER 2014

13 Diego Costa's hat-trick in Chelsea's 4-2 victory over Swansea makes him the first player to score seven goals in his first four Premier League appearances. Loic Remy comes off the bench for his first appearance for the club to complete the scoring. Southampton also hit four, without reply, to increase the pressure on Newcastle manager Alan Pardew, Graziano Pelle netting two of them. One is enough for Aston Villa to continue a successful run against Liverpool at Anfield, with Gabriel Agbonlahor, fresh from signing a new four-year contract, making it eight points accumulated from their last four visits. And one would probably have been sufficient for Burnley at Crystal Palace had Julian Speroni not been equal to Scott Arfield's 84th minute penalty. Romelu Lukaku also has a day to remember in Everton's 2-0 success away to West Bromwich Albion, with his first Premier League goal for a club that owns him after scoring 32 during loan spells with the two teams. In the day's big match, a Martin Demichelis header seven minutes from the end of normal time earns Manchester City a 2-2 draw at Arsenal.

14 Record signing Angel di Maria scores on his home debut and has a hand in three more goals as Manchester United overcome Queens Park Rangers 4-0. Ander Herrera is also on the mark for the first time in Louis van Gaal's first competitive win as manager.

15 Abel Hernandez, Hull's record buy, and Mohamed Diame mark their debuts with a goal each in a 2-2 draw with West Ham, for whom Enner Valencia scores for the first time.

20 Four players score for the first time for their clubs. Danny Welbeck nets the second of three Arsenal goals in the space of four first-half minutes which deliver a 3-0 away success against Aston Villa; substitute Victor Wanyama maintains Southampton's impressive start to the season with the only one at Swansea, who have Wilfried Bony sent off for a second booking; Morgan Amalfitano also comes off the bench to complete West Ham's 3-1 victory over Liverpool; Steven Caulker is on the mark for Queens Park Rangers, who share four goals with Stoke. Alan Pardew is facing another defeat when Newcastle trail Hull 2-0, but he brings on Papiss Cisse for his first appearance of the season after injury and the substitute scores twice to secure a point.

21 Manchester United are back in the doldrums after surrendering a two-goal lead for the first time in the Premier League and losing 5-3 at Leicester. Jamie Vardy, a non-league player two years ago, rounds off his side's comeback after having a hand in all their other goals, one of which is Esteban Cambiasso's first for the club. A straight red card for Tyler Blackett compounds United's woes. On one of the most eventual days of the whole season, on-loan Frank Lampard's 85th minute strike gives ten-man Manchester City a 1-1 draw against his former club Chelsea after Pablo Zabaleta's second yellow card. Alan Irvine celebrates his first league win as West Bromwich Albion manager, courtesy of the only goal of the game from James Morrison at Tottenham, while Fraizer Campbell's first for Crystal Palace comes in another surprise away win – 3-2 against Everton.

27 Wayne Rooney puts Manchester United on the way to a 2-1 win over West Ham and moves into third place in the all-time Premier League scoring list behind Alan Shearer and Andrew Cole. Rooney is then shown a straight red card for hacking down Stewart Downing. Also sent off, for two yellow cards, is Swansea's Angel Rangel in a goalless draw at Sunderland. The two big derby matches end 1-1. At Anfield, both captains are on the mark. Steven Gerrard's free-kick puts Liverpool ahead and Phil Jagielka levels in stoppage-time with an early contender for goal of the season – a 25-yard volley. At the Emirates, Nacer Chadli's opener for Tottenham is cancelled out for Arsenal by Alex Oxlade-Chamberlain. Chelsea end the month on top after beating Aston Villa 3-0. They are three points ahead of Southampton, who maintain their best start to a Premier League season by defeating Queens Park Rangers 2-1, with on-loan Ryan Bertrand scoring his first goal for the club. Frank Lampard's goal in Manchester City's 4-2 success at Hull is his fourth in a week in league and cup games.

28 Craig Dawson opens his account for West Bromwich Albion in a 4-0 victory over Burnley, who are goalless for the fifth successive time.

OCTOBER 2014

4 Steven Fletcher scores twice and lays one on for Connor Wickham as Sunderland register their first victory of the season – 3-1 against Stoke. Papiss Cisse also nets a brace as Newcastle twice come from behind for a 2-2 draw at Swansea. Burnley do the same at Leicester to end their goal drought, their second equaliser from substitute Ross Wallace coming in the 96th minute. Adam Lallana gets off the mark for Liverpool in a 2-1 win over West Bromwich Albion, while Manchester City finally break Aston Villa's resistance through Yaya Toure (82) and Sergio Aguero (88).

5 Arsene Wenger pushes Jose Mourinho in a touchline confrontation between the two managers during Chelsea's 2-0 win over Arsenal earned by Eden Hazard's penalty and Diego Costa's ninth goal in seven games. David de Gea saves a Leighton Baines penalty in a man-of-the-match performance and Radamel Falcao scores for the first time for the club as Manchester United defeat Everton 2-1. It's the first failure by Baines after 14 successful Premier League spot-kicks. Former United defender Rio Ferdinand makes his 500th appearance, but Queens Park Rangers stay bottom after losing 2-0 at West Ham.

18 Southampton savour the team headlines and Sergio Aguero takes the individual honours. Ronald Koeman's side overwhelm Sunderland 8-0, a scoreline equalling the best and worst records for the respective clubs. There are three own goals, by Santiago Vergini, Liam Bridcutt and Patrick van Aanholt, while Graziano Pelle maintains his impressive start to the season with a brace. Aguero nets all four in a 4-1 victory over Tottenham to overtake Carlos Tevez as Manchester City's leading Premier League marksman with 61 in 95 games. Two of them are penalties – one conceded by Federico Fazio who is sent off on his debut – and Aguero has a third saved by Hugo Lloris. Another spot-kick, from Roberto Soldado, is kept out by Joe Hart as Tottenham's goals against column in three matches against City rises to 15. Cesar Azpilicueta also receives a straight red card as Chelsea, with John Terry wearing the captain's armband for the 500th time, are 2-1 away winners over Crystal Palace, who lose Damien Delaney to a second yellow card two minutes later. Gabriel Obertan's first Premier League goal since February 2012 enables Newcastle to record their first win of the season at Leicester's expense in a match starting an hour late after canvas protecting the big TV screen comes loose in high winds. Arsenal need a stoppage-time equaliser from Danny Welbeck to salvage a 2-2 draw against Hull, while George Boyd's first goal for Burnley is not enough to prevent a 3-1 home defeat by West Ham, who go fourth.

19 Four goals are scored in the last eight minutes at Loftus Road. Eduardo Vargas opens his account for Queens Park Rangers, but his side pay the price for own goals by Richard Dunne and Steven Caulker as Liverpool emerge 3-2 winners.

20 Marouane Fellaini and Daley Blind score for the first time for Manchester United in a 2-2 draw with West Bromwich Albion.

25 Two Senegalese make their mark. Diafra Sakho becomes the first West Ham player to score in six successive Premier League games with his strike in a 2-1 success against Manchester City. Sadio Mane's goal is enough for Southampton to see off Stoke, having had his effort against Sunderland the previous week taken away by the Dubious Goals Panel. Sunderland struggle again, this time losing 2-0 at home to two Alexis Sanchez goals for Arsenal. Wilfried Bony also gets two as Swansea overcome Leicester by the same scoreline. West Bromwich Albion retrieve a two-goal deficit for a point against Crystal Palace, Saido Berahino equalising from the penalty spot in added time.

26 Chelsea go into stoppage-time leading at Old Trafford through Didier Drogba's first Premier League goal since rejoining the club. But Branislav Ivanovic is sent off for a second yellow card, Robin van Persie equalises for Manchester United from the resulting free-kick and Chelsea incur a £25,000 fine for seven bookings. They end the month still on top, four points ahead of Southampton and six clear of Manchester City. Substitute Sammy Ameobi scores eight seconds into the second-half and Ayoze Perez registers his first goal for the club to give Newcastle a 2-1 victory over Tottenham. Everton also win away, 3-1 against Burnley, with Samuel Eto'o on the mark twice.

27 Two Charlie Austin goals give Queens Park Rangers the verdict by 2-0 against Aston Villa, who lose for the fifth successive match without scoring for the first time in the top flight.

NOVEMBER 2014

1 Alan Pardew continues to win back the Newcastle fans, his side following up a midweek League Cup success against Manchester City by beating Liverpool with the only goal of the game from Ayoze Perez in front of more than 52,000 at St James' Park. Chelsea need a 75th minute penalty from Eden Hazard to overcome Queens Park Rangers 2-1, but Jose Mourinho is more concerned about a lack of atmosphere at Stamford Bridge, insisting it is like 'playing in an empty stadium.' Southampton's tenth win in 11 league and cup games is delivered by a spectacular goal from Victor Wanyama, who returns a clearance from Eldin Jakupovic over the Hull goalkeeper's head and into the net from nearly 45 yards. Two players score for the first time for their clubs. Calum Chambers backs up a brace by Alexis Sanchez as Arsenal break down Burnley in the final 20 minutes to win 3-0. On-loan Victor Moses is on the mark for Stoke against West Ham, who come from 2-0 down for an away point. Swansea's Jonjo Shelvey is sent off for a second yellow card in a goalless draw at Everton.

2 Sergio Aguero hits the only goal of the Manchester derby, giving City a fourth successive league win over their neighbours for the first time since 1970. United have Chris Smalling sent off for two yellow cards and lose Marcos Rojo with a dislocated shoulder, adding to the club's substantial casualty list. After Andreas Weimann ends Aston Villa's goal drought, they have Christian Benteke shown a straight red card and lose 2-1 to substitute Harry Kane's 90th minute goal for Tottenham.

3 Two goals by Steven Fletcher point Sunderland to a first win in 21 games on a Monday – 3-1 away to Crystal Palace, who have Mile Jedinak dismissed for a second yellow.

8 Chelsea come from behind to win 2-1 at Anfield with the help of goalline technology which indicates Gary Cahill's equaliser is over the line. The defeat leaves Liverpool 15 points adrift of the leaders and effectively out of the title running. The day gets better for Chelsea when Manchester City are held 2-2 by Queens Park Rangers at Loftus Road, where Sergio Aguero's two goals take him to 12 in the first 11 Premier League games. Shane Long comes off the bench to fire his first two in the league for Southampton, who defeat Leicester 2-0. At the bottom, Burnley win for the first time thanks to the only one of the game from Ashley Barnes against Hull.

9 Arsene Wenger admits Arsenal's championship chances are virtually over as the result of a 2-1 defeat at Swansea, whose winner from Bafetimbi Gomis, 90 seconds after coming on, is his first in the league, watched by a record Liberty Stadium crowd of 20,812. This reversal in a game of ten bookings – five for each side – leaves the FA Cup holders 12 points adrift, while Tottenham are also resigned to seeking a top four place after falling 15 points off the pace with a fourth home defeat in five games. They lose Kyle Naughton to a straight red card when going down 2-1 to Stoke, for whom Bojan Krkic scores his first goal in English football. Newcastle maintain their momentum by winning 2-0 away to West Bromwich Albion, with Ayoze Perez again on the mark

22 Newcastle's sixth successive win in all competitions, achieved by the only goal of the game from Moussa Sissoko against Queens Park Rangers, is marred when injury-dogged Ryan Taylor limps off on his first Premier League start for 32 months. Two goals in two minutes by Danny Ings earn Burnley their first away success, at Stoke's expense. Leon Osman also has a good day, making his 400th appearance for Everton and marking it with the winner against West Ham. Two more games end 2-1 – Manchester City coming from behind to overcome Swansea and Manchester United prevailing at the Emirates thanks to Wayne Rooney's record 11th goal against Arsenal in the 85th minute. At the top, Chelsea are 2-0 winners over West Bromwich Albion, who have Claudio Yacob shown a straight red card.

23 Although Rickie Lambert scores for the first time for Liverpool, after 91 seconds, his side experience another nightmare at Selhurst Park, where their title bid collapsed the previous

season when surrendering a three-goal lead. This time, Mile Jedinak rounds off a 3-1 victory for Crystal Palace with a 25-yard free-kick. Jake Livermore puts Hull ahead against his former club, but they have Gaston Ramirez shown a straight red and lose 2-1 to Christian Eriksen's 90th minute goal for Tottenham.

24 The lowest Premier League crowd at Villa Park for 15 years, 25,311, see the team's eighth successive match without a win - a 1-1 draw with Southampton.

29 Three players score for the first time for their clubs, among them Joe Cole making his first Premier League start for Aston Villa in a 1-1 draw at Burnley. Aaron Cresswell nets the only goal of the game for West Ham to end the winning run of Newcastle, who lose Moussa Sissoko to two bookings in the space of a minute. Leroy Fer also opens his account as Queens Park Rangers overcome Leicester 3-2. Chelsea fail to score for the first time, sharing a goalless draw at Sunderland, while Steve Bruce has nothing to show for his 700th match as a manager, faltering Hull losing 3-0 to Manchester United.

30 Gael Clichy opens his account for Manchester City, rounding off a 3-0 success at Southampton, achieved despite the dismissal of Eliaquim Mangala for a second yellow card. City move up to second, six points behind Chelsea, with Southampton a point further back.

DECEMBER 2014

2 Christian Benteke, back from a three-match suspension, scores the only goal of the game at Crystal Palace to give Aston Villa their first win in ten games. Steven Gerrard, subject of speculation about his future after dropping to the bench in the previous game against Stoke, is also on the mark on his return to Liverpool's starting line-up. They come from behind to win 3-1 at Leicester, who lose West Morgan to a straight red card. Stoke's 2-1 defeat by Manchester United is their 12th successive reversal at Old Trafford.

3 Sergio Aguero's two goals in Manchester City's 4-1 victory at Sunderland takes his Premier League tally to 30 in his last 33 appearances. Chelsea make light of the absence of the suspended Diego Costa, with cover strikers Didier Drogba and Loic Remy both on the mark in their 3-0 success against Tottenham. It looks to be a two-horse race for the title after Southampton's 1-0 defeat by Arsenal, whose 89th minute strike by Alexis Sanchez is their seventh goal of the season in the final five minutes.

6 Chelsea's unbeaten record in 14 Premier League games, five in the Champions League, and two in the Capital One Cup comes to an end at St James' Park. Despite having to bring on debut goalkeeper Jak Alnwick for the second half and finishing with ten men after Steven Taylor is shown a straight red card, Newcastle beat the leaders 2-1 with two goals from substitute Papiss Cisse. Manchester City close the gap when a disputed penalty from Yaya Toure sees off Everton, but they lose Sergio Aguero with a knee ligament injury which rules him out for five matches. Jon Walters hits his 100th career goal in a 3-2 success for Stoke against Arsenal, who have Calum Chambers sent off. Charlie Austin is also shown a second yellow card after wrapping up a 2-0 victory for Queens Park Rangers against Burnley. Allan McGregor earns Hull a point by saving a Graham Dorrans penalty in the goalless draw with West Bromwich Albion.

7 West Ham move into the top three – albeit briefly – for the first time since 1999 as Andy Carroll powers in two trademark headers and sets up Diafra Sakho for the third goal in a 3-1 win over Swansea, who have goalkeeper Lukasz Fabianski dismissed. Another straight red is shown to Leicester's Paul Konchesky in a 2-1 defeat at Villa Park, where Alan Hutton scores his first goal for the home side.

8 Robin van Persie hits both goals as Manchester United take over third place with a 2-1 victory at Southampton.

13 Chelsea's 2-0 win over Hull is marred when Willian and Diego Costa are booked for diving and Gary Cahill escapes a second yellow card for another tumble. Hull have Tom Huddlestone sent off and there is another straight red shown to Aston Villa's Kieran Richardson. Villa lose 1-0 to Craig Gardner's first goal for West Bromwich Albion. James McArthur is also on the mark for the first time, for Crystal Palace, who draw 1-1 with Stoke. Frank Lampard continues to flourish during his loan spell with Manchester City, scoring the only goal at

Leicester to draw level with Thierry Henry on 175 Premier League strikes. Arsenal match their midweek 4-1 Champions League success against Galatasaray when overcoming Newcastle. Santi Cazorla, on his 30th birthday, and Olivier Giroud share the spoils. Burnley move out of the bottom three for the first time with the only goal against Southampton from Ashley Barnes. Tom Heaton's save from a Dusan Tadic penalty ends Southampton's run of 29 successful Premier League spot-kicks, dating back to 1997 when Jim Magilton missed against West Ham.

14 Manchester United are 3-0 winners over Liverpool, but are indebted to a man-of-the-match display by goalkeeper David de Gea, who makes a series of outstanding saves.

20 Charlie Austin's hat-trick points Queens Park Rangers to a 3-2 victory after West Bromwich Albion establish a 2-0 lead at Loftus Road through first goals for the club from Joleon Lescott and on-loan Silvestre Varela. Austin's first is a penalty and all three stem from corners. David Silva marks his 200th appearance for the club with a brace in Manchester City's sixth successive victory, 3-0 against Crystal Palace. But Manchester United's bid to extend their 100 per cent run to seven games comes unstuck at Villa Park, where the home side secure a 1-1 draw despite a straight red card for Gabriel Agbonlahor, which is later rescinded. Southampton end a four-match losing streak by beating Everton 3-0.

21 Martin Skrtel's header in the sixth minute of time added on earns ten-man Liverpool a 2-2 draw against Arsenal after Fabio Borini is sent off for a second yellow card. Mathieu Debuchy's opener for Arsenal is his first goal for the club. Sunderland register a record fourth successive victory over Newcastle with the only goal of the Tyne-Wear derby from Adam Johnson in the 90th minute at St James' Park.

22 John Terry scores after two minutes to set Chelsea on the way to a 2-0 victory at Stoke.

26 Wayne Rooney and Alexis Sanchez land knockout blows on Boxing Day. Rooney scores twice and sets up one for Robin van Persie as Manchester United master Newcastle 3-1. Sanchez has a penalty saved by Robert Green, but puts Arsenal ahead against Queens Park Rangers and lays on a second for Tomas Rosicky, making his first full appearance of the season. Arsene Wenger shakes his head in dismay as the 2-1 success is marred by a straight red card for Olivier Giroud. John Terry is again on the mark for Chelsea, who defeat West Ham 2-0, while Manchester City equal a club record with a ninth straight victory in all competitions, the Brazilian Fernando launching a 3-1 success away to West Bromwich Albion with his first goal for the team. Belgian Toby Alderweireld celebrates his first goal as Southampton win by the same scoreline at Crystal Palace in what proves to be Neil Warnock's final game in charge at Selhurst Park. So too does on-loan Uruguayan Gaston Ramirez in Hull's 3-1 victory at Sunderland – their first in 11 games. Everton's Gareth Barry is somewhat less enamoured in a 1-0 home defeat by Stoke, having become the first player to pick up 100 bookings in the Premier League.

28 Burnley retrieve a 2-0 half-time deficit with goals by George Boyd and Ashley Barnes to hold Manchester City at the Etihad. Chelsea also drop points, in a 1-1 draw at Southampton, so enter the New Year three points ahead of City at the top. Southampton have Morgan Schneiderlin dismissed for two bookable offences and three other players are sent off. At Hull, Leicester's Paul Konchesky receives a second yellow card as his side win for the first time in 14 games, thanks to the only goal of the game from Riyad Mahrez. The home team lose Stephen Quinn in a separate incident, while Aston Villa's Fabian Delph is also shown a straight red in a goalless draw with Sunderland. Three players score for the first time their clubs – Jack Colback in Newcastle's 3-2 victory over Everton in Alan Pardew's last game as manager; Arouna Kone on his first league start for Everton after 14 months out with a knee injury; Cheikhou Kouyate in West Ham's 2-1 defeat by Arsenal. Mame Biram Diouf nets both for Stoke, whose 2-0 defeat of West Bromwich Albion is followed by the sacking of Albion's Alan Irvine.

29 Adam Lallana doubles his tally for the season with two goals in Liverpool's 4-1 win over Swansea.

JANUARY 2015

1 Tottenham and their 21-year-old striker Harry Kane launch the New Year in style against Chelsea. Kane scores twice, wins a penalty and creates their final goal in a 5-3 victory – the first time his club had scored five times in the league against Chelsea since 1961. Manchester City surrender another two-goal lead, but draw level at the top when substitute Frank Lampard's header secures a 3-2 victory against Sunderland and takes him ahead of Thierrry Henry into fourth place in the Premier League's all-time scoring list with 176 goals. On the day he announces his intention to leave Anfield at the end of the season, Steven Gerrard converts two penalties – one disputed – against Leicester, who recover the deficit with goals by David Nugent and Jeffrey Schlupp for a point. In a game of more contentious refereeing decisions, Queens Park Rangers goalkeeper Robert Green escapes a red card for handling outside the penalty against Swansea. Garry Monk's side are also angered by a straight red card – later overturned – for Wayne Routledge, but come away with a point courtesy of substitute Wilfried Bony's stoppage-time equaliser for 1-1. Antolin Alcaraz is dismissed for a second yellow in a 2-0 at defeat at Hull, leaving Everton as the only pointless team from four games over the holiday programme. Burnley continue to show commendable powers of recovery, despite having to make three substitutions in the first 37 minutes and hitting the woodwork three times. They come from behind three times for a 3-3 draw at Newcastle, who lose Steven Taylor for the remainder of the season with an achilles injury.

10 Alan Pardew and Tony Pulis make successful starts to the task of keeping their new clubs in the division. Pardew's Crystal Palace end a run of eight league games without a win by beating Tottenham 2-1 with goals by Dwight Gayle, from the penalty spot, and Jason Puncheon. West Bromwich Albion's Pulis sees Saido Berahino score the only one against Hull, who lose strikers Nikica Jelavic and Abel Hernandez to first-half injuries. Leicester are also 1-0 winners, against Aston Villa, thanks to Paul Konchesky's first in the top flight for five years. This match produces two dismissals in stoppage-time – a straight red for the home side's Matty James and a second yellow for Villa's Ciaran Clark. Sunderland lose to Liverpool by the same scoreline and have Liam Bridcutt sent off for a second yellow. In the meeting of two struggling sides, Burnley are 2-1 winners over Queens Park Rangers, whose record of ten successive away defeats is the worst in the top tier for 50 years. Chelsea see off Newcastle 2-0, while Manchester City are held 1-1 by Everton, for whom Leighton Baines sets a record for a defender with his 45th Premier League assist, this time a free-kick for Steven Naismith's equaliser.

11 Southampton defeat Manchester United at Old Trafford for the first time since 1988, substitute Dusan Tadic netting the only goal. Alexis Sanchez supplies the cross for Laurent Koscielny to put Arsenal ahead against Stoke, then scores twice himself in a 3-0 victory.

17 Four players score twice in matches at the top and bottom of the table. Oscar and Diego Costa share four goals in Chelsea's 5-0 success at Swansea, described by Jose Mourinho as the 'perfect' performance. On his second appearance for Southampton, on-loan Eljero Elia sets up a 2-1 victory at Newcastle. Dwight Gale's brace helps Crystal Palace win 3-2 at Burnley, who surrender a 2-0 lead for the second time in four days after losing to Tottenham in an FA Cup replay. Spurs are again indebted to Christian Eriksen, whose 88th minute strike for 2-1 against Sunderland is his fourth late winner of the season.

18 Arsenal's best performance of this season – and arguably several others – delivers a 2-0 win over Manchester City at the Etihad with Santi Cazorla's penalty and a header by Olivier Giroud.

19 Everton's Kevin Mirallas is widely criticised after a goalless draw with West Bromwich Albion for insisting on taking a penalty – instead of regular taker Leighton Baines – and missing it.

31 In the biggest match of the season so far, Loic Remy puts Chelsea ahead at Stamford Bridge and David Silva equalises for Manchester City four minutes later. A 1-1 scoreline leaves Chelsea five points ahead of their rivals, with Manchester United a further five points behind after beating Leicester 3-1. Leicester's consolation from Marcin Wasilewski is his first for the club and two other players open their accounts. Jermain Defoe, back in English football after a brief spell playing for Toronto, is on the mark in Sunderland's 2-0 defeat of Burnley, while Remy Cabella sets Newcastle on the way to a 3-0 success at Hull. Jon Walters marks his 200th appearance for Stoke with the club's first Premier League hat-trick – a 'perfect' treble of right foot, left foot and header – in the 3-1 win over Queens Park Rangers, who have Harry Redknapp in charge for the last time. Daniel Sturridge also has cause to celebrate, returning to the Liverpool side after five months out through injury and coming off the bench to complete a 2-0 victory over West Ham. A good day, too, for Harry Kane, who brings his season's tally in all competitions to 20 with two goals, one a penalty, as Tottenham win 3-0 away to West Bromwich Albion.

FEBRUARY 2015

1   Hector Bellerin scores his first goal for Arsenal in a 5-0 victory over Aston Villa. Ryan Bertrand is shown a straight red card as Southampton lose 1-0 at home to Swansea.

7   Harry Kane's season touches a new peak. Watched by England manager Roy Hodgson, Kane scores twice in his first north London derby, with an 86th minute header giving Tottenham a 2-1 victory over Arsenal. The Merseyside derby – Steven Gerrard's last – is goalless as Everton and Liverpool share the honours for the fifth time in six meetings. Jores Okore ends Aston Villa's run of six league games without a goal with his first for the club, but it's not enough to prevent Chelsea giving Jose Mourinho a first victory at Villa Park – 2-1. It extends their lead at the top after Manchester City falter at home against Hull, needing a stoppage-time goal from James Milner, his first in the league in 36 games, for a 1-1 draw. Another in added time – Sadio Mane's fourth in his last four starts for Southampton – delivers a 1-0 success away to Queens Park Rangers.

8   The spate of stoppage-time goals continues at Upton Park and St James' Park. Daley Blind gives Manchester United a 1-1 draw with West Ham and there is still time for a second yellow card for team-mate Luke Shaw. Peter Crouch earns Stoke the same scoreline against Newcastle. Burnley's costly habit of surrendering a two-goal lead continues, this time against West Bromwich Albion, who reply through Chris Brunt and substitute Brown Ideye for 2-2.

10   Deadline-day signing Dame N'Doye marks his first start with a goal and an assist for Nikica Jelavic as Hull beat Aston Villa 2-0. Villa slip into the bottom three and manager Paul Lambert is sacked. Andrej Kramaric, Leicester's record signing, opens his account in the 2-1 defeat at Arsenal, while Mario Balotelli comes off the bench to net his first Premier League goal in Liverpool colours – the decider for a 3-2 victory over Tottenham. Leroy Fer and Bobby Zamora are on the mark as Queens Park Rangers break their 11-match losing sequence away from home by defeating Sunderland 2-0 in a match which brings Rangers captain Joey Barton his seventh successive booking – a Premier League record.

11   The top two have contrasting victories. Manchester City win 4-1 at Stoke with a brace from Sergio Aguero, who is on the mark for the first time since returning from injury, his second goal coming from the penalty spot. Chelsea are frustrated by Everton until Gareth Barry is shown a second yellow card and Willian makes the break through after 89 minutes. Also dismissed is West Ham goalkeeper Adrian in a goalless draw at Southampton, a red card later rescinded. Chris Smalling is on the mark 22 seconds after coming off the bench, then heads a second as Manchester United are 3-1 winners over Burnley.

21   Chelsea appear to be on course for a routine victory when Branislav Ivanovic puts them ahead against Burnley. Instead, Nemanja Matic is sent off for retaliation after a nasty challenge by Ashley Barnes and Ben Mee equalises in the 81st minute. With Yaya Toure back from the Africa Cup of Nations, Manchester City overwhelm Newcastle 5-0. Sergio Aguero converts a penalty, awarded after 28 seconds, while David Silva is on the mark twice. Tim Sherwood's first match in charge of Aston Villa ends in defeat after Ron Vlaar receives a second yellow card for conceding a stoppage-time penalty which Victor Moses puts away to give Stoke a 2-1 away success. Also dismissed, for the ninth time in his career, is Joey Barton, shown a straight red as Queens Park Rangers lose 2-1 to an 89th minute header by Dame N'Doye at Hull. Manchester United go down by the same scoreline at Swansea – only their second defeat in 20 league and cup games – when Jonjo Shelvey's shot deflects in off Bafetimbi Gomis.

22 Tottenham, trailing 2-0 at home to West Ham, pull a goal back through Danny Rose after 81 minutes and draw level in the sixth minute of stoppage-time when Harry Kane converts the rebound after his penalty is saved by Adrian. Liverpool, the form team of 2015 so far, win 2-0 at Southampton, keeping a clean sheet for the fifth successive away league game.

28 West Bromwich Albion and Crystal Palace continue to move away from the relegation zone. Albion's fifth clean sheet in seven games under Tony Pulis, along with a goal after 71 seconds from Saido Berahino, bring victory over Southampton. Palace take their points tally to 13 in seven matches under Alan Pardew by winning 3-1 at West Ham. Jason Puncheon creates all three goals from set-piece deliveries, two of them converted by Glenn Murray, who is then sent off for a second yellow card. Wes Brown is mistakenly shown a straight red by Roger East at Old Trafford after team-mate John O'Shea fouls Radamel Falcao and is later cleared on appeal. Wayne Rooney nets both United goals in a 2-0 victory, one from the penalty spot, to become the first player to score ten or more in 11 successive Premier League seasons.

MARCH 2015

1 The title race swings firmly in Chelsea's favour – on the day they beat Tottenham in the League Cup Final, Manchester City lose 2-1 to Liverpool and trail by five points from an extra game played. Spectacular strikes from Jordan Henderson and Philippe Countinho extend City's run of matches without a win at Anfield to 12.

3 A stoppage-time penalty by Christian Benteke ends Aston Villa's run of 12 games without a victory. They defeat West Bromwich Albion 2-1 – Tim Sherwood's first win as manager. Sunderland manager Gus Poyet is sent to the stands for kicking a bucket of water bottles and becomes involved in an altercation with Hull's Steve Bruce before leaving the touchline during the teams' 1-1 draw. Sunderland incur a £25,000 fine for six bookings.

4 A crowd of nearly 50,000 at St James' Park give a great reception to Jonas Gutierrez, who comes off the bench for his first Newcastle appearance in 17 months after beating testicular cancer. Manchester United win the game 1-0 with an 89th minute goal by Ashley Young, his first since January 2014. Eden Hazard's header is enough to give Chelsea three points at West Ham. James Milner's third goal in four games, after 88 minutes, completes Manchester City's 2-0 win over Leicester. Ryan Mason scores his first in the Premier League as Tottenham defeat Swansea 3-2.

7 Harry Kane sustains Tottenham's bid for a Champions League place and condemns Queens Park Rangers to a seventh defeat in eight games. Kane nets both their goals, while Sandro replies with his first for Rangers.

14 Burnley and Aston Villa look anything like relegation candidates with outstanding performances. Sean Dyche's team defeat Manchester City 1-0 thanks to a sweet strike from George Boyd. Frank Lampard comes off the City bench for his 600th Premier League appearance, while Gabriel Agbonlahor marks his 300th game with two goals as Villa double their tally away from home for the whole season by winning 4-0 at Sunderland, whose manager Gus Poyet is sacked two days later. Christian Benteke also nets twice. Joel Ward scores his first for Crystal Palace in their 3-1 victory over Queens Park Rangers, whose consolation from Matt Phillips is struck from 40 yards. Hull's Tom Huddlestone is sent off for a second yellow card in the goalless draw at Leicester.

15 Chelsea, knocked out of the Champions League by Paris St-Germain in midweek, are frustrated again at Stamford Bridge, this time by Southampton, who earn a 1-1 draw. Manchester United match Arsenal's 3-0 Saturday success against West Ham with one of their best displays of the season to overcome Tottenham – victories which bring the two London clubs within striking range of second-place Manchester City. Everton are also 3-0 winners, against Newcastle, who have Fabricio Coloccini shown a straight red card.

16 In front of a record crowd for the Liberty Stadium of 20,828, Jordan Henderson scores for the third successive game to give Liverpool a 1-0 win over Swansea.

21 Harry Kane celebrates his first England call-up with his first Premier League hat-trick as Tottenham edge out Leicester 4-3. Kane, who takes his tally in all competitions to 29, shares the headlines with another case of mistaken identity, this time involving West Bromwich Albion's Gareth McAuley, who is sent off after 89 seconds by Neil Swarbrick for a foul committed by team-mate Craig Dawson. The red card is later transferred by the FA to Dawson. Albion lose 3-0 to Manchester City, for whom Wilfried Bony scores his first goal. Glenn Murray makes it four in four matches – after one in his previous 19 – with a penalty in a 2-1 success for Crystal Palace at Stoke. Olivier Giroud's brace for Arsenal in their win at Newcastle by the same scoreline stretches his productive run to eight in nine league matches. Dick Advocaat's first game in charge of Sunderland is a 1-0 defeat at West Ham, inflicted by Diafra Sakho's 88th minute strike.

22   Steven Gerrard apologises publicly for being sent off 38 seconds after coming off the bench against Manchester United at Anfield. The Liverpool captain, facing United for the last time before joining LA Galaxy, is shown a red card for stamping on Ander Herrera and his side lose 2-1 to two Juan Mata goals. Substitute Loic Remy scores with his first touch to give Chelsea a 3-2 win at Hull after they surrender a two-goal lead established in the first nine minutes. On-loan Aaron Lennon nets his first for Everton in their 2-1 victory away to Queens Park Rangers, who lose for the ninth time in ten games.

APRIL 2015

4   On a day of spectacular goals, Charlie Adam joins an exclusive list of players scoring from inside their own half when his 66-yard strike sails over the head of Chelsea's 6ft 6in goalkeeper Thibaut Courtois at Stamford Bridge. It is not enough for Stoke, who lose 2-1 and face a £25,000 fine for six bookings. Wayne Rooney brings Angel di Maria's cross under control with his first touch, spins and fires in a volley in Manchester United's 3-1 home win over Aston Villa, which also features a brace from Ander Herrera. At The Hawthorns, Bobby Zamora scores with the outside of his boot from an angle and while under pressure from a defender. It helps Queens Park Rangers win 4-1 – the first time they have scored four away from home in the Premier League since 1994 – against West Bromwich Albion, who have substitute Youssouf Mulumbu sent off. Also shown a straight red is Hull's David Meyler in a 3-1 defeat at Swansea, for whom Bafetimbi Gomis nets twice. Emre Can receives a second yellow in Liverpool's 4-1 defeat at Arsenal – one which forces manager Brendan Rodgers to write off their chances of a Champions League place. David Nugent has a penalty saved by Adrian, but Leicester achieve their first win in nine league games with an 86th minute Andy King goal for 2-1 against West Ham.

5   Another glorious goal settles the Wear-Tyne derby as Jermain Defoe's 22-yard volley with his weaker foot enables Sunderland to extend their record run of victories over Newcastle to five.

6   Manchester City's title defence looks to be over after a 2-1 defeat at Crystal Palace. It leaves them nine points behind Chelsea (70) and down to fourth place behind Arsenal (63) and Manchester United 62.

7   Christian Benteke completes a hat-trick in the 83rd minute to earn Aston Villa a 3-3 draw against Queens Park Rangers. Clint Hill scores his first Premier League goal for Rangers.

11   Yannick Bolasie's hat-trick in 11 minutes in the second half gives Crystal Palace a 4-1 win at Sunderland. The Congolese, previously with only one goal to his credit all season, becomes the first Palace player to achieve the treble in the Premier League. Bolasie also sets up their other goal for Glenn Murray, his sixth in six matches. Christian Benteke takes his tally to eight in six games for Aston Villa with the only one at White Hart Lane – a result providing extra satisfaction for Tim Sherwood after his sacking by Tottenham at the end of the previous season. Not so happy is Carlos Sanchez, who is shown a second yellow card and misses his side's FA Cup semi-final against Liverpool. While Villa move up, Leicester keep alive their survival chances with another late winner. This one, from Jamie Vardy in stoppage time, secures a 3-2 success away to West Bromwich Albion after on-loan Robert Huth's first goal for the club brings them level. Darren Fletcher opens his account for Albion. Two other sides in trouble are beaten. Burnley go down 1-0 at home to Arsenal, who win for the eighth successive time. Hull lose 2-0 at Southampton, where Graziano Pelle scores his first league goal since before Christmas. At Upton Park, persistence pays off for Marko Arnautovic,

whose equaliser for Stoke against West Ham in the fifth minute of time added on comes after two previous efforts are disallowed for offside.

12 Manchester United regain local bragging rights after four successive defeats by Manchester City. They win 4-2 with Ashley Young scoring one of the goals and setting up two more for Marouane Fellaini and Chris Smalling. Sergio Aguero nets both City goals to reach 100 in 158 games – a club record. Chelsea close in on the title when a goal by Cesc Fabregas, wearing a protective mask after breaking his nose, is enough to defeat Queens Park Rangers.

13 Joe Allen scores his first goal of the season in Liverpool's 2-0 victory over Newcastle, who have Moussa Sissoko sent off for two yellow cards.

18 Manchester United fail to halt the Chelsea bandwagon, despite enjoying the lion's share of the game at Stamford Bridge. Eden Hazard scores the only goal to stretch his side's lead to ten points. At the bottom, Leicester's revival continues when goals by Leonardo Ulloa and Andy King see off Swansea 2-0. But Burnley are unable to profit from Tom Heaton's penalty save from Ross Barkley at Goodison Park. They are goalless for the sixth time in seven matches, lose 1-0 to Everton and have Ashley Barnes sent off for a second yellow card.

19 Harry Kane becomes the first Tottenham player to score 30 goals in a season since Gary Lineker in 1991-92 when completing a 3-1 victory by his team at Newcastle.

25 Two penalty misses impact on the fight for survival. Burnley's Matt Taylor strikes a post and Leicester break away to score the only goal of the game through Jamie Vardy, record their fourth successive win in top flight football for the first time since 1966 and move out of the bottom three. West Ham goalkeeper Adrian saves his third successive spot-kick, this time from Charlie Austin, forcing Queens Park Rangers to settle for a goalless draw. Two goals by Dame N'Doye enable Hull to end a six-match lean run with a 2-0 victory at Crystal Palace, while Tom Cleverley and Carlos Sanchez both net their first for Aston Villa, who retrieve a 2-0 deficit at the Etihad but go down to Fernandinho's 89th minute effort for Manchester City. Jack Cork and on-loan Nelson Oliveira also open their accounts for Swansea, whose 3-2 success at Newcastle takes their points tally in the Premier League to 50 for the first time. Siem de Jong scores his first for Newcastle, who suffer a seventh successive defeat in the top division for the first time since the 1977-78 season. Southampton also top their best Premier League total of 56 points, recorded under Mauricio Pochettino, when two goals by Graziano Pelle earn a 2-2 draw against Pochettino's Tottenham. At The Hawthorns, Steven Gerrard makes his 500th Premier League appearance for Liverpool in a goalless draw against West Bromwich Albion, joining former team-mate Jamie Carragher (508) and Manchester United's Ryan Giggs (632) as the only players to reach that milestone with a single club.

26 John Stones heads his first goal for Everton, who master Manchester United 3-0. Arsenal and Chelsea are goalless at the Emirates.

27 Captain Michael Dawson's first goal for Hull proves the only one of the game against Liverpool.

29 Chelsea move to within one victory of the title when coming from behind to beat Leicester 3-1.

MAY 2015

2 With tension rising at the foot of the table, Sunderland's Jordi Gomez holds his nerve to convert two penalties for a 2-1 win over Southampton, who have James Ward-Prowse shown a straight red card for conceding the second one. Leonardo Ulloa is also on the mark from the spot in Leicester's 3-0 victory over Newcastle, having previously given his side the lead after 36 seconds. Newcastle's Mike Williamson and Daryl Janmaat are both dismissed for two yellow cards as their club record run of defeats in the Premier League extends to eight. Another two-goal marksman is Aston Villa's Christian Benteke, who takes his tally to ten in eight games in the 3-2 defeat of Everton. There are two other dismissals. Nedum Onuoha, of Queens Park Rangers, receives a second yellow at Liverpool, where Steven Gerrard makes amends for a penalty saved by Robert Green with an 87th minute winner for 2-1. Rangers look doomed, along with Burnley, who go down 1-0 at West Ham to a penalty conceded by Michael Duff, who is shown a straight red. This is later rescinded. West Bromwich Albion's

1-0 success at Old Trafford gives Tony Pulis his first victory over Manchester United as a manager and leaves United with a third successive defeat without scoring for the first time since 1989 after Robin van Persie's penalty is saved by Boaz Myhill. Swansea's 2-0 success against Stoke brings Jefferson Montero his first goal for the club.

3 Chelsea become champions when Eden Hazard heads the only goal against Crystal Palace after Julian Speroni saves his penalty.

4 Two goals by Alexis Sanchez point Arsenal to a 3-1 victory at Hull, who slip back into trouble – one of five teams separated by two points.

9 Burnley end a run of six goalless games by winning 1-0 at Hull, with Danny Ings on target for the first time for nearly three months. But results elsewhere send them down and Hull face the prospect of joining them after conceding the goal with Michael Dawson on the pitch changing a bloodied shirt and twice hitting he bar. Danny Graham's first goal for Sunderland paves the way for a 2-0 victory at Everton and two by Riyad Mahrez enable resurgent Leicester to register the same scoreline again Southampton. Tom Cleverly is on the mark for the third successive game – after not scoring in the previous 37 – to give Aston Villa a 1-0 win over West Ham, while Newcastle end their miserable sequence in a 1-1 draw against West Bromwich Albion. Stoke achieve their first-ever double over Tottenham, who have Vlad Chiriches dismissed for a second yellow card in a 3-0 defeat.

10 Queens Park Rangers also make an immediate return to the Championship, surrendering 6-0 to Manchester City, for whom Sergio Aguero completes a hat-trick from the penalty spot. John Terry becomes the highest scoring defender in the history of the Premier League, overtaking David Unsworth with his 39th goal for Chelsea in a 1-1 draw against Liverpool.

16 Sadio Mane scores the Premier League's fastest-ever hat-trick as Southampton overwhelm Aston Villa's 6-1. The Senegal winger, signed from Salzburg for £11.8m in September 2014, takes just two minutes and 56 seconds, overtaking Robbie Fowler's mark of four minutes 33 seconds for Liverpool against Arsenal in 1994. Southampton also go into the record books as the first Premier League team to score five first-half goals in a match and five in the second-half (against Sunderland in October) in the same season. Despite the defeat, Villa are safe because of results elsewhere. Leicester's great escape is confirmed in a goalless draw with Sunderland, who remain in danger, along with Newcastle, who lose 2-1 to Queens Park Rangers. Hull are favourites to join Rangers and Burnley in the Championship after a 2-0 defeat by Tottenham at the end of a traumatic week in which Jake Livermore is suspended by the club following a positive test for cocaine. Steven Gerrard is acclaimed by Liverpool supporters on his final appearance at Anfield before joining LA Galaxy, but Crystal Palace interrupt the celebrations by coming from behind to win 3-1. Stoke's goalless draw at Burnley takes their points total to 51 – the club's highest in the Premier League era.

17 Joe Hart pulls off arguably the save of the season, from a Federico Fernandez header as Manchester City win 4-2 at Swansea, with Yaya Toure on the mark twice.

18 Chelsea are beaten in the league for the first time since New Year's Day, going down 3-0 to West Bromwich Albion, for whom Saido Berahino is on the mark twice, including a penalty. The champions also lose Cesc Fabregas to the season's most bizarre red card – Fabregas booting the ball into a group of players as referee Mike Jones tries to sort out a penalty box melee and hitting Albion's Chris Brunt. His three match-ban is later reduced to one game.

20 Sunderland gain the point needed to ensure staying up in a goalless draw with Arsenal at the Emirates.

24 Agony for Hull, ecstasy for Newcastle on the final day of the season. Steve Bruce's side, needing to win to stand a chance of staying up, share a goalless draw with Manchester United, who have Marouane Fellaini shown a straight red card. Newcastle end a run of nine defeats and a draw by beating West Ham 2-0 in what turns out to be Sam Allardyce's last game as manager. Jonas Gutierrez has a hand in Moussa Sissoko's opening goal and scores the second himself. Elsewhere, Steven Gerrard and Frank Lampard experience sharply contrasting fortunes when bidding farewell to the Premier League to continue their careers in the United States. Gerrard's 186th goal in his 710th appearance for Liverpool comes in a 6-1 defeat at Stoke – the club's biggest defeat since 1963. Peter Crouch completes the scoring with a Premier League record 47th headed goal, overtaking Alan Shearer's mark, and Mame Biram Diouf is on the mark twice. Lampard takes his tally to 177 in 609 Premier League matches in Manchester City's 2-0 win over Southampton. Didier Drogba captains Chelsea on his final appearance for the club – a 3-1 success against Sunderland in which Loic Remy scores twice. Theo Walcott's 37-minute hat-trick in a 4-1 victory over West Bromwich comes at the end of an injury-plagued campaign and puts him in contention for a place in Arsenal's FA Cup Final team against Aston Villa.

HOW CHELSEA WON THE TITLE

AUGUST 2014

18   Burnley 1 (Arfield 14) Chelsea 3 (Diego Costa 17, Schurrle 21, Ivanovic 34).
        Att: 20,699
23   Chelsea 2 (Diego Costa 63, Hazard 77) Leicester 0. Att: 41,604
30   Everton 3 (Mirallas 45, Naismith 69, Eto'o 76) Chelsea 6 (Diego Costa 1, 90,
        Ivanovic 3, Coleman 67 og, Matic 74, Ramires 77). Att: 39,402

SEPTEMBER 2014

13   Chelsea 4 (Diego Costa 45, 56, 67, Remy 81) Swansea 2 (Terry 11 og, Shelvey
        86). Att: 41,400
21   Manchester City 1 (Lampard 85) Chelsea 1 (Schurrle 71). Att: 45,602
27   Chelsea 3 (Oscar 7, Diego Costa 59, Willian 79) Aston Villa 0. Att: 41,616

OCTOBER 2014

5   Chelsea 2 (Hazard 27 pen, Diego Costa 78) Arsenal 0. Att: 41,607
18   Crystal Palace 1 (Campbell 90) Chelsea 2 (Oscar 6, Fabregas 51). Att: 24,451
26   Manchester Utd 1 (Van Persie 90) Chelsea 1 (Drogba 53). Att: 75,327

NOVEMBER 2014

1   Chelsea 2 (Oscar 32, Hazard 75 pen) QPR 1 (Austin 62). Att: 41,486
8   Liverpool 1 (Emre Can 9) Chelsea 2 (Cahill 14, Diego Costa 67). Att: 44,698
22   Chelsea 2 (Diego Costa 11, Hazard 25) WBA 0. Att: 41,600
29   Sunderland 0 Chelsea 0. Att: 45,232

DECEMBER 2014

3   Chelsea 3 (Hazard 19, Drogba 22, Remy 73) Tottenham 0. Att: 41,518
6   Newcastle 2 (Cisse 57, 78) Chelsea 1 (Drogba 83). Att: 52,019
13   Chelsea 2 (Hazard 7, Diego Costa 68) Hull 0. Att: 41,626
22   Stoke 0 Chelsea 2 (Terry 2, Fabregas 78). Att: 27,550
26   Chelsea 2 (Terry 31, Diego Costa 62) West Ham 0. Att: 41,589
28   Southampton 1 (Mane 17) Chelsea 1 (Hazard 45). Att: 31,641

JANUARY 2015

1   Tottenham 5 (Kane 30, 52, Rose 44, Townsend 45 pen, Chadli 78) Chelsea 3
        (Diego Costa 18, Hazard 61, Terry 87). Att: 35,903
10   Chelsea 2 (Oscar 43, Diego Costa 59) Newcastle 0. Att: 41,612
17   Swansea 0 Chelsea 5 (Oscar 1, 36, Diego Costa 20, 34, Schurrle 79).
        Att: 20,785
31   Chelsea 1 (Remy 41) Manchester City 1 (Silva 45). Att: 41,620

FEBRUARY 2015

7	Aston Villa 1 (Okore 48) Chelsea 2 (Hazard 8, Ivanovic 66). Att: 35,969
11	Chelsea 1 (Willian 89) Everton 0. Att: 41,592
21	Chelsea 1 (Ivanovic 14) Burnley 1 (Mee 81). Att: 41,629

MARCH 2015

4	West Ham 0 Chelsea 1 (Hazard 22). Att: 34,927
15	Chelsea 1 (Diego Costa 11) Southampton 1 (Tadic 19 pen). Att: 41,624
22	Hull 2 (Elmohamady 26, Hernandez 28) Chelsea 3 (Hazard 2, Diego Costa 9, Remy 77). Att: 24,598

APRIL 2015

4	Chelsea 2 (Hazard 39 pen, Remy 62) Stoke 1 (Adam 44). Att: 41,098
12	QPR 0 Chelsea 1 (Fabregas 88). Att: 17,939
18	Chelsea 1 (Hazard 38) Manchester Utd 0. Att: 41,422
26	Arsenal 0 Chelsea 0. Att: 60,066
29	Leicester 1 (Albrighton 45) Chelsea 3 (Drogba 48, Terry 79, Ramires 83). Att: 32,021

MAY 2015

3	Chelsea 1 (Hazard 45) Crystal Palace 0. Att: 41,566 (clinched title)
10	Chelsea 1 (Terry 5) Liverpool 1 (Gerrard 44). Att: 41,547
18	WBA 3 (Berahino 9, 47 pen, Brunt 60) Chelsea 0. Att: 24,750
24	Chelsea 3 (Diego Costa 37 pen, Remy 70, 88) Sunderland 1 (Fletcher 26). Att: 41,620

FOOTBALL LEAGUE PLAY-OFFS 2015

More often than not, the play-offs tend to be cagey affairs. In the Championship, with so much at stake for the winners, the end-of-season lottery can be particularly tight and tense. Not so this time as **Norwich** were rewarded for a flying start at Wembley with a return to the Premier League at the first attempt. Cameron Jerome put them ahead against Middlesbrough after 12 minutes and Nathan Redmond made it 2-0 three minutes later, a scoreline they maintained to the final whistle without too many problems. Both took advantage of uncharacteristic defensive uncertainty by a side who went into the final with the division's best goals against record – 37 conceded in 46 matches. Manager Aitor Karanka had no complaints about the result, blaming individual errors and arguing that his team's late arrival at Wembley was to reduce pre-match nerves and had no affect on the result. He also maintained that subdued leading scorer Patrick Bamford was fit to play after an ankle injury. For Alex Neil, Norwich manager for just four months, it was a stunning conclusion to a season which had started with a Scottish Communities Cup tie for his Hamilton side against Arbroath in front of 730 supporters. At 33, he became the youngest in the Premier League. The League One Final featured a hat-trick by Jermaine Beckford in **Preston**'s record 4-0 win over Swindon. Paul Huntington was also on the mark for a club beaten in all of their nine previous appearances in the play-offs. **Southend**, like Preston, were denied automatic promotion on the final day of the regular season and it looked as if they would also lose out in the League Two Final. But with seconds of extra-time remaining, substitute Joe Pigott equalised against Wycombe and his side won the penalty shoot-out 7-6. **Bristol Rovers** were also penalty winners in the Conference Final, beating Grimsby 5-3 after a 1-1 scoreline to make an immediate return to the Football League.

SEMI-FINALS, FIRST LEG
CHAMPIONSHIP

Brentford 1 (Gray 54) **Middlesbrough** 2 (Vossen 26, Amorebieta 90). Att: 11,691. **Ipswich** 1 (Anderson 45) **Norwich** 1 (Howson 41). Att: 29,166

LEAGUE ONE

Chesterfield 0 **Preston** 1 (Beckford 6). Att: 8,409. **Sheffield Utd** 1 (Freeman 19) **Swindon** 2 (Ricketts 51, Byrne 90). Att: 20,890

LEAGUE TWO

Plymouth 2 (Ansah 86, Banton 89) **Wycombe** 3 (Hayes 10, Amadi-Holloway 22, Craig 52). Att: 14,175. **Stevenage** 1 (Parrett 51) **Southend** 1 (Corr 60). Att: 5,183

CONFERENCE

Eastleigh 1 (Odubade 62) **Grimsby** 2 (Arnold 3, 72). Att: 3,251; **Forest Green** 0 **Bristol Rov** 1 (Taylor 17). Att: 3,336.

SEMI-FINALS, SECOND LEG
CHAMPIONSHIP

Middlesbrough 3 (Tomlin 23, Kike 55, Adomah 78) **Brentford** 0. Att: 33,266 (Middlesborough won 5-1 on agg). **Norwich** 3 (Hoolahan 50 pen, Redmond 64, Jerome 76) **Ipswich** 1 (Smith 60). Att: 26,994 (Norwich won 4-2 on agg)

LEAGUE ONE

Preston 3 (Beckford 38, 87, Garner 62 pen) **Chesterfield** 0. Att: 15,643 (Preston won 4-0 on agg). **Swindon** 5 (Gladwin 4, 10, M Smith 18, 59 pen, Obika 84) **Sheffield Utd** 5 (Thompson 19 og, Basham 39, S Davies 65, Done 88, Adams 90). Att: 13,065 (Swindon won 7-6 on agg)

LEAGUE TWO

Southend 3 (Leonard 67, McLaughlin 108, Timlin 120) **Stevenage** 1 (Pett 55). Att: 8,998 (aet, Southend won 4-2 on agg). **Wycombe** 2 (Hayes 8, Mawson 35) **Plymouth** 1 (Brunt 71). Att: 7,750 (Wycombe won 5-3 on agg)

CONFERENCE

Bristol Rov 2 (Lines 24, Taylor 88) **Forest Green** 0. Att: 10,563 (Bristol Rov won 3-0 on agg). **Grimsby** 3 (Palmer 35, 71, John-Lewis 44) **Eastleigh** 0. Att: 6,286 (Grimsby won 5-1 on agg)

FINALS
CHAMPIONSHIP – MONDAY, MAY 25 2015

Middlesbrough 0 **Norwich City** 2 (Jerome 12, Redmond 15). Att: 85,656 (Wembley)
Middlesbrough (4-2-3-1): Konstantopoulos, Whitehead (Nsue 46), Ayala, Gibson, Friend, Leadbitter (capt), Clayton, Adomah, Vossen (Kike 68), Tomlin, Bamford. **Subs not used:** Ripley, Forshaw, Reach, Amorebieta, Woodgate. **Booked:** Vossen. **Manager:** Aitor Karanka
Norwich (4-2-3-1): Ruddy, Whittaker, Martin (capt), Bassong, Olsson, Tettey, Howson, Redmond (O'Neil 87), Hoolahan (Dorrans 74), Johnson, Jerome (Grabban 74). **Subs not used:** Rudd, E Bennett, R Bennett, Hooper. **Booked:** Howson. **Manager:** Alex Neil
Referee: M Dean (Merseyside). **Half-time:** 0-2

LEAGUE ONE – SUNDAY, MAY 24 2015

Preston North End 4 (Beckford 3, 44, 57, Huntington 13) **Swindon Town** 0. Att: 48,236 (Wembley)
Preston (4-4-2): Johnstone, Clarke (capt), Wright, Huntington, Woods, Kilkenny, Johnson (Laird 82), Welsh, Gallagher (Browne 37), Beckford (Davies 67), Garner. **Subs not used**: Stuckmann, Humphrey, Reid, Hugill. **Manager**: Simon Grayson
Swindon (3-5-2): Foderingham, N Thompson (capt) (Ricketts 5), Stephens, Turnbull, Byrne, Luongo, Kasim, Gladwin (L Thompson 58), Toffolo (Williams 66), Smith, Obita. **Subs not used**: Belford, Branco, Rodgers, Hylton. **Booked**: Kasim. **Manager**: Mark Cooper
Referee: A Madley (Yorks). **Half-time**: 3-0

LEAGUE TWO – SATURDAY, MAY 23 2015

Southend United 1 (Pigott 120) **Wycombe Wanderers** 1 (Bentley 95 og) – aet, Southend won 7-6 on pens). Att: 38,252 (Wembley)
Southend (4-2-3-1): Bentley, White (capt), Bolger, Barrett, Coker, Timlin, Leonard,Worrall (Payne 97), Atkinson (Weston 80), McLaughlin (Pigott 60), Corr. **Subs not used**: Smith, Prosser, Deegan, Cassidy. **Booked**: Bolger, Leonard. **Manager**: Phil Brown
Wycombe (4-3-3): Lynch Bean, Mawson, Pierre, Jacobson, Yennaris (Murphy 111), Saunders (Bloomfield 4), Wood, Hayes (capt), Amadi-Holloway, Ephraim (Craig 85). **Subs not used**: Horlock, McClure, Kretzschmar, Onyedinma. **Booked**: Hayes, Mawson, Wood. **Manager**: Gareth Ainsworth.
Referee: S Hooper (Wilts). **Half-time**: 0-0

CONFERENCE – SUNDAY, MAY 17 2015

Bristol Rovers 1 (Harrison 29) **Grimsby Town** 1 (John-Lewis 2) – aet, Bristol Rovers won 5-3 on pens). Att: 47,029 (Conference record)
Bristol Rovers (4-4-2): Puddy (Mildenhall 120), Lockyer, McChrystal (capt), Parkes, Brown, Gosling (Balanta 75), Lines, Mansell, Monkhouse, Taylor, Harrison (Blissett 77). **Subs not used**: Leadbitter, Clarke. **Booked**: Puddy, Taylor. **Manager**: Darrell Clarke
Grimsby (4-4-2): McKeown, Nsiala, Pearson, Magnay, Robertson (Parslow 74), Mackreth, Disley (capt), Brown (Clay 99), Arnold, John-Lewis, Palmer (Pittman 70). **Subs not used**: Hannah, Jolle. **Booked**: Magnay, Brown. **Manager**: Paul Hurst
Referee: R Joyce (Cleveland). **Half-time**: 1-1

PLAY-OFF FINALS – HOME & AWAY

1987: Divs 1/2: Charlton beat Leeds 2-1 in replay (Birmingham) after 1-1 agg (1-0h, 0-1a). Charlton remained in Div 1 Losing semi-finalists: Ipswich and Oldham. **Divs 2/3: Swindon** beat Gillingham 2-0 in replay (Crystal Palace) after 2-2 agg (0-1a, 2-1h). Swindon promoted to Div 2. Losing semi-finalists: Sunderland and Wigan; Sunderland relegated to Div 3. **Divs 3/4:** **Aldershot** beat Wolves 3-0 on agg (2-0h, 1-0a) and promoted to Div 3. Losing semi-finalists: Bolton and Colchester; Bolton relegated to Div 4.

1988: Divs 1/2: Middlesbrough beat Chelsea 2-1 on agg (2-0h, 0-1a) and promoted to Div 1; Chelsea relegated to Div 2. Losing semi-finalists: Blackburn and Bradford City. **Divs 2/3: Walsall** beat Bristol City 4-0 in replay (h) after 3-3 agg (3-1a, 0-2h) and promoted to Div 2. Losing semi-finalists: Sheffield Utd and Notts County; Sheffield Utd relegated to Div 3. **Divs 3/4:** **Swansea** beat Torquay 5-4 on agg (2-1h, 3-3a) and promoted to Div 3. Losing semi-finalists: Rotherham and Scunthorpe.; Rotherham relegated to Div 4

1989: Div 2: Crystal Palace beat Blackburn 4-3 on agg (1-3a, 3-0h). Losing semi-finalists: Watford and Swindon. **Div 3: Port Vale** beat Bristol Rovers 2-1 on agg (1-1a, 1-0h). Losing semi-finalists: Fulham and Preston **Div.4: Leyton Orient** beat Wrexham 2-1 on agg (0-0a, 2-1h). Losing semi-finalists: Scarborough and Scunthorpe

PLAY-OFF FINALS AT WEMBLEY

1990: Div 2: Swindon 1 Sunderland 0 (att: 72,873). Swindon promoted, then demoted for financial irregularities; Sunderland promoted. Losing semi-finalists: Blackburn and Newcastle Utd **Div 3: Notts County** 2 Tranmere 0 (att: 29,252). Losing semi-finalists: Bolton and Bury. **Div 4: Cambridge Utd** 1 Chesterfield 0 (att: 26,404). Losing semi-finalists: Maidstone and Stockport County

1991: Div 2: Notts County 3 Brighton 1 (att: 59,940). Losing semi-finalists: Middlesbrough and Millwall. **Div 3: Tranmere** 1 Bolton 0 (att: 30,217). Losing semi-finalists: Brentford and Bury. **Div 4: Torquay 1** Blackpool 2 – Torquay won 5-4 on pens (att: 21,615). Losing semi-finalists: Burnley and Scunthorpe

1992: Div 2: Blackburn 1 Leicester 0 (att: 68,147). Losing semi-finalists: Derby and Cambridge Utd. **Div 3: Peterborough** 2 Stockport 1 (att: 35,087). Losing semi-finalists: Huddersfield and Stoke. **Div 4: Blackpool** 1 Scunthorpe 1 aet, Blackpool won 4-3 on pens (att: 22,741). Losing semi-finalists: Barnet and Crewe

1993: Div 1: Swindon 4 Leicester 3 (att: 73,802). Losing semi-finalists: Portsmouth and Tranmere. **Div 2: WBA** 3 Port Vale 0 (att: 53,471). Losing semi-finalists: Stockport and Swansea. **Div 3: York** 1 Crewe 1 aet, York won 5-3 on pens (att: 22,416). Losing semi-finalists: Bury and Walsall

1994: Div 1: Leicester 2 Derby 1 (att: 73,671). Losing semi-finalists: Millwall and Tranmere. **Div 2: Burnley** 2 Stockport 1 (att: 44,806). Losing semi-finalists: Plymouth Argyle and York. **Div 3: Wycombe** 4 Preston 2 (att: 40,109). Losing semi-finalists: Carlisle and Torquay

1995: Div 1: Bolton 4 Reading 3 (att: 64,107). Losing semi-finalists: Tranmere and Wolves. **Div 2: Huddersfield** 2 Bristol Rov 1 (att: 59,175). Losing semi-finalists: Brentford and Crewe. **Div 3: Chesterfield** 2 Bury 0 (att: 22,814). Losing semi-finalists: Mansfield and Preston

1996: Div 1: Leicester 2 Crystal Palace 1 aet (att: 73,573). Losing semi-finalists: Charlton and Stoke. **Div 2: Bradford City** 2 Notts Co 0 (att: 39,972). Losing semi-finalists: Blackpool and Crewe. **Div 3: Plymouth Argyle** 1 Darlington 0 (att: 43,431). Losing semi-finalists: Colchester and Hereford

1997: Div 1: Crystal Palace 1 Sheffield Utd 0 (att: 64,383). Losing semi-finalists: Ipswich and Wolves. **Div 2: Crewe** 1 Brentford 0 (att: 34,149). Losing semi-finalists: Bristol City and Luton. **Div 3: Northampton** 1 Swansea 0 (att: 46,804). Losing semi-finalists: Cardiff and Chester

1998: Div 1: Charlton 4 Sunderland 4 aet, Charlton won 7-6 on pens (att: 77, 739). Losing semi-finalists: Ipswich and Sheffield Utd. **Div 2: Grimsby** 1 Northampton 0 (att: 62,988). Losing semi-finalists: Bristol Rov and Fulham. **Div 3: Colchester** 1 Torquay 0 (att: 19,486). Losing semi-finalists: Barnet and Scarborough

1999: Div 1: Watford 2 Bolton 0 (att: 70,343). Losing semi-finalists: Ipswich and Birmingham. **Div 2: Manchester City** 2 Gillingham 2 aet, Manchester City won 3-1 on pens (att: 76,935). Losing semi-finalists: Preston and Wigan. **Div 3: Scunthorpe** 1 Leyton Orient 0 (att: 36,985). Losing semi-finalists: Rotherham and Swansea

2000: Div 1: Ipswich 4 Barnsley 2 (att: 73,427). Losing semi-finalists: Birmingham and Bolton. **Div 2: Gillingham** 3 Wigan 2 aet (att: 53,764). Losing semi-finalists: Millwall and Stoke. **Div 3: Peterborough** 1 Darlington 0 (att: 33,383). Losing semi-finalists: Barnet and Hartlepool

PLAY-OFF FINALS AT MILLENNIUM STADIUM

2001: Div 1: Bolton 3 Preston 0 (att: 54,328). Losing semi-finalists: Birmingham and WBA. **Div 2: Walsall** 3 Reading 2 aet (att: 50,496). Losing semi-finalists: Stoke and Wigan. **Div 3: Blackpool** 4 Leyton Orient 2 (att: 23,600). Losing semi-finalists: Hartlepool and Hull.

2002: Div 1: Birmingham 1 Norwich 1 aet, Birmingham won 4-2 on pens, (att: 71,597). Losing semi-finalists: Millwall and Wolves. **Div 2: Stoke** 2 Brentford 0 (att: 42,523). Losing semi-finalists: Cardiff and Huddersfield. **Div 3: Cheltenham** 3 Rushden & Diamonds 1 (att: 24,368). Losing semi-finalists: Hartlepool and Rochdale

2003: Div 1: Wolves 3 Sheffield Utd 0 (att: 69,473). Losing semi-finalists: Nott'm Forest and Reading. **Div 2: Cardiff** 1 QPR. 0 aet (att: 66,096). Losing semi-finalists: Bristol City and Oldham. **Div 3: Bournemouth** 5 Lincoln 2 (att: 32,148). Losing semi-finalists: Bury and Scunthorpe

2004: Div 1: Crystal Palace 1 West Ham 0 (att: 72,523). Losing semi-finalists: Ipswich and Sunderland. **Div 2: Brighton** 1 Bristol City 0 (att: 65,167). Losing semi-finalists: Hartlepool and Swindon. **Div 3: Huddersfield** 0 Mansfield 0 aet, Huddersfield won 4-1 on pens (att: 37,298). Losing semi-finalists: Lincoln and Northampton

2005: Championship: West Ham 1 Preston 0 (att: 70,275). Losing semifinalists: Derby Co and Ipswich. **League 1: Sheffield Wed** 4 Hartlepool 2 aet (att: 59,808). Losing semi-finalists: Brentford and Tranmere **League 2: Southend** 2 Lincoln 0 aet (att: 19532). Losing semi-finalists: Macclesfield and Northampton

2006: Championship: Watford 3 Leeds 0 (att: 64,736). Losing semi-finalists: Crystal Palace and Preston. **League 1: Barnsley** 2 Swansea 2 aet (att: 55,419), Barnsley won 4-3 on pens. Losing semi-finalists: Huddersfield and Brentford. **League 2: Cheltenham** 1 Grimsby 0 (att: 29,196). Losing semi-finalists: Wycombe and Lincoln

PLAY-OFF FINALS AT WEMBLEY

2007: Championship: Derby 1 WBA 0 (att: 74,993). Losing semi-finalists: Southampton and Wolves. **League 1: Blackpool** 2 Yeovil 0 (att: 59,313). Losing semi-finalists: Nottm Forest and Oldham. **League 2: Bristol Rov** 3 Shrewsbury 1 (att: 61,589). Losing semi-finalists: Lincoln and MK Dons

2008: Championship: Hull 1 Bristol City 0 (att: 86,703). Losing semi-finalists: Crystal Palace and Watford. **League 1: Doncaster** 1 Leeds 0 (att: 75,132). Losing semi-finalists: Carlisle and Southend. **League 2: Stockport** 3 Rochdale 2 (att: 35,715). Losing semi-finalists: Darlington and Wycombe

2009: Championship: Burnley 1 Sheffield Utd 0 (att: 80,518). Losing semi-finalists: Preston and Reading. **League 1: Scunthorpe** 3 Millwall 2 (att: 59,661). Losing semi-finalists: Leeds and MK Dons. **League 2: Gillingham** 1 Shrewsbury 0 (att: 53,706). Losing semi-finalists: Bury and Rochdale

2010: Championship: Blackpool 3 Cardiff 2 (att: 82,244). Losing semi-finalists: Leicester and Nottm Forest. **League 1: Millwall** 1 Swindon 0 (att:73,108). Losing semi-finalists: Charlton and Huddersfield. **League 2: Dagenham & Redbridge** 3 Rotherham 2 (att: 32,054). Losing semi-finalists: Aldershot and Morecambe

2011: Championship: Swansea 4 Reading 2 (att: 86,581). Losing semi-finalists: Cardiff and Nottm Forest. **League 1: Peterborough** 3 Huddersfield 0 (Old Trafford, att:48,410). Losing semi-finalists: Bournemouth and MK Dons. **League 2: Stevenage** 1 Torquay 0 (Old Trafford, att: 11,484. Losing semi-finalists: Accrington and Shrewsbury

2012: Championship: West Ham 2 Blackpool 1 (att: 78,523). Losing semi-finalists: Birmingham and Cardiff. **League 1: Huddersfield** 0 Sheffield Utd 0 aet, Huddersfield won 8-7 on pens (att: 52,100). Losing semi-finalists: MK Dons and Stevenage. **League 2: Crewe** 2 Cheltenham 0 (att: 24,029). Losing semi-finalists: Southend and Torquay

2013: Championship: Crystal Palace 1 Watford 0 (att: 82,025). Losing semi-finalists: Brighton and Leicester. **League 1: Yeovil** 2 Brentford 1 (att: 41,955). Losing semi-finalists: Sheffield Utd and Swindon. **League 2: Bradford** 3 Northampton 0 (att: 47,127). Losing semi-finalists: Burton and Cheltenham

2014: Championship: QPR 1 Derby 0 (att: 87,348). Losing semi-finalists: Brighton and Wigan. **League 1: Rotherham** 2 Leyton Orient 2 aet, Rotherham won 4-3 on pens (att: 43,401). Losing semi-finalists: Peterborough and Preston. **League 2: Fleetwood** 1 Burton 0 (att: 14,007). Losing semi-finalists: Southend and York)

HISTORY OF THE PLAY-OFFS

Play-off matches were introduced by the Football League to decide final promotion and relegation issues at the end of season 1986-87. A similar series styled 'Test Matches' had operated between Divisions One and Two for six seasons from 1893-98, and was abolished when both divisions were increased from 16 to 18 clubs.

Eighty-eight years later, the play-offs were back in vogue. In the first three seasons (1987-88-89), the Finals were played home-and-away, and since they were made one-off matches in 1990, they have featured regularly in Wembley's spring calendar, until the old stadium closed its doors and the action switched to the Millennium Stadium in Cardiff in 2001.

Through the years, these have been the ups and downs of the play-offs:

1987: Initially, the 12 clubs involved comprised the one that finished directly above those relegated in Divisions One, Two and Three and the three who followed the sides automatically promoted in each section. Two of the home-and-away Finals went to neutral-ground replays, in which **Charlton** clung to First Division status by denying Leeds promotion while **Swindon** beat Gillingham to complete their climb from Fourth Division to Second in successive seasons, via the play-offs. Sunderland fell into the Third and Bolton into Division Four, both for the first time. **Aldershot** went up after finishing only sixth in Division Four; in their Final, they beat Wolves, who had finished nine points higher and missed automatic promotion by one point.

1988: Chelsea were relegated from the First Division after losing on aggregate to **Middlesbrough**, who had finished third in Division Two. So Middlesbrough, managed by Bruce Rioch, completed the rise from Third Division to First in successive seasons, only two years after their very existence had been threatened by the bailiffs. Also promoted via the play-offs: **Walsall** from Division Three and **Swansea** from the Fourth. Relegated, besides Chelsea: Sheffield Utd (to Division Three) and Rotherham (to Division Four).

1989: After two seasons of promotion-relegation play-offs, the system was changed to involve the four clubs who had just missed automatic promotion. That format has remained. Steve Coppell's **Crystal Palace**, third in Division Two, returned to the top flight after eight years, beating Blackburn 4-3 on aggregate after extra time. Similarly, **Port Vale** confirmed third place in Division Three with promotion via the play-offs. For **Leyton Orient**, promotion seemed out of the question in Division Four when they stood 15th on March 1. But eight wins and a draw in the last nine home games swept them to sixth in the final table, and two more home victories in the play-offs completed their season in triumph.

1990: The play-off Finals now moved to Wembley over three days of the Spring Holiday weekend. On successive afternoons, **Cambridge Utd** won promotion from Division Four and **Notts Co** from the Third. Then, on Bank Holiday Monday, the biggest crowd for years at a Football League fixture (72,873) saw Ossie Ardiles' **Swindon** beat Sunderland 1-0 to reach the First Division for the first time. A few weeks later, however, Wembley losers **Sunderland** were promoted instead, by default; Swindon were found guilty of "financial irregularities" and stayed in Division Two.

1991: Again, the season's biggest League crowd (59,940) gathered at Wembley for the First Division Final in which **Notts Co** (having missed promotion by one point) still fulfilled their ambition, beating Brighton 3-1. In successive years, County had climbed from Third Division to First via the play-offs – the first club to achieve double promotion by this route. Bolton were denied automatic promotion in Division Three on goal difference, and lost at Wembley to an extra-time goal by Tranmere. The Fourth Division Final made history, with Blackpool beaten 5-4 on penalties by Torquay – first instance of promotion being decided by a shoot-out. In the table, Blackpool had finished seven points ahead of Torquay.

1992: Wembley that Spring Bank Holiday was the turning point in the history of **Blackburn.** Bolstered by Kenny Dalglish's return to management and owner Jack Walker's millions, they beat Leicester 1-0 by Mike Newell's 45th-minute penalty to achieve their objective – a place in the new Premier League. Newell, who also missed a second-half penalty, had recovered from a broken leg just in time for the play-offs. In the Fourth Division Final **Blackpool** (denied by penalties the previous year) this time won a shoot-out 4-3 against Scunthorpe., who were unlucky in the play-offs for the fourth time in five years. **Peterborough** climbed out of the Third Division for the first time, beating Stockport County 2-1 at Wembley.

1993: The crowd of 73,802 at Wembley to see **Swindon** beat Leicester 4-3 in the First Division Final was 11,000 bigger than that for the FA Cup Final replay between Arsenal and Sheffield Wed Leicester rallied from three down to 3-3 before Paul Bodin's late penalty wiped away **Swindon**'s bitter memories of three years earlier, when they were denied promotion after winning at Wembley. In the Third Division Final, **York** beat Crewe 5-3 in a shoot-out after a 1-1 draw, and in the Second Division decider, **WBA** beat Port Vale 3-0. That was tough on Vale, who had finished third in the table with 89 points – the highest total never to earn promotion in any division. They had beaten Albion twice in the League, too.

1994: Wembley's record turn-out of 158,586 spectators at the three Finals started with a crowd of 40,109 to see Martin O'Neill's **Wycombe** beat Preston 4-2. They thus climbed from Conference to Second Division with successive promotions. **Burnley**'s 2-1 victory in the Second Division Final was marred by the sending-off of two Stockport players, and in the First Division decider **Leicester** came from behind to beat Derby Co and end the worst Wembley record of any club. They had lost on all six previous appearances there – four times in the FA Cup Final and in the play-offs of 1992 and 1993.

1995: Two months after losing the Coca-Cola Cup Final to Liverpool, Bruce Rioch's **Bolton** were back at Wembley for the First Division play-off final. From two goals down to Reading in front of a crowd of 64,107, they returned to the top company after 15 years, winning 4-3 with two extra-time goals. **Huddersfield** ended the first season at their new £15m. home with promotion to the First Division via a 2-1 victory against Bristol Rov – manager Neil Warnock's third play-off success (after two with Notts Co). Of the three clubs who missed automatic promotion by one place, only **Chesterfield** achieved it in the play-offs, comfortably beating Bury 2-0.

1996: Under new manager Martin O'Neill (a Wembley play-off winner with Wycombe in 1994), **Leicester** returned to the Premiership a year after leaving it. They had finished fifth in the table, but in the Final came from behind to beat third-placed Crystal Palace by Steve Claridge's shot in the last seconds of extra time. In the Second Division **Bradford City** came sixth, nine points behind Blackpool (3rd), but beat them (from two down in the semi-final first leg) and then clinched promotion by 2-0 v Notts County at Wembley. It was City's greatest day since they won the Cup in 1911. **Plymouth Argyle** beat Darlington in the Third Division Final to earn promotion a year after being relegated. It was manager Neil Warnock's fourth play-off triumph in seven seasons after two with Notts County (1990 and 1991) and a third with Huddersfield in 1995.

1997: High drama at Wembley as **Crystal Palace** left it late against Sheffield Utd in the First Division play-off final. The match was scoreless until the last 10 seconds when David Hopkin lobbed Blades' keeper Simon Tracey from 25 yards to send the Eagles back to the Premiership after two seasons of Nationwide action. In the Second Division play-off final, **Crewe** beat Brentford 1-0 courtesy of a Shaun Smith goal. **Northampton** celebrated their first Wembley appearance with a 1-0 victory over Swansea thanks to John Frain's injury-time free-kick in the Third Division play-off final.

1998: In one of the finest games ever seen at Wembley, **Charlton** eventually triumphed 7-6 on penalties over Sunderland. For Charlton, Wearside-born Clive Mendonca scored a hat-trick and Richard Rufus his first career goal in a match that lurched between joy and despair for both sides as it ended 4-4. Sunderland defender Michael Gray's superb performance ill-deserved to end with his weakly struck spot kick being saved by Sasa Ilic. In the Third Division, the penalty spot also had a role to play, as **Colchester**'s David Gregory scored the only goal to defeat Torquay, while in the Second Division a Kevin Donovan goal gave **Grimsby** victory over Northampton.

1999: Elton John, watching via a personal satellite link in Seattle, saw his **Watford** side overcome Bolton 2-0 to reach the Premiership. Against technically superior opponents, Watford prevailed with application and teamwork. They also gave Bolton a lesson in finishing through match-winners by Nick Wright and Allan Smart. **Manchester City** staged a remarkable comeback to win the Second Division Final after trailing to goals by Carl Asaba and Robert Taylor for Gillingham. Kevin Horlock and Paul Dickov scored in stoppage time and City went on to win on penalties. A goal by Spaniard Alex Calvo-Garcia earned **Scunthorpe** a 1-0 success against Leyton Orient in the Third Division Final.

2000: After three successive play-off failures, **Ipswich** finally secured a place in the Premiership. They overcame the injury loss of leading scorer David Johnson to beat Barnsley 4-2 with goals by 36-year-old Tony Mowbray, Marcus Stewart and substitutes Richard Naylor and Martijn Reuser. With six minutes left of extra-time in the Second Division Final, **Gillingham** trailed Wigan 2-1. But headers by 38-year-old player-coach Steve Butler and fellow substitute Andy Thomson gave them a 3-2 victory. Andy Clarke, approaching his 33rd birthday, scored the only goal of the Third Division decider for **Peterborough** against Darlington.

2001: Bolton, unsuccessful play-off contenders in the two previous seasons, made no mistake at the third attempt. They flourished in the new surroundings of the Millennium Stadium to beat Preston 3-0 with goals by Gareth Farrelly, Michael Ricketts – his 24th of the season – and Ricardo Gardner to reach the Premiership. **Walsall**, relegated 12 months earlier, scored twice in a three-minute spell of extra time to win 3-2 against Reading in the Second Division Final, while **Blackpool** capped a marked improvement in the second half of the season by overcoming Leyton Orient 4-2 in the Third Division Final.

2002: Holding their nerve to win a penalty shoot-out 4-2, **Birmingham** wiped away the memory of three successive defeats in the semi-finals of the play-offs to return to the top division after an absence of 16 years. Substitute Darren Carter completed a fairy-tale first season as a professional by scoring the fourth spot-kick against Norwich. **Stoke** became the first successful team to come from the south dressing room in 12 finals since football was adopted by the home of Welsh rugby, beating Brentford 2-0 in the Second Division Final with Deon Burton's strike and a Ben Burgess own goal. Julian Alsop's 26th goal of the season helped **Cheltenham** defeat League newcomers Rushden & Diamonds 3-1 in the Third Division decider.

2003: Wolves benefactor Sir Jack Hayward finally saw his £60m investment pay dividends when the club he first supported as a boy returned to the top flight after an absence of 19 years by beating Sheffield Utd 3-0. It was also a moment to savour for manager Dave Jones, who was forced to leave his previous club Southampton because of child abuse allegations, which were later found to be groundless. **Cardiff**, away from the game's second tier for 18 years, returned with an extra-time winner from substitute Andy Campbell against QPR after a goalless 90 minutes in the Division Two Final. **Bournemouth**, relegated 12 months earlier, became the first team to score five in the end-of-season deciders, beating Lincoln 5-2 in the Division Three Final.

2004: Three tight, tense Finals produced only two goals, the lowest number since the Play-offs were introduced. One of them, scored by Neil Shipperley, gave **Crystal Palace** victory over West Ham, the much-travelled striker tapping in a rebound after Stephen Bywater parried Andy Johnson's shot. It completed a remarkable transformation for Crystal Palace, who were 19th in the table when Iain Dowie left Oldham to become their manager. **Brighton** made an immediate return to Division One in a poor game against Bristol City which looked set for extra-time until Leon Knight netted his 27th goal of the campaign from the penalty spot after 84 minutes. **Huddersfield** also went back up at the first attempt, winning the Division Three Final in a penalty shoot-out after a goalless 120 minutes against Mansfield.

2005: Goals were few and far between for Bobby Zamora during **West Ham**'s Championship season – but what a difference in the Play-offs. The former Brighton and Tottenham striker scored three times in the 4-2 aggregate win over Ipswich in the semi-finals and was on the mark again with the only goal against Preston at the Millennium Stadium. **Sheffield Wed** were eight minute away from defeat against Hartlepool in the League One decider when Steven MacLean made it 2-2 from the penalty spot and they went on to win 4-2 in extra-time. **Southend**, edged out of an automatic promotion place, won the League Two Final 2-0 against Lincoln, Freddy Eastwood scoring their first in extra-time and making the second for Duncan Jupp. **Carlisle** beat Stevenage 1-0 with a goal by Peter Murphy in the Conference Final to regain their League place 12 months after being relegated.

2006: From the moment Marlon King scored his 22nd goal of the season to set up a 3-0 win over Crystal Palace in the semi-final first leg, **Watford** had the conviction of a team going places. Sure enough, they went on to beat Leeds just as comfortably in the final. Jay DeMerit, who was playing non-league football 18 months earlier, headed his side in front. James Chambers fired in a shot that hit a post and went in off goalkeeper Neil Sullivan. Then Darius Henderson put away a penalty after King was brought down by Shaun Derry, the man whose tackle had ended Boothroyd's playing career at the age of 26. **Barnsley** beat Swansea on penalties in the League One Final, Nick Colgan making the vital save from Alan Tate, while Steve Guinan's goal earned **Cheltenham** a 1-0 win over Grimsby in the League Two Final. **Hereford** returned to the Football League after a nine-year absence with Ryan Green's extra-time winner against Halifax in the Conference Final.

2007: Record crowds, plenty of goals and a return to Wembley for the finals made for some eventful and entertaining matches. Stephen Pearson, signed from Celtic for £650,000 in the January transfer window, took **Derby** back to the Premier League after an absence of five seasons with a 61st minute winner, his first goal for the club, against accounted for West Bromwich Albion. It was third time lucky for manager Billy Davies, who had led Preston into the play-offs, without success, in the two previous seasons. **Blackpool** claimed a place in the game's second tier for the first time for 30 years by beating Yeovil 2-0 – their tenth successive victory in a remarkable end-of-season run. Richard Walker took his tally for the season to 23 with two goals for **Bristol Rov**, who beat Shrewsbury 3-1 in the League Two Final. Sammy McIlroy, who led Macclesfield into the league in 1997, saw his Morecambe side fall behind in the Conference Final against Exeter, but they recovered to win 2-1.

2008: Wembley has produced some unlikely heroes down the years, but rarely one to match 39-year-old Dean Windass. The **Hull** striker took his home-town club into the top-flight for the first time with the only goal of the Championship Final against Bristol City – and it was a goal fit to grace any game. In front of a record crowd for the final of 86,703, Fraizer Campbell, his 20-year-old partner up front, picked out Windass on the edge of the penalty box and a sweetly-struck volley flew into the net. **Doncaster**, who like Hull faced an uncertain future a few years earlier, beat Leeds 1-0 in the League One Final with a header by James Hayer from Brian Stock's corner. Jim Gannon had lost four Wembley finals with **Stockport** as a player, but his first as manager brought a 3-2 win against Rochdale in the League Two Final with goals by Anthony Pilkington and Liam Dickinson and a Nathan Stanton own goal. Exeter's 1-0 win over Cambridge United in the Conference Final took them back into the Football League after an absence of five years.

2009: Delight for Burnley, back in the big time after 33 years thanks to a fine goal from 20 yards by Wade Elliott, and for their town which became the smallest to host Premier League football. Despair for Sheffield Utd, whose bid to regain a top-flight place ended with two players, Jamie Ward and Lee Hendrie, sent off by referee Mike Dean. Martyn Woolford capped a man-of-the match performance with an 85th minute winner for Scunthorpe, who beat Millwall 3-2 to make an immediate return to the Championship, Matt Sparrow having scored their first two goals. Gillingham also went back up at the first attempt, beating Shrewsbury with Simeon Jackson's header seconds from the end of normal time in the League Two Final. Torquay returned to the Football League after a two-year absence by beating Cambridge United 2-0 in the Conference Final.

2010: Blackpool, under the eccentric yet shrewd Ian Holloway, claimed the big prize two years almost to the day after the manager was sacked from his previous job at Leicester. On a scorching afternoon, with temperatures reaching 106 degrees, they twice came back from a goal down to draw level against Cardiff through Charlie Adam and Gary Taylor-Fletcher, then scored what proved to be the winner through Brett Ormerod at the end of a pulsating first half. **Millwall**, beaten in five previous play-offs, reached the Championship with the only goal of the game against Swindon from captain Paul Robinson. **Dagenham & Redbridge** defeated Rotherham 3-2 in the League Two Final, Jon Nurse scoring the winner 20 minutes from the end. **Oxford** returned to the Football League after an absence of four years with a 3-1 over York in the Conference Final.

2011: Scott Sinclair scored a hat-trick as **Swansea** reached the top flight, just eight years after almost going out of the Football League. Two of his goals came from the penalty spot as Reading were beaten 4-2 in the Championship Final, with Stephen Dobbie netting their other goal. The day after his father's side lost to Barcelona in the Champions League Final, Darren Ferguson led **Peterborough** back to the Championship at the first attempt with goals by Tommy Rowe, Craig Mackail-Smith and Grant McCann in the final 12 minutes against Huddersfield. John Mousinho scored the only one of the League Two Final for **Stevenage**, who won a second successive promotion by beating Torquay. **AFC Wimbledon**, formed by supporters in 2002 after the former FA Cup-winning club relocated to Milton Keynes, completed their rise from the Combined Counties to the Football League by winning a penalty shoot-out against Luton after a goalless draw in the Conference Final.

2012: **West Ham** were third in the Championship and second best to Blackpool in the final. But they passed the post first at Wembley, thanks to an 87th minute goal from Ricardo Vaz Te which gave Sam Allardyce's side a 2-1 victory. Allardyce brought the Portuguese striker to Upton Park from Barnsley for £500,000 – a fee dwarfed by the millions his goal was worth to the club. Goalkeepers took centre stage in the League One Final, with **Huddersfield** and Sheffield United still locked in a marathon shoot-out after a goalless 120 minutes. Alex Smithies put the 21st penalty past his opposite number Steve Simonsen, who then drove over the crossbar to give Huddersfield victory by 8-7. Nick Powell, 18, lit up the League Two Final with a spectacular volley as **Crewe** beat Cheltenham 2-0. **York** regained a Football League place after an absence of eight years by beating Luton 2-1 in the Conference decider.

2013: Veteran Kevin Phillips, a loser in three previous finals, came off the bench to fire **Crystal Palace** into the Premier League with an extra-time penalty. Wilfried Zaha was brought down by Marco Cassetti and 39-year-old Phillips showed nerves of steel to convert the spot-kick. A goalline clearance by Joel Ward then denied Fernando Forestieri as Watford sought an equaliser. **Yeovil** upset the odds by reaching the Championship for the first time. They defeated Brentford 2-1, Paddy Madden scoring his 23rd goal of the season and on-loan Dan Burn adding the second. **Bradford**, back at Wembley three months after their Capital One Cup adventure, swept aside Northampton 3-0 in the League Two Final with goals from James Hanson, Rory McArdle and Nahki Wells. **Newport** returned to the Football League after a 25-year absence by defeating Wrexham 2-0 in the Conference Final.

2014: An immediate return to the Premier League for **Queens Park Rangers** seemed unlikely when Gary O'Neil was sent off for bringing down Derby's Johnny Russell. There was still more than half-an-hour to go of a match Derby had dominated. But Rangers held on and with 90 minutes nearly up Bobby Zamora punished a mistake by captain Richard Keogh to score the only goal. **Rotherham** retrieved a 2-0 deficit against Leyton Orient with two goals by Alex Revell in the League One Final and won the eventual penalty shoot-out 4-3 for a second successive promotion. **Fleetwood** achieved their sixth promotion in ten seasons with a 1-0 victory over Burton, courtesy of a free-kick from Antoni Sarcevic in the League Two Final. Liam Hughes and Ryan Donaldson were on the mark as **Cambridge United** returned to the Football League after a nine-year absence by beating Gateshead 2-1 in the Conference Final, two months after winning the FA Trophy at Wembley

Year	Matches	Agg. Att
1987	20	310,000
1988	19	305,817
1989	18	234,393
1990	15	291,428
1991	15	266,442
1992	15	277,684

1993	15	319,907
1994	15	314,817
1995	15	295,317
1996	15	308,515
1997	15	309,085
1998	15	320,795
1999	15	372,969
2000	15	333,999
2001	15	317,745
2002	15	327,894
2003	15	374,461
2004	15	388,675
2005	15	353,330
2006	15	340,804
2007	15	405,278 (record)
2008	15	382,032
2009	15	380,329
2010	15	370,055
2011	15	310,998
2012	15	332,930
2013	15	346,062
2014	15	307,011
2015	15	367,374

COPA AMERICA

Alexis Sanchez, an FA Cup winner with Arsenal, scored the decisive penalty as Chile won the Copa America – their first major trophy. They beat Argentina in a shoot-out after the final in Santiago ended goalless.

QUARTER-FINALS

Argentina 0 Colombia 0 – aet, Argentina won 5-4 on pens; Brazil 1 (Robinho 15) Paraguay 1 (Gonzalez 72 pen) – aet, Paraguay won 4-3 on pens; Bolivia 1 (Moreno 84 pen) Peru 3 (Guerrero 20, 23, 74); Chile 1 (Isla 81) Uruguay 0

SEMI-FINALS

Argentina 6 (Rojo 15, Pastore 27, Di Maria 47, 53, Aguero 80, Higuain 83) Paraguay 1 (Barrios 43); Chile 2 (Vargas 42, 64) Peru 1 (Medel 60 og)

THIRD/FOURTH PLACE PLAY-OFF

Peru 2 (Carrillo 48, Guerrero 89) Paraguay 0

FINAL

Chile 0 Argentina 0 – aet, Chile won 4-1 on pens
Santiago (45,000); Saturday July 4 2015
Chile (4-3-1-2): Bravo, Isla, Silva, Medel, Beausejour, Vidal, Diaz, Aranguiz, Valdivia (Fernandez 75), Sanchez, Vargas (Henriquez 95). **Booked**: Silva, Medel, Diaz, Aranguiz. **Coach**: Jorge Luis Sampaoli
Argentina (4-3-3): Romero, Zabaleta, Demichelis, Otamendi, Rojo, Biglia, Mascherano, Pastore (Banega 81), Messi, Aguero (Higuain 74), Di M aria (Lavezzi 29). **Booked**: Rojo, Mascherano, Banega. **Coach**: Gerardo Martino
Referee: W Roldan (Colombia)

FA WOMEN'S PREMIER LEAGUE - NORTH

	P	W	D	L	F	A	GD	Pts
Sheffield FC	22	19	1	2	76	19	57	58
Coventry*	22	18	2	2	64	16	48	50
Blackburn	22	13	3	6	46	34	12	42
Bradford	22	11	6	5	49	28	21	39
Huddersfield	22	8	5	9	53	65	-12	29
Derby	22	8	3	11	45	56	-11	27
Stoke	22	8	2	12	38	38	0	26
Preston	22	7	5	10	41	46	-5	26
Nottm Forest	22	7	2	13	34	52	-18	23
Sporting	22	5	6	11	23	36	-13	21
Newcastle	22	5	5	12	33	50	-17	20
Wolves	22	2	2	18	17	79	-62	8

*6 pts deducted for ineligible players

SOUTH

	P	W	D	L	F	A	GD	Pts
Portsmouth	22	18	2	2	62	25	37	56
Brighton	22	17	2	3	63	22	41	53
Charlton	22	15	3	4	88	34	54	48
Cardiff	22	14	3	5	69	26	43	45
Tottenham	22	12	3	7	60	40	20	39
West Ham	22	10	5	7	39	30	9	35
Lewes	22	6	3	13	31	37	-6	21
Copsewood	22	6	2	14	23	66	-43	20
QPR*	22	6	4	12	28	42	-14	19
Plymouth	22	4	6	12	25	60	-35	18
Gillingham	22	4	3	15	28	65	-37	15
Keynsham	22	1	2	19	26	95	-69	5

*3pts deducted for late cancellation

Cup Final: Charlton 0 Sheffield FC 0 (aet, Charlton won 4-2 on pens)

FA WOMEN'S SUPER LEAGUE 2014

	P	W	D	L	F	A	GD	Pts
Liverpool	14	7	5	2	19	10	9	26
Chelsea	14	8	2	4	23	16	7	26
Birmingham	14	7	4	3	20	14	6	25
Arsenal	14	6	3	5	24	21	3	21
Manchester City	14	6	1	7	13	16	-3	19
Notts Co	14	4	6	4	12	8	4	18
Bristol Acad	14	5	1	8	18	24	-6	16
Everton	14	0	4	10	10	30	-20	4

Continental Cup Final: Manchester City 1 Arsenal 0

ENGLISH HONOURS LIST

PREMIER LEAGUE

	First	Pts	Second	Pts	Third	Pts
1992–3a	Manchester Utd	84	Aston Villa	74	Norwich	72
1993–4a	Manchester Utd	92	Blackburn	84	Newcastle	77
1994–5a	Blackburn	89	Manchester Utd	88	Nottm Forest	77
1995–6b	Manchester Utd	82	Newcastle	78	Liverpool	71
1996–7b	Manchester Utd	75	Newcastle	68	Arsenal	68
1997–8b	Arsenal	78	Manchester Utd	77	Liverpool	65
1998–9b	Manchester Utd	79	Arsenal	78	Chelsea	75
1999–00b	Manchester Utd	91	Arsenal	73	Leeds	69
2000–01b	Manchester Utd	80	Arsenal	70	Liverpool	69
2001–02b	Arsenal	87	Liverpool	80	Manchester Utd	77
2002–03b	Manchester Utd	83	Arsenal	78	Newcastle	69
2003–04b	Arsenal	90	Chelsea	79	Manchester Utd	75
2004–05b	Chelsea	95	Arsenal	83	Manchester Utd	77
2005–06b	Chelsea	91	Manchester Utd	83	Liverpool	82
2006–07b	Manchester Utd	89	Chelsea	83	Liverpool	68
2007–08b	Manchester Utd	87	Chelsea	85	Arsenal	83
2008–09b	Manchester Utd	90	Liverpool	86	Chelsea	83
2009–10b	Chelsea	86	Manchester Utd	85	Arsenal	75
2010–11b	Manchester Utd	80	Chelsea	71	Manchester City	71
2011–12b	*Manchester City	89	Manchester Utd	89	Arsenal	70
2012–13b	Manchester Utd	89	Manchester City	78	Chelsea	75
2013–14b	Manchester City	86	Liverpool	84	Chelsea	82
2014–15b	Chelsea	87	Manchester City	79	Arsenal	75

* won on goal difference. Maximum points: a, 126; b, 114

FOOTBALL LEAGUE

FIRST DIVISION

1992–3	Newcastle	96	West Ham	88	††Portsmouth	88
1993–4	Crystal Palace	90	Nottm Forest	83	††Millwall	74
1994–5	Middlesbrough	82	††Reading	79	Bolton	77
1995–6	Sunderland	83	Derby	79	††Crystal Palace	75
1996–7	Bolton	98	Barnsley	80	††Wolves	76
1997–8	Nottm Forest	94	Middlesbrough	91	††Sunderland	90
1998–9	Sunderland	105	Bradford City	87	††Ipswich	86
1999–00	Charlton	91	Manchester City	89	Ipswich	87
2000–01	Fulham	101	Blackburn	91	Bolton	87
2001–02	Manchester City	99	WBA	89	††Wolves	86
2002–03	Portsmouth	98	Leicester	92	††Sheffield Utd	80
2003–04	Norwich	94	WBA	86	††Sunderland	79

CHAMPIONSHIP

2004–05	Sunderland	94	Wigan	87	††Ipswich	85
2005–06	Reading	106	Sheffield Utd	90	Watford	81
2006–07	Sunderland	88	Birmingham	86	Derby	84
2007–08	WBA	81	Stoke	79	Hull	75
2008–09	Wolves	90	Birmingham	83	††Sheffield Utd	80
2009–10	Newcastle	102	WBA	91	††Nottm Forest	79
2010–11	QPR	88	Norwich	84	Swansea	80
2011–12	Reading	89	Southampton	88	West Ham	86
2012–13	Cardiff	87	Hull	79	††Watford	77
2013–14	Leicester	102	Burnley	93	††Derby	85

| 2014-15 | Bournemouth | 90 | Watford | 89 | Norwich | 86 |

Maximum points: 138 ††Not promoted after play-offs

SECOND DIVISION

1992–3	Stoke	93	Bolton	90	††Port Vale	89
1993–4	Reading	89	Port Vale	88	††Plymouth Argyle	85
1994–5	Birmingham	89	††Brentford	85	††Crewe	83
1995–6	Swindon	92	Oxford Utd	83	††Blackpool	82
1996–7	Bury	84	Stockport	82	††Luton	78
1997–8	Watford	88	Bristol City	85	Grimsby	72
1998–9	Fulham	101	Walsall	87	Manchester City	82
1999–00	Preston	95	Burnley	88	Gillingham	85
2000–01	Millwall	93	Rotherham	91	††Reading	86
2001–02	Brighton	90	Reading	84	††Brentford	83
2002–03	Wigan	100	Crewe	86	††Bristol City	83
2003–04	Plymouth Argyle	90	QPR	83	††Bristol City	82

LEAGUE ONE

2004–05	Luton	98	Hull	86	††Tranmere	79
2005–06	Southend	82	Colchester	79	††Brentford	76
2006–07	Scunthorpe	91	Bristol City	85	Blackpool	83
2007-08	Swansea	92	Nottm Forest	82	Doncaster	80
2008-09	Leicester	96	Peterborough	89	††MK Dons	87
2009–10	Norwich	95	Leeds	86	Millwall	85
2010–11	Brighton	95	Southampton	92	††Huddersfield	87
2011–12	Charlton	101	Sheffield Wed	93	††Sheffield Utd	90
2012–13	Doncaster	84	Bournemouth	83	††Brentford	79
2013-14	Wolves	103	Brentford	94	††Leyton Orient	86
2014-15	Bristol City	99	MK Dons	91	Preston	89

Maximum points: 138 †† Not promoted after play-offs

THIRD DIVISION

1992–3a	Cardiff	83	Wrexham	80	Barnet	79
1993–4a	Shrewsbury	79	Chester	74	Crewe	73
1994–5a	Carlisle	91	Walsall	83	Chesterfield	81
1995–6b	Preston	86	Gillingham	83	Bury	79
1996–7b	Wigan	87	Fulham	87	Carlisle	84
1997–8b	Notts Co	99	Macclesfield	82	Lincoln	75
1998–9b	Brentford	85	Cambridge Utd	81	Cardiff	80
1999–00b	Swansea	85	Rotherham	84	Northampton	82
2000–01b	Brighton	92	Cardiff	82	*Chesterfield	80
2001–02b	Plymouth Argyle	102	Luton	97	Mansfield	79
2002–03b	Rushden & D	87	Hartlepool Utd	85	Wrexham	84
2003–04b	Doncaster	92	Hull	88	Torquay	81

* Deducted 9 points for financial irregularities

LEAGUE TWO

2004–05b	Yeovil	83	Scunthorpe	80	Swansea	80
2005–06b	Carlisle	86	Northampton	83	Leyton Orient	81
2006–07b	Walsall	89	Hartlepool	88	Swindon	85
2007-08b	MK Dons	97	Peterborough	92	Hereford	88
2008-09b	Brentford	85	Exeter	79	Wycombe	78
2009–10b	Notts Co	93	Bournemouth	83	Rochdale	82
2010–11b	Chesterfield	86	Bury	81	Wycombe	80
2011–12b	Swindon	93	Shrewsbury	88	Crawley	84
2012–13b	Gillingham	83	Rotherham	79	Port Vale	78

| 2013-14*b* | Chesterfield | 84 | Scunthorpe | 81 | Rochdale | 81 |
| 2014-15*b* | Burton | 94 | Shrewsbury | 89 | Bury | 85 |

Maximum points: *a*, 126; *b*, 138;

FOOTBALL LEAGUE 1888–1992

1888–89*a*	Preston	40	Aston Villa	29	Wolves	28
1889–90*a*	Preston	33	Everton	31	Blackburn	27
1890–1*a*	Everton	29	Preston	27	Notts Co	26
1891–2*b*	Sunderland	42	Preston	37	Bolton	36

OLD FIRST DIVISION

1892–3*c*	Sunderland	48	Preston	37	Everton	36
1893–4*c*	Aston Villa	44	Sunderland	38	Derby	36
1894–5*c*	Sunderland	47	Everton	42	Aston Villa	39
1895–6*c*	Aston Villa	45	Derby	41	Everton	39
1896–7*c*	Aston Villa	47	Sheffield Utd	36	Derby	36
1897–8*c*	Sheffield Utd	42	Sunderland	39	Wolves	35
1898–9*d*	Aston Villa	45	Liverpool	43	Burnley	39
1899–1900*d*	Aston Villa	50	Sheffield Utd	48	Sunderland	41
1900–1*d*	Liverpool	45	Sunderland	43	Notts Co	40
1901–2*d*	Sunderland	44	Everton	41	Newcastle	37
1902–3*d*	The Wednesday	42	Aston Villa	41	Sunderland	41
1903–4*d*	The Wednesday	47	Manchester City	44	Everton	43
1904–5*d*	Newcastle	48	Everton	47	Manchester City	46
1905–6*e*	Liverpool	51	Preston	47	The Wednesday	44
1906–7*e*	Newcastle	51	Bristol City	48	Everton	45
1907–8*e*	Manchester Utd	52	Aston Villa	43	Manchester City	43
1908–9*e*	Newcastle	53	Everton	46	Sunderland	44
1909–10*e*	Aston Villa	53	Liverpool	48	Blackburn	45
1910–11*e*	Manchester Utd	52	Aston Villa	51	Sunderland	45
1911–12*e*	Blackburn	49	Everton	46	Newcastle	44
1912–13*e*	Sunderland	54	Aston Villa	50	Sheffield Wed	49
1913–14*e*	Blackburn	51	Aston Villa	44	Middlesbrough	43
1914–15*e*	Everton	46	Oldham	45	Blackburn	43
1919–20*f*	WBA	60	Burnley	51	Chelsea	49
1920–1*f*	Burnley	59	Manchester City	54	Bolton	52
1921–2*f*	Liverpool	57	Tottenham	51	Burnley	49
1922–3*f*	Liverpool	60	Sunderland	54	Huddersfield	53
1923–4*f*	*Huddersfield	57	Cardiff	57	Sunderland	53
1924–5*f*	Huddersfield	58	WBA	56	Bolton	55
1925–6*f*	Huddersfield	57	Arsenal	52	Sunderland	48
1926–7*f*	Newcastle	56	Huddersfield	51	Sunderland	49
1927–8*f*	Everton	53	Huddersfield	51	Leicester	48
1928–9*f*	Sheffield Wed	52	Leicester	51	Aston Villa	50
1929–30*f*	Sheffield Wed	60	Derby	50	Manchester City	47
1930–1*f*	Arsenal	66	Aston Villa	59	Sheffield Wed	52
1931–2*f*	Everton	56	Arsenal	54	Sheffield Wed	50
1932–3*f*	Arsenal	58	Aston Villa	54	Sheffield Wed	51
1933–4*f*	Arsenal	59	Huddersfield	56	Tottenham	49
1934–5*f*	Arsenal	58	Sunderland	54	Sheffield Wed	49
1935–6*f*	Sunderland	56	Derby	48	Huddersfield	48
1936–7*f*	Manchester City	57	Charlton	54	Arsenal	52
1937–8*f*	Arsenal	52	Wolves	51	Preston	49
1938–9*f*	Everton	59	Wolves	55	Charlton	50

1946–7f	Liverpool	57	Manchester Utd	56	Wolves	56
1947–8f	Arsenal	59	Manchester Utd	52	Burnley	52
1948–9f	Portsmouth	58	Manchester Utd	53	Derby	53
1949–50f	*Portsmouth	53	Wolves	53	Sunderland	52
1950–1f	Tottenham	60	Manchester Utd	56	Blackpool	50
1951–2f	Manchester Utd	57	Tottenham	53	Arsenal	53
1952–3f	*Arsenal	54	Preston	54	Wolves	51
1953–4f	Wolves	57	WBA	53	Huddersfield	51
1954–5f	Chelsea	52	Wolves	48	Portsmouth	48
1955–6f	Manchester Utd	60	Blackpool	49	Wolves	49
1956–7f	Manchester Utd	64	Tottenham	56	Preston	56
1957–8f	Wolves	64	Preston	59	Tottenham	51
1958–9f	Wolves	61	Manchester Utd	55	Arsenal	50
1959–60f	Burnley	55	Wolves	54	Tottenham	53
1960–1f	Tottenham	66	Sheffield Wed	58	Wolves	57
1961–2f	Ipswich	56	Burnley	53	Tottenham	52
1962–3f	Everton	61	Tottenham	55	Burnley	54
1963–4f	Liverpool	57	Manchester Utd	53	Everton	52
1964–5f	*Manchester Utd	61	Leeds	61	Chelsea	56
1965–6f	Liverpool	61	Leeds	55	Burnley	55
1966–7f	Manchester Utd	60	Nottm Forest	56	Tottenham	56
1967–8f	Manchester City	58	Manchester Utd	56	Liverpool	55
1968–9f	Leeds	67	Liverpool	61	Everton	57
1969–70f	Everton	66	Leeds	57	Chelsea	55
1970–1f	Arsenal	65	Leeds	64	Tottenham	52
1971–2f	Derby	58	Leeds	57	Liverpool	57
1972–3f	Liverpool	60	Arsenal	57	Leeds	53
1973–4f	Leeds	62	Liverpool	57	Derby	48
1974–5f	Derby	53	Liverpool	51	Ipswich	51
1975–6f	Liverpool	60	QPR	59	Manchester Utd	56
1976–7f	Liverpool	57	Manchester City	56	Ipswich	52
1977–8f	Nottm Forest	64	Liverpool	57	Everton	55
1978–9f	Liverpool	68	Nottm Forest	60	WBA	59
1979–80f	Liverpool	60	Manchester Utd	58	Ipswich	53
1980–1f	Aston Villa	60	Ipswich	56	Arsenal	53
1981–2g	Liverpool	87	Ipswich	83	Manchester Utd	78
1982–3g	Liverpool	82	Watford	71	Manchester Utd	70
1983–4g	Liverpool	80	Southampton	77	Nottm Forest	74
1984–5g	Everton	90	Liverpool	77	Tottenham	77
1985–6g	Liverpool	88	Everton	86	West Ham	84
1986–7g	Everton	86	Liverpool	77	Tottenham	71
1987–8h	Liverpool	90	Manchester Utd	81	Nottm Forest	73
1988–9j	††Arsenal	76	Liverpool	76	Nottm Forest	64
1989–90j	Liverpool	79	Aston Villa	70	Tottenham	63
1990–1j	Arsenal	83	Liverpool	76	Crystal Palace	69
1991–2g	Leeds	82	Manchester Utd	78	Sheffield Wed	75

Maximum points: a, 44; b, 52; c, 60; d, 68; e, 76; f, 84; g, 126; h, 120; j, 114
*Won on goal average †Won on goal diff ††Won on goals scored No comp 1915–19 –1939–46

OLD SECOND DIVISION 1892–1992

1892–3a	Small Heath	36	Sheffield Utd	35	Darwen	30
1893–4b	Liverpool	50	Small Heath	42	Notts Co	39
1894–5c	Bury	48	Notts Co	39	Newton Heath	38
1895–6c	*Liverpool	46	Manchester City	46	Grimsby	42
1896–7c	Notts Co	42	Newton Heath	39	Grimsby	38

Season	First	Pts	Second	Pts	Third	Pts
1897–8*c*	Burnley	48	Newcastle	45	Manchester City	39
1898–9*d*	Manchester City	52	Glossop	46	Leicester Fosse	45
1899–1900*d*	The Wednesday	54	Bolton	52	Small Heath	46
1900–1*d*	Grimsby	49	Small Heath	48	Burnley	44
1901–2*d*	WBA	55	Middlesbrough	51	Preston	42
1902–3*d*	Manchester City	54	Small Heath	51	Woolwich Arsenal	48
1903–4*d*	Preston	50	Woolwich Arsenal	49	Manchester Utd	48
1904–5*d*	Liverpool	58	Bolton	56	Manchester Utd	53
1905–6*e*	Bristol City	66	Manchester Utd	62	Chelsea	53
1906–7*e*	Nottm Forest	60	Chelsea	57	Leicester Fosse	48
1907–8*e*	Bradford City	54	Leicester Fosse	52	Oldham	50
1908–9*e*	Bolton	52	Tottenham	51	WBA	51
1909–10*e*	Manchester City	54	Oldham	53	Hull	53
1910–11*e*	WBA	53	Bolton	51	Chelsea	49
1911–12*e*	*Derby	54	Chelsea	54	Burnley	52
1912–13*e*	Preston	53	Burnley	50	Birmingham	46
1913–14*e*	Notts Co	53	Bradford PA	49	Woolwich Arsenal	49
1914–15*e*	Derby	53	Preston	50	Barnsley	47
1919–20*f*	Tottenham	70	Huddersfield	64	Birmingham	56
1920–1*f*	*Birmingham	58	Cardiff	58	Bristol City	51
1921–2*f*	Nottm Forest	56	Stoke	52	Barnsley	52
1922–3*f*	Notts Co	53	West Ham	51	Leicester	51
1923–4*f*	Leeds	54	Bury	51	Derby	51
1924–5*f*	Leicester	59	Manchester Utd	57	Derby	55
1925–6*f*	Sheffield Wed	60	Derby	57	Chelsea	52
1926–7*f*	Middlesbrough	62	Portsmouth	54	Manchester City	54
1927–8*f*	Manchester City	59	Leeds	57	Chelsea	54
1928–9*f*	Middlesbrough	55	Grimsby	53	Bradford City	48
1929–30*f*	Blackpool	58	Chelsea	55	Oldham	53
1930–1*f*	Everton	61	WBA	54	Tottenham	51
1931–2*f*	Wolves	56	Leeds	54	Stoke	52
1932–3*f*	Stoke	56	Tottenham	55	Fulham	50
1933–4*f*	Grimsby	59	Preston	52	Bolton	51
1934–5*f*	Brentford	61	Bolton	56	West Ham	56
1935–6*f*	Manchester Utd	56	Charlton	55	Sheffield Utd	52
1936–7*f*	Leicester	56	Blackpool	55	Bury	52
1937–8*f*	Aston Villa	57	Manchester Utd	53	Sheffield Utd	53
1938–9*f*	Blackburn	55	Sheffield Utd	54	Sheffield Wed	53
1946–7*f*	Manchester City	62	Burnley	58	Birmingham	55
1947–8*f*	Birmingham	59	Newcastle	56	Southampton	52
1948–9*f*	Fulham	57	WBA	56	Southampton	55
1949–50*f*	Tottenham	61	Sheffield Wed	52	Sheffield Utd	52
1950–1*f*	Preston	57	Manchester City	52	Cardiff	50
1951–2*f*	Sheffield Wed	53	Cardiff	51	Birmingham	51
1952–3*f*	Sheffield Utd	60	Huddersfield	58	Luton	52
1953–4*f*	*Leicester	56	Everton	56	Blackburn	55
1954–5*f*	*Birmingham	54	Luton	54	Rotherham	54
1955–6*f*	Sheffield Wed	55	Leeds	52	Liverpool	48
1956–7*f*	Leicester	61	Nottm Forest	54	Liverpool	53
1957–8*f*	West Ham	57	Blackburn	56	Charlton	55
1958–9*f*	Sheffield Wed	62	Fulham	60	Sheffield Utd	53
1959–60*f*	Aston Villa	59	Cardiff	58	Liverpool	50
1960–1*f*	Ipswich	59	Sheffield Utd	58	Liverpool	52
1961–2*f*	Liverpool	62	Leyton Orient	54	Sunderland	53

1962–3f	Stoke	53	Chelsea	52	Sunderland	52
1963–4f	Leeds	63	Sunderland	61	Preston	56
1964–5f	Newcastle	57	Northampton	56	Bolton	50
1965–6f	Manchester City	59	Southampton	54	Coventry	53
1966–7f	Coventry	59	Wolves	58	Carlisle	52
1967–8f	Ipswich	59	QPR	58	Blackpool	58
1968–9f	Derby	63	Crystal Palace	56	Charlton	50
1969–70f	Huddersfield	60	Blackpool	53	Leicester	51
1970–1f	Leicester	59	Sheffield Utd	53	Cardiff	53
1971–2f	Norwich	57	Birmingham	56	Millwall	55
1972–3f	Burnley	62	QPR	61	Aston Villa	50
1973–4f	Middlesbrough	65	Luton	50	Carlisle	49
1974–5f	Manchester Utd	61	Aston Villa	58	Norwich	53
1975–6f	Sunderland	56	Bristol City	53	WBA	53
1976–7f	Wolves	57	Chelsea	55	Nottm Forest	52
1977–8f	Bolton	58	Southampton	57	Tottenham	56
1978–9f	Crystal Palace	57	Brighton	56	Stoke	56
1979–80f	Leicester	55	Sunderland	54	Birmingham	53
1980–1f	West Ham	66	Notts Co	53	Swansea	50
1981–2g	Luton	88	Watford	80	Norwich	71
1982–3g	QPR	85	Wolves	75	Leicester	70
1983–4g	†Chelsea	88	Sheffield Wed	88	Newcastle	80
1984–5g	Oxford Utd	84	Birmingham	82	Manchester City	74
1985–6g	Norwich	84	Charlton	77	Wimbledon	76
1986–7g	Derby	84	Portsmouth	78	††Oldham	75
1987–8h	Millwall	82	Aston Villa	78	Middlesbrough	78
1988–9j	Chelsea	99	Manchester City	82	Crystal Palace	81
1989–90j	†Leeds	85	Sheffield Utd	85	†† Newcastle	80
1990–1j	Oldham	88	West Ham	87	Sheffield Wed	82
1991–2j	Ipswich	84	Middlesbrough	80	†† Derby	78

Maximum points: a, 44; b, 56; c, 60; d, 68; e, 76; f, 84; g, 126; h, 132; j, 138 * Won on goal average † Won on goal difference †† Not promoted after play–offs

THIRD DIVISION 1958–92

1958–9	Plymouth Argyle	62	Hull	61	Brentford	57
1959–60	Southampton	61	Norwich	59	Shrewsbury	52
1960–1	Bury	68	Walsall	62	QPR	60
1961–2	Portsmouth	65	Grimsby	62	Bournemouth	59
1962–3	Northampton	62	Swindon	58	Port Vale	54
1963–4	*Coventry	60	Crystal Palace	60	Watford	58
1964–5	Carlisle	60	Bristol City	59	Mansfield	59
1965–6	Hull	69	Millwall	65	QPR	57
1966–7	QPR	67	Middlesbrough	55	Watford	54
1967–8	Oxford Utd	57	Bury	56	Shrewsbury	55
1968–9	*Watford	64	Swindon	64	Luton	61
1969–70	Orient	62	Luton	60	Bristol Rov	56
1970–1	Preston	61	Fulham	60	Halifax	56
1971–2	Aston Villa	70	Brighton	65	Bournemouth	62
1972–3	Bolton	61	Notts Co	57	Blackburn	55
1973–4	Oldham	62	Bristol Rov	61	York	61
1974–5	Blackburn	60	Plymouth Argyle	59	Charlton	55
1975–6	Hereford	63	Cardiff	57	Millwall	56
1976–7	Mansfield	64	Brighton	61	Crystal Palace	59
1977–8	Wrexham	61	Cambridge Utd	58	Preston	56
1978–9	Shrewsbury	61	Watford	60	Swansea	60
1979–80	Grimsby	62	Blackburn	59	Sheffield Wed	58

1980–1	Rotherham	61	Barnsley	59	Charlton	59
†1981–2	**Burnley	80	Carlisle	80	Fulham	78
†1982–3	Portsmouth	91	Cardiff	86	Huddersfield	82
†1983–4	Oxford Utd	95	Wimbledon	87	Sheffield Utd	83
†1984–5	Bradford City	94	Millwall	90	Hull	87
†1985–6	Reading	94	Plymouth Argyle	87	Derby	84
†1986–7	Bournemouth	97	Middlesbrough	94	Swindon	87
†1987–8	Sunderland	93	Brighton	84	Walsall	82
†1988–9	Wolves	92	Sheffield Utd	84	Port Vale	84
†1989–90	Bristol Rov	93	Bristol City	91	Notts Co	87
†1990–1	Cambridge Utd	86	Southend	85	Grimsby	83
†1991–2	Brentford	82	Birmingham	81	††Huddersfield	78

* Won on goal average ** Won on goal difference † Maximum points 138 (previously 92) †† Not promoted after play-offs

FOURTH DIVISION 1958–92

1958–9	Port Vale	64	Coventry	60	York	60	Shrewsbury	58
1959–60	Walsall	65	Notts Co	60	Torquay	60	Watford	57
1960–1	Peterborough	66	Crystal Palace	64	Northampton	60	Bradford PA	60
1961–2	Millwall	56	Colchester	55	Wrexham	53	Carlisle	52
1962–3	Brentford	62	Oldham	59	Crewe	59	Mansfield	57
1963–4	*Gillingham	60	Carlisle	60	Workington	59	Exeter	58
1964–5	Brighton	63	Millwall	62	York	62	Oxford Utd	61
1965–6	*Doncaster	59	Darlington	59	Torquay	58	Colchester	56
1966–7	Stockport	64	Southport	59	Barrow	59	Tranmere	58
1967–8	Luton	66	Barnsley	61	Hartlepool Utd	60	Crewe	58
1968–9	Doncaster	59	Halifax	57	Rochdale	56	Bradford City	56
1969–70	Chesterfield	64	Wrexham	61	Swansea	60	Port Vale	59
1970–1	Notts Co	69	Bournemouth	60	Oldham	59	York	56
1971–2	Grimsby	63	Southend	60	Brentford	59	Scunthorpe	57
1972–3	Southport	62	Hereford	58	Cambridge Utd	57	Aldershot	56
1973–4	Peterborough	65	Gillingham	62	Colchester	60	Bury	59
1974–5	Mansfield	68	Shrewsbury	62	Rotherham	58	Chester	57
1975–6	Lincoln	74	Northampton	68	Reading	60	Tranmere	58
1976–7	Cambridge Utd	65	Exeter	62	Colchester	59	Bradford City	59
1977–8	Watford	71	Southend	60	Swansea	56	Brentford	59
1978–9	Reading	65	Grimsby	61	Wimbledon	61	Barnsley	61
1979–80	Huddersfield	66	Walsall	64	Newport	61	Portsmouth	60
1980–1	Southend	67	Lincoln	65	Doncaster	56	Wimbledon	55
†1981–2	Sheffield Utd	96	Bradford City	91	Wigan	91	Bournemouth	88
†1982–3	Wimbledon	98	Hull	90	Port Vale	88	Scunthorpe	83
†1983–4	York	101	Doncaster	85	Reading	82	Bristol City	82
†1984–5	Chesterfield	91	Blackpool	86	Darlington	85	Bury	84
†1985–6	Swindon	102	Chester	84	Mansfield	81	Port Vale	79
†1986–7	Northampton	99	Preston	90	Southend	80	††Wolves	79
†1987–8	Wolves	90	Cardiff	85	Bolton	78	††Scunthorpe	77
†1988–9	Rotherham	82	Tranmere	80	Crewe	78	††Scunthorpe	77
†1989–90	Exeter	89	Grimsby	79	Southend	75	††Stockport	74
†1990–1	Darlington	83	Stockport	82	Hartlepool Utd	82	Peterborough	80
1991–2a	Burnley	83	Rotherham	77	Mansfield	77	Blackpool	76

* Won on goal average Maximum points: †, 138; a, 126; previously 92 †† Not promoted after play-offs

THIRD DIVISION – SOUTH 1920–58

1920–1a	Crystal Palace	59	Southampton	54	QPR	53
1921–2a	*Southampton	61	Plymouth Argyle	61	Portsmouth	53
1922–3a	Bristol City	59	Plymouth Argyle	53	Swansea	53
1923–4a	Portsmouth	59	Plymouth Argyle	55	Millwall	54
1924–5a	Swansea	57	Plymouth Argyle	56	Bristol City	53

1925-6a	Reading	57	Plymouth Argyle	56	Millwall	53
1926-7a	Bristol City	62	Plymouth Argyle	60	Millwall	56
1927-8a	Millwall	65	Northampton	55	Plymouth Argyle	53
1928-9a	*Charlton	54	Crystal Palace	54	Northampton	52
1929-30a	Plymouth Argyle	68	Brentford	61	QPR	51
1930-31a	Notts Co	59	Crystal Palace	51	Brentford	50
1931-2a	Fulham	57	Reading	55	Southend	53
1932-3a	Brentford	62	Exeter	58	Norwich	57
1933-4a	Norwich	61	Coventry	54	Reading	54
1934-5a	Charlton	61	Reading	53	Coventry	51
1935-6a	Coventry	57	Luton	56	Reading	54
1936-7a	Luton	58	Notts Co	56	Brighton	53
1937-8a	Millwall	56	Bristol City	55	QPR	53
1938-9a	Newport	55	Crystal Palace	52	Brighton	49
1946-7a	Cardiff	66	QPR	57	Bristol City	51
1947-8a	QPR	61	Bournemouth	57	Walsall	51
1948-9a	Swansea	62	Reading	55	Bournemouth	52
1949-50a	Notts Co	58	Northampton	51	Southend	51
1950-1d	Nottm Forest	70	Norwich	64	Reading	57
1951-2d	Plymouth Argyle	66	Reading	61	Norwich	61
1952-3d	Bristol Rov	64	Millwall	62	Northampton	62
1953-4d	Ipswich	64	Brighton	61	Bristol City	56
1954-5d	Bristol City	70	Leyton Orient	61	Southampton	59
1955-6d	Leyton Orient	66	Brighton	65	Ipswich	64
1956-7d	*Ipswich	59	Torquay	59	Colchester	58
1957-8d	Brighton	60	Brentford	58	Plymouth Argyle	58

THIRD DIVISION – NORTH 1921-58

1921-2b	Stockport	56	Darlington	50	Grimsby	50
1922-3b	Nelson	51	Bradford PA	47	Walsall	46
1923-4a	Wolves	63	Rochdale	62	Chesterfield	54
1924-5a	Darlington	58	Nelson	53	New Brighton	53
1925-6a	Grimsby	61	Bradford PA	60	Rochdale	59
1926-7a	Stoke	63	Rochdale	58	Bradford PA	57
1927-8a	Bradford PA	63	Lincoln	55	Stockport	54
1928-9a	Bradford City	63	Stockport	62	Wrexham	52
1929-30a	Port Vale	67	Stockport	63	Darlington	50
1930-1a	Chesterfield	58	Lincoln	57	Wrexham	54
1931-2c	*Lincoln	57	Gateshead	57	Chester	50
1932-3a	Hull	59	Wrexham	57	Stockport	54
1933-4a	Barnsley	62	Chesterfield	61	Stockport	59
1934-5a	Doncaster	57	Halifax	55	Chester	54
1935-6a	Chesterfield	60	Chester	55	Tranmere	54
1936-7a	Stockport	60	Lincoln	57	Chester	53
1937-8a	Tranmere	56	Doncaster	54	Hull	53
1938-9a	Barnsley	67	Doncaster	56	Bradford City	52
1946-7a	Doncaster	72	Rotherham	64	Chester	56
1947-8a	Lincoln	60	Rotherham	59	Wrexham	50
1948-9a	Hull	65	Rotherham	62	Doncaster	50
1949-50a	Doncaster	55	Gateshead	53	Rochdale	51
1950-1d	Rotherham	71	Mansfield	64	Carlisle	62
1951-2d	Lincoln	69	Grimsby	66	Stockport	59
1952-3d	Oldham	59	Port Vale	58	Wrexham	56
1953-4d	Port Vale	69	Barnsley	58	Scunthorpe	57
1954-5d	Barnsley	65	Accrington	61	Scunthorpe	58
1955-6d	Grimsby	68	Derby	63	Accrington	59
1956-7d	Derby	63	Hartlepool Utd	59	Accrington	58
1957-8d	Scunthorpe	66	Accrington	59	Bradford City	57

Maximum points: a, 84; b, 76; c, 80; d, 92 * Won on goal average

TITLE WINNERS

PREMIER LEAGUE
Manchester Utd 13
Chelsea 4
Arsenal 3
Manchester City 2
Blackburn 1

FOOTBALL LEAGUE CHAMPIONSHIP
Reading 2
Sunderland 2
Bournemouth 1
Cardiff 1
Leicester 1
Newcastle 1
QPR 1
WBA 1
Wolves 1

DIV 1 (NEW)
Sunderland 2
Bolton 1
Brighton 1
Charlton 1
Crystal Palace 1
Fulham 1
Manchester City 1
Middlesbrough 1
Newcastle 1
Norwich 1
Nottm Forest 1
Portsmouth 1

DIV 1 (ORIGINAL)
Liverpool 18
Arsenal 10
Everton 9
Aston Villa 7
Manchester Utd 7
Sunderland 6
Newcastle 4
Sheffield Wed 4
Huddersfield 3
Leeds 3
Wolves 3
Blackburn 2
Burnley 2

Derby 2
Manchester City 2
Portsmouth 2
Preston 2
Tottenham 2
Chelsea 1
Ipswich 1
Nottm Forest 1
Sheffield Utd 1
WBA 1

LEAGUE ONE
Brighton 1
Bristol City 1
Charlton 1
Doncaster 1
Leicester 1
Luton 1
Norwich 1
Scunthorpe 1
Southend 1
Swansea 1
Wolves 1

DIV 2 (NEW)
Birmingham 1
Brighton 1
Bury 1
Chesterfield 1
Fulham 1
Millwall 1
Plymouth Argyle 1
Preston 1
Reading 1
Stoke 1
Swindon 1
Watford 1
Wigan 1
Notts Co 1

DIV 2 (ORIGINAL)
Leicester 6
Manchester City 6
Sheffield Wed 5
Birmingham 4
Derby 4
Liverpool 4
Ipswich 3
Leeds 3

Middlesbrough 3
Notts County 3
Preston 3
Aston Villa 2
Bolton 2
Burnley 2
Chelsea 2
Grimsby 2
Manchester Utd 2
Norwich 2
Nottm Forest 2
Stoke 2
Tottenham 2
WBA 2
West Ham 2
Wolves 2
Blackburn 1
Blackpool 1
Bradford City 1
Brentford 1
Bristol City 1
Bury 1
Coventry 1
Crystal Palace 1
Everton 1
Fulham 1
Huddersfield 1
Luton 1
Millwall 1
Newcastle 1
Oldham 1
Oxford Utd 1
QPR 1
Sheffield Utd 1
Sunderland 1

LEAGUE TWO
Chesterfield 2
Brentford 1
Burton 1
Carlisle 1
Gillingham 1
MK Dons 1
Notts County 1
Swindon 1
Walsall 1
Yeovil 1

APPLICATIONS FOR RE-ELECTION (System discontinued 1987)

14	Hartlepool	7	Chester	4	Bradford PA
12	Halifax	7	Walsall	4	Northampton
11	Barrow	7	Workington	4	Norwich
11	Southport	6	York	3	Aldershot
10	Crewe	5	Stockport	3	Bradford City
10	Newport	5	Accrington	3	Crystal Palace
10	Rochdale	5	Gillingham	3	Doncaster
8	Darlington	5	Lincoln	3	Hereford
8	Exeter	5	New Brighton	3	Merthyr

3	Swindon	2	Millwall	1	Cambridge Utd
3	Torquay	2	Nelson	1	Cardiff
3	Tranmere	2	Oldham	1	Carlisle
2	Aberdare	2	QPR	1	Charlton
2	Ashington	2	Rotherham	1	Mansfield
2	Bournemouth	2	Scunthorpe	1	Port Vale
2	Brentford	2	Southend	1	Preston
2	Colchester	2	Watford	1	Shrewsbury
2	Durham	1	Blackpool	1	Swansea
2	Gateshead	1	Brighton	1	Thames
2	Grimsby	1	Bristol Rov	1	Wrexham

RELEGATED CLUBS (TO 1992)

1892–3 In Test matches, Darwen and Sheffield Utd won promotion in place of
 Accrington and Notts Co
1893–4 Tests, Liverpool and Small Heath won promotion Darwen and Newton Heath relegated
1894–5 After Tests, Bury promoted, Liverpool relegated
1895–6 After Tests, Liverpool promoted, Small Heath relegated
1896–7 After Tests, Notts Co promoted, Burnley relegated
1897–8 Test system abolished after success of Burnley and Stoke, League extended Blackburn
and Newcastle elected to First Division
Automatic promotion and relegation introduced

FIRST DIVISION TO SECOND DIVISION

1898–9 Bolton, Sheffield Wed
1899–00 Burnley, Glossop
1900–1 Preston, WBA
1901–2 Small Heath, Manchester City
1902–3 Grimsby, Bolton
1903–4 Liverpool, WBA
1904–5 League extended Bury and Notts Co, two bottom clubs in First Division, re–elected
1905–6 Nottm Forest, Wolves
1906–7 Derby, Stoke
1907–8 Bolton, Birmingham
1908–9 Manchester City, Leicester Fosse
1909–10 Bolton, Chelsea
1910–11 Bristol City, Nottm Forest
1911–12 Preston, Bury
1912–13 Notts Co, Woolwich Arsenal
1913–14 Preston, Derby
1914–15 Tottenham, *Chelsea
1919–20 Notts Co, Sheffield Wed
1920–1 Derby, Bradford PA
1921–2 Bradford City, Manchester Utd
1922–3 Stoke, Oldham
1923–4 Chelsea, Middlesbrough
1924–5 Preston, Nottm Forest
1925–6 Manchester City, Notts Co
1926–7 Leeds, WBA
1927–8 Tottenham, Middlesbrough
1928–9 Bury, Cardiff
1929–30 Burnley, Everton
1930–1 Leeds, Manchester Utd
1931–2 Grimsby, West Ham
1932–3 Bolton, Blackpool
1933–4 Newcastle, Sheffield Utd
1934–5 Leicester, Tottenham
1935–6 Aston Villa, Blackburn
1936–7 Manchester Utd, Sheffield Wed

1937–8	Manchester City, WBA
1938–9	Birmingham, Leicester
1946–7	Brentford, Leeds
1947–8	Blackburn, Grimsby
1948–9	Preston, Sheffield Utd
1949–50	Manchester City, Birmingham
1950–1	Sheffield Wed, Everton
1951–2	Huddersfield, Fulham
1952–3	Stoke, Derby
1953–4	Middlesbrough, Liverpool
1954–5	Leicester, Sheffield Wed
1955–6	Huddersfield, Sheffield Utd
1956–7	Charlton, Cardiff
1957–8	Sheffield Wed, Sunderland
1958–9	Portsmouth, Aston Villa
1959–60	Luton, Leeds
1960–61	Preston, Newcastle
1961–2	Chelsea, Cardiff
1962–3	Manchester City, Leyton Orient
1963–4	Bolton, Ipswich
1964–5	Wolves, Birmingham
1965–6	Northampton, Blackburn
1966–7	Aston Villa, Blackpool
1967–8	Fulham, Sheffield Utd
1968–9	Leicester, QPR
1969–70	Sheffield Wed, Sunderland
1970–1	Burnley, Blackpool
1971–2	Nottm Forest, Huddersfield
1972–3	WBA, Crystal Palace
1973–4	Norwich, Manchester Utd, Southampton
1974–5	Chelsea, Luton, Carlisle
1975–6	Sheffield Utd, Burnley, Wolves
1976–7	Tottenham, Stoke, Sunderland
1977–8	Leicester, West Ham, Newcastle
1978–9	QPR, Birmingham, Chelsea
1979–80	Bristol City, Derby, Bolton
1980–1	Norwich, Leicester, Crystal Palace
1981–2	Leeds, Wolves, Middlesbrough
1982–3	Manchester City, Swansea, Brighton
1983–4	Birmingham, Notts Co, Wolves
1984–5	Norwich, Sunderland, Stoke
1985–6	Ipswich, Birmingham, WBA
1986–7	Leicester, Manchester City, Aston Villa
1987–8	Chelsea**, Portsmouth, Watford, Oxford Utd
1988–9	Middlesbrough, West Ham, Newcastle
1989–90	Sheffield Wed, Charlton, Millwall
1990–1	Sunderland, Derby
1991–2	Luton, Notts Co, West Ham

* Subsequently re–elected to First Division when League extended after the war
** Relegated after play–offs

SECOND DIVISION TO THIRD DIVISION

1920–1	Stockport
1921–2	Bradford City, Bristol City
1922–3	Rotherham, Wolves
1923–4	Nelson, Bristol City
1924–5	Crystal Palace, Coventry
1925–6	Stoke, Stockport
1926–7	Darlington, Bradford City
1927–8	Fulham, South Shields
1928–9	Port Vale, Clapton Orient

1929–30	Hull, Notts County
1930–1	Reading, Cardiff
1931–2	Barnsley, Bristol City
1932–3	Chesterfield, Charlton
1933–4	Millwall, Lincoln
1934–5	Oldham, Notts Co
1935–6	Port Vale, Hull
1936–7	Doncaster, Bradford City
1937–8	Barnsley, Stockport
1938–9	Norwich, Tranmere
1946–7	Swansea, Newport
1947–8	Doncaster, Millwall
1948–9	Nottm Forest, Lincoln
1949–50	Plymouth Argyle, Bradford PA
1950–1	Grimsby, Chesterfield
1951–2	Coventry, QPR
1952–3	Southampton, Barnsley
1953–4	Brentford, Oldham
1954–5	Ipswich, Derby
1955–6	Plymouth Argyle, Hull
1956–7	Port Vale, Bury
1957–8	Doncaster, Notts Co
1958–9	Barnsley, Grimsby
1959–60	Bristol City, Hull
1960–1	Lincoln, Portsmouth
1961–2	Brighton, Bristol Rov
1962–3	Walsall, Luton
1963–4	Grimsby, Scunthorpe
1964–5	Swindon, Swansea
1965–6	Middlesbrough, Leyton Orient
1966–7	Northampton, Bury
1967–8	Plymouth Argyle, Rotherham
1968–9	Fulham, Bury
1969–70	Preston, Aston Villa
1970–1	Blackburn, Bolton
1971–2	Charlton, Watford
1972–3	Huddersfield, Brighton
1973–4	Crystal Palace, Preston, Swindon
1974–5	Millwall, Cardiff, Sheffield Wed
1975–6	Portsmouth, Oxford Utd, York
1976–7	Carlisle, Plymouth Argyle, Hereford
1977–8	Hull, Mansfield, Blackpool
1978–9	Sheffield Utd, Millwall, Blackburn
1979–80	Fulham, Burnley, Charlton
1980–1	Preston, Bristol City, Bristol Rov
1981–2	Cardiff, Wrexham, Orient
1982–3	Rotherham, Burnley, Bolton
1983–4	Derby, Swansea, Cambridge Utd
1984–5	Notts Co, Cardiff, Wolves
1985–6	Carlisle, Middlesbrough, Fulham
1986–7	Sunderland**, Grimsby, Brighton
1987–8	Sheffield Utd**, Reading, Huddersfield
1988–9	Shrewsbury, Birmingham, Walsall
1989–90	Bournemouth, Bradford City, Stoke
1990–1	WBA, Hull
1991–2	Plymouth Argyle, Brighton, Port Vale

** Relegated after play–offs

THIRD DIVISION TO FOURTH DIVISION

| 1958–9 | Rochdale, Notts Co, Doncaster, Stockport |
| 1959–60 | Accrington, Wrexham, Mansfield, York |

1960–1	Chesterfield, Colchester, Bradford City, Tranmere
1961–2	Newport, Brentford, Lincoln, Torquay
1962–3	Bradford PA, Brighton, Carlisle, Halifax
1963–4	Millwall, Crewe, Wrexham, Notts Co
1964–5	Luton, Port Vale, Colchester, Barnsley
1965–6	Southend, Exeter, Brentford, York
1966–7	Doncaster, Workington, Darlington, Swansea
1967–8	Scunthorpe, Colchester, Grimsby, Peterborough (demoted)
1968–9	Oldham, Crewe, Hartlepool Utd, Northampton
1969–70	Bournemouth, Southport, Barrow, Stockport
1970–1	Gillingham, Doncaster, Bury, Reading
1971–2	Mansfield, Barnsley, Torquay, Bradford City
1972–3	Scunthorpe, Swansea, Brentford, Rotherham
1973–4	Cambridge Utd, Shrewsbury, Rochdale, Southport
1974–5	Bournemouth, Watford, Tranmere, Huddersfield
1975–6	Aldershot, Colchester, Southend, Halifax
1976–7	Reading, Northampton, Grimsby, York
1977–8	Port Vale, Bradford City, Hereford, Portsmouth
1978–9	Peterborough, Walsall, Tranmere, Lincoln
1979–80	Bury, Southend, Mansfield, Wimbledon
1980–1	Sheffield Utd, Colchester, Blackpool, Hull
1981–2	Wimbledon, Swindon, Bristol City, Chester
1982–3	Reading, Wrexham, Doncaster, Chesterfield
1983–4	Scunthorpe, Southend, Port Vale, Exeter
1984–5	Burnley, Orient, Preston, Cambridge Utd
1985–6	Lincoln, Cardiff, Wolves, Swansea
1986–7	Bolton**, Carlisle, Darlington, Newport
1987–8	Doncaster, York, Grimsby, Rotherham**
1988–9	Southend, Chesterfield, Gillingham, Aldershot
1989–90	Cardiff, Northampton, Blackpool, Walsall
1990–1	Crewe, Rotherham, Mansfield
1991–2	Bury, Shrewsbury, Torquay, Darlington

** Relegated after plays–offs

DEMOTED FROM FOURTH DIVISION TO CONFERENCE

1987	Lincoln
1988	Newport
1989	Darlington
1990	Colchester
1991	No demotion
1992	No demotion

DEMOTED FROM THIRD DIVISION TO CONFERENCE

1993	Halifax
1994–6	No demotion
1997	Hereford
1998	Doncaster
1999	Scarborough
2000	Chester
2001	Barnet
2002	Halifax
2003	Exeter, Shrewsbury
2004	Carlisle, York

DEMOTED FROM LEAGUE TWO TO CONFERENCE

2005	Kidderminster, Cambridge Utd
2006	Oxford Utd, Rushden & Diamonds

2007	Boston, Torquay
2008	Mansfield, Wrexham
2009	Chester Luton
2010	Grimsby, Darlington
2011	Lincoln, Stockport
2012	Hereford, Macclesfield
2013	Barnet, Aldershot
2014	Bristol Rov, Torquay
2015	Cheltenham, Tranmere

RELEGATED CLUBS (SINCE 1993)

1993
Premier League to Div 1: Crystal Palace, Middlesbrough, Nottm Forest
Div 1 to Div 2: Brentford, Cambridge Utd, Bristol Rov
Div 2 to Div 3: Preston, Mansfield, Wigan, Chester

1994
Premier League to Div 1: Sheffield Utd, Oldham, Swindon
Div 1 to Div 2: Birmingham, Oxford Utd, Peterborough
Div 2 to Div 3: Fulham, Exeter, Hartlepool Utd, Barnet

1995
Premier League to Div 1: Crystal Palace, Norwich, Leicester, Ipswich
Div 1 to Div 2: Swindon, Burnley, Bristol City, Notts Co
Div 2 to Div 3: Cambridge Utd, Plymouth Argyle, Cardiff, Chester, Leyton Orient

1996
Premier League to Div 1: Manchester City, QPR, Bolton
Div 1 to Div 2: Millwall, Watford, Luton
Div 2 to Div 3: Carlisle, Swansea, Brighton, Hull

1997
Premier League to Div 1: Sunderland, Middlesbrough, Nottm Forest
Div 1 to Div 2: Grimsby, Oldham, Southend
Div 2 to Div 3: Peterborough, Shrewsbury, Rotherham, Notts Co

1998
Premier League to Div 1: Bolton, Barnsley, Crystal Palace
Div 1 to Div 2: Manchester City, Stoke, Reading
Div 2 to Div 3: Brentford, Plymouth Argyle, Carlisle, Southend

1999
Premier League to Div 1: Charlton, Blackburn, Nottm Forest
Div 1 to Div 2: Bury, Oxford Utd, Bristol City
Div 2 to Div 3: York, Northampton, Lincoln, Macclesfield

2000
Premier League to Div 1: Wimbledon, Sheffield Wed, Watford
Div 1 to Div 2: Walsall, Port Vale, Swindon
Div 2 to Div 3: Cardiff, Blackpool, Scunthorpe, Chesterfield

2001
Premier League to Div 1: Manchester City, Coventry, Bradford City
Div 1 to Div 2: Huddersfield, QPR, Tranmere
Div 2 to Div 3: Bristol Rov, Luton, Swansea, Oxford Utd

2002
Premier League to Div 1: Ipswich, Derby, Leicester
Div 1 to Div 2: Crewe, Barnsley, Stockport
Div 2 to Div 3: Bournemouth, Bury, Wrexham, Cambridge Utd

2003
Premier League to Div 1: West Ham, WBA, Sunderland
Div 1 to Div 2: Sheffield Wed, Brighton, Grimsby
Div 2 to Div 3: Cheltenham, Huddersfield, Mansfield, Northampton

2004
Premier League to Div 1: Leicester, Leeds, Wolves
Div 1 to Div 2: Walsall, Bradford City, Wimbledon
Div 2 to Div 3: Grimsby, Rushden & Diamonds, Notts Co, Wycombe

2005
Premier League to Championship: Crystal Palace, Norwich, Southampton
Championship to League 1: Gillingham, Nottm Forest, Rotherham
League 1 to League 2: Torquay, Wrexham, Peterborough, Stockport

2006
Premier League to Championship: Birmingham, WBA, Sunderland
Championship to League 1: Crewe, Millwall, Brighton
League 1 to League 2: Hartlepool Utd, MK Dons, Swindon, Walsall

2007
Premier League to Championship: Sheffield Utd, Charlton, Watford
Championship to League 1: Southend, Luton, Leeds
League 1 to League 2: Chesterfield, Bradford City, Rotherham, Brentford

2008
Premier League to Championship: Reading, Birmingham, Derby
Championship to League 1: Leicester, Scunthorpe, Colchester
League 1 to League 2: Bournemouth, Gillingham, Port Vale, Luton

2009
Premier League to Championship: Newcastle, Middlesbrough, WBA
Championship to League 1: Norwich, Southampton, Charlton
League 1 to League 2: Northampton, Crewe, Cheltenham, Hereford

2010
Premier League to Championship: Burnley, Hull, Portsmouth
Championship to League 1: Sheffield Wed, Plymouth, Peterborough
League 1 to League 2: Gillingham, Wycombe, Southend, Stockport

2011
Premier League to Championship: Birmingham, Blackpool, West Ham
Championship to League 1: Preston, Sheffield Utd, Scunthorpe
League 1 to League 2: Dagenham & Redbridge, Bristol Rov, Plymouth, Swindon

2012
Premier League to Championship: Bolton, Blackburn, Wolves
Championship to League 1: Portsmouth, Coventry, Doncaster
League 1 to League 2: Wycombe, Chesterfield, Exeter, Rochdale

2013
Premier League to Championship: Wigan, Reading, QPR
Championship to League 1: Peterborough, Wolves, Bristol City
League 1 to League 2: Scunthorpe, Bury, Hartlepool, Portsmouth

2014
Premier League to Championship: Norwich, Fulham, Cardiff
Championship to League 1: Doncaster, Barnsley, Yeovil
League 1 to League 2: Tranmere, Carlisle, Shrewsbury, Stevenage

2015
Premier League to Championship: Hull, Burnley QPR
Championship to League 1: Millwall, Wigan, Blackpool
League 1 to League 2: Notts Co, Crawley, Leyton Orient, Yeovil

ANNUAL AWARDS

FOOTBALL WRITERS' ASSOCIATION

Footballer of the Year: 1948 Stanley Matthews (Blackpool); 1949 Johnny Carey (Manchester Utd); 1950 Joe Mercer (Arsenal); 1951 Harry Johnston (Blackpool); 1952 Billy Wright (Wolves); 1953 Nat Lofthouse (Bolton); 1954 Tom Finney (Preston); 1955 Don Revie (Manchester City); 1956 Bert Trautmann (Manchester City); 1957 Tom Finney (Preston); 1958 Danny Blanchflower (Tottenham); 1959 Syd Owen (Luton); 1960 Bill Slater (Wolves); 1961 Danny Blanchflower (Tottenham); 1962 Jimmy Adamson (Burnley); 1963 Stanley Matthews (Stoke); 1964 Bobby Moore (West Ham); 1965 Bobby Collins (Leeds); 1966 Bobby Charlton (Manchester Utd); 1967 Jack Charlton (Leeds); 1968 George Best (Manchester Utd); 1969 Tony Book (Manchester City) & Dave Mackay (Derby) – shared; 1970 Billy Bremner (Leeds); 1971 Frank McLintock (Arsenal); 1972 Gordon Banks (Stoke); 1973 Pat Jennings (Tottenham); 1974 Ian Callaghan (Liverpool); 1975 Alan Mullery (Fulham); 1976 Kevin Keegan (Liverpool); 1977 Emlyn Hughes (Liverpool); 1978 Kenny Burns (Nott'm Forest); 1979 Kenny Dalglish (Liverpool); 1980 Terry McDermott (Liverpool); 1981 Frans Thijssen (Ipswich); 1982 Steve Perryman (Tottenham); 1983 Kenny Dalglish (Liverpool); 1984 Ian Rush (Liverpool); 1985 Neville Southall (Everton); 1986 Gary Lineker (Everton); 1987 Clive Allen (Tottenham); 1988 John Barnes (Liverpool); 1989 Steve Nicol (Liverpool); Special award to the Liverpool players for the compassion shown to bereaved families after the Hillsborough Disaster; 1990 John Barnes (Liverpool); 1991 Gordon Strachan (Leeds); 1992 Gary Lineker (Tottenham); 1993 Chris Waddle (Sheffield Wed); 1994 Alan Shearer (Blackburn); 1995 Jurgen Klinsmann (Tottenham); 1996 Eric Cantona (Manchester Utd); 1997 Gianfranco Zola (Chelsea); 1998 Dennis Bergkamp (Arsenal); 1999 David Ginola (Tottenham); 2000 Roy Keane (Manchester Utd); 2001 Teddy Sheringham (Manchester Utd); 2002 Robert Pires (Arsenal); 2003 Thierry Henry (Arsenal); 2004 Thierry Henry (Arsenal); 2005 Frank Lampard (Chelsea); 2006 Thierry Henry (Arsenal); 2007 Cristiano Ronaldo (Manchester Utd); 2008 Cristiano Ronaldo (Manchester Utd); 2009 Steven Gerrard (Liverpool); 2010 Wayne Rooney (Manchester Utd); 2011 Scott Parker (West Ham); 2012 Robin van Persie (Arsenal); 2013 Gareth Bale (Tottenham); 2014 Luis Suarez (Liverpool); 2015 Eden Hazard (Chelsea)

PROFESSIONAL FOOTBALLERS' ASSOCIATION

Player of the Year: 1974 Norman Hunter (Leeds); 1975 Colin Todd (Derby); 1976 Pat Jennings (Tottenham); 1977 Andy Gray (Aston Villa); 1978 Peter Shilton (Nott'm Forest); 1979 Liam Brady (Arsenal); 1980 Terry McDermott (Liverpool); 1981 John Wark (Ipswich); 1982 Kevin Keegan (Southampton); 1983 Kenny Dalglish (Liverpool); 1984 Ian Rush (Liverpool); 1985 Peter Reid (Everton); 1986 Gary Lineker (Everton); 1987 Clive Allen (Tottenham); 1988 John Barnes (Liverpool); 1989 Mark Hughes (Manchester Utd); 1990 David Platt (Aston Villa); 1991 Mark Hughes (Manchester Utd); 1992 Gary Pallister (Manchester Utd); 1993 Paul McGrath (Aston Villa); 1994 Eric Cantona (Manchester Utd); 1995 Alan Shearer (Blackburn); 1996 Les Ferdinand (Newcastle); 1997 Alan Shearer (Newcastle); 1998 Dennis Bergkamp (Arsenal); 1999 David Ginola (Tottenham); 2000 Roy Keane (Manchester Utd); 2001 Teddy Sheringham (Manchester Utd); 2002 Ruud van Nistelrooy (Manchester Utd); 2003 Thierry Henry (Arsenal); 2004 Thierry Henry (Arsenal); 2005 John Terry (Chelsea); 2006 Steven Gerrard (Liverpool); 2007 Cristiano Ronaldo (Manchester Utd); 2008 Cristiano Ronaldo (Manchester Utd); 2009 Ryan Giggs (Manchester Utd); 2010 Wayne Rooney (Manchester Utd); 2011 Gareth Bale (Tottenham); 2012 Robin van Persie (Arsenal); 2013 Gareth Bale (Tottenham); 2014 Luis Suarez (Liverpool); 2015 Eden Hazard (Chelsea)

Young Player of the Year: 1974 Kevin Beattie (Ipswich); 1975 Mervyn Day (West Ham); 1976 Peter Barnes (Manchester City); 1977 Andy Gray (Aston Villa); 1978 Tony Woodcock (Nott'm Forest); 1979 Cyrille Regis (WBA); 1980 Glenn Hoddle (Tottenham); 1981 Gary Shaw (Aston Villa); 1982 Steve Moran (Southampton); 1983 Ian Rush (Liverpool); 1984 Paul Walsh (Luton); 1985 Mark Hughes (Manchester Utd); 1986 Tony Cottee (West Ham); 1987 Tony

Adams (Arsenal); **1988** Paul Gascoigne (Newcastle); **1989** Paul Merson (Arsenal); **1990** Matthew Le Tissier (Southampton); **1991** Lee Sharpe (Manchester Utd); **1992** Ryan Giggs (Manchester Utd); **1993** Ryan Giggs (Manchester Utd); **1994** Andy Cole (Newcastle); **1995** Robbie Fowler (Liverpool); **1996** Robbie Fowler (Liverpool); **1997** David Beckham (Manchester Utd); **1998** Michael Owen (Liverpool); **1999** Nicolas Anelka (Arsenal); **2000** Harry Kewell (Leeds); **2001** Steven Gerrard (Liverpool); **2002** Craig Bellamy (Newcastle); **2003** Jermaine Jenas (Newcastle); **2004** Scott Parker (Chelsea); **2005** Wayne Rooney (Manchester Utd); **2006** Wayne Rooney (Manchester Utd); **2007** Cristiano Ronaldo (Manchester Utd); **2008** Cesc Fabregas (Arsenal), **2009** Ashley Young (Aston Villa), **2010** James Milner (Aston Villa), **2011** Jack Wilshere (Arsenal), **2012** Kyle Walker (Tottenham), **2013** Gareth Bale (Tottenham), **2014** Eden Hazard (Chelsea), **2015** Harry Kane (Tottenham)

Merit Awards: 1974 Bobby Charlton & Cliff Lloyd; **1975** Denis Law; **1976** George Eastham; **1977** Jack Taylor; **1978** Bill Shankly; **1979** Tom Finney; **1980** Sir Matt Busby; **1981** John Trollope; **1982** Joe Mercer; **1983** Bob Paisley; **1984** Bill Nicholson; **1985** Ron Greenwood; **1986** England 1966 World Cup-winning team; **1987** Sir Stanley Matthews; **1988** Billy Bonds; **1989** Nat Lofthouse; **1990** Peter Shilton; **1991** Tommy Hutchison; **1992** Brian Clough; **1993** Manchester Utd, 1968 European Champions; Eusebio; **1994** Billy Bingham; **1995** Gordon Strachan; **1996** Pele; **1997** Peter Beardsley; **1998** Steve Ogrizovic; **1999** Tony Ford; **2000** Gary Mabbutt; **2001** Jimmy Hill; **2002** Niall Quinn; **2003** Sir Bobby Robson; **2004** Dario Gradi; **2005** Shaka Hislop; **2006** George Best; **2007** Sir Alex Ferguson; **2008** Jimmy Armfield; **2009** John McDermott, **2010** Lucas Radebe, **2011** Howard Webb, **2012** Graham Alexander, **2013** Eric Harrison/Manchester Utd Class of '92, **2014** Donald Bell (posthumously; only footballer to win Victoria Cross, World War 1), **2015** Steven Gerrard & Frank Lampard

MANAGER OF THE YEAR (chosen by media and sponsors)

1966 Jock Stein (Celtic); **1967** Jock Stein (Celtic); **1968** Matt Busby (Manchester Utd); **1969** Don Revie (Leeds); **1970** Don Revie (Leeds); **1971** Bertie Mee (Arsenal); **1972** Don Revie (Leeds); **1973** Bill Shankly (Liverpool); **1974** Jack Charlton (Middlesbrough); **1975** Ron Saunders (Aston Villa); **1976** Bob Paisley (Liverpool); **1977** Bob Paisley (Liverpool); **1978** Brian Clough (Nott'm Forest); **1979** Bob Paisley (Liverpool); **1980** Bob Paisley (Liverpool); **1981** Ron Saunders (Aston Villa); **1982** Bob Paisley (Liverpool); **1983** Bob Paisley (Liverpool); **1984** Joe Fagan (Liverpool); **1985** Howard Kendall (Everton); **1986** Kenny Dalglish (Liverpool); **1987** Howard Kendall (Everton); **1988** Kenny Dalglish (Liverpool); **1989** George Graham (Arsenal); **1990** Kenny Dalglish (Liverpool); **1991** George Graham (Arsenal); **1992** Howard Wilkinson (Leeds); **1993** Alex Ferguson (Manchester Utd); **1994** Alex Ferguson (Manchester Utd); **1995** Kenny Dalglish (Blackburn); **1996** Alex Ferguson (Manchester Utd); **1997** Alex Ferguson (Manchester Utd); **1998** Arsene Wenger (Arsenal); **1999** Alex Ferguson (Manchester Utd); **2000** Sir Alex Ferguson (Manchester Utd); **2001** George Burley (Ipswich); **2002** Arsene Wenger (Arsenal); **2003** Sir Alex Ferguson (Manchester Utd); **2004** Arsene Wenger (Arsenal); **2005** Jose Mourinho (Chelsea); **2006** Jose Mourinho (Chelsea); **2007** Sir Alex Ferguson (Manchester Utd); **2008** Sir Alex Ferguson (Manchester Utd); **2009** Sir Alex Ferguson (Manchester Utd); **2010** Harry Redknapp (Tottenham), **2011** Sir Alex Ferguson (Manchester Utd); **2012**: Alan Pardew (Newcastle); **2013** Sir Alex Ferguson (Manchester Utd); **2014** Tony Pulis (Crystal Palace), **2015** Jose Mourinho (Chelsea)

MANAGER OF THE YEAR (2)

(Chosen by the League Managers' Association)
1993 Dave Bassett (Sheffield Utd); **1994** Joe Kinnear (Wimbledon); **1995** Frank Clark (Nott'm Forest); **1996** Peter Reid (Sunderland); **1997** Danny Wilson (Barnsley); **1998** David Jones (Southampton); **1999** Alex Ferguson (Manchester Utd); **2000** Alan Curbishley (Charlton Athletic); **2001** George Burley (Ipswich); **2002** Arsene Wenger (Arsenal); **2003** David Moyes (Everton); **2004** Arsene Wenger (Arsenal); **2005** David Moyes (Everton); **2006** Steve Coppell (Reading); **2007** Steve Coppell (Reading); **2008** Sir Alex Ferguson (Manchester Utd); **2009** David Moyes (Everton), **2010** Roy Hodgson (Fulham), **2011** Sir Alex Ferguson (Manchester

Utd), **2012**: Alan Pardew (Newcastle), **2013** Sir Alex Ferguson (Manchester Utd), **2014** Brendan Rodgers (Liverpool), **2015** Eddie Howe (Bournemouth)

SCOTTISH FOOTBALL WRITERS' ASSOCIATION

Footballer of the Year: 1965 Billy McNeill (Celtic); **1966** John Greig (Rangers); **1967** Ronnie Simpson (Celtic); **1968** Gordon Wallace (Raith); **1969** Bobby Murdoch (Celtic); **1970** Pat Stanton (Hibernian); **1971** Martin Buchan (Aberdeen); **1972** David Smith (Rangers); **1973** George Connelly (Celtic); **1974** World Cup Squad; **1975** Sandy Jardine (Rangers); **1976** John Greig (Rangers); **1977** Danny McGrain (Celtic); **1978** Derek Johnstone (Rangers); **1979** Andy Ritchie (Morton); **1980** Gordon Strachan (Aberdeen); **1981** Alan Rough (Partick Thistle); **1982** Paul Sturrock (Dundee Utd); **1983** Charlie Nicholas (Celtic); **1984** Willie Miller (Aberdeen); **1985** Hamish McAlpine (Dundee Utd); **1986** Sandy Jardine (Hearts); **1987** Brian McClair (Celtic); **1988** Paul McStay (Celtic); **1989** Richard Gough (Rangers); **1990** Alex McLeish (Aberdeen); **1991** Maurice Malpas (Dundee Utd); **1992** Ally McCoist (Rangers); **1993** Andy Goram (Rangers); **1994** Mark Hateley (Rangers); **1995** Brian Laudrup (Rangers); **1996** Paul Gascoigne (Rangers); **1997** Brian Laudrup (Rangers); **1998** Craig Burley (Celtic); **1999** Henrik Larsson (Celtic); **2000** Barry Ferguson (Rangers); **2001** Henrik Larsson (Celtic); **2002** Paul Lambert (Celtic); **2003** Barry Ferguson (Rangers); **2004** Jackie McNamara (Celtic); **2005** John Hartson (Celtic); **2006** Craig Gordon (Hearts); **2007** Shunsuke Nakamura (Celtic); **2008** Carlos Cuellar (Rangers); **2009** Gary Caldwell (Celtic); **2010** David Weir (Rangers); **2011** Emilio Izaguirre (Celtic); **2012** Charlie Mulgrew (Celtic); **2013** Leigh Griffiths (Hibernian); **2014** Kris Commons (Celtic); **2015** Craig Gordon (Celtic)

PROFESSIONAL FOOTBALLERS' ASSOCIATION SCOTLAND

Player of the Year: 1978 Derek Johnstone (Rangers); **1979** Paul Hegarty (Dundee Utd); **1980** Davie Provan (Celtic); **1981** Mark McGhee (Aberdeen); **1982** Sandy Clarke (Airdrieonians); **1983** Charlie Nicholas (Celtic); **1984** Willie Miller (Aberdeen); **1985** Jim Duffy (Morton); **1986** Richard Gough (Dundee Utd); **1987** Brian McClair (Celtic); **1988** Paul McStay (Celtic); **1989** Theo Snelders (Aberdeen); **1990** Jim Bett (Aberdeen); **1991** Paul Elliott (Celtic); **1992** Ally McCoist (Rangers); **1993** Andy Goram (Rangers); **1994** Mark Hateley (Rangers); **1995** Brian Laudrup (Rangers); **1996** Paul Gascoigne (Rangers); **1997** Paolo Di Canio (Celtic) **1998** Jackie McNamara (Celtic); **1999** Henrik Larsson (Celtic); **2000** Mark Viduka (Celtic); **2001** Henrik Larsson (Celtic); **2002** Lorenzo Amoruso (Rangers); **2003** Barry Ferguson (Rangers); **2004** Chris Sutton (Celtic); **2005** John Hartson (Celtic) and Fernando Ricksen (Rangers); **2006** Shaun Maloney (Celtic); **2007** Shunsuke Nakamura (Celtic); **2008** Aiden McGeady (Celtic); **2009** Scott Brown (Celtic); **2010** Steven Davis (Rangers); **2011** Emilio Izaguirre (Celtic); **2012** Charlie Mulgrew (Celtic), **2013** Michael Higdon (Motherwell); **2014** Kris Commons (Celtic), **2015** Stefan Johansen (Celtic)

Young Player of the Year: 1978 Graeme Payne (Dundee Utd); **1979** Ray Stewart (Dundee Utd); **1980** John McDonald (Rangers); **1981** Charlie Nicholas (Celtic); **1982** Frank McAvennie (St Mirren); **1983** Paul McStay (Celtic); **1984** John Robertson (Hearts); **1985** Craig Levein (Hearts); **1986** Craig Levein (Hearts); **1987** Robert Fleck (Rangers); **1988** John Collins (Hibernian); **1989** Billy McKinlay (Dundee Utd); **1990** Scott Crabbe (Hearts); **1991** Eoin Jess (Aberdeen); **1992** Phil O'Donnell (Motherwell); **1993** Eoin Jess (Aberdeen); **1994** Phil O'Donnell (Motherwell); **1995** Charlie Miller (Rangers); **1996** Jackie McNamara (Celtic); **1997** Robbie Winters (Dundee Utd); **1998** Gary Naysmith (Hearts); **1999** Barry Ferguson (Rangers); **2000** Kenny Miller (Hibernian); **2001** Stilian Petrov (Celtic); **2002** Kevin McNaughton (Aberdeen); **2003** James McFadden (Motherwell); **2004** Stephen Pearson (Celtic); **2005** Derek Riordan (Hibernian); **2006** Shaun Maloney (Celtic); **2007** Steven Naismith (Kilmarnock); **2008** Aiden McGeady (Celtic); **2009** James McCarthy (Hamilton), **2010** Danny Wilson (Rangers), **2011:** David Goodwillie (Dundee Utd), **2012** James Forrest (Celtic), **2013** Leigh Griffiths (Hibernian), **2014** Andy Robertson (Dundee Utd), **2015** Jason Denayer (Celtic)

SCOTTISH MANAGER OF THE YEAR

1987 Jim McLean (Dundee Utd); **1988** Billy McNeill (Celtic); **1989** Graeme Souness (Rangers); **1990** Andy Roxburgh (Scotland); **1991** Alex Totten (St Johnstone); **1992** Walter Smith (Rangers); **1993** Walter Smith (Rangers); **1994** Walter Smith (Rangers); **1995** Jimmy Nicholl (Raith); **1996** Walter Smith (Rangers); **1997** Walter Smith (Rangers); **1998** Wim Jansen (Celtic); **1999** Dick Advocaat (Rangers); **2000** Dick Advocaat (Rangers); **2001** Martin O'Neill (Celtic); **2002** John Lambie (Partick Thistle); **2003** Alex McLeish (Rangers); **2004** Martin O'Neill (Celtic); **2005** Alex McLeish (Rangers); **2006** Gordon Strachan (Celtic); **2007** Gordon Strachan (Celtic); **2008** Billy Reid (Hamilton); **2009** Csaba Laszlo (Hearts), **2010** Walter Smith (Rangers), **2011:** Mixu Paatelainen (Kilmarnock), **2012** Neil Lennon (Celtic), **2013** Neil Lennon (Celtic), **2014** Derek McInnes (Aberdeen), **2015** John Hughes (Inverness)

EUROPEAN FOOTBALLER OF THE YEAR

1956 Stanley Matthews (Blackpool); **1957** Alfredo di Stefano (Real Madrid); **1958** Raymond Kopa (Real Madrid); **1959** Alfredo di Stefano (Real Madrid); **1960** Luis Suarez (Barcelona); **1961** Omar Sivori (Juventus); **1962** Josef Masopust (Dukla Prague); **1963** Lev Yashin (Moscow Dynamo); **1964** Denis Law (Manchester Utd); **1965** Eusebio (Benfica); **1966** Bobby Charlton (Manchester Utd); **1967** Florian Albert (Ferencvaros); **1968** George Best (Manchester Utd); **1969** Gianni Rivera (AC Milan); **1970** Gerd Muller (Bayern Munich); **1971** Johan Cruyff (Ajax); **1972** Franz Beckenbauer (Bayern Munich); **1973** Johan Cruyff (Barcelona); **1974** Johan Cruyff (Barcelona); **1975** Oleg Blokhin (Dynamo Kiev); **1976** Franz Beckenbauer (Bayern Munich); **1977** Allan Simonsen (Borussia Moenchengladbach); **1978** Kevin Keegan (SV Hamburg); **1979** Kevin Keegan (SV Hamburg); **1980** Karl-Heinz Rummenigge (Bayern Munich); **1981** Karl-Heinz Rummenigge (Bayern Munich); **1982** Paolo Rossi (Juventus); **1983** Michel Platini (Juventus); **1984** Michel Platini (Juventus); **1985** Michel Platini (Juventus); **1986** Igor Belanov (Dynamo Kiev); **1987** Ruud Gullit (AC Milan); **1988** Marco van Basten (AC Milan); **1989** Marco van Basten (AC Milan); **1990** Lothar Matthaus (Inter Milan); **1991** Jean-Pierre Papin (Marseille); **1992** Marco van Basten (AC Milan); **1993** Roberto Baggio (Juventus); **1994** Hristo Stoichkov (Barcelona); **1995** George Weah (AC Milan); **1996** Matthias Sammer (Borussia Dortmund); **1997** Ronaldo (Inter Milan); **1998** Zinedine Zidane (Juventus); **1999** Rivaldo (Barcelona); **2000** Luis Figo (Real Madrid); **2001** Michael Owen (Liverpool); **2002** Ronaldo (Real Madrid); **2003** Pavel Nedved (Juventus); **2004** Andriy Shevchenko (AC Milan); **2005** Ronaldinho (Barcelona); **2006** Fabio Cannavaro (Real Madrid); **2007** Kaka (AC Milan); **2008** Cristiano Ronaldo (Manchester United); **2009** Lionel Messi (Barcelona)

WORLD FOOTBALLER OF YEAR

1991 Lothar Matthaus (Inter Milan and Germany); **1992** Marco van Basten (AC Milan and Holland); **1993** Roberto Baggio (Juventus and Italy); **1994** Romario (Barcelona and Brazil); **1995** George Weah (AC Milan and Liberia); **1996** Ronaldo (Barcelona and Brazil); **1997** Ronaldo (Inter Milan and Brazil); **1998** Zinedine Zidane (Juventus and France); **1999** Rivaldo (Barcelona and Brazil); **2000** Zinedine Zidane (Juventus and France); **2001** Luis Figo (Real Madrid and Portugal); **2002** Ronaldo (Real Madrid and Brazil); **2003** Zinedine Zidane (Real Madrid and France); **2004** Ronaldinho (Barcelona and Brazil); **2005** Ronaldinho (Barcelona and Brazil); **2006** Fabio Cannavaro (Real Madrid and Italy); **2007** Kaka (AC Milan and Brazil); **2008** Cristiano Ronaldo (Manchester United and Portugal), **2009** Lionel Messi (Barcelona and Argentina)

FIFA BALLON D'OR

(replaces European and World Footballer of the Year)
2010: Lionel Messi (Barcelona). **2011** Lionel Messi (Barcelona), **2012** Lionel Messi (Barcelona), **2013** Cristiano Ronaldo (Real Madrid), **2014:** Cristiano Ronaldo (Real Madrid)

FIFA WORLD COACH OF THE YEAR

2010: Jose Mourinho (Inter Milan). **2011** Pep Guardiola (Barcelona), **2012** Vicente del Bosque (Spain), **2013** Jupp Heynckes (Bayern Munich), **2014** Joachim Low (Germany)

PREMIER LEAGUE

REVIEWS, APPEARANCES, SCORERS 2014–15

(Figures in brackets denote appearances as substitute)

ARSENAL

Will this be the season when Arsenal launch a meaningful challenge for their first Premier League success since 2004? Or will they again fall by the wayside as Chelsea, Manchester United or Manchester City continue to exclude them from the title reckoning? The question has been a recurring one, but perhaps is more pertinent now with Arsene Wenger having shown signs of developing a team capable of contesting the big prize. Certainly, the manager and his players expressed confidence in taking the big step up after a second successive FA Cup triumph. A 4-0 victory needed to be put into perspective because of Aston Villa's abject performance at Wembley. Yet there was a sense that the impact made throughout the last campaign by Alexis Sanchez, the emergence of Francis Coquelin in a defensive midfield role and the form of right-back Hector Bellerin has given the team added impetus. Arsenal need to have better luck when it comes to injuries, having been without Jack Wilshere, Theo Walcott, Mesut Ozil, Olivier Giroud and Mikel Arteta, for lengthy spells. They also have to improve on the poor start which effectively ruled out their chances after just eight games, by which time they trailed Chelsea by 11 points. At the half-way stage, Arsenal were down in sixth place, but 11 wins in the next 12 fixtures effectively sealed Champions League football for the 18th successive season, while not enough threaten Chelsea's dominance. There was a blip at the end with the failure to score in three successive home games, before Walcott's hat-trick against West Bromwich Albion persuaded Wenger to prefer him to Giroud for the final. Another lapse at the Emirates brought an end to the latest European campaign – a 3-1 first leg defeat by Monaco in the last 16.

Akpom C	– (3)	Gibbs K	18 (4)	Podolski L	– (7)
Arteta M	6 (1)	Giroud O	21 (6)	Ramsey A	23 (6)
Bellerin H	17 (3)	Koscielny L	26 (1)	Rosicky T	5 (10)
Campbell J	– (4)	Maitland-Niles A	– (1)	Sanchez A	34 (1)
Cazorla S	33 (4)	Martinez E	3 (1)	Sanogo Y	2 (1)
Chambers C	17 (6)	Mertesacker P	35	Szczesny W	17
Coquelin F	19 (3)	Monreal N	26 (2)	Walcott T	4 (10)
Debuchy M	10	Ospina D	18	Welbeck D	18 (7)
Flamini M	15 (8)	Oxlade-Chamberlain A	17 (6)	Wilshere J	9 (5)
Gabriel	4 (2)	Ozil M	21 (1)		

League goals (71): Sanchez 16, Giroud 14, Cazorla 7, Ramsey 6, Walcott 5, Ozil 4, Welbeck 4, Koscielny 3, Bellerin 2, Rosicky 2, Wilshere 2, Chambers 1, Debuchy 1, Flamini 1, Oxlade-Chamberlain 1, Opponents 2

FA Cup goals (15): Sanchez 4, Giroud 3, Mertesacker 2, Walcott 2, Monreal 1, Ozil 1, Rosicky 1, Welbeck 1. **Capital One Cup goals (1):** Sanchez 1. **Community Shield goals (3):** Cazorla 1, Giroud 1, Ramsey 1

Champions League goals (19): Sanchez 4, Podolski 3, Ramsey 3, Welbeck 3, Oxlade-Chamberlain 2, Arteta 1, Gibbs 1, Giroud 1, Sanogo 1

Average home league attendance: 59,992. **Player of Year:** Alexis Sanchez

ASTON VILLA

Tim Sherwood experienced a mixture of delight and despair after becoming manager. He took over a side third from bottom and led them to safety, while at the same time reaching the FA Cup Final. But a 4-0 defeat by Arsenal at Wembley, and the manner of it, cast a shadow over the end of the season. It was an eventful introduction to the job for Sherwood, who came in when Paul Lambert was sacked in mid-February after a promising start to the season turned sour. Lambert signed a contract extension through to 2018 on the back of ten points accumulated from the first four games. The next six were lost – the club's worst run in the top flight since 1964 – and problems mounted when a sequence of ten games without a win was accompanied by a slide into the relegation zone. The picture changed as Sherwood successfully coaxed much-needed goals out of Christian Benteke, just as he had done with Emmanuel Adebayor in his previous job at Tottenham. Benteke netted 11 in nine games, including a hat-trick against Queens Park Rangers, a brace against Sunderland and Everton and one in the semi-final victory over Liverpool. Villa then conceded five in a nightmare first-half at Southampton, losing 6-1, but results elsewhere meant they survived, albeit with the club's poorest finish since 1995 of 17th place, along with the lowest-ever total of league goals in a single season – 31. It was a bitter-sweet record to take to the final in which a poor performance left Sherwood contemplating changes of personnel during the summer.

Agbonlahor G 30 (4)	Cole J 3 (9)	Okore J 22 (1)
Bacuna L 10 (9)	Delph F 27 (1)	Richardson K 16 (6)
Baker N 8 (3)	Given S 3	Sanchez C 20 (8)
Bent D ....– (7)	Grealish J 7 (10)	Senderos P 7 (1)
Benteke C 26 (3)	Guzan B 34	Sinclair S 5 (4)
Gil C 4 (1)	Hepburn-Murphy R ......– (1)	Steer J 1
Cissokho A 24 (1)	Hutton A 27 (3)	Vlaar R 19 (1)
Clark C 22 (3)	Lowton M 8 (4)	Weimann A 20 (11)
Cleverley T 31	N'Zogbia C 19 (8)	Westwood A 25 (2)

League goals (31): Benteke 13, Agbonlahor 6, Cleverley 3, Weimann 3, Clark 1, Cole 1, Hutton 1, Okore 1, Sanchez 1, Sinclair 1. **FA Cup goals** (9): Benteke 2, Delph 2, Sinclair 2, Bacuna 1, Gil 1, Weimann 1. **Capital One Cup goals**: None
Average home league attendance: 34,133   **Player of Year**: Fabian Delph

BURNLEY

They won plenty of admirers for their approach to Premier League football and the application displayed in trying to survive against the odds. Sean Dyche's side could also point to remaining competitive throughout the season, with a 4-0 defeat by West Bromwich Albion the nearest thing to a hiding. In truth, however, Burnley lacked that bit of quality to supplement resilience and hard work. They were susceptible to conceding headed goals, while the failure to hold on to 2-0 leads against Crystal Palace and at home to Albion proved costly. The decision not to enter the transfer market in the January window was also open to question. On the plus side, Dyche and his players will remember holding Chelsea to 1-1 at Stamford Bridge and, most notably, both games against defending champions Manchester City. At the Etihad, a two-goal deficit was transformed into a point by goals from George Boyd and Ashley Barnes. In the return fixture, the sweetest of strikes from Boyd delivered a 1-0 victory. That success stirred thoughts of beating the drop. Instead, Burnley failed score in the next six games and were cut adrift. Danny Ings ended a personal three-month drought with the only goal against Hull. But wins for Aston Villa, Leicester and Sunderland, along with a point for Newcastle, ended their chances with two fixtures remaining. At least they bowed out in the right manner with another away win, this time against Villa, with Ings again on the mark.

Arfield S 36 (1)	Jutkiewicz L 10 (15)	Shackell J 38
Barnes A 28 (7)	Keane M 17 (4)	Sordell M 2 (12)
Boyd G 35	Kightly M 10 (7)	Taylor M 7 (3)
Chalobah N ....– (4)	Lafferty D ....– (1)	Trippier K 38
Duff M 21	Long K ....– (1)	Ulvestad F 1 (1)
Heaton T 38	Marney D 20	Vokes S 5 (10)
Ings D 35	Mee B 32 (1)	Wallace R 1 (14)
Jones D 36	Reid S 1 (6)	Ward S 7 (2)

League goals (28): Ings 11, Barnes 5, Boyd 5, Arfield 2, Mee 2, Kightly 1, Wallace 1, Opponents 1. **FA Cup goals** (3): Sordell 1, Vokes 1, Wallace 1. **Capital One Cup goals**: None
Average home league attendance: 19,131. **Player of Year**: George Boyd

CHELSEA

A season planned meticulously by Jose Mourinho and executed perfectly by his players was rewarded with an emphatic title success. The manager made key signings in Diego Costa and Cesc Fabregas, re-signed Didier Droga as an important back-up and decided that Thibaut Courtois, not Petr Cech, should be his No 1 goalkeeper. The impact was instant – 15 goals in the first four matches, seven of them from Costa and Chelsea in pole position. It was one they never relinquished. A 5-3 defeat at Tottenham on New Year's Day enabled Manchester City to threaten, but the defending champions hit a bad patch soon after and never came close again. After a 5-0 win over Swansea opened up a five-point gap, Mourinho was forced by injuries to Costa and Loic Remy to adopt a more conservative approach. There was no loss of impetus – indeed the lead was extended and they remained unbeaten until the penultimate fixture against West Bromwich Albion. It just resulted in a string of victories by a single-goal margin, culminating in the 1-0 defeat of Crystal Palace which ensured top spot with three games remaining. Fittingly, the goal came from Eden Hazard, who capped an outstanding season with both major Player of the Year awards and, along with his manager, the individual Premier League prize. Chelsea went on to finish eight points ahead of City. It was Mourinho's eighth league title as a manager – three of them with Chelsea – and a fourth with the club for Droga and John Terry. There was the bonus of Capital One Cup success, delivered with a 2-0 victory over Tottenham at Wembley, but also two major disappointments. A 4-2 defeat at home to Bradford City, who came from two goals down, represented one of the biggest shocks in the history of the FA Cup. And defeat by Paris Saint-Germain in the last 16 of the Champions League left Mourinho still with plenty to achieve in this competition.

Ake N ....– (1)	Drogba D.................. 8 (20)	Ramires 11 (12)
Azpilicueta C..................29	Fabregas C 33 (1)	Remy L 6 (13)
Brown I...........................– (1)	Filipe Luis 9 (6)	Salah M ....– (3)
Cahill G 33 (3)	Hazard E 38	Schurrle A 5 (9)
Cech P 6 (1)	Ivanovic B....................38	Terry J................................38
Diego Costa 24 (2)	Loftus-Cheek R 2 (1)	Willian 28 (8)
Christensen A..............– (1)	Matic N....................35 (1)	Zouma K 7 (8)
Courtois I.....................32	Mikel J O..................... 6 (12)	
Cuadrado J..................4 (8)	Oscar 26 (2)	

League goals (73): Diego Costa 20, Hazard 14, Remy 7, Oscar 6, Terry 5, Drogba 4, Ivanovic 4, Fabregas 3, Schurrle 3, Ramires 2, Willian 2, Cahill·1, Matic 1, Opponents 1
FA Cup goals (5): Cahill 1, Ramires 1, Remy 1, Willian 1, Zouma 1. **Capital One Cup goals** (11): Hazard 2, Drogba 1, Filipe Luis 1, Ivanovic 1, Oscar 1, Schurrle 1, Terry 1, Zouma 1, Opponents 2
Champions League goals (20): Hazard 3, Drogba 2, Fabregas 2, Matic 2, Terry 2, Cahill 1, Ivanovic 1, Mikel 1, Ramires 1, Remy 1, Schurrle 1, Willian 1, Opponents 2
Average home league attendance: 41,546. **Player of Year**: Eden Hazard

CRYSTAL PALACE

Alan Pardew was a popular choice to take over as manager at Selhurst Park, fondly remembered by supporters for scoring the winning goal in an FA Cup semi-final against Liverpool. He rose even further in their estimation after guiding Palace away from the threat of relegation and towards the club's highest Premier League position of tenth.They were third from bottom going into the New Year and had already gone through two managers, Tony Pulis leaving 48 hours before the start of the season over a disagreement with chairman Steve Parish on transfer policy and his replacement, Neil Warnock, sacked after four months into his second spell in charge.

After a gentle introduction, an FA Cup tie against Dover, Pardew began with a 2-1 victory over Tottenham. Palace accumulated ten points from his first five games to move clear of trouble and continued to flourish, scoring freely from set-piece situations and showing the character to come from behind when needed. Yannick Bolasie fired a hat-trick in 11 minutes in the second-half for a 4-1 success at Sunderland, having scored only once previously, to become the club's first player to register a Premier League treble. And after a lean patch which brought three successive defeats, his side finished strongly, winning 3-1 at Anfield in Steven Gerrard's last game for Liverpool and overcoming Swansea. That lifted them to mid-table and brought Pardew his tenth win in 18 games.

Ameobi S. .... – (4)	Guedioura A .... – (7)	Mutch J 4 (3)
Bannan B 2 (5)	Hangeland B............ 12 (2)	Souare P 7 (2)
Bolasie Y 31 (3)	Hennessey W 2 (1)	O'Keefe S.................... 1 (1)
Campbell F 13 (7)	Jedinak M 24	Puncheon J 31 (6)
Chamakh M.............. 15 (3)	Kelly M 27 (4)	Sanogo Y 3 (7)
Dann S 34	Ledley J 30 (2)	Speroni J........................36
Delaney D 28 (1)	Lee Chung-Yong 1 (2)	Thomas J .... – (1)
Doyle K.................... – (3)	Mariappa A................. 8 (4)	Ward J 37
Fryers E.................... – (1)	McArthur J 29 (3)	Williams J .... – (2)
Gayle D. 11 (14)	Murray G 9 (8)	Zaha W 23 (8)

League goals (47): Murray 7, Puncheon 6, Gayle 5, Jedinak 5, Bolasie 4, Campbell 4, Zaha 4, Chamakh 2, Dann 2, Hangeland 2, Ledley 2, McArthur 2, Ward 1, Opponents 1. **FA Cup goals (8):** Chamakh 2, Dann 2, Campbell 1, Doyle 1, Gayle 1, Sanogo 1. **Capital One Cup goals (5):** Gayle 4, Kaikai S 1
Average home league attendance: 24,421. **Player of Year:** Scott Dann

EVERTON

How much did the involvement in the Europa League contribute to a rare indifferent season for the club? The question has been asked before of teams caught up in the demands of Thursday night football and it was Everton's turn this time after their lowest Premier League position for nine years. Expectation of another top-four challenge was high after a strong showing in the previous campaign. But it never materialised and it needed an improvement in the closing stages to avoid the prospect of finishing in the lower reaches of the table. Perhaps significantly, it came after the European campaign ended with defeat by Dynamo Kiev. After topping their group and overcoming the Swiss side Young Boys in the last 32, Everton took a 2-1 advantage to the Ukraine, where it disappeared in a 5-2 defeat. Back home, they began to address a slide to 14th in the table by beating Queens Park Rangers, Southampton and Burnley. There was a handsome 3-0 victory over Manchester United in which John Stones scored his first goal for the club, then Romelu Lukaku's stoppage-time winner at West Ham. But home defeats by relegation-threatened Sunderland and Tottenham underlined a disappointing campaign which ended in 11th place.

Alcaraz A 6 (2)	Galloway B 2	McGeady A............ 10 (6)
Atsu C 1 (4)	Garbutt L 3 (1)	Miralias K.............. 18 (11)
Baines L.........................31	Gibson D 3 (6)	Naismith S 22 (9)
Barkley R 22 (7)	Hibbert T 4	Osman J 13 (8)
Barry G 33	Howard T 32	Oviedo B 2 (4)
Besic M 15 (8)	Jagielka P......................37	Pienaar S 3 (6)
Browning T .... – (2)	Klone A 7 (5)	Robles J 6 (1)
Coleman S 34 (1)	Lennon A 12 (2)	Stones J 23
Distin S 12 (1)	Lukaku R 32 (4)	
Eto'o S 8 (6)	McCarthy J 27 (1)	

League goals (48): Lukaku 10, Mirallas 7, Naismith 6, Jagielka 4, Coleman 3, Eto'o 3, Baines 2, Barkley 2, Lennon 2, McCarthy 2, Osman 2, Kone 1, McGeady 1, Stones 1, Opponents 2
FA Cup goals (3): Lukaku 2, Mirallas 1. **Capital One Cup goals:** None

Europa League goals (20): Lukaku 8, Mirallas 3. Coleman 2, Jagielka 2, Naismith 2, Baines 1, Eto'o 1, Osman 1
Average home league attendance: 38,406. **Player of Year:** Phil Jagielka

HULL CITY

A sizeable investment in new players, the confidence gained from finishing runners-up in the FA Cup and a first taste of European football for the club left Steve Bruce looking ahead to the season with some optimism. Nine months later, all that confidence had evaporated as Hull were relegated and Newcastle survived on a nerve-shredding final afternoon. Bruce's side, two points adrift, had to beat Manchester United and hope events at St James' Park went in their favour. As it turned out, Newcastle's victory over West Ham was rendered irrelevant because of a 0-0 draw at the KC Stadium. It was the 17th time Hull had failed to score - a familiar story of chances being created and not taken. The most crucial chapter was written a fortnight earlier when a home game against Burnley presented a golden opportunity to ease the pressure. Instead, they conceded the only goal of the game after central-half Michael Dawson was ordered off for attention to a bloodied nose. Robbie Brady twice struck the bar and his side were again out of luck in the penultimate fixture when Nikica Jelavic hit the woodwork before Tottenham scored their two goals. Before that game, the club had suspended midfielder Jake Livermore following a positive test for cocaine, the last thing they needed at such a crucial time. It was another example of a big-money summer signing turning sour. Robert Snodgrass suffered a knee injury in the opening game against Queens Park Rangers and never played again, while £10m record buy Abel Hernandez managed only four goals, one of them a penalty. There was disappointment, too, in the Europa League, with a defeat by the Belgian club Lokeren in the play-offs for the group stage.

Aluko S.	13 (12)	Figueroa M	2 (1)	McShane P.	19 (1)
Ben Arfa H.	5 (3)	Harper S	10	Meyler D	19 (9)
Boyd G	– (1)	Hernandez A.	15 (10)	N'Doye D.	13 (2)
Brady R	17 (10)	Huddlestone T	30 (1)	Quinn S	17 (11)
Bruce A	17 (5)	Ince T.	3 (4)	Ramirez G	11 (11)
Chester J	23	Jakupovic E	2 (1)	Robertson A.	18 (6)
Davies C	21	Jelavic N	21 (5)	Rosenior L.	5 (8)
Dawson M	28	Livermore J.	35	Sagbo Y	– (4)
Diame M.	10 (2)	Maguire H	– (3)	Snodgrass R	1
Elmohamady A	38	McGregor A	26		

League goals (33): Jelavic 8, N'Doye 5, Diame 4, Hernandez 4, Chester 2, Elmohamady 2, Aluko 1, Dawson 1, Livermore 1, McShane 1, Meyler 1, Quinn 1, Ramirez 1, Opponents 1
FA Cup goals: None. **Capital One Cup goals** (2): Brady 1, Ince 1
Europa League goals (4): Brady 2, Aluko 1, Elmohamady 1
Average home league attendance: 23,557. **Player of Year:** Michael Dawson

LEICESTER CITY

When Nigel Pearson called on his struggling side to win half of their final ten matches, it seemed a challenge based on hope rather than expectation. Leicester had been bottom of the table for more than three months, were seven points from safety and despite commendable attempts to play their way out of trouble, time was beginning to run out. Even supporters who had continued to pack the King Power Stadium through the leanest of times were becoming resigned to an immediate return to the Championship. Yet the manager's faith in his players to turn things around was borne out in remarkable fashion. An 86th minute winner from Andy King against West Ham set the ball rolling. When West Bromwich Albion, Swansea and Burnley were subsequently overcome, one of the greatest escapes in Premier League history had taken shape. A home defeat by Chelsea proved a setback, but one which gave way to a 3-0 victory over Newcastle, then a 2-0 success against Southampton, courtesy of two goals from Riyad Mahrez.

By then, Leicester had justified Pearson's belief – and even exceeded his target with six victories out of seven. A goalless draw at Sunderland in the penultimate fixture guaranteed survival and while that dour affair may not have been in keeping with what had gone before, it took nothing away from their achievement. Pearson's overriding feeling was one of relief at the end of a demanding season which also involved incidents on the touchline and with the media. There were special mentions for the contributions of former Inter Milan midfielder Esteban Cambiasso and on-loan defender Robert Huth. After Leicester finished with a 5-1 win over Queens Park Rangers, there were many who felt the manager should have been recognised, too, with one of the Manager of the Year awards. Not so the club's Thai owners, who sacked him in mid-summer, citing 'fundamental differences' – a decision that came out of the blue.

Albrighton M 10 (8)	Konchesky P.................26	Schwarzer M.................... 6
Cambiasso E 27 (4)	Kramaric J............... 6 (7)	Simpson D 13 (1)
De Laet R 20 (6)	Lawrence T................ – (3)	Taylor-Fletcher G......... – (1)
Drinkwater D 16 (7)	Mahrez R 25 (5)	Ulloa L..................... 29 (8)
Hamer B...........................8	Moore L 10 (1)	Upson M 5
Hammond D.............. 9 (3)	Morgan W.......................37	Vardy J..................... 26 (8)
Huth R 14	Nugent D 16 (13)	Wasilewski M 22 (3)
James M 20 (7)	Powell N .... – (3)	Wood C .... – (7)
King A 16 (8)	Schlupp J 30 (2)	
Knockaert A 3 (6)	Schmeichel K 24	

League goals (46): Ulloa 11, Cambiasso 5, Nugent 5, Vardy 5, Mahrez 4, Schlupp 3, Albrighton 2, King 2, Kramaric 2, Morgan 2, Huth 1, Konchesky 1, Wasilewski 1, Wood 1, Opponents 1
FA Cup goals (4): Ulloa 2, Kramaric 1, Schlupp 1. **Capital One Cup goals:** None
Average home league attendance: 31,693. **Player of Year:** Esteban Cambiasso

LIVERPOOL

Another alarming end-of-season slump left a cloud over Anfield and a question mark about the future of manager Brendan Rodgers. In 2014, his side cracked under the pressure with a first title since 1990 beckoning. This time, a switch to a back three following a 3-0 defeat by Manchester United was rewarded with an unbeaten run of 13 games which took them to within reach of retaining a place in the Champions League. The run ended with a home defeat by United in which Steven Gerrard was sent off 38 seconds after coming off the bench. It was followed by a 4-1 beating at Arsenal, an FA Cup semi-final defeat by Aston Villa and just two victories in the final nine fixtures, resulting in a return to the Europa League. The last of those was a 6-1 defeat at Stoke – the club's biggest since 1963 – in which Gerrard made his 710th and final appearance for the club before continuing his career in the United States. Accompany that slide was a dispute with Raheem Sterling, who publicly expressed his wish to leave while Rodgers insisted he would have to see out his contract. The difference of opinion echoed the Luis Suarez affair before he left to join Barcelona for £75m. Rodgers could do little about that, or the absence for much of the season through injury of Daniel Sturridge. But the manager was on the defensive over some of the players brought in with the money received for Suarez, notably £16m Mario Balotelli who scored a single league goal. He also had to defend his team selection for the return Champions League group game against Real Madrid when accused of 'throwing in the towel' after a 3-0 defeat at Anfield.

Allen J..................... 16 (5)	Jones B......................3	Moreno A 26 (2)
Balotelli M 10 (6)	Jose Enrique............ 2 (2)	Sakho M.................. 15 (1)
Borini F 3 (9)	Lallana A................. 23 (4)	Sinclair J.................... – (2)
Coutinho P.............. 32 (3)	Lambert R 7 (18)	Skrtel M 33
Emre Can 23 (4)	Lovren D 22 (4)	Sterling R 34 (1)
Gerrard S 25 (4)	Lucas Leiva 16 (4)	Sturridge D............... 7 (5)
Henderson J............. 36 (1)	Manquillo J 10	Toure K 7 (5)
Ibe J 7 (5)	Markovic L 11 (8)	
Johnson G............... 15 (4)	Mignolet S................ 35 (1)	

League goals (52): Gerrard 9, Sterling 7, Henderson 6, Coutinho 5, Lallana 5, Sturridge 4, Lambert 2, Markovic 2, Moreno 2, Allen 1, Balotelli 1, Borini 1, Emre Can 1, Johnson 1, Skrtel 1, Opponents 1
FA Cup goals (8): Coutinho 3, Gerrard 2, Lallana 1, Sterling 1, Sturridge 1. **Capital One Cup goals** (8): Sterling 3, Balotelli 1, Lovren 1, Markovic 1, Rossiter 1, Suso 1
Champions League goals (5): Gerrard 2, Balotelli 1, Henderson 1, Lambert 1. **Europa League goals** (1): Balotelli 1
Average home league attendance: 44,659. **Player of Year**: Philippe Coutinho

MANCHESTER CITY

Manuel Pellegrini was spot-on with a prediction that the title would be won with 87 points. The manager's contention that his own side could achieve it was not so accurate. They finished a distance behind Chelsea in the runners-up spot after a season which also brought more Champions League disappointment, along with an embarrassing FA Cup defeat. Pellegrini's forecast came at the turn of the year with City having roared back into contention on the back of seven straight wins. They shared identical records with their rivals, who remained on top on alphabetical order only. A month later, however, the gap had opened up again after a run of three points from four matches, along with a 2-0 home loss to Middlesbrough in the Cup. The sequence coincided with captain Yaya Toure on duty at the Africa Cup of Nations and leading marksman Sergio Aguero easing his way back after a knee injury. This time there was no way back. Aguero recovered his thirst for goals as City scored five against Newcastle and four against Stoke, but there were defeats by Liverpool, Burnley, Crystal Palace and, worst of all, against Manchester United. They slipped to fourth before a strong finish brought 18 goals in six matches and a return to second place. Aguero bagged a hat-trick against Queens Park Rangers and won the Premier League's Golden Boot with 26 goals, including all four in a win over Tottenham. There was another hat-trick in a group game against Bayern Munich before City bowed out to Barcelona for the second successive year at the last 16 stage of the Champions League.

Aguero S.............. 30 (3)	Fernando.............. 22 (3)	Milner J 18 (14)
Bony W.............. 2 (8)	Hart J.............. 36	Nasri S.............. 18 (6)
Boyata D.............. 1 (1)	Jesus Navas.......... 23 (12)	Pozo J.............. 1 (2)
Caballero W.............. 2	Jovetic S 9 (8)	Sagna B.............. 8 (1)
Clichy G.............. 23	Kolarov A 16 (5)	Silva D.............. 32
Demichelis M 28 (3)	Kompany V.............. 23 (2)	Sinclair S .... – (2)
Dzeko E.............. 11 (11)	Lampard F.............. 10 (22)	Toure Y.............. 27 (2)
Fernandinho.............. 25 (8)	Mangala E 24 (1)	Zabaleta P.............. 29

League goals (83): Aguero 26, Silva 12, Toure 10, Lampard 6, Jovetic 5, Milner 5, Dzeko 4, Fernandinho 3, Bony 2, Fernando 2, Kolarov 2, Nasri 2, Clichy 1, Demichelis 1, Zabaleta 1, Opponents 1
FA Cup goals (2): Milner 2. **Capital One Cup goals** (7): Dzeko 2, Lampard 2, Jesus Navas 1, Pozo 1, Toure 1
Champions League goals (10): Aguero 6, Milner 1, Nasri 1, Toure 1, Zabaleta 1. **Community Shield goals**: None
Average home league attendance: 45,365. **Player of Year**: Sergio Aguero

MANCHESTER UNITED

It quickly became clear that a summer spending spree of £150m by Louis van Gaal would not deliver instant dividends. Thirteen points from the opening ten matches represented the club's poorest start to a domestic season since 1986. By then, they were already 13 behind Chelsea and a title challenge was out of the question. So the new manager's No 1 priority was straightforward – bring back Champions League football to Old Trafford, with any cup success a bonus. An embarrassing 4-0 loss to MK Dons quickly ended interest in the League Cup and there was a home defeat by Arsenal in the sixth round of the FA Cup. But the main target was achieved, even, if it meant an early start to the new season with a play-off round to be negotiated before thoughts can turn to the group stage. After the early stutters, which also included a 5-3 beating by promoted Leicester, they hit a seven-game winning streak to secure a top-four spot which was retained for the rest of the campaign, despite a succession of injuries sustained by new signings Di Maria, Blind, Shaw, Rojo and Falcao – among others. United completed a satisfying double over Liverpool with two goals from Juan Mata at Anfield, then beat Manchester City 4-2 before experiencing three successive defeats without scoring – against Chelsea, Everton and West Bromwich Albion – for the first time since 1989. Liverpool were offered a glimpse of fourth place as a result, but United won at Crystal Palace to close the door.

Anderson .... – (1)	Hernandez J .... – (1)	Rojo M 20 (2)
Blackett T 6 (5)	Herrera A 19 (7)	Rooney W 33
Blind D 25	Januzaj A 7 (11)	Shaw L 15 (1)
Carrick M 16 (2)	Jones P 22	Smalling C 21 (4)
Cleverley T 1	Keane M .... – (1)	Thorpe T .... – (1)
De Gea D 37	Lingard J 1	Valdes V 1 (1)
Di Maria A 20 (7)	Mata J 27 (6)	Valencia A 29 (3)
Evans J 12 (2)	McNair P 12 (4)	Van Persie R 25 (2)
Falcao R 14 (12)	Nani .... – (1)	Welbeck D .... – (2)
Fellaini M 19 (8)	Pereira A .... – (1)	Wilson J 2 (11)
Fletcher D 4 (7)	Rafael 6 (4)	Young A 23 (3)

League goals (62): Rooney 12, Van Persie 10, Mata 9, Fellaini 6, Herrera 6, Falcao 4, Smalling 4, Di Maria 3, Blind 2, Young 2, Carrick 1, Wilson 1, Opponents 2
FA Cup goals (9): Herrera 2, Rooney 2, Di Maria 1, Fellaini 1, Mata 1, Rojo 1, Wilson 1. **Capital One Cup goals:** None
Average home league attendance: 75,335. **Player of Year:** David de Gea

NEWCASTLE UNITED

Sheer relief was palpable in the 52,000 crowd watching – or rather enduring – a make-or-break last game at St James' Park. Relief that Newcastle had survived, despite the club's worst run of results for 38 years; relief that a season of turmoil on and off the pitch was finally over. Jonas Gutierrez, the player who twice beat testicular cancer, scored one goal and made another for Moussa Sissoko in a 2-0 victory over West Ham which ended a nightmare sequence of nine defeats and a draw. In the end, it wasn't needed because of Hull's failure to beat Manchester United in the other crucial relegation match. Newcastle even climbed to sixth from bottom with the victory. But that was no consolation for supporters continuing to protest against owner Mike Ashley and calling for the appointment of a manager capable of restoring the club's fortunes, with the transfer funds to do so. Alan Pardew, tired of the financial constraints placed on him, had given up on the job to join Crystal Palace midway through the season, having taken the team as high as fifth. They were also the first to beat Chelsea. Under coach John Carver, the interim manager, that momentum melted away. The goals dried up, pressure built and the fans' anger reached a new level with a 3-0 defeat at Leicester after which Carver accused defender Mike Williamson of deliberately getting himself sent off – an allegation the player denied. Carver lost his job and in came former England manager Steve McClaren, himself dismissed by Derby at the end of the Championship season.

Aarons R .... – (4)	Coloccini F 32	Obertan G 8 (5)
Abeid M 7 (6)	De Jong S 1 (3)	Perez A 25 (11)
Alnwick J 5 (1)	Dummett P 24 (1)	Riviere E 15 (8)
Ameobi S 15 (10)	Elliot R 3	Sissoko M 34
Anita V 17 (2)	Gouffran Y 24 (7)	Taylor R 11 (3)
Armstrong A 1 (10)	Gutierrez J 6 (4)	Taylor S 7 (3)
Cabella R 21 (10)	Haidara M 12 (3)	Tiote C 10 (1)
Cisse P 11 (11)	Janmaat D 37	Vuckic H .... – (1)
Colback J 35	Krul T 30	Williamson M 27 (4)

League goals (40): Cisse 11, Perez 7, Colback 4, Sissoko 4, Ameobi 2, Gouffran 2, Aarons 1, Cabella 1, Coloccini 1, De Jong 1, Gutierrez 1, Janmaat 1, Obertan 1, Riviere 1, Taylor S 1, Williamson 1
FA Cup goals: None. **Capital One Cup goals** (6): Riviere 2, Aarons 1, Dummett 1, Sissoko 1, Opponents 1
Average home league attendance: 50,359. **Player of Year**: No award

QUEENS PARK RANGERS

With Harry Redknapp's survival instincts and Charlie Austin's goals, Rangers seemed to have a chance of beating the drop. Without them, an immediate return to the Championship was always on the cards. Chris Ramsey, promoted from Academy manager to take over when Redknapp resigned in early February after being told he needed knee surgery, gave it his best shot. But it proved a thankless task. His side were already into a run of defeats which extended to nine in ten matches and ultimately proved decisive. Austin's productive season had dried up after a purple patch of 11 goals in 12 games and there was a distinct shortage elsewhere in the team. A 4-1 win over West Bromwich Albion offered some hope – the first time Rangers had scored four away from home in the Premier League since 1994 and a result which left them just two points adrift. Instead, Austin's penalty miss meant a frustrating goalless draw with West Ham. Steven Gerrard's 87th minute goal brought Liverpool a 2-1 win at Loftus Road and relegation was confirmed by a 6-0 capitulation against Manchester City – a result which brought to the surface dressing room divisions as accusations were made of a lack of commitment shown by some players. There was another heavy defeat to finish on, 5-1 at Leicester, in which Austin took his tally to the season to 18. He moved on, but Ramsey remained after being given the job on a permanent basis.

Austin C	35	Grego-Cox R	1 (3)	Remy L	2
Barton J	27 (1)	Henry K	27 (6)	Sandro	17
Caulker S	34 (1)	Hill C	15 (4)	Simpson D	1
Doughty M	– (3)	Hoilett J	9 (13)	Taarabt A	3 (4)
Dunne R	22 (1)	Isla M	24 (2)	Traore A	7 (9)
Faurlin A	1 (1)	Kranjcar N	11 (11)	Vargas E	16 (5)
Fer L	27 (2)	McCarthy A	2 (1)	Wright-Phillips S	1 (3)
Ferdinand R	11	Mutch J	6 (3)	Yun Suk-Young	19 (4)
Furlong D	3	Onuoha N	22 (1)	Zamora B	19 (12)
Green R	36	Phillips M	20 (5)	Zarate M	– (4)

League goals (42): Austin 18, Fer 6, Phillips 3, Vargas 3, Zamora 3, Kranjcar 2, Barton 1, Caulker 1, Hill 1, Sandro 1, Opponents 3
FA Cup goals: None. **Capital One Cup goals**: None
Average home league attendance: 17,809. **Player of Year**: Charlie Austin

SOUTHAMPTON

A summer of turmoil at St Mary's was followed, quite remarkably, by a season of significant achievement. Supporters feared the worst when five of their best players moved to bigger clubs, followed by manager Mauricio Pochettino. How would the incoming Ronald Koeman cope with the loss of Adam Lallana, Dejan Lovren, Luke Shaw, Calum Chambers and Rickie Lambert? The answer came with a succession of shrewd signings who integrated immediately and set a record-breaking standard, rewarded with a place in Europe. It was evident from the start, Southampton's best in the Premier League, which yielded 13 points from the opening six fixtures, along with a place in the top four. They retained it for five months, during which an 8-0 win over Sunderland represented their biggest in the top flight and even prompted talk of Champions League football. That dream faded in February when the goals dried up, particularly for leading scorer Graziano Pelle, with Southampton up to third behind Chelsea and Manchester City. Five games produced a single goal, but worries about the bubble bursting were allayed by victory over Crystal Palace, followed by a point gained at Stamford Bridge. With Pelle ending his personal drought, Southampton stabilised, defeating relegation candidates Burnley and Hull, then trouncing Aston Villa 6-1 in an amazing game. Sadio

Mane scored the Premier League's fastest-ever hat-trick in two minutes and 56 seconds, while his team became the first to score five first-half goals in a match and five in the second-half (against Sunderland) in the same season. They went on to qualify for the Europa League with the club's best finish of 60 points in seventh position.

Alderweireld T 26	Gape D.......................– (1)	Ramirez G ....– (1)
Bertrand R 34	Gardos F 5 (6)	Reed H 5 (4)
Clyne N 35	Gazzaniga P..................2	Schneiderlin M 24 (2)
Cork J.....................5 (7)	Hesketh J.............. 1 (1)	Seager R ....– (1)
Davis K...................6 (1)	Isgrove L..................–(1)	Tadic D 24 (7)
Davis S 32 (3)	Long S 16 (16)	Targett M..................3 (3)
Djuricic F.............. 3 (6)	Mane S 24 (6)	Wanyama V.............26 (4)
Elia E 9 (7)	Mayuka E................–(5)	Ward-Prowse J 16 (9)
Fonte J........................37	McCarthy J ....– (2)	Yoshida M 18 (4)
Forster F....................30	Pelle G................... 37 (1)	

League goals (54): Pelle 12, Mane 10, Long 5, Schneiderlin 4, Tadic 4, Wanyama 3, Bertrand 2, Clyne 2, Cork 2, Elia 2, Alderweireld 1, Schneiderlin 1, Ward-Prowse 1, Yoshida 1, Opponents 5
FA Cup goals (4): Long 1, Pelle 1, Schneiderlin 1, Opponents 1. **Capital One Cup goals** (7): Pelle 3, Clyne 1, Cork 1, Long 1, Tadic 1
Average home league attendance: 30,652. **Player of Year**: Jose Fonte

STOKE CITY

Charlie Adam's wonder goal and a Jon Walters hat-trick were major moments for Stoke. But it was the collective effort of Mark Hughes's side which left the biggest imprint on the season. Hughes had them playing progressive, purposeful football which delivered the club's highest Premier League points total of 54. These qualities also brought a repeat of the ninth-place finish of 2014, together with a hint along the way that this record might also be beaten. It came when Stoke responded to a disappointing FA Cup defeat at Blackburn with three successive wins over Aston Villa, Hull and Everton. The opportunity was lost when three straight defeats followed, but with Adam proving an influential figure, they came good again. The Scot scored four times in six matches, including a belter against Sunderland and a rare header as Stoke achieved a first-ever double over Tottenham. Adam's most eye-catching goal was in the defeat at Stamford Bridge when he joined an exclusive list of players scoring from inside their own half with a 66-yard strike over the head of Chelsea's 6ft 6in goalkeeper Thibaut Courtois. There were milestones, too, for Walters, who scored his 100th career goal in a 3-2 win against Arsenal and marked his 200th appearance with the club's first Premier League hat-trick – a 'perfect' treble of right foot, left foot and header – in the 3-1 victory over Queens Park Rangers. He was also on the mark as Stoke finished on a high by crushing Liverpool 6-1, Peter Crouch completing the scoring with a Premier League record 47th headed goal.

Adam C 15 (14)	Crouch P 17 (16)	Shenton O ....– (1)
Arnautovic M............20 (9)	Huth R....................–(1)	Sidwell S.................5 (7)
Assaidi O 1 (8)	Ireland S.............. 11 (7)	Teixeira D ....– (1)
Bardsley P 24 (1)	Moses V 19	Walters J 28 (4)
Begovic A...................35	Muniesa M 14 (5)	Whelan G 26 (2)
Biram Diouf M......... 28 (6)	Nzonzi S...................38	Wilson M 25 (2)
Bojan 14 (2)	Odemwingie P............ 1 (6)	Wollscheid P...............12
Butland J....................3	Pieters E 29 (2)	
Cameron G.............. 21 (6)	Shawcross R...................32	

League goals (48): Biram Diouf 11, Crouch 8, Walters 8, Adam 7, Bojan 4, Moses 3, Nzonzi 3, Shawcross 2, Arnautovic 1, Opponents 1
FA Cup goals (8): Ireland 3, Arnautovic 1, Bojan 1, Crouch 1, Moses 1, Walters 1. **Capital One Cup goals** (7): Muniesa 2, Walters 2, Biram Diouf 1, Crouch 1, Nzonzi 1
Average home league attendance: 27,081. **Player of Year**: Steven Nzonzi

SUNDERLAND

It wasn't quite on a par with what Gus Poyet described as a 'miracle' escape from relegation in 2014. But Sunderland's survival was still a close-run affair and it was touch and go until a goalless draw against Arsenal in their penultimate match ensured survival. This time, they were led to safety by Dick Advocaat, who took over when Poyet was sacked following a 4-0 home defeat by Aston Villa with two months of another difficult season left. The former Holland manager quickly had the fans behind him – a 1-0 win over Newcastle, achieved by Jermain Defoe's magnificent finish, extending a record run of success against their bitter rivals to five games. Euphoria was dampened by a 4-1 home defeat by Crystal Palace. Then, back-to-back victories proved crucial. Jordi Gomez held his nerve to convert two penalties against Southampton, while Danny Graham scored his first goal for the club at Everton. A goalless draw against Leicester meant Sunderland were still in danger, faced with fixtures at the Emirates and against Chelsea. That they did not have to face the champions on the final afternoon with everything at stake was down to a resilient performance against Arsenal and some fine goalkeeping by Costel Pantilimon. The fourth straight win over Newcastle had come courtesy of Adam Johnson 90th minute goal at St James' Park. After that, his side won only one of 13 matches, conceding too many points from leading positions. Advocaat declined an offer to stay on, then changed his mind, saying he wanted to establish Sunderland as a top-ten club.

Altidore J	2 (9)	Giaccherini E	2 (6)	Pantilimon C	28
Alvarez R	5 (8)	Gomez J	22 (7)	Reveillere A	15 (1)
Bridcutt L	10 (8)	Graham D	7 (7)	Roberge V	1
Brown W	23 (2)	Johnson A	23 (9)	Rodwell J	17 (6)
Buckley W	9 (13)	Jones B	14	Vergini S	28 (3)
Cattermole L	26 (2)	Larsson S	36	Wickham C	31 (5)
Coates S	9 (1)	Mandron M	– (1)	Van Aanholt P	26 (2)
Defoe J	17	Mannone V	10		
Fletcher S	20 (10)	O'Shea J	37		

League goals (31): Wickham 5, Fletcher 5, Defoe 4, Gomez 4, Johnson 4, Larsson 3, Rodwell 3, Cattermole 1, Graham 1, Opponents 1
FA Cup goals (4): Alvarez 1, Gomez 1, Van Aanholt 1, Opponents 1. **Capital One Cup goals (4):** Altidore 1, Gomez 1, Johnson 1, Wickham 1
Average home league attendance: 43,157. **Player of Year:** Seb Larsson

SWANSEA CITY

Onwards and upwards went Swansea under Garry Monk. The 36-year-old surrendered his status as the Premier League's youngest manager to Alex Neil, who led Norwich back to the big time via the play-offs. But Monk was a winner in his first full season in charge, delivering the club's highest Premier League position of eighth and the biggest points total – 56. Four straight victories, including one in the League Cup, represented their best start in 91 years and Monk's side remained in the top half of the table for the whole campaign. All this was achieved despite the potentially damaging loss of Wilfried Bony, who joined Manchester City for a club record £28m in the January transfer window. With Bony in the side, Swansea counted Manchester United and Arsenal among their victims. Shorn of the leading scorer, they achieved notable doubles against both sides, with Bafetimbi Gomis scoring the winning goal each time. The Frenchman successfully shouldered the principal striker's role, recording another winner against Aston Villa and netting twice against Hull. Nine points adrift of a potential Europa League place with a month remaining, Swansea closed the gap to one courtesy of straight wins over Newcastle, Stoke and in the return fixture with Arsenal. But despite retrieving a two-goal deficit through Gylfi Sigurdsson and Gomis against Manchester City, they conceded two more – the second to Bony on his first return to the Liberty Stadium – and lost the chance.

Amat J 7 (3)	Fernandez F 27 (1)	Richards A 7 (3)
Barrow M 1 (10)	Fulton J 1 (1)	Routledge W 27 (2)
Bartley K 7	Gomis B 18 (14)	Shelvey J 28 (3)
Bony W 16 (4)	Gorre K ....– (1)	Sigurdsson G 32
Britton L 7 (2)	Grimes M ....– (3)	Taylor N 34
Carroll T 8 (5)	Ki Sung-yueng 30 (3)	Tiendalli D 1 (2)
Cork J 15	Montero J 15 (15)	Tremmel M 1 (1)
Dyer N 23 (9)	Naughton K 10	Williams A 37
Emnes M 3 (14)	Oliveria N 4 (6)	
Fabianski L 37	Rangel A 22 (5)	

League goals (46): Bony 9, Ki Sung-yueng 8, Gomis 7, Sigurdsson 7, Dyer 3, Routledge 3, Shelvey 3, Cork 1, Montero 1, Oliveira 1, Opponents 3
FA Cup goals (7): Gomis 2, Barrow 1, Carroll 1, Dyer 1, Routledge 1, Sigurdsson 1. **Capital One Cup goals** (5): Emnes 2, Dyer 1, Gomis 1, Sigurdsson 1
Average home league attendance: 20,555. **Player of Year**: Ki Sung-yueng

TOTTENHAM HOTSPUR

The emergence of Harry Kane as a prolific scorer was the biggest plus of a mixed season at White Hart Lane. The 21-year-old became the first Tottenham player to score 30 goals in a season since Gary Lineker in 1991-92 when completing a 3-1 victory at Newcastle. One more, the winner at Everton in the final match, took his tally in the Premier League to 21, including a hat-trick against Leicester. There were seven in the Europa League, among them a hat-trick against the Greek side Asteras, and three in the League Cup in which his side lost the final 2-0 to Chelsea. He also announced himself on the international stage, scoring with a header 79 seconds after coming off the bench for his England debut in a European Championship qualifier against Lithuania. Mauricio Pochettino, in his first season at the club, managed Kane's progress, although the goals were not enough to achieve the target of a Champions League place. Tottenham started the New Year two points away off the top four after beating Chelsea 5-3, with Kane netting twice, winning a penalty and setting up their final goal. It was the first time Spurs had scored five in the league against Chelsea since 1961. They remained within striking distance until mid-March when failing to score against Manchester United, Burnley and Aston Villa in the space of four matches. That meant another appearance in Europe's second-tier competition which ended this time in defeat by Fiorentina in the first knock-out round.

Adebayor E 9 (4)	Fazio F 20	Paulinho 3 (12)
Bentaleb N 25 (1)	Holtby L ....– (1)	Rose D 27 (1)
Capoue E 11 (1)	Kaboul Y 11	Soldado R 7 (17)
Chadli N 28 (7)	Kane H 28 (6)	Stambouli B 4 (8)
Chiriches V 8 (2)	Lamela E 25 (8)	Townsend A 10 (7)
Davies B 9 (5)	Lennon A 3 (6)	Vertonghen J 31 (1)
Dembele M 10 (16)	Lloris H 35	Vorm M 3 (1)
Dier E 25 (3)	Mason N 29 (2)	Walker K 15
Eriksen C 37 (1)	Naughton K 5	Yedlin D 1

League goals (58): Kane 21, Chadli 11, Eriksen 10, Rose 3, Adebayor 2, Dier 2, Lamela 2, Townsend 2, Dembele 1, Mason 1, Soldado 1, Opponents 2
FA Cup goals (6): Capoue 1, Chadli 1, Chiriches 1, Paulinho 1, Rose 1, Townsend 1. **Capital One Cup goals** (12): Kane 3, Eriksen 2, Soldado 2, Bentaleb 1, Chadli 1, Lamela 1, Mason 1, Townsend 1
Europa League goals (15): Kane 7, Lamela 2, Soldado 2, Townsend 2, Paulinho 1, Stambouli 1
Average home league attendance: 35,728. **Player of Year**: Harry Kane

WEST BROMWICH ALBION

Tony Pulis delivered a second successive rescue operation on his return to management at The

Hawthorns. Pulis, who led Crystal Palace out of trouble in 2014 before leaving the club on the eve of the new season, took over a side fourth from bottom when Alan Irvine was dismissed after six months in charge. He immediately overhauled a defence breached eight times in the preceding three matches and Saido Berahino's goal for a 1-0 victory over Hull set the pattern for a move away from the danger zone. It was the first of five clean sheets in seven games, an improvement helped by the signing of Manchester United's Darren Fletcher, who was immediately installed as captain. There were victories over Palace and another of Pulis's former clubs, Stoke, interrupted by a worrying ten goals conceded against Manchester City, Queens Park Rangers and Leicester. He reminded his players of the danger of thinking they were safe and defensive order was restored against Liverpool and Manchester United. A 1-0 victory at Old Trafford was earned by Jonas Olsson's goal and Boaz Myhill's penalty save from Robin van Persie was his first against United as a manager. Albion then wound up their home programme on a high by inflicting champions Chelsea's first defeat since New Year's Day, Berahino bringing his tally in all competitions to 20 with two goals in a 3-0 success.

Anichebe V 11 (10)	Fletcher D 15	Myhill B 10 (1)
Baird C 9 (10)	Foster B 28	Olsson J 9 (4)
Berahino S 32 (6)	Gamboa C 1 (9)	Pocognoli S 15
Bianco S .... – (3)	Gardner C 30 (5)	Samaras G .... – (5)
Brown I 13 (11)	Lescott J 34	Sessegnon S .... 20(8)
Brunt C 33 (1)	McAuley G 24	Varela J 3 (4)
Davidson J 1 (1)	McManaman C 5 (3)	Wisdom A 22 (2)
Dawson C 29	Morrison J 29 (4)	Yacob C 16 (4)
Dorrans G 19 (2)	Mulumbu Y 10 (7)	

League goals (38): Berahino 14, Brown 4, Anichebe 3, Gardner 3, Brunt 2, Dawson 2, Morrison 2, Dorrans 2, Fletcher 1, Lescott 1, McAuley 1, Olsson 1, Sessegnon 1, Varela 1, Opponents 1
FA Cup goals (13): Berahino 5, Anichebe 3, Brown 2, Morrison 2, Brunt 1. **Capital One Cup goals (5):** Berahino 1, Brown 1, McAuley 1, Opponents 2
Average home league attendance: 25,064. **Player of Year:** Joleon Lescott

WEST HAM UNITED

Things were looking rosy for Sam Allardyce and his side throughout the first half of the season. Diafra Sakho made a flying start with six goals in six games after a move from the French club Metz, two of them in victories over Liverpool and Manchester City. Andy Carroll's return from an ankle injury was another boost, his two goals against Swansea hinting at a productive partnership with the Senegal international. Together, they helped secure fourth place in the table in the run-up to Christmas. But defeats by Chelsea and Arsenal over the holiday period halted progress and were followed by another setback for Carroll, who needed surgery on a damaged knee and did not play again. After that, West Ham struggled for goals, while at the same time developing a habit of conceding late ones. That cost seven points against Manchester United, Tottenham, Leicester and Stoke, ruled out any chance of a highly-placed finish and put the manager under pressure. There were just three victories in the second-half of the campaign, resulting in a 12th place finish and the decision not to renew Allardyce's contract, which the manager maintained he would not have signed anyway. Ironically, two days later, the club won a Europa League place by topping the Premier League's fair play table. In came Slaven Bilic, former Besiktas and Croatia coach, who played for the club between 1996-97.

Adrian 38	Demel G 3 (3)	Lee E ....– (1)
Amalfitano M......... 14 (10)	Diame M .... – (3)	Morrison R ....– (1)
Burke R 4 (1)	Downing S 37	Nene .... – (8)
Carroll A 12 (2)	Jaaskelainen J.............– (1)	Noble M 27 (1)
Cole C 8 (15)	Jarvis M 4 (7)	Nolan K 19 (10)
Collins J 21 (6)	Jenkinson C 29 (3)	O'Brien J 6 (3)
Cresswell A 38	Kouyate C 30 (1)	Poyet D.................... 1 (2)

Reid W 29 (1)	Tomkins J 20 (2)	Zarate M.................... 5 (2)
Sakho D................. 20 (3)	Valencia E............... 25 (7)	
Song A 25 (3)	Vaz Te R 3 (1)	

League goals (44): Sakho 10, Downing 6, Carroll 5, Kouyate 4, Valencia 4, Amalfitano 3, Cole 2, Cresswell 2, Noble 2, Zarate 2, Nolan 1, Reid 1, Tomkins 1, Opponents 1
FA Cup goals (4): Cole 1, Collins 1, Sakho 1, Valencia 1. **Capital One Cup goals** (1): Sakho 1
Average home league attendance: 34,871. **Player of Year**: Aaron Cresswell

CHAMPIONSHIP

BIRMINGHAM CITY

Gary Rowett returned to St Andrew's to dispel fears of another relegation struggle. Birmingham survived on goal difference on the final day of the previous season and manager Lee Clark undertook a mass rebuilding of his squad during the summer. They continued to struggle and Clark became the ninth managerial casualty of a campaign little more than two months old after two wins in the first 12 matches. Five days after his dismissal, there was an 8-0 trouncing by Bournemouth, the club's biggest-ever home defeat and one which equalled their highest anywhere. Burton manager Rowett turned down an approach from Blackpool, but agreed to take charge of a club he served as a player – and the effect was immediate. His first eight games yielded 17 points and lifted the club from second to third from bottom towards mid-table. The run included a 6-1 victory over Reading in which teenager winger Demarai Gray scored a first-half hat-trick. Birmingham ran into a New Year sequence of eight matches without a victory, before accounting for Brentford and Blackpool in the space of four days. Then, they scored twice in stoppage-time through a Paul Caddis penalty and Clayton Donaldson for a 2-2 draw at Derby. Finishing with three straight wins, Birmingham were up to 10th.

Arthur K 7 (2)	Edgar D.................... 14 (2)	Packwood W .... – (1)
Brown R ....– (1)	Fabbrini D 5	Randolph D 45
Caddis P 44 (1)	Gleeson S 34 (5)	Reilly C 4 (13)
Cotterill D 42	Gray D 28 (13)	Robinson P...............30 (4)
Davis D 36 (6)	Grounds J....................45	Shea B 2 (4)
Donaldson C 44 (2)	Hall G 7	Shinnie A 24 (3)
Doyle C..........................1	Kiernan R............... 11 (1)	Spector J..................20 (4)
Duffy M 1 (3)	Morrison M....................21	Tesche R 12
Dyer L 7 (11)	Moussi G...................– (2)	Thomas W 9 (24)
Eardley N.......................4	Novak L 9 (12)	Zigic N....................... – (9)

League goals (54): Donaldson 15, Cotterill 9, Caddis 6, Gray 6, Thomas 4, Davis 3, Shinnie 2, Tesche 2, Dyer 1, Edgar 1, Grounds 1, Kiernan 1, Novak 1, Reilly 1, Opponents 1.
FA Cup goals (4): Thomas 2, Grounds 1, Novak 1. **Capital One Cup goals** (3): Caddis 1, Donaldson 1, Duffy 1
Average home league attendance: 16,111. **Player of Year**: Clayton Donaldson

BLACKBURN ROVERS

The prolific strike partnership of Jordan Rhodes and Rudy Gestede was not enough for a sustained promotion challenge. They became the club's first pair to both reach 20 goals for a season since Kevin Gallacher and Chris Sutton in the 1997-98 season. Rhodes was the first to record 20 in the league three times in genuine succession since Alan Shearer earlier in that decade. Yet only once did Rovers look like genuine contenders. Late autumn wins over Birmingham, Nottingham Forest, Reading and Leeds in a six-match run netting 14 points took them up to sixth place. The next three months were riddled with inconsistency and by the time another successful run was assembled – victories over Sheffield Wednesday, Bolton and Charlton – they were too far adrift of the leading pack. Rovers finished 11 points away from a play-off place, even with Gestede highlighting his personal campaign with a hat-trick of headers against Nottingham Forest. Rovers were more consistent in the FA Cup, knocking out Stoke 4-1 with a hat-trick from Josh King, and defeating Swansea 3-1. They also held Liverpool at Anfield in the sixth round, losing to the only goal of the replay.

Baptiste A	Henley A	Robinson P
Brown C	Henry D	Spearing J
Cairney T	Kilgallon M	Spurr T
Conway C	King J	Steele J
Duffy S	Lenihan D	Sullivan J
Dunn D	Lowe J	Taylor C
Eastwood S	Marshall B	Taylor P
Evans C	Olsson M	Tunnicliffe R
Gestede R	Raya D	Varney L
Hanley G	Rhodes J	Williamson L

Baptiste A 29 (3)
Brown C .... 11(9)
Cairney T 32 (7)
Conway C 29 (9)
Duffy S 18 (1)
Dunn D 1 (8)
Eastwood S 6
Evans C 37 (1)
Gestede R 31 (8)
Hanley G 31

Henley A 15 (3)
Henry D 3
Kilgallon M 22
King J 5 (11)
Lenihan D 2 (1)
Lowe J 11 (1)
Marshall B 37 (5)
Olsson M 41
Raya D 2
Rhodes J 40 (5)

Robinson P 7
Spearing J 12 (3)
Spurr T 10 (2)
Steele J 31
Sullivan J 1 (1)
Taylor C 7 (9)
Taylor P 2 (3)
Tunnicliffe R 10 (7)
Varney L .... – (11)
Williamson L 23 (5)

League goals (66): Rhodes 21, Gestede 20, Marshall 7, Baptiste 3, Cairney 3, Conway 3, Duff 1, Evans 1, Hanley 1, Henley 1, Kilgallon 1, King 1, Spearing 1, Taylor C 1, Tunnicliffe 1
FA Cup goals (9): King 3, Taylor C 3, Gestede 2, Conway 1. **Capital One Cup goals**: None
Average home league attendance: 14,912. **Player of Year**: Markus Olsson

BLACKPOOL

A season which started in disarray, and quickly got worse, ended in anarchy when the final match against Huddersfield was abandoned after supporters invaded the pitch protesting at the owners of the club – the Oyston family. Premier League football seemed a distant memory as Blackpool finished bottom, 21 points from safety, having won just four out of 46 matches. They were regarded as certainties to drop into League One before a ball had been kicked, and Jose Riga having taken over a squad of just six. Although cobbling together a bunch of free transfers and loanees, the new manager was able to name only four of the permitted seven substitutes for the opening game against Nottingham Forest. He managed to sign 17 players, but six successive league and cup defeats represented the club's worst-ever start and it was not until the 12th fixture that a win was recorded - 1-0 against Cardiff. Riga was dismissed after five months in the job with the team already seven points adrift. Ten days after himself being sacked by Birmingham, Lee Clark took over, bringing in more new faces while accepting the odds were stacked against him. So it proved. Blackpool conceded six at home to Bournemouth, lost 7-2 at Watford and long before the end of the season Clark was making plans for a complete overhaul. He eventually decided enough was enough and resigned. Blackpool used 50 players during the course of the season and went down with six games remaining. The Football League declared the abandoned fixture a 0-0 draw.

Addison M 6
Aldred T 6
Barkhuizen T 4 (3)
Blackman A 2 (1)
Cameron H 10 (1)
Clarke P 37 (2)
Cubero J 10 (2)
Cywka T 5 (1)
Daniels D 19
Davies S 11 (6)
Delfouneso N 21 (17)
Dielna J 1 (1)
Dunne C 21 (1)
Eagles C 2
Ferguson D 6 (4)
Feruz I .... – (2)
Foley K 4

Hall G 11 (1)
Henshall A .... – (2)
Jacobs M 5
Oriol J 11
Kennedy T 5
Lenihan B 2
Lewis J 34
Lundstram J 16 (1)
Madine G 14 (1)
Maher N 6 (4)
McMahon T 28 (4)
Mellis J 4 (9)
Mendy F 1 (2)
Miller I 16 (6)
Murphy J 8 (1)
Nosworthy N 5
O'Dea D 16 (3)

O'Hara J 26 (1)
O'Keefe S 3 (1)
Oliver C 4 (2)
Oriol E 8 (2)
Orlandi A 23 (5)
Osavi-Samuel B 1 (5)
Parish E 12 (1)
Perkins D 45
Ranger N 5 (9)
Rentmeister J 7 (1)
Rothwell J 1 (2)
Sene S .... – (1)
Telford D 9 (5)
Waddington M 1 (2)
Zenjov S 2 (6)
Zoko F 7 (7)

League goals (36): Davies 5, Orlandi 4, Delfouneso 3, Madine 3, Clarke 2, Miller 2, Murphy 2, O'Hara 2, Ranger 2, Cameron 1, Cywka 1, Daniels 1, Eagles 1, Ferguson 1, Hall 1, Jacobs 1, McMahon 1, Telford 1, Zoko 1, Opponents 1
FA Cup goals: None. **Capital One Cup goals**: None
Average home league attendance: 10,928. **Player of Year**: Jamie O'Hara

BOLTON WANDERERS

For the second successive season, a miserable start ruled out any prospect of progress. Bolton failed to win any of their opening ten games in 2014. This time, there was just one victory, 3-2 against Rotherham, achieved by a hat-trick in 24 minutes by on-loan Joe Mason. Manager Dougie Freedman left by mutual consent and Neil Lennon took charge of a side bottom-of-the-table. Lennon made an eventful start – victory at Birmingham along with a touchline dismissal for leaving the technical area. The former Celtic manager enjoyed further success when his new team scored three each time to defeat Brentford, Cardiff and Wigan. They stayed clear of trouble, but never got beyond half-way in the table, partly through a tendency to concede costly late goals. One bright spot was the scoring start Zach Clough made to his senior career. The 19-year-old was on the mark on his debut against Wigan in an FA Cup third round tie, netted twice on his league debut against Wolves and had scored six in nine games before a dislocated shoulder ruled him out for the remainder of the season. At the other end of the age scale, Eidur Gudjohnsen (36) returned to the club and Lennon also brought in 37-year-old Emile Heskey. Both featured in the goalless draw Bolton earned in the fourth round at Anfield, while Gudjohnsen scored from the penalty spot in 2-1 defeat by Liverpool in the replay.

Amos B	8 (1)	Hall R	2 (7)	Ream T	42 (2)
Bannan B	15 (1)	Herd C	2	Rochina	4
Beckford J	5 (8)	Heskey E	11 (5)	Slavchev S	– (1)
Bogdan A	10	Janko S	6 (4)	Spearing J	15 (6)
Clayton M	5 (4)	Kellett A	1	Taylor Q	1
Clough Z	6 (2)	Le Fondre A	16 (1)	Threlkeld O	3 (1)
Coke G	3 (1)	Lee Chung-Yong	22 (1)	Trotter L	7 (7)
Danns N	36 (5)	Lonergan A	28 (1)	Twardzik F	1 (2)
Davies C	17 (10)	Mason J	9 (3)	Vela J	25 (4)
Davies M	9 (6)	McCarthy P	5	Walker T	9 (2)
Dervitie J	34 (3)	McNaughton K	8 (1)	Wheater D	13 (4)
Eaves T	– (1)	Medo	4 (1)	White H	2 (1)
Feeney L	35 (6)	Mills M	37	Wilkinson C	2 (2)
Garvan O	3	Moxey D	14 (6)	Woolery K	– (1)
Gudjohnsen E	12 (9)	Pratley D	19 (3)		

League goals (54): Le Fondre 8, Davies C 6, Clough 5, Gudjohnsen 5, Mason 4, Mills 4, Pratley 4, Feeney 3, Lee Chung-Yong 3, Davies M 2, Clayton 1, Danns 1, Heskey 1, Janko 1, Moxey 1, Spearing 1, Trotter 1, Twardzik 1, Walker 1, Wheater 1
FA Cup goals (2): Clough 1, Gudjohnsen 1. **Capital One Cup goals** (7): Beckford 2, Danns 2, Davies C 1, Mills 1, Pratley 1
Average home league attendance: 15,413. **Player of Year**: Tim Ream

BOURNEMOUTH

Football fairytales don't come better than the one which unfolded at the Goldsands Stadium. Seven years after almost going out of business, Bournemouth defied the odds to win promotion to the Premier League – and they did it in style. Eddie Howe and his players not only took on and overcame all the big clubs in an ultra-competitive Championship, they delivered a club record 98 goals in the process, holding their nerve amid the end-of-season pressures when a host of rivals were jostling for a top-two spot. A 4-0 win at Huddersfield on the opening day of the season was a taste of things to come, with Callum Wilson, the replacement for Norwich-bound leading scorer Lewis Grabban, netting twice and missing a penalty. Another record came with an

8-0 victory over Birmingham and Bournemouth were top at Christmas after beating Blackpool 6-1. There was a wobble in February – a run of five games without a victory taking them down to fourth place. But a 5-1 success at Fulham was part of another productive run which took the team to the brink. Crucially, they overcame the disappointment of conceding an extra-time equaliser to Sheffield Wednesday to record a decisive 3-0 success against Bolton with goals by Marc Pugh, Matt Ritchie and Wilson, his 20th of the campaign. Although one match remained, a goal difference 19 superior to that of Middlesbrough meant they were up. On that final day came the icing on the cake – a 3-0 win at Charlton and with it the title after Watford dropped points.

Arter H	43	Fraser R	.... 6 (15)	Pugh M	............35 (7)
Boruc A	37	Gosling D	.... 1 (17)	Rantie T	.... – (12)
Camp L	9	Harte I	4	Ritchie M	............44 (2)
Cook S	46	Jones K	.... – (6)	Smith A	.... 6 (23)
Daniels C	.... 41 (1)	Kermorgant Y	.... 26 (12)	Stanislas J	...................6 (7)
Elphick T	46	MacDonald S	.... 3 (2)	Surman A	............40 (1)
Flahavan D	.... – (1)	O'Kane E	.... 8 (3)	Ward E	.... – (2)
Francis S	42	Pitman B	.... 18 (16)	Wilson C	45

League goals (98): Wilson 20, Kermorgant 15, Ritchie 15, Pitman 13, Arter 9, Pugh 9, Cook 5, Surman 3, Rantie 2, Daniels 1, Elphick 1, Francis 1, Fraser 1, Jones 1, Stanislas 1, Opponents 1
FA Cup goals (6): Kermorgant 2, Fraser 1, MacDonald 1, Stanislas 1, Wilson 1. **Capital One Cup goals** (11): Gosling 5, Wilson 2, Daniels 1, O'Kane 1, Pitman 1, Opponents 1
Average home league attendance: 10,265. **Player of Year**: Harry Arter

BRENTFORD

The dream died but the memory lived on for supporters, players – and the manager who led his club to within sight of the Premier League knowing that he would not be in charge even if they made it. With Brentford on the fringe of a play-off place in mid-February, owner Matthew Benham told Mark Warburton he intended to replace him at the end of the season – whatever happened. Benham said the management would be 'remodelled to ensure long-term prosperity.' The reasoning and timing of his decision were questioned in many quarters. Commendably, Warburton – who took his side up from League One in 2014 – and his team were able to maintain a promotion challenge, sparked initially by five successive victories in November. That purple patch equalled the club record in the game's second tier and earned Warburton and his leading scorer Andre Gray Manager and Player of the Month awards. Going into the final game of the regular season, they were in danger of missing out when trailing Derby in sixth place by two points. But while Derby collapsed at home to Reading, Brentford defeated Wigan by the same 3-0 scoreline to keep the dream alive. The semi-final first leg was a tight, tense affair, settled by Middlesbrough's stoppage-time goal for a 2-1 win. In the return, Warburton's side were second best to the tune of 3-0, a fact he acknowledged while at the same time paying tribute to his players for their efforts. He was replaced by Marinus Dijkhuizen, coach of the Dutch club Excelsior.

Betinho	.... – (1)	Hogan S	.... – (1)	Proschwitz N	...........1 (17)
Bidwell J	.... 42 (1)	Jota	.... 37 (5)	Saunders S	.... – (5)
Button D	46	Judge A	.... 33 (4)	Smith T	...................1 (27)
Craig T	.... 22 (1)	Long C	.... 2 (8)	Tarkowski J	34
Dallas S	.... 23 (15)	McCormack A	.... 14 (4)	Tebar M	.... 1 (3)
Dean H	.... 33 (2)	Moore L	3	Toral J-M	...............8 (26)
Diagouraga T	.... 31 (7)	O'Connell J	.... – (1)	Yennaris N	 1
Douglas J	44	Odubajo M	.... 44 (1)		
Gray A	.... 43 (2)	Pritchard A	.... 43 (2)		

Play-offs – appearances: Bidwell 2, Button 2, Dean 2, Diagouraga 2, Douglas 2, Gray 2, Jota 2, Judge 2, Odubajo 2, Pritchard 2, Tarkowski 2, Dallas – (2), Smith – (1), Long – (1), Toral – (1)
League goals (78): Gray 16, Pritchard 12, Jota 11, Douglas 8, Dallas 6, Toral 6, Long 4, Judge 3,

Odubajo 3, Saunders 2, Dean 1, McCormack 1, Proschwitz 1, Smith 1, Tarkowski 1, Opponents 2. **Play-offs – goals** (1): Gray 1
FA Cup goals: None. **Capital One Cup goals** (6): Dallas 2, Dean 1, Gray 1, Moore M 1, Proschwitz 1
Average home league attendance: 10,822. **Player of Year**: Toumani Diagouraga

BRIGHTON AND HOVE ALBION

A season spent in the lower reaches of the table contrasted sharply with the previous one when a place in the semi-finals of the play-offs was achieved and the chance of going further unluckily undermined by injuries. New manager Sami Hyypia, the former Liverpool stalwart, made a reasonable start with two wins in his first four games. But after a run of one in 18 left his side third from bottom, Hyypia resigned after six months in the job. Chris Hughton, former Newcastle, Birmingham and Norwich manager, came in and also enjoyed some early success with victories over Charlton and Ipswich, along with FA Cup progress against Brentford. Brighton also stretched Arsenal in front of a record Amex Stadium crowd of 30,278 before going down 3-2 in a fourth round tie. But league form remained inconsistent. There was a suggestion of a late surge with home success against Birmingham, Leeds and Derby in quick succession. But it never materialised and a single win in the final 11 fixtures, with just four goals scored, left Hughton planning to reshape his squad after a 20th place finish.

Agustien K 1 (1)	Chicksen A 4 (1)	Kayal B 17 (1)
Al Habsi A 1	Colunga A 11 (6)	Ledesma E 2 (2)
Baldock S 19 (1)	Crofts A 7	LuaLua K 15 (19)
Bennett E 7	Dunk L 38	Mackail-Smith C 15 (15)
Bennett J 41	Fenelon S 1 (1)	March S 6 (5)
Bent D 5	Gardner G 14 (3)	McCourt P .... – (10)
Best L 6 (7)	Greer G 37	O'Grady C 15 (13)
Bruno 33 (2)	Halford G 14 (5)	Stephens D 10 (6)
Buckley W .... – (1)	Holla D 23 (1)	Stockdale D 42
Calderon I 30 (5)	Hughes A 7 (3)	Tilley J .... – (1)
Carayol M 4 (1)	Ince R 23 (9)	Walton C 3
Caskey J 28 (1)	Teixeira J 27 (5)	

League goals (44): Teixeira 6, Dunk 5, Calderon 4, Baldock 3, Bruno 3, Colunga 3, LuaLua 3, Bent 2, Gardner 2, Greer 2, Stephens 2, Bennett J 1, Caskey 1, Holla 1, Ince 1, Kayal 1, Mackail-Smith 1, March 1, O'Grady 1, Opponents 1
FA Cup goals (4): O'Grady 2, Baldock 1, Dunk 1. **Capital One Cup goals** (9): Caskey 2, Ince 2, Mackail-Smith 2, Colunga 1, Dunk 1, LuaLua 1
Average home league attendance: 25,645. **Player of Year**: Inigo Calderon

CARDIFF CITY

Cardiff returned to their blue kit after owner Vincent Tan bowed to pressure from supporters unhappy about the team playing in red. And the first match back in the traditional shirt brought an end to a five-game league run without a win when Fulham were beaten. But there was to be no subsequent impetus for a return to the Premier League at the first attempt in a season riddled with inconsistency. Ole Gunnar Solskjaer paid the price as early as mid-September, sacked after nine months as manager. Russell Slade eventually succeeded him a month later after legal negotiations with former club Leyton Orient and the international break held up the appointment. Slade won three of his first four matches, against Nottingham Forest, Ipswich and Leeds, to raise hopes of a promotion challenge. Further success against Reading and Watford elevated his new side to within two points of a play-off place, only for a run of one victory in 13 matches to follow. It left as the only target a place in the top half of the table, which was achieved when Blackpool and Forest were beaten in the final two fixtures for a rise of three places to 11th. Cardiff finished 16 points adrift of a play-off spot.

Adeyemi T	11 (9)	
Brayford J	2	
Burgstaller G	1 (2)	
Cala	1	
Connolly M	20 (3)	
Daehli M	7 (2)	
Dikgacoi K	1 (1)	
Doyle E	11 (5)	
Da Silva F	22 (6)	
Gabbidon D	– (1)	
Guerra J	– (3)	
Gunnarsson A	43 (2)	
Harris K	3 (11)	
Hudson M	3	
John D	2 (4)	
Jones K	25 (9)	
Kennedy M	9 (5)	
Kim Bo-Kyung	2	
Le Fondre A	19 (4)	
Macheda F	13 (8)	
Malone S	12 (1)	
Manga B	29	
Marshall D	38	
Mason J	5 (2)	
Maynard N	3 (7)	
McAleny C	6 (2)	
Moore S	8 (2)	
Morrison R	1 (6)	
Morrison S	41	
Noone A	33 (4)	
O'Keefe S	4 (2)	
Peltier L	15	
Pilkington A	15 (5)	
Ralls J	15 (13)	
Revell A	8 (8)	
Turner B	11	
Whittingham P	43	

League goals (57): Jones 11, Macheda 6, Morrison S 6, Whittingham 6, Doyle 5, Gunnarsson 4, Ecuele Manga 3, Le Fondre 3, McAleny 2, Ralls 2, Revell 2, Adeyemi 1, Harris 1, Mason 1, Maynard 1, Noone 1, Pilkington 1, Opponents 1
FA Cup goals (4): Jones 2, Harris 1, Ralls 1. **Capital One Cup goals (5):** Macheda 2, Burgstaller 1, Ralls 1, Opponents 1
Average home league attendance: 21,124. **Player of Year:** Bruno Manga

CHARLTON ATHLETIC

Along with Nottingham Forest, Charlton were able to boast an unbeaten record going into the 12th round of fixtures. And for a few hours they held it outright following Forest's lunchtime defeat by Cardiff. But a 1-0 reversal at Bournemouth ended a run of four victories and seven draws – and soon after that bright start began to fade. A single win in 12 games brought the dismissal of Bob Peeters after eight months as manager. His replacement, former Standard Liege coach Guy Luzon, saw that run extend to one in 17 in the league, resulting in a fall to within three points of a relegation place. Then, the new man began to make a significant mark. Charlton won seven of their next nine games, scored three goals in five of them and climbed into the top half of the table. A favourable-looking run-in suggested they might go higher. Instead, Chris Solly was sent off and an 87th minute winner conceded to relegation-threatened Millwall. After that wins were hard to come by, apart from a 2-1 success against Leeds in which Yoni Buyens scored his eighth penalty of the season and they finished at the midway point.

Ahearne-Grant K	2 (3)	
Ben Haim T	37	
Bikey A	29 (2)	
Bulot F	19 (9)	
Buyens Y	38 (2)	
Church S	3 (14)	
Coquelin F	3 (2)	
Cousins J	43 (1)	
Diarra A	8 (4)	
Dmitrovic M	4 (1)	
Eagles C	5 (10)	
Etheridge N	4	
Fox M	23 (8)	
Gomez J	16 (5)	
Gudmundsson J B	38 (3)	
Harriott C	11 (10)	
Henderson S	31	
Jackson C	25 (1)	
Johnson R	1	
Lepoint C	1 (5)	
Morrison M	1 (1)	
Moussa F	4 (10)	
Onyewu O	1 (2)	
Pigott J	– (1)	
Pope N	7 (1)	
Solly C	38	
Tucudean G	14 (6)	
Veljkovic M	3	
Vetokele I	37 (4)	
Watt T	16 (6)	
Wiggins R	21	
Wilson L	10 (14)	

League goals (54): Vetokele 11, Gudmundsson 10, Buyens 8, Bulot 5, Watt 5, Cousins 3, Church 2, Eagles 2, Jackson 2, Tucudean 2, Bikey 1, Diarra 1, Harriott 1, Moussa 1
FA Cup goals (1): Gudmundsson 1. **Capital One Cup goals (4):** Wilson 2, Buyens 1, Church 1,
Average home league attendance: 16,708. **Player of Year:** Jordan Cousins

DERBY COUNTY

The Premier League beckoned for a second successive season – and again Steve McClaren and his players experienced crushing disappointment. They were unlucky to lose the Play-off Final to

Queens Park Rangers in 2014. This time, there were few excuses for a slump which proved so costly. Derby did lose leading scorer Chris Martin for nine games with a hamstring injury and may have suffered from speculation that McClaren was a target for struggling Newcastle. But the way they fell apart after being such a dominant force throughout the campaign was puzzling. This collective strength was reflected in a five-point cushion the leaders opened up over third-placed Ipswich with 13 games remaining. What followed was a seven-match run without a victory which left them six points adrift of an automatic promotion place. Even then, a top-six place looked a solid bet after victories over struggling Wigan and Blackpool restored some momentum. Instead, Derby were held by struggling Millwall, then succumbed 3-0 at home to Reading in the final match in which Darren Bent had a penalty saved with the score 1-0. It meant they were overtaken by Brentford and finished a single point away. McClaren was blamed for the fall from grace and sacked. Former Real Madrid assistant coach Paul Clement took over.

Albentosa R 7 (1)	Eustace J 13	Mascarell O 18 (5)
Bennett M.................– (2)	Forsyth C..................44	Russell J 27 (12)
Bent D 11 (4)	Grant L 40	Sammon C 1
Best L ....–(15)	Hanson J 2	Shotton R 23 (2)
Bryson C 25 (13)	Hendrick J.............. 34 (7)	Thomas K .... – (4)
Butland J.......................6	Hughes W 37 (5)	Thorne G 3
Buxton J 18 (1)	Ibe J 13 (7)	Ward J 21 (4)
Calero I.....................–(2)	Ince T 18	Warnock S 6 (1)
Christie C.............. 34 (4)	Keogh R.....................45	Whitbread Z................8 (1)
Coutts P ....–(7)	Lingard J 6 (8)	
Dawkins S.............. 15 (19)	Martin C.................. 31 (4)	

League goals (85): Martin 18, Ince 11, Bent 10, Hendrick 7, Russell 6, Ward 6, Ibe 5, Bryson 4, Buxton 3, Dawkins 3, Hughes 2, Lingard 2, Shotton 2, Eustace 1, Forsyth 1, Opponents 4
FA Cup goals (4): Bent 2, Hughes 1, Martin 1. **Capital One Cup goals** (11): Dawkins 2, Hendrick 2, Martin 2, Russell 2, Bryson 1, Calero 1, Opponents 1
Average home league attendance: 29,232. **Player of Year**: Will Hughes

FULHAM

Felix Magath's thoughts of an immediate return to the Premier League disappeared inside seven matches. His reshaped side, including £11m signing Ross McCormack from Leeds, gathered a single point, conceded five goals to Derby and Nottingham Forest and were left propping up the division. Magath was sacked after seven months as manager and Kit Symons appointed caretaker. The former defender made his mark with 13 points from his seven games in temporary charge and owner Shahid Khan made the appointment permanent on the recommendation of a 'search' committee which included former captains Danny Murphy and Brian McBride. After that, fortunes were mixed. Back-to-back wins over Reading and Nottingham Forest hinted at mid-table security; 12 goals conceded in three home games to Bournemouth, Leeds and Brentford meant they were still in danger. Eventually, victory over relegated Blackpool removed the threat. Then, in the final match at Craven Cottage, McCormack recorded his second hat-trick of the campaign, converting two penalties and scoring in stoppage-time to upset upset Middlesbrough's automatic promotion chances in a 4-3 thriller.

Bettinelli M..................39	Fotheringham M 2	Kiraly G 3 (1)
Bodurov N............... 36 (2)	Grimmer J..................13	McCormack R........... 43 (1)
Burgess C 4	Guthrie D....................6	Parker S 35 (2)
Burn D 20	Hoogland T 22 (3)	Richards A..................14
Chihi A .... – (1)	Husband J 5	Roberts P 2 (15)
Christensen L V 24 (1)	Hutchinson S 25	Rodallega H 30 (3)
David C 3 (2)	Hyndman E 9	Ruiz B 23 (6)
Dembele M 2 (9)	Joronen J 4	Smith M 8 (7)
Eisfeld T 2 (5)	Kacaniklic A............ 8 (6)	Stafylidis K 34 (4)
Fofana S 13 (8)	Kavanagh S 14 (5)	Tunnicliffe R 22

| Turner M | 9 | Williams G | 7 (7) | Woodrow C | 10 (19) |
| Voser K | 2 (1) | Williams R | 1 (1) | Zverotic E | 5 (5) |

League goals (62): McCormack 17, Rodallega 10, Christensen 5, Smith 5, Hoogland 4, Ruiz 4, Parker 3, Woodrow 3, Hutchinson 2, Kacaniklic 2, Amorebieta 1, Bodurov 1, Burn 1, Fofana 1, Kavanagh 1, Turner 1, Opponents 1

FA Cup goals (4): Woodrow 2, McCormack 1, Rodallega1. **Capital One Cup goals** (5): Dembele 2, Burn 1, McCormick 1, Ruiz 1

Average home league attendance: 18,276. **Player of the Year**: Ross McCormack

HUDDERSFIELD TOWN

Rarely can a club's season have started and finished in such eventful fashion. It opened with a 4-0 home defeat by the eventual champions Bournemouth and the departure of manager Mark Robins. It closed with the match at Blackpool being abandoned early in the second-half following a pitch invasion by supporters protesting against the home club's owners. The Football League ruled that the match should not be replayed because no promotion or relegation issue was involved and it was declared a goalless draw. That meant Huddersfield closed with an unbeaten run of seven matches and achieved their highest league place for 15 years – 16th. Former Charlton manager Chris Powell succeeded Robins to supervise a course through the middle reaches of the division, neither troubling the leading group nor succumbing to the threat of relegation. Early on, his team suggested something better after wins over Millwall, Wolves away and Blackpool in the space of four matches. But further progress was stifled by defensive failings, with 75 goals conceded in all, including 11 matches in which three or more were leaked.

Boyle W	– (1)	Hogg J	23 (3)	Poyet D	2
Bunn H	24 (6)	Holt G	14 (1)	Robinson J	30
Butterfield J	45	Hudson M	41	Scannell S	37 (5)
Carroll J	1 (1)	James R	6	Sinnott J	– (1)
Charles J	– (1)	Lolley J	3 (14)	Smith T	40 (1)
Coady C	42 (3)	Lynch J	34	Smithies A	44
Crooks M	1	Majewski R	3 (5)	Stead J	2 (5)
Dixon P	8 (3)	Miller I	9 (7)	Vaughan J	21 (5)
Edgar D	9 (3)	Murphy J	2	Wallace M	15 (11)
Gerrard A	1 (2)	Norwood O	1	Ward D	2 (10)
Gobern O	7 (5)	Paterson M	– (3)	Wells N	29 (6)
Hammill A	1 (4)	Peltier L	8 (3)	Wilkinson J	1

League goals (58): Wells 11, Bunn 9, Vaughan 7, Butterfield 6, Scannell 4, Coady 3, Lynch 3, Miller 3, Holt 2, Hudson 2, Lolley 2, Wallace 2, Gobern 1, James 1, Stead 1, Opponents 1

FA Cup goals: None. **Capital One Cup goals** (5): Wells 3, Lolley 1, Stead 1,

Average home league attendance: 13,613. **Player of Year**: Jacob Butterfield

IPSWICH TOWN

East Anglian derby games are always intense affairs, but none has ever matched the importance of the one which decided who went through to face Middlesbrough in the Play-off Final. Ipswich were beaten home and away by Norwich in the regular season and the first leg of their semi-final at Portman Road resulted in a 1-1 draw. In the return match, they were more than holding their own until Christophe Berra handled a shot on the line early in the second-half, was sent off and Wes Hoolahan converted the resulting penalty. Although Tommy Smith equalised, Mick McCarthy's side were behind again soon after and finally went down 3-1. McCarthy would not criticise Scotland international Berra, maintaining that defenders are 'programmed' to stop the ball going into the net in such situations. Instead, he praised his players for the consistency shown throughout the campaign when they were rarely out of the top six. Ipswich enjoyed a spell in the runners-up spot after a productive mid-winter run which delivered wins over promotion rivals Watford, Middlesbrough, Brentford and Wolves, with Daryl Murphy's goals a key asset. But such was the competitive nature of the Championship – McCarthy called it a 'bonkers' division – that two of the play-off places remained in doubt until the final round of fixtures, with the four teams in contention separated by a single point. Murphy was the division's top marksman with 27.

Ambrose D 1 (5)	Gerken D 16	Sammon C 8 (11)
Anderson P 20 (16)	Henshall A ....– (4)	Sears F 14 (7)
Bajner B 1 (4)	Hewitt E 2 (1)	Skuse C 40
Berra C...........................45	Hunt N..................... 3 (8)	Smith T...................39 (3)
Bialkowski B 30 (1)	Hunt S 10 (7)	Tabb J...................33 (7)
Bishop E 23 (10)	Hyam L 14 (2)	Varney L 5 (5)
Bru K 16 (15)	McGoldrick D....... 24 (2)	Williams J 4 (3)
Chambers L...................45	Mings T 38 (2)	Wood C 3 (5)
Chaplow R 3 (3)	Murphy D 43 (1)	Wordsworth A........... – (1)
Clarke M ....– (4)	Nouble F ....– (1)	
Fryers E 2 (1)	Parr J 24 (7)	

Play-offs – appearances: Berra 2, Bialkowski 2, Bishop 2, Bru 2, Chambers 2, Mings 2, Murphy 2, Sears 2, Skuse 2, Smith 2, Anderson 1 (1), Varney 1, Tabb – (2), McGoldrick – (1), Hunt N – (1), Parr – (1).
League goals (72): Murphy 27, Sears 9, McGoldrick 7, Berra 6, Smith 4, Hunt N 3, Parr 2, Tabb 2, Anderson 1, Bishop 1, Bru 1, Chambers 1, Chaplow 1, Hyam 1, Mings 1, Sammon 1, Skuse 1, Varney 1, Williams 1, Opponents 1. **Play-offs – goals (2):** Anderson 1, Smith 1
FA Cup goals (1) Ambrose 1. **Capital One Cup goals:** None
Average home league attendance: 19,603. **Player of Year:** Daryl Murphy

LEEDS UNITED

Another season of managerial upheaval and modest achievement left Leeds as far away as ever from challenging for a return to the top flight. Summer appointment Dave Hockaday was sacked after 70 days and six games in charge, to be replaced by former Slovenia international Darko Milanic. He was dismissed by owner Massimo Cellino after six games and 32 days at the helm. Neil Redfearn returned as caretaker, then got the job on a permanent basis. More problems followed with a transfer ban imposed for the January window for a breach of the Football League's financial fair play rules. At that point Leeds were fifth from bottom, four points above the relegation zone. They lost in the FA Cup to Sunderland in the teams' first meeting in the competition since Sunderland's shock win in the 1973 Wembley final, but improved their position in the table with seven victories in a run of ten matches. But the momentum was lost during the run-in, along with the opportunity of a top-half finish. They closed in 15th place, the same as in 2014, and following 14th and 13th finishes in previous campaigns. Redfearn was replaced by former Brentford and Wigan manager Uwe Rosler, the fifth man to take the Elland Road hot-seat in less than 12 months.

Ajose N..................... 2 (1)	Dawson C ....– (3)	Sharp B 17 (16)
Antenucci M 24 (12)	Doukara S 17 (8)	Silvestri M 43
Austin R 24 (6)	Hunt N.....................1	Sloth C........................7 (6)
Bamba S.....................19	Montenegro B............– (5)	Smith M..................1 (2)
Bellusci G 29 (1)	Morison S 17 (9)	Taylor C................22 (1)
Benedicic Z...............– (1)	Mowatt A 37 (1)	Taylor S.........................3
Berardi G 19 (3)	Murphy L 26 (4)	Tonge M 4 (6)
Bianchi T....................24	Ngoyi G.....................1	Warnock S 21
Byram S 36 (3)	Tavares A 9 (3)	White A ....– (1)
Cani E ....– (4)	Pearce J 20 (1)	Wootton S 23
Cook L 33 (4)	Phillips K 2	
Cooper L 25 (4)	Poleon D ....– (4)	

League goals (50): Antenucci 10, Mowatt 9, Doukara 5, Sharp 5, Austin 3, Byram 3, Murphy

3, Bellusci 2, Morison 2, Taylor C 2, Bamba 1, Cooper 1, Phillips 1, Warnock 1, Opponents 2
FA Cup goals: None. **Capital One Cup goals** (3): Doukara 2, Smith 1
Average home league attendance: 24,051. **Player of Year**: Alex Mowatt

MIDDLESBROUGH

Middlesbrough took the Championship's best defensive record into the Play-off Final against Norwich. They also brought two victories over their rivals during the regular season. If anything, it made them marginally the favourites to prevail in a tight affair. Instead, it all went wrong in the opening 15 minutes, with uncertainty at the back costing two goals, along with the chance of a return to the Premier League after an absence of six years. They rarely looked like finding a way back into the game, particularly with leading scorer Patrick Bamford unable to make an impression. Manager Aitor Karanka maintained that the Championship's Player of the Year was fit. But Bamford, on loan from Chelsea, had been carrying an ankle problem in previous weeks and did not look the same threat. His goals had been a key factor in Middlesbrough developing a serious challenge for automatic promotion after a mixed start to the campaign. They were one of four teams disputing the top two places and looked to be holding their nerve by beating Wolves and winning at Carrow Road. Then, a 4-3 defeat at Fulham in the penultimate fixture proved costly. Down to ten men after the dismissal of George Friend, they retrieved a 3-1 deficit and were chasing a winner when 6ft 5in goalkeeper Dimitrios Konstantopoulos went up for a 94th minute corner. But he was caught upfield when the ball was cleared and Fulham broke to make it 4-3.

Adomah A	40 (3)	Hines S	3	Reach A	27 (12)
Amorebieta F	2 (2)	Husband J	2 (1)	Tiendalli D	2
Ayala D	29 (1)	Kalas T	16 (1)	Tomlin L	32 (10)
Bamford P	32(6)	Kike	25 (17)	Veljkovic M	1 (2)
Clayton A	37 (4)	Konstantopoulos D	40	Vossen J	20 (13)
Damia	6	Leadbitter G	40 (3)	Whitehead D	11 (7)
Forshaw A	6 (12)	Ledesma E	1	Wildschut Y	3 (8)
Fredericks R	16 (1)	Mejias T	6 (1)	Williams L	– (4)
Friend G	42	Nsue E	12 (14)	Williams R	– (1)
Gibson B	33 (3)	Omeruo K	17 (2)	Woodgate J	5 (2)

Play-offs – appearances: Adomah 3, Ayala 3, Clayton 3, Friend 3, Gibson 3, Konstantopoulos 3, Leadbitter 3, Tomlin 3, Vossen 3, Whitehead 3, Bamford 2, Kike 1 (2), Forshaw – (2), Amorebieta – (1), Nsue – (1), Reach – (1)
League goals (68): Bamford 17, Leadbitter 12, Kike 9, Tomlin 7, Vossen 7, Adomah 5, Ayala 4, Reach 2, Wildschut 2, Friend 1, Woodgate 1, Opponents 1. **Play-offs – goals** (5): Adomah 1, Amorebieta 1, Kike 1, Tomlin 1, Vossen 1.
FA Cup goals (4): Ayala 1, Bamford 1, Kike 1, Vossen 1. **Capital One Cup goals** (8): Tomlin 2, Bamford 1, Fewster B 1, Kikel 1, Leadbitter 1, Reach 1, Williams L 1
Average home league attendance: 19,562. **Player of Year**: George Friend

MILLWALL

Ian Holloway steered the club away from relegation in 2014 on the back of an unbeaten run of eight matches. This time, there was no Holloway – or any escape. The manager was sacked with ten matches remaining and his side second from bottom, eight points from safety. The margin was too much for coach Neil Harris to bridge in his caretaker role, even after fellow-strugglers Rotherham were docked three points for fielding an ineligible player. A glimmer of hope came with victories over Charlton and Wigan. Lee Gregory then scored a hat-trick, including two penalties, to establish a 3-1 lead over promotion-chasing Derby in the penultimate match. But his side surrendered the advantage and the last hope went when Rotherham won their game in hand against Reading to make sure of staying up. The following day, Harris was given the job on a permanent basis. Millwall had started the campaign by defeating Leeds and Fulham and drew further encouragement when transforming a 3-0 deficit against Wolves into a point with goals by Ricardo Fuller (2) and Gregory. But they slipped into the bottom three midway through the season and the signing of eight players during the winter transfer window delivered little improvement.

Abdou N	29 (4)	Gregory L	28 (11)	Philpot J	– (1)
Angel	4	Gueye M	9 (23)	Powell J	5
Bailey N	5 (3)	Harding D	20	Ranegie M	3 (4)
Beevers M	24 (1)	Hooiveld J	15	Shittu D	7 (1)
Briggs M	7 (1)	Hoyte J	1 (1)	Taylor-Fletcher G	6 (4)
Chaplow R	6 (1)	Maierhofer S	6 (4)	Tonge M	5 (1)
Cowan-Hall P	– (5)	Malone C	17 (3)	Upson E	15 (11)
Cummings S	12	Marquis J	1	Webster B	9 (2)
Dunne A	35 (4)	Martin L	22 (5)	Wilkinson A	9
Easter J	2 (7)	McDonald S	23 (1)	Williams S	38
Edwards C	8	Nelson S	14	Woolford M	33 (5)
Fabbrini D	11 (1)	O'Brien A	13 (6)	Wright J	1
Forde D	46	Onyedinma F	1 (1)		
Fuller R	16 (22)	Pavey A	– (1)		

League goals (42): Gregory 9, Gueye 5, Fuller 4, Woolford 3, Beevers 2, Dunn 2, McDonald 2, O'Brien 2, Upson 2, Williams 2, Abdou 1, Easter 1, Fabbrini 1, Hooiveld 1, Maierhofer 1, Malone 1, Martin 1, Philpot 1, Shittu 1
FA Cup goals (3): Fuller 2, McDonald 1. **Capital One Cup goals (1):** Briggs 1
Average home league attendance: 10,902. **Player of Year:** Jimmy Abdou

NORWICH CITY

Alex Neil started the season watching his Hamilton side defeat Arbroath 2-1 in the Scottish Communities Cup in front of 730 spectators. He finished it by leading Norwich to victory over Middlesbrough in the Championship Play-off Final before a crowd of more than 85,000 at Wembley. Rarely has such a low-profile manager made such a huge impact so soon. And rarely has an appointment that appeared at the time to be a gamble by the club turned out to be such a masterstroke. The final against a side with the best defensive record in the division had all the makings of a tight, tense affair. Instead, Norwich controlled it by scoring twice in the opening 15 minutes through Cameron Jerome and Nathan Redmond and sustained their lead to win an instant return to the Premier League in which Neil, at 34, will be the youngest manager. He was appointed in early January when Neil Adams resigned, after nine months in charge, in the wake of an FA Cup defeat by Preston. The Scot's first game was a 2-1 away win over leaders Bournemouth, despite the sending-off of Jonny Howson. The first ten matches yielded eight victories, including completion of a double over Ipswich. When Norwich faced Middlesbrough in the penultimate home game of the regular season, they were up to second place. That was surrendered to an own goal by Alex Tettey, followed by an 86th minute equaliser conceded at Rotherham. Five points dropped ruled out automatic promotion and meant renewed rivalry with Ipswich in the biggest of all East Anglian derbies. The teams drew 1-1 in the first leg of the semi-final at Portman Road, with Norwich 3-1 victors in the return and Jerome and Redmond again on the mark.

Andreu A	– (6)	Hoolahan W	27 (9)	Murphy J	1 (12)
Bassong S	18	Hooper G	16 (14)	O'Neil G	10 (11)
Bennett E	3 (6)	Howson J	32 (2)	Odjidja-Ofoe V	1 (4)
Bennett R	3 (4)	Jerome C	32 (9)	Olsson M	42\
Cuellar J	8	Johnson B	40 (1)	Redmond N	33 (10)
Dorrans G	12 (3)	Lafferty K	11 (7)	Ruddy J	46
Fer L	– (1)	Loza J	– (2)	Surman A	1
Garrido J	3 (4)	Martin R	45	Tettey A	34 (2)
Grabban L	23 (12)	McGrandles C	– (1)	Turner M	22 (1)
Hooiveld J	6	Morris C	– (1)	Whittaker S	37

Play-offs – appearances: Bassong 3, Howson 3, Jerome 3, Johnson 3, Martin 3, Olsson 3, Redmond 3, Ruddy 3, Tettey 3, Whittaker 3, Hoolahan 2 (1), Dorrans 1 (2), Hooper – (2), Bennett E – (1), Grabban – (1), O'Neil – (1)
League goals (88): Jerome 18, Johnson 15, Grabban 12, Hooper 12, Howson 8, Hoolahan 4, Redmond 4, Dorrans 3, Martin 2, Tettey 2, Whittaker 2, Lafferty 1, Loza 1, Murphy 1, Olsson 1, Turner 1, Opponents 1. **Play-offs – goals** (6): Jerome 2, Redmond 2, Howson 1, Hoolahan 1
FA Cup goals: None. **Capital One Cup goals** (3): Murphy 2, Jerome 1
Average home league attendance: 26,342. **Player of Year:** Bradley Johnson

NOTTINGHAM FOREST

The return of Stuart Pearce to the City Ground as manager was regarded by many as the ideal appointment for a club in need of some managerial stability. Instead, it was a player with a less distinguished record there who went some way to achieving that. Pearce certainly made a flying start, with his side top after eight games. The next eight yielded only four points before a 2-1 win over Norwich with goals in last five minutes from Britt Assombalonga and Michail Antonio. A 3-0 victory over Wolves followed and seemed to have put Forest back on the right track. Instead, they had a transfer ban imposed for breaching the Football League's financial fair play rules and struggled again over Christmas and New Year. Despite an away success against arch-rivals Derby, earned by Assombalonga and 20-year-old Ben Osborn with his first professional goal in stoppage-time in front of a 32,000 crowd, it was the only one in 11 league and cup games. Pearce was sacked and in came Dougie Freedman, the club's sixth manager in less than three years. His first six games yielded 16 points and 19 goals, including 4-1 win over his former team Bolton. During that run, Freedman lost leading scorer Assombalonga with a knee injury and his side eventually lost momentum. After beating Rotherham to consolidate ninth place, they finished the season poorly and dropped to 14th.

Akpom C............... 5 (2)	Fox D............... 25 (2)	Lichaj E 37 (5)
Antonio M.......................46	Fryatt M 17 (8)	Mancienne M............34 (2)
Assombalonga B 27 (2)	Gardner G............. 16 (2)	McLaughlin S 1 (5)
Barrow M...................... 2 (2)	Grant J..................– (1)	Osborn B...............27 (10)
Blackstock D........... 11 (8)	Harding D.............. 6 (2)	Paterson J 4 (17)
Burke C 34 (7)	Hobbs J..................17	Reid A 6
Burke O...................– (2)	Hunt J 15 (2)	Tesche R 18 (4)
Cohen C.........................6	Ince T.............. 4 (2)	Vaughan D............... 10 (3)
Collins D................. 7 (1)	Kane T 7 (1)	Veldwijk L .... – (11)
Darlow K......................42	Lansbury H 36 (3)	Walker T...................– (7)
De Vries D....................4	Lascelles J 20 (6)	Wilson K 22 (1)

League goals (71): Assombalonga 15, Antonio 14, Lansbury 10, Burke C 6, Fryatt 6, Blackstock 5, Gardner 4, Osborn 3, Tesche 2, Collins 1, Kane 1, Lascelles 1, Paterson 1, Walker 1, Opponents 1
FA Cup goals: None. **Capital One Cup goals** (4): Antonio 1, Grant 1, Lansbury 1, Opponents 1
Average home league attendance: 23,492. **Player of the Year:** Michail Antonio

READING

A poor league season was offset to some extent by a successful FA Cup run which delivered a semi-final place for the first time since 1927 and a performance above and beyond what Steve Clarke's team had shown in the Championship. Reading were expected to play second fiddle to Arsenal at Wembley. Instead, organisation and resilience, rewarded by a goal from Garath McCleary, took the holders to extra-time. And it was anyone's game until a mistake by Adam Federici presented Alexis Sanchez with his second goal for a 2-1 victory. It was an uncharacteristic mistake by the long-serving goalkeeper, who was later voted the club's Player of the Year. There was widespread praise for a performance which posed the question as to why the campaign overall had been so inconsistent. Reading came within a point of a play-off place the previous season and there were hopes of another challenge this time under

Nigel Adkins. But Adkins was sacked following a 6-1 defeat at Birmingham – the club's worst in the league for 15 years. By then, they were 16th and needing something special to make up lost ground in the second half of the campaign with former West Bromwich Albion manager Clarke at the helm. Instead, there was little improvement in results, home form continuing to be particularly poor with a failure to score in 11 of the last 15 games at the Madejski.

Ake N 5	Gunter C 38	Novakovich A .... – (2)
Akpan H 14 (6)	Guthrie D 2 (7)	Obita J 43
Anderson M 3	Hector M 40 (1)	Pearce A 39 (1)
Appiah K 2 (4)	Karacan J 5 (3)	Pogrebnyak P 17 (9)
Blackman N 16 (21)	Kelly S 14 (1)	Robson-Kanu H 26 (3)
Chalobah N 15	Keown N 1 (1)	Stacey J 2 (4)
Cooper J 9 (6)	Knight Z 2	Tanner C .... – (3)
Cox S 28 (9)	Kuhl A 3 (3)	Taylor J 14 (8)
Cummings S 4 (1)	Mackie J 18 (14)	Travner J 1
Edwards R 4 (3)	McCleary G .... 22 (4)\	Tshibola A .... – (1)
Federici A 43	Morrison S 1	Williams D 21 (4)
Ferdinand A 1 (1)	Murray G 18	Yakubu 3 (4)
Fosu-Henry T .... – (1)	Norwood O 32 (6)	

League goals (48): Cox 8, Murray 8, Pogrebnyak 6, Mackie 5, Blackman 3, Hector 3, Cooper 2, Taylor 2, Appiah 1, Chalobah 1, Cummings 1, Karacan 1, McCleary 1, Morrison 1, Norwood 1, Robson-Kanu 1, Williams 1, Opponents 2
FA Cup goals (9): Robson-Kanu 3, McCleary 2, Blackman 1, Mackie 1, Norwood 1, Yakubu 1
Capital One Cup goals (4): Blackman 1, Pogrebnyak 1, Tanner 1, Taylor 1
Average home league attendance: 17,022. **Player of Year:** Adam Federici

ROTHERHAM UNITED

A points deduction put added pressure on a side battling to avoid an immediate return to League One. Rotherham were docked three, and fined £30,000, for fielding an ineligible player, on-loan Derby defender Farrend Rawson in a 1-0 win over Brighton. The decision left them a single point above the relegation zone on the eve of the penultimate home game against promotion-chasing Norwich. But an 86th minute goal by Jordan Bowery earned a point and they made sure of staying up by beating Reading 2-1 in their match in hand with strikes from Matt Derbyshire and Lee Frecklington. The result spared Rotherham from a make-or-break last day of the season and sent Millwall and Wigan down. Manager Steve Evans had reshaped his squad to try to meet the demands of Championship football and they kept out of trouble until a run of nine matches without a win in the run-up to Christmas. After that, they were always looking over their shoulder. There was a big over Millwall, with an 85th minute goal by Karl Arnason and Huddersfield were also beaten, despite the dismissal of Frecklington. Those victories provided a nine-point cushion, but there was more danger after two goals conceded in stoppage time resulted in a 3-2 home defeat by Sheffield Wednesday.

Agard K 1 (1)	Fryers E 10	Morgan C 34 (1)
Arnason K 42 (1)	Green P 34 (3)	Newton C 6 (7)
Barmby J 2	Hall R 2 (1)	Pringle B 39 (1)
Becchio L 3 (2)	Hammill A 4 (10)	Rawson F 4
Bowery J 6 (27)	Hunt J 14 (2)	Revell A 20 (4)
Brandy F .... – (1)	James R 7	Richardson F 19 (4)
Brindley R 1 (1)	Lafferty T 11	Sammon C 11 (4)
Broadfoot K 24 (1)	Lawrence T 6	Skarz J 17
Clarke-Harris J 5 (10)	Ledesma E 6 (1)	Smallwood R 37 (4)
Collin A .... 36\	Loach S 2	Swift J 1 (2)
Derbyshire M 28 (6)	Martinez E 8	Taylor P 13 (4)
Frecklington L 24 (5)	Milsom R 3 (5)	Tidser M .... – (1)

| Ward D .... 10 (6) | Wood R .... 3 (3) | Wordsworth A .... 3 (3) |
| Wilson L ....3 | Wootton S .... 7 | Yates J .... - (1) |

League goals (46): Derbyshire 9, Bowery 5, Revell 4, Arnason 3, Clarke-Harris 3, Green 3, Pringle 3, Sammon 3, Ward 3, Becchio 2, Frecklington 2, Hall 1, Lawrence 1, Ledesma 1, Smallwood 1, Wordsworth 1, Opponents 1
FA Cup goals (1): Brindley 1. **Capital One Cup goals (1):** Derbyshire 1
Average home league attendance: 10,240. **Player of Year:** Richie Smallwood

SHEFFIELD WEDNESDAY

A bitter-sweet season ended with Wednesday intervening dramatically in the Championship promotion race. At Dean Court, Chris McGuire's stopping-time penalty for a 2-2 draw disrupted Bournemouth's promotion charge. A fortnight later at Vicarage Road, Atdhe Nuhiu's equaliser, again in time added on, denied Watford the title and handed it to Bournemouth. In between, Wednesday's last fixture at Hillsborough was a reminder of what a poor campaign it had been in front of their own supporters. A 2-1 defeat by Leeds meant only five victories had been recorded, with a mere 16 goals scored in 23 games. Stuart Gray's side needed the nine wins recorded on their travels to stay clear of the relegation zone amid the sale of the club by Milan Mandaric to Thai businessman Dejphon Chansiri for a reported £30m. As it was, they finished 13th, an improvement of three places on 2014, and were able to equal a club record with one of the meanest defences in the division. They matched the feat of Jack Charlton's side in 1978-79 by keeping a clean sheet in 17 matches. And the total of 49 goals conceded was bettered by only three teams – Bournemouth, Norwich and Middlesbrough. But it proved unlucky 13 for Gray, who was sacked for not mounting a promotion challenge. He was replaced by Carlos Carvalhal, former Sporting Lisbon and Besiktas coach.

Baker L 2 (2)	Keane W 12 (1)	McCabe R .... – (1)
Bus S 2 (5)	Kirkland C 3 (1)	McGugan A 21 (1)
Buxton L 7 (2)	Lavery C 7 (6)	Nuhiu A 31 (12)
Coke G 9 (4)	Lee K 28 (5)	Palmer L 35
Dielna C 14 (9)	Lees T 44	Semedo J 27 (3)
Drenthe R 7 (8)	Loovens G 26	Taylor-Fletcher G 2 (2)
Melo F 4 (2)	Madine G 1 (9)	Vermijl M 8 (3)
Helan J 25 (13)	Maghoma J 28 (4)	Westwood K 43
Hope H 1 (3)	Maguire C 35 (7)	Zayatte K 11
Hutchinson S 16 (4)	Mattock J 24 (3)	
Isgrove L................... 7 (1)	May S 26 (13)	

League goals (43): Maguire 8, Nuhiu 8, May 7, Lee 6, Keane 3, McGugan 3, Lavery 2, Bus 1, Coke 1, Dielna 1, Drenthe 1, Helan 1, Opponents 1
FA Cup goals (1): Nuhiu 1. **Capital One Cup goals (4):** Nuhiu 2, Madine 1, Maghoma 1
Average home league attendance: 21,993. **Player of Year:** Liam Palmer

WATFORD

Watford returned to the Premier League after an absence of eight seasons – and provided a question for future sporting quizzes: which club won promotion to the top flight with four managers? First up was Giuseppe Sannino, who resigned after five matches, maintaining he had gone as far as he could at the club. His replacement, former Brighton manager Oscar Garcia, stepped down after 27 days for health reasons. In came Billy McKinlay, who was sacked after just two games. Finally, there was stability in the shape of Slavisa Jokanovic, former Chelsea midfielder and Partizan Belgrade coach. It was a bewildering turnover, yet the team proved a model of consistency, none more so than Nigerian striker Odion Ighalo, who became the club's first player in 83 years to score eight goals in four successive league matches. Four of them came in a 7-2 victory over Blackpool and by the time Watford had won three times in eight days, against Blackburn, Brentford and Bolton to climb to fifth place, his tally was 12 in eight fixtures. His side turned a two-goal deficit into a 3-2 victory at Leeds, slipped back after losing at home to Ipswich, then struck a decisive purple patch.

Five successive victories lifted them above the pack, with a 2-0 success at Brighton clinching promotion and Troy Deeney becoming the first Watford player to score 20 goals in three successive seasons. They were on course for the title until the 91st minute of the final game when an equaliser conceded to Sheffield Wednesday presented it to Bournemouth. The summer brought another change of manager. Jokanovic was unable to agree new terms and in came former Valencia and Atletico Madrid coach Quique Sanchez Flores.

Abdi A 28 (4)	Dyer L 4 (10)	Motta M 7 (2)
Andrews K 4 (5)	Ekstrand J 23 (1)	Munari G 21 (7)
Angella G 32 (3)	Fabbrini D 2	Murray S 2 (4)
Anya A 27 (8)	Forestieri F 10 (14)	Paredes J C 32 (7)
Bassong S 11	Gomes H 44	Pudil D 19 (4)
Bond J 2 (1)	Guedioura A 13 (4)	Tamas G 6 (1)
Byers G ....– (1)	Hoban T 20 (7)	Tozser D 34 (11)
Cathcart C 28 (1)	Ighalo O 22 (13)	Vydra M 31 (11)
Connolly M 4 (2)	Layun M ....14 (3)\	Watson B 19 (1)
Deeney T 37 (5)	McGugan L 5 (1)	....
Doyley L 5 (1)	Mensah B ....– (1)	....

League goals (91): Deeney 21, Ighalo 20, Vydra 16, Abdi 9, Forestieri 5, Tozser 5, Cathcart 3, Guedioura 3, Munari 3, Angella 2, Andrews 1, Connolly 1, Dyer 1, Ekstrand 1
FA Cup goals: None. **Capital One Cup goals** (2): Dyer 2.
Average home league attendance: 16,664. **Player of Year**: Troy Deeney

WIGAN ATHLETIC

Wigan's fall from grace continued in a traumatic season of three managers, two chairmen and a second relegation in three years. They were among the favourites to go up and had a decent enough start. But a single win in 12 games left them third from bottom and was followed by the sacking of Uwe Rosler, who had accused his players of 'giving up' when conceding three goals in 11 second-half minutes against Bolton. They remained in the relegation zone for the remainder of the campaign. Rosler's successor, former Cardiff manager Malky Mackay, won just one of his first 14 league and cup games and owner Dave Whelan came under fire for having appointed him. Whelan himself was banned from football-related activities for six weeks and fined £50,000 by the FA for offensive comments about Jewish and Chinese people and stepped down after 20 years as chairman. His grandson, 23-year-old David Sharpe, succeeded him and saw successive away wins over Blackpool and Norwich raise hopes of survival. It proved a false dawn. Mackay was dismissed after four-and-a-half-months in charge with his side eight points from safety and five games to play. Club captain Gary Caldwell took over to supervise the first home win for more than seven months, 2-1 against Brighton. But although there a slim chance of survival following Rotherham's three-point deduction for fielding an ineligible player, the Yorkshire side won their game in hand against Reading to stay up.

Al Habsi A 11	Herd C 3	Ojo S 7 (4)
Barnett L 16 (4)	Huws E 15 (1)	Pearce J 16
Bong G 14	Kiernan R 16 (1)	Pennant J.................. 12 (1)
Boyce E 26 (1)	Kim Bo-Kyung 17 (1)	Perch J 39 (2)
Carson S......................34	Kvist W 18 (8)	Ramis I 17 (1)
Chow T 3 (1)	Maguire H 16	Ridgewell L 6
Clarke L 9 (1)	Maloney S 10 (10)	Riera O 6 (7)
Cowie D 24 (8)	McArthur J 5	Robles L ....– (1)
Delort A 4 (7)	McCann C 11 (6)	Sinclair J ....– (1)
Espinoza R 6 (6)	McClean J 30 (6)	Tavernier J 7 (4)
Figueroa M......................	McKay B 1 (8)	Taylor A 26
Flores J......................– (1)	McManaman C 19 (4)	Waghorn M 6 (17)
Forshaw A 13 (3)	Murphy J 2 (3)	Watson B 7 (2)
Fortune M-A 27 (8)	Nicholls L.......................1	

League goals (39): McClean 6, McManaman 5, Pennant 3, Perch 3, Waghorn 3, Kim Bo-Kyung 2, Maloney 2, McCann 2, Pearce 2, Chow 1, Clarke 1, Espinoza 1, Forshaw 1, Fortune 1, Maguire 1, McArthur 1, Riera 1, Taylor 1, Watson 1, Opponents 1
FA Cup goals: None. **Capital One Cup goals** (1): Fortune 1
Average home league attendance: 12,882. **Player of Year:** James McClean

WOLVERHAMPTON WANDERERS

In such a competitive division, it was always likely there would be a victim of the thin line that can separate success from failure. Wolves were that team, missing out on the play-offs, along with the chance of a second successive promotion, on goal difference in a tense finish to the season. They had knocked on the door to the play-offs throughout the second half of the season after recovering from a potentially-damaging run of five straight defeats. They finally made it into the top six when an 88th minute header by Dave Edwards secured a 4-3 victory over Leeds at a packed Molineux. But successive defeats by Birmingham and Middlesbrough, followed by a 1-1 draw with Ipswich, left them trailing by three points. Benik Afobe, signed from Arsenal in the January transfer window scored his 13th goal in 21 appearances for victory against Wigan, leaving his side in a four-horse race for two places going into the final round of matches. Wolves were 4-2 winners over relegated Millwall, with two goals by Nouha Dicko bringing his tally to 14. But crucially so too were Brentford, who claimed the final spot with a superior record of plus-five.

Afobe B 20 (1)	Golbourne S 23 (4)	McDonald K 45 (1)
Batth D.......................44	Graham D......................5	Price J 19 (4)
Clarke L 5 (11)	Hause K 15 (2)	Ricketts S 4
Dicko N 30 (7)	Henry J 23 (14)	Rowe T...................... 7 (7)
Doherty M................ 26 (7)	Ikeme C 33	Sagbo Y 1 (3)
Doyle K......................– (6)	Iorfa D 20	Sako B 39 (7)
Ebanks-Landell E....... 9 (5)	Jacobs M.................. 3 (9)	Saville G 5 (2)
Edwards D 32 (9)	Kuszczak T...................13	Stearman R 38 (4)
Evans J 17 (1)	McAlinden L............ 1 (5)	Van La Parra R........29 (11)

League goals (70): Sako 15, Dicko 14, Afobe 13, Edwards 6, Henry 5, Batth 4, Clarke 2, Ebanks-Landell 2, Evans 1 Graham 1 Price 1, Van La Parra 1, Opponents 5
FA Cup goals (3): Edwards 2, Van La Parra 1. **Capital One Cup goals** (2): Dicko 1, Ricketts 1
Average home league attendance: 22,419. **Player of Year:** Richard Stearman

LEAGUE ONE

BARNSLEY

Danny Wilson's dismissal, two months after his 1,000th game, was one of the more contentious of the season's managerial changes. The club argued that in light of one of the biggest budgets in the division results had been disappointing. Yet Wilson's side were still in with a chance of developing a challenge for a return to the Championship at the first attempt, despite their position in the bottom half of the table. The immediate fall-out was an embarrassing 5-1 defeat at Crawley. The next two games were won under joint-caretakers Mark Burton and Paul Heckingbottom, before Lee Johnson left Oldham to take over. He made an instant impact with four more victories as Barnsley conceded just one goal in that six-game purple patch unmatched since 1980. It took them into the top six on goal difference with ten matches remaining. They then ran into a demanding run of fixtures against promoting-chasing teams, momentum was lost and the challenge faded. Nine games came and went without a win and it was not until the final fixture that the run was halted, a resounding 5-0 victory over Rochdale resulting in a return to the top half.

Abbott B	4 (1)	Holgate M	18 (2)	Phenix B	– (2)
Kiwomya A	3 (2)	Hourihane C	45 (1)	Ramage P	19
Bailey J	19 (6)	Ibehre J	4 (5)	Rose D	1
Berry L	25 (6)	Jennings D	9 (11)	Scowen J	19 (2)
Boakye-Yiadom N	– (1)	John D	8 (1)	Smith G	16 (2)
Bree J	6 (5)	Lalkovic M	13 (4)	Stewart C	3 (1)
Brown R	10 (3)	Lita L	11 (8)	Treacy K	6 (6)
Cole D	15 (4)	Maris G	– (1)	Trotta M	3 (2)
Cowgill J	1 (1)	Mvoto J-Y	13 (2)	Turnbull R	22
Cranie M	39	Noble-Lazarus R	– (1)	Waring G	17 (2)
Davies A	22 (1)	Nyatanga L	45	Wildsmith J	2
Digby P	5 (6)	O'Sullivan J	7 (1)	Williams G	1 (3)
Dudgeon J	14	Oates R	– (9)	Williams R	5
Hemmings K	11 (12)	Pearson B	21 (1)	Winnall S	23 (9)

League goals (62): Hourihane 13, Winnall 9, Waring 6, Cole 5, Nyatanga 5, Scowen 4, Hemmings 3, Ramage 3, Ibehre 2, Lita 2, Berry 1, Cranie 1, Holgate 1, Jennings 1, Pearson 1, Treacy 1, Trotta 1, Opponents 3
FA Cup goals (8): Winnall 3, Jennings 2, Cole 1, Hemmings 1, Hourihane 1. **Capital One Cup goals:** None. **Johnstone's Paint Trophy goals (4):** Berry 1, Cole 1 Hemmings 1, Winnall 1
Average home league attendance: 9,768. **Player of Year:** Conor Hourihane

BRADFORD CITY

Supporters could never have imagined a performance to match, or even surpass, their team's progress to the 2013 League Cup Final. Yet here it was – an FA Cup fourth round tie against Chelsea at Stamford Bridge which will go down not just in the annals of the club but also form part of the fabric of the grand old competition. Bradford delivered one of the finest giant-killing displays of all time by transforming a 2-0 deficit into a 4-2 victory with goals from Jon Stead, former Chelsea youngster Filipe Morais, Andy Halliday and Mark Yeates . For good measure, they despatched another Premier League side, Sunderland, 2-0 in round five, before falling 3-0 to Reading after a goalless draw at Valley Parade. Phil Parkinson's side did their best to keep alive a promotion bid amid this run to the quarter-finals. They succeeded until the final month of the season, remaining within a handful of points of a play-off place. Then, heavy home defeats by the top two, Bristol City (6-0) and Preston (3-0), put paid to their chances and they finished four points adrift in seventh place. A run of five matches without a win was ended on an emotional afternoon when England manager Roy Hodgson was among those present to mark the 30th anniversary of the fire which claimed the lives of 56 people at the ground.

Alnwick J	1	Knott B	31 (9)	Pickford J	33
Bennett M	4 (7)	Liddle G	39(2)	Routis C	16 (2)
Burke O	2	MacKenzie G	9 (3)	Sharif M	– (1)
Clarke B	32 (4)	McArdle R	43	Sheehan A	13 (10)
Darby S	45	McBurnie O	– (7)	Stead J	27 (5)
Davies A	28	Mclean A	7 (6)	Webb-Foster R	– (1)
Dolan M	3 (10)	McMahon T	4 (4)	Williams B	12 (2)
Halliday A	20 (5)	Meredith J	38 (2)	Yeates M	26 (15)
Hanson J	31 (7)	Morais F	22 (8)	Zoko F	3 (13)
Kennedy J	17 (3)	Mottley-Henry D	– (1)		

League goals (55): Clarke 13, Hanson 9, Stead 6, Knott 3, McArdle 3, Morais 3, Yeates 3, Kennedy 2, Mclean 2, Routis 2, Bennett 1, Halliday 1, Liddle 1, MacKenzie 1, McMahon 1, Sheehan 1, Zoko 1, Opponents 2
FA Cup goals (19): Stead 5, Knott 3, Morais 3, Halliday 2, Yeates 2, Clarke 1, Hanson 1, Opponents 1. **Capital One Cup goals (3):** Hanson 1, Knott 1, Mclean 1. **Johnstone's Paint Trophy goals:** None
Average home league attendance: 13,353. **Player of Year:** Roy McArdle

BRISTOL CITY

Steve Cotterill's team delivered a tremendous Double-winning season in keeping with the £45m redevelopment turning Ashton Gate into a high-class stadium, They were a model of consistency to become undisputed champions, while at the same time mastering the art of knock-out football to win the Johnstone's Paint Trophy. City opened with 16 league and cup games unbeaten – the club's best start to a season since 1906 – and led the division throughout the first-half. They were overtaken by Swindon on goal difference early in the New Year, regained top spot as their rivals faltered and went on to build an unassailable lead. Promotion was clinched in grand style – 6-0 at Bradford where there had not been a league victory since 1908. The title, their first for 60 years, followed four days later in a goalless draw against Coventry. With another undefeated sequence of 16 games to close the campaign, City finished eight points ahead of runners-up MK Dons, bringing down the curtain in style with an 8-2 win over Walsall in which central defender Aden Flint – one of five players named in the League One Team of the Year – scored a hat-trick. That run included a 2-0 victory over Walsall at Wembley when goals by Flint and Mark Little brought the Football League Trophy for a record third time. Nearly 40,000 supporters were there to see it, further evidence that City could have everything in place to make an impact on the Championship.

Agard K 34 (5)	Emmanuel-Thomas J10 (26)	Reid B .... – (2)
Ayling L.....................46	Fielding F.......................46	Saville G 1 (6)
Baldock S.....................4	Flint A 46	Smith K 44
Bryan J.................. 39 (2)	Freeman L............... 44 (2)	Smith M.................. 11 (3)
Burns W ....– (3)	Kane T .... 1(4)	Tavernier J 9 (3)
Cunningham G 9 (15)	Little M 35 (2)	Wagstaff S.............. 2 (24)
El-Abd A ....– (2)	Osborne K ....– (1)	Wilbraham A.............. 33 (4)
Elliott W 26 (10)	Pack M 22 (12)	Williams D.................... 44

League goals (96): Wilbraham 18, Flint 14, Agard 13, Emmanuel-Thomas 9, Freeman 7, Smith M 7, Bryan 6, Ayling 4, Pack 3, Tavernier 3, Cunningham 2, Elliott 2, Wagstaff 2, Williams 2, Burns 1, Little 1, Saville 1, Opponents 1
FA Cup goals (6): Emmanuel-Thomas 3, Agard 1, Cunningham 1, Smith M 1. **Capital One Cup goals (1):** Bryan 1. **Johnstone's Paint Trophy goals (14):** Smith M 5, Wilbraham 3, Smith K 2, Burns 1, Flint 1, Little 1, Williams 1
Average home league attendance: 12,056. **Player of Year:** Aden Flint

CHESTERFIELD

A successful season turned sour with defeat in the play-offs followed by the departure of manager Paul Cook. Despite enjoying plenty of possession, his side lost both legs of the semi-final to Preston, who had finished 20 points ahead in the table. They were beaten 1-0 at home and went down 3-0 in the return, with their opponents' greater attacking threat the major factor. The following day, Cook was named as Portsmouth's new manager. He led Chesterfield to the League Two title in 2014 and this time twice brought them back into contention for a top-six place after lean spells threatened their chances. There was a run of seven games without a victory in the autumn. Then, the sale of leading scorer Eoin Doyle to Cardiff in the winter transfer window was followed soon after by four successive defeats. On each occasion they regained momentum to finish with a four-point cushion in sixth place. Doyle scored 21 goals in 26 league games and four more in cup ties. They included two hat-tricks in four days against Scunthorpe and Preston. Cook was succeeded by former Wolves manager Dean Saunders, whose latest job had been trying unsuccessfully to keep Crawley from being relegated.

Ariyibi G 5 (12)	Clucas S 40 (1)	Duffy M 1 (2)
Banks O................ 11 (13)	Cooper L...........................1	Evatt I 38 (1)
Boco R 11 (2)	Darikwa T 46	Gardner D 8 (9)
Broadhead J.............. - (1)	Dieseruvwe E............ - (9)	Gnanduillet A 12 (14)
Carter A 2	Doyle E..........................26	Gobern O 3

Harrison B 4 (8)	Lee T.............................46	Roberts G 33 (1)
Hird S 28	Margreitter G............ 11 (2)	Ryan J 42 (2)
Humphreys R 9 (10)	Morsy S 39	Talbot D...................... 8 (1)
Johnson D.............. 7 (4)	O'Shea J................ 27 (14)	Wright M..................... - (1)
Jones D 27 (6)	Onowigun M .... - (2)	
Lavery C 6 (2)	Raglan C............... 15 (3)	

Play-offs – appearances: Clucas 2, Darikwa 2, Evatt 2, Hird 2, Jones 2, Morsy 2, O'Shea 2, Roberts 2, Ryan 2, Banks 1 (1), Gardner 1 (1), Lee 1, Murphy 1, Gnanduillet – (2), Ariyibi – (1) **League goals** (68): Doyle 21, Clucas 9, O'Shea 7, Roberts 6, Ryan 4, Hird 3, Lavery 3, Gnanduillet 2, Morsy 2, Ariyibi 2, Boco 1, Darikwa 1, Evatt 1, Gardner 1, Harrison 1, Margreitter 1, Raglan 1, Opponents 3. **Play-offs – goals:** None
FA Cup goals (12): Clucas 3, Doyle 3, O'Shea 2, Roberts 2, Gnanduillet 1, Opponents 1. **Capital One Cup goals** (3): Banks 1, Doyle 1, Humphreys 1. **Johnstone's Paint Trophy goals:** None
Average home league attendance: 6,925. **Player of Year:** Tendayi Darikwa

COLCHESTER UNITED

Against all the odds, Colchester beat the drop in a dramatic end to the season. They were four points from safety with three tough matches remaining and looked a good bet to go down. Instead, there was a lifeline when two goals in the final ten minutes by Gavin Massey and Chris Porter, with a penalty, delivered a 3-2 victory at Fleetwood. A goal after 37 seconds by Jacob Murphy against Swindon provided a further boost. But his side had to settle for a point, so for the second time in three years Colchester went into the final fixture not knowing their fate. When Porter wasted a penalty against a Preston side seeking the division's second automatic promotion spot, the pressure was back on. Porter then made up for the mistake by setting up George Moncur for an 82nd minute winner, which together with defeats for fellow-strugglers Crawley and Notts County took them clear. It had been a tough campaign after the club's worst start for 63 years – two points from first six games. Manager Joe Dunne lost his job and was replaced by head of youth Tony Humes, whose task was made more demanding by the sale of leading scorer Freddie Sears to Ipswich in the January transfer window.

Bean M..........................3	Ibehre J 5	Packwood W 1
Bonne M................... 3 (7)	Kent F 9 (1)	Porter C 20 (1)
Briggs M 17 (1)	Khumalo B 10	Roofe K....................... – (2)
Brindley R............... 7 (1)	Kpekawa C 3 (1)	Sears F 24
Clohessy S 31 (1)	Lapslie T 11	Sembie-Ferris D 2 (8)
Eastman T 46	Lawrence B .... – (1)	Smith D .... – (1)
Eastmond C 6 (4)	Lewington C 11	Szmodics S 17 (14)
Fox D 29 (1)	Marriott J .... – (5)	Vose D 2 (5)
Gilbey A................. 32 (2)	Massey G 39 (7)	Walker S 45
Gordon B 16 (2)	McEvoy K .... – (1)	Watt S.................... 17 (4)
Gorkss K.......................7	Moncur G 34 (7)	Wright David............. – (2)
Harney J .... – (1)	Murphy J......................11	Wright Drey 1 (4)
Healey R................ 7 (14)	O'Donoghue M 1	Wynter A 16 (2)
Hewitt E 21	Okuonghae M 8 (1)	
Holman D .... – (4)	Osborne K 4	

League goals (58): Sears 10, Moncur 8, Massey 7, Porter 7, Healey 4, Murphy 4, Szmodics 4, Watt 3, Fox 2, Bonne 1, Eastman 1, Eastmond 1, Gilbey 1, Gorkss 1, Hewitt 1, Lapslie 1, Marriott 1, Okuonghae 1
FA Cup goals (8): Sears 3, Gilbey 1, Massey 1, Moncur 1, Szmodics 1, Watt 1. **Capital One Cup goals:** None. **Johnstone's Paint Trophy goals** (3): Sears 1, Watt 1, Wright Drey 1
Average home league attendance: 3,886. **Player of Year:** Tom Eastman

COVENTRY CITY

A return to the Ricoh Arena, along with a solid start to the season, augured well for the club. But fortunes faded, a change of manager brought no significant improvement and Coventry went into the last game of the season at Crawley in danger of going down. They were only two points off the bottom four and the pressure built when Nick Proschwitz had a penalty saved and the home side went ahead early in the second-half. Marcus Tudgay levelled, then a last-minute winner from James Maddison ensured safety for a side who had initially thrived on their return home after playing home games at Northampton since the start of the 2013-14 season. A deal was agreed with the owners of the stadium and the first game back drew a crowd of more than 27,000. Victory over Gillingham was followed by a new four-year contract for manager Steven Pressley. But after climbing to eighth, Coventry fell into the relegation zone on the back of seven games without a win. Pressley was sacked and replaced by Tony Mowbray, former Middlesbrough and Celtic manager, who enjoyed early victories over Chesterfield, Fleetwood and Peterborough before another slump.

Allsop R	24	Jones J	4	Pugh D	5
Barton A	24 (3)	Maddison J	2 (10)	Samuel D	12 (1)
Burge L	18	Madine G	11	Stokes C	16
Clarke J	10 (1)	Martin A	26 (1)	Swanson D	8 (7)
Coulibaly M	1 (3)	McQuoid J	12 (2)	Thomas C	13 (3)
Daniels B	– (2)	Miller S	1 (11)	Thomas G	– (6)
Finch J	8 (8)	Nouble F	28 (3)	Tudgay M	18 (4)
Fleck J	43 (1)	O'Brien J	43 (1)	Turgott B	– (3)
Haynes R	20 (6)	Odelusi S	4 (10)	Ward G	11
Hines S	6 (3)	Pennington M	24	Webster A	25 (5)
Jackson S	12 (16)	Phillips A	14 (5)	Williams L	4 (1)
Johnson R	20	Proschwitz N	6 (3)	Willis J	33 (1)

League goals (49): Nouble 6, O'Brien 6, Samuel 6, Johnson 5, Tudgay 4, Jackson 3, Madine 3, McQuoid 3, Odelusi 3, Maddison 2, Clarke 1, Haynes 1, Miller 1, Proschwitz 1, Stokes 1, Turgott 1, Opponents 2
FA Cup goals (1): Johnson 1. **Capital One Cup goals** (1): Miller 1. **Johnstone's Paint Trophy goals** (6): McQuoid 2, Phillips 2, Madine 1, Nouble 1
Average home league attendance: 9,332. **Player of Year**: Jim O'Brien

CRAWLEY TOWN

Crawley experienced to their cost the fine line that separates preservation from relegation and went down after three seasons in League One. Leading 3-2 in the penultimate fixture at Peterborough, Dean Saunders and his side were set for a victory which would keep them up. Instead, goals were conceded in the 87th and 90th minutes, they dropped back in the bottom four and stayed there after a 2-1 home defeat by Coventry a week later. This time, Brian Jensen saved a first-half penalty and Mathias Pogba put them ahead. But again they were unable to maintain the advantage and finished two points adrift. The defeats underlined season-long defensive frailty, which resulted in four or more goals being conceded on eight occasions. A productive season for Izale McLeod – 19 goals including a hat-trick in a 5-1 victory over Barnsley – was not enough to offset this weakness. Saunders, formerly in charge at Doncaster and Wolves, took over as interim manager when John Gregory stepped down shortly after Christmas to undergo open heart surgery. After a tough start – one win in eight games – he had the boost of 16 points from the next eight, before another change of fortune brought back-to-back defeats at Scunthorpe and Walsall. Saunders later moved on to manage Chesterfield and Crawley appointed former Cheltenham manager Martin Yates.

Anderson B	.... – (1)	Henderson C	.... 13 (4)	Sadler M	 10
Ashdown J	9	Jensen B	.... 19 (1)	Simpson J	 8
Banya C	.... – (9)	Keane K	12	Smith J	.... 28 (8)
Bawling B	.... 13 (15)	Leacock D	23	Tomlin G	.... 29 (6)
Bradley S	.... 25 (1)	McLeod I	.... 41 (1)	Walsh J	 28
Cofie J	.... – (1)	Miller S	.... 4 (1)	Ward D	.... 17 (1)
Dickson R	.... 30 (2)	Morgan D	.... 3 (11)	Wood R	 10
Edwards G	.... 29 (8)	O'Connor E	.... 1 (3)	Wordsworth A	 18
Elliott M	.... 22 (5)	Oyebanjo L	.... 26 (5)	Wright J	.... 2 (2)
Fowler L	.... 16 (3)	Pogba M	.... 14 (3)	Youga K	 5
Harrold M	.... 4 (16)	Price L	18	Young J	.... 29 (9)

League goals (53): McLeod 19, Elliott 6, Edwards 4, Wordsworth 4, Tomlin 3, Wood 3, Henderson 2, Pogba 2, Bradley 1, Dickson 1, Fowler 1, Harrold 1, Leacock 1, Simpson 1, Smith 1, Walsh 1, Ward 1, Youga 1
FA Cup goals: None. **Capital One Cup goals** (2): McLeod 1, Opponents 1. **Johnstone's Paint Trophy goals** (4): Banya 1, Edwards 1, McLeod 1, Opponents 1
Average home league attendance: 2,709. **Player of Year**: Ryan Dickson

CREWE ALEXANDRA

A second successive season-long struggle against relegation again ended in survival in the final fixture. Crewe went into it with a two-point cushion after an excellent 3-1 victory at Coventry a week earlier. During a see-saw 90 minutes against Bradford, they twice dropped into bottom four as fellow-strugglers Crawley and Notts County led in their matches. But both lost and the 1-0 defeat at Gresty Road did not prove costly. Five successive defeats to start with had set the pattern. There was a single victory in the first 11 games and Crewe were bottom approaching the midway point, before their best spell of the campaign netted 13 points from six games. The sequence included victory over leaders Bristol City and the completion of a first-ever league double over local rivals Port Vale. They slipped back when losing 5-0 to MK Dons, conceded five more against Preston and shipped four against Rochdale. Those defeats were followed by a crucial 2-1 win against Sheffield United, their first at Bramall Lane. Ryan Colclough, out for 18 months with hip and hernia injuries, scored the decisive goal winner seconds after the four minutes of stoppage-time had been signalled.

Ajose N	.... 23 (4)	Grant A	.... 42 (1)	Oliver V	.... 6 (3)
Atkinson C	.... 8 (11)	Guthrie J	.... 21 (4)	Rachubka P	.... 14 (1)
Audel T	2	Haber M	.... 25 (11)	Ray G	 35
Baillie J	.... 12 (1)	Haynes D	.... 2 (1)	Saunders C	.... 1 (3)
Brandy F	.... 6 (2)	Ikpeazu U	.... 11 (6)	Shearer S	 2
Colclough R	.... 3 (4)	Inman B	.... 12 (9)	Stewart A	.... 2 (8)
Cooper G	.... 5 (17)	Jones J	.... 21 (3)	Tate A	 26
Dalla Valle L	.... 10 (7)	Leigh G	.... 36 (2)	Tootle M	 15
Davis H	31	Molyneux L	.... 2 (1)	Turton O	.... 39 (5)
Dugdale A	.... 16 (2)	Ness J	.... 31 (3)	Waters B	.... 11 (5)
Garratt B	30	Nolan L	.... 6 (7)		

League goals (43): Ajose 8, Haber 7, Dalla Valle 4, Cooper 3, Colclough 2, Grant 2, Ikpeazu 2, Ness 2, Ray 2, Waters 2, Brandy 1, Davis 1, Dugdale 1, Inman 1, Jones 1, Leigh 1, Oliver 1, Turton 1, Opponents 1
FA Cup goals: None. **Capital One Cup goals** (4): Haber 1, Inman 1, Tootle 1, Waters 1. **Johnstone's Paint Trophy goals**: None
Average home league attendance: 4,732. **Player of Year**: Ben Garratt

DONCASTER ROVERS

With teams lining up to stake a claim for a place in the play-offs, there was little room for error in a tightly-packed division. Rovers, relegated the previous season, were among them, having briefly put aside indifferent form at the Keepmoat to beat Yeovil and Crewe in the wake of a 5-0 victory at Crawley. Those three successes took them into sixth place and they remained in, or just outside, a play-off position until a loss of momentum proved costly. They won only twice in 11 matches, falling right off the pace and dropping into the bottom half of the table with just seven home wins to their credit, two fewer than secured on their travels. The pattern was set from the start – a 3-0 success at Yeovil on the opening day, followed by a 3-1 reversal against Port Vale in front of their own supporters. At least Rovers ended the season on a high, defeating Scunthorpe 5-2 with Nathan Tyson scoring his first hat-trick since 2006 with the help of two penalties.

Bennett K	31 (11)	Jones R	10	Razak A	5 (4)
Butler M	33	Keegan P	30 (2)	Robinson T	13 (19)
Bywater S	21	Lund M	4	Steer J	13
Clarke-Harris J	2 (6)	Main C	23 (15)	Stevens E	27 (1)
Coppinger J	33 (1)	Mandeville L	– (3)	Tyson N	31 (8)
De Val M	8 (3)	Marosi M	2 (1)	Wabara R	42 (1)
Evina C	17 (2)	McCombe J	16 (2)	Wakefield L	3 (3)
Forrester H	24 (16)	McCullough L	33	Wellens R	37 (2)
Furman D	32 (2)	McKay J	1 (3)	Whitehouse B	– (4)
Ikpeazu U	3 (4)	Middleton H	1 (3)		
Johnstone S	10	Peterson A	– (1)		

League goals (58): Tyson 12, Bennett 8, Main 8, Forrester 7, Coppinger 4, Robinson 4, Butler 3, Wellens 3, Furman 2, Jones 2, Clarke-Harris 1, McCombe 1, Stevens 1, Wabara 1, Opponents 1
FA Cup goals (6): Main 2, Coppinger 1, McCullough 1, Wellens 1, Opponents 1. **Capital One Cup goals** (4): Coppinger 1, Forrester 1, Tyson 1, Wakefield 1. **Johnstone's Paint Trophy goals** (3): Forrester 1, Tyson 1, Wellens 1
Average home league attendance: 6,884. **Player of Year**: Nathan Tyson

FLEETWOOD TOWN

Any suggestion that Graham Alexander's promoted side would be overawed by their first appearance in League One was quickly dispelled. They beat Crewe, Notts County and Scunthorpe to head the table after three matches. The wins provided momentum for the task ahead and although it would have been too much to expect a continuation of that start, Fleetwood went on to more than hold their own in a competitive division featuring some big clubs vying for a return to the Championship. There were lean spells, seven games without a win after that flying start, then five without success around Christmas. Each time they put things right. Indeed, after the biggest win of the season, 4-0 against Yeovil with two goals from David Ball in early April, they were just four points away from a play-off place. Three goalless games set them back, along with a 3-2 defeat by relegation-threatened Colchester when two goals were conceded in the final ten minutes. But Fleetwood finished with their ninth away success, 2-1 against Port Vale, to claim a highly respectable tenth place.

Andrew D	6 (1)	Hitchcock T	4 (2)	Morris J	43 (2)
Ball D	20 (12)	Hogan L	4	Murdoch S	5 (6)
Blair M	3 (5)	Hornby-Forbes T	11 (6)	Paterson M	3
Campbell A	– (2)	Hughes J	20 (2)	Pond N	24 (3)
Chicksen A	13	Hughes M	2 (4)	Proctor J	32 (9)
Crainey S	26 (2)	Hunter A	3 (9)	Roberts M	27
Cresswell R	– (1)	Jordan A	40 (2)	Sarcevic A	29 (8)
Dobbie S	18 (9)	Maxwell C	46	Schumacher S	27 (5)
Evans G	40 (3)	McAlinden L	10 (9)	Southern K	1 (1)
Haughton N	11 (11)	McLaughlin C	38 (1)		

League goals (49): Ball 8, Morris 8, Proctor 8, Dobbie 4, McAlinden 4, Evans 3, Roberts 3, Sarcevic 2, Haughton 1, Hitchcock 1, Hughes J 1, Hunter 1, Jordan 1, McLaughlin 1, Pond 1, Opponents 2

FA Cup goals: None. Capital One Cup goals: None. Johnstone's Paint Trophy goals (1): Evans 1
Average home league attendance: 3,522. Player of Year: Chris Maxwell

GILLINGHAM

A change of manager brought a change in fortunes at Priestfield. Peter Taylor's side were two points away from the relegation zone when his second spell at the club was ended midway through the season. Their predicament got worse with two more defeats after his dismissal. A four-man caretaker management team turned the tide and Newport's Justin Edinburgh came in to complete the recovery. Edinburgh watched from the stands as his new team defeated Sheffield United 2-0. When he took over, they defeated two more promotion contenders, MK Dons (4-2) and Swindon (3-0), with Cody McDonald on the mark in all three games. Gillingham also held the eventual champions, Bristol City, and Preston away from home and in a tightly-packed division closed to within three points of a play-off place. But they couldn't quite find the consistency required to close the gap and had to be satisfied with 12th place in the table, the club's highest for ten years. A grandstand finish brought a 3-1 win over Notts County – John Egan equalising after 88 minutes and Brennan Dickenson and Luke Norris scoring in stoppage-time to relegate their opponents.

Bell A	6 (1)	Galbraith D	3 (4)	Loft D	36
Bywater S	13	Garmston B	7 (1)	Marquis J	18 (3)
Chicksen A	3	German A	1 (9)	Martin J	22 (3)
Dack B	35 (7)	Hare J	2	McDonald C	38 (5)
Davies C	5	Hause K	14	McGlashan J	23 (17)
Dickenson B	17 (17)	Hessenthaler J	35 (22)	Morris G	9 (1)
Doughty M	9	Hoyte G	26 (4)	Morris A	20 (3)
Egan J	45	Kedwell D	10 (4)	Muldoon O	3
Ehmer M	27	Legge L	21 (1)	Nelson S	24
Fish M	2 (1)	Lennon H	2	Norris L	13 (24)
Freiter M	– (1)	Linganzi A	3 (4)	Pritchard J	14 (11)

League goals (65): McDonald 16, Dack 9, Marquis 8, Norris 6, McGlashan 5, Egan 4, Kedwell 4, Legge 4, Martin 2, Dickenson 1, Ehmer 1, Garmston 1, German 1, Hause 1, Hessenthaler 1, Loft 1
FA Cup goals (1): Kedwell 1. Capital One Cup goals (2): Dickenson 1, Morris 1. Johnstone's Paint Trophy goals (10): McDonald 2, McGlashan 2, Dack 1, Dickenson 1, Egan 1, German 1, Loft 1, Norris 1
Average home league attendance: 5,694. Player of Year: John Egan

LEYTON ORIENT

Orient experienced bitter disappointment for the second successive year. In 2014, it came with a defeat on penalties in the Play-off Final against Rotherham. This time, the club were relegated at the end of a season which had seen three different managers – and a fourth about to be appointed. Russell Slade, League One's longest-serving boss, resigned after four years to take over at Cardiff. Mauro Milanese, the club's sporting director and a former Queens Park Rangers defender, lasted for 43 days before returning to his previous role and making way for Fabio Liverani. Under the former Genoa coach, Orient ended the year by beating Crawley 4-1 and Yeovil 3-0 to move out of the bottom four. But the first five matches of 2015 delivered a single point and they slipped into the bottom spot – four points from safety. They remained in – or on the fringes of – the relegation zone, their situation becoming more precarious with successive defeats by Doncaster, MK Dons and Rochdale. Orient were two points from safety going into the final game at Swindon, where a 2-2 draw, coupled with Colchester's victory against Preston, sent them down. Liverani then left my mutual consent to be replaced by West Ham coach Ian Hendon, a former Orient player.

Adeboyejo V ....– (1)	Hedges R 11 (6)	Omozusi E.................24 (1)
Agyemang M ....– (1)	Henderson D............ 16 (7)	Petrasso M 2 (1)
Bartley M.................. 17 (5)	James L 10 (3)	Plasmati G 7 (7)
Batt S...................... 5 (11)	Kashket S....................– (1)	Price J 4 (1)
Baudry M.................. 28 (3)	Lee H........................– (2)	Pritchard B.............22 (9)
Cisak A.........................19	Legzdins A.................11	Sawyer G 12 (1)
Clarke N 31 (2)	Lisbie K 5 (2)	Simpson J 12 (16)
Cox D 27 (10)	Lowry S................... 31 (3)	Taylor J 3
Cuthbert S 36 (2)	Lundstram J 3 (1)	Vincelot R 27
Dagnall C.................. 34 (4)	McAnuff J 25 (9)	Woods G.................. 16 (1)
Dossena A................. 13 (2)	Mooney D 20 (13)	Wright J..................26 (3)
Eardley N...........................1	O'Neill L 8	

League goals (59): Dagnall 11, Mooney 9, Henderson 8, Cox 6, Simpson 5, McAnuff 3, Cuthbert 2, Hedges 2, Lisbie 2, Plasmati 2, Vincelot 2, Wright 2, Batt 1, Baudry 1, Dossena 1, James 1, Opponents 1
FA Cup goals: None. **Capital One Cup goals (4):** Vincelot 2, Baudry 1, Cox 1. **Johnstone's Paint Trophy goals (7):** Simpson 3, Dagnall 2, Bartley 1, Pritchard 1
Average home league attendance: 5,042. **Player of Year:** Chris Dagnall

MILTON KEYNES DONS

A remarkable scoring streak at the end of a record-breaking season was rewarded with the runners-up spot behind Bristol City and a long-awaited promotion. Dons had been losing semi-finalists in the play-offs three times in the previous six years and seemed to be heading there again when falling six points behind Preston after losing 2-0 at home to their rivals. But 32 goals in the last ten matches delivered nine victories, the most significant coming in the final fixture against relegated Yeovil. While Preston were losing at Colchester, Dons won 5-1 to overtake them, with captain Dean Lewington scoring twice and providing two assists for Darren Potter and Will Grigg – all from the left-back position. This took their tally for the campaign to a new high of 101, achieved by scoring four goals or more in nine games and including a 7-0 rout of Oldham, another record. There were two more new marks. A crowd of nearly 27,000 saw Manchester United defeated 4-0 in the Capital One Cup, with on-loan Benik Afobe scoring two of his 19 goals in the second round tie before a permanent move from Arsenal to Wolves during the winter transfer winter. Dele Alli, Dons 18-year-old midfield player, was sold to Tottenham for £5m and loaned back for the remainder of a season which brought him the Football League's Young Player of the Year award.

Afobe B 11 (11)	Flanagan T 3 (3)	McLoughlin I 7 (1)
Alli D...........................39	Green D 4 (10)	Potter D 40
Andrews K 2 (3)	Grigg W 31 (13)	Powell D..............30 (12)
Baker C 24 (8)	Hall R 5 (2)	Randall M 2 (7)
Baker L.................... 8 (4)	Hitchcock T............. 1 (11)	Reeves B 25 (5)
Baldock G 6 (3)	Hodson L 12 (2)	Spence J 33 (5)
Bowditch D 26 (9)	Kay A............................45	Walsh J 2
Carruthers S........... 20 (12)	Lewington D...............41	Williams G 2 (2)
Clarke-Harris J............ 2 (3)	Martin D.......................39	
Cole D 5 (10)	McFadzean K..............41	

League goals (101): Grigg 20, Alli 16, Afobe 10, Baker C 9, Powell 8, Bowditch 7, Reeves 7, Baker L 3, Cole 3, Hall 3, Lewington 3, McFadzean 3, Carruthers 2, Potter 2, Green 1, Hodson 1, Kay 1, Opponents 2
FA Cup goals (4): Afobe 2, Baker C 1, Green 1. **Capital One Cup goals (10):** Afobe 6, Grigg 2, McFadzean 1, Powell 1. **Johnstone's Paint Trophy goals (2):** Afobe 1, Powell 1
Average home league attendance: 9,452. **Player of Year:** Carl Baker

NOTTS COUNTY

Delight turned into despair for County who were relegated in a dramatic climax to the last match of the season. With two minutes of normal time remaining, they led at Priestfield through a goal by Graham Burke and were poised retain their League One status. Instead, Gillingham equalised and scored twice more in stoppage-time for a 3-1 victory. Ricardo Moniz looked on in horror as his side's collapse meant they were overtaken by Colchester, winners against Preston with a late goal of their own. It was a tough introduction to management for the former Tottenham coach, who took over with six games remaining, having initially turning down the job for family reasons. There were two draws and two defeats before County climbed out of the bottom four with a 2-1 win over Doncaster, earned by goals from Garry Thompson and Liam Noble. Moniz became the club's 13th manager in less than ten years after replacing Shaun Derry, who had beaten the drop against all the odds the previous season. This time, his side were promotion contenders at the turn of the year, helped by a run of five successive victories and 13 goals scored. After that, they struggled and Derry was sacked in late March.

Adams B.................. 31 (3)	Harrad S 4 (8)	Noble L..................... 30 (3)
Bajner B 8 (11)	Hayhurst W................. 8 (4)	Petrasso M 5 (3)
Balmy J ....– (1)	Haynes D 1 (1)	Pilkington K 1 (1)
Bishop C 2 (1)	Hollis H 41	Santos A 1 (2)
Brown R 3	Ismail Z 10 (4)	Smith A 20 (3)
Burke G 6 (1)	Jones G 39 (4)	Spencer J 8 (1)
Campbell-Ryce J.......... 3 (1)	Keane C 2	Thomas K...................2 (3)
Carroll R 45	Laing L 10	Thompson C 20 (11)
Cassidy J 15 (1)	Lita L 3 (3)	Thompson G 36 (5)
Cranston J.......................9	McCourt P 11 (1)	Traore D 2 (2)
Daniels B................. 1 (3)	McKenzie T 2 (2)	White H 2 (1)
Dawson A................. 1 (1)	McLaughlin S 13	Whitehouse E 3 (4)
Dumbuya M 27 (2)	Mullins H 32	Williams J 8
Edwards M............. 17 (10	Murray R 7 (13)	Woolery K 3 (2)
Hall R...................... 2 (2)	Newton S 6 (2)	Wroe N......................6 (6)

League goals (45): Thompson G 12, Noble 5, Cassidy 4, Ismail 4, Bajner 3, Edwards 3, Jones 3, Petrasso 3, Adams 1, Burke 1, Daniels 1, Harrad 1, McCourt 1, Murray 1, Spencer 1, Whitehouse 1
FA Cup goals (1): Murray 1. **Capital One Cup goals**: None. **Johnstone's Paint Trophy goals** (5): Murray 2, Cassidy 1, McLaughlin 1, Noble 1
Average home league attendance: 5,351. **Player of Year**: Roy Carroll

OLDHAM ATHLETIC

A season of some promise fell victim to a controversial transfer bid, managerial upheaval and eventually a predictable conclusion. Lee Johnson's side picked up after an indifferent start to climb to sixth on the back of some free-scoring performances before a bleak December of four league and cup defeats. They included a 7-0 trouncing by MK Dons and were followed a bitter row over attempts to sign former Sheffield United striker Ched Evans on his release from prison. Club directors and employees were subject to abuse and key sponsors threatened to withdraw support, forcing the club to abandon the bid. On the pitch, Oldham regrouped and had moved back to within two points of the top six when manager Lee Johnson left to take over at Barnsley. Former defender Dean Holden replaced him, initially as caretaker and then until the end of the campaign. But momentum was again lost, along with a fall back into mid-table. There was still a chance of ending a run of five successive finishes in the bottom half. Instead, a 3-0 victory over Rochdale gave way to eight matches without a win and 15th place. Sunderland coach Darren Kelly was appointed permanent manager, with Holden his assistant.

Bove J ....– (5)	Jones M 45	Poleon D 21 (14)
Brown C 22 (2)	Kean J 11	Rachubka P 22
Clarke-Harris J..................5	Kelly L........................37	Sadler M 7 (1)
Coleman J 10 (1)	Kenny P 3	Tidser M 1 (4)
Dayton J 5 (12)	Kusunga G 12 (6)	Tuohy J ....– (1)
Dieng T 15 (7)	Lockwood A 11 (1)	Turner R 9 (5)
Elokobi G 20 (4)	Mellis J 2 (5)	Wilkinson C 10 (7)
Forte J 32 (2)	Mellor D.................1 (1)	Wilson B 33
Gerrard A...................6	Mills J 28 (2)	Wilson J 40 (1)
Gros W ....– (1)	Morgan-Smith A........3 (10)	Winchester C 36 (5)
Ibehre J 8 (3)	Murphy R 3 (8)	Woodland L 6
Jacobs D....................– (2)	Noble D ....– (2)	
Johnson D..................5 (1)	Philliskirk D.............37 (6)	

League goals (54): Forte 15, Jones 6, Philliskirk 4, Poleon 4, Winchester 4, Elokobi 3, Johnson 3, Turner 3, Wilkinson 3, Ibehre 2, Morgan-Smith 2, Clarke-Harris 1, Dayton 1, Kelly 1, Kusunga 1, Wilson J 1
FA Cup goals (1): Jones 1. **Capital One Cup goals**: None. **Johnstone's Paint Trophy goals** (5): Philliskirk 2, Poleon 2, Bove 1.
Average home league attendance: 4,349. **Player of Year**: Carl Winchester

PETERBOROUGH UNITED

Peterborough made a flying start to the season, despite selling 33-goal Britt Assombalonga to Nottingham Forest for a record £5.5m. But they were grounded by the end of it and fell short of a second successive appearance in the play-offs. Darren Ferguson's team won five of the first six matches and were in the top two for two months until a major loss of momentum. One victory in a run of 12 games was accompanied by a slide into the bottom half of the table, leading to Ferguson's departure from the club for the second time. Dave Robertson, academy and youth team manager, took over on a caretaker basis, starting with wins over Bradford, Sheffield United, Leyton Orient and Doncaster. That restored a place in the play-offs, but again Peterborough fell away, scoring just twice in six games. They returned to winning ways with two goals in the final four minutes to beat Crawley, although by then they had lost touch with the leading group and had to satisfied with a ninth-place finish. Robertson was given the job on a three-year contract, with the club's former Northern Ireland midfielder Grant McCann as assistant.

Alnwick B 41	Ferdinand K 2 (10)	Ntlhe K 25 (3)
Anderson J 19 (5)	James L 21 (11)	Oztumer E.............11 (9)
Anderson H 6 (4)	Loach S 5	Payne J 38 (3)
Baldwin J....................11	Mackail-Smith C 3	Santos R 22 (2)
Barnett T ....– (4)	Maddison M 23 (6)	Sheehan A................1 (1)
Beautyman H 15 (3)	McCann G 2 (4)	Smith M 40 (3)
Bostwick M 37 (1)	McEvoy K 2 (5)	Taylor J 22 (2)
Brisley S 11 (4)	Mclean A 10 (8)	Vassell K 12 (5)
Burgess C 28 (2)	Mendez-Laing N........6 (8)	Washington C 31 (9)
Da Silva L....................2	Newell J 35 (4)	Williams L 1 (1)
Edwards J 1 (2)	Norris D 3 (5)	Zakuani G.............20 (2)

League goals (53): Washington 13, Bostwick 7, Maddison 7, Vassell 5, Payne 3, Taylor 3, Beautyman 2, Burgess 2, Newell 2, Anderson 1, Brisley 1, James 1, McEvoy 1, Mclean 1, Ntlhe 1, Oztumer 1, Smith 1, Zakuani 1
FA Cup goals (2): Burgess 2. **Capital One Cup goals**: None. **Johnstone's Paint Trophy goals** (2): James 1, Maddison 1
Average home league attendance: 6,227. **Player of Year**: Joe Newell

PORT VALE

In a tightly-packed division, Vale went from promotion possibles to relegation candidates within a few weeks. A first taste of management for former Wales defender Robert Page was going well when his side closed to within two points of a play-off place with a run of four wins out of five. They then lost six on the trot and with a month of the season remaining were two points away from the bottom four. Home draws against promotion-chasing MK Dons and Preston, along with a stoppage-time equaliser conceded at Scunthorpe, kept the pressure on. But goals by Tom Pope and Michael Brown delivered a 2-1 victory away to relegated Yeovil, their first in ten games, and put them four points clear. Vale then lost to Fleetwood to round off a disappointing campaign overall after the ninth-place finish in 2014. Page, given a coaching job at the club by manager Micky Adams, took over when Adams resigned in September in the wake of six successive league and cup defeats. He was given the job on a permanent basis after a spell as caretaker.

Birchall C	12 (15)	Jennings S	1 (3)	O'Sullivan T	1 (4)
Brown M	30 (6)	Johnson S	6 (1)	Pope T	28 (5)
Campion A	4 (8)	Lines C	19 (8)	Robertson C	21 (3)
Collins N	7	Luer G	– (2)	Slew J	5 (4)
Coulibaly M	1 (3)	Marshall M	45 (1)	Streete R	1 (1)
Daniel C	8 (20)	McGivern R	18 (2)	Veseli F	37
Dickinson C	43	Moore D	9 (6)	Williamson B	33 (10)
Dodds L	24 (13)	N'Guessan D	10 (1)	Yates A	24 (1)
Duffy R	27	Neal C	40	Zubar S	2
Franciso Junior	1	Nimely A	– (1)		
Inniss R	5	O'Connor M	44		

League goals (55): Pope 8, Marshall 7, O'Connor 6, Williamson 6, Brown 4, Daniel 4, Dodds 4, Birchall 3, Lines 2, N'Guessan 2, Slew 2, Campion 1, Dickinson 1, Duffy 1, Moore 1, Veseli 1, Yates 1, Opponents 1

FA Cup goals (3): N'Guessan 2, Williamson 1. **Capital One Cup goals (8):** Williamson 3, Brown 2, Pope 2, O'Connor 1. **Johnstone's Paint Trophy goals (2):** Pope 2
Average home league attendance: 5,313. **Player of Year:** Michael O'Connor

PRESTON NORTH END

Simon Grayson's side showed admirable resilience to shake off the disappointment of missing out on automatic promotion, surge through the play-offs and return to the Championship in style after a four-year absence. Jermaine Beckford's hat-trick and a goal by Paul Huntington delivered a 4-0 victory over Swindon in the final, so ending the club's jinx in the end-of- season lottery which had brought defeat in all nine appearances. Beckford, on loan from Bolton, also scored three times in the two-leg semi-final win over Chesterfield after his partnership with Joe Garner had taken Preston to the brink of the runners-up spot behind Bristol City. They had stalled early in the New Year, with points dropped against struggling Leyton Orient, Yeovil and Crawley, before Garner's return after after surgery to repair a shin injury brought an unbeaten run of 18 matches. His hat-trick in a 3-0 win over Swindon in the reverse fixture left them a point ahead of third-place Colchester going into the last match away to relegation-threatened Colchester. But they lost to an 82nd minute goal, which kept Colchester up, and were overtaken by Dons' 5-1 victory over Yeovil. Garner had previously scored four against Crewe and three against Fleetwood. He finished the division's top marksman with 25 goals and was voted League One's Player of the Year. Preston's success brought owner Trevor Hemmings a notable sporting double, with his horse Many Clouds having won the Grand National.

Beckford J	19 (4)	Davies B	4	Hayhurst W	2 (5)
Browne A	14 (6)	Davies K	8 (24)	Hugill J	– (3)
Brownhill J	13 (5)	Ebanks-Blake S	1 (8)	Humphrey C	32 (12)
Buchanan D	17	Gallagher P	45 (1)	Huntington P	32
Clarke T	42 (1)	Garner J	36 (1)	Johnson D	20

Johnstone S 22	Little A 5 (7)	Welsh J 30 (2)
Jones J 17	Reid K 5 (9)	Wiseman S 17 (5)
Kilkenny N............ 24 (11)	Robinson C 18 (7)	Woods C 12 (6)
King J.................... 10 (8)	Ryan J .... - (1)	Wright B 27
Laird S 27 (4)	Stuckmann T.................7	

Play-offs – appearances: Beckford 3, Clarke 3, Gallagher 3, Garner 3, Huntington 3, Johnson 3, Johnstone 3, Welsh 3, Wright 3, Kilkenny 2 (1), Woods 2 (1), Laird 1 (2), Humphrey 1 (1), Browne – (2), Davies – (1), Robinson – (1)
League goals (79): Garner 25, Beckford 12, Johnson 8, Gallagher 7, Huntington 5, Humphrey 4, Robinson 4, Browne 3, Brownhill 2, Wiseman 2, Clarke 1, Davies K 1, Ebanks-Blake 1, King 1, Little 1, Wright 1, Opponents 1. **Play-offs – goals (8):** Beckford 6, Garner 1, Huntington 1
FA Cup goals (11): Gallagher 5, Robinson 3, Huntington 2, Laird 1. **Capital One Cup goals (3):** Hugill 1, Kilkenny 1, Little 1. **Johnstone's Paint Trophy goals (7):** Clarke 1, Gallagher 1, Garner 1, Hugill 1, Humphrey 1, Huntington 1, Laird 1
Average home league attendance: 10,852. **Player of Year:** Paul Huntington

ROCHDALE

Keith Hill led his side to a record-breaking season which would have shone even brighter with a better finish. Rochdale, promoted in 2014, recorded their highest-ever league place, surpassing by one the ninth spot achieved by Hill in his first spell with the club in 2011. They also recorded more wins, 19, and scored more goals, 72, than previously at this level. There was even a slim chance of promotion going into the final fixtures. The first, in which Ian Henderson scored his 22nd goal – all in the league – brought a 3-2 home defeat by promotion-chasing MK Dons. The second was a 5-0 defeat at Barnsley in which all the goals were conceded in a 23-minute spell following the sending-off of Joe Rafferty. Rochdale had overcome a sticky start – three successive defeats in league and cup – to set the ball rolling by winning 5-2 at Crewe. They went on to score three or more times in ten other games, overcoming the sale of leading marksman Matt Done to Sheffield United during the winter transfer window, which Hill insisted was right for the club and the player. Done scored hat-tricks against Crewe and in an FA Cup win over Aldershot which paved the way for a 1-0 third round victory over Nottingham Forest.

Allen J...................... 33 (2)	Donnelly G 1 (2)	Lund M 12 (2)
Andrew C 5 (27)	Eastham A 40 (1)	Muldoon J 2 (1)
Bell N........................– (3)	Fenelon S..................... – (4)	Musangu J .... – (1)
Bennett R 33 (6)	Henderson I.................44	Noble-Lazarus R 7 (12)
Brandy F..................... 1 (3)	Hery B 12 (9)	O'Connell J 28 (1)
Bunney J 10 (9)	Jones J............................13	Rafferty J 28 (3)
Camps C 6 (6)	Kennedy T 22 (1)	Rose M 26 (6)
Cannon A 16 (2)	Lancashire O 16 (5)	Tanser S 27 (3)
Cywka T 1 (2)	Lillis J..................... 14 (2)	Vincenti P 36 (1)
Dawson S................. 27 (3)	Logan C 19	
Done M........................23	Logan J 4 (4)	

League goals (72): Henderson 22, Vincenti 13, Done 10, Andrew 5, O'Connell 5, Bennett 2, Bunney 2, Eastham 2, Lund 2, Camps 1, Hery 1, Noble-Lazarus 1, Rafferty 1, Rose 1, Tanser 1, Opponents 3
FA Cup goals (8): Done 3, Vincenti 2, Bennett 1, Lancashire 1, Noble-Lazarus 1. **Capital One Cup goals:** None. **Johnstone's Paint Trophy goals (3):** Andrew 1, Done 1, Vincenti 1
Average home league attendance: 3,309. **Player of Year:** Ian Henderson

SCUNTHORPE UNITED

Mark Robins started the season out of a job after Huddersfield's 4-0 home defeat by Bournemouth on the opening day; he finished it having lifted a relegation cloud over Glanford Park. Robins took over when Russ Wilcox, who led Scunthorpe to promotion in 2014 with a league record of 28 unbeaten matches as a new manager, was dismissed with his side second from bottom after 11 games. Boosted by some shrewd loan signings, they climbed out of the bottom four for first time by beating Crewe in the run-up to Christmas. The improvement continued with four goals against Walsall and Leyton Orient, followed by victories over promotion-minded Swindon and Chesterfield in the space of four days. There were even whispers of a promotion bid in a tightly-packed division. Scunthorpe were just five points away from a play-off place, with games in hand over the teams directly above them. But a failure to win any of the next nine matches landed them back in trouble, before wins over Peterborough and Crawley broke the sequence. Then, stoppage-time equalisers against Port Vale and Colchester took them clear, with 18-year-old Kyle Wootton on the mark against Vale for his first senior goal.

Addison M 3	Hawkridge T 10 (1)	Osbourne I 24 (4)
Adelakun H.............. 7 (25)	Hopper T.......................12	Robinson T................... 8
Bishop N 34 (1)	Kee B ....– (12)	Severn I 1 (1)
Boyce A 25 (4)	Llera M 15	Slocombe S 9
Brindley R....................3	Lundstram J 5 (2)	Sparrow M 6 (3)
Brisley S 6 (1)	Madden P.......................46	Syers D 1 (5)
Burton D................... 1 (4)	McAllister S 13 (10)	Taylor L 11 (7)
Canavan N 31 (1)	McSheffrey G........... 35 (6)	Townsend C 5 (1)
Clarke J 24	Murphy J.........................3	Williams L 6
Daniels L 23	Myrie-Williams J 7 (8)	Williams M 40
Davey A 13	Nolan E 4 (2)	Wootton K 1 (11)
Dawson A.....................3	O'Neil L 21 (1)	Van Veen K 11 (9)
Evans G 9 (7)	O'Neill L 13	
Fallon R.........................4	Olejnik B 13	

League goals (62): Madden 14, McSheffrey 7, Adelakun 6, Bishop 4, Hopper 4, Canavan 3, Fallon 3, Robinson 3, Taylor 3, O'Neil 2, Williams L 2, Van Veen 2, Boyce 1, Evans 1, Llera 1, Sparrow 1, Wootton 1, Opponents 1
FA Cup goals (6): Madden 2, McSheffrey 2, Davey 1, Taylor 1. **Capital One Cup goals** (1): Bishop 1. **Johnstone's Paint Trophy goals** (3): Madden 1, McAllister 1, McSheffrey 1
Average home league attendance: 3,646. **Player of Year**: Paddy Madden

SHEFFIELD UNITED

For the fourth time in seven years, United lost in the play-offs – this time in a remarkable, record-breaking tie with Swindon. After losing the first leg 2-1 to a stoppage-time goal at Bramall Lane, they conceded three in the first 20 minutes of the return and looked a spent force. Instead, Nigel Clough's team refused to give up, even while trailing 5-3 on the night. Matt Done (88) and Che Adams (90) brought the scores level for an aggregate score of 7-6 – the highest score ever recorded in the semi-finals. United had overcome an indifferent start to the regular season to climb to a top-six place by half-way. They cemented it by mid-February with successive wins over Colchester, eventual champions Bristol City and Notts County, although there was never a hint of a challenge to the leaders who were way in front. United's promotion bid was accompanied by a second successive cup semi-final. After knocking out West Ham and Southampton in the Capital One Cup, they led Tottenham 2-1 in the second leg with two goals from Adams before an 88th minute equaliser from Christian Eriksen put the Premier League side through 3-2 on aggregate. Off the field, the club were mired in controversy following an offer to their former striker Ched Evans to resume training on his release from prison – an offer withdrawn when supporters, the general public and sponsors voiced protests. Clough was sacked at the end of the season and replaced by former Reading, Southampton and Scunthorpe manager Nigel Adkins.

Adams C 5 (5)	Campbell-Ryce J....... 14 (5)	Done M 12 (3)
Alcock C 17 (7)	Collins N.........................8	Doyle M 35 (8)
Basham C 35 (2)	Coutts P 19 (1)	Flynn R 18 (14)
Baxter J 28 (6)	Cuvelier F 1 (2)	Freeman K 13 (6)
Brayford J 22	Davies R 11 (3)	Harris R 35 (45)
Calvert-Lewin D .... – (2)	Davies S 10 (3)	Higdon M 9 (4)

124

Holt J 11 (5)	McGahey H 11 (4)	Reed L 10 (9)
Howard M 35	McNulty M 11 (20)	Scougall S 20 (5)
Kennedy T 10 (1)	Murphy J 41 (2)	Turner I 11
McCarthy P 10 (1)	O'Grady C 4	Wallace K 2 (2)
McEveley J 31 (3)	Porter C .... - (1)	Wallace J 7 (3)

Play-offs – appearances: Basham 2, Coutts 2, Flynn 2, Freeman 2, Harris 2, Howard 2, McEveley 2, Murphy 2, Davies S 1 (1), Done 1 (1), Alcock 1, Brayford 1, Holt 1, McNulty 1, Adams – (1), Doyle – (1), Scougall – (1)

League goals (66): Murphy 11, Baxter 10, McNulty 9, Done 7, Holt 5, Campbell-Ryce 4, Davies B 4, Harris 3, Davies S 2, Higdon 2, Brayford 1, Collins 1, Doyle 1, Flynn 1, Freeman 1, McCarthy 1, McEveley 1, O'Grady 1, Scougall 1. **Play-offs – goals (6)**: Adams 1, Basham 1, Done 1, Freeman 1, Davies S 1, Opponents 1

FA Cup goals (10): Baxter 2, Campbell-Ryce 2, Flynn 2, McNulty 2, De Girolamo D 1, Murphy 1. **Capital One Cup goals (9)**: Higdon 3, Adams 2, McNulty 2, Butler 1, Opponents 1. **Johnstone's Paint Trophy goals (2)**: Baxter 1, Campbell-Ryce 1

Average home league attendance: 19,805. **Player of Year**: Jamie Murphy

SWINDON TOWN

The manner of their Wembley defeat by Preston was disappointing, yet Swindon were able to look back with some satisfaction on the season as a whole. They were in the thick of the promotion race for much of the time, while a 13,000 crowd who witnessed the second leg of their semi-final against Sheffield United will never forget it. In the highest scoring match in the history of the play-offs, the teams drew 5-5 at the County Ground, with the home side going through on a record 7-6 aggregate. They were up against it from the start of the final, losing captain Nathan Thompson through injury after five minutes, trailing 2-0 after 13 minutes and eventually going down 4-0 to the strike power of Jermaine Beckford and Joe Garner. Beckford scored a hat-trick, while Garner got three when the teams met near the end of the regular campaign. Swindon finished in fourth place, ten points behind Preston, having spent the best part of three months in the top two alongside the eventual champions Bristol City. A run of three successive defeats eventually set them back, but they came again to close to within two points of an automatic promotion spot before 3-0 losses to City and fast-finishing MK Dons in the space of four days early in April meant they had to settle for the play-offs.

Agombar H 1	Hylton J 1 (10)	Smith M.................... 32 (8)
Barker G 1 (4)	Kasim Y 28 (7)	Smith T....................... - (1)
Barthram J................. 3 (2)	Lelan J 2 (3)	Stephens J 36 (1)
Belford C .... – (1)	Luongo M 33 (1)	Swift J 12 (6)
Belford T 2	Marshall L................. 1 (1)	Thompson L 30 (2)
Bell A 7 (3)	Obika J 21 (11)	Thompson N 35
Branco R 26 (3)	Randall W 2 (2)	Toffolo H 22 (6)
Byrne N 42	Reeves J 1 (9)	Turnbull J 44
Cooke J 1 (1)	Ricketts S 8 (1)	Waldon C.........................1
Foderingham W 44	Rodgers J 7 (3)	Williams A 28 (18)
Gladwin B 28 (6)	Smith B 7	

Play-offs – appearances: Byrne 3, Foderingham 3, Gladwin 3, Kasim 3, Luongo 3, Smith M 3, Stephens 3, Thompson N 3, Turnbull 3, Ricketts 2 (1), Hylton 2, Obika 1 (2), Toffolo 1, Williams – (2), Branco – (1), Rodgers – (1), Swift – (1), Thompson L – (1)

League goals (76): Williams 21, Smith M 13, Gladwin 8, Obika 8, Luongo 6, Branco 3, Byrne 3, Kasim 2, Rodgers 2, Swift 2, Thompson L 2, Hylton 1, Reeves 1, Stephens 1, Toffolo 1, Turnbull 1, Opponents 1. **Play-offs – goals (7)**: Gladwin 2, Smith M 2, Byrne 1, Obika 1, Ricketts 1

FA Cup goals: None. **Capital One Cup goals (4)**: Smith M 2, Kasim 1, Thompson L 1. **Johnstone's Paint Trophy goals (4)**: Gladwin 1, Obika 1, Smith M 1, Williams 1

Average home league attendance: 7,940. **Player of Year**: Jordan Turnbull

WALSALL

Reaching Wembley for the first time in the club's history was the highlight of Walsall's season. They overcame tough opposition in Sheffield United and Preston on the way to the final of the Johnstone's Paint Trophy – but were unable to reproduce that form against Bristol City, losing 2-0. Manager Dean Smith felt the occasion, along with a 72,000 crowd, got to his players. The teams met again on the final day of the league programme and this time Smith's side had no excuses for collapsing after two goals by Jordy Hiwula, on loan from Manchester City, left them level at half-time on 2-2. Conceding four in one ten-minute spell, Walsall crashed 8-2 to the League One champions and dropped into the bottom half of the table as a result. They had been on course for a good finish once the threat of slipping into the relegation zone had been averted after a single win in 11 games left them two points above the drop zone. Hiwula was on the mark twice in a 5-0 win over Crawley, while Tom Bradshaw netted two as Oldham were beaten 2-0 to reach 20 in all competitions.

Bakayoko A .... – (8)	Downing P. 33 (2)	Mantom S 6 (6)
Baxendale J 17 (11)	Flanagan R 9 (7)	Morris K 9 (5)
Benning M 11 (9)	Forde A 24 (13)	Murphy J .... – (2)
Bradshaw T 29	Grimes A 11 (16)	O'Connor J 30 (2)
Butler A 7	Henry R 4 (5)	O'Donnell R 44
Cain M 28 (4)	Hiwula J 17 (2)	Preston M .... – (1)
Chambers A 45	Holden D 2 (2)	Purkiss R 31 (1)
Chambers J 31	Kinsella L 4	Sawyers R 37 (5)
Clifford B 7 (6)	MacGillivray C 2	Taylor A 37 (2)
Cook J 27 (5)	Manset M 4 (15)	

League goals (50): Bradshaw 17, Hiwula 9, Cook 5, Sawyers 4, Forde 3, Cain 2, Grimes 2, Morris 2, Baxendale 1, Downing 1, O'Connor 1, Taylor 1, Opponents 2
FA Cup goals (2): Bradshaw 2. **Capital One Cup goals (2):** Benning 1, Morris 1. **Johnstone's Paint Trophy goals (6):** Forde 2, Bradshaw 1, Cain 1, Manset 1, Sawyers 1
Average home league attendance: 4,392. **Player of Year:** Richard O'Donnell

YEOVIL TOWN

A fleeting acquaintance with the Championship was followed by another relegation and a return to League Two. With a much-changed side including seven new signings, Yeovil lost their opening three league and cup matches, before wins over Walsall, Bradford and Peterborough suggested they might be steadying the ship. Instead, a mere two points gained from a run of eight games left them bottom and it was hard going from then on. They were rooted in the bottom four, manager Gary Johnson was sacked in early February and his assistant, Terry Skiverton, fared no better when stepping up. The die was cast by six successive defeats, which brought another change when Paul Sturrock came in after originally deciding to join Torquay as an advisor. Sturrock, taking charge of his sixth club in England and Scotland, had the dubious distinction of seeing them relegated two days after being appointed, although ironically it was followed by the first back-to-back victories of the season, with promotion-chasing Sheffield United and Swindon both beaten.

Arthurworrey S 29	Gillett S 14 (3)	Loach S 6
Bell F 1 (1)	Grant J 15 (6)	Loza J 4 (1)
Berrett J 18 (10)	Hayter J 23 (15)	Martin A 12
Clarke J 5	Hiwula J 7 (1)	Moloney S 4 (1)
Davis L 8	Hoskins S 2 (10)	Moore K 20 (10)
Dawson K 12 (5)	Inniss R 4 (2)	Morgan A 3 (3)
Eastmond C .... – (1)	Kean J 5	Nugent B 23
Eaves T 4 (1)	Kingsley S 12	Ofori-Twumasi N 18 (18)
Edwards J 33 (1)	Krysiak A 15	Price J 5 (1)
Foley S 37 (3)	Leitch-Smith AJ 21 (12)	Ralph N 9 (12)

Sheehan J 12 (1)	Sokolik J 11	Weale C 8
Shephard L 20	Steer J 12	Webster B 14
Smith A 3 (3)	Stewart G .... - (1)	
Smith N.................. 36 (5)	Ugwu G 21 (1)	

League goals (36): Hayter 5, Ugwu 5, Grant 3, Martin 3, Moore 3, Arthurworrey 2, Clarke 2, Foley 2, Leitch-Smith 2, Berrett 1, Dawson 1, Gillett 1, Hoskins 1, Morgan 1, Nugent 1, Opponents 3
FA Cup goals (4): Clarke 1, Gillett 1, Hiwula 1, Moore 1. **Capital One Cup goals** (1): Gillett 1.
Johnstone's Paint Trophy goals (1): Ralph 1
Average home league attendance: 4,346. **Player of Year**: Sam Foley

LEAGUE TWO

ACCRINGTON STANLEY

How many new managers – if any – have won their first game 5-4? John Coleman had the statisticians delving through the record books after returning to the club for a second spell in charge and overseeing victory at Northampton in a remarkable start. Five of the goals came in the final 15 minutes, with Accrington forced to hold on at the end after leading 5-2. Coleman, who came in when James Beattie left by mutual agreement after a poor start to the season, made it a hat-trick of wins to start with against Plymouth and Mansfield, this time in tight games settled by the odd goal. By the midway point of the campaign, Accrington were relatively secure in mid-table. But five successive defeats sent them sliding, one of them a 5-1 reversal in the reverse fixture with ten-man Northampton, before Terry Gornell, beginning a third spell with the club, was on the mark in successive wins over Oxford and Southend. Accrington stayed clear of trouble from then on, despite finishing with the worst defensive record in the division, conceding 77 goals. During that time they used eight different goalkeepers, with a succession of loanees coming in.

Alabi J 1 (1)	Gornell T 14 (1)	McCartan S 11 (20)
Aldred T 25	Gray J 10 (7)	Mingoia P.................34 (2)
Atkinson R 44	Hatfield W 2 (5)	Molyneux L 7 (3)
Barry A 9 (4)	Hazeldine M ....– (1)	Mustoe J 4
Bowerman G 2 (1)	Hunt N 28 (1)	Naismith K 25 (10)
Bruna G.........................6	Jones L 11	O'Sullivan J 13
Buxton A................. 15 (2)	Joronen J 4	Procter A.......................29
Carver M 6 (11)	Joyce L 45	Rose J...........................4
Chapman A 3	Liddle M 7 (8)	Simpson L................. 6 (2)
Conneely S 12 (4)	Lumley J 5	Whitehead D...............1 (1)
Crooks M 11 (5)	Lynch J 1 (1)	Windass J.................23 (12)
Davies S 6	Macey M 4	Winnard D.................35 (2)
Gilchrist J 1 (4)	Maguire S................ 29 (4)	

League goals (58): Mingoia 8, Maguire 7, McCartan 6, Windass 6, Gornell 4, Gray 4, Naismith 4, O'Sullivan 4, Atkinson 3, Conneely 3, Joyce 3, Aldred 1, Buxton 1, Carver 1, Jones 1, Molyneux 1, Lumley
FA Cup goals (3): Aldred 1, Carver 1, Joyce 1. **Capital One Cup goals** (1): Gray 1. **Johnstone's Paint Trophy goals** (1): Carver 1, Opponents 1
Average home league attendance: 1,478. **Player of Year**: Piero Mingoia

AFC WIMBLEDON

Wimbledon achieved their highest position of the four seasons back in the Football League and would have climbed further with a better finish. Victory over Portsmouth lifted them to 12th after 38 games, with teams directly above them within striking distance. But they failed to win any of the final eight fixtures – drawing six and losing two – and had to be satisfied with 15th place. Neal Ardley's side found goals harder to come by after the loss of on-loan leading marksman Matt

Tubbs in the January transfer window. After scoring 12, Tubbs returned to Bournemouth and then joined Portsmouth on a permanent move. He also netted twice in the FA Cup to help Wimbledon to the third round, where they were drawn against Liverpool, evoking memories of the old club's famous victory in the 1988 final. Adebayo Akinfenwa sparked the possibility of another upset by cancelling out Steven Gerrard's early header and although Liverpool's captain won the tie with a trademark free-kick, the League Two side received widespread praise for their efforts.

Akinfenwa A.............. 43 (2)	Goodman J 13 (2)	Reeves J.......................... 23
Azeez A 12 (31)	Harrison B.................. 5 (2)	Rigg S.......................39 (5)
Barrett A...........................23	Kennedy C................. 20 (6)	Sainte-Luce K..............1 (8)
Beere T................... 6 (12)	McDonnell J 3 (1)	O'Shea J 38
Bennett A 16	Moore S 25 (5)	Smith J 21
Bulman D 40 (1)	Nicholson J 2	Sutherland F...............4 (3)
Connolly D 2 (6)	Nightingale W 3 (1)	Sweeney R 2 (1)
Fitzpatrick D ....– (3)	Oakley G .... – (6)	Tanner C 16 (3)
Frampton A............... 3 (1)	Oshilaja A...................23	Tubbs M 22
Francomb G 31 (6)	Pell H 1 (8)	Winfield D 5
Fuller B 45	Phillips M 2 (3)	Worner R......................5
Gallagher D...................– (1)	Potter A 10 (5)	

League goals (54): Akinfenwa 13, Tubbs 12, Azeez 6, Rigg 5, Francomb 3, Smith 3, Reeves 2, Barrett 1, Bulman 1, Connolly 1, Fuller 1, Goodman 1, Oshilaja 1, Potter 1, Sutherland 1, Opponents 3
FA Cup goals (6): Tubbs 2, Akinfenwa 1, Frampton 1, Rigg 1, Smith 1. **Capital One Cup goals (1):** Tubbs 1. **Johnstone's Paint Trophy goals (6):** Akinfenwa 1, Azeez 1, Barrett 1, Francomb 1, Rigg 1, Sainte-Luce 1.
Average home league attendance: 4,073. **Player of Year:** Adebayo Akinfenwa

BURTON ALBION

Jimmy Floyd Hasselbaink graced the game for club and country and could now be on the way to making his mark as a manager. The former Chelsea and Holland striker led Burton to their first Football League promotion after taking over from Gary Rowett, who turned down an approach from one Championship club, Blackpool, but accepted another, from Birmingham with three months of the season gone. Hasselbaink started with a 3-1 away win over Wycombe and lost just one of his first 16 games. Successive defeats by Accrington and Newport proved a temporary blip, as four successive wins to follow lifted them back on top at Shrewsbury's expense. Burton stayed there, effectively making sure of going up with two goals from Lucas Akins, one a penalty, at Morecambe. Hasselbaink called on his players to finish the job and they became champions on the final day when extending an unbeaten record to 12 games. Kevin Stewart's 88th minute goal brought a 3-2 victory at Cambridge – despite the loss of goalkeeper Jon McLaughlin, who was sent off after conceding a penalty. Afterwards, he paid tribute to Rowett's work in laying the foundation for success by taking the club to the play-offs in the two previous seasons.

Akins L 32 (3)	Harness M.................. 1 (17)	Morris B......................3 (2)
Antoine-Curier M 1 (4)	Johnstone D 2 (3)	Mousinho J....................42
Austin S ....–(1)	Kee B ....–(2)	Naylor T 13 (4)
Bell L 3 (2)	Knowles D 4 (7)	Palmer M 21 (12)
Blyth J 15 (7)	Lenihan D 15 (2)	Phillips J......................– (1)
Calero I 3 (3)	Lyness D 1	Reilly C 1 (1)
Cansdell-Sherriff S.........`37	MacDonald A 20 (1)	Sharps I 16 (3)
Cuvelier F .... – (1)	Maynard K.................. 5 (5)	Shearer S ....– (1)
Dunn J ....– (1)	McCrory A 32 (2)	Slade L ....– (6)
Edwards P.....................45	McFadzean C 7 (2)	Stewart K ....4(3)
El Khayati A 9 (9)	McGurk A 27 (10)	Taft G 22 (8)
	McLaughlin J.....................45	Weir R 39 (2)

League goals (69): Akins 9, Beavon 6, Edwards 6, MacDonald 6, McGurk 6, Blyth 5, McCrory 5, Palmer 4, El Khayati 3, Cansdell-Sherriff 2, Kee 2, Mousinho 2, Stewart 2, Bell 1, Cuvelier 1, Johnstone 1, Lenihan 1, Maynard 1, McFadzean 1, Taft 1, Opponents 4
FA Cup goals: None. **Capital One Cup goals (3):** Beavon 1, Knowles 1, McGurk 1. **Johnstone's Paint Trophy goals:** None
Average home league attendance: 3,237. **Player of Year:** Stuart Beavon

BURY

In his first full season as manager, David Flitcroft delivered promotion in a dramatic final round of matches. His side started the day two points behind Southend, who had won at the J D Stadium a fortnight earlier in front of an 8,000-plus crowd given free entry after the original fixture was abandoned through rain. That result put them in pole position for third place behind Burton and Shrewsbury. But Bury had the last word. Tom Soares scored the only goal at relegated Tranmere, while Southend went down 3-1 to Morecambe and had to start preparing for the play-offs. Flitcroft, who took charge in December 2013 when the club were struggling to stay in the Football League, supervised a decisive run of 13 victories, with 11 clean sheets, in the last 16 games. The sequence included a record seventh successive away win, at Portsmouth. Midfielder Danny Mayor played a key role and was voted League Two's Player of the Year. Bury had started successfully, winning six of their first nine matches to go top. But they hit a sticky patch in the run-up to Christmas, losing four on the trot and dropping out of the play-off places.

Adams N	29 (9)	Jalal S	5	Platt C	– (2)
Cameron N	45 (1)	Jones C	25 (15)	Poole J	– (4)
Dudley A	– (1)	Kennedy T	1 (1)	Pope N	22
Duffus C	1 (2)	Lainton R	17	Riley J	16 (1)
Eaves T	7 (2)	Loach S	2	Rose D	19 (16)
El-Abd A	24	Lowe R	23 (11)	Sedgwick C	1 (19)
Etuhu K	43	Mayor D	43 (1)	Soares T	43
Holding R	– (1)	McNulty J	22 (3)	Thompson J	– (1)
Holmes D	– (6)	Mills P	18	Tutte A	37 (5)
Hope H	10 (9)	Milsom R	2	White H	2
Hussey C	30 (8)	Nardiello D	19 (13)	Widdowson J	– (1)

League goals (60): Nardiello 10, Rose 10, Lowe 9, Mayor 8, Soares 8, Jones 3, Tutte 3, Cameron 2, Etuhu 2, Adams 1, Eaves 1, El-Abd 1, Riley 1, Opponents 1
FA Cup goals (4): Nardiello 2, Cameron 1, Tutte 1. **Capital One Cup goals (2):** Lowe 1, McNulty 1. **Johnstone's Paint Trophy goals (4):** Nardiello 2, Cameron 1, Lowe 1
Average home league attendance: 3,774. **Player of Year:** Nathan Cameron

CAMBRIDGE UNITED

Back in the Football League after a nine-year absence, Cambridge were progressing steadily in the middle reaches of the table when a dream FA Cup tie introduced a whole new perspective to the season. The Abbey Stadium suddenly became the centre of attention with the visit of Manchester United for a fourth round tie and Richard Money's side rose to the occasion in a goalless draw. Then, they were far from disgraced by a 3-0 defeat in the replay in front of a 74,000-plus crowd at Old Trafford. That enabled the club to bank around £1m – big money in League Two. The repercussions of the tie, however, were not so welcoming – a single win in 15 league games, including a 6-2 home defeat by Portsmouth. The sequence was accompanied by a fall to within five points of the bottom two and the threat of an immediate return to non-league football if there was no improvement. But a second minute goal by Harrison Dunk secured victory at Northampton to allay those fears. It was followed by a point against Accrington, then a 3-1 win over Mansfield which ensured survival and featured two goals by on-loan Sullay Kaikai – his first a 35-yard free-kick.

Akintunde J..............– (1)	Donaldson R 38	Miller I...........................8
Appiah K 19	Dunk H 21 (11)	Morrissey G 3 (5)
Atkinson W ....– (2)	Dunn C 43	Naylor T 5 (3)
Austin M..........................1	Elliott T...........................30	Nelson M 33
Ball D.........................9 (2)	Harrold M....................6 (1)	Norris W 3
Bird R 10 (14)	Hughes L 26 (4)	Sam-Yorke D...............– (2)
Blair M 1 (1)	Hunt J 4 (5)	Simpson R 23 (12)
Bonner T..........................4	Hurst L:...................– (4)	Slew J......................9 (4)
Chadwick L 8 (14)	Kaikai S 11 (14)	Stockley J...................1 (2)
Champion T 38	Lanzoni M 3	Tait R....................34 (3)
Chiedozie J 2 (4)	Lennon H ....– (2)	Taylor B-J..................1 (6)
Coulson J.......................46	Margetts J ....– (1)	Taylor G...................41 (2)
Cunnington A 4 (3)	McGeehan C...................4	Whittall S ....– (2)
Diallo I 7 (1)	Mendez-Laing N.......10 (1)	

League goals (61): Elliott 8, Simpson 8, Appiah 6, Bird 6, Donaldson 5, Kaikai 5, Hughes 3, McGeehan 3, Nelson 3, Cunnington 2, Dunk 2, Stockley 2, Chadwick 1, Coulson 1, Diallo 1, Harrold 1, Hunt 1, Mendez-Laing 1, Slew 1, Opponents 1

FA Cup goals (6): Appiah 2, Chadwick 1, Donaldson 1, Kaikai 1, Simpson 1. **Capital One Cup goals** (1): Donaldson 1. **Johnstone's Paint Trophy goals:** None

Average home league attendance: 5,108. **Player of Year:** Josh Coulson

CARLISLE UNITED

A nervy season came to a head with five matches remaining and a second successive relegation beckoning. Carlisle were fighting for their Football League place, three points away from the bottom two, when on-loan Jason Kennedy scored the only goal against Dagenham and Redbridge in a match which ended in an 18-player scuffle during six minutes of added time. A 1-1 draw away to eventual champions Burton followed. Then, a 2-0 victory over Plymouth ensured safety with an impressive performance out of keeping with much of what had gone before. The scorers were Gary Dicker and Billy Paynter, who earlier in the season had been in a training dispute with manager Keith Curle which had involved the players' union, the PFA. Curle, formerly with Mansfield, Chester, Torquay and Notts County, had replaced Graham Kavanagh, who was sacked after two points from the opening five games. Curle started with three straight wins, but his team often struggled defensively, finishing with the second worst record in the division, having conceded 74 goals.

Amoo D 12 (15)	Gillespie M.....................19	O'Hanlon S..............28 (1)
Anderson T ....– (2)	Gillies J 3 (3)	Paynter B ....9(9)
Archibald-Henville T 24	Grainger D.....................41	Potts B 34 (5)
Asamoah D 13 (14)	Griffith A 10 (1)	Rigg S.....................19 (9)
Atkinson D 6 (1)	Hammell C ....– (3)	Robson M 5 (6)
Beck M 11 (16)	Hanford D 25	Spiegel R 2
Brough P 27 (2)	Iliev G..............................4	Sweeney A...............26 (3)
Brown C............................8	Kearns D 3 (7)	Symington D 9 (3)
Buddle N 1 (2)	Kennedy J......................11	Taylor C ....– (1)
Corry P 4 (2)	Marriott J 3 (1)	Thirlwell P...............14 (4)
Dempsey K 41 (2)	Marrow A........................–	White H 8
Dicker G 16 (4)	Meppen-Walters C 17 (2)	Wyke C....................16 (1)
Elliott S 4 (11)	Monakana J 1	Young M 20

League goals (56): Dempsey 10, Potts 7, Rigg 6, Wyke 6, Amoo 5, Asamoah 4, Beck 3, Grainger 3, Kennedy 3, Archibald-Henville 1, Corry 1, Dicker 1, Elliott 1, Gillies 1, Meppen-Walters 1, O'Hanlon 1, Paynter 1, Sweeney 1

FA Cup goals (1): Asamoah 1. **Capital One Cup goals:** None. **Johnstone's Paint Trophy goals** (4): Dempsey 1, Paynter 1, Potts 1, Sweeney 1

Average home league attendance: 4,376. **Player of Year:** Kyle Dempsey

CHELTENHAM TOWN

Four different managers tried and failed to arrest the slump at Whaddon Road. As a result, Cheltenham were relegated on the penultimate day of the season after 16 years of Football League membership. What a contrast to the start of the campaign when four of their opening six fixtures brought victories, including a 3-2 success at Tranmere, where a 2-0 deficit was turned around. The two other games were drawn, the early leadership of the division shared with Burton and a successful season looked to be beckoning. Although unable to maintain that early pace, Mark Yates's side returned to winning wins by beating Northampton and Cambridge in the space of four days. Then the wheels came off – four successive defeats resulting in the dismissal of Yates, English football's third longest-serving manager behind Arsenal's Arsene Wenger and Exeter's Paul Tisdale, after nearly five years in charge. In came former Luton boss Paul Buckle, who managed a single win in 13 matches and was dismissed after 79 days. Youth team manager Russell Milton was given a chance as caretaker, but won only one of his nine matches. So a last throw of the dice brought in Gary Johnson, himself fired by relegation-bound Yeovil two months previously. Johnson had seven games to arrest the slide, but found the problems too deep rooted and defeat at home to Shrewsbury sent Cheltenham down – after a total of 42 players had been used over the course of the season.

Arthur K 1 (6)	Ferdinand K 15 (1)	Marquis J 8 (5)
Bancessi E 2 (2)	Gornell T 18 (7)	McDonald S 3 (1)
Berry D 8 (5)	Gray J 3 (1)	Mills P 8
Black P 3	Hall A 1	Packwood W 5
Bowen J 1 (2)	Hanks J 16 (17)	Richards E 6 (3)
Braham-Barrett C 45	Harrad S 10 (2)	Richards M 44 (1)
Brown T 42 (1)	Harrison B 17 (6)	Sparrow M 11
Burns W 14	Haworth A .... – (5)	Sterling-James O 9 (13)
Carson T 46	Haynes D 5 (3)	Stewart K 4
Dale B 1 (1)	Johnstone D 4 (1)	Taylor M 31 (2)
De Vita R 7 (3)	Jones L 5 (1)	Taylor J 16
Deaman J 13 (6)	Kotwica Z 8 (9)	Vaughan L 31 (1)
Dunn J 5	Lawrence J .... – (1)	Williams H 3 (5)
Elliott S 17	Manset M 8 (4)	Wynter J 12 (4)

League goals (40): Burns 4, Harrison 4, Arthur 3, Dunn 3, Gornell 3, Berry 2, Hanks 2, Kotwica 2, Richards M 2, Brown 1, Elliott 1, Harrad 1, Haynes 1, Johnstone 1, Marquis 1, Packwood 1, Richards E 1, Sparrow 1, Sterling-James 1, Stewart 1, Taylor M 1, Wynter 1, Opponents 2
FA Cup goals (5): Harrison 3, Gornell 1, Richards M 1. **Capital One Cup goals:** None.
Johnstone's Paint Trophy goals (3): Arthur 1, Gornell 1, Marquis 1
Average home league attendance: 2,864. **Player of Year:** Trevor Carson

DAGENHAM AND REDBRIDGE

Evergreen Jamie Cureton reached another milestone as he continued to show that age is no barrier to scoring goals. The 39-year-old striker netted his 250th in the league during the course of a season with his 13th different club. At the end of it, he had accumulated 278 in all competitions and now wants to reach 300 after signing a new contract. Cureton, who made his senior debut with Norwich in November 1994, finished with 19 in the league and one in a remarkable 6-6 Capital One Cup tie against Brentford which his latest side lost on penalties. He was named Player of the Year after playing a major role in Dagenham resisting the threat of a relegation struggle. They were second from bottom early in the New Year after scoring just once in seven matches. But a productive run of 16 points from eight matches, in which Cureton netted six times, took them out of trouble. He went on to record a hat-trick the 4-0 victory over Wimbledon – a scoreline repeated against Accrington in the final home fixture when he was again on the scoring sheet, alongside three players scoring their first senior goals – Frankie Raymond, Matt Partridge and Jodi Jones.

Agyemang P 2 (2)	Enigbokan-Bloomfield M– (1)	O'Brien L 9 (1)
Batt D 24 (4)	Fenelon S 3 (1)	Obileye A 25 (1)
Bingham B............... 32 (2)	Gayle I 6	Ogogo A 28 (4)
Boucard A 36 (5)	Goldbury B .... – (5)	Partridge M 20 (4)
Carr D...........................– (6)	Green N 6 (1)	Porter G 7 (12)
Chambers A 27 (5)	Hemmings A 36 (5)	Raymond F 2
Connors J.................. 14 (3)	Howell L 29 (2)	Saah B 22 (1)
Cousins M....................37	Jakubiak A 6 (17)	Widdowson J............. 20 (1)
Cureton J 40 (5)	Jones J..................... 2 (6)	Yusuff A 9 (9)
Doe S.........................39	Labadie J 16 (8)	
Doidge C................... 3 (8)	Murphy R 6 (3)	

League goals (58): Cureton 19, Hemmings 5, Howell 5, Bingham 4, Jakubiak 4, Ogogo 4, Chambers 2, Doidge 2, Labadie 2, Obileye 2, Yusuff 2, Doe 1, Jones 1, Murphy 1, Partridge 1, Porter 1, Raymond 1, Opponents 1
FA Cup goals: None. **Capital One Cup goals** (6): Hemmings 2, Boucard 1, Chambers 1, Cureton 1, Porter 1. **Johnstone's Paint Trophy goals**: None
Average home league attendance: 2,041. **Player of Year**: Jamie Cureton

EXETER CITY

A two-month transfer embargo cast a shadow over preparations for the season at St James Park. It was lifted following the repayment of a short-term loan to the PFA and the club were able to bring in players. But early results suggested another difficult campaign following the relegation scare in 2014. Exeter were bottom after the opening six fixtures yielded only two points. Things began to pick up, with four successive 2-1 victories over Cambridge, Tranmere, Bury and Dagenham. And by the half-way point, they had climbed to within goal difference of a top-seven place. With a month remaining, they were still in contention for the play-offs, a single point away. Then, a 4-0 defeat at Shrewsbury was followed by three more losses, putting an end to that target, and they had to be satisfied with tenth place when the sequence was broken with a 2-1 win over Dagenham in the final match. The season proved a washout in the knock-out competitions with defeats at the first hurdle in all three, including a 1-0 reversal against Northern Premier League Warrington, the lowest ranked team in the first round of the FA Cup.

Baldwin P 6 (1)	Jay M............................ 1 (2)	Pym C.............................25
Bennett S 26 (2)	Keohane J 11 (12)	Ribeiro C................... 33 (4)
Butterfield D 26 (4)	McAllister J 13 (1)	Riley-Lowe C......................3
Cummins G 26 (9)	McCready T 1 (2)	Sercombe L 39 (1)
Davies A 34 (5)	Moore-Taylor J 25 (1)	Tillson J 3
Dawson A................... 2 (1)	Morrison C............. 13 (12)	Watkins O.................... – (2)
Grimes M 22 (1)	Nicholls A 27 (5)	Wheeler D 14 (31)
Hamon J.......................21	Nichols T 24 (12)	Woodman C 31 (1)
Harley R 22 (3)	Noble D 8 (7)	
Holmes L 6 (2)	Oakley M.................. 44 (1)	

League goals (61): Nichols 15, Cummins 7, Wheeler 7, Nicholls 5, Davies 4, Grimes 4, Harley 4, Sercombe 4, Bennett 3, Keohane 3, Moore-Taylor 2, Ribeiro 2, Opponents 1
FA Cup goals: None. **Capital One Cup goals**: None. **Johnstone's Paint Trophy goals** (1): Watkins 1
Average home league attendance: 3,873. **Player of Year**: Christian Ribeiro

HARTLEPOOL UNITED

Every season is full of irony and none more so this time than the events involving manager Ronnie Moore, who led Hartlepool to safety against all the odds while the club that sacked him was relegated to the Conference. Moore, dismissed by Tranmere in April 2014 for breaching betting rules, was brought in midway through an ever-worrying campaign. He followed Colin Cooper, who resigned in the wake of a 3-0 home defeat by fellow-strugglers Carlisle, and Cooper's successor, former player Paul Murray, sacked after 45 days with his side bottom and beaten at home by Blyth in the FA Cup. Moore took over a team six points adrift. With 11 games to play, they were eight points from safety and looked to have little chance of survival. Then, three wins in eight days over Morecambe, Oxford and Mansfield transformed their fortunes. A fourth victory, against Cambridge, took them out of the bottom two for the first time in four months. Moore warned there was plenty of work to still do – and so it proved with the next four fixtures yielding just two points. But their rivals in distress were also having a hard time of so, so when goals by Scott Fenwick and Jordan Hugill earned a 2-1 win over Exeter in the penultimate fixture, the great escape was complete. In a final flourish, Hugill scored twice as his side came back from 3-0 down at half-time at Carlisle to draw 3-3.

Austin N	46	Flinders S	46	Miller T	14 (1)
Bates M	25	Franks J	38 (7)	Mirfin D	15
Bingham R	5	Green K	– (1)	Morgan M	4 (1)
Bird R	6	Harewood M	17 (17)	Nelson-Addy E	1 (1)
Brobbel B	13 (2)	Harrison S	36	Parnaby S	5
Campbell A	1 (1)	Hawkins L	4 (8)	Richards J	5 (4)
Collins S	7	Holden D	7 (4)	Schmelz S	2 (3)
Compton J	17 (4)	Hugill J	8	Smith C	3 (5)
Crooks M	2 (1)	Ironside J	3 (1)	Tshibola A	23
Dolan M	2	James L	3 (1)	Walker B	25 (3)
Duckworth M	37	Jones D	23 (2)	Woods M	16 (7)
Featherstone N	22 (3)	Jones J	1 (10)	Wyke C	13
Fenwick S	10 (9)	Lanzoni M	1		

League goals (39): Fenwick 6, Walker 5, Hugill 4, Wyke 4, Duckworth 3, Harewood 3, Austin 2, Bird 2, Franks 2, Bates 1, Bingham 1, Harrison 1, Ironside 1, Morgan 1, Woods 1, Opponents 2
FA Cup goals (3): Franks 3. **Capital One Cup goals** (2): Austin 1, Franks 1. **Johnstone's Paint Trophy goals** (1): Duckworth 1
Average home league attendance: 3,736. **Player of Year:** Scott Harrison

LUTON TOWN

At the start of their season back in the Football League after five years in the Conference, Luton would probably have settled for a place in the top half of the table. At the end of it, satisfaction was tinged with disappointment at not managing to sustain a promotion challenge. After an indifferent opening – one win out of six – John Still's side stepped up the pace to reel off seven successive games to go top. The leadership was shortlived, but Luton settled into a play-off position, looked to be playing well enough to retain it and after beating Accrington 2-0 at the end of February came within two points of regaining a position in the top three. The wheels then came off with seven successive defeats leaving them off the pace. If there was any consolation, it came with the fact that six were by the odd goal and, more significantly, that they had not fallen too far behind. Luton returned to winning ways against Tranmere and Hartlepool and with two fixtures remaining trailed Plymouth in sixth place only on goal difference. But a mistake by goalkeeper Elliot Justham presented Southend with the only goal of the game in the 81st minute. The result left Plymouth in the driving seat and they made sure by winning their final game.

Benson P	16 (5)	Hall R	4 (3)	Lee E	9 (2)
Connolly P	4	Harriman M	35	McGeehan C	13 (2)
Cullen M	33 (9)	Howells J	28 (8)	McNulty S	41
Doyle N	27	Justham E	15	Miller R	2 (10)
Drury A	30 (5)	Kinsella L	2 (1)	Oduwa N	3 (8)
Franks F	10 (3)	Lacey A	10 (8)	Robinson M	7 (2)
Griffiths S	35	Lafayette R	1 (10)	Rooney L	8 (3)
Guttridge L	17 (10)	Lawless A	7 (8)	Ruddock P	10 (6)

Smith J	35	Tyler M	31	Whalley S	14 (4)
Stevenson J	2 (9)	Walker C	- (3)	Wilkinson L	42
Stockley J	11 (2)	Wall A	1 (6)	Williams C	3

League goals (54): Cullen 13, Howells 4, Wilkinson 4, Guttridge 3, Lawless 3, Lee 3, McGeehan 3, Rooney 3, Stockley 3, Whalley 3, Drury 2, Griffiths 2, Smith 2, Benson 1, Harriman 1, Miller 1, Ruddock 1, Stevenson 1, Wall 1
FA Cup goals (7): Benson 1, Cullen 1, Guttridge 1, Harriman 1, Howells 1, Miller 1, Rooney 1.
Capital One Cup goals (1): Rooney 1. **Johnstone's Paint Trophy goals:** None
Average home league attendance: 8,702. **Player of Year:** Nathan Doyle

MANSFIELD TOWN

Adam Murray had a tough baptism after becoming the youngest manager in the four divisions. The 33-year--old team captain won his first game as caretaker, 1-0 against Plymouth, and was given the job on a permanent basis a fortnight later. But it was hard going as Mansfield remained on the fringes of the relegation zone through to the end of the season. Murray, who took over when Paul Cox stepped down by mutual consent in November after eight matches without a win, saw his side drop into the bottom two on goal difference after losing at Carlisle early in the New Year. They were out of it a week later when beating Stevenage and, after six signings in the winter transfer window, recorded three wins out of four against Luton, Dagenham and Newport for a much-needed cushion. Mansfield stayed out of trouble, despite losing eight out of nine matches at the end of the season, because of the failings of the teams below them. Murray then set about strengthening his squard in the summer, while expressing confidence in his younger players to provide a solid platform for the new season.

Beevers L	33 (2)	Freeman K	11	Raynes M	10
Bell F	10 (6)	Hawkridge T	4 (1)	Rhead M	16 (16)
Bingham R	15 (13)	Hearn L	– (3)	Riley M	31 (2)
Blair M	2 (1)	Heslop S	21 (4)	Sendles-White J	7
Brown J	21 (3)	Kee B	8 (5)	Shires C	– (1)
Carr R	3 (1)	Lambe R	20 (20)	Smith A	4
Clements C	30 (4)	Marsden L	9 (1)	Studer A	17
Clucas S	2 (3)	McGuire J	25 (4)	Sutton R	34
Dempster J	4	Monakana J	2 (4)	Tafazolli R	35 (1)
Elder C	21	Murray A	11 (3)	Taylor R	10 (6)
Evtimov D	10	Oliver V	28 (2)	Thomas J	11 (1)
Fisher A	6 (8)	Palmer O	2 (14)	Waterfall L	5
Fitzpatrick J	1 (2)	Pidgeley L	15		
Fletcher D	– (1)	Ravenhill R	12 (1)		

League goals (38): Oliver 7, Bingham 6, Lambe 5, Rhead 3, Beevers 2, Brown 2, Heslop 2, Kee 2, Bell 1, Carr 1, Clements 1, Fisher 1, McGuire 1, Murray 1, Palmer 1, Tafazolli 1, Thomas 1
FA Cup goals (3): Bingham 1, Palmer 1, Opponents 1. **Capital One Cup goals (1):** Fisher 1.
Johnstone's Paint Trophy goals: None
Average home league attendance: 3,064. **Player of Year:** Jack Thomas

MORECAMBE

A rousing finish to the season confirmed Morecambe's place in the top half of the table and gave midfielder Stewart Drummond the perfect send-off. The 39-year-old made the 622nd and final appearance of his career in a 3-1 home win over Southend, who missed out on automatic promotion as a result. One of his team's best performances of the campaign was achieved with goals from Jack Redshaw, Aaron Wildig and Jamie Devitt. Drummond played more than 500 games in two spells for the club, having also served Chester and Shrewsbury in between. An equally damaging victory had been delivered in the final away game a week earlier against Wycombe, who also dropped out of the top three after conceding the only goal of the game to Paul Mullin in the 86th minute. Morecambe had made a flying start with victories over Dagenham, Newport, Oxford and Cambridge to lead the division after four matches. They were unable to maintain that sort of momentum, but unlike the previous season had no relegation worries. One low point was a defeat by non-league Dover in the first round of the FA Cup.

Amond P 17 (20)	Fleming A 31 (4)	Sampson J 3 (13)
Arestidou A 17	Goodall A 22 (6)	Stewart T .... – (1)
Barkhuizen T 1 (4)	Hughes M 40	Ward D 5
Beeley S 41 (1)	Kenyon A 29 (8)	Widdowson J 8
Davies S 10	McCready T 1 (6)	Wildig A 9
Devitt J 30 (6)	McGowan A 4 (4)	Williams R 9 (3)
Doyle C 1 (1)	Mullin P 20 (22)	Wilson L 34
Drummond S 11 (3)	Parrish A 45	Wright A 10 (7)
Edwards R 31	Redshaw J 28 (12)	
Ellison K 35 (8)	Roche B 14	

League goals (53): Ellison 11, Redshaw 11, Amond 8, Mullin 8, Devitt 3, Hughes 3, Kenyon 3, Fleming 2, McGowan 1, Wildig 1, Wilson 1, Opponents 1
FA Cup goals: None. **Capital One Cup goals**: None. **Johnstone's Paint Trophy goals** (4): Amond 2, Beeley 1, Redshaw 1
Average home league attendance: 1,998. **Player of Year**: Shaun Beeley

NEWPORT COUNTY

Faltering at a critical time of the season, Newport lost the chance of a second promotion in three years. With a month remaining, they looked a good bet for the play-offs, holding down sixth place with a three-point cushion. But four successive losses proved costly. They were beaten 2-0 by Exeter, Bury and Southend. Then, the day after the club sacked jailed striker Chris Zebroski, there was a 3-2 home defeat by Dagenham. Although Newport returned to winnings ways at York, Plymouth edged them out with a better finish to the campaign, coupled to a superior goal difference. Nevertheless, there was cause to be reasonably satisfied with ninth place, achieved despite a poor start to the campaign when the opening four fixtures yielded a single point and considering the loss of manager Justin Edinburgh, who led a return to the Football League in 2013. Edinburgh took over at Gillingham in early February after the two clubs had agreed compensation and was replaced by his assistant Jimmy Dack, who took charge until the end of the season when the club appointed former England captain and Hibernian manager Terry Butcher.

Byrne M 39 (3)	Jolley C .... – (5)	Pigott J 6 (4)
Chapman A 27 (9)	Jones D 43	Poole R 11
Collins A .... – (2)	Klukowski Y 24 (14)	Porter M 21 (6)
Crow D .... – (2)	Loveridge J 2 (5)	Sandell A 32 (6)
Day J 36	Minshull L 34 (5)	Stephens J 6 (1)
Feely K 17 (5)	O'Connor A 32 (7)	Storey M 14 (4)
Flynn M 3 (8)	Obeng C 4 (1)	Tancock S 4
Howe R 5 (9)	Owen-Evans T .... – (1)	Tutonda D 10 (2)
Hughes A 16	Parker J .... – (4)	Willmott R 14 (2)
Jackson R 31 (3)	Pattern K .... – (1)	Yakubu I 32 (1)
Jeffers S 11 (10)	Pidgeley J 4	Zebroski C 28 (3)

League goals (51): O'Connor 10, Zebroski 7, Byrne 4, Jones 4, Klukowski 4, Chapman 3, Minshull 3, Pigott 3, Jeffers 2, Storey 2, Tutonda 2, Yakubu 2, Hughes 1, Porter 1, Sandell 1, Willmott 1, Opponents 1
FA Cup goals (2): O'Connor 1, Klukowski 1. **Capital One Cup goals** (1): Jeffers 1. **Johnstone's Paint Trophy goals** (1): Klukowski 1
Average home league attendance: 3,213. **Player of Year**: Darren Jones

NORTHAMPTON TOWN

A much-needed improvement in the second half of the season kept it alive at Sixfields until the penultimate match. Northampton's bright start to the campaign, including a 5-1 win over Hartlepool, had been rewarded with a place in the top six after ten matches. But it gave way to four successive defeats, sent them sliding and raised the prospect of a second successive struggle to stay in the Football League. At the midway point, they were two points off a relegation place, before five successive wins steadied the ship. The run included a 5-1 victory at Accrington, a side who had previously beaten them 5-4. The momentum was maintained with another productive run, four wins out of five, to close the gap on the leading group to three points. And there was still a chance of breaking through when Northampton took on promoted Burton in their final away fixture. Instead, three goals were conceded in a first-half performance described as 'embarrassing' by manager Chris Wilder and a 3-1 reversal cast them adrift. Closing with a last-minute defeat by Wycombe, his side finished in mid-table.

Alfei D....................... 9 (2)	Gray J 7 (1)	Nicholls A 4 (2)
Archer J......................13	Hackett C 20 (18)	O'Toole J 24 (11)
Banks O.......................3	Holmes R....................21`	Ravenhill R............... 8 (4)
Bodin B .... (4)	Horwood E................ 23 (2)	Richards M.............. 26 (5)
Byrom J 37 (2)	Jalal S 4	Robertson G 20 (1)
Carter D 12 (11)	Langmead K 4 (3)	Sinclair E 1 (1)
Collins L 36 (1)	Mohamed K 17 (6)	Stevens E.......................4
Cresswell R 31 (1)	Moloney B 22	Taylor J 21
D'Ath L 31 (10)	Morris I .... – (2)	Toney I 23 (17)
De Girolamo D............ 5 (1)	Moyo D .... – (3)	Tozer B 15 (7)
Diamond Z............... 18 (3)	Murdoch S 8	Watson R.......................5
Duke M 29 (1)	Newey T 5 (4)	

League goals (67): Richards 18, Toney 8, D'Ath 7, Cresswell 5, Holmes 5, Mohamed 4, Byrom 3, Gray 3, Hackett 3, O'Toole 3, Carter 1, Diamond 1, Moloney 1, Moyo 1, Murdoch 1, Nicholls 1, Sinclair 1, Stevens 1, Opponents 1
FA Cup goals (1): Toney 1. **Capital One Cup goals** (3): D'Ath 2, Toney 1. **Johnstone's Paint Trophy goals** (2): Mohamed 1, Moyo 1
Average home league attendance: 4,599. **Player of year**: Marc Richards

OXFORD UNITED

A season which started with a whimper ended with a bang – leaving manager Michael Appleton wishing it could have gone on for another month. His side finished with an eight-match unbeaten run which yielded 18 points and included five clean sheets. Kemar Roofe, on loan from West Bromwich Albion, scored six goals, two of them in a 3-2 away win which dented Wycombe's chances of automatic promotion. He also netted twice in a 3-0 scoreline which pushed bottom-of-the-table Tranmere nearer to non-league football. After further goals against Cambridge and Newport, Roofe delighted Appleton by signing on a permanent basis. This finishing flourish contrasted sharply to how Oxford opened, four defeats following four losses at the end of the previous campaign and resulting in an unwanted club record of eight on the trot. Against that, Oxford knocked Bristol City out of the League Cup and took West Bromwich Albion to penalties in the next round. Their first league success came at the eighth attempt against Accrington. Results improved marginally after that, but they remained in the lower reaches of the table until that final burst which carried them to just below mid-table.

Ashby J........................2	Burns W 6 (3)	Hawtin A.................... - (1)
Ashdown J 5	Campbell J................ 1 (2)	Hoban P 15 (5)
Baldock G 12	Clarke R 31	Holmes-Dennis T...........14
Barnett T 11 (1)	Collins M 38 (1)	Hoskins W.............. 2 (2)
Brindley R....................3	Dunkley C 7 (2)	Howard B.......................2
Brown J 6 (5)	Gnanduillet A.............. - (4)	Hunt D 2 (1)

Hylton D ... 41 (3)	Newey T ... 12	Rose D ... 25 (4)
Jakubiak A ... 2 (7)	O'Dowda C ... 20 (19)	Ruffles J ... 29 (4)
Long G ... 10	Potter A ... 9 (6)	Humphreys S ... - (1)
Long S ... 8 (2)	Rasulo G ... - (1)	Skarz J ... 18
MacDonald A ... 14 (1)	Raynes M ... 3 (1)	Vassell K ... 2 (4)
Meades L ... 5 (2)	Riley J ... 22	Whing A ... 18 (3)
Morris C ... 5 (2)	Roberts J ... 5 (20)	Wright J ... 42
Mullins J ... 42 (2)	Roofe K ... 12 (4)	

League goals (50): Hylton 14, Roofe 6, Barnett 4, O'Dowda 4, MacDonald 3, Roberts 3, Collins 2, Mullins 2, Potter 2, Rose 2, Baldock 1, Burns 1, Campbell 1, Hoban 1, Jakubiak 1, Long 1, Vassell 1, Opponents 1
FA Cup goals (6): Barnett 2, Roberts 2, Potter 1, Rose 1. **Capital One Cup goals (3):** Hylton 2, Morris 1. **Johnstone's Paint Trophy goals:** None
Average home league attendance: 6,154. **Player of Year:** Danny Hylton

PLYMOUTH ARGYLE

Nine months spent building a promotion platform were wasted in little more than 20 minutes of the play-offs. In that time, Plymouth trailed Wycombe 2-0 at Home Park, conceded a third goal early in the second-half and it needed a late rally to retain a measure of hope for the second leg of the semi-final. On-loan Zak Ansah and Jason Banton scored in the final four minutes of normal time to cut the deficit. But their side were again left on the back foot as Wycombe extended the advantage to 5-2 in the return match before Ryan Brunt replied with 20 minutes remaining. Amid the disappointment, manager John Sheridan was left considering his future after questioning whether he was the right man to take the club forward. Plymouth had edged into the knock-out phase – 13 points behind Wycombe – after disputing seventh place with three other teams. Exeter and Newport fell away and with two games remaining they were level on points with Luton. A 3-2 victory over Tranmere, which sent the home side into the Conference, along with a superior goal difference effectively sealed the issue. Then, goals by Bobby Reid and Kelvin Mellor for a 2-0 away win against runners-up Shrewsbury confirmed their place. Sheridan departed by mutual consent. He was succeeded by former Ross County manager Derek Adams.

Alessandra L ... 43 (1)	Flanagan T ... 4	Morgan M ... 5 (11)
Allen R ... - (3)	Hartley P ... 38 (1)	Nelson C ... 42
Ansah Z ... 2 (6)	Harvey T ... 3 (10)	Norburn O ... 7 (7)
Banton J ... 11 (14)	Holmes-Dennis T ... 17	O'Connor A ... 40
Bentley A ... 3	Jones G ... 4 (2)	Purrington B ... 4 (4)
Bittner J ... - (1)	Kellett A ... 12	Reid B ... 33
Blizzard D ... 24 (7)	Lee O ... 9 (6)	Reid R ... 42
Bray A ... - (1)	McCormick L ... 46	Smalley D ... 3 (13)
Brunt R ... 4 (12)	McHugh C ... 43 (1)	Talbot D ... 9
Cox L ... 21 (11)	Mellor K ... 36 (1)	Thomas N ... 1 (8)

Play-offs – appearances: Alessandra 2, Hartley 2, Holmes-Dennis 2, McHugh 2, McCormick 2, Mellor 2, Nelson 2, O'Connor 2, Reid B 2, Reid R 2, Blizzard 1, Jones 1, Ansah – (2), Banton – (2), Brunt – (2)
League goals (55): Reid R 18, Alessandra 11, Hartley 4, O'Connor 3, Reid B 3, Brunt 2, Lee 2, McHugh 2, Ansah 1, Blizzard 1, Harvey 1, Holmes-Dennis 1, Kellett 1, Mellor 1, Morgan 1, Nelson 1, Smalley 1, Thomas 1. **Play-offs – goals (3):** Ansah 1, Banton 1, Brunt 1
FA Cup goals (2): Hartley 1, Morgan 1. **Capital One Cup goals (3):** Reid R 2, McHugh 1.
Johnstone's Paint Trophy goals (3): Alessandra 2, Smalley 1.
Average home league attendance: 7,412. **Player of Year:** Luke McCormick

PORTSMOUTH

Portsmouth scored one notable victory off the field during the season – but are still trying to strike the right balance on it. The club that almost went into liquidation during a plunge through the divisions are now debt-free, well ahead of schedule, following the Supporters' Trust takeover. Announcing the news, the club said 'they could now look forwards, not backwards.' The immediate target is to launch a meaningful promotion challenge after missing out by some distance this time, despite being among the favourites to do well. A promising start of ten points from the opening four fixtures was not maintained and Andy Awford's team were always off the pace. Not even a productive February which brought four victories and a hat-trick for Matt Tubbs in the 6-2 defeat of Cambridge, was enough to bridge the gap. Awford, who led them away from the threat of non-league football in 2014, won the Manager of the Month award, but lost his job following a 3-1 defeat at Morecambe. His assistant, Gary Waddock, saw out the four remaining fixture. The club then appointed Paul Cook, fresh from taking Chesterfield to the League One play-offs.

Agyemang P 3 (5)	East D...................... 2 (2)	Robinson P................... 33
Atangana N............ 16 (14)	Ertl J 7 (7)	Shorey N 19 (1)
Awford N 1	Fish M 3	Storey M 10 (7)
Barcham A 6 (13)	Fogden W 3 (6)	Tarbuck B.................. – (2)
Bean M..........................6	Hollands D 39 (5)	Taylor R.................. 31 (6)
Bird R ....– (2)	Holmes L 3 (2)	Tubbs M 23
Butler D.................. 26 (4)	Holmes R 9 (4)	Wallace J............... 43 (1)
Chaplin C............... 1 (8)	Jones P......................46	Webster A............... 12 (3)
Chorley B 15 (1)	Kpekawa C 2	Westcarr C 21 (12)
Close B 3 (3)	May A .... – (1)	Whatmaugh J.......... 21 (1)
Devera J 37 (2)	McCallum P............... – (7)	Wynter A 10
Drennan M 3 (1)	Nosworthy N 6 (1)	
Dunne J.................. 34 (2)	Passley J....................12	

League goals (52): Wallace 14, Taylor 9, Tubbs 9, Westcarr 6, Robinson 2, Storey 2, Atangana 1, Barcham 1, Bean 1, Chaplin 1, Devera 1, Dunne 1, Ertl 1, Hollands 1, Webster 1, Opponents 1
FA Cup goals (2): Hollands 1, Wallace 1. **Capital One Cup goals (1):** Storey 1. **Johnstone's Paint Trophy goals (4):** Wallace 2, Taylor 1, Westcarr 1
Average home league attendance: 15,242. **Player of Year:** Jed Wallace

SHREWSBURY TOWN

The meanest defence in the Football League kept Shrewsbury on the right track for an immediate return to League One. They conceded just 31 goals and had a club record 23 clean sheets to finish runners-up to Burton. These qualities came right to the fore during the run-in after a six-point cushion had been halved by three defeats in five matches. A 4-1 success at Morecambe eased the pressure and launched a sequence of eight wins out of nine in which only two goals were given away. The last of these victories, 1-0 at Cheltenham, made sure of automatic promotion – and sent their opponents into the Conference. The goal was scored by French striker Jean-Louis Akpa Akpro, who early in the campaign netted a hat-trick in his side's biggest win – 5-0 against Bury. Akpa Akpro, leading scorer James Collins and former Republic of Ireland international Liam Lawrence as captain were among the players Micky Mellon brought in during a major overhaul of the squad that went down in 2014. In addition to being promoted, Shrewsbury defeated Blackpool, Leicester and Norwich in the League Cup, before giving Chelsea a run for their money in the fourth round, a 2-1 defeat watched by a record Greenhous Meadow Stadium crowd of 10,210

Akpa Akpro J-L... 26 (19)	Demetriou M 40 (2)	Grandison J.............. 32 (4)
Barnett T 8 (10)	Ellis M...........................32	Grant R................... 28 (4)
Caton J...................... - (2)	Gayle C.................. 27 (1)	Griffith A................. 1 (4)
Clark J..................... 18 (9)	Ginnelly J .... - (3)	Grimmer J.......................6
Collins J 42 (3)	Goldson C 44	Halstead M .... - (1)

138

Knight-Percival N 28	Passley J...................6	Vernon S................ 12 (10)
Lawrence L 30 (3)	Randall C.................. - (1)	Vincent A................ 4 (4)
Leutwiler J 46	Robinson A .... - (2)	Wesolowski J............ 18 (3)
Mandron M 2 (1)	Sharpe R 2 (1)	Wildig A.................... - (1)
Mangan A 10 (20)	Southern K 3 (3)	Woods R 41 (2)

League goals (67): Collins 15, Akpa Akpro 9, Mangan 8, Goldson 7, Grant 6, Lawrence 5, Barnett 4, Clark 3, Demetriou 3, Ellis 2, Grandison 2, Knight-Percival 1, Vernon 1, Wesolowski 1
FA Cup goals (3): Collins 1, Ellis 1, Lawrence 1. **Capital One Cup goals (4):** Mangan 2, Collins 1, Vernon 1. **Johnstone's Paint Trophy goals:** None
Average home league attendance: 5,343. **Player of Year:** Connor Goldson

SOUTHEND UNITED

They lost the chance of automatic promotion on the final day of the regular season and it looked as if Southend would also be denied in the Play-off Final. With seconds of extra-time remaining, Phil Brown's side trailed Wycombe 1-0. Many of their fans were on the way out of Wembley, resigned to another season in League Two. But they hurried back after being told that substitute Joe Pigott had equalised and were celebrating when two saves by Daniel Bentley delivered a 7-6 win in the penalty shoot-out. Bentley had earlier conceded an own goal when Joe Jacobson's free-kick struck the bar and the ball bounced off him into the net. It was a bitter-sweet match for the goalkeeper, who had kept 21 clean sheets during the regular season, been named the club's Player of the Year and won a place in the PFA's divisional Team of the Year. Seven of those shut-outs brought successive victories in April to leave Southend in third place, two points clear of Bury, going into the final fixture at Morecambe. But a 3-1 defeat, coupled to Bury's win at Tranmere, meant a third play-off place in four years, with defeats having been suffered in 2012 and 2014. Before that late surge, they had lost some momentum – beaten at home by Accrington and conceding three late goals to go down at Stevenage. But they were back on track after Barry Corr scored nine goals in 11 games.

Atkinson W 26 (10)	Coulthirst S 12 (10)	Smith T............................4
Barnard L 2 (7)	Deegan G 19 (3)	Sokolik J 1
Barrett A 9 (1)	Hurst K 19 (9)	Thompson A 27 (1)
Bentley D.......................42	Ibenfeldt M ....– (1)	Timlin M 29 (3)
Binnom-Williams J.... 18 (3)	Leonard R 39 (2)	Weston M 17 (17)
Bolger C 21 (2)	McLaughlin S 6	White J..................... 40 (2)
Cassidy J 12 (5)	O'Toole J 2	Williams J .... – (2)
Clifford C 10 (2)	Payne J 20 (14)	Worrall D................ 23 (15)
Coker B 32	Pigott J 17 (3)	
Corr B...................... 30 (9)	Prosser L 29 (1)	

Play-offs – appearances: Atkinson 3, Barrett 3, Bentley 3, Bolger 3, Coker 3, Corr 3, Leonard 3, Timlin 3, White 3, Worrall 3, McLaughlin 2 (1), Pigott 1 (2), Weston – (3), Deegan – (2), Payne – (1)
 League goals (54): Corr 14, Payne 6, Pigott 6, Worrall 6, Coulthirst 4, Leonard 3, Timlin 3, Atkinson 2, Clifford 2, Weston 2, Barnard 1, Bolger 1, Coker 1, Hurst 1, McLaughlin 1, Opponents 1. **Play-offs – goals (5):** Corr 1, Leonard 1, McLaughlin 1, Pigott 1, Timlin 1
FA Cup goals (1): Corr 1. **Capital One Cup goals (1):** Leonard 1. **Johnstone's Paint Trophy goals (2):** Payne 2
Average home league attendance: 6,024. **Player of Year:** Daniel Bentley

STEVENAGE

Defeat in the play-offs was followed by the high-profile appointment of Teddy Sheringham as manager. The former England striker left West Ham, where he was the forwards' coach, to take over from Graham Westley, whose contract was not renewed. The change was made a week after a 3-1 defeat at Southend in the second leg of the semi-finals. A goal by Tom Pett ten minutes into the second-half put Stevenage in pole position for a crack at returning to League One at the first attempt. But the advantage lasted just 12 minutes, the tie went into extra-time and Southend proved the stronger, scoring twice for a 4-2 aggregate success. Westley's much-changed squad, put together after relegation in 2014, spent most of the first half of the season in the bottom half of the table, before making an impact over the Christmas and New Year period. Five victories in six games were rewarded with a top-seven place and they stayed there or thereabouts for the remainder of the campaign. Another productive run – four wins in five – included a 4-2 victory over Southend in the return fixture of the regular season. Then, Stevenage cemented their position with Dean Parrett's winner against Carlisle in the penultimate match.

Adams C................ 5 (4)	Day C.....................38	Marriott A................8 (5)
Andrade B............. 5 (11)	Deacon R 11 (13)	Martin D...................9 (1)
Ashton J 15 (2)	Dembele B 25 (2)	McAllister D 13 (3)
Barnard L 6	Henry R 34	Okimo J 26 (3)
Beardsley C............. 23 (6)	Jebb J.................... 4 (5)	Parrett D 28 (2)
Beasant S 8	Johnson D 1 (3)	Pett T 28 (6)
Bond A 16 (4)	Johnson R .... – (4)	Richens M 2
Brunt R 3 (2)	Keane K 5 (2)	Walton S 25 (4)
Calcutt C .... – (8)	Kennedy B 6 (9)	Wells D 43
Charles D...................29	Lancaster C 4 (1)	Whelpdale C 35 (4)
Clarke J ....– (1)	Lee C 38 (6)	Worley H 3
Conlon T 6 (7)	Lisbie K 3	Zola C 1 (6)

Play-offs – appearances: Beardsley 2, Bond 2, Day 2, Lee 2, Okimo 2, Parrett 2, Wells 2, Whelpdale 2, Deacon 1 (1), Kennedy 1 (1), Pett 1 (1), Dembele 1, Martin 1, Walton 1, Ashton – (1), Conlon – (1), Henry – (1)
League goals (62): Lee 9, Pett 7, Whelpdale 7, Walton 5, Beardsley 4, Kennedy 4, Parrett 4, Wells 4, Barnard 3, Marriott 3, Charles 2, Dembele 2, Andrade 1, Calcutt 1, Deacon 1, Lancaster 1, Martin 1, Opponents 3. **Play-offs – goals** (2): Parrett 1, Pett 1
FA Cup goals (1): Charles 1. **Capital One Cup goals**: None. **Johnstone's Paint Trophy goals**: None
Average home league attendance: 3,191. **Player of the Year**: Dean Wells

TRANMERE ROVERS

Ninety four years of Football League membership came to an end as Tranmere suffered a second successive relegation. A club that had topped League One as recently as January 2013 went down on the penultimate day of the season when a 3-2 defeat at Plymouth ended all hope of escaping. It was their fifth in succession and came six days after manager Micky Adams left the club, reportedly by mutual consent. Adams was given the job when Rob Edwards was sacked in mid-October after five months in charge, with a battle to beat the drop already on the cards. The appointment was made in the hope that his greater experience would deliver a change of fortunes. A run of 13 league games without a win was ended when Portsmouth were beaten 3-1 and the turn of the year brought further success against Northampton, Accrington and Exeter. Tranmere were then reaching out for mid-table security, but failed to maintain momentum and slipped back into trouble amid continued changes of personnel. Nearly 50 players were used during the season, many making only fleeting contributions, and this lack of togetherness proved a major factor in the demise. By a supreme irony, relegation rivals Hartlepool were led to safety by Ronnie Moore, the manager sacked at Prenton Park in April 2014 for breaching betting rules.

Aimson W 2	Donnelly R 15 (5)	Gill M...........................8
Barker G 4	Dugdale A................ 15 (1)	Gnanduillet A 4
Bell-Baggie A 8 (4)	Duggan M................ – (1)	Green G 5 (10)
Brezovan P...................8	Fanimo M .... – (1)	Gumbs E............... – (1)
Davies B 3	Fenelon S 9 (1)	Hill M.................. 9 (2)
Donacien J...................31	Fon Williams O............38	Holmes D................ 33 (3)
Donnelly G............. 4 (7)	Gardner D 2 (2)	Holness M.............. 15 (2)

Hugill J.....	4 (2)	Laird M.....	27 (7)	Richards E.....	9 (4)
Hume I.....	3 (9)	Madjo G.....	- (2)	Ridehalgh L.....	13 (5)
Ihiekwe M.....	37 (1)	McDonald C.....	- (1)	Rowe J.....	3 (4)
Jago B.....	- (2)	McGahey H.....	2 (2)	Shuker C.....	1 (2)
Jahraldo-Martin J.......	1 (1)	Molyneux L.....	7 (4)	Stockton C.....	15 (7)
Jennings S.....	30	Myrie-Williams J.....	16 (2)	Taylor R.....	15
Johnson D.....	4	Odejayi K.....	27 (13)	Thompson J.....	15
Kirby J.....	7 (10)	Omotola T.....	- (1)	Woodards D.....	4 (1)
Koumas J.....	8 (12)	Power M.....	45		

League goals (45): Power 7, Odejayi 6, Donnelly 5, Stockton 4, Bell-Baggie 3, Myrie-Williams 3, Fenelon 2, Gardner 2, Gnandulliet 2, Holmes 2, Rowe 2, Green 1, Hugill 1, Ihiekwe 1, Jennings 1, Kirby 1, Laird 1, Richards 1
FA Cup goals (7): Power 3, Stockton 2, Koumas 1, Odejayi 1. **Capital One Cup goals:** None.
Johnstone's Paint Trophy goals (5): Power 3, Johnson 1, Odejayi 1
Average home league attendance: 5,192. **Player of Year:** Max Power

WYCOMBE WANDERERS

Football can be a cruel game, especially when there is so much at stake. With seconds of extra-time in the Play-off Final remaining, Wycombe led Southend by a goal from substitute Joe Pigott and were within touching distance of a place in League One. Instead, they conceded an equaliser, lost a penalty shoot-out 7-6 and saw a season's hard work count for nothing. It was a crushing finish for Gareth Ainsworth's side – after a heartbreaking start for on-loan midfield player Sam Saunders, who was injured in the first few seconds and unable to take any further part in the game. If there was any degree of consolation for him and his players, it came with the fact that 12 months earlier only a superior goal difference had prevented the club from falling out of the Football League. Nine summer signings brought a major change in fortunes, with Wycombe sharing the leadership of the division for lengthy spells with Burton and Shrewsbury, before their rivals pulled away in early April. They were still third going into the final home game against Morecambe. But a 1-0 defeat proved costly and Alfie Mawson's stoppage-time winner at Northampton a week later was not enough, with Bury's victory at Tranmere giving them the third automatic promotion place.

Amadi-Holloway A...	12 (17)	Jacobson J.....	42	Onyedinma F.....	20 (5)
Bean M.....	16 (1)	Jombati S.....	35	Pierre A.....	42
Bloomfield M.....	23 (10)	Kretzschmar M.....	8 (8)	Rowe D.....	10 (6)
Cowan-Hall P.....	18 (2)	Lewis S.....	1 (5)	Saunders S.....	11
Craig S.....	14 (17)	Lynch A.....	0 (1)	Scowen J.....	18
Ephraim H.....	5 (9)	Mawson A.....	45	Senior C.....	- (1)
Hayes P.....	38 (1)	McClure M.....	13 (14)	Wood S.....	43 (1)
Ingram M.....	46	Murphy P.....	32 (10)	Yennaris Y.....	14

Play-offs – appearances: Amadi-Holloway 3, Bean 3, Hayes 3, Jacobson 3, Lynch 3, Mawson 3, Pierre 3, Saunders 3, Wood 3, Yennaris 3, Ephraim 2, Craig 1 (1), Bloomfield – (2), Onyedinma – (2), Murphy – (2), McClure – (1)
League goals (67): Hayes 12, Onyedinma 8, Murphy 7, Cowan-Hall 6, Mawson 6, McClure 5, Wood 5, Pierre 4, Holloway 3, Jacobson 3, Craig 2, Saunders 2, Bloomfield 1, Ephraim 1, Scowen 1, Yennaris 1. **Play-off goals (6):** Hayes 2, Amadi-Holloway 1, Craig 1, Mawson 1, Opponents 1
FA Cup goals (3): Hayes 1, Pierre 1, Wood 1. **Capital One Cup goals:** None. **Johnstone's Paint Trophy goals:** None
Average home league attendance: 4,044. **Player of Year:** Alfie Mawson

YORK CITY

In his first managerial job, Russ Wilcox steered Scunthorpe to promotion. In his first second, he led York away from the threat of a return to non-league football. Wilcox was sacked at Glanford Park after a poor start to life in League One, but was back in work a week later succeeding Nigel Worthington, who resigned with York third from bottom. They finished 2014 well, beating Accrington and Carlisle to climb to five places clear of the relegation zone. But a return of just three points from seven games put them back in trouble. The pressure mounted with a last-minute equaliser conceded to Accrington, before confidence was restored with a 4-1 victory at Mansfield, achieved despite a red card for goalkeeper Bobby Olejnik for handling outside the penalty area with almost an hour still to play. It proved the turning point. Cheltenham and Hartlepool were both beaten 1-0 and safety was achieved when they came from behind to win 2-1 at Morecambe with goals by Stephane Zubar and Russell Penn.

Benning M	9	Hyde J 32 (7)	Morris C .... – (8)
Brunt R	5 (1)	Ilesanmi F 29 (4)	O'Hanlon J .... – (3)
Burton D	1	Ingham M................. 17 (2)	Olejnik B 16
Carson J	18 (4)	Jarvis R..................... 5 (3)	Penn R....................... 45
Cisak A	10	Lowe K......................46	Platt T 7 (13)
Coulson M	43	McCombe J 27 (4)	Sinclair E 9 (3)
Coulthirst S	10 (1)	McCoy M 30 (1)	Straker A.................7 (5)
De Girolamo D	9 (3)	Meikle L 13 (15)	Summerfield L 26 (5)
Fletcher W	22 (7)	Miller S 2 (4)	Winfield D 9 (1)
Halliday B	24	Montrose L 10 (4)	Zubar S..................22 (1)
Hirst B	– (3)	Mooney J................. 3 (1)	

League goals (46): Hyde 9, Fletcher 6, Lowe 6, Coulson 4, De Girolamo 4, Summerfield 4, Carson 2, Coulthirst 2, Penn 2, Sinclair 2, Winfield 2, Zubar 2, Halliday 1
FA Cup goals (2): Fletcher 1, Hyde 1. **Capital One Cup goals**: None. **Johnstone's Paint Trophy goals**: None
Average home league attendance: 3,555. **Player of Year**: Keith Lowe

SUCCESS FOR MANCHESTER UNITED 'OFFSHOOT' TEAMS

The club set up by Manchester United supporters protesting at the Glazer family's takeover at Old Trafford celebrated their tenth anniversary by moving nearer to a place in the Football League. FC United won the Northern Premier title, their fourth promotion, to reach the northern section of the National League – formerly the Conference. A month later, the club moved into their own ground in the Moston district of the city after a nomadic existence spent on the road. Portuguese champions Benfica, United's opponents in the 1968 European Cup Final, sent a team for a match to mark the official opening of the Broadhurst Park Stadium, watched by a crowd of more than 4,000. Another United 'offshoot' team were also title winners last season. Salford City, partly owned by Phil and Gary Neville, Ryan Giggs, Paul Scholes and Nicky Butt, became champions of the Northern First Division.

ENGLAND THROUGH AFTER REPLAY LASTING 76 SECONDS

England reached the European Under 19 Women's Championship in a bizarre replay lasting 76 seconds. UEFA took the unprecedented step of ordering it because of a refereeing error in their original qualifying match against Norway. A penalty by Leah Williamson in the sixth minute of stoppage-time was disallowed for encroachment and Norway played out the remaining time for a 2-1 win. German official Marija Kurtes should have ordered the spot-kick to be retaken and the governing body said there was no alternative to the closing stages of the game being restaged. The teams faced each other again at the Seavue Stadium in Belfast five days later with a different referee, Kurtes having been sent home from the qualifying event. Williamson held her nerve to score, enabling England to go through the finals in Israel.

THE THINGS THEY SAY...

'This is the World Cup of fraud and today we're issuing FIFA a red card' – **Richard Weber**, United States criminal investigator, after seven officials of the world governing body were arrested on suspicion of bribery and corruption.

'There can't be a more deplorable organisation on earth than FIFA' – **Gary Lineker**, Match of the Day presenter.

'There seems to be a huge disconnect between the sense of fair play that guides those playing and supporting the game and the allegations of corruption that have long lingered around the management of the sport internationally' – **The Duke of Cambridge**, president of the FA,

'There are signs which cannot be mistaken. The Americans were candidates for the 2022 World Cup and they lost. It doesn't smell good' – **Sepp Blatter**, FIFA president.

'While I have a mandate from the membership of FIFA, I do not feel I have a mandate from the entire world of football – the fans, the players, the clubs, the people who live, breathe and love football' – **Sepp Blatter** on his resignation, four days after being elected for a fifth term.

'This is great news for football, It should have happened years ago. There now has to be a root-and-branch investigation of FIFA. It has all got to be transparent in the future' – **Greg Dyke**, chairman of the FA.

'I told him how I felt about him. There were some expletives used. We came to an agreement' – **John Delaney**, chief executive of the FAI, on FIFA's payment of more than £3m, agreed by Sepp Blatter, to avoid potential legal action over the infamous handball by France striker Thierry Henry which cost the Republic the chance of place in the 2010 World Cup Finals.

'The FIFA president, secretary-general and communications director are in a car. Who's driving? .... the police' – **Walter De Gregorio**, one of Sepp Blatter's senior aides, who lost his job after telling this joke.

'The move will create massive disruption to global domestic seasons for years' – **Richard Scudamore**, chief executive of the Premier League, on FIFA's decision to stage the 2022 World Cup in Qatar between the end of November and late December.

'It's a disaster and could not be more disruptive. The only saving grace is that we don't have to think about it for a long time' – **Peter Coates**, Stoke chairman.

'The Premier League will be disrupted for a year, every 24 or 28 years, for a continent to have a World Cup. We have to get over it. Football is a world game' – **Gary Neville**, England coach and former Manchester United captain, offering a rare voice in favour.

'Six years ago, we were on the edge of the abyss. We could not afford a first-class stamp. We had to use bucket collections to keep the club afloat' – **Jeff Mostyn**, Bournemouth chairman, on the club's remarkable rise to the Premier League.

'We just tried to win the games and not look too far ahead. The Championship is such an intense league that people were waiting for us to slip away. They were saying our squad might not be deep enough' – **Eddie Howe**, Bournemouth's manager.

LEAGUE CLUB MANAGERS 2015–16

Figure in brackets = number of managerial changes at club since the War

PREMIER LEAGUE

Arsenal (11)	Arsene Wenger	October 1996
Aston Villa (23)	Tim Sherwood	February 2015
Bournemouth (24)	Eddie Howe+	October 2012
Chelsea (27)	Jose Mourinho+	June 2013
Crystal Palace (40)	Alan Pardew	January 2015
Everton (17)	Roberto Martinez	June 2013
Leicester (27)		
Liverpool (13)	Brendan Rodgers	May 2012
Manchester City (29)	Manuel Pellegrini	June 2013
Manchester Utd (10)	Louis van Gaal	May 2014
Newcastle (26)	Steve McClaren	June 2015
Norwich (28)	Alex Neil	January 2015
Southampton (25)	Ronald Koeman	June 2014
Stoke (23)	Mark Hughes	May 2013
Sunderland (27)	Dick Advocaat	March 2015
Swansea (32)	Garry Monk	May 2014
Tottenham (23)	Mauricio Pochettino	May 2014
Watford (33)	Quique Flores	June 2015
WBA (32)	Tony Pulis	January 2015
West Ham (14)	Slaven Bilic	June 2015
+ Second spell at club		

CHAMPIONSHIP

Birmingham (25)	Gary Rowett	October 2014
Blackburn (28)	Gary Bowyer	May 2013
Bolton (22)	Neil Lennon	October 2014
Brentford (32)	Marinus Dijkhuizen	June 2015
Brighton (33)	Chris Hughton	December 2014
Bristol City (25)	Steve Cotterill	December 2013
Burnley (24)	Sean Dyche	October 2012
Cardiff (29)	Russell Slade	October 2014
Charlton (20)	Guy Luzon	January 2015
Derby (23)	Paul Clement	May 2015
Fulham (31)	Kit Symons	October 2014
Huddersfield (27)	Chris Powell	September 2014
Hull (26)	Steve Bruce	June 2012
Ipswich (13)	Mick McCarthy	November 2012
Leeds (28)	Uwe Rosler	May 2015
Middlesbrough (20)	Aitor Karanka	November 2013
MK Dons (15)	Karl Robinson	April 2010
Nottm Forest (22)	Dougie Freedman	February 2015
Preston (28)	Simon Grayson	February 2013
QPR (32)	Chris Ramsey	May 2015
Reading (20)	Steve Clarke	December 2014
Rotherham (23)	Steve Evans	April 2012
Sheffield Wed (29)	Carlos Carvalhal	June 2015
Wolves (23)	Kenny Jackett	May 2013

LEAGUE ONE

Barnsley (24)	Lee Johnson	February 2015
Blackpool (30)	Neil McDonald	June 2015

Bradford (33)	Phil Parkinson	August 2011
Burton (2)	Jimmy Floyd Hasselbaink	November 2014
Bury (25)	David Flitcroft	December 2013
Chesterfield (20)	Dean Saunders	May 2015
Colchester (26)	Tony Humes	September 2014
Coventry (33)	Tony Mowbray	March 2015
Crewe (21)	Steve Davis	November 2011
Doncaster (2)	Paul Dickov	May 2013
Fleetwood (1)	Graham Alexander	December 2012
Gillingham (24)	Justin Edinburgh	February 2015
Millwall (31)	Neil Harris	April 2015
Oldham (27)	Darren Kelly	May 2015
Peterborough (28)	Dave Robertson	May 2015
Port Vale (24)	Robert Page	October 2014
Rochdale (32)	Keith Hill+	January 2013
Scunthorpe (27)	Mark Robins	October 2014
Sheffield Utd (37)	Nigel Adkins	June 2015
Shrewsbury (4)	Micky Mellon	May 2014
Southend (28)	Phil Brown	March 2013
Swindon (28)	Mark Cooper	August 2013
Walsall (33)	Dean Smith	January 2011
Wigan (22)	Gary Caldwell	April 2015

+ Second spell at club. Number of changes since elected to Football League: Peterborough 1960, Wigan 1978, Burton 2009, Fleetwood 2012. Since returning: Shrewsbury 2004

LEAGUE TWO

AFC Wimbledon (1)	Neal Ardley	October 2012
Accrington (4)	John Coleman	September 2014
Barnet (-)	Martin Allen	March 2014
Bristol Rov (-)	Darrell Clarke	March 2014
Cambridge (-)	Richard Money	October 2012
Carlisle (5)	Keith Curle	September 2014
Crawley (5)	Mark Yates	May 2015
Dagenham (1)	Wayne Burnett	May 2013
Exeter (-)	Paul Tisdale	June 2006
Hartlepool (36)	Ronnie Moore	December 2014
Leyton Orient (25)	Ian Hendon	May 2015
Luton (-)	John Still	February 2013
Mansfield (1)	Adam Murray	December 2014
Morecambe (1)	Jim Bentley	May 2011
Newport (1)	Terry Butcher	April 2015
Northampton (31)	Chris Wilder	January 2014
Notts Co (39)	Ricardo Moniz	April 2015
Oxford (2)	Michael Appleton	July 2014
Plymouth (34)	Derek Adams	June 2015
Portsmouth (33)	Paul Cook	May 2015
Stevenage (3)	Teddy Sheringham	May 2015
Wycombe (10)	Gareth Ainsworth	November 2012
Yeovil (5)	Paul Sturrock	April 2015
York (2)	Russ Wilcox	October 2014

Number of changes since elected to Football League: Wycombe 1993, Dagenham 2007, Morecambe 2007, Stevenage 2010, AFC Wimbledon 2011, Crawley 2011. Since returning: Carlisle 2005, Accrington 2006, Exeter 2008, Oxford 2010, York 2012, Mansfield 2013, Newport 2013, Cambridge 2014, Luton 2014, Barnet 2015, Bristol Rov 2015

MANAGERIAL INS AND OUTS 2014–15

PREMIER LEAGUE

Aston Villa: Out – Paul Lambert (Feb 2015); In – Tim Sherwood
Crystal Palace: Out – Tony Pulis (Aug 2014); In – Neil Warnock; Out (Dec 2014); In – Alan Pardew
Leicester: Out – Nigel Pearson (Jun 2015)
Newcastle: Out – Alan Pardew (Dec 2014); In – Steve McClaren
QPR: Out – Harry Redknapp (Jan 2015); In – Chris Ramsey
Sunderland: Out – Gus Poyet (Mar 2015); In – Dick Advocaat
WBA: Out – Alan Irvine (Dec 2014); In – Tony Pulis
West Ham: Out – Sam Allardyce (May 2015); In - Slaven Bilic

CHAMPIONSHIP

Birmingham: Out – Lee Clark (Oct 2014); In – Gary Rowett
Blackpool: Out – Jose Riga (Oct 2014); In – Lee Clark; Out (May 2015); In – Neil McDonald
Bolton: Out – Dougie Freedman (Oct 2014); In – Neil Lennon
Brentford: Out – Mark Warburton (May 2015); In – Marinus Dijkhuizen
Brighton: Out – Sami Hyypia (Dec 2014); In – Chris Hughton
Cardiff: Out – Ole Gunnar Solskjaer (Sep 2014); In – Russell Slade
Charlton: Out – Bob Peeters (Jan 2015); In – Guy Luzon
Derby: Out – Steve McClaren (May 2015); In – Paul Clement
Fulham: Out – Felix Magath (Sep 2014); In – Kit Symons
Huddersfield: Out – Mark Robins (Aug 2014); In – Chris Powell
Leeds: Out – Dave Hockaday (Aug 2014); In – Darko Milanic (Oct 2014); In – Neil Redfearn; Out (May 2015); In – Uwe Rosler
Millwall: Out – Ian Holloway (Mar 2015); In – Neil Harris
Norwich: Out – Neil Adams (Jan 2015); In – Alex Neil
Nottm Forest: Out – Stuart Pearce (Feb 2015); In – Dougie Freedman
Reading: Out – Nigel Adkins (Dec 2014); In – Steve Clarke
Sheffield Wed: Out – Stuart Gray (Jun 2015); In – Carlos Carvalhal
Watford: Out – Beppe Sannino (Aug 2014); In – Oscar Garcia; Out (Sep 2014); In – Billy McKinlay; Out (Oct 2014); In – Slavisa Jokanovic; Out - (Jun 2015); In – Quique Flores
Wigan: Out – Uwe Rosler (Nov 2014); In – Malky Mackay; Out (Apr 2015); In – Gary Caldwell

LEAGUE ONE

Barnsley: Out – Danny Wilson (Feb 2015); In – Lee Johnson
Chesterfield: Out – Paul Cook (May 2015); In – Dean Saunders
Colchester: Out – Joe Dunne (Sep 2014); In – Tony Humes
Coventry: Out – Steven Pressley (Feb 2015); In – Tony Mowbray
Crawley: Out – John Gregory (Dec 2014); In – Dean Saunders; Out (May 2015); In – Mark Yates
Gillingham: Out – Peter Taylor (Dec 2014); In – Justin Edinburgh
Leyton Orient: Out – Russell Slade (Sep 2014); In – Mauro Milanese; Out (Dec 2014); In – Fabio Liverani; Out (May 2015); In – Ian Hendon
Notts Co: Out – Shaun Derry (Mar 2015); In – Ricardo Moniz
Oldham: Out – Lee Johnson (Feb 2015); In – Darren Kelly
Peterborough: Out – Darren Ferguson (Feb 2015); In – Dave Robertson
Port Vale: Out – Micky Adams (Sep 2014); In – Robert Page
Scunthorpe: Out – Russ Wilcox (Oct 2014); In – Mark Robins
Sheffield Utd: Out – Nigel Clough (May 2015); In – Nigel Adkins
Yeovil: Out – Gary Johnson (Feb 2015); In – Paul Sturrock

LEAGUE TWO

Accrington: Out – James Beattie (Sep 2014); In – John Coleman
Burton: Out – Gary Rowett (Oct 2014); In – Jimmy Floyd Hasselbaink
Carlisle: Out – Graham Kavanagh (Sep 2014); In – Keith Curle
Cheltenham: Out – Mark Yates (Nov 2014); In – Paul Buckle; Out (Feb 2015); In – Gary Johnson
Hartlepool: Out – Colin Cooper (Oct 2014); In – Paul Murray; Out (Dec 2014); In – Ronnie Moore
Mansfield: Out – Paul Cox (Nov 2014); In – Adam Murray
Newport: Out – Justin Edinburgh (Feb 2015); In – Terry Butcher
Plymouth: Out – John Sheridan (May 2015); In – Derek Adams
Portsmouth: Out – Andy Awford (Apr 2015); In – Paul Cook
Stevenage: Out – Graham Westley (May 2015); In – Teddy Sheringham
Tranmere: Out – Rob Edwards (Nov 2014); In – Micky Adams; Out (Apr 2015); In – Gary Brabin
York: Out – Nigel Worthington (Oct 2014); In – Russ Wilcox

FA CUP 2014–15
(with Budweiser)

FIRST ROUND

Barnet 1 Wycombe 3
Barnsley 5 Burton 0
Basingstoke 1 Telford 1
Blyth 4 Altrincham 1
Braintree 0 Chesterfield 6
Bromley 3 Dartford 4
Bury 3 Hemel Hempstead 1
Cambridge 1 Fleetwood 0
Cheltenham 5 Swindon 0
Coventry 1 Worcester 2
Crewe 0 Sheffield Utd 0
Dagenham 0 Southport 0
Dover 1 Morecambe 0
Eastleigh 2 Lincoln 1
Forest Green 0 Scunthorpe 2
Gillingham 1 Bristol City 2
Gosport 3 Colchester 6
Grimsby 1 Oxford 3
Halifax 1 Bradford 2
Hartlepool 2 East Thurrock 0
Havant 0 Preston 3
Luton 4 Newport 2
Mansfield 1 Concord 1
Northampton 0 Rochdale 0
Norton 0 Gateshead 4
Notts Co 0 Accrington 0
Oldham 1 Leyton Orient 0
Peterborough 2 Carlisle 1
Plymouth 2 Fylde 0
Portsmouth 2 Aldershot 2
Port Vale 3 MK Dons 4
Southend 1 Chester 2
Stevenage 0 Maidstone 0
Tranmere 1 Bristol Rov 0
Walsall 2 Shrewsbury 2
Warrington 1 Exeter 0
Weston SM 1 Doncaster 4
Wrexham 3 Woking 0
Yeovil 1 Crawley 0
York 1 Wimbledon 1

FIRST ROUND REPLAYS

Accrington 2 Notts Co 1
Aldershot 1 Portsmouth 0

Concord 0 Mansfield 1
Maidstone 2 Stevenage 1
Rochdale 2 Northampton 1
Sheffield Utd 2 Crewe 0
Shrewsbury 1 Walsall 0
Southport 2 Dagenham 0
Telford 2 Basingstoke 1
Wimbledon 3 York 1

SECOND ROUND

Accrington 1 Yeovil 1
Aldershot 0 Rochdale 0
Barnsley 0 Chester 0
Bradford 4 Dartford 1
Bristol City 1 Telford 0
Bury 1 Luton 1
Cambridge 2 Mansfield 2
Cheltenham 0 Dover 1
Colchester 1 Peterborough 0
Gateshead 2 Warrington 0
Hartlepool 1 Blyth 2
*MK Dons 0 Chesterfield 1
Oldham 0 Doncaster 1
Oxford 2 Tranmere 2
Preston 1 Shrewsbury 0
Scunthorpe 1 Worcester 1
Sheffield Utd 3 Plymouth 0
Southport 2 Eastleigh 1
Wrexham 3 Maidstone 1
Wycombe 0 Wimbledon 1
*Replay ordered by FA
after Chesterfield fielded
ineligible player

SECOND ROUND REPLAYS

Chester 0 Barnsley 3
Luton 1 Bury 0
Mansfield 0 Cambridge 1
MK Dons 0 Chesterfield 1
Rochdale 4 Aldershot 1
Tranmere 2 Oxford 1
Worcester 1 Scunthorpe 1
(aet, Scunthorpe won 14-13 on pens)
Yeovil 2 Accrington 0

ARSENAL RETAIN TROPHY – VILLA OUTPLAYED

THIRD ROUND	FOURTH ROUND	FIFTH ROUND	SIXTH ROUND	SEMI-FINALS	FINAL
*Arsenal....2	Arsenal....3				
Hull....0		*Arsenal....2			
*Brentford....0	*Brighton....2				
Brighton....2			Arsenal....2		
*Manchester City....2	*Manchester City....0	Middlesbrough....0			
Sheffield Wed....1					
*Barnsley....0	Middlesbrough....2			Arsenal....+2	
Middlesbrough....2					
*Preston....2	*Preston....1:3				
Norwich....0		*Preston....1			
*QPR....0	Sheffield Utd....1:1				
Sheffield Utd....3			*Manchester Utd....1		
*Cambridge....2	*Cambridge....0:0	Manchester Utd....3			
Luton....1					
*Yeovil....0	Manchester Utd....0:3				Arsenal....4
Manchester Utd....0:3					
*Chelsea....3	*Chelsea....2				
Watford....0		*Bradford....2			
*Millwall....3:0	Bradford....4				
Bradford....3:4			*Bradford....0:0		
*Sunderland....1	*Sunderland....0:3	Sunderland....0			
Leeds....0					
*Fulham....0+A2	Fulham....0:1			Reading....1	
Wolves....0:2					
*Derby....1	*Derby....2				
Southport....0		*Derby....1			
*Scunthorpe....2:0	Chesterfield....0				
Chesterfield....2:+2			Reading....0:3		
*Cardiff....3	*Cardiff....1	Reading....2			
Colchester....1					
*Huddersfield....0	Reading....2				
Reading....1					

148

*Southampton......1:1					
Ipswich......1:0	*Southampton......2				
*Dover......0		*Crystal Palace......1			
Crystal Palace......4	Crystal Palace......3				
*Wimbledon......1			*Liverpool......0:1		
Liverpool......2	*Liverpool......0:2				
*Bolton......1		Liverpool......2			
Wigan......0	Bolton......0:1			Liverpool......1	
*Charlton......1					
Blackburn......2	*Blackburn......3				
*Tranmere......2		*Blackburn......4			
Swansea......6	Swansea......1				
*Rochdale......1			Blackburn......0:0		
Nottm Forest......0	*Rochdale......1				
*Stoke......3		Rochdale......1			
Wrexham......4	Stoke......1				Aston Villa......0
*Blyth......2					
Birmingham......3	*Birmingham......1				
*WBA......7		*WBA......4			
Gateshead......0	WBA......2				
*Doncaster......1:0			WBA......0		
Bristol City......1:2	*Bristol City......0				
*Everton......1:2		West Ham......0			
West Ham......1+B2	West Ham......1			Aston Villa......2	
*Burnley......1:2					
Tottenham......1:4	*Tottenham......1				
*Leicester......2		Leicester......1			
Newcastle......0	Leicester......1				
*Rotherham......1			*Aston Villa......2		
Bournemouth......5	Bournemouth......1				
Blackpool......0		*Aston Villa......2			
*Aston Villa 1	*Aston Villa......2				

*Drawn at home. +After extra-time. A – Fulham won 5-3 on pens. B – West Ham won 9-8 on pens. Both semi-finals at Wembley

ROUND BY ROUND HIGHLIGHTS

FIRST ROUND

Midfielder Craig Mahon enjoys a double celebration. He becomes the father of twin boys and the following day scores the winner for Chester at Southend. The Conference side go through 2-1, with Ben Heneghan scoring their other goal. Six other clubs are knocked out by non-league opposition. Worcester enjoy their finest moment since defeating Liverpool in 1959 as Sean Geddes nets both goals – one from the penalty spot – to oust Coventry 2-1 at the Ricoh Arena. Craig Robinson delivers the only goal of the tie for Warrington against Exeter, watched by brother Karl, the MK Dons manager, whose team put Manchester United out of the League Cup earlier in the season. Also 1-0 winners are Dover, who overcome Morecambe with a goal by Stefan Payne, and Aldershot in a replay against Portsmouth, thanks to Mark Molesley's strike. In other replays, an 87th minute header by Frannie Collin, his second goal of the game, earns Maidstone a 2-1 victory over Stevenage, while Southport beat Dagenham and Redbridge 2-0 (John Marsden and Danny Hattersley). Four players deliver hat-tricks – Sam Winnall for Barnsley (5-0 v Burton); Callum Robinson for Preston (3-0 at Havant); Byron Harrison for Cheltenham (5-0 v Swindon); Rob Ramshaw for Gateshead (4-0 at Norton).

SECOND ROUND

Worcester's consolation for losing a replay on penalties to Scunthorpe is a place in the record books after the longest shoot-out in FA Cup history. The League One side go through 14-13 when Miguel Llera converts the 32nd spot-kick. The previous record was Macclesfield's 11-10 win against Forest Green in 2001. Dover reach the third round for the second time in four years with an 83rd minute goal from captain Connor Essam, the only one of the game, at Cheltenham. Blyth join them, coming from behind to succeed 2-1 at Hartlepool through an equaliser by Stephen Turnbull and a 90th minute goal from Jarrett Rivers. In all non-league ties, Wrexham beat Maidstone 3-1, Gateshead see off Warrington 2-0 and Southport get the better of Eastleigh 2-1. Matt Done's hat-trick points Rochdale to a 4-1 success against Aldershot in a replay, while Chesterfield repeat a 1-0 away victory over MK Dons after being ordered to replay because of an ineligible player in the first meeting of the teams.

THIRD ROUND

Sheffield United take pride of place by beating Queens Park Rangers 3-0 at Loftus Road. Two goals by Jamal Campbell-Ryce and one from Marc McNulty deliver United's fifth victory over Premier League sides in cup competitions in 12 months under Nigel Clough. Three managers make successful starts with new clubs. Tony Pulis sees Saido Berahino score four times in West Bromwich Albion's 7-0 win over Gateshead, who hold out for 40 minutes before their defence is breached. Alan Pardew's Crystal Palace overcome Dover 4-0, Scott Dann netting two headers, while Brighton, under Chris Hughton, are 2-0 away winners over Brentford with late efforts from Lewis Dunk (88) and Chris O'Grady (90). The three other non-league teams give Premier League and Championship opposition a fright. Wrexham lead at Stoke through Mark Carrington before conceding three goals in the final ten minutes, two of them to substitute Stephen Ireland. Skipper Robbie Dale puts Blyth 2-0 up against Birmingham, who reply with three second-half goals, two of them from Wes Thomas. Southport look to have earned a replay at Derby until Chris Martin's penalty in stoppage-time sends them home empty-handed. Both Manchester clubs make hard work of going through. City need a stoppage-time goal from James Milner, his second of the tie on his 29th birthday, to account for Sheffield Wednesday 2-1. United require a last-minute strike from Angel di Maria to confirm a 2-0 win at Yeovil. Sunderland and Leeds meet for the first time in the competition since the 1973 final, with Sunderland again 1-0 winners, this time courtesy of on-loan Patrick van Aanholt's first goal for the club.

FOURTH ROUND

Stamford Bridge witnesses one of the biggest upsets in the competition's history. Bradford, trailing Chelsea 2-0, shock a 41,000 crowd with goals from Jon Stead, former Chelsea youngster Filipe Morais, Andy Halliday and Mark Yeates for a 4-2 victory. Afterwards, Jose Mourinho visits their dressing room to compliment the League One players and their manager Phil Parkinson. Manchester City, chasing Mourinho's team for the title, are also beaten on their own ground as Patrick Bamford, on loan from Chelsea, and Spanish substitute Kike give Middlesbrough a 2-0 success. City manager Manuel Pellegrini refuses to blame the defeat on his squad arriving back from a training trip to Abu Dhabi on the eve of the tie. Southampton's 3-2 home defeat by Crystal Palace leaves Manchester United as the only one of the top four in the Premier League to go through. United survive an uncomfortable goalless draw at Cambridge to win the replay 3-0 in front of a 74,000 crowd at Old Trafford which swells the League Two club's earnings from their run to more than £1m. Bolton hold Liverpool 0-0 at Anfield, lead through Eidur Gudjohnsen's penalty in the replay and are clinging on after a second yellow card for Neil Danns. But resistence is broken by Raheem Sterling after 85 minutes, followed by Philippe Countinho's winner in added time. Swansea also lead at Blackburn, but have Kyle Bartley and Gylfi Sigurdson sent off and go down 3-1. A record crowd for the Amex Stadium of 30,278 see Brighton stretch Arsenal all the way before losing 3-2.

FIFTH ROUND

Jon Stead clinches another famous win for Bradford, this time against former club Sunderland, his strike adding to John O'Shea's own goal for a 2-0 success before a 24,000 crowd at Valley Parade. Preston threaten another shock when Scott Laird puts them ahead at Deepdale, but Manchester United respond well to go through 3-1. Josh King, a former Manchester United trainee, scores a hat-trick and Rudy Gestede converts a penalty as Blackburn come from behind to beat Stoke 4-1. West Bromwich Albion's Brown Ideye also has a productive match, scoring twice and setting up a goal for Saido Berahino in their 4-0 win over West Ham. Back in English football with Reading, Yakubu delivers an 82nd minute winner for 2-1 against Derby, whose manager Steve McClaren once paid £7.5m to bring the Nigerian striker to Middlesbrough.

SIXTH ROUND

Danny Welbeck, sold by Manchester United manager Louis van Gaal early in the season, fires Arsenal through against his former team at Old Trafford. Nacho Monreal puts the holders ahead, Wayne Rooney equalises and Welbeck nets the winner. United have Angel di Maria sent off for grabbing referee Michael Oliver. Two players are dismissed and there are ugly crowd scenes at Villa Park, where the home side overcome West Bromwich Albion 2-0 with goals by Fabian Delph and Scott Sinclair. Villa's Jack Grealish and Albion's Claudio Yacob both receive second yellow cards. Bradford's run ends with a 3-0 defeat in a replay at Reading, who reach the semi-finals for the first time since 1927. Hal Robson-Kanu and Garath McCleary are on the mark in the first ten minutes and Jamie Mackie completes the scoring. Bradford have Filipe Morais shown a straight red card. Liverpool are held at home by Blackburn, but Philippe Coutinho scores the only goal in the replay, which is delayed for a month by European matches and the international break taking precedence.

SEMI-FINALS

Steven Gerrard's hopes of bringing down the curtain on his Anfield career with a Wembley final are boosted when Philippe Coutinho puts Liverpool ahead. But the dream dies as Christian Benteke scores his ninth goal in seven games under new manager Tim Sherwood and Fabian Delph delivers the winner for Aston Villa. Bitter disappointment, too, for Reading goalkeeper Adam Federici, whose extra-time mistake presents Alexis Sanchez with his second goal and along with it a 2-1 victory for Arsenal. Garath McCleary cancels out his first and the Championship side earn widespread praise for going so close.

FINAL

It normally takes centre stage at the conclusion of the domestic season, commanding wall-to-wall coverage beforehand, eager expectation among supporters across the country and an unrivalled spectacle on the big day. Not this time. A potentially intriguing clash between Arsenal master Arsene Wenger's team and apprentice Tim Sherwood's Aston Villa fell an unfortunate victim of the bribery and corruption bombshell engulfing FIFA; overshadowed by calls to oust the world governing body's beleaguered president, Sepp Blatter, not least from FA chairman Greg Dyke. It just did not feel like a normal FA Cup Final week – and neither did the match. There was no denying the quality Arsenal brought to the occasion, both in terms of their overall play and the goals scored. Theo Walcott's volley was an object lesson in precision, while Alexis Sanchez delivered one of the great Wembley strikes. Equally impressive was how Wenger set up his side, preferring Walcott to Olivier Giroud after his hat-trick against West Bromwich Albion in the final Premier League game, ensuring there was no chance for Fabian Delph and the precocious Jack Grealish to make an impression in midfield and isolating the potential threat of Christian Benteke. Even at the end, with the issue beyond doubt, the manager got it right with the introduction of Giroud bringing the fourth goal. Yet so poor were Villa that this was one of the most one-sided finals of modern times. At least a hint of a challenge to Arsenal's authority might have been expected. But it never came and Sherwood's annoyance cast doubt on the future of some of his players at Villa Park.

ARSENAL 4 ASTON VILLA 0
Wembley (89,283); Saturday, May 30 2015

Arsenal (4-2-3-1): Szczesny, Bellerin, Koscielny, Mertesacker (capt), Monreal, Coquelin, Cazorla, Ramsey, Ozil (Wilshere 77), A Sanchez (Oxlade-Chamberlain 90), Walcott (Giroud 77). **Subs not used**: Ospina, Gibbs, Gabriel, Flamini. **Scorers**: Walcott (40), A Sanchez (50), Mertesacker (62), Giroud (90). **Manager**: Arsene Wenger

Aston Villa (4-3-3): Given, Hutton, Okore, Vlaar, Richardson (Bacuna 68), Cleverley, Westwood (C Sanchez 71), Delph (capt), N'Zogbia (Agbonlahor 53), Benteke, Grealish. **Subs not used**: Guzan, Baker, Sinclair, Cole. **Booked**: Cleverley, Hutton, Delph, Westwood, Agbonlahor. **Manager**: Tim Sherwood

Referee: J Moss (Yorks). **Half-time**: 1-0

HOW THEY REACHED THE FINAL

Arsenal
Round 3: 2-0 home to Hull (Mertesacker, Sanchez)
Round 4: 3-2 away to Brighton (Walcott, Ozil, Rosicky)
Round 5: 2-0 home to Middlesbrough (Giroud 2)
Round 6: 2-1 away to Manchester Utd (Monreal, Welbeck)
Semi-finals: 2-1 v Reading – aet (Sanchez 2)

Aston Villa
Round 3: 1-0 home to Blackpool (Benteke)
Round 4: 2-1 home to Bournemouth (Gil, Weimann)
Round 5: 2-1 home to Leicester (Bacuna, Sinclair)
Round 6: 2-0 home to WBA (Delph, Sinclair)
Semi-finals: 2-1 v Liverpool (Benteke, Delph)

Leading scorers (from first round): 5 Berahino (WBA), Gallagher (Preston), Stead (Bradford); 4 Dale (Blyth), Sanchez (Arsenal)

FINAL FACTS AND FIGUIRES

• Arsenal won the trophy for a record 12th time and made a record 19th appearance in the final.

• Arsene Wenger became the most successful FA Cup manager of the modern era with a sixth win, one more than Sir Alex Ferguson. George Ramsay achieved six victories in his role as Aston Villa's manager/secretary between 1887-1920 before the role of a manager was defined.

• Villa were beaten 1-0 by Chelsea in their last appearances in the final in 2000 – the last one held at the old Wembley.

• Arsenal's margin of victory was the biggest since Manchester United's 4-0 win over Chelsea in 1994.

• The previous eight finals had all been decided by a single-goal margin, including Arsenal's 3-2 win over Hull in 2014.

• Alexis Sanchez became the second Chilean player to score in an FA Cup Final after George Robledo, who netted the winner for Newcastle against Arsenal in 1952.

• Sanchez scored both goals in the semi-final against Reading and netted both for Chile in their win over England in a friendly international at Wembley in November, 2013.

• Two of Arsenal's other three scorers, England's Theo Walcott and Germany's Per Mertesacker, have also been on the mark at Wembley for club and country

• Villa had Shay Given, 39, in goal, 17 years after his first FA Cup Final – Newcastle's 2-0 defeat by Arsenal.

• The Duke of Cambridge, president of the FA, had to put a brave face on presenting the trophy – he is a Villa supporter. He sat next to Randy Lerner in the Royal Box, commiserating with the Villa owner as the goals went in.

• The FA Cup will be rebranded for the new season following a three-year deal the FA signed with Dubai-based airline Emirates – the first title sponsorship of the game's oldest knock-out tournament. It will be known as the Emirates FA Cup.

THE THINGS THEY SAY ...

'This has been the toughest decision of my life and one which both me and my family have agonised over for a good deal of time. Liverpool Football Club has been such a huge part of all our lives for so long and saying goodbye is going to be difficult. But I feel it's something that is in the best interests of all involved' – **Steven Gerrard** on his decision to leave Anfield at the end of the season.

'I never thought he would leave Liverpool. I always envisaged that, like me, he would finish his career as a one-club man. I'm struggling to work out how it has come to this' – **Jamie Carragher**, Gerrard's former team-mate.

'If you don't know the answer to that question you are an ostrich. Your head must be in the sand' – **Nigel Pearson**, former Leicester manager, responding to a reporter asking about criticism of his players.

FA CUP FINAL SCORES & TEAMS

1872 **Wanderers 1** (Betts) Bowen, Alcock, Bonsor, Welch; Betts, Crake, Hooman, Lubbock, Thompson, Vidal, Wollaston. Note: Betts played under the pseudonym 'AH Chequer' on the day of the match **Royal Engineers 0** Capt Merriman; Capt Marindin; Lieut Addison, Lieut Cresswell, Lieut Mitchell, Lieut Renny-Tailyour, Lieut Rich, Lieut George Goodwyn, Lieut Muirhead, Lieut Cotter, Lieut Bogle

1873 **Wanderers 2** (Wollaston, Kinnaird) Bowen; Thompson, Welch, Kinnaird, Howell, Wollaston, Sturgis, Rev Stewart, Kenyon-Slaney, Kingsford, Bonsor **Oxford University 0** Kirke-Smith; Leach, Mackarness, Birley, Longman, Chappell-Maddison Dixon, Paton, Vidal, Sumner, Ottaway. March 29; 3,000; A Stair

1874 **Oxford University 2** (Mackarness, Patton) Neapean; Mackarness, Birley, Green, Vidal, Ottaway, Benson, Patton, Rawson, Chappell-Maddison, Rev Johnson **Royal Engineers 0** Capt Merriman; Major Marindin, Lieut W Addison, Gerald Onslow, Lieut Oliver, Lieut Digby, Lieut Renny-Tailyour, Lieut Rawson, Lieut Blackman Lieut Wood, Lieut von Donop. March 14; 2,000; A Stair

1875 **Royal Engineers 1** (Renny-Tailyour) Capt Merriman; Lieut Sim, Lieut Onslow, Lieut (later Sir) Ruck, Lieut Von Donop, Lieut Wood, Lieut Rawson, Lieut Stafford, Capt Renny-Tailyour, Lieut Mein, Lieut Wingfield-Stratford **Old Etonians 1** (Bonsor) Thompson; Benson, Lubbock, Wilson, Kinnaird, (Sir) Stronge, Patton, Farmer, Bonsor, Ottaway, Kenyon-Slaney. March 13; 2,000; CW Alcock. aet **Replay – Royal Engineers 2** (Renny-Tailyour, Stafford) Capt Merriman; Lieut Sim, Lieut Onslow, Lieut (later Sir) Ruck, Lieut Von Donop, Lieut Wood, Lieut Rawson, Lieut Stafford, Capt Renny-Tailyour, Lieut Mein, Lieut Wingfield-Stratford **Old Etonians 0** Capt Drummond-Moray; Kinnaird, (Sir) Stronge, Hammond, Lubbock, Patton, Farrer, Bonsor, Lubbock, Wilson, Farmer. March 16; 3,000; CW Alcock

1876 **Wanderers 1** (Edwards) Greig; Stratford, Lindsay, Chappell-Maddison, Birley, Wollaston, C Heron, G Heron, Edwards, Kenrick, Hughes **Old Etonians 1** (Bonsor) Hogg; Rev Welldon, Lyttleton, Thompson, Kinnaird, Meysey, Kenyon-Slaney, Lyttleton, Sturgis, Bonsor, Allene. March 11; 3,500; WS Rawson aet **Replay – Wanderers 3** (Wollaston, Hughes 2) Greig, Stratford, Lindsay, Chappel-Maddison, Birley, Wollaston, C Heron, G Heron, Edwards, Kenrick, Hughes **Old Etonians 0** Hogg, Lubbock, Lyttleton, Farrer, Kinnaird, (Sir) Stronge, Kenyon-Slaney, Lyttleton, Sturgis, Bonsor, Allene. March 18; 1,500; WS Rawson

1877 **Wanderers 2** (Kenrick, Lindsay) Kinnaird; Birley, Denton, Green, Heron, Hughes, Kenrick, Lindsay, Stratford, Wace, Wollaston **Oxford University 1** (Kinnaird og) Allington; Bain, Dunnell, Rev Savory, Todd, Waddington, Rev Fernandez, Otter, Parry, Rawson. March 24; 3,000; SH Wright, aet

1878 **Wanderers 3** (Kinnaird, Kenrick 2) (Sir) Kirkpatrick; Stratford, Lindsay, Kinnaird, Green, Wollaston, Heron, Wylie, Wace, Denton, Kenrick **Royal Engineers 1** (Morris) Friend; Cowan, (Sir) Morris, Mayne, Heath, Haynes, Lindsay, Hedley, (Sir) Bond, Barnet, Ruck. March 23; 4,500; SR Bastard

1879 **Old Etonians 1** (Clerke) Hawtrey; Edward, Bury, Kinnaird, Lubbock, Clerke, Pares, Goodhart, Whitfield, Chevalier, Beaufoy **Clapham Rovers 0** Birkett; Ogilvie, Field, Bailey, Prinsep, Rawson, Stanley, Scott, Bevington, Growse, Keith-Falconer. March 29; 5,000; CW Alcock

1880 **Clapham Rovers 1** (Lloyd-Jones) Birkett; Ogilvie, Field, Weston, Bailey, Stanley, Brougham, Sparkes, Barry, Ram, Lloyd-Jones **Oxford University 0** Parr; Wilson, King, Phillips, Rogers, Heygate, Rev Childs, Eyre, (Dr) Crowdy, Hill, Lubbock. April 10; 6,000; Major Marindin

1881 **Old Carthusians 3** (Page, Wynyard, Parry) Gillett; Norris, (Sir) Colvin, Prinsep, (Sir) Vintcent, Hansell, Richards, Page, Wynyard, Parry, Todd **Old Etonians 0** Rawlinson; Foley, French, Kinnaird, Farrer, Macauley, Goodhart, Whitfield, Novelli, Anderson, Chevallier. April 9; 4,000; W Pierce-Dix

1882 **Old Etonians 1** (Macauley) Rawlinson; French, de Paravicini, Kinnaird, Foley, Novelli, Dunn, Macauley, Goodhart, Chevallier, Anderson **Blackburn Rov 0** Howarth; McIntyre, Suter, Hargreaves, Sharples, Hargreaves, Avery, Brown, Strachan, Douglas, Duckworth. March 25; 6,500; JC Clegg

1883 **Blackburn Olympic 2** (Matthews, Costley) Hacking; Ward, Warburton, Gibson, Astley, Hunter, Dewhurst, Matthews, Wilson, Costley, Yates **Old Etonians 1** (Goodhart) Rawlinson; French, de

154

Paravicini, Kinnaird, Foley, Dunn, Bainbridge, Chevallier, Anderson, Goodhart, Macauley. March 31; 8,000; Major Marindin, aet

1884 **Blackburn Rov 2** (Sowerbutts, Forrest) Arthur; Suter, Beverley, McIntyre, Forrest, Hargreaves, Brown, Inglis Sowerbutts, Douglas, Lofthouse **Queen's Park 1** (Christie) Gillespie; MacDonald, Arnott, Gow, Campbell, Allan, Harrower, (Dr) Smith, Anderson, Watt, Christie. March 29; 4,000; Major Marindin

1885 **Blackburn Rov 2** (Forrest, Brown) Arthur; Turner, Suter, Haworth, McIntyre, Forrest, Sowerbutts, Lofthouse, Douglas, Brown, Fecitt **Queen's Park 0** Gillespie; Arnott, MacLeod, MacDonald, Campbell, Sellar, Anderson, McWhammel, Hamilton, Allan, Gray. April 4; 12,500; Major Marindin

1886 **Blackburn Rov 0** Arthur; Turner, Suter, Heyes, Forrest, McIntyre, Douglas, Strachan, Sowerbutts, Fecitt, Brown **WBA 0** Roberts; Green, Bell, Horton, Perry, Timmins, Woodhall, Green, Bayliss, Loach, Bell. April 3; 15,000; Major Marindin **Replay – Blackburn Rov 2** (Sowerbutts, Brown) Arthur; Turner, Suter, Walton, Forrest, McIntyre, Douglas, Strachan, Sowerbutts, Fecitt, Brown **WBA 0** Roberts; Green, Bell, Horton, Perry, Timmins, Woodhall, Green, Bayliss, Loach, Bell. April 10; 12,000; Major Marindin

1887 **Aston Villa 2** (Hodgetts, Hunter) Warner; Coulton, Simmonds, Yates, Dawson, Burton, Davis, Albert Brown, Hunter, Vaughton, Hodgetts **WBA 0** Roberts; Green, Aldridge, Horton, Perry, Timmins, Woodhall, Green, Bayliss, Paddock, Pearson. April 2; 15,500; Major Marindin

1888 **WBA 2** (Bayliss), Woodhall) Roberts; Aldridge, Green, Horton, Perry, Timmins, Woodhall, Bassett, Bayliss, Wilson, Pearson **Preston 1** (Dewhurst) Mills-Roberts; Howarth, Holmes, Ross, Russell, Gordon, Ross, Goodall, Drummond, Graham. March 24; 19,000; Major Marindin

1889 **Preston 3** (Dewhurst, Ross, Thomson) Mills-Roberts; Howarth, Holmes, Drummond, Russell, Graham, Gordon, Goodall, Dewhurst, Thompson, Ross **Wolves 0** Baynton; Baugh, Mason, Fletcher, Allen, Lowder, Hunter, Wykes, Brodie, Wood, Knight. March 30; 22,000; Major Marindin

1890 **Blackburn Rov 6** (Lofthouse, Jack Southworth, Walton, Townley 3) Horne; James Southworth, Forbes, Barton, Dewar, Forrest, Lofthouse, Campbell, Jack Southworth, Walton, Townley **Sheffield Wed 1** (Bennett) Smith; Morley, Brayshaw, Dungworth, Betts, Waller, Ingram, Woolhouse, Bennett, Mumford, Cawley. March 29; 20,000; Major Marindin

1891 **Blackburn Rov 3** (Dewar, Jack Southworth, Townley) Pennington; Brandon, Forbes, Barton, Dewar, Forrest, Lofthouse, Walton, Southworth, Hall, Townley **Notts Co 1** (Oswald) Thraves; Ferguson, Hendry, Osborne, Calderhead, Shelton, McGregror, McInnes Oswald, Locker, Daft. March 21; 23,000; CJ Hughes

1892 **WBA 3** (Geddes, Nicholls, Reynolds) Reader; Nicholson, McCulloch, Reynolds, Perry, Groves, Bassett, McLeod, Nicholls, Pearson, Geddes **Aston Villa 0** Warner; Evans, Cox, Devey, Cowan, Baird, Athersmith, Devey, Dickson, Hodgetts, Campbell. March 19; 32,810; JC Clegg

1893 **Wolves 1** (Allen) Rose; Baugh, Swift, Malpass, Allen, Kinsey, Topham, Wykes, Butcher, Griffin, Wood **Everton 0** Williams; Kelso, Howarth, Boyle, Holt, Stewart, Latta, Gordon, Maxwell, Chadwick, Milward. March 25; 45,000; CJ Hughes

1894 **Notts Co 4** (Watson, Logan 3) Toone; Harper, Hendry, Bramley, Calderhead, Shelton, Watson, Donnelly, Logan Bruce, Daft **Bolton 1** (Cassidy) Sutcliffe; Somerville, Jones , Gardiner, Paton, Hughes, Tannahill, Wilson, Cassidy, Bentley, Dickenson. March 31; 37,000; CJ Hughes

1895 **Aston Villa 1** (Chatt) Wilkes; Spencer, Welford, Reynolds, Cowan, Russell, Athersmith Chatt, Devey, Hodgetts, Smith **WBA 0** Reader; Williams, Horton, Perry, Higgins, Taggart, Bassett, McLeod, Richards, Hutchinson, Banks. April 20; 42,560; J Lewis

1896 **Sheffield Wed 2** (Spikesley 2) Massey; Earp, Langley, Brandon, Crawshaw, Petrie, Brash, Brady, Bell, Davis, Spikesley **Wolves 1** (Black) Tennant; Baugh, Dunn, Owen, Malpass, Griffiths, Tonks, Henderson, Beats, Wood, Black. April 18; 48,836; Lieut Simpson

1897 **Aston Villa 3** (Campbell, Wheldon, Crabtree) Whitehouse; Spencer, Reynolds, Evans, Cowan, Crabtree, Athersmith, Devey, Campbell, Wheldon, Cowan **Everton 2** (Bell, Boyle) Menham; Meechan,

155

Storrier, Boyle, Holt, Stewart, Taylor, Bell, Hartley, Chadwick, Milward. April 10; 65,891; J Lewis

1898 Nottm Forest 3 (Capes 2, McPherson) Allsop; Ritchie, Scott, Forman, McPherson, Wragg, McInnes, Richards, Benbow, Capes, Spouncer **Derby 1** (Bloomer) Fryer; Methven, Leiper, Cox, Goodall, Bloomer, Boag, Stevenson, McQueen. April 16; 62,017; J Lewis

1899 Sheffield Utd 4 (Bennett, Beers, Almond, Priest) Foulke; Thickett, Boyle, Johnson, Morren, Needham, Bennett, Beers, Hedley, Almond, Priest **Derby 1** (Boag) Fryer; Methven, Staley, Cox, Paterson, May, Arkesden, Bloomer, Boag, McDonald, Allen. April 15; 73,833; A Scragg

1900 Bury 4 (McLuckie 2, Wood, Plant) Thompson; Darroch, Davidson, Pray, Leeming, Ross, Richards, Wood, McLuckie, Sagar, Plant **Southampton 0** Robinson; Meechan, Durber, Meston, Chadwick, Petrie, Turner, Yates, Farrell, Wood, Milward. April 21; 68,945; A Kingscott

1901 Tottenham 2 (Brown 2) Clawley; Erentz, Tait, Morris, Hughes, Jones, Smith, Cameron, Brown, Copeland, Kirwan **Sheffield Utd 2** (Priest, Bennett) Foulke; Thickett, Boyle, Johnson, Morren, Needham, Bennett, Field, Hedley, Priest, Lipsham. April 20; 110,820; A Kingscott **Replay – Tottenham 3** (Cameron, Smith, Brown) Clawley; Erentz, Tait, Morris, Hughes, Jones, Smith, Cameron, Brown, Copeland, Kirwan. **Sheffield Utd 1** (Priest) Foulke; Thickett, Boyle, Johnson, Morren, Needham, Bennett, Field, Hedley, Priest, Lipsham. April 27; 20,470; A Kingscott

1902 Sheffield Utd 1 (Common) Foulke; Thickett, Boyle, Needham, Wilkinson, Johnson, Bennett, Common, Hedley, Priest, Lipsham **Southampton 1** (Wood) Robinson; Fry, Molyneux, Meston, Bowman, Lee, Turner, Wood Brown, Chadwick, Turner. April 19; 76,914; T Kirkham. **Replay – Sheffield Utd 2** (Hedley, Barnes) Foulke; Thickett, Boyle, Needham, Wilkinson, Johnson, Barnes, Common, Hedley, Priest, Lipsham **Southampton 1** (Brown) Robinson; Fry, Molyneux, Meston, Bowman, Lee, Turner, Wood, Brown, Chadwick, Turner. April 26; 33,068; T Kirkham

1903 Bury 6 (Leeming 2, Ross, Sagar, Wood, Plant) Monteith; Lindsey, McEwen, Johnston, Thorpe, Ross, Richards, Wood, Sagar Leeming, Plant **Derby 0** Fryer; Methven, Morris, Warren, Goodall, May, Warrington, York, Boag, Richards, Davis. April 18; 63,102; J Adams

1904 Manchester City 1 (Meredith) Hillman; McMahon, Burgess, Frost, Hynds, Ashworth, Meredith, Livingstone, Gillespie, Turnbull, Booth **Bolton 0** Davies; Brown, Struthers, Clifford, Greenhalgh, Freebairn, Stokes, Marsh, Yenson, White, Taylor. April 23; 61,374; AJ Barker

1905 Aston Villa 2 (Hampton 2) George; Spencer, Miles, Pearson, Leake, Windmill, Brawn, Garratty, Hampton, Bache, Hall **Newcastle 0** Lawrence; McCombie, Carr, Gardner, Aitken, McWilliam, Rutherford, Howie, Appleyard, Veitch, Gosnell. April 15; 101,117; PR Harrower

1906 Everton 1 (Young) Scott; Crelley, W Balmer, Makepeace, Taylor, Abbott, Sharp, Bolton, Young, Settle, Hardman **Newcastle 0** Lawrence; McCombie, Carr, Gardner, Aitken, McWilliam, Rutherford, Howie, Orr, Veitch, Gosnell. April 21; 75,609; F Kirkham

1907 Sheffield Wed 2 (Stewart, Simpson) Lyall; Layton, Burton, Brittleton, Crawshaw, Bartlett, Chapman, Bradshaw, Wilson, Stewart, Simpson **Everton 1** (Sharp) Scott; W Balmer, B Balmer, Makepeace, Taylor, Abbott, Sharp, Bolton, Young, Settle, Hardman. April 20; 84,594; N Whittaker

1908 Wolves 3 (Hunt, Hedley, Harrison) Lunn; Jones, Collins, Rev Hunt, Wooldridge, Bishop, Harrison, Shelton, Hedley, Radford, Pedley **Newcastle 1** (Howie) Lawrence; McCracken, Pudan, Gardner, Veitch, McWilliam, Rutherford, Howie, Appleyard, Speedie, Wilson. April 25; 74,697; TP Campbell

1909 Manchester Utd 1 (Sandy Turnbull) Moger; Stacey, Hayes, Duckworth, Roberts, Bell, Meredith, Halse, J Turnbull, S Turnbull, Wall **Bristol City 0** Clay; Annan, Cottle, Hanlin, Wedlock, Spear, Staniforth, Hardy, Gilligan, Burton, Hilton. April 24; 71,401; J Mason

1910 Newcastle 1 (Rutherford) Lawrence; McCracken, Whitson, Veitch, Low, McWilliam, Rutherford, Howie, Higgins, Shepherd, Wilson **Barnsley 1** (Tufnell) Mearns; Downs, Ness, Glendinning, Boyle, Utley, Tufnell, Lillycrop, Gadsby, Forman, Bartrop. April 23; 77,747; JT Ibbotson **Replay – Newcastle 2** (Shepherd 2, 1pen) Lawrence; McCracken, Carr, Veitch, Low, McWilliam, Rutherford, Howie, Higgins, Shepherd, Wilson **Barnsley 0** Mearns; Downs, Ness, Glendinning, Boyle, Utley, Tufnell, Lillycrop, Gadsby, Forman, Bartrop. April 28; 69,000; JT Ibbotson.

1911 Bradford City 0 Mellors; Campbell, Taylor, Robinson, Gildea, McDonald, Logan, Speirs, O'Rourke, Devine, Thompson **Newcastle 0** Lawrence; McCracken, Whitson, Veitch, Low, Willis, Rutherford, Jobey, Stewart, Higgins, Wilson. April 22; 69,068; JH Pearson **Replay – Bradford City 1** (Speirs) Mellors; Campbell, Taylor, Robinson, Torrance, McDonald, Logan, Speirs, O'Rourke, Devine, Thompson **Newcastle 0** Lawrence; McCracken, Whitson, Veitch, Low, Willis, Rutherford, Jobey, Stewart, Higgins, Wilson. April 26; 58,000; JH Pearson

1912 Barnsley 0 Cooper; Downs, Taylor, Glendinning, Bratley, Utley, Bartrop, Tufnell, Lillycrop, Travers, Moore **WBA 0** Pearson; Cook, Pennington, Baddeley, Buck, McNeal, Jephcott, Wright, Pailor, Bowser, Shearman. April 20; 54,556; JR Shumacher **Replay – Barnsley 1** (Tufnell) Cooper; Downs, Taylor, Glendinning, Bratley, Utley, Bartrop, Harry, Lillycrop, Travers, Jimmy Moore **WBA 0** Pearson; Cook, Pennington, Baddeley, Buck, McNeal, Jephcott, Wright, Pailor, Bowser, Shearman. April 24; 38,555; JR Schumacher. aet

1913 Aston Villa 1 (Barber) Hardy; Lyons, Weston, Barber, Harrop, Leach, Wallace, Halse, Hampton, Stephenson, Bache **Sunderland 0** Butler; Gladwin, Ness, Cuggy, Thomson, Low, Mordue, Buchan, Richardson, Holley, Martin. April 19; 120,081; A Adams

1914 Burnley 1 (Freeman) Sewell; Bamford, Taylor, Halley, Boyle, Watson, Nesbit, Lindley, Freeman, Hodgson, Mosscrop **Liverpool 0** Campbell; Longworth, Pursell, Fairfoul, Ferguson, McKinley, Sheldon, Metcalfe, Miller, Lacey, Nicholl. April 25; 72,778; HS Bamlett

1915 Sheffield Utd 3 (Simmons, Fazackerly, Kitchen) Gough; Cook, English, Sturgess, Brelsford, Utley, Simmons, Fazackerly, Kitchen, Masterman, Evans **Chelsea 0** Molyneux; Bettridge, Harrow, Taylor, Logan, Walker, Ford, Halse, Thomson, Croal, McNeil. April 24; 49,557; HH Taylor

1920 Aston Villa 1 (Kirton) Hardy; Smart, Weston, Ducat, Barson, Moss, Wallace, Kirton, Walker, Stephenson, Dorrell **Huddersfield 0** Mutch; Wood, Bullock, Slade, Wilson, Watson, Richardson, Mann, Taylor, Swann, Islip. April 24; 50,018; JT Howcroft. aet

1921 Tottenham 1 (Dimmock) Hunter; Clay, McDonald, Smith, Walters, Grimsdell, Banks, Seed, Cantrell, Bliss, Dimmock **Wolves 0** George; Woodward, Marshall, Gregory, Hodnett, Riley, Lea, Burrill, Edmonds, Potts, Brooks. April 23; 72,805; S Davies

1922 Huddersfield 1 (Smith pen) Mutch; Wood, Wadsworth, Slade, Wilson, Watson, Richardson, Mann, Islip, Stephenson, Billy Smith **Preston 0** Mitchell; Hamilton, Doolan, Duxbury, McCall, Williamson, Rawlings, Jefferis, Roberts, Woodhouse, Quinn. April 29; 53,000; JWP Fowler

1923 Bolton 2 (Jack, JR Smith) Pym; Haworth, Finney, Nuttall, Seddon, Jennings, Butler, Jack, JR Smith, Joe Smith, Vizard **West Ham 0** Hufton; Henderson, Young, Bishop, Kay, Tresadern, Richards, Brown, Watson, Moore, Ruffell. April 28; 126,047; DH Asson

1924 Newcastle 2 (Harris, Seymour) Bradley; Hampson, Hudspeth, Mooney, Spencer, Gibson, Low, Cowan, Harris, McDonald, Seymour **Aston Villa 0** Jackson; Smart, Mort, Moss, Milne, Blackburn, York, Kirton, Capewell, Walker, Dorrell. April 26; 91,695; WE Russell

1925 Sheffield Utd 1 (Tunstall) Sutcliffe; Cook, Milton, Pantling, King, Green, Mercer, Boyle, Johnson, Gillespie, Tunstall **Cardiff 0** Farquharson; Nelson, Blair, Wake, Keenor, Hardy, Davies, Gill, Nicholson, Beadles, Evans. April 25; 91,763; GN Watson

1926 Bolton 1 (Jack) Pym; Haworth, Greenhalgh, Nuttall, Seddon, Jennings, Butler, JR Smith, Jack, Joe Smith, Vizard **Manchester City 0** Goodchild; Cookson, McCloy, Pringle, Cowan, McMullan, Austin, Browell, Roberts, Johnson, Hicks. April 24; 91,447; I Baker

1927 Cardiff 1 (Ferguson) Farquharson; Nelson, Watson, Keenor, Sloan, Hardy, Curtis, Irving, Ferguson, Davies, McLachlan **Arsenal 0** Lewis; Parker, Kennedy, Baker, Butler, John, Hulme, Buchan, Brain, Blythe, Hoar. April 23; 91,206; WF Bunnell

1928 Blackburn 3 (Roscamp 2, McLean) Crawford; Hutton, Jones, Healless, Rankin, Campbell, Thornewell, Puddefoot, Roscamp, McLean, Rigby **Huddersfield 1** (Jackson) Mercer; Goodall, Barkas,

Redfern, Wilson, Steele, Jackson, Kelly, Brown, Stephenson, Smith. April 21; 92,041; TG Bryan

1929 Bolton 2 (Butler, Blackmore) Pym; Haworth, Finney, Kean, Seddon, Nuttall, Butler, McClelland, Blackmore, Gibson, Cook **Portsmouth 0** Gilfillan; Mackie, Bell, Nichol, McIlwaine, Thackeray, Forward, Smith, Weddle, Watson, Cook. April 27; 92,576; A Josephs

1930 Arsenal 2 (James, Lambert) Preedy; Parker, Hapgood, Baker, Seddon, John, Hulme, Jack, Lambert, James, Bastin **Huddersfield 0** Turner; Goodall, Spence, Naylor, Wilson, Campbell, Jackson, Kelly, Davies, Raw, Smith. April 26; 92,488; T Crew

1931 WBA 2 (WG Richardson 2) Pearson; Shaw, Trentham, Magee, Bill Richardson, Edwards, Glidden, Carter, WG Richardson, Sandford, Wood **Birmingham 1** (Bradford) Hibbs; Liddell, Barkas, Cringan, Morrall, Leslie, Briggs, Crosbie, Bradford, Gregg, Curtis. April 25; 92,406; AH Kingscott

1932 Newcastle 2 (Allen 2) McInroy; Nelson, Fairhurst, McKenzie, Davidson, Weaver, Boyd, Richardson, Allen, McMenemy, Lang **Arsenal 1** (John) Moss; Parker, Hapgood, Jones, Roberts, Male, Hulme, Jack, Lambert, Bastin, John. April 23; 92,298; WP Harper

1933 Everton 3 (Stein, Dean, Dunn) Sagar; Cook, Cresswell, Britton, White, Thomson, Geldard, Dunn, Dean, Johnson, Stein **Manchester City 0** Langford; Cann, Dale, Busby, Cowan, Bray, Toseland, Marshall, Herd, McMullan, Eric Brook. April 29; 92,950; E Wood

1934 Manchester City 2 (Tilson 2) Swift; Barnett, Dale, Busby, Cowan, Bray, Toseland, Marshall, Tilson, Herd, Brook **Portsmouth 1** (Rutherford) Gilfillan; Mackie, Smith, Nichol, Allen, Thackeray, Worrall, Smith, Weddle, Easson, Rutherford. April 28; 93,258; Stanley Rous

1935 Sheffield Wed 4 (Rimmer 2, Palethorpe, Hooper) Brown; Nibloe, Catlin, Sharp, Millership, Burrows, Hooper, Surtees, Palethorpe, Starling, Rimmer **WBA 2** (Boyes, Sandford) Pearson; Shaw, Trentham, Murphy, Bill Richardson, Edwards, Glidden, Carter, WG Richardson, Sandford, Wally. April 27; 93,204; AE Fogg

1936 Arsenal 1 (Drake) Wilson; Male, Hapgood, Crayston, Roberts, Copping, Hulme, Bowden, Drake, James, Bastin **Sheffield Utd 0** Smith; Hooper, Wilkinson, Jackson, Johnson, McPherson, Barton, Barclay, Dodds, Pickering, Williams. April 25; 93,384; H Nattrass

1937 Sunderland 3 (Gurney, Carter, Burbanks) Mapson; Gorman, Hall, Thomson, Johnston, McNab, Duns, Carter, Gurney, Gallacher, Burbanks **Preston 1** (Frank O'Donnell) Burns; Gallimore, Beattie, Shankly, Tremelling, Milne, Dougal, Beresford, O'Donnell, Fagan, O'Donnell. May 1; 93,495; RG Rudd

1938 Preston 1 (Mutch pen) Holdcroft; Gallimore, Beattie, Shankly, Smith, Batey, Watmough, Mutch, Maxwell, Beattie, O'Donnell **Huddersfield 0** Hesford; Craig, Mountford, Willingham, Young, Boot, Hulme, Issac, MacFadyen, Barclay, Beasley. April 30; 93,497; AJ Jewell. aet

1939 Portsmouth 4 (Parker 2, Barlow, Anderson) Walker; Morgan, Rochford, Guthrie, Rowe, Wharton, Worrall, McAlinden, Anderson, Barlow, Parker **Wolves 1** (Dorsett) Scott; Morris, Taylor, Galley, Cullis, Gardiner, Burton, McIntosh, Westcott, Dorsett, Maguire. April 29; 99,370; T Thompson

1946 Derby 4 (Stamps 2. Doherty, B Turner og) Woodley; Nicholas, Howe, Bullions, Leuty, Musson, Harrison, Carter, Stamps, Doherty, Duncan **Charlton Athletic 1** (B Turner) Bartram; Phipps, Shreeve, Turner, Oakes, Johnson, Fell, Brown, Turner, Welsh, Duffy. April 27; 98,000; ED Smith. aet

1947 Charlton Athletic 1 (Duffy) Bartram; Croker, Shreeve, Johnson, Phipps, Whittaker, Hurst, Dawson, Robinson, Welsh, Duffy **Burnley 0** Strong; Woodruff, Mather, Attwell, Brown, Bray, Chew, Morris, Harrison, Potts, Kippax. April 26; 99,000; JM Wiltshire. aet

1948 Manchester Utd 4 (Rowley 2, Pearson, Anderson) Crompton; Carey, Aston, Anderson, Chilton, Cockburn, Delaney, Morris, Rowley, Pearson, Mitten **Blackpool 2** (Shimwell pen, Mortensen) Robinson; Shimwell, Crosland, Johnston, Hayward, Kelly, Matthews, Munro, Mortensen, Dick, Rickett. April 24; 99,000; CJ Barrick

1949 Wolves 3 (Pye 2, Smyth) Williams; Pritchard, Springthorpe Crook, Shorthouse, Wright, Hancocks, Smyth, Pye, Dunn, Mullen **Leicester 1** (Griffiths) Bradley; Jelly, Scott, Harrison, Plummer, King,

158

Griffiths, Lee, Harrison, Chisholm, Adam. April 30; 99,500; RA Mortimer

1950 **Arsenal 2** (Lewis 2) Swindin; Scott, Barnes, Forbes, L Compton, Mercer, Cox, Logie, Goring, Lewis, D Compton **Liverpool 0** Sidlow; Lambert, Spicer, Taylor, Hughes, Jones, Payne, Baron, Stubbins, Fagan, Liddell. April 29; 100,000; H Pearce

1951 **Newcastle 2** (Milburn 2) Fairbrother; Cowell, Corbett, Harvey, Brennan, Crowe, Walker, Taylor, Milburn, Jorge Robledo, Mitchell **Blackpool 0** Farm; Shimwell, Garrett, Johnston, Hayward, Kelly, Matthews, Mudie, Mortensen, Slater, Perry. April 28; 100,000; W Ling

1952 **Newcastle 1** (G Robledo) Simpson; Cowell, McMichael, Harvey, Brennan, Eduardo Robledo, Walker, Foulkes, Milburn, Jorge Robledo, Mitchell **Arsenal 0** Swindin; Barnes, Smith, Forbes, Daniel Mercer, Cox, Logie, Holton, Lishman, Roper. May 3; 100,000; A Ellis

1953 **Blackpool 4** (Mortensen 3, Perry) Farm; Shimwell, Garrett, Fenton, Johnston, Robinson, Matthews, Taylor, Mortensen, Mudie, Perry **Bolton 3** (Lofthouse, Moir, Bell) Hanson; Ball, Banks, Wheeler, Barrass, Bell, Holden, Moir, Lofthouse, Hassall, Langton. May 2; 100,000; M Griffiths

1954 **WBA 3** (Allen 2 [1pen], Griffin) Sanders; Kennedy, Millard, Dudley, Dugdale, Barlow, Griffin, Ryan, Allen, Nicholls, Lee **Preston 2** (Morrison, Wayman) Thompson; Cunningham, Walton, Docherty, Marston, Forbes, Finney, Foster, Wayman, Baxter, Morrison. May 1; 100,000; A Luty

1955 **Newcastle 3** (Milburn, Mitchell, Hannah) Simpson; Cowell, Batty, Scoular, Stokoe, Casey, White, Milburn, Keeble, Hannah, Mitchell **Manchester City 1** (Johnstone) Trautmann; Meadows, Little, Barnes, Ewing, Paul, Spurdle, Hayes, Revie, Johnstone, Fagan. May 7; 100,000; R Leafe

1956 **Manchester City 3** (Hayes, Dyson, Johnstone) Trautmann; Leivers, Little, Barnes, Ewing, Paul, Johnstone, Hayes, Revie, Dyson, Clarke **Birmingham 1** (Kinsey) Merrick; Hall, Green, Newman, Smith, Boyd, Astall, Kinsey, Brown, Murphy, Govan. May 5; 100,000; A Bond

1957 **Aston Villa 2** (McParland 2) Sims; Lynn, Aldis, Crowther, Dugdale, Saward, Smith, Sewell, Myerscough, Dixon, McParland **Manchester Utd 1** (Taylor) Wood; Foulkes, Byrne, Colman, Blanchflower, Edwards, Berry, Whelan, Taylor, Charlton, Pegg. May 4; 100,000; F Coultas

1958 **Bolton 2** (Lofthouse 2) Hopkinson; Hartle, Banks, Hennin, Higgins, Edwards, Birch, Stevens, Lofthouse, Parry, Holden **Manchester Utd 0** Gregg; Foulkes, Greaves, Goodwin, Cope, Crowther, Dawson, Taylor, Charlton, Viollet, Webster. May 3; 100,000; J Sherlock

1959 **Nottingham Forest 2** (Dwight, Wilson) Thomson; Whare, McDonald, Whitefoot, McKinlay, Burkitt, Dwight, Quigley, Wilson, Gray, Imlach **Luton Town 1** (Pacey) Baynham; McNally, Hawkes, Groves, Owen, Pacey, Bingham, Brown, Morton, Cummins, Gregory. May 2; 100,000; J Clough

1960 **Wolves 3** (McGrath og, Deeley 2) Finlayson; Showell, Harris, Clamp, Slater, Flowers, Deeley, Stobart, Murray, Broadbent, Horne **Blackburn 0** Leyland; Bray, Whelan, Clayton, Woods, McGrath, Bimpson, Dobing, Dougan, Douglas, McLeod. May 7; 100,000; K Howley

1961 **Tottenham 2** (Smith, Dyson) Brown; Baker, Henry, Blanchflower, Norman, Mackay, Jones, White, Smith, Allen, Dyson **Leicester 0** Banks; Chalmers, Norman, McLintock, King, Appleton, Riley, Walsh, McIlmoyle, Keyworth, Cheesebrough. May 6; 100,000; J Kelly

1962 **Tottenham 3** (Greaves, Smith, Blanchflower pen) Brown; Baker, Henry, Blanchflower, Norman, Mackay, Medwin, White, Smith, Greaves, Jones **Burnley 1** (Robson) Blacklaw; Angus, Elder, Adamson, Cummings, Miller, Connelly, McIlroy, Pointer, Robson, Harris. May 5; 100,000; J Finney

1963 **Manchester Utd 3** (Law, Herd 2) Gaskell; Dunne, Cantwell, Crerand, Foulkes, Setters, Giles, Quixall, Herd, Law, Charlton **Leicester 1** (Keyworth) Banks; Sjoberg, Norman, McLintock, King, Appleton, Riley, Cross, Keyworth, Gibson, Stringfellow. May 25; 100,000; K Aston

1964 **West Ham 3** (Sissons, Hurst, Boyce) Standen; Bond, Burkett, Bovington, Brown, Moore, Brabrook, Boyce, Byrne, Hurst, Sissons **Preston 2** (Holden, Dawson) Kelly; Ross, Lawton, Smith, Singleton,

Kendall, Wilson, Ashworth, Dawson, Spavin, Holden. May 2; 100,000; A Holland

1965 **Liverpool 2** (Hunt, St John) Lawrence; Lawler, Byrne, Strong, Yeats, Stevenson, Callaghan, Hunt, St John, Smith, Thompson **Leeds 1** (Bremner) Sprake; Reaney, Bell, Bremner, Charlton, Hunter, Giles, Storrie, Peacock, Collins, Johanneson. May 1; 100,000; W Clements. aet

1966 **Everton 3** (Trebilcock 2, Temple) West; Wright, Wilson, Gabriel, Labone, Harris, Scott, Trebilcock, Young, Harvey, Temple **Sheffield Wed 2** (McCalliog, Ford) Springett; Smith, Megson, Eustace, Ellis, Young, Pugh, Fantham, McCalliog, Ford, Quinn. May 14; 100,000; JK Taylor

1967 **Tottenham 2** (Robertson, Saul) Jennings; Kinnear, Knowles, Mullery, England, Mackay, Robertson, Greaves, Gilzean, Venables, Saul. Unused sub: Jones **Chelsea 1** (Tambling) Bonetti; Allan Harris, McCreadie, Hollins, Hinton, Ron Harris, Cooke, Baldwin, Hateley, Tambling, Boyle. Unused sub: Kirkup. May 20; 100,000; K Dagnall

1968 **WBA 1** (Astle) John Osborne; Fraser, Williams, Brown, Talbut, Kaye, Lovett, Collard, Astle Hope, Clark Sub: Clarke rep Kaye 91 **Everton 0** West; Wright, Wilson, Kendall, Labone, Harvey, Husband, Ball, Royle, Hurst, Morrissey. Unused sub: Kenyon. May 18; 100,000; L Callaghan. aet

1969 **Manchester City 1** (Young) Dowd; Book, Pardoe, Doyle, Booth, Oakes, Summerbee, Bell, Lee, Young, Coleman. Unused sub: Connor **Leicester 0** Shilton; Rodrigues, Nish, Roberts, Woollett, Cross, Fern, Gibson, Lochhead, Clarke, Glover. Sub: Manley rep Glover 70. April 26; 100,000; G McCabe

1970 **Chelsea 2** (Houseman, Hutchinson) Bonetti; Webb, McCreadie, Hollins, Dempsey, R Harris, Baldwin, Houseman, Osgood, Hutchinson, Cooke. Sub: Hinton rep Harris 91 **Leeds 2** (Charlton, Jones) Sprake; Madeley, Cooper, Bremner, Charlton, Hunter, Lorimer, Clarke, Jones, Giles, Gray Unused sub: Bates. April 11; 100,000; E Jennings. aet **Replay – Chelsea 2** (Osgood, Webb) Bonetti; Webb, McCreadie, Hollins, Dempsey, R Harris, Baldwin, Houseman, Osgood, Hutchinson, Cooke. Sub: Hinton rep Osgood 105 **Leeds 1** (Jones) Harvey; Madeley, Cooper, Bremner, Charlton, Hunter, Lorimer, Clarke, Jones, Giles, Gray Unused sub: Bates. April 29; 62,078; E Jennings. aet

1971 **Arsenal 2** (Kelly, George) Wilson; Rice, McNab, Storey, McLintock Simpson, Armstrong, Graham, Radford, Kennedy, George. Sub: Kelly rep Storey 70 **Liverpool 1** (Heighway) Clemence; Lawler, Lindsay, Smith, Lloyd, Hughes, Callaghan, Evans, Heighway, Toshack, Hall. Sub: Thompson rep Evans 70. May 8; 100,000; N Burtenshaw. aet

1972 **Leeds 1** (Clarke) Harvey; Reaney, Madeley, Bremner, Charlton, Hunter, Lorimer, Clarke, Jones, Giles, Gray. Unused sub: Bates **Arsenal 0** Barnett; Rice, McNab, Storey, McLintock, Simpson, Armstrong, Ball, George, Radford, Graham. Sub: Kennedy rep Radford 80. May 6; 100,000; DW Smith

1973 **Sunderland 1** (Porterfield) Montgomery; Malone, Guthrie, Horswill, Watson, Pitt, Kerr, Hughes, Halom, Porterfield, Tueart. Unused sub: Young **Leeds 0** Harvey; Reaney, Cherry, Bremner, Madeley, Hunter, Lorimer, Clarke, Jones, Giles, Gray. Sub: Yorath rep Gray 75. May 5; 100,000; K Burns

1974 **Liverpool 3** (Keegan 2, Heighway) Clemence; Smith, Lindsay, Thompson, Cormack, Hughes, Keegan, Hall, Heighway, Toshack, Callaghan. Unused sub: Lawler **Newcastle 0** McFaul; Clark, Kennedy, McDermott, Howard, Moncur, Smith, Cassidy, Macdonald, Tudor, Hibbitt. Sub: Gibb rep Smith 70. May 4; 100,000; GC Kew

1975 **West Ham 2** (Taylor 2) Day; McDowell, Taylor, Lock, Lampard, Bonds, Paddon, Brooking, Jennings, Taylor, Holland. Unused sub: Gould **Fulham 0** Mellor; Cutbush, Lacy, Moore, Fraser, Mullery, Conway, Slough, Mitchell, Busby, Barrett. Unused sub: Lloyd. May 3; 100,000; P Partridge

1976 **Southampton 1** (Stokes) Turner; Rodrigues, Peach, Holmes, Blyth, Steele, Gilchrist, Channon, Osgood, McCalliog, Stokes. Unused sub: Fisher **Manchester Utd 0** Stepney; Forsyth, Houston, Daly, Greenhoff, Buchan, Coppell, McIlroy, Pearson, Macari, Hill. Sub: McCreery rep Hill 66. May 1; 100,000; C Thomas

1977 **Manchester Utd 2** (Pearson, J Greenhoff) Stepney; Nicholl, Albiston, McIlroy, B Greenhoff, Buchan, Coppell, J Greenhoff, Pearson, Macari, Hill. Sub: McCreery rep Hill 81 **Liverpool 1** (Case)

Clemence; Neal, Jones, Smith, Kennedy, Hughes, Keegan, Case, Heighway, Johnson, McDermott. Sub: Callaghan rep Johnson 64. May 21; 100,000; R Matthewson

1978 **Ipswich Town 1** (Osborne) Cooper; Burley, Mills, Talbot, Hunter, Beattie, Osborne, Wark, Mariner, Geddis, Woods. Sub: Lambert rep Osborne 79 **Arsenal 0** Jennings; Rice, Nelson, Price, Young, O'Leary, Brady, Hudson, Macdonald, Stapleton, Sunderland. Sub: Rix rep Brady 65. May 6; 100,000; D Nippard

1979 **Arsenal 3** (Talbot, Stapleton, Sunderland) Jennings; Rice, Nelson, Talbot, O'Leary, Young, Brady, Sunderland, Stapleton, Price, Rix. Sub: Walford rep Rix 83 **Manchester Utd 2** (McQueen, McIlroy) Bailey; Nicholl, Albiston, McIlroy, McQueen, Buchan, Coppell, J Greenhoff, Jordan, Macari, Thomas. Unused sub: Greenhoff. May 12; 100,000; R Challis

1980 **West Ham 1** (Brooking) Parkes; Stewart, Lampard, Bonds, Martin, Devonshire, Allen, Pearson, Cross, Brooking, Pike. Unused sub: Brush **Arsenal 0** Jennings; Rice, Devine, Talbot, O'Leary, Young, Brady, Sunderland, Stapleton, Price, Rix. Sub: Nelson rep Devine 61. May 10; 100,000; G Courtney

1981 **Tottenham 1** (Hutchinson og) Aleksic; Hughton, Miller, Roberts, Perryman, Villa, Ardiles, Archibald, Galvin, Hoddle, Crooks. Sub: Brooke rep Villa 68. **Manchester City 1** (Hutchinson) Corrigan; Ranson, McDonald, Reid, Power, Caton, Bennett, Gow, Mackenzie, Hutchison Reeves. Sub: Henry rep Hutchison 82. May 9; 100,000; K Hackett. aet **Replay – Tottenham 3** (Villa 2, Crooks) Aleksic; Hughton, Miller, Roberts, Perryman, Villa, Ardiles, Archibald, Galvin, Hoddle, Crooks. Unused sub: Brooke **Manchester City 2** (Mackenzie, Reeves pen) Corrigan; Ranson, McDonald, Reid, Power, Caton, Bennett, Gow, Mackenzie, Hutchison Reeves. Sub: Tueart rep McDonald 79. May 14; 92,000; K Hackett

1982 **Tottenham 1** (Hoddle) Clemence; Hughton, Miller, Price, Hazard, Perryman, Roberts, Archibald, Galvin, Hoddle, Crooks. Sub: Brooke rep Hazard 104 **Queens Park Rangers 1** (Fenwick) Hucker; Fenwick, Gillard, Waddock, Hazell, Roeder, Currie, Flanagan, Allen, Stainrod, Gregory. Sub: Micklewhite rep Allen 50. May 22; 100,000; C White. aet **Replay – Tottenham 1** (Hoddle pen) Clemence; Hughton, Miller, Price, Hazard, Perryman, Roberts, Archibald, Galvin, Hoddle, Crooks. Sub: Brooke rep Hazard 67 **Queens Park Rangers 0** Hucker; Fenwick, Gillard, Waddock, Hazell, Neill, Currie, Flanagan, Micklewhite, Stainrod, Gregory. Sub: Burke rep Micklewhite 84. May 27; 90,000; C White

1983 **Manchester Utd 2** (Stapleton, Wilkins) Bailey; Duxbury, Moran, McQueen, Albiston, Davies, Wilkins, Robson, Muhren, Stapleton, Whiteside. Unused sub: Grimes **Brighton 2** (Smith, Stevens) Moseley; Ramsey, Gary A Stevens, Pearce, Gatting, Smillie, Case, Grealish, Howlett, Robinson, Smith. Sub: Ryan rep Ramsey 56. May 21; 100,000; AW Grey, aet **Replay – Manchester Utd 4** (Robson 2, Whiteside, Muhren pen) Bailey; Duxbury, Moran, McQueen, Albiston, Davies, Wilkins, Robson, Muhren, Stapleton, Whiteside. Unused sub: Grimes **Brighton 0** Moseley; Gary A Stevens, Pearce, Foster, Gatting, Smillie, Case, Grealish, Howlett, Robinson, Smith. Sub: Ryan rep Howlett 74. May 26; 100,000; AW Grey

1984 **Everton 2** (Sharp, Gray) Southall; Gary M Stevens, Bailey, Ratcliffe, Mountfield, Reid, Steven, Heath, Sharp, Gray, Richardson. Unused sub: Harper **Watford 0** Sherwood; Bardsley, Price, Taylor, Terry, Sinnott, Callaghan, Johnston, Reilly, Jackett, Barnes. Sub: Atkinson rep Price 58. May 19; 100,000; J Hunting

1985 **Manchester Utd 1** (Whiteside) Bailey; Gidman, Albiston, Whiteside, McGrath, Moran, Robson, Strachan, Hughes, Stapleton, Olsen. Sub: Duxbury rep Albiston 91. Moran sent off 77. **Everton 0** Southall; Gary M Stevens, Van den Hauwe, Ratcliffe, Mountfield, Reid, Steven, Sharp, Gray, Bracewell, Sheedy. Unused sub: Harper. May 18; 100,000; P Willis. aet

1986 **Liverpool 3** (Rush 2, Johnston) Grobbelaar; Lawrenson, Beglin, Nicol, Whelan, Hansen, Dalglish, Johnston, Rush, Molby, MacDonald. Sub: McMahon **Everton 1** (Lineker) Mimms; Gary M Stevens, Van den Hauwe, Ratcliffe, Mountfield, Reid, Steven, Lineker, Sharp, Bracewell, Sheedy. Sub: Heath rep Stevens 65. May 10; 98,000; A Robinson

1987 **Coventry City 3** (Bennett, Houchen, Mabbutt og) Ogrizovic; Phillips, Downs, McGrath, Kilcline, Peake, Bennett, Gynn, Regis, Houchen, Pickering. Sub: Rodger rep Kilcline 88. Unused sub: Sedgley **Tottenham 2** (Allen, Mabbutt) Clemence; Hughton Thomas, Hodge, Gough, Mabbutt, C Allen, P Allen,

Waddle, Hoddle, Ardiles. Subs: Gary A Stevens rep Ardiles 91; Claesen rep Hughton 97. May 16; 98,000; N Midgley. aet

1988 **Wimbledon 1** (Sanchez) Beasant; Goodyear, Phelan, Jones, Young, Thorn, Gibson Cork, Fashanu, Sanchez, Wise. Subs: Cunningham rep Cork 56; Scales rep Gibson 63 **Liverpool 0** Grobbelaar; Gillespie, Ablett, Nicol, Spackman, Hansen, Beardsley, Aldridge, Houghton, Barnes, McMahon. Subs: Johnston rep Aldridge 63; Molby rep Spackman 72. May 14; 98,203; B Hill

1989 **Liverpool 3** (Aldridge, Rush 2) Grobbelaar; Ablett, Staunton, Nichol, Whelan, Hansen, Beardsley, Aldridge Houghton, Barnes, McMahon. Subs: Rush rep Aldridge 72; Venison rep Staunton 91 **Everton 2** (McCall 2) Southall; McDonald, Van den Hauwe, Ratcliffe, Watson, Bracewell, Nevin, Trevor Steven, Cottee, Sharp, Sheedy. Subs: McCall rep Bracewell 58; Wilson rep Sheedy 77. May 20; 82,500; J Worrall. aet

1990 **Manchester Utd 3** (Robson, Hughes 2) Leighton; Ince, Martin, Bruce, Phelan, Pallister, Robson, Webb, McClair, Hughes, Wallace. Subs: Blackmore rep Martin 88; Robins rep Pallister 93. **Crystal Palace 3** (O'Reilly, Wright 2) Martyn; Pemberton, Shaw, Gray, O'Reilly, Thorn, Barber, Thomas, Bright, Salako, Pardew. Subs: Wright rep Barber 69; Madden rep Gray 117. May 12; 80,000; A Gunn. aet **Replay – Manchester Utd 1** (Martin) Sealey; Ince, Martin, Bruce, Phelan, Pallister, Robson, Webb, McClair, Hughes, Wallace. Unused subs: Robins, Blackmore **Crystal Palace 0** Martyn; Pemberton, Shaw, Gray, O'Reilly, Thorn, Barber, Thomas, Bright, Salako, Pardew. Subs: Wright rep Barber 64; Madden rep Salako 79. May 17; 80,000; A Gunn

1991 **Tottenham 2** (Stewart, Walker og) Thorstvedt; Edinburgh, Van den Hauwe, Sedgley, Howells, Mabbutt, Stewart, Gascoigne, Samways, Lineker, Allen. Subs: Nayim rep Gascoigne 18; Walsh rep Samways 82. **Nottingham Forest 1** (Pearce) Crossley; Charles, Pearce, Walker, Chettle, Keane, Crosby, Parker, Clough, Glover, Woan. Subs: Hodge rep Woan 62; Laws rep Glover 108. May 18; 80,000; R Milford. aet

1992 **Liverpool 2** (Thomas, Rush) Grobbelaar; Jones, Burrows, Nicol, Molby, Wright, Saunders, Houghton, Rush, McManaman, Thomas. Unused subs: Marsh, Walters **Sunderland 0** Norman; Owers, Ball, Bennett, Rogan, Rush, Bracewell, Davenport, Armstrong, Byrne, Atkinson. Subs: Hardyman rep Rush 69; Hawke rep Armstrong 77. May 9; 80,000; P Don

1993 **Arsenal 1** (Wright) Seaman; Dixon, Winterburn, Linighan, Adams, Jensen, Davis, Parlour, Merson, Campbell, Wright. Subs: Smith rep Parlour 66; O'Leary rep Wright 90. **Sheffield Wed 1** (Hirst) Woods; Nilsson Worthington, Palmer, Hirst, Anderson, Waddle, Warhurst, Bright, Sheridan, Harkes. Subs: Hyde rep Anderson 85; Bart-Williams rep Waddle 112. May 15; 79,347; K Barratt. aet **Replay – Arsenal 2** (Wright, Linighan) Seaman; Dixon, Winterburn, Linighan, Adams, Jensen, Davis, Smith, Merson, Campbell, Wright. Subs: O'Leary rep Wright 81. Unused sub: Selley **Sheffield Wed 1** (Waddle) Woods; Nilsson, Worthington, Palmer, Hirst, Wilson, Waddle, Warhurst, Bright, Sheridan, Harkes. Subs: Hyde rep Wilson 62; Bart-Williams rep Nilsson 118. May 20; 62,267; K Barratt. aet

1994 **Manchester Utd 4** (Cantona 2 [2pens], Hughes, McClair) Schmeichel; Parker, Bruce, Pallister, Irwin, Kanchelskis, Keane, Ince, Giggs, Cantona, Hughes. Subs: Sharpe rep Irwin 84; McClair rep Kanchelskis 84. Unused sub: Walsh (gk) **Chelsea 0** Kharine; Clarke, Sinclair, Kjeldberg, Johnsen, Burley, Spencer, Newton, Stein, Peacock, Wise Substitutions Hoddle rep Burley 65; Cascarino rep Stein 78. Unused sub: Kevin Hitchcock (gk) May 14; 79,634; D Elleray

1995 **Everton 1** (Rideout) Southall; Jackson, Hinchcliffe, Ablett, Watson, Parkinson, Unsworth, Horne, Stuart, Rideout, Limpar. Subs: Ferguson rep Rideout 51; Amokachi rep Limpar 69. Unused sub: Kearton (gk) **Manchester Utd 0** Schmeichel; Neville, Irwin, Bruce, Sharpe, Pallister, Keane, Ince, Brian McClair, Hughes, Butt. Subs: Giggs rep Bruce 46; Scholes rep Sharpe 72. Unused sub: Gary Walsh (gk) May 20; 79,592; G Ashby

1996 **Manchester Utd 1** (Cantona) Schmeichel; Irwin, P Neville, May, Keane, Pallister, Cantona, Beckham, Cole, Butt, Giggs. Subs: Scholes rep Cole 65; G Neville rep Beckham 89. Unused sub: Sharpe **Liverpool 0** James; McAteer, Scales, Wright, Babb, Jones, McManaman, Barnes, Redknapp, Collymore, Fowler. Subs: Rush rep Collymore 74; Thomas rep Jones 85. Unused sub: Warner (gk) May 11; 79,007; D Gallagher

1997 **Chelsea 2** (Di Matteo, Newton) Grodas; Petrescu, Minto, Sinclair, Lebouef, Clarke, Zola, Di Matteo, Newton, Hughes, Wise. Sub: Vialli rep Zola 89. Unused subs: Hitchcock (gk), Myers **Middlesbrough 0** Roberts; Blackmore, Fleming, Stamp, Pearson, Festa, Emerson, Mustoe, Ravanelli, Juninho, Hignett. Subs: Beck rep Ravanelli 24; Vickers rep Mustoe 29; Kinder, rep Hignett 74. May 17; 79,160; S Lodge

1998 **Arsenal 2** (Overmars, Anelka) Seaman; Dixon, Winterburn, Vieira, Keown, Adams, Parlour, Anelka, Petit, Wreh, Overmars. Sub: Platt rep Wreh 63. Unused subs: Manninger (gk); Bould, Wright, Grimandi **Newcastle 0** Given; Pistone, Pearce, Batty, Dabizas, Howey, Lee, Barton, Shearer, Ketsbaia, Speed. Subs: Andersson rep Pearce 72; Watson rep Barton 77; Barnes rep Ketsbaia 85. Unused subs: Hislop (gk); Albert. May 16; 79,183; P Durkin

1999 **Manchester Utd 2** (Sheringham, Scholes) Schmeichel; G Neville, Johnsen, May, P Neville, Beckham, Scholes, Keane, Giggs, Cole, Solskjaer. Subs: Sheringham rep Keane 9; Yorke rep Cole 61; Stam rep Scholes 77. Unused subs: Blomqvist, Van Der Gouw **Newcastle 0** Harper; Griffin, Charvet, Dabizas, Domi, Lee, Hamann, Speed, Solano, Ketsbaia, Shearer. Subs: Ferguson rep Hamann 46; Maric rep Solano 68; Glass rep Ketsbaia 79. Unused subs: Given (gk); Barton. May 22; 79,101; P Jones

2000 **Chelsea 1** (Di Matteo) de Goey; Melchiot Desailly, Lebouef, Babayaro, Di Matteo, Wise, Deschamps, Poyet, Weah, Zola. Subs: Flo rep Weah 87; Morris rep Zola 90. Unused subs: Cudicini (gk), Terry , Harley **Aston Villa 0** James; Ehiogu, Southgate, Barry, Delaney, Taylor, Boateng, Merson, Wright, Dublin, Carbone. Subs: Stone rep Taylor 79; Joachim rep Carbone 79; Hendrie rep Wright 88. Unused subs: Enckelman (gk); Samuel May 20; 78,217; G Poll

2001 **Liverpool 2** (Owen 2) Westerveld; Babbel, Henchoz, Hyypia, Carragher, Murphy, Hamann, Gerrard, Smicer, Heskey, Owen. Subs: McAllister rep Hamann 60; Fowler rep Smicer 77; Berger rep Murphy 77. Unused subs: Arphexad (gk); Vignal **Arsenal 1** (Ljungberg) Seaman; Dixon, Keown, Adams, Cole, Ljungberg, Grimandi, Vieira, Pires, Henry, Wiltord Subs: Parlour rep Wiltord 76; Kanu rep Ljungberg 85; Bergkamp rep Dixon 90. Unused subs: Manninger (gk); Lauren. May 12; 72,500; S Dunn

2002 **Arsenal 2** (Parlour, Ljungberg) Seaman; Lauren, Campbell, Adams, Cole, Parlour, Wiltord, Vieira, Ljungberg, Bergkamp, Henry Subs: Edu rep Bergkamp 72; Kanu rep Henry 81; Keown rep Wiltord 90. Unused subs: Wright (gk); Dixon **Chelsea 0** Cudicini; Melchiot, Desailly, Gallas, Babayaro, Gronkjaer, Lampard, Petit, Le Saux, Floyd Hasselbaink, Gudjohnsen. Subs: Terry rep Babayaro 46; Zola rep Hasselbaink 68; Zenden rep Melchiot 77. Unused subs: de Goey (gk); Jokanovic. May 4; 73,963; M Riley

2003 **Arsenal 1** (Pires) Seaman; Lauren, Luzhny, Keown, Cole, Ljungberg, Parlour, Gilberto, Pires, Bergkamp, Henry. Sub: Wiltord rep Bergkamp 77. Unused subs: Taylor (gk); Kanu, Toure, van Bronckhorst **Southampton 0** Niemi; Baird, Svensson, Lundekvam, Bridge, Telfer, Svensson, Oakley, Marsden, Beattie, Ormerod. Subs: Jones rep Niemi 66; Fernandes rep Baird 87; Tessem rep Svensson 75. Unused subs: Williams, Higginbotham. May 17; 73,726; G Barber

2004 **Manchester Utd 3** (Van Nistelrooy [2, 1 pen], Ronaldo) Howard; G Neville, Brown, Silvestre, O'Shea, Fletcher, Keane, Ronaldo, Scholes, Giggs, Van Nistelrooy. Subs: Carroll rep Howard, Butt rep Fletcher, Solskjaer rep Ronaldo 84. Unused subs: P Neville, Djemba-Djemba **Millwall 0** Marshall; Elliott, Lawrence, Ward, Ryan, Wise, Ifill, Cahill, Livermore, Sweeney, Harris. Subs: Cogan rep Ryan, McCammon rep Harris 74 Weston rep Wise 88. Unused subs: Gueret (gk); Dunne. May 22; 71,350; J Winter

2005 **Arsenal 0** Lehmann; Lauren, Toure, Senderos, Cole, Fabregas, Gilberto, Vieira, Pires, Reyes, Bergkamp Subs: Ljungberg rep Bergkamp 65, Van Persie rep Fabregas 86, Edu rep Pires 105. Unused subs: Almunia (gk); Campbell. Reyes sent off 90. **Manchester Utd 0** Carroll; Brown, Ferdinand, Silvestre, O'Shea, Fletcher, Keane, Scholes, Rooney, Van Nistelrooy, Ronaldo. Subs: Fortune rep O'Shea 77, Giggs rep Fletcher 91. Unused subs: Howard (gk); G Neville, Smith. **Arsenal** (Lauren, Ljungberg, van Persie, Cole, Vieira) beat Manchester Utd (van Nistelrooy, Scholes [missed], Ronaldo, Rooney, Keane) 5-4 on penalties

2006 **Liverpool 3** (Gerrard 2, Cisse) Reina; Finnan, Carragher, Hyypiä, Riise, Gerrard, Xabi, Sissoko, Kewell, Cisse, Crouch. Subs: Morientes rep Kewell 48, Kromkamp rep Alonso 67, Hamman rep Crouch 71. Unused subs: Dudek (gk); Traoré **West Ham 3** (Ashton, Konchesky, Carragher (og)) Hislop; Scaloni, Ferdinand, Gabbidon, Konchesky, Benayoun, Fletcher, Reo-Coker, Etherington, Ashton, Harewood. Subs:

Zamora rep Ashton 71, Dailly rep Fletcher, Sheringham rep Etherington 85. Unused subs: Walker (gk); Collins. **Liverpool** (Hamann, Hyypiä [missed], Gerrard, Riise) beat **West Ham** (Zamora [missed], Sheringham, Konchesky [missed], Ferdinand [missed]) 3-1 on penalties. May 13; 71,140; A Wiley

2007   Chelsea 1 (Drogba) Cech, Ferreira, Essien, Terry, Bridge, Mikel, Makelele, Lampard, Wright-Phillips, Drogba, J Cole Subs: Robben rep J Cole 45, Kalou rep Wright-Phillips 93, A Cole rep Robben 108. Unused subs: Cudicini (gk); Diarra. **Manchester Utd 0** Van der Sar, Brown, Ferdinand, Vidic, Heinze, Fletcher, Scholes, Carrick, Ronaldo, Rooney, Giggs Subs: Smith rep Fletcher 92, O'Shea rep Carrick, Solskjaer rep Giggs 112. Unused subs: Kuszczak (gk); Evra. May 19; 89,826; S Bennett

2008 Portsmouth 1 (Kanu) James; Johnson, Campbell, Distin, Hreidarsson, Utaka, Muntari, Mendes, Diarra, Kranjcar, Kanu. Subs: Nugent rep Utaka 69, Diop rep Mendes 78, Baros rep Kanu 87. Unused subs: Ashdown (gk); Pamarot. **Cardiff 0** Enckelman; McNaughton, Johnson, Loovens, Capaldi, Whittingham, Rae, McPhail, Ledley, Hasselbaink, Parry. Subs: Ramsey rep Whittingham 62, Thompson rep Hasselbaink 70, Sinclair rep Rae 87. Unused subs: Oakes (gk); Purse. May 17; 89,874; M Dean

2009 Chelsea 2 (Drogba, Lampard); Cech; Bosingwa, Alex, Terry, A Cole, Essien, Mikel, Lampard, Drogba, Anelka, Malouda. Subs: Ballack rep Essien 61. Unused subs: Hilario (gk), Ivanovic, Di Santo, Kalou, Belletti, Mancienne. **Everton** 1 (Saha) Howard; Hibbert, Yobo, Lescott, Baines, Osman, Neville, Cahill, Pienaar, Fellaini, Saha. Subs: Jacobsen rep Hibbert 46, Vaughan rep Saha 77, Gosling rep Osman 83. Unused subs: Nash, Castillo, Rodwell, Baxter. May 30; 89,391; H Webb

2010 Chelsea 1 (Drogba) Cech; Ivanovic, Alex, Terry, A Cole, Lampard, Ballack, Malouda, Kalou, Drogba, Anelka. Subs: Belletti rep Ballack 44, J Cole rep Kalou 71, Sturridge rep Anelka 90. Unused subs: Hilario (gk), Zhirkov, Paulo Ferreira, Matic. **Portsmouth 0** James; Finnan, Mokoena, Rocha, Mullins, Dindane, Brown, Diop, Boateng, O'Hara, Piquionne. Subs: Utaka rep Boateng 73, Belhadj rep Mullins 81, Kanu rep Diop 81. Unused subs: Ashdown (gk), Vanden Borre, Hughes, Ben Haim. May 15; 88,335; C Foy

2011 Manchester City 1 (Y Toure) Hart; Richards, Kompany, Lescott, Kolarov, De Jong, Barry, Silva, Y Toure, Balotelli, Tevez. Subs: Johnson rep Barry73, Zabaleta rep Tevez 87, Vieira rep Silva 90. Unused subs: Given (gk), Boyata, Milner, Dzeko. **Stoke 0** Sorensen; Wilkinson, Shawcross, Huth, Wilson, Pennant, Whelan, Delap, Etherington, Walters, Jones. Subs: Whitehead rep Etherington 62, Carew rep Delap 80, Pugh rep Whelan 84. Unused subs: Nash (gk), Collins, Faye, Diao. May 14; 88,643; M Atkinson

2012 Chelsea 2 (Ramires, Drogba) Cech; Bosingwa, Ivanovic, Terry, Cole, Mikel, Lampard, Ramires, Mata, Kalou, Drogba. Subs: Meireles rep Ramires76, Malouda rep Mata 90. Unused subs: Turnbull (gk), Paulo Ferreira, Essien, Torres, Sturridge. **Liverpool 1** (Carroll) Reina; Johnson, Skrtel, Agger, Luis Enrique, Spearing, Bellamy, Henderson, Gerrard, Downing, Suarez. Subs Carroll rep Spearing 55, Kuyt rep Bellamy 78. Unused subs: Doni (gk), Carragher, Kelly, Shelvey, Rodriguez. May 5; 89,102; P Dowd

2013 Wigan 1 (Watson) Robles; Boyce, Alcaraz, Scharner, McCarthy, McArthur, McManaman, Maloney, Gomez, Espinoza, Kone. Subs: Watson rep Gomez 81. Unused subs: Al Habsi (gk), Caldwell, Golobart, Fyvie, Henriquez, Di Santo. **Manchester City 0** Hart; Zabaleta, Kompany, Nastasic, Clichy, Toure, Barry, Silva, Tevez, Nasri, Aguero. Subs: Milner rep Nasri 54, Rodwell rep Tevez 69, Dzeko rep Barry 90. Unused subs: Pantilimon (gk), Lescott, Kolarov, Garcia. Sent off Zabaleta (84). May 11; 86,254; A Marriner

2014 Arsenal 3 (Cazorla, Koscielny, Ramsey) Fabianski; Sagna, Koscielny, Mertesacker, Gibbs, Arteta, Ramsey, Cazorla, Ozil, Podolski, Giroud. Subs: Sanogo rep Podolski 61, Rosicky rep Cazorla 106, Wilshire rep Ozil 106. Unused subs: Szczesny (gk), Vermaelen, Monreal, Flamini. **Hull 2** (Chester, Davies) McGregor; Davies, Bruce, Chester, Elmohamady, Livermore, Huddlestone, Meyler, Rosenior, Quinn, Fryatt. Subs: McShane rep Bruce 67, Aluko rep Quinn 71, Boyd rep Rosenior 102. Unused subs: Harper (gk), Figueroa, Koren, Sagbo. May 17; 89,345; L Probert. aet

VENUES

Kennington Oval 1872; **Lillie Bridge** 1873; **Kennington Oval** 1874 – 1892 (1886 replay at the **Racecourse Ground, Derby**); **Fallowfield**, Manchester, 1893; **Goodison Park** 1894; **Crystal

Palace 1895 – 1915 (1901 replay at **Burden Park**; 1910 replay at **Goodison Park**; 1912 replay at **Bramall Lane**); **Old Trafford** 1915; **Stamford Bridge** 1920 – 1922; **Wembley** 1923 – 2000 (1970 replay at **Old Trafford**; all replays after 1981 at **Wembley**); **Millennium Stadium** 2001 – 2006; **Wembley** 2007 – 2015

SUMMARY OF FA CUP WINS

Arsenal	12	Wolves	4	Cardiff	1
Manchester Utd	11	Sheffield Wed	3	Charlton	1
Tottenham	8	West Ham	3	Clapham Rov	1
Aston Villa	7	Bury	2	Coventry	1
Liverpool	7	Nottm Forest	2	Derby	1
Chelsea	7	Old Etonians	2	Huddersfield	1
Blackburn Rov	6	Portsmouth	2	Ipswich	1
Newcastle	6	Preston	2	Leeds	1
Everton	5	Sunderland	2	Notts Co	1
Manchester City	5	Barnsley	1	Old Carthusians	1
The Wanderers	5	Blackburn Olympic	1	Oxford University	1
WBA	5	Blackpool	1	Royal Engineers	1
Bolton	4	Bradford City	1	Southampton	1
Sheffield Utd	4	Burnley	1	Wigan	1
				Wimbledon	1

APPEARANCES IN FINALS

(Figures do not include replays)

Arsenal	19	The Wanderers*	5	Queen's Park (Glas)	2
Manchester Utd	18	West Ham	5	Blackburn Olympic*	1
Liverpool	14	Derby	4	Bradford City*	1
Everton	13	Leeds	4	Brighton	1
Newcastle	13	Leicester	4	Bristol City	1
Aston Villa	11	Oxford University	4	Coventry*	1
Chelsea	11	Royal Engineers	4	Crystal Palace	1
Manchester City	10	Southampton	4	Fulham	1
WBA	10	Sunderland	4	Hull	1
Tottenham	9	Blackpool	3	Ipswich*	1
Blackburn Rov	8	Burnley	3	Luton	1
Wolves	8	Cardiff	3	Middlesbrough	1
Bolton	7	Nottm Forest	3	Millwall	1
Preston	7	Barnsley	2	Old Carthusians*	1
Old Etonians	6	Birmingham	2	QPR	1
Sheffield Utd	6	Bury*	2	Stoke	1
Sheffield Wed	6	Charlton	2	Watford	1
Huddersfield	5	Clapham Rov	2	Wigan	1
Portsmouth	5	Notts Co	2	Wimbledon*	1

(* Denotes undefeated)

APPEARANCES IN SEMI-FINALS

(Figures do not include replays)

Arsenal 28, Manchester Utd 27, Everton 25, Liverpool 24, Aston Villa 21, Chelsea 21, WBA 20, Tottenham 19, Blackburn 18, Newcastle 17, Sheffield Wed 16, Bolton 14, Sheffield Utd 14, Wolves 14, Derby 13, Manchester City 12, Nottm Forest 12, Sunderland 12, Southampton 11, Preston 10, Birmingham 9, Burnley 8, Leeds 8, Huddersfield 7, Leicester 7, Portsmouth 7, West Ham 7, Fulham 6, Old Etonians 6, Oxford University 6, Millwall 5, Notts Co 5, The Wanderers 5, Watford 5, Cardiff 4, Luton 4, Queen's Park (Glasgow) 4, Royal Engineers 4, Stoke 4, Barnsley 3, Blackpool 3, Clapham Rov 3, *Crystal Palace 3, Ipswich Town 3, Middlesbrough 3, Norwich 3, Old Carthusians 3, Oldham 3, The Swifts 3, Blackburn Olympic 2, Bristol City 2, Bury 2, Charlton 2, Grimsby Town 2, Hull 2, Reading 2, Swansea 2, Swindon 2, Wigan 2, Wimbledon 2, Bradford City 1, Brighton 1, Cambridge University 1, Chesterfield 1, Coventry 1, Crewe 1, Darwen 1, Derby Junction 1, Marlow 1, Old Harrovians 1, Orient 1, Plymouth Argyle 1, Port Vale 1, QPR 1, Rangers (Glasgow) 1, Shropshire Wand 1, Wycombe 1, York 1
(*A previous and different Crystal Palace club also reached the semi-final in season 1871–72)

MOURINHO GAMBLE PAYS OFF WITH LEAGUE CUP SUCCESS

THIRD ROUND	FOURTH ROUND	FIFTH ROUND	SEMI-FINALS	FINAL
*Chelsea 2				
Bolton 1	Chelsea 2			
*Shrewsbury............1		Chelsea 3		
Norwich............0	*Shrewsbury............1			
			Chelsea ....1+1	
*Fulham............2				
Doncaster............1	*Fulham............2			
*Derby............2		*Derby............1		
Reading............0	Derby 5			
				Chelsea............2
*Cardiff............0				
Bournemouth 3	*Bournemouth............2			
*WBA............3		*Bournemouth............1		
Hull............2	WBA............1			
			*Liverpool 1:0	
*Liverpool ....+A2				
Middlesbrough............2	*Liverpool............2			
*Swansea............3		Liverpool............3		
Everton............0	Swansea............1			
*MK Dons............2				
Bradford............0	*MK Dons............1			
*Leyton Orient............0		*Sheffield Utd............1		
Sheffield Utd............1	Sheffield Utd............2			

*Sunderland............1
Stoke............2

*Arsenal............1
Southampton............2

*Manchester City............7
Sheffield Wed............0

*Crystal Palace............2
Newcastle............+3

*Burton............0
Brighton............3

Nottm Forest............1
*Tottenham............3

*Stoke............2

Southampton............3

*Manchester City............0

Newcastle............2

Brighton............0

*Tottenham............2

Sheffield Utd............0.2

Southampton............0

Newcastle............0

*Tottenham............1:2

*Tottenham............4

Tottenham............0

*Drawn at home; in semi-finals, first leg; + After extra-time; A – Liverpool won 14-13 on pens

FIRST ROUND: Barnsley 0 Crewe 2; Birmingham 3 Cambridge 1 (aet); Blackburn 0 Scunthorpe 1; Bolton 3 Bury 2 (aet); Brighton 2 Cheltenham 0; Bristol City 1 Oxford 2; Burton 2 Wigan 1; Carlisle 0 Derby 2; Charlton 4 Colchester 0; Chesterfield 3 Huddersfield 5 (aet); Coventry 1 Cardiff 2; Crawley 1 Ipswich 0 (aet); Dagenham 6 Brentford 6 (aet, Brentford won 4-2 on pens); Exeter 0 Bournemouth 2; Leeds 2 Accrington 1; Luton 1 Swindon 2; Millwall 1 Wycombe 0; MK Dons 3 AFC Wimbledon 1; Morecambe 0 Bradford 1; Oldham 0 Middlesbrough 3; Plymouth 3 Leyton Orient 3 (aet, Leyton Orient won 6-5 on pens); Port Vale 6 Hartlepool 2; Portsmouth 1 Peterborough 0; Reading 3 Newport 1; Rochdale 0 Preston 2; Rotherham 1 Fleetwood 0 (aet); Sheffield Utd 2 Mansfield 1; Sheffield Wed 3 Notts Co 0; Shrewsbury 1 Blackpool 0; Southend 1 Walsall 2; Stevenage 0 Watford 1; Tranmere 0 Nottm Forest 1; Wolves 2 Yeovil 1 Gillingham 2; York 0 Doncaster 1

SECOND ROUND: Aston Villa 0 Leyton Orient 1; Birmingham 0 Sunderland 3; Bournemouth 3 Northampton 0; Bradford 2 Leeds 1; Brentford 0 Fulham 1; Burnley 0 Sheffield Wed 1; Burton 1 QPR 0; Crewe 2 Bolton 3 (aet); Derby 1 Charlton 0; Gillingham 0 Newcastle 1; Huddersfield 0 Nottm Forest 2; Leicester 0 Shrewsbury 1; Middlesbrough 3 Preston 1; Millwall 0 Southampton 2; MK Dons 4 Manchester Utd 0; Norwich 3 Crawley 1; Port Vale 2 Cardiff 1; Scunthorpe 0 Reading 1; Stoke 3 Portsmouth 0; Swansea 1 Rotherham 0; Swindon 2 Brighton 4 (aet); Walsall 0 Crystal Palace 3; Watford 1 Doncaster 2; WBA 1 Oxford 1 (aet, WBA won 7-6 on pens); West Ham 1 Sheffield Utd 1 (aet, Sheffield Utd won 5-4 on pens)

167

CAPITAL ONE CUP FINAL

CHELSEA 2 TOTTENHAM HOTSPUR 0
Wembley (89,294): Sunday, March 1 2015

Chelsea (4-3-3): Cech, Ivanovic, Cahill, Terry (capt), Azpilicueta, Ramires, Zouma, Fabregas (Oscar 88), Hazard, Diego Costa (Drogba 93), Willian (Cuadrado 76). **Subs not used**: Courtois, Filipe Luis, Ake, Remy. **Scorers**: Terry (45), Diego Costa (56). **Booked**: Willian, Cahill, Cuadrado. **Manager**: Jose Mourinho

Tottenham Hotspur (4-2-3-1): Lloris (capt), Walker, Dier, Vertonghen, Rose, Bentaleb, Mason (Lamela 71), Chadli (Soldado 80), Eriksen, Townsend (Dembele 62), Kane. **Subs not used**: Vorm, Davies, Fazio, Stambouli. **Booked**: Dier, Bentaleb. **Manager**: Mauricio Pochettino

Referee: A Taylor (Cheshire). **Half-time**: 1-0

For Jose Mourinho, the first trophy of his second spell as manager at Stamford Bridge and the reward for a typically bold selection decision for the big occasion. For Harry Kane, disappointment in his first major final after a rare blank afternoon of a thrilling first full season in Tottenham's attack. With his key midfielder anchor Nemanja Matic suspended, the Chelsea manager surprised everyone – including the player himself – by giving the role to 20-year-old Frenchman Kurt Zouma, a central defender regarded by many as the eventual replacement for John Terry. For a while, the gamble look like it might backfire, with Zouma struggling to adjust to his new role against the mobility of Christian Eriksen – who struck the bar with a free-kick – and Ryan Mason. But he gradually exerted his own influence, Terry's scrambled effort went in on the stroke of half-time and a second deflected goal from Diego Costa after 56 minutes made sure of the trophy. It was Chelsea's fifth League Cup success – and a good day all round as their position at the top of the Premier League strengthened with Manchester City's defeat at Liverpool. They had the advantage of a full week to prepare for the final, whereas their opponents were involved in a Europa League match in Italy against Fiorentina three days earlier. Tottenham were also beaten in that one, leaving a Champions League place as the one remaining target for the campaign. Kane, who had scored twice in his side's 5-3 victory over Chelsea on New Year's Day, was subdued by Terry and Gary Cahill this time. But the goals were soon flowing again – two against Queens Park Rangers, a hat-trick against Leicester and one on his England debut underlining a huge talent and suggesting there are more chances of silverware to come.

HOW THEY REACHED THE FINAL

CHELSEA
Round 3: 2-1 home to Bolton (Zouma, Oscar)
Round 4: 2-1 away to Shrewsbury (Drogba, Grandison og)
Round 5: 3-1 away to Derby (Hazard, Filipe Luis, Schurrle)
Semi-finals: v Liverpool – first leg, 1-1 away (Hazard pen); second leg, 1-0 home (Ivanovic) – aet

TOTTENHAM HOTSPUR
Round 3: 3-1 home to Nottm Forest (Mason, Soldado, Kane)
Round 4: 2-0 home to Brighton (Lamela, Kane)
Round 5: 4-0 away to Newcastle (Bentaleb, Chadli, Kane, Soldado)
Semi-finals: v Sheffield Utd – first leg, 1-0 home (Townsend pen); second leg, 2-2 away (Eriksen 2)

LEAGUE CUP – COMPLETE RESULTS

LEAGUE CUP FINALS

1961*	Aston Villa beat Rotherham 3-2 on agg (0-2a, 3-0h)
1962	Norwich beat Rochdale 4-0 on agg (3-0a, 1-0h)
1963	Birmingham beat Aston Villa 3-1 o agg (3-1h, 0-0a)
1964	Leicester beat Stoke 4-3 on agg (1-1a, 3-2h)
1965	Chelsea beat Leicester 3-2 on agg (3-2h, 0-0a)
1966	WBA beat West Ham 5-3 on agg (1-2a, 4-1h)

AT WEMBLEY

1967	QPR beat WBA (3-2)
1968	Leeds beat Arsenal (1-0)
1969*	Swindon beat Arsenal (3-1)
1970*	Man City beat WBA (2-1)
1971	Tottenham beat Aston Villa (2-0)
1972	Stoke beat Chelsea (2-1)
1973	Tottenham beat Norwich (1-0)
1974	Wolves beat Man City (2-1)
1975	Aston Villa beat Norwich (1-0)
1976	Man City beat Newcastle (2-1)
1977†*	Aston Villa beat Everton (3-2 after 0-0 and 1-1 draws)
1978††	Nottm Forest beat Liverpool (1-0 after 0-0 draw)
1979	Nottm Forest beat Southampton (3-2)
1980	Wolves beat Nottm Forest (1-0)
1981†††	Liverpool beat West Ham (2-1 after 1-1 draw)

MILK CUP

1982*	Liverpool beat Tottenham (3-1)
1983*	Liverpool beat Man Utd (2-1)
1984**	Liverpool beat Everton (1-0 after *0-0 draw)
1985	Norwich beat Sunderland (1-0)
1986	Oxford Utd beat QPR (3-0)

LITTLEWOODS CUP

1987	Arsenal beat Liverpool (2-1)
1988	Luton beat Arsenal (3-2)
1989	Nottm Forest beat Luton (3-1)
1990	Nottm Forest beat Oldham (1-0)

RUMBELOWS CUP

| 1991 | Sheffield Wed beat Man Utd (1-0) |
| 1992 | Man Utd beat Nottm Forest (1-0) |

COCA-COLA CUP

1993	Arsenal beat Sheffield Wed (2-1)
1994	Aston Villa beat Man Utd (3-1)
1995	Liverpool beat Bolton (2-1)
1996	Aston Villa beat Leeds (3-0)
1997***	Leicester beat Middlesbrough (*1-0 after *1-1 draw)
1998	Chelsea beat Middlesbrough (2-0)

WORTHINGTON CUP (at Millennium Stadium from 2001)

1999	Tottenham beat Leicester (1-0)
2000	Leicester beat Tranmere (2-1)
2001	Liverpool beat Birmingham (5-4 on pens after *1-1 draw)
2002	Blackburn beat Tottenham (2-1)
2003	Liverpool beat Man Utd (2-0)

CARLING CUP (at Wembley from 2008)

2004	Middlesbrough beat Bolton (2-1)
2005*	Chelsea beat Liverpool (3-2)
2006	Man Utd beat Wigan (4-0)
2007	Chelsea beat Arsenal (2-1)
2008*	Tottenham beat Chelsea (2-1)
2009	Man Utd beat Tottenham (4-1 on pens after *0-0 draw)
2010	Man Utd beat Aston Villa (2-1)
2011	Birmingham beat Arsenal (2-1)
2012	Liverpool beat Cardiff (3-2 on pens after *2-2 draw)

CAPITAL ONE CUP (at Wembley from 2013)

2013	Swansea beat Bradford (5-0)
2014	Manchester City beat Sunderland (3-1)
2015	Chelsea beat Tottenham (2-0)

* After extra time. † First replay at Hillsborough, second replay at Old Trafford. †† Replayed at Old Trafford. ††† Replayed at Villa Park. ** Replayed at Maine Road. *** Replayed at Hillsborough

SUMMARY OF LEAGUE CUP WINNERS

Liverpool 8	Arsenal.....................2	Oxford Utd 1
Aston Villa 5	Birmingham 2	QPR............................1
Chelsea 5	Norwich 2	Sheffield Wed 1
Nottm Forest 4	Wolves 2	Stoke 1
Tottenham 4	Blackburn 1	Swansea....................1
Manchester Utd...........4	Leeds........................1	Swindon 1
Leicester...................3	Luton 1	WBA 1
Manchester City 3	Middlesbrough 1	

LEAGUE CUP FINAL APPEARANCES

11 Liverpool; **8** Aston Villa, Manchester Utd, Tottenham; **7** Arsenal, Chelsea; **6** Nottm Forest; **5** Leicester; **4** Manchester City, Norwich; **3** Birmingham, Middlesbrough, WBA; **2** Bolton, Everton, Leeds, Luton, QPR, Sheffield Wed, Stoke, Sunderland, West Ham, Wolves; **1** Blackburn, Bradford, Cardiff, Newcastle, Oldham, Oxford Utd, Rochdale, Rotherham, Southampton, Swansea, Swindon, Tranmere, Wigan (Figures do not include replays).

LEAGUE CUP SEMI-FINAL APPEARANCES

15 Liverpool, Tottenham; **14** Arsenal, Aston Villa, **13** Manchester Utd **12** Chelsea; **9** West Ham; **8** Manchester City; **6** Nottm Forest, **5** Birmingham, Leeds, Leicester, Middlesbrough, Norwich; **4** Bolton, Burnley, Crystal Palace, Everton, Ipswich, Sheffield Wed, Sunderland, WBA; **3**, QPR, Swindon, Wolves; **2** Bristol City, Cardiff, Coventry, Derby, Luton, Oxford Utd, Plymouth, Sheffield Utd, Southampton, Stoke City, Tranmere, Watford, Wimbledon; **1** Blackpool, Bradford, Bury, Carlisle, Chester, Huddersfield, Newcastle, Oldham, Peterborough, Rochdale, Rotherham, Shrewsbury, Stockport, Swansea, Walsall, Wigan, Wycombe (Figures do not include replays).

OTHER COMPETITIONS 2014–15

FA COMMUNITY SHIELD

ARSENAL 3 MANCHESTER CITY 0
Wembley (71,523); Sunday, August 10 2014

Arsenal (4-3-2-1): Szczesny, Debuchy, Chambers, Koscielny (Monreal 46), Gibbs, Arteta (capt), Ramsey (Campbell 86), Wilshere (Flamini 46), Sanchez (Oxlade-Chamberlain 46), Cazorla (Rosicky 70), Sanogo (Giroud 46). **Sub not used**: Martinez. **Scorers**: Cazorla (21), Ramsey (42), Giroud (60). **Manager**: Arsene Wenger

Manchester City (4-4-2): Caballero, Clichy, Boyata, Nastasic, Kolarov (Richards 76), Jesus Navas (Sinclair 86), Toure (capt) (Zuculini 60), Fernando, Nasri (Silva 46), Dzeko (Milner 60), Jovetic. **Subs not used**: Hart, Rekik. **Booked**: Fernando. **Manager**: Manuel Pellegrini

Referee: M Oliver (Northumberland). **Half-time**: 2-0

JOHNSTONE'S PAINT TROPHY

FIRST ROUND
Northern: Accrington 1 Carlisle 3; Barnsley 2 York 0; Crewe 0 Rochdale 3; Fleetwood 2 Morecambe 3; Notts Co 2 Mansfield 0; Oldham 1 Bradford 0; Preston 1 Shrewsbury 0; Scunthorpe 2 Chesterfield 0

Southern: AFC Wimbledon 2 Southend 2 (AFC Wimbledon won 4-2 on pens); Cheltenham 2 Oxford 0; Crawley 2 Cambridge 0; Newport 1 Swindon 2; Peterborough 2 Leyton Orient 3; Stevenage 0 Gillingham 1; Wycombe 0 Coventry 1; Yeovil 1 Portsmouth 3

SECOND ROUND
Northern: Burton 0 Doncaster 3; Bury 3 Morecambe 1; Hartlepool 1 Sheffield Utd 2; Oldham

2 Barnsley 2 (Oldham won 4-2 on pens); Preston 3 Port Vale 2; Rochdale 0 Walsall 1; Scunthorpe 1 Notts Co 2; Tranmere 1 Carlisle 1 (Tranmere won 5-4 on pens)
Southern: Cheltenham 1 Bristol City 3; Colchester 3 Gillingham 3 (Gillingham won 4-2 on pens); Coventry 3 Exeter 1; Dagenham 0 Leyton Orient 2; Luton 0 Crawley 1; MK Dons 2 AFC Wimbledon 3; Plymouth 3 Swindon 2; Portsmouth 1 Northampton 2

THIRD ROUND
Northern: Bury 1 Tranmere 2; Doncaster 0 Notts Co 1; Oldham 2 Preston 2 (Preston won 10-9 on pens); Walsall 1 Sheffield Utd 0
Southern: Bristol City 2 AFC Wimbledon 1; Coventry 2 Plymouth 0; Crawley 1 Gillingham 2; Leyton Orient 2 Northampton 0

SEMI-FINALS
Northern: Notts Co 0 Preston 1; Tranmere 2 Walsall 2 (Walsall won 5-4 on pens)
Southern: Bristol City 2 Coventry 0; Gillingham 1 Leyton Orient 0

AREA FINALS
Northern first leg: Preston 0 Walsall 2 (Forde 84, Bradshaw 88). Att: 8,561. **Second leg**: Walsall 0 Preston 0. Att: 10,038 (Walsall won 2-0 on agg)
Southern first leg: Gillingham 2 (McDonald 6, 70) Bristol City 4 (M Smith 18, 27, 50, 77). Att: 2,368. **Second leg**: Bristol City 1 (M Smith 17) Gillingham 1 (McGlashan 32). Att: 2,368 (Bristol City won 5-3 on agg)

FINAL

BRISTOL CITY 2 WALSALL 0
Wembley (72,315); Sunday, March 22 2015
Bristol City (3-5-2): Fielding, Ayling, Flint, Williams, Little, K Smith, Pack, Freeman (Elliott 90), Bryan (Cunningham 87), Wilbraham (capt), Agard (Emmanuel-Thomas 88). **Subs not used**: Richards, Tavernier, Saville, Wagstaff. **Scorers**: Flint (15), Little (51). **Manager**: Steve Cotterill
Walsall (4-2-3-1): O'Donnell, Purkiss, Downing, J Chambers, Taylor, Mantom, A Chambers (capt), Forde (Grimes 74), Sawyers, Cook (Baxendale 80), Bradshaw (Hiwula 61). **Subs not used**: MacGillivray, O'Connor, Cain, Flanagan. **Booked**: Sawyers. **Manager**: Dean Smith
Referee: M Russell (Herts). **Half-time**: 1-0

FA TROPHY

FIRST ROUND: Aldershot 0 Burgess Hill 1; Altrincham 1 Macclesfield 0; Basingstoke 2 Gosport 2; Bishop's Stortford 1 Torquay 5; Bradford PA 1 Kidderminster 4; Braintree 1 Sudbury 0; Bristol Rov 0 Bath 2; Bromley 2 Leiston 0; Concord 0 Barnet 0; Dartford 2 Solihull 0; Ebbsfleet 1 Welling 1; FC United 4 Harrogate 0; Forest Green 2 Didcot 2; Fylde 3 Gainsborough 0; Gateshead 2 Halesowen 0; Guiseley 0 Chorley 2; Hemel Hempstead 1 Sutton 0; Hyde 4 Spennymoor 0; Lincoln 0 Alfreton 2; Lowestoft 1 Dover 3; Maidenhead 2 Poole 1; North Ferriby 1 Boston 1; Nuneaton 0 Grimsby 2; Ramsbottom 3 Stockport 3; Southport 1 Wrexham 1; Telford 1 Chester 1; Wealdstone 1 Hayes 0; Weston SM 1 Farnborough 3; Weymouth 1 Havant 1; Wimborne 0 Oxford City 3; Woking 2 Eastleigh 1; Worcester 0 Halifax 1. **Replays**: Barnet 2 Concord 6; Boston 0 North Ferriby 2; Chester 1 Telford 1 (aet, Telford won 4-3 on pens); Didcot 0 Forest Green 3; Gosport 2 Basingstoke 1; Havant 5 Weymouth 0; Welling 2 Ebbsfleet 3; Wrexham 2 Southport 0

SECOND ROUND: Burgess Hill 1 Dartford 2; Chorley 3 FC United 3; Ebbsfleet 1 Forest Green 0; Fylde 4 Telford 0; Gosport 0 Braintree 2; Grimsby 0 Gateshead 0; Halifax 5 Alfreton 3; Havant 0 Dover 1; Hemel Hempstead 3 Concord 1; Kidderminster 0 Altrincham 1; Maidenhead 2 Farnborough 2; North Ferriby 2 Hyde 0; Oxford City 2 Woking 0; Stockport 2 Wrexham 2; Torquay 4 Bromley 0; Wealdstone 1 Bath 3. **Replays**: Farnborough 1 Maidenhead 0; FC United 1 Chorley 0; Gateshead 3 Grimsby 2; Woking 2 Oxford City 1; Wrexham 6 Stockport 1

THIRD ROUND: Bath 1 Altrincham 0; Braintree 1 Ebbsfleet 1; Dartford 2 Halifax 2; Farnborough 0 North Ferriby 2; FC United 3 Fylde 1; Hemel Hempstead 0 Torquay 2; Woking 3 Dover 3; Wrexham 1 Gateshead 1. **Replays**: Dover 1 Woking 0; Ebbsfleet 2 Braintree 0; Gateshead 2 Wrexham 2 (aet, Wrexham won 5-3 on pens); Halifax 3 Dartford 1

FOURTH ROUND: Dover 3 Bath 3; Halifax 0 Wrexham 1; North Ferriby 1 Ebbsfleet 0; Torquay 1 FC United 0. **Replay**: Bath 2 Dover 1

SEMI-FINALS, FIRST LEG: Bath 2 (Pratt 61 pen, McCootie 85) North Ferriby 2 (Ball 25 og, St Juste 50). Att: 1,738. Wrexham 2 (Clarke 27, Moult 65) Torquay 1 (Bowman 78). Att: 2,866

SEMI-FINALS, SECOND LEG: North Ferriby 1 (King 64 pen) Bath 1 (McCootie 1). Att: 1,871 (aet, agg 3-3, North Ferriby won 4-2 on pens). Torquay 0 Wrexham 3 (Moult 61, Morris 73, 75). Att: 3,255 (Wrexham won 5-1 on agg)

FINAL

NORTH FERRIBY UNITED 3 WREXHAM 3 (aet, North Ferriby United won 5-4 on pens)
Wembley (14,585); Sunday, March 29 2015

North Ferriby United (4-1-4-1); Nicklin, Topliss, Hone, Wilson, Wilde (Peat 89), Fry (Kendall 79), D Clarke, King (capt), Bolder (Jarman 61), St Juste, Denton. **Subs not used**: Nicholson, Gray. **Scorers**: King (76 pen), Kendall (86, 101). **Manager**: Billy Heath
Wrexham (4-2-3-1): Coughlin, Tomassen, Smith, Hudson, Ashton, Harris, Keates (capt) (Evans 72), Morris (York 87) J Clarke (Bishop 102), Jennings, Moult. **Subs not used**: Carrington, Waterfall. **Scorers**: Moult (11, 118), Harris (60). **Manager**: Kevin Wilkin
Referee: M Oliver (Northumberland). **Half-time**: 0-1

WELSH CUP FINAL
New Saints 2 (Williams 54, 85 pen) Newtown 0 – Latham Park, Newtown

FA VASE FINAL
North Shields 2 (Bainbridge 80, Forster 96) Glossop North End 1 (Bailey 55) aet – Wembley. Att: 9,674

FA SUNDAY CUP FINAL
Campfield (Liverpool) 2 (Jones 2) OJM (Birmingham) 0 – Ewood Park, Blackburn

FINALS – RESULTS

Associated Members' Cup
1984 (Hull) Bournemouth 2 Hull 1

Freight Rover Trophy – Wembley
1985 Wigan 3 Brentford 1
1986 Bristol City 3 Bolton 0
1987 Mansfield 1 Bristol City 1
(aet; Mansfield won 5-4 on pens)

Sherpa Van Trophy – Wembley
1988 Wolves 2 Burnley 0
1989 Bolton 4 Torquay 1

Leyland Daf Cup – Wembley
1990 Tranmere 2 Bristol Rov 1
1991 Birmingham 3 Tranmere 2

Autoglass Trophy – Wembley
1992 Stoke 1 Stockport 0
1993 Port Vale 2 Stockport 1
1994 Huddersfield 1 Swansea 1
(aet; Swansea won 3-1 on pens)

Auto Windscreens Shield – Wembley
1995 Birmingham 1 Carlisle 0
(Birmingham won in sudden-death overtime)
1996 Rotherham 2 Shrewsbury 1
1997 Carlisle 0 Colchester 0
(aet; Carlisle won 4-3 on pens)
1998 Grimsby 2 Bournemouth 1
(Grimsby won with golden goal in extra-time)
1999 Wigan 1 Millwall 0
2000 Stoke 2 Bristol City 1

LDV Vans Trophy – Millennium Stadium
2001 Port Vale 2 Brentford 1
2002 Blackpool 4 Cambridge Utd 1
2003 Bristol City 2 Carlisle 0
2004 Blackpool 2 Southend 0
2005 Wrexham 2 Southend 0

Football League Trophy – Millennium Stadium
2006 Swansea 2 Carlisle 1

Johnstone's Paint Trophy – Wembley

2007	Doncaster 3 Bristol Rov 2 (aet) (Millennium Stadium)
2008	MK Dons 2 Grimsby 0
2009	Luton 3 Scunthorpe 2 (aet)
2010	Southampton 4 Carlisle 1
2011	Carlisle 1 Brentford 0
2012	Chesterfield 2 Swindon 0
2013	Crewe 2 Southend 0
2014	Peterborough 3 Chesterfield 1
2015	Bristol City 2 Walsall 0

OTHER LEAGUE CLUBS' CUP COMPETITIONS

FINALS – AT WEMBLEY

Full Members' Cup (Discontinued after 1992)

1985–86	Chelsea 5 Man City 4
1986–87	Blackburn 1 Charlton 0

Simod Cup

1987–88	Reading 4 Luton 1
1988–89	Nottm Forest 4 Everton 3

Zenith Data Systems Cup

1989–90	Chelsea 1 Middlesbrough 0
1990–91	Crystal Palace 4 Everton 1
1991–92	Nottm Forest 3 Southampton 2

Anglo-Italian Cup (Discontinued after 1996
* Home club)

1970	*Napoli 0 Swindon 3
1971	*Bologna 1 Blackpool 2 (aet)
1972	*AS Roma 3 Blackpool 1
1973	*Fiorentina 1 Newcastle 2
1993	Derby 1 Cremonese 3 (at Wembley)
1994	Notts Co 0 Brescia 1 (at Wembley)
1995	Ascoli 1 Notts Co 2 (at Wembley)
1996	Port Vale 2 Genoa 5 (at Wembley)

FA Vase

At Wembley (until 2000 and from 2007)

1975	Hoddesdon 2 Epsom & Ewell 1
1976	Billericay 1 Stamford 0*
1977	Billericay 2 Sheffield 1 (replay Nottingham after a 1-1 at Wembley)
1978	Blue Star 2 Barton Rov 1
1979	Billericay 4 Almondsbury Greenway 1
1980	Stamford 2 Guisborough Town 0
1981	Whickham 3 Willenhall 2*
1982	Forest Green 3 Rainworth MF Welfare 0
1983	VS Rugby 1 Halesowen 0
1984	Stansted 3 Stamford 2
1985	Halesowen 3 Fleetwood 1
1986	Halesowen 3 Southall 0
1987	St Helens 3 Warrington 2
1988	Colne Dynamoes 1 Emley 0*
1989	Tamworth 3 Sudbury 0 (replay Peterborough after a 1-1 at Wembley)
1990	Yeading 1 Bridlington 0 (replay Leeds after 0-0 at Wembley)
1991	Guiseley 3 Gresley Rov 1 (replay Bramall Lane Sheffield after a 4-4

	at Wembley)
1992	Wimborne 5 Guiseley 3
1993	Bridlington 1 Tiverton 0
1994	Diss 2 Taunton 1*
1995	Arlesey 2 Oxford City 1
1996	Brigg Town 3 Clitheroe 0
1997	Whitby Town 3 North Ferriby 0
1998	Tiverton 1 Tow Law 0
1999	Tiverton 1 Bedlington 0
2000	Deal 1 Chippenham 0
2001	Taunton 2 Berkhamsted 1 (Villa Park)
2002	Whitley Bay 1 Tiptree 0* (Villa Park)
2003	Brigg 2 AFC Sudbury 1 (Upton Park)
2004	Winchester 2 AFC Sudbury 0 (St Andrews)
2005	Didcot 3 AFC Sudbury 2 (White Hart Lane)
2006	Nantwich 3 Hillingdon 1 (St Andrews)
2007	Truro 3 AFC Totton 1
2008	Kirkham & Wesham (Fylde) 2 Lowestoft 1
2009	Whitley Bay 2 Glossop 0
2010	Whitley Bay 6 Wroxham 1
2011	Whitley Bay 3 Coalville 2
2012	Dunston 2 West Auckland 0
2013	Spennymoor 2 Tunbridge Wells 1
2014	Sholing 1 West Auckland 0
2015	North Shields 2 Glossop North End 1*

* After extra-time

FA Trophy Finals

At Wembley

1970	Macclesfield 2 Telford 0
1971	Telford 3 Hillingdon 2
1972	Stafford 3 Barnet 0
1973	Scarborough 2 Wigan 1*
1974	Morecambe 2 Dartford 1
1975	Matlock 4 Scarborough 0
1976	Scarborough 3 Stafford 2*
1977	Scarborough 2 Dag & Red 1
1978	Altrincham 3 Leatherhead 1
1979	Stafford 2 Kettering 0
1980	Dag & Red 2 Mossley 1
1981	Bishop's Stortford 1 Sutton 0
1982	Enfield 1 Altrincham 0*
1983	Telford 2 Northwich 1

1984	Northwich 2 Bangor 1 (replay Stoke after a 1-1 at Wembley)
1985	Wealdstone 2 Boston 1
1986	Altrincham 1 Runcorn 0
1987	Kidderminster 2 Burton 1 (replay WBA after a 0-0 at Wembley)
1988	Enfield 3 Telford 2 (replay WBA after a 0-0 at Wembley)
1989	Telford 1 Macclesfield 0*
1990	Barrow 3 Leek 0
1991	Wycombe 2 Kidderminster 1
1992	Colchester 3 Witton 1
1993	Wycombe 4 Runcorn 1
1994	Woking 2 Runcorn 1
1995	Woking 2 Kidderminster 1
1996	Macclesfield 3 Northwich 1
1997	Woking 1 Dag & Red & Redbridge 0*
1998	Cheltenham 1 Southport 0
1999	Kingstonian 1 Forest Green 0
2000	Kingstonian 3 Kettering 2
2015	North Ferriby 3 Wrexham 3* (North Ferriby won 5-4 on pens)

At Villa Park

2001	Canvey 1 Forest Green 0
2002	Yeovil 2 Stevenage 0
2003	Burscough 2 Tamworth 1
2004	Hednesford 3 Canvey 2
2005	Grays 1 Hucknall 1* (Grays won 6-5 on pens)

At Upton Park

2006	Grays 2 Woking 0

At Wembley

2007	Stevenage 3 Kidderminster 2
2008	Ebbsfleet 1 Torquay 0
2009	Stevenage 2 York 0
2010	Barrow 2 Stevenage 1*
2011	Darlington 1 Mansfield 0 *
2012	York 2 Newport 0
2013	Wrexham 1 Grimsby 1 * Wrexham won 4-1 on pens)
2014	Cambridge Utd 4 Gosport 0

(*After extra-time)

FA Youth Cup Winners

Year	Winners	Runners-up	Agg
1953	Man Utd	Wolves	9-3
1954	Man Utd	Wolves	5-4
1955	Man Utd	WBA	7-1
1956	Man Utd	Chesterfield	4-3
1957	Man Utd	West Ham	8-2
1958	Wolves	Chelsea	7-6
1959	Blackburn	West Ham	2-1
1960	Chelsea	Preston	5-2
1961	Chelsea	Everton	5-3
1962	Newcastle	Wolves	2-1

1963	West Ham	Liverpool	6-5
1964	Man Utd	Swindon	5-2
1965	Everton	Arsenal	3-2
1966	Arsenal	Sunderland	5-3
1967	Sunderland	Birmingham	2-0
1968	Burnley	Coventry	3-2
1969	Sunderland	WBA	6-3
1970	Tottenham	Coventry	4-3
1971	Arsenal	Cardiff	2-0
1972	Aston Villa	Liverpool	5-2
1973	Ipswich	Bristol City	4-1
1974	Tottenham	Huddersfield	2-1
1975	Ipswich	West Ham	5-1
1976	WBA	Wolves	5-0
1977	Crystal Palace	Everton	1-0
1978	Crystal Palace	Aston Villa	*1-0
1979	Millwall	Man City	2-0
1980	Aston Villa	Man City	3-2
1981	West Ham	Tottenham	2-1
1982	Watford	Man Utd	7-6
1983	Norwich	Everton	6-5
1984	Everton	Stoke	4-2
1985	Newcastle	Watford	4-1
1986	Man City	Man Utd	3-1
1987	Coventry	Charlton	2-1
1988	Arsenal	Doncaster	6-1
1989	Watford	Man City	2-1
1990	Tottenham	Middlesbrough	3-2
1991	Millwall	Sheffield Wed	3-0
1992	Man Utd	Crystal Palace	6-3
1993	Leeds	Man Utd	4-1
1994	Arsenal	Millwall	5-3
1995	Man Utd	Tottenham	†2-2
1996	Liverpool	West Ham	4-1
1997	Leeds	Crystal Palace	3-1
1998	Everton	Blackburn	5-3
1999	West Ham	Coventry	9-0
2000	Arsenal	Coventry	5-1
2001	Arsenal	Blackburn	6-3
2002	Aston Villa	Everton	4-2
2003	Man Utd	Middlesbrough	3-1
2004	Middlesbrough	Aston Villa	4-0
2005	Ipswich	Southampton	3-2
2006	Liverpool	Man City	3-2
2007	Liverpool	Man Utd	††2-2
2008	Man City	Chelsea	4-2
2009	Arsenal	Liverpool	6-2
2010	Chelsea	Aston Villa	3-2
2011	Man Utd	Sheffield Utd	6-3
2012	Chelsea	Blackburn	4-1
2013	Norwich	Chelsea	4-2
2014	Chelsea	Fulham	7-6
2015	Chelsea	Man City	5-2

(*One match only; †Manchester Utd won 4-3 on pens; ††Liverpool won 4-3 on pens)

CHARITY/COMMUNITY SHIELD RESULTS (POST WAR)
[CHARITY SHIELD]

Year	Winners	Runners-up	Score
1948	Arsenal	Manchester Utd	4-3
1949	Portsmouth	Wolves	*1-1
1950	England World Cup XI	FA Canadian Tour Team	4-2
1951	Tottenham	Newcastle	2-1
1952	Manchester Utd	Newcastle	4-2
1953	Arsenal	Blackpool	3-1
1954	Wolves	WBA	*4-4
1955	Chelsea	Newcastle	3-0
1956	Manchester Utd	Manchester City	1-0
1957	Manchester Utd	Aston Villa	4-0
1958	Bolton	Wolves	4-1
1959	Wolves	Nottm Forest	3-1
1960	Burnley	Wolves	*2-2
1961	Tottenham	FA XI	3-2
1962	Tottenham	Ipswich Town	5-1
1963	Everton	Manchester Utd	4-0
1964	Liverpool	West Ham	*2-2
1965	Manchester Utd	Liverpool	*2-2
1966	Liverpool	Everton	1-0
1967	Manchester Utd	Tottenham	*3-3
1968	Manchester City	WBA	6-1
1969	Leeds	Manchester City	2-1
1970	Everton	Chelsea	2-1
1971	Leicester	Liverpool	1-0
1972	Manchester City	Aston Villa	1-0
1973	Burnley	Manchester City	1-0
1974	Liverpool	Leeds	1-1
	(Liverpool won 6-5 on penalties)		
1975	Derby Co	West Ham	2-0
1976	Liverpool	Southampton	1-0
1977	Liverpool	Manchester Utd	*0-0
1978	Nottm Forest	Ipswich	5-0
1979	Liverpool	Arsenal	3-1
1980	Liverpool	West Ham	1-0
1981	Aston Villa	Tottenham	*2-2
1982	Liverpool	Tottenham	1-0
1983	Manchester Utd	Liverpool	2-0
1984	Everton	Liverpool	1-0
1985	Everton	Manchester Utd	2-0
1986	Everton	Liverpool	*1-1
1987	Everton	Coventry	1-0
1988	Liverpool	Wimbledon	2-1
1989	Liverpool	Arsenal	1-0
1990	Liverpool	Manchester Utd	*1-1
1991	Arsenal	Tottenham	*0-0
1992	Leeds	Liverpool	4-3
1993	Manchester Utd	Arsenal	1-1
	(Manchester Utd won 5-4 on penalties)		
1994	Manchester Utd	Blackburn	2-0
1995	Everton	Blackburn	1-0

1996	Manchester Utd	Newcastle	4-0
1997	Manchester Utd	Chelsea	1-1
	(Manchester Utd won 4-2 on penalties)		
1998	Arsenal	Manchester Utd	3-0
1999	Arsenal	Manchester Utd	2-1
2000	Chelsea	Manchester Utd	2-0
2001	Liverpool	Manchester Utd	2-1

COMMUNITY SHIELD

Year	Winners	Runners-up	Score
2002	Arsenal	Liverpool	1-0
2003	Manchester Utd	Arsenal	1-1
	(Manchester Utd won 4-3 on penalties)		
2004	Arsenal	Manchester Utd	3-1
2005	Chelsea	Arsenal	2-1
2006	Liverpool	Chelsea	2-1
2007	Manchester Utd	Chelsea	1-1
	(Manchester Utd won 3-0 on penalties)		
2008	Manchester Utd	Portsmouth	0-0
	(Manchester Utd won 3-1 on pens)		
2009	Chelsea	Manchester Utd	2-2
	(Chelsea won 4-1 on pens)		
2010	Manchester Utd	Chelsea	3-1
2011	Manchester Utd	Manchester City	3-2
2012	Manchester City	Chelsea	3-2
2013	Manchester Utd	Wigan	2-0
2014	Arsenal	Manchester City	3-0

(Fixture played at Wembley 1974–2000 and from 2007); Millennium Stadium 2001–06; Villa Park 2012) * Trophy shared

THE THINGS THEY SAY ...

'The days of walking in, shouting and screaming and throwing teacups at players, are gone. There is no point effing and blinding at a player who can hardly speak English' – **Harry Redknapp**, former Queens Park Rangers manager.

'Crisis is what is happening to people who go out to work for Christian Aid and lose their life' – **Ian Holloway**, former Millwall manager, asked about his side's poor results.

'It was like two heavyweight boxers trying to knock each other out' – **Mark Cooper**, Swindon manager, after a 5-5 draw with Sheffield United in the League One play-offs.

'It was an absolutely shocking, awful, woeful, disgraceful, abject decision... there are no other words I can use for it' – **Steve Evans**, Rotherham manager, after the sending-off of Jordan Bowery against Middlesbrough, a red card later rescinded.

'The stuff that has been said to me over the years, even from ex team-mates, is a pack of lies and sometimes you just say "listen, I have got to defend myself a little bit"' – **Roy Keane**, former Manchester United captain, in a controversial second autobiography.

FOOTBALL'S CHANGING HOMES

Chelsea have joined **Tottenham** and **West Ham** in preparing for a new stadium. The club decided to build it at Stamford Bridge, rather than continue searching for a new site, in order to raise the capacity from just under 42,000 to 60,000. They explored a move to Battersea Power Station or Earls Court, both within a three-mile radius of their home since 1905. But feasibility studies led owner Roman Abramovich and his senior executives to favour clearing the present site and possibly lower the pitch below street level, with an extra tier of seating similar to Real Madrid's Bernabeu Stadium. The cost could be as high as £500m and result in home games being played at a temporary home for up to three years. Twickenham would be an ideal solution, but there is opposition to having football at rugby HQ. Wembley also presents problems because of a limit on the number of live events there. Meanwhile, the club have been consulting with local residents and supporters about what is best.

Tottenham are now much closer to starting work on a new 56,000-seater arena at White Hart Lane after acquiring the final piece of land needed. Plans were on hold because a sheet metal company refused to relocate. But the business decided not to appeal against a High Court order to find new premises and reached a private agreement with the club to leave next year. Tottenham, whose present capacity is 36,000, will also have to move out while work takes place, with Wembley, the Olympic Stadium and MK Dons' ground in Milton Keynes among the possibilities. West Ham, meanwhile, will offer some of the cheapest tickets in the Premier League in a bid to fill the 54,000-capacity Olympic Stadium when moving from Upton Park for the 2016-17 season. Co-chairmen David Gold and David Sullivan are using enhanced television money to pass on savings to supporters.

Liverpool plan to complete expansion of the main stand at Anfield during the course of next season. It incorporates an extra 8,500 seats and takes the capacity to around 54,000. It will be one of the largest all-seater single stands in Europe, adding another major landmark to the city skyline. The redevelopment is part of a £260m scheme for regeneration of the whole Anfield area. **Everton** say there is no question of jeopardising the stability of the club to build a new ground at Walton Hall Park. In a message to supporters, chief executive Robert Elstone declared: 'Goodison remains an intense and intimidating stadium very dear to all of our hearts. However, as has been widely debated, a new stadium could be the catalyst for a significant step-change in progress. When our funding plans become clearer, we can move quickly if the deal makes sense for the club.'

Manchester City aim to have their extended south stand open for the first home match of the season against defending champions Chelsea. With a new capacity of nearly 55,000 at the Etihad, City could have their biggest attendance since the 1970s. **Bournemouth** announced they would not be increasing the 11,700 capacity of the Goldsands Stadium, smallest by some way in the Premier League, following promotion to the top division. The club considered expanding the south stand, but with so much other work needed during the summer to improve the ground and the pitch, it was regarded as impractical.

Scunthorpe have received council approval for a new 12,000-seater stadium close to Glanford Park and hope it will be ready for the start of the 2016-17 campaign. Plans include a multi-use indoor arena, community sports pitches and a 100-bedroom hotel. The third and most complex phase of **Bristol City's** £45m rebuild of Ashton Gate started with demolition of the Williams stand. It meant that three phases of work were under way simultaneously – pulling down the 60-year-old building, demolishing the Wedlock stand and complete remodelling of the Dolman stand to include conference and exhibition facilities. Once finished, the ground will have a capacity of 27,000 and become the largest conference and events venue in the south-west. **Celtic** have been given permission to introduce a safe standing area, accommodating up to 2,600 spectators, for 2016-17. Scotland is not bound by the law that banned standing following the 1989 Hillsborough disaster.

SCOTTISH TABLES 2014–2015

PREMIERSHIP

			Home					Away					
		P	W	D	L	F	A	W	D	L	F	A	Gd	Pts
1	Celtic	38	15	2	2	50	8	14	3	2	34	9	67	92
2	Aberdeen	38	12	3	4	32	15	11	3	5	25	18	24	75
3	Inverness	38	10	6	3	29	19	9	2	8	23	23	10	65
4	St Johnstone	38	8	5	6	19	17	8	4	7	15	17	0	57
5	Dundee Utd	38	12	2	5	32	20	5	3	11	26	36	2	56
6	Dundee	38	5	8	7	25	27	6	4	8	21	30	-11	45
7	Hamilton	38	8	6	5	30	20	7	2	10	20	33	-3	53
8	Partick	38	8	4	7	32	22	4	6	9	16	22	4	46
9	Ross Co	38	7	0	12	21	31	5	8	6	25	32	-17	44
10	Kilmarnock	38	7	1	10	23	17	4	7	9	21	32	-15	41
11	Motherwell	38	7	5	7	23	21	3	1	15	15	42	-25	36
12	St Mirren	38	3	2	14	14	30	6	1	12	16	36	-36	30

League split after 33 games, with teams staying in top six and bottom six regardless of points. Celtic into Champions League second qualifying round; Inverness into Europa League second qualifying round, Aberdeen and St Johnstone into first qualifying round

Play-offs (on agg) – **Quarter-final**: Rangers 3 Queen of South 2. **Semi-final**: Rangers 2 Hibernian 1. **Final**: Motherwell 6 Rangers 1
Player of Year: Stefan Johansen
PFA Team of Year: Gordon (Celtic), Logan (Aberdeen), Denayer (Celtic), Van Dijk (Celtic), Shinnie (Inverness), Armstrong (Celtic), Brown (Celtic), Johansen (Celtic), Ciftci (Dundee Utd), Rooney (Aberdeen), Stewart (Dundee)
Leading scorers (all competitions): 28 Rooney (Aberdeen); 20 Griffiths (Celtic); 16 Ciftci (Dundee Utd), Commons (Celtic); 15 Guidetti (Celtic), Stewart (Dundee); 13 Andreu (Hamilton), Johansen (Celtic), Sutton (Motherwell); 11 Boyce (Ross Co), Crawford (Hamilton); 10 Doolan (Partick), Graham (St Johnstone), McKay (Inverness), O'Halloran (St Johnstone)

CHAMPIONSHIP

			Home					Away					
		P	W	D	L	F	A	W	D	L	F	A	Gd	Pts
1	Hearts	36	15	2	1	57	12	14	2	2	39	14	70	91
2	Hibernian	36	9	6	3	33	15	12	1	5	37	17	38	70
3	Rangers	36	10	5	3	43	21	9	5	4	26	18	30	67
4	Queen of South	36	13	1	4	32	14	4	8	6	26	27	17	60
5	Falkirk	36	7	6	5	22	19	7	5	6	26	29	0	53
6	Raith	36	6	3	9	25	40	6	4	8	17	25	-23	43
7	Dumbarton	36	5	4	9	18	37	4	3	11	18	42	-43	34
8	Livingston*	36	4	4	10	18	26	4	4	10	23	27	-12	27
9	Alloa	36	4	5	9	21	25	2	4	12	13	31	-22	27
10	Cowdenbeath	36	3	2	13	13	34	4	2	12	18	52	-55	25

* 5pts deducted for financial irregularities

Play-offs (on agg) – **Semi-finals**: Alloa 2 Brechin 1; Forfar 4 Stranraer 1. **Final**: Alloa 4 Forfar 3
Player of Year: Scott Allan (Hibernian)
PFA Team of Year: Alexander (Hearts), Gray (Hibernian), Ozturk (Hearts), Wilson (Hearts), Stevenson (Hibernian), Allan (Hibernian), Gomis (Hearts), Walker (Hearts), Reilly (Queen of South), Loy (Falkirk), Sow (Hearts)
Leading league scorers: 18 Cummings (Hibernian); 15 Lyle (Queen of South); 14 Buchanan (Alloa); 13 Malonga (Hibernian), Reilly (Queen of South); 12 Zeefuik (Hearts); 11 Keatings (Hearts), Sow (Hearts), Walker (Hearts), White (Livingston)

LEAGUE ONE

			Home					Away					
		P	W	D	L	F	A	W	D	L	F	A	Gd	Pts
1	Morton	36	12	1	5	33	16	10	2	6	32	24	25	69
2	Stranraer	36	12	2	4	34	17	8	5	5	25	21	21	67
3	Forfar	36	13	2	3	32	14	7	4	7	27	27	18	66
4	Brechin	36	7	7	4	30	26	8	7	3	28	20	12	59
5	Airdrieonians	36	10	4	4	35	20	6	6	6	18	19	14	58
6	Peterhead	36	8	5	5	25	20	6	4	8	26	34	-3	51
7	Dunfermline	36	8	5	5	28	20	5	4	9	18	28	-2	48
8	Ayr	36	4	5	9	22	28	5	2	11	23	32	-15	34
9	Stenhousemuir	36	5	4	9	22	30	3	1	14	20	33	-21	29
10	Stirling	36	2	4	12	19	42	2	4	12	16	42	-49	20

Play-offs (on agg) – Semi-finals: Queen's Park 3 Arbroath 2 (aet), Stenhousemuir 4 East Fife 2 (aet). **Final**: Stenhousemuir 2 Queen's Park 1
Player of Year: Declan McManus (Morton)
PFA Team of Year: Douglas (Forfar), Russell (Morton), Malcolm (Forfar), McKeown (Stranraer), Boyle (Airdrie), Trouten (Brechin), Stevenson (Peterhead), Gibson (Stranraer), Swankie (Forfar), McManus (Morton), Barr (Brechin)
Leading league scorers: 20 McManus (Morton); 15 McMenamin (Stenhousemuir), Trouten (Brechin); 14 Prunty (Airdrie); 11 Jackson (Brechin), Longworth (Stranraer), Swankie (Forfar); 10 Hilson (Forfar), Malcolm (Stranraer)

LEAGUE TWO

			Home					Away					
		P	W	D	L	F	A	W	D	L	F	A	Gd	Pts
1	Albion	36	10	3	5	27	18	12	2	4	34	15	28	71
2	Queen's Park	36	10	4	4	27	13	7	6	5	24	21	17	61
3	Arbroath	36	9	5	4	35	19	7	3	8	30	27	19	56
4	East Fife	36	8	6	4	28	22	7	2	9	28	26	8	53
5	Annan	36	11	2	5	37	28	3	6	9	19	28	0	50
6	Clyde	36	6	4	8	22	27	7	4	7	18	23	-10	47
7	Elgin	36	7	4	7	28	29	5	5	8	27	29	-3	45
8	Berwick	36	5	8	5	30	23	6	2	10	30	34	3	43
9	East Stirling	36	7	1	10	22	31	6	3	9	18	35	-26	43
10	Montrose	36	6	1	11	24	36	3	5	10	18	42	-36	33

Play-off (on agg): Final – Montrose 3 Brora 2
Player of Year: Bobby Linn (Arbroath)
PFA Team of Year: Parry (Albion Rov), Rooney (Queen's Park), Dunlop (Albion Rov), Andrews (Montrose), Dunlop (Albion Rov), Linn (Arbroath), Miller (Queen's Park), Woods (Queen's Park), Sutherland (Elgin), Weatherson (Annan), Murray (Arbroath)
Leading league scorers: 22 Weatherson (Annan); 19 Murray (Arbroath); 13 Gunn (Elgin), Linn (Arbroath); 12 McKenna (East Stirling), Smith (East Fife); 11 McGuigan (Albion Rov), McManus (Arbroath); 10 Austin (East Fife), Chaplain (Albion Rov), Lavery (Berwick), Wood (Montrose)

SCOTTISH LEAGUE RESULTS 2014–2015

PREMIERSHIP

	Aberdeen	Celtic	Dundee	Dundee Urd	Hamilton	Inverness	Kilmarnock	Motherwell	Partick	Ross Co	St Johnstone	St Mirren
Aberdeen	–	1-2	3-3	0-3	3-0	3-2	1-0	1-0	2-0	3-0	2-0	2-2
		0-1		1-0		1-0		2-1	0-0	4-0	0-1	3-0
Celtic	2-1	–	2-1	6-1	0-1	1-0	2-0	1-1	1-0	0-0	0-1	4-1
	4-0		5-0	3-0	4-0	5-0	4-1	4-0	2-0			
Dundee	2-3	1-1	–	1-4	2-0	1-2	1-1	4-1	1-1	1-1	1-1	1-3
	1-1	1-2		3-1	1-1	0-1	1-0		1-0		0-2	
Dundee Utd	0-2	2-1	6-2	–	2-2	1-1	3-1	1-0	1-0	2-1	2-0	3-0
	1-0	0-3	3-0		1-0			3-1	0-2	1-2	0-2	
Hamilton	3-0	0-2	2-1	2-3	–	0-2	0-0	5-0	3-3	4-0	1-0	3-0
	0-3					0-2	0-0	2-0	1-1	2-2	1-1	1-0
Inverness	0-1	1-0	0-0	1-0	4-2	–	2-0	3-1	0-4	1-1	2-1	1-0
	1-2	1-1	1-1	2-1			3-3			1-1	2-0	
				3-0								
Kilmarnock	0-2	0-2	1-3	2-0	1-0	1-2	–	2-0	3-0	0-3	0-1	2-1
	1-2		3-2	2-3				1-2	2-2	1-2		1-0
Motherwell	0-2	0-1	1-3	1-0	0-4	0-2	1-1	–	1-0	2-2	0-1	1-0
		0-1		4-0	2-1	3-1			0-0	1-1	1-1	5-0
Partick	0-1	0-3	1-1	2-2	1-2	3-1	1-1	3-1	–	4-0	0-0	1-2
					5-0	1-0	1-4	2-0		1-3	3-0	0-1
												3-0
Ross	0-1	0-5	2-1	2-3	0-1	1-3	1-2	1-2	1-0	–	1-2	1-2
		0-1	1-0		2-1		2-1	3-2	1-2		1-0	1-2
St Johnstone	1-0	0-3	0-1	2-1	0-1	1-0	1-2	2-1	2-0	2-1	–	1-2
	1-1	1-2	1-0	1-1		1-1	0-0					2-0
		0-0										
St Mirren	0-2	1-2	0-1	0-3	0-2	0-1	1-2	0-1	0-1	2-2	0-1	–
		0-2	1-2	1-1	1-0	1-2	4-1	2-1		0-3		

CHAMPIONSHIP

	Alloa	Cowdenbeath	Dumbarton	Falkirk	Hearts	Hibernian	Livingston	Queen of South	Raith	Rangers
Alloa	–	2-3	0-1	2-3	0-1	2-1	1-0	1-1	0-1	1-1
		3-0	3-0	1-3	1-4	0-1	2-2	2-2	0-0	0-1
Cowdenbeath	0-3	–	1-3	2-2	0-2	1-2	1-0	2-1	1-3	0-3
	0-2	–	3-0	0-1	1-2	0-2	1-2	0-5	0-1	0-0
Dumbarton	3-1	0-0	–	0-3	0-0	3-6	1-0	0-4	2-1	0-3
	1-0	1-2	–	1-0	1-5	1-2	1-5	0-0	2-2	1-3
Falkirk	2-1	6-0	1-1	–	1-2	1-0	0-0	1-1	0-1	0-2
	1-0	1-0	3-3	–	0-3	0-3	2-0	1-1	1-0	1-1
Hearts	2-0	5-1	5-1	4-1	–	2-1	5-0	4-1	1-0	2-0
	3-0	10-0	4-0	2-3	–	1-1	1-0	2-0	2-1	2-2
Hibernian	2-0	3-2	0-0	0-1	1-1	–	2-1	0-0	1-1	4-0
	4-1	5-0	3-0	3-3	2-0	–	2-1	0-1	1-1	0-2
Livingston	4-0	2-1	1-2	0-1	0-1	0-4	–	2-2	0-1	0-1
	0-0	1-1	1-2	2-1	2-3	1-3	–	1-0	0-2	1-1
Queen of South	2-0	1-2	3-0	3-0	0-3	1-0	1-1	–	2-0	2-0
	1-0	4-1	2-1	1-0	1-2	0-2	3-1	–	2-1	3-0
Raith	1-1	2-1	3-1	0-0	0-4	1-3	1-5	3-4	–	0-4
	2-1	1-3	2-1	2-2	1-3	2-1	0-4	3-0	–	1-2
Rangers	1-1	1-0	4-1	4-0	1-2	1-3	2-0	4-2	6-1	–
	2-2	4-1	3-1	2-2	2-1	0-2	1-1	1-1	4-0	–

LEAGUE ONE

	Airdrie	Ayr	Brechin	Dunferline	Forfar	Morton	Peterhead	Stenhousemuir	Stirling	Stranraer
Airdrie	–	3-0	4-0	3-1	1-2	0-1	0-2	2-0	0-0	3-3
	–	2-0	1-1	3-2	3-1	2-1	1-3	2-1	4-1	1-1
Ayr	2-3	–	0-2	0-1	2-0	1-0	3-3	2-3	2-2	0-2
	0-1	–	2-2	0-2	1-0	1-1	2-4	0-0	4-0	0-2
Brechin	1-1	2-4	–	1-1	3-3	3-1	1-1	1-0	2-1	1-2
	0-0	2-1	–	3-0	2-3	1-1	2-2	2-1	2-1	1-3
Dunfermline	3-0	4-2	0-0	–	0-0	1-2	3-0	2-0	4-0	0-1
	2-2	2-1	0-1	–	1-3	0-4	1-1	3-2	1-1	1-0
Forfar	1-1	2-0	3-1	2-0	–	3-2	1-0	3-0	2-1	1-1
	2-0	1-3	0-2	1-0	–	1-2	3-1	1-0	4-0	1-0
Morton	2-1	0-1	2-2	2-1	2-0	–	0-1	3-1	2-0	4-0
	0-1	2-1	0-2	2-0	0-2	–	3-1	3-2	4-0	2-0
Peterhead	1-1	2-0	1-1	1-1	3-2	1-2	–	1-0	1-1	1-4
	0-1	2-0	3-0	1-1	1-0	1-3	–	2-0	2-1	1-2
Stenhousemuir	1-0	1-1	0-2	1-0	0-2	2-1	1-2	–	4-5	2-2
	0-2	1-1	2-2	0-1	1-3	2-3	2-1	–	1-2	1-0
Stirling	2-2	1-3	0-5	0-2	2-2	3-4	2-3	0-4	–	1-1
	0-2	1-4	0-1	2-2	0-1	0-2	2-1	3-2	–	0-1
Stranraer	1-0	3-1	2-2	1-2	1-1	2-0	5-0	0-2	2-0	–
	1-0	1-0	0-2	5-1	4-2	0-2	2-0	3-2	1-0	–

LEAGUE TWO

	Albion	Annan	Arbroath	Berwick	Clyde	East Fife	East Stirling	Elgin	Montrose	Queen's Park
Albion	–	2-1	2-1	2-1	2-2	2-0	1-2	3-0	0-0	1-0
	–	2-0	1-1	2-0	0-2	2-3	0-1	0-3	3-0	2-1
Annan	2-1	–	0-1	2-0	2-1	2-1	4-3	3-3	2-2	0-1
	1-3	–	2-0	4-2	0-1	2-1	3-2	2-3	4-3	2-0
Arbroath	1-0	3-2	–	2-0	4-0	0-2	4-0	1-0	3-1	1-2
	0-2	1-1	–	5-0	3-1	1-1	0-1	3-3	2-2	1-1
Berwick	1-1	2-0	1-2	–	4-0	2-3	5-0	1-1	2-2	0-0
	0-2	2-2	3-1	–	0-0	0-3	3-0	0-2	3-3	1-1
Clyde	0-1	1-1	2-5	3-3	–	3-1	0-1	2-1	1-2	0-2
	2-3	1-0	1-1	0-3	–	1-0	1-1	0-2	2-0	2-0
East Fife	0-0	1-1	1-5	2-3	0-1	–	3-1	1-1	3-0	2-2
	1-0	2-1	2-0	1-4	1-1	–	2-1	3-1	3-0	0-0
East Stirling	1-4	0-1	2-3	0-2	1-0	1-1	–	2-1	4-0	1-3
	1-5	1-3	1-0	0-4	1-2	2-0	–	1-0	0-1	3-1
Elgin	0-4	0-0	1-1	2-1	1-0	1-0	1-2	–	0-1	1-4
	2-0	4-5	2-1	3-3	2-0	3-5	0-0	–	4-0	1-2
Montrose	0-2	2-0	1-5	2-1	0-3	0-4	4-1	2-3	–	1-2
	3-4	2-1	3-0	0-2	0-1	0-3	0-1	2-1	–	2-2
Queen's Park	0-1	0-0	0-2	2-0	1-2	3-0	3-0	2-1	2-0	–
	0-1	2-0	2-1	2-1	1-1	1-0	1-1	1-1	4-1	–

HOW CELTIC WON A FOURTH SUCCESSIVE TITLE

AUGUST 2014

13   St Johnstone 0 Celtic 3 (Stokes 55, Biton 76 pen, McGregor 84). Att: 6,890
16   Celtic 6 (Denayer 4, Commons 27, Johansen 34, Stokes 54, Inge Berget 62, 90) Dundee Utd 1 (Rankin 71). Att: 44,484
23   Inverness 1 (O'Connell 65 og) Celtic 0. Att: 5,862
31   Dundee 1 (McPake 1) Celtic 1 (Griffiths 55). Att: 9,276

SEPTEMBER 2014

13   Celtic 2 (Denayer 7, Commons 46) Aberdeen 1 (Goodwillie 60). Att: 43,640
21   Celtic 1 (Commons 68 pen) Motherwell 1 (Sutton 19). Att: 41,719
27   St Mirren 1 (McLean 49) Celtic 2 (Guidetti 42, 63). Att: 5,280

OCTOBER 2014

5   Celtic 0 Hamilton 1 (Crawford 49). Att: 42,412
18   Ross Co 0 Celtic 5 (Guidetti 11, McGregor 14, Stokes 29, 56, Denayer 35). Att: 5,693
26   Celtic 2 (Guidetti 35, Scepovic 64) Kilmarnock 0. Att: 42,800

NOVEMBER 2014

1   Celtic 1 (Guidetti 49) Inverness 0. Att: 42,553
9   Aberdeen 1 (Rooney 71) Celtic 2 (Johansen 38, Van Dijk 90). Att: 19,051
22   Celtic 2 (Stokes 45, Guidetti 54) Dundee 1 (Clarkson 58). Att: 43,787

DECEMBER 2014

3   Celtic 1 (Van Dijk 60) Partick 0. Att: 40,633
6   Motherwell 0 Celtic 1 (Stokes 6). Att: 7,740
14   Celtic 4 (Brown 4, 18, Forrest 15, Stokes 67) St Mirren 1 (Kelly 10). Att: 44,827
21   Dundee Utd 2 (Ciftci 5, Armstrong 65) Celtic 1 (Griffiths 87). Att: 12,098
27   Celtic 0 Ross Co 0. Att: 45,798

JANUARY 2015

5   Kilmarnock 0 Celtic 2 (Izaguirre 36, Scepovic 72). Att: 5,329
17   Hamilton 0 Celtic 2 (Matthews 33, Henderson 50). Att: 6,007
21   Celtic 4 (Van Dijk 26, Griffiths 42, Lustig 76, 81) Motherwell 0. Att: 42,296
24   Ross Co 0 Celtic 1 (Commons 52). Att: 5,289

FEBRUARY 2015

11   Partick 0 Celtic 3 (Mackay-Steven 1, Armstrong 30, Johansen 66). Att: 5,776
14   St Johnstone 1 (O'Halloran 72) Celtic 2 (Griffiths 1, Johansen 52). Att: 6,727
22   Celtic 4 (Commons 57, 82, Johansen 64, Guidetti 78) Hamilton 0. Att: 47,989

MARCH 2015

1   Celtic 4 (Denayer 37, Griffiths 63 pen, Mackay-Steven 69, Johansen 80) Aberdeen 0. Att: 50,256
4   Celtic 0 St Johnstone 1 (Swanson 54). Att: 41,849
21   Celtic 3 (Mackay-Steven 16, Guidetti 33, Denayer 45) Dundee Utd 0. Att: 45,884

APRIL 2015

3	St Mirren 0 Celtic 2 (Forrest 64, Johansen 80 pen). Att: 5,784
8	Celtic 2 (Commons 45 pen, Johansen 63) Partick 0. Att: 43,784
11	Inverness 1 (Ofere 5) Celtic 1 (Griffiths 3). Att: 6,059
15	Celtic 4 (Commons 58, Griffiths 66, 80, 85) Kilmarnock 1 (Westlake 50). Att: 42,464
22	Dundee 1 (McAlister 87) Celtic 2 (Mackay-Steven 32, Van Dijk 63). Att: 8,908
26	Dundee Utd 0 Celtic 3 (Griffiths 47, 65, 84 pen). Att: 8,329

MAY 2015

1	Celtic 5 (Grifiths 30, Brown 37, Commons 71 pen, Forrest 77, Biton 88) Dundee 0. Att: 44,299 (clinched title May 2 after Aberdeen's defeat by Dundee Utd)
10	Aberdeen 0 Celtic 1 (Brown 49). Att: 16,742
15	St Johnstone 0 Celtic 0. Att: 6,984
24	Celtic 5 (Scepovic 5, 70, Johansen 18, Griffiths 80, Commons 90) Inverness 0. Att: 55,638

SCOTTISH HONOURS LIST

PREMIER DIVISION

	First	Pts	Second	Pts	Third	Pts
1975–6	Rangers	54	Celtic	48	Hibernian	43
1976–7	Celtic	55	Rangers	46	Aberdeen	43
1977–8	Rangers	55	Aberdeen	53	Dundee Utd	40
1978–9	Celtic	48	Rangers	45	Dundee Utd	44
1979–80	Aberdeen	48	Celtic	47	St Mirren	42
1980–81	Celtic	56	Aberdeen	49	Rangers	44
1981–2	Celtic	55	Aberdeen	53	Rangers	43
1982–3	Dundee Utd	56	Celtic	55	Aberdeen	55
1983–4	Aberdeen	57	Celtic	50	Dundee Utd	47
1984–5	Aberdeen	59	Celtic	52	Dundee Utd	47
1985–6	*Celtic	50	Hearts	50	Dundee Utd	47
1986–7	Rangers	69	Celtic	63	Dundee Utd	60
1987–8	Celtic	72	Hearts	62	Rangers	60
1988–9	Rangers	56	Aberdeen	50	Celtic	46
1989–90	Rangers	51	Aberdeen	44	Hearts	44
1990–1	Rangers	55	Aberdeen	53	Celtic	41
1991–2	Rangers	72	Hearts	63	Celtic	62
1992–3	Rangers	73	Aberdeen	64	Celtic	60
1993–4	Rangers	58	Aberdeen	55	Motherwell	54
1994–5	Rangers	69	Motherwell	54	Hibernian	53
1995–6	Rangers	87	Celtic	83	Aberdeen	55
1996–7	Rangers	80	Celtic	75	Dundee Utd	60
1997–8	Celtic	74	Rangers	72	Hearts	67

PREMIER LEAGUE

	First	Pts	Second	Pts	Third	Pts
1998–99	Rangers	77	Celtic	71	St Johnstone	57
1999–2000	Rangers	90	Celtic	69	Hearts	54
2000–01	Celtic	97	Rangers	82	Hibernian	66
2001–02	Celtic	103	Rangers	85	Livingston	58
2002–03	*Rangers	97	Celtic	97	Hearts	63
2003–04	Celtic	98	Rangers	81	Hearts	68

	First	Pts	Second	Pts	Third	Pts
2004–05	Rangers	93	Celtic	92	Hibernian	61
2005–06	Celtic	91	Hearts	74	Rangers	73
2006–07	Celtic	84	Rangers	72	Aberdeen	65
2007–08	Celtic	89	Rangers	86	Motherwell	60
2008–09	Rangers	86	Celtic	82	Hearts	59
2009–10	Rangers	87	Celtic	81	Dundee Utd	63
2010–11	Rangers	93	Celtic	92	Hearts	63
2011–12	Celtic	93	**Rangers	73	Motherwell	62
2012–13	Celtic	79	Motherwell	63	St Johnstone	56

Maximum points: 72 except 1986–8, 1991–4 (88), 1994–2000 (108), 2001–10 (114)
* Won on goal difference. **Deducted 10 pts for administration

PREMIERSHIP

	First	Pts	Second	Pts	Third	Pts
2013–14	Celtic	99	Motherwell	70	Aberdeen	68
2014–15	Celtic	92	Aberdeen	75	Inverness	65

FIRST DIVISION (Scottish Championship until 1975–76)

	First	Pts	Second	Pts	Third	Pts
1890–1a	††Dumbarton	29	Rangers	29	Celtic	24
1891–2b	Dumbarton	37	Celtic	35	Hearts	30
1892–3a	Celtic	29	Rangers	28	St Mirren	23
1893–4a	Celtic	29	Hearts	26	St Bernard's	22
1894–5a	Hearts	31	Celtic	26	Rangers	21
1895–6a	Celtic	30	Rangers	26	Hibernian	24
1896–7a	Hearts	28	Hibernian	26	Rangers	25
1897–8a	Celtic	33	Rangers	29	Hibernian	22
1898–9a	Rangers	36	Hearts	26	Celtic	24
1899–1900a	Rangers	32	Celtic	25	Hibernian	24
1900–1c	Rangers	35	Celtic	29	Hibernian	25
1901–2a	Rangers	28	Celtic	26	Hearts	22
1902–3b	Hibernian	37	Dundee	31	Rangers	29
1903–4d	Third Lanark	43	Hearts	39	Rangers	38
1904–5a	†Celtic	41	Rangers	41	Third Lanark	35
1905–6a	Celtic	46	Hearts	39	Rangers	38
1906–7f	Celtic	55	Dundee	48	Rangers	45
1907–8f	Celtic	55	Falkirk	51	Rangers	50
1908–9f	Celtic	51	Dundee	50	Clyde	48
1909–10f	Celtic	54	Falkirk	52	Rangers	49
1910–11f	Rangers	52	Aberdeen	48	Falkirk	44
1911–12f	Rangers	51	Celtic	45	Clyde	42
1912–13f	Rangers	53	Celtic	49	Hearts	41
1913–14g	Celtic	65	Rangers	59	Hearts	54
1914–15g	Celtic	65	Hearts	61	Rangers	50
1915–16g	Celtic	67	Rangers	56	Morton	51
1916–17g	Celtic	64	Morton	54	Rangers	53
1917–18f	Rangers	56	Celtic	55	Kilmarnock	43
1918–19f	Celtic	58	Rangers	57	Morton	47
1919–20h	Rangers	71	Celtic	68	Motherwell	57
1920–1h	Rangers	76	Celtic	66	Hearts	56
1921–2h	Celtic	67	Rangers	66	Raith	56
1922–3g	Rangers	55	Airdrieonians	50	Celtic	40
1923–4g	Rangers	59	Airdrieonians	50	Celtic	41
1924–5g	Rangers	60	Airdrieonians	57	Hibernian	52
1925–6g	Celtic	58	Airdrieonians	50	Hearts	50
1926–7g	Rangers	56	Motherwell	51	Celtic	49
1927–8g	Rangers	60	Celtic	55	Motherwell	55
1928–9g	Rangers	67	Celtic	55	Motherwell	50
1929–30g	Rangers	60	Motherwell	55	Aberdeen	53
1930–1g	Rangers	60	Celtic	58	Motherwell	56

	First		Second		Third	
1931–2g	Motherwell	66	Rangers	61	Celtic	48
1932–3g	Rangers	62	Motherwell	59	Hearts	50
1933–4g	Rangers	66	Motherwell	62	Celtic	47
1934–5g	Rangers	55	Celtic	52	Hearts	50
1935–6g	Celtic	68	Rangers	61	Aberdeen	61
1936–7g	Rangers	61	Aberdeen	54	Celtic	52
1937–8g	Celtic	61	Hearts	58	Rangers	49
1938–9f	Rangers	59	Celtic	48	Aberdeen	46
1946–7f	Rangers	46	Hibernian	44	Aberdeen	39
1947–8g	Hibernian	48	Rangers	46	Partick	46
1948–9i	Rangers	46	Dundee	45	Hibernian	39
1949–50i	Rangers	50	Hibernian	49	Hearts	43
1950–1i	Hibernian	48	Rangers	38	Dundee	38
1951–2i	Hibernian	45	Rangers	41	East Fife	37
1952–3i	*Rangers	43	Hibernian	43	East Fife	39
1953–4i	Celtic	43	Hearts	38	Partick	35
1954–5f	Aberdeen	49	Celtic	46	Rangers	41
1955–6f	Rangers	52	Aberdeen	46	Hearts	45
1956–7f	Rangers	55	Hearts	53	Kilmarnock	42
1957–8f	Hearts	62	Rangers	49	Celtic	46
1958–9f	Rangers	50	Hearts	48	Motherwell	44
1959–60f	Hearts	54	Kilmarnock	50	Rangers	42
1960–1f	Rangers	51	Kilmarnock	50	Third Lanark	42
1961–2f	Dundee	54	Rangers	51	Celtic	46
1962–3f	Rangers	57	Kilmarnock	48	Partick	46
1963–4f	Rangers	55	Kilmarnock	49	Celtic	47
1964–5f	*Kilmarnock	50	Hearts	50	Dunfermline	49
1965–6f	Celtic	57	Rangers	55	Kilmarnock	45
1966–7f	Celtic	58	Rangers	55	Clyde	46
1967–8f	Celtic	63	Rangers	61	Hibernian	45
1968–9f	Celtic	54	Rangers	49	Dunfermline	45
1969–70f	Celtic	57	Rangers	45	Hibernian	44
1970–1f	Celtic	56	Aberdeen	54	St Johnstone	44
1971–2f	Celtic	60	Aberdeen	50	Rangers	44
1972–3f	Celtic	57	Rangers	56	Hibernian	45
1973–4f	Celtic	53	Hibernian	49	Rangers	48
1974–5f	Rangers	56	Hibernian	49	Celtic	45

*Won on goal average †Won on deciding match ††Title shared. Competition suspended 1940–46 (Second World War)

SCOTTISH CHAMPIONSHIP WINS

Rangers	*54	Hibernian	4	Kilmarnock	1
Celtic	46	Dumbarton	*2	Motherwell	1
Aberdeen	4	Dundee	1	Third Lanark	1
Hearts	4	Dundee Utd	1	(*Incl 1 shared)	

FIRST DIVISION (Since formation of Premier Division)

	First	Pts	Second	Pts	Third	Pts
1975–6d	Partick	41	Kilmarnock	35	Montrose	30
1976–7j	St Mirren	62	Clydebank	58	Dundee	51
1977–8j	*Morton	58	Hearts	58	Dundee	57
1978–9j	Dundee	55	Kilmarnock	54	Clydebank	54
1979–80j	Hearts	53	Airdrieonians	51	Ayr	44
1980–1j	Hibernian	57	Dundee	52	St Johnstone	51
1981–2j	Motherwell	61	Kilmarnock	51	Hearts	50
1982–3j	St Johnstone	55	Hearts	54	Clydebank	50
1983–4j	Morton	54	Dumbarton	51	Partick	46
1984–5j	Motherwell	50	Clydebank	48	Falkirk	45
1985–6j	Hamilton	56	Falkirk	54	Kilmarnock	44
1986–7k	Morton	57	Dunfermline	56	Dumbarton	53

	First	Pts	Second	Pts	Third	Pts
1987–8k	Hamilton	56	Meadowbank	52	Clydebank	49
1988–9j	Dunfermline	54	Falkirk	52	Clydebank	48
1989–90j	St Johnstone	58	Airdrieonians	54	Clydebank	44
1990–1j	Falkirk	54	Airdrieonians	53	Dundee	52
1991–2k	Dundee	58	Partick	57	Hamilton	57
1992–3k	Raith	65	Kilmarnock	54	Dunfermline	52
1993–4k	Falkirk	66	Dunfermline	65	Airdrieonians	54
1994–5l	Raith	69	Dunfermline	68	Dundee	68
1995–6l	Dunfermline	71	Dundee Utd.	67	Morton	67
1996–7l	St Johnstone	80	Airdrieonians	60	Dundee	58
1997–8l	Dundee	70	Falkirk	65	Raith	60
1998–9l	Hibernian	89	Falkirk	66	Ayr	62
1999–2000l	St Mirren	76	Dunfermline	71	Falkirk	68
2000–01l	Livingston	76	Ayr	69	Falkirk	56
2001–02l	Partick	66	Airdie	56	Ayr	52
2002–03l	Falkirk	81	Clyde	72	St Johnstone	67
2003–04l	Inverness	70	Clyde	69	St Johnstone	57
2004–05l	Falkirk	75	St Mirren	60	Clyde	60
2005–06l	St Mirren	76	St Johnstone	66	Hamilton	59
2006–07l	Gretna	66	St Johnstone	58	Dundee	53
2007–08l	Hamilton	76	Dundee	69	St Johnstone	58
2008–09l	St Johnstone	65	Partick	55	Dunfermline	51
2009–10l	Inverness	73	Dundee	61	Dunfermline	58
2010–11l	Dunfermline	70	Raith	60	Falkirk	58
2011–12l	Ross	79	Dundee	55	Falkirk	52
2012–13l	Partick	78	Morton	67	Falkirk	53

CHAMPIONSHIP

	First	Pts	Second	Pts	Third	Pts
2013–14l	Dundee	69	Hamilton	67	Falkirk	66
2014–15l	Hearts	91	Hibernian	70	Rangers	67

Maximum points: a, 36; b, 44; c,.40; d 52; e, 60; f, 68; g, 76; h, 84; i, 60; j, 78; k, 88; l, 108
*Won on goal difference

SECOND DIVISION

	First	Pts	Second	Pts	Third	Pts
1921–2a	Alloa	60	Cowdenbeath	47	Armadale	45
1922–3a	Queen's Park	57	Clydebank	52	St Johnstone	50
1923–4a	St Johnstone	56	Cowdenbeath	55	Bathgate	44
1924–5a	Dundee Utd	50	Clydebank	48	Clyde	47
1925–6a	Dunfermline	59	Clyde	53	Ayr	52
1926–7a	Bo'ness	56	Raith	49	Clydebank	45
1927–8a	Ayr	54	Third Lanark	45	King'sPark	44
1928–9b	Dundee Utd	51	Morton	50	Arbroath	47
1929–30a	*LeithAthletic	57	East Fife	57	Albion	54
1930–1a	Third Lanark	61	Dundee Utd	50	Dunfermline	47
1931–2a	*E Stirling	55	St Johnstone	55	Stenhousemuir	46
1932–3c	Hibernian	55	Queen of South	49	Dunfermline	47
1933–4c	Albion	45	Dunfermline	44	Arbroath	44
1934–5c	Third Lanark	52	Arbroath	50	St Bernard's	47
1935–6c	Falkirk	59	St Mirren	52	Morton	48
1936–7c	Ayr	54	Morton	51	St Bernard's	48
1937–8c	Raith	59	Albion	48	Airdrieonians	47
1938–9c	Cowdenbeath	60	Alloa	48	East Fife	48
1946–7d	Dundee Utd	45	Airdrieonians	42	East Fife	31
1947–8e	East Fife	53	Albion	42	Hamilton	40
1948–9e	*Raith	42	Stirling	42	Airdrieonians	41
1949–50e	Morton	47	Airdrieonians	44	St Johnstone	36

	First	Pts	Second	Pts	Third	Pts
1950–1e	*Queen of South	45	Stirling	45	Ayr	36
1951–2e	Clyde	44	Falkirk	43	Ayr	39
1952–3	E Stirling	44	Hamilton	43	Queen's Park	37
1953–4e	Motherwell	45	Kilmarnock	42	Third Lanark	36
1954–5e	Airdrieonians	46	Dunfermline	42	Hamilton	39
1955–6b	Queen's Park	54	Ayr	51	St Johnstone	49
1956–7b	Clyde	64	Third Lanark	51	Cowdenbeath	45
1957–8b	Stirling	55	Dunfermline	53	Arbroath	47
1958–9b	Ayr	60	Arbroath	51	Stenhousemuir	46
1959–60b	St Johnstone	53	Dundee Utd	50	Queen of South	49
1960–1b	Stirling	55	Falkirk	54	Stenhousemuir	50
1961–2b	Clyde	54	Queen of South	53	Morton	44
1962–3b	St Johnstone	55	E Stirling	49	Morton	48
1963–4b	Morton	67	Clyde	53	Arbroath	46
1964–5b	Stirling	59	Hamilton	50	Queen of South	45
1965–6b	Ayr	53	Airdrieonians	50	Queen of South	47
1966–7b	Morton	69	Raith	58	Arbroath	57
1967–8b	St Mirren	62	Arbroath	53	East Fife	49
1968–9b	Motherwell	64	Ayr	53	East Fife	48
1969–70b	Falkirk	56	Cowdenbeath	55	Queen of South	50
1970–1b	Partick	56	East Fife	51	Arbroath	46
1971–2b	*Dumbarton	52	Arbroath	52	Stirling	50
1972–3b	Clyde	56	Dunfermline	52	Raith	47
1973–4b	Airdrieonians	60	Kilmarnock	58	Hamilton	55
1974–5b	Falkirk	54	Queen of South	53	Montrose	53

SECOND DIVISION (MODERN)

	First	Pts	Second	Pts	Third	Pts
1975–6d	*Clydebank	40	Raith	40	Alloa	35
1976–7f	Stirling	55	Alloa	51	Dunfermline	50
1977–8f	*Clyde	53	Raith	53	Dunfermline	48
1978–9f	Berwick	54	Dunfermline	52	Falkirk	50
1979–80f	Falkirk	50	E Stirling	49	Forfar	46
1980–1f	Queen's Park	50	Queen of South	46	Cowdenbeath	45
1981–2f	Clyde	59	Alloa	50	Arbroath	50
1982–3f	Brechin	55	Meadowbank	54	Arbroath	49
1983–4f	Forfar	63	East Fife	47	Berwick	43
1984–5f	Montrose	53	Alloa	50	Dunfermline	49
1985–6f	Dunfermline	57	Queen of South	55	Meadowbank	49
1986–7f	Meadowbank	55	Raith	52	Stirling	52
1987–8f	Ayr	61	St Johnstone	59	Queen's Park	51
1988–9f	Albion	50	Alloa	45	Brechin	43
1989–90f	Brechin	49	Kilmarnock	48	Stirling	47
1990–1f	Stirling	54	Montrose	46	Cowdenbeath	45
1991–2f	Dumbarton	52	Cowdenbeath	51	Alloa	50
1992–3f	Clyde	54	Brechin	53	Stranraer	53
1993–4f	Stranraer	56	Berwick	48	Stenhousemuir	47
1994–5g	Morton	64	Dumbarton	60	Stirling	58
1995–6g	Stirling	81	East Fife	67	Berwick	60
1996–7g	Ayr	77	Hamilton	74	Livingston	64
1997–8g	Stranraer	61	Clydebank	60	Livingston	59
1998–9g	Livingston	77	Inverness	72	Clyde	53
1999–2000g	Clyde	65	Alloa	64	Ross Co	62
2000–01g	Partick	75	Arbroath	58	Berwick	54
2001–02g	Queen of South	67	Alloa	59	Forfar Athletic	53
2002–03g	Raith	59	Brechin	55	Airdrie	54
2003–04g	Airdrie	70	Hamilton	62	Dumbarton	60
2004–05g	Brechin	72	Stranraer	63	Morton	62
2005–06g	Gretna	88	Morton	70	Peterhead	57

2006–07g	Morton	77	Stirling	69	Raith	62
2007–08g	Ross	73	Airdrie	66	Raith	60
2008–09g	Raith	76	Ayr	74	Brechin	62
2009–10g	*Stirling	65	Alloa	65	Cowdenbeath	59
2010–11g	Livingston	82	*Ayr	59	Forfar	59
2011–12g	Cowdenbeath	71	Arbroath	63	Dumbarton	58
2012–13g	Queen of South	92	Alloa	67	Brechin	61

LEAGUE ONE

	First	Pts	Second	Pts	Third	Pts
2013–14g	Rangers	102	Dunfermline	63	Stranraer	51
2014–15g	Morton	69	Stranraer	67	Forfar	66

Maximum points: a, 76; b, 72; c, 68; d, 52 difference   e,.60;.f..78;.108 *Won on goal average/goal

THIRD DIVISION (MODERN)

1994–5	Forfar	80	Montrose	67	Ross Co	60
1995–6	Livingston	72	Brechin	63	Caledonian Th	57
1996–7	Inverness	76	Forfar	67	Ross Co	77
1997–8	Alloa	76	Arbroath	68	Ross Co	67
1998–9	Ross Co	77	Stenhousemuir	64	Brechin	59
1999–2000	Queen's Park	69	Berwick	66	Forfar	61
2000–01	*Hamilton	76	Cowdenbeath	76	Brechin	72
2001–02	Brechin	73	Dumbarton	61	Albion	59
2002–03	Morton	72	East Fife	71	Albion	70
2003–05	Stranraer	79	Stirling	77	Gretna	68
2004–05	Gretna	98	Peterhead	78	Cowdenbeath	51
2005–06	*Cowdenbeath	76	Berwick	76	Stenhousemuir	73
2006–07	Berwick	75	Arbroath	70	Queen's Park	68
2007–08	East Fife	88	Stranraer	65	Montrose	59
2008–09	Dumbarton	67	Cowdenbeath	63	East Stirling	61
2009–10	Livingston	78	Forfar	63	East Stirling	61
2010–11	Arbroath	66	Albion	61	Queen's Park	59
2011–12	Alloa	77	Queen's Park	63	Stranraer	58
2012–13	Rangers	83	Peterhead	59	Queen's Park	56

LEAGUE TWO

	First	Pts	Second	Pts	Third	Pts
2013–14	Peterhead	76	Annan	63	Stirling	58
2014–15	Albion	71	Queen's Park	61	Arbroath	56

Maximum points: 108 * Won on goal difference

RELEGATED FROM PREMIER DIVISION/PREMIER LEAGUE/PREMIERSHIP

1975–6	Dundee,	St Johnstone	1985–6	No relegation
1976–7	Kilmarnock,	Hearts	1986–7	Clydebank, Hamilton
1977–8	Ayr,	Clydebank	1987–8	Falkirk, Dunfermline, Morton
1978–9	Hearts,	Motherwell	1988–9	Hamilton
1979–80	Dundee,	Hibernian	1989–90	Dundee
1980–1	Kilmarnock,	Hearts	1990–1	No relegation
1981–2	Partick,	Airdrieonians	1991–2	St Mirren, Dunfermline
1982–3	Morton,	Kilmarnock	1992–3	Falkirk, Airdrieonians
1983–4	St Johnstone,	Motherwell	1993–4	St J'stone, Raith, Dundee
1984–5	Dumbarton,	Morton	1994–5	Dundee Utd

1995–6	Falkirk, Partick	2007–08	Gretna
1996–7	Raith	2008–09	Inverness
1997–8	Hibernian	2009–10	Falkirk
1998–9	Dunfermline	2010–11	Hamilton
1999–2000	No relegation	2011–12	Dunfermline, *Rangers
2000–01	St Mirren	2012–13	Dundee
2001–02	St Johnstone	2013–14	Hibernian, **Hearts
2002–03	No relegation	2014–15	St Mirren
2003–04	Partick		*Following administration, liquidation and new
2004–05	Dundee		club formed.
2005–06	Livingston		**Deducted 15 points for administration
2006–07	Dunfermline		

RELEGATED FROM FIRST DIVISION/CHAMPIONSHIP

1975–6	Dunfermline, Clyde	1997–8	Partick, Stirling
1976–7	Raith, Falkirk	1998–9	Hamilton, Stranraer
1977–8	Alloa, East Fife	1999–2000	Clydebank
1978–9	Montrose, Queen of South	2000–01	Morton, Alloa
1979–80	Arbroath, Clyde	2001–02	Raith
1980–1	Stirling, Berwick	2002–03	Alloa Athletic, Arbroath
1981–2	E Stirling, Queen of South	2003–04	Ayr, Brechin
1982–3	Dunfermline, Queen's Park	2004–05	Partick, Raith
1983–4	Raith, Alloa	2005–06	Brechin, Stranraer
1984–5	Meadowbank, St Johnstone	2006–07	Airdrie Utd, Ross Co
1985–6	Ayr, Alloa	2007–08	Stirling
1986–7	Brechin, Montrose	2008–09	*Livingston, Clyde
1987–8	East Fife, Dumbarton	2009–10	Airdrie, Ayr
1988–9	Kilmarnock, Queen of South	2010–11	Cowdenbeath, Stirling
1989–90	Albion, Alloa	2011–12	Ayr, Queen of South
1990–1	Clyde, Brechin	2012–13	Dunfermline, Airdrie
1991–2	Montrose, Forfar	2013–14	Morton
1992–3	Meadowbank, Cowdenbeath	2014–15	Cowdenbeath
1993–4	Dumbarton, Stirling, Clyde, Morton, Brechin		*relegated to Division Three for breaching insolvency rules
1994–5	Ayr, Stranraer		
1995–6	Hamilton, Dumbarton		
1996–7	Clydebank, East Fife		

RELEGATED FROM SECOND DIVISION/LEAGUE ONE

1993–4	Alloa, Forfar, E Stirling, Montrose, Queen's Park, Arbroath, Albion, Cowdenbeath	2003–04	East Fife, Stenhousemuir
		2004–05	Arbroath, Berwick
		2005–06	Dumbarton
		2006–07	Stranraer, Forfar
1994–5	Meadowbank, Brechin	2007–08	Cowdenbeath, Berwick
1995–6	Forfar, Montrose	2008–09	Queen's Park, Stranraer
1996–7	Dumbarton, Berwick	2009–10	Arbroath, Clyde
1997–8	Stenhousemuir, Brechin	2010–11	Alloa, Peterhead
1998–9	East Fife, Forfar	2011–12	Stirling
1999–2000	Hamilton	2012–13	Albion
2000–01	Queen's Park, Stirling	2013–14	East Fife, Arbroath
2001–02	Morton	2014–15	Stirling
2002–03	Stranraer, Cowdenbeath		

SCOTTISH PREMIERSHIP 2014–2015

(appearances and scorers)

ABERDEEN

Anderson R 2	Langfield J 13	Robson B 9 (11)
Brown S.................25	Logan S.................35	Rooney A 32 (5)
Considine A 36 (1)	Low N.................3 (4)	Ross F ....- (2)
Daniels D 7 (2)	McGinn N 34 (2)	Shankland L.........2 (15)
Driver A 1	McLean K 11 (2)	Shaughnessy J.........1 (2)
Flood W 22 (3)	Monakana J........... - (10)	Smith C 5 (19)
Gibbons K............ - (1)	Murray C 1 (1)	Taylor A 31 (1)
Goodwillie D.......... 21 (10)	Pawlett P 28 (8)	Wright S ....- (1)
Hayes J.................32	Reynolds M.................37	
Jack R 30 (2)	Robertson C ....- (1)	

League goals (57): Rooney 18, Goodwillie 6, Pawlett 6, McGinn 5, Hayes 3, Jack 3, Logan 3, Taylor 3, Considine 2, Reynolds 2, Smith 2, Low 1, Opponents 3
Scottish Cup goals (1): Opponents 1. **Communities Cup goals (6):** Rooney 4, Daniels 1, Taylor 1. **Europa League goals (12):** Rooney 6, McGinn 2, Hayes 1, Logan 1, Pawlett 1, Reynolds 1
Average home league attendance: 13,359. **Player of Year:** Adam Rooney

CELTIC

Ambrose E 21 (6)	Griffiths L 14 (10)	Mubarak W 4 (1)
Armstrong S.............12 (3)	Guidetti J 19 (5)	Mulgrew C.................7 (3)
Berget J I.................2 (2)	Henderson L 4 (5)	O'Connell E.................2 (1)
Biton N.................24 (7)	Izaguirre E 34 (1)	Pukki T.................1
Boerrigter D ....- (1)	Johansen S 33 (4)	Scepovic S.................4 (14)
Brown S.................31 (1)	Kayal B.................2 (4)	Stokes A 18 (3)
Commons K 20 (9)	Lustig M 3 (2)	Tierney K 1 (1)
Denayer J.................29	Mackay-Steven G.... 10 (3)	Tonev A 3 (3)
Fisher D.................1 (4)	Matthews A 24 (5)	Twardzik F.................1
Forrest J 12 (7)	McGeouch D 1	Zaluska L.................5
Gordon C.................33	McGregor C 8 (10)	Van Dijk V.................35

League goals (84): Griffiths 14, Commons 10, Johansen 9, Guidetti 8, Stokes 7, Denayer 5, Brown 4, Mackay-Steven 4, Scepovic 4, Van Dijk 4, Forrest 3, Berget 2, Biton 2, Lustig 2, McGregor 2, Armstrong 1, Henderson 1, Izaguirre 1, Matthews 1
Scottish Cup goals (13): Van Dijk 4, Griffiths 3, Guidetti 2, Commons 1, Denayer 1, Johansen 1, Stokes 1. **Communities Cup goals (13):** Guidetti 4, Commons 3, Griffiths 3, Forrest 1, Izaguirre 1, Opponents 1.
Champions League goals (7): McGregor 3, Pukki 2, Van Dijk 2. **Europa League goals (13):** Johansen 3, Commons 2, Scepovic 2, Armstrong 1, Brown 1, Guidetti 1, Mubarak 1, Opponents 2
Average home league attendance: 44,585. **Player of Year:** Stefan Johansen

DUNDEE

Bain S.................22	Harkins G 21 (7)	McGinn P.................34
Black A.................- (1)	Harris A 11 (5)	McGinn S 11 (2)
Boyle M 6 (12)	Heffernan P 4 (3)	McGowan P.................30
Carreiro D ....- (1)	Irvine G 25 (1)	McPake J.................34
Clarkson D 18 (5)	Kerr C.................- (2)	Roberts P.................4 (3)
Colquhoun C 1 (1)	Konrad T.................30 (3)	Schenk A 1
Davidson I.................8 (5)	Letheren K.................15	Stewart G 32 (2)
Dyer W 18 (3)	MacDonald P.................2 (5)	Tankulic L 12 (14)
Ferry S 14 (5)	McAlister J.................34 (3)	Thomson K 20 (4)
Gadzhalov K.................6 (2)	McBride K 4 (2)	Wighton C.................1 (15)

League goals (46): Stewart 13, Clarkson 8, Harkins 4, Irvine 4, McAlister 2, McPake 2, Tankulic 2, Davidson 1, Harris 1, Heffernan 1, Konrad 1, MacDonald 1, McGinn P 1, McGinn S 1, McGowan 1, Wighton 1, Opponents 2
Scottish Cup goals (2): Clarkson 1, Konrad 1. **Communities Cup goals** (8): MacDonald 2, Stewart 2, Boyle 1, Ferry 1, McGinn P 1, Tankulic 1
Average home league attendance: 6,966. **Player of Year**: Greg Stewart

DUNDEE UNITED

Adeyemo O .... - (1)	Dixon P..................15	Paton P 22 (2)
Anier H..................... 4 (8)	Dow R 17 (7)	Rankin J...............29 (1)
Armstrong S............. 17 (3)	Erskine C 27 (7)	Smith S .... - (3)
Bilate M 6 (8)	Fojut J....................36	Souttar J..................13
Butcher C...............15	Graham R .... - (1)	Spark E .... - (2)
Cierzniak R 36 (1)	Johnson J .... - (1)	Spittal B 13 (12)
Ciftci N................... 34 (2)	Mackay-Steven G...... 14 (7)	Szromnik M............. 2 (2)
Connolly A .... - (10)	McGowan R.............12	Telfer C 13 (8)
Coote A................... - (3)	Morris C 23 (2)	Townsend C 16 (1)
Dillon S 26 (1)	Muirhead R 6 (7)	Watson K 14

League goals (58): Ciftci 14, Armstrong 6, Erskine 6, Mackay-Steven 5, Fojut 4, Telfer 4, Bilate 2, Dow 2, Muirhead 2, Paton 2, Rankin 2, Spittal 2, Anier 1, Butcher 1, Connolly 1, Dillon 1, McGowan 1, Morris 1, Watson 1
Scottish Cup goals (6): Dow 2, Ciftci 1, Erskine 1, Souttar 1, Watson 1. **Communities Cup goals** (6): Ciftci 1, Connolly 1, Dow 1, Erskine 1, Fojut 1, Morris 1
Average home league attendance: 8,113. **Player of Year**: Nadir Ciftci

HAMILTON ACADEMICAL

Andreu A 21 (2)	Hasselbaink N............ 4 (6)	McMahon S................. - (1)
Antoine-Curier M 20 (2)	Hendrie S 26 (4)	Neil A.......................7
Boyd S .... - (1)	Imrie D 33 (1)	Redmond D.............. 20 (3)
Brophy E.................. 2 (14)	Jesus Garcia........... 25 (1)	Routledge J........... 12 (3)
Canning M 22 (1)	Longridge L 9 (23)	Ryan A .... - (7)
Crawford A 37 (1)	Lucas 2 (4)	Scotland J.............. 12 (12)
Devlin M 25 (3)	Lyon D.................... 8 (6)	Sumsky N .... - (1)
Docherty C 1 (6)	MacDonald K 7 (1)	Watson C .... - (2)
Gillespie G 36	MacKinnon D 27 (3)	
Gordon Z..................24	McGovern M................38	

League goals (50): Andreu 12, Crawford 11, Antoine-Curier 8, Scotland 5, Canning 3, MacKinnon 3, Imrie 2, Redmond 2, Docherty 1, Hasselbaink 1, Jesus Garcia 1, Lucas 1
Scottish Cup goals: None. **Communities Cup goals** (6): Longridge 2, Andreu 1, Brophy 1, Canning 1, Imrie 1
Average home league attendance: 2,877

INVERNESS CALEDONIAN THISTLE

Brill D 24	Mackay C..................... - (1)	Sutherland A................ - (2)
Christie R 26 (9)	McKay B 22 (1)	Tansey G.....................36
Devine D................... 6 (2)	Meekings J.................37	Tremarco C............ 9 (2)
Doran A 15 (18)	Ofere E 7 (3)	Vincent J 13 (7)
Draper R 31 (1)	Polworth L 1 (4)	Warren G 36
Esson R 14 (2)	Raven D....................33	Watkins M 29 (4)
Ferguson C............... - (2)	Ross N 13 (13)	Williams D 27 (7)
Horner L 1 (1)	Sekajja I .... - (4)	
Kink T 1 (4)	Shinnie G 37	

League goals (52): McKay 10, Watkins 7, Doran 6, Ofere 5, Christie 4, Tansey 4, Meekings 3,

Ross 3, Shinnie 2, Warren 2, Williams 2, Vincent 1, Opponents 3
Scottish Cup goals (13): Tansey 5, Watkins 2, Devine 1, Meekings 1, Ofere 1, Raven 1, Shinnie 1, Vincent 1, Warren 1, Williams 1. **Communities Cup goals**: None
Average home league attendance: 3,733. **Player of Year**: Graeme Shinnie

KILMARNOCK

Ashcroft L............... 20 (2)	Hamill J.................... 20 (1)	Obadeyi T 28 (1)
Barbour R 28 (2)	Johnston C............ 19 (11)	Pascali M................ 29 (2)
Brennan C................. 3 (1)	Kiltie G.................... 2 (6)	Samson C.....................35
Cairney P 3 (13)	Magennis J.....................38	Slater C 23 (3)
Chantler C.....................26	McKenzie R 21 (7)	Splaine A...........................1
Clingan S 22 (2)	Miller L.................... 9 (10)	Syme C..................... 3 (2)
Connolly M.............. 25 (1)	Muirhead R 7 (13)	Westlake D.............. 16 (1)
Eccleston N 6 (4)	Ngoo M..................... 3 (3)	
Eremenko A 17 (10)	O'Hara M 14 (4)	

League goals (44): Obadeyi 9, Magennis 8, Eremenko 4, Slater 4, Pascali 3, Ashcroft 2, Clingan 2, Connolly 2, Kiltie 2, Muirhead 2, Eccleston 1, Hamill 1, Johnston 1, Miller 1, Westlake 1, Opponents 1
Scottish Cup goals: None. **Communities Cup goals** (1): McKenzie 1
Average home league attendance: 4,076. **Player of Year**: Mark Connolly

MOTHERWELL

Ainsworth L........... 19 (15)	Lasley K.......................33	Ojamaa H 16 (2)
Cadden C.................. - (3)	Law J 28 (6)	Pearson S 13
Carswell S 14 (5)	Lawson P 3	Ramsden S 20 (2)
Erwin L................... 20 (14)	Leitch J 4 (3)	Reid C 19 (1)
Ferguson D 3 (3)	Long G 13	Straker A 11 (1)
Francis-Angol Z 10 (1)	MacLean R .... - (1)	Sutton J 27 (11)
Grant C 10 (1)	McDonald S..................11	Thomas D 2 (13)
Hammell S......................8	McHugh R 1 (3)	Thomas N 1 (1)
Johnson M 10 (1)	McManus S.....................36	Twardzik D....................25
Kerr F 16 (5)	Moore C 2 (7)	Vigurs I................... 10 (1)
Laing L........................11	O'Brien M 17 (2)	Watt L 5

Play-offs – appearances: Ainsworth 2, Erwin 2, Hammell 2, Johnson 2, Laing 2, Lasley 2, Law 2, Long 2, McDonald 2, McManus 2, Pearson 2, Ramsden – (2), Grant – (1), Moore – (1), Straker – (1), Sutton – (1)
League goals (38): Sutton 12, Ainsworth 6, Erwin 5, McDonald 5, Ojamaa 3, Vigurs 2, Grant 1, Kerr 1, Laing 1, Pearson 1, Ramsden 1. **Play-offs – goals** (6): Ainsworth 2, Erwin 1, Johnson 1, McManus 1, Sutton 1
Scottish Cup goals (1): Ojamaa 1. **Communities Cup goals**: None. **Europa League goals** (4): Law 2, Ainsworth 1, Hammell 1
Average home league attendance: 4,286. **Player of Year**: Lee Erwin

PARTICK THISTLE

Balatoni C.....................32	Fraser G 13 (10)	Muirhead A 3 (2)
Bannigan S 34 (2)	Gallacher P 16 (2)	O'Donnell S....................34
Booth C 14	Hendry J 1	Osman A........................34
Carroll J 8 (2)	Higginbotham K 24 (6)	Richards-Everton B 1 (1)
Craigen J 19 (7)	Keenan D 4 (1)	Seaborne D 18
Doolan K................ 18 (17)	Lawless S 28 (5)	Stevenson R 28 (4)
Eccleston N .... - (9)	Lindsay L 1	Taylor L 10 (5)
Elliott C 18 (8)	McDaid D 5 (11)	Welsh S 1 (2)
Fox S...........................22	McLaughlin N .... - (1)	Wilson D 1 (5)
Frans F 20	McMillan J.....................11	

League goals (48): Doolan 9, O'Donnell 5, Stevenson 5, Balatoni 3, Bannigan 3, Fraser 3, Lawless 3, Taylor 3, Craigen 2, Elliott 2, Frans 2, Higginbotham 2, Eccleston 1, McMillan 1, Osman 1, Seaborne 1, Opponents 2
Scottish Cup goals (3): Stevenson 2, Taylor 1. **Communities Cup goals** (2): Doolan 1, Eccleston 1
Average home league attendance: 3,777. **Player of Year**: Abdul Osman

ROSS COUNTY

Arquin Y 14 (3)	De Vita R 13 (1)	Palazuelos R 1 (4)
Balk J.................................4	Dingwall T................ 10 (9)	Quinn P 28 (1)
Barr D 5 (1)	Dreesen T 3	Quinn R 8 (5)
Boyce L 17 (13)	Dunfield T........................4	Reckord J 26
Boyd S 31 (1)	Fenlon J 4	Reguero A 16
Brittain R.............. 18 (3)	Fraser M 16	Ross S 2 (3)
Brown M..........................22	Frempah B 4 (2)	Saunders S 6 (1)
Cardle J 11 (11)	Gardyne M 22 (2)	Sernas D .... - (5)
Carey G................... 17 (5)	Irvine J 27 (1)	Toshney L 7 (2)
Celcer U 5	Jervis J 10 (17)	Woods M 26 (1)
Curran C 17 (2)	Kiss F 21 (10)	
De Leeuw M 3 (3)	Maatsen D .... - (8)	

League goals (46): Boyce 10, Gardyne 6, Curran 5, Jervis 4, De Vita 3, Quinn P 3, Arquin 2, Carey 2, Dingwall 2, Irvine 2, Maatsen 2, Woods 2, Fraser 1, Quinn R 1, Reckord 1
Scottish Cup goals (1): Jervis 1. **Communities Cup goals** (2): Boyce 1, De Leeuw 1
Average home league attendance: 3,525. **Player of Year**: Liam Boyce

ST JOHNSTONE

Anderson S 37	Lappin S 19 (8)	Morgan A 1 (4)
Brown S................... 8 (2)	Mackay D........................34	O'Halloran M 30 (8)
Caddis L 6 (9)	MacLean S 23 (1)	Scobbie T 17 (3)
Croft L 17 (10)	Mannus A 38	Swanson D 8 (3)
Davidson M 17 (6)	McDonald G 10 (6)	Wotherspoon D 30 (5)
Easton B........................31	McFadden J 8 (9)	Wright F 23 (1)
Graham B 17 (7)	Millar C 32	
Kane C 4 (11)	Miller G 8 (12)	

League goals (34): Graham 9, O'Halloran 9, Anderson 3, Davidson 3, MacLean 2, Swanson 2, Kane 1, Lappin 1, MacKay 1, McFadden 1, Millar 1, Wotherspoon 1
Scottish Cup goals (2): McFadden 1, O'Halloran 1. **Communities Cup goals** (1): Graham 1.
Europa League goals (4): May S 2, Mackay 1, MacLean 1
Average home league attendance: 4,592. **Player of Year**: Chris Millar

ST MIRREN

Arquin Y 8 (4)	Kello M............................15	Plummer E.........................6
Baird J 7 (1)	Kelly S 28 (3)	Reilly T 14 (6)
Ball C 11 (9)	Mallan S 24 (1)	Ridgers M 23
Brown A.................... 1 (6)	Marwood J 10 (3)	Sadlier K 5 (6)
Caldwell R 2 (11)	McAusland M 28 (1)	Sonupe E .... - (4)
Cuddihy B................. - (3)	McGinn J..........................30	Stewart J .... - (1)
Dayton J..........................13	McLean K 25	Teale G 3 (2)
Drury A 10 (2)	Mclear L 6 (5)	Tesselaar J 32
Genev V 6	Morgan L 1 (7)	Thompson S 15 (3)
Goodwin J........................28	Naismith J 38	Wylde G 11 (16)
Gow A 5 (3)	Osbourne I 13 (1)	

League goals (30): McLean 7, Mallan 4, Thompson 4, Drury 3, Kelly 3, Ball 2, Naismith 2, Dayton 1, Goodwin 1, Sadlier 1, Tesselaar 1, Wylde 1
Scottish Cup goals (1): McAusland 1. **Communities Cup goals** (2): Caldwell 2
Average home league attendance: 3,869. **Player of Year**: Jim Goodwin

195

FIRST CELTIC TROPHY FOR MANAGER RONNY DEILA

SECOND ROUND	THIRD ROUND	FOURTH ROUND	SEMI-FINALS	FINAL
Bye	*Dundee Utd.....1			
*Dundee.....4		Dundee Utd.....+C3		
Raith.....0	Dundee.....0		Dundee Utd.....2	
*Stranraer.....1	*Ross Co.....0			
Ross Co.....2		*Hibernian.....3		
*Hibernian.....3	Hibernian.....2			Dundee Utd.....0
Dumbarton.....2				
Bye	*Aberdeen.....4	*Aberdeen.....1		
*Livingston.....+1	Livingston.....0		Aberdeen.....1	
Queen of South.....0				
*Hamilton.....4	*Hamilton.....+B0	Hamilton.....0		
Alloa.....1				
Bye	Motherwell.....0			
*Falkirk.....+A0	*Falkirk.....1	*Rangers.....1		
Cowdenbeath.....0			Rangers.....0	
*Rangers.....1	Rangers.....3			
Inverness.....0				
*Kilmarnock.....1	*Kilmarnock.....0			
Ayr.....0				

Bye

Morton 0
*Partick 1

*Partick .... +1

St Johnstone 1

St Johnstone 0

*St Mirren 2
Dunfermline 1

St Mirren 0
Partick 0

Partick 0

Celtic 2

Celtic 2

*Stenhousemuir 1
Hearts 2

Hearts 0

*Celtic 6

*Celtic 3

Bye

Celtic 2

*Drawn at home; +after extra-time; A – Falkirk won 4-3 on pens; B – Hamilton won 6-5 on pens; C – Dundee Utd won 7-6 on pens; both semi-finals at Hampden Park

FIRST ROUND: Airdrie 1 Stenhousemuir 3; Albion Rov 0 Livingston 0 (aet, Livingston won 4-3 on pens); Alloa 1 Stirling Alb 0; Brechin 0 Dumbarton 1; Clyde 1 Cowdenbeath 2; Dundee 4 Peterhead 0; Dunfermline 5 Annan 1; East Stirling 0 Ayr 4; Hamilton 2 Arbroath 1; Montrose 1 Falkirk 3; Morton 2 Berwick 1; Queen of South 5 Elgin 0; Queen's Park 1 Rangers 2; Raith 4 Forfar 2 (aet); Stranraer 1 East Fife 0

SCOTTISH COMMUNITIES LEAGUE CUP FINAL

DUNDEE UNITED 0 CELTIC 2

Hampden Park (49,259); Sunday, March 15 2015

Dundee Utd (4-3-2-1): Cierzniak, Dillon (capt), Morris, Fojut, Dixon, Telfer, Connolly, Spittal. **Booked:** McGowan, Paton. **Sent off:** Dillon (56). **Manager:** Jackie McNamara

Subs not used: Gordon, Ambrose, Van Dijk, Denayer, Izaguirre, Bitton (Henderson 81), Brown (capt), Stokes, Johansen, Commons (Forrest 67), McGowan, Dow, Bilate (Anier 59).

Celtic (4-2-3-1): Szromnik, Souttar, Telfer, Connolly, Spittal. **Booked:** McGowan, Paton. **Sent off:** Dillon (56). **Manager:** Jackie McNamara

Subs not used: Zaluska, Scepovic, Fisher, McGregor. **Scorers:** Commons (28), Forrest (79). **Manager:** Ronny Deila

Griffiths (Guidetti 67).

Referee: R Madden. **Half-time:** 1-0

197

SCOTTISH LEAGUE CUP FINALS

1946 Aberdeen beat Rangers (3-2)
1947 Rangers beat Aberdeen (4-0)
1948 East Fife beat Falkirk (4-1 after 0-0 draw)
1949 Rangers beat Raith Rov (2-0)
1950 East Fife beat Dunfermline Athletic (3-0)
1951 Motherwell beat Hibernian (3-0)
1952 Dundee beat Rangers (3-2)
1953 Dundee beat Kilmarnock (2-0)
1954 East Fife beat Partick (3-2)
1955 Hearts beat Motherwell (4-2)
1956 Aberdeen beat St Mirren (2-1)
1957 Celtic beat Partick (3-0 after 0-0 draw)
1958 Celtic beat Rangers (7-1)
1959 Hearts beat Partick (5-1)
1960 Hearts beat Third Lanark (2-1)
1961 Rangers beat Kilmarnock (2-0)
1962 Rangers beat Hearts (3-1 after 1-1 draw)
1963 Hearts beat Kilmarnock (1-0)
1964 Rangers beat Morton (5-0)
1965 Rangers beat Celtic (2-1)
1966 Celtic beat Rangers (2-1)
1967 Celtic beat Rangers (1-0)
1968 Celtic beat Dundee (5-3)
1969 Celtic beat Hibernian (6-2)
1970 Celtic beat St Johnstone (1-0)
1971 Rangers beat Celtic (1-0)
1972 Partick beat Celtic (4-1)
1973 Hibernian beat Celtic (2-1)
1974 Dundee beat Celtic (1-0)
1975 Celtic beat Hibernian (6-3)
1976 Rangers beat Celtic (1-0)
1977† Aberdeen beat Celtic (2-1)
1978† Rangers beat Celtic (2-1)
1979 Rangers beat Aberdeen (2-1)
1980 Dundee Utd beat Aberdeen (3-0 after 0-0 draw)
1981 Dundee Utd beat Dundee (3-0)
1982 Rangers beat Dundee Utd (2-1)
1983 Celtic beat Rangers (2-1)
1984† Rangers beat Celtic (3-2)
1985 Rangers beat Dundee Utd (1-0)
1986 Aberdeen beat Hibernian (3-0)
1987 Rangers beat Celtic (2-1)
1988† Rangers beat Aberdeen (5-3 on pens after 3-3 draw)
1989 Rangers beat Aberdeen (3-2)
1990† Aberdeen beat Rangers (2-1)
1991† Rangers beat Celtic (2-1)
1992 Hibernian beat Dunfermline Athletic (2-0)
1993† Rangers beat Aberdeen (2-1)
1994 Rangers beat Hibernian (2-1)
1995 Raith Rov beat Celtic (6-5 on pens after 2-2 draw)
1996 Aberdeen beat Dundee (2-0)
1997 Rangers beat Hearts (4-3)

1998 Celtic beat Dundee Utd (3-0)
1999 Rangers beat St Johnstone (2-1)
2000 Celtic beat Aberdeen (2-0)
2001 Celtic beat Kilmarnock (3-0)
2002 Rangers beat Ayr (4-0)
2003 Rangers beat Celtic (2-1)
2004 Livingston beat Hibernian (2-0)
2005 Rangers beat Motherwell (5-1)
2006 Celtic beat Dunfermline Athletic (3-0)
2007 Hibernian beat Kilmarnock (5-1)
2008 Rangers beat Dundee Utd (3-2 on pens after 2-2 draw)
2009† Celtic beat Rangers (2-0)
2010 Rangers beat St Mirren (1-0)
2011† Rangers beat Celtic (2-1)
2012 Kilmarnock beat Celtic (1-0)
2013 St Mirren beat Hearts (3-2)
2014 Aberdeen beat Inverness Caledonian Thistle (4-2 on pens after 0-0 draw)
2015 Celtic beat Dundee Utd (2-0)
 († After extra time; Skol Cup 1985-93, Coca-Cola Cup 1995-97, Co-operative Insurance Cup 1999 onwards)

SUMMARY OF SCOTTISH LEAGUE CUP WINNERS

Rangers 27	East Fife 3	Motherwell 1
Celtic 15	Hibernian................ 3	Partick 1
Aberdeen 7	Dundee Utd 2	Raith Rov 1
Hearts 4	Kilmarnock 2	St Mirren 1
Dundee.............. 3	Livingston 1	

PETROFAC TRAINING CUP 2014-15

First round: Airdrie 2 Albion Rov 2 (aet, Albion Rov won 4-2 on pens); Arbroath 1 Alloa 4; Brora 3 Stenhousemuir 1; Clyde 2 Ayr 0; Cowdenbeath 1 Brechin 3; Dunfermline 1 Raith 0; East Fife 2 Forfar 1; East Stirling 1 Falkirk 7; Elgin 0 Stirling Alb 3; Hearts 3 Annan 1; Montrose 2 Peterhead 3; Morton 1 Spartans 0; Queen of South 3 Livingston 4; Queen's Park 1 Berwick 1 (aet, Berwick won 4-3 on pens); Rangers 2 Hibernian 1, Stranraer 3 Dumbarton 2 **Second round**: Brechin 0 Peterhead 2; Brora 2 East Fife 3; Dunfermline 1 Falkirk 2; Livingston 4 Hearts 1; Morton 5 Berwick 2 (aet); Rangers 8 Clyde 1; Stirling Alb 1 Alloa 2; Stranraer 2 Albion Rov 1
Third round: Morton 0 Alloa 1; Peterhead 0 Livingston 1 (aet); Stranraer 1 Falkirk 0; East Fife 0 Rangers 2
Semi-finals: Alloa 3 Rangers 2; Livingston 1 Stranraer 1 (aet, Livingston won 5-4 on pen)

FINAL

LIVINGSTON 4 ALLOA ATHLETIC 0
McDiarmid Park, Perth (2,869); Sunday, April 5 2015
Livingston (4-4-2): Jamieson, Cole, Gallagher, Fordyce, Talbot (capt), Mullen (White 69), Keaghan Jacobs (Beaumont 88), Kyle Jacobs, O'Brien, Hippolyte (Glen 84), Pittman.
Subs not used: Walker, McKenna, Sekajja, Donaldson. **Scorers**: Pittman (21), Fordyce (61), White (86, 90). **Booked**: O'Brien. **Manager**: Mark Burchill
Alloa Athletic (4-4-2): McDowall, Doyle, Gordon (capt), Benedictus, Meggatt, Holmes, Docherty (Flannigan 69), Cawley, McCord (Spence 82), Chopra (Layne 69), Buchanan. **Subs not used**: Gibson, Tiffoney, Rutherford, Ferguson. **Booked**: Chopra, Benedictus. **Manager**: Paddy Connolly
Referee: J Beaton. **Half-time**: 1-0

FIRST SCOTTISH CUP FOR INVERNESS CALEY

FOURTH ROUND	FIFTH ROUND	SIXTH ROUND	SEMI-FINALS	FINAL
*Falkirk...........1				
Cowdenbeath.....0	*Falkirk...........2			
		Falkirk...........1		
*Annan.........1:2	Brechin...........1			
Brechin........1:4			Falkirk...........1	
*Queen of South...4	*Queen of South...2			Falkirk...........1
Brora............1		*Queen of South.....0		
	St Johnstone......0			
*St Johnstone......2				
Ross Co..........1			Hibernian........0	
		*Hibernian........4		
*Alloa..........1	*Hibernian........3			
Hibernian......2				
	Arbroath.........1			
*Bo'ness.........0				
Arbroath.........5		Berwick..........0		
	*Spartans......1:0			
*Spartans.......2				
Morton..........1	Berwick.......1:1			
*Berwick......1:1				
Albion Rov.....1:0	*Stranraer.......0			
		*Dundee Utd......1:0		
*Stranraer....2:3	Dundee Utd.......3			
Dunfermline...2:1			Celtic...........2	
*Motherwell......1	*Dundee..........0			
Dundee Utd......2				
*Dundee..........2				
Aberdeen.........1				

```
*Hearts .......... 0
Celtic ........... 4
                        Celtic ........... 2
*Rangers ......... 3
Kilmarnock ....... 0                          Celtic ........... 1:4
                        *Rangers ......... 1
*Stirling Alb .... 2
Raith ............ 2
                        Raith ............ 0
                                                                         Inverness .......... 2
*Partick ......... 2    *Partick ......... 1
Hamilton ......... 0                          *Inverness ........ 1
                                              Inverness ........ +3
*St Mirren ....... 1:0
Inverness ........ 1:4  Inverness ........ 2
```

*Drawn at home. Both semi-finals at Hampden Park.

WILLIAM HILL SCOTTISH CUP FINAL

FALKIRK 1 INVERNESS CALEDONIAN THISTLE 2
Hampden Park (37,149); Saturday, May 30 2015

FIRST ROUND: Auchinleck 5 Buckie 0; Clachnacuddin 1 Hurford 7; Cove 9 Hawick 0; Cutler 4 Strathspey 2; Deveronvale 0 Nairn 1; Edinburgh City 2 Coldstream 1; Forres 4 Civil Service 1; Fraserburgh 0 Linlithgow 0; Golspie 1 Dalbeattie 4; Gretna 2 Gala 1; Huntly 2 Wick 1; Keith 1 Formartine 3; Lossiemouth 0 Turriff 4; Lothian 0 East Kilbride 1; Preston 1 Threave 2; Rothes 0 Banks O'Dee 4; Selkirk 0 Bo'ness 4; Whitehill 3 Girvan 1. **Replay:** Linlithgow 2 Fraserburgh 1

SECOND ROUND: Arbroath 2 Montrose 0; Berwick 2 Formartine 0; Bo'ness 7 Cutler 1; Brora 5 Banks O'Dee 0; Cove 1 Annan 2; East Fife 7 Threave 0; Edinburgh City 2 Auchinleck 1; Elgin 0 Forres 0; Gretna 0 Queen's Park 1; Inverurie 0 Hurford 3; Linlithgow 5 Dalbeattie 1; Nairn 2 Huntly 1; Spartans 3 East Kilbride 3; Stirling Univ 1 Albion Rov 4; Turriff 0 Clyde 3; Whitehill 0 East Stirling 1. **Replays:** East Kilbride 1 Spartans 5; Forres 1 Elgin 3; Montrose 1 Arbroath 3 (aet)

THIRD ROUND: Annan 3 Livingston 2; Arbroath 2 Nairn 1; Ayr 1 Alloa 1; Dumbarton 0 Rangers 1; East Fife 2 Berwick 3; East Stirling 1 Dunfermline 4; Edinburgh City 2 Brora 3; Elgin 4 Bo'ness 4; Forfar 1 Cowdenbeath 3; Hurford 1 Stirling Alb 1; Linlithgow 0 Raith 2; Morton 0 Airdrie 0; Peterhead 0 Stranraer 1; Queen's Park 1 Albion Rov 2; Spartans 2 Clyde 0; Stenhousemuir 1 Brechin 2. **Replays:** Airdrie 0 Morton 2; Alloa 4 Ayr 0; Bo'ness 5 Elgin 4; Stirling Alb 2 Hurford 2 (aet, Stirling Alb won 13-12 on pens)

Falkirk (4-4-2): MacDonald, Duffie, McCracken (capt), Grant, Leahy, Alston, Vaulks, Taiwo, Sibbald, Smith (Bia Bi 63), Loy (Morgan 90). **Subs not used:** Bowman, Muirhead, Dick, Cooper, Blair. **Scorer:** Grant (80). **Booked:** Taiwo. **Manager:** Peter Houston

Inverness (4-2-3-1): Esson, Shinnie (capt), Devine, Meekings, Tremarco, Tansey, Draper, Watkins (Ross 90), Doran (Williams 78), Christie (Vincent 72), Ofere. **Subs not used:** Mackay, Horner, Polworth, Kink. **Scorers:** Watkins (38), Vincent (86). **Sent off:** Tremarco (75). **Manager:** John Hughes

Referee: W Collum. **Half-time:** 0-1

SCOTTISH FA CUP FINALS

1874 Queen's Park beat Clydesdale (2-0)
1875 Queen's Park beat Renton (3-0)
1876 Queen's Park beat Third Lanark (2-0 after 1-1 draw)
1877 Vale of Leven beat Rangers (3-2 after 0-0, 1-1 draws)
1878 Vale of Leven beat Third Lanark (1-0)
1879 Vale of Leven awarded Cup (Rangers withdrew after 1-1 draw)
1880 Queen's Park beat Thornliebank (3-0)
1881 Queen's Park beat Dumbarton (3-1)
1882 Queen's Park beat Dumbarton (4-1 after 2-2 draw)
1883 Dumbarton beat Vale of Leven (2-1 after 2-2 draw)
1884 Queen's Park awarded Cup (Vale of Leven withdrew from Final)
1885 Renton beat Vale of Leven (3-1 after 0-0 draw)
1886 Queen's Park beat Renton (3-1)
1887 Hibernian beat Dumbarton (2-1)
1888 Renton beat Cambuslang (6-1)
1889 Third Lanark beat Celtic (2-1)
1890 Queen's Park beat Vale of Leven (2-1 after 1-1 draw)
1891 Hearts beat Dumbarton (1-0)
1892 Celtic beat Queen's Park (5-1)
1893 Queen's Park beat Celtic (2-1)
1894 Rangers beat Celtic (3-1)
1895 St Bernard's beat Renton (2-1)
1896 Hearts beat Hibernian (3-1)
1897 Rangers beat Dumbarton (5-1)
1898 Rangers beat Kilmarnock (2-0)
1899 Celtic beat Rangers (2-0)
1900 Celtic beat Queen's Park (4-3)
1901 Hearts beat Celtic (4-3)
1902 Hibernian beat Celtic (1-0)
1903 Rangers beat Hearts (2-0 after 0-0, 1-1 draws)
1904 Celtic beat Rangers (3-2)
1905 Third Lanark beat Rangers (3-1 after 0-0 draw)
1906 Hearts beat Third Lanark (1-0)
1907 Celtic beat Hearts (3-0)
1908 Celtic beat St Mirren (5-1)
1909 Cup withheld because of riot after two drawn games in final
between Celtic and Rangers (2-2, 1-1)
1910 Dundee beat Clyde (2-1 after 2-2, 0-0 draws)
1911 Celtic beat Hamilton (2-0 after 0-0 draw)
1912 Celtic beat Clyde (2-0)
1913 Falkirk beat Raith (2-0)
1914 Celtic beat Hibernian (4-1 after 0-0 draw)
1915–19 No competition (World War 1)
1920 Kilmarnock beat Albion (3-2)
1921 Partick beat Rangers (1-0)
1922 Morton beat Rangers (1-0)
1923 Celtic beat Hibernian (1-0)
1924 Airdrieonians beat Hibernian (2-0)
1925 Celtic beat Dundee (2-1)
1926 St Mirren beat Celtic (2-0)
1927 Celtic beat East Fife (3-1)
1928 Rangers beat Celtic (4-0)
1929 Kilmarnock beat Rangers (2-0)
1930 Rangers beat Partick (2-1 after 0-0 draw)

1931 Celtic beat Motherwell (4-2 after 2-2 draw)
1932 Rangers beat Kilmarnock (3-0 after 1-1 draw)
1933 Celtic beat Motherwell (1-0)
1934 Rangers beat St Mirren (5-0)
1935 Rangers beat Hamilton (2-1)
1936 Rangers beat Third Lanark (1-0)
1937 Celtic beat Aberdeen (2-1)
1938 East Fife beat Kilmarnock (4-2 after 1-1 draw)
1939 Clyde beat Motherwell (4-0)
1940-6 No competition (World War 2)
1947 Aberdeen beat Hibernian (2-1)
1948† Rangers beat Morton (1-0 after 1-1 draw)
1949 Rangers beat Clyde (4-1)
1950 Rangers beat East Fife (3-0)
1951 Celtic beat Motherwell (1-0)
1952 Motherwell beat Dundee (4-0)
1953 Rangers beat Aberdeen (1-0 after 1-1 draw)
1954 Celtic beat Aberdeen (2-1)
1955 Clyde beat Celtic (1-0 after 1-1 draw)
1956 Hearts beat Celtic (3-1)
1957† Falkirk beat Kilmarnock (2-1 after 1-1 draw)
1958 Clyde beat Hibernian (1-0)
1959 St Mirren beat Aberdeen (3-1)
1960 Rangers beat Kilmarnock (2-0)
1961 Dunfermline beat Celtic (2-0 after 0-0 draw)
1962 Rangers beat St Mirren (2-0)
1963 Rangers beat Celtic (3-0 after 1-1 draw)
1964 Rangers beat Dundee (3-1)
1965 Celtic beat Dunfermline (3-2)
1966 Rangers beat Celtic (1-0 after 0-0 draw)
1967 Celtic beat Aberdeen (2-0)
1968 Dunfermline beat Hearts (3-1)
1969 Celtic beat Rangers (4-0)
1970 Aberdeen beat Celtic (3-1)
1971 Celtic beat Rangers (2-1 after 1-1 draw)
1972 Celtic beat Hibernian (6-1)
1973 Rangers beat Celtic (3-2)
1974 Celtic beat Dundee Utd (3-0)
1975 Celtic beat Airdrieonians (3-1)
1976 Rangers beat Hearts (3-1)
1977 Celtic beat Rangers (1-0)
1978 Rangers beat Aberdeen (2-1)
1979† Rangers beat Hibernian (3-2 after two 0-0 draws)
1980† Celtic beat Rangers (1-0)
1981 Rangers beat Dundee Utd (4-1 after 0-0 draw)
1982† Aberdeen beat Rangers (4-1)
1983† Aberdeen beat Rangers (1-0)
1984† Aberdeen beat Celtic (2-1)
1985 Celtic beat Dundee Utd (2-1)
1986 Aberdeen beat Hearts (3-0)
1987† St Mirren beat Dundee Utd (1-0)
1988 Celtic beat Dundee Utd (2-1)
1989 Celtic beat Rangers (1-0)
1990† Aberdeen beat Celtic (9-8 on pens after 0-0 draw)
1991† Motherwell beat Dundee Utd (4-3)
1992 Rangers beat Airdrieonians (2-1)

1993 Rangers beat Aberdeen (2-1)
1994 Dundee Utd beat Rangers (1-0)
1995 Celtic beat Airdrieonians (1-0)
1996 Rangers beat Hearts (5-1)
1997 Kilmarnock beat Falkirk (1-0)
1998 Hearts beat Rangers (2-1)
1999 Rangers beat Celtic (1-0)
2000 Rangers beat Aberdeen (4-0)
2001 Celtic beat Hibernian (3-0)
2002 Rangers beat Celtic (3-2)
2003 Rangers beat Dundee (1-0)
2004 Celtic beat Dunfermline (3-1)
2005 Celtic beat Dundee Utd (1-0)
2006† Hearts beat Gretna (4-2 on pens after 1-1 draw)
2007 Celtic beat Dunfermline (1-0)
2008 Rangers beat Queen of the South (3-2)
2009 Rangers beat Falkirk (1-0)
2010 Dundee Utd beat Ross Co (3-0)
2011 Celtic beat Motherwell (3-0)
2012 Hearts beat Hibernian (5-1)
2013 Celtic beat Hibernian (3-0)
2014 St Johnstone beat Dundee Utd (2-0)
2015 Inverness beat Falkirk (2-1)
† After extra time

SUMMARY OF SCOTTISH CUP WINNERS

Celtic 36, Rangers 33, Queen's Park 10, Hearts 8, Aberdeen 7, Clyde 3, Kilmarnock 3, St Mirren 3, Vale of Leven 3, Dundee Utd 2, Dunfermline 2, Falkirk 2, Hibernian 2, Motherwell 2, Renton 2, Third Lanark 2, Airdrieonians 1, Dumbarton 1, Dundee 1, East Fife 1, Inverness 1, Morton 1, Partick 1, St Bernard's 1, St Johnstone 1

THE THINGS THEY SAY...

'Goal of the day? That was goal of the season, maybe goal of the century' – **Glenn Hoddle**, former England manager, on Charlie Adam's 66-yard strike for Stoke against Chelsea.

'I'd been looking at the keeper's position all game. You never know with these balls – they swerve about so much. But I never knew I had the power to beat a quality keeper like that' – **Charlie Adam** on beating Chelsea's Thibaut Courtois.

'We have been open-minded about things like the goal-decision system which has made a great difference. Now we need to see whether what other technology can be used to get refereeing decisions more accurate' **Mike Riley**, referees' chief, after Sunderland's Wes Brown and West Bromwich Albion's Gareth McAuley were sent off in cases of mistaken identity.

'It's no good moaning about the referees. I would have two calls for each manager when the referee can take 30 seconds to consult via a video link' – **Tony Pulis**, West Bromwich Albion manager.

'The pressure on players, physically and mentally, is greater than ever. Not only do they travel at international level across the world, but the Premier League is faster and more demanding. The time they have to rest is fewer and further between and they end up never really recovering fully enough to go into the next game' – **Sam Allardyce**, former West Ham manager, calling for a fortnight's winter break.

VANARAMA PREMIER LEAGUE 2014–2015

				Home				Away					
		P	W	D	L	F	A	W	D	L	F	A	GD	PTS
1	Barnet	46	16	2	5	54	21	12	6	5	40	25	48	92
2	Bristol Rov*	46	17	4	2	47	14	8	12	3	26	20	39	91
3	Grimsby	46	12	4	7	36	20	13	7	3	38	20	34	86
4	Eastleigh	46	12	6	5	45	28	12	4	7	42	33	26	82
5	Forest Green**	46	12	7	4	42	27	10	9	4	38	27	26	79
6	Macclesfield	46	14	7	2	34	14	7	8	8	26	32	14	78
7	Woking	46	11	7	5	39	24	10	6	7	38	28	25	76
8	Dover	46	13	4	6	38	18	6	7	10	31	40	11	68
9	Halifax	46	11	7	5	38	27	6	8	9	22	27	6	66
10	Gateshead	46	10	6	7	38	34	7	9	7	28	28	4	66
11	Wrexham	46	9	8	6	27	22	8	7	8	29	30	4	66
12	Chester	46	11	3	9	35	36	8	3	12	29	40	-12	63
13	Torquay	46	10	7	6	35	26	6	6	11	29	34	4	61
14	Braintree	46	10	4	9	28	25	8	1	14	28	32	-1	59
15	Lincoln	46	11	4	8	35	28	5	6	12	27	43	-9	58
16	Kidderminster	46	9	6	8	31	30	6	6	11	20	30	-9	57
17	Altrincham	46	9	5	9	29	34	7	3	13	25	39	-19	56
18	Aldershot	46	8	5	10	27	28	6	6	11	24	33	-10	53
19	Southport	46	6	6	11	21	33	7	6	10	26	39	-25	51
20	Welling	46	7	8	8	29	27	4	4	15	23	46	-21	45
21	Alfreton	46	6	8	9	33	40	6	1	16	16	50	-41	45
22	Telford	46	3	5	15	27	44	7	4	12	31	40	-26	39
23	Dartford	46	4	9	10	26	34	4	6	13	18	40	-30	39
24	Nuneaton**	46	7	6	10	25	33	3	3	17	13	43	-38	36

*also promoted; **3 pts deducted for ineligible player

Leading league scorers: 31 Akinde (Barnet); 25 Parkin (Forest Green); 24 Rendell (Woking); 18 Constable (Eastleigh), Gray (Telford), Reeves (Altrincham), Taylor (Bristol Rov); 16 John-Lewis (Grimsby), Moult (Wrexham); 15 Payne (Dover), Williams (Aldershot)

Team of Year: Stack (Barnet), Brown (Bristol Rov), Parkes (Bristol Rov), Yiadom (Barnet), Pearson (Grimsby), Disley (Grimsby), Betsy (Woking), Arnold (Grimsby), Mansell (Bristol Rov), Akinde (Barnet), Parkin (Forest Green)

Player of Year: John Akinde (Barnet). **Manager of Year:** Darrell Clarke (Bristol Rov)

CHAMPIONS

1979–80	Altrincham	1993–94	Kidderminster	2007–08*	Aldershot
1980–81	Altrincham	1994–95	Macclesfield	2008–09*	Burton
1981–82	Runcorn	1995–96	Stevenage	2009–10*	Stevenage
1982–83	Enfield	1996–97*	Macclesfield	2010–11*	Crawley
1983–84	Maidstone	1997–98*	Halifax	2011–2012*	Fleetwood
1984–85	Wealdstone	1998–99*	Cheltenham	2012–13*	Mansfield
1985–86	Enfield	1999–2000*	Kidderminster	2013–14*	Luton
1986–87*	Scarborough	2000–01*	Rushden	2014–15*	Barnet
1987–88*	Lincoln	2001–02*	Boston	*Promoted to Football League
1988–89*	Maidstone	2002–03*	Yeovil	
1989–90*	Darlington	2003–04*	Chester	Conference – Record
1990–91*	Barnet	2004–05*	Barnet	attendance: 11,085 Bristol
1991–92*	Colchester	2005–06*	Accrington	Rov v Alfreton, April 25,
1992–93*	Wycombe	2006–07*	Dagenham	2015

VANARAMA PREMIER LEAGUE RESULTS 2014–2015

	AFC Telford	Aldershot	Alfreton	Altrincham	Barnet	Braintree	Bristol Rov	Chester	Dartford	Dover	Eastleigh	Halifax	Forest Green	Gateshead	Grimsby	K'minster	Lincoln	Macclesfield	Nuneaton	Southport	Torquay	Welling	Woking	Wrexham
AFC Telford	–	0-2	0-1	2-1	2-2	1-3	0-1	1-2	2-3	1-4	3-4	0-1	0-1	0-1	1-1	1-1	1-0	2-3	0-0	3-3	4-3	1-2	1-3	1-2
Aldershot	1-2	–	2-3	1-1	1-3	1-3	2-2	0-1	2-3	2-0	0-2	1-1	1-0	1-1	2-1	2-0	1-0	2-3	1-0	1-2	4-2	2-2	0-1	1-1
Alfreton	3-2	2-0	–	1-1	1-1	0-2	0-0	0-1	2-3	2-3	3-2	1-1	2-2	1-2	2-1	0-0	0-0	1-5	1-0	4-2	2-2	2-1	1-3	1-0
Altrincham	1-2	1-0	1-1	–	1-3	1-0	0-2	4-1	2-1	2-2	3-3	0-0	2-2	1-0	2-1	2-1	1-2	1-0	0-1	2-1	2-1	0-4	0-3	1-0
Barnet	3-1	2-1	5-0	3-0	–	3-0	2-0	1-3	3-0	4-0	3-2	1-0	3-0	1-3	2-0	1-3	3-3	1-2	3-1	1-0	4-0	2-3	5-0	2-1
Braintree	0-2	1-1	0-2	1-0	3-0	–	2-0	1-3	3-0	1-5	1-0	3-0	1-3	2-1	1-1	1-2	2-0	1-1	0-2	0-2	1-1	2-1	0-1	1-0
Bristol Rov	1-0	3-1	7-0	1-0	2-1	2-1	–	5-1	1-1	1-1	2-1	2-1	0-1	1-1	2-2	1-1	2-0	4-0	3-1	2-0	1-1	2-0	2-0	1-0
Chester	2-0	1-0	2-1	0-2	0-5	2-3	1-2	–	1-2	3-1	0-1	2-1	1-4	0-3	0-0	2-0	0-1	4-0	5-3	2-0	0-2	2-0	2-0	1-1
Dartford	1-0	1-1	0-2	0-3	0-1	2-3	2-2	1-2	–	1-1	1-1	0-1	1-4	0-1	2-0	2-0	2-0	1-1	3-1	2-0	0-2	3-0	2-0	3-0
Dover	1-0	3-0	1-2	1-2	1-2	2-0	2-2	3-2	6-1	–	1-0	4-1	1-0	0-1	2-1	2-3	1-2	2-1	5-0	2-2	0-0	4-0	1-3	1-1
Eastleigh	3-3	3-1	3-1	3-3	0-1	2-0	2-1	0-1	2-2	0-1	–	4-1	1-0	1-2	4-0	1-0	4-0	2-2	2-0	2-1	1-2	3-1	2-2	2-1
Halifax	5-0	2-0	1-0	1-1	1-2	1-1	3-1	0-1	2-0	3-2	1-0	–	2-1	1-1	0-1	2-1	2-2	2-2	2-0	2-1	2-1	0-0	0-0	4-1
Forest Green	3-0	1-3	2-0	1-2	1-1	1-1	2-1	1-0	2-4	0-2	1-0	2-0	–	1-1	2-1	2-3	3-3	2-2	2-4	1-0	1-2	3-0	0-3	2-2
Gateshead	4-1	1-1	2-0	1-0	1-1	3-1	0-1	1-2	1-0	1-0	2-3	1-6	2-4	–	3-2	0-0	3-3	0-2	0-0	0-1	3-1	0-2	3-1	0-0
Grimsby	1-0	3-1	7-0	3-1	1-0	1-0	3-0	2-1	1-1	1-0	1-3	1-0	2-1	1-0	–	1-3	3-0	3-1	1-0	0-1	0-2	3-1	0-0	3-1
K'minster	1-1	0-2	3-0	4-0	3-2	1-2	2-3	1-1	2-0	3-0	0-0	1-1	0-2	0-0	0-2	–	3-0	2-0	3-1	0-1	2-1	3-2	3-1	0-1
Lincoln	2-0	3-0	3-2	1-1	4-1	2-1	1-1	0-0	2-1	1-0	3-0	1-1	1-1	2-1	1-2	3-0	–	0-0	3-1	0-1	1-3	2-1	1-0	1-1
Macclesfield	0-0	0-0	2-1	1-1	2-1	2-1	0-2	3-2	1-0	0-1	0-2	0-0	1-0	1-1	2-1	3-0	2-1	–	1-1	2-3	1-0	1-0	0-2	2-0
Nuneaton	4-4	0-1	0-1	2-1	1-2	0-1	0-2	3-2	1-2	3-2	0-3	1-2	1-0	0-0	0-1	2-1	1-1	3-3	–	2-3	2-1	1-0	0-0	1-1
Southport	0-3	1-3	0-2	0-2	0-1	1-1	2-0	0-1	1-1	2-0	0-1	1-1	2-1	1-0	3-0	3-3	1-1	0-0	2-3	–	2-1	1-0	1-0	1-0
Torquay	1-1	1-1	1-1	1-2	2-0	2-0	1-1	0-1	2-0	0-2	2-0	3-0	3-3	1-1	3-0	0-0	3-3	4-0	0-0	4-0	–	3-0	2-5	1-0
Welling	1-1	3-1	1-2	1-2	2-1	1-0	0-0	1-3	2-2	3-0	2-0	2-0	0-0	0-0	4-1	3-0	2-0	0-4	4-0	0-0	3-0	–	1-1	1-1
Woking	1-3	1-2	3-0	1-0	1-1	0-0	3-1	0-0	2-2	2-3	0-1	1-2	1-2	0-2	2-3	3-1	3-0	4-1	1-0	1-2	3-2	2-2	–	2-1
Wrexham	0-4	3-1	4-0	2-3	0-1	3-0	0-0	1-1	1-1	1-1	3-0	0-0	0-0	0-3	0-1	1-1	1-1	2-2	1-0	1-0	2-1	2-1	1-2	–

VANARAMA NORTH

		Home					Away						
		P	W	D	L	F	A	W	D	L	F	A	GD	PTS
1	Barrow	42	16	3	2	45	16	10	6	5	36	27	38	87
2	Fylde	42	14	5	2	51	23	11	5	5	42	20	50	85
3	Boston	42	12	5	4	47	25	8	7	6	28	26	24	72
4	Chorley	42	11	8	2	42	19	9	3	9	34	36	21	71
5	Guiseley*	42	12	2	7	40	27	8	8	5	28	22	19	70
6	Oxford City	42	9	7	5	29	32	11	2	8	52	35	14	69
7	Tamworth	42	13	4	4	40	23	6	8	7	26	34	9	69
8	Hednesford	42	9	5	7	34	28	8	5	8	29	22	13	61
9	Worcester	42	9	6	6	32	30	7	6	8	22	24	0	60
10	North Ferriby	42	8	8	5	38	31	6	8	7	27	32	2	58
11	Stockport	42	12	2	7	37	28	4	7	10	19	31	-3	57
12	Solihull	42	6	4	11	31	36	10	3	8	37	27	5	55
13	Bradford PA	42	8	6	7	27	31	6	5	10	25	35	-14	53
14	Gloucester	42	8	6	7	26	28	6	4	11	37	47	-12	52
15	Harrogate	42	9	6	6	30	27	5	4	12	20	35	-12	52
16	Lowestoft	42	8	9	4	31	24	4	6	11	23	42	-12	51
17	Gainsborough	42	8	6	7	33	27	6	2	13	26	40	-8	50
18	Brackley	42	9	4	8	17	23	4	4	13	22	39	-23	47
19	Stalybridge	42	6	4	11	31	39	6	5	10	23	31	-16	45
20	Colwyn Bay	42	4	3	14	22	43	7	9	5	37	39	-23	45
21	Leamington	42	7	5	9	33	35	3	5	13	26	39	-15	40
22	Hyde	42	3	8	10	31	42	0	4	17	18	64	-57	21

* Also promoted. Play-off Final: Guiseley 3 Chorley 2

VANARAMA SOUTH

		Home					Away						
		P	W	D	L	F	A	W	D	L	F	A	GD	PTS
1	Bromley	40	11	2	7	33	23	12	6	2	46	23	33	77
2	Boreham Wood*	40	12	4	4	39	20	11	2	7	40	24	35	75
3	Basingstoke	40	10	4	6	27	22	12	3	5	40	21	24	73
4	Whitehawk	40	12	3	5	32	18	10	4	7	30	29	15	72
5	Havant	40	12	3	5	34	21	9	4	7	27	20	20	70
6	Gosport	40	9	7	4	30	19	10	3	7	33	21	23	67
7	Concord	40	10	5	5	39	24	8	6	6	21	20	16	65
8	Ebbsfleet	40	9	5	6	29	20	8	4	8	31	21	19	60
9	Hemel	40	6	8	6	30	33	10	4	6	34	27	4	60
10	Chelmsford	40	8	4	8	36	34	9	1	10	29	37	-6	56
11	Eastbourne	40	11	5	4	33	21	3	8	9	18	29	1	55
12	Wealdstone	40	5	5	10	22	32	9	7	4	34	24	0	54
13	St Albans	40	9	4	7	29	25	7	2	11	24	28	0	54
14	Bath	40	9	4	7	31	26	6	4	10	28	31	2	53
15	Sutton	40	7	4	9	25	28	8	7	7	25	26	-4	50
16	Bishop's St	40	4	8	8	29	38	8	2	10	26	31	-14	46
17	Weston SM	40	6	3	11	30	45	7	2	11	25	41	-31	44
18	Maidenhead	40	5	4	11	24	35	5	9	6	30	35	-16	43
19	Hayes	40	6	3	11	21	29	5	6	9	18	29	-19	42
20	Farnborough	40	4	3	13	19	46	4	3	13	23	55	-59	30
21	Staines	40	3	1	16	18	44	4	3	13	21	38	-43	25

* Also promoted. Play-off Final: Boreham Wood 2 Whitehawk 1 (aet)

OTHER LEAGUES 2014–15

CORBETT SPORTS WELSH PREMIER LEAGUE

	P	W	D	L	F	A	GD	Pts
New Saints	32	23	8	1	90	24	66	77
Bala	32	18	5	9	67	42	25	59
Airbus	32	18	4	10	62	34	28	58
Aberystwyth	32	14	10	8	69	61	8	52
Port Talbot	32	13	4	15	54	59	-5	43
Newtown	32	10	8	14	52	65	-13	38
Connah's Quay	32	11	10	11	44	53	-9	43
Rhyl	32	11	9	12	41	49	-8	42
Carmarthen	32	12	6	14	48	57	-9	42
Bangor	32	9	8	15	48	62	-14	35
Cefn Druids	32	7	6	19	38	64	-26	27
Prestatyn	32	4	6	22	43	86	-43	8

League split after 22 games, with teams playing ten further games
Cup Final: New Saints 3 Bala 0

RYMAN PREMIER LEAGUE

	P	W	D	L	F	A	GD	Pts
Maidstone	46	29	11	6	85	41	44	98
Hendon	46	27	14	5	82	55	27	95
Margate*	46	25	10	11	94	58	36	85
Dulwich Hamlet	46	21	13	12	66	51	15	76
Enfield	46	24	4	18	70	56	14	76
Met Police	46	21	12	13	72	51	21	75
Grays	46	22	8	16	70	57	13	74
Billericay	46	20	8	18	73	65	8	68
Leiston	46	18	13	15	73	58	15	67
Leatherhead	46	19	10	17	72	62	10	67
Kingstonian	46	18	13	15	63	56	7	67
Wingate	46	20	7	19	72	70	2	67
East Thurrock	46	17	15	14	66	71	-5	66
Bognor Regis	46	17	12	17	71	64	7	63
Hampton	46	16	9	21	62	79	-17	57
Harrow	46	15	8	23	64	77	-13	53
Canvey Is	46	14	11	21	61	77	-16	53
VCD	46	14	11	21	53	70	-17	53
Lewes	46	14	11	21	45	67	-22	53
Tonbridge	46	13	13	20	63	67	-4	52
Peacehaven	46	13	9	24	58	85	-27	48
Witham	46	9	15	22	61	84	-23	42
Hornchurch	46	10	10	26	46	70	-24	40
Bury	46	7	11	28	35	86	-51	32

*Also promoted. Play-off Final: Margate 1 Hendon 0

EVOSTICK NORTH PREMIER LEAGUE

	P	W	D	L	F	A	GD	Pts
FC United	46	26	14	6	78	37	41	92
Workington	46	27	9	10	63	39	24	90
Ashton	46	24	12	10	75	54	21	84
Curzon*	46	23	14	9	79	46	33	83
Ilkeston	46	22	15	9	79	56	23	81
Blyth	46	21	16	9	84	54	30	79
Skelmersdale	46	21	10	15	58	48	10	73
Barwell	46	21	10	15	69	63	6	73
Rushall	46	21	9	16	76	64	12	72
Buxton	46	18	17	11	70	57	13	71
Halesowen	46	13	20	13	56	48	8	59
Granthan	46	15	14	17	64	72	-8	59
Whitby	46	14	16	16	56	63	-7	58
Matlock	46	15	11	20	57	60	-3	56
Nantwich	46	16	7	23	61	76	-15	55
Stourbridge	46	14	11	21	59	72	-13	53
Ramsbottom	46	15	8	23	66	80	-14	53
King's Lynn	46	14	10	22	60	81	-21	52
Frickley	46	12	14	20	60	73	-13	50
Stamford	46	13	11	22	56	75	-19	50
Marine	46	11	16	19	58	69	-11	49
Witton	46	14	7	25	58	86	-28	49
Trafford	46	6	15	25	58	93	-35	33
Belper	46	6	14	26	62	96	-34	32

*Also promoted. Play-off Final: Curzon 1 Ilkeston 0

EVOSTICK SOUTH PREMIER LEAGUE

	P	W	D	L	F	A	GD	Pts
Corby	44	29	7	8	86	47	39	94
Poole	44	28	7	9	84	35	49	91
Truro*	44	27	5	12	83	58	25	86
Hungerford	44	22	13	9	64	36	28	79
St Neots	44	20	16	8	82	58	24	76
Redditch	44	21	12	11	73	44	29	75
Weymouth	44	22	7	15	71	71	0	73
Cirencester	44	20	12	12	77	54	23	72
Hitchin	44	20	10	14	78	63	15	70
Paulton	44	18	10	16	65	62	3	64
Chippenham	44	16	13	15	54	54	0	61
Chesham	44	16	12	16	79	72	7	60
Cambridge	44	14	15	15	71	62	9	57
Dunstable	44	16	9	19	71	78	-7	57
Bideford	44	16	7	21	66	85	-19	55
Slough	44	13	12	19	66	88	-22	51
Dorchester	44	14	8	22	63	74	-11	50
Histon	44	13	10	21	53	74	-21	49
Biggleswade	44	11	12	21	57	75	-18	45
Frome	44	10	11	23	49	80	-31	41
Banbury	44	9	10	25	53	86	-33	37
Arlesey	44	10	6	28	43	84	-41	36
Burnham**	44	5	8	31	41	89	-48	20

*Also promoted. **3 pts deducted for ineligible player. Play-off Final: Truro 1 St Neots 0

PRESS AND JOURNAL HIGHLAND LEAGUE

	P	W	D	L	F	A	GD	Pts
Brora	34	30	4	0	134	13	121	94
Turriff*	34	27	2	5	90	40	50	80
Cove	34	22	7	5	103	40	63	73
Wick	34	23	3	8	94	43	51	72
Fraserburgh	34	19	8	7	91	48	43	65
Formartine	34	19	7	8	85	59	26	64
Inverurie	34	20	3	11	93	51	42	63
Nairn	34	18	3	13	88	43	45	57
Forres	34	18	3	13	71	59	12	57
Buckie	34	15	5	14	71	66	5	50
Clachnacuddin	34	14	3	17	63	74	-11	45
Deveronvale	34	9	9	16	53	82	-29	36
Fort William	34	8	3	23	52	98	-46	27
Keith	34	7	3	24	42	97	-55	24
Lossiemouth	34	7	2	25	50	105	-55	23
Huntly	34	5	5	24	37	100	-63	20
Strathspey	34	3	5	26	36	125	-89	14
Rothes	34	2	5	27	32	142	-110	11

*3 pts deducted for ineligible player. Cup Final: Cove 4 Wick 0

BARCLAYS UNDER-21 PREMIER LEAGUE
DIVISION ONE

	P	W	D	L	F	A	GD	Pts
Manchester Utd	22	11	7	4	39	23	16	40
Liverpool	22	11	3	8	45	35	10	36
Chelsea	22	10	5	7	37	25	12	35
Sunderland	22	10	5	7	26	24	2	35
Manchester City	22	10	3	9	44	40	4	33
Leicester	22	9	5	8	39	37	2	32
Norwich	22	8	8	6	32	30	2	32
Southampton	22	9	4	9	32	34	-2	31
Tottenham	22	8	5	9	30	30	0	29
Everton	22	8	3	11	32	37	-5	27
Fulham	22	6	4	12	27	45	-18	22
West Ham	22	5	2	15	20	43	-23	17

DIVISION TWO

	P	W	D	L	F	A	GD	Pts
Middlesbrough	22	16	2	4	39	23	16	50
Reading	22	13	2	7	38	30	8	41
Derby	22	12	4	6	39	20	19	40
Arsenal	22	11	4	7	38	25	13	37
WBA	22	10	7	5	37	27	10	37
Newcastle	22	9	5	8	43	39	4	32
Aston Villa	22	8	3	11	25	36	-11	27
Brighton	22	6	5	11	19	23	-4	23
Bolton	22	5	8	9	26	33	-7	23
Blackburn	22	5	6	11	23	31	-8	21
Stoke	22	4	6	12	23	50	-27	18
Wolves	22	3	8	11	24	37	-13	17

Cup Final (on agg): Southampton 2 Blackburn 1 (aet)

IRISH FOOTBALL 2014–15

SSE AIRTRICITY LEAGUE OF IRELAND

PREMIER DIVISION

	P	W	D	L	F	A	Pts
Dundalk	33	22	8	3	73	24	74
Cork City	33	22	6	5	51	25	72
St Patrick's Ath	33	19	8	6	66	37	65
Shamrock Rov	33	18	8	7	43	26	62
Sligo Rov	33	12	7	14	44	36	43
Limerick	33	12	5	16	37	45	41
Bohemians	33	9	13	11	42	43	40
Derry City	33	9	11	13	42	41	38
Drogheda Utd	33	10	6	17	40	63	36
Bray Wdrs	33	5	11	17	28	61	26
UCD	33	6	7	20	27	71	25
Athlone Town	33	4	10	19	35	56	22

Leading scorer: 20 Christy Fagan (St Patrick's Ath), Pat Hoban (Dundalk). **Player of Year**: Christy Fagan. **Young Player of Year**: Daryl Horgan (Dundalk). **Goalkeeper of Year**: Mark McNulty (Cork City). **Personality of Year**: Stephen Kenny (Dundalk).

FIRST DIVISION

	P	W	D	L	F	A	Pts
Longford Town	28	18	6	4	56	19	60
Shelbourne	28	14	10	4	46	30	52
Galway*	28	13	10	5	47	23	49
Wexford Youths	28	13	7	8	45	35	46
Finn Harps	28	7	11	10	26	28	32
Shamrock Rov'B'	28	7	5	16	25	50	26
Waterford Utd	28	6	7	15	25	43	25
Cobh Ramblers	28	2	8	18	24	66	14

*Galway also promoted after beating Shelbourne in First Division play-off and UCD in promotion/relegation play-off
Leading scorer: 21 David O'Sullivan (Longford Town). **Player of Year**: David O'Sullivan

FAI FORD CUP FINAL

St Patrick's Athletic 2 (Fagan 2) **Derry City** 0. Aviva Stadium, November 2, 2014

St Patrick's Athletic: Clarke, O'Brien (McCormack), Hoare, Browne, Bermingham, Bolger, Fahey (Chambers), Brennan, Byrne, Fagan, Forrester (Fitzgerald)
Derry City: Doherty, Ventre, McBride (McNamee), Barry, Jarvis; Lowry, Molloy, Dooley, McEleney (Houston), Duffy, Patterson
Referee: P Sutton (Ennis)

EA SPORTS LEAGUE CUP FINAL

Dundalk 3 (Massey 2, Hoban) **Shamrock Rovers** 2 (McGuinness, Kilduff). Oriel Park, Dundalk, September 20, 2014

SETANTA SPORTS CUP FINAL

Sligo Rovers 1 (O'Connor) **Dundalk** 0. Tallaght Stadium, Dublin, May 14, 2014

DANSKE BANK PREMIERSHIP

	P	W	D	L	F	A	Pts
Crusaders	38	25	7	6	93	43	82
Linfield	38	21	9	8	67	46	72
Glenavon	38	20	6	12	82	65	66
Portadown	38	17	11	10	65	56	62
Cliftonville	38	16	13	9	71	47	61
Glentoran	38	16	10	12	67	51	58
Ballymena Utd	38	15	6	17	62	75	51
Coleraine	38	13	7	18	48	55	46
Ballinamallard Utd	38	10	9	19	40	71	39
Dungannon Swifts	38	8	13	17	38	56	37
Warrenpoint Town	38	6	12	20	50	76	30
Institute	38	4	9	25	36	84	21

Leading scorer: 31 Joe Gormley (Cliftonville). **Manager of Year**: Stephen Baxter (Crusaders).
Player of Year: Paul Heatley (Crusaders). **Young Player of Year**: Gavin Whyte (Crusaders)

BELFAST TELEGRAPH CHAMPIONSHIP – DIVISION ONE

	P	W	D	L	F	A	Pts
Carrick Rgrs	26	19	5	2	54	22	62
Bangor	26	18	6	2	71	32	60
Ards	26	16	8	2	61	30	56
H&W Welders	26	15	5	6	59	37	50
Larne	26	13	3	10	52	36	42
Dergview	26	8	9	9	40	43	33
Armagh City	26	9	5	12	38	48	32
Knockbreda	26	9	3	14	31	43	30
Ballyclare Comrades	26	8	4	14	46	48	28
Lisburn Distillery	26	8	4	14	38	58	28
Loughall	26	7	6	13	36	54	27
Donegal Celtic	26	5	9	12	35	42	24
PSNI	26	6	5	15	27	64	23
Dundela	26	3	4	19	34	65	13

Leading scorer: 19 Michael McLellan (H&W Welders). **Player of Year**: Jordan Forsythe (Bangor)

MARIE CURIE IRISH CUP FINAL

Glentoran 1 (Scullion) **Portadown** 0. The Oval, Belfast, May 2, 2015
Glentoran: Morris, Garrett, Kane, Birney, McAlorum, Holland, Henderson (Addis), Gordon, Stewart (Nelson), Allen, Scullion (McCaffrey)
Portadown: Miskelly, Casement, Redman, O'Hara, Breen, McMahon, Mackle, McAllister (Murray), Gault, Twigg, Garrett.
Referee: R Dunlop (Carrigfergus)

WASP SOLUTIONS LEAGUE CUP FINAL

Cliftonville 3 (Gormley 2, Martin Donnelly) **Ballymena United** 2 (Cushley 2). Windsor Park, January 25, 2015

COUNTY ANTRIM SHIELD FINAL

Cliftonville 1 (Winchester) **Bangor** 0. Solitude, Belfast, January 13, 2015.

UEFA CHAMPIONS LEAGUE 2014–15

FIRST QUALIFYING ROUND, ON AGGREGATE

Levadia Tallinn 8 Fiorita 0; Santa Coloma 3 Banants Yerevan 3 (Santa Coloma won on away goals); Torshavn 6 Lincoln 3

SECOND QUALIFYING ROUND, FIRST LEG

Cliftonville 0 Debrecen 0. Att: 1,750; Legia Warsaw 1 (Radovic 90) **St Patrick's** 1 (Fagan 39). Att: 11,075. Reykjavik 0 **Celtic** 1 (McGregor 84). Att: 2,781. Slovan Bratislava 1 (Cikos 53) **New Saints** 0. Att: 4,828

SECOND QUALIFYING ROUND, SECOND LEG

Celtic 4 (Van Dijk 14, 20, Pukki 27, 71) Reykjavik 0. Att: 39,099 (Celtic won 5-0 on agg). Debrecen 2 (Mihelic 56, Sidibe 80) **Cliftonville** 0. Att: 9,457 (Debrecen won 2-0 on agg). **New Saints** 0 Slovan Bratislava 2 (Milinkovic 75, 90). Att: 1,140 (Slovan Bratislava won 3-0 on agg). **St Patrick's** 0 Legia Warsaw 5 (Radovic 26, 83, Zyro 70, Saganowski 88, Byrne 90 og). Att: 4,213 (Legia Warsaw won 6-1 on agg)

SECOND QUALIFYING ROUND, ON AGGREGATE

Aktobe 4 Dynamo Tbilisi 0; Bate Borisov 1 Skenderbeu 1 (Bate Borisov won on away goal); Dinamo Zagreb 4 Zalgiris 0; HJK Helsinki 2 Radotnicki 1; Ludogorets 5 Dudelange 1; Maccabi Tel Aviv 3 Santa Coloma 0; Malmo 1 Ventspils 0; Maribor 2 Zrinjski Mostar 0; Partizan Belgrade 6 Torshavn 1; Qarabag 5 Valletta 0; Sheriff Tiraspol 5 Sutjeska 0; Sparta Prague 8 Levadia Tallinn 1; Steaua Bucharest 3 Stromsgodset 0

THIRD QUALIFYING ROUND, FIRST LEG

Legia Warsaw 4 (Radovic 10, 36, Zyro 84, Kosecki 90) **Celtic** 1 (McGregor 7). Att: 22,265

THIRD QUALIFYING ROUND, SECOND LEG

Celtic 0 Legia Warsaw 2 (Zyro 36, Kucharczyk 61). Att: 30,000 (Legia Warsaw, 6-1 winners on aggregate, expelled for fielding ineligible player – Celtic reinstated)

THIRD QUALIFYING ROUND, ON AGGREGATE

Aalborg 2 Dinamo Zagreb 1; Apoel Nicosia 4 HJK Helsinki 2; Bate Borisov 3 Debrecen 2; Besiktas 5 Feyenoord 2; Copenhagen 2 Dnipro 0; Grasshoppers 1 Lille 1 (Grasshoppers won on away goal); Ludogorets 2 Partizan Belgrade 2 (Ludogorets won on away goals); Malmo 4 Sparta Prague 4 (Malmo won on away goals); Maribor 3 Maccabi Tel Aviv 2; Salzburg 3 Qarabag 2; Slovan Bratislava 2 Sheriff Tiraspol 1; Standard Liege 2 Panathinaikos 1; Steaua Bucharest 4 Aktobe 3; Zenit St Petersburg 3 AEL 1

PLAY-OFFS, FIRST LEG

Besiktas 0 Arsenal 0. Att: 41,531. Maribor 1 (Bohar 14) **Celtic** 1 (McGregor 6). Att: 11,400

PLAY-OFFS, SECOND LEG

Arsenal 1 (Sanchez 45) Besiktas 0. Att: 59,946 (Arsenal won 1-0 on agg). **Celtic** 0 Maribor 1 (Tavares 75). Att: 55,415 (Maribor won 2-1 on agg)

PLAY-OFFS, ON AGGREGATE

Apoel Nicosia 5 Aalborg 1; Athletic Bilbao 4 Napoli 2; Bate Borisov 4 Slovan Bratislava 1; Bayer Leverkusen 7 Copenhagen 2; Ludogorets 1 Steaua Bucharest 1 (aet, Ludogorets won 6-5 on pens); Malmo 4 Salzburg 2; Porto 3 Lille 0; Zenit St Petersburg 4 Standard Liege 0

GROUP A

September 16, 2014
Juventus 2 (Tevez 59, 89) **Malmo** 0. Att: 31,218
Olympiacos 3 (Masuaku 13, Afellay 31, Mitroglou 73) **Atletico Madrid** 2 (Mandzukic 38, Griezmann 86). Att: 31,946

October 1, 2014
Atletico Madrid 1 (Turan 75) **Juventus** 0. Att: 44,322
Malmo 2 (Rosenberg 42, 82) **Olympiacos** 0. Att: 20,500

October 22, 2014
Atletico Madrid 5 (Koke 48, Mandzukic 61, Griezmann 63, Godin 87, Cerci 90) **Malmo** 0. Att: 34,502
Olympiacos 1 (Kasami 35) **Juventus** 0: Att: 31,411

November 4, 2014
Juventus 3 (Pirlo 21, Roberto 65 og, Pogba 66) **Olympiacos** 2 (Botia 24, Ndinga 61). Att: 39,091
Malmo 0 **Atletico Madrid** 2 (Koke 30, Raul Garcia 78). Att: 20,500

November 26, 2014
Atletico Madrid 4 (Raul Garcia 9, Mandzukic 38, 62, 65) **Olympiacos** 0. Att: 40,121
Malmo 0 **Juventus** 2 (Llorente 49, Tevez 88). Att: 20,500

December 9, 2014
Juventus 0 **Atletico Madrid** 0. Att: 39,219
Olympiacos 4 (Fuster 23, Dominguez 63, Mitroglou 87, Afellay 90) **Malmo** 2 (Kroon 59, Rosenberg 81). Att: 27,562

FINAL TABLE

	P	W	D	L	F	A	Pts
Atletico Madrid Q	6	4	1	1	14	3	13
Juventus Q	6	3	1	2	7	4	10
Olympiacos	6	3	0	3	10	13	9
Malmo	6	1	0	5	4	15	3

GROUP B

September 16, 2014
Liverpool 2 (Balotelli 82, Gerrard 90 pen) **Ludogorets** 1 (Dani Abalo 90). Att: 43,307
Liverpool (4-3-3): Mignolet, Manquillo, Lovren, Sakho, Moreno, Henderson, Gerrard, Lallana (Borini 67), Sterling, Coutinho (Lucas 67), Balotelli
Real Madrid 5 (Suchy 14 og, Bale 30, Ronaldo 31, Rodriguez 36, Benzema 80) **Basle** 1 (Gonzalez 38). Att: 80,454

October 1, 2014
Basle 1 (Streller 52) **Liverpool** 0. Att: 36,000
Liverpool (4-3-3): Mignolet, Manquillo, Lovren, Skrtel, Jose Enrique, Henderson, Gerrard, Markovic (Lambert 81), Sterling, Balotelli, Coutinho (Lallana 70). **Booked**: Sterling, Gerrard, Balotelli
Ludogorets 1 (Marcelinho 7) **Real Madrid** 2 (Ronaldo 24 pen, Benzema 77). Att: 41,484

October 22, 2014
Liverpool 0 **Real Madrid** 3 (Ronaldo 23, Benzema 30, 41). Att: 43,521
Liverpool (4-3-3): Mignolet, Johnson, Lovren, Skrtel, Moreno, Henderson (Emre Can 67), Gerrard, Allen, Sterling, Coutinho (Markovic 67), Balotelli (Lallana 46)
Ludogorets 1 (Minev 90) **Basle** 0. Att: 29,150

November 4, 2014
Basle 4 (Embolo 34, Gonzalez 41, Gashi 58, Suchy 65) **Ludogorets** 0. Att: 35,272
Real Madrid 1 (Benzema 27) **Liverpool** 0: Att: 79,283
Liverpool (4-2-3-1): Mignolet, Manquillo, Toure, Skrtel, Moreno, Emre Can (Coutinho 75),
Lucas (Gerrard 69), Lallana, Allen, Markovic (Sterling 69), Borini. **Booked**: Skrtel, Moreno

November 26, 2014
Basle 0 **Real Madrid** 1 (Ronaldo 35). Att: 36,000
Ludogorets 2 (Dani Abalo 3, Terziev 88) **Liverpool** 2 (Lambert 8, Henderson 37). Att: 37,143
Liverpool (4-2-3-1): Mignolet, Manquillo, Skrtel, Toure, Johnson, Lucas, Allen, Henderson,
Gerrard, Sterling (Moreno 82), Lambert

December 9, 2014
Liverpool 1 (Gerrard 81) **Basle** 1 (Frei 25). Att: 43,290
Liverpool (4-2-3-1): Mignolet, Johnson, Lovren, Skrtel, Jose Enrique (Moreno 46), Lucas
(Coutinho 74), Allen, Sterling, Gerrard, Henderson, Lambert (Markovic 46). **Booked**: Lucas,
Lovren, Moreno. **Sent off**: Markovic (61)
Real Madrid 4 (Ronaldo 21 pen, Bale 38, Arbeloa 80, Medran 88) **Ludogorets** 0. Att: 58,393

FNAL TABLE

	P	W	D	L	F	A	Pts
Real Madrid Q	6	6	0	0	16	2	18
Basle Q	6	2	1	3	7	8	7
Liverpool	6	1	2	3	5	9	5
Ludogorets	6	1	1	4	5	14	4

GROUP C

September 16, 2014
Benfica 0 **Zenit St Petersburg** 2 (Hulk 5, Witsel 22). Att: 35,294
Monaco 1 (Joao Moutinho 61) **Bayer Leverkusen** 0. Att: 8,130

October 1, 2014
Bayer Leverkusen 3 (Kiessling 25, Son 34, Calhanoglu 64 pen) **Benfica** 1 (Salvio 61). Att:
25,202
Zenit St Petersburg 0 **Monaco** 0. Att: 13,817

October 22, 2014
Bayer Leverkusen 2 (Donati 58, Papadopoulos 63) **Zenit St Petersburg** 0. Att: 27,254
Monaco 0 **Benfica** 0. Att: 12,776

November 4, 2014
Benfica 1 (Anderson Talisca 82) **Monaco** 0. Att: 32,565
Zenit St Petersburg 1 (Rondon 89) **Bayer Leverkusen** 2 (Son 68, 73). Att: 17,010

November 26, 2014
Bayer Leverkusen 0 **Monaco** 1 (Ocampos 72). Att: 26,230
Zenit St Petersburg 1 (Danny 79) **Benfica** 0. Att: 14,123

December 9, 2014
Benfica 0 **Bayer Leverkusen** 0. Att: 17,564
Monaco 2 (Abdennour 63, Fabinho 89) **Zenit St Petersburg** 0. Att: 11,319

FINAL TABLE

	P	W	D	L	F	A	Pts
Monaco Q	6	3	2	1	4	1	11
Bayer Leverkusen Q	6	3	1	2	7	4	10
Zenit St Petersburg	6	2	1	3	4	6	7
Benfica	6	1	2	3	2	6	5

GROUP D

September 16, 2014
Borussia Dortmund 2 (Immobile 45, Aubameyang 48) **Arsenal** 0. Att: 65,851
Arsenal (4-1-4-1): Szczesny, Bellerin, Mertesacker, Koscielny, Gibbs, Arteta (Podolski 77), Sanchez, Ramsey (Cazorla 62), Wilshire, Ozil (Oxlade-Chamberlain 62), Welbeck. **Booked:** Ozil, Wilshere
Galatasaray 1 (Yilmaz 90) **Anderlecht** 1 (Praet 52). Att: 28,553

October 1, 2014
Anderlecht 0 **Borussia Dortmund** 3 (Immobile 3, Ramos 69, 79). Att: 18,649
Arsenal 4 (Welbeck 22, 30, 52, Sanchez 41) **Galatasaray** 1 (Yilmaz 63 pen). Att: 59,803
Arsenal (4-2-3-1): Szczesny, Chambers, Mertesacker, Koscielny, Gibbs, Flamini, Cazorla, Oxlade-Chamberlain (Rosicky 68), Ozil (Wilshere 77), Sanchez (Ospina 62), Welbeck. **Booked:** Flamini. **Sent off:** Szczesny (60)

October 22, 2014
Anderlecht 1 (Najar 71) **Arsenal** 2 (Gibbs 89, Podolski 90). Att: 19,881
Arsenal (4-3-3): Martinez, Chambers, Mertesacker, Monreal, Gibbs, Ramsey, Flamini (Oxlade-Chamberlain 75), Wilshire (Podolski 84), Sanchez, Welbeck (Campbell 75), Cazorla. **Booked:** Monreal, Welbeck
Galatasaray 0 **Borussia Dortmund** 4 (Aubameyang 6, 18, Reus 41, Ramos 83). Att: 36,324

November 4, 2014
Arsenal 3 (Arteta 25 pen, Sanchez 29, Oxlade-Chamberlain 58) **Anderlecht** 3 (Vanden Borre 61, 73 pen, Mitrovic 90). Att: 59,872
Arsenal (4-2-3-1): Szczesny, Chambers, Mertesacker, Monreal, Gibbs, Ramsey, Arteta (Flamini 62), Oxlade-Chamberlain (Rosicky 81), Sanchez, Cazorla, Welbeck (Podolski 82). **Booked:** Monreal
Borussia Dortmund 4 (Reus 39, Papastathopoulos 55, Immobile 73, Kaya 84 og) **Galatasaray** 1 (Balta 69) Att: 65,851

November 26, 2014
Anderlecht 2 (Mbemba 44, 86) **Galatasaray** 0. Att: 19,857
Arsenal 2 (Sanogo 2, Sanchez 57) **Borussia Dortmund** 0. Att: 59, 902
Arsenal (4-2-3-1): Martinez, Chambers, Mertesacker, Monreal, Gibbs, Arteta (Flamini 67), Ramsey, Oxlade-Chamberlain (Campbell 90), Sanchez, Cazorla, Sanogo (Podolski 79). **Booked:** Arteta

December 9, 2014
Borussia Dortmund 1 (Immobile 58) **Anderlecht** 1 (Mitrovic 84). Att: 65,851
Galatasaray 1 (Sneijder 88) **Arsenal** 4 (Podolski 3, 90, Ramsey 11, 29). Att: 20,590
Arsenal (4-3-3): Szczesny, Debuchy (O'Connor 77), Mertesacker, Chambers, Bellerin, Oxlade-Chamberlain, Flamini (Zelalem 46), Ramsey (Maitland-Niles 46), Campbell, Sanogo, Podolski. **Booked:** Flamini, Debuchy, Podolski

FINAL TABLE

		P	W	D	L	F	A	Pts
Borussia Dortmund	Q	6	4	1	1	14	4	13
Arsenal	Q	6	4	1	1	15	8	13
Anderlecht		6	1	3	2	8	10	6
Galatasaray		6	0	1	5	4	19	1

GROUP E

September 17, 2014
Bayern Munich 1 (Boateng 89) **Manchester City** 0. Att: 68,000
Manchester City (4-4-1-1): Hart, Sagna, Kompany, Demichelis, Clichy, Jesus Navas (Kolarov

88), Toure, Fernandinho, Nasri (Milner 58), Silva, Dzeko (Aguero 74). **Booked:** Dzeko, Kompany, Clichy, Demichelis
Roma 5 (Iturbe 6, Gervinho 10, 31, Maicon 20, Ignashevich 50 og) **CSKA Moscow** 1 (Musa 82) Att: 40,888

September 30, 2014
CSKA Moscow 0 **Bayern Munich** 1 (Muller 22 pen). Played behind closed doors – previous crowd trouble
Manchester City 1 (Aguero 4 pen) **Roma** 1 (Totti 29). Att: 37,509
Manchester City (4-4-2): Hart, Zabaleta, Kompany, Demichelis, Clichy, Jesus Navas (Milner 46), Toure, Fernandinho, Silva, Aguero (Jovetic 84), Dzeko (Lampard 57). **Booked:** Zabaleta

October 21, 2014
CSKA Moscow 2 (Doumbia 64, Natcho 86 pen). **Manchester City** 2 (Aguero 29, Milner 37). Played behind closed doors – previous crowd trouble
Manchester City (4-2-3-1): Hart, Zabaleta, Kompany, Mangala, Kolarov, Toure, Fernando, Milner, Dzeko (Jesus Navas 7), Silva (Fernandinho 77), Aguero. **Booked:** Fernando
Roma 1 (Gervinho 66) **Bayern Munich** 7 (Robben 9, 30, Gotze 23, Lewandowski 25, Muller 36 pen, Ribery 78, Shaqiri 80). Att: 70,544

November 5, 2014
Bayern Munich 2 (Ribery 38, Gotze 64) **Roma** 0. Att: 68,000
Manchester City 1 (Toure 8) **CSKA Moscow** 2 (Doumbia 2, 34). Att: 45,143
Manchester City (4-4-2): Hart, Zabaleta, Kompany, Demichelis, Clichy, Jesus Navas (Nasri 46), Toure, Fernando (Dzeko 65), Milner, Aguero, Jovetic (Fernandinho 46). **Booked:** Fernandinho, Toure, Aguero. **Sent off:** Fernandinho (70), Toure (81)

November 25, 2014
CSKA Moscow 1 (Berezutski 90) **Roma** 1 (Totti 43). Played behind closed doors – previous crowd trouble
Manchester City 3 (Aguero 22 pen, 85, 90) **Bayern Munich** 2 (Xabi Alonso 40, Lewandowski 45). Att: 47,726
Manchester City (4-2-3-1): Hart, Sagna (Zabaleta 66), Kompany, Mangala, Clichy, Milner (Jovetic 66), Fernando, Jesus Navas, Lampard, Nasri, Aguero (Demichelis 90). **Booked:** Clichy, Zabaleta, Aguero

December 10, 2014
Bayern Munich 3 (Muller 18 pen, Rode 83, Gotze 90) **CSKA Moscow** 0. Att: 68,000
Roma 0 **Manchester City** 2 (Nasri 60, Zabaleta 86). Att: 54,119
Manchester City (4-2-3-1): Hart, Zabaleta, Demichelis, Mangala, Clichy, Fernandinho, Fernando, Jesus Navas (Silva 67), Nasri (Kolarov 89), Milner, Dzeko (Jovetic 78). **Booked:** Dzeko, Nasri

FINAL TABLE

	P	W	D	L	F	A	Pts
Bayern Munich Q	6	5	0	1	16	4	15
Manchester City Q	6	2	2	2	9	8	8
Roma	6	1	2	3	8	14	5
CSKA Moscow	6	1	2	3	6	13	5

GROUP F

September 17, 2014
Ajax 1 (Schone 74) **Paris SG** 1 (Cavani 14). Att: 50,430
Barcelona 1 (Pique 28) **Apoel Nicosia** 0. Att: 62,832

September 30, 2014
Apoel Nicosia 1 (Manduca 32 pen) **Ajax** 1 (Andersen 28). Att: 17,190

Paris SG 3 (Luiz 10, Verratti 26, Matuidi 54) **Barcelona** 2 (Messi 11, Neymar 56). Att: 46,400

October 21, 2014
Apoel Nicosia 0 **Paris SG** 1 (Cavani 87). Att: 18,659
Barcelona 3 (Neymar 7, Messi 24, Sandro 90) **Ajax** 1 (El Ghazi 88). Att: 79,357

November 5, 2014
Ajax 0 **Barcelona** 2 (Messi 36, 76). Att: 52,116
Paris SG 1 (Cavani 1) **Apoel Nicosia** 0. Att: 45,816

November 25, 2014
Apoel Nicosia 0 **Barcelona** 4 (Suarez 27, Messi 38, 58, 87). Att: 20,626
Paris SG 3 (Cavani 33, 83, Ibrahimovic 79) **Ajax** 1 (Klaassen 67). Att: 46,130

December 10, 2014
Ajax 4 (Schone 45 pen, 50, Klaassen 53, Milik 74) **Apoel Nicosia** 0. Att: 51,796
Barcelona 3 (Messi 19, Neymar 42, Suarez 77) **Paris SG** 0. Att: 82,570

FINAL TABLE

	P	W	D	L	F	A	Pts
Barcelona Q	6	5	0	1	15	5	15
Paris SG Q	6	4	1	1	10	7	13
Ajax	6	1	2	3	8	10	5
Apoel Nicosia	6	0	1	5	1	12	1

GROUP G

September 17, 2014
Chelsea 1 (Fabregas 11) **Schalke** 1 (Huntelaar 62). Att: 40,648
Chelsea (4-2-3-1): Courtois, Ivanovic, Cahill, Terry, Filipe Luis, Fabregas, Matic, Ramires (Oscar 67), Willian (Remy 74), Hazard, Drogba (Diego Costa 74). **Booked**: Terry, Willian
Maribor 1 (Zahovic 90) **Sporting** 1 (Da Cunha 80). Att: 12,211

September 30, 2014
Schalke 1 (Huntelaar 56) **Maribor** 1 (Bohar 37). Att: 47,997
Sporting 0 **Chelsea** 1 (Matic 34). Att: 40,734
Chelsea (4-2-3-1): Courtois, Ivanovic, Cahill, Terry, Filipe Luis, Fabregas, Matic, Schurrle (Willian 58), Oscar (Mikel 71), Hazard (Salah 84), Diego Costa. **Booked**: Ivanovic, Hazard, Filipe Luis, Fabregas

October 21, 2014
Chelsea 6 (Remy 13, Drogba 23 pen, Terry 31, Viler 54 og, Hazard 77 pen, 90) **Maribor** 0. Att: 41,126
Chelsea (4-2-3-1): Cech, Ivanovic, Zouma, Terry, Filipe Luis, Fabregas (Ake 60), Matic, Hazard, Oscar (Solanke 73), Willian, Remy (Drogba 16)
Schalke 4 (Obasi Ogbuke 34, Huntelaar 51, Howedes 60, Choupo-Moting 90 pen) **Sporting** 3 (Nani 16, Adrien Silva 64 pen, 78). Att: 49,943

November 5, 2014
Maribor 1 (Ibraimi 50) **Chelsea** 1 (Matic 73). Att: 12,646
Chelsea (4-2-3-1): Cech, Ivanovic, Zouma, Terry, Filipe Luis (Ramires 56), Fabregas, Matic, Schurrle (Diego Costa 46), Willian (Oscar 46), Hazard. Drogba. **Booked**: Filipe Luis
Sporting 4 (Sarr 26, Jefferson 52, Nani 72, Slimani 90) **Schalke** 2 (Slimani 17 og, Aogo 87). Att: 35,473

November 25, 2014
Schalke 0 **Chelsea** 5 (Terry 2, Willian 29, Kirchoff 44 og, Drogba 76, Ramires 78). Att: 54,442
Chelsea (4-2-3-1): Courtois, Ivanovic, Cahill, Terry, Azpilicueta, Fabregas (Schurrle 79), Matic, Willian, Oscar (Ramires 75), Hazard, Diego Costa (Drogba 66).

Sporting 3 (Carlos Mane 10, Nani 35, Slimani 65) **Maribor** 1 (Jefferson 42 og). Att: 32,739

December 10, 2014
Chelsea 3 (Fabregas 8 pen, Schurrle 16, Mikel 57) **Sporting** 1 (Silva 50). Att: 41,089
Chelsea (4-2-3-1): Cech, Azpilicueta, Zouma, Cahill, Filipe Luis, Mikel, Matic, Schurrle (Ramires 74), Fabregas (Loftus-Cheek 83), Salah (Remy 71), Diego Costa. **Booked**: Azpilicueta
Maribor 0 **Schalke** 1 (Meyer 62). Att: 12,516

FINAL TABLE

	P	W	D	L	F	A	Pts
Chelsea Q	6	4	2	0	17	3	14
Schalke Q	6	2	2	2	9	14	8
Sporting	6	2	1	3	12	12	7
Maribor	6	0	3	3	4	13	3

GROUP H

September 17, 2014
Athletic Bilbao 0 **Shakhtar Donetsk** 0. Att: 48,357
Porto 6 (Brahimi 5, 32, 57, Martinez 37, Adrian 61, Aboubakar 76) **Bate Borisov** 0. Att: 35,108

September 30, 2014
Bate Borisov 2 (Palyakow 19, Karnitskiy 41) **Athletic Bilbao** 1 (Aduriz 45). Att: 11,886
Shakhtar Donetsk 2 (Teixeira 52, Luiz Adriano 85) **Porto** 2 (Martinez 89 pen, 90). Att: 33,217

October 21, 2014
Bate Borisov 0 **Shakhtar Donetsk** 7 (Teixeira 11, Luiz Adriano 28 pen, 37, 40, 44, 82 pen, Douglas Costa 35). Att: 12,113
Porto 2 (Herrera 45, Quaresma 75) **Athletic Bilbao** 1 (Guillermo 58). Att: 38,116

November 5, 2014
Athletic Bilbao 0 **Porto** 2 (Martinez 55, Brahimi 73). Att: 47,243
Shakhtar Donetsk 5 (Srna 19, Teixeira 48, Luiz Adriano 58 pen, 83, 90) **Bate Borisov** 0. Att: 29,173

November 25, 2014
Bate Borisov 0 **Porto** 3 (Herrera 56, Martinez 65, Tello 89). Att: 10,147
Shakhtar Donetsk 0 **Athletic Bilbao** 1 (San Jose 68). Att: 33,489

December 10, 2014
Athletic Bilbao 2 (San Jose 47, Susaeta 88) **Bate Borisov** 0. Att: 42,852
Porto 1 (Aboubakar 87) **Shakhtar Donetsk** 1 (Stepanenko 50). Att: 28,010

FINAL TABLE

	P	W	D	L	F	A	Pts
Porto Q	6	4	2	0	16	4	14
Shakhtar Donetsk Q	6	2	3	1	15	4	9
Athletic Bilbao	6	2	1	3	5	6	7
Bate Borisov	6	1	0	5	2	24	3

ROUND OF 16, FIRST LEG

February 17, 2015
Paris SG 1 (Cavani 54) **Chelsea** 1 (Ivanovic 36). Att: 46,146
Chelsea (4-2-3-1): Courtois, Ivanovic, Cahill, Terry, Azpilicueta, Ramires, Matic, Willian (Cuadrado 79), Fabregas (Oscar 83), Hazard, Diego Costa (Remy 81). **Booked**: Ivanovic, Fabregas

Shakhtar Donetsk 0 **Bayern Munich** 0. Att: 34,187

February 18, 2015
Basle 1 (Gonzalez 11) **Porto** 1 (Danilo 79 pen). Att: 34,464
Schalke 0 **Real Madrid** 2 (Ronaldo 26, Marcelo 79). Att: 54,442

February 24, 2015
Juventus 2 (Tevez 13, Morata 43) **Borussia Dortmund** 1 (Reus 18). Att: 41,182
Manchester City 1 (Aguero 69) **Barcelona** 2 (Suarez 16, 30). Att: 45,081
Manchester City (4-4-2): Hart, Zabaleta, Kompany, Demichelis, Clichy, Nasri (Fernandinho 62), Milner, Fernando, Silva (Sagna 78), Dzeko (Bony 68), Aguero. **Booked**: Clichy, Fernando. **Sent off**: Clichy (74)

February 25, 2015
Arsenal 1 (Oxlade-Chamberlain 90) **Monaco** 3 (Kondogbia 38, Berbatov 53, Carrasco 90). Att: 59,868
Arsenal (4-2-3-1): Ospina, Bellerin, Mertesacker, Koscielny, Gibbs, Coquelin (Oxlade-Chamberlain 68), Cazorla (Rosicky 82), Welbeck, Ozil, Sanchez, Giroud (Walcott 60). **Booked**: Coquelin, Bellerin, Ozil
Bayer Leverkusen 1 (Calhanoglu 57) **Atletico Madrid** 0. Att: 30,210

ROUND OF 16, SECOND LEG
March 10, 2015
Porto 4 (Brahimi 14, Herrera 47, Casemiro 56, Aboubakar 76) **Basle** 0. Att: 43,108 (Porto won 5-1 on agg)
Real Madrid 3 (Ronaldo 25, 45, Benzema 53) **Schalke** 4 (Fuchs 20, Huntelaar 40, 84, Sane 57). Att: 69,986 (Real Madrid won 5-4 on agg)

March 11, 2015
Bayern Munich 7 (Muller 4 pen, 51, Boateng 34, Ribery 49, Badstuber 63, Lewandowski 75, Gotze 87) **Shakhtar Donetsk** 0. Att: 68,000 (Bayern Munich won 7-0 on agg)
Chelsea 2 (Cahill 81, Hazard 96 pen) **Paris SG** 2 (Luiz 86, Thiago Silva 114). Att: 37,692 (aet, agg 3-3, Paris SG won on away goals)
Chelsea (4-2-3-1): Courtois, Ivanovic, Cahill, Terry, Azpilicueta, Fabregas, Matic (Zouma 84), Ramires (Drogba 90), Oscar (Willian 46), Hazard, Diego Costa. **Booked**: Oscar, Ramires, Diego Costa

March 17, 2015
Atletico Madrid 1 (Suarez 27) **Bayer Leverkusen** 0. Att: 48,273 (aet, agg 1-1, Atletico Madrid won 3-2 on pens)
Monaco 0 **Arsenal** 2 (Giroud 36, Ramsey 79). Att: 17,263 (agg 3-3, Monaco won on away goals)
Arsenal: (4-2-3-1): Ospina, Bellerin, Mertesacker, Koscielny, Monreal (Gibbs 83), Coquelin (Ramsey 63), Cazorla, Welbeck (Walcott 72), Ozil, Sanchez, Giroud. **Booked**: Sanchez

March 18, 2015
Barcelona 1 (Rakitic 31) **Manchester City** 0. Att: 92,551 (Barcelona won 3-1 on agg)
Manchester City (4-4-1-1): Hart, Sagna, Kompany, Demichelis, Kolarov, Nasri (Jesus Navas 46), Fernandinho, Toure (Bony 72), Milner (Lampard 87), Silva, Aguero. **Booked**: Fernandinho, Kolarov, Silva, Nasri, Demichelis
Borussia Dortmund 0 **Juventus** 3 (Tevez 3, 79, Morata 70). Att: 65,851 (Juventus won 5-1 on agg)

QUARTER-FINALS, FIRST LEG
April 14, 2015
Atletico Madrid 0 **Real Madrid** 0. Att: 52,553
Juventus 1 (Vidal 57 pen) **Monaco** 0. Att: 40,801

April 15, 2015
Paris SG 1 (Ver der Wiel 82) **Barcelona** 3 (Neymar 18, Suarez 67, 79). Att: 45,713
Porto 3 (Quaresma 3 pen, 10, Martinez 65) **Bayern Munich** 1 (Thiago Alcantara 28). Att: 50,092

QUARTER-FINALS, SECOND LEG

April 21, 2015
Barcelona 2 (Neymar 14, 34) **Paris SG** 0. Att: 84,477 (Barcelona won 5-1 on agg)
Bayern Munich 6 (Thiago Alcantara 14, Boateng 22, Lewandowski 27, 40, Muller 36, Xabi Alonso 88) **Porto** 1 (Martinez 73). Att: 70,000 (Bayern Munich won 7-4 on agg)

April 22, 2015
Monaco 0 **Juventus** 0. Att: 16,889 (Juventus won 1-0 on agg)
Real Madrid 1 (Hernandez 88) **Atletico Madrid** 0. Att: 78,300 (Real Madrid won 1-0 on agg)

SEMI-FINALS, FIRST LEG

May 5, 2015
Juventus 2 (Morata 8, Tevez 57 pen) **Real Madrid** 1 (Ronaldo 27). Att: 41,011
May 6, 2015
Barcelona 3 (Messi 77, 80, Neymar 90) **Bayern Munich** 0. Att: 95,639

SEMI-FINALS, SECOND LEG

May 12, 2015
Bayern Munich 3 (Benatia 7, Lewandowski 59, Muller 74) **Barcelona** 2 (Neymar 15, 29). Att: 70,000 (Barcelona won 5-3 on agg)

May 13, 2015
Real Madrid 1 (Ronaldo 23 pen) **Juventus** 1 (Morata 57). Att: 78,300 (Juventus won 3-2 on agg)

FINAL

JUVENTUS 1 BARCELONA 3
Olympiastadion, Berlin (70,442); Saturday, June 6 2015

Juventus (4-3-1-2): Buffon (capt), Lichtsteiner, Bonucci, Barzagli, Evra (Coman 89), Marchisio, Pirlo, Pogba, Vidal (Pereyra 79), Tevez, Morata (Llorente 85). **Subs not used**: Storari, Ogbonna, Padoin, Sturaro. **Scorer**: Morata (55). **Booked**: Vidal, Pogba. **Coach**: Massimiliano Allegri
Barcelona (4-3-3): Ter Stegen, Dani Alves, Pique, Mascherano, Jordi Alba, Rakitic (Mathieu 90), Busquets, Iniesta (capt) (Xavi 78), Messi, Suarez (Pedro 90), Neymar. **Subs not used**: Bravo, Rafinha, Bartra, Correia. **Scorers**: Rakitic (4), Suarez (68), Neymar (90). **Booked**: Suarez. **Coach**: Luis Enrique
Referee: C Cakir (Turkey). **Half-time**: 0-1

Leading scorers: 10 Messi (Barcelona), Neymar (Barcelona), Ronaldo (Real Madrid); 9 Luiz Adriano (Shakhtar Donetsk); 7 Martinez (Porto), Muller (Bayern Munich), Suarez (Barcelona), Tevez (Juventus); 6 Aguero (Manchester City), Benzema (Real Madrid), Cavani (Paris SG), Lewandowski (Bayern Munich); 5 Brahimi (Porto), Huntelaar (Schalke), Morata (Juventus)

FINAL FACTS AND FIGURES

- This was Barcelona's fifth victory in the tournament, with four of them coming in the last ten years.

- They became the first club to twice achieve the treble of European Cup/ Champions League, domestic league and domestic cup, having first won all three in 2009.

- Six other clubs have recorded the treble once – Celtic (1967), Ajax (1972), PSV Eindhoven (1988), Manchester United (1999), Inter Milan (2010) and Bayern Munich (2013).

- Coach Luis Enrique achieved the feat in his first season as coach at the Nou Camp. As a player at the club, he won the 1997 European Cup-Winners' Cup under Bobby Robson and two La Liga titles.

- Massimiliano Allegri was also in his first season as the Juventus coach.

- Xavi made a winning farewell to the club when Andres Iniesta handed him the captain's armband as a 78th minute substitute. The Barcelona midfielder, who is moving to the Qatar club Al Sadd, appeared in two previous winning finals (2009 and 2011) and was an unused substitute in the 2006 success against Arsenal.

- Neymar, with his stoppage-time goal, joined team-mate Lionel Messi and Real Madrid's Cristiano Ronaldo at the top of the tournament's scoring list for the season.

- Juventus have now lost six of their eight finals. One of the victories was against Liverpool on the night of the Heysel Stadium disaster in Brussels in 1985.

EUROPEAN CUP/CHAMPIONS LEAGUE FINALS

1956	Real Madrid 4 Reims 3 (Paris)
1957	Real Madrid 2 Fiorentina 0 (Madrid)
1958†	Real Madrid 3 AC Milan 2 (Brussels)
1959	Real Madrid 2 Reims 0 (Stuttgart)
1960	Real Madrid 7 Eintracht Frankfurt 3 (Glasgow)
1961	Benfica 3 Barcelona 2 (Berne)
1962	Benfica 5 Real Madrid 3 (Amsterdam)
1963	AC Milan 2 Benfica 1 (Wembley)
1964	Inter Milan 3 Real Madrid 1 (Vienna)
1965	Inter Milan 1 Benfica 0 (Milan)
1966	Real Madrid 2 Partizan Belgrade 1 (Brussels)
1967	Celtic 2 Inter Milan 1 (Lisbon)
1968†	Manchester Utd 4 Benfica 1 (Wembley)
1969	AC Milan 4 Ajax 1 (Madrid)
1970†	Feyenoord 2 Celtic 1 (Milan)
1971	Ajax 2 Panathinaikos 0 (Wembley)
1972	Ajax 2 Inter Milan 0 (Rotterdam)
1973	Ajax 1 Juventus 0 (Belgrade)
1974	Bayern Munich 4 Atletico Madrid 0 (replay Brussels after a 1-1 draw Brussels)
1975	Bayern Munich 2 Leeds Utd 0 (Paris)
1976	Bayern Munich 1 St. Etienne 0 (Glasgow)
1977	Liverpool 3 Borussia Moenchengladbach 1 (Rome)
1978	Liverpool 1 Brugge 0 (Wembley)
1979	Nottm Forest 1 Malmo 0 (Munich)
1980	Nottm Forest 1 Hamburg 0 (Madrid)
1981	Liverpool 1 Real Madrid 0 (Paris)
1982	Aston Villa 1 Bayern Munich 0 (Rotterdam)
1983	SV Hamburg 1 Juventus 0 (Athens)
1984†	Liverpool 1 AS Roma 1 (Liverpool won 4-2 on penalties) (Rome)
1985	Juventus 1 Liverpool 0 (Brussels)
1986†	Steaua Bucharest 0 Barcelona 0 (Steaua won 2-0 on penalties) (Seville)
1987	Porto 2 Bayern Munich 1 (Vienna)
1988†	PSV Eindhoven 0 Benfica 0 (PSV won 6-5 on penalties) (Stuttgart)
1989	AC Milan 4 Steaua Bucharest 0 (Barcelona)
1990	AC Milan 1 Benfica 0 (Vienna)
1991†	Red Star Belgrade 0 Marseille 0 (Red Star won 5-3 on penalties) (Bari)
1992	Barcelona 1 Sampdoria 0 (Wembley)
1993	Marseille 1 AC Milan 0 (Munich)

1994	AC Milan 4 Barcelona 0 (Athens)
1995	Ajax 1 AC Milan 0 (Vienna)
1996†	Juventus 1 Ajax 1 (Juventus won 4-2 on penalties) (Rome)
1997	Borussia Dortmund 3 Juventus 1 (Munich)
1998	Real Madrid 1 Juventus 0 (Amsterdam)
1999	Manchester Utd 2 Bayern Munich 1 (Barcelona)
2000	Real Madrid 3 Valencia 0 (Paris)
2001	Bayern Munich 1 Valencia 1 (Bayern Munich won 5-4 on penalties) (Milan)
2002	Real Madrid 2 Bayer Leverkusen 1 (Glasgow)
2003†	AC Milan 0 Juventus 0 (AC Milan won 3-2 on penalties) (Manchester)
2004	FC Porto 3 Monaco 0 (Gelsenkirchen)
2005†	Liverpool 3 AC Milan 3 (Liverpool won 3-2 on penalties) (Istanbul)
2006	Barcelona 2 Arsenal 1 (Paris)
2007	AC Milan 2 Liverpool 1 (Athens)
2008†	Manchester Utd 1 Chelsea 1 (Manchester Utd won 6-5 on penalties) (Moscow)
2009	Barcelona 2 Manchester Utd 0 (Rome)
2010	Inter Milan 2 Bayern Munich 0 (Madrid)
2011	Barcelona 3 Manchester Utd 1 (Wembley)
2012†	Chelsea 1 Bayern Munich 1 (Chelsea won 4-3 on pens) (Munich)
2013	Bayern Munich 3 Borussia Dortmund 1 (Wembley)
2014†	Real Madrid 4 Atletico Madrid 1 (Lisbon)
2015	Barcelona 3 Juventus 1 (Berlin)

(† After extra time)
● Champions League since 1993

UEFA EUROPA LEAGUE 2014–15

FIRST QUALIFYING ROUND (selected results)

FIRST LEG

Aberdeen 5 (Logan 33, McGinn 49, Rooney 52 pen, 90, Hayes 73) Daugava 0. Att: 15,184. **Airbus** 1 (Johnson 30), Haugesund 1 (Bamberg 44). Att: 595. **Crusaders** 3 (Cockcroft 23, Owens 43, Coates 58) Ekranas 1 (Susnjar 88). Att: 998

Banga 0 **Sligo** 0. Att: 2,000. **Derry** 4 (McEleney 16, Patterson 26 pen, Timlin 48, McNamee 87) **Aberystwyth** 0. Att: 1,980. Hafnarfjardar 3 (Oskarsson 83, Gudnason 90, 90) **Glenavon** 0. Att: 643

Jeuness Esch 0 **Dundalk** 2 (Towell 60 pen, 72). Att: 759. Stjarnan 4 (Finsen 14, 54, Gunnarsson 16, Bjorgvinsson 70) **Bangor** 0. Att: 908. Torshavn 1 (Lawal 73) **Linfield** 2 (Mulgrew 39, Carvill 89). Att: 786

SECOND LEG

Aberystwyth 0 **Derry** 5 (Duffy 12, McNamee 15, Patterson 61, 85, 87 pen). Att: 1,046 (Derry won 9-0 on agg). **Bangor** 0 Stjarnan 4 (Rauschenberg 54, Bjorgvinsson 69, 82, Johansson 86). Att: 805 (Stjarnan won 8-0 on agg). Daugava 0 **Aberdeen** 3 (Rooney 22, 40, 45). Att: 600 (Aberdeen won 8-0 on agg)

Dundalk 3 (Gartland 9, Byrne 38, Mountney 45) Jeuness Esch 1 (Zydko 56). Att: 2,534 (Dundalk won 5-1 on agg). Ekranas 1 (Kochanauskas 61) **Crusaders** 2 (Heatley 57, 72). Att: 1,400 (Crusaders won 5-2 on agg). **Glenavon** 2 (Braniff 59, Bradley 61) Hafnarfjardar 3 (Oskarsson 4, Emilsson 38, 70 pen). Att: 1,634 (Hafnarfjardar won 6-2 on agg)

Haugesund 2 (Agdestein 8, Sema 57) **Airbus** 1 (Pearson 15). Att: 3,079 (Haugesund won 3-2 on agg). **Linfield** 1 (Carvill 18) Torshavn 1 (Lawal 49 pen). Att: 1,150 (Linfield won 3-2 on agg). **Sligo** 4 (Keane 45, Greene 73, North 84, Crawley 90) Banga 0. Att: 2,169 (Sligo won 4-0 on agg)

SECOND QUALIFYING ROUND (selected results)

FIRST LEG

Aberdeen 0 Groningen 0. Att: 16,523. Brommapojkarna 4 (Rexhepi 10, Albornoz 28, Larsson 63, Barkroth 66 pen) **Crusaders** 0. Att: 524. **Derry** 0 Shakhter 1 (Yanush 29). Att: 1,837. **Dundalk** 0 Hajduk Split 2 (Caktas 10, Vlasic 74). Att: 3,014

Linfield 1 (Waterworth 88) AIK 0. Att: 1,741. Lucerne 1 (Schneuwly 68) **St Johnstone** 1 (MacLean 48). Att: 8,902. **Motherwell** 2 (Law 9, 19) Stjarnan 2 (Finsen 35 pen, 90 pen). Att: 4,877. Rosenborg 1 (Diskerud 82) **Sligo** 2 (Keane 57, North 71). Att: 2,902

SECOND LEG

AIK 2 (Igboananike 57, Goitom 73) **Linfield** 0. Att: 9,570 (AIK won 2-1 on agg). **Crusaders** 1 (Coates 18) Brommapojkarna 1 (Rexhepi 28). Att: 798 (Brommapojkarna won 5-1 on agg). Groningen 1 (Kieftenbeld 44) **Aberdeen** 2 (Rooney 26 pen, McGinn 33). Att: 22,550 (Aberdeen won 2-1 on agg), Hajduk Split 1 (Kouassi 26) **Dundalk** 2 (Holborn 67, Byrne 75). Att: 15,000 (Hajduk Split won 3-2 on agg)

St Johnstone 1 (May 23 pen) Lucerne 1 (Schneuwly 59). Att: 8,486 (aet, agg 2-2, St Johnstone won 5-4 on pens). Shakhter 5 (Balanovich 10, Guruli 29, Osipenko 69, Yanush 82, Galyuza 90) **Derry** 1 (Duffy 7). Att: 2,900 (Shakhter won 6-1 on agg). **Sligo** 1 (North 14) Rosenborg 3 (Helland 17, Jensen 49, 65). Att: 3,792 (Rosenborg won 4-3 on agg). Stjarnan 3 (Finsen 37 pen, Toft 85, Johannsson 113) **Motherwell** 2 (Hammell 11, Ainsworth 66). Att: 1,021 (aet, Stjarnan won 5-4 on agg)

THIRD QUALIFYING ROUND (selected results)

FIRST LEG

Real Sociedad 2 (Zurutuza 53, Canales 68) **Aberdeen** 0. Att: 21,147. St Johnstone 1 (Mackay 90) Spartak Trnava 2 (Schranz 34, 64). Att: 7,001. Trenchin 0 **Hull** 0. Att: 8,254

SECOND LEG

Aberdeen 2 (Pawlett 44, Reynolds 57) Real Sociedad 3 (Prieto 28, 86 pen, Bergara 90). Att: 17,676 (Real Sociedad won 5-2 on agg). **Hull** 2 (Elmohamady 27, Aluko 80) Trenchin 1 (Malek 2. Att: 21,156 (Hull won 2-1 on agg). Spartak Trnava 1 (Mikovic 82) **St Johnstone** 1 (May 42). Att: 3,884 (Spartak Trnava won 3-2 on agg)

PLAY-OFFS

FIRST LEG

AEL Limassol 1 (Sardinero 14) **Tottenham** 2 (Soldado 74, Kane 80). Att: 8,350. Lokeren 1 (Vanaken 58) **Hull** 0. Att: 7,935

SECOND LEG

Hull 2 (Brady 6, 56 pen) Lokeren 1 (Remacle 49). Att: 18,149 (agg 2-2, Lokeren won on away goal). **Tottenham** 3 (Kane 45, Paulinho 49, Townsend 66 pen) AEL Limassol 0. Att: 29,976 (Tottenham won 5-1 on agg)

ON AGGREGATE

Apollon Limassol 1 Lokomotiv Moscow 2; Asteras Tripolis 3 Maccabi Tel Aviv 3 (Asteras Tripoli won on away goal); Astra Giurgiu 2 Lyon 2 (Astra Giugiu won on away goals); Borussia Monchengladbach 10 Sarajevo 2; Club Bruges 3 Grasshoppers 1

Dinamo Minsk 5 Nacional 2; Dinamo Zagreb 5 Petrolul Ploiesti 2; Dnipro 2 Hajduk Split 1; Dynamo Moscow 4 Omonia Nicosia 3; Feyenoord 5 Zorya Luhansk 4; HJK Helsinki 5 Rapid Vienna 4

Inter Milan 9 Stjarnan 0; Krasnodar 3 Real Sociedad 1; Legia Warsaw 3 Aktobe 0; Metalist

Kharkiv 1 Ruch Chorzow 0 (aet); Panathinaikos 6 Midtjylland 2; PAOK Salonika 4 Zimbru Chisinau 1
Partizan 5 Neftchi 3; PSV 3 Shakhter 0; Qarabag 1 Twente 1 (Qarabag won on away goal); Rijeka 4 Sheriff Tiraspol 0; Rio Ave 2 Elfsborg 2 (Rio Ave won on away goal); Sparta Prague 4 Zwolle 2
St Etienne 1 Karabukspor 1 (aet, St Etienne won 4-3 on pens); Torino 1 RNK Split 0; Trabzonspor 2 Rostov 0; Villarreal 7 Astana 0; Young Boys 3 Debrecen 1; Zurich 4 Spartak Trnava 2

GROUP STAGE

GROUP A

Match-day 1: Apollon Limassol 3 (Papoulis 9, Gullon 40, Koch 87 og) Zurich 2 (Reikan 50, Yapi Yapo 53). Att: 5,662. Borussia Monchengladbach 1 (Herrmann 21) Villarreal 1 (Uche 68). Att: 39,128
Match-day 2: Villarreal 4 (Gerard 8, 82, Espinosa 44, 51) Apollon Limassol 0. Att: 12,630 Zurich 1 (Etoundi 23) Borussia Monchengladbach 1 (Nordtveit 25). Att: 18,422
Match-day 3: Borussia Monchengladbach 5 (Traore 11, 67, Hrgota 56, Herrmann 83, Charalambous 90 og) Apollon Limassol 0. Att: 38,182. Villarreal 4 (Cani 6, Vietto 57, Bruno 60, Dos Santos 77) Zurich 1 (Schonbachler 43). Att: 14,092
Match-day 4: Apollon Limassol 0 Borussia Monchengladbach 2 (Raffael 56, Herrmann 90). Att: 5,258. Zurich 3 (Etoundi 21, Buff 28, Chikhaoui 29) Villarreal 2 (Pina 19, Gerard 24). Att: 2,300
Match-day 5: Villarreal 2 (Vietto 26, Cheryshev 63) Borussia Monchengladbach 2 (Raffael 55, Xhaka 67). Att: 16,000. Zurich 3 (Djimsiti 31, Chikhaoui 38 pen, 60 pen) Apollon Limassol 1 (Rosa 23). Att: 7,999
Match-day 6: Apollon Limassol 0 Villarreal 2 (Gerard 35, Vietto 40). Att: 1,615. Borussia Monchengladbach 3 (Herrmann 31, Hrgota 58, 64) Zurich 0. Att: 44,323

FINAL TABLE

	P	W	D	L	F	A	Pts
Borussia M'bach Q	6	3	3	0	14	4	12
Villarreal Q	6	3	2	1	15	7	11
Zurich	6	2	1	3	10	14	7
Apollon Limassol	6	1	0	5	4	18	3

GROUP B

Match-day 1: Club Bruges 0 Torino 0. Att: 11,894. Copenhagen 2 (Jorgensen 68, 81) HJK Helsinki 0. Att: 12,191
Match-day 2: HJK Helsinki 0 Club Bruges 3 (Heikkinen 19 og, De Sutter 70, De Bock 78). Att: 8,055. Torino 1 (Quagliarella 90 pen) Copenhagen 0. Att: 13,734
Match-day 3: Club Bruges 1 (Vazquez 90) Copenhagen 1 (Amartey 89). Att: 13,999. Torino 2 (Molinaro 35, Amauri 58) HJK Helsinki 0. Att: 14,759
Match-day 4: Copenhagen 0 Club Bruges 4 (Refaelov 7, 30, 36, Vormer 60). Att: 14,810. HJK Helsinki 2 (Baah 60, Moren 81) Torino 1 (Quagliarella 90). Att: 6,562
Match-day 5: HJK Helsinki 2 (Baah 28, Kandji 90) Copenhagen 1 (Nilsson 90). Att: 6,752. Torino 0 Club Bruges 0. Att: 10,000
Match-day 6: Club Bruges 2 (Felipe Gedoz 28 pen, Refaelov 88) HJK Helsinki 1 (Kandji 51). Att: 11,894. Copenhagen 1 (Amartey 6) Torino 5 (Martinez 15, 47, Amauri 41 pen, Darmian 49, Silva 53). Att: 9,202

	P	W	D	L	F	A	Pts
Club Bruges Q	6	3	3	0	10	2	12
Torino Q	6	3	2	1	9	3	11
HJK Helsinki	6	2	0	4	5	11	6
Copenhagen	6	1	1	4	4	5	4

GROUP C

Match-day 1: Besiktas 1 (Tore 33) Asteras Tripolis 1 (Parra 88). Att: 7,760. Partizan 0 **Tottenham** 0. Att: 22,112

 Match-day 2: Asteras Tripolis 2 (Usero 22, Parra 52) Partizan 0. Att: 3,601. **Tottenham** 1 (Kane 27) Besiktas 1 (Demba Ba 89 pen). Att: 24,300

Match-day 3: Partizan 0 Besiktas 4 (Kavlak 18, Demba Ba 44, Ozyakup 52, Tore 54). Att: 7,855. **Tottenham** 5 (Kane 13, 75, 81, Lamela 29, 66) Asteras Tripolis 1 (Barrales 89). Att: 21,428

Match-day 4: Asteras Tripolis 1 (Barrales 90 pen) **Tottenham** 2 (Townsend 37 pen, Kane 42). Att: 5,130. Besiktas 2 (Demba Ba 57 pen, 62) Partizan 1 (Markovic 78). Att: 11,938

Match-day 5: Asteras Tripolis 2 (Barrales 72, Parra 83) Besiktas 2 (Demba Ba 15, Tore 61 pen). Att: 2,858. **Tottenham** 1 (Stambouli 49) Partizan 0. Att: 28,362

Match-day 6: Besiktas 1 (Tosun 59) **Tottenham** 0. Att: 19,511. Partizan 0 Asteras Tripolis 0. Att: 6,750

FINAL TABLE

	P	W	D	L	F	A	Pts
Besiktas Q	6	3	3	0	11	5	12
Tottenham Q	6	3	2	1	9	4	11
Asteras Tripolis	6	1	3	2	7	10	6
Partizan	6	0	2	4	1	9	2

GROUP D

Match-day 1: Dinamo Zagreb 5 (Soudani 16, 23, 45, Henriquez 70, Coric 90) Astra Giurgiu 1 (Chitu 82). Att: 10,383. Salzburg 2 (Alan 36, Soriano 78) **Celtic** 2 (Mubarak 14, Brown 60). Att: 17,886

Match-day 2: Astra Giurgiu 1 (Seto 15) Salzburg 2 (Kampl 36, Soriano 42). Att: 3,298. **Celtic** 1 (Commons 6) Dinamo Zagreb 0. Att: 28,132

Match-day 3: **Celtic** 2 (Scepovic 73, Johansen 79) Astra Giurgiu 1 (Enache 81). Att: 28,281. Salzburg 4 (Alan 13, 45, 52, Ramalho 49) Dinamo Zagreb 2 (Ademi 81, Henriquez 89). Att: 12,872

Match-day 4: Astra Giurgiu 1 (Amorim 79) **Celtic** 1 (Johansen 32). Att: 3,400. Dinamo Zagreb 1 (Henriquez 60) Salzburg 5 (Soriano 40, 64, 85, Kampl 59, Bruno 72). Att: 10,769

Match-day 5: Astra Giurgui 1 (Bukari 50) Dinamo Zagreb 0. Att: 2,520. **Celtic** 1 (Johansen 30) Salzburg 3 (Alan 8, 14, Keita 90). Att: 32,414

Match-day 6: Dinamo Zagreb 4 (Pjaca 14, 39, 50, Brozovic 48) **Celtic** 3 (Commons 23, Scepovic 30, Pivaric 82 og). Att: 4,054. Salzburg 5 (Sabitzer 9, Kampl 34, 90, Alan 45, 70) Astra Giurgiu 1 (Florescu 51). Att: 8,258

FINAL TABLE

	P	W	D	L	F	A	Pts
Salzburg Q	6	5	1	0	21	8	16
Celtic Q	6	2	2	2	10	11	8
Dinamo Zagreb	6	2	0	4	12	15	6
Astra Giurgiu	6	1	1	4	6	15	4

GROUP E

Match-day 1: PSV 1 (De Jong 26 pen) Estoril 0. Att: 14,200. Panathinaikos 1 (Dinas 64) Dynamo Moscow 2 (Kokorin 40, Ionov 50). Att: 13,073
Match-day 2: Dynamo Moscow 1 (Zhirkov 90) PSV 0. Att: 7,872. Estoril 2 (Kleber 52, Amado 66) Panathinaikos 0. Att: 1,985
Match-day 3: Estoril 1 (Tavares 90) Dynamo Moscow 2 (Kokorin 52, Zhirkov 81). Att: 2,164. PSV 1 (Depay 43) Panathinaikos 1 (Karelis 87). Att: 21,800
Match-day 4: Dynamo Moscow 1 (Kuranyi 78) Estoril 0. Att: 5,374. Panathinaikos 2 (Ajagun 12, Petric 43) PSV 3 (Depay 27, De Jong 65, Wijnaldum 78). Att: 14,240
Match-day 5: Dynamo Moscow 2 (Triantafyllopoulos 55 og, Ionov 61) Panathinaikos 1 (Berg 14). Att: 4,207. Estoril 0 PSV (abandoned at half-time – waterlogged pitch). Replay: Estoril 3 (De Carvalho 12, Miranda 30, Amado 39) PSV 3 (Depay 6, Narsingh 14, Wijnaldum 82). Att: 3,700
Match-day 6: PSV 0 Dynamo Moscow 1 (Ionov 90). Att: 25,000. Panathinaikos 1 (Karelis 55) Estoril 1 (Kleber 87). Att: 8,200

FINAL TABLE

	P	W	D	L	F	A	Pts
Dynamo Moscow Q	6	6	0	0	9	3	18
PSV Q	6	2	2	2	8	8	8
Estoril	6	1	2	3	7	8	5
Panathinaikos	6	0	2	4	6	11	2

GROUP F

Match-day 1: Dnipro 0 Inter Milan 1 (D'Ambrosio 71). Att: 11,000. Qarabag 0 St Etienne 0. Att: 28,786
Match-day 2: Inter Milan 2 (D'Ambrosio 18, Icardi 85) Qarabag 0. Att: 28,435. St Etienne 0 Dnipro 0. Att: 28,207
Match-day 3: Dnipro 0 Qarabag 1 (Muarem 21). Att: 3,120. Inter Milan 0 St Etienne 0. Att: 33,379
Match-day 4: Qarabag 1 (George 36) Dnipro 2 (Kalinic 15, 73). Att: 31,000. St Etienne 1 (Bayal Sall 50) Inter Milan 1 (Dodo 33). Att: 36,411
Match-day 5: Inter Milan 2 (Kuzmanovic 30, Osvaldo 50). Dnipro 1 (Rotan 16). Att: 14,415. St Etienne 1 (Van Wolfswinkel 21) Qarabag 1 (Nadirov 15). Att: 29,769
Match-day 6: Dnipro 1 (Fedetskiy 66) St Etienne 0. Att: 2,579. Qarabag 0 Inter Milan 0. Att: 31,200

FINAL TABLE

	P	W	D	L	F	A	Pts
Inter Milan Q	6	3	3	0	6	2	12
Dnipro Q	6	2	1	3	4	5	7
Qarabag	6	1	3	2	3	5	6
St Etienne	6	0	5	1	2	3	5

GROUP G

Match-day 1: Sevilla 2 (Krychowiak 8, Mbia 31) Feyenoord 0. Att: 27,624. Standard Liege 2 (Ciman 74, Araujo 87) Rijeka 0. Att: 8,884
Match-day 2: Feyenoord 2 (Van Beek 47, Manu 83) Standard Liege 1 (Viera 63). Att: 33,000. Rijeka 2 (Kramaric 52 pen, Kvrzic 66) Sevilla 2 (Aspas 26, Mbia 90). Att: 9,256
Match-day 3: Rijeka 3 (Kramaric 63, 70, 76 pen) Feyenoord 1 (Toornstra 66). Att: 9,326. Standard Liege 0 Sevilla 0. Att: 10,365
Match-day 4: Feyenoord 2 (El Ahmadi 8, Immers 20) Rijeka 0. Att: 30,800. Sevilla 3 (Gameiro 19, Reyes 42, Bacca 90) Standard Liege 1 (M'Poku 32). Att: 26,850
Match-day 5: Feyenoord 2 (Toornstra 55, El Ahmadi 83) Sevilla 0. Att: 19,500. Rijeka 2

(Moises 25, Kramaric 34 pen) Standard Liege 0. Att: 8,950
Match-day 6: Sevilla 1 (Suarez 20) Rijeka 0. Att: 24,967. Standard Liege 0 Feyenoord 3
(Toornstra 16, Boetius 60, Manu 89). Att: 11,913

FINAL TABLE

	P	W	D	L	F	A	Pts
Feyenoord Q	6	4	0	2	10	6	12
Sevilla Q	6	3	2	1	8	5	11
Rijeka	6	2	1	3	7	8	7
Standard Liege	6	1	1	4	4	10	4

GROUP H

Match-day 1: **Everton** 4 (Rodriguez 15 og, Coleman 45, Baines 48 pen, Mirallas 89) Wolfsburg
1 (Rodriguez 90). Att: 29,593. Lille 1 (Kjaer 63) Krasnodar (Laborde 35). Att: 25,465
Match-day 2: Krasnodar 1 (Ari 43) **Everton** 1 (Eto'o 82). Att: 31,050. Wolfsburg 1 (De Bruyne
82) Lille 1 (Origi 77 pen). Att: 16,097
Match-day 3: Krasnador 2 (Granqvist 51 pen, Wanderson 86) Wolfsburg 4 (Granqvist 38 og, De
Bruyne 45, 79, Gustavo 64). Att: 22,500. Lille 0 **Everton** 0. Att: 41,057
Match-day 4: **Everton** 3 (Osman 27, Jagielka 42, Naismith 61)) Lille 0. Att: 28,844. Wolfsburg
5 (Hunt 47, 57, Guilavogui 73, Bendtner 89 pen, 90) Krasnodar 1 (Wanderson 72). Att:
16,674
Match-day 5: Krasnodar 1 (Ari 35) Lille 1 (Roux 79). Att: 13,450. Wolfsburg 0 **Everton** 2
(Lukaku 43, Mirallas 75). Att: 23,625
Match-day 6: **Everton** 0 Krasnador 1 (Laborde 30). Att: 20,260. Lille 0 Wolfsburg 3 (Vieirinha
45, Rodriguez 65, 89 pen). Att: 33,559

FINAL TABLE

	P	W	D	L	F	A	Pts
Everton Q	6	3	2	1	10	3	11
Wolfsburg Q	6	3	1	2	14	10	10
Krasnodar	6	1	3	2	7	12	6
Lille	6	0	4	2	3	9	4

GROUP I

Match-day 1: Napoli 3 (Higuain 23 pen, Mertens 51, 81) Sparta Prague 1 (Husbauer 14).
Att: 14,933. Young Boys 5 (Lecjaks 5, Steffen 29, Nuzzolo 63, Nikci 80, Hoarau 90) Slovan
Bratislava 0. Att: 10,010
Match-day 2: Slovan Bratislava 0 Napoli 2 (Hamsik 35, Higuain 74). Att: 10,738. Sparta
Prague 3 (Vacha 26, Lafata 28, 85) Young Boys 1 (Hoarau 52). Att: 10,205
Match-day 3: Young Boys 2 (Hoarau 52, Bertone 96) Napoli 0. Att: 24,024. Slovan Bratislava
0 Sparta Prague 3 (Lafata 56, Konate 61, Krejci 81). Att: 6,891
Match-day 4: Napoli 3 (De Guzman 45, 65, 83) Young Boys 0. Att: 12,283. Sparta Prague 4
(Lafata 29, 84, Krejci 32, Nhamoinesu 75) Slovan Bratislava 0. Att: 13,805
Match-day 5: Slovan Bratislava 1 (Soumah 12) Young Boys 3 (Hoarau 9 pen, Kubo 18, 63).
Att: 3,495. Sparta Prague 0 Napoli 0. Att: 16,111
Match-day 6: Young Boys 2 (Hoarau 76 pen, Steffen 90) Sparta Prague 0. Att: 15,150. Napoli
3 (Mertens 6, Hamsik 16, Zapata 75) Slovan Bratislava 0. Att: 6,490

FINAL TABLE

	P	W	D	L	F	A	Pts
Napoli Q	6	4	1	1	11	3	13
Young Boys Q	6	4	0	2	13	7	12
Sparta Prague	6	3	1	2	11	6	10
Slovan Bratislava	6	0	0	6	1	20	0

GROUP J

Match-day 1: Rio Ave 0 Dynamo Kiev 3 (Yarmolenko 20, Belhanda 25, Kravets 71). Att: 2,310. Steaua Bucharest 6 (Sanmartean 51, Rusescu 60 pen, 73, Keseru 61, 65, 72) Aalborg 0. Played behind closed doors – fans' previous racist behaviour
Match-day 2: Aalborg 1 (Helenius 47) Rio Ave 0. Att: 4,741. Dynamo Kiev 3 (Yarmolenko 40, Kravets 66, Teodorczyk 90) Steaua Bucharest 1 (Rusescu 89). Att: 28,280
Match-day 3: Aalborg 3 (Enevoldsen 11, Thomsen 39, 90) Dynamo Kiev 0. Att: 6,043. Steaua Bucharest 2 (Rusescu 17, 45) Rio Ave 1 (Del Valle 48). Att: 15,753
Match-day 4: Dynamo Kiev 2 (Vida 70, Gusev 90) Aalborg 0. Att: 25,230. Rio Ave 2 (Diego Lopes 35, 77 pen) Steaua Bucharest 2 (Keseru 60, Filip 90). Att: 3,232
Match-day 5: Aalborg 1 (Enevoldsen 72) Steaua Bucharest 0. Att: 7,515. Dynamo Kiev 2 (Lens 53, Veloso 78) Rio Ave 0. Att: 14,054
Match-day 6: Steaua Bucharest 0 Dynamo Kiev 2 (Yarmolenko 71, Lens 90). Att: 7,620. Rio Ave 2 (Del Valle 59, 79) Aalborg 0. Att: 2,672

FINAL TABLE

	P	W	D	L	F	A	Pts
Dynamo Kiev Q	6	5	0	1	12	4	15
Aalborg Q	6	3	0	3	5	10	9
Steaua Bucharest	6	2	1	3	11	9	7
Rio Ave	6	1	1	4	5	10	4

GROUP K

Match-day 1: Fiorentina 3 (Manuel Vargas 34, Cuadrado 67, Bernarderschi 88) Guingamp 0. Att: 15,712. PAOK Salonika 6 (Nikolic 4 og, Athanasiadis 11, 16, 27, Papadopoulos 50, Tzandaris 90) Dinamo Minsk 1 (Nikolic 80). Att: 13,416
Match-day 2: Dinamo Minsk 0 Fiorentina 3 (Aquilani 33, Ilicic 61, Bernarderschi 67). Att: 5,097. Guingamp 2 (Marveaux 47, 50) PAOK Salonika 0. Att: 8,783
Match-day 3: Dinamo Minsk 0 Guingamp 0. Att: 4,511. PAOK Salonika 0 Fiorentina 1 (Manuel Vargas 38). Att: 22,612
Match-day 4: Fiorentina 1 (Pasqual 88) PAOK Salonika 1 (Martens 81). Att: 15,316. Guingamp 2 (Beauvue 44, Mandanne 86) Dinamo Minsk 0. Att: 8,372
Match-day 5: Dinamo Minsk 0 PAOK Salonika 2 (Athanasiadis 82, 88). Att: 1,502. Guingamp 1 (Beauvue 45 pen) Fiorentina 2 (Marin 6, Babacar 13). Att: 5,519
Match-day 6: Fiorentina 1 (Marin 87) Dinamo Minsk 2 (Kantsavy 39, Nikolic 55). Att: 7,562. PAOK Salonika 1 (Athanasiadis 22 pen) Guingamp 2 (Beauvue 8, 83). Att: 12,101

FINAL TABLE

	P	W	D	L	F	A	Pts
Fiorentina Q	6	4	1	1	11	4	13
Guingamp Q	6	3	1	2	7	6	10
PAOK Salonika	6	2	1	3	10	7	7
Dinamo Minsk	6	1	1	4	3	14	4

GROUP L

Match-day 1: Legia Warsaw 1 (Radovic 58) Lokeren 0. Att: 21,475. Metalist Kharkiv 1 (Gomeniuk 61) Trabzonspor 2 (Constant 26, Papadopoulos 90). Att: 6,834
Match-day 2: Lokeren 1 (De Pauw 74) Metalist Kharkiv 0. Att: 4,638. Trabzonspor 0 Legia Warsaw 1 (Kucharczyk 17). Att: 9,051
Match-day 3: Metalist Kharkiv 0 Legia Warsaw 1 (Duda 28). Att: 2,374. Trabzonspor 2 (Yatabare 55, Constant 87) Lokeren 0. Att: 7,600
Match-day 4: Legia Warsaw 2 (Saganowski 29, Duda 84) Metalist Kharkiv 1 (Kobin 22). Att: 25,809. Lokeren 1 (Patosi 4) Trabzonspor 1 (Majeed Waris 45). Att: 6,879
Match-day 5: Lokeren 1 (Vanaken 7) Legia Warsaw 0. Att: 6,592. Trabzonspor 3 (Belkalem 37,

Ekici 86, Yilmaz 90) Metalist Kharkiv 1 (Gomeniuk 68). Attr: 10,767
Match-day 6: Legia Warsaw 2 (Ozturk 22 og, Sa 55) Trabzonspopr 0. Played behind closed doors – fans' previous racist behaviour. Metalist Kharkiv 0 Lokeren 1 (Leye 16). Att: 1,386

FINAL TABLE

	P	W	D	L	F	A	Pts
Legia Warsaw Q	6	5	0	1	7	2	15
Trabzonspor Q	6	3	1	2	8	6	10
Lokeren	6	3	1	2	4	4	10
Metalist Kharkiv	6	0	0	6	3	10	0

ROUND OF 32

FIRST LEG

Aalborg 1 (Helenius 71 pen) Club Bruges 3 (Oulare 25, Refaelov 29, Petersen 61 og). Att: 8,115. Ajax 1 (Milik 34) Legia Warsaw 0. Att: 46,761. Anderlecht 0 Dynamo Moscow 0. Att: 17,317. **Celtic** 3 (Armstrong 24, Campagnaro 25 og, Guidetti 90) Inter Milan 3 (Shaqiri 4, Palacio 13, 45). Att: 58,500
Dnipro 2 (Kankava 50, Rotan 55) Olympiacos 0. Att: 5,837. Guingamp 2 (Beauvue 72, Diallo 75) Dynamo Kiev 1 (Veloso). Att: 16,191. **Liverpool** 0 Besiktas 0 (Balotelli 85 pen) Besiktas 0. Att: 43,353. PSV 0 Zenit St Petersburg 1 (Hulk 64). Att: 21,000
Roma 1 (Gervinho 22) Feyenoord 1 (Kazim-Richards 55). Att: 29,292. Sevilla 1 (Iborra 70) Borussia Monchengladbach 0. Att: 26,850. Torino 2 (Lopez 18, 43) Athletic Bilbao 2 (Williams 9, Gurpegui 73). Att: 25,725. **Tottenham** 1 (Soldado 6) Fiorentina 1 (Basanta 36). Att: 34,235.
Trabzonspor 0 Napoli 4 (Henrique 6, Higuain 20, Gabbiadini 27, Zapata 90). Att: 23,760
Villarreal 2 (Uche 32, Cheryshev 90) Salzburg 1 (Soriano 49 pen). Att: 16,000. Wolfsburg 2 (Dost 45, 64) Sporting 0. Att: 19,207. Young Boys 1 (Hoarau 10) **Everton** 4 (Lukaku 24, 39, 58, Coleman 28). Att: 20,835

SECOND LEG

Athletic Bilbao 2 (Iraola 44, De Marcos 61) Torino 3 (Quagliarella 16 pen, Lopez 45, Darmian 67). Att: 44,180 (Torino won 5-4 on agg). Besiktas 1 (Arslan 72) Liverpool 0. Att: 63,324 (aet, agg 1-1, Besiktas won 5-4 on pens). Borussia Monchengladbach 2 (Xhaka 19, Hazard 29) Sevilla 3 (Bacca 8, Vitolo 26, 79). Att: 45,337 (Sevilla won 4-2 on agg)
Club Bruges 3 (Vazquez 11, Oulare 64, Mbombo 74) Aalborg 0. Att: 11,804 (Club Bruges won 6-1 on agg). Dynamo Kiev 3 (Teodorczyk 31, Buyalsky 45, Gyusev 75 pen) Guingamp 1 (Mandanne 66). Att: 54,308 (Dynamo Kiev won 4-3 on agg). Dynamo Moscow 3 (Kozlov 47, Yusupov 63, Kuranyi 90) Anderlecht 1 (Mitrovic 28). Att: 12,316 (Dynamo Moscow won 3-1 on agg)
Everton 3 (Lukaku 25 pen, 30, Mirallas 42) Young Boys 1 (Sanogo 13). Att: 25,058 (Everton won 7-2 on agg). Feyenoord 1 (Manu 57) Roma 2 (Ljajic 45, Gervinho 60). Att: 45,000 (Roma won 3-2 on agg). Fiorentina 2 (Gomez 54, Salah 71) **Tottenham** 0. Att: 29,886 (Fiorentina won 3-1 on agg)
Inter Milan 1 (Guarin 88) **Celtic** 0. Att: 37,133 (Inter Milan won 4-3 on agg). Legia Warsaw 0 Ajax 3 (Milik 11, 43, Viergever 13). Played behind closed doors – fans' previous racist behaviour (Ajax won 4-0 on agg). Napoli 1 (De Guzman 19) Trabzonspor 0. Att: 14,410 (Napoli won 5-0 on agg)
Olympiacos 2 (Mitroglou 14, Dominguez 90 pen) Dnipro 2 (Fedetskiy 23, Kalinic 90). Att: 24,854 (Dnipro won 4-2 on agg). Salzburg 1 (Djuricin 18) Villarreal 3 (Vietto 33, 76, Dos Santos 79). Att: 26,020 (Villarreal won 5-2 on agg). Sporting 0 Wolfsburg 0. Att: 23,097 (Wolfsburg won 2-0 on agg). Zenit St Petersburg 3 (Rondon 28, 67, Hulk 48) PSV 0. Att: 17,194 (Zenit St Petersburg won 4-0 on agg)

ROUND OF 16

FIRST LEG

Club Bruges 2 (De Sutter 62, Refaelov 79 pen) Besiktas 1 (Tore 45). Att: 12,977. Dnipro 1 (Zozulya 30) Ajax 0. Att: 10,581. **Everton** 2 (Naismith 39, Lukaku 82 pen) Dynamo Kiev 1 (Gusev 14). Att: 26,150
Fiorentina 1 (Ilicic 17) Roma 1 (Keita 77). Att: 23,557. Napoli 3 (Higuain 25, 31 pen, 55) Dynamo Moscow 1 (Kuranyi 2). Att: 17,727. Villarreal 1 (Vietto 48) Sevilla 3 (Vitolo 1, Mbia 26, Gameiro 50). Att: 19,930.
Wolfsburg 3 (Naldo 28, De Bruyne 63, 75) Inter Milan 1 (Palacio 5). Att: 25,374. Zenit St Petersburg 2 (Witsel 38, Criscito 53 pen) Torino 0. Att: 17,271

SECOND LEG

Ajax 2 (Bazoer 60, Van der Hoorn 117) Dnipro 1 (Konoplyanka 97). Att: 51,756 (aet, agg 2-2, Dnipro won on away goal). Besiktas 1 (Ramon 48) Club Bruges 3 (De Sutter 61, Mbombo 90, 90). Att: 65,110 (Club Bruges won 5-2 on agg). Dynamo Kiev 5 (Yarmolenko 21 Teodorczyk 35, Veloso 37, Gusev 56, Antunes 76) **Everton** 2 (Lukaku 29, Jagielka 82). Att: 67,553 (Dynamo Kiev won 6-4 on agg
Dynamo Moscow 0 Napoli 0. Att: 17,356 (Napoli won 3-1 on agg). Inter Milan 1 (Palacio 71) Wolfsburg 2 (Caligiuri 24, Bendtner 89). Att: 38,800 (Wolfsburg won 5-2 on agg). Roma 0 Fiorentina 3 (Gonzalo 9 pen, Alonso 18, Basanta 21). Att: 30,591 (Fiorentina won 4-1 on agg) Sevilla 2 (Iborra 69, Suarez 83) Villarreal 1 (Dos Santos 73). Att: 28,784 (Sevilla won 5-2 on agg). Torino 1 (Glik 90) Zenit St Petersburg 0. Att: 24,736 (Zenit St Petersburg won 2-1 on agg)

QUARTER-FINALS, FIRST LEG

Club Bruges 0 Dnipro 0. Att: 29,000. Dynamo Kiev 1 (Lens 36) Fiorentina 1 (Babacar 90). Att: 65,535. Sevilla 2 (Bacca 73, Suarez 88) Zenit St Petersburg 1 (Ryazantsev 29). Att: 28,450. Wolfsburg 1 (Bendtner 80) Napoli 4 (Higuain 15, Hamsik 23, 64, Gabbiadini 77). Att: 25,112

QUARTER-FINALS, SECOND LEG

Dnipro 1 Club Bruges 0 (Shakhov 82). Att: 16,234 (Dnipro won 1-0 on agg). Fiorentina 2 (Gomez 43, Vargas 90) Dynamo Kiev 0. Att: 28,058 (Fiorentina won 3-1 on agg). Napoli 2 (Callejon 49, Mertens 65) Wolfsburg 2 (Klose 71, Perisic 73). Att: 27,262 (Napoli won 6-3 on agg). Zenit St Petersburg 2 (Rondon 48, Hulk 72) Sevilla 2 (Bacca 6 pen, Gameiro 85). Att: 21,050 (Sevilla won 4-3 on agg)

SEMI-FINALS, FIRST LEG

Napoli 1 (Lopez 50) Dnipro 1 (Seleznyov 81). Att: 41,095. Sevilla 3 (Vidal 17, 52, Gameiro 75) Fiorentina 0. Att: 35,840

SEMI-FINALS, SECOND LEG

Dnipro 1 (Seleznyov 58) Napoli 0. Att: 62,344 (Dnipro won 2-1 on agg). Fiorentina 0 Sevilla 2 (Bacca 22, Carrico 27). Att: 32,466 (Sevilla won 5-0 on agg)

FINAL

DNIPRO 2 SEVILLA 3
Narodowy Stadium, Warsaw (45,000); Wednesday, May 27 2015

Dnipro (4-2-3-1): Boyko, Fedetskiy, Douglas, Cheberyachko, Matos, Kankava (Shakhov 85), Fedorchuk (Bezus 68), Matheus, Rotan (capt), Konoplyanka, Kalinic (Seleznyov 78). **Subs not used**: Lastukva, Vlad, Bruno Gama, Luchkevych. **Scorers**: Kalinic (7), Rotan (44). **Booked**: Kankava, Kalinic, Bezus, Rotan, Matos. **Coach**: Myron Markevych
Sevilla (4-2-3-1): Sergio Rico, Vidal, Carrico, Kolodziejczak, Tremoulinas, Mbia, Krychowiak,

Reyes (capt) (Coke 59), Banega (Iborra 89), Vitolo, Bacca (Gameiro 82). **Subs not used**: Beto, Fernando Navarro, Figueiras, Suarez. **Scorers**: Krychowiak (28), Bacca (31, 73). **Booked**: Krychowiak, Carrico, Bacca. **Coach**: Unai Emery
Referee: M Atkinson (England). **Half-time**: 2-2

Leading scorers: 8 Alan (Salzburg), Lukaku (Everton); 7 Bacca (Sevilla), Higuain (Napoli); 6 Athanasiadis (PAOK Salonika), Hoarau (Young Boys), Refaelov (Club Bruges), Soriano (Salzburg), Vietto (Villarreal)

CLUB WORLD CUP – MOROCCO 2014

QUALIFYING MATCHES

Crul Azul (Mex) 3 (Torrado 90 pen, 119 pen, Pavone 109) Western Sydney (Aus) 1 (La Rocca 66) – aet, Rabat; ES Setif (Alg) 0 Auckland City (NZ) 1 (Irving 53) – Rabat

SEMI-FINALS

Cruz Azul 0 Real Madrid 4 (Sergio Ramos 16, Benzema 37, Bale 51, Isco 75) – Marrakech (Att: 34,862); San Lorenzo (Arg) 2 (Barrientos 45, Matos 93) Auckland City (Berlanga 67) – aet, Marrakech (Att: 18,458)

FINAL

REAL MADRID 2 SAN LORENZO 0
Marrakech (38,345); Saturday, December 20, 2014

Real Madrid (4-3-3): Casillas (capt), Carvajal (Arbeloa 73), Pepe, Sergio Ramos (Varane 89), Marcelo (Fabio Coentrao 44), Isco, Kroos, Rodriguez, Bale, Benzema, Ronaldo. **Subs not used**: Navas, Pacheco, Khedira, Hernandez, Nacho, Illarramendi, Madran. **Scorers**: Sergio Ramos (37), Bale (51). **Booked**: Sergio Ramos, Carvajal. **Coach**: Carlo Ancelotti
San Lorenzo (4-2-3-1): Torrico, Buffarini, Kannemann, Yepes (Cetto 61), Mas, Ortigoza, Mercier (capt), Veron (Romagnoli 67), Kalinski, Barrientos, Cauteruccio (Matos 68). **Subs not used**: Franco, Arias, Villalba, Blandi, Cavallaro, Catalan, Fontanini, Quignon, Devecchi. **Booked**: Ortigoza, Barrientos, Buffarini, Kannemann. **Coach**: Edgardo Bauza
Referee: W Lopez (Guatemala). **Half-time**: 1-0

EUROPEAN SUPER CUP

REAL MADRID 2 SEVILLA 0
Cardiff City Stadium (30,844); Tuesday, August 12 2014

Real Madrid (4-3-3): Casillas (capt), Carvajal, Carvajal, Pepe, Sergio Ramos, Fabio Coentrao (Marcelo 84), Kroos, Rodriguez (Isco 72), Modric (Illarramendi 86), Bale, Benzema, Ronaldo. **Subs not used**: Navas, Varane, Arbeloa, Di Maria. **Scorer**: Ronaldo (30, 49). **Booked**: Carvajal, Kroos. **Coach**: Carlo Ancelotti
Sevilla (4-2-3-1): Beto, Coke (Figueiras 84), Pareja, Fazio (capt), Fernando Navarro, Krychowiak, Carrico, Parreu (Aspas 66), Suarez (Reyes 78), Vitolo, Bacca. **Subs not used**: Barbosa, Samperio, Iborra, Luismi. **Booked**: Vitolo, Navarro. **Coach**: Unai Emery
Referee: M Clattenburg (England). **Half-time**: 1-0

UEFA CUP FINALS

1972	Tottenham beat Wolves 3-2 on agg (2-1a, 1-1h)
1973	Liverpool beat Borussia Moenchengladbach 3-2 on agg (3-0h, 0-2a)
1974	Feyenoord beat Tottenham 4-2 on agg (2-2a, 2-0h)
1975	Borussia Moenchengladbach beat Twente Enschede 5-1 on agg (0-0h, 5-1a)
1976	Liverpool beat Brugge 4-3 on agg (3-2h, 1-1a)

1977	Juventus beat Atletico Bilbao on away goals after 2-2 agg (1-0h, 1-2a)
1978	PSV Eindhoven beat Bastia 3-0 on agg (0-0a, 3-0h)
1979	Borussia Moenchengladbach beat Red Star Belgrade 2-1 on agg (1-1a, 1-0h)
1980	Eintracht Frankfurt beat Borussia Moenchengladbach on away goals after 3-3 agg (2-3a, 1-0h)
1981	Ipswich Town beat AZ 67 Alkmaar 5-4 on agg (3-0h, 2-4a)
1982	IFK Gothenburg beat SV Hamburg 4-0 on agg (1-0h, 3-0a)
1983	Anderlecht beat Benfica 2-1 on agg (1-0h, 1-1a)
1984	Tottenham beat Anderlecht 4-3 on penalties after 2-2 agg (1-1a, 1-1h)
1985	Real Madrid beat Videoton 3-1 on agg (3-0a, 0-1h)
1986	Real Madrid beat Cologne 5-3 on agg (5-1h, 0-2a)
1987	IFK Gothenburg beat Dundee Utd 2-1 on agg (1-0h, 1-1a)
1988	Bayer Leverkusen beat Espanol 3-2 on penalties after 3-3 agg (0-3a, 3-0h)
1989	Napoli beat VfB Stuttgart 5-4 on agg (2-1h, 3-3a)
1990	Juventus beat Fiorentina 3-1 on agg (3-1h, 0-0a)
1991	Inter Milan beat AS Roma 2-1 on agg (2-0h, 0-1a)
1992	Ajax beat Torino on away goals after 2-2 agg (2-2a, 0-0h)
1993	Juventus beat Borussia Dortmund 6-1 on agg (3-1a, 3-0h)
1994	Inter Milan beat Salzburg 2-0 on agg (1-0a, 1-0h)
1995	Parma beat Juventus 2-1 on agg (1-0h, 1-1a)
1996	Bayern Munich beat Bordeaux 5-1 on agg (2-0h, 3-1a)
1997	FC Schalke beat Inter Milan 4-1 on penalties after 1-1 agg (1-0h, 0-1a)
1998	Inter Milan beat Lazio 3-0 (one match) – Paris
1999	Parma beat Marseille 3-0 (one match) – Moscow
2000	Galatasaray beat Arsenal 4-1 on penalties after 0-0 (one match) – Copenhagen
2001	Liverpool beat Alaves 5-4 on golden goal (one match) – Dortmund
2002	Feyenoord beat Borussia Dortmund 3-2 (one match) – Rotterdam
2003	FC Porto beat Celtic 3-2 on silver goal (one match) – Seville
2004	Valencia beat Marseille 2-0 (one match) – Gothenburg
2005	CSKA Moscow beat Sporting Lisbon 3-1 (one match) – Lisbon
2006	Sevilla beat Middlesbrough 4-0 (one match) – Eindhoven
2007	Sevilla beat Espanyol 3-1 on penalties after 2-2 (one match) – Hampden Park
2008	Zenit St Petersburg beat Rangers 2-0 (one match) – City of Manchester Stadium
2009†	Shakhtar Donetsk beat Werder Bremen 2-1 (one match) – Istanbul

EUROPA LEAGUE FINALS

2010†	Atletico Madrid beat Fulham 2-1 (one match) – Hamburg
2011	Porto beat Braga 1-0 (one match) – Dublin
2012	Atletico Madrid beat Athletic Bilbao 3-0 (one match) – Bucharest
2013	Chelsea beat Benfica 2-1 (one match) – Amsterdam
2014	Sevilla beat Benfica 4-2 on penalties after 0-0 (one match) – Turin
2015	Sevilla beat Dnipro 3-2 (one match) - Warsaw

(† After extra-time)

FAIRS CUP FINALS

(As UEFA Cup previously known)

1958	Barcelona beat London 8-2 on agg (2-2a, 6-0h)
1960	Barcelona beat Birmingham 4-1 on agg (0-0a, 4-1h)
1961	AS Roma beat Birmingham City 4-2 on agg (2-2a, 2-0h)
1962	Valencia beat Barcelona 7-3 on agg (6-2h, 1-1a)
1963	Valencia beat Dynamo Zagreb 4-1 on agg (2-1a, 2-0h)
1964	Real Zaragoza beat Valencia 2-1 (Barcelona)

1965	Ferencvaros beat Juventus 1-0 (Turin)
1966	Barcelona beat Real Zaragoza 4-3 on agg (0-1h, 4-2a)
1967	Dinamo Zagreb beat Leeds Utd 2-0 on agg (2-0h, 0-0a)
1968	Leeds Utd beat Ferencvaros 1-0 on agg (1-0h, 0-0a)
1969	Newcastle Utd beat Ujpest Dozsa 6-2 on agg (3-0h, 3-2a)
1970	Arsenal beat Anderlecht 4-3 on agg (1-3a, 3-0h)
1971	Leeds Utd beat Juventus on away goals after 3-3 agg (2-2a, 1-1h)

CUP-WINNERS' CUP FINALS

1961	Fiorentina beat Rangers 4-1 on agg (2-0 Glasgow first leg, 2-1 Florence second leg)
1962	Atletico Madrid beat Fiorentina 3-0 (replay Stuttgart, after a 1-1 draw, Glasgow)
1963	Tottenham beat Atletico Madrid 5-1 (Rotterdam)
1964	Sporting Lisbon beat MTK Budapest 1-0 (replay Antwerp, after a 3-3 draw, Brussels)
1965	West Ham Utd beat Munich 1860 2-0 (Wembley)
1966†	Borussia Dortmund beat Liverpool 2-1 (Glasgow)
1967†	Bayern Munich beat Rangers 1-0 (Nuremberg)
1968	AC Milan beat SV Hamburg 2-0 (Rotterdam)
1969	Slovan Bratislava beat Barcelona 3-2 (Basle)
1970	Manchester City beat Gornik Zabrze 2-1 (Vienna)
1971†	Chelsea beat Real Madrid 2-1 (replay Athens, after a 1-1 draw, Athens)
1972	Rangers beat Moscow Dynamo 3-2 (Barcelona)
1973	AC Milan beat Leeds Utd 1-0 (Salonika)
1974	Magdeburg beat AC Milan 2-0 (Rotterdam)
1975	Dynamo Kiev beat Ferencvaros 3-0 (Basle)
1976	Anderlecht beat West Ham Utd 4-2 (Brussels)
1977	SV Hamburg beat Anderlecht 2-0 (Amsterdam)
1978	Anderlecht beat Austria WAC 4-0 (Paris)
1979†	Barcelona beat Fortuna Dusseldorf 4-3 (Basle)
1980†	Valencia beat Arsenal 5-4 on penalties after a 0-0 draw (Brussels)
1981	Dinamo Tbilisi beat Carl Zeiss Jena 2-1 (Dusseldorf)
1982	Barcelona beat Standard Liege 2-1 (Barcelona)
1983†	Aberdeen beat Real Madrid 2-1 (Gothenburg)
1984	Juventus beat Porto 2-1 (Basle)
1985	Everton beat Rapid Vienna 3-1 (Rotterdam)
1986	Dynamo Kiev beat Atletico Madrid 3-0 (Lyon)
1987	Ajax beat Lokomotiv Leipzig 1-0 (Athens)
1988	Mechelen beat Ajax 1-0 (Strasbourg)
1989	Barcelona beat Sampdoria 2-0 (Berne)
1990	Sampdoria beat Anderlecht 2-0 (Gothenburg)
1991	Manchester Utd beat Barcelona 2-1 (Rotterdam)
1992	Werder Bremen beat Monaco 2-0 (Lisbon)
1993	Parma beat Royal Antwerp 3-1 (Wembley)
1994	Arsenal beat Parma 1-0 (Copenhagen)
1995†	Real Zaragoza beat Arsenal 2-1 (Paris)
1996	Paris St Germain beat Rapid Vienna 1-0 (Brussels)
1997	Barcelona beat Paris St Germain 1-0 (Rotterdam)
1998	Chelsea beat VfB Stuttgart 1-0 (Stockholm)
1999	Lazio beat Real Mallorca 2-1 (Villa Park, Birmingham)

(† After extra time)

EUROPEAN SUPER CUP RESULTS

| 1972* | Ajax beat Rangers 6-3 on agg (3-1, 3-2) |
| 1973 | Ajax beat AC Milan 6-1 on agg (0-1, 6-0) |

1974	Bayern Munich and Magdeburg did not play
1975	Dynamo Kiev beat Bayern Munich 3-0 on agg (1-0, 2-0)
1976	Anderlecht beat Bayern Munich 5-3 on agg (1-2, 4-1)
1977	Liverpool beat Hamburg 7-1 on agg (1-1, 6-0)
1978	Anderlecht beat Liverpool 4-3 on agg (3-1, 1-2)
1979	Nottm Forest beat Barcelona 2-1 on agg (1-0, 1-1)
1980	Valencia beat Nottm Forest on away goal after 2-2 agg (1-2, 1-0)
1981	Liverpool and Dinamo Tbilisi did not play
1982	Aston Villa beat Barcelona 3-1 on agg (0-1, 3-0 aet)
1983	Aberdeen beat Hamburg 2-0 on agg (0-0, 2-0)
1984	Juventus beat Liverpool 2-0 - one match (Turin)
1985	Juventus and Everton did not play
1986	Steaua Bucharest beat Dynamo Kiev 1-0 – one match (Monaco)
1987	Porto beat Ajax 2-0 on agg (1-0, 1-0)
1988	Mechelen beat PSV Eindhoven 3-1 on agg (3-0, 0-1)
1989	AC Milan beat Barcelona 2-1 on agg (1-1, 1-0)
1990	AC Milan beat Sampdoria 3-1 on agg (1-1, 2-0)
1991	Manchester Utd beat Red Star Belgrade 1-0 – one match (Old Trafford)
1992	Barcelona beat Werder Bremen 3-2 on agg (1-1, 2-1)
1993	Parma beat AC Milan 2-1 on agg (0-1, 2-0 aet)
1994	AC Milan beat Arsenal 2-0 on agg (0-0, 2-0)
1995	Ajax beat Real Zaragoza 5-1 on agg (1-1, 4-0)
1996	Juventus beat Paris St Germain 9-2 on agg (6-1, 3-1)
1997	Barcelona beat Borussia Dortmund 3-1 on agg (2-0, 1-1)
1998	Chelsea beat Real Madrid 1-0 (Monaco)
1999	Lazio beat Manchester Utd 1-0 (Monaco)
2000	Galatasaray beat Real Madrid 2-1 – aet, golden goal (Monaco)
2001	Liverpool beat Bayern Munich 3-2 (Monaco)
2002	Real Madrid beat Feyenoord 3-1 (Monaco)
2003	AC Milan beat Porto 1-0 (Monaco)
2004	Valencia beat Porto 2-1 (Monaco)
2005	Liverpool beat CSKA Moscow 3-1 – aet (Monaco)
2006	Sevilla beat Barcelona 3-0 (Monaco)
2007	AC Milan beat Sevilla 3-1 (Monaco)
2008	Zenit St Petersburg beat Manchester Utd 2-1 (Monaco)
2009	Barcelona beat Shakhtar Donetsk 1-0 – aet (Monaco)
2010	Atletico Madrid beat Inter Milan 2-0 (Monaco)
2011	Barcelona beat Porto 2-0 (Monaco)
2012	Atletico Madrid beat Chelsea 4-1 (Monaco)
2013	Bayern Munich beat Chelsea 5-4 on pens, aet – 2-2 (Prague)
2014	Real Madrid beat Sevilla 2-0 (Cardiff)

*not recognised by UEFA; from 1998 one match

INTER-CONTINENTAL CUP

Year	Winners	Runners-up	Score
1960	Real Madrid (Spa)	Penarol (Uru)	0-0 5-1
1961	Penarol (Uru)	Benfica (Por)	0-1 2-1 5-0
1962	Santos (Bra)	Benfica (Por)	3-2 5-2
1963	Santos (Bra)	AC Milan (Ita)	2-4 4-2 1-0
1964	Inter Milan (Ita)	Independiente (Arg)	0-1 2-0 1-0
1965	Inter Milan (Ita)	Independiente (Arg)	3-0 0-0
1966	Penarol (Uru)	Real Madrid (Spa)	2-0 2-0
1967	Racing (Arg)	Celtic (Sco)	0-1 2-1 1-0
1968	Estudiantes (Arg)	Manchester Utd (Eng)	1-0 1-1

1969	AC Milan (Ita)	Estudiantes (Arg)	3-0 1-2
1970	Feyenoord (Hol)	Estudiantes (Arg)	2-2 1-0
1971	Nacional (Uru)	Panathanaikos (Gre)	* 1-1 2-1
1972	Ajax (Hol)	Independiente (Arg)	1-1 3-0
1973	Independiente (Arg)	Juventus* (Ita)	1-0 #
1974	Atletico Madrid (Spa)*	Independiente (Arg)	0-1 2-0
1975	Not played		
1976	Bayern Munich (WGer)	Cruzeiro (Bra)	2-0 0-0
1977	Boca Juniors (Arg)	Borussia Mönchengladbach* (WGer)	2-2 3-0
1978	Not played		
1979	Olimpia Asuncion (Par)	Malmö* (Swe)	1-0 2-1
1980	Nacional (Arg)	Nott'm Forest (Eng)	1-0
1981	Flamengo (Bra)	Liverpool (Eng)	3-0
1982	Penarol (Uru)	Aston Villa (Eng)	2-0
1983	Porto Alegre (Bra)	SV Hamburg (WGer)	2-1
1984	Independiente (Arg)	Liverpool (Eng)	1-0
1985	Juventus (Ita)	Argentinos Juniors (Arg)	2-2 (aet)
	(Juventus won 4-2 on penalties)		
1986	River Plate (Arg)	Steaua Bucharest (Rom)	1-0
1987	Porto (Por)	Penarol (Uru)	2-1 (aet)
1988	Nacional (Uru)	PSV Eindhoven (Hol)	1-1 (aet)
	(Nacional won 7-6 on penalties)		
1989	AC Milan (Ita)	Nacional (Col)	1-0 (aet)
1990	AC Milan (Ita)	Olimpia Asuncion (Par)	3-0
1991	Red Star (Yug)	Colo Colo (Chi)	3-0
1992	Sao Paulo (Bra)	Barcelona (Spa)	2-1
1993	Sao Paulo (Bra)	AC Milan (Ita)	3-2
1994	Velez Sarsfield (Arg)	AC Milan (Ita)	2-0
1995	Ajax (Hol)	Gremio (Bra)	0-0 (aet)
	(Ajax won 4-3 on penalties)		
1996	Juventus (Ita)	River Plate (Arg)	1-0
1997	Borussia Dortmund (Ger)	Cruzeiro (Arg)	2-0
1998	Real Madrid (Spa)	Vasco da Gama (Bra)	2-1
1999	Manchester Utd (Eng)	Palmeiras (Bra)	1-0
2000	Boca Juniors (Arg)	Real Madrid (Spa)	2-1
2001	Bayern Munich (Ger)	Boca Juniors (Arg)	1-0
2002	Real Madrid (Spa)	Olimpia Ascuncion (Par)	2-0
2003	Boca Juniors (Arg)	AC Milan (Ita)	1-1
	(Boca Juniors won 3-1 on penalties)		
2004	FC Porto (Por)	Caldas (Col)	0-0
	(FC Porto won 8-7 on penalties)		

Played as a single match in Japan since 1980
* European Cup runners-up # One match only
Summary: 43 contests; South America 22 wins, Europe 23 wins

CLUB WORLD CHAMPIONSHIP

2005	Sao Paulo beat Liverpool	1-0
2006	Internacional (Bra) beat Barcelona	1-0
2007	AC Milan beat Boca Juniors (Arg)	4-2

CLUB WORLD CUP

2008	Manchester Utd beat Liga de Quito	1-0

2009	Barcelona beat Estudiantes	2-1 (aet)
2010	Inter Milan beat TP Mazembe	3-0
2011	Barcelona beat Santos	4-0
2012	Corinthians beat Chelsea	1-0
2013	Bayern Munich beat Raja Casablanca	2-0
2014	Real Madrid beat San Lorenzo	2-0

THE THINGS THEY SAY ...

'Billions of pounds have fallen into the clubs' laps and there's a real chance for them to do something positive. Three per cent of the increase from the latest deal would pay for a £20 away ticket cap. It's time for the fans to benefit' – **Malcolm Clarke**, chairman of the Football Supporters' Federation, calling for a greater share-out of the Premier League's £5.13bn TV contract with Sky and BT.

'We are not set up for charitable purposes. We are set up to be the best football competition in the world. In any talent industry, the talent gets paid a disproportionately high amount compared to the rest' – **Richard Scudamore**, chief executive of the Premier League.

'Diving is like a disease which is spreading through football' – **John Hartson**, BBC pundit, on a day when several Premier League players were guilty of simulation.

'It was like something out of Swan Lake' – **Steve Bruce**, Hull manager, on Gary Cahill's tumble during his side's match against Chelsea

'It could end up like the Dog & Duck against the Red Lion' – **Gary Neville**, former Manchester United stalwart turned pundit, on their match against a Liverpool side also struggling for form.

'He can say everything as he is an ex-legend. But as an ex-legend, or legend, you have to know what you are saying' – **Louis van Gaal**, Manchester United manager.

'99.9 per cent of the people in this country treat me with respect. I can take the other 0.1 per cent' – **Arsene Wenger**, Arsenal manager, on being abused after a defeat at Stoke.

'I owe him everything in my career, but he rose to a different level in the way he supported me through this' – **Darren Fletcher**, thanking his former Manchester United manager Sir Alex Ferguson after recovering from a debilitating bowel condition.

'As a player, you take anything off the ball – pinching and kicks that are meant to wind you up. But if someone spat at me then I think he'd be eating through a straw. It's the lowest of the low' – **Jon Walters**, Stoke striker, after Newcastle's Papiss Cisse and Manchester United's Jonny Evans were banned by the FA for spitting at each other.

'This is the beauty of the FA Cup, with the best team and the best players losing to a team with a completely different potential' – **Jose Mourinho**, Chelsea manager, on the fourth round defeat by Bradford at Stamford Bridge.

'It was a choice I felt was good for myself, my career and my family. Every time I've come back here there was a lovely welcome and a nice feeling. I knew at some point I would work in this club' – **Alan Pardew** on why he resigned as Newcastle manager to take charge at Crystal Palace.

EUROPEAN TABLES 2014–2015

FRANCE – LIGUE 1

	P	W	D	L	F	A	GD	Pts
Paris SG	38	24	11	3	83	36	47	83
Lyon	38	22	9	7	72	33	39	75
Monaco	38	20	11	7	51	26	25	71
Marseille	38	21	6	11	76	42	34	69
St Etienne	38	19	12	7	51	30	21	69
Bordeaux	38	17	12	9	47	44	3	63
Montpellier	38	16	8	14	46	39	7	56
Lille	38	16	8	14	43	42	1	56
Rennes	38	13	11	14	35	42	-7	50
Guingamp	38	15	4	19	41	55	-14	49
Nice	38	13	9	16	44	53	-9	48
Bastia	38	12	11	15	37	46	-9	47
Caen	38	12	10	16	54	55	-1	46
Nantes	38	11	12	15	29	40	-11	45
Reims	38	12	8	18	47	66	-19	44
Lorient	38	12	7	19	44	50	-6	43
Toulouse	38	12	6	20	43	64	-21	42
Evian	38	11	4	23	41	62	-21	37
Metz	38	7	9	22	31	61	-30	30
Lens	38	7	8	23	32	61	-29	29

Leading league scorers: 27 Lacazette (Lyon); 21 Gignac (Marseille); 19 Ibrahimovic (Paris SG); 18 Cavani (Paris SG); 17 Beauvue (Guingamp), Gradel (St Etienne); 15 Rolan (Bordeaux); 14 Ben Yedder (Toulouse); 13 Fekir (Lyon); 12 Ayew (Lorient)
Cup Final: Paris SG 1 (Cavani 65) Auxerre 0

HOLLAND – EREDIVISIE

	P	W	D	L	F	A	GD	Pts
PSV Eindhoven	34	29	1	4	92	31	61	88
Ajax	34	21	8	5	69	29	40	71
Alkmaar	34	19	5	10	63	56	7	62
Feyenoord	34	17	8	9	56	39	17	59
Vitesse Arnhem	34	16	10	8	66	43	23	58
Zwolle	34	16	5	13	59	43	16	53
Heerenveen	34	13	11	10	53	46	7	50
Groningen	34	11	13	10	49	53	-4	46
Willem	34	13	7	14	46	50	-4	46
Twente*	34	13	10	11	56	51	5	43
Utrecht	34	11	8	15	60	62	-2	41
Cambuur	34	11	8	15	46	56	-10	41
Den Haag	34	9	10	15	44	53	-9	37
Heracles	34	11	4	19	47	64	-17	37
Excelsior	34	6	14	14	47	63	-16	32
Breda	34	6	10	18	36	68	-32	28
Go Ahead	34	7	6	21	29	59	-30	27
Dordrecht	34	8	8	22	24	76	-52	20

*6 pts deducted for financial breaches
Leading league scorers: 22 Depay (PSV); 20 De Jong (PSV); 17 De Leeuw (Groningen), Kramer (Den Haag); 15 Chery (Groningen), Uth (Heerenveen); 14 Tighadouini (Breda), Wijnaldum (PSV); 13 Ogbeche (Cambuur), Traore (Vitesse Arnhem), Ziyech (Twente)
Cup Final: Groningen 2 (Rusnak 65, 75) Zwolle 0

GERMANY – BUNDESLIGA

	P	W	D	L	F	A	GD	Pts
Bayern Munich	34	25	4	5	80	18	62	79
Wolfsburg	34	20	9	5	72	38	34	69
Borusssia M'gladbach	34	19	9	6	53	26	27	66
Bayer Leverkusen	34	17	10	7	62	37	25	61
Augsburg	34	15	4	15	43	43	0	49
Schalke	34	13	9	12	42	40	2	48
Borussia Dortmund	34	13	7	14	47	42	5	46
Hoffenhaim	34	12	8	14	49	55	-6	44
Eintracht Frankfurt	34	11	10	13	56	62	-6	43
Werder Bremen	34	11	10	13	50	65	-15	43
Mainz	34	9	13	12	45	47	-2	40
Cologne	34	9	13	12	34	40	-6	40
Hannover	34	9	10	15	40	56	-16	37
Stuttgart	34	9	9	16	42	60	-18	36
Hertha Berlin	34	9	8	17	36	52	-16	35
Hamburg	34	9	8	17	25	50	-25	35
Freiburg	34	7	13	14	36	47	-11	34
Paderborn	34	7	10	17	31	65	-34	31

Leading league scorers: 19 Meier (Eintracht Frankfurt); 17 Lewandowski (Bayern Munich), Robben (Bayern Munich); 16 Aubameyang (Borussia Dortmund), Bas Dost (Wolfsburg); 13 Di Santo (Werder Bremen), Muller (Bayern Munich); 12 Bellarabi (Bayer Leverkusen), Okazaki (Mainz), Raffael (Borussia M'gladbach)
Cup Final: Wolfsburg 3 (Luiz Gustavo 22, De Bruyne 33, Bas Dost 38) Borussia Dortmund 1 (Aubameyang 5)

ITALY – SERIE A

	P	W	D	L	F	A	GD	Pts
Juventus	38	26	9	3	72	24	48	87
Roma	38	19	13	6	54	31	23	70
Lazio	38	21	6	11	71	38	33	69
Fiorentina	38	18	10	10	61	46	15	64
Napoli	38	18	9	11	70	54	16	63
Genoa	38	16	11	11	62	47	15	59
Sampdoria	38	13	17	8	48	42	6	56
Inter Milan	38	14	13	11	59	48	11	55
Torino	38	14	12	12	48	45	3	54
AC Milan	38	13	13	12	56	50	6	52
Palermo	38	12	13	13	53	55	-2	49
Sassuolo	38	12	13	13	49	57	-8	49
Verona	38	11	13	14	49	65	-16	46
Chievo	38	10	13	15	28	41	-13	43
Empoli	38	8	18	12	46	52	-6	42
Udinese	38	10	11	17	43	56	-13	41
Atalanta	38	7	16	15	38	57	-19	37
Cagliari	38	8	10	20	48	68	-20	34
Cesnena	38	4	12	22	36	73	-37	24
Parma*	38	6	8	24	33	75	-42	19

*7 pts deducted for financial irregularities
Leading league scorers: 22 Icardi (Inter Milan), Toni (Verona); 20 Tevez (Juventus); 18 Higuain (Napoli); 16 Menez (AC Milan); 15 Berardi (Sassuolo), Gabbiadini (Napoli); 14 Di Natale (Udinese); 13 Dybala (Palermo), Falque (Genoa), Klose (Lazio), Quagliarella (Torino)
Cup Final: Juventus 2 (Chiellini 11, Matri 97) Lazio 1 (Radu 4) - aet

PORTUGAL – PRIMEIRA LIGA

	P	W	D	L	F	A	GD	Pts
Benfica	34	27	4	3	86	16	70	85
Porto	34	25	7	2	74	13	61	82
Sporting Lisbon	34	22	10	2	67	29	38	76
Braga	34	17	7	10	55	28	27	58
Guimaraes	34	15	10	9	50	35	15	55
Belenenses	34	12	12	10	34	35	-1	48
Nacional	34	13	8	13	45	46	-1	47
Pacos Ferreira	34	12	11	11	40	45	-5	47
Maritimo	34	12	8	14	46	45	1	44
Rio Ave	34	10	13	11	38	42	-4	43
Moreirense	34	11	10	13	33	42	-9	43
Estoril	34	9	13	12	38	56	-18	40
Boavista	34	9	7	18	27	50	-23	34
Vitoria Setubal	34	7	8	19	24	56	-32	29
Academica	34	4	17	13	26	46	-20	29
Arouca	34	7	7	20	26	50	-24	28
Gil Vicente	34	4	11	19	25	60	-35	23
Penafiel	34	5	7	22	29	69	-40	22

Leading league scorers: 21 Jackson Martinez (Porto); 20 Jonas (Benfica); 19 Lima (Benfica); 17 Matias (Nacional); 12 Hassan (Rio Ave), Slimani (Sporting Lisbon); 11 Andre (Guimaraes), Montero (Sporting Lisbon); 10 Bruno Moreira (Pacos Ferreira), Eder (Braga)
Cup Final: Sporting Lisbon 2 (Slimani 84, Montero 90) Braga 2 (Eder 15 pen, Rafa 25) – aet (Sporting Lisbon won 3-1 on pens)

SPAIN – LA LIGA

	P	W	D	L	F	A	GD	Pts
Barcelona	38	30	4	4	110	21	89	94
Real Madrid	38	30	2	6	118	38	80	92
Atletico Madrid	38	23	9	6	67	29	38	78
Valencia	38	22	11	5	70	32	38	77
Sevilla	38	23	7	8	71	45	26	76
Villarreal	38	16	12	10	48	37	11	60
Athletic Bilbao	38	15	10	13	42	41	1	55
Celta Vigo	38	13	12	13	47	44	3	51
Malaga	38	14	8	16	42	48	-6	50
Espanyol	38	13	10	15	47	51	-4	49
Rayo Vallecano	38	15	4	19	46	68	-22	49
Real Sociedad	38	11	13	14	44	51	-7	46
Elche*	38	11	8	19	35	62	-27	41
Levante	38	9	10	19	34	67	-33	37
Getafe	38	10	7	21	33	64	-31	37
Deportivo La Coruna	38	7	14	17	35	60	-25	35
Granada	38	7	14	17	29	64	-35	35
Eibar	38	9	8	21	34	55	-21	35
Almeria	38	8	8	22	35	64	-29	32
Cordoba	38	3	11	24	22	68	-46	20

*Relegated for unpaid debts
Leading league scorers: 48 Ronaldo (Real Madrid); 43 Messi (Barcelona); 22 Griezmann (Atletico Madrid), Neymar (Barcelona); 20 Bacca (Sevilla); 18 Aduriz (Athletic Bilbao); 17 Bueno (Rayo Vallecano); 16 Suarez (Barcelona); 15 Benzema (Real Madrid); 14 Jonathas (Elche), Sergio Garcia (Espanyol); 13 Bale (Real Madrid)
Cup Final: Barcelona 3 (Messi 20, 74, Neymar 36) Athletic Bilbao 1 (Williams 79)

BRITISH & IRISH INTERNATIONALS 2014–2015

* denotes new cap

EUROPEAN CHAMPIONSHIP 2016 QUALIFYING

GERMANY 2 SCOTLAND 1
Group D: Dortmund (60,209); Sunday, September 7 2014
Germany (4-2-3-1): Neuer, Rudy, Boateng, Howedes, Durm, Kramer, Kroos, Muller, Reus (Ginter 90), Schurrle (Podolski 84), Gotze. **Scorer**: Muller (18, 70). **Booked**: Durm, Muller
Scotland (4-2-3-1): Marshall (Cardiff), Hutton (Aston Villa), Martin (Norwich), Hanley (Blackburn), Whittaker (Norwich), D Fletcher (Manchester Utd) (McArthur, Crystal Palace 58), Mulgrew (Celtic), Bannan (Crystal Palace) (S Fletcher, Sunderland 58), Morrison (WBA), Anya (Watford), Naismith (Everton) (Maloney, Wigan 82). **Scorer**: Anya (66). **Booked**: Hanley, Morrison, Mulgrew. **Sent off**: Mulgrew (90)
Referee: S Moen (Norway). **Half-time**: 1-0

HUNGARY 1 NORTHERN IRELAND 2
Group F: Budapest (20,672); Sunday, September 7 2014
Hungary (3-4-1-2): Gulacsi, Vanczak, Liptak, Juhasz, Gyurcso (Lovrecsics 59), Varga, Tozser, Balogh, Nikolic (Priskin 46), Rudolf (Kovacs 70), Dzsudzsak. **Scorer**: Priskin (75). **Booked**: Vanczak
Northern Ireland (4-5-1): Carroll (Notts Co), McLaughlin (Fleetwood), McAuley (WBA) (Cathcart, Watford 72), Hughes (Brighton), Brunt (WBA), Evans (Blackburn), Davis (Southampton), Norwood (Reading) (McKay, Inverness 79), Baird (WBA), Ward (Derby) (McGinn, Aberdeen 79), Lafferty (Norwich). **Scorers**: McGinn (81), Lafferty (88). **Booked**: Norwood
Referee: D Aytekin (Germany). **Half-time**: 0-0

GEORGIA 1 REPUBLIC OF IRELAND 2
Group D: Tbilisi (22,000); Sunday, September 7 2014
Georgia (4-3-2-1): Loria (Kvaskhvadze 46), Lobzhanidze, Kverkvelia, Khubutia, Kvirkvelia, Daushvili, Kashia, Kankava, Okriashvili (Mchedlidze 88), Ananidze (Targamadze 63), Gelashvili. **Scorer**: Okriashvili (38). **Booked**: Kvirkvelia, Khubutia, Daushvili
Republic of Ireland (4-3-2-1): Forde (Millwall), Coleman (Everton), O'Shea (Sunderland), Wilson (Stoke), Ward (Burnley), Whelan (Stoke), McCarthy (Everton) (Meyler, Hull 90), Quinn (Hull) (Brady, Hull 76), Walters (Stoke), McGeady (Everton), Keane (LA Galaxy) (Long, Southampton 76). **Scorer**: McGeady (24, 90). **Booked**: Walters
Referee: K Blom (Holland). **Half-time**: 1-1

SWITZERLAND 0 ENGLAND 2
Group E: Basle (35,500); Monday, September 8 2014
Switzerland (4-3-2-1): Sommer, Lichsteiner, Djourou, Von Bergen, Rodriguez, Behrami, Inler, Mehmedi (Drmic 64), Xhaka (Dzemaili 74), Shaqiri, Seferovic
England (4-4-2): Hart (Manchester City), Stones (Everton), Cahill (Chelsea), Jones (Manchester Utd) (Jagielka, Everton 78), Baines (Everton), Wilshere (Arsenal) (Milner, Manchester City 73), Henderson (Liverpool), Delph (Aston Villa), Sterling (Liverpool), Rooney (Manchester Utd) (Lambert, Liverpool 90), Welbeck (Arsenal). **Scorer**: Welbeck (59, 90). **Booked**: Delph, Lambert
Referee: C Cakir (Turkey). **Half-time**: 0-0

ANDORRA 1 WALES 2
Group B: La Vella (3,150); Tuesday, September 9 2014
Andorra (4-2-3-1): Pol, Rubio, Garcia, Lima, Maneiro, Vales, Ayala (Sanchez 86), Lorenzo, Peppe (Vieira 53), Martinez (Sonejee 83), Riera. **Scorer**: Lima (6 pen). **Booked**: Peppe, Maneiro, Lorenzo, Vieira, Riera, Vales
Wales (3-5-1-1): Hennessey (Crystal Palace), Chester (Hull), A Williams (Swansea), Davies (Tottenham), Gunter (Reading), King (Leicester) (G Williams, Fulham 76), Allen (Liverpool), Ramsey (Arsenal) (Huws, Manchester City 90), Taylor (Swansea), Bale (Real Madrid), Church

241

(Charlton) (Ledley, Crystal Palace 62). **Scorer:** Bale (22, 81). **Booked:** Allen, Church
Referee: S Vincic (Slovenia). **Half-time:** 1-1

ENGLAND 5 SAN MARINO 0
Group E: Wembley (55,990); Thursday, October 9 2014
England (4-3-1-2): Hart (Manchester City), Chambers (Arsenal), Cahill (Chelsea), Jagielka (Everton), Gibbs (Arsenal), Henderson (Liverpool) (Oxlade-Chamberlain, Arsenal 46), Wilshere (Arsenal), Milner (Manchester City), Sterling (Liverpool) (Lallana, Liverpool 46), Welbeck (Arsenal) (Townsend, Tottenham 66) Rooney (Manchester Utd). **Scorers:** Jagielka (24), Rooney (43 pen), Welbeck (49), Townsend (72), Della Valle (77 og). **Booked:** Milner
San Marino (5-4-1): Simoncini, Palazzi (Buscarini 73), F Vitaioli, Della Valle, Brolli, Battistini, Hirsch, Tosi (Gasperoni 63), Chiaruzzi, M Vitaioli, Selva (Rinaldi 87)
Referee: M Borski (Poland). **Half-time:** 2-0

WALES 0 BOSNIA-HERZEGOVINA 0
Group B: Cardiff City Stadium (30,741); Friday, October 10 2014
Wales (3-5-1-1): Hennessey (Crystal Palace), Chester (Hull), A Williams (Swansea), Davies (Tottenham), Gunter (Reading), King (Leicester), J Williams (Crystal Palace) (G Williams, Fulham 83), Ledley (Crystal Palace), Taylor (Swansea), Bale (Real Madrid), Church (Charlton) (Robson-Kanu, Reading 65). **Booked:** Taylor, Chester, A Williams
Bosnia-Herzegovina (4-3-1-2): Begovic, Mujdza, Hadzic, Sunjic, Lulic, Susic, Besic, Medunjanin, Pjanic, Dzeko, Ibisevic (Hajrovic 83). **Booked:** Hadzic, Pjanic, Dzeko
Referee: V Bezborodov (Russia)

SCOTLAND 1 GEORGIA 0
Group D: Ibrox Park (34,719); Saturday, October 11 2014
Scotland (4-3-1-2): Marshall (Cardiff), Hutton (Aston Villa), R Martin (Norwich), Hanley (Blackburn), Robertson (Hull), Anya (Watford), Brown (Celtic), Maloney (Wigan), Morrison (WBA), Naismith (Everton) (McArthur, Crystal Palace 80), Fletcher (Sunderland) (C Martin, Derby 90). **Scorer:** Khubutia (28 og). **Booked:** Morrison, Maloney
Georgia (4-4-2): Loria, Kvirkvelia (Okriashvili 46), Grigalava, Khubutia, Lobzhanidze, Kverkvelia, Kankava, Daushvili, Papava (Dzaria 70) Kazaishvili (Chanturia 80), Gelashvili. **Booked:** Grigalava, Daushvili
Referee: M Zelinka (Czech Republic). **Half-time:** 1-0

NORTHERN IRELAND 2 FAROE ISLANDS 0
Group F: Windsor Park (10,049); Saturday, October 11 2014
Northern Ireland (4-3-2-1): Carroll (Notts Co), McLaughlin (Fleetwood), McAuley (WBA) (McCullough, Doncaster 56), Hughes (Brighton), Ferguson (Newcastle), Davis (Southampton), Baird (WBA), Norwood (Reading), McGinn (Aberdeen) (McCourt, Brighton 67), Ward (Derby), Lafferty (Norwich) (Magennis, Kilmarnock 83). **Scorers:** McAuley (6), Lafferty (20). **Booked:** Ferguson
Faroe Islands (4-3-3): Nielsen, Gregersen, Nattestad, Justinussen (Baralsstovu 90), Davidsen, Naes, Benjaminsen, Hansson, Holst (Olsen 81), Edmundsson, Klettskard (Hannsen 75).
Booked: Naes
Referee: A Yefet (Israel). **Half-time:** 2-0

REPUBLIC OF IRELAND 7 GIBRALTAR 0
Group D: Aviva Stadium (35,123); Saturday, October 11 2014
Republic of Ireland (4-4-2-1): Forde (Millwall), Meyler (Hull), O'Shea (Sunderland), Wilson (Stoke), Ward (Burnley), Brady, Hull 70), McGeady (Everton), Hendrick (Derby), Gibson (Everton), McClean (Wigan), Hoolahan (Norwich) (Doyle, Wolves 64), Keane (LA Galaxy) (Murphy, Ipswich 63). **Scorers:** Keane (6, 14, 18 pen), McClean (46, 53), Perez (51 og), Hoolahan (56)
Gibraltar (4-5-1): J Perez (Robba 60), Wiseman, R Casciaro, R Chipolina (Santos 58), J Chipolina, B Perez, Bado (Guilling 46), Payas, Walker, Gosling, L Casciaro
Referee: L Trattou (Cyprus). **Half-time:** 3-0

ESTONIA 0 ENGLAND 1
Group E: Tallin (10,195); Sunday, October 12 2014

Estonia (4-1-4-1): Parelko, Jaager, Morozov, Klavan, Pikk, Mets, Antonov, Vassilijev (Lindpere 46), Vunk (Kruglov 84), Zenjov (Ojamaa 80), Anier. **Booked:** Klavan. **Sent off:** Klavan (48)
England (4-3-1-2): Hart (Manchester City), Chambers (Arsenal), Cahill (Chelsea), Jagielka (Everton), Baines (Everton), Henderson (Liverpool) (Sterling, Liverpool 64), Wilshere (Arsenal), Delph (Aston Villa) (Oxlade-Chamberlain, Arsenal 61), Lallana (Liverpool), Rooney (Manchester Utd), Welbeck (Arsenal) (Lambert, Liverpool 80). **Scorer:** Rooney (73). **Booked:** Baines, Henderson, Wilshere
Referee: M Strahonja (Croatia). **Half-time:** 0-0

WALES 2 CYPRUS 1
Group B: Cardiff City Stadium (21,273); Monday, October 13 2014

Wales (4-4-1-1): Hennessey (Crystal Palace), Gunter (Reading), Chester (Hull), A Williams (Swansea), N Taylor (Swansea), Robson-Kanu (Reading) (*J Taylor, Reading 85), King (Leicester), Ledley (Crystal Palace), G Williams (Fulham) (Edwards, Wolves 58), Bale (Real Madrid), Church (Charlton) (Cotterill, Birmingham 6). **Scorers:** Cotterill (13), Robson-Kanu (23). **Booked:** Ledley, Cotterill, Bale, Edwards. **Sent off:** King (47)
Cyprus (4-2-3-1): Kissas, Kyriakou, Merkis, Dossa (Angeli 29), Antoniades, Nikolaou (Alexandrou 68), Laban, Efrem, Makrides, Sotiriou, Christofi. **Scorer:** Laban (36). **Booked:** Nikolaou, Angeli, Sotiriou, Kyriakou, Merkis
Referee: M Grafe (Germany). **Half-time:** 2-1

POLAND 2 SCOTLAND 2
Group D: Warsaw (55,197); Tuesday, October 14 2014

Poland (4-4-2): Szczesny, Piszczek, Szukala, Glik, Jedrzejczyk, Grosicki (Zyro 88), Krychowiak, Maczynski, Sobota (Mila 63), Milik, Lewandowski. **Scorers:** Maczynski (11), Milik (76). **Booked:** Krychowiak, Mila
Scotland (4-2-3-1): Marshall (Cardiff), Hutton (Aston Villa), R Martin (Norwich), Greer (Brighton), Whittaker (Norwich), Brown (Celtic), Morrison (WBA), Naismith (Everton) (C Martin, Derby 70), Maloney (Wigan), Anya (Watford), S Fletcher (Sunderland) (D Fletcher, Manchester Utd 70). **Scorers:** Maloney (18), Naismith (57). **Booked:** Greer
Referee: A Mallenco (Spain). **Half-time:** 1-1

GREECE 0 NORTHERN IRELAND 2
Group F: Piraeus (18,726); Tuesday, October 14 2014

Greece (4-4-2): Karnezis, Torosidis, Papastathapoulos, Manolas, Vyntra (Stafylidis 16), Tachtsidis, Maniatis, Karelis, Athanasiadis (Samaris 46), Samaras (Salpingidis 67), Mitroglu. **Booked:** Samaras, Maniatis, Samaras
Northern Ireland (4-5-1): Carroll (Notts Co), McLaughlin (Fleetwood), McAuley (WBA), Hughes (Brighton), Ferguson (Newcastle) (*Reeves, MK Dons 78), Evans (Blackburn), Davis (Southampton), Baird (WBA), Norwood (Reading), Ward (Derby) (McGivern, Port Vale 60), Lafferty (Norwich) (Magennis, Kilmarnock 72). **Scorers:** Ward (9), Lafferty (51). **Booked:** Lafferty
Referee: S Lannoy (France). **Half-time:** 0-1

GERMANY 1 REPUBLIC OF IRELAND 1
Group D: Gelsenkirchen (51,204); Tuesday, October 14 2014

Germany (4-2-3-1): Neuer, Rudiger, Boateng, Hummels, Durm, Ginter (Podolski 46), Kroos, Bellarabi (Rudy 87), Gotze, Draxler (Kruse 70), Muller. **Scorer:** Kroos (71). **Booked:** Hummels
Republic of Ireland (4-4-2): Forde (Millwall), Meyler (Hull), O'Shea (Sunderland), Wilson (Stoke), Ward (Burnley), McGeady (Everton), Quinn (Hull) (Hoolahan, Norwich 76), Whelan (Stoke) (Hendrick, Derby 54), McClean (Wigan), Walters (Stoke), Keane (LA Galaxy) (Gibson, Everton 62). **Scorer:** O'Shea (90). **Booked:** Whelan, Wilson
Referee: D Skomina (Slovenia): **Half-time:** 0-0
(John O'Shea's 100th Republic of Ireland cap)

SCOTLAND 1 REPUBLIC OF IRELAND 0
Group D: Celtic Park (59,239); Friday, November 14 2014

Scotland (4-4-1-1): Marshall (Cardiff), Whittaker (Norwich), R Martin (Norwich), Hanley (Blackburn), Robertson (Hull), Maloney (Wigan), Mulgrew (Celtic), Brown (Celtic), Anya (Watford) (D Fletcher, Manchester Utd 88), Naismith (Everton), S Fletcher (Sunderland) (C Martin, Derby 56). **Scorer:** Maloney (75). **Booked:** Hanley, Robertson

Republic of Ireland (4-2-3-1): Forde (Millwall), Coleman (Everton), O'Shea (Sunderland), Keogh (Derby), Ward (Burnley), Gibson (Everton) (Quinn, Hull 69), Hendrick (Derby) (Keane, LA Galaxy 78), McGeady (Everton), Walters (Stoke), McClean (Wigan), Long (Southampton) (Brady, Hull 68). **Booked:** McGeady, Hendrick, Coleman, Quinn
Referee: M Mazic (Serbia). **Half-time:** 0-0

ROMANIA 2 NORTHERN IRELAND 0
Group F: Bucharest (28,892); Friday, November 14 2014

Romania (4-2-3-1): Tatarusanu, Papp, Chiriches, Grigore, Rat, Pintilii, Sanmartean, Torje (Hoban 81), Chipciu, Tanase (Maximov 58), Stancu (Keseru 46). **Scorer:** Papp (74, 79). **Booked:** Pintilii, Chipciu, Maximov

Northern Ireland (4-5-1): Carroll (Notts Co), McLaughlin (Fleetwood), McAuley (WBA), Hughes (Brighton), McGivern (Port Vale), McGinn (Aberdeen) (Clingan, Kilmarnock), Baird (WBA), Norwood (Reading), Evans (Blackburn) (McKay, Inverness 78), Brunt (WBA), Lafferty (Norwich). **Booked:** McLaughlin, Lafferty
Referee: J Eriksson (Sweden). **Half-time:** 0-0

ENGLAND 3 SLOVENIA 1
Group E: Wembley (82,305); Saturday, November 14

England (4-1-2-1-2): Hart (Manchester City), *Clyne (Southampton), Cahill (Chelsea), Jagielka (Everton) (Smalling, Manchester Utd 89), Gibbs (Arsenal), Wilshere (Arsenal), Henderson (Liverpool), Lallana (Liverpool) (Milner, Manchester City 80), Sterling (Liverpool) (Oxlade-Chamberlain, Arsenal 85), Rooney (Manchester Utd), Welbeck (Arsenal). **Scorers:** Rooney (59 pen), Welbeck (65, 72). **Booked:** Gibbs, Clyne, Sterling, Jagielka

Slovenia (4-2-3-1): Handanovic, Brecko, Ilic, Cesar, Sturna, Mertelj, Kurtic (Rotman 75), Birsa (Lazarevic 63), Kampl, Kirm (Ljubijankic 78), Novakovic. **Scorer:** Henderson (57 og). **Booked:** Cesar
Referee: O Benquerenca (Portugal). **Half-time:** 0-0
(Wayne Rooney's 100th England cap)

BELGIUM 0 WALES 0
Group B: Brussels (41,535); Sunday, November 16 2014

Belgium (4-2-3-1): Courtois, Vanden Borre, Alderweireld, Lombaerts, Vertonghen, Fellaini, Witsel, De Bruyne, Chadli (Benteke 62), Hazard, Origi (Mertens 73, Januzaj 89)

Wales (4-3-2-1): Hennessey (Crystal Palace), Gunter (Reading), Chester (Hull), A Williams (Swansea), Taylor (Swansea), Allen (Liverpool), Ledley (Crystal Palace), Ramsey (Arsenal), Cotterill (Birmingham) (G Williams, Fulham 46), Bale (Real Madrid), Robson-Kanu (Reading) (Huws, Manchester City 90). **Booked:** Ledley, Allen, G Williams, Hennessey
Referee: P Kralovec (Czech Rep)

ENGLAND 4 LITHUANIA 0
Group E: Wembley (83,671); Friday, March 27 2015

England (4-3-3): Hart (Manchester City), Clyne (Southampton), Cahill (Chelsea), Jones (Manchester Utd), Baines (Everton), Carrick (Manchester Utd), Delph (Aston Villa), Henderson (Liverpool) (Barkley, Everton 71), Sterling (Liverpool), Rooney (Manchester Utd) (*Kane, Tottenham 72), Welbeck (Arsenal) (Walcott, Arsenal 77). **Scorers:** Rooney (6), Welbeck (45), Sterling (58), Kane (73). **Booked:** Sterling

Lithuania (4-4-1-1): Arlauskis, Freldgelmas, Zaliukas, Kijanskas, Andriuskevicius (Slavickas 83), Chvedukas, Zulpa, Mikuckis (Stankevicius 66), Mikoliunas (Kazlauskas 88), Cernych, Matulevicius. **Booked:** Zaliukas, Kazlauskas
Referee: P Kralovec (Czech Republic). **Half-time:** 2-0

ISRAEL 0 WALES 3
Group B: Haifa (30,200): Saturday, March 28 2015
Israel (4-3-3): Marciano, Dgani, Ben Haim (1), Tibi, Ben Harush, Yeini, Natcho, Refaelov, Ben Haim (2) (Bitton 60), Zahavi (Sahar 71), Damari (Hemed 44). **Booked**: Refaelov, Tibi. **Sent off**: Tibi (51)
Wales (5-3-1-1): Hennessey (Crystal Palace), Gunter (Reading), Collins (West Ham), Williams (Swansea), Davies (Tottenham), Taylor (Swansea), Ramsey (Arsenal) (MacDonald, Bournemouth 86), Allen (Liverpool), Ledley (Crystal Palace) (Vaughan, Nottm Forest 48), Bale (Real Madrid), Robson-Kanu (Reading) (Vokes, Burnley 69). **Scorers**: Ramsey (45), Bale (50, 77).
Referee: M Mazic (Serbia). **Half-time**: 0-1

SCOTLAND 6 GIBRALTAR 1
Group D: Hampden Park (34,255): Sunday, March 29 2015
Scotland (3-4-3): Marshall (Cardiff), Hutton (Aston Villa), Martin (Norwich), Robertson (Hull), Ritchie (Bournemouth) (Greer, Brighton 46), Brown (Celtic), Maloney (Wigan), Morrison (WBA), Anya (Watford) (Bannan, Crystal Palace 74), Naismith (Everton) (Rhodes, Blackburn 66), Fletcher (Sunderland). **Scorers**: Maloney (18 pen, 34 pen), Fletcher (29, 77, 90), Naismith (39)
Gibraltar (4-5-1): Robba, Wiseman, J Chipolina, Artell (Gracia 53), R Casciaro, R Chipolina (Gosling 74), L Casciaro, Payas, Walker, Priestly, Bardon (Duarte 82). **Scorer**: L Casciaro (19)
Referee: M Grestranius (Finland). **Half-time**: 4-1

NORTHERN IRELAND 2 FINLAND 1
Group F: Windsor Park (10,264); Sunday, March 29 2015
Northern Ireland (4-1-4-1): Carroll (Notts Co), McLaughlin (Fleetwood), McAuley (WBA), J Evans (Manchester Utd), Brunt (WBA), Baird (WBA), Ward (Derby), Davis (Southampton) (C Evans, Blackburn 46), Norwood (Reading), McGinn (Aberdeen) (Dallas, Brentford 64), Lafferty (Norwich) (Magennis, Kilmarnock 79). **Scorer**: Lafferty (33, 38). **Booked**: Baird, Brunt
Finland (4-3-2-1): Hradecky, Sorsa, Toivio (Arajuuri 46), Moisander, Uronen, Ring, Mattila, Sparv, Hamalainen (Pohjanpalo 42), Eremenko, Pukki (Sadik 70). **Scorer**: Sadik (90). **Booked**: Pohjanpalo, Arajuuri
Referee: S Marciniak (Poland). **Half-time**: 2-0

REPUBLIC OF IRELAND 1 POLAND 1
Group D: Aviva Stadium (50,500); Sunday, March 29 2015
Republic of Ireland (4-4-1-1): Given (Aston Villa), Coleman (Everton), O'Shea (Sunderland), Wilson (Stoke), Brady (Hull), Walters (Stoke), Whelan (Stoke) (Long, Southampton 83), McCarthy (Everton), McGeady (Everton) (McClean, Wigan 67), Hoolahan (Norwich), Keane (LA Galaxy). **Scorer**: Long (90). **Booked**: Hoolahan, O'Shea, Coleman, Wilson, McCarthy
Poland (4-4-2): Fabianski, Olkowski, Glik, Szukala, Wawrzyniak, Peszko (Kucharczyk 87), Krychowiak, Jodlowiec, Rybus, Milik (Mila 84), Lewandowski. **Scorer**: Peszko (26). **Booked**: Glik, Szukala, Peszko
Referee: J Eriksson (Sweden). **Half-time**: 0-1

WALES 1 BELGIUM 0
Group B: Cardiff City Stadium (33,280); Friday, June 12 2015
Wales (5-2-2-1): Hennessey (Crystal Palace), Richards (Swansea), Gunter (Reading), Williams (Swansea), Chester (Hull), Taylor (Swansea), Allen (Liverpool), Ledley (Crystal Palace), Bale (Real Madrid) (Vokes, Burnley 88), Ramsey (Arsenal), Robson-Kanu (Reading) (King, Leicester 90). **Scorer**: Bale (25). **Booked**: Allen
Belgium (4-2-3-1): Courtois, Alderweireld (Ferreira Carrasco 76), Denayer, Lombaerts, Vertonghen, Nainggolan, Witsel, Mertens (Lukaku 46), De Bruyne, Hazard, Benteke. **Booked**: Lombaerts
Referee: F Brych (Germany). **Half-time**: 1-0

REPUBLIC OF IRELAND 1 SCOTLAND 1
Group D: Aviva Stadium (49,063): Saturday, June 13 2015

Republic of Ireland (4-4-1-1): Given (Aston Villa), Coleman (Everton), O'Shea (Sunderland), Wilson (Stoke), Brady (Hull), Walters (Stoke), Hendrick (Derby), McCarthy (Everton), Whelan (Stoke) (McClean, Wigan 67), Hoolahan (Norwich) (Keane, LA Galaxy 73), Murphy (Ipswich) (Long, Southampton 80). **Scorer:** Walters (38). **Booked:** Whelan, McCarthy, McClean
Scotland (4-4-1-1): Marshall (Cardiff), Hutton (Aston Villa), Martin (Norwich), Mulgrew (Celtic), Forsyth (Derby), Ritchie (Bournemouth) (Anya, Watford 46), Brown (Celtic) (McArthur, Crystal Palace 85), Morrison (WBA), Naismith (Everton) (Berra, Ipswich 90), Maloney (Chicago), Fletcher (Sunderland). **Scorer:** O'Shea (47 og). **Booked:** Naismith
Referee: N Rizzoli (Italy). **Half-time:** 1-0

NORTHERN IRELAND 0 ROMANIA 0
Group F: Windsor Park (10,000): Saturday, June 13 2015

Northern Ireland (4-4-2): McGovern (Hamilton), McLaughlin (Fleetwood), McAuley (unatt), J Evans (Manchester Utd) (Cathcart, Watford 80), Brunt (WBA), Davis (Southampton), Norwood (Reading), Baird (unatt), Ward (unatt) (C Evans, Blackburn 79), Lafferty (Norwich), Dallas (Brentford). **Booked:** Brunt
Romania (4-2-3-1): Tatarusanu, Papp, Grigore, Chiriches, Sepsi, Prepalita, Pintilii, Torje, Maxim (Tamas 90), Chipciu (Stancu 61), Keseru (Andone 72). **Booked:** Pintilii, Sepsi, Torje
Referee: C Velasco (Spain)

SLOVENIA 2 ENGLAND 3
Group E: Ljubljana (15,796): Sunday, June 14 2015

Slovenia (4-2-3-1): Handanovic, Brecko, Ilic, Cesar, Jokic, Mertelj, Kurtic (Lazarevic 79), Ilicic (Birsa 61), Kampl, Kirm (Pecnik 72), Novakovic. **Scorers:** Novakovic (37), Pecnik (84). **Booked:** Brecko, Kampl
England (4-3-3): Hart (Manchester City), Jones (Manchester Utd) (Lallana, Liverpool 46), Cahill (Chelsea), Smalling (Manchester Utd), Gibbs (Arsenal), Henderson (Liverpool), Wilshere (Arsenal), Delph (Aston Villa) (Clyne, Southampton 86), Townsend (Tottenham) (Walcott, Arsenal 74), Rooney (Manchester Utd), Sterling (Liverpool). **Scorers:** Wilshere (57, 73), Rooney (86)
Referee: A Mallenco (Spain). **Half-time:** 1-0

FRIENDLY INTERNATIONALS
ENGLAND 1 NORWAY 0
Wembley (40,181); Wednesday, September 3 2014

England (4-2-3-1): Hart (Manchester City), Stones (Everton) (*Chambers, Arsenal 81), Cahill (Chelsea) (Jagielka, Everton 84), Jones (Manchester Utd), Baines (Everton), Henderson (Liverpool), Wilshere (Arsenal) (Milner, Manchester City 70), Oxlade-Chamberlain (Arsenal) (*Delph, Aston Villa 70), Rooney (Manchester Utd) (Welbeck, Arsenal 70), Sterling (Liverpool), Sturridge (Liverpool) (Lambert, Liverpool 89). **Scorer:** Rooney (68 pen)
Norway (4-3-2-1): Nyland, Elabdellaoui, Nordtvelt, Forren, Linnes (Flo 36), Skjelbred (M Elyounoussi 69), Johansen, Jenssen (Pedersen 88), Daehli (Konradsen 57), T Elyounoussi (Kamara 78), King (Nielsen 77)
Referee: J de Sousa (Portugal). **Half-time:** 0-0

REPUBLIC OF IRELAND 2 OMAN 0
Aviva Stadium (14,376); Wednesday, September 3 2014

Republic of Ireland (4-4-1-1): Given (Aston Villa) (Elliot, Newcastle 46), Meyler (Hull) (Murphy, Ipswich 85), Keogh (Derby), Pearce (Reading), Ward (Burnley), Pilkington (Cardiff) (McGeady, Everton 59), Gibson (Everton) (Whelan, Stoke 70), Quinn (Hull), Brady (Hull), Hoolahan (Norwich) (Keane, LA Galaxy 59), Doyle (Wolves) (Long, Southampton 59). **Scorers:** Doyle (20), Pearce (82). **Booked:** Gibson

Oman (3-4-3): Al Habsi, Amur, Al Owaisi, Al Musalami, Suhail, Kano (Al Jabri 60), Mohammed (Muqbali 81), Mudhafar (Al Busaidi 60), Saleh (Al Maashari 87), Said (Karim 60), Al Seyabi (Al Hadhri 76)
Referee: I Spathos (Greece). **Half-time:** 1-0

SCOTLAND 1 ENGLAND 3
Celtic Park (49,526); Tuesday, November 18 2014

Scotland (4-2-3-1): Marshall (Cardiff) (Gordon, Celtic 46), Whittaker (Norwich), R Martin (Norwich), Hanley (Blackburn) (*May, Sheffield Wed 66), Robertson (Hull), Brown (Celtic) (Fletcher, Manchester Utd 46), Mulgrew (Celtic), Maloney (Wigan) (*Russell, Derby 81), Naismith (Everton), Anya (Watford) (Bannan, Crystal Palace 61), C Martin (Derby) (Morrison, WBA 46). **Scorer:** Robertson (83). **Booked:** Mulgrew
England (4-1-3-2): Forster (Southampton), Clyne (Southampton), Cahill (Chelsea) (Jagielka, Everton 46), Smalling (Manchester Utd), Shaw (Manchester Utd) (Gibbs, Arsenal 66), Wilshere (Arsenal) (Barkley, Everton 87), Oxlade-Chamberlain (Arsenal) (Lambert, Liverpool 80), Downing (West Ham) (Lallana, Liverpool 46), Milner (Manchester City), Rooney (Manchester Utd), Welbeck (Arsenal) (Sterling, Liverpool 66). **Scorers:** Oxlade-Chamberlain (32), Rooney (47, 85)
Referee: J Eriksson (Sweden). **Half-time:** 0-1

REPUBLIC OF IRELAND 4 USA 1
Aviva Stadium (33,332); Tuesday, November 18 2014

Republic of Ireland (4-4-2): Given (Aston Villa) (Elliot, Newcastle 84), *Christie (Derby), Pearce (Reading), Clark (Aston Villa), Brady (Hull), Pilkington (Cardiff) (McClean, Wigan 64), Meyler (Hull), Quinn (Hull), Stokes (Celtic) (McGeady, Everton 59), McGoldrick (Ipswich) (Long, Southampton 77), Murphy (Ipswich) (Hendrick, Derby 77). **Scorers:** Pilkington (8), Brady (56, 88), McClean (82). **Booked:** McGeady, Meyler
USA (4-4-2): Hamid, Chandler (Morris 76), Cameron, Besler, Morales (Garza 64), Bedoya, Beckerman (Ream 87), Johnson, Diskerud (Rubin 76), Altidore, Wondolowski (Wood 46). **Scorer:** Diskerud (39). **Booked:** Beckerman, Altidore, Cameron, Johnson
Referee: P Raczkowski (Poland). **Half-time:** 1-1

SCOTLAND 1 NORTHERN IRELAND 0
Hampden Park (28,000); Wednesday, March 25 2015

Scotland (4-2-3-1): Gordon (Celtic) (McGregor, Hull 46), Whittaker (Norwich) (Russell, Derby 77), Martin (Norwich) (Berra, Ipswich 46), Greer (Brighton), Forsyth (Derby), McArthur (Crystal Palace) (Morrison (WBA, 62), D Fletcher (WBA), *Ritchie (Bournemouth), Maloney (Chicago. Fire) (Naismith, Everton 46), Anya (Watford), S Fletcher (Sunderland) (Rhodes, Blackburn 62). **Scorer:** Berra (85)
Northern Ireland (4-2-3-1): McGovern (Hamilton), *McNair (Manchester Utd), Hughes (Brighton), Evans (Manchester Utd) (McCullough, Doncaster 81), Lafferty (Burnley), Baird (WBA) (Hodson, MK Dons 55), Norwood (Reading) (Davis, Southampton 69), Magennis (Kilmarnock) (McKay, Wigan 75), Reeves (MK Dons) (McLaughlin, Liverpool 70), Dallas (Brentford), Grigg (Brentford) (McCourt, Brighton 55)
Referee: M Atkinson (England). **Half-time:** 0-0

ITALY 1 ENGLAND 1
Turin (31,138); Tuesday, March 31 2015

Italy (3-5-2): Buffon, Ranocchia, Bonucci, Chiellini (Moretti 72), Florenzi (Abate 60), Parolo, Valdiflori (Verratti 67), Soriano, Darmian (Antonelli 73), Pelle (Immobile 61), Eder (Vazquez 61). **Scorer:** Pelle (29)
England (4-1-2-1-2): Hart (Manchester City), Clyne (Southampton) (Walker, Tottenham 46), Smalling (Manchester Utd) (Carrick, Manchester Utd 44), Jagielka (Everton), Gibbs (Arsenal) (Bertrand, Southampton 88), Jones (Manchester Utd), Henderson (Liverpool) (*Mason, Tottenham 74), Delph (Aston Villa) (Townsend, Tottenham 70), Rooney (Manchester Utd), Kane (Tottenham) Walcott (Arsenal) (Barkley, Everton 55). **Scorer:** Townsend (79). **Booked:** Gibbs, Jones
Referee: F Brych (Germany). **Half-time:** 1-0

NORTHERN IRELAND 1 QATAR 1
Alexandra Stadium, Crewe (3,022); Sunday, May31 2015

Northern Ireland (4-2-3-1): Carroll (Notts Co) (McGovern, Hamilton 46), Lafferty (Burnley), McLaughlin (Fleetwood), Cathcart (Watford), Hughes (unatt) (J Evans, Manchester Utd 61), Norwood (Reading), McNair (Manchester Utd) (Magennis, Kilmarnock 82), C Evans (Blackburn), Dallas (Brentford) (Boyce, Ross Co 73), McGinn (Aberdeen) (Ward, unatt 61), Grigg (Brentford) (McCourt, unatt 73). **Scorer:** Dallas (46)
Qatar (4-4-2): Lecomte-Addani, Kasola, Ismaeil, Traore (Hassan 56), Yasser, Siddiq (Assadalla 65, El Sayed, Musa, Hatem (Boudiaf 56), Mohammad (Khalid 56), Muntari (Jeedo 81). **Scorer:** Boudiaf (70)
Referee: M Oliver (England). **Half-time:** 0-0

SCOTLAND 1 QATAR 0
Easter Road, Edinburgh (14,270); Friday, June 5 2015

Scotland (4-2-3-1): Marshall (Cardiff) (Gordon, Celtic 46), Anya (Watford) (Adam, Stoke 60), Greer (Brighton), Mulgrew (Celtic), Forsyth (Derby), Brown (Celtic) (D Fletcher, WBA 60), McArthur (Crystal Palace) (Morrison, WBA, 46), Ritchie (Bournemouth) Maloney (Chicago), Forrest (Celtic) (Russell, Derby 73), Naismith (Everton) (Griffiths, Celtic 60). **Scorer:** Ritchie (41)
Qatar (4-3-2-1): Lecomte-Addani, Tresor (Ismaeil 78), Kasola, Yasser, Hassan, Boudiaf, Hatem (Ali 54), Assadalla (Mohd 68), El Sayed, Khalid (Hassan 86), Muntari (Ilyas 78). **Booked:** Tresor, El Sayed
Referee: S Delferiere (Belgium). **Half-time:** 1-0

REPUBLIC OF IRELAND 0 ENGLAND 0
Aviva Stadium, Dublin (43,486); Sunday, June 7 2015

Republic of Ireland (4-4-2): Westwood (Sheffield Wed) (Given, Aston Villa 61), Coleman (Everton), O'Shea (Sunderland) (McShane, Hull, 72) Wilson (Stoke), Brady (Hull), Hendrick (Derby), McCarthy (Everton) (McClean, Wigan 46), Whelan (Stoke) (*Arter, Bournemouth 63), McGeady (Everton), McGoldrick (Ipswich) (Long, Southampton 46), Murphy (Ipswich) (Walters, Stoke 56). **Booked:** McCarthy
England (4-3-2-1): Hart (Manchester City), Jones (Manchester Utd), Cahill (Chelsea) (Jagielka, (Everton 74), Smalling (Manchester Utd), Bertrand (Southampton), Milner (Liverpool), Henderson (Liverpool), Wilshere (Arsenal) (Barkley, Everton 66), Sterling (Liverpool) (Townsend, Tottenham 65), Rooney (Manchester Utd) (*Vardy, Leicester 75), Lallana (Liverpool) (Walcott, Arsenal 82)
Referee: A Hunter (Northern Ireland)

THE THINGS THEY SAY ...

'The England bid team sought to curry favour with a member of the FIFA executive committee in order to influence his vote, thereby damaging the image of FIFA and the bidding process' – **FIFA** report criticising the FA for its relationship with Jack Warner while attempting to host the 2018 World Cup.

'We do not accept any criticism regarding the integrity of England's bid. We conducted a transparent bid and, as the report demonstrates with its reference to the team's "full and valuable co-operation," willingly complied with the investigation' – **FA** statement rejecting the accusation.

OTHER BRITISH & IRISH INTERNATIONAL RESULTS

ENGLAND

v ALBANIA

		E	A
1989	Tirana (WC)	2	0
1989	Wembley (WC)	5	0
2001	Tirana (WC)	3	1
2001	Newcastle (WC)	2	0

v ALGERIA

		E	A
2010	Cape Town (WC)	0	0

v ANDORRA

		E	A
2006	Old Trafford (EC)	5	0
2007	Barcelona (EC)	3	0
2008	Barcelona (WC)	2	0
2009	Wembley (WC)	6	0

v ARGENTINA

		E	A
1951	Wembley	2	1
1953*	Buenos Aires	0	0
1962	Rancagua (WC)	3	1
1964	Rio de Janeiro	0	1
1966	Wembley (WC)	1	0
1974	Wembley	2	2
1977	Buenos Aires	1	1
1980	Wembley	3	1
1986	Mexico City (WC)	1	2
1991	Wembley	2	2
1998†	St Etienne (WC)	2	2
2000	Wembley	0	0
2002	Sapporo (WC)	1	0
2005	Geneva	3	2

(*Abandoned after 21 mins – rain)
(† England lost 3-4 on pens)

v AUSTRALIA

		E	A
1980	Sydney	2	1
1983	Sydney	0	0
1983	Brisbane	1	0
1983	Melbourne	1	1
1991	Sydney	1	0
2003	West Ham	1	3

v AUSTRIA

		E	A
1908	Vienna	6	1
1908	Vienna	11	1
1909	Vienna	8	1
1930	Vienna	0	0
1932	Stamford Bridge	4	3
1936	Vienna	1	2
1951	Wembley	2	2
1952	Vienna	3	2
1958	Boras (WC)	2	2
1961	Vienna	1	3
1962	Wembley	3	1
1965	Wembley	2	3
1967	Vienna	1	0
1973	Wembley	7	0
1979	Vienna	3	4

2004	Vienna (WC)	2	2
2005	Old Trafford (WC)	1	0
2007	Vienna	1	0

v AZERBAIJAN

		E	A
2004	Baku (WC)	1	0
2005	Newcastle (WC)	2	0

v BELARUS

		E	B
2008	Minsk (WC)	3	1
2009	Wembley (WC)	3	0

v BELGIUM

		E	B
1921	Brussels	2	0
1923	Highbury	6	1
1923	Antwerp	2	2
1924	West Bromwich	4	0
1926	Antwerp	5	3
1927	Brussels	9	1
1928	Antwerp	3	1
1929	Brussels	5	1
1931	Brussels	4	1
1936	Brussels	2	3
1947	Brussels	5	2
1950	Brussels	4	1
1952	Wembley	5	0
1954	Basle (WC)	4	4
1964	Wembley	2	2
1970	Brussels	3	1
1980	Turin (EC)	1	1
1990	Bologna (WC)	1	0
1998*	Casablanca	0	0
1999	Sunderland	2	1
2012	Wembley	1	0

(*England lost 3-4 on pens)

v BOHEMIA

		E	B
1908	Prague	4	0

v BRAZIL

		E	B
1956	Wembley	4	2
1958	Gothenburg (WC)	0	0
1959	Rio de Janeiro	0	2
1962	Vina del Mar (WC)	1	3
1963	Wembley	1	1
1964	Rio de Janeiro	1	5
1969	Rio de Janeiro	1	2
1970	Guadalajara (WC)	0	1
1976	Los Angeles	0	1
1977	Rio de Janeiro	0	0
1978	Wembley	1	1
1981	Wembley	0	1
1984	Rio de Janeiro	2	0
1987	Wembley	1	1
1990	Wembley	1	0
1992	Wembley	1	1
1993	Washington	1	1
1995	Wembley	1	3
1997	Paris (TF)	0	1
2000	Wembley	1	1

2002	Shizuoka (WC)	1	2
2007	Wembley	1	1
2009	Doha	0	1
2013	Wembley	2	1
2013	Rio de Janeiro	2	2

v BULGARIA

		E	B
1962	Rancagua (WC)	0	0
1968	Wembley	1	1
1974	Sofia	1	0
1979	Sofia (EC)	3	0
1979	Wembley (EC)	2	0
1996	Wembley	1	0
1998	Wembley (EC)	0	0
1999	Sofia (EC)	1	1
2010	Wembley (EC)	4	0
2011	Sofia (EC)	3	0

v CAMEROON

		E	C
1990	Naples (WC)	3	2
1991	Wembley	2	0
1997	Wembley	2	0
2002	Kobe (Japan)	2	2

v CANADA

		E	C
1986	Vancouver	1	0

v CHILE

		E	C
1950	Rio de Janeiro (WC)	2	0
1953	Santiago	2	1
1984	Santiago	0	0
1989	Wembley	0	0
1998	Wembley	0	2
2013	Wembley	0	2

v CHINA

		E	C
1996	Beijing	3	0

v CIS
(formerly Soviet Union)

		E	CIS
1992	Moscow	2	2

v COLOMBIA

		E	C
1970	Bogota	4	0
1988	Wembley	1	1
1995	Wembley	0	0
1998	Lens (WC)	2	0
2005	New York	3	2

v COSTA RICA

		E	CR
2014	Belo Horizonte (WC)	0	0

v CROATIA

		E	C
1995	Wembley	0	0
2003	Ipswich	3	1
2004	Lisbon (EC)	4	2
2006	Zagreb (EC)	0	2
2007	Wembley (EC)	2	3
2008	Zagreb (WC)	4	1
2009	Wembley (WC)	5	1

v CYPRUS

		E	C
1975	Wembley (EC)	5	0
1975	Limassol (EC)	1	0

v CZECH REPUBLIC

		E	C
1998	Wembley	2	0
2008	Wembley	2	2

v CZECHOSLOVAKIA

		E	C
1934	Prague	1	2
1937	White Hart Lane	5	4
1963	Bratislava	4	2
1966	Wembley	0	0
1970	Guadalajara (WC)	1	0
1973	Prague	1	1
1974	Wembley (EC)	3	0
1975*	Bratislava (EC)	1	2
1978	Wembley (EC)	1	0
1982	Bilbao (WC)	2	0
1990	Wembley	4	2
1992	Prague	2	2

(* Aband 0-0, 17 mins prev day – fog)

v DENMARK

		E	D
1948	Copenhagen	0	0
1955	Copenhagen	5	1
1956	W'hampton (WC)	5	2
1957	Copenhagen (WC)	4	1
1966	Copenhagen	2	0
1978	Copenhagen (EC)	4	3
1979	Wembley (EC)	1	0
1982	Copenhagen (EC)	2	2
1983	Wembley (EC)	0	1
1988	Wembley	1	0
1989	Copenhagen	1	1
1990	Wembley	1	0
1992	Malmo (EC)	0	0
1994	Wembley	1	0
2002	Niigata (WC)	3	0
2003	Old Trafford	2	3
2005	Copenhagen	1	4
2011	Copenhagen	2	1
2014	Wembley	1	0

v EAST GERMANY

		E	EG
1963	Leipzig	2	1
1970	Wembley	3	1
1974	Leipzig	1	1
1984	Wembley	1	0

v ECUADOR

		E	Ec
1970	Quito	2	0
2006	Stuttgart (WC)	1	0
2014	Miami	2	2

v EGYPT

		E	Eg
1986	Cairo	4	0
1990	Cagliari (WC)	1	0
2010	Wembley	3	1

v ESTONIA

		E	Est
2007	Tallinn (EC)	3	0
2007	Wembley (EC)	3	0
2014	Tallinn (EC)	1	0

v FIFA

		E	F
1938	Highbury	3	0
1953	Wembley	4	4
1963	Wembley	2	1

v FINLAND

		E	F
1937	Helsinki	8	0
1956	Helsinki	5	1
1966	Helsinki	3	0
1976	Helsinki (WC)	4	1
1976	Wembley (WC)	2	1
1982	Helsinki	4	1
1984	Wembley (WC)	5	0
1985	Helsinki (WC)	1	1
1992	Helsinki	2	1
2000	Helsinki (WC)	0	0
2001	Liverpool (WC)	2	1

v FRANCE

		E	F
1923	Paris	4	1
1924	Paris	3	1
1925	Paris	3	2
1927	Paris	6	0
1928	Paris	5	1
1929	Paris	4	1
1931	Paris	2	5
1933	White Hart Lane	4	1
1938	Paris	4	2
1947	Highbury	3	0
1949	Paris	3	1
1951	Highbury	2	2
1955	Paris	0	1
1957	Wembley	4	0
1962	Hillsborough (EC)	1	1
1963	Paris (EC)	2	5
1966	Wembley (WC)	2	0
1969	Wembley	5	0
1982	Bilbao (WC)	3	1
1984	Paris	0	2
1992	Wembley	2	0
1992	Malmo (EC)	0	0
1997	Montpellier (TF)	1	0
1999	Wembley	0	2
2000	Paris	1	1
2004	Lisbon (EC)	1	2
2008	Paris	0	1
2010	Wembley	1	2
2012	Donetsk (EC)	1	1

v GEORGIA

		E	G
1996	Tbilisi (WC)	2	0
1997	Wembley (WC)	2	0

v GERMANY/WEST GERMANY

		E	G
1930	Berlin	3	3
1935	White Hart Lane	3	0
1938	Berlin	6	3
1954	Wembley	3	1
1956	Berlin	3	1
1965	Nuremberg	1	0
1966	Wembley	1	0
1966	Wembley (WCF)	4	2
1968	Hanover	0	1
1970	Leon (WC)	2	3
1972	Wembley (EC)	1	3
1972	Berlin (EC)	0	0
1975	Wembley	2	0
1978	Munich	1	2
1982	Madrid (WC)	0	0
1982	Wembley	1	2
1985	Mexico City	3	0
1987	Dusseldorf	1	3
1990*	Turin (WC)	1	1
1991	Wembley	0	1
1993	Detroit	1	2
1996†	Wembley (EC)	1	1
2000	Charleroi (EC)	1	0
2000	Wembley (WC)	0	1
2001	Munich (WC)	5	1
2007	Wembley	1	2
2008	Berlin	2	1
2010	Bloemfontein (WC)	1	4
2012	Donetsk (EC)	1	1
2013	Wembley	0	1

(*England lost 3-4 on pens)
(† England lost 5-6 on pens)

v GHANA

		E	G
2011	Wembley	1	1

v GREECE

		E	G
1971	Wembley (EC)	3	0
1971	Athens (EC)	2	0
1982	Salonika (EC)	3	0
1983	Wembley (EC)	0	0
1989	Athens	2	1
1994	Wembley	5	0
2001	Athens (WC)	2	0
2001	Old Trafford (WC)	2	2
2006	Old Trafford	4	0

v HOLLAND

		E	H
1935	Amsterdam	1	0
1946	Huddersfield	8	2
1964	Amsterdam	1	1
1969	Amsterdam	1	0
1970	Wembley	0	0
1977	Wembley	0	2
1982	Wembley	2	0
1988	Wembley	2	2
1988	Dusseldorf (EC)	1	3
1990	Cagliari (WC)	0	0
1993	Wembley (WC)	2	2
1993	Rotterdam (WC)	0	2
1996	Wembley (EC)	4	1
2001	White Hart Lane	0	2
2002	Amsterdam	1	1
2005	Villa Park	0	0
2006	Amsterdam	1	1

| 2009 | Amsterdam | 2 | 2 |
| 2012 | Wembley | 2 | 3 |

v HONDURAS

		E	H
2014	Miami	0	0

v HUNGARY

		E	H
1908	Budapest	7	0
1909	Budapest	4	2
1909	Budapest	8	2
1934	Budapest	1	2
1936	Highbury	6	2
1953	Wembley	3	6
1954	Budapest	1	7
1960	Budapest	0	2
1962	Rancagua (WC)	1	2
1965	Wembley	1	0
1978	Wembley	4	1
1981	Budapest (WC)	3	1
1981	Wembley (WC)	1	0
1983	Wembley (EC)	2	0
1983	Budapest (EC)	3	0
1988	Budapest	0	0
1990	Wembley	1	0
1992	Budapest	1	0
1996	Wembley	3	0
1999	Budapest	1	1
2006	Old Trafford	3	1
2010	Wembley	2	1

v ICELAND

		E	I
1982	Reykjavik	1	1
2004	City of Manchester	6	1

v ISRAEL

		E	I
1986	Tel Aviv	2	1
1988	Tel Aviv	0	0
2006	Tel Aviv (EC)	0	0
2007	Wembley (EC)	3	0

v ITALY

		E	I
1933	Rome	1	1
1934	Highbury	3	2
1939	Milan	2	2
1948	Turin	4	0
1949	White Hart Lane	2	0
1952	Florence	1	1
1959	Wembley	2	2
1961	Rome	3	2
1973	Turin	0	2
1973	Wembley	0	1
1976	New York	3	2
1976	Rome (WC)	0	2
1977	Wembley (WC)	2	0
1980	Turin (EC)	0	1
1985	Mexico City	1	2
1989	Wembley	0	0
1990	Bari (WC)	1	2
1996	Wembley (WC)	0	1
1997	Nantes (TF)	2	0
1997	Rome (WC)	0	0
2000	Turin	0	1
2002	Leeds	1	2
2012*	Kiev (EC)	0	0
2012	Berne	2	1
2014	Manaus (WC)	1	2
2015	Turin	1	1

(*England lost 2-4 on pens)

v JAMAICA

		E	J
2006	Old Trafford	6	0

v JAPAN

		E	J
1995	Wembley	2	1
2004	City of Manchester	1	1
2010	Graz	2	1

v KAZAKHSTAN

		E	K
2008	Wembley (WC)	5	1
2009	Almaty (WC)	4	0

v KUWAIT

		E	K
1982	Bilbao (WC)	1	0

v LIECHTENSTEIN

		E	L
2003	Vaduz (EC)	2	0
2003	Old Trafford (EC)	2	0

v LITHUANIA

		E	L
2015	Wembley (EC)	4	0

v LUXEMBOURG

		E	L
1927	Luxembourg	5	2
1960	Luxembourg (WC)	9	0
1961	Highbury (WC)	4	1
1977	Wembley (WC)	5	0
1977	Luxembourg (WC)	2	0
1982	Wembley (EC)	9	0
1983	Luxembourg (EC)	4	0
1998	Luxembourg (EC)	3	0
1999	Wembley (EC)	6	0

v MACEDONIA

		E	M
2002	Southampton (EC)	2	2
2003	Skopje (EC)	2	1
2006	Skopje (EC)	1	0
2006	Old Trafford (EC)	0	0

v MALAYSIA

		E	M
1991	Kuala Lumpur	4	2

v MALTA

		E	M
1971	Valletta (EC)	1	0
1971	Wembley (EC)	5	0
2000	Valletta	2	1

v MEXICO

		E	M
1959	Mexico City	1	2
1961	Wembley	8	0
1966	Wembley (WC)	2	0
1969	Mexico City	0	0
1985	Mexico City	0	1
1986	Los Angeles	3	0

		E	M
1997	Wembley	2	0
2001	Derby	4	0
2010	Wembley	3	1

v MOLDOVA

		E	M
1996	Kishinev	3	0
1997	Wembley (WC)	4	0
2012	Chisinu (WC)	5	0
2013	Wembley (WC)	4	0

v MONTENEGRO

		E	M
2010	Wembley (EC)	0	0
2011	Podgorica (EC)	2	2
2013	Podgorica (WC)	1	1
2013	Wembley (WC)	4	1

v MOROCCO

		E	M
1986	Monterrey (WC)	0	0
1998	Casablanca	1	0

v NEW ZEALAND

		E	NZ
1991	Auckland	1	0
1991	Wellington	2	0

v NIGERIA

		E	NZ
1994	Wembley	1	0
2002	Osaka (WC)	0	0

v NORWAY

		E	NZ
1937	Oslo	6	0
1938	Newcastle	4	0
1949	Oslo	4	1
1966	Oslo	6	1
1980	Wembley (WC)	4	0
1981	Oslo (WC)	1	2
1992	Wembley (WC)	1	1
1993	Oslo (WC)	0	2
1994	Wembley	0	0
1995	Oslo	0	0
2012	Oslo	1	0
2014	Wembley	1	0

v PARAGUAY

		E	P
1986	Mexico City (WC)	3	0
2002	Anfield	4	0
2006	Frankfurt (WC)	1	0

v PERU

		E	P
1959	Lima	1	4
1961	Lima	4	0
2014	Wembley	3	0

v POLAND

		E	P
1966	Goodison Park	1	1
1966	Chorzow	1	0
1973	Chorzow (WC)	0	2
1973	Wembley (WC)	1	1
1986	Monterrey (WC)	3	0
1989	Wembley (WC)	3	0
1989	Katowice (WC)	0	0
1990	Wembley (EC)	2	0
1991	Poznan (EC)	1	1
1993	Chorzow (WC)	1	1
1993	Wembley (WC)	3	0
1996	Wembley (WC)	2	1
1997	Katowice (WC)	2	0
1999	Wembley (EC)	3	1
1999	Warsaw (EC)	0	0
2004	Katowice (WC)	2	1
2005	Old Trafford (WC)	2	1
2012	Warsaw (WC)	1	1
2013	Wembley (WC)	2	0

v PORTUGAL

		E	P
1947	Lisbon	10	0
1950	Lisbon	5	3
1951	Goodison Park	5	2
1955	Oporto	1	3
1958	Wembley	2	1
1961	Lisbon (WC)	1	1
1961	Wembley (WC)	2	0
1964	Lisbon	4	3
1964	Sao Paulo	1	1
1966	Wembley (WC)	2	1
1969	Wembley	1	0
1974	Lisbon	0	0
1974	Wembley (EC)	0	0
1975	Lisbon (EC)	1	1
1986	Monterrey (WC)	0	1
1995	Wembley	1	1
1998	Wembley	3	0
2000	Eindhoven (EC)	2	3
2002	Villa Park	1	1
2004	Faro	1	1
2004*	Lisbon (EC)	2	2
2006†	Gelsenkirchen (WC)	0	0

(† England lost 1–3 on pens)
(*England lost 5–6 on pens)

v REPUBLIC OF IRELAND

		E	RoI
1946	Dublin	1	0
1949	Goodison Park	0	2
1957	Wembley (WC)	5	1
1957	Dublin (WC)	1	1
1964	Dublin	3	1
1977	Wembley	1	1
1978	Dublin (EC)	1	1
1980	Wembley (EC)	2	0
1985	Wembley	2	1
1988	Stuttgart (EC)	1	1
1990	Cagliari (WC)	1	1
1990	Dublin (EC)	1	1
1991	Wembley (EC)	1	1
1995*	Dublin	0	1
2013	Wembley	1	1
2015	Dublin	0	0

(*Abandoned 27 mins – crowd riot)

v ROMANIA

		E	R
1939	Bucharest	2	0
1968	Bucharest	0	0
1969	Wembley	1	1
1970	Guadalajara (WC)	1	0
1980	Bucharest (WC)	1	2

1981	Wembley (WC)	0	0
1985	Bucharest (WC)	0	0
1985	Wembley (WC)	1	1
1994	Wembley	1	1
1998	Toulouse (WC)	1	2
2000	Charleroi (EC)	2	3

v RUSSIA

		E	R
2007	Wembley (EC)	3	0
2007	Moscow (EC)	1	2

v SAN MARINO

		E	SM
1992	Wembley (WC)	6	0
1993	Bologna (WC)	7	1
2012	Wembley (WC)	5	0
2013	Serravalle (WC)	8	0
2014	Wembley (EC)	5	0

v SAUDI ARABIA

		E	SA
1988	Riyadh	1	1
1998	Wembley	0	0

v SERBIA-MONTENEGRO

		E	S-M
2003	Leicester	2	1

v SLOVAKIA

		E	S
2002	Bratislava (EC)	2	1
2003	Middlesbrough (EC)	2	1
2009	Wembley	4	0

v SLOVENIA

		E	S
2009	Wembley	2	1
2010	Port Elizabeth (WC)	1	0
2014	Wembley (EC)	3	1
2015	Ljubljana (EC)	3	2

v SOUTH AFRICA

		E	SA
1997	Old Trafford	2	1
2003	Durban	2	1

v SOUTH KOREA

		E	SK
2002	Seoguipo	1	1

v SOVIET UNION (see also CIS)

		E	SU
1958	Moscow	1	1
1958	Gothenburg (WC)	2	2
1958	Gothenburg (WC)	0	0
1958	Wembley	5	0
1967	Wembley	2	2
1968	Rome (EC)	2	0
1973	Moscow	2	1
1984	Wembley	0	2
1986	Tbilisi	1	0
1988	Frankfurt (EC)	1	3
1991	Wembley	3	1

v SPAIN

		E	S
1929	Madrid	3	4
1931	Highbury	7	1
1950	Rio de Janeiro (WC)	0	1
1955	Madrid	1	1
1955	Wembley	4	1
1960	Madrid	0	3
1960	Wembley	4	2
1965	Madrid	2	0
1967	Wembley	2	0
1968	Wembley (EC)	1	0
1968	Madrid (EC)	2	1
1980	Barcelona	2	0
1980	Naples (EC)	2	1
1981	Wembley	1	2
1982	Madrid (WC)	0	0
1987	Madrid	4	2
1992	Santander	0	1
1996*	Wembley (EC)	0	0
2001	Villa Park	3	0
2004	Madrid	0	1
2007	Old Trafford	0	1
2009	Seville	0	2
2011	Wembley	1	0

(*England won 4-2 on pens)

v SWEDEN

		E	S
1923	Stockholm	4	2
1923	Stockholm	3	1
1937	Stockholm	4	0
1948	Highbury	4	2
1949	Stockholm	1	3
1956	Stockholm	0	0
1959	Wembley	2	3
1965	Gothenburg	2	1
1968	Wembley	3	1
1979	Stockholm	0	0
1986	Stockholm	0	1
1988	Wembley (WC)	0	0
1989	Stockholm (WC)	0	0
1992	Stockholm (EC)	1	2
1995	Leeds	3	3
1998	Stockholm (EC)	1	2
1999	Wembley (EC)	0	0
2001	Old Trafford	1	1
2002	Saitama (WC)	1	1
2004	Gothenburg	0	1
2006	Cologne (WC)	2	2
2011	Wembley	1	0
2012	Kiev (EC)	3	2
2012	Stockholm	2	4

v SWITZERLAND

		E	S
1933	Berne	4	0
1938	Zurich	1	2
1947	Zurich	0	1
1949	Highbury	6	0
1952	Zurich	3	0
1954	Berne (WC)	2	0
1962	Wembley	3	1
1963	Basle	8	1
1971	Basle (EC)	3	2
1971	Wembley (EC)	1	1
1975	Basle	2	1
1977	Wembley	0	0
1980	Wembley (WC)	2	1
1981	Basle (WC)	1	2
1988	Lausanne	1	0

1995	Wembley	3	1
1996	Wembley (EC)	1	1
1998	Berne	1	1
2004	Coimbra (EC)	3	0
2008	Wembley	2	1
2010	Basle (EC)	3	1
2011	Wembley (EC)	2	2
2014	Basle (EC)	2	0

v TRINIDAD & TOBAGO

		E	T
2006	Nuremberg (WC)	2	0
2008	Port of Spain	3	0

v TUNISIA

		E	T
1990	Tunis	1	1
1998	Marseille (WC)	2	0

v TURKEY

		E	T
1984	Istanbul (WC)	8	0
1985	Wembley (WC)	5	0
1987	Izmir (EC)	0	0
1987	Wembley (EC)	8	0
1991	Izmir (EC)	1	0
1991	Wembley (EC)	1	0
1992	Wembley (WC)	4	0
1993	Izmir (WC)	2	0
2003	Sunderland (EC)	2	0
2003	Istanbul (EC)	0	0

v UKRAINE

		E	U
2000	Wembley	2	0
2004	Newcastle	3	0
2009	Wembley (WC)	2	1
2009	Dnipropetrovski (WC)	0	1
2012	Donetsk (EC)	1	0
2012	Wembley (EC)	1	1
2013	Kiev (WC)	0	0

v URUGUAY

		E	U
1953	Montevideo	1	2
1954	Basle (WC)	2	4
1964	Wembley	2	1
1966	Wembley (WC)	0	0
1969	Montevideo	2	1
1977	Montevideo	0	0
1984	Montevideo	0	2
1990	Wembley	1	2
1995	Wembley	0	0
2006	Anfield	2	1
2014	Sao Paulo (WC)	1	2

v USA

		E	USA
1950	Belo Horizonte (WC)	0	1
1953	New York	6	3
1959	Los Angeles	8	1
1964	New York	10	0
1985	Los Angeles	5	0
1993	Boston	0	2
1994	Wembley	2	0
2005	Chicago	2	1
2008	Wembley	2	0
2010	Rustenburg (WC)	1	1

v YUGOSLAVIA

		E	Y
1939	Belgrade	1	2
1950	Highbury	2	2
1954	Belgrade	0	1
1956	Wembley	3	0
1958	Belgrade	0	5
1960	Wembley	3	3
1965	Belgrade	1	1
1966	Wembley	2	0
1968	Florence (EC)	0	1
1972	Wembley	1	1
1974	Belgrade	2	2

ENGLAND'S RECORD

England's first international was a 0-0 draw against Scotland in Glasgow, on the West of Scotland cricket ground, Partick, on November 30, 1872 Their complete record at the start of 2014–15 is:

P	W	D	L	F	A
944	535	231	178	2083	938

ENGLAND'S 'B' TEAM RESULTS

England scores first

1986	Wembley (EC)	2	0	1995	Leeds	3	3
1987	Belgrade (EC)	4	1	1998	Stockholm (EC)	1	2
1989	Wembley	2	1	1999	Wembley (EC)	0	0
1937	Stockholm	4	0	2001	Old Trafford	1	1
1948	Highbury	4	2	2002	Saitama (WC)	1	1
1949	Stockholm	1	3	2004	Gothenburg	0	1
1956	Stockholm	0	0	2006	Cologne (WC)	2	2
1959	Wembley	2	3	1949	Finland (A)	4	0
1965	Gothenburg	2	1	1949	Holland (A)	4	0
1968	Wembley	3	1	1950	Italy (A)	0	5
1979	Stockholm	0	0	1950	Holland (H)	1	0
1986	Stockholm	0	1	1950	Holland (A)	0	3
1988	Wembley (WC)	0	0	1950	Luxembourg (A)	2	1
1989	Stockholm (WC)	0	0	1950	Switzerland (H)	5	0
1992	Stockholm (EC)	1	2	1952	Holland (A)	1	0

1952	France (A)	1	7
1953	Scotland (A)	2	2
1954	Scotland (H)	1	1
1954	Germany (A)	4	0
1954	Yugoslavia (A)	1	2
1954	Switzerland (A)	0	2
1955	Germany (H)	1	1
1955	Yugoslavia (H)	5	1
1956	Switzerland (H)	4	1
1956	Scotland (A)	2	2
1957	Scotland (H)	4	1
1978	W Germany (A)	2	1
1978	Czechoslovakia (A)	1	0
1978	Singapore (A)	8	0
1978	Malaysia (A)	1	1
1978	N Zealand (A)	4	0
1978	N Zealand (A)	3	1
1978	N Zealand (A)	4	0
1979	Austria (A)	1	0
1979	N Zealand (H)	4	1
1980	USA (H)	1	0
1980	Spain (H)	1	0
1980	Australia (H)	1	0
1981	Spain (A)	2	3
1984	N Zealand (H)	2	0
1987	Malta (A)	2	0
1989	Switzerland (A)	2	0
1989	Iceland (A) .	2	0
1989	Norway (A)	1	0
1989	Italy (H)	1	1
1989	Yugoslavia (H)	2	1
1990	Rep of Ireland (A)	1	4
1990	Czechoslovakia (H)	2	0
1990	Algeria (A)	0	0
1991	Wales (A)	1	0
1991	Iceland (H)	1	0
1991	Switzerland (H)	2	1
1991	Spanish XI (A)	1	0
1992	France (A)	3	0
1992	Czechoslovakia (A)	1	0
1992	CIS (A)	1	1
1994	N Ireland (H)	4	2
1995	Rep of Ireland (H)	2	0
1998	Chile (H)	1	2
1998	Russia (H)	4	1
2006	Belarus (H)	1	2
2007	Albania	3	1

GREAT BRITAIN v REST OF EUROPE (FIFA)

		GB	RofE				GB	RofE
1947	Glasgow	6	1		1955	Belfast	1	4

SCOTLAND

v ARGENTINA

		S	A
1977	Buenos Aires	1	1
1979	Glasgow	1	3
1990	Glasgow	1	0
2008	Glasgow	0	1

v AUSTRALIA

		S	A
1985*	Glasgow (WC)	2	0
1985*	Melbourne (WC)	0	0
1996	Glasgow	1	0
2000	Glasgow	0	2
2012	Edinburgh	3	1
(* World Cup play-off)			

v AUSTRIA

		S	A
1931	Vienna	0	5
1933	Glasgow	2	2
1937	Vienna	1	1
1950	Glasgow	0	1
1951	Vienna	0	4
1954	Zurich (WC)	0	1
1955	Vienna	4	1
1956	Glasgow	1	1
1960	Vienna	1	4
1963*	Glasgow	4	1
1968	Glasgow (WC)	2	1
1969	Vienna (WC)	0	2
1978	Vienna (EC)	2	3
1979	Glasgow (EC)	1	1
1994	Vienna	2	1
1996	Vienna (WC)	0	0
1997	Glasgow (WC)	2	0
(* Abandoned after 79 minutes)			
2003	Glasgow	0	2
2005	Graz	2	2
2007	Vienna	1	0

v BELARUS

		S	B
1997	Minsk (WC)	1	0
1997	Aberdeen (WC)	4	1
2005	Minsk (WC)	0	0
2005	Glasgow (WC)	0	1

v BELGIUM

		S	B
1947	Brussels	1	2
1948	Glasgow	2	0
1951	Brussels	5	0
1971	Liege (EC)	0	3
1971	Aberdeen (EC)	1	0
1974	Brugge	1	2
1979	Brussels (EC)	0	2
1979	Glasgow (EC)	1	3
1982	Brussels (EC)	2	3
1983	Glasgow (EC)	1	1
1987	Brussels (EC)	1	4
1987	Glasgow (EC)	2	0
2001	Glasgow (WC)	2	2
2001	Brussels (WC)	0	2

| 2012 | Brussels (WC) | 0 | 2 |
| 2013 | Glasgow (WC) | 0 | 2 |

v BOSNIA

		S	B
1999	Sarajevo (EC)	2	1
1999	Glasgow (EC)	1	0

v BRAZIL

		S	B
1966	Glasgow	1	1
1972	Rio de Janeiro	0	1
1973	Glasgow	0	1
1974	Frankfurt (WC)	0	0
1977	Rio de Janeiro	0	2
1982	Seville (WC)	1	4
1987	Glasgow	0	2
1990	Turin (WC)	0	1
1998	St Denis (WC)	1	2
2011	Arsenal	0	2

v BULGARIA

		S	B
1978	Glasgow	2	1
1986	Glasgow (EC)	0	0
1987	Sofia (EC)	1	0
1990	Sofia (EC)	1	1
1991	Glasgow (EC)	1	1
2006	Kobe	5	1

v CANADA

		S	C
1983	Vancouver	2	0
1983	Edmonton	3	0
1983	Toronto	2	0
1992	Toronto	3	1
2002	Edinburgh	3	1

v CHILE

		S	C
1977	Santiago	4	2
1989	Glasgow	2	0

v CIS (formerly Soviet Union)

		S	C
1992	Norrkoping (EC)	3	0

v COLOMBIA

		S	C
1988	Glasgow	0	0
1996	Miami	0	1
1998	New York	2	2

v COSTA RICA

		S	C
1990	Genoa (WC)	0	1

v CROATIA

		S	C
2000	Zagreb (WC)	1	1
2001	Glasgow (WC)	0	0
2008	Glasgow	1	1
2013	Zagreb (WC)	1	0
2013	Glasgow (WC)	2	0

v CYPRUS

		S	C
1968	Nicosia (WC)	5	0
1969	Glasgow (WC)	8	0
1989	Limassol (WC)	3	2
1989	Glasgow (WC)	2	1

| 2011 | Larnaca | 2 | 1 |

v CZECH REPUBLIC

		S	C
1999	Glasgow (EC)	1	2
1999	Prague (EC)	2	3
2008	Prague	1	3
2010	Glasgow	1	0
2010	Prague (EC)	0	1
2011	Glasgow (EC)	2	2

v CZECHOSLOVAKIA

		S	C
1937	Prague	3	1
1937	Glasgow	5	0
1961	Bratislava (WC)	0	4
1961	Glasgow (WC)	3	2
1961*	Brussels (WC)	2	4
1972	Porto Alegre	0	0
1973	Glasgow (WC)	2	1
1973	Bratislava (WC)	0	1
1976	Prague (WC)	0	2
1977	Glasgow (WC)	3	1

(*World Cup play-off)

v DENMARK

		S	D
1951	Glasgow	3	1
1952	Copenhagen	2	1
1968	Copenhagen	1	0
1970	Glasgow (EC)	1	0
1971	Copenhagen (EC)	0	1
1972	Copenhagen (WC)	4	1
1972	Glasgow (WC)	2	0
1975	Copenhagen (EC)	1	0
1975	Glasgow (EC)	3	1
1986	Neza (WC)	0	1
1996	Copenhagen	0	2
1998	Glasgow	0	1
2002	Glasgow	0	1
2004	Copenhagen	0	1
2011	Glasgow	2	1

v EAST GERMANY

		S	EG
1974	Glasgow	3	0
1977	East Berlin	0	1
1982	Glasgow (EC)	2	0
1983	Halle (EC)	1	2
1986	Glasgow	0	0
1990	Glasgow	0	1

v ECUADOR

		S	E
1995	Toyama, Japan	2	1

v EGYPT

		S	E
1990	Aberdeen	1	3

v ESTONIA

		S	E
1993	Tallinn (WC)	3	0
1993	Aberdeen	3	1
1996	Tallinn (WC)	*No result	
1997	Monaco (WC)	0	0
1997	Kilmarnock (WC)	2	0
1998	Edinburgh (EC)	3	2
1999	Tallinn (EC)	0	0

(* Estonia absent)

| 2004 | Tallinn | 1 | 0 |
| 2013 | Aberdeen | 1 | 0 |

v FAROE ISLANDS

		S	F
1994	Glasgow (EC)	5	1
1995	Toftir (EC)	2	0
1998	Aberdeen (EC)	2	1
1999	Toftir (EC)	1	1
2002	Toftir (EC)	2	2
2003	Glasgow (EC)	3	1
2006	Glasgow (EC)	6	0
2007	Toftir (EC)	2	0
2010	Aberdeen	3	0

v FINLAND

		S	F
1954	Helsinki	2	1
1964	Glasgow (WC)	3	1
1965	Helsinki (WC)	2	1
1976	Glasgow	6	0
1992	Glasgow	1	1
1994	Helsinki (EC)	2	0
1995	Glasgow (EC)	1	0
1998	Edinburgh	1	1

v FRANCE

		S	F
1930	Paris	2	0
1932	Paris	3	1
1948	Paris	0	3
1949	Glasgow	2	0
1950	Paris	1	0
1951	Glasgow	1	0
1958	Orebro (WC)	1	2
1984	Marseilles	0	2
1989	Glasgow (WC)	2	0
1990	Paris (WC)	0	3
1997	St Etienne	1	2
2000	Glasgow	0	2
2002	Paris	0	5
2006	Glasgow (EC)	1	0
2007	Paris (EC)	1	0

v GEORGIA

		S	G
2007	Glasgow (EC)	2	1
2007	Tbilisi (EC)	0	2
2014	Glasgow (EC)	1	0

v GERMANY/WEST GERMANY

		S	G
1929	Berlin	1	1
1936	Glasgow	2	0
1957	Stuttgart	3	1
1959	Glasgow	3	2
1964	Hanover	2	2
1969	Glasgow (WC)	1	1
1969	Hamburg (WC)	2	3
1973	Glasgow	1	1
1974	Frankfurt	1	2
1986	Queretaro (WC)	1	2
1992	Norrkoping (EC)	0	2
1993	Glasgow	0	1
1999	Bremen	1	0
2003	Glasgow (EC)	1	1
2003	Dortmund (EC)	1	2

| 2014 | Dortmund (EC) | 1 | 2 |

v GIBRALTAR

		S	G
2015	Glasgow (EC)	6	1

v GREECE

		S	G
1994	Athens (EC)	0	1
1995	Glasgow	1	0

v HOLLAND

		S	H
1929	Amsterdam	2	0
1938	Amsterdam	3	1
1959	Amsterdam	2	1
1966	Glasgow	0	3
1968	Amsterdam	0	0
1971	Amsterdam	1	2
1978	Mendoza (WC)	3	2
1982	Glasgow	2	1
1986	Eindhoven	0	0
1992	Gothenburg (EC)	0	1
1994	Glasgow	0	1
1994	Utrecht	1	3
1996	Birmingham (EC)	0	0
2000	Arnhem	0	0
2003*	Glasgow (EC)	1	0
2003*	Amsterdam (EC)	0	6
2009	Amsterdam (WC)	0	3
2009	Glasgow (WC)	0	1

(*Qual Round play-off)

v HUNGARY

		S	H
1938	Glasgow	3	1
1955	Glasgow	2	4
1955	Budapest	1	3
1958	Glasgow	1	1
1960	Budapest	3	3
1980	Budapest	1	3
1987	Glasgow	2	0
2004	Glasgow	0	3

v ICELAND

		S	I
1984	Glasgow (WC)	3	0
1985	Reykjavik (WC)	1	0
2002	Reykjavik (EC)	2	0
2003	Glasgow (EC)	2	1
2008	Reykjavik (WC)	2	1
2009	Glasgow (WC)	2	1

v IRAN

		S	I
1978	Cordoba (WC)	1	1

v ISRAEL

		S	I
1981	Tel Aviv (WC)	1	0
1981	Glasgow (WC)	3	1
1986	Tel Aviv	1	0

v ITALY

		S	I
1931	Rome	0	3
1965	Glasgow (WC)	1	0
1965	Naples (WC)	0	3
1988	Perugia	0	2

		S	
1992	Glasgow (WC)	0	0
1993	Rome (WC)	1	3
2005	Milan (WC)	0	2
2005	Glasgow (WC)	1	1
2007	Bari (EC)	0	2
2007	Glasgow (EC)	1	2

v JAPAN

		S	J
1995	Hiroshima	0	0
2006	Saitama	0	0
2009	Yokohama	0	2

v LATVIA

		S	L
1996	Riga (WC)	2	0
1997	Glasgow (WC)	2	0
2000	Riga (WC)	1	0
2001	Glasgow (WC)	2	1

v LIECHTENSTEIN

		S	L
2010	Glasgow (EC)	2	1
2011	Vaduz (EC)	1	0

v LITHUANIA

		S	L
1998	Vilnius (EC)	0	0
1999	Glasgow (EC)	3	0
2003	Kaunus (EC)	0	1
2003	Glasgow (EC)	1	0
2006	Kaunas (EC)	2	1
2007	Glasgow (EC)	3	1
2010	Kaunas (EC)	0	0
2011	Glasgow (EC)	1	0

v LUXEMBOURG

		S	L
1947	Luxembourg	6	0
1986	Glasgow (EC)	3	0
1987	Esch (EC)	0	0
2012	Josy Barthel	2	1

v MACEDONIA

		S	M
2008	Skopje (WC)	0	1
2009	Glasgow (WC)	2	0
2012	Glasgow (WC)	1	1
2013	Skopje (WC)	2	1

v MALTA

		S	M
1988	Valletta	1	1
1990	Valletta	2	1
1993	Glasgow (WC)	3	0
1993	Valletta (WC)	2	0
1997	Valletta	3	2

v MOLDOVA

		S	M
2004	Chisinau (WC)	1	1
2005	Glasgow (WC)	2	0

v MOROCCO

		S	M
1998	St Etienne (WC)	0	3

v NEW ZEALAND

		S	NZ
1982	Malaga (WC)	5	2
2003	Edinburgh	1	1

v NIGERIA

		S	N
2002	Aberdeen	1	2
2014	Fulham	2	2

v NORWAY

		S	N
1929	Bergen	7	3
1954	Glasgow	1	0
1954	Oslo	1	1
1963	Bergen	3	4
1963	Glasgow	6	1
1974	Oslo	2	1
1978	Glasgow (EC)	3	2
1979	Oslo (EC)	4	0
1988	Oslo (WC)	2	1
1989	Glasgow (WC)	1	1
1992	Oslo	0	0
1998	Bordeaux (WC)	1	1
2003	Oslo	0	0
2004	Glasgow (WC)	0	1
2005	Oslo (WC)	2	1
2008	Glasgow (WC)	0	0
2009	Oslo (WC)	0	4
2013	Molde	1	0

v PARAGUAY

		S	P
1958	Norrkoping (WC)	2	3

v PERU

		S	P
1972	Glasgow	2	0
1978	Cordoba (WC)	1	3
1979	Glasgow	1	1

v POLAND

		S	P
1958	Warsaw	2	1
1960	Glasgow	2	3
1965	Chorzow (WC)	1	1
1965	Glasgow (WC)	1	2
1980	Poznan	0	1
1990	Glasgow	1	1
2001	Bydgoszcz	1	1
2014	Warsaw	1	0
2014	Warsaw (EC)	2	2

v PORTUGAL

		S	P
1950	Lisbon	2	2
1955	Glasgow	3	0
1959	Lisbon	0	1
1966	Glasgow	0	1
1971	Lisbon (EC)	0	2
1971	Glasgow (EC)	2	1
1975	Glasgow	1	0
1978	Lisbon (EC)	0	1
1980	Glasgow (EC)	4	1
1980	Glasgow (WC)	0	0
1981	Lisbon (WC)	1	2
1992	Glasgow (WC)	0	0
1993	Lisbon (WC)	0	5
2002	Braga	0	2

v QATAR

		S	Q
2015	Edinburgh	1	0

v REPUBLIC OF IRELAND

		S	RoI
1961	Glasgow (WC)	4	1
1961	Dublin (WC)	3	0
1963	Dublin	0	1
1969	Dublin	1	1
1986	Dublin (EC)	0	0
1987	Glasgow (EC)	0	1
2000	Dublin	2	1
2003	Glasgow (EC)	0	2
2011	Dublin (CC)	0	1
2014	Glasgow (EC)	1	0
2015	Dublin (EC)	1	1

v ROMANIA

		S	R
1975	Bucharest (EC)	1	1
1975	Glasgow (EC)	1	1
1986	Glasgow	3	0
1990	Glasgow (EC)	2	1
1991	Bucharest (EC)	0	1
2004	Glasgow	1	2

v RUSSIA

		S	R
1994	Glasgow (EC)	1	1
1995	Moscow (EC)	0	0

v SAN MARINO

		S	SM
1991	Serravalle (EC)	2	0
1991	Glasgow (EC)	4	0
1995	Serravalle (EC)	2	0
1995	Glasgow (EC)	5	0
2000	Serravalle (WC)	2	0
2001	Glasgow (WC)	4	0

v SAUDI ARABIA

		S	SA
1988	Riyadh	2	2

v SERBIA

		S	Se
2012	Glasgow (WC)	0	0
2013	Novi Sad (WC)	0	2

v SLOVENIA

		S	SL
2004	Glasgow (WC)	0	0
2005	Celje (WC)	3	0
2012	Koper	1	1

v SOUTH AFRICA

		S	SA
2002	Hong Kong	0	2
2007	Aberdeen	1	0

v SOUTH KOREA

		S	SK
2002	Busan	1	4

v SOVIET UNION (see also CIS and RUSSIA)

		S	SU
1967	Glasgow	0	2
1971	Moscow	0	1
1982	Malaga (WC)	2	2
1991	Glasgow	0	1

v SPAIN

		S	Sp
1957	Glasgow (WC)	4	2
1957	Madrid (WC)	1	4
1963	Madrid	6	2
1965	Glasgow	0	0
1975	Glasgow (EC)	1	2
1975	Valencia (EC)	1	1
1982	Valencia	0	3
1985	Glasgow (WC)	3	1
1985	Seville (WC)	0	1
1988	Madrid	0	0
2004*	Valencia	1	1

(*Abandoned after 59 mins – floodlight failure)

		S	Sp
2010	Glasgow (EC)	2	3
2011	Alicante (EC)	1	3

v SWEDEN

		S	Swe
1952	Stockholm	1	3
1953	Glasgow	1	2
1975	Gothenburg	1	1
1977	Glasgow	3	1
1980	Stockholm (WC)	1	0
1981	Glasgow (WC)	2	0
1990	Genoa (WC)	2	1
1995	Solna	0	2
1996	Glasgow (WC)	1	0
1997	Gothenburg (WC)	1	2
2004	Edinburgh	1	4
2010	Stockholm	0	3

v SWITZERLAND

		S	Sw
1931	Geneva	3	2
1948	Berne	1	2
1950	Glasgow	3	1
1957	Basle (WC)	2	1
1957	Glasgow (WC)	3	2
1973	Berne	0	1
1976	Glasgow	1	0
1982	Berne (EC)	0	2
1983	Glasgow (EC)	2	2
1990	Glasgow (EC)	2	1
1991	Berne (EC)	2	2
1992	Berne (WC)	1	3
1993	Aberdeen (WC)	1	1
1996	Birmingham (EC)	1	0
2006	Glasgow	1	3

v TRINIDAD & TOBAGO

		S	T
2004	Hibernian	4	1

v TURKEY

		S	T
1960	Ankara	2	4

v UKRAINE

		S	U
2006	Kiev (EC)	0	2
2007	Glasgow (EC)	3	1

v USA

		S	USA
1952	Glasgow	6	0
1992	Denver	1	0
1996	New Britain, Conn	1	2
1998	Washington	0	0
2005	Glasgow	1	1
2012	Jacksonville	1	5

2013	Glasgow	0	0

v URUGUAY

		S	U
1954	Basle (WC)	0	7
1962	Glasgow	2	3
1983	Glasgow	2	0
1986	Neza (WC)	0	0

v YUGOSLAVIA

		S	Y
1955	Belgrade	2	2
1956	Glasgow	2	0

1958	Vaasteras (WC)	1	1
1972	Belo Horizonte	2	2
1974	Frankfurt (WC)	1	1
1984	Glasgow	6	1
1988	Glasgow (WC)	1	1
1989	Zagreb (WC)	1	3

v ZAIRE

		S	Z
1974	Dortmund (WC)	2	0

WALES

v ALBANIA

		W	A
1994	Cardiff (EC)	2	0
1995	Tirana (EC)	1	1

v ANDORRA

		W	A
2014	La Vella (EC)	2	1

v ARGENTINA

		W	A
1992	Gifu (Japan)	0	1
2002	Cardiff	1	1

v ARMENIA

		W	A
2001	Yerevan (WC)	2	2
2001	Cardiff (WC)	0	0

v AUSTRALIA

		W	A
2011	Cardiff	1	2

v AUSTRIA

		W	A
1954	Vienna	0	2
1955	Wrexham	1	2
1975	Vienna (EC)	1	2
1975	Wrexham (EC)	1	0
1992	Vienna	1	1
2005	Cardiff	0	2
2005	Vienna	0	1
2013	Swansea	2	1

v AZERBAIJAN

		W	A
2002	Baku (EC)	2	0
2003	Cardiff (EC)	4	0
2004	Baku (WC)	1	1
2005	Cardiff (WC)	2	0
2008	Cardiff (WC)	1	0
2009	Baku (WC)	1	0

v BELARUS

		W	B
1998	Cardiff (EC)	3	2
1999	Minsk (EC)	2	1
2000	Minsk (WC)	1	2
2001	Cardiff (WC)	1	0

v BELGIUM

		W	B
1949	Liege	1	3
1949	Cardiff	5	1
1990	Cardiff (EC)	3	1
1991	Brussels (EC)	1	1
1992	Brussels (WC)	0	2
1993	Cardiff (WC)	2	0
1997	Cardiff (WC)	1	2
1997	Brussels (WC)	2	3
2012	Cardiff (WC)	0	2
2013	Brussels (WC)	1	1
2014	Brussels (EC)	0	0
2015	Cardiff (EC)	1	0

v BOSNIA-HERZEGOVINA

		W	B-H
2003	Cardiff	2	2
2012	Llanelli	0	2
2014	Cardiff (EC)	0	0

v BRAZIL

		W	B
1958	Gothenburg (WC)	0	1
1962	Rio de Janeiro	1	3
1962	Sao Paulo	1	3
1966	Rio de Janeiro	1	3
1966	Belo Horizonte	0	1
1983	Cardiff	1	1
1991	Cardiff	1	0
1997	Brasilia	0	3
2000	Cardiff	0	3
2006	White Hart Lane	0	2

v BULGARIA

		W	B
1983	Wrexham (EC)	1	0
1983	Sofia (EC)	0	1
1994	Cardiff (EC)	0	3
1995	Sofia (EC)	1	3
2006	Swansea	0	0
2007	Bourgas	1	0
2010	Cardiff (EC)	0	1
2011	Sofia (EC)	1	0

v CANADA

		W	C
1986	Toronto	0	2
1986	Vancouver	3	0
2004	Wrexham	1	0

v CHILE

		W	C
1966	Santiago	0	2

v COSTA RICA

		W	C
1990	Cardiff	1	0
2012	Cardiff	0	1

v CROATIA

		W	C
2002	Varazdin	1	1
2010	Osijek	0	2
2012	Osijek (WC)	0	2
2013	Swansea (WC)	1	2

v CYPRUS

		W	C
1992	Limassol (WC)	1	0
1993	Cardiff (WC)	2	0
2005	Limassol	0	1
2006	Cardiff (EC)	3	1
2007	Nicosia (EC)	1	3
2014	Cardiff (EC)	2	1

v CZECHOSLOVAKIA (see also RCS)

		W	C
1957	Cardiff (WC)	1	0
1957	Prague (WC)	0	2
1971	Swansea (EC)	1	3
1971	Prague (EC)	0	1
1977	Wrexham (WC)	3	0
1977	Prague (WC)	0	1
1980	Cardiff (WC)	1	0
1981	Prague (WC)	0	2
1987	Wrexham (EC)	1	1
1987	Prague (EC)	0	2

v CZECH REPUBLIC

		W	CR
2002	Cardiff	0	0
2006	Teplice (EC)	1	2
2007	Cardiff (EC)	0	0

v DENMARK

		W	D
1964	Copenhagen (WC)	0	1
1965	Wrexham (WC)	4	2
1987	Cardiff (EC)	1	0
1987	Copenhagen (EC)	0	1
1990	Copenhagen	0	1
1998	Copenhagen (EC)	2	1
1999	Anfield	0	2
2008	Copenhagen	1	0

v EAST GERMANY

		W	EG
1957	Leipzig (WC)	1	2
1957	Cardiff (WC)	4	1
1969	Dresden (WC)	1	2
1969	Cardiff (WC)	1	3

v ESTONIA

		W	E
1994	Tallinn	2	1
2009	Llanelli	1	0

v FAROE ISLANDS

		W	FI
1992	Cardiff (WC)	6	0
1993	Toftir (WC)	3	0

v FINLAND

		W	F
1971	Helsinki (EC)	1	0
1971	Swansea (EC)	3	0
1986	Helsinki (EC)	1	1
1987	Wrexham (EC)	4	0
1988	Swansea (WC)	2	2

1989	Helsinki (WC)	0	1
2000	Cardiff	1	2
2002	Helsinki (EC)	2	0
2003	Cardiff (EC)	1	1
2009	Cardiff (WC)	0	2
2009	Helsinki (WC)	1	2
2013	Cardiff	1	1

v FRANCE

		W	F
1933	Paris	1	1
1939	Paris	1	2
1953	Paris	1	6
1982	Toulouse	1	0

v GEORGIA

		W	G
1994	Tbilisi (EC)	0	5
1995	Cardiff (EC)	0	1
2008	Swansea	1	2

v GERMANY/WEST GERMANY

		W	G
1968	Cardiff	1	1
1969	Frankfurt	1	1
1977	Cardiff	0	2
1977	Dortmund	1	1
1979	Wrexham (EC)	0	2
1979	Cologne (EC)	1	5
1989	Cardiff (WC)	0	0
1989	Cologne (WC)	1	2
1991	Cardiff (EC)	1	0
1991	Nuremberg (EC)	1	4
1995	Dusseldorf (EC)	1	1
1995	Cardiff (EC)	1	2
2002	Cardiff	1	0
2007	Cardiff (EC)	0	2
2007	Frankfurt (EC)	0	0
2008	Moenchengladbach (WC)	0	1
2009	Cardiff (WC)	0	2

v GREECE

		W	G
1964	Athens (WC)	0	2
1965	Cardiff (WC)	4	1

v HOLLAND

		W	H
1988	Amsterdam (WC)	0	1
1989	Wrexham (WC)	1	2
1992	Utrecht	0	4
1996	Cardiff (WC)	1	3
1996	Eindhoven (WC)	1	7
2008	Rotterdam	0	2
2014	Amsterdam	0	2

v HUNGARY

		W	H
1958	Sanviken (WC)	1	1
1958	Stockholm (WC)	2	1
1961	Budapest	2	3
1963	Budapest (EC)	1	3
1963	Cardiff (EC)	1	1
1974	Cardiff (EC)	2	0
1975	Budapest (EC)	2	1
1986	Cardiff	0	3
2004	Budapest	2	1
2005	Cardiff	2	0

v ICELAND

		W	I
1980	Reykjavik (WC)	4	0
1981	Swansea (WC)	2	2
1984	Reykjavik (WC)	0	1
1984	Cardiff (WC)	2	1
1991	Cardiff	1	0
2008	Reykjavik	1	0
2014	Cardiff	3	1

v IRAN

		W	I
1978	Tehran	1	0

v ISRAEL

		W	I
1958	Tel Aviv (WC)	2	0
1958	Cardiff (WC)	2	0
1984	Tel Aviv	0	0
1989	Tel Aviv	3	3
2015	Haifa (EC)	3	0

v ITALY

		W	I
1965	Florence	1	4
1968	Cardiff (WC)	0	1
1969	Rome (WC)	1	4
1988	Brescia	1	0
1996	Terni	0	3
1998	Anfield (EC)	0	2
1999	Bologna (EC)	0	4
2002	Cardiff (EC)	2	1
2003	Milan (EC)	0	4

v JAMAICA

		W	J
1998	Cardiff	0	0

v JAPAN

		W	J
1992	Matsuyama	1	0

v KUWAIT

		W	K
1977	Wrexham	0	0
1977	Kuwait City	0	0

v LATVIA

		W	L
2004	Riga	2	0

v LIECHTENSTEIN

		W	L
2006	Wrexham	4	0
2008	Cardiff (WC)	2	0
2009	Vaduz (WC)	2	0

v LUXEMBOURG

		W	L
1974	Swansea (EC)	5	0
1975	Luxembourg (EC)	3	1
1990	Luxembourg (EC)	1	0
1991	Luxembourg (EC)	1	0
2008	Luxembourg	2	0
2010	Llanelli	5	1

v MACEDONIA

		W	M
2013	Skopje (WC)	1	2
2013	Cardiff (WC)	1	0

v MALTA

		W	M
1978	Wrexham (EC)	7	0
1979	Valletta (EC)	2	0
1988	Valletta	3	2
1998	Valletta	3	0

v MEXICO

		W	M
1958	Stockholm (WC)	1	1
1962	Mexico City	1	2
2012	New York	0	2

v MOLDOVA

		W	M
1994	Kishinev (EC)	2	3
1995	Cardiff (EC)	1	0

v MONTENEGRO

		W	M
2009	Podgorica	1	2
2010	Podgorica (EC)	0	1
2011	Cardiff (EC)	2	1

v NEW ZEALAND

		W	NZ
2007	Wrexham	2	2

v NORWAY

		W	N
1982	Swansea (EC)	1	0
1983	Oslo (EC)	0	0
1984	Trondheim	0	1
1985	Wrexham	1	1
1985	Bergen	2	4
1994	Cardiff	1	3
2000	Cardiff (WC)	1	1
2001	Oslo (WC)	2	3
2004	Oslo	0	0
2008	Wrexham	3	0
2011	Cardiff	4	1

v PARAGUAY

		W	P
2006	Cardiff	0	0

v POLAND

		W	P
1973	Cardiff (WC)	2	0
1973	Katowice (WC)	0	3
1991	Radom	0	0
2000	Warsaw (WC)	0	0
2001	Cardiff (WC)	1	2
2004	Cardiff (WC)	2	3
2005	Warsaw (WC)	0	1
2009	Vila-Real (Por)	0	1

v PORTUGAL

		W	P
1949	Lisbon	2	3
1951	Cardiff	2	1
2000	Chaves	0	3

v QATAR

		W	Q
2000	Doha	1	0

v RCS (formerly Czechoslovakia)

		W	RCS
1993	Ostrava (WC)	1	1
1993	Cardiff (WC)	2	2

v REPUBLIC OF IRELAND

		W	RI
1960	Dublin	3	2
1979	Swansea	2	1
1981	Dublin	3	1
1986	Dublin	1	0
1990	Dublin	0	1
1991	Wrexham	0	3
1992	Dublin	1	0
1993	Dublin	1	2
1997	Cardiff	0	0
2007	Dublin (EC)	0	1
2007	Cardiff (EC)	2	2
2011	Dublin (CC)	0	3
2013	Cardiff	0	0

v REST OF UNITED KINGDOM

		W	UK
1951	Cardiff	3	2
1969	Cardiff	0	1

v ROMANIA

		W	R
1970	Cardiff (EC)	0	0
1971	Bucharest (EC)	0	2
1983	Wrexham	5	0
1992	Bucharest (WC)	1	5
1993	Cardiff (WC)	1	2

v RUSSIA (See also Soviet Union)

		W	R
2003*	Moscow (EC)	0	0
2003*	Cardiff (EC)	0	1
2008	Moscow (WC)	1	2
2009	Cardiff (WC)	1	3
(*Qual Round play-offs)			

v SAN MARINO

		W	SM
1996	Serravalle (WC)	5	0
1996	Cardiff (WC)	6	0
2007	Cardiff (EC)	3	0
2007	Serravalle (EC)	2	1

v SAUDI ARABIA

		W	SA
1986	Dahran	2	1

v SERBIA

		W	S
2012	Novi Sad (WC)	1	6
2013	Cardiff (WC)	0	3

v SERBIA & MONTENEGRO

		W	S
2003	Belgrade (EC)	0	1
2003	Cardiff (EC)	2	3

v SLOVAKIA

		W	S
2006	Cardiff (EC)	1	5
2007	Trnava (EC)	5	2

v SLOVENIA

		W	S
2005	Swansea	0	0

v SOVIET UNION (See also Russia)

		W	SU
1965	Moscow (WC)	1	2
1965	Cardiff (WC)	2	1

1981	Wrexham (WC)	0	0
1981	Tbilisi (WC)	0	3
1987	Swansea	0	0

v SPAIN

		W	S
1961	Cardiff (WC)	1	2
1961	Madrid (WC)	1	1
1982	Valencia	1	1
1984	Seville (WC)	0	3
1985	Wrexham (WC)	3	0

v SWEDEN

		W	S
1958	Stockholm (WC)	0	0
1988	Stockholm	1	4
1989	Wrexham	0	2
1990	Stockholm	2	4
1994	Wrexham	0	2
2010	Swansea	0	1

v SWITZERLAND

		W	S
1949	Berne	0	4
1951	Wrexham	3	2
1996	Lugano	0	2
1999	Zurich (EC)	0	2
1999	Wrexham (EC)	0	2
2010	Basle (EC)	1	4
2011	Swansea (EC)	2	0

v TRINIDAD & TOBAGO

		W	T
2006	Graz	2	1

v TUNISIA

		W	T
1998	Tunis	0	4

v TURKEY

		W	T
1978	Wrexham (EC)	1	0
1979	Izmir (EC)	0	1
1980	Cardiff (WC)	4	0
1981	Ankara (WC)	1	0
1996	Cardiff (WC)	0	0
1997	Istanbul (WC)	4	6

v UKRAINE

		W	U
2001	Cardiff (WC)	1	1
2001	Kiev (WC)	1	1

v URUGUAY

		W	U
1986	Wrexham	0	0

v USA

		W	USA
2003	San Jose	0	2

v YUGOSLAVIA

		W	Y
1953	Belgrade	2	5
1954	Cardiff	1	3
1976	Zagreb (EC)	0	2
1976	Cardiff (EC)	1	1
1982	Titograd (EC)	4	4
1983	Cardiff (EC)	1	1
1988	Swansea	1	2

NORTHERN IRELAND

v ALBANIA

		NI	A
1965	Belfast (WC)	4	1
1965	Tirana (WC)	1	1
1983	Tirana (EC)	0	0
1983	Belfast (EC)	1	0
1992	Belfast (WC)	3	0
1993	Tirana (WC)	2	1
1996	Belfast (WC)	2	0
1997	Zurich (WC)	0	1
2010	Tirana	0	1

v ALGERIA

		NI	A
1986	Guadalajara (WC)	1	1

v ARGENTINA

		NI	A
1958	Halmstad (WC)	1	3

v ARMENIA

		NI	A
1996	Belfast (WC)	1	1
1997	Yerevan (WC)	0	0
2003	Yerevan (EC)	0	1
2003	Belfast (EC)	0	1

v AUSTRALIA

		NI	A
1980	Sydney	2	1
1980	Melbourne	1	1
1980	Adelaide	2	1

v AUSTRIA

		NI	A
1982	Madrid (WC)	2	2
1982	Vienna (EC)	0	2
1983	Belfast (EC)	3	1
1990	Vienna (EC)	0	0
1991	Belfast (EC)	2	1
1994	Vienna (EC)	2	1
1995	Belfast (EC)	5	3
2004	Belfast (WC)	3	3
2005	Vienna (WC)	0	2

v AZERBAIJAN

		NI	A
2004	Baku (WC)	0	0
2005	Belfast (WC)	2	0
2012	Belfast (WC)	1	1
2013	Baku (WC)	0	2

v BARBADOS

		NI	B
2004	Bridgetown	1	1

v BELGIUM

		NI	B
1976	Liege (WC)	0	2
1977	Belfast (WC)	3	0
1997	Belfast	3	0

v BRAZIL

		NI	B
1986	Guadalajara (WC)	0	3

v BULGARIA

		NI	B
1972	Sofia (WC)	0	3
1973	Sheffield (WC)	0	0
1978	Sofia (EC)	2	0
1979	Belfast (EC)	2	0
2001	Sofia (WC)	3	4
2001	Belfast (WC)	0	1
2008	Belfast	0	1

v CANADA

		NI	C
1995	Edmonton	0	2
1999	Belfast	1	1
2005	Belfast	0	1

v CHILE

		NI	C
1989	Belfast	0	1
1995	Edmonton, Canada	0	2
2010	Chillan	0	1
2014	Valparaiso	0	2

v COLOMBIA

		NI	C
1994	Boston, USA	0	2

v CYPRUS

		NI	C
1971	Nicosia (EC)	3	0
1971	Belfast (EC)	5	0
1973	Nicosia (WC)	0	1
1973	Fulham (WC)	3	0
2002	Belfast	0	0
2014	Nicosia	0	0

v CZECHOSLOVAKIA/CZECH REP

		NI	C
1958	Halmstad (WC)	1	0
1958	Malmo (WC)	2	1
2001	Belfast (WC)	0	1
2001	Teplice (WC)	1	3
2008	Belfast (WC)	0	0
2009	Prague (WC)	0	0

v DENMARK

		NI	D
1978	Belfast (EC)	2	1
1979	Copenhagen (EC)	0	4
1986	Belfast	1	1
1990	Belfast (EC)	1	1
1991	Odense (EC)	1	2
1992	Belfast (WC)	0	1
1993	Copenhagen (WC)	0	1
2000	Belfast (WC)	1	1
2001	Copenhagen (WC)	1	1
2006	Copenhagen (EC)	0	0
2007	Belfast (EC)	2	1

v ESTONIA

		NI	E
2004	Tallinn	1	0
2006	Belfast	1	0
2011	Tallinn (EC)	1	4
2011	Belfast (EC)	1	2

v FAROE ISLANDS

		NI	FI
1991	Belfast (EC)	1	1
1991	Landskrona, Sw (EC)	5	0
2010	Toftir (EC)	1	1
2011	Belfast (EC)	4	0
2014	Belfast (EC)	2	0

v FINLAND

		NI	F
1984	Pori (WC)	0	1
1984	Belfast (WC)	2	1
1998	Belfast (EC)	1	0
1999	Helsinki (EC)	1	4
2003	Belfast	0	1
2006	Helsinki	2	1
2012	Belfast	3	3
2015	Belfast (EC)	2	1

v FRANCE

		NI	F
1951	Belfast	2	2
1952	Paris	1	3
1958	Norrkoping (WC)	0	4
1982	Paris	0	4
1982	Madrid (WC)	1	4
1986	Paris	0	0
1988	Belfast	0	0
1999	Belfast	0	1

v GEORGIA

		NI	G
2008	Belfast	4	1

v GERMANY/WEST GERMANY

		NI	G
1958	Malmo (WC)	2	2
1960	Belfast (WC)	3	4
1961	Berlin (WC)	1	2
1966	Belfast	0	2
1977	Cologne	0	5
1982	Belfast (EC)	1	0
1983	Hamburg (EC)	1	0
1992	Bremen	1	1
1996	Belfast	1	1
1997	Nuremberg (WC)	1	1
1997	Belfast (WC)	1	3
1999	Belfast (EC)	0	3
1999	Dortmund (EC)	0	4
2005	Belfast	1	4

v GREECE

		NI	G
1961	Athens (WC)	1	2
1961	Belfast (WC)	2	0
1988	Athens	2	3
2003	Belfast (EC)	0	2
2003	Athens (EC)	0	1
2014	Piraeus (EC)	2	0

v HOLLAND

		NI	H
1962	Rotterdam	0	4
1965	Belfast (WC)	2	1
1965	Rotterdam (WC)	0	0
1976	Rotterdam (WC)	2	2
1977	Belfast (WC)	0	1
2012	Amsterdam	0	6

v HONDURAS

		NI	H
1982	Zaragoza (WC)	1	1

v HUNGARY

		NI	H
1988	Budapest (WC)	0	1
1989	Belfast (WC)	1	2
2000	Belfast	0	1
2008	Belfast	0	2
2014	Budapest (EC)	2	1

v ICELAND

		NI	I
1977	Reykjavik (WC)	0	1
1977	Belfast (WC)	2	0
2000	Reykjavik (WC)	0	1
2001	Belfast (WC)	3	0
2006	Belfast (EC)	0	3
2007	Reykjavik (EC)	1	2

v ISRAEL

		NI	I
1968	Jaffa	3	2
1976	Tel Aviv	1	1
1980	Tel Aviv (WC)	0	0
1981	Belfast (WC)	1	0
1984	Belfast	3	0
1987	Tel Aviv	1	1
2009	Belfast	1	1
2013	Belfast (WC)	0	2
2013	Ramat Gan (WC)	1	1

v ITALY

		NI	I
1957	Rome (WC)	0	1
1957	Belfast	2	2
1958	Belfast (WC)	2	1
1961	Bologna	2	3
1997	Palermo	0	2
2003	Campobasso	0	2
2009	Pisa	0	3
2010	Belfast (EC)	0	0
2011	Pescara (EC)	0	3

v LATVIA

		NI	L
1993	Riga (WC)	2	1
1993	Belfast (WC)	2	0
1995	Riga (EC)	1	0
1995	Belfast (EC)	1	2
2006	Belfast (EC)	1	0
2007	Riga (EC)	0	1

v LIECHTENSTEIN

		NI	L
1994	Belfast (EC)	4	1
1995	Eschen (EC)	4	0
2002	Vaduz	0	0
2007	Vaduz (EC)	4	1
2007	Belfast (EC)	3	1

v LITHUANIA

		NI	L
1992	Belfast (EC)	2	2

v LUXEMBOURG

		NI	L
2000	Luxembourg	3	1
2012	Belfast (WC)	1	1

2013 Luxembourg (WC) 2 3

v MALTA

		NI	M
1988	Belfast (WC)	3	0
1989	Valletta (WC)	2	0
2000	Ta'Qali	3	0
2000	Belfast (WC)	1	0
2001	Valletta (WC)	1	0
2005	Valletta	1	1
2013	Ta'Qali	0	0

v MEXICO

		NI	M
1966	Belfast	4	1
1994	Miami	0	3

v MOLDOVA

		NI	M
1998	Belfast (EC)	2	2
1999	Kishinev (EC)	0	0

v MONTENEGRO

		W	M
2010	Podgorica	0	2

v MOROCCO

		NI	M
1986	Belfast	2	1
2010	Belfast	1	1

v NORWAY

		NI	N
1974	Oslo (EC)	1	2
1975	Belfast (EC)	3	0
1990	Belfast	2	3
1996	Belfast	0	2
2001	Belfast	0	4
2004	Belfast	1	4
2012	Belfast	0	3

v POLAND

		NI	P
1962	Katowice (EC)	2	0
1962	Belfast (EC)	2	0
1988	Belfast	1	1
1991	Belfast	3	1
2002	Limassol (Cyprus)	1	4
2004	Belfast (WC)	0	3
2005	Warsaw (WC)	0	1
2009	Belfast (WC)	3	2
2009	Chorzow (WC)	1	1

v PORTUGAL

		NI	P
1957	Lisbon (WC)	1	1
1957	Belfast (WC)	3	0
1973	Coventry (WC)	1	1
1973	Lisbon (WC)	1	1
1980	Lisbon (WC)	0	1
1981	Belfast (WC)	1	0
1994	Belfast (EC)	1	2
1995	Oporto (EC)	1	1
1997	Belfast (WC)	0	0
1997	Lisbon (WC)	0	1
2005	Belfast	1	1
2012	Porto (WC)	1	1
2013	Belfast (WC)	2	4

v QATAR

		NI	Q
2015	Crewe	1	1

v REPUBLIC OF IRELAND

		NI	RI
1978	Dublin (EC)	0	0
1979	Belfast (EC)	1	0
1988	Belfast (WC)	0	0
1989	Dublin (WC)	0	3
1993	Dublin (WC)	0	3
1993	Belfast (WC)	1	1
1994	Belfast (EC)	0	4
1995	Dublin (EC)	1	1
1999	Dublin	1	0
2011	Dublin (CC)	0	5

v ROMANIA

		NI	R
1984	Belfast (WC)	3	2
1985	Bucharest (WC)	1	0
1994	Belfast	2	0
2006	Chicago	0	2
2014	Bucharest (EC)	0	2
2015	Belfast (EC)	0	0

v RUSSIA

		NI	R
2012	Moscow (WC)	0	2
2013	Belfast (WC)	1	0

v SAN MARINO

		NI	SM
2008	Belfast (WC)	4	0
2009	Serravalle (WC)	3	0

v SERBIA & MONTENEGRO

		NI	S
2004	Belfast	1	1

v SERBIA

		NI	S
2009	Belfast	0	1
2011	Belgrade (EC)	1	2
2011	Belfast (EC)	0	1

v SLOVAKIA

		NI	S
1998	Belfast	1	0
2008	Bratislava (WC)	1	2
2009	Belfast (WC)	0	2

v SLOVENIA

		NI	S
2008	Maribor (WC)	0	2
2009	Belfast (WC)	1	0
2010	Maribor (EC)	1	0
2011	Belfast (EC)	0	0

v SOVIET UNION

		NI	SU
1969	Belfast (WC)	0	0
1969	Moscow (WC)	0	2
1971	Moscow (EC)	0	1
1971	Belfast (EC)	1	1

v SPAIN

		NI	S
1958	Madrid	2	6
1963	Bilbao	1	1
1963	Belfast	0	1

1970	Seville (EC)	0	3
1972	Hull (EC)	1	1
1982	Valencia (WC)	1	0
1985	Palma, Majorca	0	0
1986	Guadalajara (WC)	1	2
1988	Seville (WC)	0	4
1989	Belfast (WC)	0	2
1992	Belfast (WC)	0	0
1993	Seville (WC)	1	3
1998	Santander	1	4
2002	Belfast	0	5
2002	Albacete (EC)	0	3
2003	Belfast (EC)	0	0
2006	Belfast (EC)	3	2
2007	Las Palmas (EC)	0	1

v ST KITTS & NEVIS

		NI	SK
2004	Basseterre	2	0

v SWEDEN

		NI	S
1974	Solna (EC)	2	0
1975	Belfast (EC)	1	2
1980	Belfast (WC)	3	0
1981	Stockholm (WC)	0	1
1996	Belfast	1	2
2007	Belfast (EC)	2	1
2007	Stockholm (EC)	1	1

v SWITZERLAND

		NI	S
1964	Belfast (WC)	1	0
1964	Lausanne (WC)	1	2
1998	Belfast	1	0
2004	Zurich	0	0
2010	Basle (EC)	1	4

v THAILAND

		NI	T
1997	Bangkok	0	0

v TRINIDAD & TOBAGO

		NI	T

2004	Port of Spain	3	0

v TURKEY

		NI	T
1968	Belfast (WC)	4	1
1968	Istanbul (WC)	3	0
1983	Belfast (EC)	2	1
1983	Ankara (EC)	0	1
1985	Belfast (WC)	2	0
1985	Izmir (WC)	0	0
1986	Izmir (EC)	0	0
1987	Belfast (EC)	1	0
1998	Istanbul (EC)	0	3
1999	Belfast (EC)	0	3
2010	Connecticut	0	2
2013	Adana	0	1

v UKRAINE

		NI	U
1996	Belfast (WC)	0	1
1997	Kiev (WC)	1	2
2002	Belfast (EC)	0	0
2003	Donetsk (EC)	0	0

v URUGUAY

		NI	U
1964	Belfast	3	0
1990	Belfast	1	0
2006	New Jersey	0	1
2014	Montevideo	0	1

v YUGOSLAVIA

		NI	Y
1975	Belfast (EC)	1	0
1975	Belgrade (EC)	0	1
1982	Zaragoza (WC)	0	0
1987	Belfast (EC)	1	2
1987	Sarajevo (EC)	0	3
1990	Belfast (EC)	0	2
1991	Belgrade (EC)	1	4
2000	Belfast	1	2

REPUBLIC OF IRELAND

v ALBANIA

		RI	A
1992	Dublin (WC)	2	0
1993	Tirana (WC)	2	1
2003	Tirana (EC)	0	0
2003	Dublin (EC)	2	1

v ALGERIA

		RI	A
1982	Algiers	0	2
2010	Dublin	3	0

v ANDORRA

		RI	A
2001	Barcelona (WC)	3	0
2001	Dublin (WC)	3	1
2010	Dublin (EC)	3	1
2011	La Vella (EC)	2	0

v ARGENTINA

		RI	A
1951	Dublin	0	1

1979*	Dublin	0	0
1980	Dublin	0	1
1998	Dublin	0	2
2010	Dublin	0	1
(*Not regarded as full Int)			

v ARMENIA

		RI	A
2010	Yerevan (EC)	1	0
2011	Dublin (EC)	2	1

v AUSTRALIA

		RI	A
2003	Dublin	2	1
2009	Limerick	0	3

v AUSTRIA

		RI	A
1952	Vienna	0	6
1953	Dublin	4	0
1958	Vienna	1	3

1962	Dublin	2	3
1963	Vienna (EC)	0	0
1963	Dublin (EC)	3	2
1966	Vienna	0	1
1968	Dublin	2	2
1971	Dublin (EC)	1	4
1971	Linz (EC)	0	6
1995	Dublin (EC)	1	3
1995	Vienna (EC)	1	3
2013	Dublin (WC)	2	2
2013	Vienna (WC)	0	1

v BELGIUM

		RI	B
1928	Liege	4	2
1929	Dublin	4	0
1930	Brussels	3	1
1934	Dublin (WC)	4	4
1949	Dublin	0	2
1950	Brussels	1	5
1965	Dublin	0	2
1966	Liege	3	2
1980	Dublin (WC)	1	1
1981	Brussels (WC)	0	1
1986	Brussels (EC)	2	2
1987	Dublin (EC)	0	0
1997*	Dublin (WC)	1	1
1997*	Brussels (WC)	1	2
(*World Cup play-off)			

v BOLIVIA

		RI	B
1994	Dublin	1	0
1996	East Rutherford, NJ	3	0
2007	Boston	1	1

v BOSNIA HERZEGOVINA

		RI	B-H
2012	Dublin	1	0

v BRAZIL

		RI	B
1974	Rio de Janeiro	1	2
1982	Uberlandia	0	7
1987	Dublin	1	0
2004	Dublin	0	0
2008	Dublin	0	1
2010	Arsenal	0	2

v BULGARIA

		RI	B
1977	Sofia (WC)	1	2
1977	Dublin (WC)	0	0
1979	Sofia (EC)	0	1
1979	Dublin (EC)	3	0
1987	Sofia (EC)	1	2
1987	Dublin (EC)	2	0
2004	Dublin	1	1
2009	Dublin (WC)	1	1
2009	Sofia (WC)	1	1

v CAMEROON

		RI	C
2002	Niigata (WC)	1	1

v CANADA

		RI	C
2003	Dublin	3	0

v CHILE

		RI	C
1960	Dublin	2	0
1972	Recife	1	2
1974	Santiago	2	1
1982	Santiago	0	1
1991	Dublin	1	1
2006	Dublin	0	1

v CHINA

		RI	C
1984	Sapporo	1	0
2005	Dublin	1	0

v COLOMBIA

		RI	C
2008	Fulham	1	0

v COSTA RICA

		RI	CR
2014	Chester, USA	1	1

v CROATIA

		RI	C
1996	Dublin	2	2
1998	Dublin (EC)	2	0
1999	Zagreb (EC)	0	1
2001	Dublin	2	2
2004	Dublin	1	0
2011	Dublin	0	0
2012	Poznan (EC)	1	3

v CYPRUS

		RI	C
1980	Nicosia (WC)	3	2
1980	Dublin (WC)	6	0
2001	Nicosia (WC)	4	0
2001	Dublin (WC)	4	0
2004	Dublin (WC)	3	0
2005	Nicosia (WC)	1	0
2006	Nicosia (EC)	2	5
2007	Dublin (EC)	1	1
2008	Dublin (WC)	1	0
2009	Nicosia (WC)	2	1

v CZECHOSLOVAKIA/CZECH REP

		RI	C
1938	Prague	2	2
1959	Dublin (EC)	2	0
1959	Bratislava (EC)	0	4
1961	Dublin (WC)	1	3
1961	Prague (WC)	1	7
1967	Dublin (EC)	0	2
1967	Prague (EC)	2	1
1969	Dublin (WC)	1	2
1969	Prague (WC)	0	3
1979	Prague	1	4
1981	Dublin	3	1
1986	Reykjavik	1	0
1994	Dublin	1	3
1996	Prague	0	2
1998	Olomouc	1	2
2000	Dublin	3	2
2004	Dublin	2	1
2006	Dublin (EC)	1	1
2007	Prague (EC)	0	1
2012	Dublin	1	1

v DENMARK

		RI	D
1956	Dublin (WC)	2	1
1957	Copenhagen (WC)	2	0
1968*	Dublin (WC)	1	1
1969	Copenhagen (WC)	0	2
1969	Dublin (WC)	1	1
1978	Copenhagen (EC)	3	3
1979	Dublin (EC)	2	0
1984	Copenhagen (WC)	0	3
1985	Dublin (WC)	1	4
1992	Copenhagen (WC)	0	0
1993	Dublin (WC)	1	1
2002	Dublin	3	0

(*Abandoned after 51 mins – fog)

| 2007 | Aarhus | 4 | 0 |

v ECUADOR

		RI	E
1972	Natal	3	2
2007	New York	1	1

v EGYPT

		RI	E
1990	Palermo (WC)	0	0

v ESTONIA

		RI	E
2000	Dublin (WC)	2	0
2001	Tallinn (WC)	2	0
2011	Tallinn (EC)	4	0
2011	Dublin (EC)	1	1

v FAROE ISLANDS

		RI	F
2004	Dublin (WC)	2	0
2005	Torshavn (WC)	2	0
2012	Torshavn (WC)	4	1
2013	Dublin (WC)	3	0

v FINLAND

		RI	F
1949	Dublin (WC)	3	0
1949	Helsinki (WC)	1	1
1990	Dublin	1	1
2000	Dublin	3	0
2002	Helsinki	3	0

v FRANCE

		RI	F
1937	Paris	2	0
1952	Dublin	1	1
1953	Dublin (WC)	3	5
1953	Paris (WC)	0	1
1972	Dublin (WC)	2	1
1973	Paris (WC)	1	1
1976	Paris (WC)	0	2
1977	Dublin (WC)	1	0
1980	Paris (WC)	0	2
1981	Dublin (WC)	3	2
1989	Dublin	0	0
2004	Paris (WC)	0	0
2005	Dublin (WC)	0	1
2009	Dublin (WC)	0	1
2009	Paris (WC)	1	1

v GEORGIA

		RI	G
2002	Tbilisi (EC)	2	1

(continued)

2003	Dublin (EC)	2	0
2008	Mainz (WC)	2	1
2009	Dublin (WC)	2	1
2013	Dublin	4	0
2014	Tbilisi (EC)	2	1

v GERMANY/WEST GERMANY

		RI	G
1935	Dortmund	1	3
1936	Dublin	5	2
1939	Bremen	1	1
1951	Dublin	3	2
1952	Cologne	0	3
1955	Hamburg	1	2
1956	Dublin	3	0
1960	Dusseldorf	1	0
1966	Dublin	0	4
1970	Berlin	1	2
1975*	Dublin	1	0
1979	Dublin	1	3
1981	Bremen	0	3
1989	Dublin	1	1
1994	Hanover	2	0
2002	Ibaraki (WC)	1	1
2006	Stuttgart (EC)	0	1
2007	Dublin (EC)	0	0
2012	Dublin (WC)	1	6
2013	Cologne (WC)	0	3
2014	Gelsenkirchen (EC)	1	1

(*v W Germany 'B')

v GIBRALTAR

		RI	G
2014	Dublin (EC)	7	0

v GREECE

		RI	G
2000	Dublin	0	1
2002	Athens	0	0
2012	Dublin	0	1

v HOLLAND

		RI	H
1932	Amsterdam	2	0
1934	Amsterdam	2	5
1935	Dublin	3	5
1955	Dublin	1	0
1956	Rotterdam	4	1
1980	Dublin (WC)	2	1
1981	Rotterdam (WC)	2	2
1982	Rotterdam (EC)	1	2
1983	Dublin (EC)	2	3
1988	Gelsenkirchen (EC)	0	1
1990	Palermo (WC)	1	1
1994	Tilburg	1	0
1994	Orlando (WC)	0	2
1995*	Liverpool (EC)	0	2
1996	Rotterdam	1	3

(*Qual Round play-off)

2000	Amsterdam (WC)	2	2
2001	Dublin (WC)	1	0
2004	Amsterdam	1	0
2006	Dublin	0	4

v HUNGARY

		RI	H
1934	Dublin	2	4

1936	Budapest	3	3
1936	Dublin	2	3
1939	Cork	2	2
1939	Budapest	2	2
1969	Dublin (WC)	1	2
1969	Budapest (WC)	0	4
1989	Budapest (WC)	0	0
1989	Dublin (WC)	2	0
1992	Gyor	2	1
2012	Budapest	0	0

v ICELAND

		RI	I
1962	Dublin (EC)	4	2
1962	Reykjavik (EC)	1	1
1982	Dublin (EC)	2	0
1983	Reykjavik (EC)	3	0
1986	Reykjavik	2	1
1996	Dublin (WC)	0	0
1997	Reykjavik (WC)	4	2

v IRAN

		RI	I
1972	Recife	2	1
2001*	Dublin (WC)	2	0
2001*	Tehran (WC)	0	1
(*Qual Round play-off)			

v ISRAEL

		RI	I
1984	Tel Aviv	0	3
1985	Tel Aviv	0	0
1987	Dublin	5	0
2005	Tel Aviv (WC)	1	1
2005	Dublin (WC)	2	2

v ITALY

		RI	I
1926	Turin	0	3
1927	Dublin	1	2
1970	Florence (EC)	0	3
1971	Dublin (EC)	1	2
1985	Dublin	1	2
1990	Rome (WC)	0	1
1992	Boston, USA	0	2
1994	New York (WC)	1	0
2005	Dublin	1	2
2009	Bari (WC)	1	1
2009	Dublin (WC)	2	2
2012	Poznan (EC)	0	2
2014	Fulham	0	0

v JAMAICA

		RI	J
2004	Charlton	1	0

v KAZAKHSTAN

		RI	K
2012	Astana (WC)	2	1
2013	Dublin (WC)	3	1

v LATVIA

		RI	L
1992	Dublin (WC)	4	0
1993	Riga (WC)	2	0
1994	Riga (EC)	3	0
1995	Dublin (EC)	2	1
2013	Dublin	3	0

v LIECHTENSTEIN

		RI	L
1994	Dublin (EC)	4	0
1995	Eschen (EC)	0	0
1996	Eschen (WC)	5	0
1997	Dublin (WC)	5	0

v LITHUANIA

		RI	L
1993	Vilnius (WC)	1	0
1993	Dublin (WC)	2	0
1997	Dublin (WC)	0	0
1997	Zalgiris (WC)	2	1

v LUXEMBOURG

		RI	L
1936	Luxembourg	5	1
1953	Dublin (WC)	4	0
1954	Luxembourg (WC)	1	0
1987	Luxembourg (EC)	2	0
1987	Luxembourg (EC)	2	1

v MACEDONIA

		RI	M
1996	Dublin (WC)	3	0
1997	Skopje (WC)	2	3
1999	Dublin (EC)	1	0
1999	Skopje (EC)	1	1
2011	Dublin (EC)	2	1
2011	Skopje (EC)	2	0

v MALTA

		RI	M
1983	Valletta (EC)	1	0
1983	Dublin (EC)	8	0
1989	Dublin (WC)	2	0
1989	Valletta (WC)	2	0
1990	Valletta	3	0
1998	Dublin (EC)	1	0
1999	Valletta (EC)	3	2

v MEXICO

		RI	M
1984	Dublin	0	0
1994	Orlando (WC)	1	2
1996	New Jersey	2	2
1998	Dublin	0	0
2000	Chicago	2	2

v MONTENEGRO

		RI	M
2008	Podgorica (WC)	0	0
2009	Dublin (WC)	0	0

v MOROCCO

		RI	M
1990	Dublin	1	0

v NIGERIA

		RI	N
2002	Dublin	1	2
2004	Charlton	0	3
2009	Fulham	1	1

v NORWAY

		RI	N
1937	Oslo (WC)	2	3
1937	Dublin (WC)	3	3
1950	Dublin	2	2
1951	Oslo	3	2

1954	Dublin	2	1
1955	Oslo	3	1
1960	Dublin	3	1
1964	Oslo	4	1
1973	Oslo	1	1
1976	Dublin	3	0
1978	Oslo	0	0
1984	Oslo (WC)	0	1
1985	Dublin (WC)	0	0
1988	Oslo	0	0
1994	New York (WC)	0	0
2003	Dublin	1	0
2008	Oslo	1	1
2010	Dublin	1	2

v OMAN

		RI	O
2012	Fulham	4	1
2014	Dublin	2	0

v PARAGUAY

		RI	P
1999	Dublin	2	0
2010	Dublin	2	1

v POLAND

		RI	P
1938	Warsaw	0	6
1938	Dublin	3	2
1958	Katowice	2	2
1958	Dublin	2	2
1964	Cracow	1	3
1964	Dublin	3	2
1968	Dublin	2	2
1968	Katowice	0	1
1970	Dublin	1	2
1970	Poznan	0	2
1973	Wroclaw	0	2
1973	Dublin	1	0
1976	Poznan	2	0
1977	Dublin	0	0
1978	Lodz	0	3
1981	Bydgoszcz	0	3
1984	Dublin	0	0
1986	Warsaw	0	1
1988	Dublin	3	1
1991	Dublin (EC)	0	0
1991	Poznan (EC)	3	3
2004	Bydgoszcz	0	0
2008	Dublin	2	3
2013	Dublin	2	0
2013	Poznan	0	0
2015	Dublin (EC)	1	1

v PORTUGAL

		RI	P
1946	Lisbon	1	3
1947	Dublin	0	2
1948	Lisbon	0	2
1949	Dublin	1	0
1972	Recife	1	2
1992	Boston, USA	2	0
1995	Dublin (EC)	1	0
1995	Lisbon (EC)	0	3
1996	Dublin	0	1
2000	Lisbon (WC)	1	1

2001	Dublin (WC)	1	1
2005	Dublin	1	0
2014	East Rutherford, USA	1	5

v ROMANIA

		RI	R
1988	Dublin	2	0
1990*	Genoa	0	0
1997	Bucharest (WC)	0	1
1997	Dublin (WC)	1	1
2004	Dublin	1	0

(*Rep won 5-4 on pens)

v RUSSIA (See also Soviet Union)

		RI	R
1994	Dublin	0	0
1996	Dublin	0	2
2002	Dublin	2	0
2002	Moscow (EC)	2	4
2003	Dublin (EC)	1	1
2010	Dublin (EC)	2	3
2011	Moscow (EC)	0	0

v SAN MARINO

		RI	SM
2006	Dublin (EC)	5	0
2007	Rimini (EC)	2	1

v SAUDI ARABIA

		RI	SA
2002	Yokohama (WC)	3	0

v SERBIA

		RI	S
2008	Dublin	1	1
2012	Belgrade	0	0
2014	Dublin	1	2

v SLOVAKIA

		RI	S
2007	Dublin (EC)	1	0
2007	Bratislava (EC)	2	2
2010	Zilina (EC)	1	1
2011	Dublin (EC)	0	0

v SOUTH AFRICA

		RI	SA
2000	New Jersey	2	1
2009	Limerick	1	0

v SOVIET UNION (See also Russia)

		RI	SU
1972	Dublin (WC)	1	2
1973	Moscow (WC)	0	1
1974	Dublin (EC)	3	0
1975	Kiev (EC)	1	2
1984	Dublin (WC)	1	0
1985	Moscow (WC)	0	2
1988	Hanover (EC)	1	1
1990	Dublin	1	0

v SPAIN

		RI	S
1931	Barcelona	1	1
1931	Dublin	0	5
1946	Madrid	1	0
1947	Dublin	3	2
1948	Barcelona	1	2
1949	Dublin	1	4
1952	Madrid	0	6

1955	Dublin	2	2
1964	Seville (EC)	1	5
1964	Dublin (EC)	0	2
1965	Dublin (WC)	1	0
1965	Seville (WC)	1	4
1965	Paris (WC)	0	1
1966	Dublin (EC)	0	0
1966	Valencia (EC)	0	2
1977	Dublin	0	1
1982	Dublin (EC)	3	3
1983	Zaragoza (EC)	0	2
1985	Cork	0	0
1988	Seville (WC)	0	2
1989	Dublin (WC)	1	0
1992	Seville (WC)	0	0
1993	Dublin (WC)	1	3
2002*	Suwon (WC)	1	1

(*Rep lost 3-2 on pens)

| 2012 | Gdansk (EC) | 0 | 4 |
| 2013 | New York | 0 | 2 |

v SWEDEN

		RI	S
1949	Stockholm (WC)	1	3
1949	Dublin (WC)	1	3
1959	Dublin	3	2
1960	Malmo	1	4
1970	Dublin (EC)	1	1
1970	Malmo (EC)	0	1
1999	Dublin	2	0
2006	Dublin	3	0
2013	Stockholm (WC)	0	0
2013	Dublin (WC)	1	2

v SWITZERLAND

		RI	S
1935	Basle	0	1
1936	Dublin	1	0
1937	Berne	1	0
1938	Dublin	4	0
1948	Dublin	0	1
1975	Dublin (EC)	2	1
1975	Berne (EC)	0	1
1980	Dublin	2	0
1985	Dublin (WC)	3	0
1985	Berne (WC)	0	0
1992	Dublin	2	1
2002	Dublin (EC)	1	2
2003	Basle (EC)	0	2

| 2004 | Basle (WC) | 1 | 1 |
| 2005 | Dublin (WC) | 0 | 0 |

v TRINIDAD & TOBAGO

		RI	T&T
1982	Port of Spain	1	2

v TUNISIA

		RI	T
1988	Dublin	4	0

v TURKEY

		RI	T
1966	Dublin (EC)	2	1
1967	Ankara (EC)	1	2
1974	Izmir (EC)	1	1
1975	Dublin (EC)	4	0
1976	Ankara	3	3
1978	Dublin	4	2
1990	Izmir	0	0
1990	Dublin (EC)	5	0
1991	Istanbul (EC)	3	1
1999	Dublin (EC)	1	1
1999	Bursa (EC)	0	0
2003	Dublin	2	2
2014	Dublin	1	2

v URUGUAY

		RI	U
1974	Montevideo	0	2
1986	Dublin	1	1
2011	Dublin	2	3

v USA

		RI	USA
1979	Dublin	3	2
1991	Boston	1	1
1992	Dublin	4	1
1992	Washington	1	3
1996	Boston	1	2
2000	Foxboro	1	1
2002	Dublin	2	1
2014	Dublin	4	1

v YUGOSLAVIA

		RI	Y
1955	Dublin	1	4
1988	Dublin	2	0
1998	Belgrade (EC)	0	1
1999	Dublin (EC)	2	1

BRITISH AND IRISH INTERNATIONAL APPEARANCES SINCE THE WAR (1946–2015)

(As at start of season 2015–16; in year shown 2015 = season 2014–15
*Also a pre-war International player. Totals include appearances as substitute)

ENGLAND

Agbonlahor G (Aston Villa, 2009–10)	3
A'Court A (Liverpool, 1958–59)	5
Adams T (Arsenal, 1987–2001)	66
Allen A (Stoke, 1960)	3
Allen C (QPR, Tottenham, 1984–88)	5
Allen R (WBA, 1952–55)	5
Anderson S (Sunderland, 1962)	2
Anderson V (Nottm Forest, Arsenal, Manchester Utd, 1979–88)	30
Anderton D (Tottenham, 1994–2002)	30
Angus J (Burnley, 1961)	1
Armfield J (Blackpool, 1959–66)	43
Armstrong D (Middlesbrough, Southampton, 1980–4)	3
Armstrong K (Chelsea, 1955)	1
Ashton D (West Ham, 2008)	1
Astall G (Birmingham, 1956)	2
Astle J (WBA, 1969–70)	5
Aston J (Manchester Utd, 1949–51)	17
Atyeo J (Bristol City, 1956–57)	6
Bailey G (Manchester Utd, 1985)	2
Bailey M (Charlton, 1964–5)	2
Baily E (Tottenham, 1950–3)	9
Baines L (Everton, 2010–15)	30
Baker J (Hibs, Arsenal, 1960–6)	8
Ball A (Blackpool, Everton, Arsenal, 1965–75)	72
Ball M (Everton, 2001)	1
Banks G (Leicester, Stoke, 1963–72)	73
Banks T (Bolton, 1958–59)	6
Bardsley D (QPR, 1993)	2
Barham M (Norwich, 1983)	2
Barkley R (Everton, 2014–15)	13
Barlow R (WBA, 1955)	1
Barmby N (Tottenham, Middlesbrough, Everton, Liverpool, 1995–2002)	23
Barnes J (Watford, Liverpool, 1983–96)	79
Barnes P (Manchester City, WBA, Leeds, 1978–82)	22
Barrass M (Bolton, 1952–53)	3
Barrett E (Oldham, Aston Villa, 1991–93)	3
Barry G (Aston Villa, Manchester City, 2000–12)	53
Barton J (Manchester City, 2007)	1
Barton W (Wimbledon, Newcastle, 1995)	3
Batty D (Leeds, Blackburn, Newcastle, Leeds, 1991–2000)	42
Baynham R (Luton, 1956)	3
Beardsley P (Newcastle, Liverpool, Newcastle, 1986–96)	59
Beasant D (Chelsea, 1990)	2
Beattie J (Southampton, 2003–04)	5
Beattie K (Ipswich, 1975–58)	9
Beckham D (Manchester Utd, Real Madrid, LA Galaxy, AC Milan 1997–2010)	115
Bell C (Manchester City, 1968–76)	48
Bent D (Charlton, Tottenham Sunderland, Aston Villa, 2006–12)	13
Bentley D (Blackburn, 2008–09)	7
Bentley R (Chelsea, 1949–55)	12
Berry J (Manchester Utd, 1953–56)	4
Bertrand R (Chelsea, Southampton 2013–15)	4
Birtles G (Nottm Forest, 1980–81)	3
Blissett L (Watford, AC Milan, 1983–84)	14
Blockley J (Arsenal, 1973)	1
Blunstone F (Chelsea, 1955–57)	5
Bonetti P (Chelsea, 1966–70)	7
Bothroyd J (Cardiff, 2011)	1
Bould S (Arsenal, 1994)	2
Bowles S (QPR, 1974–77)	5
Bowyer L (Leeds, 2003)	1
Boyer P (Norwich, 1976)	1
Brabrook P (Chelsea, 1958–60)	3
Bracewell P (Everton, 1985–86)	3
Bradford G (Bristol Rov, 1956)	1
Bradley W (Manchester Utd, 1959)	3
Bridge W (Southampton, Chelsea, Manchester City 2002–10)	36
Bridges B (Chelsea, 1965–66)	4
Broadbent P (Wolves, 1958–60)	7
Broadis I (Manchester City, Newcastle, 1952–54)	14
Brooking T (West Ham, 1974–82)	47
Brooks J (Tottenham, 1957)	3
Brown A (WBA, 1971)	1
Brown K (West Ham, 1960)	1
Brown W (Manchester Utd, 1999–2010)	23
Bull S (Wolves, 1989–91)	13
Butcher T (Ipswich, Rangers, 1980–90)	77
Butland J (Birmingham, 2013)	1
Butt N (Manchester Utd, Newcastle, 1997–2005)	39
Byrne G (Liverpool, 1963–66)	2
Byrne J (Crystal Palace, West Ham, 1962–65)	11
Byrne R (Manchester Utd, 1954–58)	33
Cahill G (Bolton, Chelsea, 2011–15)	36
Callaghan I (Liverpool, 1966–78)	4
Campbell F (Sunderland, 2012)	1
Campbell S (Tottenham, Arsenal, Portsmouth, 1996–2008)	73
Carragher J (Liverpool, 1999–2010)	38
Carrick M (West Ham, Tottenham, Manchester Utd, 2001–15)	33
Carroll A (Newcastle, Liverpool 2011–13)	9
Carson S (Liverpool, Aston Villa WBA, Bursaspor 2008–12)	4

*Carter H (Derby, 1947)	7
Caulker S (Tottenham, 2013)	1
Chamberlain M (Stoke, 1983–85)	8
Chambers C (Arsenal, 2015)	3
Channon M (Southampton, Manchester City, 1973–78)	46
Charles G (Nottm Forest, 1991)	2
Charlton, J (Leeds, 1965–70)	35
Charlton, R (Manchester Utd, 1958–70)	106
Charnley R (Blackpool, 1963)	1
Cherry T (Leeds, 1976–80)	27
Chilton A (Manchester Utd, 1951–52)	2
Chivers M (Tottenham, 1971–74)	24
Clamp E (Wolves, 1958)	4
Clapton D (Arsenal, 1959)	1
Clarke A (Leeds, 1970–6)	19
Clarke H (Tottenham, 1954)	1
Clayton R (Blackburn, 1956–60)	35
Clemence R (Liverpool, Tottenham, 1973–84)	61
Clement D (QPR, 1976–7)	5
Cleverley T (Manchester Utd, 2013–14)	13
Clough B (Middlesbrough, 1960)	2
Clough N (Nottm Forest, Liverpool, 1989–93)	14
Clyne N (Southampton, 2015)	5
Coates R (Burnley, Tottenham, 1970–71)	4
Cockburn H (Manchester Utd, 1947–52)	13
Cohen G (Fulham, 1964–68)	37
Cole Andy (Manchester Utd, 1995–2002)	15
Cole Ashley (Arsenal, Chelsea, 2001–14)	107
Cole C (West Ham, 2009–10)	7
Cole J (West Ham, Chelsea, 2001–10)	56
Collymore S (Nottm Forest, Aston Villa, 1995–97)	3
Compton L (Arsenal, 1951)	2
Connelly J (Burnley, Manchester Utd, 1960–66)	20
Cooper C (Nottm Forest, 1995)	2
Cooper T (Leeds, 1969–75)	20
Coppell S (Manchester Utd, 1978–83)	42
Corrigan J (Manchester City, 1976–82)	9
Cottee T (West Ham, Everton, 1987–89)	7
Cowans G (Aston Villa, Bari, Aston Villa, 1983–91)	10
Crawford R (Ipswich, 1962)	2
Crouch P (Southampton, Liverpool, Portsmouth, Tottenham, 2005–11)	42
Crowe C (Wolves, 1963)	1
Cunningham L (WBA, Real Madrid, 1979–81)	6
Currie K (Manchester City, 1992)	3
Currie A (Sheffield Utd, Leeds, 1972–79)	17
Daley T (Aston Villa, 1992)	7
Davenport P (Nottm Forest, 1985)	1
Davies K (Bolton, 2011)	1
Dawson M (Tottenham 2011)	4
Deane B (Sheffield Utd, 1991–93)	3
Deeley N (Wolves, 1959)	2
Defoe J (Tottenham, Portsmouth, Tottenham, 2004–14)	55
Delph F (Aston Villa, 2015)	6
Devonshire A (West Ham, 1980–84)	8

Dickinson J (Portsmouth, 1949–57)	48
Ditchburn E (Tottenham, 1949–57)	6
Dixon K (Chelsea, 1985–87)	8
Dixon L (Arsenal, 1990–99)	22
Dobson M (Burnley, Everton, 1974–75)	5
Dorigo T (Chelsea, Leeds, 1990–94)	15
Douglas B (Blackburn, 1959–63)	36
Downing S (Middlesbrough, Aston Villa, Liverpool, West Ham, 2005–15)	35
Doyle M (Manchester City, 1976–77)	5
Dublin D (Coventry, Aston Villa, 1998–99)	4
Dunn D (Blackburn, 2003)	1
Duxbury, M (Manchester Utd, 1984–85)	10
Dyer K (Newcastle, West Ham, 2000–08)	33
Eastham G (Arsenal, 1963–66)	19
Eckersley W (Blackburn, 1950–54)	17
Edwards, D (Manchester Utd, 1955–58)	18
Ehiogu U (Aston Villa, Middlesbrough, 1996–2002)	4
Ellerington W (Southampton, 1949)	2
Elliott W (Burnley, 1952–53)	5
Fantham J (Sheffield Wed, 1962)	1
Fashanu J (Wimbledon, 1989)	2
Fenwick T (QPR, 1984–88)	20
Ferdinand L (QPR, Newcastle, Tottenham, 1993–98)	17
Ferdinand R (West Ham, Leeds, Manchester Utd, 1997–2011)	81
Finney T (Preston, 1947–59)	76
Flanagan J (Liverpool, 2014)	1
Flowers R (Wolves, 1955–66)	49
Flowers T (Southampton, Blackburn, 1993–98)	11
Forster F (Celtic, Southampton, 2014–15)	3
Foster B (Manchester Utd, Birmingham, WBA, 2007–14)	8
Foster S (Brighton, 1982)	3
Foulkes W (Manchester Utd, 1955)	1
Fowler R (Liverpool, Leeds, 1996–2002)	26
Francis G (QPR, 1975–76)	12
Francis T (Birmingham, Nottm Forest, Man City, Sampdoria, 1977–86)	52
Franklin N (Stoke, 1947–50)	27
Froggatt J (Portsmouth, 1950–53)	13
Froggatt R (Sheffield Wed, 1953)	4
Gardner A (Tottenham, 2004)	1
Garrett T (Blackpool, 1952–54)	3
Gascoigne P (Tottenham, Lazio, Rangers, Middlesbrough, 1989–98)	57
Gates E (Ipswich, 1981)	2
George C (Derby, 1977)	1
Gerrard S (Liverpool, 2000–14)	114
Gibbs K (Arsenal, 2011–15)	8
Gidman J (Aston Villa, 1977)	1
Gillard I (QPR, 1975–76)	3
Goddard P (West Ham, 1982)	1
Grainger C (Sheffield Utd, Sunderland, 1956–57)	7
Gray A (Crystal Palace, 1992)	1

Ripley S (Blackburn, 1994–97) 2
Rix G (Arsenal, 1981–84) 17
Robb G (Tottenham, 1954) 1
Roberts G (Tottenham, 1983–84) 6
Robinson P (Leeds, Tottenham, 2003–08) 41
Robson B (WBA, Manchester Utd, 1980–92) 90
Robson R (WBA, 1958–62) 20
Rocastle D (Arsenal, 1989–92) 14
Rodriguez J (Southampton, 2014) 1
Rodwell J (Everton, Manchester City, 2012–13) 3
Rooney W (Everton, Manchester Utd, 2003–15) 105
Rowley J (Manchester Utd, 1949–52) 6
Royle J (Everton, Manchester City, 1971–77) 6
Ruddock N (Liverpool, 1995) 1
Ruddy J (Norwich, 2013) 1

Sadler D (Manchester Utd, 1968–71) 4
Salako J (Crystal Palace, 1991–92) 5
Sansom K (Crystal Palace, Arsenal, 1979–88) 86
Scales J (Liverpool, 1995) 3
Scholes P (Manchester Utd, 1997–2004) 66
Scott L (Arsenal, 1947–49) 17
Seaman D (QPR, Arsenal, 1989–2003) 75
Sewell J (Sheffield Wed, 1952–54) 6
Shackleton L (Sunderland, 1949–55) 5
Sharpe L (Manchester Utd, 1991–94) 8
Shaw G (Sheffield Utd, 1959–63) 5
Shaw L (Southampton, Manchester Utd, 2014–15) 4
Shawcross, R (Stoke, 2013) 1
Shearer A (Southampton, Blackburn, Newcastle, 1992–2000) 63
Shellito K (Chelsea, 1963) 1
Shelvey J (Liverpool, 2013) 1
Sheringham E (Tottenham, Manchester Utd, Tottenham, 1993–2002) 51
Sherwood T (Tottenham, 1999) 3
Shilton P (Leicester, Stoke, Nottm Forest, Southampton, Derby, 1971–90) 125
Shimwell E (Blackpool, 1949) 1
Shorey N (Reading, 2007) 2
Sillett P (Chelsea, 1955) 3
Sinclair T (West Ham, Manchester City, 2002–04) 12
Sinton A (QPR, Sheffield Wed, 1992–94) 12
Slater W (Wolves, 1955–60) 12
Smalling C (Manchester Utd, 2012–15) 18
Smith A (Arsenal, 1989–92) 13
Smith A (Leeds, Manchester Utd, Newcastle, 2001–08) 19
Smith L (Arsenal, 1951–53) 6
Smith R (Tottenham, 1961–64) 15
Smith T (Birmingham, 1960) 2
Smith T (Liverpool, 1971) 1
Southgate G (Aston Villa, Middlesbrough, 1996–2004) 57
Spink A (Aston Villa, 1983) 1
Springett R (Sheffield Wed, 1960–66) 33
Staniforth R (Huddersfield, 1954–55) 8

Statham D (WBA, 1983) 3
Stein B (Luton, 1984) 1
Stepney A (Manchester Utd, 1968) 1
Sterland M (Sheffield Wed, 1989) 1
Sterling R (Liverpool, 2013–15) 16
Steven T (Everton, Rangers, Marseille, 1985–92) 36
Stevens G (Everton, Rangers, 1985–92) 46
Stevens G (Tottenham, 1985–86) 7
Stewart P (Tottenham, 1992) 3
Stiles N (Manchester Utd, 1965–70) 28
Stone S (Nottm Forest, 1996) 9
Stones J (Everton, 2014–15) 4
Storey P (Arsenal, 1971–73) 19
Storey-Moore I (Nottm Forest, 1970) 1
Streten B (Luton, 1950) 1
Sturridge D (Chelsea, Liverpool, 2012–15) 16
Summerbee M (Manchester City, 1968–73) 8
Sunderland, A (Arsenal, 1980) 1
Sutton C (Blackburn, 1997) 1
Swan P (Sheffield Wed, 1960–62) 19
Swift F (Manchester City, 1947–79) 19

Talbot B (Ipswich, Arsenal, 1977–80) 6
Tambling R (Chelsea, 1963–66) 3
Taylor E (Blackpool, 1954) 1
Taylor J (Fulham, 1951) 2
Taylor P (Liverpool, 1948) 3
Taylor P (Crystal Palace, 1976) 4
Taylor T (Manchester Utd, 1953–58) 19
Temple D (Everton, 1965) 1
Terry J (Chelsea, 2003–13) 78
Thomas D (QPR, 1975–76) 8
Thomas D (Coventry, 1983) 2
Thomas G (Crystal Palace, 1991–92) 9
Thomas M (Arsenal, 1989–90) 2
Thompson A (Celtic, 2004) 1
Thompson Peter (Liverpool, 1964–70) 16
Thompson Phil (Liverpool, 1976–83) 42
Thompson T (Aston Villa, Preston, 1952–57) 2
Thomson R (Wolves, 1964–65) 8
Todd C (Derby, 1972–77) 27
Towers A (Sunderland, 1978) 3
Townsend A (Tottenham, 2014–15) 9
Tueart D (Manchester City, 1975–77) 6

Ufton D (Charlton, 1954) 1
Unsworth D (Everton, 1995) 1
Upson M (Birmingham, West Ham, 2003–10) 21

Vardy J (Leicester, 2015) 1
Vassell D (Aston Villa, 2002–04) 22
Venables T (Chelsea, 1965) 2
Venison B (Newcastle, 1995) 2
Viljoen C (Ipswich, 1975) 2
Viollet D (Manchester Utd, 1960) 2

Waddle C (Newcastle, Tottenham, Marseille, 1985–92) 62
Waiters A (Blackpool, 1964–65) 5

SCOTLAND

Brown H (Partick, 1947) 3
Brown J (Sheffield Utd, 1975) 1
Brown R (Rangers, 1947–52) 3
Brown S (Hibernian, Celtic, 2007–15) 45
Brown W (Dundee, Tottenham, 1958–66) 28
Brownlie J (Hibs, 1971–76) 7
Bryson C (Kilmarnock, Derby, 2011–14) 2
Buchan M (Aberdeen, Manchester Utd, 1972–8) 34
Buckley P (Aberdeen, 1954–55) 3
Burchill M (Celtic, 2000) 6
Burke C (Rangers, Birmingham, 2006–14) 7
Burley C (Chelsea, Celtic, Derby, 1995–2003) 46
Burley G (Ipswich, 1979–82) 11
Burns F (Manchester Utd, 1970) 1
Burns K (Birmingham, Nottm Forest, 1974–81) 20
Burns T (Celtic, 1981–88) 8

Calderwood C (Tottenham, Aston Villa, 1995–2000) 36
Caldow E (Rangers, 1957–63) 40
Caldwell G (Newcastle, Sunderland, Hibs, Wigan, 2002–13) 55
Caldwell S (Newcastle, Sunderland, Celtic, Wigan, 2001–11) 12
Callaghan T (Dunfermline, 1970) 2
Cameron C (Hearts, Wolves, 1999–2005) 28
Campbell J (Falkirk, Chelsea, 1947–50) 5
Campbell W (Morton, 1947–48) 5
Canero P (Leicester, 2004) 1
Carr W (Coventry, 1970–73) 6
Chalmers S (Celtic, 1965–67) 5
Clark J (Celtic, 1966–67) 4
Clark R (Aberdeen, 1968–73) 17
Clarke S (Chelsea, 1988–94) 6
Clarkson D (Motherwell, 2008–09) 2
Collins J (Hibs, Celtic, Monaco, Everton, 1988–2000) 58
Collins R (Celtic, Everton, Leeds, 1951–65) 31
Colquhoun E (Sheffield Utd, 1972–73) 9
Colquhoun J (Hearts, 1988) 2
Combe J (Hibs, 1948) 3
Commons K (Derby, Celtic, 2009–13) 12
Conn A (Hearts, 1956) 1
Conn A (Tottenham, 1975) 2
Connachan E (Dunfermline, 1962) 2
Connelly G (Celtic, 1974) 2
Connolly J (Everton, 1973) 1
Connor R (Dundee, Aberdeen, 1986–91) 4
Conway C (Dundee Utd, Cardiff, 2010–14) 7
Cooke C (Dundee, Chelsea, 1966–75) 16
Cooper D (Rangers, Motherwell, 1980–90) 22
Cormack P (Hibs, 1966–72) 9
Cowan J (Morton, 1948–52) 25
Cowie D (Dundee, 1953–58) 20
Cowie D (Watford, 2010–12) 10

Cox C (Hearts, 1948) 1
Cox S (Rangers, 1948–54) 25
Craig JP (Celtic, 1968) 1
Craig J (Celtic, 1977) 1
Craig T (Newcastle, 1976) 1
Crainey S (Celtic, Southampton, Blackpool, 2002–12) 12
Crawford S (Raith, Dunfermline, Plymouth Argyle, 1995–2005) 25
Crerand P (Celtic, Manchester Utd, 1961–66) 16
Cropley A (Hibs, 1972) 2
Cruickshank J (Hearts, 1964–76) 6
Cullen M (Luton, 1956) 1
Cumming J (Hearts, 1955–60) 9
Cummings W (Chelsea, 2002) 1
Cunningham W (Preston, 1954–55) 8
Curran H (Wolves, 1970–71) 5

Dailly C (Derby, Blackburn, West Ham, 1997–2008) 67
Dalglish K (Celtic, Liverpool, 1972–87) 102
Davidson C (Blackburn, Leicester, Preston, 1999–2010) 19
Davidson M (St Johnstone, 2013) 1`
Davidson J (Partick, 1954–55) 8
Dawson A (Rangers, 1980–83) 5
Deans J (Celtic, 1975) 2
*Delaney J (Manchester Utd, 1947–48) 4
Devlin P (Birmingham, 2003–04) 10
Dick J (West Ham, 1959) 1
Dickov P (Manchester City, Leicester, Blackburn, 2001–05) 10
Dickson W (Kilmarnock, 1970–71) 5
Dixon P (Huddersfield, 2013) 3
Dobie S (WBA, 2002–03) 6
Docherty T (Preston, Arsenal, 1952–59) 25
Dodds D (Dundee Utd, 1984) 2
Dodds W (Aberdeen, Dundee Utd, Rangers, 1997–2002) 26
Donachie W (Manchester City, 1972–79) 35
Donnelly S (Celtic, 1997–99) 10
Dorrans G (WBA, 2010–14) 10
Dougall C (Birmingham, 1947) 1
Dougan R (Hearts, 1950) 1
Douglas R (Celtic, Leicester, 2002–06) 19
Doyle J (Ayr, 1976) 1
Duncan A (Hibs, 1975–76) 6
Duncan D (East Fife, 1948) 3
Duncanson J (Rangers, 1947) 1
Durie G (Chelsea, Tottenham, Rangers, 1988–98) 43
Durrant I (Rangers, Kilmarnock, 1988–2000) 20

Elliott M (Leicester, 1997–2002) 18
Evans A (Aston Villa, 1982) 4
Evans R (Celtic, Chelsea, 1949–60) 48
Ewing T (Partick, 1958) 2

Farm G (Blackpool, 1953–59) 10
Ferguson B (Rangers, Blackburn, Rangers, 1999–2009) 45

Ferguson D (Dundee Utd, Everton, 1992–97)	7
Ferguson D (Rangers, 1988)	2
Ferguson I (Rangers, 1989–97)	9
Ferguson R (Kilmarnock, 1966–67)	7
Fernie W (Celtic, 1954–58)	12
Flavell R (Airdrie, 1947)	2
Fleck R (Norwich, 1990–91)	4
Fleming C (East Fife, 1954)	1
Fletcher D (Manchester Utd, WBA, 2004–07)	68
Fletcher S (Hibernian, Burnley, Wolves, Sunderland, 2008–15)	21
Forbes A (Sheffield Utd, Arsenal, 1947–52)	14
Ford D (Hearts, 1974)	3
Forrest J (Motherwell, 1958)	1
Forrest J (Rangers, Aberdeen, 1966–71)	5
Forrest J (Celtic, 2011–15)	10
Forsyth A (Partick, Manchester Utd, 1972–76)	10
Forsyth C (Kilmarnock, 1964)	4
Forsyth C (Derby, 2014–15)	4
Forsyth T (Motherwell, Rangers, 1971–78)	22
Fox D (Burnley, Southampton, 2010–13)	4
Fraser D (WBA, 1968–69)	2
Fraser W (Sunderland, 1955)	2
Freedman D (Crystal Palace, 2002)	2
Gabriel J (Everton, 1961–64)	2
Gallacher K (Dundee Utd, Coventry, Blackburn, Newcastle, 1988–2001)	53
Gallacher P (Dundee Utd, 2003–04)	8
Gallagher P (Blackburn, 2004)	1
Galloway M (Celtic, 1992)	1
Gardiner I (Motherwell, 1958)	1
Gemmell T (St Mirren, 1955)	2
Gemmell T (Celtic, 1966–71)	18
Gemmill A (Derby, Nottm Forest, Birmingham, 1971–81)	43
Gemmill S (Nottm Forest, Everton, 1995–2003)	26
Gibson D (Leicester, 1963–65)	7
Gilks M (Blackpool, 2013–14)	3
Gillespie G (Liverpool, 1988–91)	13
Gilzean A (Dundee, Tottenham, 1964–71)	22
Glass S (Newcastle Utd 1999)	1
Glavin R (Celtic, 1977)	1
Glen A (Aberdeen, 1956)	2
Goodwillie D (Dundee Utd, Blackburn, 2011–12)	3
Goram A (Oldham, Hibs, Rangers, 1986–98)	43
Gordon C (Hearts, Sunderland, Celtic, 2004–15)	43
Gough R (Dundee Utd, Tottenham, Rangers, 1983–93)	61
Gould J (Celtic, 2000–01)	2
Govan J (Hibs, 1948–49)	6
Graham A (Leeds, 1978–81)	10
Graham G (Arsenal, Manchester Utd, 1972–73)	12
Gray A (Aston Villa, Wolves, Everton, 1976–85)	20

Gray A (Bradford City, 2003)	2
Gray E (Leeds, 1969–77)	12
Gray F (Leeds, Nottm Forest, 1976–83)	32
Grant J (Hibs, 1958)	2
Grant P (Celtic, 1989)	2
Green A (Blackpool, Newcastle, 1971–72)	6
Greer G (Brighton, 2014–15)	8
Greig J (Rangers, 1964–76)	44
Griffiths L (Wolves, Celtic 2013–15)	5
Gunn B (Norwich, 1990–94)	6
Haddock H (Clyde, 1955–58)	6
Haffey F (Celtic, 1960–61)	2
Hamilton A (Dundee, 1962–66)	24
Hamilton G (Aberdeen, 1947–54)	5
Hamilton W (Hibs, 1965)	1
Hammell S (Motherwell, 2005)	1
Hanley G (Blackburn, 2011–15)	17
Hansen A (Liverpool, 1979–87)	26
Hansen J (Partick, 1972)	2
Harper J (Aberdeen, Hibs, 1973–78)	4
Hartford A (WBA, Manchester City, Everton, 1972–82)	50
Hartley P (Hearts, Celtic, Bristol City, 2005–10)	25
Harvey D (Leeds, 1973–77)	16
Haughney M (Celtic, 1954)	1
Hay D (Celtic, 1970–74)	27
Hegarty P (Dundee Utd, 1979–83)	8
Henderson J (Portsmouth, Arsenal, 1953–59)	7
Henderson W (Rangers, 1963–71)	29
Hendry C (Blackburn, Rangers, Coventry, Bolton, 1994–2001)	51
Herd D (Arsenal, 1959–61)	5
Herd G (Clyde, 1958–61)	5
Herriot J (Birmingham, 1969–70)	8
Hewie J (Charlton, 1956–60)	19
Holt D (Hearts, 1963–64)	5
Holt G (Kilmarnock, Norwich, 2001–05)	10
Holton J (Manchester Utd, 1973–75)	15
Hope R (WBA, 1968–69)	2
Hopkin D (Crystal Palace, Leeds, 1997–2000)	7
Houliston W (Queen of the South, 1949)	3
Houston S (Manchester Utd, 1976)	1
Howie H (Hibs, 1949)	1
Hughes J (Celtic, 1965–70)	8
Hughes R (Portsmouth, 2004–06)	5
Hughes S (Norwich, 2010)	1
Hughes W (Sunderland, 1975)	1
Humphries W (Motherwell, 1952)	1
Hunter A (Kilmarnock, Celtic, 1972–74)	4
Hunter W (Motherwell, 1960–61)	3
Husband J (Partick, 1947)	1
Hutchison D (Everton, Sunderland, West Ham, 1999–2004)	26
Hutchison T (Coventry, 1974–76)	17
Hutton A (Rangers, Tottenham, Aston Villa, 2007–15)	45

Imlach S (Nottm Forest, 1958) 4
Irvine B (Aberdeen, 1991–94) 9
Iwelumo C (Wolves, Burnley, 2009–11) 4

Jackson C (Rangers, 1975–77) 8
Jackson D (Hibs, Celtic, 1995–99) 28
Jardine A (Rangers, 1971–80) 38
Jarvie A (Airdrie, 1971) 3
Jess E (Aberdeen, Coventry,
  Aberdeen, 1993–99) 17
Johnston A (Sunderland, Rangers,
  Middlesbrough, 1999–2003) 18
Johnston M (Watford, Celtic, Nantes,
  Rangers, 1984–92) 38
Johnston W (Rangers, WBA, 1966–78) 21
Johnstone D (Rangers, 1973–80) 14
Johnstone J (Celtic, 1965–75) 23
Johnstone L (Clyde, 1948) 2
Johnstone R (Hibs, Manchester City,
  1951–56) 17
Jordan J (Leeds, Manchester Utd, AC Milan,
  1973–82) 52

Kelly H (Blackpool, 1952) 1
Kelly J (Barnsley, 1949) 2
Kelly L (Kilmarnock, 2013) 1
Kennedy J (Celtic, 1964–65) 6
Kennedy J (Celtic, 2004) 1
Kennedy S (Rangers, 1975) 5
Kennedy S (Aberdeen, 1978–82) 8
Kenneth G (Dundee Utd, 2011) 2
Kerr A (Partick, 1955) 2
Kerr B (Newcastle, 2003–04) 3
Kyle K (Sunderland, Kilmarnock,
  2002–10) 10

Lambert P (Motherwell, Borussia Dortmund,
  Celtic, 1995–2003) 40
Law D (Huddersfield, Manchester City,
  Torino, Manchester Utd, 1959–74) 55
Lawrence T (Liverpool, 1963–69) 3
Leggat G (Aberdeen, Fulham, 1956–60) 18
Leighton J (Aberdeen, Manchester Utd,
  Hibs, Aberdeen, 1983–99) 91
Lennox R (Celtic, 1967–70) 10
Leslie L (Airdrie, 1961) 5
Levein C (Hearts, 1990–95) 16
Liddell W (Liverpool, 1947–55) 28
Linwood A (Clyde, 1950) 1
Little R (Rangers, 1953) 1
Logie J (Arsenal, 1953) 1
Long H (Clyde, 1947) 1
Lorimer P (Leeds, 1970–76) 21

Macari L (Celtic, Manchester Utd, 1972–78) 24
Macaulay A (Brentford, Arsenal, 1947–48) 7
MacDonald A (Rangers, 1976) 1
MacDougall E (Norwich, 1975–76) 7
Mackail-Smith C (Peterborough, Brighton
  2011–12) 7
Mackay D (Hearts, Tottenham, 1957–66) 22
Mackay G (Hearts, 1988) 4

Mackay M (Norwich, 2004–05) 5
Mackay–Steven G (Dundee Utd, 2014) 1
Mackie J (QPR, 2011–13) 9
MacLeod J (Hibs, 1961) 4
MacLeod M (Celtic, Borussia Dortmund,
  Hibs, 1985–91) 20
Maguire C (Aberdeen, 2011) 2
Maloney S (Celtic, Aston Villa, Celtic,
  Wigan, Chicago, 2006–15) 41
Malpas M (Dundee Utd, 1984–93) 55
Marshall D (Celtic, Cardiff, 2005–15) 19
Marshall G (Celtic, 1992) 1
Martin B (Motherwell, 1995) 2
Martin C (Derby, 2014–15) 5
Martin F (Aberdeen, 1954–55) 6
Martin N (Hibs, Sunderland, 1965–66) 3
Martin R (Norwich, 2011–15) 19
Martis J (Motherwell, 1961) 1
Mason J (Third Lanark 1949–51) 7
Masson D (QPR, Derby, 1976–78) 17
Mathers D (Partick, 1954) 1
Matteo D (Leeds, 2001–02) 6
May S (Sheffield Wed, 2015) 1
McAllister B (Wimbledon, 1997) 3
McAllister G (Leicester, Leeds,
  Coventry, 1990–99) 57
McAllister J (Livingston, 2004) 1
McArthur J (Wigan, Crystal Palace, 2011–15) 20
McAvennie F (West Ham, Celtic, 1986–88) 5
McBride J (Celtic, 1967) 2
McCall S (Everton, Rangers, 1990–98) 40
McCalliog J (Sheffield Wed, Wolves,
  1967–71) 5
McCann N (Hearts, Rangers,
  Southampton, 1999–2006) 26
McCann R (Motherwell, 1959–61) 5
McClair B (Celtic, Manchester Utd,
  1987–93) 30
McCloy P (Rangers, 1973) 4
McCoist A (Rangers, Kilmarnock,
  1986–99) 61
McColl I (Rangers, 1950–58) 14
McCormack R (Motherwell, Cardiff,
  Leeds, 2008–14) 11
McCreadie E (Chelsea, 1965–9) 23
McCulloch R (Wigan, Rangers, 2005–11) 18
McDonald J (Sunderland, 1956) 2
McEveley J (Derby, 2008) 3
McFadden J (Motherwell, Everton,
  Birmingham, 2002–11) 48
McFarlane W (Hearts, 1947) 1
McGarr E (Aberdeen, 1970) 2
McGarvey F (Liverpool, Celtic, 1979–84) 7
McGhee M (Aberdeen, 1983–84) 4
McGinlay J (Bolton, 1995–97) 14
McGrain D (Celtic, 1973–82) 62
McGregor A (Rangers, Besiktas, Hull, 2007–15) 33
McGrory J (Kilmarnock, 1965–66) 3
McInally A (Aston Villa, Bayern Munich,
  1989–90) 8
McInally J (Dundee Utd, 1987–93) 10
McInnes D (WBA, 2003) 2

McKay D (Celtic, 1959–62) — 14
McKean R (Rangers, 1976) — 1
McKenzie J (Partick, 1954–56) — 9
McKimmie S (Aberdeen, 1989–96) — 40
McKinlay T (Celtic, 1996–98) — 22
McKinlay W (Dundee Utd, Blackburn, 1994–99) — 29
McKinnon R (Rangers, 1966–71) — 28
McKinnon R (Motherwell, 1994–95) — 3
McLaren A (Preston, 1947–48) — 4
McLaren A (Hearts, Rangers, 1992–96) — 24
McLaren A (Kilmarnock, 2001) — 1
McLean G (Dundee, 1968) — 1
McLean T (Kilmarnock, Rangers, 1969–71) — 6
McLeish A (Aberdeen, 1980–93) — 77
McLintock F (Leicester, Arsenal, 1963–71) — 9
McManus S (Celtic, Middlesbrough, 2007–11) — 26
McMillan I (Airdrie, 1952–61) — 6
McNamara J (Celtic, Wolves, 1997–2006) — 33
McNamee D (Livingston, 2004–06) — 4
McNaught W (Raith, 1951–55) — 5
McNaughton K (Aberdeen, Cardiff, 2002–08) — 4
McNeill W (Celtic, 1961–72) — 29
McPhail J (Celtic, 1950–54) — 5
McPherson D (Hearts, Rangers, 1989–93) — 27
McQueen G (Leeds, Manchester Utd, 1974–81) — 30
McStay P (Celtic, 1984–97) — 76
McSwegan G (Hearts, 2000) — 2
Millar J (Rangers, 1963) — 2
Miller C (Dundee Utd, 2001) — 1
Miller K (Rangers, Wolves, Celtic, Derby, Rangers, Bursaspor, Cardiff, Vancouver, 2001–14) — 69
Miller L (Dundee Utd, Aberdeen 2006–10) — 3
Miller W (Celtic, 1946–47) — 6
Miller W (Aberdeen, 1975–90) — 65
Mitchell R (Newcastle, 1951) — 2
Mochan N (Celtic, 1954) — 3
Moir W (Bolton, 1950) — 1
Moncur R (Newcastle, 1968–72) — 16
Morgan W (Burnley, Manchester Utd, 1968–74) — 21
Morris H (East Fife, 1950) — 1
Morrison J (WBA, 2008–15) — 39
Mudie J (Blackpool, 1957–58) — 17
Mulgrew C (Celtic, 20012–15) — 18
Mulhall G (Aberdeen, Sunderland, 1960–64) — 3
Munro F (Wolves, 1971–75) — 9
Munro I (St Mirren, 1979–80) — 7
Murdoch R (Celtic, 1966–70) — 12
Murray I (Hibs, Rangers, 2003–06) — 6
Murray J (Hearts, 1958) — 5
Murray S (Aberdeen, 1972) — 1
Murty G (Reading, 2004–08) — 4

Naismith S (Kilmarnock, Rangers, Everton, 2007–15) — 38
Narey D (Dundee Utd, 1977–89) — 35
Naysmith G (Hearts, Everton, Sheffield Utd, 2000–09) — 46
Neilson R (Hearts, 2007) — 1
Nevin P (Chelsea, Everton, Tranmere, 1987–96) — 28
Nicholas C (Celtic, Arsenal, Aberdeen, 1983–89) — 20
Nicholson B (Dunfermline, 2001–05) — 3
Nicol S (Liverpool, 1985–92) — 27
O'Connor G (Hibs, Lokomotiv Moscow, Birmingham, 2002–10) — 16
O'Donnell P (Motherwell, 1994) — 1
O'Hare J (Derby, 1970–72) — 13
O'Neil B (Celtic, VfL Wolfsburg, Derby, Preston, 1996–2006) — 7
O'Neil J (Hibs, 2001) — 1
Ormond W (Hibs, 1954–59) — 6
Orr T (Morton, 1952) — 2
Parker A (Falkirk, Everton, 1955–56) — 15
Parlane D (Rangers, 1973–77) — 12
Paton A (Motherwell, 1952) — 2
Pearson S (Motherwell, Celtic, Derby, 2004–07) — 10
Pearson T (Newcastle, 1947) — 2
Penman A (Durdee, 1966) — 1
Pettigrew W (Motherwell, 1976–77) — 5
Phillips M (Blackpool, 2012–13) — 2
Plenderleith J (Manchester City, 1961) — 1
Pressley S (Hearts, 2000–07) — 32
Provan D (Rangers, 1964–66) — 5
Provan D (Celtic, 1980–82) — 10
Quashie N (Portsmouth, Southampton, WBA, 2004–07) — 14
Quinn P (Motherwell, 1961–62) — 9
Rae G (Dundee, Rangers, Cardiff, 2001–09) — 14
Redpath W (Motherwell, 1949–52) — 9
Reilly L (Hibs, 1949–57) — 38
Rhodes J (Huddersfield, Blackburn, 2012–15) — 13
Ring T (Clyde, 1953–58) — 12
Rioch B (Derby, Everton, 1975–78) — 24
Riordan D (Hibs, 2006–10) — 3
Ritchie M (Bournemouth, 2015) — 4
Ritchie P (Hearts, Bolton, 1999–2000) — 6
Ritchie W (Rangers, 1962) — 1
Robb D (Aberdeen, 1971) — 5
Robertson A (Clyde, 1955) — 5
Robertson A (Dundee Utd, Hull, 2014–15) — 6
Robertson D (Rangers, 1992–94) — 3
Robertson H (Dundee, 1962) — 1
Robertson J (Tottenham, 1964) — 1
Robertson J (Nottm Forest, Derby, 1978–84) — 28
Robertson J (Hearts, 1991–96) — 16
Robertson S (Dundee Utd, 2009–11) — 2
Robinson R (Dundee, 1974–75) — 4
Robson B (Celtic, Middlesbrough, 2008–12) — 17
Ross M (Rangers, 2002–04) — 12

Rough A (Partick, Hibs, 1976–86) 53
Rougvie D (Aberdeen, 1984) 1
Russell J (Derby, 2015) 3
Rutherford E (Rangers, 1948) 1

Saunders S (Motherwell, 2011) 1
Schaedler E (Hibs, 1974) 1
Scott A (Rangers, Everton, 1957–66) 16
Scott J (Hibs, 1966) 1
Scott J (Dundee, 1971) 2
Scoular J (Portsmouth, 1951–53) 9
Severin S (Hearts, Aberdeen, 2002–07) 15
Sharp G (Everton, 1985–88) 12
Shaw D (Hibs, 1947–49) 8
Shaw J (Rangers, 1947) 4
Shearer D (Aberdeen, 1994–96) 7
Shearer R (Rangers, 1961) 4
Shinnie A (Inverness, 2013) 1
Simpson N (Aberdeen, 1983–88) 4
Simpson R (Celtic, 1967–69) 5
Sinclair J (Leicester, 1966) 1
Smith D (Aberdeen, Rangers, 1966–68) 2
Smith G (Hibs, 1947–57) 18
Smith H (Hearts, 1988–92) 3
Smith JE (Celtic, 1959) 2
Smith J (Aberdeen, Newcastle, 1968–74) 4
Smith J (Celtic, 2003) 2
Snodgrass R (Leeds, Norwich, 2011–14) 15
Souness G (Middlesbrough, Liverpool, Sampdoria, Rangers, 1975–86) 54
Speedie D (Chelsea, Coventry, 1985–89) 10
Spencer J (Chelsea, QPR, 1995–97) 14
Stanton P (Hibs, 1966–74) 16
Steel W (Morton, Derby, Dundee, 1947–53) 30
Stein C (Rangers, Coventry, 1969–73) 21
Stephen J (Bradford City, 1947–48) 2
Stewart D (Leeds, 1978) 1
Stewart J (Kilmarnock, Middlesbrough, 1977–79) 2
Stewart M (Manchester Utd, Hearts 2002–09) 4
Stewart R (West Ham, 1981–7) 10
St John I (Motherwell, Liverpool, 1959–65) 21
Stockdale R (Middlesbrough, 2002–03) 5
Strachan G (Aberdeen, Manchester Utd, Leeds, 1980–92) 50
Sturrock P (Dundee Utd, 1981–87) 20
Sullivan N (Wimbledon, Tottenham, 1997–2003) 28

WALES

Aizlewood M (Charlton, Leeds, Bradford City, Bristol City, Cardiff, 1986–95) 39
Allchurch I (Swansea City, Newcastle, Cardiff, 1951–66) 68
Allchurch L (Swansea City, Sheffield Utd, 1955–64) 11

Teale G (Wigan, Derby, 2006–09) 13
Telfer P (Coventry, 2000) 1
Telfer W (St Mirren, 1954) 1
Thomson K (Rangers, Middlesbrough, 2009–11) 3
Thompson S (Dundee Utd, Rangers, 2002–05) 16
Thomson W (St Mirren, 1980–84) 7
Thornton W (Rangers, 1947–52) 7
Toner W (Kilmarnock, 1959) 2
Turnbull E (Hibs, 1948–58) 8

Ure I (Dundee, Arsenal, 1962–68) 11

Waddell W (Rangers, 1947–55) 17
Walker A (Celtic, 1988–95) 3
Walker N (Hearts, 1993–96) 2
Wallace I (Coventry, 1978–79) 3
Wallace L (Hearts, Rangers, 2010–14) 8
Wallace R (Preston, 2010) 1
Wallace W (Hearts, Celtic, 1965–69) 7
Wardhaugh J (Hearts, 1955–57) 2
Wark J (Ipswich, Liverpool, 1979–85) 29
Watson J (Motherwell, Huddersfield, 1948–54) 2
Watson R (Motherwell, 1971) 1
Webster A (Hearts, Rangers, Hearts, 2003–13) 28
Weir A (Motherwell, 1959–60) 6
Weir D (Hearts, Everton, Rangers, 1997–2011) 69
Weir P (St Mirren, Aberdeen, 1980–84) 6
White J (Falkirk, Tottenham, 1959–64) 22
Whittaker S (Rangers, Norwich, 2010–15) 29
Whyte D (Celtic, Middlesbrough, Aberdeen, 1988–99) 12
Wilkie L (Dundee, 2002–03) 11
Williams G (Nottm Forest, 2002–03) 5
Wilson A (Portsmouth, 1954) 1
Wilson D (Liverpool, 2011–12) 5
Wilson D (Rangers, 1961–65) 22
Wilson I (Leicester, Everton, 1987–8) 5
Wilson M (Celtic, 2011) 1
Wilson P (Celtic, 1975) 1
Wilson R (Arsenal, 1972) 2
Wood G (Everton, Arsenal, 1978–82) 4
Woodburn W (Rangers, 1947–52) 24
Wright K (Hibs, 1992) 1
Wright S (Aberdeen, 1993) 2
Wright T (Sunderland, 1953) 3

Yeats R (Liverpool, 1965–66) 2
Yorston H (Aberdeen, 1955) 1
Young A (Hearts, Everton, 1960–6) 8
Young G (Rangers, 1947–57) 53
Younger T (Hibs, Liverpool, 1955–58) 24

Allen B (Coventry, 1951) 2
Allen J (Swansea, Liverpool, 2009–15) 21
Allen M (Watford, Norwich, Millwall, Newcastle, 1986–94) 14

Baker C (Cardiff, 1958–62) 7

284

MacDonald S (Swansea, Bournemouth 2011–2015) 2
Maguire G (Portsmouth, 1990–92) 7
Mahoney J (Stoke, Middlesbrough, Swansea, 1968–83) 51
Mardon P (WBA, 1996) 1
Margetson M (Cardiff, 2004) 1
Marriott A (Wrexham, 1996–98) 5
Marustik C (Swansea, 1982–83) 6
Matthews A (Cardiff, Celtic, 2011–14) 12
Medwin T (Swansea, Tottenham, 1953–63) 29
Melville A (Swansea, Oxford Utd, Sunderland, Fulham, West Ham, 1990–2005) 65
Mielczarek R (Rotherham, 1971) 1
Millington A (WBA, Peterborough, Swansea, 1963–72) 21
Moore G (Cardiff, Chelsea, Manchester Utd, Northampton, Charlton, 1960–71) 21
Morgan C (MK Dons, Peterborough, Preston, 2007–11) 23
Morison S (Millwall, Norwich, 2011–13) 20
Morris W (Burnley, 1947–52) 5
Myhill B (Hull, WBA, 2008–14) 20

Nardiello D (Coventry, 1978) 2
Nardiello D (Barnsley, QPR, 2007–08) 3
Neilson G (Newcastle, Southampton, 1992–97) 5
Nicholas P (Crystal Palace, Arsenal, Crystal Palace, Luton, Aberdeen, Chelsea, Watford, 1979–92) 73
Niedzwiecki E (Chelsea, 1985–88) 2
Nogan L (Watford, Reading, 1991–96) 2
Norman T (Hull, 1986–88) 5
Nurse M (Swansea, Middlesbrough, 1960–63) 12
Nyatanga L (Derby, Bristol City, 2006–11) 34

O'Sullivan P (Brighton, 1973–78) 3
Oster J (Everton, Sunderland, 1997–2005) 13
Page M (Birmingham, 1971–79) 28
Page R (Watford, Sheffield Utd, Cardiff, Coventry, 1997–2006) 41
Palmer D (Swansea, 1957) 3
Parry J (Swansea, 1951) 1
Parry P (Cardiff, 2004–07) 11
Partridge D (Motherwell, Bristol City, 2005–06) 7
Pascoe C (Swansea, Sunderland, 1984–92) 10
Paul R (Swansea, Manchester City, 1949–56) 33
Pembridge M (Luton, Derby, Sheffield Wed, Benfica, Everton, Fulham, 1992–2005) 54
Perry J (Cardiff, 1994) 1
Phillips D (Plymouth Argyle, Manchester City, Coventry, Norwich, Nottm Forest, 1984–96) 62

Phillips J (Chelsea, 1973–78) 4
Phillips L (Cardiff, Aston Villa, Swansea, Charlton, 1971–82) 58
Pipe D (Coventry, 2003) 1
Pontin K (Cardiff, 1980) 2
Powell A (Leeds, Everton, Birmingham, 1947–51) 8
Powell D (Wrexham, Sheffield Utd, 1968–71) 11
Powell I (QPR, Aston Villa, 1947–51) 8
Price L (Ipswich, Derby, Crystal Palace, 2006–13) 11
Price P (Luton, Tottenham, 1980–84) 25
Pring K (Rotherham, 1966–67) 3
Pritchard H (Bristol City, 1985) 1

Ramsey A (Arsenal, 2009–15) 34
Rankmore F (Peterborough, 1966) 1
Ratcliffe K (Everton, Cardiff, 1981–93) 59
Ready K (QPR, 1997–98) 5
Reece G (Sheffield Utd, Cardiff, 1966–75) 29
Reed W (Ipswich, 1955) 2
Rees A (Birmingham, 1984) 1
Rees J (Luton, 1992) 1
Rees R (Coventry, WBA, Nottm Forest, 1965–72) 39
Rees W (Cardiff, Tottenham, 1949–50) 4
Ribeiro C (Bristol City, 2010–11) 2
Richards A (Swansea, 2012–15) 5
Richards J (Swansea, 2012) 1
Richards, S (Cardiff, 1947) 1
Ricketts S (Swansea, Hull, Bolton, Wolves, 2005–14) 52
Roberts A (QPR, 1993) 1
Roberts D (Oxford Utd, Hull, 1973–78) 17
Roberts G (Tranmere, 2000–06) 8
Roberts I (Watford, Huddersfield, Leicester, Norwich, 1990–2002) 15
Roberts J (Arsenal, Birmingham, 1971–76) 21
Roberts J (Bolton, 1949) 1
Roberts M (QPR, 1997) 1
Roberts N (Wrexham, Wigan, 2000–04) 4
Roberts P (Portsmouth, 1974) 4
Roberts S (Wrexham, 2005) 1
Robinson C (Wolves, Portsmouth, Sunderland, Norwich, Toronto 2000–08) 46
Robinson J (Charlton, 1996–2002) 30
Robson-Kanu H (Reading, 2010–15) 26
Rodrigues P (Cardiff, Leicester, City Sheffield Wed, 1965–74) 40
Rouse V (Crystal Palace, 1959) 1
Rowley T (Tranmere, 1959) 1
Rush I (Liverpool, Juventus, Liverpool, 1980–96) 73

Saunders D (Brighton, Oxford Utd, Derby, Liverpool, Aston Villa, Galatasaray, Nottm Forest, Sheffield Utd, Benfica, Bradford City, 1986–2001) 75
Savage R (Crewe, Leicester, Birmingham, 1996–2005) 39

Sayer P (Cardiff, 1977–8) 7
Scrine F (Swansea, 1950) 2
Sear C (Manchester City, 1963) 1
Sherwood A (Cardiff, Newport, 1947–57) 41
Shortt W (Plymouth Argyle, 1947–53) 12
Showers D (Cardiff, 1975) 2
Sidlow C (Liverpool, 1947–50) 7
Slatter N (Bristol Rov, Oxford Utd, 1983–89) 22
Smallman D (Wrexham, Everton, 1974–6) 7
Southall N (Everton, 1982–97) 92
Speed G (Leeds, Everton, Newcastle, 1990–2004) 85
Sprake G (Leeds, Birmingham, 1964–75) 37
Stansfield F (Cardiff, 1949) 1
Stevenson B (Leeds, Birmingham, 1978–82) 15
Stevenson N (Swansea, 1982–83) 4
Stitfall R (Cardiff, 1953–57) 2
Stock B (Doncaster, 2010–11) 3
Sullivan D (Cardiff, 1953–60) 17
Symons K (Portsmouth, Manchester City, Fulham, Crystal Palace, 1992–2004) 37

Tapscott D (Arsenal, Cardiff, 1954–59) 14
Taylor G (Crystal Palace, Sheffield Utd, Burnley, Nottm Forest, 1996–2005) 15
Taylor J (Reading, 2015) 1
Taylor N (Wrexham, Swansea, 2010–15) 22
Thatcher B (Leicester, Manchester City, 2004–05) 7
Thomas D (Swansea, 1957–58) 2
Thomas M (Wrexham, Manchester Utd, Everton, Brighton, Stoke, Chelsea, WBA, 1977–86) 51
Thomas M (Newcastle, 1987) 1
Thomas R (Swindon, Derby, Cardiff, 1967–78) 50
Thomas S (Fulham, 1948–49) 4
Toshack J (Cardiff, Liverpool, Swansea, 1969–80) 40
Trollope P (Derby, Fulham, Northampton, 1997–2003) 9

Tudur Jones O (Swansea, Norwich, Hibs, 2008–14) 7
Van den Hauwe P (Everton, 1985–89) 13
Vaughan D (Crewe, Real Sociedad, Blackpool, Sunderland, Nottm Forest, 2003–15) 39
Vaughan N (Newport, Cardiff, 1983–85) 10
Vearncombe G (Cardiff, 1958–61) 2
Vernon R (Blackburn, Everton, Stoke, 1957–68) 32
Villars A (Cardiff, 1974) 3
Vokes S (Wolves, Burnley, 2008–15) 33

Walley T (Watford, 1971) 1
Walsh I (Crystal Palace, 1980–82) 18
Ward D (Bristol Rov, Cardiff, 1959–62) 2
Ward D (Notts Co, Nottm Forest, 2000–04) 5
Webster C (Manchester Utd, 1957–58) 4
Weston R (Arsenal, Cardiff, 2000–05) 7
Williams A (Stockport, Swansea, 2008–15) 51
Williams A (Reading, Wolves, Reading, 1994–2003) 13
Williams A (Southampton, 1997–98) 2
Williams D (Norwich, 1986–87) 5
Williams G (Cardiff, 1951) 1
Williams G (Derby, Ipswich, 1988–96) 13
Williams G (West Ham, 2006) 2
Williams G (Fulham, 2014–15) 5
Williams GE (WBA, 1960–69) 26
Williams GG (Swansea, 1961–62) 5
Williams HJ (Swansea, 1965–72) 3
Williams HT (Newport, Leeds, 1949–50) 4
Williams J (Crystal Palace, 2013–15) 7
Williams S (WBA, Southampton, 1954–66) 43
Wilson H (Liverpool, 2014) 1
Wilson J (Oldham, 2014) 1
Witcomb D (WBA, Sheffield Wed, 1947) 3
Woosnam P (Leyton Orient, West Ham, Aston Villa, 1959–63) 17
Yorath T (Leeds, Coventry, Tottenham, Vancouver Whitecaps 1970–81) 59
Young E (Wimbledon, Crystal Palace, Wolves, 1990–96) 21

NORTHERN IRELAND

Aherne T (Belfast Celtic, Luton, 1947–50) 4
Anderson T (Manchester Utd, Swindon, Peterborough, 1973–79) 22
Armstrong G (Tottenham, Watford, Real Mallorca, WBA, 1977–86) 63
Baird C (Southampton, Fulham, Burnley, WBA, 2003–15) 72
Barr H (Linfield, Coventry, 1962–63) 3
Barton A (Preston, 2011) 1
Best G (Manchester Utd, Fulham, 1964–77) 37
Bingham W (Sunderland, Luton, Everton, Port Vale, 1951–64) 56
Black K (Luton, Nottm Forest, 1988–94) 30

Blair R (Oldham, 1975–76) 5
Blanchflower RD (Barnsley, Aston Villa, Tottenham, 1950–63) 56
Blanchflower J (Manchester Utd, 1954–58) 12
Blayney A (Doncaster, Linfield, 2006–11) 5
Bowler G (Hull, 1950) 3
Boyce L (Werder Bremen, Ross Co, 2011–15) 5
Braithwaite R (Linfield, Middlesbrough, 1962–65) 10
Braniff K (Portadown, 2010) 2
Brennan R (Luton, Birmingham, Fulham, 1949–51) 5
Briggs W (Manchester Utd, Swansea, 1962–65) 2
Brotherston N (Blackburn, 1980–85) 27
Bruce A (Hull, 2013–14) 2

288

Bruce W (Glentoran, 1961–67) 2
Brunt C (Sheffield Wed, WBA, 2005–15) 50
Bryan, M (Watford, 2010) 2

Camp L (Nottm Forest, 2011–13) 9
Campbell D (Nottm Forest, Charlton,
    1987–88) 2
Campbell J (Fulham, 1951) 1
Campbell R (Crusaders, 1963–65) 2
Campbell R (Bradford City, 1982) 2
Campbell W (Dundee, 1968–70) 6
Capaldi A (Plymouth Argyle,
    Cardiff, 2004–08) 22
Carey J (Manchester Utd, 1947–49) 7
Carroll R (Wigan, Manchester Utd, West Ham,
    Olympiacos, Notts Co, 1997–2015) 41
Carson J (Ipswich, 2011–13) 4
Carson S (Coleraine, 2009) 1
Casey T (Newcastle, Portsmouth,
    1955–59) 12
Casement C (Ipswich, 2009) 1
Caskey W (Derby, Tulsa, Roughnecks,
    1979–82) 7
Cassidy T (Newcastle, Burnley,
    1971–82) 24
Cathcart C (Blackpool, Watford, 2011–15) 21
Caughey M (Linfield, 1986) 2
Clarke C (Bournemouth, Southampton,
    QPR, Portsmouth, 1986–93) 38
Cleary J (Glentoran, 1982–85) 5
Clements D (Coventry, Sheffield Wed,
    Everton, New York Cosmos,
    1965–76) 48
Clingan S (Nottm Forest, Norwich, Coventry,
    Kilmarnock, 2006–15) 39
Clyde, M (Wolves, 2005) 3
Coates C (Crusaders, 2009–11) 6
Cochrane A (Coleraine, Burnley,
    Middlesbrough, Gillingham, 1976–84) 26
Cochrane D (Leeds, 1947–50) 10
Connell T (Coleraine, 1978) 1
Coote A (Norwich, 1999–2000) 6
Cowan J (Newcastle, 1970) 1
Coyle F (Coleraine, Nottm Forest,
    1956–58) 4
Coyle L (Derry City, 1989) 1
Coyle R (Sheffield Wed, 1973–74) 5
Craig D (Newcastle, 1967–75) 25
Craigan S (Partick, Motherwell, 2003–11) 54
Crossan E (Blackburn, 1950–55) 3
Crossan J (Sparta Rotterdam,
    Sunderland, Manchester City,
    Middlesbrough, 1960–68) 24
Cunningham W (St Mirren, Leicester,
    Dunfermline, 1951–62) 30
Cush W (Glenavon, Leeds, Portadown,
    1951–62) 26

Dallas S (Crusaders, Brentford, 2011–15) 5
D'Arcy S (Chelsea, Brentford, 1952–53) 5
Davis S (Aston Villa, Fulham, Rangers,
    Southampton, 2005–15) 74

Davison A (Bolton, Bradford City,
    Grimsby, 1996–97) 3
Dennison R (Wolves, 1988–97) 18
Devine J (Glentoran, 1990) 1
Dickson D (Coleraine, 1970–73) 4
Dickson T (Linfield, 1957) 1
Dickson W (Chelsea, Arsenal, 1951–55) 12
Doherty L (Linfield, 1985–88) 2
*Doherty P (Derby, Huddersfield,
    Doncaster, 1946–50) 6
Doherty T (Bristol City, 2003–05) 9
Donaghy M (Luton, Manchester Utd,
    Chelsea, 1980–94) 91
Donnelly L (Fulham, 2014) 1
Donnelly M (Crusaders, 2009) 1
Dougan D (Portsmouth, Blackburn, Aston
    Villa, Leicester, Wolves, 1958–73) 43
Douglas J (Belfast Celtic, 1947) 1
Dowd H (Glenavon, 1974) 3
Dowie I (Luton, Southampton, Crystal Palace,
    West Ham, QPR, 1990–2000) 59
Duff M (Cheltenham, Burnley, 2002–12) 24
Dunlop G (Linfield, 1985–90) 4

Eglington T (Everton, 1947–49) 6
Elder A (Burnley, Stoke, 1960–70) 40
Elliott S (Motherwell, Hull, 2001–08) 38
Evans C (Manchester Utd, Hull,
    Blackburn, 2009–15) 29
Evans J (Manchester Utd 2007–15) 42

Farrell P (Everton, 1947–49) 7
Feeney J (Linfield, Swansea, 1947–50) 2
Feeney W (Glentoran, 1976) 1
Feeney W (Bournemouth, Luton, Cardiff,
    Oldham, Plymouth 2002–12) 46
Ferguson G (Linfield, 1999–2001) 5
Ferguson S (Newcastle, 2009–15) 18
Ferguson W (Linfield, 1966–67) 2
Ferris R (Birmingham, 1950–52) 3
Fettis A (Hull, Nottm Forest, Blackburn,
    1992–99) 25
Finney T (Sunderland, Cambridge Utd,
    1975–80) 14
Fleming G (Nottm Forest, Manchester City,
    Barnsley, 1987–95) 31
Forde J (Ards, 1959–61) 4

Gallogly C (Huddersfield, 1951) 2
Garrett R (Stoke, Linfield, 2009–11) 5
Gaston R (Coleraine, 1969) 1
Gault M (Linfield, 2008) 1
Gillespie K (Manchester Utd, Newcastle,
    Blackburn, Leicester, Sheffield Utd,
    1995–2009) 86
Gorman J (Wolves, 2010–12) 9
Gorman W (Brentford, 1947–48) 4
Graham W (Doncaster, 1951–99) 14
Gray P (Luton, Sunderland, Nancy,
    Burnley, Oxford Utd, 1993–2001) 25
Gregg H (Doncaster, Manchester Utd,
    1954–64) 25

Griffin D (St Johnstone, Dundee Utd, Stockport, 1996–2004) — 29
Grigg W (Walsall, Brentford, 2012–15) — 7

Hamill R (Glentoran, 1999) — 1
Hamilton B (Linfield, Ipswich, Everton, Millwall, Swindon, 1969–80) — 50
Hamilton G (Glentoran, Portadown, 2003–08) — 5
Hamilton W (QPR, Burnley, Oxford Utd, 1978–86) — 41
Harkin J (Southport, Shrewsbury, 1968–70) — 5
Harvey M (Sunderland, 1961–71) — 34
Hatton S (Linfield, 1963) — 2
Healy D (Manchester Utd, Preston, Leeds, Fulham, Sunderland, Rangers, Bury, 2000–13) — 95
Healy F (Coleraine, Glentoran, 1982–83) — 4
Hegan D (WBA, Wolves, 1970–73) — 7
Hill C (Sheffield Utd, Leicester, Trelleborg, Northampton, 1990–99) — 27
Hill J (Norwich, Everton, 1959–64) — 7
Hinton E (Fulham, Millwall, 1947–51) — 7
Hodson L (Watford, MK Dons, 2011–15) — 15
Holmes S (Wrexham, 2002) — 1
Horlock K (Swindon, Manchester City, 1995–2003) — 32
Hughes A (Newcastle, Aston Villa, Fulham, QPR, Brighton, 1997–2015) — 96
Hughes J (Lincoln, 2006) — 2
Hughes M (Oldham, 2006) — 1
Hughes M (Manchester City, Strasbourg, West Ham, Wimbledon, Crystal Palace, 1992–2005) — 71
Hughes P (Bury, 1987) — 3
Hughes W (Bolton, 1951) — 1
Humphries W (Ards, Coventry, Swansea, 1962–65) — 14
Hunter A (Blackburn, Ipswich, 1970–80) — 53
Hunter B (Wrexham, Reading, 1995–2000) — 15
Hunter V (Coleraine, 1962) — 2
Ingham M (Sunderland, Wrexham, 2005–07) — 3
Irvine R (Linfield, Stoke, 1962–5) — 8
Irvine W (Burnley, Preston, Brighton, 1963–72) — 23

Jackson T (Everton, Nottm Forest, Manchester Utd, 1969–77) — 35
Jamison J (Glentoran, 1976) — 1
Jenkins I (Chester, Dundee Utd, 1997–2000) — 6
Jennings P (Watford, Tottenham, Arsenal, Tottenham, 1964–86) — 119
Johnson D (Blackburn, Birmingham, 1999–2010) — 56
Johnston W (Glenavon, Oldham, 1962–66) — 2
Jones J (Glenavon, 1956–57) — 3
Jones S (Crewe, Burnley, 2003–08) — 29
Keane T (Swansea, 1949) — 1
Kee P (Oxford Utd, Ards, 1990–95) — 9
Keith R (Newcastle, 1958–62) — 23
Kelly H (Fulham, Southampton, 1950–51) — 4

Kelly P (Barnsley, 1950) — 1
Kennedy P (Watford, Wigan, 1999–2004) — 20
Kirk A (Hearts, Boston, Northampton, Dunfermline, 2000–10) — 11

Lafferty D (Burnley 2012–14) — 11
Lafferty K (Burnley, Rangers, Sion, Palermo, Norwich 2006–15) — 44
Lawrie J (Port Vale, 2009–10) — 3
Lawther W (Sunderland, Blackburn, 1960–62) — 4
Lennon N (Crewe, Leicester, Celtic, 1994–2002) — 40
Little A (Rangers, 2009–13) — 9
Lockhart N (Linfield, Coventry, Aston Villa, 1947–56) — 8
Lomas S (Manchester City, West Ham, 1994–2003) — 45
Lutton B (Wolves, West Ham, 1970–4) — 6

Magennis J (Cardiff, Aberdeeen, Kilmarnock, 2010–15) — 11
Magill E (Arsenal, Brighton, 1962–66) — 26
Magilton J (Oxford Utd, Southampton, Sheffield Wed, Ipswich, 1991–2002) — 52
Mannus A (Linfield, St Johnstone, 2004–14) — 7
Martin C (Glentoran, Leeds, Aston Villa, 1947–50) — 6
McAdams W (Manchester City, Bolton, Leeds, 1954–62) — 15
*McAlinden J (Portsmouth, Southend, 1947–49) — 2
McArdle R (Rochdale, Aberdeen, Bradford, 2010–14) — 7
McAuley G (Lincoln, Leicester, Ipswich, WBA, 2005–15) — 53
McBride S (Glenavon, 1991–92) — 4
McCabe J (Leeds, 1949–54) — 6
McCann G (West Ham, Cheltenham, Barnsley, Scunthorpe, Peterborough, 2002–12) — 39
McCarthy J (Port Vale, Birmingham, 1996–2001) — 18
McCartney G (Sunderland, West Ham, Sunderland 2002–10) — 34
McCavana T (Coleraine, 1954–55) — 3
McCleary J (Cliftonville, 1955) — 1
McClelland J (Arsenal, Fulham, 1961–67) — 6
McClelland J (Mansfield, Rangers, Watford, Leeds, 1980–90) — 53
McCourt F (Manchester City, 1952–53) — 6
McCourt P (Rochdale, Celtic, Barnsley, Brighton, 2002–15) — 17
McCoy R (Coleraine, 1987) — 1
McCreery D (Manchester Utd, QPR, Tulsa, Newcastle, 1976–90) — 67
McCrory S (Southend, 1958) — 1
McCullough L (Doncaster, 2014–15) — 4
McCullough W (Arsenal, Millwall, 1961–67) — 10
McCurdy C (Linfield, 1980) — 1
McDonald A (QPR, 1986–96) — 52
McElhinney G (Bolton, 1984–85) — 6
McEvilly L (Rochdale, 2002) — 1
McFaul W (Linfield, Newcastle, 1967–74) — 6

McGarry J (Cliftonville, 1951) 3
McGaughey M (Linfield, 1985) 1
McGibbon P (Manchester Utd, Wigan, 1995–2000) 7
McGinn N (Derry, Celtic, Aberdeen, 2009–15) 36
McGivern R (Manchester City, Hibernian, Port Vale, 2009–15) 23
McGovern M (Ross Co, Hamilton, 2010–15) 4
McGrath C (Tottenham, Manchester 1974–79) 21
McIlroy J (Burnley, Stoke, 1952–66) 55
McIlroy S (Manchester Utd, Stoke, Manchester City, 1972–87) 88
McKay N (Inverness, Wigan, 2013–15) 10
McKeag W (Glentoran, 1968) 2
McKenna J (Huddersfield, 1950–52) 7
McKenzie R (Airdrie, 1967) 1
McKinney W (Falkirk, 1966) 1
McKnight A (Celtic, West Ham, 1988–89) 10
McLaughlin C (Preston, Fleetwood, 2012–15) 10
McLaughlin J (Shrewsbury, Swansea, 1962–66) 12
McLaughlin R (Liverpool, 2014–15) 3
McLean B (Motherwell, 2006) 1
McMahon G (Tottenham, Stoke, 1995–98) 17
McMichael A (Newcastle, 1950–60) 40
McMillan S (Manchester Utd, 1963) 2
McMordie A (Middlesbrough, 1969–73) 21
McMorran E (Belfast Celtic, Barnsley, Doncaster, 1947–57) 15
McNair P (Manchester Utd, 2015) 2
McNally B (Shrewsbury, 1987–88) 5
McPake J (Coventry, 2012) 1
McParland P (Aston Villa, Wolves, 1954–62) 34
McQuoid J (Millwall, 2011–12) 5
McVeigh P (Tottenham, Norwich, 1999–2005) 20
Montgomery F (Coleraine, 1955) 1
Moore C (Glentoran, 1949) 1
Moreland V (Derby, 1979–80) 6
Morgan S (Port Vale, Aston Villa, Brighton, Sparta Rotterdam, 1972–99) 18
Morrow S (Arsenal, QPR, 1990–2000) 39
Mulgrew J (Linfield, 2010) 2
Mullan G (Glentoran, 1983) 5
Mulryne P (Manchester Utd, Norwich, 1997–2005) 26
Murdock C (Preston, Hibs, Crewe, Rotherham, 2000–06) 34

Napier R (Bolton, 1966) 1
Neill T (Arsenal, Hull, 1961–73) 59
Nelson S (Arsenal, Brighton, 1970–82) 51
Nicholl C (Aston Villa, Southampton, Grimsby, 1975–83) 51
Nicholl J (Manchester Utd, Toronto, Sunderland, Rangers, WBA, 1976–86) 73
Nicholson J (Manchester Utd, Huddersfield, 1961–72) 41
Nolan I (Sheffield Wed, Bradford City, Wigan, 1997–2002) 18

Norwood O (Manchester Utd, Huddersfield, Reading, 2011–15) 25
O'Boyle G (Dunfermline, St Johnstone, 1994–99) 13
O'Connor M (Crewe, Scunthorpe, Rotherham, 2008–14) 11
O'Doherty A (Coleraine, 1970) 2
O'Driscoll J (Swansea, 1949) 3
O'Kane W (Nottm Forest, 1970–75) 20
O'Neill C (Motherwell, 1989–91) 3
O'Neill J (Sunderland, 1962) 1
O'Neill J (Leicester, 1980–86) 39
O'Neill M (Distillery, Nottm Forest, Norwich, Manchester City, Notts Co, 1972–85) 64
O'Neill M (Newcastle, Dundee Utd, Hibs, Coventry, 1989–97) 31
Owens J (Crusaders, 2011) 1

Parke J (Linfield, Hibs, Sunderland, 1964–68) 14
Paterson M (Scunthorpe, Burnley, Huddersfield, 2008–14) 22
Paton P (Dundee Utd, 2014) 1
Patterson D (Crystal Palace, Luton, Dundee Utd, 1994–99) 17
Patterson R (Coleraine, Plymouth, 2010–11) 5
Peacock R (Celtic, Coleraine, 1952–62) 31
Penney S (Brighton, 1985–89) 17
Platt J (Middlesbrough, Ballymena, Coleraine, 1976–86) 23
Quinn J (Blackburn, Swindon, Leicester, Bradford City, West Ham, Bournemouth, Reading, 1985–96) 46
Quinn SJ (Blackpool, WBA, Willem 11, Sheffield Wed, Peterborough, Northampton, 1996–2007) 50

Rafferty W (Wolves, 1980) 1
Ramsey P (Leicester, 1984–89) 14
Reeves B (MK Dons, 2015) 2
Rice P (Arsenal, 1969–80) 49
Robinson S (Bournemouth, Luton, 1997–2008) 7
Rogan A (Celtic, Sunderland, Millwall, 1988–97) 17
Ross W (Newcastle, 1969) 1
Rowland K (West Ham, QPR, 1994–99) 19
Russell A (Linfield, 1947) 1
Ryan R (WBA, 1950) 1

Sanchez L (Wimbledon, 1987–89) 3
Scott J (Grimsby, 1958) 2
Scott P (Everton, York, Aldershot, 1976–79) 10
Sharkey P (Ipswich, 1976) 1
Shields J (Southampton, 1957) 1
Shiels D (Hibs, Doncaster, Kilmarnock, Rangers, 2006–13) 14
Simpson W (Rangers, 1951–59) 12

Sloan D (Oxford Utd, 1969–71) — 2
Sloan J (Arsenal, 1947) — 1
Sloan T (Manchester Utd, 1979) — 3
Smith A (Glentoran, Preston, 2003–05) — 18
Smyth S (Wolves, Stoke, 1948–52) — 9
Smyth W (Distillery, 1949–54) — 4
Sonner D (Ipswich, Sheffield Wed, Birmingham, Nottm Forest, Peterborough, 1997–2005) — 13
Spence D (Bury, Blackpool, Southend, 1975–82) — 27
Sproule I (Hibs, 2006–08) — 11
*Stevenson A (Everton, 1947–48) — 3
Steele J (New York Bulls, 2014) — 3
Stewart A (Glentoran, Derby, 1967–69) — 7
Stewart D (Hull, 1978) — 1
Stewart I (QPR, Newcastle, 1982–87) — 31
Stewart T (Linfield, 1961) — 1

Taggart G (Barnsley, Bolton, Leicester, 1990–2003) — 51
Taylor M (Fulham, Birmingham, 1999–2012) — 88
Thompson A (Watford, 2011[1]) — 2
Thompson P (Linfield, 2006–08) — 7
Todd S (Burnley, Sheffield Wed, 1966–71) — 11
Toner C (Leyton Orient, 2003) — 2
Trainor D (Crusaders, 1967) — 1
Tuffey J (Partick, Inverness, 2009–11) — 8
Tully C (Celtic, 1949–59) — 10
Uprichard W (Swindon, Portsmouth, 1952–59) — 18

Vernon J (Belfast Celtic, WBA, 1947–52) — 17

Walker J (Doncaster, 1955) — 1
Walsh D (WBA, 1947–50) — 9
Walsh W (Manchester City, 1948–49) — 5
Ward J (Derby, 2012–15) — 16
Watson P (Distillery, 1971) — 1
Webb S (Ross Co, 2006–07) — 4
Welsh E (Carlisle, 1966–67) — 4
Whiteside N (Manchester Utd, Everton, 1982–90) — 38
Whitley Jeff (Manchester City, Sunderland, Cardiff, 1997–2006) — 20
Whitley Jim (Manchester City, 1998–2000) — 3
Williams M (Chesterfield, Watford, Wimbledon, Stoke, Wimbledon, MK Dons, 1999–2005) — 36
Williams P (WBA, 1991) — 1
Wilson D (Brighton, Luton, Sheffield Wed, 1987–92) — 24
Wilson K (Ipswich, Chelsea, Notts Co, Walsall, 1987–95) — 42
Wilson S (Glenavon, Falkirk, Dundee, 1962–68) — 12
Winchester C (Oldham, 2011) — 1
Wood T (Walsall, 1996) — 1
Worthington N (Sheffield Wed, Leeds, Stoke, 1984–97) — 66
Wright T (Newcastle, Nottm Forest, Reading, Manchester City, 1989–2000) — 31

REPUBLIC OF IRELAND

Aherne T (Belfast Celtic, Luton, 1946–54) — 16
Aldridge J (Oxford Utd, Liverpool, Real Sociedad, Tranmere, 1986–97) — 69
Ambrose P (Shamrock R, 1955–64) — 5
Anderson J (Preston, Newcastle, 1980–89) — 16
Andrews K (Blackburn, WBA, 2009–13) — 35
Arter H (Bournemouth, 2015) — 1
Babb P (Coventry, Liverpool, Sunderland, 1994–2003) — 35
Bailham E (Shamrock R, 1964) — 1
Barber E (Bohemians, Birmingham, 1966) — 2
Barrett G (Arsenal, Coventry, 2003–05) — 6
Beglin J (Liverpool, 1984–87) — 15
Bennett A (Reading, 2007) — 2
Best L (Coventry, 2009–10) — 7
Braddish S (Dundalk, 1978) — 2
Branagan K (Bolton, 1997) — 1
Bonner P (Celtic, 1981–96) — 80
Brady L (Arsenal, Juventus, Sampdoria, Inter-Milan, Ascoli, West Ham, 1975–90) — 72
Brady R (QPR, 1964) — 6
Brady R (Manchester Utd, Hull, 2013–15) — 14
Breen G (Birmingham, Coventry, West Ham, Sunderland, 1996–2006) — 63
*Breen T (Shamrock R, 1947) — 3
Brennan F (Drumcondra, 1965) — 1
Brennan S (Manchester Utd, Waterford, 1965–71) — 19
Browne W (Bohemians, 1964) — 3
Bruce A (Ipswich, 2007–09) — 2
Buckley L (Shamrock R, Waregem, 1984–85) — 2
Burke F (Cork Ath, 1952) — 1
Butler P (Sunderland, 2000) — 1
Butler T (Sunderland, 2003) — 2
Byrne A (Southampton, 1970–74) — 14
Byrne J (Shelbourne, 2004–06) — 2
Byrne J (QPR, Le Havre, Brighton, Sunderland, Millwall, 1985–93) — 23
Byrne P (Shamrock R, 1984–86) — 8

Campbell A (Santander, 1985) — 3
Campbell N (St Patrick's Ath, Fortuna Cologne, 1971–77) — 11
Cantwell N (West Ham, Manchester Utd, 1954–67) — 36
Carey B (Manchester Utd, Leicester, 1992–94) — 3
*Carey J (Manchester Utd, 1946–53) — 21
Carolan J (Manchester Utd, 1960) — 2

Carr S (Tottenham, Newcastle, 1999–2008) 43
Carroll B (Shelbourne, 1949–50) 2
Carroll T (Ipswich, 1968–73) 17
Carsley L (Derby, Blackburn, Coventry, Everton, 1997–2008) 39
Cascarino A (Gillingham, Millwall, Aston Villa, Chelsea, Marseille, Nancy, 1986–2000) 88
Chandler J (Leeds, 1980) 2
Christie C (Derby, 2015) 1
Clark C (Aston Villa, 2011–15) 11
Clarke C (Stoke, 2004) 2
Clarke J (Drogheda, 1978) 1
Clarke K (Drumcondra, 1948) 2
Clarke M (Shamrock R, 1950) 1
Clinton T (Everton, 1951–54) 3
Coad P (Shamrock R, 1947–52) 11
Coffey T (Drumcondra, 1950) 1
Colfer M (Shelbourne, 1950–51) 2
Coleman S (Everton, 2011–15) 28
Colgan N (Hibs, 2002–07) 9
Conmy O (Peterborough, 1965–70) 5
Connolly D (Watford, Feyenoord, Excelsior Feyenoord, Wimbledon, West Ham, Wigan, 1996–2006) 41
Conroy G (Stoke, 1970–77) 27
Conway J (Fulham, Manchester City, 1967–7) 20
Corr P (Everton, 1949–50) 4
Courtney E (Cork Utd, 1946) 1
Cox S (WBA, Nottm Forest, 2011–14) 30
Coyle O (Bolton, 1994) 1
Coyne T (Celtic, Tranmere, Motherwell, 1992–98) 22
Crowe G (Bohemians, 2003) 2
Cummins G (Luton, 1954–61) 19
Cuneen T (Limerick, 1951) 1
Cunningham G (Man City, Bristol City, 2010–13) 4
Cunningham K (Wimbledon, Birmingham, 1996–2006) 72
Curtis D (Shelbourne, Bristol City, Ipswich, Exeter, 1956–63) 17
Cusack S (Limerick, 1953) 1

Daish L (Cambridge Utd, Coventry, 1992–96) 5
Daly G (Manchester Utd, Derby, Coventry, Birmingham, Shrewsbury, 1973–87) 48
Daly M (Wolves, 1978) 2
Daly P (Shamrock R, 1950) 1
Deacy E (Aston Villa, 1982) 4
Delaney D (QPR, Ipswich, Crystal Palace, 2008–14) 9
Delap R (Derby, Southampton, 1998–2004) 11
De Mange K (Liverpool, Hull, 1987–89) 2
Dempsey J (Fulham, Chelsea, 1967–72) 19
Dennehy J (Cork Hibs, Nottm Forest, Walsall, 1972–77) 11
Desmond P (Middlesbrough, 1950) 4
Devine J (Arsenal, 1980–85) 13
Doherty G (Tottenham, Norwich, 2000–06) 34
Donovan D (Everton, 1955–57) 5
Donovan T (Aston Villa, 1980) 2
Douglas J (Blackburn, Leeds, 2004–08) 8
Doyle C (Shelbourne, 1959) 1
Doyle C (Birmingham, 2007) 1
Doyle K (Reading, Wolves, 2006–15) 61
Doyle M (Coventry, 2004) 1
Duff D (Blackburn, Chelsea, Newcastle, Fulham, 1998–2012) 100
Duffy B (Shamrock R, 1950) 1
Duffy S (Everton, 2014) 1
Dunne A (Manchester Utd, Bolton,1962–76) 33
Dunne J (Fulham, 1971) 1
Dunne P (Manchester Utd, 1965–67) 5
Dunne R (Everton, Manchester City, Aston Villa, 2000–14) 80
Dunne S (Luton, 1953–60) 15
Dunne T (Bolton, 1975) 1
Dunning P (Shelbourne, 1971) 2
Dunphy E (York, Millwall, 1966–71) 23
Dwyer N (West Ham, Swansea, 1960–65) 14

Eccles P (Shamrock R, 1986) 1
Eglington T (Shamrock R, Everton, 1946–56) 24
Elliot R (Newcastle, 2014–15) 3
Elliott S (Sunderland, 2005–07) 9
Evans M (Southampton, 1997) 1

Fagan E (Shamrock R, 1973) 1
Fagan F (Manchester City, Derby, 1955–61) 8
Fahey K (Birmingham, 2010–13) 16
Fairclough M (Dundalk, 1982) 2
Fallon S (Celtic, 1951–55) 8
Farrell P (Shamrock R, Everton, 1946–57) 28
Farrelly G (Aston Villa, Everton, Bolton, 1996–2000) 6
Finnan S (Fulham, Liverpool, Espanyol 2000–09) 53
Finucane A (Limerick, 1967–72) 11
Fitzgerald F (Waterford, 1955–6) 2
Fitzgerald P (Leeds, 1961–2) 5
Fitzpatrick K (Limerick, 1970) 1
Fitzsimons A (Middlesbrough, Lincoln, 1950–59) 26
Fleming C (Middlesbrough, 1996–8) 10
Fogarty A (Sunderland, Hartlepool Utd, 1960–64) 11
Folan C (Hull, 2009–10) 7
Foley D (Watford, 2000–01) 6
Foley K (Wolves, 2009–11) 8
Foley T (Northampton, 1964–67) 9
Fullam J (Preston, Shamrock R, 1961–70) 11
Forde D (Millwall, 2011–15) 23

Gallagher C (Celtic, 1967) 2
Gallagher M (Hibs, 1954) 1
Galvin A (Tottenham, Sheffield Wed, Swindon, 1983–90) 29
Gamble J (Cork City, 2007) 2

Lawrence L (Stoke, Portsmouth, 2009–11) 15
Lawrenson M (Preston, Brighton, Liverpool,
  1977–88) 39
Lee A (Rotherham, Cardiff, Ipswich,
  2003–07) 9
Leech M (Shamrock R, 1969–73) 8
Long S (Reading WBA, Hull, Southampton,
  2007–15) 54
Lowry D (St Patrick's Ath, 1962) 1
McAlinden J (Portsmouth, 1946) 2
McAteer J (Bolton, Liverpool, Blackburn,
  Sunderland, 1994–2004) 52
McCann J (Shamrock R, 1957) 1
McCarthy J (Wigan, Everton, 2011–15) 27
McCarthy M (Manchester City, Celtic,
  Lyon, Millwall, 1984–92) 57
McClean J (Sunderland, Wigan, 2012–15) 30
McConville T (Dundalk, Waterford,
  1972–73) 6
McDonagh J (Everton, Bolton, Sunderland,
  Notts Co, 1981–86) 25
McDonagh J (Shamrock R, 1984–85) 3
McEvoy A (Blackburn, 1961–67) 17
McGeady A (Celtic, Spartak Moscow,
  Everton, 2004–15) 76
McGee P (QPR, Preston, 1978–81) 15
McGoldrick E (Crystal Palace, Arsenal,
  1992–95) 15
McGoldrick D (Ipswich, 2015) 1
McGowan D (West Ham, 1949) 3
McGowan J (Cork Utd, 1947) 1
McGrath M (Blackburn, Bradford PA,
  1958–66) 22
McGrath P (Manchester Utd, Aston Villa,
  Derby, 1985–97) 83
Macken J (Manchester City, 2005) 1
Mackey G (Shamrock R, 1957) 3
McLoughlin A (Swindon, Southampton,
  Portsmouth, 1990–2000) 42
McMillan W (Belfast Celtic, 1946) 2
McNally B (Luton, 1959–63) 3
McPhail S (Leeds, 2000–04) 10
McShane P (WBA, Sunderland, Hull, 2006–15) 32
Macken A (Derby, 1977) 1
Madden P (Yeovil, 2014) 1
Mahon A (Tranmere, 2000) 3
Malone G (Shelbourne, 1949) 1
Mancini T (QPR, Arsenal, 1974–75) 5
Martin C (Glentoran, Leeds, Aston Villa,
  1946–56) 30
Martin M (Bohemians, Manchester Utd,
  1972–83) 52
Maybury A (Leeds, Hearts, Leicester,
  1998–2005) 10
Meagan M (Everton, Huddersfield,
  Drogheda, 1961–70) 17
Meyler D (Sunderland, Hull, 2013–15) 13
Miller L (Celtic, Manchester Utd,
  Sunderland, QPR 2004–10) 21
Milligan J (Oldham, 1992) 1
Mooney J (Shamrock R, 1965) 2
Moore A (Middlesbrough, 1996–97) 8

Moran K (Manchester Utd, Sporting Gijon,
  Blackburn, 1980–94) 71
Moroney T (West Ham, 1948–54) 12
Morris C (Celtic, Middlesbrough,
  1988–93) 35
Morrison C (Crystal Palace, Birmingham,
  Crystal Palace, 2002–07) 36
Moulson G (Lincoln, 1948–49) 3
Mucklan C (Drogheda, 1978) 1
Mulligan P (Shamrock R, Chelsea,
  Crystal Palace, WBA, Shamrock R,
  1969–80) 50
Munroe L (Shamrock R, 1954) 1
Murphy A (Clyde, 1956) 1
Murphy B (Bohemians, 1986) 1
Murphy D (Sunderland, Ipswich, 2007–15) 16
Murphy J (Crystal Palace, 1980) 3
Murphy J (Scunthorpe, 2009–10) 2
Murphy J (WBA, 2004) 1
Murphy P (Carlisle, 2007) 1
Murray T (Dundalk, 1950) 1

Newman W (Shelbourne, 1969) 1
Nolan E (Preston, 2009–10) 3
Nolan R (Shamrock R, 1957–63) 10

O'Brien Alan (Newcastle, 2007) 5
O'Brien Andy (Newcastle, Portsmouth,
  2001–07) 26
O'Brien F (Philadelphia Forest, 1980) 3
O'Brien J (Bolton, West Ham, 2006–13) 5
O'Brien L (Shamrock R, Manchester Utd,
  Newcastle, Tranmere, 1986–97) 16
O'Brien R (Notts Co, 1976–77) 5
O'Byrne L (Shamrock R, 1949) 1
O'Callaghan B (Stoke, 1979–82) 6
O'Callaghan K (Ipswich, Portsmouth,
  1981–87) 21
O'Cearuill J (Arsenal, 2007) 2
O'Connell A (Dundalk, Bohemians,
  1967–71) 2
O'Connor T (Shamrock R, 1950) 4
O'Connor T (Fulham, Dundalk, Bohemians,
  1968–73) 8
O'Dea D (Celtic, Toronto,
  Metalurh Donetsk, 2010–14) 20
O'Driscoll J (Swansea, 1949) 3
O'Driscoll S (Fulham, 1982) 3
O'Farrell F (West Ham, Preston, 1952–59) 9
*O'Flanagan Dr K (Arsenal, 1947) 3
O'Flanagan M (Bohemians, 1947) 1
O'Halloran A (Aston Villa, 2007) 2
O'Hanlon K (Rotherham, 1988) 1
O'Keefe E (Everton, Port Vale, 1981–85) 5
O'Leary D (Arsenal, 1977–93) 68
O'Leary P (Shamrock R, 1980–1) 7
O'Neill F (Shamrock R, 1962–72) 20
O'Neill J (Everton, 1952–59) 17
O'Neill J (Preston, 1961) 1
O'Neill K (Norwich, Middlesbrough,
  1996–2000) 13
O'Regan K (Brighton, 1984–85) 4

O'Reilly J (Cork Utd, 1946) — 3
O'Shea J (Manchester Utd, Sunderland, 2002–15) — 104

Pearce A (Reading, 2013–15) — 5
Peyton G (Fulham, Bournemouth, Everton, 1977–92) — 33
Peyton N (Shamrock R, Leeds, 1957–61) — 6
Phelan T (Wimbledon, Manchester City, Chelsea, Everton, Fulham, 1992–2000) — 42
Pilkington A (Norwich, Cardiff, 2014–15) — 8
Potter D (Wolves, 2007–08) — 5

Quinn A (Sheffield Wed, Sheffield Utd, 2003–07) — 7
Quinn B (Coventry, 2000) — 4
Quinn N (Arsenal, Manchester City, Sunderland, 1986–2002) — 92
Quinn S (Hull, 2013–15) — 12

Randolph D (Motherwell, 2013) — 2
Reid A (Nottm Forest, Tottenham, Charlton, Sunderland, Nottm Forest, 2004–14) — 29
Reid S (Millwall, Blackburn, 2002–09) — 23
Richardson D (Shamrock R, Gillingham, 1972–80) — 3
Ringstead A (Sheffield Utd, 1951–59) — 20
Robinson M (Brighton, Liverpool, QPR, 1981–86) — 24
Roche P (Shelbourne, Manchester Utd, 1972–76) — 8
Rogers E (Blackburn, Charlton, 1968–73) — 19
Rowlands M (QPR, 2004–10) — 5
Ryan G (Derby, Brighton, 1978–85) — 18
Ryan R (WBA, Derby, 1950–56) — 16

Sadlier R (Millwall, 2002) — 1
Sammon C (Derby, 2013–14) — 9
Savage D (Millwall, 1996) — 5
Saward P (Millwall, Aston Villa, Huddersfield, 1954–63) — 18
Scannell T (Southend, 1954) — 1
Scully P (Arsenal, 1989) — 1
Sheedy K (Everton, Newcastle, 1984–93) — 46
Sheridan C (Celtic, CSKA Sofia, 2010–11) — 3
Sheridan J (Leeds, Sheffield Wed, 1988–96) — 34

Slaven B (Middlesbrough, 1990–93) — 7
Sloan P (Arsenal, 1946) — 2
Smyth M (Shamrock R, 1969) — 1
St Ledger S (Preston, Leicester, 2009–14) — 37
Stapleton F (Arsenal, Manchester Utd, Ajax Derby, Le Havre, Blackburn, 1977–90) — 71
Staunton S (Liverpool, Aston Villa, Liverpool, Crystal Palace, Aston Villa, 1989–2002) — 102
*Stevenson A (Everton, 1947–49) — 6
Stokes A (Sunderland, Celtic, 2007–15) — 9
Strahan F (Shelbourne, 1964–65) — 5
Swan M (Drumcondra, 1960) — 1
Synnott N (Shamrock R, 1978–79) — 3

Thomas P (Waterford, 1974) — 2
Thompson J (Nottm Forest, 2004) — 1
Townsend A (Norwich, Chelsea, Aston Villa, Middlesbrough, 1989–97) — 70
Traynor T (Southampton, 1954–64) — 8
Treacy K (Preston, Burnley 2011–12) — 6
Treacy R (WBA, Charlton, Swindon, Preston, Shamrock R, 1966–80) — 42
Tuohy L (Shamrock R, Newcastle, Shamrock R, 1956–65) — 8
Turner A (Celtic, 1963) — 2

Vernon J (Belfast Celtic, 1946) — 2

Waddock G (QPR, Millwall, 1980–90) — 21
Walsh D (WBA, Aston Villa, 1946–54) — 20
Walsh J (Limerick, 1982) — 1
Walsh M (Blackpool, Everton, QPR, Porto, 1976–85) — 21
Walsh M (Everton, Norwich, 1982–83) — 4
Walsh W (Manchester City, 1947–50) — 9
Walters J (Stoke, 2011–15) — 33
Ward S (Wolves, Burnley, 2011–15) — 29
Waters J (Grimsby, 1977–80) — 2
Westwood K (Coventry, Sunderland, Sheffield Wed, 2009–15) — 17
Whelan G (Stoke, 2009–15) — 64
Whelan R (St Patrick's Ath, 1964) — 2
Whelan R (Liverpool, Southend, 1981–95) — 53
Whelan L (Manchester Utd, 1956–57) — 4
Whittaker R (Chelsea, 1959) — 1
Wilson M (Stoke, 2011–15) — 23

INTERNATIONAL GOALSCORERS 1946–2015

(start of season 2015–16)

ENGLAND

Charlton R	49
Lineker	48
Rooney	48
Greaves	44
Owen	40
Finney	30
Lofthouse	30
Shearer	30
Lampard Frank jnr	29
Platt	27
Robson B	26
Hurst	24
Mortensen	23
Crouch	22
Channon	21
Gerrard	21
Keegan	21
Peters	20
Defoe	19
Haynes	18
Hunt R	18
Beckham	17
Lawton	16
Taylor T	16
Woodcock	16
Scholes	14
Welbeck	14
Chivers	13
Mariner	13
Smith R	13
Francis T	12
Barnes J	11
Douglas	11
Mannion	11
Sheringham	11
Clarke A	10
Cole J	10
Flowers R	10
Gascoigne	10
Lee F.	10
Milburn	10
Wilshaw	10
Beardsley	9
Bell	9
Bentley	9
Hateley	9
Wright I	9
Ball	8
Broadis	8
Byrne J.	8
Hoddle	8
Kevan	8
Anderton	7
Connelly	7
Coppell	7
Fowler	7
Heskey	7
Paine	7
Young A	7
Charlton J	6
Johnson D	6
Macdonald	6
Mullen	6
Rowley	6
Terry	6
Vassell	6
Waddle	6
Wright-Phillips S	6
Adams	5
Atyeo	5
Baily	5
Brooking	5
Carter	5
Edwards	5
Ferdinand L	5
Hitchens	5
Latchford	5
Neal	5
Pearce	5
Pearson Stan	5
Pearson Stuart	5
Pickering F	5
Sturridge	5
Barmby	4
Barnes P	4
Bent	4
Bull	4
Dixon K	4
Hassall	4
Oxlade-Chamberlain	4
Revie	4
Robson R	4
Steven	4
Walcott	4
Watson Dave (Sunderland)	4
Webb	4
Baker	3
Barry	3
Blissett	3
Butcher	3
Cahill	3
Currie	3
Elliott	3
Ferdinand R	3
Francis G	3
Grainger	3
Jagielka	3
Kennedy R	3
Lambert	3
McDermott	3
McManaman	3
Matthews S	3
Merson	3
Morris	3
O'Grady	3
Peacock	3
Ramsey	3
Sewell	3
Townsend	3
Wilkins	3
Wright W	3
Allen R	2
Anderson	2
Bradley	2
Broadbent	2
Brooks	2
Carroll	2
Cowans	2
Eastham	2
Froggatt J	2
Froggatt R	2
Haines	2
Hancocks	2
Hunter	2
Ince	2
Johnson A	2
Keown	2
King	2
Lee R	2
Lee S	2
Moore	2
Perry	2
Pointer	2
Richardson	2
Royle	2
Smith A (1989–92)	2
Southgate	2
Stone	2
Taylor P	2
Tueart	2
Upson	2
Wignall	2
Wilshere	2
Worthington	2
A'Court	1
Astall	1
Baines	1
Beattie K	1
Bowles	1
Bradford	1
Bridge	1
Bridges	1
Brown	1
Campbell	1

Caulker	1	
Chamberlain	1	
Cole Andy	1	
Crawford	1	
Dixon L	1	
Ehiogu	1	
Goddard	1	
Hirst	1	
Hughes E	1	
Jeffers	1	
Jenas	1	
Johnson G	1	
Kane	1	
Kay	1	
Kidd	1	
Langton	1	
Lawler	1	
Lee J	1	
Lescott	1	
Le Saux	1	
Mabbutt	1	
Marsh	1	
Medley	1	
Melia	1	
Milner	1	
Mullery	1	
Murphy	1	
Nicholls	1	
Nicholson	1	
Nugent	1	
Palmer	1	
Parry	1	
Redknapp	1	
Richards	1	
Sansom	1	
Shackleton	1	
Smith A (2001–5)	1	
Sterling	1	
Stiles	1	
Summerbee	1	
Tambling	1	
Thompson Phil	1	
Viollet	1	
Wallace	1	
Walsh	1	
Weller	1	
Wise	1	
Withe	1	
Wright M	1	

SCOTLAND

Dalglish	30
Law	30
Reilly	22
McCoist	19
Miller K	18
McFadden	15
Johnston M	14

Collins J	12	
Gilzean	12	
Steel	12	
Jordan	11	
Collins R	10	
Johnstone R	10	
Stein	10	
Gallacher	9	
McStay	9	
Mudie	9	
St John	9	
Brand	8	
Gemmill A	8	
Leggat	8	
Robertson J (1978–84)	8	
Wilson Davie	8	
Boyd K	7	
Dodds	7	
Durie	7	
Gray A	7	
Wark	7	
Booth	6	
Brown A	6	
Cooper	6	
Daily	6	
Gough	6	
Liddell	6	
Maloney	6	
Murdoch	6	
Rioch	6	
Waddell	6	
Fletcher D	5	
Henderson W	5	
Hutchison	5	
Macari	5	
Masson	5	
McAllister G	5	
McQueen	5	
Naismith	5	
Nevin	5	
Nicholas	5	
O'Hare	5	
Scott A	5	
Strachan	5	
Young A	5	
Archibald	4	
Brown S	4	
Caldow	4	
Crawford	4	
Fletcher S	4	
Hamilton	4	
Hartford	4	
Herd D	4	
Jackson D	4	
Johnstone J	4	
Lorimer	4	
Mackay D	4	
Mason	4	

McGinlay	4	
McKinlay W	4	
McLaren	4	
O'Connor	4	
Smith G	4	
Souness	4	
Baxter	3	
Berra	3	
Bremner W	3	
Burley C	3	
Chalmers	3	
Ferguson B	3	
Gibson	3	
Graham G	3	
Gray E	3	
Greig	3	
Hendry	3	
Lennox	3	
MacDougall	3	
McCann	3	
McInally A	3	
McNeill	3	
McPhail	3	
Morris	3	
Morrison	3	
Rhodes	3	
Robertson J (1991–5)	3	
Snodgrass	3	
Sturrock	3	
Thompson	3	
White	3	
Anya	2	
Baird S	2	
Bauld	2	
Burke	2	
Caldwell G	2	
Cameron	2	
Commons	2	
Flavell	2	
Fleming	2	
Graham A	2	
Harper	2	
Hewie	2	
Holton	2	
Hopkin	2	
Houliston	2	
Jess	2	
Johnstone A	2	
Johnstone D	2	
Mackie	2	
McClair	2	
McCormack	2	
McGhee	2	
McMillan	2	
McManus	2	
Mulgrew	2	
Pettigrew	2	
Ring	2	

Robertson Archie 2
Shearer D 2
Aitken R 1
Bannon.......................... 1
Beattie 1
Bett 1
Bone 1
Boyd T 1
Brazil 1
Broadfoot....................... 1
Buckley 1
Burns 1
Calderwood 1
Campbell R 1
Clarkson 1
Combe 1
Conn 1
Craig 1
Curran 1
Davidson 1
Dickov 1
Dobie 1
Docherty 1
Duncan M 1
Elliott 1
Fernie 1
Freedman 1
Goodwillie....................... 1
Gray F 1
Gemmell T 1
Hanley............................ 1
Hartley 1
Henderson J 1
Holt 1
Howie 1
Hughes J 1
Hunter W 1
Hutchison T 1
Goodwillie....................... 1
Jackson C 1
Jardine 1
Johnstone L 1
Kyle 1
Lambert.......................... 1
Linwood.......................... 1
Mackail-Smith.................. 1
Mackay G 1
MacLeod 1
McAvennie 1
McCall 1
McCalliog 1
McArthur 1
McCulloch 1
McKenzie 1
McKimmie 1
McKinnon 1
McLean 1
McLintock 1

McSwegan 1
Miller W 1
Mitchell 1
Morgan 1
Mulhall 1
Murray J 1
Narey 1
Naysmith 1
Ormond 1
Orr 1
Parlane 1
Provan D 1
Quashie.......................... 1
Quinn 1
Ritchie M 1
Ritchie P 1
Robertson Andrew............ 1
Sharp 1
Stewart R 1
Thornton......................... 1
Wallace I 1
Webster.......................... 1
Weir A 1
Weir D 1
Wilkie 1
Wilson Danny 1

WALES

Rush 28
Allchurch I 23
Ford 23
Saunders 22
Bellamy 19
Bale 17
Earnshaw 16
Hughes M 16
Charles John 15
Jones C 15
Hartson 14
Toshack 13
Giggs 12
James L 10
Koumas 10
Davies RT 9
Ramsey 9
James R 8
Vernon 8
Davies RW 7
Flynn 7
Speed 7
Walsh I 7
Charles M 6
Curtis A 6
Davies S 6
Griffiths A 6
Medwin 6
Pembridge 6
Vokes 6
Clarke R 5

Leek 5
Blake............................. 4
Coleman 4
Deacy 4
Eastwood........................ 4
Edwards I 4
Tapscott.......................... 4
Thomas M 4
Woosnam 4
Allen M........................... 3
Bodin 3
Bowen M 3
Collins J 3
Edwards D 3
England 3
Ledley............................ 3
Melville 3
Palmer D 3
Rees R 3
Robinson J 3
Church 2
Cotterill 2
Davies G 2
Durban A 2
Dwyer 2
Edwards G 2
Evans C 2
Giles D 2
Godfrey........................... 2
Griffiths M 2
Hodges 2
Horne 2
Jones Barrie 2
Jones Bryn 2
King 2
Lowrie 2
Nicholas 2
Phillips D 2
Reece G 2
Robson-Kanu 2
Savage 2
Slatter 2
Symons 2
Yorath 2
Barnes 1
Blackmore 1
Blake.............................. 1
Bowen D 1
Boyle T 1
Burgess R 1
Charles Jeremy 1
Evans I 1
Fletcher 1
Foulkes........................... 1
Harris C 1
Hewitt R 1
Hockey 1
Jones A........................... 1

Jones D ... 1
Jones J ... 1
Krzywicki ... 1
Llewellyn ... 1
Lovell ... 1
Mahoney ... 1
Moore G ... 1
Morison ... 1
O'Sullivan ... 1
Parry ... 1
Paul ... 1
Powell A ... 1
Powell D ... 1
Price P ... 1
Roberts P ... 1
Robinson C ... 1
Smallman ... 1
Taylor ... 1
Vaughan ... 1
Williams Adrian ... 1
Williams Ashley ... 1
Williams GE ... 1
Williams GG ... 1
Young ... 1

N IRELAND

Healy ... 36
Lafferty ... 14
Clarke ... 13
Armstrong ... 12
Quinn JM ... 12
Dowie ... 11
Bingham ... 10
Crossan J ... 10
McIlroy J ... 10
McParland ... 10
Best ... 9
Whiteside ... 9
Dougan ... 8
Irvine W ... 8
O'Neill M (1972–85) ... 8
McAdams ... 7
Taggart G ... 7
Wilson S ... 7
Gray ... 6
McLaughlin ... 6
Nicholson J ... 6
Wilson K ... 6
Cush ... 5
Davis ... 5
Feeney ((2002–9)) ... 5
Hamilton W ... 5
Hughes M ... 5
Magilton ... 5
McAuley ... 5
McIlroy S ... 5
Simpson ... 5
Smyth S ... 5
Walsh D ... 5

Anderson T ... 4
Elliott ... 4
Hamilton B ... 4
McCann ... 4
McGrath ... 4
McMorran ... 4
O'Neill M (1989–96) ... 4
Quinn SJ ... 4
Brotherston ... 3
Harvey M ... 3
Lockhart ... 3
Lomas ... 3
McDonald ... 3
McMordie ... 3
Morgan S ... 3
Mulryne ... 3
Nicholl C ... 3
Paterson ... 3
Spence D ... 3
Tully ... 3
Blanchflower D ... 2
Casey ... 2
Clements ... 2
Doherty P ... 2
Finney ... 2
Gillespie ... 2
Harkin ... 2
Lennon ... 2
McCourt ... 2
McGinn ... 2
McMahon ... 2
Neill W ... 2
O'Neill J ... 2
Peacock ... 2
Penney ... 2
Stewart I ... 2
Ward ... 2
Whitley ... 2
Barr ... 1
Black ... 1
Blanchflower J ... 1
Brennan ... 1
Brunt ... 1
Campbell W ... 1
Caskey ... 1
Cassidy ... 1
Cochrane T ... 1
Crossan E ... 1
Dallas ... 1
D'Arcy ... 1
Doherty L ... 1
Elder ... 1
Evans C ... 1
Evans J ... 1
Ferguson S ... 1
Ferguson W ... 1
Ferris ... 1
Griffin ... 1
Hill C ... 1

Hughes ... 1
Humphries ... 1
Hunter A ... 1
Hunter B ... 1
Johnston ... 1
Jones J ... 1
Jones, S. ... 1
McCartney ... 1
McClelland (1961) ... 1
McCrory ... 1
McCurdy ... 1
McGarry ... 1
McVeigh ... 1
Moreland ... 1
Morrow ... 1
Murdock ... 1
Nelson ... 1
Nicholl J ... 1
O'Boyle ... 1
O'Kane ... 1
Patterson D ... 1
Patterson R ... 1
Rowland ... 1
Shiels ... 1
Sproule ... 1
Stevenson ... 1
Thompson ... 1
Walker ... 1
Welsh ... 1
Williams ... 1
Wilson D ... 1

REP OF IRELAND

Keane Robbie ... 65
Quinn N ... 21
Stapleton ... 20
Aldridge ... 19
Cascarino ... 19
Givens ... 19
Cantwell ... 14
Doyle ... 14
Daly ... 13
Harte ... 11
Long ... 11
Brady L ... 9
Connolly ... 9
Duff ... 9
Keane Roy ... 9
Kelly D ... 9
Morrison ... 9
Sheedy ... 9
Curtis ... 8
Dunne R ... 8
Grealish ... 8
Kilbane ... 8
McGrath P ... 8
Staunton ... 8
Breen G ... 7
Fitzsimons ... 7

Ringstead	7	Kennedy Mark	3	Dempsey	1
Townsend	7	Kinsella	3	Duffy	1
Coyne	6	McAteer	3	Elliott	1
Houghton	6	O'Shea	3	Fitzgerald J	1
McEvoy	6	Ryan R	3	Fullam J	1
Martin C	6	St Ledger S	3	Galvin	1
Moran	6	Waddock	3	Gibson	1
Cummins	5	Walsh M	3	Glynn	1
Fagan F	5	Whelan R	3	Green	1
Giles	5	Barrett	2	Grimes	1
Holland	5	Conroy	2	Healy	1
Lawrenson	5	Dennehy	2	Holmes	1
McGeady	5	Eglington	2	Hughton	1
Rogers	5	Fallon	2	Hunt	1
Sheridan	5	Finnan	2	Gibson	1
Treacy	5	Fitzgerald P	2	Kavanagh	1
Walsh D	5	Foley	2	Keogh R	1
Walters	5	Gavin	2	Kernaghan	1
Byrne J	4	Hale	2	Mancini	1
Cox	4	Hand	2	McCann	1
Doherty	4	Hoolahan	2	McPhail	1
Ireland	4	Hurley	2	Miller	1
Irwin	4	Kelly G	2	Mooney	1
McClean	4	Keogh A	2	Moroney	1
McGee	4	Lawrence	2	Mulligan	1
Martin M	4	Leech	2	O'Brien A	1
O'Neill K	4	McCarthy	2	O'Dea	1
Reid A	4	McLoughlin	2	O'Callaghan K	1
Robinson	4	O'Connor	2	O'Keefe	1
Tuohy	4	O'Farrell	2	O'Leary	1
Andrews	3	O'Reilly J	2	O'Neill F	1
Brady R	3	Pearce	2	Pilkington	1
Carey J	3	Whelan G	2	Ryan G	1
Coad	3	Reid S	2	Slaven	1
Conway	3	Ward	2	Sloan	1
Fahey	3	Ambrose	1	Strahan	1
Farrell	3	Anderson	1	Waters	1
Fogarty	3	Carroll	1	Wilson	1
Haverty	3	Clark	1		

HOME INTERNATIONAL RESULTS

Note: In the results that follow, WC = World Cup, EC = European Championship, CC = Carling Cup
TF = Tournoi de France For Northern Ireland read Ireland before 1921

ENGLAND V SCOTLAND

Played 112; England won 47; Scotland 41; drawn 24 Goals: England 198, Scotland 172

		E	S				
1872	Glasgow	0	0	1885	The Oval	1	1
1873	The Oval	4	2	1886	Glasgow	1	1
1874	Glasgow	1	2	1887	Blackburn	2	3
1875	The Oval	2	2	1888	Glasgow	5	0
1876	Glasgow	0	3	1889	The Oval	2	3
1877	The Oval	1	3	1890	Glasgow	1	1
1878	Glasgow	2	7	1891	Blackburn	2	1
1879	The Oval	5	4	1892	Glasgow	4	1
1880	Glasgow	4	5	1893	Richmond	5	2
1881	The Oval	1	6	1894	Glasgow	2	2
1882	Glasgow	1	5	1895	Goodison Park	3	0
1883	Sheffield	2	3	1896	Glasgow	1	2
1884	Glasgow	0	1	1897	Crystal Palace	1	2
				1898	Glasgow	3	1

1899	Birmingham	2	1
1900	Glasgow	1	4
1901	Crystal Palace	2	2
1902	Birmingham	2	2
1903	Sheffield	1	2
1904	Glasgow	1	0
1905	Crystal Palace	1	0
1906	Glasgow	1	2
1907	Newcastle	1	1
1908	Glasgow	1	1
1909	Crystal Palace	2	0
1910	Glasgow	0	2
1911	Goodison Park	1	1
1912	Glasgow	1	1
1913	Stamford Bridge	1	0
1914	Glasgow	1	3
1920	Sheffield	5	4
1921	Glasgow	0	3
1922	Birmingham	0	1
1923	Glasgow	2	2
1924	Wembley	1	1
1925	Glasgow	0	2
1926	Manchester	0	1
1927	Glasgow	2	1
1928	Wembley	1	5
1929	Glasgow	0	1
1930	Wembley	5	2
1931	Glasgow	0	2
1932	Wembley	3	0
1933	Glasgow	1	2
1934	Wembley	3	0
1935	Glasgow	0	2
1936	Wembley	1	1
1937	Glasgow	1	3
1938	Wembley	0	1
1939	Glasgow	2	1
1947	Wembley	1	1
1948	Glasgow	2	0
1949	Wembley	1	3
1950	Glasgow (WC)	1	0
1951	Wembley	2	3
1952	Glasgow	2	1
1953	Wembley	2	2
1954	Glasgow (WC)	4	2
1955	Wembley	7	2
1956	Glasgow	1	1
1957	Wembley	2	1
1958	Glasgow	4	0
1959	Wembley	1	0
1960	Glasgow	1	1
1961	Wembley	9	3
1962	Glasgow	0	2
1963	Wembley	1	2
1964	Glasgow	0	1
1965	Wembley	2	2
1966	Glasgow	4	3
1967	Wembley (EC)	2	3
1968	Glasgow (EC)	1	1
1969	Wembley	4	1
1970	Glasgow	0	0
1971	Wembley	3	1
1972	Glasgow	1	0
1973	Glasgow	5	0
1973	Wembley	1	0
1974	Glasgow	0	2
1975	Wembley	5	1
1976	Glasgow	1	2
1977	Wembley	1	2
1978	Glasgow	1	0
1979	Wembley	3	1
1980	Glasgow	2	0
1981	Wembley	0	1
1982	Glasgow	1	0
1983	Wembley	2	.0
1984	Glasgow	1	1
1985	Glasgow	0	1
1986	Wembley	2	1
1987	Glasgow	0	0
1988	Wembley	1	0
1989	Glasgow	2	0
1996	Wembley (EC)	2	0
1999	Glasgow (EC)	2	0
1999	Wembley (EC)	0	1
2013	Wembley	3	2
2014	Glasgow	3	1

ENGLAND v WALES

Played 101; England won 66; Wales 14; drawn 21; Goals: England 245 Wales 90

		E	W
1879	The Oval	2	1
1880	Wrexham	3	2
1881	Blackburn	0	1
1882	Wrexham	3	5
1883	The Oval	5	0
1884	Wrexham	4	0
1885	Blackburn	1	1
1886	Wrexham	3	1
1887	The Oval	4	0
1888	Crewe	5	1
1889	Stoke	4	1
1890	Wrexham	3	1
1891	Sunderland	4	1
1892	Wrexham	2	0
1893	Stoke	6	0
1894	Wrexham	5	1
1895	Queens Club, London	1	1
1896	Cardiff	9	1
1897	Bramall Lane	4	0
1898	Wrexham	3	0
1899	Bristol	4	0
1900	Cardiff	1	1
1901	Newcastle	6	0
1902	Wrexham	0	0
1903	Portsmouth	2	1
1904	Wrexham	2	2
1905	Anfield	3	1
1906	Cardiff	1	0
1907	Fulham	1	1
1908	Wrexham	7	1
1909	Nottingham	2	0
1910	Cardiff	1	0
1911	Millwall	3	0

Year	Venue		
1912	Wrexham	2	0
1913	Bristol	4	3
1914	Cardiff	2	0
1920	Highbury	1	2
1921	Cardiff	0	0
1922	Anfield	1	0
1923	Cardiff	2	2
1924	Blackburn	1	2
1925	Swansea	2	1
1926	Selhurst Park	1	3
1927	Wrexham	3	3
1927	Burnley	1	2
1928	Swansea	3	2
1929	Stamford Bridge	6	0
1930	Wrexham	4	0
1931	Anfield	3	1
1932	Wrexham	0	0
1933	Newcastle	1	2
1934	Cardiff	4	0
1935	Wolverhampton	1	2
1936	Cardiff	1	2
1937	Middlesbrough	2	1
1938	Cardiff	2	4
1946	Maine Road	3	0
1947	Cardiff	3	0
1948	Villa Park	1	0
1949	Cardiff (WC)	4	1
1950	Sunderland	4	2
1951	Cardiff	1	1
1952	Wembley	5	2
1953	Cardiff (WC)	4	1
1954	Wembley	3	2
1955	Cardiff	1	2
1956	Wembley	3	1
1957	Cardiff	4	0
1958	Villa Park	2	2
1959	Cardiff	1	1
1960	Wembley	5	1
1961	Cardiff	1	1
1962	Wembley	4	0
1963	Cardiff	4	0
1964	Wembley	2	1
1965	Cardiff	0	0
1966	Wembley (EC)	5	1
1967	Cardiff (EC)	3	0
1969	Wembley	2	1
1970	Cardiff	1	1
1971	Wembley	0	0
1972	Cardiff	3	0
1972	Cardiff (WC)	1	0
1973	Wembley (WC)	1	1
1973	Wembley	3	0
1974	Cardiff	2	0
1975	Wembley	2	2
1976	Wrexham	2	1
1976	Cardiff	1	0
1977	Wembley	0	1
1978	Cardiff	3	1
1979	Wembley	0	0
1980	Wrexham	1	4
1981	Wembley	0	0
1982	Cardiff	1	0
1983	Wembley	2	1
1984	Wrexham	0	1
2004	Old Trafford (WC)	2	0
2005	Cardiff (WC)	1	0
2011	Cardiff (EC)	2	0
2011	Wembley (EC)	1	0
		E	*I*

ENGLAND v N IRELAND

Played 98; England won 75; Ireland 7; drawn 16 Goals: England 323, Ireland 81

Year	Venue		
1882	Belfast	13	0
1883	Aigburth, Liverpool	7	0
1884	Belfast	8	1
1885	Whalley Range	4	0
1886	Belfast	6	1
1887	Bramall Lane	7	0
1888	Belfast	5	1
1889	Goodison Park	6	1
1890	Belfast	9	1
1891	Wolverhampton	6	1
1892	Belfast	2	0
1893	Perry Barr	6	1
1894	Belfast	2	2
1895	Derby	9	0
1896	Belfast	2	0
1897	Nottingham	6	0
1898	Belfast	3	2
1899	Sunderland	13	2
1900	Dublin	2	0
1901	Southampton	3	0
1902	Belfast	1	0
1903	Wolverhampton	4	0
1904	Belfast	3	1
1905	Middlesbrough	1	1
1906	Belfast	5	0
1907	Goodison Park	1	0
1908	Belfast	3	1
1909	Bradford PA	4	0
1910	Belfast	1	1
1911	Derby	2	1
1912	Dublin	6	1
1913	Belfast	1	2
1914	Middlesbrough	0	3
1919	Belfast	1	1
1920	Sunderland	2	0
1921	Belfast	1	1
1922	West Bromwich	2	0
1923	Belfast	1	2
1924	Goodison Park	3	1
1925	Belfast	0	0
1926	Anfield	3	3
1927	Belfast	0	2
1928	Goodison Park	2	1
1929	Belfast	3	0
1930	Bramall Lane	5	1
1931	Belfast	6	2
1932	Blackpool	1	0
1933	Belfast	3	0
1935	Goodison Park	2	1
1935	Belfast	3	1

Year	Venue			Year	Venue		
1936	Stoke	3	1	1969	Belfast	3	1
1937	Belfast	5	1	1970	Wembley	3	1
1938	Old Trafford	7	0	1971	Belfast	1	0
1946	Belfast	7	2	1972	Wembley	0	1
1947	Goodison Park	2	2	1973	*Goodison Park	2	1
1948	Belfast	6	2	1974	Wembley	1	0
1949	Maine Road (WC)	9	2	1975	Belfast	0	0
1950	Belfast	4	1	1976	Wembley	4	0
1951	Villa Park	2	0	1977	Belfast	2	1
1952	Belfast	2	2	1978	Wembley	1	0
1953	Goodison Park (WC)	3	1	1979	Wembley (EC)	4	0
1954	Belfast	2	0	1979	Belfast	2	0
1955	Wembley	3	0	1979	Belfast (EC)	5	1
1956	Belfast	1	1	1980	Wembley	1	1
1957	Wembley	2	3	1982	Wembley	4	0
1958	Belfast	3	3	1983	Belfast	0	0
1959	Wembley	2	1	1984	Wembley	1	0
1960	Belfast	5	2	1985	Belfast (WC)	1	0
1961	Wembley	1	1	1985	Wembley (WC)	0	0
1962	Belfast	3	1	1986	Wembley (EC)	3	0
1963	Wembley	8	3	1987	Belfast (EC)	2	0
1964	Belfast	4	3	2005	Old Trafford (WC)	4	0
1965	Wembley	2	1	2005	Belfast (WC)	0	1
1966	Belfast (EC)	2	0	(*Switched from Belfast because of political situation)			
1967	Wembley (EC)	2	0				

SCOTLAND v WALES
Played 107; Scotland won 61; Wales 23; drawn 23; Goals: Scotland 243, Wales 124

Year	Venue	S	W	Year	Venue	S	W
1876	Glasgow	4	0	1910	Kilmarnock	1	0
1877	Wrexham	2	0	1911	Cardiff	2	2
1878	Glasgow	9	0	1912	Tynecastle	1	0
1879	Wrexham	3	0	1913	Wrexham	0	0
1880	Glasgow	5	1	1914	Glasgow	0	0
1881	Wrexham	5	1	1920	Cardiff	1	1
1882	Glasgow	5	0	1921	Aberdeen	2	1
1883	Wrexham	3	0	1922	Wrexham	1	2
1884	Glasgow	4	1	1923	Paisley	2	0
1885	Wrexham	8	1	1924	Cardiff	0	2
1886	Glasgow	4	1	1925	Tynecastle	3	1
1887	Wrexham	2	0	1926	Cardiff	3	0
1888	Edinburgh	5	1	1927	Glasgow	3	0
1889	Wrexham	0	0	1928	Wrexham	2	2
1890	Paisley	5	0	1929	Glasgow	4	2
1891	Wrexham	4	3	1930	Cardiff	4	2
1892	Edinburgh	6	1	1931	Glasgow	1	1
1893	Wrexham	8	0	1932	Wrexham	3	2
1894	Kilmarnock	5	2	1933	Edinburgh	2	5
1895	Wrexham	2	2	1934	Cardiff	2	3
1896	Dundee	4	0	1935	Aberdeen	3	2
1897	Wrexham	2	2	1936	Cardiff	1	1
1898	Motherwell	5	2	1937	Dundee	1	2
1899	Wrexham	6	0	1938	Cardiff	1	2
1900	Aberdeen	5	2	1939	Edinburgh	3	2
1901	Wrexham	1	1	1946	Wrexham	1	3
1902	Greenock	5	1	1947	Glasgow	1	2
1903	Cardiff	1	0	1948	Cardiff (WC)	3	1
1904	Dundee	1	1	1949	Glasgow	2	0
1905	Wrexham	1	3	1950	Cardiff	3	1
1906	Edinburgh	0	2	1951	Glasgow	0	1
1907	Wrexham	0	1	1952	Cardiff (WC)	2	1
1908	Dundee	2	1	1953	Glasgow	3	3
1909	Wrexham	2	3	1954	Cardiff	1	0
				1955	Glasgow	2	0

Year	Venue			Year	Venue		
1956	Cardiff	2	2	1976	Glasgow	3	1
1957	Glasgow	1	1	1977	Glasgow (WC)	1	0
1958	Cardiff	3	0	1977	Wrexham	0	0
1959	Glasgow	1	1	1977	Anfield (WC)	2	0
1960	Cardiff	0	2	1978	Glasgow	1	1
1961	Glasgow	2	0	1979	Cardiff	0	3
1962	Cardiff	3	2	1980	Glasgow	1	0
1963	Glasgow	2	1	1981	Swansea	0	2
1964	Cardiff	2	3	1982	Glasgow	1	0
1965	Glasgow (EC)	4	1	1983	Cardiff	2	0
1966	Cardiff (EC)	1	1	1984	Glasgow	2	1
1967	Glasgow	3	2	1985	Glasgow (WC)	0	1
1969	Wrexham	5	3	1985	Cardiff (WC)	1	1
1970	Glasgow	0	0	1997	Kilmarnock	0	1
1971	Cardiff	0	0	2004	Cardiff	0	4
1972	Glasgow	1	0	2009	Cardiff	0	3
1973	Wrexham	2	0	2011	Dublin (CC)	3	1
1974	Glasgow	2	0	2012	Cardiff (WC)	1	2
1975	Cardiff	2	2	2013	Glasgow (WC	1	2

SCOTLAND v NORTHERN IRELAND

Played 96; Scotland won 64; Northern Ireland 15; drawn 17; Goals: Scotland 258, Northern Ireland 80

Year	Venue	S	I	Year	Venue	S	I
1884	Belfast	5	0	1927	Belfast	2	0
1885	Glasgow	8	2	1928	Glasgow	0	1
1886	Belfast	7	2	1929	Belfast	7	3
1887	Belfast	4	1	1930	Glasgow	3	1
1888	Belfast	10	2	1931	Belfast	0	0
1889	Glasgow	7	0	1932	Glasgow	3	1
1890	Belfast	4	1	1933	Belfast	4	0
1891	Glasgow	2	1	1934	Glasgow	1	2
1892	Belfast	3	2	1935	Belfast	1	2
1893	Glasgow	6	1	1936	Edinburgh	2	1
1894	Belfast	2	1	1937	Belfast	3	1
1895	Glasgow	3	1	1938	Aberdeen	1	1
1896	Belfast	3	3	1939	Belfast	2	0
1897	Glasgow	5	1	1946	Glasgow	0	0
1898	Belfast	3	0	1947	Belfast	0	2
1899	Glasgow	9	1	1948	Glasgow	3	2
1900	Belfast	3	0	1949	Belfast	8	2
1901	Glasgow	11	0	1950	Glasgow	6	1
1902	Belfast	5	1	1951	Belfast	3	0
1902	Belfast	3	0	1952	Glasgow	1	1
1903	Belfast	0	2	1953	Belfast	3	1
1904	Dublin	1	1	1954	Glasgow	2	2
1905	Glasgow	4	0	1955	Belfast	1	2
1906	Dublin	1	0	1956	Glasgow	1	0
1907	Glasgow	3	0	1957	Belfast	1	1
1908	Dublin	5	0	1958	Glasgow	2	2
1909	Glasgow	5	0	1959	Belfast	4	0
1910	Belfast	0	1	1960	Glasgow	5	1
1911	Glasgow	2	0	1961	Belfast	6	1
1912	Belfast	4	1	1962	Glasgow	5	1
1913	Dublin	2	1	1963	Belfast	1	2
1914	Belfast	1	1	1964	Glasgow	3	2
1920	Glasgow	3	0	1965	Belfast	2	3
1921	Belfast	2	0	1966	Glasgow	2	1
1922	Glasgow	2	1	1967	Belfast	0	1
1923	Belfast	1	0	1969	Glasgow	1	1
1924	Glasgow	2	0	1970	Belfast	1	0
1925	Belfast	3	0	1971	Glasgow	0	1
1926	Glasgow	4	0	1972	Glasgow	2	0
				1973	Glasgow	1	2

1974	Glasgow	0 1	1981	Belfast (WC)	0 0
1975	Glasgow	3 0	1982	Belfast	1 1
1976	Glasgow	3 0	1983	Glasgow	1 0
1977	Glasgow	3 0	1984	Belfast	0 2
1978	Glasgow	1 1	1992	Glasgow	1 0
1979	Glasgow	1 0	2008	Glasgow	0 0
1980	Belfast	0 1	2011	Dublin (CC)	3 0
1981	Glasgow (WC)	1 1	2015	Glasgow	1 0
1981	Glasgow	2 0			

WALES v NORTHERN IRELAND

Played 95; Wales won 44; Northern Ireland won 27; drawn 24; Goals: Wales 189, Northern Ireland 131

Year	Venue	W	l	Year	Venue	W	l
1882	Wrexham	7	1	1935	Wrexham	3	1
1883	Belfast	1	1	1936	Belfast	2	3
1884	Wrexham	6	0	1937	Wrexham	4	1
1885	Belfast	8	2	1938	Belfast	0	1
1886	Wrexham	5	0	1939	Wrexham	3	1
1887	Belfast	1	4	1947	Belfast	1	2
1888	Wrexham	11	0	1948	Wrexham	2	0
1889	Belfast	3	1	1949	Belfast	2	0
1890	Shrewsbury	5	2	1950	Wrexham (WC)	0	0
1891	Belfast	2	7	1951	Belfast	2	1
1892	Bangor	1	1	1952	Swansea	3	0
1893	Belfast	3	4	1953	Belfast	3	2
1894	Swansea	4	1	1954	Wrexham (WC)	1	2
1895	Belfast	2	2	1955	Belfast	3	2
1896	Wrexham	6	1	1956	Cardiff	1	1
1897	Belfast	3	4	1957	Belfast	0	0
1898	Llandudno	0	1	1958	Cardiff	1	1
1899	Belfast	0	1	1959	Belfast	1	4
1900	Llandudno	2	0	1960	Wrexham	3	2
1901	Belfast	1	0	1961	Belfast	5	1
1902	Cardiff	0	3	1962	Cardiff	4	0
1903	Belfast	0	2	1963	Belfast	4	1
1904	Bangor	0	1	1964	Swansea	2	3
1905	Belfast	2	2	1965	Belfast	5	0
1906	Wrexham	4	4	1966	Cardiff	1	4
1907	Belfast	3	2	1967	Belfast (EC)	0	0
1908	Aberdare	0	1	1968	Wrexham (EC)	2	0
1909	Belfast	3	2	1969	Belfast	0	0
1910	Wrexham	4	1	1970	Swansea	1	0
1911	Belfast	2	1	1971	Belfast	0	1
1912	Cardiff	2	3	1972	Wrexham	0	0
1913	Belfast	1	0	1973	*Goodison Park	0	1
1914	Wrexham	1	2	1974	Wrexham	1	0
1920	Belfast	2	2	1975	Belfast	0	1
1921	Swansea	2	1	1976	Swansea	1	0
1922	Belfast	1	1	1977	Belfast	1	1
1923	Wrexham	0	3	1978	Wrexham	1	0
1924	Belfast	1	0	1979	Belfast	1	1
1925	Wrexham	0	0	1980	Cardiff	0	1
1926	Belfast	0	3	1982	Wrexham	3	0
1927	Cardiff	2	2	1983	Belfast	1	0
1928	Belfast	2	1	1984	Swansea	1	1
1929	Wrexham	2	2	2004	Cardiff (WC)	2	2
1930	Belfast	0	7	2005	Belfast (WC)	3	2
1931	Wrexham	3	2	2007	Belfast	0	0
1932	Belfast	0	4	2008	Glasgow	0	0
1933	Wrexham	4	1	2011	Dublin (CC)	2	0
1934	Belfast	1	1				

(*Switched from Belfast because of political situation in N Ireland)

WORLD CUP SUMMARIES 1930–2014

1930 – URUGUAY

WINNERS: Uruguay RUNNERS-UP: Argentina THIRD: USA FOURTH: Yugoslavia
Other countries taking part: Belgium, Bolivia, Brazil, Chile, France, Mexico, Paraguay, Peru, Romania. **Total entries:** 13
Venue: All matches played in Montevideo
Top scorer: Stabile (Argentina) 8 goals
Final (30/7/30): **Uruguay 4** (Dorado 12, Cea 55, Iriarte 64, Castro 89) **Argentina 2** (Peucelle 29, Stabile 35). **Att:** 90,000
Uruguay: Ballesteros; Nasazzi (capt), Mascheroni, Andrade, Fernandez, Gestido, Dorado, Scarone, Castro, Cea, Iriarte
Argentina: Botasso; Della Torre, Paternoster, J Evaristo, Monti, Suarez, Peucelle, Varallo, Stabile, Ferreira (capt), M Evaristo
Referee: Langenus (Belgium). **Half-time:** 1-2

1934 – ITALY

WINNERS: Italy RUNNERS-UP: Czechoslovakia THIRD: Germany FOURTH: Austria
Other countries in finals: Argentina, Belgium, Brazil, Egypt, France, Holland, Hungary, Romania, Spain, Sweden, Switzerland, USA. **Total entries:** 29 (16 qualifiers)
Venues: Bologna, Florence, Genoa, Milan, Naples, Rome, Trieste, Turin
Top scorers: Conen (Germany), Nejedly (Czechoslovakia), Schiavio (Italy), each 4 goals. **Final** (Rome, 10/6/34): **Italy 2** (Orsi 82, Schiavio 97) **Czechoslovakia 1** (Puc 70) after extra-time.
Att: 50,000
Italy: Combi (capt); Monzeglio, Allemandi, Ferraris, Monti, Bertolini, Guaita, Meazza, Schiavio, Ferrari, Orsi
Czechoslovakia: Planicka (capt); Zenisek, Ctyroky, Kostalek, Cambal, Krcil, Junek, Svoboda, Sobotka, Nejedly, Puc
Referee: Eklind (Sweden). **Half-time:** 0-0 (90 mins: 1-1)

1938 – FRANCE

WINNERS: Italy RUNNERS-UP: Hungary THIRD: Brazil FOURTH: Sweden
Other countries in finals: Belgium, Cuba, Czechoslovakia, Dutch East Indies, France, Germany, Holland, Norway, Poland, Romania, Switzerland. **Total entries:** 25 (15 qualifiers)
Venues: Antibes, Bordeaux, Le Havre, Lille, Marseille, Paris, Reims, Strasbourg, Toulouse
Top scorer: Leonidas (Brazil) 8 goals
Final (Paris, 19/6/38): **Italy 4** (Colaussi 6, 36, Piola 15, 81) **Hungary 2** (Titkos 7, Sarosi 65).
Att: 45,000
Italy: Olivieri; Foni, Rava, Serantoni, Andreolo, Locatelli, Biavati, Meazza (capt), Piola, Ferrari, Colaussi
Hungary: Szabo; Polgar, Biro, Szalay, Szucs, Lazar, Sas, Vincze, Sarosi (capt), Szengeller, Titkos
Referee: Capdeville (France). **Half-time:** 3-1

1950 – BRAZIL

WINNERS: Uruguay RUNNERS-UP: Brazil THIRD: Sweden FOURTH: Spain
Other countries in finals: Bolivia, Chile, England, Italy, Mexico, Paraguay, Switzerland, USA, Yugoslavia. **Total entries:** 29 (13 qualifiers)
Venues: Belo Horizonte, Curitiba, Porto Alegre, Recife, Rio de Janeiro, Sao Paulo
Top scorer: Ademir (Brazil) 9 goals
Deciding Match (Rio de Janeiro, 16/7/50): **Uruguay 2** (Schiaffino 64, Ghiggia 79) **Brazil 1** (Friaca 47). **Att:** 199,850
(For the only time, the World Cup was decided on a final pool system, in which the winners of the four qualifying groups met in a six-match series So, unlike previous and subsequent

307

tournaments, there was no official final as such, but Uruguay v Brazil was the deciding match in the final pool)

Uruguay: Maspoli; Gonzales, Tejera, Gambetta, Varela (capt), Andrade, Ghiggia, Perez, Miguez, Schiaffino, Moran

Brazil: Barbosa; Augusto (capt), Juvenal, Bauer, Danilo, Bigode, Friaca, Zizinho, Ademir, Jair, Chico

Referee: Reader (England). **Half-time:** 0-0

1954 – SWITZERLAND

WINNERS: West Germany RUNNERS-UP: Hungary THIRD: Austria FOURTH: Uruguay
Other countries in finals: Belgium, Brazil, Czechoslovakia, England, France, Italy, Korea, Mexico, Scotland, Switzerland, Turkey, Yugoslavia. **Total entries:** 35 (16 qualifiers)
Venues: Basle, Berne, Geneva, Lausanne, Lugano, Zurich
Top scorer: Kocsis (Hungary) 11 goals
Final (Berne, 4/7/54): **West Germany 3** (Morlock 12, Rahn 17, 84) **Hungary 2** (Puskas 4, Czibor 9). **Att:** 60,000
West Germany: Turek; Posipal, Kohlmeyer, Eckel, Liebrich, Mai, Rahn, Morlock, O Walter, F Walter (capt), Schaefer
Hungary: Grosics; Buzansky, Lantos, Bozsik, Lorant, Zakarias, Czibor, Kocsis, Hidegkuti, Puskas (capt), J Toth
Referee: Ling (England). **Half-time:** 2-2

1958 – SWEDEN

WINNERS: Brazil RUNNERS-UP: Sweden THIRD: France FOURTH: West Germany
Other countries in finals: Argentina, Austria, Czechoslovakia, England, Hungary, Mexico, Northern Ireland, Paraguay, Scotland, Soviet Union, Wales, Yugoslavia. **Total entries:** 47 (16 qualifiers)
Venues: Boras, Eskilstuna, Gothenburg, Halmstad, Helsingborgs, Malmo, Norrkoping, Orebro, Sandviken, Stockholm, Vasteras
Top scorer: Fontaine (France) 13 goals
Final (Stockholm, 29/6/58): **Brazil 5** (Vava 10, 32, Pele 55, 88, Zagalo 76) **Sweden 2** (Liedholm 4, Simonsson 83). **Att:** 49,737
Brazil: Gilmar; D Santos, N Santos, Zito, Bellini (capt), Orlando, Garrincha, Didi, Vava, Pele, Zagalo
Sweden: Svensson; Bergmark, Axbom, Boerjesson, Gustavsson, Parling, Hamrin, Gren, Simonsson, Liedholm (capt), Skoglund
Referee: Guigue (France). **Half-time:** 2-1

1962 – CHILE

WINNERS: Brazil RUNNERS-UP: Czechoslovakia THIRD: Chile FOURTH: Yugoslavia
Other countries in finals: Argentina, Bulgaria, Colombia, England, Hungary, Italy, Mexico, Soviet Union, Spain, Switzerland, Uruguay, West Germany. **Total entries:** 53 (16 qualifiers)
Venues: Arica, Rancagua, Santiago, Vina del Mar
Top scorer: Jerkovic (Yugoslavia) 5 goals
Final (Santiago, 17/6/62): **Brazil 3** (Amarildo 17, Zito 69, Vava 77) **Czechoslovakia 1** (Masopust 16). **Att:** 68,679
Brazil: Gilmar; D Santos, Mauro (capt), Zozimo, N Santos, Zito, Didi, Garrincha, Vava, Amarildo, Zagalo
Czechoslovakia: Schroiff; Tichy, Novak, Pluskal, Popluhar, Masopust (capt), Pospichal, Scherer, Kvasnak, Kadraba, Jelinek
Referee: Latychev (Soviet Union). **Half-time:** 1-1

1966 – ENGLAND

WINNERS: England RUNNERS-UP: West Germany THIRD: Portugal FOURTH: USSR
Other countries in finals: Argentina, Brazil, Bulgaria, Chile, France, Hungary, Italy, Mexico, North Korea, Spain, Switzerland, Uruguay. **Total entries:** 53 (16 qualifiers)

Venues: Birmingham (Villa Park), Liverpool (Goodison Park), London (Wembley and White City), Manchester (Old Trafford), Middlesbrough (Ayresome Park), Sheffield (Hillsborough), Sunderland (Roker Park)
Top scorer: Eusebio (Portugal) 9 goals
Final (Wembley, 30/7/66): **England 4** (Hurst 19, 100, 120, Peters 78) **West Germany 2** (Haller 13, Weber 89) after extra-time. **Att:** 93,802
England: Banks; Cohen, Wilson, Stiles, J Charlton, Moore (capt), Ball, Hurst, Hunt, R Charlton, Peters
West Germany: Tilkowski; Hottges, Schnellinger, Beckenbauer, Schulz, Weber, Haller, Held, Seeler (capt), Overath, Emmerich
Referee: Dienst (Switzerland). **Half-time:** 1-1 (90 mins: 2-2)

1970 – MEXICO

WINNERS: Brazil RUNNERS-UP: Italy THIRD: West Germany FOURTH: Uruguay
Other countries in finals: Belgium, Bulgaria, Czechoslovakia, El Salvador, England, Israel, Mexico, Morocco, Peru, Romania, Soviet Union, Sweden. **Total entries:** 68 (16 qualifiers)
Venues: Guadalajara, Leon, Mexico City, Puebla, Toluca
Top scorer: Muller (West Germany) 10 goals
Final (Mexico City, 21/6/70): **Brazil 4** (Pele 18, Gerson 66, Jairzinho 71, Carlos Alberto 87) **Italy 1** (Boninsegna 38). **Att:** 107,412
Brazil: Felix; Carlos Alberto (capt), Brito, Piazza, Everaldo, Clodoaldo, Gerson, Jairzinho, Tostao, Pele, Rivelino
Italy: Albertosi; Burgnich, Facchetti (capt), Cera, Rosato, Bertini (Juliano 72), Domenghini, De Sisti, Mazzola, Boninsegna (Rivera 84), Riva
Referee: Glockner (East Germany). **Half-time:** 1-1

1974 – WEST GERMANY

WINNERS: West Germany RUNNERS-UP: Holland THIRD: Poland FOURTH: Brazil
Other countries in finals: Argentina, Australia, Bulgaria, Chile, East Germany, Haiti, Italy, Scotland, Sweden, Uruguay, Yugoslavia, Zaire. **Total entries:** 98 (16 qualifiers)
Venues: Berlin, Dortmund, Dusseldorf, Frankfurt, Gelsenkirchen, Hamburg, Hanover, Munich, Stuttgart
Top scorer: Lato (Poland) 7 goals
Final (Munich, 7/7/74): **West Germany 2** (Breitner 25 pen, Muller 43) **Holland 1** (Neeskens 2 pen). **Att:** 77,833
West Germany: Maier; Vogts, Schwarzenbeck, Beckenbauer (capt), Breitner, Bonhof, Hoeness, Overath, Grabowski, Muller, Holzenbein
Holland: Jongbloed; Suurbier, Rijsbergen (De Jong 69), Haan, Krol, Jansen, Van Hanegem, Neeskens, Rep, Cruyff (capt), Rensenbrink (R Van der Kerkhof 46)
Referee: Taylor (England). **Half-time:** 2-1

1978 – ARGENTINA

WINNERS: Argentina RUNNERS-UP: Holland THIRD: Brazil FOURTH: Italy
Other countries in finals: Austria, France, Hungary, Iran, Mexico, Peru, Poland, Scotland, Spain, Sweden, Tunisia, West Germany. **Total entries:** 102 (16 qualifiers)
Venues: Buenos Aires, Cordoba, Mar del Plata, Mendoza, Rosario
Top scorer: Kempes (Argentina) 6 goals
Final (Buenos Aires, 25/6/78): **Argentina 3** (Kempes 38, 104, Bertoni 115) **Holland 1** (Nanninga 82) after extra-time. **Att:** 77,000
Argentina: Fillol; Passarella (capt), Olguin, Galvan, Tarantini, Ardiles (Larrosa 66), Gallego, Ortiz (Houseman 74), Bertoni, Luque, Kempes
Holland: Jongbloed; Krol (capt), Poortvliet, Brandts, Jansen (Suurbier 73), Haan, Neeskens, W Van der Kerkhof, Rep (Nanninga 58), R Van der Kerkhof, Rensenbrink
Referee: Gonella (Italy). **Half-time:** 1-0 (90 mins: 1-1)

1982 – SPAIN

WINNERS: Italy RUNNERS-UP: West Germany THIRD: Poland FOURTH: France
Other countries in finals: Algeria, Argentina, Austria, Belgium, Brazil, Cameroon, Chile, Czechoslovakia, El Salvador, England, Honduras, Hungary, Kuwait, New Zealand, Northern Ireland, Peru, Scotland, Soviet Union, Spain, Yugoslavia. **Total entries:** 109 (24 qualifiers)
Venues: Alicante, Barcelona, Bilbao, Coruna, Elche, Gijon, Madrid, Malaga, Oviedo, Seville, Valencia, Valladolid, Vigo, Zaragoza
Top scorer: Rossi (Italy) 6 goals
Final (Madrid, 11/7/82): **Italy** 3 (Rossi 57, Tardelli 69, Altobelli 81) **West Germany** 1 (Breitner 84). **Att:** 90,089
Italy: Zoff (capt); Bergomi, Scirea, Collovati, Cabrini, Oriali, Gentile, Tardelli, Conti, Rossi, Graziani (Altobelli 18 – Causio 88)
West Germany: Schumacher; Kaltz, Stielike, K-H Forster, B Forster, Dremmler (Hrubesch 63), Breitner, Briegel, Rummenigge (capt) (Muller 70), Fischer, Littbarski
Referee: Coelho (Brazil). **Half-time:** 0-0

1986 – MEXICO

WINNERS: Argentina RUNNERS-UP: West Germany THIRD: France FOURTH: Belgium
Other countries in finals: Algeria, Brazil, Bulgaria, Canada, Denmark, England, Hungary, Iraq, Italy, Mexico, Morocco, Northern Ireland, Paraguay, Poland, Portugal, Scotland, South Korea, Soviet Union, Spain, Uruguay. **Total entries:** 118 (24 qualifiers)
Venues: Guadalajara, Irapuato, Leon, Mexico City, Monterrey, Nezahualcoyotl, Puebla, Queretaro, Toluca
Top scorer: Lineker (England) 6 goals
Final (Mexico City, 29/6/86): **Argentina** 3 (Brown 23, Valdano 56, Burruchaga 85) **West Germany** 2 (Rummenigge 74, Voller 82). **Att:** 115,026
Argentina: Pumpido; Cuciuffo, Brown, Ruggeri, Olarticoechea, Batista, Giusti, Maradona (capt), Burruchaga (Trobbiani 89), Enrique, Valdano
West Germany: Schumacher; Berthold, K-H Forster, Jakobs, Brehme, Briegel, Eder, Matthaus, Magath (Hoeness 62), Allofs (Voller 45), Rummenigge (capt)
Referee: Filho (Brazil). **Half-time:** 1-0

1990 – ITALY

WINNERS: West Germany RUNNERS-UP: Argentina THIRD: Italy FOURTH: England
Other countries in finals: Austria, Belgium, Brazil, Cameroon, Colombia, Costa Rica, Czechoslovakia, Egypt, Holland, Republic of Ireland, Romania, Scotland, Spain, South Korea, Soviet Union, Sweden, United Arab Emirates, USA, Uruguay, Yugoslavia. **Total entries:** 103 (24 qualifiers)
Venues: Bari, Bologna, Cagliari, Florence, Genoa, Milan, Naples, Palermo, Rome, Turin, Udine, Verona
Top scorer: Schillaci (Italy) 6 goals
Final (Rome, 8/7/90): **Argentina** 0 **West Germany** 1 (Brehme 85 pen). **Att:** 73,603
Argentina: Goycochea; Ruggeri (Monzon 45), Simon, Serrizuela, Lorenzo, Basualdo, Troglio, Burruchaga (Calderon 53), Sensini, Maradona (capt), Dezotti **Sent-off:** Monzon (65), Dezotti (86) – first players ever to be sent off in World Cup Final
West Germany: Illgner; Berthold (Reuter 75), Buchwald, Augenthaler, Kohler, Brehme, Matthaus (capt), Littbarski, Hassler, Klinsmann, Voller
Referee: Codesal (Mexico). **Half-time:** 0-0

1994 – USA

WINNERS: Brazil RUNNERS-UP: Italy THIRD: Sweden FOURTH: Bulgaria
Other countries in finals: Argentina, Belgium, Bolivia, Cameroon, Colombia, Germany, Greece, Holland, Mexico, Morocco, Nigeria, Norway, Republic of Ireland, Romania, Russia, Saudi Arabia, South Korea, Spain, Switzerland, USA. **Total entries:** 144 (24 qualifiers)

Venues: Boston, Chicago, Dallas, Detroit, Los Angeles, New York City, Orlando, San Francisco, Washington

Top scorers: Salenko (Russia), Stoichkov (Bulgaria), each 6 goals

Final (Los Angeles, 17/7/94): **Brazil** 0 **Italy** 0 after extra-time; Brazil won 3-2 on pens

Att: 94,194

Brazil: Taffarel; Jorginho (Cafu 21), Aldair, Marcio Santos, Branco, Mazinho, Mauro Silva, Dunga (capt), Zinho (Viola 105), Romario, Bebeto

Italy: Pagliuca; Mussi (Apolloni 35), Baresi (capt), Maldini, Benarrivo, Berti, Albertini, D Baggio (Evani 95), Donadoni, R Baggio, Massaro

Referee: Puhl (Hungary)

Shoot-out: Baresi missed, Marco Santos saved, Albertini 1-0, Romario 1-1, Evani 2-1, Branco 2-2, Massaro saved, Dunga 2-3, R Baggio missed

1998 – FRANCE

WINNERS: France RUNNERS-UP: Brazil THIRD: Croatia FOURTH: Holland

Other countries in finals: Argentina, Austria, Belgium, Bulgaria, Cameroon, Chile, Colombia, Denmark, England, Germany, Iran, Italy, Jamaica, Japan, Mexico, Morocco, Nigeria, Norway, Paraguay, Romania, Saudi Arabia, Scotland, South Africa, South Korea, Spain, Tunisia, USA, Yugoslavia. **Total entries:** 172 (32 qualifiers)

Venues: Bordeaux, Lens, Lyon, Marseille, Montpellier, Nantes, Paris (St Denis, Parc des Princes), Saint-Etienne, Toulouse

Top scorer: Davor Suker (Croatia) 6 goals

Final (Paris St Denis, 12/7/98): **Brazil** 0 **France** 3 (Zidane 27, 45, Petit 90). **Att:** 75,000

Brazil: Taffarel; Cafu, Junior Baiano, Aldair, Roberto Carlos; Dunga (capt), Leonardo (Denilson 46), Cesar Sampaio (Edmundo 74), Rivaldo; Bebeto, Ronaldo

France: Barthez; Thuram, Leboeuf, Desailly, Lizarazu; Karembeu (Boghossian 56), Deschamps (capt), Petit, Zidane, Djorkaeff (Viera 75); Guivarc'h (Dugarry 66) **Sent-off:** Desailly (68)

Referee: Belqola (Morocco). **Half-time:** 0-2

2002 – JAPAN/SOUTH KOREA

WINNERS: Brazil RUNNERS-UP: Germany THIRD: Turkey FOURTH: South Korea

Other countries in finals: Argentina, Belgium, Cameroon, China, Costa Rica, Croatia, Denmark, Ecuador, England, France, Italy, Japan, Mexico, Nigeria, Paraguay, Poland, Portugal, Republic of Ireland, Russia, Saudi Arabia, Senegal, Slovenia, South Africa, Spain, Sweden, Tunisia, USA, Uruguay. **Total entries:** 195 (32 qualifiers)

Venues: Japan – Ibaraki, Kobe, Miyagi, Niigata, Oita, Osaka, Saitama, Sapporo, Shizuoka, Yokohama. **South Korea** – Daegu, Daejeon, Gwangju, Incheon, Jeonju, Busan, Seogwipo, Seoul, Suwon Ulsan

Top scorer: Ronaldo (Brazil) 8 goals

Final (Yokohama, 30/6/02): **Germany** 0, **Brazil** 2 (Ronaldo 67, 79). **Att:** 69,029

Germany: Kahn (capt), Linke, Ramelow, Metzelder, Frings, Jeremies (Asamoah 77), Hamann, Schneider, Bode (Zeige 84), Klose (Bierhoff 74), Neuville

Brazil: Marcos, Lucio, Edmilson, Roque Junior, Cafu (capt) Kleberson, Gilberto Silva, Roberto Carlos, Ronaldinho (Juninho 85), Rivaldo, Ronaldo (Denilson 90)

Referee: Collina (Italy). **Half-time:** 0-0

2006 – GERMANY

WINNERS: Italy RUNNERS-UP: France THIRD: Germany FOURTH: Portugal

Other countries in finals: Angola, Argentina, Australia, Brazil, Costa Rica, Croatia, Czech Republic, Ecuador, England, Ghana, Holland, Iran, Ivory Coast, Japan, Mexico, Paraguay, Poland, Saudi Arabia, Serbia & Montenegro, South Korea, Spain, Sweden, Switzerland, Trinidad & Tobago, Togo, Tunisia, Ukraine, USA. **Total entries:** 198 (32 qualifiers)

Venues: Berlin, Cologne, Dortmund, Frankfurt, Gelsenkirchen, Hamburg, Hanover, Kaiserslautern, Leipzig, Munich, Nuremberg, Stuttgart

Top scorer: Klose (Germany) 5 goals
Final (Berlin, 9/7/06): **Italy** 1 (Materazzi 19) **France** 1 (Zidane 7 pen) after extra-time: Italy won 5-3 on pens. **Att:** 69,000
Italy: Buffon; Zambrotta, Cannavaro (capt), Materazzi, Grosso, Perrotta (De Rossi 61), Pirlo, Gattuso, Camoranesi (Del Piero 86), Totti (Iaquinta 61), Toni
France: Barthez; Sagnol, Thuram, Gallas, Abidal, Makelele, Vieira (Diarra 56), Ribery (Trezeguet 100), Malouda, Zidane (capt), Henry (Wiltord 107) **Sent-off:** Zidane (110)
Referee: Elizondo (Argentina). **Half-time:** 1-1 90 mins: 1-1
Shoot-out: Pirlo 1-0, Wiltord 1-1, Materazzi 2-1, Trezeguet missed, De Rossi 3-1, Abidal 3-2, Del Piero 4-2, Sagnol 4-3, Grosso 5-3

2010 – SOUTH AFRICA

WINNERS: Spain RUNNERS-UP: Holland THIRD: Germany FOURTH: Uruguay
Other countries in finals: Algeria, Argentina, Australia, Brazil, Cameroon, Chile, Denmark, England, France, Ghana, Greece, Honduras, Italy, Ivory Coast, Japan, Mexico, New Zealand, Nigeria, North Korea, Paraguay, Portugal, Serbia, Slovakia, Slovenia, South Africa, South Korea, Switzerland, USA. **Total entries:** 204 (32 qualifiers)
Venues: Bloemfontein, Cape Town, Durban, Johannesburg (Ellis Park), Johannesburg (Soccer City), Nelspruit, Polokwane, Port Elizabeth, Pretoria, Rustenburg
Top scorers: Forlan (Uruguay), Muller (Germany), Sneijder (Holland), Villa (Spain) 5 goals
Final (Johannesburg, Soccer City, 11/7/10): **Holland** 0 **Spain** 1 (Iniesta 116) after extra-time; **Att:** 84,490
Holland: Stekelenburg; Van der Wiel, Heitinga, Mathijsen, Van Bronckhorst (capt) (Braafheid 105), Van Bommel, De Jong (Van der Vaart 99), Robben, Sneijder, Kuyt (Elia 71), Van Persie. **Sent off:** Heitinga (109)
Spain: Casillas (capt); Sergio Ramos, Puyol, Piquet, Capdevila, Busquets, Xabi Alonso (Fabregas 87), Iniesta, Xavi, Pedro (Jesus Navas 60), Villa (Torres 106)
Referee: Webb (England). **Half-time:** 0-0

2014 – BRAZIL

WINNERS: Germany RUNNERS-UP: Argentina THIRD: Holland FOURTH: Brazil
Other countries in finals: Algeria, Argentina, Australia, Belgium, Bosnia-Herzegovina, Brazil, Cameroon, Chile, Colombia, Costa Rica, Croatia, Ecuador, England, France, Germany, Ghana, Greece, Holland, Honduras, Iran, Italy, Ivory Coast, Japan, Mexico, Nigeria, Portugal, Russia, South Korea, Spain, Switzerland, Uruguay, USA. **Total entries:** 204 (32 qualifiers)
Venues: Belo Horizonte, Brasilia, Cuiaba, Curitiba, Fortaleza, Manaus, Natal, Porto Alegre, Recife, Rio de Janeiro, Salvador, Sao Paulo
Top scorer: Rodriguez (Colombia) 6 goals
Final (Rio de Janeiro, 13/7/14): **Germany** 1 (Gotze 113) **Argentina** 0 after extra-time; **Att:** 74,738
Germany: Neuer; Lahm (capt), Boateng, Hummels, Howedes, Kramer (Schurrle 32), Schweinsteiger, Muller, Kroos, Ozil (Mertesacker 120), Klose (Gotze 88)
Argentina: Romero; Zabaleta, Demichelis, Garay, Rojo, Biglia, Mascherano, Perez (Gago 86), Messi (capt), Lavezzi (Aguero 46), Higuain (Palacio 78)
Referee: Rizzoli (Italy). **Half-time:** 0-0

BRITISH AND IRISH UNDER-21 INTERNATIONALS 2014–15

EUROPEAN CHAMPIONSHIP 2015 QUALIFYING

SLOVAKIA 1 SCOTLAND 1
Group 3: Senec (1,263): September 4 2014

Scotland: Archer (Tottenham), Jack (Aberdeen), Findlay (Celtic), McGhee (Hearts), Robertson (Aberdeen) (Hendrie, Hamilton 26), Macleod (Rangers), Slater (Kilmarnock), McGinn (St Mirren), Gauld (Sporting) (M Fraser, Celtic 88), R Fraser (Bournemouth) (McKenzie, Kilmarnock 82), May (Sheffield Wed). **Booked**: Gauld
Scorers – Slovakia: Duda (89). **Scotland**: R Fraser (67). **Half-time**: 0-0

LITHUANIA 0 ENGLAND 1
Group 1: Kaunas (3,500); September 5 2014

England: Butland (Stoke), Keane (Manchester Utd), Gibson (Middlesbrough) (Kane, Tottenham 55), Moore (Leicester), Garbutt (Everton), Ward-Prowse (Southampton), Chalobah (Chelsea), Ince (Hull) (Hughes, Derby 79), Carroll (Tottenham), Redmond (Norwich) (Pritchard, Tottenham 79), Berahino (WBA). **Booked**: Chalobah, Ward-Prowse
Scorer – England: Kane (81). **Half-time**: 0-0

FINLAND 2 WALES 2
Group 1: Turku (5,096); September 5 2014

Wales: Ward (Liverpool), Jones (Everton), Ray (Crewe), Walsh (Crawley), Fox (Charlton), Edwards (Crawley), Sheehan (Swansea), Evans (Wolves), Harrison (Bristol Rov) (Hedges, Swansea 65), O'Sullivan (Cardiff), Burns (Bristol City). **Booked**: Ray, Burns
Scorers – Finland: Lod (20), Vayrynen (88). **Wales**: Burns (66), Evans (70). **Half-time**: 1-0

GERMANY 2 REPUBLIC OF IRELAND 0
Group 6: Halle (3,969); September 5 2014

Republic of Ireland: Lawlor (Manchester City), Long (Reading), Hoban (Watford), Watkins-Clark (Stoke), Griffin (Reading), Byrne (Manchester City) (Sweeney, Reading 61), Lenihan (Blackburn), Sadlier (West Ham) (Garmston, WBA 65), Grealish (Aston Villa), Connors (Dagenham), Wilkinson (Bolton). **Booked**: Wilkinson
Scorers – Germany: P Hofmann (48), J Hofmann (51). **Half-time**: 0-0

LUXEMBOURG 0 SCOTLAND 3
Group 3: Differdange (243); September 8 2014

Scotland: Hamilton (Hearts), Jack (Aberdeen), Findlay (Celtic), McGhee (Hearts), Hendrie (Hamilton), Macleod (Rangers) (Christie, Inverness 72), Slater (Kilmarnock) (M Fraser, Celtic 63), McGinn (St Mirren), Gauld (Sporting) (McKenzie, Kilmarnock 85), R Fraser (Bournemouth), May (Sheffield Wed). **Booked**: Slater, M Fraser
Scorers – Scotland: Gauld (32, 63), Macleod (36). **Half-time**: 0-2

MOLDOVA 0 ENGLAND 3
Group 1: Tiraspol (2,654); September 9 2014

England: Bond (Watford), Keane (Manchester Utd), Moore (Leicester), Lascelles (Newcastle), Garbutt, Manchester Utd 81), Forster-Caskey (Brighton), Carroll (Tottenham), Redmond (Norwich) (Ings, Burnley 81), Hughes (Derby), Berahino (WBA) (Pritchard, Tottenham 86), Kane (Tottenham)
Scorers – England: Berahino (16, 52), Kane (85). **Half-time**: 0-1

LITHUANIA 1 WALES 1
Group 1: Alytus (550); September 9 2014
Wales: Ward (Liverpool), Hewitt (Ipswich), Williams (Liverpool), Walsh (Crawley), Fox (Charlton), Edwards (Crawley) (J Evans, Fulham 58), Sheehan (Swansea), L Evans (Wolves), O'Sullivan (Cardiff) (Wharton, Cardiff 74), Hedges (Swansea), Reid (Wolves) (Harrison, Bristol Rov 62).
Booked: L Evans, Hedges, Hewitt
Scorers – Lithuania: Tamulevicius (82). **Wales**: L Evans (90). **Half-time**: 0-0

NORTHERN IRELAND 1 SERBIA 4
Group 9: Shamrock Park, Portadown (285); September 9 2014
Northern Ireland: Johns (Southampton), Dummigan (Burnley), Conlan (Burnley) (Burns, Linfield 80), Sendles-White (QPR), Harney (West Ham), McNair (Manchester Utd) (McGeehan, Norwich 83), Winchester (Oldham), Doherty (Watford) (Millar, Linfield 58), Brobbel (Middlesbrough), Gray (Accrington), Duffy (Derry). **Booked**: Gray, Burns
Scorers – Northern Ireland: Brobbel (68). **Serbia**: Pesic (35), Srnic (37, 57), Kostic (59).
Half-time: 0-2

FINAL QUALIFYING TABLES

(Group winners and four best runners-up to two-leg play-offs to determine seven finalists. Czech Republic qualify as hosts

GROUP 1

	P	W	D	L	F	A	Pts
England	10	9	1	0	31	2	28
Finland	10	4	4	2	17	10	16
Moldova	10	5	1	4	12	6	16
Wales	10	3	3	4	12	13	12
Lithuania	10	2	2	6	6	19	8
San Marino	10	1	1	8	2	30	4

GROUP 2

	P	W	D	L	F	A	Pts
Denmark	10	8	2	0	37	9	26
Russia	10	7	1	2	22	12	22
Slovenia	10	5	2	3	29	11	17
Bulgaria	10	2	3	5	18	26	9
Estonia	10	2	3	5	9	23	9
Andorra	10	0	1	9	1	35	1

GROUP 3

	P	W	D	L	F	A	Pts
Slovakia	8	5	2	1	19	7	17
Holland	8	5	1	2	22	6	16
Scotland	8	3	2	3	12	15	11
Georgia	8	3	1	4	8	15	10
Luxembourg	8	1	0	7	5	23	3

GROUP 4

	P	W	D	L	F	A	Pts
Spain	8	7	1	0	24	6	22
Austria	8	5	1	2	15	12	16
Hungary	8	3	0	5	12	13	9
Bosnia-Herz	8	2	0	6	10	22	6
Albania	8	2	0	6	7	15	6

GROUP 5

	P	W	D	L	F	A	Pts
Croatia	8	6	1	1	20	5	19
Ukraine	8	6	1	1	20	8	19
Switzerland	8	5	0	3	23	8	15
Latvia	8	2	0	6	11	22	6
Liechtenstein	8	0	0	8	3	34	0

GROUP 6

	P	W	D	L	F	A	Pts
Germany	8	6	2	0	25	5	20
Romania	8	3	3	2	14	19	12
Montenegro	8	3	2	3	12	11	11
Republic of Ireland	8	2	2	4	10	12	8
Faroe Is	8	1	1	6	9	23	4

GROUP 7

	P	W	D	L	F	A	Pts
Sweden	8	5	1	2	20	14	16
Greece	8	5	0	3	20	10	15
Poland	8	5	0	3	17	10	15
Turkey	8	4	1	3	16	11	13
Malta	8	0	0	8	2	30	0

GROUP 8

	P	W	D	L	F	A	Pts
Portugal	8	8	0	0	22	6	24
Israel	8	5	0	3	22	15	15
Norway	8	3	0	5	11	19	9
Azerbaijan	8	2	1	5	9	15	7
Macedonia	8	1	1	6	4	13	4

GROUP 9

	P	W	D	L	F	A	Pts
Italy	8	6	0	2	19	7	18
Serbia	8	5	1	2	18	10	16
Belgium	8	5	1	2	15	7	16
Cyprus	8	2	0	6	7	21	6
Northern Ireland	8	1	0	7	3	17	3

GROUP 10

	P	W	D	L	F	A	Pts
France	8	7	1	0	28	7	22
Iceland	8	5	1	2	20	11	16
Kazakhstan	8	3	0	5	8	18	9
Armenia	8	3	0	5	7	19	9
Belarus	8	1	0	7	6	14	3

PLAY-OFFS

ENGLAND 2 CROATIA 1
First leg: Molineux (23,107); October 10, 2014

England: Butland (Stoke), Keane (Manchester Utd) (Dier, Tottenham 46), Moore (Leicester), Gibson (Middlesbrough), Shaw (Manchester Utd), Forster-Caskey (Brighton), Hughes (Derby), Redmond (Norwich), Carroll (Tottenham) (Ince, Hull 56), Berahino (WBA), Kane (Tottenham).
Booked: Dier, Moore
Scorers – England: Kane (58), Berahino (85 pen). **Croatia**: Livaja (13). **Half-time**: 0-1

315

CROATIA 1 ENGLAND 2 (England won 4-2 on agg)
Second leg: Vinkovci (6,000); October 14 2014
England: Butland (Stoke), Dier (Tottenham), Moore (Leicester), Gibson (Middlesbrough), Shaw (Manchester Utd), Forster-Caskey (Brighton), Hughes (Derby), Redmond (Norwich) (Ince, Hull 85), Carroll (Tottenham), Berahino (WBA), Kane (Tottenham). **Booked**: Hughes
Scorers – Croatia: Livaja (38). **England**: Moore (9), Hughes (73). **Half-time**: 1-1

ON AGGREGATE
Denmark 1 Iceland 1 (Denmark won on away goal); Germany 5 Ukraine 0; Italy 4 Slovakia 2; Portugal 7 Holland 4; Serbia 2 Spain 1; Sweden 4 France 3

EUROPEAN CHAMPIONSHIP 2017 – QUALIFYING

REPUBLIC OF IRELAND 1 ANDORRA 0
Group 2: RSC Waterford (1,588), March 26, 2015
Republic of Ireland: Rogers (Aberdeen), Connors (Dagenham), Lenihan (Blackburn), Hoban (Watford), Kavanagh (Fulham), Rea (Brighton), Byrne (Manchester City), Connolly (Ipswich) (Maguire, West Ham 90), McEvoy (Tottenham) (Browne, Preston, 86), O'Dowda (Oxford), Wilkinson (Bolton) (Goodwin, Brighton 72). **Scorer**: Connolly (31). **Half-time**: 1-0. **Booked**: Wilkinson, Rea, Connolly

WALES 3 BULGARIA 1
Group 5: Cardiff City Stadium (1,175): March 31, 2015
Wales: Dibble (Barnsley), Jones (Everton), Yorwerth (Cardiff), Wright (Huddersfield) (Smith, Shrewsbury 55), John (Cardiff), Sheehan (Swansea), Hedges (Swansea), Evans (Fulham), O'Sullivan (Cardiff) (Weeks, Wolves 46), Harrison (Bristol Rov) (Wilson, Liverpool 82), Burns (Bristol City). **Booked**: Burns, Weeks, Sheehan
Scorers – Wales: O'Sullivan (9, 13), Yorwerth (25). **Bulgaria**: Kolev (51). **Half-time**: 3-0

INTERNATIONAL FRIENDLIES

NORWAY 4 REPUBLIC OF IRELAND 1
Drammen (503); October 9, 2014
Republic of Ireland: Lawlor (Manchester City) (Rogers, Aberdeen 60), Long (Reading), Hoban (Watford), Sweeney (Reading) (Kavanagh, Fulham 46), Griffin (Reading) (Connolly, Shelbourne 60), O'Connell (Celtic), J Byrne (Manchester City), Lenihan (Blackburn) (Watkins-Clark, Stoke 46), Sadlier (West Ham) (Browne, Preston 46), Connors (Dagenham) (McEvoy, Tottenham 46), S Byrne (Everton) (Roberts, Dundee 60)
Scorers – Norway: Elyounoussi (27), Finne (33), Strand (53), Hansen (56). **Republic of Ireland**: Browne (75 pen). **Half-time**: 2-0

ENGLAND 3 PORTUGAL 1
Turf Moor, Burnley (10,711); November 13, 2014
England: Butland (Stoke), Jenkinson (Arsenal), Keane (Manchester Utd), Gibson (Middlesbrough), Garbutt (Everton) (Robinson, QPR 80), Ince (Hull), Hughes (Derby) (Chalobah, Chelsea 56), Forster-Caskey (Brighton), Carroll (Tottenham), Ings (Burnley) (Bamford, Chelsea 79), Redmond (Norwich) (Pritchard,Tottenham 73)
Scorers – England: Ings (6, 58), Jenkinson (44). **Portugal**: Bernardo-Silva (48). **Half-time**: 2-0

REPUBLIC OF IRELAND 0 USA 1
Marbella; November 15, 2014
Republic of Ireland: Rogers (Aberdeen), Long (Reading) (Lenihan, Blackburn 46), Hoban (Watford), Watkins-Clark (Stoke), Griffin (Reading), J Byrne (Manchester City) (Connolly, Shelbourne 90), Rea (Brighton), Kelly (Reading) (Hamilton, Wigan 46), Connors (Dagenham) (Hayhurst, Preston 46), Wilkinson (Bolton), McEvoy (Tottenham) (S Byrne (Everton) 46)
Scorer – USA: Yomba (13). **Half-time**: 0-1

FRANCE 3 ENGLAND 2
Brest (5,000); November 17, 2014
England: Bond (Watford); Lascelles (Newcastle), Keane (Manchester Utd), Gibson (Middlesbrough) (Jenkinson, Arsenal 42), Garbutt (Everton), Chalobah (Chelsea) (Forster-Caskey, Brighton 33), Carroll (Tottenham), Pritchard (Tottenham) (Ings, Burnley 46), Ince (Hull), Redmond (Norwich), Kane (Tottenham) (Wilson, Bournemouth 65)
Scorers – France: Sanogo (29, 44), Coman (73). **England**: Kane (20, 22). **Half-time**: 2-2

REPUBLIC OF IRELAND 2 RUSSIA 2
Marbella; November 17, 2014
Republic of Ireland: Rogers (Aberdeen) (Grimes, Leeds 46), Connors (Dagenham), Hoban (Watford), Lenihan (Blackburn) (Hoare, St Patrick's 73), Griffin (Reading), McEvoy (Tottenham), Connolly (Shelbourne) (Hayhurst, Preston 81), Desmond (Shelbourne) (O'Connell, Celtic 85), Hamilton (Wigan), Rea (Brighton), Browne (Preston) (Sadlier, West Ham 76)
Scorers – Republic of Ireland: Rea (5), Connolly (47). **Russia**: Morgunov (65), Sheydaev (77) **Half-time**: 1-0

SWITZERLAND 1 SCOTLAND 1
Thun (837); November 18, 2014
Scotland: Hamilton (Hearts) (Henly, Reading 56), M Fraser (Celtic) (Naismith, St Mirren 72), McGhee (Hearts) (Hyam, Reading, 56), Findlay (Celtic), Hendrie (Hamilton), Slater (Kilmarnock), Fulton (Swansea) (Handling, Hibernian) 56), A King (Swansea) (C King, Norwich 80), Gauld (Sporting), R Fraser (Bournemouth) (Christie, Inverness 72), McManus (Aberdeen) (Cardwell (Reading 72)
Scorers – Switzerland: Araz (43). **Scotland**: C King (90). **Half-time**: 1-0

HUNGARY 1 SCOTLAND 2
Tatabanya (650); March 26, 2015
Scotland: Hamilton (Hearts), Paterson (Hearts) (Love, Manchester Utd 46), McFadzean (Sheffield Utd) (Kingsley, Swansea 63), McGhee (Hearts), Findlay (Celtic) (Hyam, Reading 46), Handling (Hibernian) (O'Hara, Kilmarnock 76), Nicholson (Hearts) (Christie, Inverness, 46), McGinn (St Mirren) (Telfer, Dundee Utd 76), McManus (Aberdeen) (Shankland, Aberdeen, 46), Gauld (Sporting) (Smith, Aberdeen 76), Fraser (Bournemouth) (King, Hearts 63)
Scorers – Hungary: Bence (62). **Scotland**: Shankland (85, 90). **Half-time**: 0-0

CZECH REPUBLIC 0 ENGLAND 1
Prague (5,126); March 27, 2015
England: Bettinelli (Fulham), Chambers (Arsenal) (Jenkinson, Arsenal 62), Keane (Burnley), Moore (Leicester) (Stones, Everton, 70), Targett (Southampton) (Garbutt, Everton 46), Ward-Prowse (Southampton), Forster-Caskey (Brighton), Redmond (Norwich), Carroll (Tottenham) (Hughes, Derby 53), Pritchard (Tottenham) (Lingard, Manchester Utd 62), Woodrow (Fulham) (Ings, Burnley 62)
Scorer – England: Carroll (47). **Half-time**: 0-0

ENGLAND 3 GERMANY 2
Riverside Stadium, Middlesbrough (30,178); March 30, 2015
England: Bond (Watford), Jenkinson (Arsenal), Stones (Everton), Gibson (Middlesbrough) (Keane, Burnley 77), Garbutt (Everton), Ward-Prowse (Southampton), Forster-Caskey (Brighton) (Chambers, Arsenal 86), Lingard (Manchester Utd), Hughes (Derby) (Pritchard, Tottenham 65), Redmond (Norwich), Ings (Burnley)
Scorers – England: Lingard (34), Redmond (79), Ward-Prowse (82). **Germany**: Hofmann (15, 50). **Half-time**: 1-1

ENGLAND 1 BELARUS 0
Oakwell Stadium, Barnsley (15,207); Thursday, June 11 2015
England: Butland (Stoke) (Bond, Watford 69), Jenkinson (Arsenal), Stones (Everton) (Chambers, Arsenal 46), Gibson (Middlesbrough), Garbutt (Everton), Ward-Prowse (Southampton) (Chalobah, Chelsea 69), Hughes (Derby) (Loftus-Cheek, Chelsea 46), Redmond (Norwich) (Ings, Liverpool 60), Carroll (Tottenham) (Forster-Caskey, Brighton 69), Pritchard (Tottenham) (Lingard, Manchester Utd 69), Berahino (WBA) (Kane, Tottenham 60). **Booked**: Garbutt
Scorer – Gibson (83). **Half-time: 0-0

317

TRANSFER TRAIL

Player	From	To	Date	£
Gareth Bale	Tottenham	Real Madrid	8/13	85,300,000
Cristiano Ronaldo	Manchester Utd	Real Madrid	7/09	80,000,000
Luis Suarez	Liverpool	Barcelona	7/14	75,000,000
Angel di Maria	Real Madrid	Manchester Utd	8/14	59,700,000
Fernando Torres	Liverpool	Chelsea	1/11	50,000,000
Mesut Ozil	Real Madrid	Arsenal	9/13	42,400,000
David Luiz	Chelsea	Paris SG	6/14	40,000,000
Sergio Aguero	Atletico Madrid	Manchester City	7/11	38,500,000
Juan Mata	Chelsea	Manchester Utd	1/14	37,100,000
Andy Carroll	Newcastle	Liverpool	1/11	35,000,000
Cesc Fabregas	Arsenal	Barcelona	8/11	35,000,000
Alexis Sanchez	Barcelona	Arsenal	7/14	35,000,000
Robinho	Real Madrid	Manchester City	9/08	32,500,000
Eden Hazard	Lille	Chelsea	6/12	32,000,000
Diego Costa	Atletico Madrid	Chelsea	7/14	32,000,000
Eliaquim Mangala	Porto	Manchester City	8/14	31,900,000
Dimitar Berbatov	Tottenham	Manchester Utd	9/08	30,750,000
Andriy Shevchenko	AC Milan	Chelsea	5/06	30,800,000
Xabi Alonso	Liverpool	Real Madrid	8/09	30,000,000
Fernandinho	Shakhtar Donetsk	Manchester City	6/13	30,000,000
Willian	Anzhi Makhachkala	Chelsea	8/13	30,000,000
Erik Lamela	Roma	Tottenham	8/13	30,000,000
Luke Shaw	Southampton	Manchester Utd	6/14	30,000,000
Rio Ferdinand	Leeds	Manchester Utd	7/02	29,100,000
Ander Herrera	Athletic Bilbao	Manchester Utd	6/14	28,800,000
Juan Sebastian Veron	Lazio	Manchester Utd	7/01	28,100,000
Romelu Lukaku	Chelsea	Everton	7/14	28,000,000
Yaya Toure	Barcelona	Manchester City	7/10	28,000,000
Wilfried Bony	Swansea	Manchester City	1/15	28,000,000
Roberto Firmino	Hoffenheim	Liverpool	6/15	28,000,000
Marouane Fellaini	Everton	Manchester Utd	9/13	27,500,000
Wayne Rooney	Everton	Manchester Utd	8/04	27,000,000
Edin Dzeko	Wolfsburg	Manchester City	1/11	27,000,000
Luka Modric	Tottenham	Real Madrid	8/12	27,000,000
Cesc Fabregas	Barcelona	Chelsea	6/14	27,000,000
Roberto Soldado	Valencia	Tottenham	8/13	26,000,000
Marc Overmars	Arsenal	Barcelona	7/00	25,000,000
Carlos Tevez	Manchester Utd	Manchester City	7/09	25,000,000
Emmanuel Adebayor	Arsenal	Manchester City	7/09	25,000,000
Samir Nasri	Arsenal	Manchester City	8/11	25,000,000
Oscar	Internacional	Chelsea	7/12	25,000,000
Adam Lallana	Southampton	Liverpool	7/14	25,000,000
Memphis Depay	PSV Eindhoven	Manchester Utd	6/15	25,000,000
Arjen Robben	Chelsea	Real Madrid	8/07	24,500,000
Michael Essien	Lyon	Chelsea	8/05	24,400,000
David Silva	Valencia	Manchester City	7/10	24,000,000
James Milner	Aston Villa	Manchester City	8/10	24,000,000
Mario Balotelli	Inter Milan	Manchester City	8/10	24,000,000
Robin van Persie	Arsenal	Manchester Utd	8/12	24,000,000
Juan Mata	Valencia	Chelsea	8/11	23,500,000
David Beckham	Manchester Utd	Real Madrid	7/03	23,300,000

Juan Cuadrado	Fiorentina	Chelsea	2/15	23,300,000
Didier Drogba	Marseille	Chelsea	7/04	23,200,000
Andre Schurrle	Chelsea	Wolfsburg	2/15	23,000,000
Luis Suarez	Ajax	Liverpool	1/11	22,700,000
Nicolas Anelka	Arsenal	Real Madrid	8/99	22,300,000
Fernando Torres	Atletico Madrid	Liverpool	7/07	22,000,000
Joleon Lescott	Everton	Manchester City	8/09	22,000,000
Stevan Jovetic	Fiorentina	Manchester City	7/13	22,000,000
David Luiz	Benfica	Chelsea	1/11	21,300,000
Shaun Wright-Phillips	Manchester City	Chelsea	7/05	21,000,000
Nemanja Matic	Benfica	Chelsea	01/14	21,000,000
Lassana Diarra	Portsmouth	Real Madrid	12/08	20,000,000
Alberto Aquilani	Roma	Liverpool	8/09	20,000,000
Stewart Downing	Aston Villa	Liverpool	7/11	20,000,000
Lazar Markovic	Benfica	Liverpool	7/14	20,000,000
Dejan Lovren	Southampton	Liverpool	7/14	20,000,000
Ricardo Carvalho	Porto	Chelsea	7/04	19,850,000
Mario Balotelli	Manchester City	AC Milan	1/13	19,500,000
Ruud van Nistelrooy	PSV Eindhoven	Manchester Utd	4/01	19,000,000
Robbie Keane	Tottenham	Liverpool	7/08	19,000,000
Michael Carrick	Tottenham	Manchester Utd	8/06	18,600,000
Javier Mascherano	Media Sports	Liverpool	2/08	18,600,000
Rio Ferdinand	West Ham	Leeds	11/00	18,000,000
Anderson	Porto	Manchester Utd	7/07	18,000,000
Jo	CSKA Moscow	Manchester City	6/08	18,000,000
Yuri Zhirkov	CSKA Moscow	Chelsea	7/09	18,000,000
Ramires	Benfica	Chelsea	8/10	18,000,000
Darren Bent	Sunderland	Aston Villa	1/11	18,000,000
Romelu Lukaku	Anderlecht	Chelsea	8/11	18,000,000
Andre Schurrle	Bayer Leverkusen	Chelsea	6/13	18,000,000
Mamadou Sakho	Paris SG	Liverpool	9/13	18,000,000
David De Gea	Atletico Madrid	Manchester Utd	6/11	17,800,000
Roque Santa Cruz	Blackburn	Manchester City	6/09	17,500,000
Jose Reyes	Sevilla	Arsenal	1/04	17,400,000
Javier Mascherano	Liverpool	Barcelona	8/10	17,250,000
Damien Duff	Blackburn	Chelsea	7/03	17,000,000
Owen Hargreaves	Bayern Munich	Manchester Utd	6/07	17,000,000
Glen Johnson	Portsmouth	Liverpool	6/09	17,000,000
Paulinho	Corinthians	Tottenham	7/13	17,000,000
Andrey Arshavin	Zenit St Petersburg	Arsenal	2/09	16,900,000
Hernan Crespo	Inter Milan	Chelsea	8/03	16,800,000
Claude Makelele	Real Madrid	Chelsea	9/03	16,600,000
Luka Modric	Dinamo Zagreb	Tottenham	6/08	16,600,000
Darren Bent	Charlton	Tottenham	6/07	16,500,000
Phil Jones	Blackburn	Manchester Utd	6/11	16,500,000
Santi Cazorla	Malaga	Arsenal	8/12	16,500,000
Jose Bosingwa	Porto	Chelsea	6/08	16,200,000
Michael Owen	Real Madrid	Newcastle	8/05	16,000,000
Thierry Henry	Arsenal	Barcelona	6/07	16,000,000
Aleksandar Kolarov	Lazio	Manchester City	7/10	16,000,000
Robinho	Manchester City	AC Milan	8/10	16,000,000
Jordan Henderson	Sunderland	Liverpool	6/11	16,000,000
Ashley Young	Aston Villa	Manchester Utd	6/11	16,000,000
Calum Chambers	Southampton	Arsenal	7/14	16,000,000

Mario Balotelli	AC Milan	Liverpool	8/14	16,000,000
Danny Welbeck	Manchester Utd	Arsenal	8/14	16,000,000
Adrian Mutu	Parma	Chelsea	8/03	15,800,000
Samir Nasri	Marseille	Arsenal	7/08	15,800,000
Javi Garcia	Benfica	Manchester City	8/12	15,800,000
Jermain Defoe	Portsmouth	Tottenham	1/09	15,750,000
Antonio Valencia	Wigan	Manchester Utd	6/09	15,250,000

BRITISH RECORD TRANSFERS FROM FIRST £1,000 DEAL

Player	From	To	Date	£
Alf Common	Sunderland	Middlesbrough	2/1905	1,000
Syd Puddefoot	West Ham	Falkirk	2/22	5,000
Warney Cresswell	South Shields	Sunderland	3/22	5,500
Bob Kelly	Burnley	Sunderland	12/25	6,500
David Jack	Bolton	Arsenal	10/28	10,890
Bryn Jones	Wolves	Arsenal	8/38	14,500
Billy Steel	Morton	Derby	9/47	15,000
Tommy Lawton	Chelsea	Notts Co	11/47	20,000
Len Shackleton	Newcastle	Sunderland	2/48	20,500
Johnny Morris	Manchester Utd	Derby	2/49	24,000
Eddie Quigley	Sheffield Wed	Preston	12/49	26,500
Trevor Ford	Aston Villa	Sunderland	10/50	30,000
Jackie Sewell	Notts Co	Sheffield Wed	3/51	34,500
Eddie Firmani	Charlton	Sampdoria	7/55	35,000
John Charles	Leeds	Juventus	4/57	65,000
Denis Law	Manchester City	Torino	6/61	100,000
Denis Law	Torino	Manchester Utd	7/62	115,000
Allan Clarke	Fulham	Leicester	6/68	150,000
Allan Clarke	Leicester	Leeds	6/69	165,000
Martin Peters	West Ham	Tottenham	3/70	200,000
Alan Ball	Everton	Arsenal	12/71	220,000
David Nish	Leicester	Derby	8/72	250,000
Bob Latchford	Birmingham	Everton	2/74	350,000
Graeme Souness	Middlesbrough	Liverpool	1/78	352,000
Kevin Keegan	Liverpool	Hamburg	6/77	500,000
David Mills	Middlesbrough	WBA	1/79	516,000
Trevor Francis	Birmingham	Nottm Forest	2/79	1,180,000
Steve Daley	Wolves	Manchester City	9/79	1,450,000
Andy Gray	Aston Villa	Wolves	9/79	1,469,000
Bryan Robson	WBA	Manchester Utd	10/81	1,500,000
Ray Wilkins	Manchester Utd	AC Milan	5/84	1,500,000
Mark Hughes	Manchester Utd	Barcelona	5/86	2,300,000
Ian Rush	Liverpool	Juventus	6/87	3,200,000
Chris Waddle	Tottenham	Marseille	7/89	4,250,000
David Platt	Aston Villa	Bari	7/91	5,500,000
Paul Gascoigne	Tottenham	Lazio	6/92	5,500,000
Andy Cole	Newcastle	Manchester Utd	1/95	7,000,000
Dennis Bergkamp	Inter Milan	Arsenal	6/95	7,500,000
Stan Collymore	Nottm Forest	Liverpool	6/95	8,500,000
Alan Shearer	Blackburn	Newcastle	7/96	15,000,000
Nicolas Anelka	Arsenal	Real Madrid	8/99	22,500,000
Juan Sebastian Veron	Lazio	Manchester Utd	7/01	28,100,000
Rio Ferdinand	Leeds	Manchester Utd	7/02	29,100,000
Andriy Shevchenko	AC Milan	Chelsea	5/06	30,800,000

Robinho	Real Madrid	Manchester City	9/08	32,500,000
Cristiano Ronaldo	Manchester Utd	Real Madrid	7/09	80,000,000
Gareth Bale	Tottenham	Real Madrid	9/13	85,300,000

• World's first £1m transfer: GuiseppeSavoldi, Bologna to Napoli, July 1975

TOP FOREIGN SIGNINGS

Player	From	To	Date	£
Zlatan Ibrahimovic	Inter Milan	Barcelona	7/09	60,300,000
James Rodriguez	Monaco	Real Madrid	7/14	60,000,000
Kaka	AC Milan	Real Madrid	6/08	56,000,000
Edinson Cavani	Napoli	Paris SG	7/13	53,000,000
Radamel Falcao	Atletico Madrid	Monaco	6/13	51,000,000
Neymar	Santos	Barcelona	6/13	48,600,000
Zinedine Zidane	Juventus	Real Madrid	7/01	47,200,000
James Rodriguez	Porto	Monaco	5/13	38,500,000
Luis Figo	Barcelona	Real Madrid	7/00	37,200,000
Javier Pastore	Palermo	Paris SG	8/11	36,600,000
Karim Benzema	Lyon	Real Madrid	7/09	35,800,000
Hernan Crespo	Parma	Lazio	7/00	35,000,000
Radamel Falcao	Porto	Atletico Madrid	8/11	34,700,000
Gonzalo Higuain	Real Madrid	Napoli	7/13	34,500,000
David Villa	Valencia	Barcelona	5/10	34,000,000
Thiago Silva	AC Milan	Paris SG	7/12	34,000,000
Lucas Moura	Sao Paulo	Paris SG	1/13	34,000,000
Asier Illarramendi	Real Sociedad	Real Madrid	7/13	34,000,000
Ronaldo	Inter Milan	Real Madrid	8/02	33,000,000
Gianluigi Buffon	Parma	Juventus	7/01	32,600,000
Axel Witsel	Benfica	Zenit St Petersburg	8/12	32,500,000
Hulk	Porto	Zenit St Petersburg	8/12	32,000,000
Javi Martinez	Athletic Bilbao	Bayern Munich	8/12	31,600,000
Mario Gotze	Borussia Dortmund	Bayern Munich	6/13	31,500,000
Christian Vieri	Lazio	Inter Milan	6/99	31,000,000
Alessandro Nesta	Lazio	AC Milan	8/02	30,200,000
Willian	Shakhtar Donetsk	Anzhi Makhachkala	1/13	30,000,000

WORLD'S MOST EXPENSIVE TEENAGER
£30m: Luke Shaw, 18, Southampton to Manchester Utd, June 2014

WORLD RECORD FOR 16-YEAR-OLD
£12m: Theo Walcott, Southampton to Arsenal, Jan 2006

RECORD FEE BETWEEN SCOTTISH CLUBS
£4.4m: Scott Brown, Hibernian to Celtic, May 2007

RECORD NON-LEAGUE FEE
£1m: Jamie Vardy, Fleetwood to Leicester, May 2012

RECORD FEE BETWEEN NON-LEAGUE CLUBS
£275,000: Richard Brodie, York to Crawley, Aug 2010

MILESTONES OF SOCCER

1848: First code of rules compiled at Cambridge University.

1857: Sheffield FC, world's oldest football club, formed.

1862: Notts Co (oldest League club) formed.

1863: Football Association founded – their first rules of game agreed.

1871: FA Cup introduced.

1872: First official International: Scotland 0 England 0. Corner-kick introduced.

1873: Scottish FA formed; Scottish Cup introduced.

1874: Shinguards introduced.

1875: Crossbar introduced (replacing tape).

1876: FA of Wales formed.

1877: Welsh Cup introduced.

1878: Referee's whistle first used.

1880: Irish FA founded; Irish Cup introduced.

1883: Two-handed throw-in introduced.

1885: Record first-class score (Arbroath 36 Bon Accord 0 – Scottish Cup). Professionalism legalised.

1886: International Board formed.

1887: Record FA Cup score (Preston 26 Hyde 0).

1888: Football League founded by William McGregor. First matches on Sept 8.

1889: Preston win Cup and League (first club to complete Double).

1890: Scottish League and Irish League formed.

1891: Goal-nets introduced. Penalty-kick introduced.

1892: Inter-League games began. Football League Second Division formed.

1893: FA Amateur Cup launched.

1894: Southern League formed.

1895: FA Cup stolen from Birmingham shop window – never recovered.

1897: First Players' Union formed. Aston Villa win Cup and League.

1898: Promotion and relegation introduced.

1901: Maximum wage rule in force (£4 a week). Tottenham first professional club to take FA Cup south. First six-figure attendance (110,802) at FA Cup Final.

1902: Ibrox Park disaster (25 killed). Welsh League formed.

1904: FIFA founded (7 member countries).

1905: First £1,000 transfer (Alf Common, Sunderland to Middlesbrough).

1907: Players' Union revived.

1908: Transfer fee limit (£350) fixed in January and withdrawn in April.

1911: New FA Cup trophy – in use to 1991. Transfer deadline introduced.

1914: King George V first reigning monarch to attend FA Cup Final.

1916: Entertainment Tax introduced.

1919: League extended to 44 clubs.

1920: Third Division (South) formed.

1921: Third Division (North) formed.

1922: Scottish League (Div II) introduced.

1923: Beginning of football pools. First Wembley Cup Final.

1924: First International at Wembley (England 1 Scotland 1). Rule change allows goals to be scored direct from corner-kicks.

1925: New offside law.

1926: Huddersfield complete first League Championship hat-trick.

1927: First League match broadcast (radio): Arsenal v Sheffield United. First radio broadcast of Cup Final (winners Cardiff City). Charles Clegg, president of FA, becomes first knight of football.

1928: First £10,000 transfer – David Jack (Bolton to Arsenal). WR ('Dixie') Dean (Everton) creates League record – 60 goals in season. Britain withdraws from FIFA

1930: Uruguay first winners of World Cup.

1931: WBA win Cup and promotion.

1933: Players numbered for first time in Cup Final (1-22).

1934: Sir Frederick Wall retires as FA secretary; successor Stanley Rous. Death of Herbert Chapman (Arsenal manager).

1935: Arsenal equal Huddersfield's Championship hat-trick record. Official two-referee trials.

1936: Joe Payne's 10-goal League record (Luton 12 Bristol Rov 0).

1937: British record attendance: 149,547 at Scotland v England match.

1938: First live TV transmission of FA Cup Final. Football League 50th Jubilee. New pitch marking – arc on edge of penalty-area. Laws of Game re-drafted by Stanley Rous. Arsenal pay record £14,500 fee for Bryn Jones (Wolves).

1939: Compulsory numbering of players in Football League. First six-figure attendance for League match (Rangers v Celtic 118,567). All normal competitions suspended for duration of Second World War.

1945: Scottish League Cup introduced.

1946: British associations rejoin FIFA. Bolton disaster (33 killed) during FA Cup tie with Stoke. Walter Winterbottom appointed England's first director of coaching.

1947: Great Britain beat Rest of Europe 6-1 at Hampden Park, Glasgow. First £20,000 transfer – Tommy Lawton, Chelsea to Notts Co

1949: Stanley Rous, secretary FA, knighted. England's first home defeat outside British Champ. (0-2 v Eire).

1950: Football League extended from 88 to 92 clubs. World record crowd (203,500) at World Cup Final, Brazil v Uruguay, in Rio. Scotland's first home defeat by foreign team (0-1 v Austria).

1951: White ball comes into official use.

1952: Newcastle first club to win FA Cup at Wembley in successive seasons.

1953: England's first Wembley defeat by foreign opponents (3-6 v Hungary).

1954: Hungary beat England 7-1 in Budapest.

1955: First FA Cup match under floodlights (prelim round replay): Kidderminster v Brierley Hill Alliance.

1956: First FA Cup ties under floodlights in competition proper. First League match by floodlight (Portsmouth v Newcastle). Real Madrid win the first European Cup.

1957: Last full Football League programme on Christmas Day. Entertainment Tax withdrawn.

1958: Manchester United air crash at Munich. League re-structured into four divisions.

1960: Record transfer fee: £55,000 for Denis Law (Huddersfield to Manchester City). Wolves win Cup, miss Double and Championship hat-trick by one goal. For fifth time in ten years FA Cup Final team reduced to ten men by injury. FA recognise Sunday football. Football League Cup launched.

1961: Tottenham complete the first Championship–FA Cup double this century. Maximum wage (£20 a week) abolished in High Court challenge by George Eastham. First British £100-a-week wage paid (by Fulham to Johnny Haynes). First £100,000 British transfer – Denis Law, Manchester City to Torino. Sir Stanley Rous elected president of FIFA

1962: Manchester United raise record British transfer fee to £115,000 for Denis Law.

1963: FA Centenary. Season extended to end of May due to severe winter. First pools panel. English "retain and transfer" system ruled illegal in High Court test case.

1964: Rangers' second great hat-trick – Scottish Cup, League Cup and League. Football League and Scottish League guaranteed £500,000 a year in new fixtures copyright agreement with Pools. First televised 'Match of the Day' (BBC2): Liverpool 3 Arsenal 2.

1965: Bribes scandal – ten players jailed (and banned for life by FA) for match-fixing 1960–63. Stanley Matthews knighted in farewell season. Arthur Rowley (Shrewsbury) retires with record of 434 League goals. Substitutes allowed for injured players in Football League matches (one per team).

1966: England win World Cup (Wembley).

1967: Alf Ramsey, England manager, knighted; OBE for captain Bobby Moore. Celtic become first British team to win European Cup. First substitutes allowed in FA Cup Final (Tottenham v Chelsea) but not used. Football League permit loan transfers (two per club).

1968: First FA Cup Final televised live in colour (BBC2 – WBA v Everton). Manchester United first English club to win European Cup.

1970: FIFA/UEFA approve penalty shoot-out in deadlocked ties.

1971: Arsenal win League Championship and FA Cup.

1973: Football League introduce 3-up, 3-down promotion/relegation between Divisions 1, 2 and 3 and 4-up, 4-down between Divisions 3 and 4.

1974: First FA Cup ties played on Sunday. League football played on Sunday for first time. Last FA Amateur Cup Final. Joao Havelange (Brazil) succeeds Sir Stanley Rous as FIFA president.

1975: Scottish Premier Division introduced.

1976: Football League introduce goal difference (replacing goal average) and red/yellow cards.

1977: Liverpool achieve the double of League Championship and European Cup. Don Revie defects to United Arab Emirates when England manager – successor Ron Greenwood.

1978: Freedom of contract for players accepted by Football League. PFA lifts ban on foreign players in English football. Football League introduce Transfer Tribunal. Viv Anderson (Nottm Forest) first black player to win a full England cap. Willie Johnston (Scotland) sent home from World Cup Finals in Argentina after failing dope test.

1979: First all-British £500,000 transfer – David Mills, Middlesbrough to WBA. First British million pound transfer (Trevor Francis – Birmingham to Nottm Forest). Andy Gray moves from Aston Villa to Wolves for a record £1,469,000 fee.

1981: Tottenham win 100th FA Cup Final. Liverpool first British side to win European Cup three times. Three points for a win introduced by Football League. QPR install Football League's first artificial pitch. Death of Bill Shankly, manager–legend of Liverpool 1959–74. Record British transfer – Bryan Robson (WBA to Manchester United), £1,500,000.

1982: Aston Villa become sixth consecutive English winners of European Cup. Tottenham retain FA Cup – first club to do so since Tottenham 1961 and 1962. Football League Cup becomes the (sponsored) Milk Cup.

1983: Liverpool complete League Championship–Milk Cup double for second year running. Manager Bob Paisley retires. Aberdeen first club to do Cup-Winners' Cup and domestic Cup double. Football League clubs vote to keep own match receipts. Football League sponsored by Canon, Japanese camera and business equipment manufacturers – 3-year agreement starting 1983–4. Football League agree two-year contract for live TV coverage of ten matches per season (5 Friday night, BBC, 5 Sunday afternoon, ITV).

1984: One FA Cup tie in rounds 3, 4, 5 and 6 shown live on TV (Friday or Sunday). Aberdeen take Scottish Cup for third successive season, win Scottish Championship, too. Tottenham win UEFA Cup on penalty shoot-out. Liverpool win European Cup on penalty shoot-out to complete unique treble with Milk Cup and League title (as well as Championship hat-trick). N Ireland win the final British Championship. France win European Championship – their first honour. FA National Soccer School opens at Lilleshall. Britain's biggest score this century: Stirling Alb 20 Selkirk 0 (Scottish Cup).

1985: Bradford City fire disaster – 56 killed. First £1m receipts from match in Britain (FA Cup Final). Kevin Moran (Manchester United) first player to be sent off in FA Cup Final. Celtic win 100th Scottish FA Cup Final. European Cup Final horror (Liverpool v Juventus, riot in Brussels) 39 die. UEFA ban all English clubs indefinitely from European competitions. No TV coverage at start of League season – first time since 1963 (resumption delayed until January 1986). Sept: first ground-sharing in League history – Charlton Athletic move from The Valley to Selhurst Park (Crystal Palace).

1986: Liverpool complete League and Cup double in player-manager Kenny Dalglish's first season in charge. Swindon (4th Div Champions) set League points record (102). League approve reduction of First Division to 20 clubs by 1988. Everton chairman Philip Carter elected president of Football League. Death of Sir Stanley Rous (91). 100th edition of News of the World Football Annual. League Cup sponsored for next three years by Littlewoods (£2m). Football League voting majority (for rule changes) reduced from three-quarters to two-thirds. Wales move HQ from Wrexham to Cardiff after 110 years. Two substitutes in FA Cup and League (Littlewoods) Cup. Two-season League/TV deal (£6.2m):- BBC and ITV each show seven live League matches per season, League Cup semi-finals and Final. Football League sponsored by Today newspaper. Luton first club to ban all visiting supporters; as sequel are themselves banned from League Cup. Oldham and Preston install artificial pitches, making four in Football League (following QPR and Luton).

1987: League introduce play-off matches to decide final promotion/relegation places in all divisions. Re-election abolished – bottom club in Div 4 replaced by winners of GM Vauxhall Conference. Two substitutes approved for Football League 1987–8. Red and yellow disciplinary cards (scrapped 1981) re-introduced by League and FA Football League sponsored by Barclays. First Div reduced to 21 clubs.

1988: Football League Centenary. First Division reduced to 20 clubs.

1989: Soccer gets £74m TV deal: £44m over 4 years, ITV; £30m over 5 years, BBC/BSB. But it costs Philip Carter the League Presidency. Ted Croker retires as FA chief executive; successor Graham Kelly, from Football League. Hillsborough disaster: 95 die at FA Cup semi-final (Liverpool v Nottm Forest). Arsenal win closest-ever Championship with last kick. Peter Shilton sets England record with 109 caps.

1990: Nottm Forest win last Littlewoods Cup Final. Both FA Cup semi-finals played on Sunday and televised live. Play-off finals move to Wembley; Swindon win place in Div 1, then relegated back to Div 2 (breach of financial regulations) – Sunderland promoted instead. England reach World Cup semi-final in Italy and win FIFA Fair Play Award. Peter Shilton retires as England goalkeeper with 125 caps (world record). Graham Taylor (Aston Villa) succeeds Bobby Robson as England manager. International Board amend offside law (player 'level' no longer offside). FIFA make "professional foul" a sending-off offence. English clubs back in Europe (Manchester United and Aston Villa) after 5-year exile.

1991: First FA Cup semi-final at Wembley (Tottenham 3 Arsenal 1). Bert Millichip (FA chairman) and Philip Carter (Everton chairman) knighted. End of artificial pitches in Div 1 (Luton, Oldham). Scottish League reverts to 12-12-14 format (as in 1987–8). Penalty shoot-out introduced to decide FA Cup ties level after one replay.

1992: FA launch Premier League (22 clubs). Football League reduced to three divisions (71 clubs). Record TV-sport deal: BSkyB/BBC to pay £304m for 5-year coverage of Premier League. ITV do £40m, 4-year deal with Football League. Channel 4 show Italian football live (Sundays). FIFA approve new back-pass rule (goalkeeper must not handle ball kicked to him by team-mate). New League of Wales formed. Record all-British transfer, £3.3m: Alan Shearer (Southampton to Blackburn). Charlton return to The Valley after 7-year absence.

1993: Barclays end 6-year sponsorship of Football League. For first time both FA Cup semi-finals at Wembley (Sat, Sun). Arsenal first club to complete League Cup/FA Cup double. Rangers pull off Scotland's domestic treble for fifth time. FA in record British sports sponsorship deal (£12m over 4 years) with brewers Bass for FA Carling Premiership, from Aug. Brian Clough retires after 18 years as Nottm Forest manager; as does Jim McLean (21 years manager of Dundee Utd). Football League agree 3-year, £3m sponsorship with Endsleigh Insurance. Premier League introduce squad numbers with players' names on shirts. Record British transfer: Duncan Ferguson, Dundee Utd to Rangers (£4m). Record English-club signing: Roy Keane, Nottm Forest to Manchester United (£3.75m). Graham Taylor resigns as England manager after World Cup exit (Nov). Death of Bobby Moore (51), England World Cup winning captain 1966.

1994: Death of Sir Matt Busby. Terry Venables appointed England coach. Manchester United complete the Double. Last artificial pitch in English football goes – Preston revert to grass, summer 1994. Bobby Charlton knighted. Scottish League format changes to four divisions of ten clubs. Record British transfer: Chris Sutton, Norwich to Blackburn (£5m). FA announce first sponsorship of FA Cup – Littlewoods Pools (4-year, £14m deal, plus

£6m for Charity Shield). Death of Billy Wright.

1995: New record British transfer: Andy Cole, Newcastle to Manchester United (£7m). First England match abandoned through crowd trouble (v Republic of Ireland, Dublin). Blackburn Champions for first time since 1914. Premiership reduced to 20 clubs. British transfer record broken again: Stan Collymore, Nottm Forest to Liverpool (£8.5m). Starting season 1995–6, teams allowed to use 3 substitutes per match, not necessarily including a goalkeeper. European Court of Justice upholds Bosman ruling, barring transfer fees for players out of contract and removing limit on number of foreign players clubs can field.

1996: Death of Bob Paisley (77), ex-Liverpool, most successful manager in English Football. FA appoint Chelsea manager Glenn Hoddle to succeed Terry Venables as England coach after Euro 96. Manchester United first English club to achieve Double twice (and in 3 seasons). Football League completes £125m, 5-year TV deal with BSkyB starting 1996–7. England stage European Championship, reach semi-finals, lose on pens to tournament winners Germany. Keith Wiseman succeeds Sir Bert Millichip as FA Chairman. Linesmen become known as 'referees' assistants'. Alan Shearer football's first £15m player (Blackburn to Newcastle). Nigeria first African country to win Olympic soccer. Nationwide Building Society sponsor Football League in initial 3-year deal worth £5.25m Peter Shilton first player to make 1000 League appearances.

1997: Howard Wilkinson appointed English football's first technical director. England's first home defeat in World Cup (0–1 v Italy). Ruud Gullit (Chelsea) first foreign coach to win FA Cup. Rangers equal Celtic's record of 9 successive League titles. Manchester United win Premier League for fourth time in 5 seasons. New record World Cup score: Iran 17, Maldives 0 (qualifying round). Season 1997–8 starts Premiership's record £36m, 4-year sponsorship extension with brewers Bass (Carling).

1998: In French manager Arsene Wenger's second season at Highbury, Arsenal become second English club to complete the Double twice. Chelsea also win two trophies under new player-manager Gianluca Vialli (Coca-Cola Cup, Cup Winners' Cup). In breakaway from Scottish League, top ten clubs form new Premiership under SFA, starting season 1998–9. Football League celebrates its 100th season, 1998–9. New FA Cup sponsors – French insurance giants AXA (25m, 4-year deal). League Cup becomes Worthington Cup in £23m, 5-year contract with brewers Bass. Nationwide Building Society's sponsorship of Football League extended to season 2000–1.

1999: FA buy Wembley Stadium (£103m) for £320m, plan rebuilding (Aug 2000–March 2003) as new national stadium (Lottery Sports fund contributes £110m) Scotland's new Premier League takes 3-week mid-season break in January. Sky screen Oxford Utd v Sunderland (Div 1) as first pay-per-view match on TV. FA sack England coach Glenn Hoddle; Fulham's Kevin Keegan replaces him at £1m a year until 2003. Sir Alf Ramsey, England's World Cup-winning manager, dies aged 79. With effect 1999, FA Cup Final to be decided on day (via penalties, if necessary). Hampden Park re-opens for Scottish Cup Final after £63m refit. Alex Ferguson knighted after Manchester United complete Premiership, FA Cup, European Cup treble. Starting season 1999–2000, UEFA increase Champions League from 24 to 32 clubs. End of Cup-Winners' Cup (merged into 121-club UEFA Cup). FA allow holders Manchester United to withdraw from FA Cup to participate in FIFA's inaugural World Club Championship in Brazil in January. Chelsea first British club to field an all-foreign line-up – at Southampton (Prem). FA vote in favour of streamlined 14-man board of directors to replace its 92-member council.

2000: Scot Adam Crozier takes over as FA chief executive. Wales move to Cardiff's £125m Millennium Stadium (v Finland). Brent Council approve plans for new £475m Wembley Stadium (completion target spring 2003); demolition of old stadium to begin after England v Germany (World Cup qual.). Fulham Ladies become Britain's first female professional team. FA Premiership and Nationwide League to introduce (season 2000–01) rule whereby referees advance free-kick by 10 yards and caution player who shows dissent, delays kick or fails to retreat 10 yards. Scottish football increased to 42 League clubs in 2000–01 (12 in Premier League and 3 divisions of ten; Peterhead and Elgin elected from Highland League). France win European Championship – first time a major international tournament has been jointly hosted (Holland/ Belgium). England's £10m bid to stage 2006 World Cup fails; vote goes to Germany. England manager Kevin Keegan resigns after 1-0 World Cup defeat by Germany in Wembley's last International. Lazio's Swedish coach Sven-Goran Eriksson agrees to become England head coach.

2001: Scottish Premier League experiment with split into two 5-game mini leagues (6 clubs in each) after 33 matches completed. New transfer system agreed by FIFA/UEFA is ratified. Barclaycard begin £48m, 3-year sponsorship of the Premiership, and Nationwide's contract with the Football League is extended by a further 3 years (£12m). ITV, after winning auction against BBC's Match of the Day, begin £183m, 3-season contract for highlights of Premiership matches; BSkyB's live coverage (66 matches per season) for next 3 years will cost £1.1bn. BBC and BSkyB pay £400m (3-year contract) for live coverage of FA Cup and England home matches. ITV and Ondigital pay £315m to screen Nationwide League and Worthington Cup matches. In new charter for referees, top men can earn up to £60,000 a season in Premiership. Real Madrid break world transfer record, buying Zinedine Zidane from Juventus for £47.2m. FA introduce prize money, round by round, in FA Cup.

2002: Scotland appoint their first foreign manager, Germany's former national coach Bertie Vogts replacing Craig Brown. Collapse of ITV Digital deal, with Football League owed £178m, threatens lower-division clubs. Arsenal complete Premiership/FA Cup Double for second time in 5 seasons, third time in all. Newcastle manager Bobby Robson knighted in Queen's Jubilee Honours. New record British transfer and world record for defender, £29.1m Rio Ferdinand (Leeds to Manchester United). Transfer window introduced to British football. FA Charity Shield renamed FA Community Shield. After 2-year delay, demolition of Wembley Stadium begins. October: Adam Crozier, FA chief executive, resigns.

2003: FA Cup draw (from 4th Round) reverts to Monday lunchtime. Scottish Premier League decide to end mid-winter shut-down. Mark Palios appointed FA chief executive. For first time, two Football League clubs demoted (replaced by two from Conference). Ban lifted on loan transfers between Premiership clubs. July: David Beckham becomes record British export (Manchester United to Real Madrid, £23.3m). Biggest takeover in British football history – Russian oil magnate Roman Abramovich buys control of Chelsea for £150m Wimbledon leave rented home at Selhurst Park, become England's first franchised club in 68-mile move to Milton Keynes.

2004: Arsenal first club to win Premiership with unbeaten record and only the third in English football history to stay undefeated through League season. Trevor Brooking knighted in Queen's Birthday Honours. Wimbledon change name to Milton Keynes Dons. Greece beat hosts Portugal to win European Championship as biggest outsiders (80-1 at start) ever to succeed in major international tournament. New contracts – Premiership in £57m deal with Barclays, seasons 2004–07. Coca-Cola replace Nationwide as Football League sponsors (£15m over 3 years), rebranding Div 1 as Football League Championship, with 2nd and 3rd Divisions, becoming Leagues 1 and 2. All-time League record of 49 unbeaten Premiership matches set by Arsenal. Under new League rule, Wrexham forfeit 10 points for going into administration.

2005: Brian Barwick, controller of ITV Sport, becomes FA chief executive. Foreign managers take all major trophies for English clubs: Chelsea, in Centenary year, win Premiership (record 95 points) and League Cup in Jose Mourinho's first season; Arsene Wenger's Arsenal win FA Cup in Final's first penalty shoot-out; and under new manager Rafael Benitez, Liverpool lift European Cup on penalties after trailing 0-3 in Champions League Final. Wigan, a League club only since 1978, promoted to Premiership. In new record British-club take-over, American tycoon Malcolm Glazer buys Manchester United for £790m Tributes are paid world-wide to George Best, who dies aged 59.

2006: Steve Staunton succeeds Brian Kerr as Republic of Ireland manager. Chelsea post record losses of £140m. Sven-Goran Eriksson agrees a settlement to step down as England coach. Steve McClaren replaces him. The Premier League announce a new 3-year TV deal worth £1.7 billion under which Sky lose their monopoly of coverage. Chelsea smash the British transfer record, paying £30.8m for Andriy Shevchenko. Clydesdale Bank replace Bank of Scotland as sponsor of the SPL.

2007: Michel Platini becomes the new president of UEFA. Walter Smith resigns as Scotland manager to return to Rangers and is replaced by Alex McLeish. The new £800m Wembley Stadium is finally completed. The BBC and Sky lose TV rights for England's home matches and FA Cup ties to ITV and Setanta. World Cup-winner Alan Ball dies aged 61. Lawrie Sanchez resigns as Northern Ireland manager to take over at Fulham. Nigel Worthington succeeds him. Lord Stevens names five clubs in his final report into alleged transfer irregularities. Steve McClaren is sacked after England fail to qualify for the European Championship Finals and is replaced by Fabio Capello. The Republic of Ireland's Steve Staunton also goes. Scotland's Alex McLeish resigns to become Birmingham manager.

2008: The Republic of Ireland follow England's lead in appointing an Italian coach – Giovanni Trapattoni. George Burley leaves Southampton to become Scotland manager. Manchester United beat Chelsea in the first all-English Champions League Final. Manchester City smash the British transfer record when signing Robinho from Real Madrid for £32.5m.

2009: Sky secure the rights to five of the six Premier League packages from 2010-13 with a bid of £1.6bn. Reading's David Beckham breaks Bobby Moore's record number of caps for an England outfield player with his 109th appearance. A British league record for not conceding a goal ends on 1,311 minutes for Manchester United's Edwin van der Sar. AC Milan's Kaka moves to Real Madrid for a world record fee of £56m. Nine days later, Manchester United agree to sell Cristiano Ronaldo to Real for £80m. Sir Bobby Robson dies aged 76 after a long battle with cancer. Shay Given and Kevin Kilbane win their 100th caps for the Republic of Ireland. The Premier League vote for clubs to have eight home-grown players in their squads. George Burley is sacked as Scotland manager and replaced by Craig Levein.

2010: npower succeed Coca-Cola as sponsors of the Football League. Portsmouth become the first Premier League club to go into administration. Chelsea achieve the club's first League and FA Cup double. Lord Triesman resigns as chairman of the FA and of England's 2018 World Cup bid. John Toshack resigns as Wales manager and is replaced by former captain Gary Speed. England are humiliated in the vote for the 2018 World Cup which goes to Russia, with the 2022 tournament awarded to Qatar.

2011: Seven club managers are sacked in a week. The transfer record between Britsh clubs is broken twice in a day, with Liverpool buying Newcastle's Andy Carroll for £35m and selling Fernando Torres to Chelsea for £50m. Vauxhall replace Nationwide as sponsors of England and the other home nations. John Terry is restored as England captain. Football League clubs vote to reduce the number of substitutes from seven to five. Nigel Worthington steps down as Northern Ireland manager and is succeeded by Michael O'Neill. Sir Alex Ferguson completes 25 years as Manchester United manager. Manchester City post record annual losses of nearly £195m. Huddersfield set a Football League record of 43 successive unbeaten league games. Football mourns Gary Speed after the Wales manager is found dead at his home.

2012: Chris Coleman is appointed the new Wales manager. Fabio Capello resigns as manager after John Terry is stripped of the England captaincy for the second time. Roy Hodgson takes over. Rangers are forced into liquidation by crippling debts and a newly-formed club are demoted from the Scottish Premier League to Division Three. Manchester City become champions for the first time since 1968 after the tightest finish to a Premier League season. Chelsea win a penalty shoot-out against Bayern Munich in the Champions League Final. Capital One replace Carling as League Cup sponsors. Steven Gerrard (England) and Damien Duff (Republic of Ireland) win their 100th caps. The FA's new £120m National Football Centre at Burton upon Trent is opened. Scotland manager Craig Levein is sacked.

2013: Gordon Strachan is appointed Scotland manager. FIFA and the Premier League announce the introduction of goal-line technology. Energy company npower end their sponsorship of the Football League and are succeeded by Sky Bet. Sir Alex Ferguson announces he is retiring after 26 years as Manchester United manager. Wigan become the first club to lift the FA Cup and be relegated in the same season. Chelsea win the Europa League. Ashley Cole and Frank Lampard win their 100th England caps. Robbie Keane becomes the most capped player in the British Isles on his 126th appearance for the Republic of Ireland. Scottish Football League clubs agree to merge with the Scottish Premier League. Greg Dyke succeeds David Bernstein as FA chairman. Real Madrid sign Tottenham's Gareth Bale for a world record £85.3m. Giovanni Trapatonni is replaced as Republic of Ireland manager by Martin O'Neill.

2014: Sir Tom Finney, one of the finest British players of all-time, dies aged 91. England experience their worst-ever World Cup, finishing bottom the group with a single point. Germany deliver one of the most remarkable scorelines in World Cup history – 7-1 against Brazil in the semi-finals. Manchester United announce a world-record kit sponsorship with adidas worth £750m. United break the incoming British transfer record by paying £59.7m for Real Madrid's Angel di Maria, part of a record £835m spending by Premier League clubs in the summer transfer window. England's Wayne Rooney and the Republic of Ireland's John O'Shea win their 100th caps.

2015: The Premier League sell live TV rights for 2016-19 to Sky and BT for a record £5.13bn. Bournemouth, a club on the brink of folding in 2008, win promotion to the Premier League. FIFA president Sepp Blatter resigns as a bribery and corruption scandal engulfs the world governing body.

THE THINGS THEY SAY ...

'I don't want to be perceived as a money-grabbing 20-year-old. It is about winning trophies throughout your career. I don't talk about how many cars I will drive or how many houses I've got' – **Raheem Sterling** on rejecting Liverpool's contract offer.

'I've let down my team-mates and the supporters. I've been in the game long enough to know that when you do something like that you get sent off. I don't know what made me do it' – **Steven Gerrard** on being sent off for stamping on Manchester United's Ander Herrera 38 seconds after coming off the Liverpool bench.

'It has been an incredible journey' – **Thierry Henry** announcing his retirement after a glittering 20-year career at club and international level.

'A run like Ricky Villa, a finish like Ricky Gervais' – **Brendan Rodgers**, Liverpool manager, after Raheem Sterling beat four Tottenham players then scuffed his shot.

'When I was told what he said I didn't understand it. But I typed in both names (to Google), so I know now what he meant' – **Raheem Sterling**.

'I use the word embarrassing because I'm trying to be respectful' – **Gus Poyet**, former Sunderland manager, after the 8-0 defeat by Southampton.

'Coaches are like watermelons. You find out about them when you open them' – **Massimo Cellino**, Leeds owner, after sacking David Hockaday, then Darko Milanic, both after six games in charge.

FINAL WHISTLE – OBITUARIES 2014–15

JULY 2014

ALEX FORBES, 89, was a tough-tackling Scotland international who played in two Championship-winning Arsenal sides. His move from Sheffield United in February, 1948 came too late to make sufficient appearances for a medal. But he played a full part in the 1952–53 campaign when they pipped Preston on goal average after finishing level on 54 points. Forbes was an FA Cup winner in 1950 when Liverpool were beaten 2-0 and featured in the 1952 final when his team lost 1-0 to Newcastle. He made 240 appearances in eight years at the club and was capped 14 times by his country. The wing-half had spells with Leyton Orient and Fulham, then returned to Arsenal as youth coach. After emigrating to South Africa, he became one of the first white managers to take charge of a major black team, Orlando Pirates, in 1975.

JEFF BOURNE, 66, was signed from local football by Brian Clough in 1969, made his Derby debut in 1971 and the following season played a key role in the reserve team's Central League title win. He went on to make 17 appearances as the club became First Division champions in the 1974–75 campaign and also scored in European Cup and UEFA Cup matches. Bourne later played for Crystal Palace and Sheffield United, then for Dallas, Atlanta and Seattle in the North American League.

RAY KING, 89, played more than 250 matches for Port Vale between 1949–57 and was widely regarded as the club's best-ever goalkeeper. In a memorable 1953–54 season, he kept a Football League record 29 clean sheets and conceded just five goals at home as Vale won the Third Division North title. They also reached the semi-finals of the FA Cup before losing 2-1 to West Bromwich Albion in front of a 68,000 crowd at Villa Park. King, who made one appearance for England B against Switzerland, began his career as a youth at Newcastle, had a spell with Leyton Orient and was player-manager of Boston.

MORRIS STEVENSON, 71, helped Morton win promotion to the top flight of Scottish football as Second Division champions in the 1963–64 season. His team scored 135 goals in 36 matches and also reached the League Cup Final, losing 5-0 to Rangers. Stevenson, an inside-forward who made 215 appearances for the club, was previously with Motherwell and Hibernian and later played for Luton, Dundee United and Berwick.

BRIAN LOUGHNANE, 83, was an amateur with Manchester City before spells as a winger for Shrewsbury and Bournemouth in the mid-1950s.

AUGUST 2014

DON CLARK, 96, made up for lost time when league football resumed after the Second World War. The centre-forward scored 42 goals in 42 games for Bristol City in the 1946–47 season – a club record that still stands. But the conflict, along with a serious injury in 1951, restricted his career to 128 games and 77 goals. Son Brian, who died in 2010 aged 67, also played for City and later for Cardiff, where he was leading marksman for three successive seasons playing alongside John Toshack.

BOBBY KINLOCH, 79, scored one of the most famous goals in Hibernian's history. It came from the penalty spot in the 85th minute of the second leg of the 1961 quarter-final of the Inter-Cities Fairs Cup – forerunner of the UEFA Cup and Europa League. The goal knocked out Barcelona and sparked angry scenes at the final whistle when Spanish players chased West German referee Johannes Malka down the tunnel. Kinloch netted twice in the second leg of the semi-final to earn a 5-5 aggregate scoreline against Roma, who won the play-off game 6-0. The inside-forward later served Morton, Berwick, Raith and Dunfermline, as well playing for Toronto and Hamilton in Canada.

ERIC BARBER, 72, was a Republic of Ireland international who had three spells with Shelbourne and became the club's record scorer with 126 league goals. He was a key figure in their

Championship-winning side of 1962, won the FAI Cup in 1960 and 1963 and managed the club during the 1979–80 season. Barber, capped against Spain and Belgium, had a spell with Birmingham and also played in the United States and Austria.

SAMMY CONN, 52, played for five Scottish clubs, including two spells at Falkirk and Albion. The midfielder spent time at Clydebank and Airdrie and captained Cowdenbeath, where he also served as player-manager.

JAMES ALEXANDER GORDON, 78, delivered Saturday football results on BBC radio for 40 years. His trademark style, using the tone of his voice to give a clue to the score, made him instantly recognisable to fans all over the country. After working in music publishing, he joined the Corporation in 1972 as an announcer and newsreader, began reading the classified results the following year and continued until retiring through illness in 2013.

SEPTEMBER 2014

DAVID WHYTE, 43, was Charlton's leading marksman in the 1994–95 season with 21 goals in all competitions – the first time one of their strikers had topped 20 since Derek Hales in the 1980–81 campaign. Whyte, who started his career with Greenwich Borough and came to The Valley initially on loan, scored 35 times in 106 appearances for the club after signing from Crystal Palace. He went on to play for Reading, Ipswich, Bristol Rovers and Southend.

WILLIE FINLAY, 88, won three post-war Scottish League Cups with East Fife. His side also led the First Division for much of the 1952–53 season before taking a single point from their final three fixtures and finishing behind Rangers and Hibernian. The centre-half made nearly 400 appearances in ten seasons at the club, then helped Clyde beat Hibernian 1-0 in the 1958 Scottish Cup Final and win the Second Division title on two occasions. He finished his career with Raith.

TIM RAWLINGS, 81, left West Bromwich Albion because of a lack of first-team opportunities to sign for Walsall, where he was involved in successive promotions. The club won the Division Four title in 1960 and were runners-up to Bury in the Third Division a year later. Rawlings, a wing-half, made 207 appearances before joining Port Vale.

HUGH 'DICK' DOHERTY, 93, was the oldest surviving former Celtic player. The Irish-born winger played for the club in the 1946–47 season before joining Blackpool, where a knee injury cut short his career. He also had spells with Irish clubs Derry and Dundalk.

LEN STEPHENSON, 84, played alongside Stanley Matthews when FA Cup holders Blackpool were knocked out by Port Vale in a fifth round tie in 1954. The centre-forward joined Vale the following year and was their leading scorer in the 1955–56 season. After losing his place in the team, he moved on to play for Oldham.

BILLY NEIL, 75, was part of the Great Britain squad for the 1960 Olympics in Rome. He made one appearance, forming all all-Scottish full-back pairing with Davie Holt in a 2-2 draw with Italy. On returning home, Neil left Airdrie for Queen's Park, where he made more than 400 appearances.

JOHN DIVERS, 74, was told by a surgeon at the age of 20 that he had the legs of a 70-year-old because of a disease affecting the veins. But he overcame the handicap to play for Celtic for ten seasons from 1956 and score 100 goals in 232 appearances. It was a period of under-achievement by his club and the inside-forward did not win a major trophy. He also had to be satisfied with a non-playing place in the Scotland squad for an international against Uruguay in 1962. Divers, whose father played for Celtic, retired at 28 to become a teacher after a spell with Partick.

OCTOBER 2014

PAT PARTRIDGE, 81, progressed through the ranks in the north-east to become a leading international referee. He was promoted to the Football League in 1965 and spent ten years on the FIFA list. His career included three major finals – West Ham v Fulham in the FA Cup, Liverpool against Nottingham Forest in the League Cup and Hamburg v Anderlecht in the Cup-Winners Cup. Another big game was the Inter-Continental Cup – forerunner of the Club World Cup – between Cruzeiro and Bayern Munich in front of a crowd of more than 123,000 in Belo Horizonte, Brazil. In 1978, he refereed Peru against Poland at the World Cup in Argentina after running the line in two group games. Partridge, who retired in 1981, was awarded the British Empire Medal in the Queen's Birthday Honours in June, 2014.

DON RATCLIFFE, 79, had a key role in Stoke's Second Division title-winning team of 1962–63. Alongside the likes of Stanley Matthews and Dennis Viollet, the versatile inside-forward was an ever-present in a side finishing a point ahead of Chelsea and Sunderland. He played the first eight games of the following season in the top flight, but was then sold to Middlesbrough for £30,000 after 260 first team appearances. Ratcliffe went on to serve two Fourth Division promotion-winning teams – Darlington and Crewe.

JIM BARRETT, 83, was Nottingham Forest's leading scorer for three successive seasons, including 1956–57 when he netted 30 goals as they finished runners-up to Leicester in Division Two. The inside-forward previously played for West Ham, where his father – centre-half Jim – had made more than 500 appearances. After a spell with Birmingham, Barrett junior returned to Upton Park in a coaching role. He also coached at Millwall.

GEORGE FRANCIS, 80, ranks second on Brentford's all-time scoring list. He scored 136 goals in 280 appearances in two spells at the club, forming a prolific partnership with Jim Towers which yielded more than 250 between them. His highest tally was 31 in the 1959–60 season. The pair were sold to Queens Park Rangers in the summer of 1961, but Francis played only two games before returning to Griffin Park. He moved on to Gillingham and scored the winner against Newport on the final day of the 1963–64 season to clinch the Division Four title on goal average from Carlisle.

JOE BROWN, 85, served Burnley as a player and manager. The wing-half joined the club from Middlesbrough in 1952, later made more than 200 appearances in six years at Bournemouth and had a spell with Aldershot. He returned to Turf Moor to join the coaching staff and spent six years as assistant to Jimmy Adamson before replacing him as manager in 1976. Brown was in charge for 13 months, during which Burnley were relegated from the First Division.

ARNOLD MITCHELL, 84, arrived at Exeter in 1952 having made a single appearance in spells with Derby, Nottingham Forest and Notts County. It was the start of a 14-year career at St James Park which brought a club record 516 appearances. High point was the 1963–64 season when Exeter gained promotion, from Division Four, for the first time in the club's history. In 2013, as part of the Football League's 125-year celebrations, the wing-half was voted the club's greatest captain by supporters.

KLAS INGESSON, 46, had two seasons in the Premiership with Sheffield Wednesday after an £800,000 move from PSV Eindhoven in 1994. The midfielder was sold to Bari for £1m, then joined Bologna and Marseille. He played for Sweden in the 1990 and 1994 World Cup Finals and later managed Elfsborg.

JIM SHARKEY, 80, scored on his debut for Celtic against Raith in 1955. The inside-forward spent three years at the club, moved on to Airdrie and Raith, then played non-league football for several clubs in England , including Cambridge United.

MALCOLM THOMPSON, 68, headed the extra-time goal which gave Scarborough a 2-1 win over Wigan in the 1973 FA Trophy Final. He previously played for Hartlepool and Goole.

NOVEMBER 2014

JOHN NEAL, 82, helped restore Chelsea's fortunes, on and off the field, at a time when financial problems were threatening to cripple the club. He replaced Geoff Hurst as manager in 1981, made significant signings like Kerry Dixon and Pat Nevin, and brought top flight football back to Stamford Bridge after four seasons in Division Two. His side were promoted as champions in 1984, pipping Sheffield Wednesday on goal difference, and they finished sixth the following season. Neal retired through ill health, but continued to serve the club as a director. He had previously led Wrexham to promotion from Division Four, to the quarter-finals of the FA Cup and into the European Cup-Winners' Cup. He then succeeded Jack Charlton as Middlesbrough manager. As a player, Neal had spells as a full-back with Hull, Swindon, Aston Villa and Southend, helping Villa become Second Division champions in 1960. They also won the inaugural League Cup the following year by beating Rotherham 3-2 on aggregate in the two-leg final.

JIM STORRIE, 74, was a free-scoring centre-forward whose goals helped Leeds, under Don Revie, become a power in English football. He was top scorer with 25 in his first season after signing from Airdrie for £15,000. His second brought a Division Two Championship medal. In 1965, Leeds finished runners-up to Manchester United on goal average and reached the FA Cup Final. They lost it 2-1 Liverpool, who a year later forced them to settle for second again in the league. Storrie scored 67 goals in 156 games for the club before joining Aberdeen, where he was among the scorers in their first European match, against Reykjavic. He later played for Rotherham, Portsmouth and St Mirren and was manager of St Johnstone between 1976–78.

MALCOLM FINLAYSON, 84, won back-to-back First Division titles and the FA Cup during a golden period for Wolves. His side were champions in 1958, finishing five points ahead of Preston, and again a year later, six clear of Manchester United. In 1960, Wolves defeated Blackburn 3-0 in the Wembley final. But Finlayson, signed initially as cover for England goalkeeper Bert Williams, missed out on international recognition because of Scotland's policy of including only home-based players. He made 203 appearances in eight years at Molineux, having joined the club after 251 matches for Millwall.

ROY HARTLE, 83, served Bolton throughout his professional career after joining the club as a 16-year-old from Bromsgrove Rovers. He played 499 games between 1952–66, forming a formidable full-back pairing with Tommy Banks. High spot was the 1958 FA Cup Final when Bolton defeated Manchester United 2-0.

ALEX BAIN, 78, scored two goals in a Second Division match which produced one of the greatest comebacks in English football. They helped Bill Shankly's Huddersfield establish a 5-1 lead over Charlton with 28 minutes remaining at The Valley in December 1957. The home side were down to ten men through injury, but fought back to win 7-6, with Johnny Summers netting five times. Bain joined the club from Motherwell and also played for Chesterfield, Falkirk and Bournemouth.

IAIN HESFORD, 54, became Blackpool's youngest-ever goalkeeper when making his league debut, aged 17, in 1977. The England Under-21 international went on to play more than 200 games for the club before spells with Sheffield Wednesday, Fulham and Notts County on loan, then Sunderland and Hull. For his last league side, Maidstone, he scored against Hereford in a Division Four match with a wind-assisted clearance in 1991. Hesford's father, Bob, was Huddersfield's goalkeeper in the 1938 FA Cup Final against Preston. Brother Bob junior was an England rugby union international, while another brother, Steve, was a prolific Rugby League points scorer for Warrington.

DEREK HOGG, 84, came to Leicester as a right-winger, switched flanks with considerable success and proved a valuable source of goals for the prolific Arthur Rowley. Their team were Second Division champions in 1954, on goal average from Everton, and again three years later with seven points to spare over runners-up Nottingham Forest. Hogg moved on to West Bromwich Albion for £20,000 in 1958 and joined Cardiff two years later for a £12,500 fee.

SAMMY REID, 75, scored the goal which delivered one of the biggest upsets in Scottish football. The winger's left-foot shot after 32 minutes gave Berwick a 1-0 victory over Rangers in the Scottish Cup first round in front of a record 13,000-plus crowd at Shielfield Park in January, 1967. Reid had previously been Bill Shankly's first signing as Liverpool manager, although he never made the first team at Anfield after arriving from Motherwell. He later played for Falkirk, Clyde and Dumbarton.

GEOFF COX, 79, made 286 appearances in ten years with Torquay, featuring in promotion from the Fourth Division in 1960 and 1966. Cox, who operated on the wing and at inside-forward, joined the club from Birmingham and later had a brief spell at Plymouth. Son Maurice also played for Torquay, as well as Huddersfield and Cambridge University, for whom he scored the fastest-ever goal at Wembley – after 20 seconds of the 1979 Varsity match against Oxford.

IVOR SEEMLEY, 85, helped Sheffield Wednesday to the semi-finals of the FA Cup in 1954, a run ended with a 2-0 defeat by Preston in front of a 75,000 crowd at Maine Road, Manchester. The left-back also played for Stockport and Chesterfield.

REG FOULKES, 91, made his debut for Walsall in 1945 against Norwich, the club he joined five years later. The former England schoolboy international centre-half played 238 games in six years at Carrow Road. One of the highspots was a 2-1 away win for the Third Division South team against Arsenal in round four of the FA Cup in 1954.

SAMMY WILSON, 82, opened the scoring in Celtic's record 7-1 win over Rangers in the 1957–58 Scottish League Cup Final. The inside-forward netted 46 goals in 70 appearances for the club after starting his career with St Mirren. He also played for Millwall, Northampton and Ross County.

SIR WILLIAM DUGDALE, 92, was chairman of Aston Villa during their most successful period in modern times – League champions in 1981 and European Cup winners the following season. The uncle of David Cameron, he took the future Prime Minister to his first Villa Park game when aged 13. Sir William presided for seven years before his great rival, Sir Doug Ellis, returned as chairman.

ARTHUR MONTFORD, 85, received the Scottish PFA Merit award in 2010 for services to football broadcasting and journalism. He was the first anchor for STV's Scotsport in 1957 and presented more than 2,000 programmes before retiring in 1989. He also served as a director of Greenock Morton.

DECEMBER 2014

RON HENRY, 80, was Tottenham's left-back in their Double-winning season of 1960–61. Bill Nicholson's side finished eight points ahead of Sheffield Wednesday in the league and beat Leicester 2-0 in the FA Cup Final. Henry, who joined the club as a centre half and switched positions when Mel Hopkins was injured, was back at Wembley 12 months later when Tottenham defeated Burnley 3-1. He also gained a European Cup' Winners Cup medal in 1963 when they overcame Atletico Madrid 5-1 in Rotterdam. During that successful period, the former Luton amateur missed just one of 188 matches. Henry made 287 appearances for the club and won one England cap, against France in Alf Ramsey's first fixture as manager of the national team. After retiring, he continued to serve in various coaching roles at White Hart Lane.

JIMMY DUNN, 91, followed in the footsteps of his father by winning the FA Cup. He was in the Wolves side that defeated Leicester 3-1 in the 1949 final, having played in every tie on the way to Wembley. Jimmy Dunn senior, also an inside-forward, scored Everton's third goal in their 3-0 victory over Manchester City in 1933. He also featured in Scotland's historic 5-1 win over England in 1928. Dunn junior joined Wolves as an apprentice, played for the club in unofficial wartime games and made his full debut in 1946. He joined Derby for a £15,000 fee in 1953 and later returned to Wembley as West Bromwich Albion trainer in the 1967 League Cup Final (2-3 v Queens Park Rangers) and the following year's FA Cup Final (1-0 v Everton).

LESLIE SILVER, 89, was chairman of Leeds from 1983–1996. He presided over the club's return to top flight football in 1990, after an absence of eight years, and their League Championship success two years later when Howard Wilkinson's side finished four points ahead of Manchester United. Wilkinson was the last English manager to win the title which came to Elland Road in the last year before the start of the Premier League

JOHN BAXTER, 78, was a Scottish Under-23 international wing-half who made 307 appearances for Hibernian. One of them was in the 1958 Scottish Cup Final when a John Coyle shot deflected off him to give Clyde the only goal of the game. Baxter also played for Falkirk and Clydebank.

JIMMY DUNCAN, 73, scored on his competitive debut for Celtic against St Mirren in the 1952–53 season. He made nine senior appearances for the club and later played for St Mirren, Albion, Dundee United and Stranraer.

PAT HOLTON, 78, started and finished his career with Hamilton, gaining promotion from the Scottish Second Division in 1965 during his second spell with the club. The left-back also played for Motherwell, Southend and St Johnstone and had a brief spell with Chelsea.

JANUARY 2015

SIR JACK HAYWARD, 91, bought Wolves in 1990 and transformed a decaying Molineux into one of the first and finest all-seater stadiums in the country. The Bahamas-based developer spent upwards of £60m on a club he first supported as a boy when he used to crawl under the turnstiles to watch the team. Sir Jack, who also donated vast sums to charity, saw his dream realised in 2003 when Wolves reached the Premier League, albeit for a single season. He sold the club to Steve Morgan in 2007 for just £10, on condition that the new owner invested £30m.

KEN FURPHY, 83, was an innovative manager – on and off the pitch and at home and abroad. He led Watford into the second tier of English football for the first time, as Division Three champions in 1969. The following season, they reached the FA Cup semi-finals for the first time, beating Liverpool and Stoke on the way, before losing to Chelsea. Furphy also became the first manager to allow his pre-match team talk to be broadcast on television – on BBC Grandstand. He later managed Blackburn and Sheffield United, coached Pele at New York Cosmos and had spells with clubs in Miami, Detroit and Washington. In his playing career, Furphy made more than 300 appearances as a full-back for Darlington and won promotion from Division Four with Workington. He also spent the first four of his seven years at Vicarage Road as player-manager.

HAROLD HASSALL, 85, won five England caps and scored four goals – two against the Irish and one each against Scotland and Portugal. He also featured in one of the most famous of all FA Cup matches – the 1953 final when his Bolton side lost 4-3 to a Stanley Matthews-inspired Blackpool after leading 3-1. The inside-forward joined Bolton from Huddersfield for a club record £27,000 the previous year. His career was cut short on New Year's Day 1955 by a knee injury sustained against Chelsea. Hassall later coached England's youth team and the Malaysian national side.

JENO BUZANSZKY, 89, was the last surviving member of the formidable Hungary team – the 'Mighty Magyars' – of the 1950s. They were unbeaten for six years, apart from a surprise 3-2 defeat by West Germany in the 1954 World Cup Final. The run included a 6-3 win over England at Wembley, a 7-1 victory in the return match in Budapest and Olympic success in Helsinki in 1952. Buzanszky, a right-back, played 49 times for his country.

KEN HALE, 75, made 450 appearances and scored 95 goals in a 17-year career spanning five clubs. The inside-forward joined Coventry from Newcastle and shared part of manager Jimmy Hill's transformation of the club, winning a Third Division championship medal in 1964. Hale went on to serve Oxford, Darlington as player-manager and Halifax, then managed Hartlepool from 1974–76.

DANNY MALLOY, 84, joined Cardiff from Dundee for a £17,000 fee in 1955 and led them into the top flight in 1960 as runners-up to Second Division champions Aston Villa. The centre-half and captain left the club at the end of the following season – in which they defeated champions Tottenham, Manchester United and Chelsea to stay up – after being refused a £10-a-week pay rise. He joined Doncaster as player-manager and the following year returned top Scotland to play for Clyde.

PETER HILL, 83, was a one-club player who made 303 appearances for Coventry, scoring 77 goals. He made his debut as a 17-year-old inside-forward in 1949 and later switched successfully to the right-wing. After retiring at 31, Hill became trainer during Jimmy Hill's 'Sky Blue revolution.' He returned to the club in the late 1980s to become kit man.

JOHN MCPHEE, 77, joined Blackpool from home-town side Motherwell in 1962 and made 291 appearances for the club. The wing-half helped them win promotion back to the top flight in 1970 and was twice Player of the Year. He moved on to Barnsley, then captained Southport to the Fourth Division title in 1973.

ALBERT MCPHERSON, 87, won back-to-back promotions in a decade with Walsall during which he made 367 appearances. His side were Division Four champions in 1960 and Third Division runners-up 12 months later. The centre-half, who joined the club from Bury, went on to become trainer-coach with West Bromwich Albion's senior side, the reserves and youth team through to 1984.

SAM MORRIS, 84, was in the Chester team that held Chelsea to a 2-2 draw in an FA Cup third round tie at Stamford Bridge in 1952. He also played in the replay which his side lost 3-2 in front of a record crowd for their Sealand Road ground of 20,378. The wing-half made 90 Football League appearances for the club before a knee injury ended his career in 1957.

IAN TOWERS, 74, joined Oldham from Burnley and scored 27 times in the 1965–66 season to keep them in Division Three. The winger went on to net 45 goals in 95 appearances before moving to Bury. Then he played for Cape Town in South Africa before a knee injury cut short his career and he went into coaching.

DEREK ROBERTSON, 65, was St Johnstone's goalkeeper when they conceded a goal five seconds after the start of a pre-season friendly against Newcastle in 1972. John Tudor tapped the ball to Malcolm Macdonald, who drove it from 50 yards into the net. Robertson spent 13 seasons with the club, making 265 appearances.

ROGER WOSAHLO, 67, was top scorer for Chelsea's youth team, but made only one senior appearance, against Stoke in 1967, before leaving for the first of two spells with Ipswich. The winger also played for Peterborough and for the Johannesburg club Rangers.

FEBRUARY 2015

ROY LITTLE, 83, featured in two successive FA Cup Finals for Manchester City. His side lost 3-1 to Newcastle in 1955. A year later, they defeated Birmingham by the same scoreline in a game notable for the heroics of City goalkeeper Bert Trautmann, who was hurt diving at the feet of Peter Murphy. Captain Roy Paul thought about putting Little in goal, but Trautmann insisted on carrying on with what proved to be a broken neck. The left-back spent nine years at Maine Road before serving Brighton and Crystal Palace, then joining Dover as player-manager.

NICK SHARKEY, 71, averaged more than a goal every other game after making his debut for Sunderland in 1961. He scored five times in a 7-1 win over Norwich at Roker Park in 1963 and totalled 20 the following season as Sunderland won promotion to the top flight as runners-up to Leeds. Another 21 followed in all competitions and Sharkey's tally was 62 in 117 appearances when he moved to Leicester in 1966. The Scotland schoolboy and under-23 international went on to play for Mansfield and Hartlepool.

ANDY KING, 72, helped Kilmarnock become Scottish champions in 1965, for the first and only time in their history. After finishing runners-up in four of the previous five seasons, they defeated Hearts 2-0 at Tynecastle on the final day of the campaign to overtake their rivals on goal average, both teams having totalled 50 points. King, a right-back, made 224 appearances in 11 years at the club.

GEOFF MORRIS, 66, was Walsall's youngest-ever player in a league match, making his debut against Scunthorpe in 1965 at the age of 16 years and 218 days. The right-winger played 201 games in nine years at the club before helping Shrewsbury regain a place in Division Three in 1975. Morris then joined Port Vale, had a spell with Kidderminster and played for Brisbane in Australia.

TOM MCQUEEN, 85, played for several Scottish League clubs between 1946–61, including Motherwell, Hibernian, Alloa, Queen of the South, East Fife, Berwick and Stranraer. The goalkeeper, who also had a spell with Accrington, was the father of former Leeds and Manchester United centre-half Gordon McQueen.

DAVID WILLIAMS, 72, played under or worked alongside 13 managers in a long association with home-town club Newport. He made his debut as a left-winger in the 1960–61 season, moved to right-back three years later and made 306 appearances before retiring in 1973. Williams then served as coach and physio, along with a spell as caretaker manager. After the club went out of business in 1989, he was involved in the new Newport AFC as trainer and a director, then served the Wales national teams as kitman.

GUS MOFFAT, 66, was a right-winger who started at Southampton in 1963 and went on to play for Motherwell, Falkirk and Dumbarton. He also had spells in American and Canadian football with Detroit, Washington and Toronto.

MARCH 2015

DAVE MACKAY, 80, was one of the most influential players of his era, a powerful, tough-tackling wing-half who won a succession of major honours north and south of the border. His biggest achievement came in the 1960–61 season as the driving force behind Tottenham becoming the first post-war team to complete the Double. They became champions by an eight-point margin from Sheffield Wednesday and beat Leicester 2-0 in the FA Cup Final. There were two further Wembley triumphs, against Burnley the following season then Chelsea in 1967, by which time he had succeeded Danny Blanchflower as captain. Mackay, described by George Best as 'the hardest man I have ever played against', was also instrumental in Tottenham reaching the 1963 European Cup Winners' Cup Final, but missed the 5-1 victory over Atletico Madrid through injury. He had previously captained Hearts to the Scottish title, along with winning the Scottish Cup and two Scottish League Cups. After leaving White Hart Lane in 1968 for Derby, he helped Brian Clough's side become Second Division champions and shared the Football Writers' Association Footballer of the Year award with Manchester City's Tony Book. The Scot, who won 22 caps for his country, then became player-manager at Swindon, where his career on the pitch ended after nearly 700 appearances. He managed Nottingham Forest before succeeding Clough at the Baseball Ground and guiding Derby to the top flight title in 1975. After that, he was in charge of Walsall, Doncaster and Birmingham and spent more than a decade with clubs in the Middle East.

RON SUART, 94, was assistant manager alongside Tommy Docherty and then Dave Sexton during a 16-year association with Chelsea. He had seven months in charge following Sexton's departure in1974, but was unable to prevent relegation and was replaced by Eddie McCreadie. There were also spells as general manager and chief scout at Stamford Bridge. Suart had previously managed Blackpool for nine years, led Scunthorpe to the Third Division North title and been player-manager at Wigan. He also played, at centre-half and full-back, for Blackpool and Blackburn.

ROY MCCROHAN, 84, was an ever-present during Norwich's famous FA Cup run in the 1958–59 season. Then in the Third Division, they knocked out Manchester United and Tottenham before losing to Luton in the semi-finals. McCrohan made 426 appearances after joining the club from Reading. His last one, after 11 years at Carrow Road, was in the second leg of the 1962 League Cup Final which Norwich won 4-0 on aggregate against Rochdale. The wing-half went on to play for Colchester and Bristol Rovers.

JIMMY MCGILL, 68, made his debut for Arsenal against Leeds at Highbury in 1966 in front of the lowest crowd for a top division game at a major ground since the War. The attendance of 4,554 was the result of live TV coverage of the Cup-Winners' Cup Final between Liverpool and Borussia Dortmund. McGill's first-team, chances at the club were limited and he joined Huddersfield for a £10,000 fee in 1967. The midfielder helped them win the Second Division title three years later, moved on to Hull, then played for Halifax. He finished his career abroad, at San Diego and Melbourne.

IAN MOIR, 71, made more than 300 appearances for five clubs, including Manchester United. The winger spent four seasons with the 'Busby Babes' before joining Blackpool for £25,000 in 1964. He had two spells with Wrexham, including their Fourth Division promotion season in 1969–70, and also played for Chester and Shrewsbury, along with a spell in South Africa.

STUART MCGRADY, 29, played for Ayr and Queen's Park before joining Scottish junior club Maybole in 2009. He died suddenly, hours after scoring in their 3-0 win over Ardeer.

APRIL 2015

HARRY DOWD, 76, was Manchester City's goalkeeper in the 1969 FA Cup Final when they defeated Leicester 1-0. He succeeded Bert Trautmann and was first-choice for almost a decade until the emergence of Joe Corrigan. During that time, he scored against Bury after sustaining a broken thumb and switching to centre-forward. Dowd had a loan spell at Stoke, as understudy to Gordon Banks, before ending his career with Oldham.

RAY TREACY, 68, won 42 caps for the Republic of Ireland, making his debut against West Germany in 1966, his final appearance against Czechoslovakia in 1979 and scoring five goals. The inside-forward played his club football for West Bromwich Albion, Charlton, Swindon, Preston and Oldham. He then scored the winner for Shamrock Rovers in the 1978 FAI Cup Final and managed the club to the title in 1994.

SIR PHILIP CARTER, 87, presided over the most successful period in Everton's history. The chairman resisted calls from supporters to sack manager Howard Kendall and was rewarded with title wins in 1985 and 1987, the FA Cup in 1984 and the European Cup Winners' Cup in 1985. He stepped down when Peter Johnson bought the club, but returned after Bill Kenwright took over. Sir Philip was made life-president in 2004 and also served as president of the Football League and vice-president of the FA.

CHRIS TURNER, 64, had a long association with Peterborough as captain, manager and chairman. The central defender made 364 appearances between 1969–78, scoring 43 goals. He also played for Luton, Swindon, Cambridge and Southend, along with spells in the United States with Connecticut. After managing Cambridge, Turner returned to London Road in 1991, winning back-to-back promotions to take the club into the game's second tier for the first time. He then led a buy-out of the club and became chairman, before leaving in 1996 when Barry Fry became the owner.

BILL ELLERINGTON, 91, served Southampton for more than 30 years and was regarded as one of their best-ever right-backs. The former England schools' captain signed for his home-town club in 1945, made 238 appearances and won two England caps, against Norway and France in 1949. Ellerington later had coaching and scouting roles and was acclaimed by FA Cup winner Mick Channon for 'the greatest piece of tactical scouting I have ever known' before Southampton's victory over Manchester United in the 1976 final.

BILLY RONSON, 58, signed for Cardiff from Blackpool in 1979 for a then club record fee of £130,000. During two seasons at Ninian Park, he scored the winner against arch-rivals Swansea. The 5ft 4in midfielder moved on to Wrexham, Barnsley and Birmingham, then played in outside and indoor leagues in the United States for Tampa Bay, Baltimore, Pittsburgh, Detroit and Washington.

TOMMY PRESTON, 82, was part of Hibernian's history-making team in 1955. They became the first British club to compete in Europe, reaching the semi-finals of the European Cup before losing to Reims. Preston was in the side beaten by Clyde in the 1958 Scottish Cup Final and during the 1960–61 season scored in each leg of an Inter-Cities Fairs Cup tie against Barcelona when Hibernian again reached the last four before losing to Roma. The inside-forward made 313 appearances and scored 50 goals in 11 years at the club before ending his career with St Mirren.

KEN BIRCH, 81, played for Everton and Southampton in the late 1950s, then led Bangor to victory in the Welsh Cup in 1962. It brought a European Cup-Winners' Cup tie against Napoli in which he scored a penalty in a famous 2-0 first leg victory. Bangor lost the second 3-1 and, with away goals not counting in those days, were beaten 2-1 in a play-off at Highbury. Birch, a wing-half, later played and managed in South Africa.

DAVE WALKER, 73, made 231 appearances for Southampton between 1965–74 after joining the club from Burnley. The wing-half finished his career in South Africa, playing and coaching in Cape Town.

MAY 2015

ANDY KING, 58, was a much-travelled goalscoring midfielder, who made 248 appearances and netted 67 times in two spells with Everton. Two of the goals came against reigning champions Derby on his second appearance. But the one he was best remembered for was a 20-yard drive at Goodison Park in 1978 – Everton's first winner in seven years against Liverpool. The England under-21 international also played for Luton, Queens Park Rangers, West Bromwich Albion, Wolves and Aldershot, along with short spells with the Dutch side Cambuur and Swedish team Orebro. King managed Mansfield, Swindon and the Irish club Waterford, coached at Sunderland and scouted for Plymouth, Colchester and most recently MK Dons.

JOHN HEWIE, 87, made 530 appearances for Charlton between 1951–66 and ranks third on the club's all-time list. The South African-born left-back was renowned for his versatility, occupying several other positions when called upon, including makeshift goalkeeper. He was in the side that staged one of the game's greatest comebacks, recovering from 5-1 down with ten men to defeat Huddersfield 7-6 at The Valley in December 1957. Hewie won 19 Scotland caps – qualifying through his parentage – and played in the 1958 World Cup Finals in Sweden, missing a penalty in the 2-1 defeat by France.

ALAN WOODWARD, 68, joined Sheffield United as an apprentice in 1962 and made his Football League debut against Liverpool at Anfield. The right-winger, an England youth international, went on to play 640 matches for his home-town club, putting him third on their all-time list. Woodward's tally of 191 goals ranked him second. He was a dead-ball specialist and many of them came from free-kicks and penalties. They included four in a 7-0 victory over Ipswich in 1971. He spent 14 years at Bramall Lane before playing for Tulsa in the United States.

TONY MCNAMARA, 85, came through the ranks at Everton and scored 22 goals before crossing Stanley Park to join Liverpool for a £4,000 fee in 1957. He was on the mark on his debut for the Anfield club against Bristol City, but made only ten appearances. The right-winger left for Crewe and moved on to Bury, becoming the first player to appear in all four divisions in the space of 12 months.

GARRY LIDDELL, 60, joined Grimsby from Leeds for a £15,000 fee in 1977 and suffered relegation to Division Four in his first season. He then helped the club to two successive promotions, but had his career interrupted by two broken legs. The forward signed for Hearts in 1981 and later moved to Doncaster, managed by Billy Bremner, before a neck injury forced him to retire.

ERNIE HANNIGAN, 72, was Noel Cantwell's first signing as Coventry manager, a £55,000 buy from Preston in 1967, and played a key role in his new side surviving their first season in Division One. He struggled to hold down a place after that, moved on to Morton and had a spell with New York Cosmos. The right-winger, who had started his career with Queen of the South, then played and coached in Western Australia, where he won a place in the state's football Hall of Fame.

COLIN WHITAKER, 82, started his career with Sheffield Wednesday in 1951 and went on to play for Bradford Park Avenue, Shrewsbury, Queens Park Rangers, Rochdale, Oldham and Barrow. During his time with Shrewsbury, the left-winger also played Minor Counties cricket for Shropshire.

TOMMY DUNNE, 83, was a Republic of Ireland international who won back-to-back League of Ireland titles with St Patrick's in 1955–56. He also captained them to FAI Cup successes in 1959 and 1961. The right-half had previously played for Shamrock Rovers, later served Sligo and won a third title with Dundalk in 1967. He gained three caps.

ERIC BAKIE, 87, combined his playing career with a job in the Civil Service. His debut for Aberdeen in 1949 came in a 5-0 win over Motherwell. The left-half spent six years with Dunfermline and also served St Johnstone.

JUNE 2015

ZITO, 82, was at the heart of two World Cup-winning Brazil sides. In 1958, he formed a powerful midfield partnership with Didi which allowed the attacking talents of Pele, Garrincha and Vava to deliver 5-2 victories over France in the semi-finals and hosts Sweden in the final. Four years later in Chile, he scored the second goal in a 3-1 victory over Czechoslovakia in the final, achieved without the injured Pele. His death left Pele and Mario Zagallo as the only survivors from the 1958 team. Zito, who won 52 caps, spent his entire club career with Santos, making 733 appearances and scoring 57 goals. He was credited with spotting the talent of the Brazil and Barcelona star Neymar, signing him for the club when aged 11.

COLIN JACKSON, 68, was an influential figure during a golden era for Rangers. The central defender won 11 trophies – three League titles, three Scottish Cups and five League Cups – and made 506 appearances for the Ibrox club between 1963–82. One that stood out was the 1979 League Cup Final against Aberdeen when he scored a 90th minute winner. Biggest disappointment was failing a fitness test before the 1972 Cup Winners' Cup Final win over Moscow Dynamo in Barcelona. Jackson, capped eight times by Scotland, also played for Morton and Partick Thistle.

IAN MCKECHNIE, 73, became the first goalkeeper in English football to make a save in a competitive penalty shoot-out. It came in Hull's pre-season Watney Cup tie against Manchester United in 1970 after FIFA had approved shoot-outs to settle deadlocked ties. McKechnie denied Denis Law, but then missed one himself to give United victory. McKechnie made 255 appearances for Hull after starting his career as a winger with Arsenal and then playing for Southend. He left Boothferry Park to join Boston in the Northern American League and later had a spell as manager of the Irish club Sligo.

BRIAN TAYLOR, 78, joined Birmingham from Walsall for £10,000 in 1958 and played First Division football before a broken leg sustained in an Inter-Cities Fairs Cup tie kept him out of the game for a year. He moved on to Rotherham, Shrewsbury and Port Vale, then helped Barnsley win promotion from the Third Division in 1968.

DENNIS FIDLER, 76, was a trophy winner at the beginning and towards the end of his career. The left-winger twice lifted the FA Youth Cup with Manchester United, turned professional with Manchester City in 1957 and went on to play for Port Vale, Grimsby, Halifax and Darlington. Then, he helped Macclesfield beat Telford in the first FA Trophy Final at Wembley in 1970.

JOHNNY FULLAM, 75, was a Republic of Ireland international who lifted the FAI Cup a record eight times – six with Shamrock Rovers and two for Bohemians. The wing-half also won a League of Ireland title with each club. Fullam, who began his career at Preston in 1958, finished it with Athlone in 1980. He won 11 caps.

HOWARD JOHNSON, 89, won a Second Division Championship medal with Sheffield United in 1953. The trained accountant, a part-timer, spent six years at the club, but his first-team chances were restricted by the consistency of long-serving centre-half Joe Shaw. He later played for York.

JOE CARR, 83, made 230 appearances and scored 70 goals for St Johnstone between 1953–62. The club awarded the winger a testimonial in 1961 and in 2013 he was inducted into their Hall of Fame.

DENIS THWAITES, 70, died along with his wife Elaine in the terrorist attack in Tunisia. He made his senior debut for Birmingham as a 16-year-old, turned professional the following year and played several times in the First Division early in the 1962-63 season. The forward suffered from severe attacks of nerves and struggled in front of big crowds. But he still made 87 appearances for the club, scoring 18 goals, and was third top scorer in the 1965-66 campaign. He retired at 27.

LARRY CARBERRY, 79, turned down the chance to sign for home-town team Liverpool after completing National Service. Instead, he joined Alf Ramsey's Ipswich and was part of the Division One championship-winning side of 1961-62 when they finished three points ahead of Burnley and four clear of third-place Tottenham. The right-back was one of five players who also won the Division Three South and Division Two titles. Carberry made 283 appearances and was inducted into the club's Hall of Fame in 2010. He also had a spell with Barrow.

KEN BARRETT, 77, scored twice on his debut for Aston Villa in a 2-1 win over Newcastle in 1958. The outside-left was also on the mark the following week in a 4-1 defeat by West Bromwich Albion. He made five appearances under manager Eric Houghton, but was never selected by Houghton's successor, Joe Mercer, and joined Lincoln. He then played for home-town club Bromsgrove.

JIMMY ROBERTSON, 86, made a single appearance for Arsenal towards the end of the 1951-52 season, before joining Brentford in a part-exchange deal for Tommy Lawton. The winger was a regular during a three-year stay at Griffin Park, then played for Gravesend in the Southern League.

JIM ROWAN, 79, was an inside-forward who started his career with Celtic in 1954 and went on to play for six other Scottish clubs -Stirling, Clyde, Dunfermline, Airdrieonians, Falkirk and Partick. Later, he had a spell as caretaker-manager of Falkirk and managed East Stirling.

SIX RED CARDS IN FOUR GAMES

Six players were sent off in four matches between Celtic and Dundee United over the course of a fortnight last season. There were three red cards during a 1-1 Scottish Cup tie – Dundee's Paul Paton and Paul Dixon and Celtic's Virgil van Dijk. Paton, on the grounds of mistaken identity, and Van Dijk had them rescinded, freeing the pair to play in the League Cup Final. Celtic won it 2-0 after United captain Sean Dillon was dismissed, followed by a 4-0 success in the quarter-final replay in which Anthony Stokes saw red, along with Dundee's Ryan McGowan. The fourth meeting, this time in the Premiership, brought another victory for the eventual champions – 3-0.

PENALTY MARATHON FOR NEW MANAGER

Stuart McLaren will always remember his first game as manager of Stirling Albion – a record Scottish Cup penalty shoot-out which his side won 13-12 after 28 spot-kicks of a third round replay against non-league Hurlford United.

RECORDS SECTION

INDEX

GOALSCORING

(†Football League pre-1992–93)

Highest: Arbroath 36 Bon Accord (Aberdeen) 0 in Scottish Cup 1, Sep 12, 1885. On same day, also in Scottish Cup 1, Dundee Harp beat Aberdeen Rov 35-0.

Internationals: France 0 England 15 in Paris, 1906 (Amateur); Ireland 0 England 13 in Belfast Feb 18, 1882 (record in UK); England 9 Scotland 3 at Wembley, Apr 15, 1961; Biggest England win at Wembley: 9-0 v Luxembourg (Euro Champ), Dec 15, 1982.

Other record wins: Scotland: 11-0 v Ireland (Glasgow, Feb 23, 1901); **Northern Ireland:** 7-0 v Wales (Belfast, Feb 1, 1930); **Wales:** 11-0 v Ireland (Wrexham, Mar 3, 1888); **Rep of Ireland:** 8-0 v Malta (Euro Champ, Dublin, Nov 16, 1983).

Record international defeats: England: 1-7 v Hungary (Budapest, May 23, 1954); **Scotland:** 3-9 v England (Wembley, Apr 15, 1961); **Ireland:** 0-13 v England (Belfast, Feb 18, 1882); **Wales:** 0-9 v Scotland (Glasgow, Mar 23, 1878); **Rep of Ireland:** 0-7 v Brazil (Uberlandia, May 27, 1982).

World Cup: Qualifying round – Australia 31 American Samoa 0, world record international score (Apr 11, 2001); Australia 22 Tonga 0 (Apr 9, 2001); Iran 19 Guam 0 (Nov 25, 2000); Maldives 0 Iran 17 (Jun 2, 1997). **Finals – highest scores:** Hungary 10 El Salvador 1 (Spain, Jun 15, 1982); Hungary 9 S Korea 0 (Switzerland, Jun 17, 1954); Yugoslavia 9 Zaire 0 (W Germany, Jun 18, 1974).

European Championship: Qualifying round – highest scorers: San Marino 0 Germany 13 (Serravalle, Sep 6, 2006). **Finals – highest score:** Holland 6 Yugoslavia 1 (quarter-final, Rotterdam, Jun 25, 2000).

Biggest England U-21 win: 9-0 v San Marino (Shrewsbury, Nov 19, 2013).

FA Cup: Preston 26 Hyde 0 1st round, Oct 15, 1887.

League Cup: West Ham 10 Bury 0 (2nd round, 2nd leg, Oct 25, 1983); Liverpool 10 Fulham 0 (2nd round, 1st leg, Sep 23, 1986). **Record aggregates:** Liverpool 13 Fulham 2 (10-0h, 3-2a), Sep 23, Oct 7, 1986; West Ham 12 Bury 1 (2-1a, 10-0h), Oct 4, 25, 1983; Liverpool 11 Exeter 0 (5-0h, 6-0a), Oct 7, 28, 1981.

League Cup - most goals in one match: 12 Reading 5 Arsenal 7 aet (4th round, Oct 30, 2012); Dagenham & Redbridge 6 Brentford 6 aet (Brentford won 4-2 on pens; 1st round, Aug 12, 2014

Premier League (beginning 1992–93): Manchester Utd 9 Ipswich 0, Mar 4, 1995. **Record away win:** Nottm Forest 1 Manchester Utd 8 Feb 6, 1999.

Highest aggregate scores in Premier League – 11: Portsmouth 7 Reading 4, Sep 29, 2007; **10:** Tottenham 4 Reading 4, Dec 29, 2007; Tottenham 9 Wigan 1, Nov 22, 2009; Manchester Utd 8 Arsenal 2, Aug 28, 2011; Arsenal 7 Newcastle 3, Dec 29, 2012; WBA 5 Manchester Utd 5, May 19, 2013.

†Football League (First Division): Aston Villa 12 Accrington 2, Mar 12, 1892; Tottenham 10 Everton 4, Oct 11, 1958 (highest Div 1 aggregate that century); WBA 12 Darwen 0, Apr 4, 1892; Nottm Forest 12 Leicester Fosse 0, Apr 21, 1909. **Record away win:** Newcastle 1 Sunderland 9, Dec 5, 1908; Cardiff 1 Wolves 9, Sep 3, 1955; Wolves 0 WBA 8, Dec 27, 1893.

New First Division (beginning 1992–93): Bolton 7 Swindon 0, Mar 8, 1997; Sunderland 7 Oxford Utd 0, Sep 19, 1998. **Record away win:** Stoke 0 Birmingham 7, Jan 10, 1998; Oxford Utd 0 Birmingham 7, Dec 12, 1998. **Record aggregate:** Grimsby 6 Burnley 5, Oct 29, 2002; Burnley 4 Watford 7, Apr 5, 2003.

Championship (beginning 2004–05): Birmingham 0 Bournemouth 8, Oct 25, 2014. **Record away win:** Birmingham 0 Bournemouth 8, Oct 25, 2014. **Record aggregate:** Leeds 4 Preston 6, Sep 29, 2010; Leeds 3 Nottm Forest 7, Mar 20, 2012.

†**Second Division:** Newcastle 13 Newport Co 0, Oct 5, 1946; Small Heath 12 Walsall Town Swifts 0, Dec 17, 1892; Darwen 12 Walsall 0, Dec 26, 1896; Woolwich Arsenal 12 Loughborough 0, Mar 12, 1900; Small Heath 12 Doncaster 0, Apr 11, 1903. **Record away win:** *Burslem Port Vale 0 Sheffield Utd 10, Dec 10, 1892. **Record aggregate:** Manchester City 11 Lincoln 3, Mar 23, 1895.

New Second Division (beginning 1992–93): Hartlepool 1 Plymouth Argyle 8, May 7, 1994; Hartlepool 8 Grimsby 1, Sep 12, 2003.

New League 1 (beginning 2004–05): MK Dons 7 Oldham 0, Dec 20, 2014. **Record aggregate:** Hartlepool 4 Wrexham 6, Mar 5, 2005; Wolves 6 Rotherham 4, Apr 18, 2014; Bristol City 8 Walsall 2, May 3, 2015.

†**Third Division:** Gillingham 10 Chesterfield 0, Sep 5, 1987; Tranmere 9 Accrington 0, Apr 18, 1959; Brentford 9 Wrexham 0, Oct 15, 1963. **Record away win:** Halifax 0 Fulham 8, Sep 16, 1969. **Record aggregate:** Doncaster 7 Reading 5, Sep 25, 1982.

New Third Division (beginning 1992–93): Barnet 1 Peterborough 9, Sep 5, 1998. **Record aggregate:** Hull 7 Swansea 4, Aug 30, 1997.

New League 2 (beginning 2004–05): Peterborough 7 Brentford 0, Nov 24, 2007 Shrewsbury 7 Gillingham 0, Sep 13, 2008; Crewe 7 Barnet 0, Aug 21, 2010; Crewe 8 Cheltenham 1, Apr 2, 2011.

Record away win: Boston 0 Grimsby 6, Feb 3, 2007; Macclesfield 0 Darlington 6, Aug 30, 2008; Lincoln 0 Rotherham 6, Mar 25, 2011. **Record aggregate:** Burton 5 Cheltenham 6, Mar 13, 2010; Accrington 7 Gillingham 4, Oct 2, 2010.

†**Third Division (North):** Stockport 13 Halifax 0 (still joint biggest win in Football League – see Div 2) Jan 6, 1934; Tranmere 13 Oldham 4, Dec 26, 1935. (17 is highest Football League aggregate score). **Record away win:** Accrington 0 Barnsley 9, Feb 3, 1934.

†**Third Division (South):** Luton 12 Bristol Rov 0, Apr 13, 1936; Bristol City 9 Gillingham 4, Jan 15, 1927; Gillingham 9 Exeter 4, Jan 7, 1951. **Record away win:** Northampton 0 Walsall 8, Apr 8, 1947.

†**Fourth Division:** Oldham 11 Southport 0, Dec 26, 1962. **Record away win:** Crewe 1 Rotherham 8, Sep 8, 1973. **Record aggregate:** Hartlepool 10 Barrow 1, Apr 4, 1959; Crystal Palace 9 Accrington 2, Aug 20, 1960; Wrexham 10 Hartlepool 1, Mar 3, 1962; Oldham 11 Southport 0, Dec 26, 1962; Torquay 8 Newport 3, Oct 19, 1963; Shrewsbury 7 Doncaster 4, Feb 1, 1975; Barnet 4 Crewe 7, Aug 17, 1991.

Scottish Premier – Highest aggregate: 12: Motherwell 6 Hibernian 6, May 5, 2010; **11:** Celtic 8 Hamilton 3, Jan 3, 1987; Motherwell 5 Aberdeen 6, Oct 20, 1999. **Other highest team scores:** Aberdeen 8 Motherwell 0 (Mar 26, 1979); Hamilton 0 Celtic 8 (Nov 5, 1988); Celtic 9 Aberdeen 0 (Nov 6, 2010).

Scottish League Div 1: Celtic 11 Dundee 0, Oct 26, 1895. **Record away win:** Hibs 11 *Airdrie 1, Oct 24, 1959.

Scottish League Div 2: Airdrieonians 15 Dundee Wanderers 1, Dec 1, 1894 (biggest win in history of League football in Britain).

Record modern Scottish League aggregate: 12 – Brechin 5 Cowdenbeath 7, Div 2, Jan 18, 2003.

Record British score since 1900: Stirling 20 Selkirk 0 (Scottish Cup 1, Dec 8, 1984). Winger Davie Thompson (7 goals) was one of 9 Stirling players to score.

LEAGUE GOALS – BEST IN SEASON (Before restructure in 1992)

Div		Goals	Games
1	WR (Dixie) Dean, Everton, 1927–28	60	39

2	George Camsell, Middlesbrough, 1926–27	59	37
3(S)	Joe Payne, Luton, 1936–37	55	39
3(N)	Ted Harston, Mansfield, 1936–37	55	41
3	Derek Reeves, Southampton, 1959–60	39	46
4	Terry Bly, Peterborough, 1960–61	52	46

(Since restructure in 1992)

Div		Goals	Games
1	Guy Whittingham, Portsmouth, 1992–93	42	46
2	Jimmy Quinn, Reading, 1993–94	35	46
3	Andy Morrell, Wrexham, 2002–03	34	45

Premier League – BEST IN SEASON
Andy Cole **34 goals** (Newcastle – 40 games, 1993–94); Alan Shearer **34 goals** (Blackburn – 42 games, 1994–95).

FOOTBALL LEAGUE – BEST MATCH HAULS

(Before restructure in 1992)

Div	Goals	
1	Ted Drake (Arsenal), away to Aston Villa, Dec 14, 1935	7
	James Ross (Preston) v Stoke, Oct 6, 1888	7
2	*Neville (Tim) Coleman (Stoke) v Lincoln, Feb 23, 1957	7
	Tommy Briggs (Blackburn) v Bristol Rov, Feb 5, 1955	7
3(S)	Joe Payne (Luton) v Bristol Rov, Apr 13, 1936	10
3(N)	Robert ('Bunny') Bell (Tranmere) v Oldham, Dec 26, 1935 he also missed a penalty	9
3	Barrie Thomas (Scunthorpe) v Luton, Apr 24, 1965	5
	Keith East (Swindon) v Mansfield, Nov 20, 1965	5
	Steve Earle (Fulham) v Halifax, Sep 16, 1969	5
	Alf Wood (Shrewsbury) v Blackburn, Oct 2, 1971	5
	Tony Caldwell (Bolton) v Walsall, Sep 10, 1983	5
	Andy Jones (Port Vale) v Newport Co., May 4, 1987	5
4	Bert Lister (Oldham) v Southport, Dec 26, 1962	6

*Scored from the wing

(Since restructure in 1992)

Div Goals

1   **4** in match – John Durnin (Oxford Utd v Luton, 1992–93); Guy Whittingham (Portsmouth v Bristol Rov 1992–93); Craig Russell (Sunderland v Millwall, 1995–96); David Connolly (Wolves at Bristol City 1998–99); Darren Byfield (Rotherham at Millwall, 2002–03); David Connolly (Wimbledon at Bradford City, 2002–03); Marlon Harewood (Nottm Forest v Stoke, 2002–03); Michael Chopra (Watford at Burnley, 2002–03); Robert Earnshaw (Cardiff v Gillingham, 2003–04).

2   **5** in match – Paul Barnes (Burnley v Stockport, 1996–97); Robert Taylor (all 5, Gillingham at Burnley, 1998–99); Lee Jones (all 5, Wrexham v Cambridge Utd, 2001–02).

3   **5** in match – Tony Naylor (Crewe v Colchester, 1992–93); Steve Butler (Cambridge Utd v Exeter, 1993–4); Guiliano Grazioli (Peterborough at Barnet, 1998–99).

Champ   **4** in match – Garath McCleary (Nottm Forest at Leeds 2011–12); Nikola Zigic (Birmingham at Leeds 2011–12); Craig Davies (Barnsley at Birmingham 2012–13; Ross McCormack (Leeds at Charlton 2013–14), Jesse Lingard (Birmingham v Sheffield Wed 2013–14); Odion Ighalo (Watford v Blackpool, 2014-15).

Lge 1   **4** in match – Jordan Rhodes (all 4, Huddersfield at Sheffield Wed, 2011–12) **5** in match – Juan Ugarte (Wrexham at Hartlepool, 2004–05); Jordan Rhodes (Huddersfield at Wycombe, 2011–12).

Last player to score 6 in English League match: Geoff Hurst (West Ham 8 Sunderland 0, Div 1 Oct 19,1968.

PREMIER LEAGUE – BEST MATCH HAULS

5 goals in match: Andy Cole (Manchester Utd v Ipswich, Mar 4, 1995); Alan Shearer (Newcastle v Sheffield Wed, Sep 19, 1999); Jermain Defoe (Tottenham v Wigan, Nov 22, 2009); Dimitar Berbatov (Manchester Utd v Blackburn, Nov 27, 2010).

SCOTTISH LEAGUE

Div		Goals
Prem	Gary Hooper (Celtic) v Hearts, May 13, 2012	5
	Kris Boyd (Rangers) v Dundee Utd, Dec 30, 2009	5
	Kris Boyd (Kilmarnock) v Dundee Utd, Sep 25, 2004	5
	Kenny Miller (Rangers) v St Mirren, Nov 4, 2000	5
	Marco Negri (Rangers) v Dundee Utd, Aug. 23, 1997	5
	Paul Sturrock (Dundee Utd) v Morton, Nov 17, 1984	5
1	Jimmy McGrory (Celtic) v Dunfermline, Jan 14, 1928	8
1	Owen McNally (Arthurlie) v Armadale, Oct 1, 1927	8
2	Jim Dyet (King's Park) v Forfar, Jan 2, 1930 on his debut for the club	8
2	John Calder (Morton) v Raith, Apr 18, 1936	8
2	Norman Haywood (Raith) v Brechin, Aug. 20, 1937	8

SCOTTISH LEAGUE – BEST IN SEASON

Prem	Brian McClair (Celtic, 1986–87) **35**	
	Henrik Larsson (Celtic, 2000–01)	35
1	William McFadyen (Motherwell, 1931–32)	53
2	*Jimmy Smith (Ayr, 1927–28 – 38 appearances)	66
	(*British record)	

CUP FOOTBALL

Scottish Cup: John Petrie (Arbroath) v Bon Accord, at Arbroath, 1st round, Sep 12, 1885 — 13

FA Cup: Ted MacDougall (Bournemouth) v Margate, 1st round, Nov 20,1971 — 9

FA Cup Final: Billy Townley (Blackburn) v Sheffield Wed, at Kennington Oval, 1890; Jimmy Logan (Notts Co) v Bolton, at Everton, 1894; Stan Mortensen (Blackpool) v Bolton, at Wembley, 1953 — 3

League Cup: Frank Bunn (Oldham) v Scarborough (3rd round), Oct 25, 1989 — 6

Scottish League Cup: Jim Fraser (Ayr) v Dumbarton, Aug. 13, 1952; Jim Forrest (Rangers) v Stirling Albion, Aug. 17, 1966 — 5

Scottish Cup: Most goals in match since war: 10 by **Gerry Baker** (St Mirren) in 15-0 win (1st round) v Glasgow Univ, Jan 30, 1960; 9 by his brother **Joe Baker** (Hibernian) in 15-1 win (2nd round) v Peebles, Feb 11, 1961.

AGGREGATE LEAGUE SCORING RECORDS

	Goals
*Arthur Rowley (1947–65, WBA, Fulham, Leicester, Shrewsbury)	434
†Jimmy McGrory (1922–38, Celtic, Clydebank)	410
Hughie Gallacher (1921–39, Airdrieonians, Newcastle, Chelsea, Derby, Notts Co, Grimsby, Gateshead)	387
William ('Dixie') Dean (1923–37, Tranmere, Everton, Notts Co)	379
Hugh Ferguson (1916–30, Motherwell, Cardiff, Dundee)	362
● Jimmy Greaves (1957–71, Chelsea, Tottenham, West Ham)	357
Steve Bloomer (1892–1914, Derby, Middlesbrough, Derby)	352
George Camsell (1923–39, Durham City, Middlesbrough)	348

Dave Halliday (1920–35, St Mirren, Dundee, Sunderland, Arsenal, Manchester City, Clapton Orient) **338**

John Aldridge (1979–98, Newport, Oxford Utd, Liverpool, Tranmere) **329**

Harry Bedford (1919–34), Nottm Forest, Blackpool, Derby, Newcastle, Sunderland, Bradford PA, Chesterfield **326**

John Atyeo (1951–66, Bristol City) **315**

Joe Smith (1908–29, Bolton, Stockport) **315**

Victor Watson (1920–36, West Ham, Southampton) **312**

Harry Johnson (1919–36, Sheffield Utd, Mansfield) **309**

Bob McPhail (1923–1939, Airdrie, Rangers) **306**

(*Rowley scored 4 for WBA, 27 for Fulham, 251 for Leicester, 152 for Shrewsbury.

• **Greaves'** 357 is record top-division total (he also scored 9 League goals for AC Milan). **Aldridge** also scored 33 League goals for Real Sociedad. †McGrory scored 397 for Celtic, 13 for Clydebank).

Most League goals for one club: 349 – Dixie Dean (Everton 1925–37); 326 – George Camsell (Middlesbrough 1925–39); 315 – John Atyeo (Bristol City 1951–66); 306 – Vic Watson (West Ham 1920–35); 291 – Steve Bloomer (Derby 1892–1906, 1910–14); 259 – Arthur Chandler (Leicester 1923–35); 255 – Nat Lofthouse (Bolton 1946–61); 251 – Arthur Rowley (Leicester 1950–58).

More than 500 goals: Jimmy McGrory (Celtic, Clydebank and Scotland) scored a total of **550** goals in his first-class career (1922–38).

More than 1,000 goals: Brazil's Pele is reputedly the game's all-time highest scorer with **1,283** goals in 1,365 matches (1956–77), but many of them were scored in friendlies for his club, Santos. He scored his 1,000th goal, a penalty, against Vasco da Gama in the Maracana Stadium, Rio, on Nov 19, 1969. • Pele (born Oct 23, 1940) played regularly for Santos from the age of 16. During his career, he was sent off only once. He played 95 'A' internationals for Brazil and in their World Cup-winning teams in 1958 and 1970. † Pele (Edson Arantes do Nascimento) was subsequently Brazil's Minister for Sport. He never played at Wembley, apart from being filmed there scoring a goal for a commercial. Aged 57, Pele received an 'honorary knighthood' (Knight Commander of the British Empire) from the Queen at Buckingham Palace on Dec 3, 1997.

Romario (retired Apr, 2008, aged 42) scored more than 1,000 goals for Vasco da Gama, Barcelona, PSV Eindhoven, Valencia and Brazil (56 in 73 internationals).

MOST LEAGUE GOALS IN SEASON: DEAN'S 60

WR ('Dixie') Dean, Everton centre-forward, created a League scoring record in 1927–28 with 60 in 39 First Division matches. He also scored three in FA Cup ties, and 19 in representative games, totalling 82 for the season.

George Camsell, of Middlesbrough, previously held the record with 59 goals in 37 Second Division matches in 1926–27, his total for the season being 75.

SHEARER'S RECORD 'FIRST'

Alan Shearer (Blackburn) is the only player to score more than 30 top-division goals in 3 successive seasons since the War: 31 in 1993–94, 34 in 1994–95, 31 in 1995–96.

Thierry Henry (Arsenal) is the first player to score more than 20 Premiership goals in five consecutive seasons (2002–06). **David Halliday** (Sunderland) topped 30 First Division goals in 4 consecutive seasons with totals of 38, 36, 36 and 49 from 1925–26 to 1928–29.

MOST GOALS IN A MATCH

Sep 12, 1885: John Petrie set the all-time British individual record for a first-class match when, in Arbroath's 36-0 win against Bon Accord (Scottish Cup 1), he scored **13**.

Apr 13, 1936: Joe Payne set the still-existing individual record on his debut as a centre-forward, for Luton v Bristol Rov (Div 3 South). In a 12-0 win he scored **10**.

ROWLEY'S ALL-TIME RECORD

Arthur Rowley is English football's top club scorer with a total of 464 goals for WBA, Fulham, Leicester and Shrewsbury (1947–65). There were 434 in the League, 26 FA Cup, 4 League Cup.

Jimmy Greaves is second with a total of 420 goals for Chelsea, AC Milan, Tottenham and West Ham, made up of 366 League, 35 FA Cup, 10 League Cup and 9 in Europe. He also scored nine goals for AC Milan.

John Aldridge retired as a player at the end of season 1997–98 with a career total of 329 League goals for Newport, Oxford Utd, Liverpool and Tranmere (1979–98). In all competitions for those clubs he scored 410 in 737 appearances. He also scored 45 in 63 games for Real Sociedad.

MOST GOALS IN INTERNATIONAL MATCHES

13 by **Archie Thompson** for Australia v American Samoa in World Cup (Oceania Group qualifier) at Coff's Harbour, New South Wales, Apr 11, 2001. Result: 31-0.

7 by **Stanley Harris** for England v France in Amateur International in Paris, Nov 1, 1906. Result: 15-0.

6 by **Nat Lofthouse** for Football League v Irish League, at Wolverhampton, Sep 24, 1952. Result: 7-1.

Joe Bambrick for Northern Ireland against Wales (7-0) in Belfast, Feb 1, 1930 – a record for a Home Nations International.

WC Jordan in Amateur International for England v France, at Park Royal, Mar 23, 1908. Result: 12-0.

Vivian Woodward for England v Holland in Amateur International, at Chelsea, Dec 11,1909. Result: 9-1.

5 by **Howard Vaughton** for England v Ireland (Belfast) Feb 18, 1882. Result: 13-0.

Steve Bloomer for England v Wales (Cardiff) Mar 16, 1896. Result: 9-1.

Hughie Gallacher for Scotland against Ireland (Belfast), Feb 23, 1929. Result: 7-3.

Willie Hall for England v Northern Ireland, at Old Trafford, Nov 16, 1938. Five in succession (first three in 3·5 mins – fastest international hat-trick). Result: 7-0.

Malcolm Macdonald for England v Cyprus (Wembley) Apr 16, 1975. Result: 5-0.

Hughie Gallacher for Scottish League against Irish League (Belfast) Nov 1925. Result: 7-3.

Barney Battles for Scottish League against Irish League (Firhill Park, Glasgow) Oct 31, 1928. Result: 8-2.

Bobby Flavell for Scottish League against Irish League (Belfast) Apr 30, 1947. Result: 7-4.

Joe Bradford for Football League v Irish League (Everton) Sep 25, 1929. Result: 7-2.

Albert Stubbins for Football League v Irish League (Blackpool) Oct 18, 1950. Result: 6-3.

Brian Clough for Football League v Irish League (Belfast) Sep 23, 1959. Result: 5-0.

LAST ENGLAND PLAYER TO SCORE …

3 goals: Jermain Defoe v Bulgaria (4-0), Euro Champ qual, Wembley, Sep 3, 2010.

4 goals: Ian Wright v San Marino (7-1), World Cup qual, Bologna, Nov 17, 1993.

5 goals: Malcolm Macdonald v Cyprus (5-0), Euro Champ qual, Wembley, Apr 16, 1975.

INTERNATIONAL TOP SHOTS

		Goals	Games
England	Bobby Charlton (1958–70)	49	106
N Ireland	David Healy (2000–13)	36	95
Scotland	Denis Law (1958–74)	30	55
	Kenny Dalglish (1971–86)	30	102
Wales	Ian Rush (1980–96)	28	73
Rep of Ire	Robbie Keane (1998–2015)	65	140

ENGLAND'S TOP MARKSMEN

(As at start of season 2015–16)

	Goals	Games
Bobby Charlton (1958–70)	49	106
Gary Lineker (1984–92)	48	80
Wayne Rooney (2003-15)	48	105
Jimmy Greaves (1959–67)	44	57
Michael Owen (1998–2008)	40	89
Tom Finney (1946–58)	30	76
Nat Lofthouse (1950–58)	30	33
Alan Shearer (1992–2000)	30	63
Vivian Woodward (1903–11)	29	23
Frank Lampard (2003–14)	29	106
Steve Bloomer (1895–1907)	28	23
David Platt (1989–96)	27	62
Bryan Robson (1979–91)	26	90
Geoff Hurst (1966–72)	24	49
Stan Mortensen (1947–53)	23	25
Tommy Lawton (1938–48)	22	23
Peter Crouch (2005–11)	22	42
Mike Channon (1972–77)	21	46
Kevin Keegan (1972–82)	21	63

CONSECUTIVE GOALS FOR ENGLAND

Steve Bloomer scored in **10** consecutive appearances (19 goals) between Mar 1895 and Mar 1899.

Jimmy Greaves scored 11 goals in five consecutive matches from the start of season 1960–61.

Paul Mariner scored in five consecutive appearances (7 goals) between Nov 1981 and Jun 1982.

Wayne Rooney scored in five consecutive appearances (6 goals) between Oct 2012 and Mar 2013.

ENGLAND'S TOP FINAL SERIES MARKSMAN

Gary Lineker with 6 goals at 1986 World Cup in Mexico.

ENGLAND TOP SCORERS IN COMPETITIVE INTERNATIONALS

Michael Owen 26 goals in 53 matches; **Gary Lineker** 22 in 39; **Alan Shearer** 20 in 31.

MOST ENGLAND GOALS IN SEASON

13 – **Jimmy Greaves** (1960–61 in 9 matches); **12** – Dixie Dean (1926–27 in 6 matches); **10** – **Gary Lineker** (1990–91 in 10 matches); **10** – **Wayne Rooney** – (2008–09 in 9 matches).

MOST ENGLAND HAT-TRICKS

Jimmy Greaves 6; **Gary Lineker** 5, **Bobby Charlton** 4, **Vivian Woodward** 4, **Stan Mortensen** 3.

MOST GOALS FOR ENGLAND U-21s

13 – Alan Shearer (11 apps) Francis Jeffers (13 apps).

GOLDEN GOAL DECIDERS

The Football League, in an experiment to avoid penalty shoot-outs, introduced a new golden goal system in the 1994–95 **Auto Windscreens Shield** to decide matches in the knock-out stages of the competition in which scores were level after 90 minutes. The first goal scored in overtime ended play.

Iain Dunn (Huddersfield) became the first player in British football to settle a match by this sudden-death method. His 107th-minute goal beat Lincoln 3-2 on Nov 30, 1994, and to mark his 'moment in history' he was presented with a golden football trophy.

The AWS Final of 1995 was decided when Paul Tait headed the only goal for Birmingham against Carlisle 13 minutes into overtime – the first time a match at Wembley had been decided by the 'golden goal' formula.

First major international tournament match to be decided by sudden death was the Final of the **1996 European Championship** at Wembley in which Germany beat Czech Rep 2-1 by **Oliver Bierhoff's** goal in the 95th minute.

In the **1998 World Cup Finals** (2nd round), host country France beat Paraguay 1-0 with **Laurent Blanc's** goal (114).

France won the **2000 European Championship** with golden goals in the semi-final, 2-1 v Portugal (Zinedine Zidane pen, 117), and in the Final, 2-1 v Italy (David Trezeguet, 103).

Galatasaray (Turkey) won the **European Super Cup** 2-1 against Real Madrid (Monaco, Aug 25, 2000) with a 103rd minute golden goal, a penalty.

Liverpool won the **UEFA Cup** 5-4 against Alaves with a 117th-min golden goal, an own goal, in the Final in Dortmund (May 19, 2001).

In the **2002 World Cup Finals**, 3 matches were decided by Golden Goals: in the 2nd round Senegal beat Sweden 2-1 (Henri Camara, 104) and South Korea beat Italy 2-1 (Ahn Jung-hwan, 117); in the quarter-final, Turkey beat Senegal 1-0 (Ilhan Mansiz, 94).

France won the 2003 **FIFA Confederations Cup Final** against Cameroon (Paris, Jun 29) with a 97th-minute golden goal by Thierry Henry.

Doncaster won promotion to Football League with a 110th-minute golden goal winner (3-2) in the Conference Play-off Final against Dagenham at Stoke (May 10, 2003).

Germany won the **Women's World Cup Final** 2-1 v Sweden (Los Angeles, Oct 12, 2003) with a 98th-minute golden goal.

GOLD TURNS TO SILVER

Starting with the 2003 Finals of the UEFA Cup and Champions League/European Cup, UEFA introduced a new rule by which a silver goal could decide the winners if the scores were level after 90 minutes.

Team leading after 15 minutes' extra time win match. If sides level, a second period of 15 minutes to be played. If still no winner, result to be decided by penalty shoot-out.

UEFA said the change was made because the golden goal put too much pressure on referees and prompted teams to play negative football.

Although both 2003 European Finals went to extra-time, neither was decided by a silver goal. The new rule applied in the 2004 European Championship Finals, and Greece won their semi-final against the Czech Republic in the 105th minute.

The **International Board** decided (Feb 28 2004) that the golden/silver goal rule was 'unfair' and that from July 1 competitive international matches level after extra-time would, when necessary, be settled on penalties.

PREMIER LEAGUE TOP SHOTS (1992–2015)

Alan Shearer	260	Robbie Keane	126
Andy Cole	187	Nicolas Anelka	125
Wayne Rooney	185	Dwight Yorke	123
Frank Lampard	177	Steven Gerrard	120
Thierry Henry	175	Ian Wright	113
Robbie Fowler	163	Dion Dublin	111
Michael Owen	150	Emile Heskey	111
Les Ferdinand	149	Ryan Giggs	109
Teddy Sheringham	146	Paul Scholes	107
Robin van Persie	144	Darren Bent	106
Jermain Defoe	128	Didier Drogba	104
Jimmy Floyd Hasselbaink	127	Matt Le Tissier	102

LEAGUE GOAL RECORDS

The highest goal-scoring aggregates in the Football League, Premier and Scottish League are as follows:

For

	Goals	Games	Club	Season
Prem	103	38	Chelsea	2009–10
Div 1	128	42	Aston Villa	1930–31
New Div 1	108	46	Manchester City	2001–02
New Champ	99	46	Reading	2005–06
Div 2	122	42	Middlesbrough	1926–27
New Div 2	89	46	Millwall	2000–01
New Lge 1	106	46	Peterborough	2010–11
Div 3(S)	127	42	Millwall	1927–28
Div 3(N)	128	42	Bradford City	1928–29
Div 3	111	46	QPR	1961–62
New Div 3	96	46	Luton	2001–02
New Lge 2	96	46	Notts Co	2009–10
Div 4	134	46	Peterborough	1960–61
Scot Prem	105	38	Celtic	2003–04
Scot L 1	132	34	Hearts	1957–58
Scot L 2	142	34	Raith Rov	1937–38
Scot L 3 (Modern)	130	36	Gretna	2004–05

Against

	Goals	Games	Club	Season
Prem	100	42	Swindon	1993–94
Div 1	125	42	Blackpool	1930–31
New Div 1	102	46	Stockport	2001–02
New Champ	86	46	Crewe	2004–05
Div 2	141	34	Darwen	1898–99
New Div 2	102	46	Chester	1992–93
New Lge 1	98	46	Stockport	2004–05
Div 3(S)	135	42	Merthyr T	1929–30
Div 3(N)	136	42	Nelson	1927–28
Div 3	123	46	Accrington Stanley	1959–60
New Div 3	113	46	Doncaster	1997–98
New Lge 2	96	46	Stockport	2010–11
Div 4	109	46	Hartlepool Utd	1959–60
Scot Prem	100	36	Morton	1984–85
Scot Prem	100	44	Morton	1987–88
Scot L 1	137	38	Leith A	1931–32
Scot L 2	146	38	Edinburgh City	1931–32
Scot L 3 (Modern)	118	36	East Stirling	2003–04

BEST DEFENSIVE RECORDS

Denotes under old offside law

Div	Goals Agst	Games	Club	Season
Prem	15	38	Chelsea	2004–05
1	16	42	Liverpool	1978–79
1	*15	22	Preston	1888–89
New Div 1	28	46	Sunderland	1998–99
New Champ	30	46	Preston	2005–06
2	18	28	Liverpool	1893–94
2	*22	34	Sheffield Wed	1899–1900
2	24	42	Birmingham	1947–48

Div	Goals Agst	Games	Club	Season
2	24	42	Crystal Palace	1978–79
New Div 2	25	46	Wigan	2002–03
New Lge 1	32	46	Nottm Forest	2007–08
3(S)	*21	42	Southampton	1921–22
3(S)	30	42	Cardiff	1946–47
3(N)	*21	38	Stockport	1921–22
3(N)	21	46	Port Vale	1953–54
3	30	46	Middlesbrough	1986–87
New Div 3	20	46	Gillingham	1995–96
New Lge 2	31	46	Notts Co	2009–10
4	25	46	Lincoln	1980–81

SCOTTISH LEAGUE

Div	Goals Agst	Games	Club	Season
Prem	17	38	Celtic	2014–15
1	*12	22	Dundee	1902–03
1	*14	38	Celtic	1913–14
2	20	38	Morton	1966–67
2	*29	38	Clydebank	1922–23
2	29	36	East Fife	1995–96
New Div 3	21	36	Brechin	1995–96

TOP SCORERS (LEAGUE ONLY)

		Goals	Div
2014–15	Daryl Murphy (Ipswich)	27	Champ
2013–14	Luis Suarez (Liverpool)	31	Prem
2012–13	Tom Pope (Port Vale)	31	Lge 2
2011–12	Jordan Rhodes (Huddersfield)	36	Lge 1
2010–11	Clayton Donaldson (Crewe)	28	Lge 2
2009–10	Rickie Lambert (Southampton)	31	Lge 1
2008– 09	Simon Cox (Swindon)		
	Rickie Lambert (Bristol Rov)	29	Lge 1
2007–08	Cristiano Ronaldo (Manchester Utd)	31	Prem
2006–07	Billy Sharp (Scunthorpe)	30	Lge 1
2005–06	Thierry Henry (Arsenal)	27	Prem
2004–05	Stuart Elliott (Hull)	27	1
	Phil Jevons (Yeovil)	27	2
	Dean Windass (Bradford City)	27	1
2003–04	Thierry Henry (Arsenal)	30	Prem
2002–03	Andy Morrell (Wrexham)	34	3
2001–02	Shaun Goater (Manchester City)	28	1
	Bobby Zamora (Brighton)	28	2
2000–01	Bobby Zamora (Brighton)	28	3
1999–00	Kevin Phillips (Sunderland)	30	Prem
1998–99	Lee Hughes (WBA)	31	1
1997–98	Pierre van Hooijdonk (Nottm Forest)	29	1
	Kevin Phillips (Sunderland)	29	1
1996–97	Graeme Jones (Wigan)	31	3
1995–96	Alan Shearer (Blackburn)	31	Prem
1994–95	Alan Shearer (Blackburn)	34	Prem
1993–94	Jimmy Quinn (Reading)	35	2
1992–93	Guy Whittingham (Portsmouth)	42	1
1991–92	Ian Wright (Crystal Palace 5, Arsenal 24)	29	1
1990–91	Teddy Sheringham (Millwall)	33	2
1989–90	Mick Quinn (Newcastle)	32	2

1988–89	Steve Bull (Wolves)	37	3
1987–88	Steve Bull (Wolves)	34	4
1986–87	Clive Allen (Tottenham)	33	1
1985–86	Gary Lineker (Everton)	30	1
1984–85	Tommy Tynan (Plymouth Argyle)	31	3
	John Clayton (Tranmere)	31	4
1983–84	Trevor Senior (Reading)	36	4
1982–83	Luther Blissett (Watford)	27	1
1981–82	Keith Edwards (Hull 1, Sheffield Utd 35)	36	4
1980–81	Tony Kellow (Exeter)	25	3
1979–80	Clive Allen (Queens Park Rangers)	28	2
1978–79	Ross Jenkins (Watford)	29	3
1977–78	Steve Phillips (Brentford)	32	4
	Alan Curtis (Swansea City)	32	4
1976–77	Peter Ward (Brighton)	32	3
1975–76	Dixie McNeil (Hereford)	35	3
1974–75	Dixie McNeil (Hereford)	31	3
1973–74	Brian Yeo (Gillingham)	31	4
1972–73	Bryan (Pop) Robson (West Ham)	28	1
1971–72	Ted MacDougall (Bournemouth)	35	3
1970–71	Ted MacDougall (Bournemouth)	42	4
1969–70	Albert Kinsey (Wrexham)	27	4
1968–69	Jimmy Greaves (Tottenham)	27	1
1967–68	George Best (Manchester Utd)	28	1
	Ron Davies (Southampton)	28	1
1966–67	Ron Davies (Southampton)	37	1
1965–66	Kevin Hector (Bradford PA)	44	4
1964–65	Alick Jeffrey (Doncaster)	36	4
1963–64	Hugh McIlmoyle (Carlisle)	39	4
1962–63	Jimmy Greaves (Tottenham)	37	1
1961–62	Roger Hunt (Liverpool)	41	2
1960–61	Terry Bly (Peterborough)	52	4

100 LEAGUE GOALS IN SEASON

Manchester City, First Div Champions in 2001–02, scored 108 goals.

Bolton, First Div Champions in 1996–97, reached 100 goals, the first side to complete a century in League football since 103 by **Northampton** (Div 4 Champions) in 1986–87.

Last League Champions to reach 100 League goals: Chelsea (103 in 2009–10). Last century of goals in the top division: 111 by runners-up **Tottenham** in 1962–63.

Clubs to score a century of Premier League goals in season: **Chelsea** 103 in 2009–10, Manchester City (102) and Liverpool (101) in 2013–14.

Wolves topped 100 goals in four successive First Division seasons (1957–58, 1958–59, 1959–60, 1960–61).

In **1930–31,** the top three all scored a century of League goals: 1 Arsenal (127), 2 Aston Villa (128), 3 Sheffield Wed (102).

Latest team to score a century of League goals: Peterborough with 106 in 2010–11 (Lge 1).

100 GOALS AGAINST

Swindon, relegated with 100 goals against in 1993–94, were the first top-division club to concede a century of League goals since **Ipswich** (121) went down in 1964. Most goals conceded in the top division: 125 by **Blackpool** in 1930–31, but they avoided relegation.

MOST LEAGUE GOALS ON ONE DAY

A record of 209 goals in the four divisions of the Football League (43 matches) was set on **Jan 2,**

1932: 56 in Div 1, 53 in Div 2, 57 in Div 3 South and 43 in Div 3 North. There were two 10-goal aggregates: Bradford City 9, Barnsley 1 in Div 2 and Coventry City 5, Fulham 5 in Div 3 South. That total of 209 League goals on one day was equalled on **Feb 1, 1936** (44 matches): 46 in Div 1, 46 in Div 2, 49 in Div 3 South and 69 in Div 3 North. Two matches in the Northern Section produced 23 of the goals: Chester 12, York 0 and Crewe 5, Chesterfield 6.

MOST GOALS IN TOP DIV ON ONE DAY

This record has stood since **Dec 26, 1963,** when 66 goals were scored in the ten First Division matches played.

MOST PREMIER LEAGUE GOALS ON ONE DAY

47, in nine matches on **May 8, 1993** (last day of season). For the first time, all 20 clubs scored in the Premier League programme over the weekend of Nov 27-28, 2010.

FEWEST PREMIER LEAGUE GOALS IN ONE WEEK-END

10, in **10** matches on **Nov 24/25, 2001.**

FEWEST FIRST DIV GOALS ON ONE DAY

For full/near full programme: **Ten goals,** all by home clubs, in ten matches on Apr 28, 1923 (day of Wembley's first FA Cup Final).

SCORER OF LEAGUE'S FIRST GOAL

Kenny Davenport (2 mins) for Bolton v Derby, Sep 8, 1888.

SCORERS IN CONSECUTIVE TOP-DIVISION MATCHES

Stan Mortensen scored in 11 consecutive Division One games for Blackpool in season 1950–51. **Ruud van Nistelrooy** (Manchester Utd) scored 13 goals in last 8 games of season 2002–03 and in first 2 of 2003–04. Since the last war, 3 other players scored in 10 successive matches in the old First Division: **Billy McAdams** (Man City, 1957–58), **Ron Davies** (Southampton, 1966–67) and **John Aldridge** (Liverpool, May–Oct 1987).

SCORERS FOR 7 PREMIER LEAGUE CLUBS

Craig Bellamy (Coventry, Newcastle, Blackburn, Liverpool, West Ham, Manchester City, Cardiff).

SCORERS FOR 6 PREMIER LEAGUE CLUBS

Les Ferdinand (QPR, Newcastle, Tottenham, West Ham, Leicester, Bolton); **Andy Cole** (Newcastle, Manchester Utd, Blackburn, Fulham, Manchester City, Portsmouth); **Marcus Bent** (Crystal Palace, Ipswich, Leicester, Everton, Charlton, Wigan); **Nick Barmby** (Tottenham, Middlesbrough, Everton, Liverpool, Leeds, Hull); **Peter Crouch** (Tottenham, Aston Villa, Southampton, Liverpool, Portsmouth, Stoke); **Robbie Keane** (Coventry, Leeds, Tottenham, Liverpool, West Ham, Aston Villa); **Nicolas Anelka** (Arsenal, Liverpool, Manchester City, Bolton, Chelsea, WBA); **Darren Bent** (Ipswich, Charlton, Tottenham, Sunderland, Aston Villa, Fulham).

SCORERS FOR 5 PREMIER LEAGUE CLUBS

Stan Collymore (Nottm Forest, Liverpool, Aston Villa, Leicester, Bradford); **Mark Hughes** (Manchester Utd, Chelsea, Southampton, Everton, Blackburn); **Benito Carbone** (Sheffield Wed, Aston Villa, Bradford, Derby, Middlesbrough); **Ashley Ward** (Norwich, Derby, Barnsley, Blackburn Bradford); **Teddy Sheringham** (Nottm Forest, Tottenham, Manchester Utd, Portsmouth, West Ham); **Chris Sutton** (Norwich, Blackburn, Chelsea, Birmingham, Aston Villa).

SCORERS IN MOST CONSECUTIVE LEAGUE MATCHES

Arsenal broke the record by scoring in 55 successive Premiership fixtures: the last match in season 2000–01, then all 38 games in winning the title in 2001–02, and the first 16 in season 2002–03. The sequence ended with a 2-0 defeat away to Manchester Utd on December 7, 2002.

Chesterfield previously held the record, having scored in 46 consecutive matches in Div 3 (North), starting on Christmas Day, 1929 and ending on December 27, 1930.

SIX-OUT-OF-SIX HEADERS

When **Oxford Utd** beat Shrewsbury 6-0 (Div 2) on Apr 23, 1996, all six goals were headers.

ALL–ROUND MARKSMEN

Alan Cork scored in four divisions of the Football League and in the Premier League in his 18-season career with Wimbledon, Sheffield Utd and Fulham (1977–95).

Brett Ormerod scored in all four divisions (2, 1, Champ and Prem Lge) for Blackpool in two spells (1997–2002, 2008–11). **Grant Holt** (Sheffield Wed, Rochdale, Nottm Forest, Shrewsbury, Norwich) has scored in four Football League divisions and in the Premier League.

MOST CUP GOALS

FA Cup – most goals in one season: 20 by **Jimmy Ross** (Preston, runners-up 1887–88); 15 by **Alex (Sandy) Brown** (Tottenham, winners 1900–01).

Most FA Cup goals in individual careers: 49 by **Harry Cursham** (Notts Co 1877–89); 20th century: **44** by **Ian Rush** (39 for Liverpool, 4 for Chester, 1 for Newcastle 1979–98). **Denis Law** was the previous highest FA Cup scorer in the 20th century with 41 goals for Huddersfield Town, Manchester City and Manchester Utd (1957–74).

Most FA Cup Final goals by individual: 5 by **Ian Rush** for Liverpool (2 in 1986, 2 in 1989, 1 in 1992).

HOTTEST CUP HOT-SHOT

Geoff Hurst scored 21 cup goals in season 1965–66: 11 League Cup, 4 FA Cup and 2 Cup-Winners' Cup for West Ham, and 4 in the World Cup for England.

SCORERS IN EVERY ROUND

Twelve players have scored in every round of the FA Cup in one season, from opening to Final inclusive: **Archie Hunter** (Aston Villa, winners 1887); **Sandy Brown** (Tottenham, winners 1901); **Harry Hampton** (Aston Villa, winners 1905); **Harold Blackmore** (Bolton, winners 1929); **Ellis Rimmer** (Sheffield Wed, winners 1935); **Frank O'Donnell** (Preston, beaten 1937); **Stan Mortensen** (Blackpool, beaten 1948); **Jackie Milburn** (Newcastle, winners 1951); **Nat Lofthouse** (Bolton, beaten 1953); **Charlie Wayman** (Preston, beaten 1954); **Jeff Astle** (WBA, winners 1968); **Peter Osgood** (Chelsea, winners 1970).

Blackmore and the next seven completed their 'set' in the Final at Wembley; Osgood did so in the Final replay at Old Trafford.

Only player to score in every **Football League Cup** round possible in one season: **Tony Brown** for WBA, winners 1965–66, with 9 goals in 10 games (after bye in Round 1).

TEN IN A ROW

Dixie McNeill scored for Wrexham in ten successive FA Cup rounds (18 goals): 11 in Rounds 1-6, 1977–78; 3 in Rounds 3-4, 1978–79; 4 in Rounds 3-4, 1979–80.

Stan Mortensen (Blackpool) scored 25 goals in 16 FA Cup rounds out of 17 (1946–51).

TOP MATCH HAULS IN FA CUP

Ted MacDougall scored nine goals, a record for the competition proper, in the FA Cup first round on Nov 20, 1971, when Bournemouth beat Margate 11-0. On Nov 23, 1970 he had scored six in an 8-1 first round replay against Oxford City.

Other six-goal FA Cup scorers include **George Hilsdon** (Chelsea v Worksop, 9-1, 1907–08), **Ronnie Rooke** (Fulham v Bury, 6-0, 1938–39), **Harold Atkinson** (Tranmere v Ashington, 8-1,

1952–53), **George Best** (Manchester Utd v Northampton 1969–70, 8-2 away), **Duane Darby** (Hull v Whitby, 8-4, 1996–97).

Denis Law scored all six for Manchester City at Luton (6-2) in an FA Cup 4th round tie on Jan 28, 1961, but none of them counted – the match was abandoned (69 mins) because of a waterlogged pitch. He also scored City's goal when the match was played again, but they lost 3-1.

Tony Philliskirk scored **five** when Peterborough beat Kingstonian 9-1 in an FA Cup 1st round replay on Nov 25, 1992, but had them wiped from the records.

With the score at 3-0, the Kingstonian goalkeeper was concussed by a coin thrown from the crowd and unable to play on. The FA ordered the match to be replayed at Peterborough behind closed doors, and Kingstonian lost 1-0.

• Two players have scored **ten goals** in FA Cup preliminary round matches: **Chris Marron** for South Shields against Radcliffe in Sep 1947; **Paul Jackson** when Sheffield-based club Stocksbridge Park Steels beat Oldham Town 17-1 on Aug 31, 2002. He scored 5 in each half and all ten with his feet – goal times 6, 10, 22, 30, 34, 68, 73, 75, 79, 84 mins.

QUICKEST GOALS AND RAPID SCORING

A goal in **4 sec** was claimed by **Jim Fryatt**, for Bradford PA v Tranmere (Div 4, Apr 25, 1965), and by **Gerry Allen** for Whitstable v Danson (Kent League, Mar 3,1989). **Damian Mori** scored in **4 sec** for Adelaide v Sydney (Australian National League, December 6, 1995).

Goals after **6 sec** – **Albert Mundy** for Aldershot v Hartlepool, Oct 25, 1958; **Barrie Jones** for Notts Co v Torquay, Mar 31, 1962; **Keith Smith** for Crystal Palace v Derby, Dec 12, 1964.

9.6 sec by **John Hewitt** for Aberdeen at Motherwell, 3rd round, Jan 23, 1982 (fastest goal in Scottish Cup history).

Colin Cowperthwaite reputedly scored in **3.5 sec** for Barrow v Kettering (Alliance Premier League) on Dec 8, 1979, but the timing was unofficial.

Phil Starbuck for Huddersfield **3 sec** after entering the field as 54th min substitute at home to Wigan (Div 2) on Easter Monday, Apr 12, 1993. Corner was delayed, awaiting his arrival and he scored with a header.

Malcolm Macdonald after **5 sec** (officially timed) in Newcastle's 7-3 win in a pre-season friendly at St Johnstone on Jul 29, 1972.

World's fastest goal: 2.8 sec, direct from kick-off, Argentinian **Ricardo Olivera** for Rio Negro v Soriano (Uruguayan League), December 26, 1998.

Fastest international goal: 8.3 sec, **Davide Gualtieri** for San Marino v England (World Cup qual, Bologna, Nov 17, 1993).

Fastest England goals: 17 sec, Tommy Lawton v Portugal in Lisbon, May 25, 1947. **27 sec, Bryan Robson** v France in World Cup at Bilbao, Spain on Jun 16, 1982; **37 sec, Gareth Southgate** v South Africa in Durban, May 22, 2003; **30 sec, Jack Cock** v Ireland, Belfast, Oct 25, 1919; **30 sec, Bill Nicholson** v Portugal at Goodison Park, May 19, 1951. **38 sec, Bryan Robson** v Yugoslavia at Wembley, Dec 13, 1989; **42 sec, Gary Lineker** v Malaysia in Kuala Lumpur, Jun 12, 1991.

Fastest international goal by substitute: 5 sec, John Jensen for Denmark v Belgium (Euro Champ), Oct 12, 1994.

Fastest England goal by substitute: 10 sec, Teddy Sheringham v Greece (World Cup qualifier) at Old Trafford, Oct 6, 2001.

Fastest FA Cup goal: 4 sec, Gareth Morris (Ashton Utd) v Skelmersdale, 1st qual round, Sep 15, 2001.

Fastest FA Cup goal (comp proper): 9.7 sec, Jimmy Kebe for Reading v WBA, 5th Round, Feb 13, 2010.

Fastest FA Cup Final goal: 25 sec, Louis Saha for Everton v Chelsea at Wembley, May 30, 2009.

Fastest goal by substitute in FA Cup Final: 96 sec, Teddy Sheringham for Manchester Utd v Newcastle at Wembley, May 22, 1999.

Fastest League Cup Final goal: 45 sec, John Arne Riise for Liverpool v Chelsea, 2005.

Fastest goal on full League debut: 7.7 sec, Freddy Eastwood for Southend v Swansea (Lge 2),

Oct 16, 2004. He went on to score hat-trick in 4-2 win.

Fastest goal in cup final: 4.07 sec, 14-year-old Owen Price for Ernest Bevin College, Tooting, beaten 3-1 by Barking Abbey in Heinz Ketchup Cup Final at Arsenal on May 18, 2000. Owen, on Tottenham's books, scored from inside his own half when the ball was played back to him from kick-off.

Fastest Premier League goals: 10 sec, Ledley King for Tottenham away to Bradford, Dec 9, 2000; **10.4 sec, Alan Shearer for** Newcastle v Manchester City, Jan 18, 2003: **11 sec, Mark Viduka** for Leeds v Charlton, Mar 17, 2001; **12.5 sec. James Beattie** for Southampton at Chelsea, Aug 28, 2004; **13 sec, Chris Sutton** for Blackburn at Everton, Apr 1, 1995; **13 sec, Dwight Yorke** for Aston Villa at Coventry, Sep 30, 1995; **13 sec Asmir Begovic** (goalkeeper) for Stoke v Southampton, Nov 2, 2013; **13 sec Jay Rodriguez** for Southampton at Chelsea, Dec 1, 2013.

Fastest top-division goal: 7 sec, Bobby Langton for Preston v Manchester City (Div 1), Aug 25, 1948.

Fastest goal in Champions League: 10 sec, Roy Makaay for Bayern Munich v Real Madrid (1st ko rd), Mar 7, 2007.

Fastest Premier League goal by substitute: 9 sec, Shaun Goater, Manchester City's equaliser away to Manchester Utd (1-1), Feb 9, 2003. In Dec, 2011, Wigan's **Ben Watson** was brought off the bench to take a penalty against Stoke and scored.

Fastest goal on Premier League debut: 36 sec, Thievy Bifouma on as sub for WBA away to Crystal Palace, Feb 8, 2014.

Fastest goal by goalkeeper in professional football: 13 sec, Asmir Begovic for Stoke v Southampton (Prem Lge), Nov 2, 2013.

Fastest goal in women's football: 7 sec, Angie Harriott for Launton v Thame (Southern League, Prem Div), season 1998–99.

Fastest hat-trick in League history: 2 min 20 sec, Bournemouth's 84th-minute substitute **James Hayter** in 6-0 home win v Wrexham (Div 2) on Feb 24, 2004 (goal times 86, 87, 88 mins).

Fastest First Division hat-tricks since war: Graham Leggat, 3 goals in 3 minutes (first half) when Fulham beat Ipswich 10-1 on Boxing Day, 1963; **Nigel Clough,** 3 goals in **4 minutes** (81, 82, 85 pen) when Nottm Forest beat QPR 4-0 on Dec 13, 1987.

Fastest Premier League hat-trick: 2 min 56 sec (13, 14, 16) by **Sadio Mane** in Southampton 6, Aston Villa 1 on May 16, 2015.

Fastest international hat-trick: 2 min 35 sec, Abdul Hamid Bassiouny for Egypt in 8-2 win over Namibia in Abdallah, Libya, (African World Cup qual), Jul 13, 2001.

Fastest international hat-trick in British matches: 3.5 min, Willie Hall for England v N Ireland at Old Trafford, Manchester, Nov 16, 1938. (Hall scored 5 in 7-0 win); **3min 30 sec, Arif Erdem** for Turkey v N Ireland, European Championship qualifier, at Windsor Park, Belfast, on Sep 4, 1999.

Fastest FA Cup hat-tricks: In 3 min, Billy Best for Southend v Brentford (2nd round, Dec 7, 1968); **2 min 20 sec, Andy Locke** for Nantwich v Droylsden (1st Qual round, Sep 9, 1995).

Fastest Scottish hat-trick: 2 min 30 sec, Ian St John for Motherwell away to Hibernian (Scottish League Cup), Aug 15, 1959.

Fastest hat-trick of headers: Dixie Dean's 5 goals in Everton's 7-2 win at home to Chelsea (Div 1) on Nov 14, 1931 included 3 headers between **5th** and **15th-min.**

Fastest all-time hat-trick: Reported at 1 min 50 sec, Eduardo Maglioni for Independiente against Gimnasia de la Plata in Argentina Div , Mar 18, 1973.

Scored first kick: Billy Foulkes (Newcastle) for Wales v England at Cardiff, Oct 20, 1951, in his first international match.

Preston scored six goals in **7 min** in record 26-0 FA Cup 1st round win v Hyde, Oct 15, 1887.

Notts Co scored six second-half goals in **12 min** (Tommy Lawton 3, Jackie Sewell 3) when beating Exeter 9-0 (Div 3 South) at Meadow Lane on Oct 16, 1948.

Arsenal scored six in **18 min** (71-89 mins) in 7-1 home win (Div 1) v Sheffield Wed, Feb 15, 1992.

Tranmere scored six in first **19 min** when beating Oldham 13-4 (Div 3 North), December 26, 1935.

Sunderland scored eight in **28 min** at Newcastle (9-1 Div 1), December 5, 1908. Newcastle went on to win the title.

Southend scored all seven goals in **29 min** in 7-0 win at home to Torquay (Leyland Daf Cup, Southern quarter-final), Feb 26, 1991. Score was 0-0 until 55th minute.

Plymouth scored five in first **18 min** in 7-0 home win v Chesterfield (Div 2), Jan 3, 2004.

Five in 20 min: Frank Keetley in Lincoln's 9-1 win over Halifax in Div 3 (North), Jan 16, 1932; **Brian Dear** for West Ham v WBA (6-1, Div 1) Apr 16, 1965. **Kevin Hector** for Bradford PA v Barnsley (7-2, Div 4), Nov 20, 1965.

Four in 5 min: John McIntyre for Blackburn v Everton (Div 1), Sep 16, 1922; **WG (Billy) Richardson** for WBA v West Ham (Div 1), Nov 7, 1931.

Three in 2'5 min: Jimmy Scarth for Gillingham v Leyton Orient (Div 3S), Nov 1, 1952.

Three in three minutes: Billy Lane for Watford v Clapton Orient (Div 3S), December 20, 1933; **Johnny Hartburn** for Leyton Orient v Shrewsbury (Div 3S), Jan 22, 1955; **Gary Roberts** for Brentford v Newport, (Freight Rover Trophy, South Final), May 17, 1985; **Gary Shaw** for Shrewsbury v Bradford City (Div 3), December 22, 1990.

Two in 9 sec: Jamie Bates with last kick of first half, **Jermaine McSporran** 9 sec into second half when Wycombe beat Peterborough 2-0 at home (Div 2) on Sep 23, 2000.

Premier League – fastest scoring: Four goals in 4 min 44 sec, Tottenham home to Southampton on Sunday, Feb 7, 1993.

Premiership – fast scoring away: When **Aston Villa** won 5-0 at Leicester (Jan 31, 2004), all goals scored in **18 second-half min** (50-68).

Four in 13 min by Premier League sub: Ole Gunnar Solskjaer for Manchester Utd away to Nottm Forest, Feb 6, 1999.

FASTEST GOALS IN WORLD CUP FINAL SERIES

10.8 sec, Hakan Sukur for Turkey against South Korea in 3rd/4th-place match at Taegu, Jun 29, 2002; **15 sec, Vaclav Masek** for Czechoslovakia v Mexico (in Vina, Chile, 1962); **27 sec, Bryan Robson** for England v France (in Bilbao, Spain, 1982).

TOP MATCH SCORES SINCE WAR

By English clubs: 13-0 by Newcastle v Newport (Div 2, Oct 1946); 13-2 by Tottenham v Crewe (FA Cup 4th. Rd replay, Feb 1960); 13-0 by Chelsea v Jeunesse Hautcharage, Lux. (Cup-Winners' Cup 1st round, 2nd leg, Sep 1971).

By Scottish club: 20-0 by Stirling v Selkirk (E. of Scotland League) in Scottish Cup 1st round. (Dec 1984). That is the highest score in British first-class football since Preston beat Hyde 26-0 in FA Cup, Oct 1887.

MOST GOALS IN CALENDAR YEAR

88 by **Lionel Messi** in 2012 (76 Barcelona, 12 Argentina).

PREMIER LEAGUE LONGEST-RANGE GOALS BY OUTFIELD PLAYERS

66 yards: Charlie Adam (Stoke at Chelsea, Apr 4, 2015)
64 yards: Xabi Alonso (Liverpool v Newcastle, Sep 20, 2006)
62 yards: Maynor Figueroa (Wigan at Stoke, Dec 12, 2009)
59 yards: David Beckham (Manchester Utd at Wimbledon, Aug 17, 1996)
55 yards: Wayne Rooney (Manchester Utd at West Ham, Mar 22, 2014)

GOALS BY GOALKEEPERS

(Long clearances unless stated)
Pat Jennings for Tottenham v Manchester Utd (goalkeeper Alex Stepney), Aug 12, 1967 (FA Charity Shield).
Peter Shilton for Leicester v Southampton (Campbell Forsyth), Oct 14, 1967 (Div 1).
Ray Cashley for Bristol City v Hull (Jeff Wealands), Sep 18, 1973 (Div 2).
Steve Sherwood for Watford v Coventry (Raddy Avramovic), Jan 14, 1984 (Div 1).
Steve Ogrizovic for Coventry v Sheffield Wed (Martin Hodge), Oct 25, 1986 (Div 1).
Andy Goram for Hibernian v Morton (David Wylie), May 7, 1988 (Scot Prem Div).

Andy McLean, on Irish League debut, for Cliftonville v Linfield (George Dunlop), Aug 20, 1988.
Alan Paterson for Glentoran v Linfield (George Dunlop), Nov 30, 1988 (Irish League Cup Final – only instance of goalkeeper scoring winner in a senior cup final in UK).
Ray Charles for East Fife v Stranraer (Bernard Duffy), Feb 28, 1990 (Scot Div 2).
Iain Hesford for Maidstone v Hereford (Tony Elliott), Nov 2, 1991 (Div 4).
Chris Mackenzie for Hereford v Barnet (Mark Taylor), Aug 12, 1995 (Div 3).
Peter Schmeichel for Manchester Utd v Rotor Volgograd, Sep 26, 1995 (header, UEFA Cup 1).
Mark Bosnich (Aston Villa) for Australia v Solomon Islands, Jun 11, 1997 (penalty in World Cup qual – 13-0).
Peter Keen for Carlisle away to Blackpool (goalkeeper John Kennedy), Oct 24, 2000 (Div 3).
Steve Mildenhall for Notts Co v Mansfield (Kevin Pilkington), Aug 21, 2001 (free-kick inside own half, League Cup 1).
Peter Schmeichel for Aston Villa v Everton (Paul Gerrard), Oct 20, 2001 (volley, first goalkeeper to score in Premiership).
Mart Poom for Sunderland v Derby (Andy Oakes), Sep 20, 2003 (header, Div 1).
Brad Friedel for Blackburn v Charlton (Dean Kiely), Feb 21, 2004 (shot, Prem).
Paul Robinson for Leeds v Swindon (Rhys Evans), Sep 24, 2003 (header, League Cup 2).
Andy Lonergan for Preston v Leicester (Kevin Pressman), Oct 2, 2004 (Champ).
Gavin Ward for Tranmere v Leyton Orient (Glenn Morris), Sep 2, 2006 (free-kick Lge 1).
Mark Crossley for Sheffield Wed v Southampton (Kelvin Davis), Dec 23, 2006 (header, Champ).
Paul Robinson for Tottenham v Watford (Ben Foster), Mar 17, 2007 (Prem).
Adam Federici for Reading v Cardiff (Peter Enckelman), Dec 28, 2008 (shot, Champ).
Chris Weale for Yeovil v Hereford (Peter Gulacsi), Apr 21, 2009 (header, Lge 1).
Scott Flinders for Hartlepool v Bournemouth (Shwan Jalal), Apr 30, 2011 (header, Lge 1).
Iain Turner for Preston v Notts Co (Stuart Nelson), Aug 27 2011 (shot, Lge 1).
Tim Howard for Everton v Bolton (Adam Bogdan), Jan 4, 2012 (Prem).
Asmir Begovic for Stoke v Southampton (Artur Boruc), Nov 2, 2013 (Prem).

MORE GOALKEEPING HEADLINES

Arthur Wilkie, sustained a hand injury in Reading's Div 3 match against Halifax on Aug 31, 1962, then played as a forward and scored twice in a 4-2 win.
Alex Stepney was Manchester Utd's joint top scorer for two months in season 1973–74 with two penalties.
Alan Fettis scored twice for Hull in 1994–95 Div 2 season, as a substitute in 3-1 home win over Oxford Utd (Dec 17) and, when selected outfield, with last-minute winner (2-1) against Blackpool on May 6.
Roger Freestone scored for Swansea with a penalty at Oxford Utd (Div 2, Apr 30, 1995) and twice from the spot the following season against Shrewsbury (Aug 12) and Chesterfield (Aug 26).
Jimmy Glass, on loan from Swindon, kept Carlisle in the Football League on May 8, 1999. With ten seconds of stoppage-time left, he went upfield for a corner and scored the winner against Plymouth that sent Scarborough down to the Conference instead.
Paul Smith, Nottm Forest goalkeeper, was allowed to run through Leicester's defence unchallenged and score direct from the kick-off of a Carling Cup second round second match on Sep 18, 2007. It replicated the 1-0 score by which Forest had led at half-time when the original match was abandoned after Leicester defender Clive Clarke suffered a heart attack. Leicester won the tie 3-2.
Tony Roberts (Dagenham), is the only known goalkeeper to score from open play in the FA Cup, his last-minute goal at Basingstoke in the fourth qualifying round on Oct 27, 2001 earning a 2-2 draw. Dagenham won the replay 3-0 and went on to reach the third round proper.
The only known instance in first-class football in Britain of a goalkeeper scoring direct from a goal-kick was in a First Division match at Roker Park on Apr 14, 1900. The kick by Manchester City's **Charlie Williams** was caught in a strong wind and Sunderland keeper J. E Doig fumbled the ball over his line.

Jose Luis Chilavert, Paraguay's international goalkeeper, scored a hat-trick of penalties when his club Velez Sarsfield beat Ferro Carril Oeste 6-1 in the Argentine League on Nov 28, 1999. In all, he scored 8 goals in 72 internationals. He also scored with a free-kick from just inside his own half for Velez Sarsfield against River Plate on Sep 20, 2000.

Most goals by a goalkeeper in a League season: 5 (all penalties) by **Arthur Birch** for Chesterfield (Div 3 North), 1923–24.

When Brazilian goalkeeper **Rogerio Ceni** (37) converted a free-kick for Sao Paulo's winner (2-1) v Corinthians in a championship match on Mar 27, 2011, it was his 100th goal (56 free-kicks, 44 pens) in a 20-season career.

OWN GOALS

Most by player in one season: 5 by **Robert Stuart** (Middlesbrough) in 1934–35.

Three in match by one team: Sheffield Wed's **Vince Kenny, Norman Curtis** and **Eddie Gannon** in 5-4 defeat at home to WBA (Div 1) on Dec 26, 1952; Rochdale's **George Underwood, Kenny Boyle** and **Danny Murphy** in 7-2 defeat at Carlisle (Div 3 North), Dec 25, 1954; Sunderland's **Stephen Wright** and **Michael Proctor** (2) at home to Charlton (1-3, Prem), Feb 1, 2003; Brighton's **Liam Bridcutt** (2) and **Lewis Dunk** in 6-1 FA Cup 5th rd defeat at Liverpool, Feb 19, 2012.; Sunderland's **Santiago Vergini, Liam Bridcutt** and **Patrick van Aanholt** in 8-0 defeat at Southampton (Prem), Oct 18, 2014.

Two in match by one player: Chris Nicholl (Aston Villa) scored all 4 goals in 2-2 draw away to Leicester (Div 1), Mar 20, 1976; **Jamie Carragher** (Liverpool) in first half at home to Manchester Utd (2-3) in Premiership, Sep 11, 1999; **Jim Goodwin** (Stockport) in 1-4 defeat away to Plymouth (Div 2), Sep 23, 2002; **Michael Proctor** (Sunderland) in 1-3 defeat at home to Charlton (Premiership), Feb 1, 2003. **Michael Duberry** (Oxford) scored two own goals against Hereford on Jan 21, 2012, then rescued a point for his side with a 90th minute equaliser. **Jonathan Walters** (Stoke) headed the first 2 Chelsea goals in their 4-0 Premier League win at the Britannia Stadium, Jan 12, 2013. He also missed a penalty.Newport's **Tom Naylor** conceded two own goals and gave away a penalty in a 3-2 defeat by Moreca\mbe on Sept 14, 2013.

Fastest own goals: 8 sec by **Pat Kruse** of Torquay, for Cambridge Utd (Div 4), Jan 3, 1977; In First Division, **16 sec** by Steve Bould (Arsenal) away to Sheffield Wed, Feb 17, 1990.

Late own-goal man: Frank Sinclair (Leicester) put through his own goal in the 90th minute of Premiership matches away to Arsenal (L1-2) and at home to Chelsea (2-2) in Aug 1999.

Half an own goal each: Chelsea's second goal in a 3-1 home win against Leicester on December 18, 1954 was uniquely recorded as 'shared own goal'. Leicester defenders **Stan Milburn** and **Jack Froggatt**, both lunging at the ball in an attempt to clear, connected simultaneously and sent it rocketing into the net.

Match of 149 own goals: When Adama, Champions of Malagasy (formerly Madagascar) won a League match 149-0 on Oct 31, 2002, all 149 were own goals scored by opponents Stade Olympique De L'Emryne. They repeatedly put the ball in their own net in protest at a refereeing decision.

MOST SCORERS IN MATCH

Liverpool set a Football League record with **eight** scorers when beating Crystal Palace 9-0 (Div 1) on Sep 12, 1989. Marksmen were: Steve Nicol (7 and 88 mins), Steve McMahon (16), Ian Rush (45), Gary Gillespie (56), Peter Beardsley (61), John Aldridge (67 pen), John Barnes (79), Glenn Hysen (82).

Fifteen years earlier, **Liverpool** had gone one better with **nine** different scorers when they achieved their record win, 11-0 at home to Stromsgodset (Norway) in the Cup-Winners' Cup 1st round, 1st leg on Sep 17, 1974.

Eight players scored for **Swansea** when they beat Sliema, Malta, 12-0 in the Cup-Winners' Cup 1st round, 1st leg on Sep 15, 1982.

Nine Stirling players scored in the 20-0 win against Selkirk in the Scottish Cup 1st Round on December 8, 1984.

Premier League record: **Seven Chelsea** scorers in 8-0 home win over Aston Villa, Dec 23, 2012. An eighth player missed a penalty.

LONG SCORING RUNS

Tom Phillipson scored in 13 consecutive matches for Wolves (Div 2) in season 1926–27, which is still an English League record. **Bill Prendergast** scored in 13 successive League and Cup appearances for Chester (Div 3 North) in season 1938–39.

Dixie Dean scored in 12 consecutive games (23 goals) for Everton in Div 2 in 1930–31.

Danish striker **Finn Dossing** scored in 15 consecutive matches (Scottish record) for Dundee Utd (Div 1) in 1964–65.

50-GOAL PLAYERS

With **52** goals for **Wolves** in 1987–78 (34 League, 12 Sherpa Van Trophy, 3 Littlewoods Cup, 3 FA Cup), **Steve Bull** became the first player to score 50 in a season for a League club since **Terry Bly** for Div 4 newcomers Peterborough in 1960–61. Bly's 54 comprised 52 League goals and 2 in the FA Cup, and included 7 hat-tricks, still a post-war League record. Bull was again the country's top scorer with 50 goals in season 1988–89: 37 League, 2 Littlewoods Cup and 11 Sherpa Van Trophy. Between Bly and Bull, the highest individual scoring total for a season was 49 by two players: **Ted MacDougall** (Bournemouth 1970–71, 42 League, 7 FA Cup) and **Clive Allen** (Tottenham 1986–87, 33 League, 12 Littlewoods Cup, 4 FA Cup).

HOT SHOTS

Jimmy Greaves was top Div 1 scorer (League goals) six times in 11 seasons: 32 for Chelsea (1958–59), 41 for Chelsea (1960–61) and, for Tottenham, 37 in 1962–63, 35 in 1963–64, 29 in 1964–65 (joint top) and 27 in 1968–69.

Brian Clough (Middlesbrough) was leading scorer in Div 2 in three successive seasons: 40 goals in 1957–58, 42 in 1958–59 and 39 in 1959–60.

John Hickton (Middlesbrough) was top Div 2 scorer three times in four seasons: 24 goals in 1967–68, 24 in 1969–70 and 25 in 1970–71.

MOST HAT-TRICKS

Nine by George Camsell (Middlesbrough) in Div 2, 1926–27, is the record for one season. Most League hat-tricks in career: 37 by **Dixie Dean** for Tranmere and Everton (1924–38).

Most top division hat-tricks in a season since last War: six by **Jimmy Greaves** for Chelsea (1960–61). **Alan Shearer** scored five hat-tricks for Blackburn in the Premier League, season 1995–96.

Frank Osborne (Tottenham) scored three consecutive hat-tricks in Div 1 in Oct–Nov 1925, against Liverpool, Leicester (away) and West Ham.

Tom Jennings (Leeds) scored hat-tricks in three successive Div 1 matches (Sep–Oct, 1926): 3 goals v Arsenal, 4 at Liverpool, 4 v Blackburn. Leeds were relegated that season.

Jack Balmer (Liverpool) scored his three hat-tricks in a 17-year career in successive Div 1 matches (Nov 1946): 3 v Portsmouth, 4 at Derby, 3 v Arsenal. No other Liverpool player scored during that 10-goal sequence by Balmer.

Gilbert Alsop scored hat-tricks in three successive matches for Walsall in Div 3 South in Apr 1939: 3 at Swindon, 3 v Bristol City and 4 v Swindon.

Alf Lythgoe scored hat-tricks in three successive games for Stockport (Div 3 North) in Mar 1934: 3 v Darlington, 3 at Southport and 4 v Wrexham.

TRIPLE HAT-TRICKS

There have been at least three **instances of 3 hat-tricks being scored for one team in a Football League match:**

Apr 21, 1909: Enoch West, Billy Hooper and **Alfred Spouncer** for Nottm Forest (12-0 v Leicester Fosse, Div 1).

Mar 3, 1962: Ron Barnes, Wyn Davies and **Roy Ambler** in Wrexham's 10-1 win against Hartlepool (Div 4).

Nov 7, 1987: Tony Adcock, Paul Stewart and **David White** for Manchester City in 10-1 win at home to Huddersfield (Div 2).

For the first time in the Premiership, **three** hat-tricks were completed on one day (Sep 23, 1995):

Tony Yeboah for Leeds at Wimbledon; **Alan Shearer** for Blackburn v Coventry; **Robbie Fowler** with 4 goals for Liverpool v Bolton.
In the FA Cup, **Jack Carr, George Elliott** and **Walter Tinsley** each scored 3 in Middlesbrough's 9-3 first round win against Goole in Jan, 1915. **Les Allen** scored 5, **Bobby Smith** 4 and **Cliff Jones** 3 when Tottenham beat Crewe 13-2 in a fourth-round replay in Feb 1960.

HAT-TRICKS v THREE 'KEEPERS

When West Ham beat Newcastle 8-1 (Div 1) on Apr 21, 1986 **Alvin Martin** scored 3 goals against different goalkeepers: Martin Thomas injured a shoulder and was replaced, in turn, by outfield players Chris Hedworth and Peter Beardsley.
Jock Dodds of Lincoln had done the same against West Ham on Dec 18, 1948, scoring past Ernie Gregory, Tommy Moroney and George Dick in 4-3 win.
David Herd (Manchester Utd) scored against Sunderland's Jim Montgomery, Charlie Hurley and Johnny Parke in 5-0 First Division home win on Nov 26, 1966.
Brian Clark, of Bournemouth, scored against Rotherham's Jim McDonagh, Conal Gilbert and Michael Leng twice in 7-2 win (Div 3) on Oct 10, 1972.
On Oct 16, 1993 (Div 3) **Chris Pike** (Hereford) scored a hat-trick in 5-0 win over Colchester, who became the first team in league history to have two keepers sent off in the same game.
On Dec 18, 2004 (Lge 1), in 6-1 defeat at Hull, Tranmere used **John Achterberg** and **Russell Howarth**, both retired injured, and defender **Theo Whitmore**.
On Mar 9, 2008, Manchester Utd had three keepers in their 0-1 FA Cup quarter-final defeat by Portsmouth. **Tomasz Kuszczak** came on at half-time for **Edwin van der Sar** but was sent off when conceding a penalty. **Rio Ferdinand** went in goal and was beaten by Sulley Muntari's spot-kick.
Derby used three keepers in a 4-1 defeat at Reading (Mar 10, 2010, Champ). **Saul Deeney**, who took over when **Stephen Bywater** was injured, was sent off for a foul and **Robbie Savage** replaced him.

EIGHT-DAY HAT-TRICK TREBLE

Joe Bradford, of Birmingham, scored three hat-tricks in eight days in Sep 1929–30 v Newcastle (won 5-1) on the 21st, 5 for the Football League v Irish League (7-2) on the 25th, and 3 in his club's 5-7 defeat away to Blackburn on the 28th.

PREMIERSHIP DOUBLE HAT-TRICK

Robert Pires and **Jermaine Pennant** each scored 3 goals in Arsenal's 6-1 win at home to Southampton (May 7, 2003).

TON UP – BOTH ENDS

Manchester City are the only club to score and concede a century of League goals in the same season. When finishing fifth in the 1957–58 season, they scored 104 and gave away 100.

TOURNAMENT TOP SHOTS

Most individual goals in a World Cup Final series: 13 by **Just Fontaine** for France, in Sweden 1958. Most in European Championship Finals: 9 by **Michel Platini** for France, in France 1984.

MOST GOALS ON CLUB DEBUT

Jim Dyet scored eight in King's Park's 12-2 win against Forfar (Scottish Div 2, Jan 2, 1930). **Len Shackleton** scored six times in Newcastle's 13-0 win v Newport (Div 2, Oct 5, 1946) in the week he joined them from Bradford Park Avenue.

MOST GOALS ON LEAGUE DEBUT

Five by **George Hilsdon**, for Chelsea (9-2) v Glossop, Div 2, Sep 1, 1906. **Alan Shearer**, with three goals for Southampton (4-2) v Arsenal, Apr 9, 1988, became, at 17, the youngest player to score a First Division hat-trick on his full debut.

FOUR-GOAL SUBSTITUTE

James Collins (Swindon), sub from 60th minute, scored 4 in 5-0 home win v Portsmouth (Lge 1) on Jan 1, 2013.

CLEAN-SHEET RECORDS

On the way to promotion in Div 3 in season 1995–96, Gillingham's ever-present goalkeeper **Jim Stannard** set a clean-sheet record. In 46 matches. He achieved 29 shut-outs (17 at home, 12 away), beating the 28 by **Ray Clemence** for Liverpool (42 matches in Div 1, 1978–79) and the previous best in a 46-match programme of 28 by Port Vale (Div 3 North, 1953–54). In conceding only 20 League goals in 1995–96, Gillingham created a defensive record for the lower divisions.

Chris Woods, Rangers' England goalkeeper, set a British record in season 1986–87 by going 1,196 minutes without conceding a goal. The sequence began in the UEFA Cup match against Borussia Moenchengladbach on Nov 26, 1986 and ended when Rangers were sensationally beaten 1-0 at home by Hamilton in the Scottish Cup 3rd round on Jan 31, 1987 with a 70th-minute goal by **Adrian Sprott**. The previous British record of 1,156 minutes without a goal conceded was held by Aberdeen goalkeeper **Bobby Clark** (season 1970–01).

Manchester Utd set a new Premier League clean-sheet record of 1,333 minutes (including 14 successive match shut-outs) in season 2008–09 (Nov 15–Feb 21). **Edwin van der Sar's** personal British league record of 1,311 minutes without conceding ended when United won 2-1 at Newcastle on Mar 4, 2009.

Most clean sheets in season in top English division: **28** by **Liverpool** (42 matches) in 1978–79; **25** by **Chelsea** (38 matches) in 2004–05.

There have been three instances of clubs keeping 11 consecutive clean sheets in the Football League: **Millwall** (Div 3 South, 1925–26), **York** (Div 3, 1973–74) and **Reading** (Div 4, 1978–79). In his sequence, Reading goalkeeper **Steve Death** set the existing League shut-out record of 1,103 minutes.

Sasa Ilic remained unbeaten for over 14 hours with 9 successive shut-outs (7 in Div 1, 2 in play-offs) to equal a Charlton club record in Apr/May 1998. He had 12 clean sheets in 17 first team games after winning promotion from the reserves with 6 successive clean sheets.

Sebastiano Rossi kept a clean sheet in 8 successive away matches for AC Milan (Nov 1993–Apr 1994).

A world record of 1,275 minutes without conceding a goal was set in 1990–01 by **Abel Resino**, the Atletico Madrid goalkeeper. He was finally beaten by Sporting Gijon's Enrique in Atletico's 3-1 win on Mar 19, 1991.

In international football, the record is held by **Dino Zoff** with a shut-out for Italy (Sep 1972 to Jun 1974) lasting 1,142 minutes.

LOW SCORING

Fewest goals by any club in season in Football League: 18 by **Loughborough** (Div 2, 34 matches, 1899–1900); in 38 matches 20 by **Derby** (Prem Lge, 2007–08); in 42 matches, 24 by **Watford** (Div 2, 1971–72) and by **Stoke** (Div 1, 1984–85)); in 46-match programme, 27 by **Stockport** (Div 3, 1969–70).

Arsenal were the lowest Premier League scorers in its opening season (1992–93) with 40 goals in 42 matches, but won both domestic cup competitions. In subsequent seasons the lowest Premier League scorers were **Ipswich** (35) in 1993–94, **Crystal Palace** (34) in 1994–95, **Manchester City** (33) in 1995–96 and **Leeds** (28) in 1996–97 until **Sunderland** set the Premiership's new fewest-goals record with only 21 in 2002–03. Then, in 2007–08, **Derby** scored just 20.

LONG TIME NO SCORE

The world international non-scoring record was set by **Northern Ireland** when they played 13 matches and 1,298 minutes without a goal. The sequence began against Poland on Feb 13, 2002 and ended 2 years and 5 days later when David Healy scored against Norway (1-4) in Belfast on Feb 18, 2004.

Longest non-scoring sequences in Football League: 11 matches by **Coventry** in 1919–20 (Div 2); 11 matches in 1992–93 (Div 2) by **Hartlepool**, who after beating Crystal Palace 1-0 in the FA Cup 3rd round on Jan 2, went 13 games and 2 months without scoring (11 League, 1 FA Cup, 1 Autoglass Trophy). The sequence ended after 1,227 blank minutes with a 1-1 draw at Blackpool (League) on Mar 6.

In the Premier League (Oct–Jan season 1994–95) **Crystal Palace** failed to score in nine consecutive matches.

The British non-scoring club record is held by **Stirling:** 14 consecutive matches (13 League, 1 Scottish Cup) and 1,292 minutes play, from Jan 31 1981 until Aug 8, 1981 (when they lost 4-1 to Falkirk in the League Cup).

In season 1971–72, **Mansfield** did not score in any of their first nine home games in Div 3. They were relegated on goal difference of minus two.

FA CUP CLEAN SHEETS

Most consecutive FA Cup matches without conceding a goal: 11 by **Bradford City.** The sequence spanned 8 rounds, from 3rd in 1910–11 to 4th. Round replay in 1911–12, and included winning the Cup in 1911.

GOALS THAT WERE WRONGLY GIVEN

Tottenham's last-minute winner at home to Huddersfield (Div 1) on Apr 2, 1952: Eddie Baily's corner-kick struck referee WR Barnes in the back, and the ball rebounded to Baily, who crossed for Len Duquemin to head into the net. Baily had infringed the Laws by playing the ball twice, but the result (1-0) stood. Those two points helped Spurs to finish Championship runners-up; Huddersfield were relegated.

The second goal (66 mins) in **Chelsea's** 2-1 home win v Ipswich (Div 1) on Sep 26, 1970: Alan Hudson's shot hit the stanchion on the outside of goal and the ball rebounded on to the pitch. But instead of the goal-kick, referee Roy Capey gave a goal, on a linesman's confirmation. TV pictures proved otherwise. The Football League quoted from the Laws of the Game: 'The referee's decision on all matters is final.'

When **Watford's** John Eustace and **Reading's** Noel Hunt challenged for a 13th minute corner at Vicarage Road on Sep 20, 2008, the ball was clearly diverted wide. But referee Stuart Attwell signalled for a goal on the instruction his assistant and it went down officially as a Eustace own goal. The Championship match ended 2-2.

Sunderland's 1-0 Premier League win over **Liverpool** on Oct 17, 2009 was decided by one of the most bizarre goals in football history when Darren Bent's shot struck a red beach ball thrown from the crowd and wrong-footed goalkeeper Jose Reina. Referee Mike Jones wrongly allowed it to stand. The Laws of the Game state: 'An outside agent interfering with play should result in play being stopped and restarted with a drop ball.'

Blackburn's 59th minute equaliser (2-2) in 3-3 draw away to Wigan (Prem) on Nov 19, 2011 was illegal. Morten Gamst Pedersen played the ball to himself from a corner and crossed for Junior Hoilett to net.

The Republic of Ireland were deprived of the chance of a World Cup place in the second leg of their play-off with France on Nov 18, 2009. They were leading 1-0 in Paris when Thierry Henry blatantly handled before setting up William Gallas to equalise in extra-time time and give his side a 2-1 aggregate victory. The FA of Ireland's call for a replay was rejected by FIFA.

• The most notorious goal in World Cup history was fisted in by Diego Maradona in **Argentina's** 2-1 quarter-final win over England in Mexico City on Jun 22, 1986.

ATTENDANCES

GREATEST WORLD CROWDS

World Cup, Maracana Stadium, Rio de Janeiro, Jul 16, 1950. Final match (Brazil v Uruguay) attendance 199,850; receipts £125,000.

Total attendance in three matches (including play-off) between Santos (Brazil) and AC Milan for the Inter-Continental Cup (World Club Championship) 1963, exceeded 375,000.

BRITISH RECORD CROWDS

Most to pay: 149,547, Scotland v England, at Hampden Park, Glasgow, Apr 17, 1937. This was the first all-ticket match in Scotland (receipts £24,000).

At Scottish FA Cup Final: 146,433, Celtic v Aberdeen, at Hampden Park, Apr 24, 1937. Estimated another 20,000 shut out.

For British club match (apart from a Cup Final): 143,470, Rangers v Hibernian, at Hampden Park, Mar 27, 1948 (Scottish Cup semi-final).

FA Cup Final: 126,047, Bolton v West Ham, Apr 28, 1923. Estimated 150,000 in ground at opening of Wembley Stadium.

New Wembley: 89,874, FA Cup Final, Cardiff v Portsmouth, May 17, 2008.

World Cup Qualifying ties: 120,000, Cameroon v Morocco, Yaounde, Nov 29, 1981; 107,580, Scotland v Poland, Hampden Park, Oct 13, 1965.

European Cup: 135,826, Celtic v Leeds (semi-final, 2nd leg) at Hampden Park, Apr 15, 1970.

European Cup Final: 127,621, Real Madrid v Eintracht Frankfurt, at Hampden Park, May 18, 1960.

European Cup-Winners' Cup Final: 100,000, West Ham v TSV Munich, at Wembley, May 19, 1965.

Scottish League: 118,567, Rangers v Celtic, Jan 2, 1939.

Scottish League Cup Final: 107,609, Celtic v Rangers, at Hampden Park, Oct 23, 1965.

Football League old format: First Div: 83,260, Manchester Utd v Arsenal, Jan 17, 1948 (at Maine Road); **Div 2** 70,302 Tottenham v Southampton, Feb 25, 1950; **Div 3S:** 51,621, Cardiff v Bristol City, Apr 7, 1947; **Div 3N:** 49,655, Hull v Rotherham, Dec 25, 1948; **Div 3:** 49,309, Sheffield Wed v Sheffield Utd, Dec 26, 1979; **Div 4:** 37,774, Crystal Palace v Millwall, Mar 31, 1961.

Premier League: 76,098, Manchester Utd v Blackburn, Mar 31, 2007.

Football League – New Div 1: 41,214, Sunderland v Stoke, Apr 25, 1998; **New Div2:** 32,471, Manchester City v York, May 8, 1999; **New Div 3:** 22,319, Hull v Hartlepool Utd, Dec 26, 2002. **New Champs:** 52,181, Newcastle v Ipswich, Apr 24, 2010; **New Lge 1:** 38,256, Leeds v Gillingham, May 3, 2008; **New Lge 2:** 17,250, MK Dons v Morecambe, May 3, 2008.

In English Provinces: 84,569, Manchester City v Stoke (FA Cup 6), Mar 3, 1934.

Record for Under-21 International: 55,700, England v Italy, first match at New Wembley, Mar 24, 2007.

Record for friendly match: 104,679, Rangers v Eintracht Frankfurt, at Hampden Park, Glasgow, Oct 17, 1961.

FA Youth Cup: 38,187, Arsenal v Manchester Utd, at Emirates Stadium, Mar 14, 2007.

Record Football League aggregate (season): 41,271,414 (1948–49) – 88 clubs.

Record Football League aggregate (single day): 1,269,934, December 27, 1949, previous day, 1,226,098.

Record average home League attendance for season: 75,691 by Manchester Utd in 2007–08.

Long-ago League attendance aggregates: 10,929,000 in 1906–07 (40 clubs); 28,132,933 in 1937–38 (88 clubs).

Last 1m crowd aggregate, League (single day): 1,007,200, December 27, 1971.

Record Amateur match attendance: 100,000 for FA Amateur Cup Final, Pegasus v Harwich & Parkeston at Wembley, April 11, 1953.

Record Cup-tie aggregate: 265,199, at two matches between Rangers and Morton, in Scottish Cup Final, 1947–48.

Abandoned match attendance records: In England – 63,480 at Newcastle v Swansea City FA Cup 3rd round, Jan 10, 1953, abandoned 8 mins (0-0), fog.

In Scotland: 94,596 at Scotland v Austria (4-1), Hampden Park, May 8, 1963. Referee Jim Finney ended play (79 minutes) after Austria had two players sent off and one carried off.

Colchester's record crowd (19,072) was for the FA Cup 1st round tie v Reading on Nov 27, 1948, abandoned 35 minutes (0-0), fog.

SMALLEST CROWDS

Smallest League attendances: 450 Rochdale v Cambridge Utd (Div 3, Feb 5, 1974); 469, Thames v Luton (Div 3 South, December 6, 1930).

Only 13 people paid to watch Stockport v Leicester (Div 2, May 7, 1921) at Old Trafford, but up to 2,000 stayed behind after Manchester Utd v Derby earlier in the day. Stockport's ground was closed.

Lowest Premier League crowd: 3,039 for Wimbledon v Everton, Jan 26, 1993 (smallest top-division attendance since War).

Lowest Saturday post-war top-division crowd: 3,231 for Wimbledon v Luton, Sep 7, 1991 (Div 1).

Lowest Football League crowds, new format – Div 1: 849 for Wimbledon v Rotherham, (Div 1) Oct 29, 2002 (smallest attendance in top two divisions since War); 1,054 Wimbledon v Wigan (Div 1), Sep 13, 2003 in club's last home match when sharing Selhurst Park; **Div 2:** 1,077, Hartlepool Utd v Cardiff, Mar 22, 1994; **Div 3:** 739, Doncaster v Barnet, Mar 3, 1998.

Lowest top-division crowd at a major ground since the war: 4,554 for Arsenal v Leeds (May 5, 1966) – fixture clashed with live TV coverage of Cup-Winners' Cup Final (Liverpool v Borussia Dortmund).

Smallest League Cup attendances: 612, Halifax v Tranmere (1st round, 2nd leg) Sep 6, 2000; 664, Wimbledon v Rotherham (3rd round), Nov 5, 2002.

Smallest League Cup attendance at top-division ground: 1,987 for Wimbledon v Bolton (2nd Round, 2nd Leg) Oct 6, 1992.

Smallest Wembley crowds for England matches: 15,628 v Chile (Rous Cup, May 23, 1989 – affected by Tube strike); 20,038 v Colombia (Friendly, Sep 6, 1995); 21,432 v Czech. (Friendly, Apr 25, 1990); 21,142 v Japan (Umbro Cup, Jun 3, 1995); 23,600 v Wales (British Championship, Feb 23, 1983); 23,659 v Greece (Friendly, May 17, 1994); 23,951 v East Germany (Friendly, Sep 12, 1984); 24,000 v N Ireland (British Championship, Apr 4, 1984); 25,756 v Colombia (Rous Cup, May 24, 1988); 25,837 v Denmark (Friendly, Sep 14, 1988).

Smallest international modern crowds: 221 for Poland v N Ireland (4-1, friendly) at Limassol, Cyprus, on Feb 13, 2002. Played at neutral venue at Poland's World Cup training base. 265 (all from N Ireland) at their Euro Champ qual against Serbia in Belgrade on Mar 25, 2011. Serbia ordered by UEFA to play behind closed doors because of previous crowd trouble.

Smallest international modern crowds at home: N Ireland: 2,500 v Chile (Belfast, May 26, 1989 – clashed with ITV live screening of Liverpool v Arsenal Championship decider); Scotland: 7,843 v N Ireland (Hampden Park, May 6, 1969); Wales: 2,315 v N Ireland (Wrexham, May 27, 1982).

Smallest attendance for post-war England match: 2,378 v San Marino (World Cup) at Bologna (Nov 17, 1993). Tie clashed with Italy v Portugal (World Cup) shown live on Italian TV.

Lowest England attendance at New Wembley: 40,181 v Norway (friendly), Sep 3, 2014

Smallest paid attendance for British first-class match: 29 for Clydebank v East Stirling, CIS Scottish League Cup 1st round, Jul 31, 1999. Played at Morton's Cappielow Park ground, shared by Clydebank. Match clashed with the Tall Ships Race which attracted 200,000 to the area.

FA CUP CROWD RECORD (OUTSIDE FINAL)

The first FA Cup-tie shown on closed-circuit TV (5th round, Saturday, Mar 11, 1967, kick-off 7pm) drew a total of 105,000 spectators to Goodison Park and Anfield. At Goodison, 64,851 watched the match 'for real', while 40,149 saw the TV version on eight giant screens at Anfield. Everton beat Liverpool 1-0.

LOWEST SEMI-FINAL CROWD

The smallest FA Cup semi-final attendance since the War was 17,987 for the Manchester Utd–Crystal Palace replay at Villa Park on Apr 12, 1995. Palace supporters largely boycotted tie after a fan died in car-park clash outside pub in Walsall before first match.

Previous lowest: 25,963 for Wimbledon v Luton, at Tottenham on Apr 9, 1988.

Lowest quarter-final crowd since the war: 8,735 for Chesterfield v Wrexham on Mar 9, 1997.

Smallest FA Cup 3rd round attendances for matches between League clubs: 1,833 for Chester v Bournemouth (at Macclesfield) Jan 5, 1991; 1,966 for Aldershot v Oxford Utd, Jan 10, 1987.

PRE-WEMBLEY CUP FINAL CROWDS

AT CRYSTAL PALACE

1895 42,560	1902 48,036	1908 74,967
1896 48,036	Replay 33,050	1909 67,651
1897 65,891	1903 64,000	1910 76,980
1898 62,017	1904 61,734	1911 69,098
1899 73,833	1905 101,117	1912 54,434
1900 68,945	1906 75,609	1913 120,028
1901 110,802	1907 84,584	1914 72,778

AT OLD TRAFFORD

1915   50,000

AT STAMFORD BRIDGE

1920 50,018	1921 72,805	1922 53,000

England women's record crowd: 45,619 v Germany, 0-3 (Wembley, Nov 23, 2014) – Karen Carney's 100th cap.

INTERNATIONAL RECORDS

MOST APPEARANCES

Peter Shilton, England goalkeeper, then aged 40, retired from international football after the 1990 World Cup Finals with the European record number of caps – 125. Previous record (119) was set by **Pat Jennings,** Northern Ireland's goalkeeper from 1964–86, who retired on his 41st birthday during the 1986 World Cup in Mexico. Shilton's England career spanned 20 seasons from his debut against East Germany at Wembley on Nov 25, 1970.

Eight players have completed a century of appearances in full international matches for England. **Billy Wright** of Wolves, was the first, retiring in 1959 with a total of 105 caps. **Bobby Charlton,** of Manchester Utd, beat Wright's record in the World Cup match against West Germany in Leon, Mexico, in Jun 1970 and **Bobby Moore,** of West Ham, overtook Charlton's 106 caps against Italy in Turin, in Jun 1973. Moore played 108 times for England, a record that stood until Shilton reached 109 against Denmark in Copenhagen (Jun 7, 1989). In season 2008–09, **David Beckham** (LA Galaxy/AC Milan) overtook Moore as England's most-capped outfield player. In the vastly different selection processes of their eras, Moore played 108 full games for his country, whereas Beckham's total of 115 to the end of season 2009–10, included 58 part matches, 14 as substitute and 44 times substituted. **Steven Gerrard** won his 100th cap against Sweden in Stockholm on Nov 14, 2012 and **Ashley Cole** reached 100 appearances against Brazil at Wembley on Feb 6, 2013. **Frank Lampard** played his 100th game against Ukraine in Kiev (World Cup qual) on Sep 10, 2013.

Robbie Keane won his 126th Republic of Ireland cap, overtaking Shay Given's record, In a World Cup qualifier against the Faroe Islands on Jun 7, 2013. Keane scored all his team's three goals in a 3-0 win.

Kenny Dalglish became Scotland's first 100-cap international v Romania (Hampden Park, Mar 26, 1986).

World's most-capped player: Ahmed Hassan, 184 for Egypt (1995–2012).

Most-capped European player: Vitalijs Astafjevs, 167 for Latvia (1992–2010).

Most-capped European goalkeeper: Thomas Ravelli, 143 Internationals for Sweden (1981–97).

Gillian Coultard, (Doncaster Belles), England Women's captain, received a special presentation from Geoff Hurst to mark 100 caps when England beat Holland 1-0 at Upton Park on Oct 30, 1997. She made her international debut at 18 in May 1981, and retired at the end of season 1999–2000 with a record 119 caps (30 goals).

BRITAIN'S MOST-CAPPED PLAYERS

(As at start of season 2015–16)

Peter Shilton	125	Paul McStay	76	David Healy	95
David Beckham	115	Tommy Boyd	72	Mal Donaghy	91
Steven Gerrard	114	**Wales**		Sammy McIlroy	88
Bobby Moore	108	Neville Southall	92	Maik Taylor	88
Ashley Cole	107	Gary Speed	85	**Republic of Ireland**	
Bobby Charlton	106	Craig Bellamy	78	Robbie Keane	140
Frank Lampard	106	Dean Saunders	75	Shay Given	130
Billy Wright	105	Peter Nicholas	73	Kevin Kilbane	110
Wayne Rooney	105	Ian Rush	73	John O'Shea	104
Scotland		**Northern Ireland**		Steve Staunton	102
Kenny Dalglish	102	Pat Jennings	119	Damien Duff	100
Jim Leighton	91	Aaron Hughes	96		
Alex McLeish	77				

ENGLAND'S MOST-CAPPED PLAYER (either gender)

Fara Williams (Liverpool midfielder) with 147 appearances for the England's women's team to end of season 2014–15.

MOST ENGLAND CAPS IN ROW

Most consecutive international appearances: 70 by **Billy Wright**, for England from Oct 1951 to May 1959. He played 105 of England's first 108 post-war matches.

England captains most times: Billy Wright and Bobby Moore, 90 each.

England captains – 4 in match (v Serbia & Montenegro at Leicester Jun 3, 2003): **Michael Owen** was captain for the first half and after the interval the armband passed to **Emile Heskey** (for 15 minutes), **Phil Neville** (26 minutes) and substitute **Jamie Carragher** (9 minutes, including time added).

MOST SUCCESSIVE ENGLAND WINS

10 (Jun 1908–Jun 1909. Modern: 8 (Oct 2005–Jun 2006).

ENGLAND'S LONGEST UNBEATEN RUN

19 matches (16 wins, 3 draws), Nov 1965–Nov 1966.

ENGLAND'S TALLEST

At **6ft 7in**, Peter Crouch became England's tallest-ever international when he made his debut against Colombia in New Jersey, USA on May 31, 2005.

MOST PLAYERS FROM ONE CLUB IN ENGLAND SIDES

Arsenal supplied seven men (a record) to the England team v Italy at Highbury on Nov 14, 1934. They were: Frank Moss, George Male, Eddie Hapgood, Wilf Copping, Ray Bowden, Ted Drake and Cliff Bastin. In addition, Arsenal's Tom Whittaker was England's trainer.

Since then until 2001, the most players from one club in an England team was six from **Liverpool** against Switzerland at Wembley in Sep 1977. The side also included a Liverpool old boy, Kevin Keegan (Hamburg).

Seven **Arsenal** men took part in the England – France (0-2) match at Wembley on Feb 10, 1999. Goalkeeper David Seaman and defenders Lee Dixon, Tony Adams and Martin Keown lined up for England. Nicolas Anelka (2 goals) and Emmanuel Petit started the match for France and Patrick Vieira replaced Anelka.

Manchester Utd equalled Arsenal's 1934 record by providing England with seven players in the World Cup qualifier away to Albania on Mar 28, 2001. Five started the match – David Beckham (captain), Gary Neville, Paul Scholes, Nicky Butt and Andy Cole – and two went on as substitutes: Wes Brown and Teddy Sheringham.

INTERNATIONAL SUBS RECORDS

Malta substituted all 11 players in their 1-2 home defeat against England on Jun 3, 2000. Six substitutes by England took the total replacements in the match to 17, then an international record.

Most substitutions in match by **England:** 11 in second half by Sven-Goran Eriksson against Holland at Tottenham on Aug 15, 2001; 11 against Italy at Leeds on Mar 27, 2002; Italy sent on 8 players from the bench – the total of 19 substitutions was then a record for an England match; 11 against Australia at Upton Park on Feb 12, 2003 (entire England team changed at half-time); 11 against Iceland at City of Manchester Stadium on Jun 5, 2004.

Forty three players, a record for an England match, were used in the international against Serbia & Montenegro at Leicester on Jun 3, 2003. England sent on 10 substitutes in the second half and their opponents changed all 11 players.

The **Republic of Ireland** sent on 12 second-half substitutes, using 23 players in all, when they beat Russia 2-0 in a friendly international in Dublin on Feb 13, 2002.

First England substitute: Wolves winger **Jimmy Mullen** replaced injured Jackie Milburn (15 mins) away to Belgium on May 18, 1950. He scored in a 4-1 win.

ENGLAND'S WORLD CUP-WINNERS

At Wembley, Jul 30, 1966, 4-2 v West Germany (2-2 after 90 mins), scorers Hurst 3, Peters. Team: Banks; Cohen, Wilson, Stiles, Jack Charlton, Moore (capt), Ball, Hurst, Bobby Charlton, Hunt, Peters. Manager **Alf Ramsey** fielded that same eleven in six successive matches (an England record): the World Cup quarter-final, semi-final and Final, and the first three games of the following season. England wore red shirts in the Final and The Queen presented the Cup to Bobby Moore. The players each received a £1,000 bonus, plus £60 World Cup Final appearance money, all less tax, and Ramsey a £6,000 bonus from the FA The match was shown live on TV (in black and white).

England's non-playing reserves – there were no substitutes – also received the £1,000 bonus, but no medals. That remained the case until FIFA finally decided that non-playing members and staff of World Cup-winning squads should be given replica medals. England's 'forgotten heroes' received theirs at a reception in Downing Street on June 10, 2009 and were later guests of honour at the World Cup qualifier against Andorra at Wembley. The 11 reserves were: Springett, Bonetti, Armfield, Byrne, Flowers, Hunter, Paine, Connelly, Callaghan, Greaves, Eastham.

BRAZIL'S RECORD RUN

Brazil hold the record for the longest unbeaten sequence in international football: 45 matches from 1993–97. The previous record of 31 was held by Hungary between Jun 1950 and Jul 1954.

ENGLAND MATCHES ABANDONED

May 17, 1953 v **Argentina** (Friendly, Buenos Aires) after 23 mins (0-0) – rain.

Oct 29, 1975 v **Czechoslovakia** (Euro Champ qual, Bratislava) after 17 mins (0-0) – fog. Played next day.

Feb 15, 1995 v **Rep of Ireland** (Friendly, Dublin) after 27 mins (1-0) – crowd disturbance.

ENGLAND POSTPONEMENTS

Nov 21; 1979 v **Bulgaria** (Euro Champ qual, Wembley, postponed for 24 hours – fog; Aug 10, 2011 v **Holland** (friendly), Wembley, postponed after rioting in London.

Oct 16, 2012 v **Poland** (World Cup qual, Warsaw) postponed to next day – pitch waterlogged. The friendly against **Honduras** (Miami, Jun 7, 2014) was suspended midway through the first half for 44 minutes – thunderstorm.

ENGLAND UNDER COVER

England played indoors for the first time when they beat Argentina 1-0 in the World Cup at the Sapporo Dome, Japan, on Jun 7, 2002.

ALL-SEATED INTERNATIONALS

The first **all-seated crowd** (30,000) for a full international in Britain saw **Wales** and **West Germany** draw 0-0 at Cardiff Arms Park on May 31, 1989. The terraces were closed.

England's first all-seated international at Wembley was against Yugoslavia (2-1) on December 13, 1989 (attendance 34,796). The terracing behind the goals was closed for conversion to seating.

The first **full-house all-seated** international at Wembley was for England v Brazil (1-0) on Mar 28, 1990, when a capacity 80,000 crowd paid record British receipts of £1,200,000.

MOST NEW CAPS IN ENGLAND TEAM

6, by Sir Alf Ramsey (v Portugal, Apr 3, 1974) and by Sven-Goran Eriksson (v Australia, Feb 12, 2003; 5 at half-time when 11 changes made).

PLAYED FOR MORE THAN ONE COUNTRY

Multi-nationals in senior international football include: **Johnny Carey** (1938–53) – caps Rep of Ireland 29, N Ireland 7; **Ferenc Puskas** (1945–62) – caps Hungary 84, Spain 4; **Alfredo di Stefano** (1950–56) – caps Argentina 7, Spain 31; **Ladislav Kubala** (1948–58) – caps, Hungary 3, Czechoslovakia 11, Spain 19, only player to win full international honours with 3 countries. Kubala also played in a fourth international team, scoring twice for FIFA v England at Wembley in 1953. Eleven players, including **Carey**, appeared for both N Ireland and the Republic of Ireland in seasons directly after the last war.

Cecil Moore, capped by N Ireland in 1949 when with Glentoran, played for USA v England in 1953.

Hawley Edwards played for England v Scotland in 1874 and for Wales v Scotland in 1876.

Jack Reynolds (Distillery and WBA) played for both Ireland (5 times) and England (8) in the 1890s.

Bobby Evans (Sheffield Utd) had played 10 times for Wales when capped for England, in 1910–11. He was born in Chester of Welsh parents.

In recent years, several players have represented USSR and one or other of the breakaway republics. The same applies to Yugoslavia and its component states. **Josip Weber** played for Croatia in 1992 and made a 5-goal debut for Belgium in 1994.

THREE-GENERATION INTERNATIONAL FAMILY

When Bournemouth striker **Warren Feeney** was capped away to Liechtenstein on Mar 27, 2002, he became the third generation of his family to play for Northern Ireland. He followed in the footsteps of his grandfather James (capped twice in 1950) and father Warren snr. (1 in 1976).

FATHERS & SONS CAPPED BY ENGLAND

George Eastham senior (pre-war) and **George Eastham junior**; **Brian Clough** and **Nigel Clough**; **Frank Lampard snr** and **Frank Lampard jnr**; **Mark Chamberlain** and **Alex Oxlade-Chamberlain**.

FATHER & SON SAME-DAY CAPS

Iceland made father-and-son international history when they beat Estonia 3-0 in Tallin on Apr 24, 1996. **Arnor Gudjohnsen** (35) started the match and was replaced (62 mins) by his 17-year-old son **Eidur**.

LONGEST UNBEATEN START TO ENGLAND CAREER

Steven Gerrard, 21 matches (W16, D5) 2000–03.

SUCCESSIVE ENGLAND HAT-TRICKS

The last player to score a hat-trick in consecutive England matches was **Dixie Dean** on the summer tour in May 1927, against Belgium (9-1) and Luxembourg (5-2).

MOST GOALS BY PLAYER v ENGLAND

4 by **Zlatan Ibrahimovic** (Sweden 4 England 2, Stockholm, Nov 14, 2012).

POST-WAR HAT-TRICKS v ENGLAND

Nov 25, 1953, **Nandor Hidegkuti** (England 3, Hungary 6, Wembley); May 11, 1958, **Aleksandar Petakovic** (Yugoslavia 5, England 0, Belgrade); May 17, 1959, **Juan Seminario** (Peru 4, England 1, Lima); Jun 15, 1988, **Marco van Basten** (Holland 3, England 1, European Championship, Dusseldorf). Six other players scored hat-tricks against England (1878–1930).

NO-SAVE GOALKEEPERS

Chris Woods did not have one save to make when England beat San Marino 6-0 (World Cup) at Wembley on Feb 17, 1993. He touched the ball only six times.

Gordon Banks had a similar no-save experience when England beat Malta 5-0 (European Championship) at Wembley on May 12, 1971. Malta did not force a goal-kick or corner, and the four times Banks touched the ball were all from back passes.

Robert Green was also idle in the 6-0 World Cup qualifying win over Andorra at Wembley on Jun 10, 2009.

Joe Hart was untroubled in England's 5-0 win over San Marino in a World Cup qualifier at Wembley on Oct 12, 2012.

WORLD/EURO MEMBERS

FIFA has 209 member countries, **UEFA** 53

FIFA WORLD YOUTH CUP (UNDER-20)

Finals: **1977** (Tunis) Soviet Union 2 Mexico 2 (Soviet won 9-8 on pens.); **1979** (Tokyo) Argentina 3 Soviet Union 1; **1981** (Sydney) W Germany 4 Qatar 0; **1983** (Mexico City) Brazil 1 Argentina 0; **1985** (Moscow) Brazil 1 Spain 0; **1987** (Santiago) Yugoslavia 1 W Germany 1 (Yugoslavia won 5-4 on pens.); **1989** (Riyadh) Portugal 2 Nigeria 0; **1991** (Lisbon) Portugal 0 Brazil 0 (Portugal won 4-2 on pens.); **1993** (Sydney) Brazil 2 Ghana 1; **1995** (Qatar) Argentina 2 Brazil 0; **1997** (Kuala Lumpur) Argentina 2 Uruguay 1; **1999** (Lagos) Spain 4 Japan 0; **2001** (Buenos Aires) Argentina 3 Ghana 0; **2003** (Dubai) Brazil 1 Spain 0; **2005** (Utrecht) Argentina 2 Nigeria 1; **2007** (Toronto) Argentina 2 Czech Republic 1; **2009** (Cairo) Ghana 0 Brazil 0 (aet, Ghana won 4-3 on pens); **2011** (Bogota) Brazil 3 Portugal 2 (aet); **2013** (Istanbul) France 0 Uruguay 0 (aet, France won 4-1 on pens), **2015** (Auckland) Serbia 2 Brazil 1 (aet).

FAMOUS CLUB FEATS

Chelsea were Premiership winners in 2004–05, their centenary season with the highest points total (95) ever recorded by England Champions. They set these other records: Most Premiership wins in season (29); most clean sheets (25) and fewest goals conceded (15) in top-division history. They also won the League Cup in 2005.

Arsenal created an all-time English League record sequence of 49 unbeaten Premiership matches (W36, D13), spanning 3 seasons, from May 7, 2003 until losing 2-0 away to Manchester Utd on Oct 24, 2004. It included all 38 games in season 2003–04.

The Double: There have been 11 instances of a club winning the Football League/Premier League title and the FA Cup in the same season. **Manchester Utd** and **Arsenal** have each done so three times: **Preston** 1888–89; **Aston Villa** 1896–97; **Tottenham** 1960–61; **Arsenal** 1970–71, 1997–98, 2001–02; **Liverpool** 1985–86; **Manchester Utd** 1993–94, 1995–96, 1998–99; **Chelsea** 2009–10.

The Treble: **Liverpool** were the first English club to win three major competitions in one season when in 1983–84, Joe Fagan's first season as manager, they were League Champions, League Cup winners and European Cup winners.

Sir Alex Ferguson's **Manchester Utd** achieved an even more prestigious treble in 1998–99, completing the domestic double of Premiership and FA Cup and then winning the European Cup. In season 2008–09, they completed another major triple success – Premier League, Carling Cup and World Club Cup.

Liverpool completed a unique treble by an English club with three cup successes under Gerard Houllier in season 2000–01: the League Cup, FA Cup and UEFA Cup.

Liverpool the first English club to win five major trophies in one calendar year (Feb– Aug 2001): League Cup, FA Cup, UEFA Cup, Charity Shield, UEFA Super Cup.

As Champions in season 2001–02, **Arsenal** set a Premiership record by winning the last 13 matches. They were the first top-division club since Preston in the League's inaugural season (1888–89) to maintain an unbeaten away record.

(See Scottish section for treble feats by Rangers and Celtic).

Record Home Runs: Liverpool went 85 competitive first-team games unbeaten at home between losing 2-3 to Birmingham on Jan 21, 1978 and 1-2 to Leicester on Jan 31, 1981. They comprised 63 in the League, 9 League Cup, 7 in European competition and 6 FA Cup.

Chelsea hold the record unbeaten home League sequence of 86 matches (W62, D24) between losing 1-2 to Arsenal, Feb 21, 2004, and 0-1 to Liverpool, Oct 26, 2008.

Third to First: Charlton, in 1936, became the first club to advance from the Third to First Division in successive seasons. **Queens Park Rangers** were the second club to achieve the feat in 1968, and **Oxford Utd** did it in 1984 and 1985 as Champions of each division. Subsequently, **Derby** (1987), **Middlesbrough** (1988), **Sheffield Utd** (1990) and **Notts Co** (1991) climbed from Third Division to First in consecutive seasons.

Watford won successive promotions from the modern Second Division to the Premier League in 1997–98, 1998–99. **Manchester City** equalled the feat in 1998–99, 1999–2000. **Norwich** climbed from League 1 to the Premier League in seasons 2009–10, 2010–11. **Southampton** did the same in 2010–11 and 2011–12.

Fourth to First: Northampton , in 1965 became the first club to rise from the Fourth to the First Division. **Swansea** climbed from the Fourth Division to the First (three promotions in four seasons), 1977–78 to 1980–81. **Wimbledon** repeated the feat, 1982–83 to 1985–86 **Watford** did it in five seasons, 1977–8 to 1981–82. **Carlisle** climbed from Fourth Division to First, 1964–74.

Non-League to First: When **Wimbledon** finished third in the Second Division in 1986, they completed the phenomenal rise from non-League football (Southern League) to the First Division in nine years. Two years later they won the FA Cup.

Tottenham, in 1960–61, not only carried off the first First Division Championship and the FA Cup for the first time that century but set up other records by opening with 11 successive wins, registering most First Division wins (31), most away wins in the League's history (16), and equalling Arsenal's First Division records of 66 points and 33 away points. They already held the Second Division record of 70 points (1919–20).

Arsenal, in 1993, became the first club to win both English domestic cup competitions (FA Cup and League Cup) in the same season. **Liverpool** repeated the feat in 2001. **Chelsea** did it in 2007.

Chelsea achieved the FA Cup/Champions League double in May 2012.

Preston, in season 1888–89, won the first League Championship without losing a match and the FA Cup without having a goal scored against them. Only other English clubs to remain unbeaten through a League season were **Liverpool** (Div 2 Champions in 1893–94) and **Arsenal** (Premiership Champions 2003–04).

Bury, in 1903, also won the FA Cup without conceding a goal.

Everton won Div 2, Div 1 and the FA Cup in successive seasons, 1930–31, 1931–32, 1932–33.

Wolves won the League Championship in 1958 and 1959 and the FA Cup in 1960.

Liverpool won the title in 1964, the FA Cup in 1965 and the title again in 1966. In 1978 they became the first British club to win the European Cup in successive seasons. Nottm Forest repeated the feat in 1979 and 1980.

Liverpool won the League Championship six times in eight seasons (1976–83) under **Bob Paisley's** management.

Sir Alex Ferguson's **Manchester Utd** won the Premier League in 13 of its 21 seasons (1992–2013). They were runners-up five times and third three times.
Most Premiership wins in season: 29 by Chelsea in 2004–05, 2005–06.
Biggest points-winning margin by League Champions: 18 by **Manchester Utd** (1999–2000).

FA CUP/PROMOTION DOUBLE
WBA are the only club to achieve this feat in the same season (1930-31).

COVENTRY UNIQUE
Coventry are the only club to have played in the Premier League, all four previous divisions of the Football League, in both sections (North and South) of the old Third Division and in the modern Championship.

FAMOUS UPS & DOWNS
Sunderland: Relegated in 1958 after maintaining First Division status since their election to the Football League in 1890. They dropped into Division 3 for the first time in 1987.
Aston Villa: Relegated with Preston to the Third Division in 1970.
Arsenal up: When the League was extended in 1919, Woolwich Arsenal (sixth in Division Two in 1914–15, last season before the war) were elected to Division One. Arsenal have been in the top division ever since.
Tottenham down: At that same meeting in 1919 Chelsea (due for relegation) retained their place in Division One but the bottom club (Tottenham) had to go down to Division Two.
Preston and **Burnley down**: Preston, the first League Champions in season 1888–89, dropped into the Fourth Division in 1985. So did Burnley, also among the League's original members in 1888. In 1986, Preston had to apply for re-election.
Wolves' fall: Wolves, another of the Football League's original members, completed the fall from First Division to Fourth in successive seasons (1984–85–86).
Lincoln out: Lincoln became the first club to suffer automatic demotion from the Football League when they finished bottom of Div 4, on goal difference, in season 1986–87. They were replaced by Scarborough, champions of the GM Vauxhall Conference. Lincoln regained their place a year later.
Swindon up and down: In the 1990 play-offs, Swindon won promotion to the First Division for the first time, but remained in the Second Division because of financial irregularities.

MOST CHAMPIONSHIP WINS
Manchester Utd have been champions of England a record 20 times (7 Football League, 13 Premier League).

LONGEST CURRENT MEMBERS OF TOP DIVISION
Arsenal (since 1919), **Everton** (1954), **Liverpool** (1962), **Manchester Utd** (1975).

CHAMPIONS: FEWEST PLAYERS
Liverpool used only **14** players (five ever-present) when they won the League Championship in season 1965–66. **Aston Villa** also called on no more than 14 players to win the title in 1980–81, with seven ever-present.

UNBEATEN CHAMPIONS
Only two clubs have become Champions of England with an unbeaten record: **Preston** as the Football League's first winners in 1888–89 (22 matches) and **Arsenal**, Premiership winners in 2003–04 (38 matches).

LEAGUE HAT-TRICKS
Huddersfield created a record in 1924–25–26 by winning the League Championship three years in succession.

Arsenal equalled this hat-trick in 1933–34–35, **Liverpool** in 1982–83–84 and **Manchester Utd** in 1999–2000–01. Sir Alex Ferguson's side became the first to complete two hat-tricks (2007–08–09).

'SUPER DOUBLE' WINNERS

Since the War, there have been three instances of players appearing in and then managing FA Cup and Championship-winning teams:

Joe Mercer: Player in Arsenal Championship teams 1948, 1953 and in their 1950 FA Cup side; manager of Manchester City when they won Championship 1968, FA Cup 1969.

Kenny Dalglish: Player in Liverpool Championship-winning teams 1979, 1980, 1982, 1983, 1984, player-manager 1986, 1988, 1990: player-manager when Liverpool won FA Cup (to complete Double) 1986; manager of Blackburn, Champions 1995.

George Graham: Played in Arsenal's Double-winning team in 1971, and as manager took them to Championship success in 1989 and 1991 and the FA Cup – League Cup double in 1993.

ORIGINAL TWELVE

The original 12 members of the Football League (formed in 1888) were: **Accrington, Aston Villa, Blackburn, Bolton, Burnley, Derby, Everton, Notts Co, Preston, Stoke, WBA** and **Wolves.**

Results on the opening day (Sep 8, 1888): Bolton 3, Derby 6; Everton 2, Accrington 1; Preston 5, Burnley 2; Stoke 0, WBA 2; Wolves 1, Aston Villa 1. Preston had the biggest first-day crowd: 6,000. Blackburn and Notts Co did not play that day. They kicked off a week later (Sep 15) – Blackburn 5, Accrington 5; Everton 2, Notts Co 1.

Accrington FC resigned from the league in 1893 and later folded. A new club, Accrington Stanley, were members of the league from 1921 until 1962 when financial problems forced their demise. The current Accrington Stanley were formed in 1968 and gained league status in 2007.

FASTEST CLIMBS

Three promotions in four seasons by two clubs – **Swansea City:** 1978 third in Div 4; 1979 third in Div 3; 1981 third in Div 2; **Wimbledon:** 1983 Champions of Div 4; 1984 second in Div 3; 1986 third in Div 2.

MERSEYSIDE RECORD

Liverpool is the only city to have staged top-division football – through Everton and/or Liverpool – **in every season** since League football began in 1888.

EARLIEST PROMOTIONS TO TOP DIVISION POST-WAR

Mar 23, 1974, **Middlesbrough;** Mar 25, 2006, **Reading.**

EARLIEST RELEGATIONS POST-WAR

From top division: **QPR** went down from the old First Division on Mar 29, 1969; **Derby** went down from the Premier League on Mar 29, 2008, with 6 matches still to play. From modern First Division: **Stockport** on Mar 16, 2002, with 7 matches still to play; **Wimbledon** on Apr 6, 2004, with 7 matches to play.

LEAGUE RECORDS

CHAMPIONS OF ENGLND 1888–2015

Football League and Premier league

Manchester Utd 20, Liverpool 18, Arsenal 13, Everton 9, Aston Villa 7, Sunderland 6, Chelsea 5, Manchester City 4, Newcastle 4, Sheffield Wed 4, Blackburn 3, Huddersfield 3, Leeds 3, Wolves 3, Burnley 2, Derby 2, Portsmouth 2, Preston 2, Tottenham 1, Ipswich 1, Nottm Forest 1, Sheffield Utd 1, WBA 1

DOUBLE CHAMPIONS

Nine men have played in and managed League Championship-winning teams:

Ted Drake Player – Arsenal 1934, 1935, 1938. Manager – Chelsea 1955.
Bill Nicholson Player – Tottenham 1951. Manager – Tottenham 1961.
Alf Ramsey Player – Tottenham 1951. Manager – Ipswich 1962.
Joe Mercer Player – Everton 1939, Arsenal 1948, 1953. Manager – Manchester City 1968.
Dave Mackay Player – Tottenham 1961. Manager – Derby 1975.
Bob Paisley Player – Liverpool 1947. Manager – Liverpool 1976, 1977, 1979, 1980, 1982, 1983.
Howard Kendall Player – Everton 1970. Manager – Everton 1985, 1987.
Kenny Dalglish Player – Liverpool 1979, 1980, 1982, 1983, 1984. Player-manager – Liverpool 1986, 1988, 1990. Manager – Blackburn 1995.
George Graham Player – Arsenal 1971. Manager – Arsenal 1989, 1991.

GIGGS RECORD COLLECTION

Ryan Giggs (Manchester Utd) has collected the most individual honours in English football with a total of 34 prizes to the end of season 2012–13. They comprise: 13 Premier League titles, 4 FA Cups, 3 League Cups, 2 European Cups, 1 UEFA Super Cup, 1 Inter-Continental Cup, 1 World Club Cup, 9 Charity Shields/Community Shields. One-club man Giggs played 24 seasons for United, making a record 963 appearances. He won 64 Wales caps and on retiring as a player, aged 40, in May 2014, became the club's assistant manager.

CANTONA'S FOUR-TIMER

Eric Cantona played in four successive Championship-winning teams: Marseille 1990–01, Leeds 1991–92, Manchester Utd 1992–93 and 1993–94.

ARRIVALS AND DEPARTURES

The following are the Football League arrivals and departures since 1923:

Year	In	Out
1923	Doncaster	Stalybridge Celtic
	New Brighton	
1927	Torquay	Aberdare Athletic
1928	Carlisle	Durham
1929	York	Ashington
1930	Thames	Merthyr Tydfil
1931	Mansfield	Newport Co
	Chester	Nelson
1932	Aldershot	Thames
	Newport Co	Wigan Borough
1938	Ipswich	Gillingham
1950	Colchester, Gillingham	
	Scunthorpe, Shrewsbury	
1951	Workington	New Brighton
1960	Peterborough	Gateshead
1962	Oxford Utd	Accrington (resigned)
1970	Cambridge Utd	Bradford PA
1972	Hereford	Barrow
1977	Wimbledon	Workington
1978	Wigan	Southport
1987	Scarborough	Lincoln
1988	Lincoln	Newport Co
1989	Maidstone	Darlington
1990	Darlington	Colchester

1991	Barnet	
1992	Colchester	Aldershot, Maidstone (resigned)
1993	Wycombe	Halifax
1997	Macclesfield	Hereford
1998	Halifax	Doncaster
1999	Cheltenham	Scarborough
2000	Kidderminster	Chester
2001	Rushden	Barnet
2002	Boston	Halifax
2003	Yeovil, Doncaster	Exeter, Shrewsbury
2004	Chester, Shrewsbury	Carlisle, York
2005	Barnet, Carlisle	Kidderminster, Cambridge Utd
2006	Accrington, Hereford	Oxford Utd, Rushden & Diamonds
2007	Dagenham, Morecambe	Torquay, Boston
2008	Aldershot, Exeter	Wrexham, Mansfield
2009	Burton, Torquay	Chester, Luton
2010	Stevenage, Oxford Utd	Grimsby, Darlington
2011	Crawley, AFC Wimbledon	Lincoln, Stockport
2012	Fleetwood, York	Hereford, Macclesfield
2013	Mansfield, Newport	Barnet, Aldershot
2014	Luton, Cambridge Utd	Bristol Rov, Torquay
2105	Barnet, Bristol Rov	Cheltenham, Tranmere

Leeds City were expelled from Div 2 in Oct, 1919; Port Vale took over their fixtures.

EXTENSIONS TO FOOTBALL LEAGUE

Clubs	Season	Clubs	Season
12 to 14	1891–92	44 to 66†	1920–21
14 to 28*	1892–93	66 to 86†	1921–22
28 to 31	1893–94	86 to 88	1923–24
31 to 32	1894–95	88 to 92	1950–51
32 to 36	1898–99	92 to 93	1991–92
36 to 40	1905–06	(Reverted to 92 when Aldershot closed, Mar 1992)	

*Second Division formed. † Third Division (South) formed from Southern League clubs.
†Third Division (North) formed.
Football League reduced to 70 clubs and three divisions on the formation of the FA Premier League in 1992; increased to 72 season 1994–95, when Premier League reduced to 20 clubs.

RECORD RUNS

Arsenal hold the record unbeaten sequence in the English League – 49 Premiership matches (36 wins, 13 draws) from May 7, 2003 until Oct 24, 2004 when beaten 2-0 away to Manchester Utd. The record previously belonged to **Nottm Forest** – 42 First Division matches (21 wins, 21 draws) from Nov 19, 1977 until beaten 2-0 at Liverpool on December 9, 1978.

Huddersfield set a new Football League record of 43 League 1 matches unbeaten from Jan 1, 2011 until Nov 28, 2011 when losing 2-0 at Charlton.

Best debuts: Ipswich won the First Division at their first attempt in 1961–62.

Peterborough in their first season in the Football League (1960–01) not only won the Fourth Division but set the all-time scoring record for the League of 134 goals. **Hereford** were promoted from the Fourth Division in their first League season, 1972–73.

Wycombe were promoted from the Third Division (via the play-offs) in their first League season, 1993–94. **Stevenage** were promoted from League 2 (via the play-offs) in their first League season, 2010–11. **Crawley** gained automatic promotion in their first season in 2011–12.

Record winning sequence in a season: 14 consecutive League victories (all in Second Division): **Manchester Utd** 1904–05, **Bristol City** 1905–06 and **Preston** 1950–51.

Best winning start to League season: 13 successive victories in Div 3 by **Reading,** season 1985–86.

Best starts in 'old' First Division: 11 consecutive victories by **Tottenham** in 1960–61; 10 by **Manchester Utd** in 1985–86. In 'new' First Division, 11 consecutive wins by **Newcastle** in 1992–93 and by **Fulham** in 2000–01.

Longest unbeaten sequence (all competitions): 40 by **Nottm Forest,** Mar–December 1978. It comprised 21 wins, 19 draws (in 29 League matches, 6 League Cup, 4 European Cup, 1 Charity Shield).

Longest unbeaten starts to League season: 38 matches (26 wins, 12 draws) in **Arsenal's** undefeated Premiership season, 2003–04; 29 matches – **Leeds,** Div 1 1973–74 (19 wins, 10 draws), **Liverpool,** Div 1 1987–88 (22 wins, 7 draws).

Most consecutive League matches unbeaten in a season: 38 **Arsenal** Premiership season 2003–04 (see above); 33 **Reading** (25 wins, 8 draws) 2005–06.

Longest winning sequence in Div 1: 13 matches by **Tottenham** – last two of season 1959–60, first 11 of 1960–61.

Longest winning one-season sequences in League Championship: 13 matches by **Preston,** 1891–92; **Sunderland,** also 1891–92; **Arsenal** 2001–02.

Longest unbeaten home League sequence in top division: 86 matches (62 wins, 24 draws) by **Chelsea** (Mar 2004–Oct 2008).

League's longest winning sequence with clean sheets: 9 matches by **Stockport** (Lge 2, 2006–07 season).

Premier League – best starts to season: Arsenal, 38 games, 2003–04; **Manchester City,** 14 games, 2011–12.

Best winning start to Premiership season: 9 consecutive victories by **Chelsea** in 2005–06.

Premier League – most consecutive wins (two seasons): 14 by **Arsenal,** Feb–Aug, 2002. Single season: 13 by **Arsenal** (Feb–May, 2002).

Premier League – most consecutive home wins: 20 by **Manchester City** (last 5 season 2010–11, first 15 season 2011–12).

Most consecutive away League wins in top flight: 11 by **Chelsea** (3 at end 2007–08 season, 8 in 2008–09).

Premier League – longest unbeaten away run: 27 matches (W17, D10) by **Arsenal** (Apr 5, 2003–Sep 25, 2004).

Record home-win sequences: Bradford Park Avenue won 25 successive home games in Div 3 North – the last 18 in 1926–27 and the first 7 the following season. Longest run of home wins in the top division is 21 by **Liverpool** – the last 9 of 1971–72 and the first 12 of 1972–73.

British record for successive League wins: 25 by **Celtic** (Scottish Premier League), 2003–04.

WORST SEQUENCES

Derby experienced the longest run without a win in League history in season 2007–08 – 32 games from Sep 22 to the end of the campaign (25 lost, 7 drawn). They finished bottom by a 24-pt margin. The sequence increased to 36 matches (28 lost, 8 drawn) at the start of the following season.

Cambridge Utd had the previous worst of 31 in 1983–84 (21 lost, 10 drawn). They were bottom of Div 2.

Worst losing start to a League season : 12 consecutive defeats by **Manchester Utd** (Div 1), 1930–31.

Worst Premier League start: QPR 16 matches without win (7 draws, 9 defeats), 2012–13.

Premier League – most consecutive defeats: 20 **Sunderland** last 15 matches, 2002–03, first five matches 2005–06.

Longest non-winning start to League season: 25 matches (4 draws, 21 defeats) by **Newport,** Div 4. Worst no-win League starts since then: 16 matches by **Burnley** (9 draws, 7 defeats in Div 2, 1979–80); 16 by **Hull** (10 draws, 6 defeats in Div 2, 1989–90); 16 by **Sheffield Utd** (4 draws, 12 defeats in Div 1, 1990–91).

Most League defeats in season: 34 by **Doncaster** (Div 3) 1997–98.

Fewest League wins in season: 1 by **Loughborough** (Div 2, season 1899–1900). They lost 27, drew 6, goals 18–100 and dropped out of the League. (See also Scottish section). 1 by **Derby** (Prem Lge, 2007–08). They lost 29, drew 8, goals 20–89.

Most consecutive League defeats in season: 18 by **Darwen** (Div 1, 1898–99); 17 by **Rochdale** (Div 3 North, 1931–32).

Fewest home League wins in season: 1 by **Loughborough** (Div 2, 1899–1900), **Notts Co** (Div 1, 1904–05), **Woolwich Arsenal** (Div 1, 1912–13), **Blackpool** (Div 1, 1966–67), **Rochdale** (Div 3, 1973–74), **Sunderland** (Prem Lge, 2005–06); **Derby** (Prem Lge, 2007–08).

Most home League defeats in season: 18 by **Cambridge Utd** (Div 3, 1984–85).

Away League defeats record: 24 in row by **Crewe** (Div 2) – all 15 in 1894–95 followed by 9 in 1895–96; by **Nelson** (Div 3 North) – 3 in Apr 1930 followed by all 21 in season 1930–31. They then dropped out of the League.

Biggest defeat in Champions' season: During **Newcastle's** title-winning season in 1908–09, they were beaten 9-1 at home by Sunderland on December 5.

WORST START BY EVENTUAL CHAMPIONS

Sunderland took only 2 points from their first 7 matches in season 1912–13 (2 draws, 5 defeats). They won 25 of the remaining 31 games to clinch their fifth League title.

DISMAL DERBY

Derby were relegated in season 2007–08 as the worst-ever team in the Premier League: fewest wins (1), fewest points (11); fewest goals (20), first club to go down in March (29th).

UNBEATEN LEAGUE SEASON

Only three clubs have completed an English League season unbeaten: **Preston** (22 matches in 1888–89, the League's first season), **Liverpool** (28 matches in Div 2, 1893–94) and **Arsenal** (38 matches in Premiership, 2003–04).

100 PER CENT HOME RECORDS

Six clubs have won every home League match in a season: **Sunderland** (13 matches)' in 1891–92 and four teams in the old Second Division: **Liverpool** (14) in 1893–94, **Bury** (15) in 1894–95, **Sheffield Wed** (17) in 1899–1900 and **Small Heath**, subsequently **Birmingham** (17) in 1902–03. The last club to do it, **Brentford**, won all 21 home games in Div 3 South in 1929–30. **Rotherham** just failed to equal that record in 1946–47. They won their first 20 home matches in Div 3 North, then drew the last 3-3 v Rochdale.

BEST HOME LEAGUE RECORDS IN TOP FLIGHT

Sunderland, 1891–92 (P13, W13); **Newcastle**, 1906–07 (P19, W18, D1); **Chelsea**, 2005–06 (P19, W18, D1); **Manchester Utd**, 2010–11 (P19, W18, D1); **Manchester City**, 2011–12 (P19, W18, D1).

MOST CONSECUTIVE CLEAN SHEETS

Premier League – 14: **Manchester Utd** (2008–09); **Football League** – 11: **Millwall** (Div 3 South 1925–26); **York** (Div 3 1973–74); **Reading** (Div 4, 1978–79).

WORST HOME RUNS

Most consecutive home League defeats: 14 **Rochdale** (Div 3 North) seasons 1931–32 and 1932–33; 10 **Birmingham** (Div 1) 1985–86; 9 **Darwen** (Div 2) 1897–98; 9 **Watford** (Div 2) 1971–72.

Between Nov 1958 and Oct 1959 **Portsmouth** drew 2 and lost 14 out of 16 consecutive home games.

West Ham did not win in the Premiership at Upton Park in season 2002–03 until the 13th home match on Jan 29.

MOST AWAY WINS IN SEASON

Doncaster won 18 of their 21 away League fixtures when winning Div 3 North in 1946–47.

AWAY WINS RECORD

Most consecutive away League wins: 11 **Chelsea** (Prem Lge) – 8 at start of 2008–09 after ending previous season with 3.

100 PER CENT HOME WINS ON ONE DAY

Div 1 – All 11 home teams won on Feb 13, 1926 and on Dec 10, 1955. **Div 2** – All 12 home teams won on Nov 26, 1988. **Div 3**, all 12 home teams won in the week-end programme of Oct 18–19, 1968.

NO HOME WINS IN DIV ON ONE DAY

Div 1 – 8 away wins, 3 draws in 11 matches on Sep 6, 1986. **Div 2** – 7 away wins, 4 draws in 11 matches on Dec 26, 1987. **Premier League** – 6 away wins, 5 draws in 11 matches on Dec 26, 1994.

The week-end **Premiership** programme on Dec 7–8–9, 1996 produced no home win in the ten games (4 aways, 6 draws). There was again no home victory (3 away wins, 7 draws) in the week-end **Premiership** fixtures on Sep 23–24, 2000.

MOST DRAWS IN A SEASON (FOOTBALL LEAGUE)

23 by **Norwich** (Div 1, 1978–79), **Exeter** (Div 4, 1986–87). **Cardiff** and **Hartlepool** (both Div 3, 1997–98). **Norwich** played 42 matches, the others 46.

MOST DRAWS IN PREMIER LEAGUE SEASON

18 (in 42 matches) by **Manchester City** (1993–94), **Sheffield Utd** (1993–94), **Southampton** (1994–95).

MOST DRAWS IN ONE DIV ON ONE DAY

On Sep 18, 1948 **nine** out of 11 First Division matches were drawn.

MOST DRAWS IN PREMIER DIV PROGRAMME

Over the week-ends of December 2–3–4, 1995, and Sep 23–24, 2000, **seven** out of the ten matches finished level.

FEWEST DRAWS IN SEASON

In 46 matches: 3 by **Reading** (Div 3 South, 1951–52); **Bradford Park Avenue** (Div 3 North, 1956–57); **Tranmere** (Div 4, 1984–85); **Southend** (Div 3, 2002–03); in 42 matches: 2 by **Reading** (Div 3 South, 1935–36); **Stockport** (Div 3 North, 1946–47); in 38 matches: 2 by **Sunderland** (Div 1, 1908–09).

HIGHEST-SCORING DRAWS IN LEAGUE

Leicester 6, **Arsenal** 6 (Div 1 Apr 21, 1930); **Charlton** 6, **Middlesbrough** 6 (Div 2. Oct 22, 1960) Latest **6-6** draw in first-class football was between **Tranmere** and **Newcastle** in the Zenith Data Systems Cup 1st round on Oct 1, 1991. The score went from 3-3 at 90 minutes to 6-6 after extra time, and Tranmere won 3-2 on penalties. In Scotland: **Queen of the South** 6, **Falkirk** 6 (Div 1, Sep 20, 1947).

Most recent **5-5** draws in top division: **Southampton** v **Coventry** (Div 1, May 4, 1982); **QPR** v **Newcastle** (Div 1, Sep 22, 1984); **WBA** v **Manchester Utd** (Prem Lge, May 19, 2013).

DRAWS RECORDS

Most consecutive drawn matches in Football League: 8 by **Torquay** (Div 3, 1969–70), **Middlesbrough** (Div 2, 1970–71), **Peterborough** (Div 4, 1971–72), **Birmingham** (Div 3 (1990–91), **Southampton** (Champ, 2005–06), **Chesterfield** (Lge 1, 2005–06), **Swansea** (Champ, 2008–09).

Longest sequence of draws by the same score: six 1-1 results by **QPR** in season 1957–58. **Tranmere** became the first club to play **five consecutive 0-0 League draws**, in season 1997–98.

IDENTICAL RECORDS

There is only **one instance** of two clubs in one division finishing a season with identical records.
In 1907–08, **Blackburn** and **Woolwich Arsenal** were bracketed equal 14th in the First Division with these figures: P38, W12, D12, L14, Goals 51-63, Pts. 36.

The total of **1195 goals** scored in the Premier League in season 1993–94 was repeated in 1994–95.

DEAD LEVEL

Millwall's record in Division Two in season 1973–74 was P42, W14, D14, L14, F51, A51, Pts 42.

CHAMPIONS OF ALL DIVISIONS

Wolves, Burnley and **Preston** are the only clubs to have won titles in the old Divisions 1, 2, 3 and 4. Wolves also won the Third Division North and the new Championship.

POINTS DEDUCTIONS

2000–01: Chesterfield 9 for breach of transfer regulations and falsifying gate receipts.
2002–03: Boston 4 for contractual irregularities.
2004–05: Wrexham, Cambridge Utd 10 for administration.
2005–06: Rotherham 10 for administration.
2006–07: Leeds, Boston 10 for administration; **Bury** 1 for unregistered player.
2007–08: Leeds 15 over insolvency rules; **Bournemouth, Luton, Rotherham** 10 for administration.
2008–09: Luton 20 for failing Insolvency rules, 10 over payments to agents; **Bournemouth, Rotherham** 17 for breaking administration rules; **Southampton, Stockport** 10 for administration – **Southampton** with effect from season 2009–10 **Crystal Palace** 1 for ineligible player.
2009–10: Portsmouth 9, **Crystal Palace** 10 for administration; **Hartlepool** 3 for ineligible player.
2010–11: Plymouth 10 for administration; **Hereford** 3, **Torquay** 1, each for ineligible player
2011–12: Portsmouth and **Port Vale** both 10 for administration – Portsmouth from following season.
2013–14: Coventry 10 for administration; **AFC Wimbledon** 3 for ineligible player.
2014–15: Rotherham 3 for ineligible player.

Among previous points penalties imposed:
Nov 1990: Arsenal 2, **Manchester Utd** 1 following mass players' brawl at Old Trafford.
Dec 1996: Brighton 2 for pitch invasions by fans.
Jan 1997: Middlesbrough 3 for refusing to play Premiership match at Blackburn because of injuries and illness.
Jun 1994: Tottenham 12 (reduced to 6) and banned from following season's FA Cup for making illegal payments to players. On appeal, points deduction annulled and club re-instated in Cup.

NIGHTMARE STARTS

Most goals conceded by a goalkeeper on League debut: 13 by **Steve Milton** when Halifax lost 13-0 at Stockport (Div 3 North) on Jan 6, 1934.

Post-war: 11 by Crewe's new goalkeeper **Dennis Murray** (Div 3 North) on Sep 29, 1951, when Lincoln won 11-1.

RELEGATION ODD SPOTS

None of the Barclays Premiership relegation places in season 2004–05 were decided until the last day (Sunday, May 15). **WBA** (bottom at kick-off) survived with a 2-0 home win against Portsmouth, and the three relegated clubs were **Southampton** (1-2 v Manchester Utd), **Norwich** (0-6 at Fulham) and **Crystal Palace** (2-2 at Charlton).

In season 1937–38, **Manchester City** were the highest-scoring team in the First Division with 80 goals (3 more than Champions Arsenal), but they finished in 21st place and were relegated – a year after winning the title. They scored more goals than they conceded (77).

That season produced the **closest relegation battle** in top-division history, with only 4 points spanning the bottom 11 clubs in Div 1. **WBA** went down with **Manchester City**.

Twelve years earlier, in 1925–26, City went down to Division 2 despite totalling 89 goals – still the most scored in any division by a relegated team. Manchester City also scored 31 FA Cup goals that season, but lost the Final 1-0 to Bolton Wanderers.

Cardiff were relegated from Div 1 in season 1928–29, despite conceding fewest goals in the division (59). They also scored fewest (43).

On their way to relegation from the First Division in season 1984–85, **Stoke** twice lost ten matches in a row.

RELEGATION TREBLES

Two Football League clubs have been relegated three seasons in succession. **Bristol City** fell from First Division to Fourth in 1980–81–82 and **Wolves** did the same in 1984–85–86.

OLDEST CLUBS

Oldest Association Football Club is **Sheffield FC** (formed in 1857). The oldest Football League clubs are **Notts Co**, 1862; **Nottm Forest**, 1865; and **Sheffield Wed**, 1866.

FOUR DIVISIONS

In **May, 1957**, the Football League decided to re-group the two sections of the Third Division into Third and Fourth Divisions in **season 1958–59**.

The Football League was reduced to three divisions on the formation of the Premier League in **1992**.

In season 2004–05, under new sponsors Coca-Cola, the titles of First, Second and Third Divisions were changed to League Championship, League One and League Two.

THREE UP – THREE DOWN

The Football League annual general meeting of Jun 1973 agreed to adopt the promotion and relegation system of three up and three down.

The **new system** came into effect in **season 1973–74** and applied only to the first three divisions; four clubs were still relegated from the Third and four promoted from the Fourth.

It was the first change in the promotion and relegation system for the top two divisions in 81 years.

MOST LEAGUE APPEARANCES

Players with more than 700 English League apps (as at end of season 2012–13)

1005   Peter Shilton 1966–97 (286 Leicester, 110 Stoke, 202 Nottm Forest, 188 Southampton, 175 Derby, 34 Plymouth Argyle, 1 Bolton, 9 Leyton Orient).

931   Tony Ford 1975–2002 (423 Grimsby, 9 Sunderland, 112 Stoke, 114 WBA, 5 Bradford City, 76 Scunthorpe, 103 Mansfield, 89 Rochdale).

840   Graham Alexander 1991–2012 (159 Scunthorpe, 152 Luton, 372 Preston, 157 Burnley)

824   Terry Paine 1956–77 (713 Southampton, 111 Hereford).

795   Tommy Hutchison 1968–91 (165 Blackpool, 314 Coventry City, 46 Manchester City, 92 Burnley, 178 Swansea). In addition, 68 Scottish League apps for Alloa 1965–68, giving career League app total of 863.

790   Neil Redfearn 1982–2004 (35 Bolton, 100 Lincoln, 46 Doncaster, 57 Crystal Palace, 24 Watford, 62 Oldham, 292 Barnsley, 30 Charlton, 17 Bradford City, 22 Wigan, 42 Halifax, 54 Boston, 9 Rochdale).

782   Robbie James 1973–94 (484 Swansea, 48 Stoke, 87 QPR, 23 Leicester, 89 Bradford City, 51 Cardiff).

777   Alan Oakes 1959–84 (565 Manchester City, 211 Chester, 1 Port Vale).

773   Dave Beasant 1980–2003 (340 Wimbledon, 20 Newcastle, 6 Grimsby, 4 Wolves, 133 Chelsea, 88 Southampton, 139 Nottm F, 27 Portsmouth, 16 Brighton).

770   John Trollope 1960–80 (all for Swindon, record total for one club).

769   David James 1990–2012 (89 Watford, 214 Liverpool, 67 Aston Villa, 91 West Ham, 93 Manchester City, 134 Portsmouth, 81 Bristol City).

764   Jimmy Dickinson 1946–65 (all for Portsmouth).

761   Roy Sproson 1950–72 (all for Port Vale).

760   Mick Tait 1974–97 (64 Oxford Utd, 106 Carlisle, 33 Hull, 240 Portsmouth, 99 Reading, 79 Darlington, 139 Hartlepool Utd).

758   Billy Bonds 1964–88 (95 Charlton, 663 West Ham).

758   Ray Clemence 1966–88 (48 Scunthorpe, 470 Liverpool, 240 Tottenham).

757   Pat Jennings 1963–86 (48 Watford, 472 Tottenham, 237 Arsenal).

757   Frank Worthington 1966–88 (171 Huddersfield Town, 210 Leicester, 84 Bolton, 75 Birmingham, 32 Leeds, 31 Sunderland, 34 Southampton, 31 Brighton, 59 Tranmere, 23 Preston, 19 Stockport).

755   Wayne Allison 1986–2008 (84 Halifax, 7 Watford, 195 Bristol City, 103 Swindon, 76 Huddersfield, 102 Tranmere, 73 Sheffield Utd, 115 Chesterfield).

749   Ernie Moss 1968–88 (469 Chesterfield, 35 Peterborough, 57 Mansfield, 74 Port Vale, 11 Lincoln, 44 Doncaster, 26 Stockport, 23 Scarborough, 10 Rochdale).

746   Les Chapman 1966–88 (263 Oldham, 133 Huddersfield Town, 70 Stockport, 139 Bradford City, 88 Rochdale, 53 Preston).

744   Asa Hartford 1967–90 (214 WBA, 260 Manchester City, 3 Nottm Forest, 81 Everton, 28 Norwich, 81 Bolton, 45 Stockport, 7 Oldham, 25 Shrewsbury).

743   Alan Ball 1963–84 (146 Blackpool, 208 Everton, 177 Arsenal, 195 Southampton, 17 Bristol Rov).

743   John Hollins 1963–84 (465 Chelsea, 151 QPR, 127 Arsenal).

743   Phil Parkes 1968–91 (52 Walsall, 344 QPR, 344 West Ham, 3 Ipswich).

737   Steve Bruce 1979–99 (205 Gillingham, 141 Norwich, 309 Manchester Utd 72 Birmingham, 10 Sheffield Utd).

734   Teddy Sheringham 1983–2007 (220 Millwall, 5 Aldershot, 42 Nottm Forest, 104 Manchester Utd, 236 Tottenham, 32 Portsmouth, 76 West Ham, 19 Colchester)

732   Mick Mills 1966–88 (591 Ipswich, 103 Southampton, 38 Stoke).

731   Ian Callaghan 1959–81 (640 Liverpool, 76 Swansea, 15 Crewe).

731   David Seaman 1982–2003 (91 Peterborough, 75 Birmingham, 141 QPR, 405 Arsenal, 19 Manchester City).

725   Steve Perryman 1969–90 (655 Tottenham, 17 Oxford Utd, 53 Brentford).

722   Martin Peters 1961–81 (302 West Ham, 189 Tottenham, 207 Norwich, 24 Sheffield Utd).

718   Mike Channon 1966–86 (511 Southampton, 72 Manchester City, 4 Newcastle, 9 Bristol Rov, 88 Norwich, 34 Portsmouth).

716   Ron Harris 1961–83 (655 Chelsea, 61 Brentford).

716   Mike Summerbee 1959–79 (218 Swindon, 357 Manchester City, 51 Burnley, 3 Blackpool, 87 Stockport).

714   Glenn Cockerill 1976–98 (186 Lincoln, 26 Swindon, 62 Sheffield Utd, 387 Southampton, 90 Leyton Orient, 40 Fulham, 23 Brentford).

705   Keith Curle 1981–2003 (32 Bristol Rov, 16 Torquay, 121 Bristol City, 40 Reading, 93 Wimbledon, 171 Manchester City, 150 Wolves, 57 Sheffield Utd, 11 Barnsley, 14 Mansfield).

705   Phil Neal 1968–89 (186 Northampton, 455 Liverpool, 64 Bolton).

705   John Wile 1968–86 (205 Peterborough, 500 WBA).

701   Neville Southall 1980–2000 (39 Bury, 578 Everton, 9 Port Vale, 9 Southend, 12 Stoke, 53 Torquay, 1 Bradford City).

● **Stanley Matthews** made 701 League apps 1932–65 (322 Stoke, 379 Blackpool), incl. 3 for Stoke at start of 1939–40 before season abandoned (war).

● Goalkeeper **John Burridge** made a total of 771 League appearances in a 28-season career in English and Scottish football (1968–96). He played 691 games for 15 English clubs (Workington, Blackpool, Aston Villa, Southend, Crystal Palace, QPR, Wolves, Derby, Sheffield

Utd, Southampton, Newcastle, Scarborough, Lincoln, Manchester City and Darlington) and
80 for 5 Scottish clubs (Hibernian, Aberdeen, Dumbarton, Falkirk and Queen of the South).

LONGEST LEAGUE APPEARANCE SEQUENCE

Harold Bell, centre-half of Tranmere, was ever-present for the first nine post-war seasons (1946–
55), achieving a League record of 401 consecutive matches. Counting FA Cup and other
games, his run of successive appearances totalled 459.

The longest League sequence since Bell's was 394 appearances by goalkeeper **Dave Beasant**
for Wimbledon, Newcastle and Chelsea. His nine-year run began on Aug 29, 1981 and was
ended by a broken finger sustained in Chelsea's League Cup-tie against Portsmouth on Oct
31, 1990. Beasant's 394 consecutive League games comprised 304 for Wimbledon (1981–
88), 20 for Newcastle (1988–89) and 70 for Chelsea (1989–90).

Phil Neal made 366 consecutive First Division appearances for Liverpool between December
1974 and Sep 1983, a remarkable sequence for an outfield player in top-division football.

MOST CONSECUTIVE PREMIER LEAGUE APPEARANCES

310 by goalkeeper **Brad Friedel** (152 Blackburn, 114 Aston Villa, 44 Tottenham, May 2004–Oct
2012). He played in 8 **ever-present seasons** (2004–12, Blackburn 4, Villa 3, Tottenham 1).

EVER-PRESENT DEFENCE

The **entire defence** of **Huddersfield** played in all 42 Second Division matches in season 1952–
53, namely, Bill Wheeler (goal), Ron Staniforth and Laurie Kelly (full-backs), Bill McGarry,
Don McEvoy and Len Quested (half-backs). In addition, Vic Metcalfe played in all 42 League
matches as outside-left.

FIRST SUBSTITUTE USED IN LEAGUE

Keith Peacock (Charlton), away to Bolton (Div 2) on Aug 21, 1965.

FROM PROMOTION TO CHAMPIONS

Clubs who have become Champions of England a year after winning promotion: **Liverpool** 1905,
1906; **Everton** 1931, 1932; **Tottenham** 1950, 1951; **Ipswich** 1961, 1962; **Nottm Forest**
1977, 1978. The first four were placed top in both seasons: Forest finished third and first.

PREMIERSHIP'S FIRST MULTI-NATIONAL LINE-UP

Chelsea made history on December 26, 1999 when starting their Premiership match at
Southampton without a single British player in the side.

Fulham's Unique XI: In the Worthington Cup 3rd round at home to Bury on Nov 6, 2002, Fulham
fielded 11 players of 11 different nationalities. Ten were full Internationals, with Lee Clark
an England U–21 cap.

On Feb 14, 2005 **Arsenal** became the first English club to select an all-foreign match squad
when Arsene Wenger named 16 non-British players at home to Crystal Palace (Premiership).

Fifteen nations were represented at Fratton Park on Dec 30, 2009 (Portsmouth 1 Arsenal 4)
when, for the first time in Premier League history, not one Englishman started the match. The
line-up comprised seven Frenchmen, two Algerians and one from each of 13 other countries.

Players from 22 nationalities (subs included) were involved in the Blackburn–WBA match at
Ewood Park on Jan 23, 2011.

PREMIER LEAGUE'S FIRST ALL-ENGLAND LINE-UP

On Feb 27, 1999 **Aston Villa** (at home to Coventry) fielded the first all-English line up seen in
the Premier League (starting 11 plus 3 subs).

ENTIRE HOME-GROWN TEAM

Crewe Alexandra's starting 11 in the 2-0 home win against Walsall (Lge 1) on Apr 27, 2013 all
graduated from the club's academy.

THREE-NATION CHAMPIONS

David Beckham won a title in four countries: with Manchester Utd six times (1996–97–99–2000–01–03), Real Madrid (2007), LA Galaxy (2011 and Paris St Germain (2013).

Trevor Steven earned eight Championship medals in three countries: two with Everton (1985, 1987); five with Rangers (1990, 1991, 1993, 1994, 1995) and one with Marseille in 1992.

LEEDS NO WIN AWAY

Leeds, in 1992–93, provided the first instance of a club failing to win an away League match as reigning Champions.

PIONEERS IN 1888 AND 1992

Three clubs among the twelve who formed the Football League in 1888 were also founder members of the Premier League: **Aston Villa, Blackburn** and **Everton.**

CHAMPIONS (MODERN) WITH TWO CLUBS – PLAYERS

Francis Lee (Manchester City 1968, Derby 1975); **Ray Kennedy** (Arsenal 1971, Liverpool 1979, 1980, 1982); **Archie Gemmill** (Derby 1972, 1975, Nottm Forest 1978); **John McGovern** (Derby 1972, Nottm Forest 1978) **Larry Lloyd** (Liverpool 1973, Nottm Forest 1978); **Peter Withe** (Nottm Forest 1978, Aston Villa 1981); **John Lukic** (Arsenal 1989, Leeds 1992); **Kevin Richardson** (Everton 1985, Arsenal 1989); **Eric Cantona (**Leeds 1992, Manchester Utd 1993, 1994, 1996, 1997); **David Batty** (Leeds 1992, Blackburn 1995); **Bobby Mimms** (Everton 1987, Blackburn 1995); **Henning Berg** (Blackburn 1995, Manchester Utd 1999, 2000); **Nicolas Anelka** (Arsenal 1998, Chelsea 2010); **Ashley Cole** (Arsenal 2002, 2004, Chelsea 2010); **Gael Clichy** (Arsenal 2004, Manchester City 2012); **Kolo Toure** (Arsenal 2004, Manchester City 2012); **Carlos Tevez** (Manchester Utd 2008, 2009, Manchester City 2012).

TITLE TURNABOUTS

In Jan 1996, **Newcastle** led the Premier League by 13 points. They finished runners-up to Manchester Utd.

At Christmas 1997, **Arsenal** were 13 points behind leaders Manchester Utd and still 11 points behind at the beginning of Mar 1998. But a run of 10 wins took the title to Highbury.

On Mar 2, 2003, **Arsenal,** with 9 games left, went 8 points clear of Manchester Utd, who had a match in hand. United won the Championship by 5 points.

In Mar 2002, **Wolves** were in second (automatic promotion) place in Nationwide Div 1, 11 points ahead of WBA, who had 2 games in hand. They were overtaken by Albion on the run-in, finished third, then failed in the play-offs. A year later they won promotion to the Premiership via the play-offs.

CLUB CLOSURES

Four clubs have left the Football League in mid-season: **Leeds City** (expelled Oct 1919); **Wigan Borough** (Oct 1931, debts of £20,000); **Accrington Stanley** (Mar 1962, debts £62,000); **Aldershot** (Mar 1992, debts £1.2m). **Maidstone,** with debts of £650,000, closed Aug 1992, on the eve of the season.

FOUR-DIVISION MEN

In season 1986–87, goalkeeper **Eric Nixon,** became the first player to appear in **all four divisions** of the Football League **in one season**. He served two clubs in Div 1: Manchester City (5 League games) and Southampton (4); in Div 2 Bradford City (3); in Div 3 Carlisle (16); and in Div 4 Wolves (16). Total appearances: 44.

Harvey McCreadie, a teenage forward, played in four divisions over two seasons inside a calendar year – from Accrington (Div 3) to Luton (Div 1) in Jan 1960, to Div 2 with Luton later that season and to Wrexham (Div 4) in Nov.

Tony Cottee played in all four divisions in season 2000–01, for Leicester (Premiership), Norwich (Div 1), Barnet (Div 3, player-manager) and Millwall (Div 2).

FATHERS AND SONS

When player-manager **Ian** (39) and **Gary** (18) **Bowyer** appeared together in the **Hereford** side at Scunthorpe (Div 4, Apr 21, 1990), they provided the first instance of father and son playing in the same team in a Football League match for 39 years. Ian played as substitute, and Gary scored Hereford's injury-time equaliser in a 3-3 draw.

Alec (39) and **David** (17) **Herd** were among previous father-and-son duos in league football – for Stockport, 2-0 winners at Hartlepool (Div 3 North) on May 5, 1951.

When Preston won 2-1 at Bury in Div 3 on Jan 13, 1990, the opposing goalkeepers were brothers: **Alan Kelly** (21) for Preston and **Gary** (23) for Bury. Their father, **Alan** (who kept goal for Preston in the 1964 FA Cup Final and won 47 Rep of Ireland caps) flew from America to watch the sons he taught to keep goal line up on opposite sides.

Other examples: **Bill Dodgin Snr** (manager, Bristol Rov) faced son **Bill Jnr** (manager of Fulham) four times between 1969 and 1971. On Apr 16, 2013 (Lge 1), Oldham, under **Lee Johnson**, won 1-0 at home to Yeovil, managed by his father **Gary**.

George Eastham Snr (manager) and son **George Eastham Jnr** were inside-forward partners for Ards in the Irish League in season 1954–55.

FATHER AND SON REFEREE PLAY-OFF FINALS

Father and son refereed two of the 2009 Play-off Finals. **Clive Oliver**, 46, took charge of Shrewsbury v Gillingham (Lge 2) and **Michael Oliver**, 26, refereed Millwall v Scunthorpe (Lge 1) the following day.

FATHER AND SON BOTH CHAMPIONS

John Aston snr won a Championship medal with Manchester Utd in 1952 and **John Aston jnr** did so with the club in 1967. **Ian Wright** won the Premier League title with Arsenal in 1998 and **Shaun Wright-Phillips** won with Chelsea in 2006.

FATHER AND SON RIVAL MANAGERS

When **Bill Dodgin snr** took Bristol Rov to Fulham for an FA Cup 1st Round tie in Nov 1971, the opposing manager was his son, **Bill jnr.** Rovers won 2-1. Oldham's new manager, **Lee Johnson**, faced his father **Gary's** Yeovil in a Lge 1 match in April, 2013. Oldham won 1-0.

FATHER AND SON ON OPPOSITE SIDES

It happened for the first time in FA Cup history (1st Qual Round on Sep 14, 1996) when 21-year-old **Nick Scaife** (Bishop Auckland) faced his father **Bobby** (41), who played for Pickering. Both were in midfield. Home side Bishops won 3-1.

THREE BROTHERS IN SAME SIDE

Southampton provided the first instance for 65 years of three brothers appearing together in a Div 1 side when **Danny Wallace** (24) and his 19-year-old twin brothers **Rodney** and **Ray** played against Sheffield Wed on Oct 22, 1988. In all, they made 25 appearances together for Southampton until Sep 1989.

A previous instance in Div 1 was provided by the Middlesbrough trio, **William**, **John** and **George Carr** with 24 League appearances together from Jan 1920 to Oct 1923.

The **Tonner** brothers, **Sam**, **James** and **Jack,** played together in 13 Second Division matches for Clapton Orient in season 1919–20.

Brothers **David**, **Donald** and **Robert Jack** played together in Plymouth's League side in 1920.

TWIN TEAM-MATES (see also Wallace twins above)

Twin brothers **David** and Peter Jackson played together for three League clubs (Wrexham, Bradford City and Tranmere) from 1954–62. The **Morgan** twins, **Ian** and **Roger**, played regularly in the QPR forward line from 1964–68. WBA's **Adam** and **James Chambers**, 18, were the first twins to represent England (v Cameroon in World Youth Championship, Apr 1999). They first played together in Albion's senior team, aged 19, in the League Cup 2nd.

Round against Derby in Sep 2000. Brazilian identical twins **Rafael** and **Fabio Da Silva** (18) made first team debuts at full-back for Manchester Utd in season 2008–09. Swedish twins **Martin** and **Marcus Olsson** played together for Blackburn in season 2011–12. **Josh** and **Jacob Murphy**, 19, played for Norwich in season 2013–2014.

SIR TOM DOES THE HONOURS

Sir Tom Finney, England and Preston legend, opened the Football League's new headquarters on their return to Preston on Feb 23, 1999. Preston had been the League's original base for 70 years before the move to Lytham St Annes in 1959.

SHORTENED MATCHES

The 0-0 score in the **Bradford City v Lincoln** Third Division fixture on May 11, 1985, abandoned through fire after 40 minutes, was subsequently confirmed as a result. It is the shortest officially- completed League match on record, and was the fourth of only five instances in Football League history of the score of an unfinished match being allowed to stand.

The other occasions: **Middlesbrough 4, Oldham 1** (Div 1, Apr 3, 1915), abandoned after 55 minutes when Oldham defender Billy Cook refused to leave the field after being sent off; **Barrow 7, Gillingham 0** (Div 4, Oct 9, 1961), abandoned after 75 minutes because of bad light, the match having started late because of Gillingham's delayed arrival.

A crucial **Manchester** derby (Div 1) was abandoned after 85 minutes, and the result stood, on Apr 27, 1974, when a pitch invasion at Old Trafford followed the only goal, scored for City by Denis Law, which relegated United, Law's former club.

The only instance of a first-class match in England being abandoned **'through shortage of players'** occurred in the First Division at Bramall Lane on Mar 16, 2002. Referee Eddie Wolstenholme halted play after 82 minutes because **Sheffield Utd** were reduced to 6 players against **WBA**. They had 3 men sent off (goalkeeper and 2 substitutes), and with all 3 substitutes used and 2 players injured, were left with fewer than the required minimum of 7 on the field. Promotion contenders WBA were leading 3-0, and the League ordered the result to stand.

The last 60 seconds of **Birmingham v Stoke** (Div 3, 1-1, on Feb 29, 1992) were played behind locked doors. The ground had been cleared after a pitch invasion.

A First Division fixture, **Sheffield Wed v Aston Villa** (Nov 26, 1898), was abandoned through bad light after 79 mins with Wednesday leading 3-1. The Football League ruled that the match should be completed, and the remaining 10.5 minutes were played four months later (Mar 13, 1899), when Wednesday added another goal to make the result 4-1.

FA CUP RECORDS

(See also Goalscoring section)

CHIEF WINNERS

12 Arsenal, **11** Manchester Utd, **8** Tottenham; **7** Aston Villa, Chelsea, Liverpool; **6** Blackburn, Newcastle.

Three times in succession: The Wanderers (1876–77–78) and Blackburn (1884–85–86).

Trophy handed back: The FA Cup became the Wanderers' absolute property in 1878, but they handed it back to the Association on condition that it was not to be won outright by any club.

In successive years by professional clubs: Blackburn (1890 and 1891); Newcastle (1951 and 1952); Tottenham (1961 and 1962); Tottenham (1981 and 1982); Arsenal (2002 and 2003); Chelsea (2009–10).

Record Final-tie score: Bury 6, Derby 0 (1903).

Most FA Cup Final wins at Wembley: Arsenal 9, Manchester Utd 9, Chelsea 6, Tottenham 6, Liverpool 5, Newcastle 5.

SECOND DIVISION WINNERS

Notts Co (1894), **Wolves** (1908), **Barnsley** (1912), **WBA** (1931), **Sunderland** (1973), **Southampton** (1976), **West Ham** (1980). When **Tottenham** won the Cup in 1901 they were a Southern League club.

'OUTSIDE' SEMI-FINALISTS

Sheffield Utd, in 2014, became the ninth team from outside the top two divisions to reach the semi-finals, following **Millwall** (1937), **Port Vale** (1954), **York** (1955), **Norwich** (1959), **Crystal Palace** (1976), **Plymouth** (1984), **Chesterfield** (1997) and **Wycombe** (2001). None reached the Final.

FOURTH DIVISION QUARTER-FINALISTS

Oxford Utd (1964), **Colchester** (1971), **Bradford City** (1976), **Cambridge Utd** (1990).

FOURTH ROUND – NO REPLAYS

No replays were necessary in the 16 fourth round ties in January 2008 (7 home wins, 9 away). This had not happened for 51 years, since 8 home and 8 away wins in season 1956–57.

FIVE TROPHIES

The trophy which Arsenal won in 2014 was the fifth in FA Cup history. These were its predecessors:

1872–95: First Cup stolen from shop in Birmingham while held by Aston Villa. Never seen again.
1910: Second trophy presented to Lord Kinnaird on completing 21 years as FA president.
1911–91: Third trophy used until replaced ('battered and fragile') after 80 years' service.
1992–2013 Fourth FA Cup lasted 21 years – now retained at FA headquarters at Wembley Stadium.
Traditionally, the Cup stays with the holders until returned to the FA in March.

FINALISTS RELEGATED

Six clubs have reached the FA Cup Final and been relegated. The first five all lost at Wembley - **Manchester City** 1926, **Leicester** 1969, **Brighton** 1983, **Middlesbrough** 1997 and **Portsmouth** 2010. **Wigan,** Cup winners for the first time in 2013, were relegated from the Premier League three days later.

FA CUP – TOP SHOCKS

(2015 = season 2014–15; rounds shown in brackets; R = replay)

1922 (1)	Everton	0	Crystal Palace	6
1933 (3)	Walsall	2	Arsenal	0
1939 (F)	Portsmouth	4	Wolves	1
1948 (3)	Arsenal	0	Bradford PA	1
1948 (3)	Colchester	1	Huddersfield	0
1949 (4)	Yeovil	2	Sunderland	1
1954 (4)	Arsenal	1	Norwich	2
1955 (5)	York	2	Tottenham	1
1957 (4)	Wolves	0	Bournemouth	1
1957 (5)	Bournemouth	3	Tottenham	1
1958 (4)	Newcastle	1	Scunthorpe	3
1959 (3)	Norwich	3	Manchester Utd	0
1959 (4)	Worcester	2	Liverpool	1
1961 (3)	Chelsea	1	Crewe	2
1964 (3)	Newcastle	2	Bedford	2
1965 (4)	Peterborough	2	Arsenal	1
1971 (5)	Colchester	3	Leeds	2
1972 (3)	Hereford	2	Newcastle	1R
1973 (F)	Sunderland	1	Leeds	0
1975 (3)	Burnley	0	Wimbledon	1
1978 (F)	Ipswich	1	Arsenal	0
1980 (3)	Chelsea	0	Wigan	1
1980 (3)	Halifax	1	Manchester City	0

1980 (F)	West Ham	1	Arsenal	0
1981 (4)	Exeter	4	Newcastle	0R
1984 (3)	Bournemouth	2	Manchester Utd	0
1985 (4)	York	1	Arsenal	0
1986 (3)	Birmingham	1	Altrincham	2
1988 (F)	Wimbledon	1	Liverpool	0
1989 (3)	Sutton	2	Coventry	1
1991 (3)	WBA	2	Woking	4
1992 (3)	Wrexham	2	Arsenal	1
1994 (3)	Liverpool	0	Bristol City	1R
1994 (3)	Birmingham	1	Kidderminster	2
1997 (5)	Chesterfield	1	Nottm Forest	0
2001 (4)	Everton	0	Tranmere	3
2003 (3)	Shrewsbury	2	Everton	1
2005 (3)	Oldham	1	Manchester City	0
2008 (6)	Barnsley	1	Chelsea	0
2009 (2)	Histon	1	Leeds	0
2010 (4)	Liverpool	1	Reading	2R
2011 (3)	Stevenage	3	Newcastle	1
2012 (3)	Macclesfield	2	Cardiff	1
2013 (3)	Norwich	0	Luton	1
2013 (4)	Oldham	3	Liverpool	2
2013 (F)	Wigan	1	Manchester City	0
2014 (3)	Rochdale	2	Leeds	0
2015 (4)	Chelsea	2	Bradford City	4
2015 (5)	Bradford City	2	Sunderland	0

YEOVIL TOP GIANT-KILLERS

Yeovil's victories over Colchester and Blackpool in season 2000–01 gave them a total of 20 FA Cup wins against League opponents. They set another non-League record by reaching the third round 13 times.

This was Yeovil's triumphant (non-League) Cup record against League clubs: 1924–25 Bournemouth 3-2; 1934–35 Crystal Palace 3-0, Exeter 4-1; 1938–39 Brighton 2-1; 1948–49 Bury 3-1, Sunderland 2-1; 1958–59 Southend 1-0; 1960–61 Walsall 1-0; 1963–64 Southend 1-0, Crystal Palace 3-1; 1970–71 Bournemouth 1-0; 1972–73 Brentford 2-1; 1987–88 Cambridge Utd 1-0; 1991–92 Walsall 1-0; 1992–93 Torquay 5-2, Hereford 2-1; 1993–94 Fulham 1-0; 1998–99 Northampton 2-0; 2000–01 Colchester 5-1, Blackpool 1-0.

NON-LEAGUE BEST

Since League football began in 1888, three non-League clubs have reached the FA Cup Final. **Sheffield Wed** (Football Alliance) were runners-up in 1890, as were **Southampton** (Southern League) in 1900 and 1902. **Tottenham** won the Cup as a Southern League team in 1901.

Otherwise, the furthest progress by non-League clubs has been to the 5th round on 7 occasions: **Colchester** 1948, **Yeovil** 1949, **Blyth** 1978, **Telford** 1985, **Kidderminster** 1994, **Crawley** 2011, **Luton** 2013.

Greatest number of non-League sides to reach the **3rd round** is 8 in 2009: **Barrow, Blyth, Eastwood, Forest Green, Histon, Kettering, Kidderminster** and **Torquay**.

Most to reach **Round 4: 3** in 1957 (**Rhyl, New Brighton, Peterborough**) and 1975 (**Leatherhead, Stafford** and **Wimbledon**).

Five non-League clubs reaching **round 3** in 2001 was a Conference record. They were **Chester, Yeovil, Dagenham, Morecambe** and **Kingstonian**.

In season 2002–03, **Team Bath** became the first University-based side to reach the FA Cup 1st Round since **Oxford University** (Finalists in 1880).

NON-LEAGUE 'LAST TIMES'

Last time no non-League club reached round 3: 1951. Last time only one did so: 1969 (**Kettering**).

TOP-DIVISION SCALPS

Victories in FA Cup by non-League clubs over top-division teams since 1900 include: 1900–01 (Final, replay): **Tottenham** 3 Sheffield Utd 1 (Tottenham then in Southern League); 1919–20 **Cardiff** 2, Oldham 0; Sheffield Wed 0, **Darlington** 2; 1923–24 **Corinthians** 1, Blackburn 0; 1947–48 **Colchester** 1, Huddersfield 0; 1948–9 **Yeovil** 2, Sunderland 1; 1971–72 **Hereford** 2, Newcastle 1; 1974–75 Burnley 0, **Wimbledon** 1; 1985–86 Birmingham 1, **Altrincham** 2; 1988–89 **Sutton** 2, Coventry 1; 2012–13 Norwich 0, **Luton** 1.

MOST WINNING MEDALS

Ashley Cole has won the trophy seven times, with (Arsenal 2002–03–05) and Chelsea (2007–09–10–12). **The Hon Arthur Kinnaird** (The Wanderers and Old Etonians), **Charles Wollaston** (The Wanderers) and **Jimmy Forrest** (Blackburn) each earned five winners' medals. Kinnaird, later president of the FA, played in nine of the first 12 FA Cup Finals, and was on the winning side three times for The Wanderers, in 1873 (captain), 1877, 1878 (captain), and twice as captain of Old Etonians (1879, 1882).

MANAGERS' MEDALS BACKDATED

In 2010, the FA agreed to award Cup Final medals to all living managers who took their teams to the Final before 1996 (when medals were first given to Wembley team bosses). Lawrie McMenemy had campaigned for the award since Southampton's victory in 1976.

MOST WINNERS' MEDALS AT WEMBLEY

4 – **Mark Hughes** (3 for Manchester Utd, 1 for Chelsea), **Petr Cech, Frank Lampard, John Terry, Didier Drogba, Ashley Cole** (all Chelsea).

3 – **Dick Pym** (3 clean sheets in Finals), **Bob Haworth, Jimmy Seddon, Harry Nuttall, Billy Butler** (all Bolton); **David Jack** (2 Bolton, 1 Arsenal); **Bob Cowell, Jack Milburn, Bobby Mitchell** (all Newcastle); **Dave Mackay** (Tottenham); **Frank Stapleton** (1 Arsenal, 2 Manchester Utd); **Bryan Robson** (3 times winning captain), **Arthur Albiston, Gary Pallister** (all Manchester Utd); **Bruce Grobbelaar, Steve Nicol, Ian Rush** (all Liverpool); **Roy Keane, Peter Schmeichel, Ryan Giggs** (all Manchester Utd); **Dennis Wise** (1 Wimbledon, 2 Chelsea).

Arsenal's **David Seaman** and **Ray Parlour** have each earned 4 winners' medals (2 at Wembley, 2 at Cardiff) as have Manchester Utd's **Roy Keane** and **Ryan Giggs** (3 at Wembley, 1 at Cardiff).

MOST WEMBLEY FINALS

Nine players appeared in five FA Cup Finals at Wembley, replays excluded:

- **Joe Hulme** (Arsenal: 1927 lost, 1930 won, 1932 lost, 1936 won; Huddersfield: 1938 lost).
- **Johnny Giles** (Manchester Utd: 1963 won; Leeds: 1965 lost, 1970 drew at Wembley, lost replay at Old Trafford, 1972 won, 1973 lost).
- **Pat Rice** (all for Arsenal: 1971 won, 1972 lost, 1978 lost, 1979 won, 1980 lost).
- **Frank Stapleton** (Arsenal: 1978 lost, 1979 won, 1980 lost; Manchester Utd: 1983 won, 1985 won).
- **Ray Clemence** (Liverpool: 1971 lost, 1974 won, 1977 lost; Tottenham: 1982 won, 1987 lost).
- **Mark Hughes** (Manchester Utd: 1985 won, 1990 won, 1994 won, 1995 lost; Chelsea: 1997 won).
- **John Barnes** (Watford: 1984 lost; Liverpool: 1988 lost, 1989 won, 1996 lost; Newcastle: 1998 sub, lost): – first player to lose Wembley FA Cup Finals with three different clubs.
- **Roy Keane** (Nottm Forest: 1991 lost; Manchester Utd: 1994 won, 1995 lost, 1996 won, 1999 won).
- **Ryan Giggs** (Manchester Utd: 1994 won, 1995 lost, 1996 won, 1999 won, 2007 lost).
- Clemence, Hughes and Stapleton also played in a replay, making six actual FA Cup Final appearances for each of them.

- **Glenn Hoddle** also made six appearances at Wembley: 5 for Tottenham (incl. 2 replays), in 1981 won, 1982 won and 1987 lost, and 1 for Chelsea as sub in 1994 lost.
- **Paul Bracewell** played in four FA Cup Finals without being on the winning side – for Everton 1985, 1986, 1989, Sunderland 1992.

MOST WEMBLEY/CARDIFF FINAL APPEARANCES

8 by **Ashley Cole** (Arsenal: 2001 lost; 2002 won; 2003 won; 2005 won; Chelsea: 2007 won; 2009 won; 2010 won, 2012 won).

7 by **Roy Keane** (Nottm Forest: 1991 lost; Manchester Utd: 1994 won; 1995 lost; 1996 won; 1999 won; 2004 won; 2005 lost).

7 by **Ryan Giggs** (Manchester Utd): 1994 won; 1995 won; 1996 won; 1999 won; 2004 won; 2005 lost; 2007 lost.

6 by **Paul Scholes** (Manchester Utd): 1995 lost; 1996 won; 1999 won; 2004 won; 2005 lost; 2007 lost.

5 by **David Seaman** and **Ray Parlour** (Arsenal): 1993 won; 1998 won; 2001 lost; 2002 won; 2003 won; **Dennis Wise** (Wimbledon 1988 won; Chelsea 1994 lost; 1997 won; 2000 won; Millwall 2004 lost); Patrick Vieira (Arsenal): 1998 won; 2001 lost; 2002 won; 2005 won; (Manchester City) 2011 won.

BIGGEST FA CUP SCORE AT WEMBLEY

5-0 by Stoke v Bolton (semi-final, Apr 17, 2011.

WINNING GOALKEEPER-CAPTAINS

1988 Dave Beasant (Wimbledon); 2003 **David Seaman** (Arsenal).

MOST WINNING MANAGERS

6 **Arsene Wenger** (Arsenal) 1998, 2002, 2003, 2005, 20014, 2015; **5 Sir Alex Ferguson** (Manchester Utd 1990, 1994, 1996, 1999, 2004).

PLAYER-MANAGERS IN FINAL

Kenny Dalglish (Liverpool, 1986); **Glenn Hoddle** (Chelsea, 1994); **Dennis Wise** (Millwall, 2004).

DEBUTS IN FINAL

Alan Davies (Manchester Utd v Brighton, 1983); **Chris Baird** (Southampton v Arsenal, 2003); **Curtis Weston** (Millwall sub v Manchester Utd, 2004).

SEMI-FINALS AT WEMBLEY

1991 Tottenham 3 Arsenal 1; **1993** Sheffield Wed 2 Sheffield Utd 1, Arsenal 1 Tottenham 0; **1994** Chelsea 2 Luton 0, Manchester Utd 1 Oldham 1; **2000** Aston Villa beat Bolton 4-1 on pens (after 0-0), Chelsea 2 Newcastle 1; **2008** Portsmouth 1 WBA 0, Cardiff 1 Barnsley 0; **2009** Chelsea 2 Arsenal 1, Everton beat Manchester Utd 4-2 on pens (after 0-0); **2010** Chelsea 3 Aston Villa 0, Portsmouth 2 Tottenham 0; **2011** Manchester City 1 Manchester Utd 0, Stoke 5 Bolton 0; **2012** Liverpool 2 Everton 1, Chelsea 5 Tottenham 1; **2013** Wigan 2 Millwall 0, Manchester City 2 Chelsea 1; **2014** Arsenal beat Wigan 4-2 on pens (after 1-1), Hull 5 Sheffield Utd 3; **2015** Arsenal 2 Reading 1, Aston Villa 2 Liverpool 1.

CHELSEA'S FA CUP MILESTONES

Their victory over Liverpool in the 2012 Final set the following records:

Captain **John Terry** first player to lift the trophy four times for one club; **Didier Drogba** first to score in four Finals; **Ashley Cole** first to earn seven winner's medals (Arsenal 3, Chelsea 4); **Roberto Di Matteo** first to score for and manage the same winning club (player for Chelsea 1997, 2000, interim manager 2012).

Chelsea's four triumphs in six seasons (2007–12) the best winning sequence since Wanderers won five of the first seven competitions (1872–78) and Blackburn won five out of eight (1884–91).

FIRST ENTRANTS (1871–72)

Barnes, Civil Service, Crystal Palace, Clapham Rov, Donnington School (Spalding), Hampstead Heathens, Harrow Chequers, Hitchin, Maidenhead, Marlow, Queen's Park (Glasgow), Reigate Priory, Royal Engineers, Upton Park and Wanderers. Total 15.

FA CUP FIRSTS

Out of country: Cardiff, by defeating Arsenal 1-0 in the 1927 Final at Wembley, became the first and only club to take the FA Cup out of England.

All-English Winning XI: First club to win the FA Cup with all-English XI: Blackburn Olympic in 1883. Others since: WBA in 1888 and 1931, Bolton (1958), Manchester City (1969), West Ham (1964 and 1975).

Non-English Winning XI: Liverpool in 1986 (Mark Lawrenson, born Preston, was a Rep of Ireland player).

Won both Cups: Old Carthusians won the FA Cup in 1881 and the FA Amateur Cup in 1894 and 1897. **Wimbledon** won Amateur Cup in 1963, FA Cup in 1988.

MOST GAMES NEEDED TO WIN

Barnsley played a record 12 matches (20 hours' football) to win the FA Cup in season 1911–12. All six replays (one in round 1, three in round 4 and one in each of semi-final and Final) were brought about by goalless draws.

Arsenal played 11 FA Cup games when winning the trophy in 1979. Five of them were in the 3rd round against Sheffield Wed.

LONGEST TIES

6 matches: (11 hours): Alvechurch v Oxford City (4th qual round, 1971–72). Alvechurch won 1-0.

5 matches: (9 hours, 22 mins – record for competition proper): Stoke v Bury (3rd round, 1954–55). Stoke won 3-2.

5 matches: Chelsea v Burnley (4th round, 1955–56). Chelsea won 2-0.

5 matches: Hull v Darlington (2nd round, 1960–61). Hull won 3-0.

5 matches: Arsenal v Sheffield Wed (3rd round, 1978–79). Arsenal won 2-0.

Other marathons (qualifying comp, all 5 matches, 9 hours): Barrow v Gillingham (last qual round, 1924–25) – winners Barrow; Leyton v Ilford (3rd qual round, 1924–25) – winners Leyton; Falmouth v Bideford (3rd qual round, 1973–74) – winners Bideford.

End of Cup Final replays: The FA decided that, with effect from 1999, there would be no Cup Final replays. In the event of a draw after extra-time, the match would be decided on penalties. This happened for the first time in 2005, when Arsenal beat Manchester Utd 5-4 on penalties after a 0-0 draw. A year later, Liverpool beat West Ham 3-1 on penalties after a 3-3 draw.

FA Cup marathons ended in season 1991–92, when the penalty shoot-out was introduced to decide ties still level after one replay and extra-time.

In 1932–33 **Brighton** (Div 3 South) played 11 FA Cup games, including replays, and scored 43 goals, without getting past round 5. They forgot to claim exemption and had to play from 1st qual round.

LONGEST ROUND

The longest round in FA Cup history was the **3rd round** in **1962–63**. It took 66 days to complete, lasting from Jan 5 to Mar 11, and included 261 postponements because of bad weather.

LONGEST UNBEATEN RUN

23 matches by Blackburn In winning the Cup in three consecutive years (1884–05–06), they won 21 ties (one in a replay), and their first Cup defeat in four seasons was in a first round replay of the next competition.

RE-STAGED TIES

Sixth round, Mar 9, 1974: Newcastle 4, Nottm Forest 3. Match declared void by FA and ordered to be replayed following a pitch invasion after Newcastle had a player sent off. Forest claimed the hold-up caused the game to change its pattern. The tie went to two further matches at Goodison Park (0-0, then 1-0 to Newcastle).

Third round, Jan 5, 1985: Burton 1, Leicester 6 (at Derby). Burton goalkeeper Paul Evans was hit on the head by a missile thrown from the crowd and continued in a daze. The FA ordered the tie to be played again, behind closed doors at Coventry (Leicester won 1-0).

First round replay, Nov 25, 1992: Peterborough 9 (Tony Philliskirk 5), Kingstonian 1. Match expunged from records because, at 3-0 after 57 mins, Kingstonian were reduced to ten men when goalkeeper Adrian Blake was concussed by a 50 pence coin thrown from the crowd. The tie was re-staged on the same ground behind closed doors (Peterborough won 1-0).

Fifth round: Within an hour of holders Arsenal beating Sheffield Utd 2-1 at Highbury on Feb 13, 1999, the FA took the unprecedented step of declaring the match void because an unwritten rule of sportsmanship had been broken. With United's Lee Morris lying injured, their goalkeeper Alan Kelly kicked the ball into touch. Play resumed with Arsenal's Ray Parlour throwing it in the direction of Kelly, but Nwankwo Kanu took possession and centred for Marc Overmars to score the 'winning' goal. After four minutes of protests by manager Steve Bruce and his players, referee Peter Jones confirmed the goal. Both managers absolved Kanu of cheating but Arsenal's Arsene Wenger offered to replay the match. With the FA immediately approving, it was re-staged at Highbury ten days later (ticket prices halved) and Arsenal again won 2-1.

PRIZE FUND

The makeover of the FA Cup competition took off in 2001–02 with the introduction of round-by-round prize-money.

FA CUP FOLLIES

1999–2000 The FA broke with tradition by deciding the 3rd round be moved from its regular Jan date and staged before Christmas. Criticism was strong, gates poor and the 3rd round in 2000–01 reverted to the New Year. By allowing the holders Manchester Utd to withdraw from the 1999–2000 competition in order to play in FIFA's inaugural World Club Championship in Brazil in Jan, the FA were left with an odd number of clubs in the 3rd round. Their solution was a 'lucky losers' draw among clubs knocked out in round 2. Darlington, beaten at Gillingham, won it to re-enter the competition, then lost 2-1 away to Aston Villa.

HAT-TRICKS IN FINAL

There have been three in the history of the competition: **Billy Townley** (Blackburn, 1890), **Jimmy Logan** (Notts Co, 1894) and **Stan Mortensen** (Blackpool, 1953).

MOST APPEARANCES

88 by **Ian Callaghan** (79 for Liverpool, 7 for Swansea City, 2 for Crewe); **87** by **John Barnes** (31 for Watford, 51 for Liverpool, 5 for Newcastle); **86** by **Stanley Matthews** (37 for Stoke, 49 for Blackpool); **84** by **Bobby Charlton** (80 for Manchester Utd, 4 for Preston); **84** by **Pat Jennings** (3 for Watford, 43 for Tottenham, 38 for Arsenal); **84** by **Peter Shilton** for seven clubs (30 for Leicester, 7 for Stoke, 18 for Nottm Forest, 17 for Southampton, 10 for Derby, 1 for Plymouth Argyle, 1 for Leyton Orient); **82** by **David Seaman** (5 for Peterborough, 5 for Birmingham, 17 for QPR, 54 for Arsenal, 1 for Manchester City).

THREE-CLUB FINALISTS

Five players have appeared in the FA Cup Final for three clubs: **Harold Halse** for Manchester Utd (1909), Aston Villa (1913) and Chelsea (1915); **Ernie Taylor** for Newcastle (1951), Blackpool (1953) and Manchester Utd (1958); **John Barnes** for Watford (1984), Liverpool

(1988, 1989, 1996) and Newcastle (1998); **Dennis Wise** for Wimbledon (1988), Chelsea (1994, 1997, 2000), Millwall (2004); **David James** for Liverpool (1996), Aston Villa (2000) and Portsmouth (2008, 2010).

CUP MAN WITH TWO CLUBS IN SAME SEASON

Stan Crowther, who played for Aston Villa against Manchester Utd in the 1957 FA Cup Final, appeared for both Villa and United in the 1957–58 competition. United signed him directly after the Munich air crash and, in the circumstances, he was given dispensation to play for them in the Cup, including the Final.

CAPTAIN'S CUP DOUBLE

Martin Buchan is the only player to have captained Scottish and English FA Cup-winning teams – Aberdeen in 1970 and Manchester Utd in 1977.

MEDALS BEFORE AND AFTER

Two players appeared in FA Cup Final teams before and after the Second World War: **Raich Carter** was twice a winner (Sunderland 1937, Derby 1946) and **Willie Fagan** twice on the losing side (Preston 1937, Liverpool 1950).

DELANEY'S COLLECTION

Scotland winger **Jimmy Delaney** uniquely earned Scottish, English, Northern Ireland and Republic of Ireland Cup medals. He was a winner with Celtic (1937), Manchester Utd (1948) and Derry City (1954) and a runner-up with Cork City (1956).

STARS WHO MISSED OUT

Internationals who never won an FA Cup winner's medal include: Tommy Lawton, Tom Finney, Johnny Haynes, Gordon Banks, George Best, Terry Butcher, Peter Shilton, Martin Peters, Nobby Stiles, Alan Ball, Malcolm Macdonald, Alan Shearer, Matthew Le Tissier, Stuart Pearce, Des Walker, Phil Neal, Ledley King.

CUP WINNERS AT NO COST

Not one member of **Bolton**'s 1958 FA Cup-winning team cost the club a transfer fee. Each joined the club for a £10 signing-on fee.

11-NATIONS LINE-UP

Liverpool fielded a team of 11 different nationalities in the FA Cup 3rd round at Yeovil on Jan 4, 2004.

HIGH-SCORING SEMI-FINALS

The **record team score** in FA Cup semi-finals is **6**: 1891–92 WBA 6, Nottm Forest 2; 1907–08 Newcastle 6, Fulham 0; 1933–34 Manchester City 6, Aston Villa 1.

Most goals in semi-finals (aggregate): 17 in 1892 (4 matches) and 1899 (5 matches). In modern times: 15 in 1958 (3 matches, including Manchester Utd 5, Fulham 3 – highest-scoring semi-final since last war); 16 in 1989–90 (Crystal Palace 4, Liverpool 3; Manchester Utd v Oldham 3-3, 2-1. All **16 goals** in those three matches were scored by **different players**.

Stoke's win against Bolton at Wembley in 2011 was the first 5-0 semi-final result since Wolves beat Grimsby at Old Trafford in 1939. In 2014, Hull defeated Sheffield Utd 5-3.

Last hat-trick in an FA Cup semi-final was scored by **Alex Dawson** for Manchester Utd in 5-3 replay win against Fulham at Highbury in 1958.

SEMI-FINAL VENUES

Villa Park has staged more such matches (55 including replays) than any other ground. Next is Hillsborough (33).

ONE IN A HUNDRED

The 2008 semi-finals included only one top-division club, Portsmouth, for the first time in 100 years – since Newcastle in 1908.

FOUR SPECIAL AWAYS

For the only time in FA Cup history, **all four quarter-finals** in season 1986–87 were won by the away team.

DRAWS RECORD

In season 1985–86, **seven** of the eight 5th round ties went to replays – a record for that stage of the competition.

SHOCK FOR TOP CLUBS

The fourth round on Jan 24, 2015 produced an astonishing set of home defeats for leading clubs. The top three in the Premier League, Chelsea, Manchester City and Southampton were all knocked out and sixth-place Tottenham also lost at home. Odds against this happening were put at 3825-1.

LUCK OF THE DRAW

In the FA Cup on Jan 11, 1947, eight of **London**'s ten Football League clubs involved in the 3rd round were drawn at home (including Chelsea v Arsenal). Only Crystal Palace played outside the capital (at Newcastle).

In the 3rd round in Jan 1992, Charlton were the only London club drawn at home (against Barnet), but the venue of the Farnborough v West Ham tie was reversed on police instruction. So Upton Park staged Cup ties on successive days, with West Ham at home on the Saturday and Charlton (who shared the ground) on Sunday.

Arsenal were drawn away in every round on the way to reaching the Finals of 1971 and 1972. **Manchester Utd** won the Cup in 1990 without playing once at home.

The 1999 finalists, **Manchester Utd** and **Newcastle,** were both drawn at home every time in Rounds 3–6.

On their way to the semi-finals of both domestic Cup competitions in season 2002–03, **Sheffield Utd** were drawn at home ten times out of ten and won all ten matches – six in the League's Worthington Cup and four in the FA Cup.

On their way to winning the Cup in 2014, **Arsenal** did not play once outside London. Home draws in rounds 3, 4, 5 and 6 were followed by the semi-final at Wembley.

ALL TOP-DIVISION VICTIMS

The only instance of an FA Cup-winning club meeting top-division opponents in every round was provided by Manchester Utd in 1947–48. They beat Aston Villa, Liverpool, Charlton, Preston, then Derby in the semi-final and Blackpool in the Final.

In contrast, these clubs have reached the Final without playing top-division opponents on the way: West Ham (1923), Bolton (1926), Blackpool (1948), Bolton (1953), Millwall (2004).

WON CUP WITHOUT CONCEDING GOAL

1873 **The Wanderers** (1 match; as holders, exempt until Final); 1889 **Preston** (5 matches); 1903 **Bury** (5 matches). In 1966 **Everton** reached Final without conceding a goal (7 matches), then beat Sheffield Wed 3-2 at Wembley.

HOME ADVANTAGE

For the first time in FA Cup history, all eight ties in the 1992–93 5th round were won (no replays) by the **clubs drawn at home.** Only other instance of eight home wins at the last 16 stage was in 1889–90, in what was then the 2nd round.

NORTH-EAST WIPE-OUT

For the first time in 54 years, since the 4th round in Jan, 1957, the North-East's 'big three' were knocked out on the same date, Jan 8, 2011 (3rd round). All lost to lower-division opponents – **Newcastle** 3-1 at Stevenage, **Sunderland** 2-1 at home to Notts County and **Middlesbrough** 2-1 at Burton.

FEWEST TOP-DIVISION CLUBS IN LAST 16 (5th ROUND)

5 in 1958; **6** in 1927, 1970, 1982; **7** in 1994, 2003; **8** in 2002, 2004.

SIXTH-ROUND ELITE

For the first time in FA Cup 6th round history, dating from 1926 when the format of the competition changed, all **eight quarter-finalists** in 1995–96 were from the top division.

SEMI-FINAL – DOUBLE DERBIES

There have been three instances of both FA Cup semi-finals in the same year being local derbies: **1950** Liverpool beat Everton 2-0 (Maine Road), Arsenal beat Chelsea 1-0 after 2-2 draw (both at Tottenham); **1993** Arsenal beat Tottenham 1-0 (Wembley), Sheffield Wed beat Sheffield Utd 2-1 (Wembley); **2012** Liverpool beat Everton 2-1 (Wembley), Chelsea beat Tottenham 5-1 (Wembley).

TOP CLUB DISTINCTION

Since the Football League began in 1888, there has never been an FA Cup Final in which **neither club** represented the top division.

CLUBS THROWN OUT

Bury expelled (Dec 2006) for fielding an ineligible player in 3-1 2nd rd replay win at Chester. **Droylsden** expelled for fielding a suspended player in 2-1 2nd rd replay win at home to Chesterfield (Dec 2008).

SPURS OUT – AND IN

Tottenham were banned, pre-season, from the 1994–95 competition because of financial irregularities, but were re-admitted on appeal and reached the semi-finals.

FATHER & SON FA CUP WINNERS

Peter Boyle (Sheffield Utd 1899, 1902) and **Tommy Boyle** (Sheffield Utd 1925); **Harry Johnson Snr** (Sheffield Utd 1899, 1902) and **Harry Johnson Jnr** (Sheffield Utd 1925); **Jimmy Dunn Snr** (Everton 1933) and **Jimmy Dunn Jnr** (Wolves 1949); **Alec Herd** (Manchester City 1934) and **David Herd** (Manchester Utd 1963); **Frank Lampard Snr** (West Ham 1975, 1980) and **Frank Lampard Jnr** (Chelsea 2007, 2009, 2010, 2012).

BROTHERS IN FA CUP FINAL TEAMS (modern times)

1950 **Denis and Leslie Compton** (Arsenal); 1952 **George and Ted Robledo** (Newcastle); 1967 **Ron and Allan Harris** (Chelsea); 1977 **Jimmy and Brian Greenhoff** (Manchester Utd); 1996 and 1999 **Gary and Phil Neville** (Manchester Utd).

FA CUP SPONSORS

Littlewoods Pools became the first sponsors of the FA Cup in season 1994–95 in a £14m, 4-year deal. French insurance giants **AXA** took over (season 1998–99) in a sponsorship worth £25m over 4 years. German energy company **E.ON** agreed a 4-year deal worth £32m from season 2006–07 and extended it for a year to 2011. American beer company **Budweiser** began a three-year sponsorship worth £24m in season 2011–12. The **Emirates** airline became the first title sponsor (2015-18) in a reported £30m deal with the FA.

FIRST GOALKEEPER-SUBSTITUTE IN FINAL

Paul Jones (Southampton), who replaced injured Antti Niemi against Arsenal in 2003.

LEAGUE CUP RECORDS

(See also Goalscoring section)

Highest scores: West Ham 10-0 v Bury (2nd round, 2nd leg 1983–84; agg 12-1); Liverpool 10-0 v Fulham (2nd round, 1st leg 1986–87; agg 13-2).

Most League Cup goals (career): 49 Geoff Hurst (43 West Ham, 6 Stoke, 1960–75); 49 Ian Rush (48 Liverpool, 1 Newcastle, 1981–98).

Highest scorer (season): 12 Clive Allen (Tottenham 1986–87 in 9 apps).

Most goals in match: 6 Frank Bunn (Oldham v Scarborough, 3rd round, 1989–90).

Most winners' medals: 5 Ian Rush (Liverpool).

Most appearances in Final: 6 Kenny Dalglish (Liverpool 1978–87), Ian Rush (Liverpool 1981–95). Emile Heskey (Leicester 1997, 1999, 2000), Liverpool (2001, 2003), Aston Villa (2010)

Biggest Final win: Swansea City 5 Bradford City 0 (2013).

League Cup sponsors: Milk Cup 1981–86, Littlewoods Cup 1987–90, Rumbelows Cup 1991–92, Coca-Cola Cup 1993–98. Worthington Cup 1999–2003, Carling Cup 2003–12; Capital One Cup from season 2012–15.

Up for the cup, then down: In 2011, Birmingham became only the second club to win a major trophy (the Carling Cup) and be relegated from the top division. It previously happened to Norwich in 1985 when they went down from the old First Division after winning the Milk Cup.

Liverpool's League Cup records: Winners a record 8 times. **Ian Rush** only player to win 5 times. Rush also first to play in 8 winning teams in Cup Finals **at Wembley**, all with Liverpool (FA Cup 1986–89/92; League Cup 1981–82–83–84/95).

Britain's first under-cover Cup Final: Worthington Cup Final between Blackburn and Tottenham at Cardiff's Millennium Stadium on Sunday, Feb 24, 2002. With rain forecast, the retractable roof was closed on the morning of the match.

Record penalty shoot-out: Liverpool beat Middlesbrough 14-13 (3rd round, Sep 23, 2014) after 2-2.

DISCIPLINE

SENDINGS-OFF

Season 2003–04 set an **all-time record** of 504 players sent off in English domestic football competitions. There were 58 in the Premiership, 390 Nationwide League, 28 FA Cup (excluding non-League dismissals), 22 League Cup, 2 in Nationwide play-offs, 4 in LDV Vans Trophy.

Most sendings-off in Premier League programme (10 matches): 9 (8 Sat, 1 Sun, Oct 31–Nov 1, 2009).

The 58 Premiership red cards was 13 fewer than the record English **top-division** total of 71 in 2002–03. **Bolton** were the only club in the English divisions without a player sent off in any first-team competition that season.

Worst day for dismissals in English football was Boxing Day, 2007, with **20 red cards** (5 Premier League and 15 Coca-Cola League). Three players, Chelsea's Ashley Cole and Ricardo Carvalho and Aston Villa's Zat Knight were sent off in a 4-4 draw at Stamford Bridge. Luton had three men dismissed in their game at Bristol Rov, but still managed a 1-1 draw.

Previous worst day was Dec 13, 2003, with **19 red cards** (2 Premiership and the 17 Nationwide League).

In the entire first season of post-war League football (1946–47) only 12 players were sent off, followed by 14 in 1949–50, and the total League dismissals for the first nine seasons after the War was 104.

The worst pre-War total was 28 in each of seasons 1921–22 and 1922–23.

ENGLAND SENDINGS-OFF

In a total of 15 England dismissals, David Beckham and Wayne Rooney have been red-carded twice. Beckham and Steven Gerrard are the only England captains to be sent off and Robert Green the only goalkeeper.

Jun 5, 1968	**Alan Mullery**	v Yugoslavia (Florence, Euro Champ)
Jun 6, 1973	**Alan Ball**	v Poland (Chorzow, World Cup qual)
Jun 12, 1977	**Trevor Cherry**	v Argentina (Buenos Aires, friendly)
Jun 6, 1986	**Ray Wilkins**	v Morocco (Monterrey, World Cup Finals)
Jun 30, 1998	**David Beckham**	v Argentina (St Etienne, World Cup Finals)
Sep 5, 1998	**Paul Ince**	v Sweden (Stockholm, Euro Champ qual)
Jun 5, 1999	**Paul Scholes**	v Sweden (Wembley, Euro Champ qual)
Sep 8, 1999	**David Batty**	v Poland (Warsaw, Euro Champ qual)
Oct 16, 2002	**Alan Smith**	v Macedonia (Southampton, Euro Champ qual)
Oct 8, 2005	**David Beckham**	v Austria (Old Trafford, World Cup qual)
Jul 1, 2006	**Wayne Rooney**	v Portugal (Gelsenkirchen, World Cup Finals)
Oct 10, 2009	**Robert Green**	v Ukraine (Dnipropetrovsk, World Cup qual)
Oct 7, 2011	**Wayne Rooney**	v Montenegro (Podgorica, Euro Champ qual)
Sep 11, 2012	**Steven Gerrard**	v Ukraine (Wembley, World Cup qual)
Jun 4, 2014	**Raheem Sterling**	v Ecuador (Miami, friendly)

Other countries: Most recent sendings-off of players representing other Home Countries:
N Ireland – Gareth McAuley (Friendly v Cyprus, Nicosia, Mar 5, 2014).
Scotland – Charlie Mulgrew (European Champ qual v Germany, Dortmund, Sep 7, 2014).
Wales – Andy King (European Champ qual v Cyprus, Cardiff, Oct 13, 2014).
Rep of Ireland– Keith Andrews (European Champ v Italy, Poznan, Jun 18, 2012).
England dismissals at other levels:
U-23: Stan Anderson (v Bulgaria, Sofia, May 19, 1957); **Alan Ball** (v Austria, Vienna, Jun 2, 1965); **Kevin Keegan** (v E Germany, Magdeburg, Jun 1, 1972); **Steve Perryman** (v Portugal, Lisbon, Nov 19, 1974).
U-21: Sammy Lee (v Hungary, Keszthely, Jun 5, 1981); **Mark Hateley** (v Scotland, Hampden Park, Apr 19, 1982); **Paul Elliott** (v Denmark, Maine Road, Manchester, Mar 26, 1986); **Tony Cottee** (v W Germany, Ludenscheid, Sep 8, 1987); **Julian Dicks** (v Mexico, Toulon, France, Jun 12, 1988); **Jason Dodd** (v Mexico, Toulon, May 29, 1991; 3 Mexico players also sent off in that match); **Matthew Jackson** (v France, Toulon, May 28, 1992); **Robbie Fowler** (v Austria, Kafkenberg, Oct 11, 1994); **Alan Thompson** (v Portugal, Oporto, Sep 2, 1995); **Terry Cooke** (v Portugal, Toulon, May 30, 1996); **Ben Thatcher** (v Italy, Rieti, Oct 10, 1997); **John Curtis** (v Greece, Heraklion, Nov 13, 1997); **Jody Morris** (v Luxembourg, Grevenmacher, Oct 13, 1998); **Stephen Wright** (v Germany, Derby, Oct 6, 2000); **Alan Smith** (v Finland, Valkeakoski, Oct 10, 2000); **Luke Young** and **John Terry** (v Greece, Athens, Jun 5, 2001); **Shola Ameobi** (v Portugal, Rio Maior, Mar 28, 2003); **Jermaine Pennant** (v Croatia, Upton Park, Aug 19, 2003); **Glen Johnson** (v Turkey, Istanbul, Oct 10, 2003); **Nigel Reo-Coker** (v Azerbaijan, Baku, Oct 12, 2004); **Glen Johnson** (v Spain, Henares, Nov 16, 2004); **Steven Taylor** (v Germany, Leverkusen, Oct 10, 2006); **Tom Huddlestone** (v Serbia & Montenegro, Nijmegen, Jun 17, 2007); **Tom Huddlestone** (v Wales, Villa Park, Oct 14, 2008); **Michael Mancienne** (v Finland, Halmstad, Jun 15, 2009); **Fraizer Campbell** (v Sweden, Gothenburg, Jun 26, 2009); **Ben Mee** (v Italy, Empoli, Feb 8, 2011); **Danny Rose** (v Serbia, Krusevac, Oct 16, 2012); **Andre Wisdom** (v Finland, Tampere, Sep 9, 2013).
England 'B' (1): **Neil Webb** (v Algeria, Algiers, Dec 11, 1990).

MOST DISMISSALS IN INTERNATIONAL MATCHES

19 (10 Chile, 9 Uruguay), Jun 25, 1975; **6** (2 Mexico, 4 Argentina), 1956; **6** (5 Ecuador, 1 Uruguay), Jan 4, 1977 (4 Ecuadorians sent off in 78th min, match abandoned, 1-1); **5** (Holland 3, Brazil 2), Jun 6, 1999 in Goianio, Brazil.

INTERNATIONAL STOPPED THROUGH DEPLETED SIDE

Portugal v Angola (5-1), friendly international in Lisbon on Nov 14, 2001, abandoned (68 mins) because Angola were down to 6 players (4 sent off, 1 carried off, no substitutes left).

MOST 'CARDS' IN WORLD CUP FINALS MATCH

20 in Portugal v Holland quarter-final, Nuremberg, Jun 25, 2006 (9 yellow, 2 red, Portugal; 7 yellow, 2 red, Holland).

FIVE OFF IN ONE MATCH

For the first time since League football began in 1888, five players were sent off in one match (two Chesterfield, three Plymouth) in Div 2 at Saltergate on **Feb 22, 1997.** Four were dismissed (two from each side) in a goalmouth brawl in the last minute. Five were sent off on Dec 2, 1997 (4 Bristol Rov, 1 Wigan) in Div 2 match at Wigan, four in the 45th minute. The third instance occurred at Exeter on **Nov 23, 2002** in Div 3 (three Exeter, two Cambridge United) all in the last minute. On **Mar 27, 2012** (Lge 2) three Bradford players and two from Crawley were shown red cards in the dressing rooms after a brawl at the final whistle at Valley Parade.

Matches with **four** Football League club players being sent off in one match:

Jan 8, 1955: Crewe v Bradford City (Div 3 North), two players from each side.

Dec 13, 1986: Sheffield Utd (1 player) v Portsmouth (3) in Div 2.

Aug 18, 1987: Port Vale v Northampton (Littlewoods Cup 1st Round, 1st Leg), two players from each side.

Dec 12, 1987: Brentford v Mansfield (Div 3), two players from each side.

Sep 6, 1992: First instance in British first-class football of four players from one side being sent off in one match. Hereford's seven survivors, away to Northampton (Div 3), held out for a 1-1 draw.

Mar 1, 1977: Norwich v Huddersfield (Div 1), two from each side.

Oct 4, 1977: Shrewsbury (1 player), Rotherham (3) in Div 3.

Aug 22, 1998: Gillingham v Bristol Rov (Div 2), two from each side, all after injury-time brawl.

Mar 16, 2001: Bristol City v Millwall (Div 2), two from each side.

Aug 17, 2002: Lincoln (1 player), Carlisle (3) in Div 3.

Aug 26, 2002: Wycombe v QPR (Div 2), two from each side.

Nov 1, 2005: Burnley (1 player) v Millwall (3) in Championship.

Nov 24, 2007: Swindon v Bristol Rov (Lge 1), two from each side.

Mar 4, 2013: Hull v Burnley (Champ) two from each side.

Four Stranraer players were sent off away to Airdrie (Scottish Div 1) on Dec 3, 1994, and that Scottish record was equalled when four Hearts men were ordered off away to Rangers (Prem Div) on Sep 14, 1996. Albion had four players sent off (3 in last 8 mins) away to Queen's Park (Scottish Div 3) on Aug 23, 1997.

In the **Island Games** in Guernsey (Jul 2003), five players (all from Rhodes) were sent off against Guernsey for violent conduct and the match was abandoned by referee Wendy Toms.

Most dismissals one team, one match: Five players of America Tres Rios in first ten minutes after disputed goal by opponents Itaperuna in Brazilian cup match in Rio de Janeiro on Nov 23, 1991. Tie then abandoned and awarded to Itaperuna.

Eight dismissals in one match: Four on each side in South American Super Cup quarter-final (Gremio, Brazil v Penarol, Uruguay) in Oct 1993.

Five dismissals in one season – Dave Caldwell (2 with Chesterfield, 3 with Torquay) in 1987–88.

First instance of four dismissals in Scottish match: three Rangers players (all English – Terry Hurlock, Mark Walters, Mark Hateley) and Celtic's Peter Grant in Scottish Cup quarter-final at Parkhead on Mar 17, 1991 (Celtic won 2-0).

Four players (3 Hamilton, 1 Airdrie) were sent off in Scottish Div 1 match on Oct 30, 1993.

Four players (3 Ayr, 1 Stranraer) were sent off in Scottish Div 1 match on Aug 27, 1994.

In Scottish Cup first round replays on Dec 16, 1996, there were two instances of three players of one side sent off: Albion Rov (away to Forfar) and Huntly (away to Clyde).

FASTEST SENDINGS-OFF

World record – 10 sec: Giuseppe Lorenzo (Bologna) for striking opponent in Italian League match v Parma, Dec 9, 1990. Goalkeeper **Preston Edwards** (Ebbsfleet) for bringing down opponent and conceding penalty in Blue Square Premier League South match v Farnborough, Feb 5, 2011.

World record (non-professional) – 3 sec: David Pratt (Chippenham) at Bashley (British Gas Southern Premier League, Dec 27, 2008).

Domestic – 13 sec: Kevin Pressman (Sheffield Wed goalkeeper at Wolves, Div 1, Sunday, Aug 14, 2000); **15 sec: Simon Rea** (Peterborough at Cardiff, Div 2, Nov 2, 2002). **19 sec: Mark Smith** (Crewe goalkeeper at Darlington, Div 3, Mar 12, 1994). **Premier League – 72 sec: Tim Flowers** (Blackburn goalkeeper v Leeds Utd, Feb 1, 1995).

In World Cup – 55 sec: Jose Batista (Uruguay v Scotland at Neza, Mexico, Jun 13, 1986).

In European competition – 90 sec: Sergei Dirkach (Dynamo Moscow v Ghent UEFA Cup 3rd round, 2nd leg, Dec 11, 1991).

Fastest FA Cup dismissal – 52 sec: Ian Culverhouse (Swindon defender, deliberate hand-ball on goal-line, away to Everton, 3rd Round, Sunday Jan 5, 1997).

Fastest League Cup dismissal – 33 sec: Jason Crowe (Arsenal substitute v Birmingham, 3rd Round, Oct 14, 1997). Also fastest sending off on debut.

Fastest Sending-off of substitute – 0 sec: Walter Boyd (Swansea City) for striking opponent before ball in play after he went on (83 mins) at home to Darlington, Div 3, Nov 23, 1999. **15 secs: Keith Gillespie** (Sheffield Utd) for striking an opponent at Reading (Premiership), Jan 20, 2007. **90 sec: Andreas Johansson** (Wigan), without kicking a ball, for shirt-pulling (penalty) away to Arsenal (Premiership), May 7, 2006.

MOST SENDINGS-OFF IN CAREER

21 **Willie Johnston** , 1964–82 (Rangers 7, WBA 6, Vancouver Whitecaps 4, Hearts 3, Scotland 1)

21 **Roy McDonough**, 1980–95 (13 in Football League – Birmingham, Walsall, Chelsea, Colchester, Southend, Exeter, Cambridge Utd plus 8 non-league)

13 **Steve Walsh** (Wigan, Leicester, Norwich, Coventry)

13 **Martin Keown** (Arsenal, Aston Villa, Everton)

13 **Alan Smith** (Leeds, Manchester Utd, Newcastle, England U–21, England)

12 **Dennis Wise** (Wimbledon, Chelsea, Leicester, Millwall)

12 **Vinnie Jones** (Wimbledon, Leeds, Sheffield Utd, Chelsea, QPR)

12 **Mark Dennis** (Birmingham, Southampton, QPR)

12 **Roy Keane** (Manchester Utd, Rep of Ireland)

10 **Patrick Vieira** (Arsenal)

10 **Paul Scholes** (Manchester Utd, England)

Most Premier League sendings-off: Patrick Vieira 9, Duncan Ferguson 8, Richard Dunne 8, Vinnie Jones 7, Roy Keane 7, Alan Smith 7. Lee Cattermole 7.

● **Carlton Palmer** holds the unique record of having been sent off with each of his five Premiership clubs: Sheffield Wed, Leeds, Southampton, Nottm Forest and Coventry.

FA CUP FINAL SENDINGS-OFF

Kevin Moran (Manchester Utd) v Everton, Wembley, 1985; **Jose Antonio Reyes** (Arsenal) v Manchester Utd, Cardiff, 2005; Pablo Zabaleta (Manchester City) v Wigan, Wembley 2013.

WEMBLEY SENDINGS-OFF

Aug 1948	**Branko Stankovic** (Yugoslavia) v Sweden, Olympic Games
Jul 1966	**Antonio Rattin** (Argentina captain) v England, World cup quarter-final
Aug 1974	**Billy Bremner** (Leeds) and **Kevin Keegan** (Liverpool), Charity Shield
Mar 1977	**Gilbert Dresch** (Luxembourg) v England, World Cup
May 1985	**Kevin Moran** (Manchester Utd) v Everton, FA Cup Final
Apr 1993	**Lee Dixon** (Arsenal) v Tottenham, FA Cup semi-final
May 1993	**Peter Swan** (Port Vale) v WBA, Div 2 Play-off Final
Mar 1994	**Andrei Kanchelskis** (Manchester Utd) v Aston Villa, League Cup Final
May 1994	**Mike Wallace, Chris Beaumont** (Stockport) v Burnley, Div 2 Play-off Final
Jun 1995	**Tetsuji Hashiratani** (Japan) v England, Umbro Cup
May 1997	**Brian Statham** (Brentford) v Crewe, Div 2 Play-off Final
Apr 1998	**Capucho** (Portugal) v England, friendly
Nov 1998	**Ray Parlour** (Arsenal) and **Tony Vareilles** (Lens), Champions League

Mar 1999	**Justin Edinburgh** (Tottenham) v Leicester, League Cup Final
Jun 1999	**Paul Scholes** (England) v Sweden, European Championship qual
Feb 2000	**Clint Hill** (Tranmere) v Leicester, League Cup Final
Apr 2000	**Mark Delaney** (Aston Villa) v Bolton, FA Cup semi-final
May 2000	**Kevin Sharp** (Wigan) v Gillingham, Div 2 Play-off Final
Aug 2000	**Roy Keane** (Manchester Utd captain) v Chelsea, Charity Shield
May 2007	**Marc Tierney** (Shrewsbury) v Bristol Rov, Lge 2 Play-off Final
May 2007	**Matt Gill** (Exeter) v Morecambe, Conf Play-off Final
May 2009	**Jamie Ward** (Sheffield Utd) and **Lee Hendrie** (Sheffield Utd) v Burnley, Champ Play-off Final (Hendrie after final whistle)
May 2009	**Phil Bolland** (Cambridge Utd) v Torquay, Blue Square Prem Lge Play-off Final
May 2010	**Robin Hulbert** (Barrow) and **David Bridges** (Stevenage), FA Trophy Final
Apr 2011	**Paul Scholes** (Manchester Utd) v Manchester City, FA Cup semi-final
Apr 2011	**Toumani Diagouraga** (Brentford) v Carlisle, Johnstone's Paint Trophy Final
Sep 2012	**Steven Gerrard** (England) v Ukraine, World Cup qual
Feb 2013	**Matt Duke** (Bradford) v Swansea, League Cup Final
May 2013	**Pablo Zabaleta** (Manchester City) v Wigan, FA Cup Final
Mar 2014	**Joe Newell** (Peterborough) v Chesterfield, Johnstone's Paint Trophy Final
May 2014	**Gary O'Neil** (QPR) v Derby, Champ Play-off Final

WEMBLEY'S SUSPENDED CAPTAINS

Suspension prevented four **club captains** playing at Wembley in modern finals, in successive years. Three were in FA Cup Finals – **Glenn Roeder** (QPR, 1982), **Steve Foster** (Brighton, 1983), **Wilf Rostron** (Watford, 1984). Sunderland's **Shaun Elliott** was banned from the 1985 Milk Cup Final. Roeder was banned from QPR's 1982 Cup Final replay against Tottenham, and Foster was ruled out of the first match in Brighton's 1983 Final against Manchester Utd.

RED CARD FOR KICKING BALL-BOY

Chelsea's **Eden Hazard** was sent off (80 mins) in the League Cup semi-final, second leg at Swansea on Jan 23, 2013 for kicking a 17-year-old ball-boy who refused to hand over the ball that had gone out of play. The FA suspended Hazard for three matches.

BOOKINGS RECORDS

Most players of one Football League club booked in one match is **TEN** – members of the Mansfield team away to Crystal Palace in FA Cup third round, Jan 1963. Most yellow cards for one team in Premier League match – **8** for West Ham away to QPR, Oct 1, 2012.

Fastest bookings – 3 seconds after kick-off, **Vinnie Jones** (Chelsea, home to Sheffield Utd, FA Cup fifth round, Feb 15, 1992); 5 seconds after kick-off: **Vinnie Jones** (Sheffield Utd, away to Manchester City, Div 1, Jan 19, 1991). He was sent-off (54 mins) for second bookable offence.

FIGHTING TEAM-MATES

Charlton's **Mike Flanagan** and **Derek Hales** were sent off for fighting each other five minutes from end of FA Cup 3rd round tie at home to Southern League Maidstone on Jan 9, 1979.

Bradford City's **Andy Myers** and **Stuart McCall** had a fight during the 1-6 Premiership defeat at Leeds on Sunday, May 13, 2001.

On Sep 28, 1994 the Scottish FA suspended Hearts players **Graeme Hogg** and **Craig Levein** for ten matches for fighting each other in a pre-season 'friendly' v Raith.

Blackburn's England players **Graeme Le Saux** and **David Batty** clashed away to Spartak Moscow (Champions League) on Nov 22, 1995. Neither was sent off.

Newcastle United's England Internationals **Lee Bowyer** and **Kieron Dyer** were sent off for fighting each other at home to Aston Villa (Premiership on Apr 2, 2005).

Arsenal's **Emmanuel Adebayor** and **Nicklas Bendtner** clashed during the 5-1 Carling Cup semi-final 2nd leg defeat at Tottenham on Jan 22, 2008. Neither was sent off; each fined by their club.

Stoke's **Richardo Fuller** was sent off for slapping his captain, Andy Griffin, at West Ham in the Premier League on Dec 28, 2008.

FOOTBALL'S FIRST BETTING SCANDAL

A Football League investigation into the First Division match which ended Manchester Utd 2, Liverpool 0 at Old Trafford on Good Friday, Apr 2, 1915 proved that the result had been 'squared' by certain players betting on the outcome. Four members of each team were suspended for life, but some of the bans were lifted when League football resumed in 1919 in recognition of the players' war service.

PLAYERS JAILED

Ten professional footballers found guilty of conspiracy to fraud by 'fixing' matches for betting purposes were given prison sentences at Nottingham Assizes on Jan 26, 1965.

Jimmy Gauld (Mansfield), described as the central figure, was given four years. Among the others sentenced, **Tony Kay** (Sheffield Wed, Everton & England), **Peter Swan** (Sheffield Wed & England) and **David 'Bronco' Layne** (Sheffield Wed) were suspended from football for life by the FA.

DRUGS BANS

Abel Xavier (Middlesbrough) was the first Premiership player found to have taken a performance-enchancing drug. He was banned by UEFA for 18 months in Nov 2005 after testing positive for an anabolic steroid. The ban was reduced to a year in Jul 2006 by the Court of Arbitration for Sport. **Paddy Kenny** (Sheffield Utd goalkeeper) was suspended by an FA commission for 9 months from July, 2009 for failing a drugs test the previous May. Kolo Toure (Manchester City) received a 6-month ban in May 2011 for a doping offence. It was backdated to Mar 2.

LONG SUSPENSIONS

The longest suspension (8 months) in modern times for a player in British football was imposed on two Manchester Utd players. First was **Eric Cantona** following his attack on a spectator as he left the pitch after being sent off at Crystal Palace (Prem League) on Jan 25, 1995. The club immediately suspended him to the end of the season and fined him 2 weeks' wages (est £20,000). Then, on a disrepute charge, the FA fined him £10,000 (Feb 1995) and extended the ban to Sep 30 (which FIFA confirmed as world-wide). A subsequent 2-weeks' jail sentence on Cantona for assault was altered, on appeal, to 120 hours' community service, which took the form of coaching schoolboys in the Manchester area.

On **Dec 19, 2003** an FA Commission, held at Bolton, suspended **Rio Ferdinand** from football for 8 months (plus £50,000 fine) for failing to take a random drug test at the club's training ground on Sep 23. The ban operated from Jan 12, 2004.

Aug 1974: Kevin Keegan (Liverpool) and **Billy Bremner** (Leeds) both suspended for 10 matches and fined £500 after being sent off in FA Charity Shield at Wembley.

Jan 1988: Mark Dennis (QPR) given 8-match ban after 11th sending-off of his career.

Oct 1988: Paul Davis (Arsenal) banned for 9 matches for breaking the jaw of Southampton's Glenn Cockerill.

Oct 1998: Paolo Di Canio (Sheff Wed) banned for 11 matches and fined £10,000 for pushing referee Paul Alcock after being sent off at home to Arsenal (Prem), Sep 26.

Mar 2005: David Prutton (Southampton) banned for 10 matches (plus 1 for red card) and fined £6,000 by FA for shoving referee Alan Wiley when sent off at home to Arsenal (Prem), Feb 26.

Aug 2006: Ben Thatcher (Manchester City) banned for 8 matches for elbowing Pedro Mendes (Portsmouth).

Sep 2008: Joey Barton (Newcastle) banned for 12 matches (6 suspended) and fined £25,000 by FA for training ground assault on former Manchester City team-mate Ousmane Dabo.

May 2012: Joey Barton (QPR) suspended for 12 matches and fined £75,000 for violent conduct when sent off against Manchester City on final day of Premier League season.

Mar 2014: Joss Labadie (Torquay) banned for 10 matches and fined £2,000 for biting Chesterfield's Ollie Banks (Lge 2) on Feb 15, 2014.

Seven-month ban: Frank Barson, 37-year-old Watford centre-half, sent off at home to Fulham (Div 3 South) on Sep 29, 1928, was suspended by the FA for the remainder of the season.

Twelve-month ban: Oldham full-back **Billy Cook** was given a 12-month suspension for refusing to leave the field when sent off at Middlesbrough (Div 1), on Apr 3, 1915. The referee abandoned the match with 35 minutes still to play, and the score (4-1 to Middlesbrough) was ordered to stand.

Long Scottish bans: Sep 1954: Willie Woodburn, Rangers and Scotland centre-half, suspended for rest of career after fifth sending-off in 6 years.

Billy McLafferty, Stenhousemuir striker, was banned (Apr 14) for 8 and a half months, to Jan 1, 1993, and fined £250 for failing to appear at a disciplinary hearing after being sent off against Arbroath on Feb 1.

Twelve-match ban: On May 12, 1994 Scottish FA suspended Rangers forward **Duncan Ferguson** for 12 matches for violent conduct v Raith on Apr 16. On Oct 11, 1995, Ferguson (then with Everton) sent to jail for 3 months for the assault (served 44 days); Feb 1, 1996 Scottish judge quashed 7 matches that remained of SFA ban on Ferguson.

On Sep 29, 2001 the SFA imposed a **17-match suspension** on Forfar's former Scottish international **Dave Bowman** for persistent foul and abusive language when sent off against Stranraer on Sep 22. As his misconduct continued, he was shown **5 red cards** by the referee.

On Apr 3, 2009, captain **Barry Ferguson** and goalkeeper **Allan McGregor** were banned for life from playing for Scotland for gestures towards photographers while on the bench for a World Cup qualifier against Iceland.

On Dec 20, 2011 Liverpool and Uruguay striker **Luis Suarez** was given an 8-match ban and fined £40,000 by the FA for making 'racially offensive comments' to Patrice Evra of Manchester Utd (Prem Lge, Oct 15).

On Apr 25, 2013 **Luis Suarez** was given a 10-match suspension by the FA for 'violent conduct' – biting Chelsea defender Branislav Ivanovic, Prem Lge, Apr 21. The Liverpool player was also fined £200,000 by Liverpool. His ban covered the last 4 games of that season and the first 6 of 2013–14. On Jun 26, 2014, Suarez, while still a Liverpool player, received the most severe punishment in World Cup history – a four-month ban from 'all football activities' and £66,000 fine from FIFA for biting Giorgio Chiellini during Uruguay's group game against Italy.

TOP FINES

Clubs: £49,000,000 (World record) Manchester City: May 2014 for breaking UEFA Financial Fair Play rules (**£32,600,000** suspended subject to City meeting certain conditions over two seasons). **£5,500,000** West Ham: Apr 2007, for breaches of regulations involving 'dishonesty and deceit' over Argentine signings Carlos Tevez and Javier Mascherano; **£1,500,000** (increased from original £600,000) Tottenham: Dec 1994, financial irregularities; **£875,000** QPR: May 2011 for breaching rules when signing Argentine Alejandro Faurlin; **£300,000** (reduced to £75,000 on appeal) Chelsea: Jun 2005, illegal approach to Arsenal's Ashley Cole; **£200,000** Aston Villa: May 2015 for fans' pitch invasion after FA Cup quarter-final v WBA; **£175,000** Arsenal: Oct 2003, players' brawl v Manchester Utd; **£150,000** Leeds: Mar 2000, players' brawl v Tottenham; **£150,000** Tottenham: Mar 2000, players brawl v Leeds; **£145,000** Hull: Feb 2015, breaching Financial Fair Play rules; **£115,000** West Ham: Aug 2009, crowd misconduct at Carling Cup; v Millwall; **£105,000** Chelsea: Jan 1991, irregular payments; **£100,000** Boston Utd: Jul 2002, contract irregularities; **£100,000** Arsenal and Chelsea: Mar 2007 for mass brawl after Carling Cup Final; **£100,000** (including suspended fine) Blackburn: Aug 2007, poor disciplinary record; **£100,000** Sunderland: May 2014, breaching agents' regulations; **£90,000** Brighton: Feb 2015, breaching rules on agents; **£71,000** West Ham: Feb 2015 for playing Diafra Sakho in FA Cup 4th round tie against Bristol City after declaring him unfit for Senegal's Africa Cup of Nations squad; **£62,000** Macclesfield: Dec 2005, funding of a stand at club's ground.

Players: £220,000 (plus 4-match ban) John Terry (Chelsea): Sep 2012, racially abusing Anton Ferdinand (QPR); **£150,000** Roy Keane (Manchester Utd): Oct 2002, disrepute offence over autobiography; **£100,000** (reduced to £75,000 on appeal) Ashley Cole (Arsenal): Jun 2005, illegal approach by Chelsea; **£90,000** Ashley Cole (Chelsea): Oct 2012, offensive Tweet against FA; **£80,000 (plus 5-match ban)** Nicolas Anelka (WBA): Feb 2014, celebrating goal at West Ham with racially-offensive 'quenelle' gesture; **£75,000 (plus 12-match ban)** Joey Barton

(QPR): May 2012, violent conduct v Manchester City; **£60,000 (plus 3-match ban)** John Obi Mikel (Chelsea): Dec 2012, abusing referee Mark Clattenburg after Prem Lge v Manchester Utd); **£60,000** Dexter Blackstock (Nottm Forest): May 2014, breaching betting rules; **£50,000** Cameron Jerome (Stoke): Aug 2013, breaching FA betting rules; **£50,000** Benoit Assou-Ekotto (Tottenham): Sep 2014, publicly backing Nicolas Anelka's controversial 'quenelle' gesture; **£45,000** Patrick Vieira (Arsenal): Oct 1999, tunnel incidents v West Ham; **£45,000** Rio Ferdinand (Manchester Utd): Aug 2012, improper comments about Ashley Cole on Twitter; **£40,000** Lauren (Arsenal): Oct 2003, players' fracas v Manchester Utd; **£40,000 (plus 8-match ban)** Luis Suarez (Liverpool): Dec 2011, racially abusing Patrice Evra (Manchester Utd); **£40,000 (plus 3-match ban)** Dani Osvaldo (Southampton): Jan 2014, violent conduct, touchline Newcastle.

*In eight seasons with Arsenal (1996–2004) **Patrick Vieira** was fined a total of £122,000 by the FA for disciplinary offences.

Managers: £200,000 (reduced to £75,000 on appeal) Jose Mourinho (Chelsea): Jun 2005, illegal approach to Arsenal's Ashley Cole; **£60,000 (plus 7-match ban)** Alan Pardew (Newcastle): head-butting Hull player David Meyler (also fined £100,000 by club); **£33,000 (plus 3-match Euro ban)** Arsene Wenger (Arsenal): Mar 2012, criticising referee after Champions League defeat by AC Milan; **£30,000** Sir Alex Ferguson (Manchester Utd): Mar 2011 criticising referee Martin Atkinson v Chelsea; **£30,000 (plus 6-match ban (plus 6-match ban reduced to 4 on appeal)** Rui Faria (Chelsea assistant): May 2014, confronting match officials v Sunderland.

• Jonathan Barnett, Ashley Cole's agent was fined **£100,000** in Sep 2006 for his role in the 'tapping up' affair involving the player and Chelsea.

*£68,000 FA: May 2003, pitch invasions and racist chanting by fans during England v Turkey, Sunderland.

£50,000 FA: Dec 2014, for Wigan owner-chairman Dave Whelan, plus 6-week ban from all football activity, for remarks about Jewish and Chinese people in newspaper interview.

MANAGERS

INTERNATIONAL RECORDS
(As at start of season 2015–16)

	P	W	D	L	F	A
Roy Hodgson (England – appointed May 2012)	41	23	13	5	81	32
Gordon Strachan (Scotland – appointed Jan 2013	21	11	4	6	28	21
Chris Coleman (Wales – appointed Jan 2012)	23	9	5	9	23	31
Michael O'Neill (Northern Ireland – appointed Oct 2011)	26	5	9	12	21	39
Martin O'Neill (Republic of Ireland) - appointed Nov 2013)	15	5	7	3	24	11

ENGLAND MANAGERS

		P	W	D	L
1946–62	**Walter Winterbottom**	139	78	33	28
1963–74	**Sir Alf Ramsey**	113	69	27	17
1974	**Joe Mercer**, caretaker	7	3	3	1
1974–77	**Don Revie**	29	14	8	7
1977–82	**Ron Greenwood**	55	33	12	10
1982–90	**Bobby Robson**	95	47	30	18
1990–93	**Graham Taylor**	38	18	13	7
1994–96	**Terry Venables**	23	11	11	1
1996–99	**Glenn Hoddle**	28	17	6	5
1999	**Howard Wilkinson**, caretaker	1	0	0	1
1999–2000	**Kevin Keegan**	18	7	7	4
2000	**Howard Wilkinson**, caretaker	1	0	1	0
2000	**Peter Taylor**, caretaker	1	0	0	1
2001–06	**Sven-Goran Eriksson**	67	40	17	10
2006–07	**Steve McClaren**	18	9	4	5
2007–12	**Fabio Capello**	42	28	8	6

INTERNATIONAL MANAGER CHANGES

England: Walter Winterbottom 1946–62 (initially coach); **Alf Ramsey** (Feb 1963–May 1974); **Joe Mercer** (caretaker May 1974); **Don Revie** (Jul 1974–Jul 1977); **Ron Greenwood** (Aug 1977–Jul 1982); **Bobby Robson** (Jul 1982–Jul 1990); **Graham Taylor** (Jul 1990–Nov 1993); **Terry Venables**, coach (Jan 1994–Jun 1996); **Glenn Hoddle**, coach (Jun 1996–Feb 1999); **Howard Wilkinson** (caretaker Feb 1999); **Kevin Keegan coach** (Feb 1999–Oct 2000); **Howard Wilkinson** (caretaker Oct 2000); **Peter Taylor** (caretaker Nov 2000); **Sven–Goran Eriksson** (Jan 2001–Aug 2006); **Steve McClaren** (Aug 2006–Nov 2007); **Fabio Capello** (Dec 2007– Feb 2012); **Roy Hodgson** (since May 2012).

Scotland (modern): Bobby Brown (Feb 1967–Jul 1971); **Tommy Docherty** (Sep 1971–Dec 1972); **Willie Ormond** (Jan 1973–May 1977); **Ally MacLeod** (May 1977–Sep 1978); **Jock Stein** (Oct 1978–Sep 1985); **Alex Ferguson** (caretaker Oct 1985–Jun 1986); **Andy Roxburgh**, coach (Jul 1986–Sep 1993); **Craig Brown** (Sep 1993–Oct 2001); **Berti Vogts** (Feb 2002–Oct 2004); **Walter Smith** (Dec 2004–Jan 2007); **Alex McLeish** (Jan 2007–Nov 2007); **George Burley** (Jan 2008–Nov 2009); **Craig Levein** (Dec 2009–Nov 2012); **Billy Stark** (caretaker Nov–Dec 2012); **Gordon Strachan** (since Jan 2013).

Northern Ireland (modern): Peter Doherty (1951–62); **Bertie Peacock** (1962–67); **Billy Bingham** (1967–Aug 1971); **Terry Neill** (Aug 1971–Mar 1975); **Dave Clements** (player-manager Mar 1975–1976); **Danny Blanchflower** (Jun 1976–Nov 1979); **Billy Bingham** (Feb 1980–Nov 1993); **Bryan Hamilton** Feb 1994–Feb 1998); **Lawrie McMenemy** (Feb 1998–Nov 1999); **Sammy McIlroy** (Jan 2000–Oct 2003); **Lawrie Sanchez** (Jan 2004–May 2007); **Nigel Worthington** (May 2007–Oct 2011); **Michael O'Neill** (since Oct 2011).

Wales (modern): Mike Smith (Jul 1974–Dec 1979); **Mike England** (Mar 1980–Feb 1988); **David Williams** (caretaker Mar 1988); **Terry Yorath** (Apr 1988–Nov 1993); **John Toshack** (Mar 1994, one match); **Mike Smith** (Mar 1994–Jun 1995); **Bobby Gould** (Aug 1995–Jun 1999); **Mark Hughes** (Aug 1999 – Oct 2004); **John Toshack** (Nov 2004–Sep 2010); Brian Flynn (caretaker Sep–Dec 2010); **Gary Speed** (Dec 2010–Nov 2011); **Chris Coleman** (since Jan 2012).

Republic of Ireland (modern): Liam Tuohy (Sep 1971–Nov 1972); **Johnny Giles** (Oct 1973– Apr 1980, initially player–manager); **Eoin Hand** (Jun 1980–Nov 1985); **Jack Charlton** (Feb 1986–Dec 1995); **Mick McCarthy** (Feb 1996–Oct 2002); **Brian Kerr** (Jan 2003–Oct 2005); **Steve Staunton** (Jan 2006–Oct 2007); **Giovanni Trapattoni** (May 2008–Sep 2013); **Martin O'Neill** (since Nov 2013).

WORLD CUP-WINNING MANAGERS

1930 Uruguay (Alberto Suppici); 1934 and 1938 Italy (Vittorio Pozzo); 1950 Uruguay (Juan Lopez Fontana); 1954 West Germany (Sepp Herberger); 1958 Brazil (Vicente Feola); 1962 Brazil (Aymore Moreira); 1966 England (Sir Alf Ramsey); 1970 Brazil (Mario Zagallo); 1974 West Germany (Helmut Schon); 1978 Argentina (Cesar Luis Menotti); 1982 Italy (Enzo Bearzot); 1986 Argentina (Carlos Bilardo); 1990 West Germany (Franz Beckenbauer); 1994 Brazil (Carlos Alberto Parreira); 1998 France (Aimee Etienne Jacquet); 2002 Brazil (Luiz Felipe Scolari); 2006 Italy (Marcello Lippi); 2010 Spain (Vicente Del Bosque); 2014 Germany (Joachim Low).

Each of the 20 winning teams had a manager/coach of that country's nationality.

YOUNGEST LEAGUE MANAGERS

Ivor Broadis, 23, appointed player-manager of Carlisle, Aug 1946; **Chris Brass**, 27, appointed player-manager of York, Jun 2003; **Terry Neill**, 28, appointed player manager of Hull, Jun 1970; **Graham Taylor**, 28, appointed manager of Lincoln, Dec 1972.

LONGEST-SERVING LEAGUE MANAGERS – ONE CLUB

Fred Everiss, secretary–manager of WBA for 46 years (1902–48); **George Ramsay**, secretary– manager of Aston Villa for 42 years (1884–1926); **John Addenbrooke**, Wolves, for 37 years (1885–1922). Since last war: **Sir Alex Ferguson** at Manchester Utd for 27 seasons (1986– 2013); **Sir Matt Busby**, in charge of Manchester Utd for 25 seasons (1945–69, 1970–71;

Dario Gradi at Crewe for 26 years (1983–2007, 2009–11); **Jimmy Seed** at Charlton for 23 years (1933–56); **Brian Clough** at Nottm Forest for 18 years (1975–93); **Arsene Wenger** at Arsenal for 18 years (1996-to-date).

LAST ENGLISH MANAGER TO WIN CHAMPIONSHIP

Howard Wilkinson (Leeds), season 1991–92.

1,000-TIME MANAGERS

Only six have managed in more than **1,000 English League games**: Alec Stock, Brian Clough, Jim Smith, Graham Taylor, Dario Gradi and Sir Alex Ferguson.

Sir Matt Busby, Dave Bassett, Lennie Lawrence, Alan Buckley, Denis Smith, Joe Royle, Ron Atkinson, Brian Horton, Neil Warnock, Harry Redknapp, Graham Turner, Steve Coppell, Roy Hodgson, Arsene Wenger, Len Ashurst, Lawrie McMenemy, Sir Bobby Robson and Danny Wilson have each managed more than **1,000 matches in all first class competitions**.

SHORT-TERM MANAGERS

Departed

3 days	Bill Lambton (Scunthorpe)	Apr 1959
7 days	Tim Ward (Exeter)	Mar 1953
7 days	Kevin Cullis (Swansea City)	Feb 1996
8 days	Billy McKinlay (Watford)	Oct 2014
10 days	Dave Cowling (Doncaster)	Oct 1997
10 days	Peter Cormack (Cowdenbeath)	Dec 2000
13 days	Johnny Cochrane (Reading)	Apr 1939
13 days	Micky Adams (Swansea City)	Oct 1997
16 days	Jimmy McIlroy (Bolton)	Nov 1970
19 days	Martin Allen (Barnet)	Apr 2011
20 days	Paul Went (Leyton Orient)	Oct 1981
27 days	Malcolm Crosby (Oxford Utd)	Jan 1998
27 days	Oscar Garcia (Watford)	Sep 2014
28 days	Tommy Docherty (QPR)	Dec 1968
28 days	Paul Hart (QPR)	Jan 2010
32 days	Steve Coppell (Manchester City)	Nov 1996
32 days	Darko Milanic (Leeds)	Oct 2014
34 days	Niall Quinn (Sunderland)	Aug 2006
36 days	Steve Claridge (Millwall)	Jul 2005
39 days	Paul Gascoigne (Kettering)	Dec 2005
40 days	Alex McLeish (Nottm Forest)	Feb 2013
41 days	Steve Wicks (Lincoln)	Oct 1995
41 days	Les Reed (Charlton)	Dec 2006
43 days	Mauro Milanese (Leyton Orient)	Dec 2014
44 days	Brian Clough (Leeds)	Sep 1974
44 days	Jock Stein (Leeds)	Oct 1978
45 days	Paul Murray (Hartlepool)	Dec 2014
48 days	John Toshack (Wales)	Mar 1994
48 days	David Platt (Sampdoria coach)	Feb 1999
49 days	Brian Little (Wolves)	Oct 1986
49 days	Terry Fenwick (Northampton)	Feb 2003
57 days	Henning Berg (Blackburn)	Dec 2012
61 days	Bill McGarry (Wolves)	Nov 1985

- In May 1984, Crystal Palace named **Dave Bassett** as manager, but he changed his mind four days later, without signing the contract, and returned to Wimbledon.
- In May 2007, **Leroy Rosenior** was reportedly appointed manager of Torquay after relegation and sacked ten minutes later when the club came under new ownership.

- **Brian Laws** lost his job at Scunthorpe on Mar 25, 2004 and was reinstated three weeks later.
- In an angry outburst after a play-off defeat in May 1992, Barnet chairman Stan Flashman sacked manager **Barry Fry** and re-instated him a day later.

EARLY-SEASON MANAGER SACKINGS

2012: Andy Thorn (Coventry) 8 days; John Sheridan (Chesterfield) 10 days; **2011:** Jim Jefferies (Hearts) 9 days; **2010** Kevin Blackwell (Sheffield Utd) 8 days; **2009** Bryan Gunn (Norwich) 6 days; **2007:** Neil McDonald (Carlisle) 2 days; Martin Allen (Leicester) 18 days; **2004:** Paul Sturrock (Southampton) 9 days; **2004:** Sir Bobby Robson (Newcastle) 16 days; **2003:** Glenn Roeder (West Ham) 15 days; **2000:** Alan Buckley (Grimsby) 10 days; **1997:** Kerry Dixon (Doncaster) 12 days; **1996:** Sammy Chung (Doncaster) on morning of season's opening League match; **1996:** Alan Ball (Manchester City) 12 days; **1994:** Kenny Hibbitt (Walsall) and Kenny Swain (Wigan) 20 days; **1993:** Peter Reid (Manchester City) 12 days; **1991:** Don Mackay (Blackburn) 14 days; **1989:** Mick Jones (Peterborough) 12 days; **1980:** Bill McGarry (Newcastle) 13 days; **1979:** Dennis Butler (Port Vale) 12 days; **1977:** George Petchey (Leyton O) 13 days; **1977:** Willie Bell (Birmingham) 16 days; **1971:** Len Richley (Darlington) 12 days.

RECORD START FOR MANAGER

Russ Wilcox, appointed by Scunthorpe in Nov 2013, remained unbeaten in his first 28 league matches (14 won, 14 drawn) and took the club to promotion from League Two. It was the most successful start to a managerial career In English football, beating the record of 23 unbeaten games by Preston's William Sudell in 1889.

RECORD TOP DIVISION START

Arsenal were unbeaten in 17 league matches from the start of season 1947-48 under new manager **Tom Whittaker**.

SACKED, REINSTATED, FINISHED

Brian McDermott was sacked as Leeds manager on Jan 31, 2014. The following day, he was reinstated. At the end of the season, with the club under new ownership, he left by 'mutual consent.'

CARETAKER SUPREME

As Chelsea's season collapsed, Andre Villas-Boas was sacked in March 2012 after eight months as manager, 2012. Roberto Di Matteo was appointed caretaker and by the season's end his team had won the FA Cup and the Champions League.

MANAGER DOUBLES

Four managers have won the League Championship with different clubs: **Tom Watson**, secretary–manager with Sunderland (1892–93–95) and **Liverpool** (1901); **Herbert Chapman** with Huddersfield (1923–24, 1924–25) and Arsenal (1930–31, 1932–33); **Brian Clough** with Derby (1971–72) and Nottm Forest (1977–78); **Kenny Dalglish** with Liverpool (1985–86, 1987–88, 1989–90) and Blackburn (1994–95).

Managers to win the FA Cup with different clubs: **Billy Walker** (Sheffield Wed 1935, Nottm Forest 1959); **Herbert Chapman** (Huddersfield 1922, Arsenal 1930).

Kenny Dalglish (Liverpool) and **George Graham** (Arsenal) completed the Championship/FA Cup double as both player and manager with a single club. **Joe Mercer** won the title as a player with Everton, the title twice and FA Cup as a player with Arsenal and both competitions as manager of Manchester City.

CHAIRMAN–MANAGER

On Dec 20, 1988, after two years on the board, Dundee Utd manager **Jim McLean** was elected chairman, too. McLean, Scotland's longest-serving manager (appointed on Nov 24, 1971), resigned at end of season 1992–93 (remained chairman).

Ron Noades was chairman-manager of Brentford from Jul 1998–Mar 2001. **John Reames** did both jobs at Lincoln from Nov 1998–Apr 2000)

Niall Quinn did both jobs for five weeks in 2006 before appointing Roy Keane as manager of Sunderland.

TOP DIVISION PLAYER–MANAGERS

Les Allen (QPR 1968–69); **Johnny Giles** (WBA 1976–77); **Howard Kendall** (Everton 1981–82); **Kenny Dalglish** (Liverpool, 1985–90); **Trevor Francis** (QPR, 1988–89); **Terry Butcher** (Coventry, 1990–91), **Peter Reid** (Manchester City, 1990–93), **Trevor Francis** (Sheffield Wed, 1991–94), **Glenn Hoddle**, (Chelsea, 1993–95), **Bryan Robson** (Middlesbrough, 1994–97), **Ray Wilkins** (QPR, 1994–96), **Ruud Gullit** (Chelsea, 1996–98), **Gianluca Vialli** (Chelsea, 1998–2000).

FIRST FOREIGN MANAGER IN ENGLISH LEAGUE

Uruguayan **Danny Bergara** (Rochdale 1988–89).

COACHING KINGS OF EUROPE

Five coaches have won the European Cup/Champions League with two different clubs: **Ernst Happel** with Feyenoord (1970) and Hamburg (1983); **Ottmar Hitzfeld** with Borussia Dortmund (1997) and Bayern Munich (2001); **Jose Mourinho** with Porto (2004) and Inter Milan (2010); **Jupp Heynckes** with Real Madrid (1998) and Bayern Munich (2013); **Carlo Ancelotti** with AC Milan (2003, 2007) and Real Madrid (2014).

FOREIGN TRIUMPH

Former Dutch star **Ruud Gullit** became the first foreign manager to win a major English competition when Chelsea took the FA Cup in 1997.

Arsene Wenger and **Gerard Houllier** became the first foreign managers to receive recognition when they were awarded honorary OBEs in the Queen's Birthday Honours in Jun 2003 'for their contribution to English football and Franco–British relations'.

MANAGERS OF POST-WAR CHAMPIONS (*Double winners)

1947 George Kay (Liverpool); **1948** Tom Whittaker (Arsenal); **1949** Bob Jackson (Portsmouth).

1950 Bob Jackson (Portsmouth); **1951** Arthur Rowe (Tottenham); **1952** Matt Busby (Manchester Utd); **1953** Tom Whittaker (Arsenal); **1954** Stan Cullis (Wolves); **1955** Ted Drake (Chelsea); **1956** Matt Busby (Manchester Utd); **1957** Matt Busby (Manchester Utd); **1958** Stan Cullis (Wolves); **1959** Stan Cullis (Wolves).

1960 Harry Potts (Burnley); **1961** *Bill Nicholson (Tottenham); **1962** Alf Ramsey (Ipswich); **1963** Harry Catterick (Everton); **1964** Bill Shankly (Liverpool); **1965** Matt Busby (Manchester Utd); **1966** Bill Shankly (Liverpool); **1967** Matt Busby (Manchester Utd); **1968** Joe Mercer (Manchester City); **1969** Don Revie (Leeds).

1970 Harry Catterick (Everton); **1971** *Bertie Mee (Arsenal); **1972** Brian Clough (Derby); **1973** Bill Shankly (Liverpool); **1974** Don Revie (Leeds); **1975** Dave Mackay (Derby); **1976** Bob Paisley (Liverpool); **1977** Bob Paisley (Liverpool); **1978** Brian Clough (Nottm Forest); **1979** Bob Paisley (Liverpool).

1980 Bob Paisley (Liverpool); **1981** Ron Saunders (Aston Villa); **1982** Bob Paisley (Liverpool); **1983** Bob Paisley (Liverpool); **1984** Joe Fagan (Liverpool); **1985** Howard Kendall (Everton); **1986** *Kenny Dalglish (Liverpool – player/manager); **1987** Howard Kendall (Everton); **1988** Kenny Dalglish (Liverpool – player/manager); **1989** George Graham (Arsenal).

1990 Kenny Dalglish (Liverpool); **1991** George Graham (Arsenal); **1992** Howard Wilkinson (Leeds); **1993** Alex Ferguson (Manchester Utd); **1994** *Alex Ferguson (Manchester Utd); **1995** Kenny Dalglish (Blackburn); **1996** *Alex Ferguson (Manchester Utd); **1997** Alex Ferguson (Manchester Utd); **1998** *Arsene Wenger (Arsenal); **1999** *Alex Ferguson (Manchester Utd).

2000 Sir Alex Ferguson (Manchester Utd); **2001** Sir Alex Ferguson (Manchester Utd); **2002** *Arsene Wenger (Arsenal); **2003** Sir Alex Ferguson (Manchester Utd); **2004** Arsene Wenger (Arsenal); **2005** Jose Mourinho (Chelsea); **2006** Jose Mourinho (Chelsea); **2007** Sir Alex Ferguson (Manchester Utd); **2008** Sir Alex Ferguson (Manchester Utd); **2009** Sir Alex

Ferguson (Manchester Utd); **2010** *Carlo Ancelotti (Chelsea); **2011** Sir Alex Ferguson (Manchester Utd); **2012** Roberto Mancini (Manchester City); **2013** Sir Alex Ferguson (Manchester Utd); **2014** Manuel Pellegrini (Manchester City); **2015** Jose Mourinho (Chelsea).

WORLD NO 1 MANAGER

When **Sir Alex Ferguson**, 71, retired in May 2013, he ended the most successful managerial career in the game's history. He took Manchester United to a total of 38 prizes - 13 Premier League titles, 5 FA Cup triumphs, 4 League Cups, 10 Charity/Community Shields (1 shared), 2 Champions League wins, 1 Cup-Winners' Cup, 1 FIFA Club World Cup, 1 Inter-Continental Cup and 1 UEFA Super Cup. Having played centre-forward for Rangers, the Glaswegian managed 3 Scottish clubs, East Stirling, St Mirren and then Aberdeen, where he broke the Celtic/Rangers duopoly with 9 successes: 3 League Championships, 4 Scottish Cups, 1 League Cup and 1 UEFA Cup. Appointed at Old Trafford in November 1986, when replacing Ron Atkinson, he did not win a prize there until his fourth season (FA Cup 1990), but thereafter the club's trophy cabinet glittered with silverware. His total of 1,500 matches in charge ended with a 5-5 draw away to West Bromwich Albion. The longest-serving manager in the club's history, he constructed 4 triumphant teams. Sir Alex was knighted in 1999 and in 2012 he received the FIFA award for services to football. On retirement from management, he became a director and club ambassador. United maintained the dynasty of long-serving Scottish managers (Sir Matt Busby for 24 seasons) by appointing David Moyes, who had been in charge at Everton for 11 years.

MANAGERS' EURO TREBLES

Two managers have won the European Cup/Champions League three times. **Bob Paisley** did it with Liverpool (1977,78, 81).
Carlo Ancelotti's successes were with AC Milan in 2003 and 2007 and with Real Madrid in 2014.

WINNER MOURINHO

In winning the Premier League and League Cup in 2015, Jose Mourinho embellished his reputation as Chelsea's most successful manager. Those achievements took his total of honours in two spells at the club to 8: 3 Premier League, 3 League Cup, 1 FA Cup, 1 Community Shield. Joining from Portuguese champions Porto, Mourinho was initially with Chelsea from June 2004 to September 2007. He then successfully coached Inter Milan and Real Madrid before returning to Stamford Bridge in June 2013. His Premier League triumph in 2015 was his eighth title In 11 years in four countries (England 3, Portugal 2, Italy 2, Spain 1). He starts season 2015-16 with the remarkable six-season Chelsea home record of only one loss in 98 Premier League matches (W76, D21, goals 207-48). That one defeat was by 2-1 against Sunderland on April 19, 2014.

WENGER'S CUP AGAIN

Holder's Arsenal's win against Aston Villa in the 2015 Final was a record 12th success for them in the FA Cup and a sixth triumph in the competition for manager Arsene Wenger, equalling the record of George Ramsay for Villa (1887-1920). With his sixth victory in seven Finals, Wenger made history as the first manager to win the Cup in successive seasons twice (previously in 2002 and 2003).

RECORD MANAGER FEE

Chelsea paid Porto a record £13.25m compensation when they appointed **Andre Villas-Boas** as manager in June 2011. He lasted less than nine months at Stamford Bridge.

FATHER AND SON MANAGERS WITH SAME CLUB

Fulham: Bill Dodgin Snr 1949-53; Bill Dodgin Jnr 1968-72. **Brentford:** Bill Dodgin Snr 1953-57; Bill Dodgin Jnr 1976-80. **Bournemouth:** John Bond 1970-73; Kevin Bond 2006-08. **Derby:** Brian Clough 1967-73; Nigel Clough 2009.

SIR BOBBY'S HAT-TRICK

Sir Bobby Robson, born and brought up in County Durham, achieved a unique hat-trick when he received the Freedom of Durham in Dec 2008. He had already been awarded the Freedom of Ipswich and Newcastle. He died in July 2009 and had an express loco named after him on the East Coast to London line.

MANAGERS WITH MOST FA CUP SUCCESSES

6 Arsene Wenger (Arsenal), George Ramsay (Aston Villa); 5 Sir Alex Ferguson (Manchester Utd); 3 Charles Foweraker (Bolton), John Nicholson (Sheffield Utd), Bill Nicholson (Tottenham).

RELEGATION 'DOUBLES'

Managers associated with two clubs relegated in same season: **John Bond** in 1985–86 (Swansea City and Birmingham); **Ron Saunders** in 1985–86 (WBA – and their reserve team – and Birmingham); **Bob Stokoe** in 1986–87 (Carlisle and Sunderland); **Billy McNeill** in 1986–87 (Manchester City and Aston Villa); **Dave Bassett** in 1987–88 (Watford and Sheffield Utd); **Mick Mills** in 1989–90 (Stoke and Colchester); **Gary Johnson** in 2014-15 (Yeovil and Cheltenham)

THREE FA CUP DEFEATS IN ONE SEASON

Manager **Michael Appleton** suffered three FA Cup defeats in season 2012-13, with Portsmouth (v Notts Co, 1st rd); Blackpool (v Fulham, 3rd rd); Blackburn (v Millwall, 6th rd).

WEMBLEY STADIUM

NEW WEMBLEY

A new era for English football began in March 2007 with the completion of the new national stadium. The 90,000-seater arena was hailed as one of the world's finest – but came at a price. Costs soared, the project fell well behind schedule and disputes involving the FA, builders Multiplex and the Government were rife. The old stadium, opened in 1923, cost £750,000. The new one, originally priced at £326m in 2000, ended up at around £800m. The first international after completion was an Under-21 match between England and Italy. The FA Cup returned to its spiritual home after being staged at the Millennium Stadium in Cardiff for six seasons. Then, England's senior team were back for a friendly against Brazil.

DROGBA'S WEMBLEY RECORD

Didier Drogba's FA Cup goal for Chelsea against Liverpool in May 2012 meant that he had scored in all his 8 competitive appearances for the club at Wembley. (7 wins, 1 defeat). They came in: 2007 FA Cup Final (1-0 v Manchester Utd); 2008 League Cup Final (1-2 v Tottenham); 2009 FA Cup semi-final (2-1 v Arsenal); 2009 FA Cup Final (2-1 v Everton); 2010 FA Cup semi-final (3-0 v Aston Villa); 2010 FA Cup Final (1-0 v Portsmouth); 2012 FA Cup semi-final (5-1 v Tottenham); 2012 FA Cup Final (2-1 v Liverpool).

INVASION DAY

Memorable scenes were witnessed at the first **FA Cup Final at Wembley**, Apr 28, 1923, between **Bolton** and **West Ham**. An accurate return of the attendance could not be made owing to thousands breaking in, but there were probably more than 200,000 spectators present. The match was delayed for 40 minutes by the crowd invading the pitch. Official attendance was 126,047. Gate receipts totalled £27,776. The two clubs and the FA each received £6,365 and the FA refunded £2,797 to ticket-holders who were unable to get to their seats. Cup Final admission has since been by ticket only.

REDUCED CAPACITY

Capacity of the all-seated Wembley Stadium was 78,000. The last 100,000 attendance was for the 1985 FA Cup Final between Manchester Utd and Everton. Crowd record for New Wembley: 89,874 for 2008 FA Cup Final (Portsmouth v Cardiff).

WEMBLEY'S FIRST UNDER LIGHTS

Nov 30, 1955 (England 4, Spain 1), when the floodlights were switched on after 73 minutes (afternoon match played in damp, foggy conditions).
First Wembley international played throughout under lights: England 8, N Ireland 3 on evening of Nov 20, 1963 (att: 55,000).

MOST WEMBLEY APPEARANCES

59 by **Tony Adams** (35 England, 24 Arsenal); 57 by **Peter Shilton** (52 England, 3 Nottm Forest, 1 Leicester, 1 Football League X1).

WEMBLEY HAT-TRICKS

Three players have scored hat-tricks in major finals at Wembley: **Stan Mortensen** for Blackpool v Bolton (FA Cup Final, 1953), **Geoff Hurst** for England v West Germany (World Cup Final, 1966) and **David Speedie** for Chelsea v Manchester City (Full Members Cup, 1985).

ENGLAND'S WEMBLEY DEFEATS

England have lost 24 matches to foreign opponents at Wembley:

Nov 1953	3-6 v Hungary	**Sep 1991**	0-1 v Germany
Oct 1959	2-3 v Sweden	**Jun 1995**	1-3 v Brazil
Oct 1965	2-3 v Austria	**Feb 1997**	0-1 v Italy
Apr 1972	1-3 v W Germany	**Feb 1998**	0-2 v Chile
Nov 1973	0-1 v Italy	**Feb 1999**	0-2 v France
Feb 1977	0-2 v Holland	**Oct 2000**	0-1 v Germany
Mar 1981	1-2 v Spain	**Aug 2007**	1-2 v Germany
May 1981	0-1 v Brazil	**Nov 2007**	2-3 v Croatia
Oct 1982	1-2 v W Germany	**Nov 2010**	1-2 v France
Sep 1983	0-1 v Denmark	**Feb 2012**	2-3 v Holland
Jun 1984	0-2 v Russia	**Nov 2013**	0-2 v Chile
May 1990	1-2 v Uruguay	**Nov 2013**	0-1 v Germany

A further defeat came in Euro 96. After drawing the semi-final with Germany 1-1, England went out 6-5 on penalties.

FASTEST GOALS AT WEMBLEY

In first-class matches: **25 sec** by **Louis Saha** for Everton in 2009 FA Cup Final against Chelsea; **38 sec** by **Bryan Robson** for England's against Yugoslavia in 1989; **42 sec** by **Roberto Di Matteo** for Chelsea in 1997 FA Cup Final v Middlesbrough; **44 sec** by **Bryan Robson** for England v Northern Ireland in 1982.
Fastest goal in **any** match at Wembley: **20 sec** by **Maurice Cox** for Cambridge University against Oxford in 1979.

FOUR WEMBLEY HEADERS

When **Wimbledon** beat Sutton 4-2 in the FA Amateur Cup Final at Wembley on May 4, 1963, Irish centre-forward **Eddie Reynolds** headed all four goals.

WEMBLEY ONE-SEASON DOUBLES

In 1989, **Nottm Forest** became the first club to win two Wembley Finals in the same season (Littlewoods Cup and Simod Cup).
In 1993, **Arsenal** made history there as the first club to win the League (Coca-Cola) Cup and the FA Cup in the same season. They beat Sheffield Wed 2-1 in both finals.
In 2012, **York** won twice at Wembley in nine days at the end of the season, beating Newport 2-0 in the FA Trophy Final and Luton 2-1 in the Conference Play-off Final to return to the Football League.

SUDDEN-DEATH DECIDERS

First Wembley Final decided on sudden death (first goal scored in overtime): Apr 23, 1995 – **Birmingham** beat Carlisle (1-0, Paul Tait 103 mins) to win Auto Windscreens Shield.

First instance of a golden goal deciding a major international tournament was at Wembley on Jun 30, 1996, when **Germany** beat the Czech Republic 2-1 in the European Championship Final with Oliver Bierhoff's goal in the 95th minute.

WEMBLEY'S MOST ONE-SIDED FINAL (in major domestic cups)

Swansea 5 **Bradford City** 0 (League Cup, Feb 24, 2013).

FOOTBALL TRAGEDIES

DAYS OF TRAGEDY – CLUBS

Season 1988–89 brought the worst disaster in the history of British sport, with the death of 96 Liverpool supporters (200 injured) at the **FA Cup semi-final** against Nottm Forest at **Hillsborough, Sheffield**, on Saturday, Apr 15. The tragedy built up in the minutes preceding kick-off, when thousands surged into the ground at the Leppings Lane end. Many were crushed in the tunnel between entrance and terracing, but most of the victims were trapped inside the perimeter fencing behind the goal. The match was abandoned without score after six minutes' play. The dead included seven women and girls, two teenage sisters and two teenage brothers. The youngest victim was a boy of ten, the oldest 67-year-old Gerard Baron, whose brother Kevin played for Liverpool in the 1950 Cup Final. (*Total became 96 in Mar 1993, when Tony Bland died after being in a coma for nearly four years).

The two worst disasters in one season in British soccer history occurred at the end of 1984–85. On May 11, the last Saturday of the League season, 56 people (two of them visiting supporters) were burned to death – and more than 200 taken to hospital – when fire destroyed the main stand at the **Bradford City–Lincoln** match at Valley Parade.

The wooden, 77-year-old stand was full for City's last fixture before which, amid scenes of celebration, the club had been presented with the Third Division Championship trophy. The fire broke out just before half-time and, within five minutes, the entire stand was engulfed.

Heysel Tragedy

Eighteen days later, on May 29, at the European Cup Final between **Liverpool** and **Juventus** at the Heysel Stadium, Brussels, 39 spectators (31 of them Italian) were crushed or trampled to death and 437 injured. The disaster occurred an hour before the scheduled kick-off, when Liverpool supporters charged a Juventus section of the crowd at one end of the stadium, and a retaining wall collapsed. The sequel was a 5-year ban by UEFA on English clubs generally in European competition, with a 6-year ban on Liverpool.

On May 26 1985 ten people were trampled to death and 29 seriously injured in a crowd panic on the way into the **Olympic Stadium, Mexico City** for the Mexican Cup Final between local clubs National University and America.

More than 100 people died and 300 were injured in a football disaster at **Nepal's national stadium** in Katmandu in Mar 1988. There was a stampede when a violent hailstorm broke over the capital. Spectators rushed for cover, but the stadium exits were locked, and hundreds were trampled in the crush.

In South Africa, on Jan 13 1991 40 black fans were trampled to death (50 injured) as they tried to escape from fighting that broke out at a match in the gold-mining town of Orkney, 80 miles from Johannesburg. The friendly, between top teams **Kaiser Chiefs** and **Orlando Pirates**, attracted a packed crowd of 20,000. Violence erupted after the referee allowed Kaiser Chiefs a disputed second-half goal to lead 1-0.

Disaster struck at the French Cup semi-final (May 5, 1992), with the death of 15 spectators and 1,300 injured when a temporary metal stand collapsed in the Corsican town of Bastia. The tie between Second Division **Bastia** and French Champions **Marseille** was cancelled. Monaco, who won the other semi-final, were allowed to compete in the next season's Cup-Winners' Cup.

A total of 318 died and 500 were seriously injured when the crowd rioted over a disallowed goal at the National Stadium in Lima, Peru, on May 24, 1964. **Peru** and **Argentina** were competing to play in the Olympic Games in Tokyo.

That remained **sport's heaviest death** toll until Oct 20, 1982, when (it was revealed only in Jul 1989) 340 Soviet fans were killed in Moscow's Lenin Stadium at the UEFA Cup second round first leg match between **Moscow Spartak** and **Haarlem** (Holland). They were crushed on an open stairway when a last-minute Spartak goal sent departing spectators surging back into the ground.

Among other crowd disasters abroad: Jun, 1968 – 74 died in Argentina. Panic broke out at the end of a goalless match between River Plate and Boca Juniors at Nunez, Buenos Aires, when Boca supporters threw lighted newspaper torches on to fans in the tiers below.

Feb 1974 – 49 killed in **Egypt** in crush of fans clamouring to see Zamalek play Dukla Prague.

Sep 1971 – 44 died in **Turkey**, when fighting among spectators over a disallowed goal (Kayseri v Siwas) led to a platform collapsing.

The then worst disaster in the history of British football, in terms of loss of life, occurred at Glasgow Rangers' ground at **Ibrox Park**, Jan 2 1971. Sixty-six people were trampled to death (100 injured) as they tumbled down Stairway 13 just before the end of the **Rangers v Celtic** New Year's match. That disaster led to the 1975 Safety of Sports Grounds legislation.

The Ibrox tragedy eclipsed even the Bolton disaster in which 33 were killed and about 500 injured when a wall and crowd barriers collapsed near a corner-flag at the **Bolton v Stoke** FA Cup sixth round tie on Mar 9 1946. The match was completed after half an hour's stoppage.

In a previous crowd disaster at **Ibrox** on Apr 5, 1902, part of the terracing collapsed during the Scotland v England international and 25 people were killed. The match, held up for 20 minutes, ended 1-1, but was never counted as an official international.

Eight leading players and three officials of **Manchester Utd** and eight newspaper representatives were among the 23 who perished in the air crash at **Munich** on Feb 6, 1958, during take-off following a European Cup-tie in Belgrade. The players were Roger Byrne, Geoffrey Bent, Eddie Colman, Duncan Edwards, Mark Jones, David Pegg, Tommy Taylor and Liam Whelan, and the officials were Walter Crickmer (secretary), Tom Curry (trainer) and Herbert Whalley (coach). The newspaper representatives were Alf Clarke, Don Davies, George Follows, Tom Jackson, Archie Ledbrooke, Henry Rose, Eric Thompson and Frank Swift (former England goalkeeper of Manchester City).

On May 14, 1949, the entire team of Italian Champions **Torino**, 8 of them Internationals, were killed when the aircraft taking them home from a match against Benfica in Lisbon crashed at Superga, near Turin. The total death toll of 28 included all the club's reserve players, the manager, trainer and coach.

On Feb 8, 1981, 24 spectators died and more than 100 were injured at a match in **Greece**. They were trampled as thousands of the 40,000 crowd tried to rush out of the stadium at Piraeus after Olympiacos beat AEK Athens 6-0.

On Nov 17, 1982; 24 people (12 of them children) were killed and 250 injured when fans stampeded at the end of a match at the Pascual Guerrero stadium in **Cali, Colombia**. Drunken spectators hurled fire crackers and broken bottles from the higher stands on to people below and started a rush to the exits.

On Dec 9, 1987, the 18-strong team squad of **Alianza Lima**, one of Peru's top clubs, were wiped out, together with 8 officials and several youth players, when a military aircraft taking them home from Puccalpa crashed into the sea off Ventillana, ten miles from Lima. The only survivor among 43 on board was a member of the crew.

On Apr 28, 1993, 18 members of **Zambia's international squad** and 5 ZFA officials died when the aircraft carrying them to a World Cup qualifying tie against Senegal crashed into the Atlantic soon after take-off from Libreville, Gabon.

On Oct 16 1996, 81 fans were crushed to death and 147 seriously injured in the '**Guatemala Disaster**' at the World Cup qualifier against Costa Rica in Mateo Flores stadium. The tragedy happened an hour before kick-off, allegedly caused by ticket forgery and overcrowding – 60,000 were reported in the 45,000-capacity ground – and safety problems related to perimeter fencing.

On Jul 9, 1996, 8 people died, 39 injured in riot after derby match between **Libya's two top clubs** in Tripoli. Al-Ahli had beaten Al-Ittihad 1-0 by a controversial goal.

On Apr 6, 1997, 5 spectators were crushed to death at **Nigeria's national stadium** in Lagos after the 2-1 World Cup qualifying victory over Guinea. Only two of five gates were reported open as the 40,000 crowd tried to leave the ground.

It was reported from the **Congo** (Oct 29, 1998) that a bolt of lightning struck a village match, killing all 11 members of the home team Benatshadi, but leaving the opposing players from Basangana unscathed. It was believed the surviving team wore better-insulated boots.

On Jan 10, 1999, eight fans died and 13 were injured in a stampede at **Egypt's Alexandria Stadium**. Some 25,000 spectators had pushed into the ground. Despite the tragedy, the cup-tie between Al-Ittihad and Al-Koroum was completed.

Three people suffocated and several were seriously injured when thousands of fans forced their way into **Liberia's national stadium** in Monrovia at a goalless World Cup qualifying match against Chad on Apr 23, 2000. The stadium (capacity 33,000) was reported 'heavily overcrowded'.

On Jul 9, 2000, 12 spectators died from crush injuries when police fired tear gas into the 50,000 crowd after South Africa scored their second goal in a World Cup group qualifier against Zimbabwe in **Harare**. A stampede broke out as fans scrambled to leave the national stadium. Players of both teams lay face down on the pitch as fumes swept over them. FIFA launched an investigation and decided that the result would stand, with South Africa leading 2-0 at the time of the 84th-minute abandonment.

On Apr 11, 2001, at one of the biggest matches of the South African season, 43 died and 155 were injured in a crush at **Ellis Park, Johannesburg**. After tearing down a fence, thousands of fans surged into a stadium already packed to its 60,000 capacity for the Premiership derby between top Soweto teams Kaizer Chiefs and Orlando Pirates. The match was abandoned at 1-1 after 33 minutes. In Jan 1991, 40 died in a crowd crush at a friendly between the same clubs at Orkney, 80 miles from Johannesburg.

On Apr 29, 2001, seven people were trampled to death and 51 injured when a riot broke out at a match between two of Congo's biggest clubs, Lupopo and Mazembe at **Lubumbashi**, southern Congo.

On May 6, 2001, two spectators were killed in Iran and hundreds were injured when a glass fibre roof collapsed at the over-crowded Mottaqi Stadium at Sari for the match between Pirouzi and Shemshak Noshahr.

On May 9, 2001, in Africa's worst football disaster, 123 died and 93 were injured in a stampede at the national stadium in **Accra, Ghana**. Home team Hearts of Oak were leading 2-1 against Asante Kotoko five minutes from time, when Asanti fans started hurling bottles on to the pitch. Police fired tear gas into the stands, and the crowd panicked in a rush for the exits, which were locked. It took the death toll on three big matches in Africa in Apr/May to 173.

On Aug 12, 2001, two players were killed by lightning and ten severely burned at a **Guatemala** Third Division match between Deportivo Culquimulilla and Pueblo Nuevo Vinas.

On Nov 1, 2002, two players died from injuries after lightning struck Deportivo Cali's training ground in **Colombia**.

On Mar 12 2004, five people were killed and more than 100 injured when spectators stampeded shortly before the Syrian Championship fixture between Al-Jihad and Al-Fatwa in **Qameshli**, Northern Syria. The match was cancelled.

On Oct 10, 2004, three spectators died in a crush at the African Zone World Cup qualifier between **Guinea** and **Morocco** (1-1) at Conakry, Guinea.

On Mar 25, 2005, five were killed as 100,000 left the Azadi Stadium, **Tehran**, after Iran's World Cup qualifying win (2-1) against Japan.

On Jun 2, 2007, 12 spectators were killed and 46 injured in a crush at the Chillabombwe Stadium, **Zambia**, after an African Nations Cup qualifier against Congo.

On Mar 29, 2009, 19 people died and 139 were injured after a wall collapsed at the Ivory Coast stadium in **Abidjan** before a World Cup qualifier against Malawi. The match went ahead, Ivory Coast winning 5-0 with two goals from Chelsea's Didier Drogba. The tragedy meant that, in

13 years, crowd disasters at club and internationals at ten different grounds across Africa had claimed the lives of 283 people.

On Jan 8, 2010, terrorists at **Cabinda**, Angola machine-gunned the Togo team buses travelling to the Africa Cup of Nations. They killed a driver, an assistant coach and a media officer and injured several players. The team were ordered by their Government to withdraw from the tournament.

On Oct 23, 2010, seven fans were trampled to death when thousands tried to force their way into the Nyayo National Stadium in **Nairobi** at a Kenya Premier League match between the Gor Mahia and AFC Leopards clubs.

On Feb 1, 2012, 74 died and nearly 250 were injured in a crowd riot at the end of the Al-Masry v Al-Ahly match in **Port Said** – the worst disaster in Egyptian sport.

DAYS OF TRAGEDY – PERSONAL

Sam Wynne, Bury right-back, collapsed five minutes before half-time in the First Division match away to Sheffield Utd on Apr 30, 1927, and died in the dressing-room.

John Thomson, Celtic and Scotland goalkeeper, sustained a fractured skull when diving at an opponent's feet in the Rangers v Celtic League match on Sep 5, 1931, and died the same evening.

Sim Raleigh (Gillingham), injured in a clash of heads at home to Brighton (Div 3 South) on Dec 1, 1934, continued to play but collapsed in second half and died in hospital the same night.

James Thorpe, Sunderland goalkeeper, was injured during the First Division match at home to Chelsea on Feb 1, 1936 and died in a diabetic coma three days later.

Derek Dooley, Sheffield Wed centre-forward and top scorer in 1951–52 in the Football League with 46 goals in 30 matches, broke a leg in the League match at Preston on Feb 14, 1953, and, after complications set in, had to lose the limb by amputation.

John White, Tottenham's Scottish international forward, was killed by lightning on a golf course at Enfield, North London in Jul, 1964.

Tony Allden, Highgate centre-half, was struck by lightning during an Amateur Cup quarter-final with Enfield on Feb 25, 1967. He died the following day. Four other players were also struck but recovered.

Roy Harper died while refereeing the York v Halifax (Div 4) match on May 5, 1969.

Jim Finn collapsed and died from a heart attack while refereeing Exeter v Stockport (Div 4) on Sep 16, 1972.

Scotland manager **Jock Stein**, 62, collapsed and died at the end of the Wales-Scotland World Cup qualifying match (1-1) at Ninian Park, Cardiff on Sep 10, 1985.

David Longhurst, York forward, died after being carried off two minutes before half-time in the Fourth Division fixture at home to Lincoln on Sep 8, 1990. The match was abandoned (0-0). The inquest revealed that Longhurst suffered from a rare heart condition.

Mike North collapsed while refereeing Southend v Mansfield (Div 3) on Apr 16, 2001 and died shortly afterwards. The match was abandoned and re-staged on May 8, with the receipts donated to his family.

Marc-Vivien Foe, on his 63rd appearance in Cameroon's midfield, collapsed unchallenged in the centre circle after 72 minutes of the FIFA Confederations Cup semi-final against Colombia in Lyon, France, on Jun 26, 2003, and despite the efforts of the stadium medical staff he could not be revived. He had been on loan to Manchester City from Olympique Lyonnais in season 2002–03, and poignantly scored the club's last goal at Maine Road.

Paul Sykes, Folkestone Invicta (Ryman League) striker, died on the pitch during the Kent Senior Cup semi-final against Margate on Apr 12, 2005. He collapsed after an innocuous off-the-ball incident.

Craig Gowans, Falkirk apprentice, was killed at the club's training ground on Jul 8, 2005 when he came into contact with power lines.

Peter Wilson, Mansfield goalkeeping coach, died of a heart attack after collapsing during the warm-up of the League Two game away to Shrewsbury on Nov 19, 2005.

Matt Gadsby, Hinckley defender, collapsed and died while playing in a Conference North match at Harrogate on Sep 9, 2006.

Phil O'Donnell, 35-year-old Motherwell captain and Scotland midfield player, collapsed when about to be substituted near the end of the SPL home game against Dundee Utd on Dec 29, 2007 and died shortly afterwards in hospital.

GREAT SERVICE

'For services to Association Football', **Stanley Matthews** (Stoke, Blackpool and England), already a CBE, became the first professional footballer to receive a knighthood. This was bestowed in 1965, his last season. Before he retired and five days after his 50th birthday, he played for Stoke to set a record as the oldest First Division footballer (v Fulham, Feb 6, 1965).

Over a brilliant span of 33 years, he played in 886 first-class matches, including 54 full Internationals (plus 31 in war time), 701 League games (including 3 at start of season 1939–40, which was abandoned on the outbreak of war) and 86 FA Cup-ties, and scored 95 goals. He was never booked in his career.

Sir Stanley died on Feb 23, 2000, three weeks after his 85th birthday. His ashes were buried under the centre circle of Stoke's Britannia Stadium. After spending a number of years in Toronto, he made his home back in the Potteries in 1989, having previously returned to his home town, Hanley in Oct, 1987 to unveil a life-size bronze statue of himself. The inscription reads: 'Sir Stanley Matthews, CBE. Born Hanley, 1 Feb 1915.

His name is symbolic of the beauty of the game, his fame timeless and international, his sportsmanship and modesty universally acclaimed. A magical player, of the people, for the people.' On his home-coming in 1989, Sir Stanley was made President of Stoke, the club he joined as a boy of 15 and served as a player for 20 years between 1931 and 1965, on either side of his spell with Blackpool.

In Jul 1992 FIFA honoured him with their 'Gold merit award' for outstanding services to the game.

Former England goalkeeper **Peter Shilton** has made more first-class appearances (1,387) than any other footballer in British history. He played his 1,000th. League game in Leyton Orient's 2-0 home win against Brighton on Dec 22, 1996 and made 9 appearances for Orient in his final season. He retired from international football after the 1990 World Cup in Italy with 125 caps, then a world record. Shilton kept a record 60 clean sheets for England.

Shilton's career spanned 32 seasons, 20 of them on the international stage. He made his League debut for Leicester in May 1966, two months before England won the World Cup.

His 1,387 first-class appearances comprise a record 1,005 in the Football League, 125 Internationals, 102 League Cup, 86 FA Cup, 13 for England U-23s, 4 for the Football League and 52 other matches (European Cup, UEFA Cup, World Club Championship, Charity Shield, European Super Cup, Full Members' Cup, Play-offs, Screen Sports Super Cup, Anglo-Italian Cup, Texaco Cup, Simod Cup, Zenith Data Systems Cup and Autoglass Trophy).

Shilton appeared 57 times at Wembley, 52 for England, 2 League Cup Finals, 1 FA Cup Final, 1 Charity Shield match, and 1 for the Football League. He passed a century of League appearances with each of his first five clubs: Leicester (286), Stoke (110), Nottm Forest (202), Southampton (188) and Derby (175) and subsequently played for Plymouth, Bolton and Leyton Orient.

He was awarded the MBE and OBE for services to football. At the Football League Awards ceremony in March 2013, he received the League's Contribution award.

Six other British footballers have made more than 1,000 first-class appearances:

Ray Clemence, formerly with Tottenham, Liverpool and England, retired through injury in season 1987–88 after a goalkeeping career of 1,119 matches starting in 1965–66.

Clemence played 50 times for his first club, Scunthorpe; 665 for Liverpool; 337 for Tottenham; his 67 representative games included 61 England caps.

A third great British goalkeeper, **Pat Jennings**, ended his career (1963–86) with a total of 1,098 first-class matches for Watford, Tottenham, Arsenal and N Ireland. They were made up of 757 in the Football League, 119 full Internationals, 84 FA Cup appearances, 72 League/Milk Cup, 55 European club matches, 2 Charity Shield, 3 Other Internationals, 1 Under-23 cap, 2 Texaco Cup, 2 Anglo-Italian Cup and 1 Super Cup. Jennings played his 119th and final international on his 41st birthday, Jun 12, 1986, against Brazil in Guadalajara in the Mexico World Cup.

Yet another outstanding 'keeper, **David Seaman**, passed the 1,000 appearances milestone for clubs and country in season 2002–03, reaching 1,004 when aged 39, he captained Arsenal to FA Cup triumph against Southampton.

With Arsenal, Seaman won 3 Championship medals, the FA Cup 4 times, the Double twice, the League Cup and Cup-Winners' Cup once each. After 13 seasons at Highbury, he joined Manchester City (Jun 2003) on a free transfer. He played 26 matches for City before a shoulder injury forced his retirement in Jan 2004, aged 40.

Seaman's 22-season career composed 1,046 first-class matches: 955 club apps (Peterborough 106, Birmingham 84, QPR 175, Arsenal 564, Manchester City 26); 75 senior caps for England, 6 'B' caps and 10 at U-21 level.

Defender **Graeme Armstrong**, 42-year-old commercial manager for an Edinburgh whisky company and part-time assistant-manager and captain of Scottish Third Division club Stenhousemuir, made the 1000th first team appearance of his career in the Scottish Cup 3rd Round against Rangers at Ibrox on Jan 23, 1999. He was presented with the Man of the Match award before kick-off.

Against East Stirling on Boxing Day, he had played his 864th League game, breaking the British record for an outfield player set by another Scot, Tommy Hutchison, with Alloa, Blackpool, Coventry, Manchester City, Burnley and Swansea City.

Armstrong's 24-year career, spent in the lower divisions of the Scottish League, began as a 1-match trialist with Meadowbank Thistle in 1975 and continued via Stirling Albion, Berwick Rangers, Meadowbank and, from 1992, Stenhousemuir.

Tony Ford became the first English outfield player to reach 1000 senior appearances in Rochdale's 1-0 win at Carlisle (Auto Windscreens Shield) on Mar 7, 2000. Grimsby-born, he began his 26-season midfield career with Grimsby and played for 7 other League clubs: Sunderland (loan), Stoke, WBA, Bradford City (loan), Scunthorpe, Mansfield and Rochdale. He retired, aged 42, in 2001 with a career record of 1072 appearances (121 goals) and his total of 931 League games is exceeded only by Peter Shilton's 1005.

On Apr 16, 2011, **Graham Alexander** reached 1,000 appearances when he came on as a sub for Burnley at home to Swansea. Alexander, 40, ended a 22-year career with the equaliser for Preston against Charlton (2-2, Lge 1) on Apr 28, 2012 – his 1,023rd appearance. He also played for Luton and Scunthorpe and was capped 40 times by Scotland.

KNIGHTS OF SOCCER

Players, managers and administrators who have been honoured for their services to football: **Charles Clegg** (1927), **Stanley Rous** (1949), **Stanley Matthews** (1965), **Alf Ramsey** (1967), **Matt Busby** (1968), **Walter Winterbottom** (1978) **Bert Millichip** (1991), **Bobby Charlton** (1994), **Tom Finney** (1998), **Geoff Hurst** (1998), **Alex Ferguson** (1999), **Bobby Robson** (2002), **Trevor Brooking** (2004), **Dave Richards** (2006), **Doug Ellis** (2011).

● On Nov 6, 2014, **Karren Brady**, vice-chairman of West Ham, was elevated to the Lords as Karren, Baroness Brady, OBE, of Knightsbridge, life peer

FOOTBALL IN STATUE

In recognition of **Brian Clough's** outstanding achievements as manager, a 9ft bronze statue was unveiled by his widow Barbara in Market Square, Nottingham on Nov 6, 2008. The bulk of the £60,000 cost was met by supporters of Forest, the club he led to back-to-back European Cup triumphs. There is also a statue of Clough in his home town, Middlesbrough, and at Derby's Pride Park stands a combined statue of the famous management team of Clough and Peter Taylor. Other leading managers and players have been honoured over the years. They include **Sir Matt Busby** (Manchester Utd), **Bill Shankly** (Liverpool), **Sir Alf Ramsey** and **Sir Bobby Robson** (Ipswich), **Stan Cullis** (Wolves), **Jackie Milburn** (Newcastle), **Bob Stokoe** (Sunderland), **Ted Bates** (Southampton), **Nat Lofthouse** (Bolton), **Don Revie** and **Billy Bremner** (both Leeds), **Tony Brown** (WBA).

Bobby Moore, England's World Cup-winning captain, is immortalised by a statue at the new Wembley, where there is a bust of Sir Alf in the tunnel corridor. There are statues of Sir Stanley Matthews and Sir Tom Finney recognising their playing achievements with Stoke and Preston, and one honouring Manchester Utd's Sir Bobby Charlton, George Best and Denis Law outside Old Trafford. At Upton Park, there is a combined statue of West Ham's World Cup-winning trio, Bobby Moore, Sir Geoff Hurst and Martin Peters. Similarly, Fulham legend Johnny Haynes and Charlton's greatest goalkeeper Sam Bartram are honoured. So, too, is Everton great William Ralph 'Dixie' Dean at Goodison Park. The original bust of Herbert Chapman remains on its plinth at Arsenal's former home at Highbury (now converted into apartments). A replica is in place at the Emirates Stadium, which also has a bust of the club's most successful manager, Arsene Wenger. A bust of Derby's record scorer, Steve Bloomer, is at Pride Park and there is one of Blackburn's former owner, Jack Walker, at Ewood Park. Chelsea honoured Peter Osgood in 2010 and Blackpool did the same for Jimmy Armfield the following year. 2011 also saw statues unveiled of Herbert Chapman, Thierry Henry and Tony Adams, as part of Arsenal's 125th anniversary, and of Jimmy Hill at Coventry. The following year, Sir Bobby Robson was honoured at Newcastle and Sir Alex Ferguson at Old Trafford. A 16ft statue of former Port Vale player and manager Roy Sproson, costing £96,000 and paid for by supporters, went up at Vale Park. In 2013, Arsenal commissioned a statue of Dennis Bergkamp, while Roy Hodgson unveiled a bust of Sir Walter Winterbottom, England's first manager (1946-62) at the National Football Centre at St George's Park on St George's Day, At Villa Park, there is a statue of William McGregor, founder of the Football League in 1888. At Cardiff city Stadium, stands a statue of Fred Keenor, captain of the club's 1927 FA Cuip-winning team. On Oct 16, 2014, an 8ft statue of Arthur Wharton, the world's first black professional footballer, was unveiled at St George's Park. He came to Britain from Ghana in 1882, aged 19, and kept goal for Darlington, Preston, Rotherham and Sheffield Utd.

PENALTIES

The penalty-kick was introduced to the game, following a proposal to the Irish FA in 1890 by William McCrum, son of the High Sheriff for Co Omagh, and approved by the International Football Board on Jun 2, 1891.

First penalty scored in a first-class match in England was by John Heath, for Wolves v Accrington Stanley (5-0 in Div 1, Sep 14, 1891).

The greatest influence of the penalty has come since the 1970s, with the introduction of the shoot-out to settle deadlocked ties in various competitions.

Manchester Utd were the first club to win a competitive match in British football via a shoot-out (4-3 away to Hull, Watney Cup semi-final, Aug 5, 1970); in that penalty contest, George Best was the first player to score, Denis Law the first to miss.

The shoot-out was adopted by FIFA and UEFA the same year (1970).

In season 1991–92, penalty shoot-outs were introduced to decide FA Cup ties still level after one replay and extra time.

Wembley saw its first penalty contest in the 1974 Charity Shield. Since then many major matches across the world have been settled in this way, including:

1976	**European Championship Final (Belgrade):** Czechoslovakia beat West Germany 5-3 (after 2-2)
1980	**Cup-Winners' Cup Final (Brussels):** Valencia beat Arsenal 5-4 (after 0-0)
1984	**European Cup Final (Rome):** Liverpool beat Roma 4-2 (after 1-1)
1984	**UEFA Cup Final:** Tottenham (home) beat Anderlecht 4-3 (2-2 agg)
1986	**European Cup Final (Seville):** Steaua Bucharest beat Barcelona 2-0 (after 0-0).
1987	**Freight Rover Trophy Final (Wembley):** Mansfield beat Bristol City 5-4 (after 1-1)
1987	**Scottish League Cup Final (Hampden Park):** Rangers beat Aberdeen 5-3 (after 3-3)
1988	**European Cup Final (Stuttgart):** PSV Eindhoven beat Benfica 6-5 (after 0-0)

1988	**UEFA Cup Final:** Bayer Leverkusen (home) beat Espanyol 3-2 after 3-3 (0-3a, 3-0h)
1990	**Scottish Cup Final (Hampden Park):** Aberdeen beat Celtic 9-8 (after 0-0)
1991	**European Cup Final (Bari):** Red Star Belgrade beat Marseille 5-3 (after 0-0)
1991	**Div 4 Play-off Final (Wembley):** Torquay beat Blackpool 5-4 (after 2-2)
1992	**Div 4 Play-off Final (Wembley):** Blackpool beat Scunthorpe 4-3 (after 1-1)
1993	**Div 3 Play-off Final (Wembley):** York beat Crewe 5-3 (after 1-1)
1994	**Autoglass Trophy Final (Wembley):** Swansea City beat Huddersfield 3-1 (after 1-1)
1994	**World Cup Final (Los Angeles):** Brazil beat Italy 3-2 (after 0-0)
1994	**Scottish League Cup Final (Ibrox Park):** Raith beat Celtic 6-5 (after 2-2)
1995	**Copa America Final (Montevideo):** Uruguay beat Brazil 5-3 (after 1-1)
1996	**European Cup Final (Rome):** Juventus beat Ajax 4-2 (after 1-1)
1996	**European U-21 Champ Final (Barcelona):** Italy beat Spain 4-2 (after 1-1)
1997	**Auto Windscreens Shield Final (Wembley):** Carlisle beat Colchester 4-3 (after 0-0)
1997	**UEFA Cup Final:** FC Schalke beat Inter Milan 4-1 (after 1-1 agg)
1998	**Div 1 Play-off Final (Wembley):** Charlton beat Sunderland 7-6 (after 4-4)
1999	**Div 2 Play-off Final (Wembley):** Manchester City beat Gillingham 3-1 (after 2-2)
1999	**Women's World Cup Final (Pasedena):** USA beat China 5-4 (after 0-0)
2000	**African Nations Cup Final (Lagos):** Cameroon beat Nigeria 4-3 (after 0-0)
2000	**UEFA Cup Final (Copenhagen):** Galatasaray beat Arsenal 4-1 (after 0-0)
2000	**Olympic Final (Sydney):** Cameroon beat Spain 5-3 (after 2-2)
2001	**League Cup Final (Millennium Stadium):** Liverpool beat Birmingham 5-4 (after 1-1)
2001	**Champions League Final (Milan):** Bayern Munich beat Valencia 5-4 (after 1-1)
2002	**Euro U-21 Champ Final (Basle):** Czech Republic beat France 3-1 (after 0-0)
2002	**Div 1 Play-off Final (Millennium Stadium):** Birmingham beat Norwich 4-2 (after 1-1)
2003	**Champions League Final (Old Trafford):** AC Milan beat Juventus 3-2 (after 0-0)
2004	**Div 3 Play-off Final (Millennium Stadium):** Huddersfield beat Mansfield 4-1 (after 0-0)
2004	**Copa America Final (Lima):** Brazil beat Argentina 4-2 (after 2-2)
2005	**FA Cup Final (Millennium Stadium):** Arsenal beat Manchester Utd 5-4 (after 0-0)
2005	**Champions League Final (Istanbul):** Liverpool beat AC Milan 3-2 (after 3-3)
2006	**African Cup of Nations Final (Cairo):** Egypt beat Ivory Coast 4-2 (after 0-0)
2006	**FA Cup Final (Millennium Stadium):** Liverpool beat West Ham 3-1 (after 3-3)
2006	**Scottish Cup Final (Hampden Park):** Hearts beat Gretna 4-2 (after 1-1)
2006	**Lge 1 Play-off Final (Millennium Stadium):** Barnsley beat Swansea City 4-3 (after 2-2)
2006	**World Cup Final (Berlin):** Italy beat France 5-3 (after 1-1)
2007	**UEFA Cup Final (Hampden Park):** Sevilla beat Espanyol 3-1 (after 2-2)
2008	**Champions League Final (Moscow):** Manchester Utd beat Chelsea 6-5 (after 1-1)
2008	**Scottish League Cup Final (Hampden Park):** Rangers beat Dundee Utd 3-2 (after 2-2)
2009	**League Cup Final (Wembley):** Manchester Utd beat Tottenham 4-1 (after 0-0)
2011	**Women's World Cup Final (Frankfurt):** Japan beat USA 3-1 (after 2-2)
2012	**League Cup Final (Wembley):** Liverpool beat Cardiff 3-2 (after 2-2)
2012	**Champions League Final (Munich):** Chelsea beat Bayern Munich 4-3 (after 1-1)
2012	**Lge 1 Play-off Final (Wembley):** Huddersfield beat Sheffield Utd 8-7 (after 0-0)
2012	**Africa Cup of Nations Final (Gabon):** Zambia beat Ivory Coast 8-7 (after 0-0)
2013	**FA Trophy Final (Wembley):** Wrexham beat Grimsby 4-1 (after 1-1)
2013	**European Super Cup (Prague):** Bayern Munich beat Chelsea 5-4 (after 2-2)
2014	**Scottish League Cup Final (Celtic Park):** Aberdeen beat Inverness 4-2 (after 0-0)
2014	**Lge 1 Play-off Final (Wembley):** Rotherheam beat Leyton Orient 4-3 (after 2-2)
2014	**Europa Lge (Turin):** Sevilla beat Benfica 4-2 (after 0-0)
2015	**Africa Cup of Nations Final (Equ Guinea):** Ivory Coast beat Ghana 9-8 (after 0-0)
2015	**Conference Play-off Final (Wembley):** Bristol Rov beat Grimsby 5-3 (after 1-1)
2015	**Lge 2 Play-off Final (Wembley):** Southend beat Wycombe 7-6 (after 1-1)
2015	**FA Trophy Final (Wembley)** North Ferriby beat Wrexham 5-4 (after3-3)
2015	**Euro U-21 Champ Final (Prague):** Sweden beat Portugal 4-3 (after 0-0)

In South America in 1992, in a 26-shot competition, **Newell's Old Boys** beat America 11-10 in the Copa Libertadores.

Longest-recorded penalty contest in first-class matches was in Argentina in 1988 – from 44 shots, **Argentinos Juniors** beat Racing Club 20-19. Genclerbirligi beat Galatasaray 17-16 in a Turkish Cup-tie in 1996. Only one penalty was missed.

Highest-scoring shoot-outs in international football: **North Korea** beat Hong Kong 11-10 (after 3-3 draw) in an Asian Cup match in 1975; and **Ivory Coast** beat Ghana 11-10 (after 0-0 draw) in African Nations Cup Final, 1992.

Most penalties needed to settle an adult game in Britain: **44** in Norfolk Primary Cup 4th round replay, Dec 2000. Aston Village side **Freethorpe** beat Foulsham 20-19 (5 kicks missed). All 22 players took 2 penalties each, watched by a crowd of 20. The sides had drawn 2-2, 4-4 in a tie of 51 goals.

Penalty that took 24 days: That was how long elapsed between the award and the taking of a penalty in an Argentine Second Division match between **Atalanta** and Defensores in 2003. A riot ended the original match with 5 minutes left. The game resumed behind closed doors with the penalty that caused the abandonment. Lucas Ferreiro scored it to give Atalanta a 1-0 win.

INTERNATIONAL PENALTIES, MISSED

Four penalties out of five were missed when **Colombia** beat Argentina 3-0 in a Copa America group tie in Paraguay in Jul 1999. Martin Palmermo missed three for Argentina and Colombia's Hamilton Ricard had one spot-kick saved.

In the European Championship semi-final against Italy in Amsterdam on Jun 29, 2000, **Holland** missed five penalties – two in normal time, three in the penalty contest which Italy won 3-1 (after 0-0). Dutch captain Frank de Boer missed twice from the spot.

ENGLAND'S SHOOT-OUT RECORD

England have been beaten in seven of nine penalty shoot-outs in major tournaments:

1990 (World Cup semi-final, Turin) 3-4 v West Germany after 1-1.
1996 (Euro Champ quarter-final, Wembley) 4-2 v Spain after 0-0.
1996 (Euro Champ semi-final, Wembley) 5-6 v Germany after 1-1.
1998 (World Cup 2nd round., St Etienne) 3-4 v Argentina after 2-2.
2004 (Euro Champ quarter-final, Lisbon) 5-6 v Portugal after 2-2.
2006 (World Cup quarter-final, Gelsenkirchen) 1-3 v Portugal after 0-0.
2007 (Euro U-21 Champ semi-final, Heerenveen) 12-13 v Holland after 1-1.
2009 (Euro U-21 Champ semi-final, Gothenburg) 5-4 v Sweden after 3-3.
2012 (Euro Champ quarter-final, Kiev) 2-4 v Italy after 0-0.

FA CUP SHOOT-OUTS

First penalty contest in the FA Cup took place in 1972. In the days of the play-off for third place, the match was delayed until the eve of the following season when losing semi-finalists Birmingham and Stoke met at St Andrew's on Aug 5. The score was 0-0 and Birmingham won 4-3 on penalties.

Highest-scoring: Preliminary round replay (Aug 30, 2005): Tunbridge Wells beat Littlehampton 16-15 after 40 spot-kicks (9 missed).

Competition proper: Scunthorpe beat Worcester 14-13 in 2nd round replay (Dec 17, 2014) after 1-1 (32 kicks).

Shoot-out abandoned: The FA Cup 1st round replay between Oxford City and Wycombe at Wycombe on Nov 9, 1999 was abandoned (1-1) after extra-time. As the penalty shoot-out was about to begin, a fire broke out under a stand. Wycombe won the second replay 1-0 at Oxford Utd's ground.

First FA Cup Final to be decided by shoot-out was in 2005 (May 21), when Arsenal beat Manchester Utd 5-4 on penalties at Cardiff's Millennium Stadium (0-0 after extra time). A year later (May 13) Liverpool beat West Ham 3-1 (3-3 after extra-time).

MARATHON SHOOT-OUT BETWEEN LEAGUE CLUBS

Highest recorded score in shoot-out between league clubs: Dagenham & Redbridge 14-13 against
  Leyton Orient (after 1-1) in Johnstone's Paint Trophy southern section on Sep 7, 2011

SHOOT-OUT RECORD WINNERS AND LOSERS

When **Bradford** beat Arsenal 3-2 on penalties in a League Cup fifth round tie, it was the club's
  ninth successive shoot-out victory in FA Cup, League Cup and Johnstone's Paint Trophy ties
  between Oct 2009 and Dec 2012.
Tottenham's 4-1 spot-kick failure against Basel in the last 16 of the Europa League was their
  seventh successive defeat in shoot-outs from Mar 1996 to Apr 2013 (FA Cup, League Cup,
  UEFA Cup, Europa League)

MISSED CUP FINAL PENALTIES

John Aldridge (Liverpool) became the first player to miss a penalty in an FA Cup Final at Wembley
  when Dave Beasant saved his shot in 1988 to help Wimbledon to a shock 1-0 win. Seven
  penalties before had been scored in the Final at Wembley.
Previously, **Charlie Wallace**, of Aston Villa, had failed from the spot in the 1913 Final against
  Sunderland at Crystal Palace, which his team won 1-0
Gary Lineker (Tottenham) had his penalty saved by Nottm Forest's Mark Crossley in the 1991 FA
  Cup Final.
For the first time, two spot-kicks were missed in an FA Cup Final. In 2010, Petr Cech saved
  from Portsmouth's **Kevin-Prince Boateng** while Chelsea's **Frank Lampard** put his kick wide.
Another miss at Wembley was by Arsenal's **Nigel Winterburn**, Luton's Andy Dibble saving his
  spot-kick in the 1988 Littlewoods Cup Final, when a goal would have put Arsenal 3-1 ahead.
  Instead, they lost 3-2.
Winterburn was the third player to fail with a League Cup Final penalty at Wembley, following **Ray
  Graydon** (Aston Villa) against Norwich in 1975 and **Clive Walker** (Sunderland), who shot wide in
  the 1985 Milk Cup Final, also against Norwich who won 1-0. Graydon had his penalty saved by
  Kevin Keelan, but scored from the rebound and won the cup for Aston Villa (1-0).
Derby's Martin Taylor saved a penalty from **Eligio Nicolini** in the Anglo-Italian Cup Final at
  Wembley on Mar 27, 1993, but Cremonese won 3-1.

LEAGUE PENALTIES RECORD

Most penalties in Football League match: Five – 4 to Crystal Palace (3 missed), 1 to Brighton
  (scored) in Div 2 match at Selhurst Park on Mar 27 (Easter Monday), 1989. Crystal Palace
  won 2-1. Three of the penalties were awarded in a 5-minute spell. The match also produced
  5 bookings and a sending-off. Other teams missing 3 penalties in a match: Burnley v Grimsby
  (Div 2), Feb 13, 1909; Manchester City v Newcastle (Div 1), Jan 17, 1912.

HOTTEST MODERN SPOT-SHOTS

Matthew Le Tissier ended his career in season 2001–02 with the distinction of having netted 48 out
  of 49 first-team penalties for Southampton. He scored the last 27 after his only miss when Nottm
  Forest keeper Mark Crossley saved in a Premier League match at The Dell on Mar 24, 1993.
Graham Alexander scored 78 out of 84 penalties in a 22-year career (Scunthorpe, Luton, Preston
  twice and Burnley) which ended in 2012.

SPOT-KICK HAT-TRICKS

Right-back **Joe Willetts** scored three penalties when Hartlepool beat Darlington 6-1 (Div 3N) on
  Good Friday 1951.
Danish international **Jan Molby's** only hat-trick in English football, for Liverpool in a 3-1 win at
  home to Coventry (Littlewoods Cup, 4th round replay, Nov 26, 1986) comprised three goals
  from the penalty spot.
It was the first such hat-trick in a major match for two years – since **Andy Blair** scored three
  penalties for Sheffield Wed against Luton (Milk Cup 4th round, Nov 20 1984).

Portsmouth's **Kevin Dillon** scored a penalty hat-trick in the Full Members Cup (2nd round) at home to Millwall (3-2) on Nov 4, 1986.

Alan Slough scored a hat-trick of penalties in an away game, but was on the losing side, when Peterborough were beaten 4-3 at Chester (Div 3, Apr 29, 1978).

Penalty hat-tricks in **international football: Dimitris Saravakos** (in 9 mins) for Greece v Egypt in 1990. He scored 5 goals in match. **Henrik Larsson**, among his 4 goals in Sweden's 6-0 home win v Moldova in World Cup qualifying match, Jun 6, 2001.

MOST PENALTY GOALS (LEAGUE) IN SEASON

13 out of 13 by **Francis Lee** for Manchester City (Div 1) in 1971–72. His goal total for the season was 33. In season 1988–89, **Graham Roberts** scored 12 League penalties for Second Division Champions Chelsea. In season 2004–05, **Andrew Johnson** scored 11 Premiership penalties for Crystal Palace, who were relegated.

PENALTY-SAVE SEQUENCES

Ipswich goalkeeper **Paul Cooper** saved eight of the ten penalties he faced in 1979–80. **Roy Brown** (Notts Co) saved six in a row in season 1972–73.

Andy **Lomas**, goalkeeper for Chesham (Diadora League) claimed a record eighth **consecutive** penalty saves – three at the end of season 1991–92 and five in 1992–93.

Mark Bosnich (Aston Villa) saved five in two consecutive matches in 1993–94: three in Coca-Cola Cup semi-final penalty shoot–out v Tranmere (Feb 26), then two in Premiership at Tottenham (Mar 2).

MISSED PENALTIES SEQUENCE

Against Wolves in Div 2 on Sep 28, 1991, **Southend** missed their seventh successive penalty (five of them the previous season).

SCOTTISH RECORDS

(See also under 'Goals' & 'Discipline')

RANGERS' MANY RECORDS

Rangers' record-breaking feats include:

League Champions: 54 times (once joint holders) – world record.

Winning every match in Scottish League (18 games, 1898–99 season).

Major hat-tricks: Rangers have completed the domestic treble (League Championship, League Cup and Scottish FA Cup) a record seven times (1948–49, 1963–64, 1975–76, 1977–78, 1992–93, 1998–99, 2002–03).

League & Cup double: 17 times.

Nine successive Championships (1989–97). Four men played in all nine sides: Richard Gough, Ally McCoist, Ian Ferguson and Ian Durrant.

115 major trophies: Championships 54, Scottish Cup 33, League Cup 27, Cup-Winners' Cup 1.

CELTIC'S GRAND SLAM

Celtic's record in 1966–67 was the most successful by a British club in one season. They won the **Scottish League**, the **Scottish Cup**, the **Scottish League Cup** and became the first British club to win the **European Cup**. They also won the **Glasgow Cup**.

Celtic have three times achieved the Scottish treble (League Championship, League Cup and FA Cup), in 1966–67, 1968–69 and 2000–01 (in Martin O'Neill's first season as their manager). They became Scottish Champions for 2000–01 with a 1-0 home win against St Mirren on Apr 7 – the earliest the title had been clinched for 26 years, since Rangers' triumph on Mar 29, 1975. They have been champions 45 times.

They have won the Scottish Cup 36 times, and have completed the League and Cup double 15 times.

Celtic won nine consecutive Scottish League titles (1966–74) under Jock Stein.
They set a **British record** of 25 consecutive League wins in season 2003–04 (Aug 15 to Mar 14). They were unbeaten for 77 matches (all competitions) at Celtic Park from Aug 22, 2001, to Apr 21, 2004. They have won the Scottish Championship 46 times.

UNBEATEN SCOTTISH CHAMPIONS

Celtic and **Rangers** have each won the Scottish Championship with an unbeaten record: Celtic in 1897–98 (P18, W15, D3), Rangers in 1898–99 (P18, W18).

FORSTER'S SHUT-OUT RECORD

Celtic goalkeeper **Fraser Forster** set a record in Scottish top-flight football by not conceding a goal for 1,256 consecutive minutes in season 2013–14.

TRIO OF TOP CLUBS MISSING

Three of Scotland's leading clubs were missing from the 2014-15 Premiership season. With **Hearts** finishing bottom and **Rangers** still working their way back through the divisions after being demoted, they were joined in the second tier by **Hibernian**, who lost the play-off final on penalties to Hamilton.

SCOTTISH CUP HAT-TRICKS

Aberdeen's feat of winning the Scottish FA Cup in 1982–83–84 made them only the third club to achieve that particular hat-trick. **Queen's Park** did it twice (1874–75–76 and 1880–81–82), and **Rangers** have won the Scottish Cup three years in succession on three occasions: 1934–35–36, 1948–49–50 and 1962–63–64.

SCOTTISH CUP FINAL DISMISSALS

Five players have been sent off in the Scottish FA Cup Final: **Jock Buchanan** (Rangers v Kilmarnock, 1929); **Roy Aitken** (Celtic v Aberdeen, 1984); **Walter Kidd** (Hearts captain v Aberdeen, 1986); **Paul Hartley** (Hearts v Gretna, 2006); **Pa Kujabi** (Hibernian v Hearts, 2012).

HIGHEST-SCORING SHOOT-OUT

In Scottish football's highest-scoring penalty shoot-out, **Stirling Albion** beat junior club Hurlford 13-12 after 28 spot-kicks in a third round replay. The tie, on Nov 8, 2014, had ended 2-2 after extra-time.

RECORD SEQUENCES

Celtic hold Britain's League record of 62 matches undefeated, from Nov 13, 1915 to Apr 21, 1917, when Kilmarnock won 2-0 at Parkhead. They won 49, drew 13 (111 points) and scored 126 goals to 26.
Greenock Morton in 1963–64 accumulated 67 points out of 72 and scored 135 goals.
Queen's Park did not have a goal scored against them during the first seven seasons of their existence (1867–74, before the Scottish League was formed).

EARLIEST PROMOTIONS IN SCOTLAND

Dundee promoted from Div 2, Feb 1, 1947; **Greenock Morton** promoted from Div 2, Mar 2, 1964; **Gretna** promoted from Div 3, Mar 5, 2005; **Hearts** promoted from Championship, Mar 21, 2015.

WORST HOME SEQUENCE

After gaining promotion to Div 1 in 1992, **Cowdenbeath** went a record 38 consecutive home League matches without a win. They ended the sequence (drew 8, lost 30) when beating Arbroath 1-0 on Apr 2, 1994, watched by a crowd of 225.

ALLY'S RECORDS

Ally McCoist became the first player to complete 200 goals in the Premier Division when he scored Rangers' winner (2-1) at Falkirk on Dec 12, 1992. His first was against Celtic in Sep 1983, and he reached 100 against Dundee on Boxing Day 1987.

When McCoist scored twice at home to Hibernian (4-3) on Dec 7, 1996, he became Scotland's record post-war League marksman, beating Gordon Wallace's 264.

Originally with St Johnstone (1978–81), he spent two seasons with Sunderland (1981–83), then joined Rangers for £200,000 in Jun 1983.

In 15 seasons at Ibrox, he scored 355 goals for Rangers (250 League), and helped them win 10 Championships (9 in succession), 3 Scottish Cups and earned a record 9 League Cup winner's medals. He won the European Golden Boot in consecutive seasons (1991–92, 1992–93).

His 9 Premier League goals in three seasons for Kilmarnock gave him a career total of 281 Scottish League goals when he retired at the end of 2000–01. McCoist succeeded Walter Smith as manager of Rangers in May 2011.

SCOTLAND'S MOST SUCCESSFUL MANAGER

Bill Struth, 30 trophies for Rangers, 1920–54 (18 Championships, 10 Scottish Cups, 2 League Cups.

SMITH'S IBROX HONOURS

Walter Smith, who retired in May, 2011, won a total of 21 trophies in two spells as Rangers manager (10 League titles, 5 Scottish Cups, 6 League Cups).

RANGERS PUNISHED

In April 2012, **Rangers** (in administration) were fined £160,000 by the Scottish FA and given a 12-month transfer ban on charges relating to their finances. The ban was later overturned in court. The club had debts estimated at around £135m and on June 12, 2012 were forced into liquidation. A new company emerged, but Rangers were voted out of the Scottish Premier League and demoted to Division Three for the start of the 2012-13 season. Dundee, runners-up in Division One, replaced them in the top flight.

FIVE IN A MATCH

Paul Sturrock set an individual scoring record for the Scottish Premier Division with 5 goals in Dundee Utd's 7-0 win at home to Morton on Nov 17, 1984. **Marco Negri** equalled the feat with all 5 when Rangers beat Dundee Utd 5-1 at Ibrox (Premier Division) on Aug 23, 1997, and **Kenny Miller** scored 5 in Rangers' 7-1 win at home to St Mirren on Nov 4, 2000. **Kris Boyd** scored all Kilmarnock's goals in a 5-2 SPL win at home to Dundee Utd on Sep 25, 2004. **Boyd** scored another 5 when Rangers beat Dundee Utd 7-1 on Dec 30, 2009. That took his total of SPL goals to a record 160. **Gary Hooper** netted all Celtic's goals in 5-0 SPL win against Hearts on May 13, 2012

NEGRI'S TEN-TIMER

Marco Negri scored in Rangers' first ten League matches (23 goals) in season 1997–98, a Premier Division record. The previous best was 8 by **Ally MacLeod** for Hibernian in 1978.

DOUBLE SCOTTISH FINAL

Rangers v Celtic drew **129,643** and **120,073** people to the Scottish Cup Final and replay at Hampden Park, Glasgow, in 1963. Receipts for the two matches totalled £50,500.

MOST SCOTTISH CHAMPIONSHIP MEDALS

13 by **Sandy Archibald** (Rangers, 1918–34). Post-war record: 10 by **Bobby Lennox** (Celtic, 1966–79).

Alan Morton won **nine** Scottish Championship medals with Rangers in 1921–23–24–25–27–28–29–30–31. **Ally McCoist** played in the Rangers side that won nine successive League titles (1989–97).

Between 1927 and 1939 **Bob McPhail** helped Rangers win nine Championships, finish second twice and third once. He scored 236 League goals but was never top scorer in a single season.

TOP SCOTTISH LEAGUE SCORERS IN SEASON

Raith Rovers (Div 2) 142 goals in 1937–38; **Morton** (Div 2) 135 goals in 1963–64; **Hearts** (Div 1) 132 goals in 1957–58; **Falkirk** (Div 2) 132 goals in 1935–36; **Gretna** (Div 3) 130 goals in 2004–05.

SCOTTISH CUP – NO DECISION

The **Scottish FA** withheld their Cup and medals in 1908–09 after Rangers and Celtic played two drawn games in the Final. Spectators rioted.

FEWEST LEAGUE WINS IN SEASON

In modern times: 1 win by **Ayr** (34 matches, Div 1, 1966–67); **Forfar** (38 matches, Div 2, 1973–74); **Clydebank** (36 matches, Div 1, 1999–2000).
Vale of Leven provided the only instance of a British team failing to win a single match in a league season (Div 1, 18 games, 1891–92).

HAMPDEN'S £63M REDEVELOPMENT

On completion of redevelopment costing £63m **Hampden Park**, home of Scottish football and the oldest first-class stadium in the world, was re-opened full scale for the Rangers-Celtic Cup Final on May 29, 1999.
Work on the 'new Hampden' (capacity 52,000) began in 1992. The North and East stands were restructured (£12m); a new South stand and improved West stand cost £51m. The Millennium Commission contributed £23m and the Lottery Sports Fund provided a grant of £3.75m.

FIRST FOR INVERNESS

Inverness Caledonian Thistle won the Scottish Cup for the Highlands for the first time when beating Falkirk 2-1 in the Final on May 30, 2015.

DEMISE OF AIRDRIE AND CLYDEBANK

In May 2002, First Division **Airdrieonians**, formed in 1878, went out of business. They had debts of £3m. Their place in the Scottish League was taken by **Gretna**, from the English Unibond League, who were voted into Div 3. Second Division **Clydebank** folded in Jul 2002 and were taken over by the new **Airdrie United** club.

FASTEST GOAL IN SPL

12.4 sec by **Anthony Stokes** for Hibernian in 4-1 home defeat by Rangers, Dec 27, 2009.

YOUNGEST SCORER IN SPL

Fraser Fyvie, aged 16 years and 306 days, for Aberdeen v Hearts (3-0) on Jan 27, 2010.

12 GOALS SHARED

There was a record aggregate score for the SPL on May 5, 2010, when **Motherwell** came from 6-2 down to draw 6-6 with **Hibernian**.

25-POINT DEDUCTION

Dundee were deducted 25 points by the Scottish Football League in November 2010 for going into administration for the second time. It left the club on minus 11 points, but they still managed to finish in mid-table in Division One.

GREAT SCOTS

In Feb 1988, the Scottish FA launched a national **Hall of Fame**, initially comprising the first 11 Scots to make 50 international appearances, to be joined by all future players to reach that number of caps. Each member receives a gold medal, invitation for life at all Scotland's home matches, and has his portrait hung at Scottish FA headquarters in Glasgow.

MORE CLUBS IN 2000

The **Scottish Premier League** increased from 10 to 12 clubs in season 2000–01. The **Scottish Football League** admitted two new clubs – Peterhead and Elgin City from the Highland League – to provide three divisions of 10 in 2000–01.

NOTABLE SCOTTISH 'FIRSTS'

- The father of League football was a Scot, **William McGregor**, a draper in Birmingham. The 12-club Football League kicked off in Sep 1888, and McGregor was its first president.
- **Hibernian** were the first British club to play in the European Cup, by invitation. They reached the semi-final when it began in 1955–56.
- **Celtic** were Britain's first winners of the European Cup, in 1967.
- Scotland's First Division became the **Premier Division** in season 1975–76.
- Football's **first international** was staged at the West of Scotland cricket ground, Partick, on Nov 30, 1872: Scotland 0, England 0.
- Scotland introduced its **League Cup** in 1945–46, the first season after the war. It was another 15 years before the Football League Cup was launched.
- Scotland pioneered the use in British football of **two subs** per team in League and Cup matches.
- The world's **record football score** belongs to Scotland: Arbroath 36, Bon Accord 0 (Scottish Cup 1st rd) on Sep 12, 1885.
- The Scottish FA introduced the penalty **shoot-out** to their Cup Final in 1990.
- On Jan 22, 1994 all six matches in the **Scottish Premier Division** ended as draws.
- Scotland's new Premier League introduced a **3-week shut-down** in Jan 1999 – first instance of British football adopting the winter break system that operates in a number of European countries. The SPL ended its New Year closure after 2003.
- **Rangers** made history at home to St Johnstone (Premier League, 0-0, Mar 4, 2000) when fielding a team entirely without Scottish players.

John Fleck, aged 16 years, 274 days, became the youngest player in a Scottish FA Cup Final when he came on as a substitute for Rangers in their 3-2 win over Queen of the South at Hampden Park on May 24, 2008

SCOTTISH CUP SHOCK RESULTS

1885–86	(1)	Arbroath 36 Bon Accord 0
1921–22	(F)	Morton 1 Rangers 0
1937–38	(F)	East Fife 4 Kilmarnock 2 (replay, after 1-1)
1960–61	(F)	Dunfermline 2 Celtic 0 (replay, after 0-0)
1966–67	(1)	Berwick 1 Rangers 0
1979–80	(3)	Hamilton 2 Keith 3
1984–85	(1)	Stirling 20 Selkirk 0
1984–85	(3)	Inverness 3 Kilmarnock 0
1986–87	(3)	Rangers 0 Hamilton 1
1994–95	(4)	Stenhousemuir 2 Aberdeen 0
1998–99	(3)	Aberdeen 0 Livingston 1
1999–2000	(3)	Celtic 1 Inverness 3
2003–04	(5)	Inverness 1 Celtic 0
2005–06	(3)	Clyde 2 Celtic 1
2008–09	(6)	St Mirren 1 Celtic 0
2009–10	(SF)	Ross Co 2 Celtic 0
2013–14	(4)	Albion 1 Motherwell 0

Scottish League (Coca-Cola) Cup Final
1994–95	Raith 2, Celtic 2 (Raith won 6-5 on pens)

MISCELLANEOUS

NATIONAL ASSOCIATIONS FORMED

FA	1863
FA of Wales	1876
Scottish FA	1873
Irish FA	1904
Federation of International Football Associations (FIFA)	1904

NATIONAL & INTERNATIONAL COMPETITIONS LAUNCHED

FA Cup	1871
Welsh Cup	1877
Scottish Cup	1873
Irish Cup	1880
Football League	1888
Premier League	1992
Scottish League	1890
Scottish Premier League	1998
Scottish League Cup	1945
Football League Cup	1960
Home International Championship	1883–84
World Cup	1930
European Championship	1958
European Cup	1955
Fairs/UEFA Cup	1955
Cup-Winners' Cup	1960
European Champions League	1992
Olympic Games Tournament, at Shepherd's Bush	1908

INNOVATIONS

Size of Ball: Fixed in **1872**.

Shinguards: Introduced and registered by Sam Weller Widdowson (Nottm Forest & England) in **1874**.

Referee's whistle: First used on Nottm Forest's ground in **1878**.

Professionalism: Legalised in England in the summer of **1885** as a result of agitation by Lancashire clubs.

Goal-nets: Invented and patented in **1890** by Mr JA Brodie of Liverpool. They were first used in the North v South match in Jan, **1891**.

Referees and linesmen: Replaced umpires and referees in Jan, **1891**.

Penalty-kick: Introduced at Irish FA's request in the season **1891–92**. The penalty law ordering the goalkeeper to remain on the goal-line came into force in Sep, **1905**, and the order to stand on his goal-line until the ball is kicked arrived in **1929–30**.

White ball: First came into official use in **1951**.

Floodlighting: First FA Cup-tie (replay), Kidderminster Harriers v Brierley Hill Alliance, **1955**. First Football League match: Portsmouth v Newcastle (Div 1), **1956**.

Heated pitch to beat frost tried by Everton at Goodison Park in **1958**.

First soccer closed-circuit TV: At Coventry ground in Oct **1965** (10,000 fans saw their team win at Cardiff, 120 miles away).

Substitutes (one per team) were first allowed in Football League matches at the start of season **1965–66**. Three substitutes (one a goalkeeper) allowed, two of which could be used, in Premier League matches, **1992–93**. The Football League introduced three substitutes for **1993–94**.

Three points for a win: Introduced by the Football League in **1981–82**, by FIFA in World Cup games in **1994**, and by the Scottish League in the same year.

Offside law amended, player 'level' no longer offside, and 'professional foul' made sending-off offence, **1990**.

Penalty shoot-outs introduced to decide FA Cup ties level after one replay and extra time, **1991– 92**.

New back-pass rule: goalkeeper must not handle ball kicked to him by team-mate, **1992**.

Linesmen became 'referees' assistants', **1998**.

Goalkeepers not to hold ball longer than 6 seconds, **2000**.

Free-kicks advanced by ten yards against opponents failing to retreat, **2000**. This experimental rule in England was scrapped in 2005).

YOUNGEST AND OLDEST

Youngest Caps

Harry Wilson (Wales v Belgium, Oct 15, 2013)	**16 years 207 days**
Norman Whiteside (N Ireland v Yugoslavia, Jun 17, 1982)	**17 years 41 days**
Theo Walcott (England v Hungary, May 30, 2006)	**17 years 75 days**
Johnny Lambie (Scotland v Ireland, Mar 20, 1886)	**17 years 92 days**
Jimmy Holmes (Rep of Ireland v Austria, May 30, 1971)	**17 years 200 days**

Youngest England scorer: Wayne Rooney (17 years, 317 days) v Macedonia, Skopje, Sep 6, 2003.

Youngest England hat-trick scorer: Theo Walcott (19 years, 178 days) v Croatia, Zagreb, Sep 10, 2008.

Youngest England captains: Bobby Moore (v Czech., Bratislava, May 29, 1963), 22 years, 47 days; Michael Owen (v Paraguay, Anfield, Apr 17, 2002), 22 years, 117 days.

Youngest England goalkeeper: Jack Butland (19 years, 158 days) v Italy, Bern, Aug 15, 2012

Youngest England players to reach 50 caps: Michael Owen (23 years, 6 months) v Slovakia at Middlesbrough, Jun 11, 2003; Bobby Moore (25 years, 7 months) v Wales at Wembley, Nov 16, 1966.

Youngest player in World Cup Final: Pele (Brazil) aged 17 years, 237 days v Sweden in Stockholm, Jun 12, 1958.

Youngest player to appear in World Cup Finals: Norman Whiteside (N Ireland v Yugoslavia in Spain – Jun 17, 1982, age 17 years and 42 days.

Youngest First Division player: Derek Forster (Sunderland goalkeeper v Leicester, Aug 22, 1964) aged 15 years, 185 days.

Youngest First Division scorer: At 16 years and 57 days, schoolboy Jason Dozzell (substitute after 30 minutes for Ipswich at home to Coventry on Feb 4, 1984). Ipswich won 3-1 and Dozzell scored their third goal.

Youngest Premier League player: Matthew Briggs (Fulham sub at Middlesbrough, May 13, 2007) aged 16 years and 65 days.

Youngest Premier League scorer: James Vaughan (Everton, home to Crystal Palace, Apr 10, 2005), 16 years, 271 days.

Youngest Premier League captain: Lee Cattermole (Middlesbrough away to Fulham, May 7, 2006) aged 18 years, 47 days.

Youngest player sent off in Premier League: Wayne Rooney (Everton, away to Birmingham, Dec 26, 2002) aged 17 years, 59 days.

Youngest First Division hat-trick scorer: Alan Shearer, aged 17 years, 240 days, in Southampton's 4-2 home win v Arsenal (Apr 9, 1988) on his full debut. Previously, Jimmy Greaves (17 years, 309 days) with 4 goals for Chelsea at home to Portsmouth (7-4), Christmas Day, 1957.

Youngest to complete 100 Football League goals: Jimmy Greaves (20 years, 261 days) when he did so for Chelsea v Manchester City, Nov 19, 1960.

Youngest players in Football League: Reuben Noble-Lazarus (Barnsley 84th minute sub at Ipswich, Sep 30, 2008, Champ) aged 15 years, 45 days; Mason Bennett (Derby at Middlesbrough, Champ, Oct 22, 2011) aged 15 years, 99 days; Albert Geldard (Bradford PA v Millwall, Div 2, Sep 16, 1929) aged 15 years, 158 days; Ken Roberts (Wrexham v Bradford Park Avenue, Div 3 North, Sep 1, 1951) also 15 years, 158 days.

Youngest Football League scorer: Ronnie Dix (for Bristol Rov v Norwich, Div 3 South, Mar 3, 1928) aged 15 years, 180 days.

Youngest player in Scottish League: Goalkeeper Ronnie Simpson (Queens Park) aged 15 in 1946.

Youngest player in FA Cup: Andy Awford, Worcester City's England Schoolboy defender, aged 15 years, 88 days when he substituted in second half away to Boreham Wood (3rd qual round) on Oct 10, 1987.

Youngest player in FA Cup proper: Luke Freeman, Gillingham substitute striker (15 years, 233 days) away to Barnet in 1st round, Nov 10, 2007.

Youngest FA Cup scorer: Sean Cato (16 years, 25 days), second half sub in Barrow Town's 7-2 win away to Rothwell Town (prelim rd), Sep 3, 2011.

Youngest Wembley Cup Final captain: Barry Venison (Sunderland v Norwich, Milk Cup Final, Mar 24, 1985 – replacing suspended captain Shaun Elliott) – aged 20 years, 220 days.

Youngest FA Cup-winning captain: Bobby Moore (West Ham, 1964, v Preston), aged 23 years, 20 days.

Youngest FA Cup Final captain: David Nish aged 21 years and 212 days old when he captained Leicester against Manchester City at Wembley on Apr 26, 1969.

Youngest FA Cup Final player: Curtis Weston (Millwall sub last 3 mins v Manchester Utd, 2004) aged 17 years, 119 days.

Youngest FA Cup Final scorer: Norman Whiteside (Manchester Utd v Brighton, 1983 replay, Wembley), aged 18 years, 19 days.

Youngest FA Cup Final managers: Stan Cullis, Wolves (32) v Leicester, 1949; Steve Coppell, Crystal Palace (34) v Manchester Utd, 1990; Ruud Gullit, Chelsea (34) v Middlesbrough, 1997.

Youngest player in Football League Cup: Chris Coward (Stockport) sub v Sheffield Wed, 2nd Round, Aug 23, 2005, aged 16 years and 31 days.

Youngest Wembley scorer: Norman Whiteside (Manchester Utd v Liverpool, Milk Cup Final, Mar 26, 1983) aged 17 years, 324 days.

Youngest Wembley Cup Final goalkeeper: Chris Woods (18 years, 125 days) for Nottm Forest v Liverpool, League Cup Final on Mar 18, 1978.

Youngest Wembley FA Cup Final goalkeeper: Peter Shilton (19 years, 219 days) for Leicester v Manchester City, Apr 26, 1969.

Youngest senior international at Wembley: Salomon Olembe (sub for Cameroon v England, Nov 15, 1997), aged 16 years, 342 days.

Youngest winning manager at Wembley: Stan Cullis, aged 32 years, 187 days, as manager of Wolves, FA Cup winners on April 30 1949.

Youngest scorer in full international: Mohamed Kallon (Sierra Leone v Congo, African Nations Cup, Apr 22, 1995), reported as aged 15 years, 192 days.

Youngest English scorer in Champions League: Alex Oxlade-Chamberlain (Arsenal v Olympiacos, Sep 28, 2011) aged 18 years 1 month, 13 days

Youngest player sent off in World Cup Final series: Rigobert Song (Cameroon v Brazil, in USA, Jun 1994) aged 17 years, 358 days.

Youngest FA Cup Final referee: Kevin Howley, of Middlesbrough, aged 35 when in charge of Wolves v Blackburn, 1960.

Youngest player in England U-23 team: Duncan Edwards (v Italy, Bologna, Jan 20, 1954), aged 17 years, 112 days.

Youngest player in England U-21 team: Theo Walcott (v Moldova, Ipswich, Aug 15, 2006), aged 17 years, 152 days.

Youngest player in Scotland U-21 team: Christian Dailly (v Romania, Hampden Park, Sep 11, 1990), aged 16 years, 330 days.

Youngest player in senior football: Cameron Campbell Buchanan, Scottish-born outside right, aged 14 years, 57 days when he played for Wolves v WBA in War-time League match, Sep 26, 1942.

Youngest player in peace-time senior match: Eamon Collins (Blackpool v Kilmarnock, Anglo-Scottish Cup quarter-final 1st leg, Sep 9, 1980) aged 14 years, 323 days.

World's youngest player in top division match: Centre-forward Fernando Rafael Garcia, aged 13, played for

23 minutes for Peruvian club Juan Aurich in 3-1 win against Estudiantes on May 19, 2001.

Oldest player to appear in Football League: New Brighton manager Neil McBain (51 years, 120 days) as emergency goalkeeper away to Hartlepool (Div 3 North, Mar 15, 1947).

Other oldest post-war League players: Sir Stanley Matthews (Stoke, 1965, 50 years, 5 days); Peter Shilton (Leyton Orient 1997, 47 years, 126 days); Kevin Poole (Burton, 2010, 46 years, 291 days); Dave Beasant (Brighton 2003, 44 years, 46 days); Alf Wood (Coventry, 1958, 43 years, 199 days); Tommy Hutchison (Swansea City, 1991, 43 years, 172 days).

Oldest Football League debutant: Andy Cunningham, for Newcastle at Leicester (Div 1) on Feb 2, 1929, aged 38 years, 2 days.

Oldest post-war debut in English League: Defender David Donaldson (35 years, 7 months, 23 days) for Wimbledon on entry to Football League (Div 4) away to Halifax, Aug 20, 1977.

Oldest player to appear in First Division: Sir Stanley Matthews (Stoke v Fulham, Feb 6, 1965), aged 50 years, 5 days – on that his last League appearance, the only 50-year-old ever to play in the top division.

Oldest players in Premier League: Goalkeepers John Burridge (Manchester City v QPR, May 14, 1995), 43 years, 5 months, 11 days; Alec Chamberlain (Watford v Newcastle, May 13, 2007) 42 years, 11 months, 23 days; Steve Ogrizovic (Coventry v Sheffield Wed, May 6, 2000), 42 years, 7 months, 24 days; Brad Friedel (Tottenham v Newcastle, Nov 10, 2013) 42 years, 4 months, 22 days; Neville Southall (Bradford City v Leeds, Mar 12, 2000), 41 years, 5 months, 26 days. Outfield: Teddy Sheringham (West Ham v Manchester City, Dec 30, 2006), 40 years, 8 months, 28 days; Ryan Giggs (Manchester Utd v Hull, May 6, 2014), 40 years, 5 months, 7 days; Gordon Strachan (Coventry City v Derby, May 3, 1997), 40 years, 2 months, 24 days.

Oldest player for British professional club: John Ryan (owner-chairman of Conference club Doncaster, played as substitute for last minute in 4-2 win at Hereford on Apr 26, 2003), aged 52 years, 11 months, 3 weeks.

Oldest FA Cup Final player: Walter (Billy) Hampson (Newcastle v Aston Villa on Apr 26, 1924), aged 41 years, 257 days.

Oldest captain and goalkeeper in FA Cup Final: David James (Portsmouth v Chelsea, May 15, 2010) aged 39 years, 287 days.

Oldest FA Cup Final scorers: Bert Turner (Charlton v Derby, Apr 27, 1946) aged 36 years, 312 days. Scored for both sides. Teddy Sheringham (West Ham v Liverpool, May 13, 2006) aged 40 years, 41 days. Scored in penalty shoot-out.

Oldest FA Cup-winning team: Arsenal 1950 (average age 31 years, 2 months). Eight of the players were over 30, with the three oldest centre-half Leslie Compton 37, and skipper Joe Mercer and goalkeeper George Swindin, both 35.

Oldest World Cup-winning captain: Dino Zoff, Italy's goalkeeper v W Germany in 1982 Final, aged 40 years, 92 days.

Oldest player capped by England: Stanley Matthews (v Denmark, Copenhagen, May 15, 1957), aged 42 years, 103 days.

Oldest England scorer: Stanley Matthews (v N Ireland, Belfast, Oct 6, 1956), aged 41 years, 248 days.

Oldest British international player: Billy Meredith (Wales v England at Highbury, Mar 15, 1920), aged 45 years, 229 days.

Oldest 'new caps': Goalkeeper Alexander Morten, aged 41 years, 113 days when earning his only England Cap against Scotland on Mar 8, 1873; Arsenal centre-half Leslie Compton, at 38 years, 64 days when he made his England debut in 4-2 win against Wales at Sunderland on Nov 15, 1950. **For Scotland:** Goalkeeper Ronnie Simpson (Celtic) at 36 years, 186 days v England at Wembley, Apr 15, 1967.

Longest Football League career: This spanned 32 years and 10 months, by Stanley Matthews (Stoke, Blackpool, Stoke) from Mar 19, 1932 until Feb 6, 1965.

Shortest FA Cup-winning captain: 5ft 4in – Bobby Kerr (Sunderland v Leeds, 1973).

SHIRT NUMBERING

Numbering players in Football League matches was made compulsory in 1939. Players wore numbered shirts (1-22) in the FA Cup Final as an experiment in 1933 (Everton 1-11 v Manchester City 12-22).

Squad numbers for players were introduced by the Premier League at the start of season 1993–94. They were optional in the Football League until made compulsory in 1999–2000.

Names on shirts: For first time, players wore names as well as numbers on shirts in League Cup and FA Cup Finals, 1993.

SUBSTITUTES

In **1965**, the Football League, by 39 votes to 10, agreed that **one substitute** be allowed for an injured player at any time during a League match. First substitute used in Football League: Keith Peacock (Charlton), away to Bolton in Div 2, Aug 21, 1965.

Two substitutes per team were approved for the League (Littlewoods) Cup and FA Cup in season 1986–87 and two were permitted in the Football League for the first time in 1987–88.

Three substitutes (one a goalkeeper), two of which could be used, introduced by the Premier League for 1992–93. The Football League followed suit for 1993–94.

Three substitutes (one a goalkeeper) were allowed at the World Cup Finals for the first time at US '94.

Three substitutes (any position) introduced by Premier League and Football League in 1995–96.

Five named substitutes (three of which could be used) introduced in Premier League in 1996–97, in FA Cup in 1997–98, League Cup in 1998–99 and Football League in 1999–2000.

Seven named substitutes for Premier League, FA Cup and League Cup in 2008–09. Still only three to be used. Football League adopted this rule for 2009–10, reverted to five in 2011–12 and went back to seven for the 2012–13 season.

First substitute to score in FA Cup Final: Eddie Kelly (Arsenal v Liverpool, 1971). The **first recorded use** of a substitute was in 1889 (Wales v Scotland at Wrexham on Apr 15) when Sam Gillam arrived late – although he was a Wrexham player – and Allen Pugh (Rhostellyn) was allowed to keep goal until he turned up. The match ended 0-0.

When **Dickie Roose**, the Welsh goalkeeper, was injured against England at Wrexham, Mar 16, 1908, **Dai Davies** (Bolton) was allowed to take his place as substitute. Thus Wales used 12 players. England won 7-1.

END OF WAGE LIMIT

Freedom from the maximum wage system – in force since the formation of the Football League in 1888 – was secured by the Professional Footballers' Association in 1961. About this time Italian clubs renewed overtures for the transfer of British stars and Fulham's **Johnny Haynes** became the first British player to earn £100 a week.

THE BOSMAN RULING

On Dec 15, 1995 the **European Court of Justice** ruled that clubs had no right to transfer fees for out-of-contract players, and the outcome of the 'Bosman case' irrevocably changed football's player-club relationship. It began in 1990, when the contract of 26-year-old **Jean-Marc Bosman**, a midfield player with FC Liege, Belgium, expired. French club Dunkirk wanted him but were unwilling to pay the £500,000 transfer fee, so Bosman was compelled to remain with Liege. He responded with a lawsuit against his club and UEFA on the grounds of 'restriction of trade', and after five years at various court levels the European Court of Justice ruled not only in favour of Bosman but of all professional footballers.

The end of restrictive labour practices revolutionised the system. It led to a proliferation of transfers, rocketed the salaries of elite players who, backed by an increasing army of agents, found themselves in a vastly improved bargaining position as they moved from team to team, league to league, nation to nation. Removing the limit on the number of foreigners clubs could field brought an increasing ratio of such signings, not least in England and Scotland.

Bosman's one-man stand opened the way for footballers to become millionaires, but ended his own career. All he received for his legal conflict was 16 million Belgian francs (£312,000) in compensation, a testimonial of poor reward and martyrdom as the man who did most to change the face of football.

By 2011, he was living on Belgian state benefits, saying: 'I have made the world of football rich and shifted the power from clubs to players. Now I find myself with nothing.'

INTERNATIONAL SHOCK RESULTS

1950	USA 1 England 0 (World Cup).
1953	England 3 Hungary 6 (friendly).
1954	Hungary 7 England 1 (friendly)
1966	North Korea 1 Italy 0 (World Cup).
1982	Spain 0, Northern Ireland 1; Algeria 2, West Germany 1 (World Cup).
1990	Cameroon 1 Argentina 0; Scotland 0 Costa Rica 1; Sweden 1 Costa Rica 2 (World Cup).
1990	Faroe Islands 1 Austria 0 (European Champ qual).
1992	Denmark 2 Germany 0 (European Champ Final).
1993	USA 2 England 0 (US Cup tournament).
1993	Argentina 0 Colombia 5 (World Cup qual).
1993	France 2 Israel 3 (World Cup qual).
1994	Bulgaria 2 Germany 1 (World Cup).
1994	Moldova 3 Wales 2; Georgia 5 Wales 0 (European Champ qual).
1995	Belarus 1 Holland 0 (European Champ qual).
1996	Nigeria 4 Brazil 3 (Olympics).
1998	USA 1 Brazil 0 (Concacaf Gold Cup).
1998	Croatia 3 Germany 0 (World Cup).
2000	Scotland 0 Australia 2 (friendly).
2001	Australia 1 France 0; Australia 1, Brazil 0 (Confederations Cup).
2001	Honduras 2 Brazil 0 (Copa America).
2001	Germany 1 England 5 (World Cup qual).
2002	France 0 Senegal 1; South Korea 2 Italy 1 (World Cup).
2003:	England 1 Australia 3 (friendly)
2004:	Portugal 0 Greece 1 (European Champ Final).
2005:	Northern Ireland 1 England 0 (World Cup qual).
2014:	Holland 5 Spain 1 (World Cup).
2014:	Brazil 1 Germany 7 (World Cup).

GREAT RECOVERIES – DOMESTIC FOOTBALL

On Dec 21, 1957, **Charlton** were losing 5-1 against Huddersfield (Div 2) at The Valley with only 28 minutes left, and from the 15th minute, had been reduced to ten men by injury, but they won 7-6, with left-winger Johnny Summers scoring five goals. **Huddersfield** (managed by Bill Shankly) remain the only team to score six times in a League match and lose. On Boxing Day, 1927 in Div 3 South, **Northampton** won 6-5 at home to Luton after being 1-5 down at half-time.

Season 2010–11 produced a Premier League record for **Newcastle**, who came from 4-0 down at home to Arsenal to draw 4-4. Previous instance of a team retrieving a four-goal deficit in the top division to draw was in 1984 when Newcastle trailed at QPR in a game which ended 5-5.

In the 2012-13 League Cup, **Arsenal** were 0-4 down in a fourth round tie at Reading, levelled at 4-4 and went on to win 7-5 in extra-time.

MATCHES OFF

Worst day for postponements: Feb 9, 1963, when 57 League fixtures in England and Scotland were frozen off. Only 7 Football League matches took place, and the entire Scottish programme was wiped out.

Other weather-hit days:

Jan 12, 1963 and Feb 2, 1963 – on both those Saturdays, only 4 out of 44 Football League matches were played.

Jan 1, 1979 – 43 out of 46 Football League fixtures postponed.

Jan 17, 1987 – 37 of 45 scheduled Football League fixtures postponed; only 2 Scottish matches survived.

Feb 8–9, 1991 – only 4 of the week-end's 44 Barclays League matches survived the freeze-up (4 of the postponements were on Friday night). In addition, 11 Scottish League matches were off. Jan 27, 1996 – 44 Cup and League matches in England and Scotland were frozen off. On the weekend of Jan 9, 10, 11, 2010, 46 League and Cup matches in England and Scotland were victims of the weather. On the weekend of Dec 18-21, 2010, 49 matches were frozen off in England and Scotland.

Fewest matches left on one day by postponements was during the Second World War – Feb 3, 1940 when, because of snow, ice and fog only one out of 56 regional league fixtures took place. It resulted Plymouth Argyle 1, Bristol City 3.

The Scottish Cup second round tie between Inverness Thistle and Falkirk in season 1978–79 was **postponed 29 times** because of snow and ice. First put off on Jan 6, it was eventually played on Feb 22. Falkirk won 4-0.

Pools Panel's busiest days: Jan 17, 1987 and Feb 9, 1991 – on both dates they gave their verdict on 48 postponed coupon matches.

FEWEST 'GAMES OFF'

Season 1947–48 was the best since the war for English League fixtures being played to schedule. Only six were postponed.

LONGEST SEASON

The latest that League football has been played in a season was **Jun 7, 1947** (six weeks after the FA Cup Final). The season was extended because of mass postponements caused by bad weather in mid-winter.

The latest the FA Cup competition has been completed was in season 2014–15 when Arsenal beat Aston Villa 4-0 in the Final on May 30, kick-off 5.30pm

Worst winter hold-up was in season 1962–63. The Big Freeze began on Boxing Day and lasted until Mar, with nearly 500 first-class matches postponed. The FA Cup 3rd round was the longest on record – it began with only three out of 32 ties playable on Jan 5 and ended 66 days and 261 postponements later on Mar 11. The Lincoln–Coventry tie was put off 15 times. The Pools Panel was launched that winter, on Jan 26, 1963.

HOTTEST DAYS

The Nationwide League kicked off season 2003–04 on Aug 9 with pitch temperatures of 102 degrees recorded at Luton v Rushden and Bradford v Norwich. On the following day, there was a pitch temperature of 100 degrees for the Community Shield match between Manchester Utd and Arsenal at Cardiff's Millennium Stadium. Wembley's pitch-side thermometer registered 107 degrees for the 2009 Chelsea–Everton FA Cup Final.

FOOTBALL ASSOCIATION SECRETARIES/CHIEF EXECUTIVES

1863–66 Ebenezer Morley; 1866–68 **Robert Willis**; 1868–70 **RG Graham**; 1870–95 **Charles Alcock** (paid from 1887); 1895–1934 **Sir Frederick Wall**; 1934–62 **Sir Stanley Rous**; 1962–73 **Denis Follows**; 1973–89 **Ted Croker** (latterly chief executive); 1989–99 **Graham Kelly** (chief executive); 2000–02 **Adam Crozier** (chief executive); 2003–04 **Mark Palios** (chief executive); 2005–08: **Brian Barwick** (chief executive); 2009–10 **Ian Watmore** (chief executive); 2010-15 **Alex Horne** (chief executive); 2015 **Martin Glenn** (chief executive).

FOOTBALL'S SPONSORS

Football League: Canon 1983–86; Today Newspaper 1986–87; Barclays 1987–93; Endsleigh Insurance 1993–96; Nationwide Building Society 1996–2004; Coca-Cola 2004–10; npower 2010–14; Sky Bet from 2014.

League Cup: Milk Cup 1982–86; Littlewoods 1987–90; Rumbelows 1991–92; Coca-Cola 1993–98; Worthington 1998–2003; Carling 2003–12; Capital One 2012–15.

Premier League: Carling 1993–2001; Barclaycard 2001–04; Barclays from 2004.

FA Cup: Littlewoods 1994–98; AXA 1998–2002; E.ON 2006–11; Budweiser 2011–15; Emirates (title sponsor) from 2015.

SOCCER HEADQUARTERS

Football Association: PO Box 1966, London SW1P 9EQ.
Premier League: 30 Gloucester Place, London W1U 8PL.
Football League: Edward VII Quay, Navigation Way, Preston PR2 2YF. London Office: 30 Gloucester Place, London W1U 8FL.
League Managers' Association: St Georges Park, Newborough Road, Burton on Trent DE13 9PD.
Professional Footballers' Association: 2 Oxford Court, Bishopsgate, Manchester M2 3WQ.
Scottish Football Association: Hampden Park, Glasgow G42 9AY.
Scottish Professional Football League: Hampden Park, Glasgow G42 9DE
Irish Football Association: 20 Windsor Avenue, Belfast BT9 6EG.
Irish Football League: Benmore House, 343-353 Lisburn Road, Belfast BT9 7EN.
League of Ireland: Sports Campus, Abbotstown, Dublin 15.
Football Association of Ireland: Sports Campus, Abbotstown, Dublin 15.
Welsh Football Association: 11/12 Neptune Court, Vanguard Way, Cardiff CF24 5PJ.
FIFA: P.O. Box 85, 8030 Zurich, Switzerland.
UEFA: Route de Geneve, CH-1260, Nyon, Geneva, Switzerland.

NEW HOMES OF SOCCER

Newly-constructed League grounds in England since the war: 1946 Hull (Boothferry Park); 1950 Port Vale (Vale Park); 1955 Southend (Roots Hall); 1988 Scunthorpe (Glanford Park); 1990 Walsall (Bescot Stadium); 1990 Wycombe (Adams Park); 1992 Chester (Deva Stadium); 1993 Millwall (New Den); 1994 Huddersfield (McAlpine Stadium); 1994 Northampton (Sixfields Stadium); 1995 Middlesbrough (Riverside Stadium); 1997 Bolton (Reebok Stadium); 1997 Derby (Pride Park); 1997 Stoke (Britannia Stadium); 1997 Sunderland (Stadium of Light); 1998 Reading (Madejski Stadium); 1999 Wigan (JJB Stadium); 2001 Southampton (St Mary's Stadium); 2001 Oxford Utd (Kassam Stadium); 2002 Leicester (Walkers Stadium); 2002 Hull (Kingston Communications Stadium); 2003 Manchester City (City of Manchester Stadium); 2003 Darlington (New Stadium); 2005 Coventry (Ricoh Arena); Swansea (Stadium of Swansea, Morfa); 2006 Arsenal (Emirates Stadium); 2007 Milton Keynes Dons (Stadium: MK); Shrewsbury (New Meadow); 2008 Colchester (Community Stadium); 2009 Cardiff City Stadium; 2010 Chesterfield (b2net Stadium); Morecambe (Globe Arena); 2011 Brighton (American Express Stadium); 2012 Rotherham (New York Stadium).

Bolton now Macron Stadium; Chesterfield now Proact Stadium; Derby now iPro Stadium; Huddersfield now John Smith's Stadium; Leicester now King Power Stadium; Manchester City now Etihad Stadium; Shrewsbury now Greenhous Meadow Stadium; Swansea now Liberty Stadium; Walsall now Banks's Stadium; Wigan now DW Stadium.

NATIONAL FOOTBALL CENTRE

The FA's new £120m centre at St George's Park, Burton upon Trent, was opened on Oct 9, 20012 by the Duke of Cambridge, president of the FA. The site covers 330 acres, has 12 full-size pitches (5 with undersoil heating and floodlighting). There are 5 gyms, a 90-seat lecture theatre, a hydrotherapy unit with swimming pool for the treatment of injuries and two hotels. It is the base for England teams, men and women, at all levels.

GROUND-SHARING

Manchester Utd played their home matches at **Manchester City's** Maine Road ground for 8 years after Old Trafford was bomb-damaged in Aug 1941. **Crystal Palace** and **Charlton** shared Selhurst Park (1985–91); **Bristol Rov** and **Bath City** (Twerton Park, Bath, 1986–96); **Partick Thistle** and **Clyde** (Firhill Park, Glasgow, 1986–91; in seasons 1990–01, 1991–92 **Chester** shared **Macclesfield's** ground (Moss Rose).

Crystal Palace and **Wimbledon** shared Selhurst Park, from season 1991–92, when **Charlton** (tenants) moved to rent Upton Park from **West Ham**, until 2003 when Wimbledon relocated to Milton Keynes. **Clyde** moved to Douglas Park, **Hamilton Academical's** home, in 1991–92. **Stirling Albion** shared **Stenhousemuir's** ground, Ochilview Park, in 1992–93. In 1993–94,

Clyde shared **Partick**'s home until moving to Cumbernauld. In 1994–95, **Celtic** shared Hampden Park with **Queen's Park** (while Celtic Park was redeveloped); **Hamilton** shared **Partick**'s ground. **Airdrie** shared **Clyde**'s Broadwood Stadium. **Bristol Rov** left **Bath City**'s ground at the start of season 1996–97, sharing Bristol Rugby Club's Memorial Ground. **Clydebank** shared **Dumbarton**'s Boghead Park from 1996–97 until renting **Greenock Morton**'s Cappielow Park in season 1999–2000. **Brighton** shared **Gillingham**'s ground in seasons 1997–98, 1998–99. **Fulham** shared **QPR**'s home at Loftus Road in seasons 2002–03, 2003–04, returning to Craven Cottage in Aug 2004. **Coventry** played home fixtures at Northampton in season 2013–14, returning to their own ground, the Ricoh Arena, in Sept 2014.

Inverness Caledonian Thistle moved to share **Aberdeen**'s Pittodrie Stadium in 2004–05 after being promoted to the SPL; **Gretna's** home matches on arrival in the SPL in 2007–08 were held at Motherwell and Livingston.

ARTIFICIAL TURF

QPR were the first British club to install an artificial pitch, in 1981. They were followed by **Luton** in 1985, and **Oldham** and **Preston** in **1986**. QPR reverted to grass in 1988, as did Luton and promoted Oldham in season 1991–92 (when artificial pitches were banned in Div 1). **Preston** were the last Football League club playing 'on plastic' in 1993–94, and their Deepdale ground was restored to grass for the start of 1994–95.

Stirling were the **first Scottish club** to play on plastic, in season 1987–88.

DOUBLE RUNNERS-UP

There have been nine instances of clubs finishing runner-up in **both the League Championship** and **FA Cup** in the same season: 1928 Huddersfield; 1932 Arsenal; 1939 Wolves; 1962 Burnley; 1965 and 1970 Leeds; 1986 Everton; 1995 Manchester Utd; 2001 Arsenal.

CORNER-KICK RECORDS

Not a single corner-kick was recorded when **Newcastle** drew 0–0 at home to **Portsmouth** (Div 1) on Dec 5, 1931.

The record for **most corners** in a match for one side is believed to be **Sheffield Utd's 28** to West Ham's 1 in Div 2 at Bramall Lane on Oct 14, 1989. For all their pressure, Sheffield Utd lost 2–0.

Nottm Forest led **Southampton** 22–2 on corners (Premier League, Nov 28, 1992) but lost the match 1–2.

Tommy Higginson (Brentford, 1960s) once passed back to his own goalkeeper from a corner kick.

When **Wigan** won 4–0 at home to Cardiff (Div 2) on Feb 16, 2002, all four goals were headed in from corners taken by N Ireland international **Peter Kennedy**.

Steve Staunton (Rep of Ireland) is believed to be the only player to score direct from a corner in **two** Internationals.

In the 2012 Champions League Final, **Bayern Munich** forced 20 corners without scoring, while **Chelsea** scored from their only one.

SACKED AT HALF-TIME

Leyton Orient sacked **Terry Howard** on his 397th appearance for the club – at half-time in a Second Division home defeat against Blackpool (Feb 7, 1995) for 'an unacceptable performance'. He was fined two weeks' wages, given a free transfer and moved to Wycombe.

Bobby Gould resigned as **Peterborough**'s head coach at half-time in their 1–0 defeat in the LDV Vans Trophy 1st round at Bristol City on Sep 29, 2004.

Harald Schumacher, former Germany goalkeeper, was sacked as Fortuna Koln coach when they were two down at half-time against Waldhof Mannheim (Dec 15, 1999). They lost 5–1.

MOST GAMES BY 'KEEPER FOR ONE CLUB

Alan Knight made 683 League appearances for Portsmouth, over 23 seasons (1978–2000), a record for a goalkeeper at one club. The previous holder was Peter Bonetti with 600 League games for Chelsea (20 seasons, 1960–79).

PLAYED TWO GAMES ON SAME DAY

Jack Kelsey played full-length matches for both club and country on Wednesday Nov 26, 1958. In the afternoon he kept goal for Wales in a 2-2 draw against England at Villa Park, and he then drove to Highbury to help Arsenal win 3-1 in a prestigious floodlit friendly against Juventus.

On the same day, winger **Danny Clapton** played for England (against Wales and Kelsey) and then in part of Arsenal's match against Juventus.

On Nov 11, 1987, **Mark Hughes** played for Wales against Czechoslovakia (European Championship) in Prague, then flew to Munich and went on as substitute that night in a winning Bayern Munich team, to whom he was on loan from Barcelona.

On Feb 16, 1993 goalkeeper **Scott Howie** played in Scotland's 3-0 U-21 win v Malta at Tannadice Park, Dundee (ko 1.30pm) and the same evening played in Clyde's 2-1 home win v Queen of South (Div 2).

Ryman League **Hornchurch**, faced by end-of-season fixture congestion, played **two matches** on the same night (May 1, 2001). They lost 2-1 at home to Ware and drew 2-2 at Clapton.

RECORD LOSS

Manchester City made a record loss of £194.9m in the 2010–11 financial year.

FIRST 'MATCH OF THE DAY'

BBC TV (recorded highlights): Liverpool 3, Arsenal 2 on Aug 22, 1964. **First complete match to be televised:** Arsenal 3, Everton 2 on Aug 29, 1936. **First League match televised in colour:** Liverpool 2, West Ham 0 on Nov 15, 1969.

'MATCH OF THE DAY' – BIGGEST SCORES

Football League: Tottenham 9, Bristol Rov 0 (Div 2, 1977–78). **Premier League:** Nottm Forest 1, Manchester Utd 8 (1998–99); Portsmouth 7 Reading 4 (2007–08).

FIRST COMMENTARY ON RADIO

Arsenal 1 Sheffield Utd 1 (Div 1) broadcast on BBC, Jan 22, 1927.

OLYMPIC FOOTBALL WINNERS

1908 Great Britain (in London); **1912** Great Britain (Stockholm); **1920** Belgium (Antwerp); **1924** Uruguay (Paris); **1928** Uruguay (Amsterdam); **1932** No soccer in Los Angeles Olympics; **1936** Italy (Berlin); **1948** Sweden (London); **1952** Hungary (Helsinki); **1956** USSR (Melbourne); **1960** Yugoslavia (Rome); **1964** Hungary (Tokyo); **1968** Hungary (Mexico City); **1972** Poland (Munich); **1976** E Germany (Montreal); **1980** Czechoslovakia (Moscow); **1984** France (Los Angeles); **1988** USSR (Seoul); **1992** Spain (Barcelona); **1996** Nigeria (Atlanta); **2000** Cameroon (Sydney); **2004** Argentina (Athens); **2008** Argentina (Beijing); **2012** Mexico (Wembley).

Highest scorer in Final tournament: Ferenc Bene (Hungary) 12 goals, 1964.

Record crowd for Olympic Soccer Final: 108,800 (France v Brazil, Los Angeles 1984).

MOST AMATEUR CUP WINS

Bishop Auckland set the FA Amateur Cup record with 10 wins, and in 1957 became the only club to carry off the trophy in three successive seasons. The competition was discontinued after the Final on Apr 20, 1974. (Bishop's Stortford 4, Ilford 1, at Wembley).

FOOTBALL FOUNDATION

This was formed (May 2000) to replace the **Football Trust**, which had been in existence since 1975 as an initiative of the Pools companies to provide financial support at all levels, from schools football to safety and ground improvement work throughout the game.

SEVEN-FIGURE TESTIMONIALS

The first was **Sir Alex Ferguson**'s at Old Trafford on Oct 11, 1999, when a full-house of 54,842 saw a Rest of the World team beat Manchester Utd 4-2. United's manager pledged that a large percentage of the estimated £1m receipts would go to charity.

Estimated receipts of £1m and over came from testimonials for **Denis Irwin** (Manchester Utd) against Manchester City at Old Trafford on Aug 16, 2000 (45,158); **Tom Boyd** (Celtic) against Manchester Utd at Celtic Park on May 15, 2001 (57,000) and **Ryan Giggs** (Manchester Utd) against Celtic on Aug 1, 2001 (66,967).

Tony Adams' second testimonial (1-1 v Celtic on May 13, 2002) two nights after Arsenal completed the Double, was watched by 38,021 spectators at Highbury. Of £1m receipts, he donated £500,000 to Sporting Chance, the charity that helps sportsmen/women with drink, drug, gambling problems.

Sunderland and a Republic of Ireland XI drew 0-0 in front of 35,702 at the Stadium of Light on May 14, 2002. The beneficiary, **Niall Quinn**, donated his testimonial proceeds, estimated at £1m, to children's hospitals in Sunderland and Dublin, and to homeless children in Africa and Asia.

A record testimonial crowd of 69,591 for **Roy Keane** at Old Trafford on May 9, 2006 netted more than £2m for charities in Dublin, Cork and Manchester. Manchester Utd beat Celtic 1-0, with Keane playing for both teams.

Alan Shearer's testimonial on May 11, 2006, watched by a crowd of 52,275 at St James' Park, raised more than £1m. The club's record scorer, in his farewell match, came off the bench in stoppage time to score the penalty that gave Newcastle a 3-2 win over Celtic. Total proceeds from his testimonial events, £1.64m, were donated to 14 charities in the north-east.

Ole Gunnar Solskjaer, who retired after 12 years as a Manchester Utd player, had a crowd of 68,868, for his testimonial on Aug 2, 2008 (United 1 Espanyol 0). He donated the estimated receipts of £2m to charity, including the opening of a dozen schools In Africa.

Liverpool's **Jamie Carragher** had his testimonial against Everton (4-1) on Sep 4, 2010. It was watched by a crowd of 35,631 and raised an estimated £1m for his foundation, which supports community projects on Merseyside.

Gary Neville donated receipts of around £1m from his testimonial against Juventus (2-1) in front of 42,000 on May 24, 2011, to charities and building a Supporters' Centre near Old Trafford.

Paul Scholes had a crowd of 75,000 for his testimonial, Manchester United against New York Cosmos, on Aug 5, 2011. Receipts were £1.5m.

Steven Gerrard, Liverpool captain, donated £500,000 from his testimonial to the local Alder Hey Children's Hospital after a match against Olympiacos was watched by a crowd of 44,362 on Aug 3, 2013. Gerrard chose the Greek champions because he scored a special goal against them in the season Liverpool won the 2005 Champions League.

WHAT IT USED TO COST

Minimum admission to League football was one shilling in 1939 After the war, it was increased to 1s 3d in 1946; 1s 6d in 1951; 1s 9d in 1952; 2s in 1955; 2s 6d; in 1960; 4s in 1965; 5s in 1968; 6s in 1970; and 8s (40p) in 1972 After that, the fixed minimum charge was dropped.

Wembley's first Cup Final programme in 1923 cost three pence ($1\frac{1}{4}$p in today's money). The programme for the 'farewell' FA Cup Final in May, 2000 was priced £10.

FA Cup Final ticket prices in 2011 reached record levels – £115, £85, £65 and £45.

WHAT THEY USED TO EARN

In the 1930s, First Division players were on £8 a week (£6 in close season) plus bonuses of £2 win, £1 draw. The maximum wage went up to £12 when football resumed post-war in 1946 and had reached £20 by the time the limit was abolished in 1961.

EUROPEAN TROPHY WINNERS

European Cup/Champions League: 10 Real Madrid; **7** AC Milan; **5** Liverpool, Barcelona, Bayern Munich; **4** Ajax; **3** Inter Milan, Manchester Utd; **2** Benfica, Juventus, Nottm Forest, Porto; **1** Aston Villa, Borussia Dortmund, Celtic, Chelsea, Feyenoord, Hamburg, Marseille, PSV Eindhoven, Red Star Belgrade, Steaua Bucharest

Cup-Winners' Cup: 4 Barcelona; **2** Anderlecht, Chelsea, Dynamo Kiev, AC Milan; **1** Aberdeen, Ajax, Arsenal, Atletico Madrid, Bayern Munich, Borussia Dortmund, Dynamo Tbilisi, Everton, Fiorentina, Hamburg, Juventus, Lazio, Magdeburg, Manchester City, Manchester Utd, Mechelen, Paris St Germain, Parma, Rangers, Real Zaragoza, Sampdoria, Slovan Bratislava, Sporting Lisbon, Tottenham, Valencia, Werder Bremen, West Ham.

UEFA Cup: 3 Barcelona, Inter Milan, Juventus, Liverpool, Valencia; **2** Borussia Moenchengladbach, Feyenoord, Gothenburg, Leeds, Parma, Real Madrid, Sevilla, Tottenham; **1** Anderlecht, Ajax, Arsenal, Bayer Leverkusen, Bayern Munich, CSKA Moscow, Dynamo Zagreb, Eintracht Frankfurt, Ferencvaros, Galatasaray, Ipswich, Napoli, Newcastle, Porto, PSV Eindhoven, Real Zaragoza, Roma, Schalke, Shakhtar Donetsk, Zenit St Petersburg.

Europa League: 2 Atletico Madrid, Sevilla; **1** Chelsea, Porto..

● The Champions League was introduced into the European Cup in 1992–93 to counter the threat of a European Super League. The UEFA Cup became the Europa League, with a new format, in season 2009–10.

BRITAIN'S 34 TROPHIES IN EUROPE

Euro Cup/Champs Lge (13)		Cup-Winners' Cup (10)		Fairs/UEFA Cup/Europa Lge (11)	
1967	Celtic	1963	Tottenham	1968	Leeds
1968	Manchester Utd	1965	West Ham	1969	Newcastle
1977	Liverpool	1970	Manchester City	1970	Arsenal
1978	Liverpool	1971	Chelsea	1971	Leeds
1979	Nottm Forest	1972	Rangers	1972	Tottenham
1980	Nottm Forest	1983	Aberdeen	1973	Liverpool
1981	Liverpool	1985	Everton	1976	Liverpool
1982	Aston Villa	1991	Manchester Utd	1981	Ipswich
1984	Liverpool	1994	Arsenal	1984	Tottenham
1999	Manchester Utd	1998	Chelsea	2001	Liverpool
2005	Liverpool			2013	Chelsea
2008	Manchester Utd				
2012	Chelsea				

ENGLAND'S EUROPEAN RECORD

Manchester Utd, Chelsea, Arsenal and Liverpool all reached the Champions League quarter-finals in season 2007–08 – the first time one country had provided four of the last eight. For the first time, England supplied both finalists in 2008 (Manchester Utd and Chelsea) and have provided three semi-finalists in 2007–08–09).

END OF CUP-WINNERS' CUP

The **European Cup-Winners' Cup**, inaugurated in 1960–61, terminated with the 1999 Final. The competition merged into a revamped **UEFA Cup**.

From its inception in 1955, the **European Cup** comprised only championship-winning clubs until 1998–99, when selected runners-up were introduced. Further expansion came in 1999–2000 with the inclusion of clubs finishing third in certain leagues and fourth in 2002.

EUROPEAN CLUB COMPETITIONS – SCORING RECORDS

European Cup – record aggregate: 18-0 by Benfica v Dudelange (Lux) (8-0a, 10-0h), prelim rd, 1965–66.

Record single-match score: 11-0 by Dinamo Bucharest v Crusaders (rd 1, 2nd leg, 1973-74 (agg 12-0).

Champions League – record single-match score: Liverpool 8-0 v Besiktas, Group A qual (Nov 6, 2007).

Highest match aggregate: 13 – Bayern Munich 12 Sporting Lisbon 1 (5-0 away, 7-1 at home, 1st ko rd, 2008–09)

Cup-Winners' Cup – *record aggregate: 21-0 by Chelsea v Jeunesse Hautcharage (Lux) (8-0a,

13-0h), 1st rd, 1971–72.

Record single-match score: 16-1 by Sporting Lisbon v Apoel Nicosia, 2nd round, 1st leg, 1963–64 (aggregate was 18-1).

UEFA Cup (prev Fairs Cup) – *Record aggregate: 21-0 by Feyenoord v US Rumelange (Lux) (9-0h, 12-0a), 1st round, 1972–73.

Record single-match score: 14-0 by Ajax Amsterdam v Red Boys (Lux) 1st rd, 2nd leg, 1984–85 (aggregate also 14-0).

Record British score in Europe: 13-0 by **Chelsea** at home to Jeunesse Hautcharage (Lux) in Cup-Winners' Cup 1st round, 2nd leg, 1971–72. Chelsea's overall 21-0 win in that tie is highest aggregate by British club in Europe.

Individual scoring record for European tie (over two legs): 10 goals (6 home, 4 away) by **Kiril Milanov** for Levski Spartak in 19-3 agg win Cup-Winners' Cup 1st round v Lahden Reipas, 1976–77. Next highest: **8** goals by Jose Altafini for AC Milan v US Luxembourg (European Cup, prelim round, 1962–63, agg 14-0) and by **Peter Osgood** for Chelsea v Jeunesse Hautcharage (Cup-Winners' Cup, 1st round 1971–72, agg 21-0). Altafini and Osgood each scored 5 goals at home, 3 away.

Individual single-match scoring record in European competition: **6** by **Mascarenhas** for Sporting Lisbon in 16-1 Cup-Winner's Cup 2nd round, 1st leg win v Apoel, 1963–64; and by **Lothar Emmerich** for Borussia Dortmund in 8-0 CWC 1st round, 2nd leg win v Floriana 1965–66; and by Kiril Milanov for Levski Spartak in 12-2 CWC 1st round, 1st leg win v Lahden Reipas, 1976–77.

Most goals in single European campaign: 15 by **Jurgen Klinsmann** for Bayern Munich (UEFA Cup 1995–96).

Most goals by British player in European competition: 30 by **Peter Lorimer** (Leeds, in 9 campaigns).

Most individual goals in Champions League match: 5 by **Lionel Messi** (Barcelona) in 7-1 win at home to Bayer Leverkusen in round of 16 second leg, 2011–12.

Most European Cup goals by individual player: 49 by **Alfredo di Stefano** in 58 apps for Real Madrid (1955–64).

(*Joint record European aggregate)

First European treble: Clarence Seedorf became the first player to win the European Cup with three clubs: Ajax in 1995, Real Madrid in 1998 and AC Milan in 2003.

EUROPEAN FOOTBALL – BIG RECOVERIES

In the most astonishing Final in the history of the European Cup/Champions League, **Liverpool** became the first club to win it from a 3-0 deficit when they beat AC Milan 3-2 on penalties after a 3-3 draw in Istanbul on May 25, 2005. Liverpool's fifth triumph in the competition meant that they would keep the trophy.

The following season, **Middlesbrough** twice recovered from three-goal aggregate deficits in the **UEFA Cup**, beating Basel 4-3 in the quarter finals and Steaua Bucharest by the same scoreline in the semi-finals. In 2010, **Fulham** beat Juventus 5-4 after trailing 1-4 on aggregate in the second leg of their Europa League, Round of 16 match at Craven Cottage.

Two Scottish clubs have won a European tie from a 3-goal, first leg deficit: **Kilmarnock** 0-3, 5-1 v Eintracht Frankfurt (Fairs Cup 1st round, 1964–65); **Hibernian** 1-4, 5-0 v Napoli (Fairs Cup 2nd Round, 1967–68).

English clubs have three times gone out of the **UEFA Cup** after leading 3-0 from the first leg: 1975–76 (2nd Rd) **Ipswich** lost 3-4 on agg to Bruges; 1976–77 (quarter-final) **QPR** lost on penalties to AEK Athens after 3-3 agg; 1977–78 (3rd round) **Ipswich** lost on penalties to Barcelona after 3-3 agg.

On Oct 16, 2012, Sweden recovered from 0-4 down to draw 4-4 with Germany (World Cup qual) in Berlin.

● In the **1966 World Cup quarter-final** (Jul 23) at Goodison Park, North Korea led Portugal 3-0, but Eusebio scored 4 times to give **Portugal** a 5-3 win.

HEAVIEST ENGLISH-CLUB DEFEATS IN EUROPE

(Single-leg scores)

European Cup: Artmedia Bratislava 5, **Celtic** 0 (2nd qual round), Jul 2005 (agg 5-4); Ajax 5, **Liverpool** 1 (2nd round), Dec 1966 (agg 7-3); Real Madrid 5, **Derby** 1 (2nd round), Nov 1975 (agg 6-5).

Cup-Winners' Cup: Sporting Lisbon 5, **Manchester Utd** 0 (quarter-final), Mar 1964 (agg 6-4).

Fairs/UEFA Cup: Bayern Munich 6, **Coventry** 1 (2nd round), Oct 1970 (agg 7-3). **Combined London** team lost 6-0 (agg 8-2) in first Fairs Cup Final in 1958. Barcelona 5, **Chelsea** 0 in Fairs Cup semi-final play-off, 1966, in Barcelona (after 2-2 agg).

SHOCK ENGLISH CLUB DEFEATS

1968–69 (Eur Cup, 1st round): **Manchester City** beaten by Fenerbahce, 1-2 agg.

1971–72 (CWC, 2nd round): **Chelsea** beaten by Atvidaberg on away goals.

1993–94 (Eur Cup, 2nd round): **Manchester Utd** beaten by Galatasaray on away goals.

1994–95 (UEFA Cup, 1st round): **Blackburn** beaten by Trelleborgs, 2-3 agg.

2000–01 (UEFA Cup, 1st round): **Chelsea** beaten by St Gallen, Switz 1-2 agg.

PFA FAIR PLAY AWARD (Bobby Moore Trophy from 1993)

1988	Liverpool	2002	Crewe
1989	Liverpool	2003	Crewe
1990	Liverpool	2004	Crewe
1991	Nottm Forest	2005	Crewe
1992	Portsmouth	2006	Crewe
1993	Norwich	2007	Crewe
1994	Crewe	2008	Crewe
1995	Crewe	2009	Stockport
1996	Crewe	2010	Rochdale
1997	Crewe	2011	Rochdale
1998	Cambridge Utd	2012	Chesterfield
1999	Grimsby	2013	Crewe
2000	Crewe	2014	Exeter
2001	Hull		

RECORD MEDAL SALES

At Sotherby's in London on Nov 11, 2014, the FA Cup winner's medal which **Sir Stanley Matthews** earned with Blackpool in 1953 was sold for £220,000 - the most expensive medal in British sporting history. At the same auction, **Ray Wilson's** 1966 World Cup winner's medal fetched £136,000, while **Jimmy Greaves**, who was left out of the winning England team, received £44,000 for the medal the FA belatedly awarded him in 2009

West Ham bought (Jun 2000) the late **Bobby Moore**'s collection of medals and trophies for £1.8m at Christie's auction. It was put up for sale by his first wife Tina and included his World Cup-winner's medal.

A No. 6 duplicate red shirt made for England captain **Bobby Moore** for the 1966 World Cup Final fetched £44,000 at an auction at Wolves' ground in Sep, 1999. Moore kept the shirt he wore in that Final and gave the replica to England physio Harold Shepherdson.

Sir Geoff Hurst's 1966 World Cup-winning shirt fetched a record £91,750 at Christie's in Sep, 2000. His World Cup Final cap fetched £37,600 and his Man of the Match trophy £18,800. Proceeds totalling £274,410 from the 129 lots went to Hurst's three daughters and charities of his choice, including the Bobby Moore Imperial Cancer Research Fund.

In Aug, 2001, Sir Geoff sold his World Cup-winner's medal to his former club West Ham Utd (for their museum) at a reported £150,000.

'The **Billy Wright** Collection' – caps, medals and other memorabilia from his illustrious career – fetched over £100,000 at Christie's in Nov, 1996.

At the sale in Oct 1993, trophies, caps and medals earned by **Ray Kennedy**, former England, Arsenal and Liverpool player, fetched a then record total of £88,407. Kennedy, suffering from

Parkinson's Disease, received £73,000 after commission. The PFA paid £31,080 for a total of 60 lots – including a record £16,000 for his 1977 European Cup winner's medal – to be exhibited at their Manchester museum. An anonymous English collector paid £17,000 for the medal and plaque commemorating Kennedy's part in the Arsenal Double in 1971.

Previous record for one player's medals, shirts etc collection: £30,000 (**Bill Foulkes**, Manchester Utd in 1992). The sale of **Dixie Dean**'s medals etc in 1991 realised £28,000.

In Mar, 2001, **Gordon Banks**' 1966 World Cup-winner's medal fetched a new record £124,750. TV's Nick Hancock, a Stoke fan, paid £23,500 for **Sir Stanley Matthews**'s 1953 FA Cup-winner's medal. He also bought one of Matthews's England caps for £3,525 and paid £2,350 for a Stoke Div 2 Championship medal (1963).

Dave Mackay's 1961 League Championship and FA Cup winner's medals sold for £18,000 at Sotherby's. Tottenham bought them for their museum.

A selection of England World Cup-winning manager **Sir Alf Ramsey**'s memorabilia – England caps, championship medals at Ipswich etc. – fetched more than £80,000 at Christie's. They were offered for sale by his family, and his former clubs Tottenham and Ipswich were among the buyers.

Ray Wilson's 1966 England World Cup-winning shirt fetched £80,750. Also in Mar, 2002, the No. 10 shirt worn by **Pele** in Brazil's World Cup triumph in 1970 was sold for a record £157,750 at Christies. It went to an anonymous telephone bidder.

In Oct, 2003, **George Best**'s European Footballer of the Year (1968) trophy was sold to an anonymous British bidder for £167,250 at Bonham's. It was the then most expensive item of sporting memorabilia ever auctioned in Britain.

England captain **Bobby Moore**'s 1970 World Cup shirt, which he swapped with Pele after Brazil's 1-0 win in Mexico, was sold for £60,000 at Christie's in Mar, 2004.

Sep, 2004: England shirt worn by tearful **Paul Gascoigne** in 1990 World Cup semi-final v Germany sold at Christie's for £28,680. At same auction, shirt worn by Brazil's **Pele** in 1958 World Cup Final in Sweden sold for £70,505.

May, 2005: The **second FA Cup** (which was presented to winning teams from 1896 to 1909) was bought for £420,000 at Christie's by Birmingham chairman David Gold, a world record for an item of football memorabilia. It was presented to the National Football Museum, Preston. At the same auction, the World Cup-winner's medal earned by England's **Alan Ball** in 1966 was sold for £164,800.

Oct, 2005: At auction at Bonham's, the medals and other memorabilia of Hungary and Real Madrid legend **Ferenc Puskas** were sold for £85,000 to help pay for hospital treatment.

Nov, 2006: A ball used in the 2006 World Cup Final and signed by the winning **Italy** team was sold for £1.2m (a world record for football memorabilia) at a charity auction in Qatar. It was bought by the Qatar Sports Academy.

Feb, 2010: A pair of boots worn by **Sir Stanley Matthews** in the 1953 FA Cup Final was sold at Bonham's for £38,400.

Oct, 2010: Trophies and memorabilia belonging to **George Best** were sold at Bonham's for £193,440. His 1968 European Cup winner's medal fetched £156,000.

Oct–Nov 2010: **Nobby Stiles** sold his 1966 World Cup winner's medal at an Edinburgh auction for a record £188,200. His old club, Manchester Utd, also paid £48,300 for his 1968 European Cup medal to go to the club's museum at Old Trafford. In London, the shirt worn by Stiles in the 1966 World Cup Final went for £75,000. A total of 45 items netted £424,438. **George Cohen** and **Martin Peters** had previously sold their medals from 1966.

Oct 2011: **Terry Paine** (who did not play in the Final) sold his 1966 World Cup medal for £27,500 at auction.

Mar 2013: **Norman Hunter** (Leeds and England) sold his honours' collection on line for nearly £100,000

Nov 2013: A collection of **Nat Lofthouse's** career memorabilia was sold at auction for £100,000. Bolton Council paid £75,000 for items including his 1958 FA Cup winner's medal to go on show at the local museum.

LONGEST UNBEATEN CUP RUN

Liverpool established the longest unbeaten Cup sequence by a Football League club: 25 successive rounds in the League/Milk Cup between semi-final defeat by Nottm Forest (1-2 agg) in 1980 and defeat at Tottenham (0-1) in the third round on Oct 31, 1984. During this period Liverpool won the tournament in four successive seasons, a feat no other Football League club has achieved in any competition.

BIG HALF-TIME SCORES

Tottenham 10, Crewe 1 (FA Cup 4th round replay, Feb 3, 1960; result 13-2); Tranmere 8, Oldham 1 (Div 3N., Dec 26, 1935; result 13-4); **Chester City 8, York 0** (Div 3N., Feb 1, 1936; result 12-0; believed to be record half-time scores in League football!)
Nine goals were scored in the first half – **Burnley 4, Watford 5** in Div 1 on Apr 5, 2003. Result: 4-7.
Stirling Albion led Selkirk 15-0 at half-time (result 20-0) in the Scottish Cup 1st round, Dec 8, 1984.
World record half-time score: **16-0** when **Australia** beat **American Samoa** 31-0 (another world record) in the World Cup Oceania qualifying group at Coff's Harbour, New South Wales, on Apr 11 2001.
• On Mar 4 1933 **Coventry** beat QPR (Div 3 South) 7-0, having led by that score at half-time. This repeated the half-time situation in Bristol City's 7-0 win over Grimsby on Dec 26, 1914.

TOP SECOND-HALF TEAM

Most goals scored by a team in one half of a League match is **11. Stockport** led Halifax 2-0 at half-time in Div 3 North on Jan 6 1934 and won 13-0.

FIVE NOT ENOUGH

Last team to score **5** in League match and lose: **Burton**, beaten 6-5 by Cheltenham (Lge 2, Mar 13, 2010).

LONG SERVICE WITH ONE CLUB

Bill Nicholson, OBE, was associated with Tottenham for 67 years – as a wing-half (1938–55), then the club's most successful manager (1958–74) with 8 major prizes, subsequently chief advisor and scout. He became club president, and an honorary freeman of the borough, had an executive suite named after him at the club, and the stretch of roadway from Tottenham High Road to the main gates has the nameplate Bill Nicholson Way. He died, aged 85, in Oct 2004.
Ted Bates, the Grand Old Man of Southampton with 66 years of unbroken service to the club, was awarded the Freedom of the City in Apr, 2001. He joined Saints as an inside-forward from Norwich in 1937, made 260 peace-time appearances for the club, became reserve-team trainer in 1953 and manager at The Dell for 18 years (1955–73), taking Southampton into the top division in 1966. He was subsequently chief executive, director and club president. He died in Oct 2003, aged 85.
Bob Paisley was associated with Liverpool for 57 years from 1939, when he joined them from Bishop Auckland, until he died in Feb 1996. He served as player, trainer, coach, assistant-manager, manager, director and vice-president. He was Liverpool's most successful manager, winning 13 major trophies for the club (1974–83).
Dario Gradi, MBE, stepped down after completing 24 seasons and more than 1,000 matches as manager of Crewe (appointed Jun 1983). Never a League player, he previously managed Wimbledon and Crystal Palace. At Crewe, his policy of finding and grooming young talent has earned the club more than £20m in transfer fees. He stayed with Crewe as technical director, and twice took charge of team affairs again following the departure of the managers who succeeded him, Steve Holland and Gudjon Thordarson.
Ronnie Moran, who joined Liverpool in as a player 1952, retired from the Anfield coaching staff in season 1998–99.
Ernie Gregory served West Ham for 52 years as goalkeeper and coach. He joined them as boy of 14 from school in 1935, retired in May 1987.

Ryan Giggs played 24 seasons for Manchester Utd (1990-2014), then became assistant manager under Louis van Gaal.

Ted Sagar, Everton goalkeeper, 23 years at Goodison Park (1929–52, but only 16 League seasons because of war).

Alan Knight, goalkeeper, played 23 seasons (1977–2000) for his only club, Portsmouth.

Sam Bartram was recognised as one of the finest goalkeepers never to play for England, apart from unofficial wartime games. He was with Charlton from 1934–56

Jack Charlton, England World Cup winner, served Leeds from 1952–73.

Roy Sproson, defender, played 21 League seasons for his only club, Port Vale (1950–71).

TIGHT AT HOME

Fewest home goals conceded in League season (modern times): 4 by **Liverpool** (Div 1, 1978–9); 4 by **Manchester Utd** (Premier League, 1994–95) – both in 21 matches.

FOOTBALL POOLS

Littlewoods launched them in 1923 with a capital of £100. Coupons were first issued (4,000 of them) outside Manchester Utd's ground, the original 35 investors staking a total of £4 7s 6d (pay-out £2 12s).

Vernons joined Littlewoods as the leading promoters. The Treble Chance, leading to bonanza dividends, was introduced in 1946 and the Pools Panel began in Jan 1963, to counter mass fixture postponements caused by the Big Freeze winter.

But business was hard hit by the launch of the National Lottery in 1994. Dividends slumped, the work-force was drastically cut and in Jun 2000 the Liverpool-based Moores family sold Littlewoods Pools in a £161m deal. After 85 years, the name Littlewoods disappeared from Pools betting in Aug 2008. The New Football Pools was formed. Vernons and Zetters continued to operate under their own name in the ownership of Sportech. The record prize remains the £2,924,622 paid to a Worsley, Manchester, syndicate in Nov 1994.

Fixed odds football – record pay-out: £654,375 by Ladbrokes (May 1993) to Jim Wright, of Teignmouth, Devon. He placed a £1,000 each-way pre-season bet on the champions of the three Football League divisions – Newcastle (8–1), Stoke (6–1) and Cardiff (9–1).

Record match accumulators: £164,776 to £4 stake on 18 correct results, Oct 5, 6, 7, 2002. The bet, with Ladbrokes in Colchester, was made by Army chef Mark Simmons; £272,629 for £2.50 stake on 9 correct scores (6 English Prem Lge, 3 Spanish Cup) on Jan 5, 2011, by an anonymous punter at Ladbrokes in Berkshire.

TRANSFER WINDOW

This was introduced to Britain in Sep 2002 via FIFA regulations to bring uniformity across Europe (the rule previously applied in a number of other countries).

The transfer of contracted players is restricted to two periods: Jun 1–Aug 31 and Jan 1–31).

On appeal, Football League clubs continued to sign/sell players (excluding deals with Premiership clubs).

PROGRAMME PIONEERS

Chelsea pioneered football's magazine-style programme by introducing a 16-page issue for the First Division match against Portsmouth on Christnmas Day 1948. It cost sixpence (2.5p). A penny programme from the 1909 FA Cup Final fetched £23,500 at a London auction in May, 2012.

WORLD'S OLDEST FOOTBALL ANNUAL

Now in its 129th edition, this publication began as the 16-page Athletic News Football Supplement & Club Directory in 1887. From the long-established Athletic News, it became the Sunday Chronicle Annual in 1946, the Empire News in 1956, the News of the World & Empire News in 1961 and the News of the World Annual from 1965 until becoming the Nationwide Annual in 2008.

PREMIER LEAGUE CLUB DETAILS AND SQUADS 2015-16

(at time of going to press)

ARSENAL

Ground: Emirates Stadium, Highbury, London, N5 IBU
Telephone: 0207 7619 5000. **Club nickname:** Gunners
Capacity: 60,272. **Colours:** Red and white. **Main sponsor:** Emirates
Record transfer fee: £42.4m to Real Madrid for Mesut Ozil, Sep 2013
Record fee received: £35m from Barcelona for Cesc Fabregas, Aug 2011
Record attendance: Highbury: 73,295 v Sunderland (Div 1) Mar 9, 1935. Wembley: 73,707 v Lens (Champ Lge) Nov 1998. Emirates Stadium: 60,161 v Manchester Utd (Prem Lge) Nov 3, 2007
League Championship: Winners 1930–31, 1932–33, 1933–34, 1934–35, 1937–38, 1947–48, 1952–53, 1970–71, 1988–89, 1990–91, 1997–98, 2001–02, 2003–04
FA Cup: Winners 1930, 1936, 1950, 1971, 1979, 1993, 1998, 2002, 2003, 2005, 2014, 2015
League Cup: Winners 1987, 1993
European competitions: Winners Fairs Cup 1969–70; Cup-Winners' Cup 1993–94
Finishing positions in Premier League: 1992–93 10th, 1993–94 4th, 1994–95 12th, 1995–96 5th, 1996–97 3rd, 1997–98 1st, 1998–99 2nd, 1999–2000 2nd, 2000–01 2nd, 2001–02 1st, 2002–03 2nd, 2003–04 1st, 2004–05 2nd, 2005–06 4th, 2006–07 4th, 2007–08 3rd, 2008–09 4th, 2009–10 3rd, 2010–11 4th, 2011–12 3rd, 2012–13 4th, 2013–14 4th, 2014–15 3rd
Biggest win: 12-0 v Loughborough (Div 2) Mar 12, 1900
Biggest defeat: 0-8 v Loughborough (Div 2) Dec 12, 1896
Highest League scorer in a season: Ted Drake 42 (1934–35)
Most League goals in aggregate: Thierry Henry 175 (1999–2007) (2012)
Longest unbeaten League sequence: 49 matches (2003–04)
Longest sequence without a League win: 23 matches (1912–13)
Most capped player: Thierry Henry (France) 81

Name	Height ft in	Previous club	Birthplace	Birthdate
Goalkeepers				
Cech, Petr	6.5	Chelsea	Plzen, Cz	20.05.82
Martinez, Damian	6.4	Independiente	Mar del Plata, Arg	02.09.92
Ospina, David	6.0	Nice	Medellin, Col	31.08.88
Szczesny, Wojciech	6.5	–	Warsaw, Pol	18.04.90
Defenders				
Bellerin, Hector	5.10	Barcelona	Barcelona, Sp	19.03.95
Chambers, Calum	6.0	Southampton	Petersfield	20.01.95
Debuchy, Mathieu	5.10	Newcastle	Fretin, Fr	28.07.85
Gabriel Paulista	6.2	Villarreal	Sao Paulo, Br	26.11.90
Gibbs, Kieran	5.10	–	Lambeth	26.09.89
Hayden, Isaac	6.1	–	Chelmsford	22.03.95
Jenkinson, Carl	6.1	Charlton	Harlow	08.02.92
Koscielny, Laurent	6.1	Lorient	Tulle, Fr	10.09.85
Mertesacker, Per	6.6	Werder Bremen	Hannover, Ger	29.09.84
Monreal, Nacho	5.10	Malaga	Pamplona, Sp	26.02.86
Midfielders				
Arteta, Mikel	5.9	Everton	San Sebastian, Sp	28.03.82
Bielik, Krystian	6.2	Legia Warsaw	Konin, Pol	04.01.98

Cazorla, Santi	5.6	Malaga	Llanera, Sp	13.12.84
Coquelin, Francis	5.10	–	Laval, Fr	13.05.91
Flamini, Mathieu	5.10	AC Milan	Marseille, Fr	07.03.84
Oxlade-Chamberlain, Alex	5.11	Southampton	Portsmouth	15.08.93
Ozil, Mesut	5.11	Real Madrid	Gelsenkirchen, Ger	15.10.88
Rosicky, Tomas	5.10	Borussia Dortmund	Prague, Cz	04.10.80
Ramsey, Aaron	5.11	Cardiff	Caerphilly	26.12.90
Wilshere, Jack	5.8	–	Stevenage	01.01.92
Zelalem, Gedion	5.11	Hertha Berlin	Berlin	26.01.97
Forwards				
Akpom, Chuba	6.0	Southend	Canning Town	09.10.95
Giroud, Olivier	6.4	Montpellier	Chambery, Fr	30.09.86
Gnabry, Serge	5.9	Stuttgart	Stuttgart, Ger	14.07.95
Sanchez, Alexis	5.7	Barcelona	Tocopilla, Chil	19.12.88
Walcott, Theo	5.8	Southampton	Newbury	16.03.89
Welbeck, Danny	5.10	Manchester Utd	Manchester	26.11.90

ASTON VILLA

Ground: Villa Park, Trinity Road, Birmingham, B6 6HE
Telephone: 0800 612 0970. **Club nickname**: Villans
Capacity: 42,682. **Colours**: Claret and blue. **Main sponsor**: Quickbooks
Record transfer fee: £18m to Sunderland for Darren Bent, Jan 2011
Record fee received: £24m from Manchester City for James Milner, Aug 2010
Record attendance: 76,588 v Derby (FA Cup 6) Mar 2, 1946
League Championship: Winners 1893–94, 1895–96, 1896–97, 1898–99, 1899–1900, 1909–10, 1980–81
FA Cup: Winners 1887, 1895, 1897, 1905, 1913, 1920, 1957
League Cup: Winners 1961, 1975, 1977, 1994, 1996
European competitions: Winners European Cup 1981–82; European Super Cup 1983
Finishing positions in Premier League: 1992–93 2nd, 1993–94 10th, 1994–95 18th, 1995–96 4th, 1996–97 5th, 1997–98 7th, 1998–99 6th, 1999–2000 6th, 2000–01 8th, 2001–02 8th, 2002–03 16th, 2003–04 6th, 2004–05 10th, 2005–06 16th, 2006–07 11th, 2007–08 6th, 2008–09 6th, 2009–10 6th, 2010–11 9th, 2011–12 16th, 2012–13 15th, 2013–14 15th, 2014–15 17th
Biggest win: 12-2 v Accrington (Div 1) Mar 12, 1892; 11-1 v Charlton (Div 2) Nov 24, 1959; 10-0 v Sheffield Wed (Div 1) Oct 5, 1912, v Burnley (Div 1) Aug 29, 1925. Also: 13-0 v Wednesbury (FA Cup 1) Oct 30, 1886
Biggest defeat: 0-8 v Chelsea (Prem Lge) Dec 23, 2012
Highest League scorer in a season: 'Pongo' Waring 49 (1930–31)
Most League goals in aggregate: Harry Hampton 215 (1904–1915)
Longest unbeaten League sequence: 15 matches (1897, 1909–10 and 1949)
Longest sequence without a League win: 12 matches (1973–74 and 1986–87)
Most capped player: Steve Staunton (Republic of Ireland) 64

Goalkeepers				
Bunn, Mark	6.0	Norwich	Southgate	16.11.84
Guzan, Brad	6.4	Chivas	Evergreen Park, US	09.09.84
Steer, Jed	6.3	Norwich	Norwich	23.09.92
Defenders				
Baker, Nathan	6.3	–	Worcester	23.04.91
Cissokho, Aly	5.11	Valencia	Blois, Fr	15.09.87
Clark, Ciaran	6.2	–	Harrow	26.09.89
Hutton, Alan	6.1	Tottenham	Glasgow	30.11.84
Okore, Jores	6.0	Nordsjaelland	Abidjan Iv C	11.08.92

Richards, Micah	5.11	Manchester City	Birmingham	24.06.88
Richardson, Kieran	5.10	Fulham	Greenwich	21.10.84
Senderos, Philippe	6.3	Valencia	Geneva, Swi	14.02.85

Midfielders

Bacuna, Leandro	6.2	Groningen	Groningen, Hol	21.08.91
Cole, Joe	5.9	West Ham	Islington	08.11.81
Delph, Fabian	5.9	Leeds	Bradford	05.05.91
Gil, Charles	5.7	Valencia	Valencia, Sp	22.11.92
Grealish, Jack	5.9	–	Solihull	10.09.95
Gueye, Idrissa	5.9	Lille	Dakar, Sen	26.09.89
N'Zogbia, Charles	5.8	Wigan	Harfleur, Fr	28.05.86
Sanchez, Carlos	6.0	Elche	Quibdo, Col	06.02.86
Sinclair, Scott	5.10	Manchester City	Bath	25.03.89
Tonev, Aleksandar	5.10	Lech Poznan	Elin Pelin, Bul	03.02.90
Westwood, Ashley	5.8	Crewe	Nantwich	01.04.90

Forwards

Agbonlahor, Gabriel	5.11	–	Birmingham	13.10.86
Benteke, Christian	6.3	Genk	Kinshasa, DR Cong	03.12.90
Kozak, Libor	6.4	Lazio	Opava, Cz	30.05.89

BOURNEMOUTH

Ground: Goldsands Stadium, Dean Court, Bournemouth BH7 7AF
Telephone: 0844 576 1910. **Club nickname**: Cherries
Capacity: 11,700. **Colours**: Red and black. **Main sponsor**: Mansion Group
Record transfer fee: £8m to Ipswich for Tyrone Mings, Jun 2015
Record fee received: £3m from Norwich for Lewis Grabban, Jun 2014
Record attendance: 28,799 v Manchester Utd (FA Cup 6) Mar 2, 1957
FA Cup: Sixth round 1957
League Cup: Fifth round 2014
Biggest win: 8-0 v Birmingham (Champ) Oct 15, 2014. Also: 11-0 v Margate (FA Cup 1) Nov 20, 1971
Biggest defeat: 0-9 v Lincoln (Div 3) Dec 18, 1982
Highest League scorer in a season: Ted MacDougall 42 (1970–71)
Most League goals in aggregate: Ron Eyre 202 (1924–33)
Longest unbeaten League sequence: 18 (1982)
Longest sequence without a League win: 14 (1974)
Most capped player: Gerry Peyton (Republic of Ireland) 7

Goalkeepers

Allsop, Ryan	6.3	Leyton Orient	Birminghanm	17.06.92
Boruc, Artur	6.4	Southampton	Siedice, Pol	20.02.80
Camp, Lee	6.1	WBA	Derby	22.08.84
Federici, Adam	6.2	Reading	Nowra, Aus	31.01.85

Defenders

Cargill, Baily	6.2	–	Winchester	05.07.95
Cook, Steve	6.1	Brighton	Hastings	19.04.91
Distin, Sylvain	6.4	Everton	Paris, Fr	16.12.77
Elphick, Tommy	5.11	Bournemouth	Brighton	07.09.87
Francis, Simon	6.0	Charlton	Nottingham	16.02.85
Mings, Tyrone	6.3	Ipswich	Bath	13.03.93
Smith, Adam	5.11	Tottenham	Leystonstone	29.04.91
Ward, Elliott	6.1	Norwich	Harrow	19.01.85

Midfielders

| Arter, Harry | 5.9 | Woking | Eltham | 28.12.89 |
| Atsu, Christian | 5.8 | Chelsea (loan) | Ada Foah, Gha | 10.01.92 |

Daniels, Charlie	5.10	Leyton Orient	Harlow	07.09.86
Gosling, Dan	5.10	Newcastle	Brixham	02.02.90
MacDonald, Shaun	6.1	Swansea	Swansea	17.06.88
O'Kane, Eunan	5.8	Torquay	Derry	10.07.90
Pugh, Marc	5.11	Hereford	Bacup	02.04.87
Ritchie, Matt	5.8	Swindon	Gosport	10.09.89
Stanislas, Junior	6.0	Burnley	Eltham	26.11.89
Surman, Andrew	5.11	Norwich	Johannesburg, SA	20.08.86
Forwards				
Kermorgant, Yann	6.1	Charlton	Vannes, Fr	08.11.81
King, Josh	5.11	Blackburn	Oslo, Nor	15.01.92
Rantie, Tokelo	5.9	Malmo	Parys, SA	08.09.90
Wilson, Callum	5.11	Coventry	Coventry	27.02.92

CHELSEA

Ground: Stamford Bridge Stadium, London SW6 1HS
Telephone: 0871 984 1905. **Club nickname**: Blues
Capacity: 41,798. **Colours**: Blue. **Main sponsor**: Yokohama Rubber
Record transfer fee: £50m to Liverpool for Fernando Torres, Jan 2011
Record fee received: £40m from Paris SG for David Luiz, Jun 2014
Record attendance: 82,905 v Arsenal (Div 1) Oct 12, 1935
League Championship: Winners 1954–55, 2004–05, 2005–06, 2009–10, 2014–15
FA Cup: Winners 1970, 1997, 2000, 2007, 2009, 2010, 2012
League Cup: Winners 1965, 1998, 2005, 2007, 2015
European competitions: Winners Champions League 2011–12; Cup-Winners' Cup 1970–71, 1997–98; Europa League 2012–13; European Super Cup 1998
Finishing positions in Premier League: 1992–93 11th, 1993–94 14th, 1994–95 11th, 1995–96 11th, 1996–97 6th, 1997–98 4th, 1998–99 3rd, 1999–2000 5th, 2000–01 6th, 2001–02 6th, 2002–03 4th, 2003–04 2nd, 2004–05 1st, 2005–06 1st, 2006–07 2nd, 2007–08 2nd, 2008–09 3rd, 2009–10 1st, 2010–11 2nd, 2011–12 6th, 2012–13 3rd, 2013–14 3rd, 2014–15 1st
Biggest win: 8-0 v Aston Villa (Prem Lge) Dec 23, 2012. Also: 13-0 v Jeunesse Hautcharage, (Cup-Winners' Cup 1) Sep 29, 1971
Biggest defeat: 1-8 v Wolves (Div 1) Sep 26, 1953; 0-7 v Leeds (Div 1) Oct 7, 1967, v Nottm Forest (Div 1) Apr 20, 1991
Highest League scorer in a season: Jimmy Greaves 41 (1960–61)
Most League goals in aggregate: Bobby Tambling 164 (1958–70)
Longest unbeaten League sequence: 40 matches (2004–05)
Longest sequence without a League win: 21 matches (1987–88)
Most capped player: Frank Lampard (England) 104

Goalkeepers				
Begovic, Asmir	6.5	Stoke	Trebinje, Bos	20.06.87
Blackman, Jamal	6.6	–	Croydon	27.10.93
Courtois, Thibaut	6.6	Genk	Bree, Bel	11.05.92
Defenders				
Ake, Nathan	5.11	Feyenoord	The Hague, Hol	18.02.95
Azpilicueta, Cesar	5.10	Marseille	Pamplona, Sp	28.08.89
Cahill, Gary	6.2	Bolton	Sheffield	19.12.85
Christensen, Andreas	6.2	Brondby	Lillerod, Den	10.04.96
Filipe Luis	6.0	Atletico Madrid	Jaragua, Br	09.08.85
Ivanovic, Branislav	6.2	Lokomotive Moscow	Mitrovica, Serb	22.02.84
Terry, John	6.1	–	Barking	07.12.80
Zouma, Kurt	6.3	St Etienne	Lyon, Fr	27.10.94

Midfielders

Cuadrado, Juan	5.10	Fiorentina	Necocli, Col	26.05.88
Fabregas, Cesc	5.11	Barcelona	Arenys de Mar, Sp	04.05.87
Hazard, Eden	5.8	Lille	La Louviere, Bel	07.01.91
Loftus-Cheek, Ruben	6.3	–	Lewisham	23.01.96
Matic, Nemanja	6.4	Benfica	Sabac, Serb	01.08.88
Mikel, John Obi	6.2	Lyn Oslo	Plato State, Nig	22.04.87
Nathan	5.10	Paranaense	Blumenau, Br	13.03.96
Oscar	5.10	Internacional	Americana, Br	09.09.91
Ramires	5.11	Benfica	Rio de Janeiro, Br	24.03.87
Willian	5.9	Anzhi Makhachkala	Ribeirao Pires, Br	09.08.88

Forwards

Brown, Isaiah	6.0	–	Peterborough	07.01.97
Diego Costa	6.2	Atletico Madrid	Lagarto, Br	07.10.88
Falcao, Radamel	5.10	Monaco (loan)	Santa Marta, Col	10.02.86
Remy, Loic	6.1	QPR	Rilleux, Fr	02.01.87

CRYSTAL PALACE

Ground: Selhurst Park, Whitehorse Lane, London SE25, 6PU
Telephone: 0208 768 6000. **Club nickname**: Eagles
Capacity: 25,073. **Colours**: Red and blue. **Main sponsor**: Neteller
Record transfer fee: £10m to Paris St-Germain for Yohan Cabaye, Jul 2015
Record fee received: £15m from Manchester Utd for Wilfried Zaha, Jan 2013
Record attendance: 51,482 v Burnley (Div 2), May 11, 1979
League Championship: 3rd 1990–91
FA Cup: Runners-up 1990
League Cup: Semi-finals 1993, 1995, 2001, 2012
Finishing positions in Premier League: 1992–93 20th, 1994–95 19th, 1997–98 20th, 2004–05 18th, 2013–14 11th, 2014–15 10th
Biggest win: 9-0 v Barrow (Div 4) Oct 10, 1959
Biggest defeat: 0-9 v Liverpool (Div 1) Sep 12, 1989. Also: 0-9 v Burnley (FA Cup 2 rep) Feb 10, 1909
Highest League scorer in a season: Peter Simpson 46 (1930–31)
Most League goals in aggregate: Peter Simpson 153 (1930–36)
Longest unbeaten League sequence: 18 matches (1969)
Longest sequence with a League win: 20 matches (1962)
Most capped player: Aki Riihilahti (Finland) 36

Goalkeepers

Hennessey, Wayne	6.5	Wolves	Bangor, Wal	24.01.87
Kettings, Chris	6.4	Blackpool	Glasgow	25.10.92
Speroni, Julian	6.1	Dundee	Buenos Aires, Arg	18.05.79

Defenders

Dann, Scott	6.2	Blackburn	Liverpool	14.02.87
Delaney, Damien	6.2	Ipswich	Cork, Ire	29.07.81
Fryers, Zeki	6.0	Tottenham	Manchester	09.09.92
Guedioura, Adlene	6.0	Wolves	La Roche, Fr	12.11.85
Kelly, Martin	6.3	Liverpool	Whiston	27.04.90
Mariappa, Adrian	5.11	Reading	Harrow	03.10.86
McCarthy, Patrick	6.1	Charlton	Dublin, Ire	31.05.83
Souare, Pape	5.10	Lille	Mbao, Sen	06.06.90
Ward, Joel	6.2	Portsmouth	Portsmouth	29.10.89

Midfielders

Bannan, Barry	5.11	Aston Villa	Airdrie	01.12.89

Bolasie, Yannick	6.2	Bristol City	Kinshasa, DR Cong	24.05.89
Cabaye, Yohan	5.9	Paris SG	Tourcoing, Fr	14.01.86
Jedinak, Mile	6.3	Genclerbirligi	Sydney, Aus	03.08.84
Kaikai, Sullay	6.0	–	Southwark	26.08.95
Ledley, Joe	6.0	Celtic	Cardiff	23.01.87
Lee Chung–Yong	5.11	Bolton	Seoul, S Kor	02.07.88
McArthur, James	5.7	Wigan	Glasgow	07.10.87
Mutch, Jordon	5.9	QPR	Birmingham	02.12.91
Puncheon, Jason	5.8	Southampton	Croydon	26.06.86
Williams, Jonathan	5.7	–	Pembury	09.10.93
Zaha, Wilfried	5.10	Manchester Utd	Abidjan, Iv C	10.11.92
Forwards				
Appiah, Kwesi	5.11	Margate	Thamesmead	12.08.90
Campbell, Fraizer	5.11	Cardiff	Huddersfield	13.09.87
Chamakh, Marouane	6.1	Arsenal	Tonneins, Fr	10.01.84
Gayle, Dwight	5.10	Peterborough	Walthamstow	20.10.90
Murray, Glenn	6.2	Brighton	Maryport	25.09.83

EVERTON

Ground: Goodison Park, Liverpool L4 4EL
Telephone: 0871 663 1878. **Club nickname**: Toffees
Capacity: 39,571. **Colours**: Blue and white. **Main sponsor**: Chang
Record transfer fee: £28m to Chelsea for Romelu Lukaku, Jul 2014
Record fee received: £27m from Manchester Utd for Wayne Rooney, Aug 2004
Record attendance: 78,299 v Liverpool (Div 1) Sep 18, 1948
League Championship: Winners 1890–91, 1914–15, 1927–28, 1931–31, 1938–39, 1962–63, 1969–70, 1984–85, 1986–87
FA Cup: Winners 1906, 1933, 1966, 1984, 1995
League Cup: Runners-up 1977, 1984
European competitions: Winners Cup-Winners' Cup 1984–85
Finishing positions in Premier League: 1992–93 13th, 1993–94 17th, 1994–95 15th, 1995–96 6th 1996–97 15th 1997–98 17th 1998–99 14th, 1999–2000 13th, 2000–01 16th, 2001–02 15th, 2002–03 7th, 2003–04 17th, 2004–05 4th, 2005–06 11th, 2006–07 6th, 2007–08 5th, 2008–09 5th, 20010–11 7th, 2011–12 7th, 2012–13 6th, 2013–14 5th, 2014–15 11th
Biggest win: 9-1 v Manchester City (Div 1) Sep 3, 1906, v Plymouth (Div 2) Dec 27, 1930. Also: 11-2 v Derby (FA Cup 1) Jan 18, 1890
Biggest defeat: 0-7 v Portsmouth (Div 1) Sep 10, 1949, v Arsenal (Prem Lge) May 11, 2005
Highest League scorer in a season: Ralph 'Dixie' Dean 60 (1927–28)
Most League goals in aggregate: Ralph 'Dixie' Dean 349 (1925–37)
Longest unbeaten League sequence: 20 matches (1978)
Longest sequence without a League win: 14 matches (1937)
Most capped player: Neville Southall (Wales) 92

Goalkeepers				
Howard, Tim	6.3	Manchester Utd	North Brunswick, US	03.06.79
Robles, Joel	6.5	Atletico Madrid	Getafe, Sp	17.06.90
Stanek, Jindrich	6.3	Sparta Prague	Strakonice, Cz	27.04.96
Defenders				
Baines, Leighton	5.7	Wigan	Liverpool	11.12.84
Browning, Tyias	5.11	–	Liverpool	27.05.94
Coleman, Seamus	5.10	Sligo	Donegal, Ire	11.10.88
Galloway, Brendan	6.2	MK Dons	Harare, Zimb	17.03.96
Garbutt, Luke	5.10	Leeds	Harrogate	21.05.93

Hibbert, Tony	5.10	–	Liverpool	20.02.81
Jagielka, Phil	5.11	Sheffield Utd	Manchester	17.08.82
Stones, John	5.10	Barnsley	Barnsley	28.05.94
Midfielders				
Barkley, Ross	6.2	–	Liverpool	05.12.93
Barry, Gareth	6.0	Manchester City	Hastings	23.02.81
Besic, Muhamed	5.10	Ferencvaros	Berlin, Ger.	10.09.92
Cleverley, Tom	5.10	Manchester Utd	Basingstoke	12.08.89
Deulofeu, Gerard	5.10	Barcelona	Riudarenes, Sp	13.03.94
Gibson, Darron	5.9	Manchester Utd	Derry	25.10.87
McCarthy, James	5.11	Wigan	Glasgow	12.11.90
McGeady, Aiden	5.11	Spartak Moscow	Paisley	04.04.86
Mirallas, Kevin	6.0	Olympiacos	Liege, Bel	05.10.87
Osman, Leon	5.8	–	Billinge	17.05.81
Oviedo, Bryan	5.8	Copenhagen	Ciudad, C Rica	18.02.90
Pienaar, Steven	5.9	Tottenham	Johannesburg, SA	17.03.82
Forwards				
Henen, David	6.1	Olympiacos	Libramont, Bel	19.04.96
Kone, Arouna	5.11	Wigan	Anyama Iv C	11.11.83
Lukaku, Romelu	6.3	Chelsea	Antwerp, Bel	13.05.93
McAleny, Conor	5.10	–	Liverpool	12.08.92
Naismith, Steven	5.10	Rangers	Irvine	14.09.86

LEICESTER CITY

Ground: King Power Stadium, Filbert Way, Leicester, LE2 7FL
Telephone: 0344 815 5000. **Club nickname**: Foxes
Capacity: 32,312. **Colours**: Blue and white. **Main sponsor**: King Power
Record transfer fee: £9m to Rijeka for Andrej Kramaric, Jan 2015
Record fee received: £11m from Liverpool for Emile Heskey, Mar 2000
Record attendance: Filbert Street: 47,298 v Tottenham (FA Cup 5) Feb 18, 1928; King Power Stadium: 32,148 v Newcastle (Prem Lge) Dec 26, 2003. Also: 32,188 v Real Madrid (friendly) Jul 30, 2011
League Championship: Runners-up 1928–29
FA Cup: Runners-up 1949, 1961, 1963, 1969
League Cup: Winners 1964, 1997, 2000
European competitions: Cup-Winners' Cup rd 1 1961–62; UEFA Cup rd 1 1997–98, 2000–01
Finishing positions in Premier League: 1994–95 21st, 1996–97 9th, 1997–98 10th, 1998–99 10th, 1999–2000 8th, 2000–01 13th, 2001–02 20th, 2003–04 18th, 2014–15 14th
Biggest win: 10-0 v Portsmouth (Div 1) Oct 20, 1928. Also: 13-0 v Notts Olympic (FA Cup) Oct 13, 1894
Biggest defeat (while Leicester Fosse): 0-12 v Nottm Forest (Div 1) Apr 21, 1909
Highest League scorer in a season: Arthur Rowley 44 (1956–57)
Most League goals in aggregate: Arthur Chandler 259 (1923–35)
Longest unbeaten League sequence: 23 matches (2008–09)
Longest sequence without a League win: 19 matches (1975)
Most capped player: John O'Neill (Northern Ireland) 39

Goalkeepers				
Hamer, Ben	6.4	Charlton	Taunton	20.11.87
Logan, Conrad	6.2	–	Ramelton, Ire	18.04.86
Schmeichel, Kasper	6.0	Leeds	Copenhagen, Den	05.11.86
Schwarzer, Mark	6.4	Chelsea	Sydney, Aus	06.10.72
Defenders				
De Laet, Ritchie	6.1	Manchester Utd	Antwerp, Bel	28.11.88
Fuchs, Christian	6.1	Schalke	Neunkirchen, Aut	07.04.86

Huth, Robert	6.3	Stoke	Berlin, Ger	18.08.84
Konchesky, Paul	5.10	Liverpool	Barking	15.05.81
Morgan, Wes	5.11	Nottm Forest	Nottingham	21.01.84
Moore, Liam	6.1	–	Leicester	31.01.93
Schlupp, Jeffrey	5.8	–	Hamburg, Ger	23.12.92
Simpson, Danny	6.0	QPR	Salford	04.01.87
Wesilewski, Marcin	6.1	Anderlecht	Krakow, Pol	09.06.80

Midfielders

Albrighton, Mark	6.1	Aston Villa	Tamworth	18.11.89
Cambiasso, Esteban	5.10	Inter Milan	Buenos Aires, Arg	18.08.80
Drinkwater, Danny	5.10	Manchester Utd	Manchester	05.03.90
Hammond, Dean	6.0	Southampton	Hastings	07.03.83
James, Matty	5.10	Manchester Utd	Bacup	22.07.91
King, Andy	6.0	–	Maidenhead	29.10.88
Knockaert, Anthony	5.10	Guingamp	Roubaix, Fr	20.11.91
Mahrez, Riyad	5.11	Le Havre	Sarcelles, Fr	21.02.91

Forwards

Kramaric, Andrej	5.11	Rijeka	Zagreb, Cro	19.06.91
Lawrence, Tom	5.10	Manchester Utd	Wrexham	13.01.94
Nugent, David	5.11	Portsmouth	Liverpool	02.05.85
Okazaki, Shinji	5.9	Mainz	Takarazuka, Jap	16.04.86
Ulloa, Leonardo	6.2	Brighton	General Roca, Arg	26.07.86
Vardy, Jamie	5.10	Fleetwood	Sheffield	11.01.87

LIVERPOOL

Ground: Anfield, Liverpool L4 0TH
Telephone: 0151 263 2361. **Club nickname**: Reds or Pool
Capacity: 45,276. **Colours**: Red. **Main sponsor**: Standard Chartered
Record transfer fee: £35m to Newcastle for Andy Carroll, Jan 2011
Record fee received: £75m from Barcelona for Luis Suarez, Jul 2014
Record attendance: 61,905 v Wolves, (FA Cup 4), Feb 2, 1952
League Championship: Winners 1900–01, 1905–06, 1921–22, 1922–23, 1946–47, 1963–64, 1965–66, 1972–73, 1975–76, 1976–77, 1978–79, 1979–80, 1981–82, 1982–83, 1983–84, 1985–86, 1987–88, 1989–90
FA Cup: Winners 1965, 1974, 1986, 1989, 1992, 2001, 2006
League Cup: Winners 1981, 1982, 1983, 1984, 1995, 2001, 2003, 2012
European competitions: Winners European Cup/Champions League 1976–77, 1977–78, 1980–81, 1983–84, 2004–05; UEFA Cup 1972–73, 1975–76, 2000–01; European Super Cup 1977, 2001, 2005
Finishing positions in Premier League: 1992–93 6th, 1993–94 8th, 1994–95 4th, 1995–96 3rd, 1996–97 4th, 1997–98 3rd, 1998–99 7th, 1999–2000 4th, 2000–01 3rd, 2001–02 2nd, 2002–03 5th, 2003–04 4th, 2004–05 5th, 2005–06 3rd, 2006–07 3rd, 2007–08 4th, 2008–09 2nd, 2009–10 7th, 2010–11 6th, 2011–12 8th, 2012–13 7th, 2013–14 2nd, 2014–15 6th
Biggest win: 10-1 v Rotherham (Div 2) Feb 18, 1896. Also: 11-0 v Stromsgodset (Cup-Winners' Cup 1) Sep 17, 1974
Biggest defeat: 1-9 v Birmingham (Div 2) Dec 11, 1954
Highest League scorer in a season: Roger Hunt 41 (1961–62)
Most League goals in aggregate: Roger Hunt 245 (1959–69)
Longest unbeaten League sequence: 31 matches (1987–88)
Longest sequence without a League win: 14 matches (1953–54))
Most capped player: Steven Gerrard (England) 114

Goalkeepers

| Bogdan, Adam | 6.4 | Stoke | Budapest, Hun | 27.09.87 |

Mignolet, Simon	6.4	Sunderland	Sint-Truiden, Bel	06.08.88
Defenders				
Clyne, Nathaniel	5.9	Southampton	Stockwell	05.04.91
Flanagan, Jon	5.11	–	Liverpool	01.01.93
Gomez, Joe	6.1	Charlton	Catford	23.05.97
Ilori, Tiago	6.3	Sporting	London	26.02.93
Jose Enrique	6.0	Newcastle	Valencia, Sp	23.01.86
Lovren, Dejan	6.2	Southampton	Zenica, Bos	05.07.89
Manquillo, Javier	5.9	Atletico Madrid (loan)	Madrid, Sp	05.05.94
McLaughlin, Ryan	5.11	–	Liverpool	21.01.93
Moreno, Alberto	5.7	Sevilla	Seville, Sp	05.07.92
Sakho, Mamadou	6.2	Paris SG	Paris, Fr	13.02.90
Skrtel, Martin	6.3	Zenit St Petersburg	Trencin, Slovak	15.12.84
Toure, Kolo	6.0	Manchester City	Bouake, Iv C	19.03.81
Wisdom, Andre	6.1	–	Leeds	09.05.93
Midfielders				
Allen, Joe	5.7	Swansea	Carmarthen	14.03.90
Can Emre	6.1	Bayer Leverkusen	Frankfurt, Ger	12.01.94
Coutinho, Philippe	5.8	Inter Milan	Rio de Janeiro, Br	12.06.92
Henderson, Jordan	5.10	Sunderland	Sunderland	17.06.90
Ibe, Jordon	5.7	Wycombe	Bermondsey	08.12.95
Lallana, Adam	5.10	Southampton	Bournemouth	10.05.88
Lucas Leiva	5.10	Gremio	Dourados, Br	09.01.87
Markovic, Lazar	5.9	Benfica	Cacak, Serb	02.03.94
Milner, James	5.11	Manchester City	Leeds	04.01.86
Sterling, Raheem	5.7	–	Kingston, Jam	08.12.94
Teixeira, Joao Carlos	5.9	Sporting	Braga, Por	18.01.93
Forwards				
Balotelli, Mario	6.3	AC Milan	Palermo, It	12.08.90
Borini, Fabio	5.11	Parma	Bentivoglio, It	29.03.91
Firmino, Roberto	6.0	Hoffenheim	Maceio, Br	02.10.91
Ings, Danny	5.10	Burnley	Winchester	16.03.92
Lambert, Rickie	5.10	Southampton	Liverpool	16.02.82
Sturridge, Daniel	6.2	Chelsea	Birmingham	01.09.89
Yesil, Samed	5.8	Bayer Leverkusen	Dusseldorf, Ger	25.05.94

MANCHESTER CITY

Ground: Etihad Stadium, Etihad Campus, Manchester M11 3FF
Telephone: 0161 444 1894. **Club nickname**: City
Capacity: 48,000. **Colours**: Sky blue and white. **Main sponsor**: Etihad
Record transfer fee: £38.5m to Atletico Madrid for Sergio Aguero, Jul 2011
Record fee received: £21m from Chelsea for Shaun Wright-Phillips, Jul 2005
Record attendance: Maine Road: 84,569 v Stoke (FA Cup 6) Mar 3, 1934 (British record for any game outside London or Glasgow). Etihad Stadium: 47,435 v QPR (Prem Lge) May 13, 2012. Also: 47,726 Zenit St Petersburg v Rangers (UEFA Cup Final) May 14, 2008
League Championship: Winners 1936–37, 1967–68, 2011–12, 2013–14
FA Cup: Winners 1904, 1934, 1956, 1969, 2011
League Cup: Winners 1970, 1976, 2014
European competitions: Winners Cup-Winners' Cup 1969–70
Finishing positions in Premier League: 1992–93 9th, 1993–94 16th, 1994–95 17th, 1995–96 18th, 2000–01: 18th, 2002–03 9th, 2003–04 16th, 2004–05 8th, 2005–06 15th, 2006–07 14th, 2007–08 9th, 2008–09 10th, 2009–10 5th, 2010–11 3rd, 2011–12 1st, 2012–13 2nd, 2013–14 1st, 2014–15 2nd
Biggest win: 10-1 Huddersfield (Div 2) Nov 7, 1987. Also: 10-1 v Swindon (FA Cup 4) Jan 29, 1930

Biggest defeat: 1-9 v Everton (Div 1) Sep 3, 1906
Highest League scorer in a season: Tommy Johnson 38 (1928–29)
Most League goals in aggregate: Tommy Johnson, 158 (1919–30)
Longest unbeaten League sequence: 22 matches (1946–47)
Longest sequence without a League win: 17 matches (1979–80)
Most capped player: Colin Bell (England) 48

Goalkeepers

Caballero, Willy	6.1	Malaga	Santa Elena, Arg	28.09.81
Hart, Joe	6.3	Shrewsbury	Shrewsbury	19.04.87
Wright, Richard	6.2	Ipswich	Ipswich	05.11.77

Defenders

Clichy, Gael	5.11	Arsenal	Paris, Fr	26.07.85
Demichelis, Martin	6.0	Atletico Madrid	Justiniano, Arg	20.12.80
Kompany, Vincent	6.4	Hamburg	Uccle, Bel	10.04.86
Kolarov, Aleksandar	6.2	Lazio	Belgrade, Serb	10.11.85
Mangala, Eliaquim	6.2	Porto	Colombes, Fr	13.02.91
Sagna, Bacary	5.9	Arsenal	Sens, Fr	14.02.83
Zabaleta, Pablo	5.10	Espanyol	Buenos Aires, Arg	16.01.85

Midfielders

Fernandinho	5.10	Shakhtar Donetsk	Londrina, Br	04.05.85
Fernando	6.0	Porto	Alto Paraiso, Br	25.07.87
Jesus Navas	5.8	Sevilla	Los Palacios, Sp	21.11.85
Lopes, Marcos	5.9	Benfica	Belem, Br	28.12.95
Nasri, Samir	5.10	Arsenal	Marseille, Fr	26.06.87
Silva, David	5.7	Valencia	Arguineguin, Sp	08.01.86
Toure, Yaya	6.3	Barcelona	Bouake, Iv C	13.05.83
Zuculini, Bruno	5.10	Racing Club	Belen, Arg	02.04.93

Forwards

Aguero, Sergio	5.8	Atletico Madrid	Quilmes, Arg	02.06.88
Bony, Wilfried	6.0	Swansea	Bingerville, Iv C	10.12.88
Dzeko, Edin	6.4	Wolfsburg	Sarajevo, Bos	17.03.86
Jovetic, Stevan	6.1	Fiorentina	Titograd, Mont	02.11.89
Negredo, Alvaro	6.1	Sevilla	Madrid, Sp	20.08.85
Unal, Enes	6.1	Bursaspor	Osmangazi, Tur	10.05.97

MANCHESTER UNITED

Ground: Old Trafford Stadium, Sir Matt Busby Way, Manchester, M16 ORA
Telephone: 0161 868 8000. **Club nickname**: Red Devils
Capacity: 75,635. **Colours**: Red and white. **Main sponsor**: Chevrolet
Record transfer fee: £59.7m to Real Madrid for Angel di Maria, Aug 2014
Record fee received: £80m from Real Madrid for Cristiano Ronaldo, Jun 2009
Record attendance: 75,811 v Blackburn (Prem Lge), Mar 31, 2007. Also: 76,962 Wolves v Grimsby (FA Cup semi-final) Mar 25, 1939. Crowd of 83,260 saw Manchester Utd v Arsenal (Div 1) Jan 17, 1948 at Maine Road – Old Trafford out of action through bomb damage
League Championship: Winners 1907–08, 1910–11, 1951–52, 1955–56, 1956–7, 1964–65, 1966–67, 1992–93, 1993–94, 1995–96, 1996–97, 1998–99, 1999–2000, 2000–01, 2002–03, 2006–07, 2007–08, 2008–09, 2010–11, 2012–13
FA Cup: Winners 1909, 1948, 1963, 1977, 1983, 1985, 1990, 1994, 1996, 1999, 2004
League Cup: Winners 1992, 2006, 2009
European competitions: Winners European Cup/Champions League 1967–68, 1998–99, 2007–08; Cup-Winners' Cup 1990–91; European Super Cup 1991
World Club Cup: Winners 2008
Finishing positions in Premier League: 1992–93 1st, 1993–94 1st, 1994–95 2nd, 1995–96 1st,

1996–97 1st, 1997–98 2nd, 1998–99 1st, 1999–2000 1st, 2000–01 1st, 2001–02 3rd, 2002–03 1st, 2003–04 3rd, 2004–05 3rd, 2005–06 2nd, 2006–07 1st, 2007–08 1st, 2008–09 1st, 2009–10 2nd, 2010–11 1st, 2011–12 2nd, 2012–13 1st, 2013–14 7th, 2014–15 4th

Biggest win: As Newton Heath: 10-1 v Wolves (Div 1) Oct 15, 1892. As Manchester Utd: 9-0 v Ipswich (Prem Lge), Mar 4, 1995. Also: 10-0 v Anderlecht (European Cup prelim rd) Sep 26, 1956
Biggest defeat: 0-7v Blackburn (Div 1) Apr 10, 1926, v Aston Villa (Div 1) Dec 27, 1930, v Wolves (Div 2) 26 Dec, 1931
Highest League scorer in a season: Dennis Viollet 32 (1959–60)
Most League goals in aggregate: Bobby Charlton 199 (1956–73)
Longest unbeaten League sequence: 29 matches (1998–99)
Longest sequence without a League win: 16 matches (1930)
Most capped player: Bobby Charlton (England) 106

Goalkeepers

De Gea, David	6.4	Atletico Madrid	Madrid, Sp	07.11.90
Johnstone, Sam	6.3	–	Preston	25.03.93
Lindegaard, Anders	6.4	Aalesund	Odense, Den	13.04.84
Valdes, Victor	6.0	Barcelona	Barcelona, Sp	14.01.82

Defenders

Blackett, Tyler	6.1	–	Manchester	02.04.94
Darmian, Matteo	6.0	Torino	Legnano, It	02.12.89
Evans, Jonny	6.2	–	Belfast	03.01.88
Jones, Phil	5.11	Blackburn	Blackburn	21.02.92
McNair, Paddy	6.0	–	Ballyclare	27.04.95
Rafael	5.6	Fluminense	Petropolis, Br	09.07.90
Rojo, Marcos	6.2	Sporting Lisbon	La Plata, Arg	20.03.90
Shaw, Luke	6.1	Southampton	Kingston	12.07.95
Smalling, Chris	6.1	Fulham	Greenwich	22.11.89

Midfielders

Blind, Daley	5.11	Ajax	Amsterdam, Hol	09.03.90
Carrick, Michael	6.0	Tottenham	Wallsend	28.07.81
Depay, Memphis	5.10	PSV Eindhoven	Moordrecht, Hol	13.02.94
Di Maria, Angel	5.11	Real Madrid	Rosario, Arg	14.02.88
Fellaini, Marouane	6.4	Everton	Etterbeek, Bel	22.11.87
Herrera, Ander	6.0	Athletic Bilbao	Bilbao, Sp	14.08.89
Januzaj, Adnan	5.11	Anderlecht	Brussels, Bel	05.02.95
Lingard, Jesse	6.2	–	Warrington	15.12.92
Mata, Juan	5.7	Chelsea	Burgos, Sp	28.04.88
Pereira, Andreas	5.10	PSV Eindhoven	Duffel, Bel	01.01.96
Schweinsteiger, Bastian	6.0	Bayern Munich	Kolbermoor, Ger	01.08.84
Valencia, Antonio	5.10	Wigan	Lago Agrio, Ec	04.08.85
Young, Ashley	5.10	Aston Villa	Stevenage	09.07.85

Forwards

Hernandez, Javier	5.8	Chivas	Guadalajara, Mex	01.06.88
Powell, Nick	6.0	Crewe	Crewe	23.03.94
Rooney, Wayne	5.10	Everton	Liverpool	24.10.85
Van Persie, Robin	6.0	Arsenal	Rotterdam, Hol	06.08.83
Wilson, James	6.1	–	Biddulph	01.12.95

NEWCASTLE UNITED

Ground: St James' Park, Newcastle-upon-Tyne, NE1 4ST
Telephone: 0844 372 1892. **Club nickname**: Magpies
Capacity: 52,338. **Colours**: Black and white. **Main sponsor**: Wonga
Record transfer fee: £16m to Real Madrid for Michael Owen, Aug 2005
Record fee received: £35m from Liverpool for Andy Carroll, Jan 2011

Record attendance: 68,386 v Chelsea (Div 1) Sep 3, 1930
League Championship: Winners 1904–05, 1906–07, 1908–09, 1926–27
FA Cup: Winners 1910, 1924, 1932, 1951, 1952, 1955
League Cup: Runners-up 1976
European competitions: Winners Fairs Cup 1968–69; Anglo-Italian Cup 1972–73
Finishing positions in Premier League: 1993–94 3rd 1994–95 6th 1995–96 2nd 1996–97 2nd 1997–98 13th 1998–99 13th, 1999–2000 11th, 2000–01 11th, 2001–02 4th, 2002–03 3rd, 2003–04 5th, 2004–05 14th, 2005–06 7th, 2006–07 13th, 2007–08 12th, 2008–09 18th, 2010–11 12th, 2011–12 5th, 2012–13 16th, 2013–14 10th, 2014–15 15th
Biggest win: 13-0 v Newport (Div 2) Oct 5, 1946
Biggest defeat: 0-9 v Burton (Div. 2) Apr 15, 1895
Highest League scorer in a season: Hughie Gallacher 36 (1926–27)
Most League goals in aggregate: Jackie Milburn 177 (1946–57)
Longest unbeaten League sequence: 14 matches (1950)
Longest sequence without a League win: 21 matches (1978)
Most capped player: Shay Given (Republic of Ireland) 83

Goalkeepers

Darlow, Karl	6.1	Nottm Forest	Northampton	08.10.90
Elliot, Rob	6.3	Charlton	Chatham	30.04.86
Krul, Tim	6.3	Den Haag	Den Haag, Hol	03.04.88

Defenders

Coloccini, Fabricio	6.0	Dep La Coruna	Cordoba, Arg	22.01.82
Dummett, Paul	6.0	–	Newcastle	26.09.91
Ferguson, Shane	5.11	–	Derry	12.07.91
Janmaat, Daryl	6.1	Feyenoord	Leidschendam, Hol	22.07.89
Haidara, Massadio	5.10	Nancy	Trappes, Fr	02.12.92
Lascelles, Jamaal	6.2	Nottm Forest	Derby	11.11.93
Mbabu, Kevin	6.0	Servette	Chene-Bougeries, Swtz	19.04.95
Taylor, Steven	6.2	–	Greenwich	23.01.86
Williamson, Mike	6.4	Portsmouth	Stoke	08.11.83

Midfielders

Aarons, Rolando	5.9	Bristol City	Kingston, Jam	16.11.95
Abeid, Mehdi	5.11	Lens	Montreuil, Fr	06.08.92
Anita, Vurnon	5.6	Ajax	Willemstad, Cur	04.04.89
Bigirimana, Gael	5.10	Coventry	Bujumbura, Bur	22.10.93
Cabella, Remy	5.8	Montpellier	Ajaccio, Fr	08.03.90
Colback, Jack	5.10	Sunderland	Killingworth	24.10.89
De Jong, Siem	6.1	Ajax	Aigle, Swi	28.01.89
Marveaux, Sylvain	5.8	Rennes	Vannes, Fr	15.04.86
Obertan, Gabriel	6.2	Manchester Utd	Pantin, Fr	26.02.89
Sissoko, Moussa	6.2	Toulouse	Paris, Fr	16.08.89
Tiote, Cheick	5.11	Twente	Yamoussoukro, Iv C	21.06.86
Vuckic, Haris	6.2	Domzale	Ljubljana, Sloven	21.08.92
Wijnaldum, Georginio	5.9	PSV Eindhoven	Rotterdam, Hol	11.11.90

Forwards

Armstrong, Adam	5.8	–	Newcastle	10.02.97
Ayoze Perez	5.11	Tenerife	Santa Cruz, Ten	23.07.93
Cisse, Papiss	6.0	Freiburg	Dakar, Sen	03.06.85
Gouffran, Yoan	5.10	Bordeaux	Villeneuve Georges, Fr	25.05.86
Riviere, Emmanuel	6.0	Monaco	Le Lamentin, Mart	03.03.90

NORWICH CITY

Ground: Carrow Road, Norwich NR1 1JE
Telephone: 01603 760760. **Club nickname**: Canaries

Capacity: 27,244. **Colours:** Yellow and green. **Main sponsor:** Dafabet
Record transfer fee: £8m to Sporting Lisbon for Ricky van Wolfswinkel, Jun 2013
Record fee received: £7.2m from West Ham for Dean Ashton, Jan 2006
Record attendance: 43,984 v Leicester City (FA Cup 6), Mar 30, 1963
League Championship: 3rd 1993
FA Cup: semi-finals 1959, 1989, 1992
League Cup: Winners 1962, 1985
European competitions: UEFA Cup rd 3 1993–94
Finishing positions in Premier League: 1992–93: 3rd, 1993–94 12th, 1994–95 20th,
2004–05 19th, 2011–12 12th, 2012–13 11th, 2013–14 18th
Biggest win: 10-2 v Coventry (Div 3S) Mar 15, 1930
Biggest defeat: 2-10 v Swindon (Southern Lge) Sep 5, 1908
Highest League scorer in a season: Ralph Hunt 31 (1955–56)
Most League goals in aggregate: Johnny Gavin 122 (1945–54, 55–58)
Longest unbeaten League sequence: 20 matches (1950)
Longest sequence without a League win: 25 matches (1956–7)
Most capped player: Mark Bowen (Wales) 35

Goalkeepers

Rudd, Declan	6.3	–	Diss	16.01.91
Ruddy, John	6.4	Everton	St Ives, Cam	24.10.86
Defenders				
Bassong, Sebastien	6.2	Tottenham	Paris, Fr	09.07.86
Bennett, Ryan	6.2	Peterborough	Orsett	06.03.90
Gafaiti, Adel	6.1	Rangers	Paris, Fr	13.09.94
Martin, Russell	6.0	Peterborough	Brighton	04.01.86
Miquel, Ignasi	6.4	Arsenal	Barcelona, Sp	28.09.92
Olsson, Martin	5.10	Blackburn	Gavle, Swe	17.05.88
Turner, Michael	6.4	Sunderland	Lewisham	09.11.83
Whittaker, Steven	6.1	Rangers	Edinburgh	16.06.84
Midfielders				
Andreu, Tony	5.10	Hamilton	Cagnes-sur-Mer, Fr	22.05.88
Bennett, Elliott	5.9	Brighton	Telford	18.12.88
Dorrans, Graham	5.9	WBA	Glasgow	05.05.87
Hoolahan, Wes	5.7	Blackpool	Dublin, Ire	10.08.83
Howson, Jonathan	5.11	Norwich	Leeds	21.05.88
Johnson, Bradley	6.0	Leeds	Hackney	28.04.87
McGrandles, Conor	6.0	Falkirk	Falkirk	24.09.95
Mulumbu, Youssouf	5.10	WBA	Kinshasa, DR Cong	25.01.87
Odjidja-Ofoe, Vadis	6.1	Club Bruges	Ghent, Bel	21.02.89
O'Neil, Gary	5.8	QPR	Beckenham	18.05.83
Redmond, Nathan	5.8	Birmingham	Birmingham	06.03.94
Tettey, Alexander	5.11	Rennes	Accra, Gh	04.04.86
Thompson, Louis	5.11	Swindon	Bristol	19.12.94
Forwards				
Grabban, Lewis	6.0	Bournemouth	Croydon	12.01.88
Hooper, Gary	5.11	Celtic	Harlow	26.01.88
Jerome, Cameron	6.1	Stoke	Huddersfield	14.08.86
Lafferty, Kyle	6.4	Palermo	Enniskillen	16.09.87
Loza, Jamar	5.8	–	Kingston, Jam	10.05.94
Murphy, Jacob	5.10	–	Wembley	24.02.95
Murphy, Josh	5.9	–	Wembley	24.02.95

SOUTHAMPTON

Ground: St Mary's Stadium, Britannia Road, Southampton, SO14 5FP
Telephone: 0845 688 9448. **Club nickname**: Saints
Capacity: 32,505. **Colours**: Red and white. **Main sponsor**: Veho
Record transfer fee: £14.6m to Roma for Pablo Osvaldo, Aug 2013
Record fee received: £30m from Manchester Utd for Luke Shaw, Jun 2014
Record attendance: The Dell: 31,044 v Manchester Utd (Div 1) Oct 8, 1969. St Mary's: 32,363 v Coventry (Champ) Apr 28, 2012
League Championship: Runners-up 1983–84
FA Cup: Winners 1976
League Cup: Runners-up 1979
European competitions: Fairs Cup rd 3 1969–70; Cup-Winners' Cup rd 3 1976–77
Finishing positions in Premier League: 1992–93 18th, 1993–94 18th, 1994–5 10th, 1995–96 17th, 1996–97 16th, 1997–98 12th, 1998–99 17th, 1999–200 15th, 2000–01 10th, 2001–02 11th, 2002–03 8th, 2003–04 12th, 2004–05 20th, 2012–13 14th, 2013–14 8th, 2014–15 7th
Biggest win: 8-0 v Northampton (Div 3S) Dec 24, 1921, v Sunderland (Prem Lge) Oct 18, 2014
Biggest defeat: 0-8 v Tottenham (Div 2) Mar 28, 1936, v Everton (Div 1) Nov 20, 1971
Highest League scorer in a season: Derek Reeves 39 (1959–60)
Most League goals in aggregate: Mick Channon 185 (1966–82)
Longest unbeaten League sequence: 19 matches (1921)
Longest unbeaten League sequence: 20 matches (1969)
Most capped player: Peter Shilton (England) 49

Goalkeepers

Davis, Kelvin	6.1	Sunderland	Bedford	29.09.76
Forster, Fraser	6.7	Celtic	Hexham	17.03.88
Gazzaniga, Paulo	6.5	Gillingham	Murphy, Arg	02.01.92
Stekelenburg, Maarten	6.6	Fulham (loan)	Haarlem, Hol	22.09.82

Defenders

Bertrand, Ryan	5.10	Chelsea	Southwark	05.08.89
Fonte, Jose	6.2	Crystal Palace	Penafiel, Por	22.12.83
Gardos, Florin	6.4	Steaua Bucharest	Satu Mare, Rom	29.10.88
Martina, Cuco	6.1	Twente	Rotterdam, Hol	25.09.89
McCarthy, Jason	6.1	–	Southampton	07.11.95
Soares, Cedric	5.8	Sporting Lisbon	Singen, Ger	31.08.91
Stephens, Jack	6.1	Plymouth	Torpoint	27.01.94
Targett, Matt	6.0	–	Eastleigh	18.09.95
Yoshida, Maya	6.2	Venlo	Nagasaki, Jap	24.08.88

Midfielders

Davis, Steven	5.8	Rangers	Ballymena	01.01.85
Gape, Dominic	5.11	–	Burton Bradstock	09.09.94
Isgrove, Lloyd	5.10	–	Yeovil	12.01.93
Mane, Sadio	5.9	Salzburg	Sedhiou, Sen	10.04.92
McQueen, Sam	5.11	–	Southampton	06.02.95
Reed, Harrison	5.7	–	Worthing	27.01.95
Schneiderlin, Morgan	5.11	Strasbourg	Zellwiller, Fr	08.11.89
Tadic, Dusan	5.11	Twente	Backa Topola, Serb	20.11.88
Wanyama, Victor	6.2	Celtic	Nairobi, Ken	25.06.91
Ward-Prowse, James	5.8	–	Portsmouth	01.11.94

Forwards

Gallagher, Sam	6.4	–	Crediton	15.09.95
Juanmi	5.8	Malaga	Coin, Sp	20.05.93
Long, Shane	5.10	Hull	Gortnahoe, Ire	22.01.87

Mayuka, Emmanuel	5.9	Young Boys	Kabwe, Zim	21.11.90
Pelle, Graziano	6.4	Feyenoord	San Cesario, It	15.07.85
Rodriguez, Jay	6.1	Burnley	Burnley	29.07.89
Seager, Ryan	5.9	–	Yeovil	05.02.96

STOKE CITY

Ground: Britannia Stadium, Stanley Matthews Way, Stoke-on-Trent ST4 7EG
Telephone: 01782 367598. **Club nickname**: Potters
Capacity: 27,740. **Colours**: Red and white. **Main sponsor**: Bet 365
Record transfer fee: £10m to Tottenham for Peter Crouch, Aug 2012
Record fee received: £4.5m from Wolfsburg for Tuncay, Jan 2011
Record attendance: Victoria Ground: 51,380 v Arsenal (Div 1) Mar 29, 1937. Britannia Stadium: 28,218 v Everton (FA Cup 3) Jan 5, 2002
League Championship: 4th 1935–36, 1946–47
FA Cup: Runners-up 2011
League Cup: Winners 1972
European competitions: Europa League rd of 32 2011–12
Finishing positions in Premier League: 2008–09 12th, 2009–10 11th, 2010–11 13th, 2011–12 14th, 2012–13 13th, 2013–14 9th, 2014–15 9th
Biggest win: 10-3 v WBA (Div 1) Feb 4, 1937
Biggest defeat: 0-10 v Preston (Div 1) Sep 14, 1889
Highest League scorer in a season: Freddie Steele 33 (1936–37)
Most League goals in aggregate: Freddie Steele 142 (1934–49)
Longest unbeaten League sequence: 25 matches (1992–93)
Longest sequence without a League win: 17 matches (1989)
Most capped player: Glenn Whelan (Republic of Ireland) 64

Goalkeepers
Butland, Jack	6.4	Birmingham	Bristol	10.03.93
Given, Shay	6.2	Aston Villa	Lifford, Ire	20.04.76
Haugaard, Jakob	6.6	Midtjylland	Sundby, Den	01.05.92

Defenders
Bardsley, Phil	5.11	Sunderland	Salford	28.06.85
Cameron, Geoff	6.3	Houston	Attleboro, US	11.07.85
Johnson, Glen	6.0	Liverpool	Greenwich	23.08.84
Muniesa, Marc	5.11	Barcelona	Lloret de Mar, Sp	27.03.92
Pieters, Erik	6.1	PSV Eindhoven	Tiel, Hol	07.08.88
Shawcross, Ryan	6.3	Manchester Utd	Chester	04.10.87
Teixeira, Dionatan	6.4	Banska Bystrica	Londrina, Br	24.07.92
Wilson, Marc	6.2	Portsmouth	Belfast	17.08.87
Wollscheid, Philipp	6.4	Bayer Leverkusen	Wadern, Ger	06.03.89

Midfielders
Adam, Charlie	6.1	Liverpool	Dundee	10.12.85
Ireland, Stephen	5.8	Aston Villa	Cork, Ire	22.08.86
Sidwell, Steve	5.10	Fulham	Wandsworth	14.12.82
Van Ginkel, Marco	6.1	Chelsea (loan)	Amersfoort, Hol	01.12.92
Whelan, Glenn	5.10	Sheffield Wed	Dublin, Ire	13.01.84

Forwards
Arnautovic, Marko	6.4	Werder Bremen	Vienna, Aut	19.04.89
Biram Diouf, Mame	6.1	Hannover	Dakar, Sen	16.12.87
Crouch, Peter	6.7	Tottenham	Macclesfield	30.01.81
Joselu	6.3	Hannover	Stuttgart, Ger	27.03.90
Krkic, Bojan	5.7	Barcelona	Linyola, Sp	28.08.90
Odemwingie, Peter	6.0	Cardiff	Tashkent, Uzbek	15.07.81
Walters, Jon	6.0	Ipswich	Birkenhead	20.09.83

SUNDERLAND

Ground: Stadium of Light, Sunderland SR5 1SU
Telephone: 0871 911 1200. **Club nickname**: Black Cats
Capacity: 48,707. **Colours**: Red and white. **Main sponsor**: Dafabet
Record transfer fee: £13m to Rennes for Asamoah Gyan, Aug 2010
Record fee received: £18m from Aston Villa for Darren Bent, Jan 2011
Record attendance: Roker Park: 75,118 v Derby (FA Cup 6 rep) Mar 8, 1933. Stadium of Light: 48,353 v Liverpool (Prem Lge) Apr 13, 2002
League Championship: Winners 1891–92, 1892–93, 1894–95, 1901–02, 1912–13, 1935–36
FA Cup: Winners 1937, 1973
League Cup: Runners-up 1985
European competitions: Cup-Winners' Cup rd 2 1973–74
Finishing positions in Premier League: 1996–97 18th, 1999–2000 7th, 2000–01 7th, 2001–02 17th, 2002–03 20th, 2005–06 20th, 2007–08 15th, 2008–09 16th, 2009–10 13th, 2010–11 10th, 2011–12 13th, 2012–13 17th, 2013–14 14th, 2014–15 16th
Biggest win: 9-1 v Newcastle (Div 1) Dec 5, 1908. Also: 11-1 v Fairfield (FA Cup 1) Feb 2, 1895
Biggest defeat: 0-8 v Sheffield Wed (Div 1) Dec 26, 1911, v West Ham (Div 1) Oct 19, 1968, v Watford (Div 1) Sep 25, 1982, v Southampton (Prem Lge) Oct 18, 2014
Highest League scorer in a season: Dave Halliday 43 (1928–29)
Most League goals in aggregate: Charlie Buchan 209 (1911–25)
Longest unbeaten League sequence: 19 matches (1998–99)
Longest sequence without a League win: 22 matches (2003–04)
Most capped player: Charlie Hurley (Republic of Ireland) 38

Goalkeepers				
Mannone, Vito	6.3	Arsenal	Desio, It	02.03.88
Pantilimon, Costel	6.8	Manchester City	Bacau, Rom	01.02.87
Pickford, Jordan	6.1	–	Washington, Co Dur	07.03.94
Defenders				
Brown, Wes	6.1	Manchester Utd	Manchester	13.10.79
Coates, Sebastian	6.5	Liverpool	Montevideo, Uru	07.10.90
Jones, Billy	5.11	WBA	Shrewsbury	24.03.87
Matthews, Adam	5.10	Celtic	Swansea	13.01.92
O'Shea, John	6.3	Manchester Utd	Waterford, Ire	30.04.81
Roberge, Valentin	6.2	Maritimo	Montreuil, Fr	09.06.87
Van Aanholt, Patrick	5.9	Chelsea	Hertogenbosch, Hol	29.08.90
Midfielders				
Bridcutt, Liam	5.9	Brighton	Reading	08.05.89
Buckley, Will	6.0	Brighton	Oldham	12.08.88
Cattermole, Lee	5.10	Wigan	Stockton	21.03.88
Giaccherini, Emanuele	5.8	Juventus	Bibbiena, It	05.05.85
Gomez, Jordi	5.10	Wigan	Barcelona, Sp	24.05.85
Johnson, Adam	5.9	Manchester City	Sunderland	14.07.87
Larsson, Sebastian	5.10	Birmingham	Eskiltuna, Swe	06.06.85
Mavrias, Charis	5.10	Panathinaikos	Zakynthos, Gre	21.02.94
Rodwell, Jack	6.1	Manchester City	Birkdale	17.09.89
Forwards				
Defoe, Jermain	5.8	Toronto	Beckton	07.10.82
Fletcher, Steven	6.1	Wolves	Shrewsbury	26.03.87
Graham, Danny	6.1	Swansea	Gateshead	12.08.85
Mandron, Mikael	6.3	–	Boulogne, Fr	11.10.94
Watmore, Duncan	5.9	Altrincham	Cheadle Hulme	08.03.94
Wickham, Connor	6.3	Ipswich	Colchester	31.03.93

SWANSEA CITY

Ground: Liberty Stadium, Morfa, Swansea SA1 2FA
Telephone: 01792 616600. **Club nickname**: Swans
Capacity: 20,827. **Colours**: White. **Main sponsor**: Goldenway
Record transfer fee: £12m to Vitesse Arnhem for Wilfried Bony, Jan 2015
Record fee received: £28m from Manchester City for Wilfried Bony, Aug 2012
Record attendance: Vetch Field: 32,796 v Arsenal (FA Cup 4) Feb 17, 1968. Liberty Stadium: 20,828 v Liverpool (Prem Lge) Mar 16, 2015
League Championship: 6th 1981–82
FA Cup: Semi-finals 1926, 1964
League Cup: Winners 2013
Finishing positions in Premier League: 2011–12 11th, 2012–13 9th, 2013–14 12th, 2014–15 8th
European competitions: Cup-winners' Cup rd 2 1982–83; Europa Lge rd of 32 2013–14
Biggest win: 8-0 v Hartlepool (Div 4) Apr 1, 1978. Also: 12-0 v Sliema (Cup-winners' Cup rd 1, 1st leg), Sep 15, 1982
Biggest defeat: 0-8 v Liverpool (FA Cup 3) Jan 9, 1990, 0-8 v Monaco (Cup-winners' Cup rd 1, 2nd leg) Oct 1, 1991
Highest League scorer in a season: Cyril Pearce 35 (1931–32)
Most League goals in aggregate: Ivor Allchuch 166 (1949–58, 1965–68)
Longest unbeaten League sequence: 19 matches (1970–71)
Longest sequence without a League win: 15 matches (1989)
Most capped player: Ivor Allchurch (Wales) 42

Goalkeepers				
Fabianski, Lukasz	6.3	Arsenal	Kostrzyn, Pol	18.04.85
Nordfeldt, Kristoffer	6.3	Heerenveen	Stockholm, Swe	23.06.89
Defenders				
Amat, Jordi	6.1	Espanyol	Canet de Mar, Sp	21.03.92
Bartley, Kyle	6.4	Arsenal	Stockport	22.05.91
Fernandez, Federico	6.3	Napoli	Tres Algarrobos, Arg	21.02.89
Naughton, Kyle	5.10	Tottenham	Sheffield	11.11.88
Rangel, Angel	5.11	Terrassa	Tortosa, Sp	28.10.82
Tabanou, Franck	5.10	St Etienne	Thiais, Fr	30.01.89
Taylor, Neil	5.9	Wrexham	St Asaph	07.02.89
Tiendalli, Dwight	5.10	Twente	Paramaribo, Sur	21.10.85
Williams, Ashley	6.0	Stockport	Wolverhampton	23.08.84
Midfielders				
Britton, Leon	5.5	Sheffield Utd	Merton	16.09.82
Cork, Jack	6.1	Southampton	Carshalton	25.06.89
Dyer, Nathan	5.10	Southampton	Trowbridge	29.11.87
Fulton, Jay	5.10	Falkirk	Bolton	04.04.94
Gorre, Kenji	5.10	Manchester Utd	Spijkenisse, Hol	29.09.94
Grimes, Matt	5.10	Exeter	Exeter	15.07.95
Ki Sung-Yeung	6.2	Celtic	Gwangju, S Kor	24.01.89
King, Adam	5.11	Hearts	Edinburgh	11.10.95
Montero, Jefferson	5.7	Morelia	Babahoyo, Ec	01.09.89
Routledge, Wayne	5.7	Newcastle	Sidcup	07.01.85
Shelvey, Jonjo	6.0	Liverpool	Romford	27.02.92
Sigurdsson, Gylfi	6.1	Tottenham	Hafnarfjordur, Ice	08.09.89
Forwards				
Ayew, Andre	5.10	Marseille	Seclin, Fr	17.12.89
Barrow, Modou	5.10	Ostersunds	Gambia	13.10.92
Eder	6.3	Sporting Braga	Bissau, Guin	22.12.87
Emnes, Marvin	5.11	Middlesbrough	Rotterdam, Hol	27.05.88
Gomis, Bafetimbi	6.0	Lyon	La Seyne, Fr	06.08.85

TOTTENHAM HOTSPUR

Ground: White Hart Lane, Tottenham, London N17 OAP
Telephone: 0844 499 5000. **Club nickname**: Spurs
Capacity: 36,284. **Colours**: White. **Main sponsor**: AIA
Record transfer fee: £30m to Roma for Erik Lamela, Aug 2013
Record fee received: £85.3m from Real Madrid for Gareth Bale, Aug 2013
Record attendance: 75,038 v Sunderland (FA Cup 6) Mar 5, 1938
League Championship: Winners 1950–51, 1960–61
FA Cup: Winners 1901, 1921, 1961, 1962, 1967, 1981, 1982, 1991
League Cup: Winners 1971, 1973, 1999, 2008
European competitions: Winners Cup-Winners' Cup 1962–63; UEFA Cup 1971–72, 1983–84
Finishing positions in Premier League: 1992–93 8th, 1993–94 15th, 1994–95 7th, 1995–96 8th, 1996–97 10th, 1997–98 14th, 1998–99 11th, 1999–2000 10th, 2000–01 12th, 2001–02 9th, 2002–03 10th, 2003–04 14th, 2004–05 9th, 2005–06 5th, 2006–07 5th, 2007–08 11th, 2008–09 8th, 2009–10 4th, 2010–11 5th, 2011–12 4th, 2012–13 5th, 2013–14 6th, 2014–15 5th
Biggest win: 9-0 v Bristol Rov (Div 2) Oct 22, 1977. Also: 13-2 v Crewe (FA Cup 4 replay) Feb 3, 1960
Biggest defeat: 0-7 v Liverpool (Div 1) Sep 2, 1979. Also: 0-8 v Cologne (Inter Toto Cup) Jul 22, 1995
Highest League scorer in a season: Jimmy Greaves 37 (1962–63)
Most League goals in aggregate: Jimmy Greaves 220 (1961–70)
Longest unbeaten League sequence: 22 matches (1949)
Longest sequence without a League win: 16 matches (1934–35)
Most capped player: Pat Jennings (Northern Ireland) 74

Goalkeepers				
Lloris, Hugo	6.2	Lyon	Nice, Fr	26.12.86
Vorm, Michel	6.0	Swansea	Nieuwegein, Hol	20.10.83
Defenders				
Alderweireld, Toby	6.2	Atletico Madrid	Antwerp, Bel	02.03.89
Chiriches, Vlad	6.1	Steaua Bucharest	Bacau, Rom	14.11.89
Davies, Ben	5.6	Swansea	Neath	24.04.93
Dier, Eric	6.2	Sporting Lisbon	Cheltenham	15.01.94
Fazio, Federico	6.5	Sevilla	Buenos Aires, Arg	17.03.87
Kaboul, Younes	6.3	Portsmouth	St Julien, Fr	04.01.86
Rose, Danny	5.8	Leeds	Doncaster	02.07.90
Trippier, Kieran	5.10	Burnley	Bury	19.09.90
Vertonghen, Jan	6.2	Ajax	Sint-Niklaas, Bel	24.04.87
Walker, Kyle	5.10	Sheffield Utd	Sheffield	28.05.90
Wimmer, Kevin	6.2	Cologne	Wels, Aut	15.11.92
Yedlin, DeAndre	5.9	Seattle	Seattle, US	09.07.93
Midfielders				
Alli, Dele	6.1	MK Dons	Milton Keynes	11.04.96
Bentaleb, Nabil	6.2	–	Lille, Fr	24.11.94
Carroll, Tom	5.10	–	Watford	28.05.92
Chadli, Nacer	6.2	Twente	Liege, Bel	02.08.89
Dembele, Mousa	6.1	Fulham	Wilrijk, Bel	16.07.87
Eriksen, Christian	5.10	Ajax	Middelfart, Den	14.02.92
Lamela, Erik	6.0	Roma	Buenos Aires, Arg	04.03.92
Lennon, Aaron	5.5	Leeds	Leeds	16.04.87
Mason, Ryan	5.9	–	Enfield	13.06.91
Stambouli, Benjamin	5.11	Montpellier	Marseille, Fr	13.08.90
Townsend, Andros	6.0	–	Leytonstone	16.07.91

Forwards

Adebayor, Emmanuel	6.3	Manchester City	Lome, Tog	24.12.84
Kane, Harry	6.2	–	Walthamstow	28.07.93
Soldado, Roberto	5.11	Valencia	Valencia, Sp	27.05.85

WATFORD

Ground: Vicarage Road Stadium, Vicarage Road, Watford WD18 OER
Telephone: 01923 496000. **Club nickname**: Hornets
Capacity: 21,400. **Colours**: Yellow and black. **Main sponsor**: 138.com
Record transfer fee: £6m to Tottenham for Etienne Capoue, Jul 2015
Record fee received: £9.65m from Aston Villa for Ashley Young, Jan 2007
Record attendance: 34,099 v Manchester Utd (FA Cup 4 rep) Feb 3, 1969
League Championship: Runners-up 1982-83
FA Cup: Runners-up 1984
League Cup: Semi-finals 1979, 2005
European competitions: UEFA Cup rd 3 1983-84
Finishing positions in Premier League: 1999-2000 20th, 2006-07 20th
Biggest win: 8-0 v Sunderland (Div 1) Sep 25, 1982. Also: 10-1 v Lowestoft (FA Cup 1) Nov 27, 1926
Biggest defeat: 0-10 v Wolves (FA Cup 1 replay) Jan 24, 1912
Highest League scorer in a season: Cliff Holton 42 (1959-60)
Most League goals in aggregate: Luther Blissett 148 (1976-83, 1984-88, 1991-92)
Longest unbeaten League sequence: 22 matches (1996-97)
Longest sequence without a League win: 19 matches (1971-72)
Most capped players: John Barnes (England) 31, Kenny Jackett (Wales) 31

Goalkeepers

Arlauskis, Giedrius	6.4	Steaua Bucharest	Telsiai, Lith	01.12.87
Gilmartin, Rene	6.5	St Patrick's	Dublin, Ire	31.05.87
Gomes, Heurelho	6.2	PSV Eindhoven	Joao Pinheiro, Br	15.12.81

Defenders

Angella, Gabriele	6.3	Udinese	Florence, It	28.04.89
Cathcart, Craig	6.2	Blackpool	Belfast	06.02.89
Doyley, Lloyd	5.10	–	Whitechapel	01.12.82
Ekstrand, Joel	6.1	Udinese	Lund, Swe	04.02.89
Hoban, Tommie	6.2	–	Waltham Forest	24.01.94
Holebas, Jose	6.0	Roma	Aschaffenburg, Ger	27.06.84
Layun, Miguel	5.10	Granada	Cordoba, Mex	25.06.88
Paredes, Juan Carlos	5.9	Granada	Esmeraldas, Ec	08.07.87
Prodl, Sebastian	6.4	Werder Bremen	Graz, Aut	21.06.87
Pudil, Daniel	6.1	Granada	Prague, Cz	27.09.85

Midfielders

Abdi, Almen	5.11	Udinese	Prizren, Kos	21.10.86
Anya, Ikechi	5.7	Granada	Glasgow	03.01.88
Behrami, Valon	6.1	Hamburg	Mitrovica, Kos	19.04.85
Capoue, Etienne	6.2	Tottenham	Niort, Fr	11.07.88
Dyer, Lloyd	5.9	Leicester	Birmingham	13.09.82
McGugan, Lewis	5.10	Nottm Forest	Long Eaton	25.10.88
Murray, Sean	5.9	–	Abbots Langley	11.10.93
Smith, Connor	5.11	–	Mullingar, Ire	18.02.93
Watson, Ben	5.10	Wigan	Camberwell	09.07.85

Forwards

Deeney, Troy	6.0	Walsall	Birmingham	29.06.88
Fabbrini, Diego	6.0	Udinese	Pisa, It	31.07.90

Forestieri, Fernando	5.8	Udinese	Rosario, Arg	15.01.90
Ighalo, Odion	6.2	Udinese	Lagos, Nig	16.06.89
Ikpeazu, Uche	6.3	–	Harrow	28.02.95
Vydra, Matej	5.11	Udinese	Chotebor, Cz	01.05.92

WEST BROMWICH ALBION

Ground: The Hawthorns, Halfords Lane, West Bromwich B71 4LF
Telephone: 0871 271 1100. **Club nickname**: Baggies
Capacity: 26,445. **Colours**: Blue and white. **Main sponsor**:
Record transfer fee: £10m to Dynamo Kiev for Brown Ideye, Jul 2014
Record fee received: £8.5m from Aston Villa for Curtis Davies, Jul 2008
Record attendance: 64,815 v Arsenal (FA Cup 6) Mar 6, 1937
League Championship: Winners 1919–20
FA Cup: Winners 1888, 1892, 1931, 1954, 1968
League Cup: Winners 1966
European competitions: Cup-Winners' Cup quarter-finals 1968–69; UEFA Cup quarter-finals 1978–79
Finishing positions in Premier League: 2002–03 19th, 2004–5 17th, 2005–6 19th; 2008–09 20th, 2010–11 11th, 2011–12 10th, 2012–13 8th, 2013–14 17th, 2014–15 13th
Biggest win: 12-0 v Darwen (Div 1) Apr 4, 1892
Biggest defeat: 3-10 v Stoke (Div 1) Feb 4, 1937
Highest League scorer in a season: William Richardson 39 (1935–36)
Most League goals in aggregate: Tony Brown 218 (1963–79)
Longest unbeaten League sequence: 17 matches (1957)
Longest sequence without a League win: 14 matches (1995)
Most capped player: Chris Brunt (Northern Ireland) 40

Goalkeepers
Foster, Ben	6.2	Birmingham	Leamington	03.04.83
Myhill, Boaz	6.3	Hull	Modesto, US	09.11.82

Defenders
Dawson, Craig	6.2	Rochdale	Rochdale	06.05.90
Gamboa, Cristian	5.10	Rosenborg	Liberia, CRica	26.01.87
Lescott, Joleon	6.2	Manchester City	Birmingham	16.08.82
McAuley, Gareth	6.3	Ipswich	Larne	05.12.79
Olsson, Jonas	6.4	Nijmegen	Landskrona, Swe	10.03.83
O'Neil, Liam	5.11	Histon	Cambridge	31.07.93
Pocognoli, Sebastien	6.0	Hannover	Liege, Bel	01.08.87

Midfielders
Brunt, Chris	6.1	Sheffield Wed	Belfast	14.12.84
Fletcher, Darren	6.0	Manchester Utd	Edinburgh	01.02.84
Gardner, Craig	5.10	Sunderland	Solihull	25.11.86
McClean, James	5.11	Wigan	Derry	22.04.89
Morrison, James	5.10	Middlesbrough	Darlington	25.05.86
Sessegnon, Stephane	5.8	Sunderland	Allahe, Benin	01.06.84
Yacob, Claudio	5.11	Racing Club	Carcarana, Arg	18.07.87

Forwards
Anichebe, Victor	6.1	Everton	Lagos, Nig	23.04.88
Berahino, Saido	5.10	–	Bujumbura, Bur	04.08.93
Brown Ideye	5.11	Dynamo Kiev	Lagos, Nig	10.10.88
McManaman, Callum	5.11	Wigan	Knowsley	25.04.91
Nabi, Adil	5.8		Birmingham	28.02.94

WEST HAM UNITED

Ground: Boleyn Ground, Upton Park, London E13 9AZ
Telephone: 0208 548 2748. **Club nickname**: Hammers
Capacity: 35,345. **Colours**: Claret and blue. **Main sponsor**: Alpari
Record transfer fee: £15m to Liverpool for Andy Carroll, Jul 2013
Record fee received: £18m from Leeds for Rio Ferdinand, Nov 2000
Record attendance: 43,322 v Tottenham (Div 1) Oct 17, 1970
League Championship: 3rd 1985–86
FA Cup: Winners 1964, 1975, 1980
League Cup: Runners-up 1966, 1981
European competitions: Winners Cup-Winners' Cup 1964–65
Finishing positions in Premier League: 1993–94 13th, 1994–95 14th, 1995–96 10th,
1996–97 14th, 1997–98 8th, 1998–99 5th, 1999–2000 9th, 2000–01 15th; 2001–02
7th, 2002–03 18th, 2005–06 9th, 2006–07 15th, 2007–08 10th, 2008–09: 9th, 2009
10 17th, 2010–11 20th, 2012–13 10th, 2013–14 13th, 2014–15 12th
Biggest win: 8-0 v Rotherham (Div 2) Mar 8, 1958, v Sunderland (Div 1) Oct 19, 1968. Also:
10-0 v Bury (League Cup 2) Oct 25, 1983
Biggest defeat: 0-7 v Barnsley (Div 2) Sep 1, 1919, v Everton (Div 1) Oct 22, 1927, v Shef-
field Wed (Div 1) Nov 28, 1959
Highest League scorer in a season: Vic Watson 42 (1929–30)
Most League goals in aggregate: Vic Watson 298 (1920–35)
Longest unbeaten League sequence: 27 matches (1980–81)
Longest sequence without a League win: 17 matches (1976)
Most capped player: Bobby Moore (England) 108

Goalkeepers

Adrian	6.3	Real Betis	Seville, Sp	03.01.87
Randolph, Darren	6.1	Birmingham	Bray, Ire	12.05.87

Defenders

Burke, Reece	6.2	–	Newham	02.09.96
Collins, James	6.2	Aston Villa	Newport	23.08.83
Cresswell, Aaron	5.7	Ipswich	Liverpool	15.12.89
Hendrie, Stephen	5.10	Hamilton	Glasgow	08.01.95
Henry, Doneil	6.2	Apollon Limassol	Brampton, Can	20.04.93
O'Brien, Joey	6.2	Bolton	Dublin, Ire	17.02.86
Ogbonna, Angelo	6.3	Juventus	Cassino, It	23.05.88
Reid, Winston	6.3	Midtjylland	Auckland, NZ	03.07.88
Tomkins, James	6.3		Basildon	29.03.89

Midfielders

Amalfitano, Morgan	5.10	Marseille	Nice, Fr	20.03.85
Downing, Stewart	6.0	Liverpool	Middlesbrough	02.07.84
Jarvis, Matt	5.8	Wolves	Middlesbrough	22.05.86
Kouyate, Cheikhou	6.4	Anderlecht	Dakar, Sen	21.12.89
Noble, Mark	5.11	–	West Ham	08.05.87
Nolan, Kevin	6.1	Newcastle	Liverpool	24.06.82
Obiang, Pedro	6.1	Sampdoria	Alcala, Sp	27.03.92
Payet, Dimitri	5.9	Marseille	St-Pierre, Reunion, Fr	29.03.87
Poyet, Diego	5.11	Charlton	Zaragoza, Sp	08.04.95

Forwards

Carroll, Andy	6.3	Liverpool	Gateshead	06.01.89
Lee, Elliot	5.11	–	Durham	16.12.94
Maiga, Modibo	6.1	Sochaux	Bamako, Mali	03.09.87
Sakho, Diafra	6.1	Metz	Guediawaye, Sen	24.12.89
Valencia, Enner	5.11	Pachuca	Esmeraldas, Ec	04.11.89
Zarate, Mauro	5.10	Velez Sarsfield	Haedo, Arg	18.03.87

CHAMPIONSHIP

BIRMINGHAM CITY

Ground: St Andrew's, Birmingham B9 4NH
Telephone: 0844 557 1875. **Club nickname**: Blues
Colours: Blue and white. **Capacity**: 30,016
Record attendance: 66,844 v Everton (FA Cup 5) Feb 11, 1939

Goalkeepers

Kuszczak, Tomasz	6.3	Wolves	Krosno, Pol	20.03.82
Legzdins, Adam	6.0	Leyton Orient	Penkridge	28.11.86
Townsend, Nick	5.11	–	Solihull	01.11.94
Trueman, Connal	6.1	–	Birmingham	26.03.96

Defenders

Caddis, Paul	5.7	Swindon	Irvine	19.04.88
Eardley, Neal	5.11	Blackpool	Llandudno	06.11.88
Edgar, David	6.2	Burnley	Kitchener, Can	19.05.87
Grounds, Jonathan	6.1	Oldham	Thornaby	02.02.88
Hancox, Mitch	5.10	–	Solihull	09.11.93
Morrison, Michael	6.1	Charlton	Bury St Edmunds	03.03.88
Robinson, Paul	5.9	Bolton	Watford	14.12.78
Spector, Jonathan	6.1	West Ham	Arlington Heights, US	03.01.86

Midfielders

Adams, Charlee	5.11	–	Redbridge	16.02.95
Arthur, Koby	5.8	–	Kumasi, Gh	31.01.96
Brown, Reece	5.9	–	Dudley	03.03.96
Cotterill, David	5.9	Doncaster	Cardiff	04.12.87
Davis, David	5.8	Wolves	Smethwick	20.02.91
Gleeson, Stephen	6.2	MK Dons	Dublin, Ire	03.08.88
Gray, Demarai	5.10	–	Birmingham	28.06.96
Maghoma, Jacques	5.11	Sheffield Wed	Lubumbashi, DR Cong	23.10.87
Shinnie, Andrew	5.11	Inverness	Aberdeen	17.07.89

Forwards

Donaldson, Clayton	6.1	Brentford	Bradford	07.02.84
Johnstone, Denny	6.2	Celtic	Dumfries	09.01.95
Novak, Lee	6.0	Huddersfield	Newcastle	28.09.88
Thomas, Wes	5.11	Rotherham	Barking	23.01.87

BLACKBURN ROVERS

Ground: Ewood Park, Blackburn BB2 4JF
Telephone: 0871 702 1875. **Club nickname**: Rovers
Colours: Blue and white. **Capacity**: 31,367
Record attendance: 62,522 v Bolton (FA Cup 6) Mar 2, 1929

Goalkeepers

Eastwood, Simon	6.2	Portsmouth	Luton	26.06.89
Kean, Jake	6.5	–	Derby	04.02.91
Raya, David	6.0	Cornella	Barcelona, Sp	15.09.95
Steele, Jason	6.2	Middlesbrough	Newton Aycliffe	18.08.90

Defenders

Duffy, Shane	6.4	Everton	Derry	01.01.92

Hanley, Grant	6.2	–	Dumfries	20.11.91
Henley, Adam	5.10	–	Knoxville, US	14.06.94
Kilgallon, Matt	6.1	Sunderland	York	08.01.84
Olsson, Markus	6.0	Halmstads	Gavle, Swe	17.05.88
Spurr, Tommy	6.1	Doncaster	Leeds	30.09.87
Midfielders				
Conway, Craig	5.8	Cardiff	Irvine	02.05.85
Evans, Corry	5.11	Hull	Belfast	30.07.90
Lowe, Jason	6.0	–	Wigan	02.09.91
Lenihan, Darragh	5.10	Belvedere	Dublin	16.03.94
Mahoney, Connor	5.9	Accrington	Blackburn	12.02.97
Marshall, Ben	6.0	Leicester	Salford	29.09.91
O'Sullivan, John	5.11	–	Dublin, Ire	18.09.93
Taylor, Chris	5.11	Millwall	Oldham	20.12.86
Williamson, Lee	5.10	Portsmouth	Derby	07.06.82
Forwards				
Brown, Chris	6.3	Doncaster	Doncaster	11.12.84
Gestede, Rudy	6.4	Cardiff	Nancy, Fr	10.10.88
Rhodes, Jordan	6.1	Huddersfield	Oldham	05.02.90

BOLTON WANDERERS

Ground: Macron Stadium, Burnden Way, Lostock, Bolton BL6 6JW
Telephone: 0844 871 2932. **Club nickname**: Trotters
Colours: White and navy. **Capacity**: 28,723
Record attendance: Burnden Park: 69,912 v Manchester City (FA Cup 5) Feb 18, 1933;
Macron Stadium: 28,353 v Leicester (Prem Lge) Dec 28, 2003

Goalkeepers				
Amos, Ben	6.2	Manchester Utd	Macclesfield	10.04.90
Fitzsimons, Ross	6.1	Crystal Palace	Hammersmith	28.05.94
Defenders				
Dervite, Dorian	6.3	Charlton	Lille, Fr	25.07.88
Moxey, Dean	5.11	Crystal Palace	Exeter	14.01.86
Osede, Derik	6.0	Real Madrid	Madrid, Sp	21.02.93
Ream, Tim	6.1	NY Red Bulls	St Louis, US	05.10.87
Taylor, Quade	6.3	Crystal Palace	Tooting	11.12.92
Threlkeld, Oscar	6.1	–	Bolton	15.02.94
Wheater, David	6.4	Middlesbrough	Redcar	14.02.87
White, Hayden	6.1	Sheffield Wed	Greenwich	15.04.95
Midfielders				
Danns, Neil	5.9	Leicester	Liverpool	23.11.82
Davies, Mark	5.11	Wolves	Wolverhampton	18.02.88
Feeney, Liam	6.0	Millwall	Hammersmith	28.04.86
Holden, Stuart	5.10	Houston	Aberdeen	01.08.85
Medo, Mohamed	5.9	Partizan Belgrade	Bo, SLeone	16.11.87
Pratley, Darren	6.0	Swansea	Barking	22.04.85
Spearing, Jay	5.7	Liverpool	Wallasey	25.11.88
Trotter, Liam	6.2	Millwall	Ipswich	24.08.88
Twardzik, Filip	6.1	Celtic	Trinec, Cz	10.02.93
Vela, Josh	5.11	–	Salford	14.12.93
Forwards				
Clayton, Max	5.9	Crewe	Crewe	09.08.94
Clough, Zach	5.8	–	Manchester	08.03.95
Eaves, Tom	6.4	Oldham	Liverpool	14.01.92
Hall, Robert	6.2	West Ham	Aylesbury	20.10.93

| Madine, Gary | 6.3 | Sheffield Wed | Gateshead | 24.08.90 |
| Woolery, Kaiyne | 5.10 | Tamworth | Hackney | 11.01.95 |

BRENTFORD

Ground: Griffin Park, Braemar Road, Brentford TW8 0NT
Telephone: 0845 345 6442. **Club nickname**: Bees
Colours: Red, white and black. **Capacity**: 12,763
Record attendance: 39,626 v Preston (FA Cup 6) Mar 5, 1938

Goalkeepers

| Bonham, Jack | 6.3 | Watford | Stevenage | 14.09.93 |
| Button, David | 6.3 | Charlton | Stevenage | 27.02.89 |

Defenders

Barbet, Yoann	6.2	Chamois	Libourne, Fr	10.05.93
Bidwell, Jake	6.0	Everton	Southport	21.03.93
Bjelland, Andreas	6.2	Twente	Vedbaek, Den	11.07.88
Calvet, Raphael	6.0	Auxerre	Auxerre, Fr	07.02.94
Dean, Harlee	5.10	Southampton	Basingstoke	26.07.91
O'Connell, Jack	6.3	Blackburn	Liverpool	29.03.94
O'Shaughnessy, Daniel	6.1	Metz	Riihimaki, Fin	14.04.94
Tarkowski, James	6.1	Oldham	Manchester	19.11.92
Yennaris, Nico	5.9	Arsenal	Leytonstone	24.05.93

Midfielders

Dallas, Stuart	6.0	Crusaders	Cookstown	19.04.91
Diagouraga, Toumani	6.3	Peterborough	Paris, Fr	09.06.87
Douglas, Jonathan	5.11	Swindon	Monaghan, Ire	22.11.81
Gogia, Akaki	5.10	Hallescher	Rustavi, Georgia	18.01.92
Jota	5.11	Celta Vigo	Pobra do Caraminal, Sp	16.06.91
Judge, Alan	6.0	Blackburn	Dublin, Ire	11.11.88
Kerschbaumer, Konstantin	5.11	Admira Wacker	Tulln Donau, Aut	01.07.92
MacLeod, Lewis	5.9	Rangers	Wishaw	16.06.94
McCormack, Alan	5.8	Swindon	Dublin, Ire	10.01.84
McEachran, Josh	5.10	Chelsea	Oxford	01.03.93
Odubajo, Moses	5.10	Leyton Orient	Greenwich	28.07.93
Saunders, Sam	5.11	Dagenham	Greenwich	29.08.83
Tebar, Marcos	6.1	Almeria	Madrid, Sp	07.02.86
Williams, Ryan	5.8	Morecambe	Birkenhead	08.04.91

Forwards

Gray, Andre	5.10	Luton	Wolverhampton	26.06.91
Grigg, Will	5.11	Walsall	Solihull	03.07.91
Hogan, Scott	5.11	Rochdale	Salford	13.04.92

BRIGHTON AND HOVE ALBION

Ground: American Express Stadium, Village Way, Brighton BN1 9BL
Telephone: 01273 878288. **Club nickname**: Seagulls
Colours: Blue and white. **Capacity**: 30,750
Record attendance: Goldstone Ground: 36,747 v Fulham (Div 2) Dec 27, 1958; Withdean Stadium: 8,729 v Manchester City (Carling Cup 2) Sep 23, 2008; Amex Stadium: 30,278 v Arsenal (FA Cup 4) Jan 25, 2015

Goalkeepers

Ankergren, Casper	6.3	Leeds	Koge, Den	09.11.79
Maenpaa, Niki	6.3	Venlo	Espoo, Fin	23.01.85
Stockdale, David	6.3	Fulham	Leeds	28.09.85
Walton Christian	6.0	Plymouth	Wadebridge	09.11.95

Defenders

Name	Height	Club	Birthplace	Date
Bong, Gaetan	6.2	Wigan	Sakbayeme, Cam	25.04.88
Calderon, Inigo	5.11	Alaves	Vitoria, Sp	04.01.82
Chicksen, Adam	5.8	MK Dons	Milton Keynes	01.11.90
Dunk, Lewis	6.4	–	Brighton	21.11.91
Greer, Gordon	6.2	Swindon	Glasgow	14.12.80
Rosenior, Liam	5.10	Hull	Wandsworth	09.07.84
Saltor, Bruno	5.11	Valencia	El Masnou, Sp	01.10.80

Midfielders

Name	Height	Club	Birthplace	Date
Crofts, Andrew	5.11	Norwich	Chatham	29.05.84
Forster-Caskey, Jake	5.10	–	Southend	25.04.94
Holla, Danny	6.0	Den Haag	Almere, Hol	31.12.87
Ince, Rohan	6.3	Chelsea	Whitechapel	08.11.92
Kayal, Beram	5.10	Celtic	Jadeidi, Isr	02.05.88
LuaLua, Kazenga	5.11	Newcastle	Kinshasa, DR Congo	10.12.90
March, Solly	5.11	–	Eastbourne	20.07.94
Monakana, Jeffrey	5.11	Preston	Edmonton	05.11.93
Stephens, Dale	5.7	Charlton	Bolton	12.06.89

Forwards

Name	Height	Club	Birthplace	Date
Akindayini, Daniel	6.0	Tottenham	Plaistow	25.10.95
Baldock, Sam	5.8	Bristol City	Bedford	15.03.89
Colunga, Adrian	5.9	Getafe	Oviedo, Sp	17.11.84
Hemed, Tomer	6.0	Almeria	Kiryat Tivon, Isr	02.05.87
O'Grady, Chris	6.1	Barnsley	Nottingham	25.01.86

BRISTOL CITY

Ground: Ashton Gate, Bristol BS3 2EJ
Telephone: 0871 222 6666. **Club nickname**: Robins
Colours: Red and white. **Capacity**: 21,479
Record attendance: 43,335 v Preston (FA Cup 5) Feb 16, 1935

Goalkeepers

Name	Height	Club	Birthplace	Date
Fielding, Frank	6.0	Derby	Blackburn	04.04.88

Defenders

Name	Height	Club	Birthplace	Date
Ayling, Luke	6.1	Yeovil	Lambeth	25.08.91
Cunningham, Greg	6.0	Manchester City	Carnmore, Ire	31.01.91
El-Abd, Adam	6.0	Bristol City	Brighton	11.09.84
Flint, Aden	6.2	Swindon	Pinxton	11.07.89
Little, Mark	6.1	Peterborough	Worcester	20.08.88
Williams, Derrick	6.2	Aston Villa	Waterford, Ire	17.01.93

Midfielders

Name	Height	Club	Birthplace	Date
Bryan, Joe	5.7	–	Bristol	17.09.93
Freeman, Luke	5.10	Stevenage	Dartford	22.03.92
Pack, Marlon	6.2	Cheltenham	Portsmouth	25.03.91
Reid, Bobby	5.7	–	Bristol	02.02.93
Smith, Korey	6.0	Oldham	Hatfield	31.01.91
Wagstaff, Scott	5.11	Charlton	Maidstone	31.03.90

Forwards

Name	Height	Club	Birthplace	Date
Agard, Kieran	5.10	Rotherham	Newham	10.10.89
Burns, Wes	5.9	–	Cardiff	28.12.95
Wilbrahan, Aaron	6.3	Crystal Palace	Knutsford	21.10.79

BURNLEY

Ground: Turf Moor, Harry Potts Way, Burnley BB10 4BX
Telephone: 0871 221 1882. **Club nickname**: Clarets

Colours: Claret and blue. **Capacity**: 21,401.
Record attendance: 54,775 v Huddersfield (FA Cup 3) Feb 23, 1924

Goalkeepers

Cisak, Alex	6.4	Oldham	Krakow, Pol	19.05.89
Gilks, Matt	6.1	Blackpool	Rochdale	04.06.82
Heaton, Tom	6.1	Bristol City	Chester	15.04.86

Defenders

Anderson, Tom	6.4	–	Burnley	02.09.93
Duff, Mike	6.1	Cheltenham	Belfast	11.01.78
Dummigan, Cameron	5.11	Cliftonville	Lurgan	02.06.96
Keane, Michael	5.10	Manchester Utd	Stockport	11.01.93
Lafferty, Danny	6.1	Derry	Derry	01.04.89
Long, Kevin	6.2	Cork	Cork, Ire	18.08.90
Lowton, Matthew	5.11	Aston Villa	Chesterfield	09.06.89
Mee, Ben	5.11	Manchester City	Sale	23.09.89
O'Neill, Luke	6.0	Mansfield	Slough	20.08.91
Shackell, Jason	6.4	Derby	Stevenage	27.09.83
Ward, Stephen	5.11	Wolves	Dublin, Ire	20.08.85

Midfielders

Arfield, Scott	5.10	Huddersfield	Livingston	01.11.88
Hewitt, Steven	5.7	–	Manchester	05.12.93
Jones, David	5.10	Wigan	Southport	04.11.84
Kightly, Michael	5.11	Stoke	Basildon	24.01.86
Marney, Dean	5.11	Hull	Barking	31.01.84
Taylor, Matt	5.10	West Ham	Oxford	27.11.81
Ulvestad, Fredrik	6.0	Aalesund	Aalesund, Nor	17.06.92

Forwards

Barnes, Ashley	6.0	Brighton	Bath	31.10.89
Boyd, George	5.10	Hull	Chatham	02.10.85
Gilchrist, Jason	5.10	Manchester City	St Helens	17.12.94
Jutkiewicz, Lukas	6.1	Middlesbrough	Southampton	20.03.89
Sordell, Marvin	5.10	Bolton	Brent	17.02.91
Vokes, Sam	5.11	Wolves	Lymington	21.10.89
Vossen, Jelle	5.11	Genk	Bilzen, Bel	22.03.89

CARDIFF CITY

Ground: Cardiff City Stadium, Leckwith Road, Cardiff CF11 8AZ
Telephone: 0845 365 1115. **Club nickname**: Bluebirds
Colours: Red and black. **Capacity**: 33,500
Record attendance: Ninian Park: 62,634 Wales v England, Oct 17, 1959; Club: 57,893 v
Arsenal (Div 1) Apr 22, 1953, Cardiff City Stadium: 33,280 (Wales v Belgium) Jun 12, 2015.
Club: 28,018 v Liverpool (Prem Lge) Mar 22, 2014.

Goalkeepers

Marshall, David	6.3	Norwich	Glasgow	05.03.85
Moore, Simon	6.3	Brentford	Sandown	19.05.90

Defenders

Ajayi, Semi	6.4	Arsenal	Crayford	09.11.93
Connolly, Matthew	6.2	QPR	Barnet	24.09.87
Fabio	5.6	Manchester Utd	Petropolis, Br	09.07.90
John, Declan	5.10	–	Merthyr Tydfil	30.06.95
Malone, Scott	6.2	Millwall	Rowley Regis	25.03.91
Manga, Bruno	6.1	Lorient	Libreville, Gab	16.07.88
Morrison, Sean	6.1	Reading	Plymouth	08.01.91

| Peltier, Lee | 5.11 | Huddersfield | Liverpool | 11.12.86 |
| Turner, Ben | 6.4 | Coventry | Birmingham | 21.08.88 |

Midfielders

Adeyemi, Tom	6.1	Birmingham	Norwich	24.10.91
Dikgacoi, Kagisho	5.11	Crystal Palace	Brandfort, SA	24.11.84
Gunnarsson, Aron	5.11	Coventry	Akureyri, Ice	22.04.89
Harris, Kadeem	5.9	Wycombe	Westminster	08.06.93
Kennedy, Matthew	5.9	Everton	Dundonald	01.11.94
Noone, Craig	6.3	Brighton	Fazakerly	17.11.87
O'Keefe, Stuart	5.8	Crystal Palace	Norwich	04.03.91
Pilkington, Anthony	6.0	Norwich	Blackburn	06.06.88
Ralls, Joe	6.0	–	Aldershot	13.10.93
Whittingham, Peter	5.10	Aston Villa	Nuneaton	08.09.84

Forwards

Ameobi, Sammy	6.3	Newcastle (loan)	Newcastle	01.05.92
Doyle, Eoin	6.0	Chesterfield	Dublin, Ire	12.03.88
Jones, Kenwyne	6.2	Stoke	Point Fortin, Trin	05.01.84
Le Fondre, Adam	5.9	Reading	Stockport	02.12.86
Macheda, Federico	6.0	Manchester Utd	Rome, It	22.08.91
Mason, Joe	5.10	Plymouth	Plymouth	13.05.91
Revell, Alex	6.3	Rotherham	Cambridge	07.07.83
Velikonja, Etien	5.10	Maribor	Sempeter, Sloven	26.12.88

CHARLTON ATHLETIC

Ground: The Valley, Floyd Road, London SE7 8BL
Telephone: 0208 333 4000. **Club nickname**: Addicks
Colours: Red and white. **Capacity**: 27,111
Record attendance: 75,031 v Aston Villa (FA Cup 5) Feb 12, 1938

Goalkeepers

Dmitrovic, Marko	6.4	Ujpest	Subotica, Serb	24.01.92
Henderson, Stephen	6.3	West Ham	Dublin, Ire	02.05.88
Pope, Nick	6.3	Bury Town	Cambridge	19.04.92

Defenders

Bauer, Patrick	6.4	Maritimo	Backnang, Ger	28.10.92
Bikey, Andre	6.0	Panetolikos	Douala, Cam	08.01.85
Fox, Morgan	6.1	–	Chelmsford	21.09.93
Lennon, Harry	6.3	–	Romford	16.12.94
Nego, Loic	6.0	Ujpest	Paris, Fr	15.01.91
Solly, Chris	5.8	–	Rochester	20.01.90
Wiggins, Rhoys	5.9	Bournemouth	Hillingdon	04.11.87

Midfielders

Ba, El Hadji	6.0	Sunderland	Paris, Fr	05.03.93
Cousins, Jordan	5.10	–	Greenwich	06.03.94
Diarra, Alou	6.3	West Ham	Villepinte, Fr	15.07.81
Gudmundsson, Johann Berg	6.1	Alkmaar	Reykjavik, Ice	27.10.90
Harriott, Callum	5.5	–	Norbury	04.03.94
Jackson, Johnnie	6.1	Notts Co	Camden	15.08.82
Moussa, Franck	5.8	Coventry	Brussels, Bel	24.07.89

Forwards

Ahearne-Grant, Karlan	6.0	–	Greenwich	19.12.97
Ansah, Zak	5.10	Arsenal	Sidcup	04.05.94
Makienok, Simon	6.7	Palermo (loan)	Naestved, Den	21.11.90
Pigott, Joe	5.10	–	Maidstone	24.11.93

| Vetokele, Igor | 5.9 | Copenhagen | Luanda, Ang | 23.03.92 |
| Watt, Tony | 6.0 | Standard Liege | Coatbridge | 29.12.93 |

DERBY COUNTY

Ground: iPro Stadium, Pride Park, Derby DE24 8XL
Telephone: 0871 472 1884. **Club nickname**: Rams
Colours: White and black. **Capacity**: 33,597
Record attendance: Baseball Ground: 41,826 v Tottenham (Div 1) Sep 20, 1969; iPro Stadium: 33,597 (England v Mexico) May 25, 2011; Club: 33,475 v Rangers (Ted McMinn testimonial) May 1, 2006

Goalkeepers

Carson, Scott	6.3	Wigan	Whitehaven	03.09.85
Grant, Lee	6.2	Burnley	Hemel Hempstead	27.01.83
Roos, Kelle	6.5	Nuneaton	Rijkevoort, Hol	31.05.92

Defenders

Albentosa, Raul	6.4	Eibar	Alzira, Sp	07.09.88
Baird, Chris	5.11	WBA	Rasharkin	25.02.82
Buxton, Jake	5.11	Burton	Sutton-in-Ashfield	04.03.85
Christie, Cyrus	6.2	Coventry	Coventry	30.09.92
Forsyth, Craig	6.0	Watford	Carnoustie	24.02.89
Keogh, Richard	6.2	Coventry	Harlow	11.08.86
Pearce, Alex	6.2	Reading	Wallingford	09.11.88
Shotton, Ryan	6.3	Stoke	Stoke	30.09.88
Warnock, Stephen	5.10	Leeds	Ormskirk	12.12.81

Midfielders

Bryson, Craig	5.8	Kilmarnock	Rutherglen	06.11.86
Bunjaku, Alban	6.0	Sevilla	Romford	20.05.94
Hendrick, Jeff	6.1	–	Dublin, Ire	31.01.92
Hughes, Will	6.1	–	Surrey	07.04.95
Ince, Thomas	5.10	Hull	Stockport	30.01.92
Thorne, George	6.2	WBA	Chatham	04.01.93

Forwards

Bent, Darren	5.11	Aston Villa	Wandsworth	06.02.84
Dawkins, Simon	5.10	Tottenham	Edgware	01.12.87
Martin, Chris	5.10	Norwich	Beccles	04.11.88
Russell, Johnny	5.10	Dundee Utd	Glasgow	08.04.90
Sammon, Conor	6.2	Wigasn	Dublin, Ire	06.11.86
Weimann, Andreas	6.2	Aston Villa	Vienna, Aut	05.08.91

FULHAM

Ground: Craven Cottage, Stevenage Road, London SW6 6HH
Telephone: 0870 442 1222. **Club nickname**: Cottagers
Colours: White and black. **Capacity**: 25,700
Record attendance: 49,335 v Millwall (Div 2) Oct 8, 1938

Goalkeepers

Bettinelli, Marcus	6.4	–	Camberwell	24.05.92
Joronen, Joronen	6.5	–	Helsinki, Fin	21.03.93
Lonergan, Andy	6.3	Bolton	Preston	19.10.83

Defenders

Amorebieta, Fernando	6.4	Athletic Bilbao	Cantaura, Ven	29.03.85
Bodurov, Nikolay	5.11	Litex Lovech	Blagoevgrad, Bul	03.05.86
Burgess, Cameron	6.4	–	Aberdeen	21.10.95
Burn, Dan	6.7	Darlington	Blyth	09.05.92
Casasola, Tiago	6.3	Boca Juniors	Argentina	11.08.95

Grimmer, Jack	6.1	Aberdeen	Aberdeen	25.01.94
Hutchinson, Shaun	6.2	Motherwell	Newcastle	23.11.90
Kavanagh, Sean	5.9	Belvedere	Dublin	24.01.94
Richards, Jazz	6.1	Swansea	Swansea	12.04.91
Midfielders				
Cairney, Tom	6.0	Blackburn	Nottingham	20.01.91
Christensen, Lasse	5.10	Midtjylland	Esbjerg, Den	15.08.94
Eisfeld, Thomas	5.10	Arsenal	Finsterwalde, Ger	18.01.93
Hyndman, Emerson	5.8	Dallas	Dallas	09.04.96
Kacaniklic, Alex	5.11	Liverpool	Helsingborg, Swe	13.08.91
O'Hara, Jamie	5.11	Blackpool	Dartford	25.09.86
Parker, Scott	5.7	Tottenham	Lambeth	13.10.80
Pringle, Ben	5.9	Rotherham	Newcastle	25.07.89
Tunnicliffe, Ryan	6.0	Manchester Utd	Heywood	30.12.92
Voser, Kay	5.6	Basle	Baden, Swi	04.01.87
Forwards				
Dembele, Moussa	6.0	Paris SG	Pontoise, Fr	12.07.96
McCormack, Ross	5.10	Leeds	Glasgow	18.08.86
Mitroglou, Kostas	6.2	Olympiacos	Kavala, Gre	12.03.88
Roberts, Patrick	5.8	–	Kingston	05.02.97
Smith, Matt	6.6	Leeds	Birmingham	07.06.89
Taggart, Adam	6.0	Newcastle Jets	Perth, Aus	02.06.93
Williams, George	5.8	MK Dons	Milton Keynes	07.09.95
Woodrow, Cauley	6.1	Luton	Hemel Hempstead	02.12.94

HUDDERSFIELD TOWN

Ground: John Smith's Stadium, Huddersfield HD1 6PX
Telephone: 0870 444 4677. **Club nickname**: Terriers
Colours: Blue and white. **Capacity**: 24,500
Record attendance: Leeds Road: 67,037 v Arsenal (FA Cup 6) Feb 27, 1932; John Smith's Stadium: 23,678 v Liverpool (FA Cup 3) Dec 12, 1999

Goalkeepers				
Murphy, Joe	6.2	Coventry	Dublin, Ire	21.08.81
Smithies, Alex	6.1	–	Huddersfield	25.03.90
Defenders				
Boyle, William	6.2	–	Garforth	01.09.95
Davidson, Jason	5.11	WBA	Melbourne, Ais	29.06.91
Hudson, Mark	6.3	Cardiff	Guildford	30.03.82
Lynch, Joel	6.1	Nottm Forest	Eastbourne	03.10.87
Smith, Tommy	6.1	Manchester City	Warrington	14.04.92
Wallace, Murray	6.2	Falkirk	Glasgow	10.01.93
Wilkinson, Joe	6.0	–	Dewsbury	02.11.95
Midfielders				
Billing, Philip	6.4	–	Esbjerg, Den	11.06.96
Butterfield, Jacob	5.11	Middlesbrough	Bradford	10.06.90
Dempsey, Kyle	5.10	Carlisle	Whitehaven	17.09.95
Hammill, Adam	5.10	Wolves	Liverpool	25.01.88
Hogg, Jonathan	5.7	Watford	Middlesbrough	06.12.88
Holmes, Duane	5.8	–	Wakefield	06.11.94
Tronstad, Sondre	5.8	IK Start	Norway	26.08.95
Whitehead, Dean	5.11	Middlesbrough	Abingdon	12.01.82
Forwards				
Bunn, Harry	5.9	Manchester City	Oldham	21.11.92
Charles, Jake	6.0	–	Garforth	16.02.96

Lolley, Joe	5.10	Kidderminster	Redditch	25.08.92
Miller, Ishmael	6.3	Blackpool	Manchester	05.03.87
Scannell, Sean	5.9	Crystal Palace	Croydon	21.03.89
Vaughan, James	5.11	Norwich	Birmingham	14.07.88
Wells, Nahki	5.7	Bradford	Bermuda	01.06.90

HULL CITY

Ground: Kingston Communications Stadium, Anlaby Road, Hull, HU3 6HU
Telephone: 01482 504600. **Club nickname**: Tigers
Colours: Amber and black. **Capacity**: 25,400.
Record attendance: Boothferry Park: 55,019 v Manchester Utd (FA Cup 6) Feb 26, 1949. KC Stadium: 25,030 v Liverpool (Prem Lge) May 9, 2010. Also: 25,280 (England U21 v Holland) Feb 17, 2004

Goalkeepers
Jakupovic, Eldin	6.3	Aris	Sarajevo, Bos	02.10.84
McGregor, Allan	6.0	Besiktas	Edinburgh	31.01.82
Watson, Rory	6.3	–	York	05.02.96

Defenders
Bruce, Alex	5.11	Leeds	Norwich	28.09.84
Chester, James	5.10	Manchester Utd	Warrington	23.01.89
Davidson, Jason	5.11	WBA	Melbourne, Aus	29.06.91
Davies, Curtis	6.2	Birmingham	Waltham Forest	15.03.85
Dawson, Michael	6.2	Tottenham	Northallerton	18.11.83
Lenihan, Brian	5.10	Cork	Cork	08.06.94
Maguire, Harry	6.2	Sheffield Utd	Sheffield	05.03.93
Robertson, Andrew	5.10	Dundee Utd	Glasgow	11.03.94

Midfielders
Brady, Robbie	5.10	Manchester Utd	Dublin, Ire	14.01.92
Diame, Mohamed	6.1	West Ham	Creteil, Fr	14.06.87
Elmohamady, Ahmed	5.11	Sunderland	Basyoun, Egy	09.09.87
Huddlestone, Tom	6.1	Tottenham	Nottingham	28.12.86
Livermore, Jake	6.2	Tottenham	Enfield	14.11.89
Meyler, David	6.2	Sunderland	Cork, Ire	29.05.89
Snodgrass, Robert	6.0	Norwich	Glasgow	07.09.87

Forwards
Aluko, Sone	5.8	Rangers	Hounslow	19.02.89
Hernandez, Abel	6.1	Palermo	Pando, Uru	08.08.90
N'Doye, Dame	6.1	Lokomotiv Moscow	Thies, Sen	21.02.85
Jelevic, Nikica	6.2	Everton	Capljina, Cro	27.08.85

IPSWICH TOWN

Ground: Portman Road, Ipswich IP1 2DA
Telephone: 01473 400500. **Club nickname**: Blues/Town
Colours: Blue and white. **Capacity**: 30,311
Record attendance: 38,010 v Leeds (FA Cup 6) Mar 8, 1975

Goalkeepers
| Bialkowski, Bartosz | 6.0 | Notts Co | Braniewo, Pol | 06.07.87 |
| Gerken, Dean | 6.2 | Bristol City | Southend | 04.08.85 |

Defenders
Berra, Christophe	6.1	Wolves	Edinburgh	31.01.85
Chambers, Luke	5.11	Nottm Forest	Kettering	29.08.85
Clarke, Matt	5.11	–	Ipswich	22.09.96
Parr, Jonathan	6.0	Crystal Palace	Oslo, Nor	21.10.88

Smith, Tommy	6.1	–	Macclesfield	31.03.90
Yorwerth, Josh	6.0	Cardiff	Bridgend	28.02.95

Midfielders

Bru, Kevin	6.0	Levski Sofia	Paris, Fr	12.12.88
Bishop, Teddy	5.11	–	Cambridge	15.07.96
Fraser, Ryan	5.4	Bournemouth (loan)	Aberdeen	24.02.94
Henshall, Alex	5.10	Manchester City	Swindon	15.02.94
Hyam, Luke	5.10	–	Ipswich	24.10.91
Skuse, Cole	5.9	Bristol City	Bristol	29.03.86
Stewart, Cameron	5.8	Hull	Manchester	08.04.91
Tabb, Jay	5.7	Reading	Tooting	21.02.84

Forwards

Maitland-Miles, Ainsley	5.10	Arsenal (loan)	Goodmayes	29.08.97
McGoldrick, David	6.1	Nottm Forest	Nottingham	29.11.87
Murphy, Daryl	6.2	Celtic	Waterford, Ire	15.03.83
Pitman, Brett	6.0	Bournemouth	St Helier, Jer	03.01.88
Sears, Freddie	5.10	Colchester	Hornchurch	27.11.89

LEEDS UNITED

Ground: Elland Road, Leeds LS11 0ES
Telephone: 0871 334 1919. **Club nickname**: Whites
Colours: White. **Capacity**: 37,890
Record attendance: 57,892 v Sunderland (FA Cup 5 rep) Mar 15, 1967

Goalkeepers

Horton, Charlie	6.3	Cardiff	Lambeth	14.09.94
Silvestri, Marco	6.3	Chievo	Castelnovo, It	02.03.91

Defenders

Bamba, Sol	6.3	Palermo	Ivry-sur-Seine, Fr	13.01.85
Bellusci, Giuseppe	6.1	Catania	Trebisacce, It	21.08.89
Berardi, Gaetano	5.11	Sampdoria	Sorengo, Swi	21.08.88
Byram, Sam	5.11	–	Thurrock	16.09.93
Cooper, Liam	6.0	Chesterfield	Hull	30.08.91
Killock, Ross	6.1	–	Huddersfield	12.07.94
Taylor, Charlie	5.9	–	York	18.09.93
Wootton, Scott	6.2	Manchester Utd	Birkenhead	12.09.91

Midfielders

Bianchi, Tommaso	6.0	Sassuolo	Piombino, It	01.11.88
Cook, Lewis	5.9	–	Leeds	28.03.97
Dawson, Chris	5.6	–	Dewsbury	02.09.94
Mowatt, Alex	5.10	–	Doncaster	13.02.95
Murphy, Luke	6.2	Crewe	Alsager	21.10.89
Sloth, Casper	6.0	Aarhus	Aarhus, Den	26.03.92

Forwards

Ajose, Nicky	5.9	Peterborough	Bury	07.10.91
Antenucci, Mirco	5.10	Ternana	Termoli, It	09.08.84
Doukara, Souleymane	6.1	Catania	Meudon, Fr	29.09.91
Erwin, Lee	6.2	Motherwell	Bellshill	19.03.94
Morison, Steve	6.2	Norwich	Enfield	29.08.83
Sharp, Billy	5.9	Southampton	Sheffield	05.02.86
Walters, Lewis	5.9	–	Harrogate	28.03.95
Wood, Chris	6.3	Leicester	Auckland, NZ	07.12.91

MIDDLESBROUGH

Ground: Riverside Stadium, Middlesbrough, TS3 6RS
Telephone: 0844 499 6789. **Club nickname**: Boro
Colours: Red. **Capacity**: 34,742
Record attendance: Ayresome Park: 53,536 v Newcastle (Div 1) Dec 27, 1949; Riverside Stadium: 35,000 (England v Slovakia) Jun 11, 2003. Club: 34,836 v Norwich (Prem Lge) Dec 28, 2004

Goalkeepers

Konstantopoulos, Dimitrios	6.5	AEK Athens	Thessaloniki, Gre	29.11.79
Mejias, Tomas	6.5	Real Madrid	Madrid, Sp	30.01.89

Defenders

Ayala, Daniel	6.3	Norwich	El Saucejo, Sp	07.11.90
Baptiste, Alex	5.11	Bolton	Sutton-in-Ashfield	31.01.86
Damia	6.2	Osasuna	Olot, Sp	15.04.82
Friend, George	6.0	Doncaster	Barnstaple	19.10.87
Gibson, Ben	6.1	–	Nunthorpe	15.01.93
Husband, James	5.11	Doncaster	Leeds	03.01.94
Williams, Rhys	6.1	Joondalup	Perth, Aus	07.07.88

Midfielders

Adomah, Albert	6.1	Bristol City	Lambeth	13.12.87
Carayol, Mustapha	5.10	Bristol Rov	Banjul, Gam	10.06.89
Clayton, Adam	5.9	Huddersfield	Manchester	14.01.89
Forshaw, Adam	6.1	Wigan	Liverpool	08.10.91
Leadbitter, Grant	5.9	Ipswich	Chester-le-Street	07.01.86
Morris, Bryn	6.0	–	Hartlepool	25.04.96
Reach, Adam	6.1	–	Gateshead	03.02.93

Forwards

Kike	6.1	Real Murcia	Motilla del Palanca, Sp	25.11.89
Nsue, Emilio	6.0	Mallorca	Palma, Sp	30.09.89
Tomlin, Lee	5.11	Peterborough	Leicester	12.01.89
Wildschut, Yanic	6.2	Heerenveen	Amsterdam, Hol	01.11.91

MILTON KEYNES DONS

Ground: stadiummk, Stadium Way West, Milton Keynes MK1 1ST
Telephone: 01908 622922. **Club nickname**: Dons
Colours: White. **Capacity**: 30,500
Record attendance: 20,516 v Wolves (Lge 1) Mar 29, 2014

Goalkeepers

Burns, Charlie	6.2	–	Croydon	27.05.95
Cropper, Cody	6.3	Southampton	Atlanta, US	16.02.93
Martin, David	6.2	Liverpool	Romford	22.01.86

Defenders

Flanagan, Tom	6.2	–	Hammersmith	30.12.91
Hodson, Lee	5.11	Watford	Borehamwood	02.10.91
Kay, Antony	5.11	Huddersfield	Barnsley	21.10.82
Lewington, Dean	5.11	Wimbledon	Kingston	18.05.84
McFadzean, Kyle	6.1	Crawley	Sheffield	28.02.87
Spence, Jordan	6.1	West Ham	Woodford	24.05.90
Walsh, Joe	5.11	Crawley	Cardiff	13.05.92

Midfielders

Baker, Carl	6.2	Coventry	Whiston	26.12.82
Carruthers, Samir	5.8	Aston Villa	Islington	04.04.93

Jennings, Dale	5.8	Barnsley	Liverpool	21.12.92
Potter, Darren	5.10	Sheffield Wed	Liverpool	21.12.84
Powell, Daniel	6.2	–	Luton	12.03.91
Randall, Mark	6.0	Ascoli	Milton Keynes	28.09.89
Reeves, Ben	5.10	Southampton	Verwood	19.11.91
Forwards				
Bowditch, Dean	5.11	Yeovil	Bishop's Stortford	15.06.86
Church, Simon	6.0	Charlton	High Wycombe	10.12.88
Hitchcock, Tom	5.11	QPR	Hemel Hempstead	01.10.92
Rasulo, Giorgio	5.10	–	Banbury	23.01.97

NOTTINGHAM FOREST

Ground: City Ground, Pavilion Road, Nottingham NG2 5FJ
Telephone: 0115 982 4444. **Club nickname**: Forest
Colours: Red and white. **Capacity**: 30,602
Record attendance: 49,946 v Manchester Utd (Div 1) Oct 28, 1967

Goalkeepers				
De Vries, Dorus	6.0	Wolves	Beverwijk, Hol	29.12.80
Erlandsson, Tim	6.3	Halmstads	Sweden	25.12.96
Evtimov, Dimitar	6.3	Etropole	Shumen, Bul	07.09.93
Defenders				
Fox, Danny	6.0	Southampton	Winsford	29.05.86
Hobbs, Jack	6.3	Hull	Portsmouth	18.08.88
Lichaj, Eric	5.10	Aston Villa	Illinois, US	17.11.88
Mancienne, Michael	6.0	Hamburg	Feltham	08.01.88
Mills, Matt	6.3	Bolton	Swindon	14.07.86
Riera, Roger	6.1	Barcelona	El Masnou, Sp	17.02.95
Wilson, Kevin	6.3	Celtic	Nottingham	03.09.85
Midfielders				
Antonio, Michail	5.11	Sheffield Wed	Wandsworth	28.03.90
Burke, Chris	5.9	Birmingham	Glasgow	02.12.83
Cohen, Chris	5.11	Yeovil	Norwich	05.03.87
Lansbury, Henri	6.0	Arsenal	Enfield	12.10.90
McLaughlin, Stephen	5.9	Derry	Donegal, Ire	14.06.90
Osborn, Ben	5.10	–	Derby	05.08.94
Reid, Andy	5.7	Blackpool	Dublin	29.07.82
Tesche, Robert	5.11	Hamburg	Wismar, Ger	27.05.87
Vaughan, David	5.7	Sunderland	Rhuddlan	18.02.83
Forwards				
Assombalonga, Britt	5.10	Peterborough	Kinshasa, DR Cong	06.12.92
Blackstock, Dexter	6.2	Nottm Forest	Oxford	20.05.86
Fryatt, Matt	5.10	Hull	Nuneaton	05.03.86
Paterson, Jamie	5.9	Walsall	Coventry	20.12.91
Walker, Tyler	5.10	–	Nottingham	07.10.96
Ward, Jamie	5.5	Derby	Birmingham	12.05.86

PRESTON NORTH END

Ground: Deepdale, Sir Tom Finney Way, Preston PR1 6RU
Telephone: 0844 856 1964. **Club nickname**: Lilywhites
Colours: White and navy. **Capacity**: 23,408
Record attendance: 42,684 v Arsenal (Div 1) Apr 23, 1938

Goalkeepers				
James, Steven	6.0	–	Southport	19.12.94

Jones, Jamie	6.0	Leyton Orient	Kirkby	18.02.89
Defenders				
Anderton, Nick	6.2	–	Preston	22.04.96
Clarke, Tom	5.11	Huddersfield	Halifax	21.12.87
Davies, Ben	5.11	–	Barrow	11.08.95
Huntington, Paul	6.2	Yeovil	Carlisle	17.09.87
Woods, Calum	5.11	Huddersfield	Liverpool	05.02.87
Wright, Bailey	5.10	VIS	Melbourne, Aus	28.07.92
Midfielders				
Browne, Alan	5.8	Cork	Cork, Ire	15.04.95
Brownhill, Josh	5.10	–	Warrington	19.12.95
Humphrey, Chris	5.9	Motherwell	St Catherine, Jam	19.09.87
Johnson, Daniel	5.8	Aston Villa	Kingston, Jam	08.10.92
Kilkenny, Neil	5.8	Bristol City	Enfield	19.12.85
Reid, Kyel	5.11	Bradford	Deptford	26.11.87
Welsh, John	6.0	Tranmere	Liverpool	10.01.84
Forwards				
Beckford, Jermaine	6.2	Bolton	Ealing	09.12.83
Gallagher, Paul	6.0	Leicester	Glasgow	09.08.84
Garner, Joe	5.10	Watford	Blackburn	12.04.88
Hugill, Jordan	6.0	Port Vale	Middlesbrough	04.06.92
Ryan, Jack	6.0	–	Barrow	05.04.96
Keane, Will	6.0	Manchester Utd (loan)	Stockport	11.01.93
Little, Andy	6.0	Rangers	Enniskillen	12.05.89

QUEENS PARK RANGERS

Ground: Loftus Road Stadium, South Africa Road, London W12 7PA
Telephone: 0208 743 0262. **Club nickname**: Hoops
Colours: Blue and white. **Capcity**: 18,000
Record attendance: 35,353 v Leeds (Div 1) 27 Apr, 1974

Goalkeepers				
Green, Rob	6.2	West Ham	Chertsey	18.01.80
McCarthy, Alex	6.4	Reading	Guildford	03.12.89
Defenders				
Caulker, Steven	6.3	Cardiff	Feltham	29.12.91
Hill, Clint	6.0	Crystal Palace	Liverpool	22.02.80
Onuoha, Nedum	6.2	Manchester City	Warri, Nig	12.11.86
Robinson, Jack	5.7	Liverpool	Warrington	01.09.93
Traore, Armand	6.1	Arsenal	Paris, Fr	08.10.89
Yun Suk-Young	6.0	Chunnam	Suwon, S Kor	13.02.90
Midfielders				
Diakite, Samba	6.1	Nancy	Montfermeil, Fr	24.01.89
Doughty, Michael	6.1	–	Westminster	20.11.92
Faurlin, Alejandro	6.1	Instituto	Rosario, Arg	09.08.86
Fer, Leroy	6.2	Norwich	Zoetermeer, Hol	05.01.90
Gladwin, Ben	6.3	Swindon	Reading	08.06.92
Henry, Karl	6.0	Wolves	Wolverhampton	26.11.82
Hoilett, Junior	5.8	Blackburn	Ottawa, Can	05.06.90
Luongo, Massimo	5.10	Swindon	Sydney, Aus	25.09.92
Phillips, Matt	6.0	Blackpool	Aylesbury	13.03.91
Sandro	6.2	Tottenham	Riachinho, Br	15.03.89
Sutherland, Frankie	5.9	–	Hillingdon	06.12.93
Forwards				
Austin, Charlie	6.2	Burnley	Hungerford	05.07.89

Emmanuel-Thomas, Jay	6.3	Bristol City	Forest Gate	27.12.90
Mackie, Jamie	5.8	Nottm Forest	Dorking	22.09.85
Polter, Sebastian	6.4	Mainz	Wilhelmshaven, Ger	01.04.91

READING

Ground: Madejski Stadium, Junction 11 M4, Reading RG2 OFL
Telephone: 0118 968 1100. **Club nickname**: Royals
Colours: Blue and white. **Capacity**: 24,200
Record attendance: Elm Park: 33,042 v Brentford (FA Cup 5) Feb 19, 1927; Madejski Stadium: 24,184 v Everton (Prem Lge) Nov 17, 2012

Goalkeepers

| Bond, Jonathan | 6.3 | Watford | Hemel Hempstead | 19.05.93 |

Defenders

Cooper, Jake	6.4	–	Bracknell	03.02.95
Ferdinand, Anton	6.0	Antalyaspor	Peckham	18.02.85
Gunter, Chris	5.11	Nottm Forest	Newport	21.07.89
Hector, Michael	6.4	Thurrock	East Ham	19.07.92
Kelly, Stephen	5.11	Fulham	Dublin, Ire	06.09.83
McShane, Paul	6.0	Hull	Kilpedder, Ire	06.01.86
Obita, Jordan	5.11	–	Oxford	08.12.93

Midfielders

Akpan, Hope	6.0	Crawley	Liverpool	14.08.91
Fosu, Tarique	5.8	–	Wandsworth	05.11.95
McCleary, Garath	5.11	Nottm Forest	Bromley	15.05.87
Norwood, Oliver	5.11	Huddersfield	Burnley	12.04.91
Quinn, Stephen	5.6	Hull	Dublin, Ire	04.04.86
Robson-Kanu, Hal	6.0	–	Acton	21.05.89
Taylor, Jake	5.10	–	Ascot	01.12.91
Williams, Danny	6.0	Hoffenheim	Karlsruhe, Ger	08.03.89

Forwards

Blackman, Nick	5.10	Sheffield Utd	Whitefield	11.11.89
Cox, Simon	5.10	Nottm Forest	Reading	28.04.87
Pogrebnyak, Pavel	6.2	Fulham	Moscow, Rus	08.11.83
Sa, Orlando	6.2	Legia Warsaw	Barcelos, Por	26.05.88

ROTHERHAM UNITED

Ground: New York Stadium, New York Way, Rotherham S60 1AH
Telephone: 08444 140733. **Club nickname**: Millers
Colours: Red and white. **Capacity**: 12,021
Record attendance: Millmoor: 25,170 v Sheffield Wed (Div 2) Jan 26, 1952 and v Sheffield Wed (Div 2) Dec 13, 1952; **Don Valley Stadium**: 7,082 v Aldershot (Lge 2 play-off semi-final, 2nd leg) May 19, 2010; **New York Stadium**: 11,758 v Sheffield Utd (Lge 1) Sep 7, 2013

Goalkeepers

| Collin, Adam | 6.1 | Carlisle | Carlisle | 09.12.84 |
| Loach, Scott | 6.2 | Ipswich | Nottingham | 14.10.79 |

Defenders

Broadfoot, Kirk	6.3	Blackpool	Irvine	08.08.84
Buxton, Lewis	6.1	Sheffield Wed	Newport, IOW	10.12.83
Collins, Danny	6.0	Nottm Forest	Chester	06.08.80
Halford, Greg	6.4	Nottm Forest	Chelmsford	08.12.84
Mattock, Joe	6.0	Sheffield Wed	Leicester	15.05.90
Richardson, Frazer	5.11	Middlesbrough	Rotherham	29.10.82
Thorpe, Tom	6.2	Manchester Utd	Manchester	13.01.93

White, Aidan	5.9	Leeds	Leeds	10.10.91
Wood, Richard	6.3	Charlton	Ossett	05.07.85
Midfielders				
Frecklington, Lee	5.8	Peterborough	Lincoln	08.09.85
Green, Paul	5.10	Leeds	Sheffield	10.04.83
Newton, Conor	5.11	Newcastle	Newcastle	17.10.91
Smallwood, Richard	5.11	Middlesbrough	Redcar	29.12.90
Ward, Danny	5.11	Huddersfield	Bradford	09.12.90
Forwards				
Bowery, Jordan	6.1	Aston Villa	Nottingham	02.07.91
Clarke-Harris, Jonson	6.0	Oldham	Leicester	20.07.94
Derbyshire, Matt	6.1	Nottm Forest	Blackburn	14.04.86
Ledesman, Emmanuel	5.11	Middlesbrough	Quilmes, Arg	24.05.88

SHEFFIELD WEDNESDAY

Ground: Hillsborough, Sheffield, S6 1SW
Telephone: 0871 995 1867. **Club nickname**: Owls
Colours: Blue and white. **Capacity**: 39,812
Record attendance: 72,841 v Manchester City (FA Cup 5) Feb 17, 1934

Goalkeepers				
Dawson, Cameron	6.0	Sheffield Utd	Sheffield	07.07.95
Price, Lewis	6.3	Crystal Palace	Bournemouth	19.07.84
Westwood, Keiren	6.1	Sunderland	Manchester	23.10.84
Defenders				
Dielna, Claude	6.1	Olympiacos	Clichy, Fr	14.12.87
Helan, Jeremy	5.11	Manchester City	Clichy, Fr	09.05.92
Hunt, Jack	5.9	Crystal Palace (loan)	Rothwell	06.12.90
Lachman, Darryl	6.3	Twente	Zaanstad, Hol	11.11.89
Lees, Tom	6.1	Leeds	Warwick	18.11.90
Loovens, Glenn	6.2	Zaragoza	Doetinchem, Hol	22.10.83
Sasso, Vincent	6.3	Braga (loan)	Saint-Cloud, Fr	16.02.91
Vermijl, Marnick	5.11	Manchester Utd	Peer, Bel	13.01.92
Midfielders				
Filipe Melo	6.2	Moreirenses	Santa Maria, Port	03.11.89
Hutchinson, Sam	6.0	Chelsea	Windsor	03.08.89
Lee, Kieran	6.1	Oldham	Tameside	22.06.88
Lopez, Alex	5.9	Celta Vigo (loan)	Ferrol, Sp	11.01.88
Palmer, Liam	6.2	–	Worksop	19.09.91
Semedo, Jose	6.0	Charlton	Setubal, Por	11.01.85
Wallace, Ross	5.6	Burnley	Dundee	23.05.85
Forwards				
Bus, Sergiu	5.11	CSKA Sofia	Cluj-Napoca, Rom	02.11.92
Lavery, Caolan	5.11	Ipswich	Alberta, Can	22.10.92
Maguire, Chris	5.8	Derby	Bellshill	16.01.89
Matias, Marco	5.10	Nacional	Barreiro, Por	10.05.89
May, Stevie	5.10	St Johnstone	Perth, Scot	03.11.92
Nuhiu, Atdhe	6.6	Rapid Vienna	Prishtina, Kos	29.07.89

WOLVERHAMPTON WANDERERS

Ground: Molineux Stadium, Waterloo Road, Wolverhampton WV1 4QR
Telephone: 0871 222 2220. **Club nickname**: Wolves
Colours: Gold and black. **Capacity**: 30,852
Record attendance: 61,315 v Liverpool (FA Cup 5) Feb 11, 1939

Goalkeepers

Ikeme, Carl	6.2	–	Sutton Coldfield	08.06.86
McCarey, Aaron	6.1	–	Monaghan, Ire	14.01.92

Defenders

Batth, Danny	6.3	–	Brierley Hill	21.09.90
Doherty, Matt	5.11	–	Dublin, Ire	16.01.92
Ebanks-Landell, Ethan	6.2	–	Smethwick	12.12.92
Golbourne, Scott	5.9	Barnsley	Bristol	29.02.88
Iorfa, Dominic	6.2	–	Southend	08.07.95
Stearman, Richard	6.2	Leicester	Wolverhampton	19.08.87

Midfielders

Coady, Conor	6.1	Huddersfield	St Helens	25.02.93
Edwards, David	5.11	Luton	Pontesbury	03.02.85
Evans, Lee		Newport	Newport	24.07.94
Henry, James	6.1	Millwall	Reading	10.06.89
Jacobs, Michael	5.9	Derby	Rothwell	04.11.91
McDonald, Kevin	6.2	Sheffield Utd	Carnoustie	04.11.88
Price, Jack	5.7	–	Shrewsbury	19.12.92
Rowe, Tommy	5.11	Peterborough	Manchester	01.05.89
Van La Parra, Rajiv	5.11	Heerenveen	Rotterdam, Hol	04.06.91
Wallace, Jed	5.10	Portsmouth	Reading	26.03.94

Forwards

Afobe, Benik	6.0	Arsenal	Waltham Forest	12.02.93
Dicko, Nouha	5.8	Wigan	Paris, Fr	14.05.92
Sigurdarson, Bjorn	6.1	Lillestrom	Akranes, Ice	26.02.91

LEAGUE ONE

BARNSLEY

Ground: Oakwell Stadium, Barnsley S71 1ET
Telephone: 01226 211211. **Club nickname**: Tykes
Colours: Red and white. **Capacity**: 23,009
Record attendance: 40,255 v Stoke (FA Cup 5) Feb 15, 1936

Goalkeepers

Davies, Adam	6.1	Sheffield Wed	Rinteln, Ger	17.07.92
Turnbull, Ross	6.1	Doncaster	Bishop Auckland	04.01.85

Defenders

Bree, James	5.10	–	Wakefield	11.10.97
Brown, Reece	6.2	Watford	Manchester	01.11.91
Cowgill, Jack	6.1	–	Wakefield	08.01.97
Holgate, Mason	5.11	–	Doncaster	22.10.96
Mawson, Alfie	6.2	Brentford	Hillingdon	19.01.94
Nyatanga, Lewin	6.2	Bristol City	Burton	18.08.88
Roberts, Marc	6.0	Halifax	Wakefield	26.07.90
Smith, George	6.0	–	Barnsley	14.08.96
Williams, George	5.9	Worcester	Hillingdon	14.04.93

Midfielders

Abbott, Brad	5.11	–	Doncaster	24.12.94
Bailey, James	6.0	Derby	Bollington	18.09.88
Digby, Paul	6.3	–	Sheffield	02.02.95
Hourihane, Conor	6.0	Plymouth	Cork, Ire	02.02.91
Scowen, Josh	5.10	Wycombe	Enfield	28.03.93

Watkins, Marley	6.1	Inverness	Lewisham	17.10.90
Forwards				
Lalkovic, Milan	5.9	Mlada Boleslav	Kosice, Slovak	09.12.92
Maris, George	5.11	–	Sheffield	06.03.96
Phenix, Mike	5.10	Telford	Manchester	15.03.89
Wilkinson, Conor	6.2	Bolton (loan)	Croydon	23.01.95
Winnall, Sam	5.11	Scunthorpe	Wolverhampton	19.01.91

BLACKPOOL

Ground: Bloomfield Road, Blackpool FY1 6JJ
Telephone: 0871 622 1953. **Club nickname**: Seasiders
Colours: Tangerine and white. **Capacity**: 17,338
Record attendance: 38,098 v Wolves (Div 1) Sep 17, 1955

Goalkeepers				
Doyle, Colin	6.5	Birmingham	Cork, Ire	12.08.85
Letheren, Kyle	6.2	Dundee	Llanelli	26.12.87
Defenders				
Aldred, Tom	6.2	Accrington	Bolton	11.09.90
Dunne, Charles	6.1	Wycombe	Lambeth	13.02.93
Ferguson, David	5.11	Sunderland	Sunderland	07.06.94
Jones, Lloyd	6.3	Liverpool (loan)	Plymouth	07.10.95
Oliver, Connor		Sunderland	Newcastle	17.02.94
Robertson, Clark	6.2	Aberdeen	Aberdeen	05.09.93
Midfielders				
Cameron, Henry	5.10	–	Lytham St Annes	28.06.97
Cubero, Jose Miguel	5.10	Herediano	Sarchi, CRica	14.02.87
Herron, John	5.10	Celtic	Coatbridge	01.02.94
Orlandi, Andrea	6.0	Brighton	Barcelona, Sp	03.08.84
Potts, Brad	6.2	Carlisle	Hexham	07.03.94
Waddington, Mark	6.0	–	Wigan	11.10.96
Forwards				
Cullen, Mark	5.9	Luton	Stakeford	21.04.92
Ranger, Nile	6.2	Swindon	Wood Green	11.04.91
Redshaw, Jack	5.7	Morecambe	Salford	20.11.90
Telford, Dom	5.9	–	Burnley	05.12.96

BRADFORD CITY

Ground: Coral Windows Stadium, Valley Parade, Bradford BD8 7DY
Telephone: 01274 773355. **Club nickname**: Bantams
Colours: Yellow and claret. **Capacity**: 25,136
Record attendance: 39,146 v Burnley (FA Cup 4) Mar 11, 1911

Goalkeepers				
Williams, Ben	6.0	Hibernian	Manchester	27.08.82
Defenders				
Darby, Stephen	5.9	Liverpool	Liverpool	06.10.88
McArdle, Rory	6.1	Aberdeen	Sheffield	01.05.87
McMahon, Tony	5.10	Blackpool	Bishop Auckland	24.03.86
Meredith, James	6.1	York	Albury, Aus	04.04.88
Routis, Christopher	6.1	Servette	Geneva, Swi	03.03.90
Sheehan, Alan	5.11	Notts Co	Athlone, Ire	14.09.86
Midfielders				
Knott, Billy	5.8	Sunderland	Canvey Is	28.11.92
Liddle, Gary	6.1	Notts Co	Middlesbrough	15.06.86
Morais, Filipe	5.9	Stevenage	Benavente, Por	21.11.85

Morris, Josh	5.10	Blackburn	Preston	30.09.91
Forwards				
Clarke, Billy	5.9	Crawley	Cork, Ire	13.12.87
Davies, Steve	6.1	Blackpool	Liverpool	29.12.87
Hanson, James	6.4	Guiseley	Bradford	09.11.87
James, Luke	6.0	Peterborough (loan)	Amble	04.11.94
McBurnie, Oliver	6.2	–	Leeds	04.06.96

BURTON ALBION

Ground: Pirelli Stadium, Princess Way, Burton upon Trent DE13 AR
Telephone: 01283 565938. **Club nickname**: Brewers
Colours: Yellow and black. **Capacity**: 6,912
Record attendance: 6,192 v Oxford Utd (Blue Square Prem Lge) Apr 17, 2009

Goalkeepers				
Matthews, Remi	6.1	Norwich (loan)	Gorleston	10.02.94
McLaughlin, Jon	6.2	Bradford	Edinburgh	09.09.87
Defenders				
Cansdell-Sherriff, Shane	6.0	Preston	Sydney, Aus	10.11.82
Charles, Darius	6.1	Stevenage	Ealing	10.12.87
Edwards, Phil	5.9	Rochdale	Bootle	08.11.85
Maynard, Kelvin	5.11	Royal Antwerp	Paramaribo, Sur	29.05.87
McCrory, Damien	6.2	Dagenham	Croom, Ire	23.02.90
Naylor, Tom	6.0	Derby	Sutton-in-Ashfield	28.06.91
Slade, Liam	6.3	–	Birmingham	14.05.95
Taft, George	6.3	Leicester	Leicester	29.07.93
Midfielders				
Butcher, Calum	6.0	Dundee Utd	Rochford	26.02.91
Duffy, Mark	5.9	Birmingham (loan)	Liverpool	07.10.85
Harness, Marcus	6.0	–	Coventry	01.08.94
Mousinho, John	6.1	Preston	Isleworth	30.04.86
Palmer, Matt	5.10	–	Derby	01.08.93
Reilly, Callum	6.1	Birmingham	Warrington	03.10.93
Weir, Robbie	5.9	Tranmere	Belfast	09.12.88
Forwards				
Akins, Lucas	6.0	Stevenage	Huddersfield	25.02.89
Beavon, Stuart	5.10	Preston	Reading	05.05.84
El Khayati, Abdenasser	6.1	Kozakken	Rotterdam, Hol	07.02.89
Knowles, Dominic	5.9	Harrogate	Accrington	13.02.92
Thiele, Timmy	6.2	Borussia Dortmund	Berlin, Ger	31.07.91

BURY

Ground: J D Stadium, Gigg Lane, Bury BL9 9HR
Telephone: 08445 790009. **Club nickname**: Shakers
Colours: White and blue. **Capacity**: 11,840
Record attendance: 35,000 v Bolton (FA Cup 3) Jan 9, 1960

Goalkeepers				
Lainton, Rob	6.2	Bolton	Ashton-under-Lyne	12.10.89
Defenders				
Cameron, Nathan	6.2	Coventry	Birmingham	21.11.91
Clarke, Peter	6.0	Blackpool	Southport	03.01.82
Hussey, Chris	6.0	Burton	Hammersmith	02.01.89
O'Brien, Keil	6.4	Chorley	Stockport	29.06.92
Riley, Joe	6.0	Bolton	Salford	13.10.91

Midfielders

Burgess, Scott	5.10	–	Warrington	27.06.96
Etuhu, Kelvin	6.1	Barnsley	Kano, Nig	30.05.88
Jones, Craig	5.8	New Saints	Chester	20.03.87
Mayor, Danny	6.0	Sheffield Wed	Leyland	18.10.90
Mellis, Jacob	5.11	Blackpool	Nottingham	08.01.91
Soares, Tom	6.0	Stoke	Reading	10.07.86
Tutte, Andrew	5.9	Rochdale	Liverpool	21.09.90

Forwards

Clarke, Leon	6.2	Wolves	Wolverhampton	10.02.85
Dudley, Anthony	5.10		Manchester	03.01.96
Hope, Hallam	5.11	Everton	Manchester	17.03.94
Lowe, Ryan	5.11	Tranmere	Liverpool	18.09.78
Nardiello, Daniel	5.11	Rotherham	Coventry	22.10.82
Pope, Tom	6.3	Port Vale	Stoke	27.08.85
Rose, Danny	5.10	Barnsley	Barnsley	10.12.93

CHESTERFIELD

Ground: Proact Stadium, Whittington Moor, Chesterfield S41 8NZ
Telephone: 01246 209765. **Club nickname**: Spireites
Colours: Blue and white. **Capacity**: 10,504
Record attendance: Saltergate: 30,561 v Tottenham (FA Cup 5) Feb 12, 1938; Proact Stadium: 10,089 v Rotherham (Lge 2) Mar 18, 2011

Goalkeepers

Chapman, Aaron	6.8	Belper	Rotherham	29.05.90
Lee, Tommy	6.2	Macclesfield	Keighley	03.01.86

Defenders

Evatt, Ian	6.3	Blackpool	Coventry	19.11.81
Hird Sam	6.0	Doncaster	Doncaster	07.09.87
Humphreys, Richie	5.11	Hartlepool	Sheffield	30.11.77
Jones, Daniel	6.2	Port Vale	Wordsley	23.12.86
Raglan, Charlie	6.0	FC United	Wythenshawe	28.04.93

Midfielders

Ariyibi, Gregory	6.0	Leeds	Virginia, US	18.01.95
Banks, Ollie	6.3	FC United	Rotherham	21.09.92
Clucas, Sam	6.2	Mansfield	Lincoln	25.09.90
Darikwa, Tendayi	6.2	–	Nottingham	13.12.91
Gardner, Dan	6.1	Halifax	Gorton	05.04.90
Morsy, Sam	5.9	Port Vale	Wolverhampton	10.09.91
Onovwigun, Michael	6.2	Brentford	Clapham	09.04.96
O'Shea, Jay	6.0	MK Dons	Dublin, Ire	10.08.88
Talbot, Drew	5.10	Luton	Barnsley	19.07.86

Forwards

Ebanks-Blake, Sylvan	5.8	Preston	Cambridge	29.03.86
Gnanduillet, Armand	6.3	Poissy	Angers, Fr	13.02.92
Harrison, Byron	6.3	Cheltenham	Wandsworth	15.06.87

COLCHESTER UNITED

Ground: Weston Homes Community Stadium, United Way, Colchester CO4 5HE
Telephone: 01206 755100. **Club nickname**: U's
Colours: Blue and white. **Capacity**: 10,105
Record attendance: Layer Road:19,072 v Reading (FA Cup 1) Nov 27, 1948; Community Stadium: 10,064 v Norwich (Lge 1) Jan 16, 2010

Goalkeepers

Lewington, Chris	6.2	Dagenham	Sidcup	23.08.88
Walker, Sam	6.6	Chelsea	Gravesend	02.10.91

Defenders

Briggs, Matthew	6.2	Millwall	Wandsworth	09.03.91
Brindley, Richard	5.11	Rotherham	Norwich	05.05.93
Eastman, Tom	6.3	Ipswich	Colchester	21.10.91
Elokobi, George	6.0	Oldham	Mamfe, Cam	31.01.86
Harney, Jamie	6.0	West Ham	Plumbridge	04.03.96
Kent, Frankie	6.2	–	Romford	21.11.95
O'Donoghue, Michael	5.11	Leyton Orient	Islington	18.01.96
Wynter, Alex	6.1	Crystal Palace	Croydon	16.09.93

Midfielders

Edwards, Joe	5.9	Yeovil	Gloucester	31.10.90
Gilbey, Alex	6.0	–	Dagenham	09.12.94
Lapslie, Tom	5.6	–	Waltham Forest	05.10.95
Lawrence, Byron	5.10	Ipswich	Cambridge	12.03.96
Moncur, George	5.9	West Ham	Swindon	18.08.93
Olufemi, Tosin	5.8	–	Hackney	13.05.94
Sembie-Ferris, Dion	5.8	St Neots	Peterborough	23.05.96
Simmons, Jack	5.7	Ipswich	Basildon	25.11.94
Szmodics, Sammie	5.7	–	Colchester	24.09.95
Wright, Drey	5.9	–	Greenwich	30.04.95

Forwards

Bonne, Macauley	5.11	Ipswich	Ipswich	26.10.95
Holman, Dan	5.11	Braintree	Northampton	05.06.90
Massey, Gavin	5.10	Watford	Watford	14.10.92
Porter, Chris	6.1	Sheffield Utd	Wigan	12.12.83

COVENTRY CITY

Ground: Ricoh Arena, Phoenix Way, Coventry CV6 6GE.
Telephone: 02476 992326. **Club nickname**: Sky Blues
Colours: Sky blue. **Capacity**: 32,609
Record attendance: Highfield Road: 51,455 v Wolves (Div 2) Apr 29, 1967; Ricoh Arena: 31,407 v Chelsea (FA Cup 6), Mar 7, 2009

Goalkeepers

Burge, Lee	5.11	–	Hereford	09.01.93
Charles-Cook, Reice	6.1	Bury	Lewisham	08.04.94

Defenders

Haynes, Ryan	5.7	–	Northampton	27.09.95
Johnson, Reda	6.3	Sheffield Wed	Marseille, Fr	21.03.88
Kelly-Evans, Dion	5.10	–	Coventry	21.09.96
Martin, Aaron	6.1	Yeovil	Newport, IOW	29.09.89
Phillips, Aaron	5.8	–	Warwick	20.11.93
Ricketts, Sam	6.1	Wolves	Aylesbury	11.10.81
Stokes, Chris	6.1	Forest Green	Trowbridge	08.03.91
Vincelot, Romain	5.10	Leyton Orient	Poitiers, Fr	29.10.85
Willis, Jordan	5.11	–	Coventry	24.08.94

Midfielders

Fleck, John	5.7	Rangers	Glasgow	24.08.91
Finch, Jack	6.1	–	Southam	06.08.96
Kelly-Evans, Devon	5.10	–	Coventry	21.09.96
Lawton, Ivor	5.11	–	Coventry	05.09.95
Maddison, James	5.10	–	Coventry	23.11.96

O'Brien, Jim	6.0	Barnsley	Vale of Leven	28.09.87
Swanson, Danny	5.7	Peterborough	Leith	28.12.86
Thomas, Conor	6.1	–	Coventry	29.10.93
Forwards				
Spence, Kyle	5.7	–	Croydon	14.01.97
Thomas, George	5.8	–	Leicester	24.03.97
Tudgay, Marcus	5.10	Nottm Forest	Shoreham	03.02.83

CREWE ALEXANDRA

Ground: Alexandra Stadium, Gresty Road, Crewe CW2 6EB
Telephone: 01270 213014. **Club nickname**: Railwaymen
Colours: Red and white. **Capacity**: 12,700
Record attendance: 20,000 v Tottenham (FA Cup 4) Jan 30, 1960

Goalkeepers				
Garratt, Ben	6.1	–	Shrewsbury	25.04.93
Rachubka, Paul	6.1	Oldham	San Luis Obispo, US	21.05.81
Defenders				
Baillie, James	5.11	–	Warrington	27.03.96
Davis, Harry	6.2	–	Burnley	24.09.91
Guthrie, Jon	5.10	–	Devizes	29.07.92
Ng, Perry	5.11	–	Liverpool	27.04.96
Ray, George	6.0	–	Warrington	13.10.93
Midfielders				
Atkinson, Chris	6.1	Huddersfield	Halifax	13.02.92
Bingham. Billy	5.11	Dagenham	Greenwich	15.07.90
Cooper, George	5.9	–	Warrington	02.11.96
Inman, Brad	5.9	Newcastle	Adelaide, Aus	10.12.91
Jones, James	5.9	–	Winsford	01.02.96
King, Adam	5.11	Swansea (loan)	Edinburgh	11.10.95
Nolan, Liam	5.9	Everton	Liverpool	20.09.94
Turton, Oliver	5.11	–	Manchester	06.12.92
Forwards				
Colclough, Ryan	6.0	–	Stoke	27.12.94
Dalla Valle, Lauri	5.11	Sint-Truiden	Kontiolahti, Fin	14.09.91
Haber, Marcus	6.3	Stevenage	Vancouver, Can	11.01.89
Murdoch, Fraser	5.11	–	Manchester	17.09.96
Saunders, Callum	5.10	–	Istanbul, Tur	26.09.95

DONCASTER ROVERS

Ground: Keepmoat Stadium, Stadium Way, Doncaster DN4 5JW
Telephone: 01302 764664. **Club nickname**: Rovers
Colours: Red and white. **Capacity**: 15,231
Record attendance: Belle Vue: 37,149 v Hull (Div 3 N) Oct 2, 1948; Keepmoat Stadium: 15,001 v Leeds (Lge 1) Apr 1, 2008

Goalkeepers				
Marosi, Marko	6.3	Wigan	Slovakia	23.10.93
Stuckmann, Thorsten	6.6	Preston	Gutersloh, Ger	17.03.81
Defenders				
Askins, Ben	5.10	–	Middlesbrough	02.01.96
Butler, Andy	6.0	Sheffield Utd	Doncaster	04.11.83
Evina, Cedric	5.9	Charlton	Cameroon	16.11.91
Jones, Rob	6.7	Sheffield Wed	Stockton	03.11.79
Lund, Mitchell	6.1	–	Leeds	27.08.96
McCullough, Luke	6.1	Manchester Utd	Portadown	15.02.94

MacKenzie, Gary	6.3	Blackpool	Lanark	15.10.85
McKay, Paul	6.2	–	Glasgow	19.11.96
Wakefield, Liam	6.0	–	Doncaster	09.04.94
Midfielders				
Chaplow, Richard	5.9	Millwall	Accrington	02.02.85
Coppinger, James	5.7	Exeter	Middlesbrough	10.01.81
Forrester, Harry	5.10	Brentford	Milton Keynes	02.01.91
Keegan, Paul	5.7	Bohemians	Dublin, Ire	05.07.84
Middleton, Harry	5.11	–	Doncaster	12.04.95
Wellens, Richie	5.9	Leicester	Manchester	26.03.80
Whitehouse, Billy	5.11	–	Rotherhanm	13.06.96
Forwards				
Main, Curtis	5.10	Middlesbrough	South Shields	20.06.92
McKay, Jack	6.2	–	Glasgow	19.11.96
Tyson, Nathan	6.1	Blackpool	Reading	04.05.82
Williams, Andy	5.10	Swindon	Hereford	14.08.86

FLEETWOOD TOWN

Ground: Highbury Stadium, Park Avenue, Fleetwod FY7 6TX
Telephone: 01253 775080. **Club nickname**: Fishermen
Colours: Red and white. **Capacity**: 5,327
Record attendance: 5,194 v York (Lge 2 play-off semi-final, 2nd leg) May 16, 2014

Goalkeepers				
Lucas, David	6.1	Birmingham	Preston	23.11.77
Maxwell, Chris	6.2	Wrexham	St Asaph	30.07.90
Defenders				
Andrew, Danny	5.11	Macclesfield	Holbeach	23.12.90
Bell, Amari'i	5.11	Birmingham	Burton	05.05.94
Cartwright, Max	6.0	–	Manchester	18.11.95
Hogan, Liam	6.0	Halifax	Salford	08.02.89
Jordan, Stephen	6.0	Dunfermline	Warrington	06.03.82
McLaughlin, Conor	6.0	Preston	Belfast	26.07.91
Pond, Nathan	6.2	Lancaster	Preston	05.01.85
Midfielders				
Evans, Gareth	6.0	Rotherham	Macclesfield	26.04.88
Jonsson, Eggert	6.2	Vestsjaelland	Reykjavik, Ice	18.08.88
Ryan, Jimmy	5.10	Chesterfield	Maghull	06.09.88
Sarcevic, Antoni	6.0	Chester	Manchester	13.03.92
Southern, Keith	5.10	Huddersfield	Gateshead	21.04.84
Forwards				
Hunter, Ashley	5.10	Ilkeston	Derby	29.09.95
Matt, Jamille	6.2	Kidderminster	Walsall	02.12.90
McManus, Declan	5.11	Aberdeen	Glasgow	03.08.94
Proctor, Jamie	6.2	Crawley	Preston	25.03.92

GILLINGHAM

Ground: Priestfield Stadium, Redfern Avenue, Gillingham ME7 4DD
Telephone: 01634 300000. **Club nickname**: Gills
Colours: Blue and white. **Capacity**: 11,582
Record attendance: 23,002 v QPR. (FA Cup 3) Jan 10, 1948

Goalkeepers				
Morris, Glenn	6.0	Aldershot	Woolwich	20.12.83
Nelson, Stuart	6.1	Notts Co	Stroud	17.09.81

Defenders

Name	Height	Previous club	Birthplace	Date
Davies, Callum	6.1	–	Chatham	08.02.93
Egan, John	6.2	Sunderland	Cork, Ire	20.10.92
Ehmer, Max	6.2	QPR	Frankfurt, Ger	03.02.92
Garmston, Bradley	5.11	WBA	Chorley	18.01.94
Hare, Josh	6.0	–	Canterbury	12.08.94
Jackson, Ryan	5.9	Newport	Streatham	31.07.90
Morris, Aaron	6.0	Wimbledon	Rumney	30.12.89

Midfielders

Name	Height	Previous club	Birthplace	Date
Dack, Bradley	5.8	–	Greenwich	31.12.93
Hessenthaler, Jake	5.10	–	Gravesend	20.04.90
Loft, Doug	6.0	Port Vale	Maidstone	25.12.86
McGlashan, Jermaine	5.7	Cheltenham	Croydon	14.04.88
Pritchard, Josh	6.0	Fulham	Stockport	23.09.92

Forwards

Name	Height	Previous club	Birthplace	Date
Dickenson, Brennan	6.0	Brighton	Ashford, Sur	26.02.93
Donnelly, Rory	6.2	Swansea	Belfast	18.02.92
McDonald, Cody	6.0	Coventry	Witham	30.05.86
Millbank, Aaron	6.0	–	Ramsgate	04.02.95
Norris, Luke	6.1	Brentford	Stevenage	03.06.93
Williamson, Ben	5.11	Port Vale	Lambeth	25.12.88

MILLWALL

Ground: The Den, Zampa Road, London SE16 3LN
Telephone: 0207 232 1222. **Club nickname**: Lions
Colours: Blue. **Capacity**: 20,146
Record attendance: The Den: 48,672 v Derby (FA Cup 5) Feb 20, 1937; New Den: 20,093 v Arsenal (FA Cup 3) Jan 10, 1994

Goalkeepers

Name	Height	Previous club	Birthplace	Date
Archer, Jordan	6.3	Tottenham	Walthamstow	12.04.93
Forde, David	6.2	Cardiff	Galway, Ire	20.12.79
King, Tom	6.1	Crystal Palace	Plymouth	09.03.95

Defenders

Name	Height	Previous club	Birthplace	Date
Beevers, Mark	6.4	Sheffield Wed	Barnsley	21.11.89
Craig, Tony	6.0	Brentford	Greenwich	20.04.85
Cummings, Shaun	6.0	Reading	Hammersmith	28.02.89
Nelson, Sid	6.1	–	Lewisham	01.01.96
Webster, Byron	6.4	Yeovil	Leeds	31.03.87

Midfielders

Name	Height	Previous club	Birthplace	Date
Abdou, Nadjim	5.10	Plymouth	Martigues, Fr	13.07.84
Cowan-Hall, Paris	5.8	Wycombe	Hillingdon	05.10.90
Martin, Joe	6.0	Gillingham	Dagenham	29.11.88
Martin, Lee	5.10	Ipswich	Taunton	09.02.87
Philpot, Jamie	5.11	–	Tunbridge Wells	02.10.96
Powell, Jack	6.1	West Ham	Newham	29.01.94
Upson, Ed	5.10	Yeovil	Bury St Edmunds	21.11.89
Williams, Shaun	6.0	MK Dons	Dublin, Ire	19.09.86

Forwards

Name	Height	Previous club	Birthplace	Date
Gregory, Lee	6.2	Halifax	Sheffield	26.08.88
Marquis, John	6.1	–	Lewisham	16.05.92
O'Brien, Aiden	5.8	–	Islington	04.10.93
Pavey, Alfie	5.11	Maidstone	Southwark	02.10.95

OLDHAM ATHLETIC

Ground: SportsDirect Park, Oldham OL1 2PA
Telephone: 0161 624 4972. **Club nickname**: Latics
Colours: Blue and white. **Capacity**: 10,638
Record attendance: 47,761 v Sheffield Wed (FA Cup 4) Jan 25, 1930

Goalkeepers

Coleman, Joel	6.4	–	Bolton	26.09.95
Cornell, David	6.0	Swansea	Swansea	28.03.91

Defenders

Brown, Connor	5.9	Sheffield Utd	Sheffield	22.08.92
Elokobi, George	5.11	Wolves	Mamfe, Cam	31.01.86
Mills, Joseph	5.9	Burnley	Swindon	30.10.89
Truelove, Jack	5.10	–	Burnley	27.12.95
Wilson, Brian	5.10	Colchester	Manchester	09.05.83
Wilson, James	6.2	Bristol City	Chepstow	26.02.89

Midfielders

Croft, Lee	5.11	St Johnstone	Wigan	21.06.85
Dieng, Timothee	6.2	Brest	Grenoble, Fr	09.04.92
Green, George	6.0	Everton	Dewsbury	02.01.96
Jones, Mike	6.0	Crawley	Birkenhead	15.08.87
Kelly, Liam	5.10	Bristol City	Milton Keynes	10.02.90
Winchester, Carl	6.0	Linfield	Belfast	12.04.93

Forwards

Bove, Jordan	5.9	–	Manchester	12.12.95
Cassidy, Jake	6.2	Wolves	Glan Conwy	09.02.93
Forte, Jonathan	6.0	Southampton	Sheffield	25.07.86
Murphy, Rhys	6.1	Dagenham	Shoreham	06.11.90
Philliskirk, Danny	5.10	Coventry	Oldham	10.04.91
Poleon, Dominic	6.2	Leeds	Newham	07.09.93
Turner, Rhys	5.11	Stockport	Preston	22.07.95

PETERBOROUGH UNITED

Ground: Abax Stadium, London Road, Peterborough PE2 8AL
Telephone: 01733 563947. **Club nickname**: Posh
Colours: Blue and white. **Capacity**: 15,315
Record attendance: 30,096 v Swansea (FA Cup 5) Feb 20, 1965

Goalkeepers

Alnwick, Ben	6.2	Leyton Orient	Prudhoe	01.01.87
Henry, Dion	5.11	–	Ipswich	12.09.97

Defenders

Baldwin, Jack	6.1	Hartlepool	Barking	30.06.93
Brisley, Shaun	6.2	Macclesfield	Macclesfield	06.05.90
Ntlhe, Kgosi	5.9	–	Pretoria, SA	21.02.94
Santos, Ricardo	6.5	Thurrock	Almada, Port	18.06.95
Smith, Michael	5.11	Bristol Rov	Ballyclare	04.09.88
Zakuani, Gabriel	6.1	Kalloni	Kinshasa, DR Cong	31.05.86

Midfielders

Adebayo-Rowling, Tobi	6.0	Eastbourne	Camden	16.11.96
Anderson, Harry	5.7	Crawley	–	09.01.97
Anderson, Jermaine	5.11	–	Camden	16.05.96
Beautyman, Harry	5.10	Welling	Newham	01.04.92
Bostwick, Michael	6.1	Stevenage	Greenwich	17.05.88

Collison, Jack	6.2	Ipswich	Watford	02.10.88
Newell, Joe	5.11	–	Tamworth	15.03.93
Oztumer, Erhun	5.3	Dulwich Hamlet	Greenwich	29.05.91
Payne, Jack	5.9	Gillingham	Gravesend	05.12.91
Taylor, Jon	5.11	Shrewsbury	Liverpool	20.07.92
Forwards				
Edwards, Jonny	5.11	–	Luton	24.11.96
Friend, Jack	5.7	Wisbech	King's Lynn	03.11.96
Gormley, Joe	6.0	Cliftonville	Belfast	26.11.90
Maddison, Marcus	5.11	Gateshead	Durham	26.09.93
Vassell, Kyle	6.0	Bishop's Stortford	Milton Keynes	07.02.93
Washington, Conor	5.9	Newport	Chatham	18.05.92

PORT VALE

Ground: Vale Park, Hamil Road, Burslem, Stoke-on-Trent ST6 1AW
Telephone: 01782 655800. **Club nickname:** Valiants
Colours: Black and white. **Capacity:** 19,052
Record attendance: 49,768 v Aston Villa (FA Cup 5) Feb 20, 1960

Goalkeepers				
Johnson, Sam	6.6	Stoke	Newcastle-u-Lyme	01.12.92
Neal, Chris	6.2	Shrewsbury	St Albans	23.10.85
Defenders				
Deen-Conteh, Aziz	5.10	Ergotelis	Bumpeh, S Leo	14.01.93
Dickinson, Carl	6.1	Watford	Swadlincote	31.03.87
Duffy, Richard	5.11	Exeter	Swansea	30.08.85
McGivern, Ryan	6.2	Hibernian	Newry	08.01.90
Purkiss, Ben	6.2	Walsall	Sheffield	01.04.84
Smith, Nathan	6.0	–	Madeley	03.04.96
Streete, Remie	6.2	Newcastle	South Shields	02.11.94
Veseli, Freddie	6.0	Ipswich	Renens, Swi	20.11.92
Yates, Adam	5.10	Morecambe	Stoke	28.05.83
Midfielders				
Andoh, Enoch	5.7	Limassol	Kumasi, Gh	01.01.93
Birchall, Chris	5.9	Columbus	Stafford	05.05.84
Brown, Michael	5.10	Leeds	Hartlepool	25.01.77
Daniel, Colin	5.11	Mansfield	Nottingham	15.02.88
Foley, Sam	6.0	Yeovil	Upton-on-Severn	17.10.86
Grant, Anthony	5.10	Crewe	Lambeth	04.06.87
Lloyd, Ryan	5.10	–	Newcastle-u-Lyme	01.02.94
O'Connor, Michael	6.1	Rotherham	Belfast	06.10.87
Forwards				
Campion, Achille	6.2	Norrby	Levallois-Perret, Fr	10.03.90
Dodds, Louis	5.10	Leicester	Sheffield	08.10.86
Moore, Byron	6.0	Crewe	Stoke	24.08.88

ROCHDALE

Ground: Spotland, Wilbutts Lane, Rochdale OL11 5DS
Telephone: 01706 644648. **Club nickname:** Dale
Colours: Blue and black. **Capacity:** 10,249
Record attendance: 24,231 v Notts Co (FA Cup 2) Dec 10, 1949

Goalkeepers				
Collis, Steve	6.3	Macclesfield	Harrow	18.03.81
Lillis, Josh	6.0	Scunthorpe	Derby	24.06.87

Defenders

Bennett, Rhys	6.3	Bolton	Manchester	01.09.91
Eastham, Ashley	6.3	Blackpool	Preston	22.03.91
Kennedy, Tom	5.11	Barnsley	Bury	24.06.85
Lancashire, Olly	6.1	Aldershot	Basingstoke	13.12.88
McNulty, Jim	6.0	Bury	Liverpool	13.02,.85
Rafferty, Joe	6.0	Liverpool	Liverpool	06.10.93
Rose, Michael	5.11	Colchester	Salford	28.07.82
Tanser, Scott	6.0	–	Blackpool	23.10.94

Midfielders

Allen, Jamie	5.11	–	Rochdale	29.01.95
Barry-Murphy, Brian	6.0	Bury	Cork, Ire	27.07.78
Camps, Callum	5.11	–	Stockport	14.03.96
Cannon, Andy	5.9	–	Tameside	14.03.96
Logan, Joel	5.11	–	Manchester	25.01.95
Lund, Matthew	6.0	Stoke	Manchester	21.11.90
Vincenti, Peter	6.2	Aldershot	St Peter, Jer	07.07.86

Forwards

Alessandra, Lewis	5.10	Plymouth	Heywood	08.02.89
Andrew, Calvin	6.2	York	Luton	19.12.86
Bell, Nyal	6.3	–	Manchester	18.01.97
Bunney, Joe	5.10	–	Northwich	26.09.93
Henderson, Ian	5.10	Colchester	Thetford	24.01.85
Noble-Lazarus, Reuben	5.11	Barnsley	Huddersfield	16.08.93
McDermott, Donal	5.10	Dundalk	Dublin, Ire	19.10.89

SCUNTHORPE UNITED

Ground: Glanford Park, Doncaster Road, Scunthorpe DN15 8TD
Telephone: 0871 221 1899. **Club nickname**: Iron
Colours: Claret and blue. **Capacity**: 9,088
Record attendance: Old Show Ground: 23,935 v Portsmouth (FA Cup 4) Jan 30, 1954;
Glanford Park: 8,921 v Newcastle (Champ) Oct 20, 2009

Goalkeepers

Anyon, Joe	6.2	Shrewsbury	Lytham St Annes	29.12.86
Daniels, Luke	6.4	WBA	Bolton	05.01.88

Defenders

Boyce, Andrew	6.2	Lincoln	Doncaster	05.11.89
Canavan, Niall	6.3	–	Leeds	11.04.91
Clarke, Jordan	6.0	Coventry	Coventry	19.11.91
King, Jack	6.0	Preston	Oxford	20.08.85
Laird, Scott	5.9	Preston	Taunton	15.05.88
Mirfin, David	6.1	Watford	Sheffield	18.04.85
Waterfall, Luke	6.2	Gainsborough	Sheffield	30.07.90
Wiseman, Scott	6.0	Preston	Hull	13.12.85

Midfielders

Bishop, Neal	6.0	Blackpool	Stockton	07.08.81
Dawson, Stephen	5.6	Rochdale	Dublin, Ire	04.12.85
Hawkridge, Terry	5.10	Gainsborough	Nottingham	23.02.90
McAllister, Sean	5.8	Cowdenbeath	Bolton	15.08.87
McSheffrey, Gary	5.8	Chesterfield	Coventry	13.08.72
Ness, Jamie	6.1	Stoke	Irvine	02.03.91
Syers, David	5.10	Doncaster	Leeds	30.11.87

Forwards

Adelakun, Hakeeb	6.0	–	Hackney	11.06.96

Hopper, Tom	6.1	Leicester	Boston	14.12.93
Madden, Paddy	6.0	Yeovil	Dublin, Ire	04.03.90
Taylor, Lyle	6.2	Sheffield Utd	Greenwich	29.03.90
Van Veen, Kevin	6.0	FC Oss	Eindhovhen, Hol	01.06.91
Williams, Luke	6.1	Middlesbrough	Middlesbrough	11.06.93
Wootton, Kyle	6.2	–	Epworth	11.10.96

SHEFFIELD UNITED

Ground: Bramall Lane, Sheffield S2 4SU
Telephone: 0871 995 1899. **Club nickname**: Blades
Colours: Red and white. **Capacity**: 32,702
Record attendance: 68,287 v Leeds (FA Cup 5) Feb 15, 1936

Goalkeepers
| Howard, Mark | 6.1 | Blackpool | Southwark | 21.09.86 |
| Willis, George | 5.11 | – | Rotherham | 30.07.95 |

Defenders
Alcock, Craig	5.8	Peterborough	Truro	08.12.87
Basham, Chris	5.11	Blackpool	Hebburn	18.02.88
Brayford, John	5.8	Cardiff	Stoke	29.12.87
Freeman, Kieron	6.1	Derby	Bestwood	21.03.92
Harris, Bob	5.8	Blackpool	Glasgow	28.08.87
Kennedy, Terry	5.10	–	Barnsley	14.11.93
McEveley, Jay	6.1	Swindon	Liverpool	11.02.85
McGahey, Harrison	6.1	Blackpool	Preston	26.09.95

Midfielders
Campbell-Ryce, Jamal	5.7	Notts Co	Lambeth	06.04.83
Coutts, Paul	6.1	Derby	Aberdeen	22.07.88
Cuvelier, Florent	6.0	Stoke	Brussels, Bel	12.09.92
Done, Matt	5.10	Rochdale	Oswestry	22.07.88
Flynn, Ryan	5.7	Falkirk	Edinburgh	04.09.88
McFadzean, Callum	5.11	–	Sheffield	01.04.94
Scougall, Stefan	5.7	Livingston	Edinburgh	07.12.92
Wallace, James	6.0	Tranmere	Fazackerley	19.12.91

Forwards
Adams, Che	5.10	Ilkeston	Leicester	13.07.96
Baxter, Jose	5.10	Oldham	Bootle	07.02.92
De Girolano, Diego	5.10	–	Chesterfield	05.10.95
Higdon, Michael	6.1	Nijmegen	Liverpool	02.09.83
McNulty, Marc	5.10	Livingston	Edinburgh	14.09.92
Murphy, Jamie	5.10	Motherwell	Glasgow	28.08.89

SHREWSBURY TOWN

Ground: Greenhous Meadow Stadium, Oteley Road, Shrewsbury SY2 6ST
Telephone: 01743 289177. **Club nickname**: Shrews
Colours: Blue and yellow. **Capacity**: 9,875
Record attendance: Gay Meadow: 18,917 v Walsall (Div 3) Apr 26, 1961; Greenhous
Meadow: 10,210 v Chelsea (Lge Cup 4) Oct 28, 2014

Goalkeepers
| Halstead, Mark | 6.3 | Blackpool | Blackpool | 01.01.90 |
| Leutwiler, Jayson | 6.4 | Middlesbrough | Switzerland | 25.04.89 |

Defenders
| Ellis, Mark | 6.2 | Crewe | Plymouth | 30.09.88 |
| Demetriou, Mickey | 5.11 | Kidderminster | Durrington | 12.03.90 |

Grandison, Jermaine	6.4	Coventry	Birmingham	15.12.90
Goldson, Connor	6.3	–	Wolverhampton	18.12.92
Knight-Percival, Nat	6.0	Peterborough	Cambridge	31.03.87
Sadler, Mat	5.11	Rotherham	Birmingham	26.02.85
Smith, Dominic	6.0	–	Shrewsbury	09.02.96
Tootle, Matt	5.9	Crewe	Knowsley	11.10.90

Midfielders

Brown, Junior	5.9	Mansfield	Crewe	07.05.89
Caton, James	5.8	Blackpool	Widnes	04.01.94
Clark, Jordan	6.0	Barnsley	Hoyland	22.09.93
Lawrence, Liam	5.11	Barnsley	Retford	14.12.81
McKnight, Darren	5.10	Barnsley	Ballyclare	27.08.95
Ogogo, Abu	5.10	Dagenham	Epsom	03.11.89
Wesolowski, James	5.9	Oldham	Sydney, Aus	25.08.87
Whalley, Shaun	5.9	Luton	Whiston	07.08.87
Woods, Martin	5.11	Ross Co	Airdrie	01.01.86
Woods, Ryan	5.8	–	Norton Canes	13.12.93

Forwards

Akpa Akpro, Jean-Louis	6.0	Tranmere	Toulouse, Fr	04.01.85
Barnett, Tyrone	6.3	Peterborough	Stevenage	28.10.85
Collins, James	6.2	Hibernian	Coventry	01.12.90
McAlinden, Liam	6.1	Wolves (loan)	Cannock	26.09.93
Vernon, Scott	6.1	Aberdeen	Manchester	13.12.83

SOUTHEND UNITED

Ground: Roots Hall, Victoria Avenue, Southend SS2 6NQ
Telephone: 01702 304050. **Club nickname**: Shrimpers
Colours: Blue and white. **Capacity**: 12,392
Record attendance: 31,090 v Liverpool (FA Cup 3) Jan 10, 1979

Goalkeepers

| Bentley, Daniel | 6.2 | – | Basildon | 13.07.93 |
| Smith, Ted | 6.1 | – | Benfleet | 18.01.96 |

Defenders

Barrett, Adam	5.10	Gillingham	Dagenham	29.11.79
Bolger, Cian	6.4	Bolton	Cellbridge, Ire	12.03.92
Coker, Ben	5.11	Colchester	Cambridge	01.07.90
Leonard, Ryan	6.1	Plymouth	Plymouth	24.05.92
Prosser, Luke	6.3	Port Vale	Enfield	28.05.88
Thompson, Adam	6.2	Watford	Harlow	28.09.92
White, John	6.0	Colchester	Colchester	25.07.86

Midfielders

Atkinson, Will	5.10	Bradford	Beverley	14.10.88
Deegan, Gary	5.9	Northampton	Dublin, Ire	28.09.87
Hurst, Kevan	6.0	Walsall	Chesterfield	27.08.85
Payne, Jack	5.6	–	Tower Hamlets	25.10.94
Timlin, Michael	5.8	Swindon	Lambeth	19.03.85
Weston, Myles	5.11	Gillingham	Lewisham	12.03.88
Wordsworth, Anthony	6.1	Ipswich	Camden	03.01.89
Worrall, David	6.0	Rotherham	Manchester	12.06.90

Forwards

SWINDON TOWN

Ground: County Ground, County Road, Swindon SN1 2ED
Telephone: 0871 423 6433. **Club nickname**: Robins

Colours: Red and white. **Capacity**: 15,728
Record attendance: 32,000 v Arsenal (FA Cup 3) Jan 15, 1972

Goalkeepers
Belford, Tyrell	6.0	Liverpool	Nuneaton	06.05.94

Defenders
Byrne, Nathan	5.10	Tottenham	St Albans	05.06.92
Ormonde-Ottewill, Brandon	5.9	Arsenal	–	21.12.95
Rossi Branco, Raphael	6.3	Whitehawk	Campinas, Br	25.07.90
Thompson, Nathan	5.10	–	Chester	22.04.91

Midfielders
Kasim, Yaser	5.11	Brighton	Baghdad, Irq	16.05.91
Marshall, Lee	5.11	–	Gloucester	21.11.97
Randall, Will	5.11	–	Swindon	02.05.97
Rodgers, Anton	5.8	Oldham	Reading	26.01.93
Williams, Jordan	6.0	Liverpool (loan)	Bangor	06.11.95

Forwards
Hylton, Jermaine	5.10	Redditch	Birmingham	28.06.93
Obika, Jonathan	6.0	Tottenham	Enfield	12.09.90
Smith, Michael	6.4	Charlton	Wallsend	17.10.91
Storey, Miles	5.11	–	West Bromwich	04.01.94

WALSALL

Ground: Banks's Stadium, Bescot Crescent, Walsall WS1 4SA
Telephone: 01922 622791. **Club nickname**: Saddlers
Colours: Red and white. **Capacity**: 11,300
Record attendance: Fellows Park: 25,453 v Newcastle (Div 2) Aug 29, 1961; Banks's
Stadium: 11,049 v Rotherham (Div 1) May 10, 2004

Goalkeepers
Etheridge, Neil	6.3	Charlton	Enfield	07.02.90
MacGillivray, Craig	6.2	Harrogate	Harrogate	12.01.93

Defenders
Chambers, James	5.10	Doncaster	Sandwell	20.11.80
Demetriou, Jason	5.11	Anorthosis Famagusta	Newham	18.11.87
Downing, Paul	6.1	WBA	Taunton	26.10.91
O'Connor, James	5.10	Derby	Birmingham	20.11.84
Preston, Matt	6.0	–	Birmingham	16.03.95
Taylor, Andy	5.11	Sheffield Utd	Blackburn	14.03.86

Midfielders
Baxendale, James	5.8	Doncaster	Thorne	16.09.92
Chambers, Adam	5.10	Leyton Orient	Sandwell	20.11.80
Forde, Anthony	5.9	Wolves	Ballingarry, Ire	16.11.93
Kinsella, Liam	5.9	–	Colchester	23.02.96
Mantom, Sam	5.9	WBA	Stourbridge	20.02.92
Morris, Kieron	5.10	–	Hereford	03.06.94
Sawyers, Romaine	5.10	WBA	Birmingham	02.11.91

Forwards
Bakayoko, Amadou	6.3	–	Sierra Leone	01.01.96
Bradshaw, Tom	5.10	Shrewsbury	Shrewsbury	27.07.92
Cook, Jordan	5.9	Charlton	Sunderland	20.03.90
Murphy, Jordan	5.8	Stourbridge	Birmingham	05.06.96

WIGAN ATHLETIC

Ground: DW Stadium, Robin Park, Wigan WN5 0UZ
Telephone: 01942 774000. **Club nickname**: Latics
Colours: Blue and white. **Capacity**: 25,133
Record attendance: Springfield Park: 27,526 v Hereford (FA Cup 2) Dec 12, 1953;
DW Stadium: 25,133 v Manchester Utd (Prem Lge) May 11, 2008

Goalkeepers

Nicholls, Lee	6.3	–	Huyton	05.10.92
O'Donnell, Richard	6.2	Walsall	Sheffield	12.09.88

Defenders

Barnett, Leon	6.1	Norwich	Luton	30.11.85
Daniels, Donervon	6.1	WBA	Montserrat	24.11.93
Morgan, Craig	6.0	Rotherham	Flint	16.06.85
Pearce, Jason	5.11	Leeds	Hillingdon	06.12.87
Perch, James	6.0	Newcastle	Mansfield	28.09.85
Tavernier, James	5.10	Newcastle	Bradford	31.10.91
Taylor, Andrew	5.10	Cardiff	Hartlepool	01.08.86
Taylor-Sinclair, Aaron	6.0	Partick	Aberdeen	08.04.91

Midfielders

Chow, Tim	5.11	–	Wigan	18.01.94
Cowie, Don	5.11	Cardiff	Inverness	15.02.83
Huws, Emyr	5.10	Manchester City	Llanelli	30.09.93
McCann, Chris	6.1	Burnley	Dublin, Ire	21.07.87
Perkins, David	5.6	Blackpool	Heysham	21.06.82
Power, Max	5.11	Tranmere	Birkenhead	27.07.93

Forwards

Davies, Craig	6.2	Bolton	Burton	09.01.86
Holt, Grant	6.0	Norwich	Carlisle	12.04.81
McKay, Billy	5.9	Inverness	Corby	22.10.88
Odelusi, Sanmi	6.0	Bolton	Dagenham	11.06.93
Riera, Oriol	6.1	Osasuna	Vic, Sp	03.07.86
Waghorn, Martyn	5.10	Leicester	South Shields	23.01.90

LEAGUE TWO

ACCRINGTON STANLEY

Ground: Store First Stadium, Livingstone Road, Accrington BB5 5BX
Telephone: 0871 434 1968. **Club nickname**: Stanley
Colours: Red and white. **Capacity**: 5,057
Record attendance: 4,368 v Colchester (FA Cup 3) Jan 3, 2004

Goalkeepers

Etheridge, Ross	6.2	Derby	–	04.09.94
Mooney, Jason	6.9	York	Belfast	26.02.89

Defenders

Buxton, Adam	6.1	Wigan	Liverpool	12.05.92
Conneely, Seamus	6.1	Sligo	Lambeth	09.07.88
Crooks, Matt	6.0	Huddersfield	Huddersfield	20.01.94
Davies, Tom	5.11	Fleetwood	Warrington	18.04.92
Pearson, Matty	6.3	Halifax	Keighley	03.08.93
Winnard, Dean	5.9	Blackburn	Wigan	20.08.89
Wright, Joe	6.4	Huddersfield (loan)	Monk Fryston	26.02.95

Midfielders

Barry, Anthony	5.7	Forest Green	Liverpool	29.05.86
Bruna, Gerardo	5.11	Whitehawk	Mendoza, Arg	29.01.91
McConville, Sean	5.11	Chester	Burscough	06.03.89
Mingoia, Piero	5.7	Watford	Enfield	20.10.91
Procter, Andy	5.11	Bury	Blackburn	13.03.83
Windass, Josh	5.10	Huddersfield	Hull	09.01.94

Forwards

Carver, Marcus	5.11	–	Blackburn	22.10.93
Gornell, Terry	5.11	Cheltenham	Liverpool	16.12.89
Hazeldine, Max	5.10	–	Stockport	13.02.97
Kee, Billy	5.9	Scunthorpe	Leicester	01.12.90
McCartan, Shay	5.10	Burnley	Newry	18.05.94
Morgan, Adam	5.10	Yeovil	Liverpool	21.04.94

AFC WIMBLEDON

Ground: Cherry Red Records Stadium, Kingston Road, Kingston upon Thames KT1 3PB
Telephone: 0208 547 3528. **Club nickname**: Dons
Colours: Blue. **Capacity**: 4,850
Record attendance: 4,749 v Exeter (Lge 2) Apr 23, 2013

Goalkeepers

McDonnell, Joe	5.11	Basingstoke	Basingstoke	19.05.94
Shea, James	5.11	Harrow	Islington	16.06.91

Defenders

Fuller, Barry	5.10	Barnet	Ashford, Kent	25.09.84
Kennedy, Callum	6.1	Scunthorpe	Chertsey	09.11.89
Meades, Jon	6.1	Oxford	Cardiff	02.03.92
Nightingale, Will	6.1	–	Wandsworth	02.08.95
Osborne, Karleigh	6.2	Bristol City (loan)	Southall	19.03.83

Midfielders

Barcham, Andy	5.10	Portsmouth	Basildon	16.12.86
Beere, Tom	5.11	–	Southwark	27.11.95
Bulman, Dannie	5.8	Crawley	Ashford, Sur	24.01.79
Francomb, George	6.0	Norwich	Hackney	08.09.91
Reeves, Jake	5.7	Swindon	Greenwich	30.05.93
Rigg, Sean	5.9	Oxford	Bristol	01.10.88

Forwards

Akinfenwa, Adebayo	6.1	Gillingham	West Ham	10.05.82
Azeez, Adebayo	6.0	Charlton	Sidcup	08.01.94
Elliott, Tom	6.4	Cambridge	Leeds	09.11.90
Oakley, George	6.2	–	Wandsworth	18.11.95

BARNET

Ground: The Hive, Camrose Avenue, London HA8 6AG
Telephone: 0208 381 3800. **Club nickname**: Bees
Colours: Gold and black. **Capacity**: 5,176
Record attendance: Underderhill: 11,026 v Wycombe (FA Amateur Cup 4) Feb 23, 1952. The Hive: 5,233 v Gateshead (Conf) Apr 25, 2015

Goalkeepers

Stack, Graham	6.2	Hibernian	Hampstead	26.09.81

Defenders

Dembele, Bira	6.3	Stevenage	Villepinte, Fr	22.03.88
Hoyte, Gavin	5.11	Gillingham	Leytonstone	06.06.90

Johnson, Elliot	5.10	Norwich	Edgware	17.08.94
Muggleton, Sam	5.11	Gillingham	Melton Mowbray	17.11.95
N'Gala, Bondz	6.0	Portsmouth	Newham	03.10.89
Yiadom, Andy	5.11	Braintree	Holloway	09.12.91
Midfielders				
Champion, Tom	6.3	Cambridge Utd	Barnet	15.05.86
Gambin, Luke	5.7	–	Sutton	16.03.93
Marsh-Brown, Keanu	5.11	Yeovil	Hammersmith	10.08.92
Togwell, Sam	5.10	Chesterfield	Maidenhead	14.10.84
Vilhete, Mauro	5.9	–	Rio de Mauro, Por	10.05.93
Weston, Curtis	5.11	Gillingham	Greenwich	24.01.87
Forwards				
Akinde, John	6.2	Alfreton	Gravesend	08.07.89
Batt, Shaun	6.2	Leyton Orient	Luton	22.02.87
Gash, Michael	5.10	Kidderminster	Cambridge	03.09.86
Lisbie, Kevin	5.10	Luton	Hackney	17.10.78
Tomlinson, Ben	5.11	Lincoln	Dinnington	31.10.89

BRISTOL ROVERS

Ground: Memorial Stadium, Filton Avenue, Horfield, Bristol BS7 0BF
Telephone: 0117 909 6648. **Club nickname**: Pirates
Colours: Blue and white. **Capacity**: 11,976
Record attendance: Eastville: 38,472 v Preston (FA Cup 4) Jan 30, 1960. Memorial Stadium: 12,011 v WBA (FA Cup 6) Mar 9, 2008

Goalkeepers				
Mildenhall, Steve	6.4	Millwall	Swindon	13.05.78
Puddy, Will	6.1	Salisbury	Salisbury	04.10.87
Defenders				
Brown, Lee	6.0	QPR	Farnborough	10.08.90
Clarke, James	6.0	Woking	Aylesbury	17.11.89
Leadbitter, Daniel	6.0	Hereford	Newcastle	24.06.91
Lockyer, Tom	6.1	–	Cardiff	03.12.94
McChrystal, Mark	6.1	Tranmere	Derry	26.06.84
Parkes, Tom	6.3	Leicester	Mansfield	15.01.92
Midfielders				
Clarke, Ollie	5.11	–	Bristol	29.06.92
Gosling, Jake	5.9	Exeter	Newquay	11.08.93
Lines, Chris	6.2	Port Vale	Bristol	30.11.85
Mansell, Lee	5.9	Torquay	Gloucester	23.09.82
Montano, Cristian	5.11	America de Cali	Cali, Col	11.12.91
Sinclair, Stuart	5.8	Salisbury	Houghton Conquest	09.11.87
Thomas, Dominic	6.1	Charlton	London	23.11.95
Forwards				
Blissett, Nathan	6.1	Kidderminster	West Bromwich	29.06.90
Easter, Jermaine	5.9	Millwall	Cardiff	15.01.82
Harrison, Ellis	5.11	–	Newport	29.01.94
Lucas, Jamie	6.2	–	Pontypridd	06.12.95
Taylor, Matt	5.9	Forest Green	–	30.03.90

CAMBRIDGE UNITED

Ground: Costings Abbey Stadium, Newmarket Road, Cambridge CB5 8LN
Telephone: 01223 566500. **Club nickname**: U's
Colours: Yellow and black. **Capacity**: 9,617

Record attendance: 14,000 v Chelsea (friendly) May 1, 1970

Goalkeepers
Beasant, Sam	6.5	Stevenage	Denham	08.04.88
Dunn, Chris	6.3	Yeovil	Brentwood	23.10.87

Defenders
Coulson, Josh	6.3	–	Cambridge	28.01.89
Legge, Leon	6.1	Gillingham	Hastings	28.04.85
Omozusi, Elliot	5.11	Leyton Orient	Hackney	15.12.88
Roberts, Mark	6.1	Stevenage	Northwich	16.10.83
Taylor, Greg	6.1	Luton	Bedford	15.01.90

Midfielders
Berry, Luke	5.9	Barnsley	Cambridge	12.07.92
Donaldson, Ryan	5.9	Gateshead	Newcastle	01.05.91
Dunk, Harrison	6.0	Bromley	London	25.10.90
Hughes, Liam	6.4	Scunthorpe	Rotherham	10.08.92
Keane, Keith	5.9	Preston	Luton	20.11.86
Morrissey, Gearoid	6.0	Cork City	Cork	17.11.91

Forwards
Carr, Danny	5.11	Huddersfield	Lambeth	30.11.93
Chiedozie, Jordan	6.1	Concord	Owerri, Nig	22.07.94
Corr, Barry	6.3	Southend	Newcastle, NI	02.04.85
Gaffney, Rory	6.0	Limerick	Tuam	23.10.89
Simpson, Robbie	6.1	Leyton Orient	Poole	15.03.85
Slew, Jordan	6.3	Cambridge	Sheffield	07.09.92

CARLISLE UNITED
Ground: Brunton Park, Warwick Road, Carlisle CA1 1LL
Telephone: 01228 526237. **Club nickname:** Cumbrians
Colours: Blue and white. **Capacity:** 18,202
Record attendance: 27,500 v Birmingham City (FA Cup 3) Jan 5, 1957, v Middlesbrough (FA Cup 5) Jan 7, 1970

Goalkeepers
Gillespie, Mark	6.0	–	Newcastle	27.03.92
Hanford, Dan	6.3	Floriana	Rochdale	06.03.91

Defenders
Archibald-Henville, Troy	6.2	Swindon	Newham	04.11.88
Grainger, Danny	5.10	Dunfermline	Penrith	28.07.86
Griffith, Anthony	6.0	Shrewsbury	Huddersfield	28.10.86
McQueen, Alexander	6.2	Tottenham	London	24.03.95
Meppen-Walter, Courtney	6.3	–	Bury	02.08.94
Miller, Tom	5.11	Lincoln	Ely	29.06.90
Raynes, Michael	6.3	Mansfield	Manchester	15.10.87

Midfielders
Brough, Patrick	6.3	–	Carlisle	20.02.96
Dicker, Gary	6.0	Crawley	Dublin, Ire	31.07.86
Hery, Bastien	5.9	Rochdale	Chantereine, Fr	23.03.92
Joyce, Luke	5.11	Accrington	Bolton	09.07.87
Kearns, Danny	5.10	Peterborough	Belfast	26.08.91
Kennedy, Jason	6.1	Bradford	Roseworth	11.09.86
Rigg, Steven	6.0	Penrith	Keswick	30.06.92
Sweeney, Anthony	6.0	Hartlepool	Stockton	05.09.83

Forwards
Asamoah, Derek	5.7	Daegu	Accra, Gh	01.05.81

Balanta, Angelo	5.10	Bristol Rov	Cali, Col	01.07.90
Beck, Mark	6.5	–	Sunderland	02.04.94
Ibehre, Jabo	6.2	Colchester	Islington	28.01.83
Wyke, Charlie	5.11	Middlesbrough	Middlesbrough	06.12.92

CRAWLEY TOWN

Ground: Checkatrade Stadium, Winfield Way, Crawley RH11 9RX
Telephone: 01293 410000. **Club nickname**: Reds
Colours: Red. **Capacity**: 6,134
Record attendance: 5,880 v Reading (FA Cup 3) Jan 5, 2013

Goalkeepers
Defenders
Bradley, Sonny	6.4	Portsmouth	Hull	13.09.91
Oyebanjo, Lanre	6.1	York	Hackney	27.04.90
Midfielders				
Ashton, Jon	6.2	Stevenage	Nuneaton	04.10.82
Bawling, Bobson	5.10	Watford	Islington	21.09.95
Edwards, Gwion	5.9	Swansea	Lampeter	01.03.93
Henderson, Conor	6.1	Hull	Sidcup	08.09.91
Rooney, Luke	5.10	Ebbsfleet	Bermondsey	28.12.90
Smith, Jimmy	6.1	Stevenage	Newham	07.01.87
Walton, Simon	6.1	Stevenage	Sherburn	13.09.87
Young, Lewis	5.9	Bury	Stevenage	27.09.89
Forwards				
Fenelon, Shamir	6.1	Brighton	Brighton	03.08.94
Harrold, Matt	6.1	Bristol Rov	Leyton	25.07.84
McLeod, Izale	6.1	MK Dons	Birmingham	15.10.84
Tomlin, Gavin	5.10	Port Vale	Lewisham	21.08.83

DAGENHAM AND REDBRIDGE

Ground: Dagenham Stadium, Victoria Road, Dagenham RM10 7XL
Telephone: 0208 592 1549. **Club nickname**: Daggers
Colours: Red and blue. **Capacity**: 6,078
Record attendance: 5,949 v Ipswich (FA Cup 3), Jan 5, 2002

Goalkeepers
Cousins, Mark	6.1	Colchester	Chelmsford	09.01.87
O'Brien, Liam	6.4	Brentford	Ruislip	30.11.91
Defenders				
Connors, Jack	5.9	–	Brent	24.10.94
Gayle, Ian	5.11	–	Welling	23.10.92
Nosworthy, Nyron	6.0	Blackpool	Brixton	11.10.80
Partridge, Matt	6.2	Reading	Reading	24.10.94
Widdowson, Joe	6.0	Bury	Forest Gate	29.03.89
Midfielders				
Boucard, Andre	5.10	Notts Co	Enfield	10.10.84
Chambers, Ashley	5.10	Cambridge Utd	Leicester	01.03.90
Howell, Luke	5.11	Lincoln	Cuckfield	05.01.87
Jones, Jodi	5.9	–	Bow	22.10.97
Labadie, Joss	6.3	Torquay	Croydon	30.08.90
Raymond, Frankie	5.10	Eastbourne	Chislehurst	18.11.92
Forwards				
Bloomfield, Mason	6.0	–	Westminster	06.11.96
Cureton, Jamie	5.8	Cheltenham	Bristol	28.08.75
Doidge, Christian	6.1	Carmarthen	Newport	25.08.92

Hemmings, Ashley	5.8	Walsall	Wolverhampton	03.03.91
Hines, Zavron	5.10	Bradford	Kingston, Jam	27.12.88
Yusuff, Ade	5.7	Chatham	Lewisham	25.05.94

EXETER CITY

Ground: St James Park, Stadium Way, Exeter EX4 6PX
Telephone: 01392 411243. **Club nickname**: Grecians
Colours: Red and white. **Capacity**: 8,541
Record attendance: 20,984 v Sunderland (FA Cup 6 replay) Mar 4, 1931

Goalkeepers
| Olejnik, Bobby | 6.0 | Peterborough | Vienna, Aut | 26.11.86 |
| Pym, Christy | 5.11 | – | Exeter | 24.04.95 |

Defenders
Brown, Troy	6.1	Cheltenham	Croydon	17.09.90
Butterfield, Danny	5.9	Carlisle	Boston	21.11.79
McAllister, Jamie	5.10	Kerala	Glasgow	26.04.78
Moore-Taylor, Jordan	5.10	–	Exeter	21.01.94
Ribeiro, Christian	6.0	Scunthorpe	Neath	14.12.89
Riley-Lowe, Connor	5.10	–	Paignton	10.01.96
Tillson, Jordan	6.0	Bristol Rov	Bath	05.03.93
Woodman, Craig	5.9	Brentford	Tiverton	22.12.82

Midfielders
Davies, Arron	5.9	Northampton	Cardiff	22.06.84
Harley, Ryan	5.9	Swindon	Bristol	22.01.85
Holmes, Lee	5.9	Preston	Mansfield	02.04.87
Keohane, Jimmy	5.11	Bristol City	Aylesbury	22.01.91
McCready, Tom	6.0	Morecambe	Chester	07.06.91
Noble, David	6.0	Oldham	Hitchin	02.02.82
Oakley, Matt	5.10	Leicester	Peterborough	17.08.77
Oyeleke, Manny	5.9	Brentford	Wandsworth	24.12.92
Wheeler, David	5.11	Staines	Brighton	04.10.90

Forwards
Jay, Matt	5.10	–	Torbay	27.02.96
Nicholls, Alex	5.10	Northampton	Stourbridge	09.12.87
Nichols, Tom	5.10	–	Taunton	28.08.93
Reid, Jamie	5.11	–	Torquay	12.07.94
Watkins, Ollie	5.10	–	Torbay	30.12.95

HARTLEPOOL UNITED

Ground: Victoria Park, Clarence Road, Hartlepool TS24 8BZ
Telephone: 01429 272584. **Club nickname**: Pool
Colours: Blue and white. **Capacity**: 7,856
Record attendance: 17,426 v Manchester Utd (FA Cup 3) Jan 5, 1957

Goalkeepers
| Bartlett, Adam | 6.0 | Gateshead | Newcastle | 27.02.86 |
| Carson, Trevor | 6.0 | Cheltenham | Killyleagh | 05.03.88 |

Defenders
Austin, Neil	5.10	Darlington	Barnsley	26.04.83
Bates, Matthew	5.10	Bradford	Stockton	10.12.86
Carroll, Jake	6.0	Huddersfield	Dublin, Ire	11.08.91
Duckworth, Michael	5.11	Bradford PA	Germany	28.04.92
Green, Kieran	5.9	–	Stockton	30.06.97
Harrison, Scott	6.2	Sunderland	Middlesbrough	03.09.93

Jones, Dan	6.0	–	Bishop Auckland	14.12.94
Magnay, Carl	6.1	Grimsby	Birtley	20.01.89
Nearney, Josh	5.11	–	Newcastle	07.09.95
Worley, Harry	6.4	Stevenage	Warrington	25.11.88
Midfielders				
Featherstone, Nicky	5.9	Harrogate	Goole	22.09.88
Hawkins, Lewis	5.10	–	Hartlepool	15.06.93
Nelson-Addy, Ebby	5.7	Brackley	Milton Keynes	13.09.92
Richards, Jordan	5.9	–	Sunderland	25.04.93
Smith, Connor	6.1	–	Stockton	14.10.96
Walker, Brad	6.1	–	Billingham	25.04.96
Woods, Michael	5.8	Harrogate	York	06.04.90
Forwards				
Bingham, Rakish	6.0	Mansfield	Newham	25.10.93
Fenwick, Scott	6.1	Dunston	Gateshead	09.04.90
Oates, Rhys	6.2	Barnsley	Pontefract	04.12.94
Oyenuga, Kudus	5.10	Dundee Utd	Walthamstow	18.03.93
Paynter, Billy	6.0	Carlisle	Liverpool	13.07.84

LEYTON ORIENT

Ground: Matchroom Stadium, Brisbane Road, London E10 5NE
Telephone: 0871 310 1881. **Club nickname**: O's
Colours: Red. **Capacity**: 9,271
Record attendance: 34,345 v West Ham (FA Cup 4) Jan 25, 1964

Goalkeepers				
Grainger, Charlie	6.2	–	Enfield	31.07.96
Woods, Gary	6.1	Watford	Kettering	01.10.90
Defenders				
Baudry, Mathieu	6.2	Bournemouth	Le Havre, Fr	24.02.88
Clarke, Nathan	6.2	Huddersfield	Halifax	30.11.83
Clohessy, Sean	5.11	Colchester	Croydon	12.12.86
Ling, Sam	5.9	–	Broxbourne	17.12.96
Lowry, Shane	6.1	Millwall	Perth, Aus	12.06.89
Midfielders				
Bartley, Marvin	5.11	Burnley	Reading	01.07.89
Cox, Dean	5.5	–	Brighton	12.08.87
James, Lloyd	5.11	Colchester	Bristol	16.02.88
Lee, Harry	5.11	–	Hackney	20.03.95
McAnuff, Jobi	5.11	Reading	Edmonton	09.11.81
Moore, Sammy	5.8	Wimbledon	Deal	07.09.87
Pritchard, Bradley	6.1	Charlton	Harare, Zim	19.12.85
Turgott, Blair	6.0	Coventry	Bromley	22.05.94
Wright, Josh	6.1	Millwall	Tower Hamlets	06.11.89
Forwards				
McCallum, Paul	6.3	West Ham	Streatham	28.07.93
Palmer, Ollie	6.2	Mansfield	Epsom	21.01.92
Simpson, Jay	5.11	Buriram	Enfield	01.12.88

LUTON TOWN

Ground: Kenilworth Stadium, Maple Road, Luton LU4 8AW
Telephone: 01582 411622. **Club nickname**: Hatters
Colours: Orange and black. **Capacity**: 10,226
Record attendance: 30,069 v Blackpool (FA Cup 6) Mar 4, 1959

Goalkeepers

Justham, Elliot	6.3	East Thurrock	Barking	18.07.90
Tyler, Mark	5.11	Peterborough	Norwich	02.04.77

Defenders

Cuthbert, Scott	6.2	Leyton Orient	Alexandria, Sco	15.06.87
Franks, Fraser	6.0	Welling	Hammersmith	22.11.90
Griffiths, Scott	5.9	Peterborough	Westminster	27.11.85
Lacey, Alex	5.11	–	Milton Keynes	31.05.93
McNulty, Steve	6.1	Fleetwood	Liverpool	26.09.83
O'Donnell, Stephen	6.0	Partick	Aberdeen	11.05.92
Okuonghae, Magnus	6.3	Colchester	Croydon	16.02.86
Parry, Andy	–	Southport	Liverpool	13.09.91
Potts, Dan	5.8	West Ham	Romford	13.04.94
Wilkinson, Luke	6.2	Dagenham	Wells	02.12.91
Williams, Curtley	6.0	Lowestoft	Ipswich	19.03.90

Midfielders

Doyle, Nathan	5.11	Bradford	Derby	12.01.87
Drury, Andy	5.11	Crawley	Chatham	28.11.83
Green, Danny	6.0	MK Dons	Harlow	09.07.88
Guttridge Luke	5.8	Northampton	Barnstaple	27.03.82
Hall, Ryan	5.10	Rotherham	Dulwich	04.01.88
Howells, Jake	5.9	–	Hemel Hempstead	18.04.91
Lawless, Alex	5.11	York	Tonypandy	05.02.83
McCourt, Paddy	6.0	Brighton	Derry	16.12.83
McGeehan, Cameron	5.11	Norwich	Kingston	06.04.95
O'Brien, Mark	5.11	Derby	Dublin, Ire	20.11.92
Robinson, Matt	6.2	Leicester	Leicester	01.06.94
Ruddock, Pelly	5.9	West Ham	Hendon	17.07.93
Smith, Jonathan	6.3	York	Preston	17.10.86

Forwards

Banton, Zane	5.6	–	Stevenage	06.09.96
Benson, Paul	6.2	Swindon	Southend	12.10.79
Marriott, Jack	5.9	Ipswich	Beverley	09.09.84
McQuoid, Josh	5.10	Bournemouth	Southampton	15.12.89

MANSFIELD TOWN

Ground: One Call Stadium, Quarry Lane, Mansfield NG18 5DA
Telephone: 01623 482482. **Club nickname**: Stags
Colours: Amber and blue. **Capacity**: 10,000
Record attendance: 24,467 v Nottm Forest (FA Cup 3) Jan 10, 1953

Goalkeepers

Jensen, Brian	6.1	Crawley	Copenhagen, Den	08.06.75
Shearer, Scott	6.3	Crewe	Glasgow	15.02.81

Defenders

Benning, Malvind	5.10	Walsall	Sandwell	02.11.93
Collins, Lee	5.11	Northampton	Telford	28.09.88
Hunt, Nicky	6.1	Accrington	Westhoughton	03.09.83
Jones, Luke	6.0	Stevenage	Blackburn	10.04.87
Marsden, Liam	5.10	Matlock	Creswell	21.11.94
Shires, Corbin	6.3	Hallam	Sheffield	31.12.97
Tafazolli, Ryan	6.5	Cambridge City	Sutton	28.09.91

Midfielders

Beardsley, Chris	6.0	Stevenage	Derby	28.02.84
Blair, Matty	5.10	Fleetwood	Warwick	30.11.87

Clements, Chris	5.9	Hednesford	Birmingham	06.02.90
Lambe, Reggie	5.8	Nykopings	Hamilton, Berm	04.02.91
McGuire, Jamie	5.7	Fleetwood	Birkenhead	13.11.83
Thomas, Jack	5.9	–	Sutton-in-Ashfield	03.06.96
Thomas, Nathan	5.9	Motherwell	Ingleby Barwick	27.09.94
Forwards				
Green, Matt	6.0	Birmingham	Bath	02.01.87
Westcarr, Craig	5.11	Portsmouth	Nottingham	29.01.85
Yussuf, Adi	6.1	Oxford City	Zanzibar, Tanz	20.02.92

MORECAMBE

Ground: Globe Arena, Christie Way, Westgate, Morecambe LA4 4TB
Telephone: 01524 411797. **Club nickname**: Shrimps
Colours: Red and white. **Capacity**: 6,476
Record attendance: Christie Park: 9,234 v Weymouth (FA Cup 3) Jan 6, 1962. Globe Arena: 5,003 v Burnley (League Cup 2) Aug 24, 2010

Goalkeepers				
Roche, Barry	6.4	Chesterfield	Dublin, Ire	06.04.82
Defenders				
Beeley, Shaun	5.10	Fleetwood	Stockport	21.11.88
Doyle, Chris	5.11	–	Liverpool	17.02.95
Dugdale, Adam	6.3	Tranmere	Liverpool	13.09.87
Edwards, Ryan	5.11	Blackburn	Liverpool	07.10.93
Goodall, Alan	5.9	Fleetwood	Birkenhead	02.12.81
McGowan, Aaron	5.9	–	Kirkby	24.07.96
Murphy, Peter	6.0	Wycombe	Liverpool	13.02.90
Parrish, Andy	6.0	Bury	Bolton	22.06.88
Wilson, Laurence	5.10	Accrington	Liverpool	10.10.86
Midfielders				
Ellison, Kevin	6.0	Rotherham	Liverpool	23.02.79
Devitt, Jamie	5.10	Chesterfield	Dublin, Ire	06.07.90
Fleming, Andy	5.11	Wrexham	Liverpool	05.10.87
Kenyon, Alex	6.0	Stockport	Euxton	17.07.92
Molyneux, Lee	6.1	Tranmere	Huyton	24.02.89
Wildig, Aaron	5.9	Shrewsbury	Hereford	15.04.92
Forwards				
Barkhuizen, Tom	5.11	Blackpool	Blackpool	04.07.93
Mullin, Paul	5.10	Huddersfield	Liverpool	06.11.94

NEWPORT COUNTY

Ground: Rodney Parade, Newport NP19 0UU
Telephone: 01633 670690. **Club nickname**: Exiles
Colours: Amber and black. **Capacity**: 9,097
Record attendance: Somerton Park: 24,268 v Cardiff (Div 3S) Oct 16, 1937. Rodney Parade: 6,615 v Grimsby (Conf play-off semi-finals 2nd leg) Apr 28, 2013

Goalkeepers				
Day, Joe	6.0	Peterborough	Brighton	13.08.90
Taylor, Rhys	6.2	Macclesfield	Neath	07.04.90
Defenders				
Barrow, Scott	5.9	Macclesfield	Swansea	19.10.88
Feely, Kevin	6.2	Charlton	Kildare, Ire	30.08.92
Holmes, Danny	6.0	Tranmere	Wirral	06.01.89
Hughes, Andrew	5.11	Cardiff	Cardiff	05.06.92
Ofori-Twumasi, Nana	5.8	Yeovil	Accra, Gha	15.05.90

Poole, Regan	6.0	–	Cardiff	18.06.98
Ralph, Nathan	5.10	Yeovil	Great Dunmow	14.02.93
Taylor, Matt	6.0	Cheltenham	Ormskirk	30.01.82

Midfielders

Byrne, Mark	5.9	Barnet	Dublin, Ire	09.11.88
Elito, Medy	6.0	Venlo	Kinshasa, Zai	20.03.90
Klukowski, Yan	6.1	Forest Green	Chippenham	01.01.87
Rodman, Alex	6.2	Gateshead	Sutton Coldfield	15.12.87

Forwards

| Collin, Aaron | 5.10 | – | Newport | 27.05.97 |
| John-Lewis, Lenell | 5.10 | Grimsby | Hammersmith | 17.05.89 |

NORTHAMPTON TOWN

Ground: Sixfields Stadium, Upton Way, Northampton NN5 5QA
Telephone: 01604 683700. **Club nickname**: Cobblers
Colours: Claret and white. **Capacity**: 7,653
Record attendance: County Ground: 24,523 v Fulham (Div 1) Apr 23, 1966; Sixfields Stadium: 7,557 v Manchester City (Div 2) Sep 26, 1998

Goalkeepers

| Clarke, Ryan | 6.3 | Oxford | Bristol | 30.04.82 |
| Smith, Adam | 5.11 | Leicester | Sunderland | 23.01.92 |

Defenders

Buchanan, David	5.9	Preston	Rochdale	06.05.86
Cresswell, Ryan	6.2	Fleetwood	Rotherham	22.12.87
Diamond, Zander	6.2	Burton	Alexandria, Sco	03.12.85
Horwood, Evan	6.0	Tranmere	Hartlepool	10.03.86
Lelan, Josh	6.0	Derby	Burton	21.12.94
Moloney, Brendan	5.10	Yeovil	Beaufort, Ire	18.01.89

Midfielders

Adams, Nicky	5.10	Bury	Bolton	16.10.86
Byrom, Joel	6.0	Preston	Oswaldtwistle	14.09.86
Clifton, Danny	5.10	–	Northampton	08.11.96
D'Ath, Lawson	5.9	Reading	Witney	24.12.92
Hackett, Chris	6.0	Millwall	Oxford	01.03.83
O'Toole, John-Joe	6.2	Bristol Rov	Harrow	30.09.88
Potter, Alfie	5.7	AFC Wimbledon	Islington	09.01.89
Taylor, Jason	6.1	Cheltenham	Ashton-u-Lyne	28.01.87

Forwards

Holmes, Ricky	6.2	Portsmouth	Uxbridge	19.06.87
Richards, Marc	5.11	Chesterfield	Wolverhampton	08.07.82
Toney, Ivan	5.10	–	Northampton	16.03.96

NOTTS COUNTY

Ground: Meadow Lane, Nottingham NG2 3HJ
Telephone: 0115 952 9000. **Club nickname**: Magpies
Colours: White and black. **Capacity**: 20,211
Record attendance: 47,310 v York (FA Cup 6) Mar 12, 1955

Goalkeepers

| Carroll, Roy | 6.2 | Olympiacos | Enniskillen | 30.09.77 |

Defenders

Adams, Blair	5.9	Coventry	South Shields	08.09.91
Amevor, Mawouna	6.3	Go Ahead	Rotterdam, Hol	16.12.91
Bennett, Scott	5.10	Exeter	Truro	30.11.90

Cranston, Jordan	5.11	Nuneaton	Wednesfield	11.11.93
Hollis, Haydn	6.4	–	Selston	14.10.92
McKenzie, Taylor	6.2	Sheffield Wed	London	30.05.94
Sharpe, Rhys	5.10	Derby	Nottingham	17.10.94
Swerts, Gill	5.10	Breda	Brasschaat, Bel	23.09.82
Midfielders				
De Silva, Kyle	5.8	Crystal Palace	Croydon	29.11.93
Hayhurst, Will	5.10	Preston	Longridge	24.02.94
Milsom, Rob	5.10	Rotherham	Redhill	02.01.87
Noble, Liam	5.8	Carlisle	Cramlington	08.05.91
Smith, Alan	5.10	MK Dons	Rothwell	28.10.80
Snijders, Genaro	5.7	FC Oss	Amsterdam, Hol	29.07.89
Thompson, Curtis	5.7	–	Nottingham	02.09.93
Valencic, Filip	6.0	Monza	Ljubljana, Sloven	07.01.92
Wroe, Nicky	5.11	Preston	Sheffield	28.09.85
Forwards				
Bishop, Colby	5.11	–	Nottingham	04.11.94
Burke, Graham	5.11	Aston Villa	Dublin, Ire	21.09.93
Campbell, Adam	5.9	Newcastle	North Shields	01.01.95
Daniels, Billy	6.0	Coventry	Bristol	03.07.94
Jenner, Julian	6.2	Diosgyor	Delft, Hol	28.02.84
Murray, Ronan	5.8	Ipswich	Mayo, Ire	12.09.91
Spencer, Jimmy	6.1	Huddersfield	Leeds	13.12.91
Stead, Jon	6.3	Huddersfield	Huddersfield	07.04.83

OXFORD UNITED

Ground: Kassam Stadium, Grenoble Road, Oxford OX4 4XP
Telephone: 01865 337500. **Club nickname**: U's
Colours: Yellow. **Capacity**: 12,500
Record attendance: Manor Ground: 22,750 v Preston (FA Cup 6) Feb 29, 1964; Kassam Stadium, 12,243 v Leyton Orient (Lge 2) May 6, 2006

Goalkeepers				
Crocombe, Max	6.4	Buckingham	Auckland, NZ	12.08.93
Slocombe, Sam	6.0	Scunthorpe Utd	Scunthorpe	05.06.88
Defenders				
Dunkley, Chey	6.2	Kidderminster	Wolverhampton	13.02.92
Long, Sam	5.10	–	Oxford	16.01.95
Mullins, John	5.11	Rotherham	Hampstead	06.11.85
Skarz, Joe	6.0	Rotherham	Huddersfield	13.07.89
Wright, Jake	5.11	Brighton	Keighley	11.03.86
Midfielders				
Ashby, Josh	5.11	–	Oxford	03.05.96
Baldock, George	5.9	MK Dons (loan)	Buckingham	26.01.93
Collins, Michael	6.0	Scunthorpe	Halifax	30.04.86
Humphreys, Sam	5.8	–	Chipping Norton	03.11.95
MacDonald, Alex	5.7	Burton	Chester	14.04.90
O'Dowda, Callum	5.11	–	Oxford	23.04.95
Roofe, Kemar	5.10	WBA	Walsall	06.01.93
Rose, Danny	5.8	Fleetwood	Bristol	21.02.88
Ruffels, Josh	5.10	Coventry	Oxford	23.10.93
Sercombe, Liam	5.10	Exeter	Exeter	25.04.90
Forwards				
Hylton, Danny	6.0	Rotherham	Camden	25.02.89

Hoban, Pat	5.11	Dundalk	Galway, Ire	28.07.91
Roberts, James	5.11	Wycombe	Stoke Mandeville	21.06.96
Taylor, Ryan	6.2	Portsmouth	Rotherham	04.05.88

PLYMOUTH ARGYLE

Ground: Home Park, Plymouth PL2 3DQ
Telephone: 01752 562561. **Club nickname**: Pilgrims
Colours: Green and white. **Capacity**: 16,906
Record attendance: 43,596 v Aston Villa (Div 2) Oct 10, 1936

Goalkeepers
| Bittner, James | 6.1 | Salisbury | Devizes | 02.02.82 |
| McCormick, Luke | 6.0 | Oxford | Coventry | 15.08.83 |

Defenders
Bentley, Aaron	5.9	–	Plymouth	08.11.95
Hartley, Peter	6.2	Stevenage	Hartlepool	03.04.88
McHugh, Carl	5.11	Bradford	Toome, Ire	05.02.93
Mellor, Kelvin	6.2	Crewe	Crewe	25.01.91
Nelson, Curtis	6.0	Stoke	Newcastle-u-Lyme	21.05.93
Purrington, Ben	5.9	–	Exeter	05.05.96
Sawyer, Gary	6.0	Leyton Orient	Bideford	05.07.85

Midfielders
Carey, Graham	6.0	Ross Co	Dublin, Ire	02.05.89
Cox, Lee	6.1	Swindon	Leicester	26.06.90
Simpson, Josh	5.10	Crawley	Cambridge	06.03.87
Wylde, Gregg	5.10	St Mirren	Kirkintilloch	23.03.91

Forwards
Brunt, Ryan	6.1	Bristol Rov	Birmingham	26.05.93
Harvey, Tyler	6.1	–	Plymouth	29.06.95
Jervis, Jake	6.3	Ross Co	Birmingham	17.09.91
Reid, Reuben	6.0	Yeovil	Bristol	26.07.88
Smalley, Deane	6.0	Oxford	Chadderton	05.09.88

PORTSMOUTH

Ground: Fratton Park, Frogmore Road, Portsmouth, PO4 8RA
Telephone: 0239 273 1204. **Club nickname**: Pompey
Colours: Blue and white. **Capacity**: 21,100
Record attendance: 51,385 v Derby (FA Cup 6) Feb 26, 1949

Goalkeepers
| Jones, Paul | 6.3 | Crawley | Maidstone | 28.06.86 |
| Poke, Michael | 6.2 | Torquay | Ashford, Sur | 21.11.85 |

Defenders
Burgess. Christian	6.5	Peterborough	Barking	07.10.91
Ertl, Johannes	6.2	Sheffield Utd	Graz, Aut	13.11.82
Robinson, Paul	6.1	Millwall	Barnet	07.01.82
Stevens, Enda	6.0	Aston Villa	Dublin, Ire	09.07.90
Webster, Adam	6.3	–	Chichester	04.01.95
Whatmough, Jack	6.0	–	Gosport	19.08.96

Midfielders
Atangana, Nigel	6.2	Havant	Corbeil-Essonnes, Fr	09.10.89
Barton, Adam	5.11	Coventry	Blackburn	07.01.91
Bennett, Kyle	5.5	Doncaster	Telford	09.09.90
Close, Ben	5.9	–	Portsmouth	08.08.96
Doyle, Michael	5.10	Sheffield Utd	Dublin, Ire	08.07.81

Dunne, James	5.11	Stevenage	Farnborough	18.09.89
Hollands, Danny	5.11	Charlton	Ashford, Kent	06.11.85
Naismith, Kal	6.1	Accrington	Glasgow	18.02.92
Roberts, Gary	5.10	Chesterfield	Chester	18.03.84
Forwards				
Chaplin, Conor	5.10	–	Worthing	16.02.97
McGurk, Adam	5.10	Burton	St Helier	24.01.89
Stockley, Jayden	6.2	Bournemouth (loan)	Poole	10.10.93
Tubbs, Matt	5.10	Bournemouth	Salisbury	15.07.84

STEVENAGE

Ground: Lamex Stadium, Broadhall Way, Stevenage SG2 8RH
Telephone: 01438 223223. **Club nickname**: Boro
Colours: White and red. **Capacity**: 6,722
Record attendance: 8,040 v Newcastle (FA Cup 4) January 25, 1998

Goalkeepers				
Day, Chris	6.2	Millwall	Walthamstow	28.07.75
Defenders				
Henry, Ronnie	5.11	Luton	Hemel Hempstead	02.01.84
Hughes, Mark	6.3	Morecambe	Kirkby	09.12.86
Johnson, Ryan	6.2	–	Birmingham	02.10.96
Okimo, Jerome	6.0	Wealdstone	Ealing	08.06.88
Wells, Dean	6.1	Braintree	Isleworth	25.05.85
Midfielders				
Conlon, Tom	5.9	Peterborough	Stoke	03.02.96
Gordon, Rohdell	5.10	–	Wandsworth	28.03.96
Lee, Charlie	5.11	Gillingham	Whitechapel	05.01.87
Martin, David	5.9	Luton	Erith	03.06.85
McAllister, David	5.11	Shrewsbury	Dublin, Ire	29.12.88
Parrett, Dean	5.9	Tottenham	Hampstead	16.11.91
Pett, Tom	5.8	Wealdstone	Hatfield	03.12.91
Schumacher, Steven	6.0	Fleetwood	Liverpool	30.04.84
Whelpdale, Chris	6.0	Gillingham	Harold Wood	27.01.87
Forwards				
Kennedy, Ben	5.10	–	Northern Ireland	12.01.97
Marriott, Adam	5.10	Cambridge City	Brandon	14.04.91
Williams, Brett	6.2	Aldershot	Southampton	01.12.87

WYCOMBE WANDERERS

Ground: Adams Park, Hillbottom Road, High Wycombe HP12 4HJ
Telephone: 01494 472100. **Club nickname**: Chairboys
Colours: Light and dark blue. **Capacity**: 10,284
Record attendance: 10,000 v Chelsea (friendly) July 13, 2005

Goalkeepers				
Ingram, Matt	6.3	–	High Wycombe	18.12.93
Lynch, Alex	5.11	Peterborough	Hoylhead	04.04.95
Defenders				
Harriman, Michael	5.7	QPR (loan)	Chichester	23.10.92
Jacobson, Joe	5.11	Shrewsbury	Cardiff	17.11.86
Jombati, Sido	6.1	Cheltenham	Lisbon, Por	20.08.87
Pierre, Aaron	6.1	Brentford	Souhall	17.02.93
Rowe, Dan	6.2	Rotherham	Middlesbrough	24.10.95

Stewart, Anthony	6.0	Crewe	Lambeth	18.09.92

Midfielders

Banton, Jason	5.11	Plymouth	Tottenham	15.12.92
Bean, Marcus	5.11	Colchester	Hammersmith	02.11.84
Bloomfield, Matt	5.8	Ipswich	Felixstowe	08.02.84
Kretzschmar, Max	5.9	–	Kingston	12.10.93
Thompson, Garry	5.11	Notts Co	Kendal	24.11.80
Wood, Sam	6.0	Brentford	Bexley	09.08.86

Forwards

Ephraim, Hogan	5.9	QPR	Islington	31.03.88
Hayes, Paul	6.0	Scunthorpe	Dagenham	20.09.83
Holloway, Aaron	6.2	Newport	Cardiff	01.02.93

YEOVIL TOWN

Ground: Huish Park, Lufton Way, Yeovil BA22 8YF
Telephone: 01935 423662. **Club nickname**: Glovers
Colours: Green and white. **Capacity**: 9,565
Record attendance: 9,527 v Leeds (Lge 1) Apr 25, 2008

Goalkeepers

Krysiak, Artur	6.4	Exeter	Lodz, Pol	11.08.89
Weale, Chris	6.2	Shrewsbury	Yeovil	09.02.82

Defenders

Arthurworrey, Stephen	6.4	Fulham (loan)	Hackney	15.10.94
Dickson, Ryan	5.10	Crawley	Saltash	14.12.86
Smith, Nathan	6.0	Chesterfield	Enfield	11.01.87
Sokolik, Jakub	6.2	Liverpool	Ostrava, Cz	28.08.93
Sowunmi, Omar	6.6	Ipswich	Colchester	07.11.95
Tozer, Ben	6.1	Northampton	Plymouth	01.03.90

Midfielders

Compton, Jack	5.11	Hartlepool	Torquay	02.09.88
Dawson, Kevin	5.11	Shelbourne	Dublin, Ire	30.06.90
Dolan, Matt	5.9	Bradford	Hartlepool	11.02.93
Gibbons, Jordan	5.10	QPR	Bromley	18./11.93
Gillett, Simon	5.6	Nottm Forest	Oxford	06.11.85
Laird, Marc	5.11	Tranmere	Edinburgh	23.01.86

Forwards

Burrows, Jamie	6.2	Rangers	St Helier, Jer	24.03.95
Jeffers, Shaun	6.1	Newport	Bedford	14.04.92

YORK CITY

Ground: Bootham Crescent, York, YO30 7AQ
Telephone: 01904 624447. **Club nickname**: Minstermen
Colours: Red and blue. **Capacity**: 7,872
Record attendance: 28,123 v Huddersfield (FA Cup 6) Mar 5, 1938

Goalkeepers

Ingham, Michael	6.4	Hereford	Preston	07.09.80
Flinders, Scott	6.4	Hartlepool	Rotherham	12.06.86

Defenders

Ilesanmi, Femi	6.1	Dagenham	Southwark	18.04.91
Lowe, Keith	6.2	Cheltenham	Wolverhampton	13.09.85
McCombe, John	6.2	Mansfield	Pontefract	07.05.85
McCoy, Marvin	6.0	Wycombe	Waltham Forest	02.10.88
Nolan, Eddie	6.1	Scunthorpe	Waterford, Ire	05.08.88

Swan, George	6.1	Wolves	Plymouth	12.09.94
Winfield, Dave	6.2	Shrewsbury	Aldershot	24.03.88
Midfielders				
Carson, Josh	5.9	Ipswich	Ballymena	03.06.93
Berrett, James	5.10	Yeovil	Halifax	13.01.89
Meikle, Lindon	5.10	Mansfield	Nottingham	21.03.88
Penn, Russell	6.0	Cheltenham	Wordsley	08.11.85
Platt, Tom	6.1	–	Pontefract	01.10.93
Straker, Antony	5.9	Southend	Ealing	23.09.88
Summerfield, Luke	6.0	Shrewsbury	Ivybridge	06.12.87
Forwards				
Coulson, Michael	5.10	Grimsby	Scarborough	04.04.88
Hirst, Ben	6.0	–	York	22.10.97
Hyde, Jake	6.1	Barnet	Maidenhead	01.07.90
Oliver, Vadaine	6.1	Crewe	Sheffield	21.10.91
Sinclair, Emile	6.0	Northampton	Leeds	29.12.87

SCOTTISH PREMIERSHIP SQUADS 2015–16

(at time of going to press)

ABERDEEN
Ground: Pittodrie Stadium, Pittodrie Street, Aberdeen AB24 5QH. **Capacity**: 20,897.
Telephone: 01224 650400. **Manager**: Derek McInnes. **Colours**: Red and white. **Nickname**: Dons
Goalkeepers: Scott Brown, Jamie Langfield, Danny Ward (loan)
Defenders: Andrew Considine, Lukas Culjak, Shaleum Logan, Mark Reynolds, Paul Quinn, Michael Rose, Graeme Shinnie, Ash Taylor
Midfielders: Willo Flood, Jonny Hayes, Ryan Jack, Kenny McLean, Peter Pawlett, Barry Robson, Craig Storie, Scott Wright
Forwards: David Goodwillie, Niall McGinn, Joe Nuttall, Adam Rooney, Lawrence Shankland, Cameron Smith

CELTIC
Ground: Celtic Park, Glasgow G40 3RE. **Capacity**: 60,355. **Telephone**: 0871 226 1888.
Manager: Ronny Deila. **Colours**: Green and white. **Nickname**: Bhoys
Goalkeepers: Logan Bailly, Craig Gordon, Leonardo Fasan
Defenders: Efe Ambrose, Dedryck Boyata, Darnell Fisher, Emilio Izaguirre, Saidy Janko, Mikael Lustig, Charlie Mulgrew, Eoghan O'Connell, Virgil van Dijk
Midfielders: Stuart Armstrong, Derk Boerrigter, Nir Biton, Scott Brown, Kris Commons, James Forrest, Liam Henderson, Jackson Irvine, Stefan Johansen, Dylan McGeouch, Callum McGregor, Gary Mackay-Steven, Tom Rogic, Kieran Tierney
Forwards: Nadir Ciftci, Leigh Griffiths, Stefan Scepovic, Anthony Stokes

DUNDEE
Ground: Dens Park, Sandeman Street, Dundee DD3 7JY. **Capacity**: 11,506. **Telephone**: 01382. 889966. **Manager**: Paul Hartley. **Colours**: Blue and white. **Nickname**: Dark Blues
Goalkeepers: Scott Bain, David Mitchell
Defenders: Julen Etxabeguren, Kostadin Gadzhalov, Kevin Holt, Gary Irvine, Cammy Kerr, Daryll Meggatt, Thomas Konrad, Paul McGinn, James McPake
Midfielders: Dylan Carreiro, Simon Ferry, Gary Harkins, Nicky Low, Nick Ross, Kevin Thomson
Forwards: Kane Hemmings, Paul McGowan, Rory Loy, Phil Roberts, Greg Stewart, Luka Tankulic

DUNDEE UNITED

Ground: Tannadice Park, Tannadice Street, Dundee DD3 7JW. **Capacity**: 14,229. **Telephone**: 01382 833166. **Manager**: Jackie McNamara. **Colours**: Orange and black. **Nickname**: Terrors
Goalkeepers: Marc McCallum, Michal Szromnik, Luis Zwick
Defenders: Sean Dillon, Paul Dixon, Mark Durnan, Ryan McGowan, Callum Morris, John Souttar
Midfielders: Chris Erskine, Scott Fraser, Justin Johnson, Paul Paton, John Rankin, Blair Spittal, Scott Smith, Charlie Telfer
Forwards: Henri Anier, Mario Bilate, Aidan Connolly, Ryan Dow, Jordan Moore, Robbie Muirhead, Simon Murray

HAMILTON ACADEMICAL

Ground: New Douglas Park, Hamilton ML3 0FT. **Capacity**: 6,078. **Telephone**: 01698 368652. **Manager**: Martin Canning. **Colours**: Red and white. **Nickname**: Accies
Goalkeepers: Darren Hill, Alan Martin, Michael McGovern
Defenders: Martin Canning, Michael Devlin, Ziggy Gordon, Scott McMann, Lucas Tagliapietra, Jesus Garcia Tena
Midfielders: Steven Boyd, Ali Crawford, Greg Docherty, Grant Gillespie, Doug Imrie, Darren Lyon, Louis Longridge, Kieran MacDonald, Danny Redmond, Nico Sumsky, Chris Turner, Craig Watson
Forwards: Eamonn Brophy, Darian MacKinnon, Andy Ryan

HEART OF MIDLOTHIAN

Ground: Tynecastle Stadium, McLeod Street Edinburgh EH11 2NL. **Capacity**: 17,590. **Telephone**: 0871 663 1874. **Manager**: Robbie Neilson. **Colours**: Maroon and white. **Nickname**: Jam Tarts
Goalkeepers: Neil Alexander, Scott Gallacher, Jack Hamilton
Defenders: Blazej Augustyn, Kevin McHattie, Jordan McGhee, Alim Ozturk, Liam Smith, Callum Paterson
Midfielders: Kenny Anderson, Angus Beith, Prince Buaben, Billy King, Morgaro Gomis, Russell McLean, Sam Nicholson, Miguel Pallardo, Jamie Walker
Forwards: Robbie Buchanan, Juanma Delgado, Soufian El Hassnaoui, Gary Oliver, Osman Sow, Gavin Reilly, Alistair Roy

INVERNESS CALEDONIAN THISTLE

Ground: Tulloch Caledonian Stadium, Stadium Road, Inverness IV1 1FF. **Capacity**: 7,800. **Telephone**: 01463 222880. **Manager**: John Hughes. **Colours**: Blue and red. **Nickname**: Caley Thistle
Goalkeepers: Dean Brill, Ryan Esson, Cameron Mackay
Defenders: Daniel Devine, Calum Howarth, Josh Meekings, David Raven, Carl Tremarco, Gary Warren
Midfielders: Jason Brown, Ryan Christie, Aaron Doran, Ross Draper, Richie Foran, Lewis Horner, Liam Polworth, Jordan Roberts, Greg Tansey, James Vincent, Nat Wedderburn, Danny Williams
Forwards: Calum Ferguson, Tarmo Kink, Alasdair Sutherland

KILMARNOCK

Ground: Rugby Park, Kilmarnock KA 1 2DP. **Capacity**: 18,128. **Telephone**: 01563 545300. **Manager**: Gary Locke. **Colours**: Blue and white. **Nickname**: Killie
Goalkeepers: Jamie MacDonald, Craig Samson
Defenders: Lee Ashcroft, Ross Barbour, Mark Connolly, Stuart Findlay, Mark O'Hara, Steven Smith, Daryl Westlake

Midfielders: Jamie Hamill, Tope Obadeyi, Scott Robinson, Craig Slater
Forwards: Kris Boyd, Dale Carrick, Kallum Higginbotham, Chris Johnston, Greg Kiltie, Josh Magennis, Rory McKenzie, Michael Ngoo

MOTHERWELL

Ground: Fir Park, Firpark Street, Motherwell ML1 2QN. **Capacity**: 13,677. **Telephone**: 01698 333333. **Manager**: Ian Baraclough. **Colours**: Clarent and amber. **Nickname**: Well
Goalkeepers: Dan Twardzik
Defenders: Joe Chalmers, David Ferguson, Steven Hammell, Louis Laing, Stephen McManus, Craig Reid, Luke Watt
Midfielders: Lionel Ainsworth, Chris Cadden, Marvin Johnson, Keith Lasley, Josh Law, Jack Leitch, Ross MacLean, Stephen Pearson, Dom Thomas
Forwards: David Clarkson, Wes Fletcher, Craig Moore, Louis Moult

PARTICK THISTLE

Ground: Firhill Stadium, Firhill Road, Glasgow G20 7BA. **Capacity**: 10,102. **Telephone**: 0141 579 1971. **Manager**: Alan Archibald. **Colours**: Yellow, red and black. **Nickname**: Jags
Goalkeepers: Paul Gallacher, Tomas Cerny, Ryan Scully
Defenders: Callum Booth, Frederic Frans, Jack Hendry, Liam Lindsay, Daniel Seaborne
Midfielders: David Amoo, Stuart Bannigan, Gary Fraser, Steve Lawless, Declan McDaid, Abdul Osman, Ryan Stevenson, Sean Welsh, David Wilson
Forwards: Kris Doolan, Chris Duggan, Christie Elliott

ROSS COUNTY

Ground: Global Energy Stadium, Victoria Park, Jubilee Road, Dingwall IV15 9QZ. **Capacity**: 6,541. **Telephone**: 01349 860860. **Manager**: Jim McIntyre. **Colours**: Blue. **Nickname**: Staggies
Goalkeepers: Scott Fox,
Defenders: Scott Boyd, Andrew Davies, Richard Foster, Darren Holden, Marcus Fraser, Jamie Reckord, Chris Robertson
Midfielders: Raffaele De Vita, Tony Dingwall, Jonathan Franks, Ian McShane, Stewart Murdoch, Rocco Quinn
Forwards: Liam Boyce, Craig Curran, Michael Gardyne, Brian Graham, Kyle Macleod

ST JOHNSTONE

Ground: McDiarmid Park, Crieff Road, Perth PH1 2SJ. **Capacity**: 10,696. **Telephone**: 01738 459090. **Manager**: Tommy Wright. **Colours**: Blue and white. **Nickname**: Saints
Goalkeepers: Steve Banks, Zander Clark, Alan Mannus
Defenders: Steven Anderson, Brian Easton, Brad McKay, Tom Scobbie, Joe Shaughnessy, Frazer Wright
Midfielders: Scott Brown, Liam Caddis, Murray Davidson, Simon Lappin, Chris Millar, David Wotherspoon
Forwards: Graham Cummins, Chris Kane, Steven MacLean, Michael O'Halloran, John Sutton

ENGLISH FIXTURES 2015–2016
Premier League and Football League

Friday, 7 August
Championship
Brighton v Nottm Forest

Saturday, 8 August
Premier League
Bournemouth v Aston Villa
Chelsea v Swansea
Everton v Watford
Leicester v Sunderland
Man Utd v Tottenham
Newcastle v Southampton
Norwich v Crystal Palace

Championship
Birmingham v Reading
Blackburn v Wolves
Bolton v Derby
Brentford v Ipswich
Cardiff v Fulham
Charlton v QPR
Hull v Huddersfield
Leeds v Burnley
Rotherham v MK Dons
Sheff Wed v Bristol City

League One
Burton v Scunthorpe
Chesterfield v Barnsley
Colchester v Blackpool
Coventry v Wigan
Crewe v Port Vale
Doncaster v Bury
Fleetwood v Southend
Gillingham v Sheff Utd
Rochdale v Peterborough
Shrewsbury v Millwall
Swindon v Bradford
Walsall v Oldham

League Two
Accrington v Luton
Bristol Rovers v Northampton
Cambridge v Newport
Exeter v Yeovil
Hartlepool v Morecambe
Leyton Orient v Barnet
Mansfield v Carlisle
Oxford v Crawley
Portsmouth v Dag & Red
Stevenage v Notts County
Wimbledon v Plymouth
Wycombe v York

Sunday, 9 August
Premier League

Arsenal v West Ham
Stoke v Liverpool
Championship
Preston v Middlesbrough

Monday, 10 August
Premier League
WBA v Man City

Friday, 14 August
Premier League
Aston Villa v Man Utd

League Two
Notts Co v Mansfield

Saturday, 15 August
Premier League
Southampton v Everton
Sunderland v Norwich
Swansea v Newcastle
Tottenham v Stoke
Watford v WBA
West Ham v Leicester

Championship
Bristol City v Brentford
Burnley v Birmingham
Derby v Charlton
Fulham v Brighton
Huddersfield v Blackburn
Ipswich v Sheff Wed
Middlesbrough v Bolton
MK Dons v Preston
Nottm Forest v Rotherham
QPR v Cardiff
Reading v Leeds

League One
Barnsley v Burton
Blackpool v Rochdale
Bradford v Shrewsbury
Bury v Swindon
Millwall v Coventry
Oldham v Fleetwood
Peterborough v Colchester
Port Vale v Gillingham
Scunthorpe v Crewe
Sheff Utd v Chesterfield
Southend v Walsall

League Two
Barnet v Wycombe
Carlisle v Cambridge
Crawley v Wimbledon
Dag & Red v Leyton Orient
Luton v Oxford

Morecambe v Accrington
Newport v Stevenage
Northampton v Exeter
Plymouth v Portsmouth
Yeovil v Bristol Rovers
York v Hartlepool

Sunday, 16 August
Premier League
Crystal Palace v Arsenal
Man City v Chelsea

Championship
Wolves v Hull
Reading v Leeds

League One
Wigan v Doncaster

Monday, 17 August
Premier League
Liverpool v Bournemouth

Tuesday, 18 August
Championship
Blackburn v Cardiff
Brentford v Birmingham
Bristol City v Leeds
Derby v Middlesbrough
Huddersfield v Brighton
Hull y Fulham
Ipswich v Burnley
MK Dons v Bolton
Nottm Forest v Charlton
Rotherham v Preston
Sheff Wed v Reading
Wolves v QPR

League One
Peterborough v Sheff Utd
Blackpool v Burton
Bradford v Gillingham
Bury v Fleetwood
Colchester v Oldham
Coventry v Crewe
Millwall v Barnsley
Rochdale v Walsall
Shrewsbury v Chesterfield
Swindon v Port Vale

League Two
Accrington v Mansfield
Barnet v Northampton
Crawley v Portsmouth
Dag & Red v Exeter
Hartlepool v Newport
Leyton Orient v Stevenage
Luton v Bristol Rovers
Morecambe v Wycombe
Oxford v Notts County
Plymouth v Carlisle

Wimbledon v Cambridge
York v Yeovil

Wednesday 19 August
League One
Doncaster v Southend
Wigan v Scunthorpe

Friday, 21 August
Championship
Birmingham v Derby

Saturday, 22 August
Premier League
Crystal Palace v Aston Villa
Leicester v Tottenham
Man Utd v Newcastle
Norwich v Stoke
Sunderland v Swansea
Watford v Southampton
West Ham v Bournemouth

Championship
Bolton v Nottm Forest
Brighton v Blackburn
Burnley v Brentford
Cardiff v Wolves
Charlton v Hull
Fulham v Huddersfield
Leeds v Sheff Wed
Middlesbrough v Bristol City
Preston v Ipswich
QPR v Rotherham
Reading v MK Dons

League One
Barnsley v Bradford
Burton v Peterborough
Chesterfield v Rochdale
Crewe v Bury
Fleetwood v Colchester
Gillingham v Wigan
Oldham v Shrewsbury
Port Vale v Doncaster
Scunthorpe v Millwall
Sheff Utd v Blackpool
Southend v Swindon
Walsall v Coventry

League Two
Bristol Rovers v Barnet
Cambridge v Crawley
Carlisle v Wimbledon
Exeter v York
Mansfield v Oxford
Newport v Leyton Orient
Northampton v Plymouth
Notts County v Accrington
Portsmouth v Morecambe
Stevenage v Hartlepool

Wycombe v Dag & Red
Yeovil v Luton

Sunday, 23 August
Premier League
Everton v Man City
WBA v Chelsea

Monday, 24 August
Premier League
Arsenal v Liverpool

Friday, 28 August
Championship
Blackburn v Bolton

Saturday, 29 August
Premier League
Aston Villa v Sunderland
Bournemouth v Leicester
Chelsea v Crystal Palace
Liverpool v West Ham
Man City v Watford
Newcastle v Arsenal
Stoke v WBA
Tottenham v Everton

Championship
Brentford v Reading
Bristol City v Burnley
Derby v Leeds
Huddersfield v QPR
Hull v Preston
Ipswich v Brighton
MK Dons v Birmingham
Nottm Forest v Cardiff
Rotherham v Fulham
Sheff Wed v Middlesbrough
Wolves v Charlton

League One
Blackpool v Walsall
Bradford v Port Vale
Bury v Oldham
Colchester v Scunthorpe
Coventry v Southend
Doncaster v Fleetwood
Millwall v Chesterfield
Peterborough v Gillingham
Rochdale v Barnsley
Shrewsbury v Burton
Swindon v Sheff Utd
Wigan v Crewe

League Two
Accrington v Northampton
Barnet v Cambridge
Crawley v Wycombe
Dag & Red v Stevenage
Hartlepool v Carlisle

Leyton Orient v Bristol Rovers
Luton v Portsmouth
Morecambe v Notts County
Oxford v Yeovil
Plymouth v Newport
Wimbledon v Exeter
York v Mansfield

Sunday, 30 August
Premier League
Southampton v Norwich
Swansea v Man Utd

Saturday, 5 September
League One
Barnsley v Shrewsbury
Chesterfield v Wigan
Crewe v Swindon
Fleetwood v Rochdale
Gillingham v Doncaster
Oldham v Bradford
Port Vale v Millwall
Scunthorpe v Blackpool
Sheff Utd v Colchester
Southend v Peterborough
Walsall v Bury

League Two
Cambridge v Luton
Carlisle v Barnet
Exeter v Leyton Orient
Mansfield v Wimbledon
Newport v York
Northampton v Dag & Red
Notts County v Crawley
Portsmouth v Accrington
Stevenage v Plymouth
Wycombe v Hartlepool
Yeovil v Morecambe

Sunday, 6 September
League One
Burton v Coventry

League Two
Bristol Rov v Oxford

Friday, 11 September
Championship
Reading v Ipswich

Saturday, 12 September
Premier League
Arsenal v Stoke
Crystal Palace v Man City
Everton v Chelsea
Man Utd v Liverpool
Norwich v Bournemouth
Watford v Swansea
WBA v Southampton

Championship

Birmingham v Bristol City
Bolton v Wolves
Brighton v Hull
Burnley v Sheff Wed
Cardiff v Huddersfield
Charlton v Rotherham
Leeds v Brentford
Middlesbrough v MK Dons
Preston v Derby
QPR v Nottm Forest

League One

Barnsley v Swindon
Burton v Rochdale
Chesterfield v Colchester
Crewe v Millwall
Fleetwood v Bradford
Gillingham v Blackpool
Oldham v Peterborough
Port Vale v Wigan
Scunthorpe v Coventry
Sheff Utd v Bury
Southend v Shrewsbury
Walsall v Doncaster

League Two

Bristol Rovers v Accrington
Cambridge v Leyton Orient
Carlisle v Dag & Red
Exeter v Hartlepool
Mansfield v Crawley
Newport v Morecambe
Northampton v Oxford
Notts County v Luton
Portsmouth v Barnet
Stevenage v York
Wycombe v Plymouth
Yeovil v Wimbledon

Sunday, 13 September
Premier League
Leicester v Aston Villa
Sunderland v Tottenham

Championship
Fulham v Blackburn

Monday, 14 September
Premier League
West Ham v Newcastle

Tuesday, 15 September
Championship
Birmingham v Nottm Forest
Brighton v Rotherham
Burnley v MK Dons
Cardiff v Hull
Charlton v Huddersfield
Fulham v Wolves

Leeds v Ipswich
Middlesbrough v Brentford
Preston v Bristol City
QPR v Blackburn
Bolton v Sheff Wed
Reading v Derby

Friday, 18 September
Championship
Ipswich v Birmingham

Saturday, 19 September
Premier League
Aston Villa v WBA
Bournemouth v Sunderland
Chelsea v Arsenal
Liverpool v Norwich
Man City v West Ham
Newcastle v Watford
Stoke v Leicester
Swansea v Everton

Championship
Blackburn v Charlton
Brentford v Preston
Bristol City v Reading
Derby v Burnley
Huddersfield v Bolton
Hull v QPR
MK Dons v Leeds
Nottm Forest v Middlesbrough
Rotherham v Cardiff
Sheff Wed v Fulham
Wolves v Brighton

League One
Blackpool v Barnsley
Bury v Port Vale
Colchester v Gillingham
Coventry v Chesterfield
Doncaster v Oldham
Millwall v Southend
Peterborough v Walsall
Rochdale v Scunthorpe
Shrewsbury v Crewe
Swindon v Burton
Wigan v Fleetwood

League Two
Accrington v Exeter
Barnet v Stevenage
Crawley v Yeovil
Dag & Red v Newport
Hartlepool v Cambridge
Leyton Orient v Wycombe
Luton v Mansfield
Morecambe v Northampton
Oxford v Portsmouth
Plymouth v Bristol Rovers
Wimbledon v Notts County

York v Carlisle

Sunday, 20 September
Premier League
Southampton v Man Utd
Tottenham v Crystal Palace

League One
Bradford v Sheff Utd

Friday, 25 September
Championship
Fulham v QPR

Saturday, 26 September
Premier League
Leicester v Arsenal
Liverpool v Aston Villa
Man Utd v Sunderland
Newcastle v Chelsea
Southampton v Swansea
Stoke v Bournemouth
Tottenham v Man City
West Ham v Norwich

Championship
Birmingham v Rotherham
Bolton v Brighton
Brentford v Sheff Wed
Burnley v Reading
Cardiff v Charlton
Huddersfield v Nottm Forest
Hull v Blackburn
Ipswich v Bristol City
MK Dons v Derby
Preston v Wolves

League One
Barnsley v Gillingham
Bradford v Peterborough
Bury v Coventry
Chesterfield v Burton
Fleetwood v Port Vale
Millwall v Rochdale
Oldham v Wigan
Sheff Utd v Doncaster
Shrewsbury v Blackpool
Southend v Scunthorpe
Swindon v Colchester
Walsall v Crewe

League Two
Barnet v Dag & Red
Bristol Rovers v Portsmouth
Cambridge v Stevenage
Carlisle v Newport
Crawley v Accrington
Exeter v Wycombe
Luton v Wimbledon
Mansfield v Plymouth
Northampton v Leyton Orient

Notts County v York
Oxford v Morecambe
Yeovil v Hartlepool

Sunday, 27 September
Premier League
Watford v Crystal Palace

Monday, 28 September
Premier League
WBA v Everton

Championship
Middlesbrough v Leeds

Tuesday, 29 September
League One
Blackpool v Chesterfield
Burton v Sheff Utd
Colchester v Bradford
Coventry v Barnsley
Crewe v Southend
Doncaster v Swindon
Gillingham v Fleetwood
Peterborough v Bury
Port Vale v Oldham
Rochdale v Shrewsbury
Scunthorpe v Walsall
Wigan v Millwall

League Two
Accrington v Yeovil
Dag & Red v Notts County
Hartlepool v Bristol Rovers
Leyton Orient v Carlisle
Morecambe v Luton
Newport v Crawley
Plymouth v Barnet
Portsmouth v Exeter
Stevenage v Mansfield
Wimbledon v Northampton
Wycombe v Cambridge
York v Oxford

Friday, 2 October
Championship
Rotherham v Burnley

Saturday, 3 October
Premier League
Arsenal v Man Utd
Aston Villa v Stoke
Bournemouth v Watford
Chelsea v Southampton
Crystal Palace v WBA
Everton v Liverpool
Man City v Newcastle
Norwich v Leicester
Sunderland v West Ham
Swansea v Tottenham

Championship

Blackburn v Ipswich
Brighton v Cardiff
Bristol City v MK Dons
Charlton v Fulham
Derby v Brentford
Leeds v Birmingham
Nottm Forest v Hull
QPR v Bolton
Reading v Middlesbrough
Sheff Wed v Preston
Wolves v Huddersfield

League One

Blackpool v Swindon
Burton v Southend
Colchester v Bury
Coventry v Shrewsbury
Crewe v Chesterfield
Doncaster v Barnsley
Gillingham v Oldham
Peterborough v Millwall
Port Vale v Sheff Utd
Rochdale v Bradford
Scunthorpe v Fleetwood
Wigan v Walsall

League Two

Accrington v Oxford
Dag & Red v Mansfield
Hartlepool v Luton
Leyton Orient v Notts County
Morecambe v Bristol Rovers
Newport v Exeter
Plymouth v Crawley
Portsmouth v Yeovil
Stevenage v Carlisle
Wimbledon v Barnet
Wycombe v Northampton
York v Cambridge

Saturday, 10 October
League One

Barnsley v Crewe
Bradford v Blackpool
Bury v Wigan
Chesterfield v Gillingham
Fleetwood v Coventry
Millwall v Doncaster
Oldham v Scunthorpe
Sheff Utd v Rochdale
Shrewsbury v Colchester
Southend v Port Vale
Swindon v Peterborough
Walsall v Burton

League Two

Barnet v Accrington
Bristol Rovers v Wycombe

Cambridge v Portsmouth
Carlisle v Morecambe
Crawley v Leyton Orient
Exeter v Stevenage
Luton v York
Mansfield v Newport
Northampton v Hartlepool
Notts County v Plymouth
Oxford v Wimbledon
Yeovil v Dag & Red

Saturday, 17 October
Premier League

Chelsea v Aston Villa
Crystal Palace v West Ham
Everton v Man Utd
Man City v Bournemouth
Newcastle v Norwich
Southampton v Leicester
Swansea v Stoke
Tottenham v Liverpool
Watford v Arsenal
WBA v Sunderland

Championship

Birmingham v QPR
Brentford v Rotherham
Bristol City v Nottm Forest
Burnley v Bolton
Derby v Wolves
Ipswich v Huddersfield
Leeds v Brighton
Middlesbrough v Fulham
MK Dons v Blackburn
Preston v Cardiff
Reading v Charlton
Sheff Wed v Hull

League One

Bury v Rochdale
Coventry v Blackpool
Crewe v Gillingham
Doncaster v Bradford
Fleetwood v Burton
Millwall v Swindon
Oldham v Sheff Utd
Port Vale v Peterborough
Scunthorpe v Shrewsbury
Southend v Barnsley
Walsall v Chesterfield
Wigan v Colchester

League Two

Barnet v York
Cambridge v Northampton
Carlisle v Exeter
Crawley v Luton
Dag & Red v Hartlepool
Leyton Orient v Oxford

Mansfield v Bristol Rovers
Newport v Portsmouth
Notts County v Yeovil
Plymouth v Accrington
Stevenage v Wycombe
Wimbledon v Morecambe

Tuesday, 20 October
Championship
Blackburn v Derby
Bolton v Birmingham
Brighton v Bristol City
Cardiff v Middlesbrough
Charlton v Preston
Huddersfield v MK Dons
Hull v Ipswich
Nottm Forest v Burnley
QPR v Sheff Wed
Rotherham v Reading
Wolves v Brentford

League Two
Accrington v Wimbledon
Bristol Rovers v Notts County
Hartlepool v Barnet
Luton v Leyton Orient
Morecambe v Crawley
Northampton v Carlisle
Oxford v Plymouth
Portsmouth v Stevenage
Wycombe v Newport
Yeovil v Mansfield
York v Dag & Red

Wednesday, 21 October
Championship
Fulham v Leeds

League Two
Exeter v Cambridge

Saturday, 24 October
Premier League
Arsenal v Everton
Aston Villa v Swansea
Bournemouth v Tottenham
Leicester v Crystal Palace
Liverpool v Southampton
Man Utd v Man City
Norwich v WBA
Stoke v Watford
Sunderland v Newcastle
West Ham v Chelsea

Championship
Blackburn v Burnley
Bolton v Leeds
Brighton v Preston
Cardiff v Bristol City
Charlton v Brentford

Fulham v Reading
Huddersfield v Derby
Hull v Birmingham
Nottm Forest v Ipswich
QPR v MK Dons
Rotherham v Sheff Wed
Wolves v Middlesbrough

League One
Barnsley v Fleetwood
Blackpool v Crewe
Bradford v Wigan
Burton v Port Vale
Chesterfield v Scunthorpe
Colchester v Walsall
Gillingham v Southend
Peterborough v Doncaster
Rochdale v Oldham
Sheff Utd v Millwall
Shrewsbury v Bury
Swindon v Coventry

League Two
Accrington v Dag & Red
Bristol Rovers v Newport
Exeter v Notts County
Hartlepool v Crawley
Luton v Plymouth
Morecambe v Leyton Orient
Northampton v Stevenage
Oxford v Barnet
Portsmouth v Mansfield
Wycombe v Carlisle
Yeovil v Cambridge
York v Wimbledon

Saturday, 31 October
Premier League
Chelsea v Liverpool
Crystal Palace v Man Utd
Everton v Sunderland
Man City v Norwich
Newcastle v Stoke
Southampton v Bournemouth
Swansea v Arsenal
Tottenham v Aston Villa
Watford v West Ham
WBA v Leicester

Championship
Birmingham v Wolves
Brentford v QPR
Bristol City v Fulham
Burnley v Huddersfield
Derby v Rotherham
Ipswich v Cardiff
Leeds v Blackburn
Middlesbrough v Charlton
MK Dons v Hull

Preston v Bolton
Reading v Brighton
Sheff Wed v Nottm Forest

League One

Bury v Blackpool
Coventry v Peterborough
Crewe v Sheff Utd
Doncaster v Colchester
Fleetwood v Chesterfield
Millwall v Bradford
Oldham v Burton
Port Vale v Shrewsbury
Scunthorpe v Barnsley
Southend v Rochdale
Walsall v Gillingham
Wigan v Swindon

League Two

Barnet v Exeter
Cambridge v Bristol Rovers
Carlisle v Yeovil
Crawley v York
Dag & Red v Luton
Leyton Orient v Accrington
Mansfield v Wycombe
Newport v Northampton
Notts County v Portsmouth
Plymouth v Morecambe
Stevenage v Oxford
Wimbledon v Hartlepool

Tuesday, 3 November
Championship

Birmingham v Blackburn
Brentford v Hull
Bristol City v Wolves
Burnley v Fulham
Derby v QPR
Ipswich v Bolton
Leeds v Cardiff
Middlesbrough v Rotherham
MK Dons v Charlton
Preston v Nottm Forest
Sheff Wed v Brighton
Reading v Huddersfield

Saturday, 7 November
Premier League

Arsenal v Tottenham
Aston Villa v Man City
Bournemouth v Newcastle
Leicester v Watford
Liverpool v Crystal Palace
Man Utd v WBA
Norwich v Swansea
Stoke v Chelsea
Sunderland v Southampton
West Ham v Everton

Championship

Blackburn v Brentford
Bolton v Bristol City
Brighton v MK Dons
Cardiff v Reading
Charlton v Sheff Wed
Fulham v Birmingham
Huddersfield v Leeds
Hull v Middlesbrough
Nottm Forest v Derby
QPR v Preston
Rotherham v Ipswich
Wolves v Burnley

Saturday, 14 November
League One

Barnsley v Port Vale
Blackpool v Doncaster
Bradford v Crewe
Burton v Millwall
Chesterfield v Oldham
Colchester v Coventry
Gillingham v Bury
Peterborough v Fleetwood
Rochdale v Wigan
Sheff Utd v Southend
Shrewsbury v Walsall
Swindon v Scunthorpe

League Two

Accrington v Newport
Bristol Rovers v Carlisle
Exeter v Crawley
Hartlepool v Leyton Orient
Luton v Barnet
Morecambe v Dag & Red
Northampton v Mansfield
Oxford v Cambridge
Portsmouth v Wimbledon
Wycombe v Notts County
Yeovil v Stevenage
York v Plymouth

Saturday, 21 November
Premier League

Chelsea v Norwich
Crystal Palace v Sunderland
Everton v Aston Villa
Man City v Liverpool
Newcastle v Leicester
Southampton v Stoke
Swansea v Bournemouth
Tottenham v West Ham
Watford v Man Utd
WBA v Arsenal

Championship

Birmingham v Charlton
Brentford v Nottm Forest

Bristol City v Hull
Burnley v Brighton
Derby v Cardiff
Ipswich v Wolves
Leeds v Rotherham
Middlesbrough v QPR
MK Dons v Fulham
Preston v Blackburn
Reading v Bolton
Sheff Wed v Huddersfield

League One
Bury v Burton
Coventry v Gillingham
Crewe v Peterborough
Doncaster v Rochdale
Fleetwood v Swindon
Millwall v Colchester
Oldham v Barnsley
Port Vale v Chesterfield
Scunthorpe v Bradford
Southend v Blackpool
Walsall v Sheff Utd
Wigan v Shrewsbury

League Two
Barnet v Morecambe
Cambridge v Accrington
Carlisle v Portsmouth
Crawley v Bristol Rovers
Dag & Red v Oxford
Leyton Orient v York
Mansfield v Hartlepool
Newport v Yeovil
Notts County v Northampton
Plymouth v Exeter
Stevenage v Luton
Wimbledon v Wycombe

Tuesday, 24 November
League One
Bradford v Coventry
Bury v Scunthorpe
Colchester v Crewe
Doncaster v Chesterfield
Fleetwood v Millwall
Gillingham v Rochdale
Oldham v Southend
Peterborough v Barnsley
Port Vale v Blackpool
Sheff Utd v Shrewsbury
Swindon v Walsall
Wigan v Burton

League Two
Accrington v Hartlepool
Bristol Rovers v Stevenage
Crawley v Northampton
Luton v Carlisle

Mansfield v Exeter
Morecambe v Cambridge
Notts County v Barnet
Oxford v Newport
Plymouth v Leyton Orient
Portsmouth v York
Wimbledon v Dag & Red
Yeovil v Wycombe

Saturday, 28 November
Premier League
Aston Villa v Watford
Bournemouth v Everton
Crystal Palace v Newcastle
Leicester v Man Utd
Liverpool v Swansea
Man City v Southampton
Norwich v Arsenal
Sunderland v Stoke
Tottenham v Chelsea
West Ham v WBA

Championship
Blackburn v Sheff Wed
Bolton v Brentford
Brighton v Birmingham
Cardiff v Burnley
Charlton v Ipswich
Fulham v Preston
Huddersfield v Middlesbrough
Hull v Derby
Nottm Forest v Reading
QPR v Leeds
Rotherham v Bristol City
Wolves v MK Dons

League One
Barnsley v Sheff Utd
Blackpool v Fleetwood
Burton v Colchester
Chesterfield v Swindon
Coventry v Doncaster
Crewe v Oldham
Millwall v Bury
Rochdale v Port Vale
Scunthorpe v Peterborough
Shrewsbury v Gillingham
Southend v Wigan
Walsall v Bradford

League Two
Barnet v Mansfield
Cambridge v Notts County
Carlisle v Crawley
Dag & Red v Plymouth
Exeter v Bristol Rovers
Hartlepool v Oxford
Leyton Orient v Wimbledon
Newport v Luton

Northampton v Yeovil
Stevenage v Morecambe
Wycombe v Portsmouth
York v Accrington

Saturday, 5 December

Premier League
Arsenal v Sunderland
Chelsea v Bournemouth
Everton v Crystal Palace
Man Utd v West Ham
Newcastle v Liverpool
Southampton v Aston Villa
Stoke v Man City
Swansea v Leicester
Watford v Norwich
WBA v Tottenham

Championship
Birmingham v Huddersfield
Bolton v Cardiff
Brentford v MK Dons
Brighton v Charlton
Bristol City v Blackburn
Burnley v Preston
Ipswich v Middlesbrough
Leeds v Hull
Nottm Forest v Fulham
Reading v QPR
Rotherham v Wolves
Sheff Wed v Derby

Saturday, 12 December

Premier League
Aston Villa v Arsenal
Bournemouth v Man Utd
Crystal Palace v Southampton
Leicester v Chelsea
Liverpool v WBA
Man City v Swansea
Norwich v Everton
Sunderland v Watford
Tottenham v Newcastle
West Ham v Stoke

Championship
Blackburn v Rotherham
Cardiff v Sheff Wed
Charlton v Leeds
Derby v Brighton
Fulham v Brentford
Huddersfield v Bristol City
Hull v Bolton
Middlesbrough v Birmingham
MK Dons v Ipswich
Preston v Reading
QPR v Burnley
Wolves v Nottm Forest

League One
Bradford v Southend
Bury v Chesterfield
Colchester v Barnsley
Doncaster v Crewe
Fleetwood v Walsall
Gillingham v Burton
Oldham v Millwall
Peterborough v Shrewsbury
Port Vale v Scunthorpe
Sheff Utd v Coventry
Swindon v Rochdale
Wigan v Blackpool

League Two
Accrington v Wycombe
Bristol Rovers v York
Crawley v Dag & Red
Luton v Northampton
Mansfield v Leyton Orient
Morecambe v Exeter
Notts County v Newport
Oxford v Carlisle
Plymouth v Cambridge
Portsmouth v Hartlepool
Wimbledon v Stevenage
Yeovil v Barnet

Tuesday, 15 December

Championship
Blackburn v Nottm Forest
Cardiff v Brentford
Charlton v Bolton
Derby v Bristol City
Fulham v Ipswich
Huddersfield v Rotherham
Hull v Reading
Middlesbrough v Burnley
MK Dons v Sheff Wed
Preston v Birmingham
QPR v Brighton
Wolves v Leeds

Friday 18 December

League One
Southend v Bury

Saturday, 19 December

Premier League
Arsenal v Man City
Chelsea v Sunderland
Everton v Leicester
Man Utd v Norwich
Newcastle v Aston Villa
Southampton v Tottenham
Stoke v Crystal Palace
Swansea v West Ham
Watford v Liverpool
WBA v Bournemouth

Championship
Birmingham v Cardiff
Bolton v Fulham
Brentford v Huddersfield
Brighton v Middlesbrough
Bristol City v QPR
Burnley v Charlton
Ipswich v Derby
Leeds v Preston
Nottm Forest v MK Dons
Reading v Blackburn
Rotherham v Hull
Sheff Wed v Wolves

League One
Barnsley v Wigan
Blackpool v Peterborough
Burton v Doncaster
Chesterfield v Bradford
Coventry v Oldham
Crewe v Fleetwood
Millwall v Gillingham
Rochdale v Colchester
Scunthorpe v Sheff Utd
Shrewsbury v Swindon
Walsall v Port Vale

League Two
Barnet v Crawley
Cambridge v Mansfield
Carlisle v Notts County
Dag & Red v Bristol Rovers
Exeter v Luton
Hartlepool v Plymouth
Leyton Orient v Yeovil
Newport v Wimbledon
Northampton v Portsmouth
Stevenage v Accrington
Wycombe v Oxford
York v Morecambe

Saturday, 26 December
Premier League
Aston Villa v West Ham
Bournemouth v Crystal Palace
Chelsea v Watford
Liverpool v Leicester
Man City v Sunderland
Newcastle v Everton
Southampton v Arsenal
Stoke v Man Utd
Swansea v WBA
Tottenham v Norwich

Championship
Blackburn v Middlesbrough
Brentford v Brighton
Bristol City v Charlton
Derby v Fulham

Huddersfield v Preston
Hull v Burnley
Ipswich v QPR
MK Dons v Cardiff
Nottm Forest v Leeds
Rotherham v Bolton
Sheff Wed v Birmingham
Wolves v Reading

League One
Blackpool v Oldham
Bradford v Burton
Bury v Barnsley
Colchester v Southend
Coventry v Port Vale
Doncaster v Scunthorpe
Millwall v Walsall
Peterborough v Chesterfield
Rochdale v Crewe
Shrewsbury v Fleetwood
Swindon v Gillingham
Wigan v Sheff Utd

League Two
Accrington v Carlisle
Barnet v Newport
Crawley v Stevenage
Dag & Red v Cambridge
Hartlepool v Notts County
Leyton Orient v Portsmouth
Luton v Wycombe
Morecambe v Mansfield
Oxford v Exeter
Plymouth v Yeovil
Wimbledon v Bristol Rovers
York v Northampton

Monday, 28 December
Premier League
Arsenal v Bournemouth
Crystal Palace v Swansea
Everton v Stoke
Leicester v Man City
Man Utd v Chelsea
Norwich v Aston Villa
Sunderland v Liverpool
Watford v Tottenham
WBA v Newcastle
West Ham v Southampton

Championship
Birmingham v MK Dons
Bolton v Blackburn
Burnley v Bristol City
Cardiff v Nottm Forest
Charlton v Wolves
Leeds v Derby
Middlesbrough v Sheff Wed
Preston v Hull

QPR v Huddersfield
Reading v Brentford

League One
Barnsley v Blackpool
Burton v Swindon
Chesterfield v Coventry
Crewe v Shrewsbury
Fleetwood v Wigan
Gillingham v Colchester
Oldham v Doncaster
Port Vale v Bury
Scunthorpe v Rochdale
Sheff Utd v Bradford
Southend v Millwall
Walsall v Peterborough

League Two
Bristol Rovers v Leyton Orient
Cambridge v Barnet
Carlisle v Hartlepool
Exeter v Wimbledon
Mansfield v York
Newport v Plymouth
Northampton v Accrington
Notts County v Morecambe
Portsmouth v Luton
Stevenage v Dag & Red
Wycombe v Crawley
Yeovil v Oxford

Tuesday, 29 December
Championship
Brighton v Ipswich
Fulham v Rotherham

Saturday, 2 January
Premier League
Arsenal v Newcastle
Crystal Palace v Chelsea
Everton v Tottenham
Leicester v Bournemouth
Man Utd v Swansea
Norwich v Southampton
Sunderland v Aston Villa
Watford v Man City
WBA v Stoke
West Ham v Liverpool

Championship
Birmingham v Brentford
Bolton v Huddersfield
Brighton v Wolves
Burnley v Ipswich
Cardiff v Blackburn
Charlton v Nottm Forest
Fulham v Sheff Wed
Leeds v MK Dons
Middlesbrough v Derby

Preston v Rotherham
QPR v Hull
Reading v Bristol City

League One
Barnsley v Millwall
Burton v Blackpool
Chesterfield v Shrewsbury
Crewe v Coventry
Fleetwood v Bury
Gillingham v Bradford
Oldham v Colchester
Port Vale v Swindon
Scunthorpe v Wigan
Sheff Utd v Peterborough
Southend v Doncaster
Walsall v Rochdale

League Two
Bristol Rovers v Luton
Cambridge v Wimbledon
Carlisle v Plymouth
Exeter v Dag & Red
Mansfield v Accrington
Newport v Hartlepool
Northampton v Barnet
Notts County v Oxford
Portsmouth v Crawley
Stevenage v Leyton Orient
Wycombe v Morecambe
Yeovil v York

Saturday, 9 January
League One
Blackpool v Sheff Utd
Bradford v Barnsley
Bury v Crewe
Colchester v Fleetwood
Coventry v Walsall
Doncaster v Port Vale
Millwall v Scunthorpe
Peterborough v Burton
Rochdale v Chesterfield
Shrewsbury v Oldham
Swindon v Southend
Wigan v Gillingham

League Two
Accrington v Notts County
Barnet v Bristol Rovers
Crawley v Cambridge
Dag & Red v Wycombe
Hartlepool v Stevenage
Leyton Orient v Newport
Luton v Yeovil
Morecambe v Portsmouth
Oxford v Mansfield
Plymouth v Northampton

Wimbledon v Carlisle
York v Exeter

Tuesday, 12 January
Premier League
Aston Villa v Crystal Palace
Bournemouth v West Ham
Swansea v Sunderland
Liverpool v Arsenal

Championship
Blackburn v QPR
Brentford v Middlesbrough
Bristol City v Preston
Derby v Reading
Huddersfield v Charlton
Hull v Cardiff
Ipswich v Leeds
MK Dons v Burnley
Nottm Forest v Birmingham
Rotherham v Brighton
Sheff Wed v Bolton
Wolves v Fulham

Wednesday, 13 January
Premier League
Chelsea v WBA
Man City v Everton
Newcastle v Man Utd
Southampton v Watford
Stoke v Norwich
Tottenham v Leicester

Saturday, 16 January
Premier League
Aston Villa v Leicester
Bournemouth v Norwich
Chelsea v Everton
Liverpool v Man Utd
Man City v Crystal Palace
Newcastle v West Ham
Southampton v WBA
Stoke v Arsenal
Swansea v Watford
Tottenham v Sunderland

Championship
Blackburn v Brighton
Brentford v Burnley
Bristol City v Middlesbrough
Derby v Birmingham
Huddersfield v Fulham
Hull v Charlton
Ipswich v Preston
MK Dons v Reading
Nottm Forest v Bolton
Rotherham v QPR
Sheff Wed v Leeds
Wolves v Cardiff

League One
Blackpool v Scunthorpe
Bradford v Oldham
Bury v Walsall
Colchester v Sheff Utd
Coventry v Burton
Doncaster v Gillingham
Millwall v Port Vale
Peterborough v Southend
Rochdale v Fleetwood
Shrewsbury v Barnsley
Swindon v Crewe
Wigan v Chesterfield

League Two
Accrington v Portsmouth
Barnet v Carlisle
Crawley v Notts County
Dag & Red v Northampton
Hartlepool v Wycombe
Leyton Orient v Exeter
Luton v Cambridge
Morecambe v Yeovil
Oxford v Bristol Rovers
Plymouth v Stevenage
Wimbledon v Mansfield
York v Newport

Saturday, 23 January
Premier League
Arsenal v Chelsea
Crystal Palace v Tottenham
Everton v Swansea
Leicester v Stoke
Man Utd v Southampton
Norwich v Liverpool
Sunderland v Bournemouth
Watford v Newcastle
WBA v Aston Villa
West Ham v Man City

Championship
Birmingham v Ipswich
Bolton v MK Dons
Brighton v Huddersfield
Burnley v Derby
Cardiff v Rotherham
Charlton v Blackburn
Fulham v Hull
Leeds v Bristol City
Middlesbrough v Nottm Forest
Preston v Brentford
QPR v Wolves
Reading v Sheff Wed

League One
Barnsley v Rochdale
Burton v Shrewsbury
Chesterfield v Millwall

Crewe v Wigan
Fleetwood v Doncaster
Gillingham v Peterborough
Oldham v Bury
Port Vale v Bradford
Scunthorpe v Colchester
Sheff Utd v Swindon
Southend v Coventry
Walsall v Blackpool

League Two
Bristol Rovers v Plymouth
Cambridge v Hartlepool
Carlisle v York
Exeter v Accrington
Mansfield v Luton
Newport v Dag & Red
Northampton v Morecambe
Notts County v Wimbledon
Portsmouth v Oxford
Stevenage v Barnet
Wycombe v Leyton Orient
Yeovil v Crawley

Saturday, 30 January
Championship
Blackburn v Fulham
Brentford v Leeds
Bristol City v Birmingham
Derby v Preston
Huddersfield v Cardiff
Hull v Brighton
Ipswich v Reading
MK Dons v Middlesbrough
Nottm Forest v QPR
Rotherham v Charlton
Sheff Wed v Burnley
Wolves v Bolton

League One
Blackpool v Gillingham
Bradford v Fleetwood
Bury v Sheff Utd
Colchester v Chesterfield
Coventry v Scunthorpe
Doncaster v Walsall
Millwall v Crewe
Peterborough v Oldham
Rochdale v Burton
Shrewsbury v Southend
Swindon v Barnsley
Wigan v Port Vale

League Two
Accrington v Bristol Rovers
Barnet v Portsmouth
Crawley v Mansfield
Dag & Red v Carlisle
Hartlepool v Exeter

Leyton Orient v Cambridge
Luton v Notts County
Morecambe v Newport
Oxford v Northampton
Plymouth v Wycombe
Wimbledon v Yeovil
York v Stevenage

Tuesday, 2 February
Premier League
Arsenal v Southampton
Leicester v Liverpool
Norwich v Tottenham
Sunderland v Man City
Watford v Chelsea
West Ham v Aston Villa
Crystal Palace v Bournemouth
Man Utd v Stoke
WBA v Swansea

Wednesday, 3 February
Premier League
Everton v Newcastle

Saturday, 6 February
Premier League
Aston Villa v Norwich
Bournemouth v Arsenal
Chelsea v Man Utd
Liverpool v Sunderland
Man City v Leicester
Newcastle v WBA
Southampton v West Ham
Stoke v Everton
Swansea v Crystal Palace
Tottenham v Watford

Championship
Birmingham v Sheff Wed
Bolton v Rotherham
Brighton v Brentford
Burnley v Hull
Cardiff v MK Dons
Charlton v Bristol City
Fulham v Derby
Leeds v Nottm Forest
Middlesbrough v Blackburn
Preston v Huddersfield
QPR v Ipswich
Reading v Wolves

League One
Barnsley v Bury
Burton v Bradford
Chesterfield v Peterborough
Crewe v Rochdale
Fleetwood v Shrewsbury
Gillingham v Swindon
Oldham v Blackpool

Port Vale v Coventry
Scunthorpe v Doncaster
Sheff Utd v Wigan
Southend v Colchester
Walsall v Millwall

League Two
Bristol Rovers v Wimbledon
Cambridge v Dag & Red
Carlisle v Accrington
Exeter v Oxford
Mansfield v Morecambe
Newport v Barnet
Northampton v York
Notts County v Hartlepool
Portsmouth v Leyton Orient
Stevenage v Crawley
Wycombe v Luton
Yeovil v Plymouth

Friday, 12 February
League One
Burton v Chesterfield

Saturday, 13 February
Premier League
Arsenal v Leicester
Aston Villa v Liverpool
Bournemouth v Stoke
Chelsea v Newcastle
Crystal Palace v Watford
Everton v WBA
Man City v Tottenham
Norwich v West Ham
Sunderland v Man Utd
Swansea v Southampton

Championship
Blackburn v Hull
Brighton v Bolton
Bristol City v Ipswich
Charlton v Cardiff
Derby v MK Dons
Leeds v Middlesbrough
Nottm Forest v Huddersfield
QPR v Fulham
Reading v Burnley
Rotherham v Birmingham
Sheff Wed v Brentford
Wolves v Preston

League One
Blackpool v Shrewsbury
Colchester v Swindon
Coventry v Bury
Crewe v Walsall
Doncaster v Sheff Utd
Gillingham v Barnsley
Peterborough v Bradford
Port Vale v Fleetwood

Rochdale v Millwall
Scunthorpe v Southend
Wigan v Oldham

League Two
Accrington v Crawley
Dag & Red v Barnet
Hartlepool v Yeovil
Leyton Orient v Northampton
Morecambe v Oxford
Newport v Carlisle
Plymouth v Mansfield
Portsmouth v Bristol Rovers
Stevenage v Cambridge
Wimbledon v Luton
Wycombe v Exeter
York v Notts County

Saturday, 20 February
Championship
Birmingham v Leeds
Bolton v QPR
Brentford v Derby
Burnley v Rotherham
Cardiff v Brighton
Fulham v Charlton
Huddersfield v Wolves
Hull v Nottm Forest
Ipswich v Blackburn
Middlesbrough v Reading
MK Dons v Bristol City
Preston v Sheff Wed

League One
Barnsley v Doncaster
Bradford v Rochdale
Bury v Colchester
Chesterfield v Crewe
Fleetwood v Scunthorpe
Millwall v Peterborough
Oldham v Gillingham
Sheff Utd v Port Vale
Shrewsbury v Coventry
Southend v Burton
Swindon v Blackpool
Walsall v Wigan

League Two
Barnet v Wimbledon
Bristol Rovers v Morecambe
Cambridge v York
Carlisle v Stevenage
Crawley v Plymouth
Exeter v Newport
Luton v Hartlepool
Mansfield v Dag & Red
Northampton v Wycombe
Notts County v Leyton Orient
Oxford v Accrington
Yeovil v Portsmouth

Tuesday, 23 February
Championship
Birmingham v Bolton
Brentford v Wolves
Bristol City v Brighton
Burnley v Nottm Forest
Derby v Blackburn
Ipswich v Hull
Leeds v Fulham
Middlesbrough v Cardiff
MK Dons v Huddersfield
Preston v Charlton
Sheff Wed v QPR
Reading v Rotherham

Saturday, 27 February
Premier League
Leicester v Norwich
Liverpool v Everton
Man Utd v Arsenal
Newcastle v Man City
Southampton v Chelsea
Stoke v Aston Villa
Tottenham v Swansea
Watford v Bournemouth
WBA v Crystal Palace
West Ham v Sunderland

Championship
Blackburn v MK Dons
Bolton v Burnley
Brighton v Leeds
Cardiff v Preston
Charlton v Reading
Fulham v Middlesbrough
Huddersfield v Ipswich
Hull v Sheff Wed
Nottm Forest v Bristol City
QPR v Birmingham
Rotherham v Brentford
Wolves v Derby

League One
Blackpool v Bradford
Burton v Walsall
Colchester v Shrewsbury
Coventry v Fleetwood
Crewe v Barnsley
Doncaster v Millwall
Gillingham v Chesterfield
Peterborough v Swindon
Port Vale v Southend
Rochdale v Sheff Utd
Scunthorpe v Oldham
Wigan v Bury

League Two
Accrington v Barnet
Dag & Red v Yeovil

Hartlepool v Northampton
Leyton Orient v Crawley
Morecambe v Carlisle
Newport v Mansfield
Plymouth v Notts County
Portsmouth v Cambridge
Stevenage v Exeter
Wimbledon v Oxford
Wycombe v Bristol Rovers
York v Luton

Tuesday, 1 March
Premier League
Arsenal v Swansea
Aston Villa v Everton
Bournemouth v Southampton
Leicester v WBA
Norwich v Chelsea
Sunderland v Crystal Palace
West Ham v Tottenham
Liverpool v Man City
Man Utd v Watford

League One
Barnsley v Coventry
Bradford v Colchester
Bury v Peterborough
Chesterfield v Blackpool
Fleetwood v Gillingham
Millwall v Wigan
Oldham v Port Vale
Sheff Utd v Burton
Shrewsbury v Rochdale
Southend v Crewe
Swindon v Doncaster
Walsall v Scunthorpe

League Two
Barnet v Plymouth
Bristol Rovers v Hartlepool
Cambridge v Wycombe
Carlisle v Leyton Orient
Crawley v Newport
Exeter v Portsmouth
Luton v Morecambe
Mansfield v Stevenage
Northampton v Wimbledon
Notts County v Dag & Red
Oxford v York
Yeovil v Accrington

Wednesday, 2 March
Premier League
Stoke v Newcastle

Saturday, 5 March
Premier League
Chelsea v Stoke
Crystal Palace v Liverpool

Everton v West Ham
Man City v Aston Villa
Newcastle v Bournemouth
Southampton v Sunderland
Swansea v Norwich
Tottenham v Arsenal
Watford v Leicester
WBA v Man Utd

Championship
Birmingham v Hull
Brentford v Charlton
Bristol City v Cardiff
Burnley v Blackburn
Derby v Huddersfield
Ipswich v Nottm Forest
Leeds v Bolton
Middlesbrough v Wolves
MK Dons v QPR
Preston v Brighton
Reading v Fulham
Sheff Wed v Rotherham

League One
Bury v Bradford
Coventry v Rochdale
Crewe v Burton
Doncaster v Shrewsbury
Fleetwood v Sheff Utd
Millwall v Blackpool
Oldham v Swindon
Port Vale v Colchester
Scunthorpe v Gillingham
Southend v Chesterfield
Walsall v Barnsley
Wigan v Peterborough

League Two
Barnet v Hartlepool
Cambridge v Exeter
Carlisle v Northampton
Crawley v Morecambe
Dag & Red v York
Leyton Orient v Luton
Mansfield v Yeovil
Newport v Wycombe
Notts County v Bristol Rovers
Plymouth v Oxford
Stevenage v Portsmouth
Wimbledon v Accrington

Tuesday, 8 March
Championship
Blackburn v Birmingham
Bolton v Ipswich
Brighton v Sheff Wed
Cardiff v Leeds
Charlton v MK Dons
Fulham v Burnley

Huddersfield v Reading
Hull v Brentford
Nottm Forest v Preston
QPR v Derby
Rotherham v Middlesbrough
Wolves v Bristol City

Saturday, 12 March
Premier League
Arsenal v WBA
Aston Villa v Tottenham
Bournemouth v Swansea
Leicester v Newcastle
Liverpool v Chelsea
Man Utd v Crystal Palace
Norwich v Man City
Stoke v Southampton
Sunderland v Everton
West Ham v Watford

Championship
Blackburn v Leeds
Bolton v Preston
Brighton v Reading
Cardiff v Ipswich
Charlton v Middlesbrough
Fulham v Bristol City
Huddersfield v Burnley
Hull v MK Dons
Nottm Forest v Sheff Wed
QPR v Brentford
Rotherham v Derby
Wolves v Birmingham

League One
Barnsley v Southend
Blackpool v Coventry
Bradford v Doncaster
Burton v Fleetwood
Chesterfield v Walsall
Colchester v Wigan
Gillingham v Crewe
Peterborough v Port Vale
Rochdale v Bury
Sheff Utd v Oldham
Shrewsbury v Scunthorpe
Swindon v Millwall

League Two
Accrington v Plymouth
Bristol Rovers v Mansfield
Exeter v Carlisle
Hartlepool v Dag & Red
Luton v Crawley
Morecambe v Wimbledon
Northampton v Cambridge
Oxford v Leyton Orient
Portsmouth v Newport
Wycombe v Stevenage

Yeovil v Notts County
York v Barnet

Saturday, 19 March
Premier League
Chelsea v West Ham
Crystal Palace v Leicester
Everton v Arsenal
Man City v Man Utd
Newcastle v Sunderland
Southampton v Liverpool
Swansea v Aston Villa
Tottenham v Bournemouth
Watford v Stoke
WBA v Norwich
Championship
Birmingham v Fulham
Brentford v Blackburn
Bristol City v Bolton
Burnley v Wolves
Derby v Nottm Forest
Ipswich v Rotherham
Leeds v Huddersfield
Middlesbrough v Hull
MK Dons v Brighton
Preston v QPR
Reading v Cardiff
Sheff Wed v Charlton

League One
Bury v Shrewsbury
Coventry v Swindon
Crewe v Blackpool
Doncaster v Peterborough
Fleetwood v Barnsley
Millwall v Sheff Utd
Oldham v Rochdale
Port Vale v Burton
Scunthorpe v Chesterfield
Southend v Gillingham
Walsall v Colchester
Wigan v Bradford

League Two
Barnet v Oxford
Cambridge v Yeovil
Carlisle v Wycombe
Crawley v Hartlepool
Dag & Red v Accrington
Leyton Orient v Morecambe
Mansfield v Portsmouth
Newport v Bristol Rovers
Notts County v Exeter
Plymouth v Luton
Stevenage v Northampton
Wimbledon v York

Friday 25 March
League One
Barnsley v Scunthorpe
Burton v Oldham
Colchester v Doncaster
Gillingham v Walsall
Peterborough v Coventry
Rochdale v Southend
Sheff Utd v Crewe
Shrewsbury v Port Vale
Swindon v Wigan

League Two
Accrington v Leyton Orient
Bristol Rovers v Cambridge
Exeter v Barnet
Hartlepool v Wimbledon
Luton v Dag & Red
Morecambe v Plymouth
Northampton v Newport
Oxford v Stevenage
Portsmouth v Notts County
Wycombe v Mansfield
Yeovil v Carlisle
York v Crawley

Saturday, 26 March
League One
Blackpool v Bury
Bradford v Millwall
Chesterfield v Fleetwood

Monday 28 March
League One
Bury v Gillingham
Crewe v Bradford
Doncaster v Blackpool
Fleetwood v Peterborough
Millwall v Burton
Oldham v Chesterfield
Port Vale v Barnsley
Scunthorpe v Swindon
Southend v Sheff Utd
Walsall v Shrewsbury
Wigan v Rochdale

League Two
Barnet v Luton
Cambridge v Oxford
Carlisle v Bristol Rovers
Crawley v Exeter
Dag & Red v Morecambe
Leyton Orient v Hartlepool
Mansfield v Northampton
Newport v Accrington
Notts County v Wycombe
Plymouth v York
Stevenage v Yeovil
Wimbledon v Portsmouth

Tuesday, 29 March
League One
Coventry v Colchester

Saturday, 2 April
Premier League
Arsenal v Watford
Aston Villa v Chelsea
Bournemouth v Man City
Leicester v Southampton
Liverpool v Tottenham
Man Utd v Everton
Norwich v Newcastle
Stoke v Swansea
Sunderland v WBA
West Ham v Crystal Palace

Championship
Blackburn v Preston
Bolton v Reading
Brighton v Burnley
Cardiff v Derby
Charlton v Birmingham
Fulham v MK Dons
Huddersfield v Sheff Wed
Hull v Bristol City
Nottm Forest v Brentford
QPR v Middlesbrough
Rotherham v Leeds
Wolves v Ipswich

League One
Barnsley v Oldham
Blackpool v Southend
Bradford v Scunthorpe
Burton v Bury
Chesterfield v Port Vale
Colchester v Millwall
Gillingham v Coventry
Peterborough v Crewe
Rochdale v Doncaster
Sheff Utd v Walsall
Shrewsbury v Wigan
Swindon v Fleetwood

League Two
Accrington v Cambridge
Bristol Rovers v Crawley
Exeter v Plymouth
Hartlepool v Mansfield
Luton v Stevenage
Morecambe v Barnet
Northampton v Notts County
Oxford v Dag & Red
Portsmouth v Carlisle
Wycombe v Wimbledon
Yeovil v Newport
York v Leyton Orient

Tuesday, 5 April
Championship
Birmingham v Brighton
Brentford v Bolton
Bristol City v Rotherham
Burnley v Cardiff
Derby v Hull
Ipswich v Charlton
Leeds v QPR
Middlesbrough v Huddersfield
MK Dons v Wolves
Preston v Fulham
Sheff Wed v Blackburn
Reading v Nottm Forest

Saturday, 9 April
Premier League
Aston Villa v Bournemouth
Crystal Palace v Norwich
Liverpool v Stoke
Man City v WBA
Southampton v Newcastle
Sunderland v Leicester
Swansea v Chelsea
Tottenham v Man Utd
Watford v Everton
West Ham v Arsenal

Championship
Bristol City v Sheff Wed
Burnley v Leeds
Derby v Bolton
Fulham v Cardiff
Huddersfield v Hull
Ipswich v Brentford
Middlesbrough v Preston
MK Dons v Rotherham
Nottm Forest v Brighton
QPR v Charlton
Reading v Birmingham
Wolves v Blackburn

League One
Barnsley v Chesterfield
Blackpool v Colchester
Bradford v Swindon
Bury v Doncaster
Millwall v Shrewsbury
Oldham v Walsall
Peterborough v Rochdale
Port Vale v Crewe
Scunthorpe v Burton
Sheff Utd v Gillingham
Southend v Fleetwood
Wigan v Coventry

League Two
Barnet v Leyton Orient
Carlisle v Mansfield

Crawley v Oxford
Dag & Red v Portsmouth
Luton v Accrington
Morecambe v Hartlepool
Newport v Cambridge
Northampton v Bristol Rovers
Notts County v Stevenage
Plymouth v Wimbledon
Yeovil v Exeter
York v Wycombe

Saturday, 16 April
Premier League
Arsenal v Crystal Palace
Bournemouth v Liverpool
Chelsea v Man City
Everton v Southampton
Leicester v West Ham
Man Utd v Aston Villa
Newcastle v Swansea
Norwich v Sunderland
Stoke v Tottenham
WBA v Watford

Championship
Birmingham v Burnley
Blackburn v Huddersfield
Bolton v Middlesbrough
Brentford v Bristol City
Brighton v Fulham
Cardiff v QPR
Charlton v Derby
Hull v Wolves
Leeds v Reading
Preston v MK Dons
Rotherham v Nottm Forest
Sheff Wed v Ipswich

League One
Burton v Barnsley
Chesterfield v Sheff Utd
Colchester v Peterborough
Coventry v Millwall
Crewe v Scunthorpe
Doncaster v Wigan
Fleetwood v Oldham
Gillingham v Port Vale
Rochdale v Blackpool
Shrewsbury v Bradford
Swindon v Bury
Walsall v Southend

League Two
Accrington v Morecambe
Bristol Rovers v Yeovil
Cambridge v Carlisle
Exeter v Northampton
Hartlepool v York
Leyton Orient v Dag & Red

Mansfield v Notts County
Oxford v Luton
Portsmouth v Plymouth
Stevenage v Newport
Wimbledon v Crawley
Wycombe v Barnet

Tuesday, 19 April
Championship
Birmingham v Preston
Brentford v Cardiff
Brighton v QPR
Bristol City v Derby
Burnley v Middlesbrough
Ipswich v Fulham
Leeds v Wolves
Nottm Forest v Blackburn
Rotherham v Huddersfield
Sheff Wed v MK Dons
Bolton v Charlton
Reading v Hull

League One
Barnsley v Peterborough
Blackpool v Port Vale
Burton v Wigan
Chesterfield v Doncaster
Coventry v Bradford
Crewe v Colchester
Millwall v Fleetwood
Rochdale v Gillingham
Scunthorpe v Bury
Shrewsbury v Sheff Utd
Southend v Oldham
Walsall v Swindon

League Two
Barnet v Notts County
Cambridge v Morecambe
Carlisle v Luton
Dag & Red v Wimbledon
Exeter v Mansfield
Hartlepool v Accrington
Leyton Orient v Plymouth
Newport v Oxford
Northampton v Crawley
Stevenage v Bristol Rovers
Wycombe v Yeovil
York v Portsmouth

Saturday, 23 April
Premier League
Aston Villa v Southampton
Bournemouth v Chelsea
Crystal Palace v Everton
Leicester v Swansea
Liverpool v Newcastle
Man City v Stoke
Norwich v Watford

Sunderland v Arsenal
Tottenham v WBA
West Ham v Man Utd

Championship
Blackburn v Bristol City
Cardiff v Bolton
Charlton v Brighton
Derby v Sheff Wed
Fulham v Nottm Forest
Huddersfield v Birmingham
Hull v Leeds
Middlesbrough v Ipswich
MK Dons v Brentford
Preston v Burnley
QPR v Reading
Wolves v Rotherham

League One
Bradford v Walsall
Bury v Millwall
Colchester v Burton
Doncaster v Coventry
Fleetwood v Blackpool
Gillingham v Shrewsbury
Oldham v Crewe
Peterborough v Scunthorpe
Port Vale v Rochdale
Sheff Utd v Barnsley
Swindon v Chesterfield
Wigan v Southend

League Two
Accrington v York
Bristol Rovers v Exeter
Crawley v Carlisle
Luton v Newport
Mansfield v Barnet
Morecambe v Stevenage
Notts County v Cambridge
Oxford v Hartlepool
Plymouth v Dag & Red
Portsmouth v Wycombe
Wimbledon v Leyton Orient
Yeovil v Northampton

Saturday, 30 April
Premier League
Arsenal v Norwich
Chelsea v Tottenham
Everton v Bournemouth
Man Utd v Leicester
Newcastle v Crystal Palace
Southampton v Man City
Stoke v Sunderland
Swansea v Liverpool
Watford v Aston Villa
WBA v West Ham

Championship
Birmingham v Middlesbrough
Bolton v Hull
Brentford v Fulham
Brighton v Derby
Bristol City v Huddersfield
Burnley v QPR
Ipswich v MK Dons
Leeds v Charlton
Nottm Forest v Wolves
Reading v Preston
Rotherham v Blackburn
Sheff Wed v Cardiff

League One
Barnsley v Colchester
Blackpool v Wigan
Burton v Gillingham
Chesterfield v Bury
Coventry v Sheff Utd
Crewe v Doncaster
Millwall v Oldham
Rochdale v Swindon
Scunthorpe v Port Vale
Shrewsbury v Peterborough
Southend v Bradford
Walsall v Fleetwood

League Two
Barnet v Yeovil
Cambridge v Plymouth
Carlisle v Oxford
Dag & Red v Crawley
Exeter v Morecambe
Hartlepool v Portsmouth
Leyton Orient v Mansfield
Newport v Notts County
Northampton v Luton
Stevenage v Wimbledon
Wycombe v Accrington
York v Bristol Rovers

Saturday, 7 May
Premier League
Aston Villa v Newcastle
Bournemouth v WBA
Crystal Palace v Stoke
Leicester v Everton
Liverpool v Watford
Man City v Arsenal
Norwich v Man Utd
Sunderland v Chelsea
Tottenham v Southampton
West Ham v Swansea

Championship
Blackburn v Reading
Cardiff v Birmingham
Charlton v Burnley

Derby v Ipswich
Fulham v Bolton
Huddersfield v Brentford
Hull v Rotherham
Middlesbrough v Brighton
MK Dons v Nottm Forest
Preston v Leeds
QPR v Bristol City
Wolves v Sheff Wed

League Two
Accrington v Stevenage
Bristol Rovers v Dag & Red
Crawley v Barnet
Luton v Exeter
Mansfield v Cambridge
Morecambe v York
Notts County v Carlisle
Oxford v Wycombe
Plymouth v Hartlepool
Portsmouth v Northampton
Wimbledon v Newport
Yeovil v Leyton Orient

Sunday 8 May
League One
Bradford v Chesterfield

Bury v Southend
Colchester v Rochdale
Doncaster v Burton
Fleetwood v Crewe
Gillingham v Millwall
Oldham v Coventry
Peterborough v Blackpool
Port Vale v Walsall
Sheff Utd v Scunthorpe
Swindon v Shrewsbury
Wigan v Barnsley

Sunday, 15 May
Premier League
Arsenal v Aston Villa
Chelsea v Leicester
Everton v Norwich
Man Utd v Bournemouth
Newcastle v Tottenham
Southampton v Crystal Palace
Stoke v West Ham
Swansea v Man City
Watford v Sunderland
WBA v Liverpool

SCOTTISH FIXTURES 2015–2016
Premiership, Championship, League One and League Two

Saturday, 1 August
Premiership
Celtic v Ross Co
Hamilton v Partick
Inverness v Motherwell
Kilmarnock v Dundee

Saturday, 2 August
Dundee Utd v Aberdeen
Hearts v St Johnstone

Saturday, 8 August
Premiership
Aberdeen v Kilmarnock
Dundee v Hearts
Motherwell v Dundee Utd
Partick v Celtic
Ross Co v Hamilton
St Johnstone v Inverness

Championship
Dumbarton v Hibernian
Morton v Falkirk
Queen of South v Alloa
Raith v Livingston
Rangers v St Mirren

League One
Airdrieonians v Forfar

Albion v Ayr
Brechin v Dunfermline
Cowdenbea v Stranraer
Peterhead v Stenhousemuir

League Two
Arbroath v Elgin
Berwick v Montrose
East Stirling v East Fife
Queen's Park v Annan
Stirling v Clyde

Wednesday, 12 August
Premiership
Aberdeen v Hamilton
Dundee Utd v Dundee
Hearts v Motherwell
Inverness v Partick
Kilmarnock v Celtic
St Johnstone v Ross Co

Saturday, 15 August
Premiership
Celtic v Inverness
Dundee v St Johnstone
Hamilton v Dundee Utd
Motherwell v Aberdeen
Partick v Kilmarnock
Ross Co v Hearts

Championship

Alloa v Rangers
Falkirk v Raith
Hibernian v Morton
Livingston v Queen of South
St Mirren v Dumbarton

League One

Ayr v Brechin
Dunfermline v Cowdenbeath
Forfar v Albion
Stenhousemuir v Airdrieonians
Stranraer v Peterhead

League Two

Annan v Stirling
Clyde v Queen's Park
East Fife v Berwick
Elgin v East Stirling
Montrose v Arbroath

Saturday, 22 August

Premiership

Aberdeen v Dundee
Dundee Utd v Celtic
Hearts v Partick
Inverness v Hamilton
Kilmarnock v Ross Co
St Johnstone v Motherwell

Championship

Dumbarton v Queen of South
Livingston v Falkirk
Morton v St Mirren
Raith v Alloa
Rangers v Hibernian

League One

Brechin v Airdrieonians
Cowdenbea v Albion
Forfar v Stenhousemuir
Peterhead v Dunfermline
Stranraer v Ayr

League Two

Arbroath v Queen's Park
East Fife v Elgin
East Stirling v Annan
Montrose v Clyde
Stirling v Berwick

Saturday, 29 August

Premiership

Celtic v St Johnstone
Dundee v Inverness
Hamilton v Hearts
Motherwell v Kilmarnock
Partick v Aberdeen
Ross Co v Dundee Utd

Championship

Alloa v Morton
Falkirk v Dumbarton
Hibernian v Raith
Queen of South v Rangers
St Mirren v Livingston

League One

Airdrieonians v Peterhead
Albion v Brechin
Ayr v Forfar
Dunfermline v Stranraer
Stenhousemuir v Cowdenbeath

League Two

Annan v Montrose
Berwick v Arbroath
Clyde v East Stirling
Elgin v Stirling
Queen's Park v East Fife

Saturday, 5 September

Championship

Dumbarton v Alloa
Falkirk v Hibernian
Livingston v Morton
Queen of South v St Mirren
Rangers v Raith

League One

Airdrieonians v Cowdenbeath
Ayr v Stenhousemuir
Forfar v Dunfermline
Peterhead v Albion
Stranraer v Brechin

League Two

Annan v East Fife
Arbroath v Clyde
Berwick v Queen's Park
East Stirling v Stirling
Montrose v Elgin

Saturday, 12 September

Premiership

Aberdeen v Celtic
Dundee Utd v Kilmarnock
Inverness v Hearts
Motherwell v Ross Co
Partick v Dundee
St Johnstone v Hamilton

Championship

Hibernian v Alloa
Morton v Dumbarton
Raith v Queen of South
Rangers v Livingston
St Mirren v Falkirk

League One

Albion v Airdrieonians

Brechin v Forfar
Cowdenbea v Peterhead
Dunfermline v Ayr
Stenhousemuir v Stranraer

League Two
Clyde v Annan
East Fife v Arbroath
Elgin v Berwick
Queen's Park v East Stirling
Stirling v Montrose

Saturday, 19 September
Premiership
Celtic v Dundee
Dundee Utd v Inverness
Hamilton v Motherwell
Hearts v Aberdeen
Kilmarnock v St Johnstone
Ross Co v Partick

Championship
Alloa v Falkirk
Dumbarton v Rangers
Livingston v Hibernian
Queen of South v Morton
St Mirren v Raith

League One
Airdrieonians v Ayr
Cowdenbea v Forfar
Peterhead v Brechin
Stenhousemuir v Dunfermline
Stranraer v Albion

League Two
Arbroath v Stirling
Berwick v Annan
East Fife v Clyde
Montrose v East Stirling
Queen's Park v Elgin

Saturday, 26 September
Premiership
Celtic v Hearts
Dundee v Ross Co
Inverness v Aberdeen
Kilmarnock v Hamilton
Motherwell v Partick
St Johnstone v Dundee Utd

Championship
Alloa v Livingston
Falkirk v Queen of South
Hibernian v St Mirren
Morton v Rangers
Raith v Dumbarton

League One
Albion v Stenhousemuir
Ayr v Peterhead

Brechin v Cowdenbeath
Dunfermline v Airdrieonians
Forfar v Stranraer

League Two
Annan v Elgin
Clyde v Berwick
East Stirling v Arbroath
Montrose v East Fife
Stirling v Queen's Park

Saturday, 3 October
Premiership
Aberdeen v St Johnstone
Dundee v Motherwell
Hamilton v Celtic
Hearts v Kilmarnock
Partick v Dundee Utd
Ross Co v Inverness

Championship
Dumbarton v Livingston
Queen of South v Hibernian
Raith v Morton
Rangers v Falkirk
St Mirren v Alloa

League One
Airdrieonians v Stranraer
Ayr v Cowdenbeath
Dunfermline v Albion
Peterhead v Forfar
Stenhousemuir v Brechin

League Two
Arbroath v Annan
Berwick v East Stirling
East Fife v Stirling
Elgin v Clyde
Queen's Park v Montrose

Saturday, 17 October
Premiership
Dundee Utd v Hearts
Hamilton v Dundee
Kilmarnock v Inverness
Motherwell v Celtic
Ross Co v Aberdeen
St Johnstone v Partick

Championship
Alloa v Raith
Falkirk v Morton
Hibernian v Dumbarton
Livingston v St Mirren
Rangers v Queen of South

League One
Airdrieonians v Brechin
Albion v Peterhead
Cowdenbea v Stenhousemuir

Forfar v Ayr
Stranraer v Dunfermline

League Two
Annan v Queen's Park
Arbroath v Montrose
Berwick v East Fife
Clyde v Stirling
East Stirling v Elgin

Saturday, 24 October
Premiership
Aberdeen v Motherwell
Celtic v Dundee Utd
Dundee v Kilmarnock
Hearts v Ross Co
Inverness v St Johnstone
Partick v Hamilton

Championship
Dumbarton v Falkirk
Morton v Alloa
Queen of South v Livingston
Raith v Hibernian
St Mirren v Rangers

League One
Brechin v Albion
Dunfermline v Forfar
Peterhead v Airdrieonians
Stenhousemuir v Ayr
Stranraer v Cowdenbeath

Saturday, 31 October
Premiership
Celtic v Aberdeen
Dundee Utd v Ross Co
Hamilton v St Johnstone
Inverness v Dundee
Kilmarnock v Motherwell
Partick v Hearts

Championship
Alloa v Queen of South
Dumbarton v Morton
Falkirk v St Mirren
Hibernian v Rangers
Livingston v Raith

League One
Airdrieonians v Albion
Ayr v Stranraer
Cowdenbea v Dunfermline
Forfar v Brechin
Stenhousemuir v Peterhead

League Two
East Fife v Annan
Elgin v Arbroath
Montrose v Berwick
Queen's Park v Clyde
Stirling v East Stirling

Saturday, 7 November
Premiership
Aberdeen v Dundee Utd
Dundee v Partick
Hearts v Hamilton
Motherwell v Inverness
Ross Co v Celtic
St Johnstone v Kilmarnock

Championship
Morton v Livingston
Queen of South v Dumbarton
Raith v Falkirk
Rangers v Alloa
St Mirren v Hibernian

League One
Albion v Cowdenbeath
Brechin v Ayr
Dunfermline v Peterhead
Forfar v Airdrieonians
Stranraer v Stenhousemuir

League Two
Arbroath v East Fife
Berwick v Stirling
Clyde v Montrose
East Stirling v Queen's Park
Elgin v Annan

Saturday, 14 November
Championship
Falkirk v Alloa
Hibernian v Livingston
Morton v Queen of South
Raith v St Mirren
Rangers v Dumbarton

League One
Airdrieonians v Dunfermline
Ayr v Albion
Cowdenbea v Brechin
Peterhead v Stranraer
Stenhousemuir v Forfar

League Two
Annan v Berwick
Clyde v Elgin
East Fife v East Stirling
Montrose v Queen's Park
Stirling v Arbroath

Saturday, 21 November
Premiership
Celtic v Kilmarnock
Dundee Utd v St Johnstone
Hamilton v Aberdeen
Hearts v Dundee
Partick v Inverness
Ross Co v Motherwell

Championship
Alloa v Hibernian
Dumbarton v Raith
Livingston v Rangers
Queen of South v Falkirk
St Mirren v Morton

League One
Albion v Dunfermline
Ayr v Airdrieonians
Brechin v Stenhousemuir
Peterhead v Cowdenbeath
Stranraer v Forfar

League Two
Annan v Arbroath
Berwick v Clyde
East Stirling v Montrose
Elgin v East Fife
Queen's Park v Stirling

Saturday, 28 November
Premiership
Aberdeen v Ross Co
Dundee Utd v Hamilton
Inverness v Celtic
Kilmarnock v Partick
Motherwell v Hearts
St Johnstone v Dundee

Saturday, 5 December
Premiership
Celtic v Hamilton
Dundee v Aberdeen
Hearts v Inverness
Kilmarnock v Dundee Utd
Partick v Motherwell
Ross Co v St Johnstone

Championship
Alloa v Dumbarton
Falkirk v Livingston
Morton v Hibernian
Raith v Rangers
St Mirren v Queen of South

League One
Airdrieonians v Stenhousemuir
Albion v Stranraer
Cowdenbea v Ayr
Dunfermline v Brechin
Forfar v Peterhead

League Two
Arbroath v Berwick
East Fife v Queen's Park
East Stirling v Clyde
Montrose v Annan
Stirling v Elgin

Saturday, 12 December
Premiership
Aberdeen v Hearts
Dundee Utd v Partick
Hamilton v Ross Co
Inverness v Kilmarnock
Motherwell v Dundee
St Johnstone v Celtic

Championship
Dumbarton v St Mirren
Hibernian v Falkirk
Livingston v Alloa
Queen of South v Raith
Rangers v Morton

League One
Ayr v Dunfermline
Brechin v Peterhead
Forfar v Cowdenbeath
Stenhousemuir v Albion
Stranraer v Airdrieonians

League Two
Annan v East Stirling
Berwick v Elgin
Clyde v East Fife
Montrose v Stirling
Queen's Park v Arbroath

Saturday, 19 December
Premiership
Celtic v Motherwell
Dundee v Hamilton
Inverness v Dundee Utd
Kilmarnock v Aberdeen
Partick v Ross Co
St Johnstone v Hearts

Championship
Alloa v St Mirren
Falkirk v Rangers
Hibernian v Queen of South
Livingston v Dumbarton
Morton v Raith

League One
Albion v Forfar
Brechin v Stranraer
Cowdenbea v Airdrieonians
Dunfermline v Stenhousemuir
Peterhead v Ayr

League Two
Clyde v Arbroath
East Fife v Montrose
East Stirling v Berwick
Elgin v Queen's Park
Stirling v Annan

Saturday, 26 December

Premiership
Aberdeen v Inverness
Dundee Utd v Motherwell
Hamilton v Kilmarnock
Hearts v Celtic
Partick v St Johnstone
Ross Co v Dundee

Championship
Falkirk v Dumbarton
Queen of South v Morton
Raith v Alloa
Rangers v Hibernian
St Mirren v Livingston

League One
Airdrieonians v Peterhead
Ayr v Brechin
Cowdenbea v Albion
Forfar v Dunfermline
Stenhousemuir v Stranraer

League Two
Annan v Clyde
Arbroath v East Stirling
Elgin v Montrose
Queen's Park v Berwick
Stirling v East Fife

Wednesday, 30 December

Premiership
Aberdeen v Partick
Dundee v Celtic
Hamilton v Inverness
Hearts v Dundee Utd
Motherwell v St Johnstone
Ross Co v Kilmarnock

Saturday, 2 January

Premiership
Celtic v Partick
Dundee v Dundee Utd
Inverness v Ross Co
Kilmarnock v Hearts
Motherwell v Hamilton
St Johnstone v Aberdeen

Championship
Alloa v Falkirk
Dumbarton v Rangers
Hibernian v Raith
Livingston v Queen of South
Morton v St Mirren

League One
Albion v Airdrieonians
Brechin v Forfar
Dunfermline v Cowdenbeath
Peterhead v Stenhousemuir
Stranraer v Ayr

League Two
Berwick v Annan
Clyde v Queen's Park
East Fife v Elgin
East Stirling v Stirling
Montrose v Arbroath

Saturday, 9 January

League Two
Arbroath v Elgin
East Fife v Berwick
Montrose v East Stirling
Queen's Park v Annan
Stirling v Clyde

Saturday, 16 January

Premiership
Dundee Utd v Celtic
Hearts v Motherwell
Kilmarnock v Inverness
Partick v Dundee
Ross Co v Aberdeen
St Johnstone v Hamilton

Championship
Alloa v Morton
Dumbarton v Queen of South
Falkirk v Hibernian
Rangers v Livingston
St Mirren v Raith

League One
Airdrieonians v Forfar
Ayr v Cowdenbeath
Dunfermline v Albion
Stenhousemuir v Brechin
Stranraer v Peterhead

League Two
Annan v East Fife
Berwick v Arbroath
Clyde v East Stirling
Elgin v Stirling
Queen's Park v Montrose

Saturday, 23 January

Premiership
Aberdeen v Dundee
Celtic v St Johnstone
Dundee Utd v Kilmarnock
Hamilton v Hearts
Inverness v Partick
Motherwell v Ross Co

Championship
Hibernian v St Mirren
Livingston v Falkirk
Morton v Rangers
Queen of South v Alloa
Raith v Dumbarton

League One
Albion v Ayr
Brechin v Airdrieonians
Cowdenbea v Stranraer
Forfar v Stenhousemuir
Peterhead v Dunfermline

League Two
Arbroath v Annan
East Stirling v East Fife
Elgin v Berwick
Montrose v Clyde
Stirling v Queen's Park

Saturday, 30 January
Premiership
Aberdeen v Celtic
Dundee v Motherwell
Kilmarnock v Hamilton
Partick v Dundee Utd
Ross Co v Hearts
St Johnstone v Inverness

Championship
Dumbarton v Livingston
Hibernian v Morton
Raith v Queen of South
Rangers v Falkirk
St Mirren v Alloa

League One
Ayr v Stenhousemuir
Cowdenbea v Forfar
Dunfermline v Airdrieonians
Peterhead v Albion
Stranraer v Brechin

League Two
Annan v Elgin
Berwick v Queen's Park
East Fife v Clyde
East Stirling v Arbroath
Stirling v Montrose

Saturday, 6 February
League One
Airdrieonians v Cowdenbeath
Albion v Brechin
Ayr v Peterhead
Forfar v Stranraer
Stenhousemuir v Dunfermline

League Two
Arbroath v Stirling
Berwick v East Stirling
Clyde v Annan
Montrose v East Fife
Queen's Park v Elgin

Saturday, 13 February
Premiership
Celtic v Ross Co
Dundee v St Johnstone
Hamilton v Dundee Utd
Hearts v Partick
Inverness v Aberdeen
Motherwell v Kilmarnock

Championship
Alloa v Rangers
Falkirk v Raith
Livingston v Hibernian
Morton v Dumbarton
Queen of South v St Mirren

League One
Brechin v Cowdenbeath
Dunfermline v Ayr
Peterhead v Forfar
Stenhousemuir v Airdrieonians
Stranraer v Albion

League Two
Annan v Montrose
East Fife v Arbroath
Elgin v Clyde
Queen's Park v East Stirling
Stirling v Berwick

Saturday, 20 February
Premiership
Celtic v Inverness
Dundee Utd v Hearts
Kilmarnock v Dundee
Partick v Aberdeen
Ross Co v Hamilton
St Johnstone v Motherwell

Championship
Hibernian v Alloa
Morton v Falkirk
Queen of South v Rangers
Raith v Livingston
St Mirren v Dumbarton

League One
Airdrieonians v Stranraer
Albion v Stenhousemuir
Ayr v Forfar
Brechin v Dunfermline
Cowdenbea v Peterhead

League Two
Arbroath v Queen's Park
Clyde v Berwick
East Fife v Stirling
East Stirling v Annan
Montrose v Elgin

Saturday, 27 February
Premiership
Aberdeen v St Johnstone
Dundee v Inverness
Hamilton v Celtic
Hearts v Kilmarnock
Motherwell v Partick
Ross Co v Dundee Utd

Championship
Alloa v Livingston
Dumbarton v Hibernian
Falkirk v Queen of South
Raith v Morton
Rangers v St Mirren

League One
Airdrieonians v Ayr
Dunfermline v Stranraer
Forfar v Albion
Peterhead v Brechin
Stenhousemuir v Cowdenbeath

League Two
Annan v Stirling
Arbroath v Clyde
Berwick v Montrose
Elgin v East Stirling
Queen's Park v East Fife

Tuesday, 1 March
Championship
Livingston v Morton
Queen of South v Hibernian
Rangers v Raith
St Mirren v Falkirk

Wednesday, 2 March
Premiership
Celtic v Dundee
Dundee Utd v Aberdeen
Hamilton v Motherwell
Inverness v Hearts
Kilmarnock v Ross Co
St Johnstone v Partick

Championship
Dumbarton v Alloa

Saturday, 5 March
Championship
Falkirk v Alloa
Hibernian v Rangers
Livingston v Dumbarton
Morton v Queen of South
Raith v St Mirren

League One
Albion v Peterhead
Brechin v Ayr
Cowdenbea v Airdrieonians

Dunfermline v Stenhousemuir
Stranraer v Forfar

League Two
Annan v Clyde
East Stirling v Montrose
Elgin v East Fife
Queen's Park v Berwick
Stirling v Arbroath

Saturday, 12 March
Premiership
Aberdeen v Kilmarnock
Dundee v Hearts
Inverness v Hamilton
Motherwell v Dundee Utd
Partick v Celtic
St Johnstone v Ross Co

League One
Airdrieonians v Brechin
Albion v Stranraer
Ayr v Dunfermline
Forfar v Cowdenbeath
Stenhousemuir v Peterhead

Championship
Alloa v Raith
Dumbarton v Falkirk
Hibernian v Livingston
Rangers v Morton
St Mirren v Queen of South

League Two
Arbroath v East Stirling
Berwick v Stirling
Clyde v Elgin
East Fife v Annan
Montrose v Queen's Park

Saturday, 19 March
Premiership
Dundee Utd v Dundee
Hamilton v Partick
Hearts v St Johnstone
Kilmarnock v Celtic
Motherwell v Aberdeen
Ross Co v Inverness

Championship
Falkirk v Rangers
Livingston v St Mirren
Morton v Alloa
Queen of South v Dumbarton
Raith v Hibernian

League One
Brechin v Albion
Cowdenbea v Dunfermline
Forfar v Ayr
Peterhead v Airdrieonians
Stranraer v Stenhousemuir

League Two
Annan v Berwick
East Stirling v Clyde
Elgin v Montrose
Queen's Park v Arbroath
Stirling v East Fife

Saturday, 26 March
Championship
Alloa v St Mirren
Falkirk v Livingston
Hibernian v Dumbarton
Morton v Raith
Rangers v Queen of South

League One
Airdrieonians v Albion
Ayr v Stranraer
Dunfermline v Brechin
Peterhead v Cowdenbeath
Stenhousemuir v Forfar

League Two
Berwick v Elgin
Clyde v Arbroath
East Fife v Queen's Park
Montrose v Annan
Stirling v East Stirling

Saturday, 2 April
Premiership
Aberdeen v Hamilton
Celtic v Hearts
Dundee v Ross Co
Inverness v Motherwell
Partick v Kilmarnock
St Johnstone v Dundee Utd

Championship
Dumbarton v Morton
Livingston v Alloa
Queen of South v Falkirk
Raith v Rangers
St Mirren v Hibernian

League One
Albion v Dunfermline
Brechin v Stenhousemuir
Cowdenbea v Ayr
Forfar v Peterhead
Stranraer v Airdrieonians

League Two
Arbroath v East Fife
Clyde v Montrose
East Stirling v Berwick
Elgin v Annan
Queen's Park v Stirling

Saturday, 9 April
Premiership
Dundee Utd v Inverness
Hamilton v Dundee
Hearts v Aberdeen
Kilmarnock v St Johnstone
Motherwell v Celtic
Ross Co v Partick

Championship
Alloa v Hibernian
Falkirk v St Mirren
Morton v Livingston
Queen of South v Raith
Rangers v Dumbarton

League One
Airdrieonians v Stenhousemuir
Ayr v Albion
Cowdenbea v Brechin
Dunfermline v Forfar
Peterhead v Stranraer

League Two
Annan v Arbroath
Berwick v Clyde
East Fife v Montrose
East Stirling v Queen's Park
Stirling v Elgin

Saturday, 16 April
Championship
Alloa v Queen of South
Dumbarton v Raith
Hibernian v Falkirk
Livingston v Rangers
St Mirren v Morton

League One
Albion v Cowdenbeath
Brechin v Peterhead
Forfar v Airdrieonians
Stenhousemuir v Ayr
Stranraer v Dunfermline

League Two
Annan v East Stirling
Arbroath v Berwick
Clyde v East Fife
Elgin v Queen's Park
Montrose v Stirling

Saturday, 23 April
Championship
Dumbarton v St Mirren
Morton v Hibernian
Queen of South v Livingston
Raith v Falkirk
Rangers v Alloa

League One
Airdrieonians v Dunfermline
Albion v Forfar
Brechin v Stranraer
Cowdenbea v Stenhousemuir
Peterhead v Ayr

League Two
Arbroath v Montrose
Berwick v East Fife
East Stirling v Elgin
Queen's Park v Clyde
Stirling v Annan

Saturday, 30 April
Championship
Alloa v Dumbarton

Falkirk v Morton
Hibernian v Queen of South
Livingston v Raith
St Mirren v Rangers

League One
Ayr v Airdrieonians
Dunfermline v Peterhead
Forfar v Brechin
Stenhousemuir v Albion
Stranraer v Cowdenbeath

League Two
Annan v Queen's Park
Clyde v Stirling
East Fife v East Stirling
Elgin v Arbroath
Montrose v Berwick

NATIONAL LEAGUE FIXTURES 2015–2016

Saturday, 8 August
Aldershot v Gateshead
Altrincham v Forest Green
Barrow v Dover
Boreham Wood v Halifax
Bromley v Wrexham
Chester v Braintree
Kidderminster v Grimsby
Lincoln v Cheltenham
Southport v Eastleigh
Torquay v Macclesfield
Tranmere v Woking
Welling v Guiseley

Tuesday, 11 August
Braintree v Lincoln
Cheltenham v Aldershot
Dover v Kidderminster
Eastleigh v Boreham Wood
Halifax v Chester
Forest Green v Welling
Gateshead v Tranmere
Grimsby v Barrow
Guiseley v Altrincham
Macclesfield v Southport
Woking v Bromley
Wrexham v Torquay

Saturday, 15 August
Braintree v Tranmere
Cheltenham v Southport
Dover v Chester
Eastleigh v Lincoln
Halifax v Torquay
Forest Green v Barrow
Gateshead v Boreham Wood
Grimsby v Bromley
Guiseley v Kidderminster

Macclesfield v Welling
Woking v Altrincham
Wrexham v Aldershot

Tuesday, 18 August
Aldershot v Dover
Altrincham v Grimsby
Barrow v Guiseley
Boreham Wood v Forest Green
Bromley v Braintree
Chester v Cheltenham
Kidderminster v Wrexham
Lincoln v Macclesfield
Southport v Gateshead
Torquay v Woking
Tranmere v Halifax
Welling v Eastleigh

Saturday, 22 August
Braintree v Southport
Cheltenham v Barrow
Dover v Altrincham
Eastleigh v Macclesfield
Halifax v Bromley
Forest Green v Lincoln
Gateshead v Kidderminster
Grimsby v Torquay
Guiseley v Aldershot
Tranmere v Boreham Wood
Woking v Chester
Wrexham v Welling

Saturday, 29 August
Aldershot v Eastleigh
Altrincham v Tranmere
Barrow v Southport
Boreham Wood v Woking
Bromley v Dover

Guiseley v Gateshead
Kidderminster v Forest Green
Lincoln v Grimsby
Macclesfield v Chester
Torquay v Cheltenham
Welling v Braintree
Wrexham v Halifax

Monday, 31 August

Braintree v Aldershot
Cheltenham v Wrexham
Chester v Guiseley
Dover v Boreham Wood
Eastleigh v Torquay
Halifax v Barrow
Forest Green v Bromley
Gateshead v Lincoln
Grimsby v Macclesfield
Southport v Altrincham
Tranmere v Kidderminster
Woking v Welling

Saturday, 5 September

Aldershot v Halifax
Altrincham v Cheltenham
Barrow v Eastleigh
Boreham Wood v Grimsby
Bromley v Gateshead
Chester v Forest Green
Kidderminster v Braintree
Lincoln v Wrexham
Macclesfield v Woking
Southport v Dover
Torquay v Guiseley
Welling v Tranmere

Saturday, 12 September

Braintree v Barrow
Bromley v Macclesfield
Cheltenham v Dover
Eastleigh v Gateshead
Halifax v Kidderminster
Forest Green v Southport
Grimsby v Aldershot
Guiseley v Woking
Lincoln v Boreham Wood
Tranmere v Chester
Welling v Torquay
Wrexham v Altrincham

Tuesday, 15 September

Aldershot v Welling
Altrincham v Eastleigh
Barrow v Lincoln
Boreham Wood v Bromley
Cheltenham v Macclesfield
Chester v Grimsby
Dover v Braintree
Gateshead v Wrexham

Guiseley v Halifax
Kidderminster v Torquay
Southport v Tranmere
Woking v Forest Green

Saturday, 19 September

Altrincham v Braintree
Barrow v Aldershot
Boreham Wood v Wrexham
Chester v Eastleigh
Dover v Guiseley
Halifax v Southport
Gateshead v Welling
Grimsby v Tranmere
Kidderminster v Lincoln
Macclesfield v Forest Green
Torquay v Bromley
Woking v Cheltenham

Tuesday, 22 September

Braintree v Woking
Bromley v Kidderminster
Eastleigh v Dover
Halifax v Gateshead
Forest Green v Cheltenham
Guiseley v Southport
Lincoln v Altrincham
Macclesfield v Barrow
Torquay v Boreham Wood
Tranmere v Aldershot
Welling v Chester
Wrexham v Grimsby

Saturday, 26 September

Aldershot v Macclesfield
Barrow v Kidderminster
Boreham Wood v Altrincham
Braintree v Guiseley
Bromley v Chester
Cheltenham v Tranmere
Dover v Woking
Forest Green v Gateshead
Lincoln v Torquay
Southport v Grimsby
Welling v Halifax
Wrexham v Eastleigh

Saturday, 3 October

Altrincham v Barrow
Chester v Wrexham
Eastleigh v Braintree
Halifax v Cheltenham
Gateshead v Dover
Grimsby v Forest Green
Guiseley v Lincoln
Kidderminster v Welling
Macclesfield v Boreham Wood
Torquay v Aldershot

Tranmere v Bromley
Woking v Southport

Tuesday, 6 October
Aldershot v Forest Green
Altrincham v Halifax
Barrow v Chester
Cheltenham v Braintree
Grimsby v Gateshead
Guiseley v Macclesfield
Kidderminster v Boreham Wood
Torquay v Dover
Welling v Bromley
Wrexham v Tranmere

Saturday, 10 October
Aldershot v Altrincham
Boreham Wood v Welling
Braintree v Grimsby
Bromley v Barrow
Chester v Lincoln
Dover v Wrexham
Halifax v Woking
Forest Green v Guiseley
Gateshead v Cheltenham
Macclesfield v Kidderminster
Southport v Torquay
Tranmere v Eastleigh

Tuesday, 13 October
Altrincham v Kidderminster
Boreham Wood v Aldershot
Braintree v Dover
Bromley v Cheltenham
Eastleigh v Forest Green
Grimsby v Halifax
Macclesfield v Gateshead
Southport v Chester
Tranmere v Barrow
Welling v Lincoln
Woking v Torquay
Wrexham v Guiseley

Saturday, 17 October
Aldershot v Bromley
Barrow v Welling
Cheltenham v Eastleigh
Chester v Halifax
Dover v Macclesfield
Forest Green v Tranmere
Gateshead v Altrincham
Guiseley v Boreham Wood
Kidderminster v Southport
Lincoln v Braintree
Torquay v Grimsby
Woking v Wrexham

Saturday, 31 October
Altrincham v Torquay

Boreham Wood v Gateshead
Braintree v Macclesfield
Eastleigh v Halifax
Forest Green v Chester
Grimsby v Cheltenham
Guiseley v Welling
Kidderminster v Woking
Lincoln v Bromley
Southport v Aldershot
Tranmere v Dover
Wrexham v Barrow

Tuesday, 10 November
Aldershot v Lincoln
Barrow v Grimsby
Bromley v Boreham Wood
Cheltenham v Guiseley
Chester v Kidderminster
Dover v Eastleigh
Gateshead v Southport
Macclesfield v Altrincham
Torquay v Wrexham
Welling v Forest Green
Woking v Braintree

Saturday, 14 November
Barrow v Torquay
Boreham Wood v Chester
Bromley v Altrincham
Halifax v Braintree
Forest Green v Dover
Grimsby v Welling
Guiseley v Eastleigh
Kidderminster v Aldershot
Lincoln v Tranmere
Southport v Cheltenham
Woking v Macclesfield
Wrexham v Gateshead

Saturday, 21 November
Aldershot v Wrexham
Altrincham v Boreham Wood
Braintree v Kidderminster
Cheltenham v Forest Green
Chester v Woking
Dover v Barrow
Eastleigh v Grimsby
Gateshead v Halifax
Macclesfield v Bromley
Torquay v Lincoln
Tranmere v Guiseley
Welling v Southport

Tuesday, 24 November
Boreham Wood v Lincoln
Chester v Dover
Guiseley v Barrow
Woking v Tranmere

541

Saturday, 28 November

Aldershot v Cheltenham
Barrow v Woking
Boreham Wood v Tranmere
Braintree v Torquay
Eastleigh v Southport
Halifax v Dover
Forest Green v Altrincham
Gateshead v Chester
Grimsby v Kidderminster
Guiseley v Bromley
Lincoln v Welling
Wrexham v Macclesfield

Saturday, 5 December

Altrincham v Wrexham
Barrow v Boreham Wood
Bromley v Grimsby
Cheltenham v Chester
Dover v Aldershot
Halifax v Guiseley
Kidderminster v Gateshead
Macclesfield v Eastleigh
Southport v Forest Green
Torquay v Welling
Tranmere v Braintree
Woking v Lincoln

Saturday, 19 December

Aldershot v Guiseley
Braintree v Wrexham
Cheltenham v Altrincham
Chester v Torquay
Eastleigh v Kidderminster
Halifax v Tranmere
Forest Green v Boreham Wood
Gateshead v Woking
Grimsby v Dover
Lincoln v Barrow
Southport v Bromley
Welling v Macclesfield

Saturday, 26 December

Aldershot v Woking
Altrincham v Chester
Barrow v Gateshead
Boreham Wood v Braintree
Bromley v Eastleigh
Guiseley v Grimsby
Kidderminster v Cheltenham
Lincoln v Halifax
Macclesfield v Tranmere
Torquay v Forest Green
Welling v Dover
Wrexham v Southport

Monday, 28 December

Braintree v Welling

Cheltenham v Torquay
Chester v Macclesfield
Dover v Bromley
Eastleigh v Aldershot
Halifax v Wrexham
Forest Green v Kidderminster
Gateshead v Guiseley
Grimsby v Lincoln
Southport v Barrow
Tranmere v Altrincham
Woking v Boreham Wood

Saturday, 2 January

Braintree v Boreham Wood
Cheltenham v Kidderminster
Chester v Altrincham
Dover v Welling
Eastleigh v Bromley
Halifax v Lincoln
Forest Green v Torquay
Gateshead v Barrow
Grimsby v Guiseley
Southport v Wrexham
Tranmere v Macclesfield
Woking v Aldershot

Saturday, 9 January

Aldershot v Chester
Altrincham v Gateshead
Barrow v Tranmere
Boreham Wood v Cheltenham
Bromley v Southport
Guiseley v Forest Green
Kidderminster v Eastleigh
Lincoln v Dover
Macclesfield v Halifax
Torquay v Braintree
Welling v Grimsby
Wrexham v Woking

Saturday, 23 January

Boreham Wood v Eastleigh
Bromley v Tranmere
Chester v Southport
Dover v Cheltenham
Forest Green v Braintree
Grimsby v Altrincham
Kidderminster v Guiseley
Macclesfield v Aldershot
Torquay v Gateshead
Welling v Barrow
Woking v Halifax
Wrexham v Lincoln

Tuesday, 26 January

Altrincham v Woking

Saturday, 30 January

Aldershot v Kidderminster

Altrincham v Dover
Braintree v Chester
Cheltenham v Bromley
Eastleigh v Wrexham
Halifax v Welling
Forest Green v Macclesfield
Gateshead v Grimsby
Lincoln v Guiseley
Southport v Boreham Wood
Tranmere v Torquay
Woking v Barrow

Saturday, 6 February
Barrow v Cheltenham
Boreham Wood v Kidderminster
Braintree v Gateshead
Bromley v Halifax
Chester v Aldershot
Dover v Southport
Grimsby v Woking
Guiseley v Tranmere
Lincoln v Eastleigh
Macclesfield v Torquay
Welling v Altrincham
Wrexham v Forest Green

Tuesday, 9 February
Tranmere v Southport

Saturday, 13 February
Aldershot v Tranmere
Altrincham v Lincoln
Cheltenham v Welling
Dover v Gateshead
Eastleigh v Barrow
Halifax v Forest Green
Grimsby v Boreham Wood
Kidderminster v Macclesfield
Southport v Braintree
Torquay v Chester
Woking v Guiseley
Wrexham v Bromley

Tuesday, 16 February
Gateshead v Eastleigh
Torquay v Halifax

Saturday, 20 February
Altrincham v Guiseley
Barrow v Braintree
Boreham Wood v Torquay
Bromley v Woking
Halifax v Grimsby
Forest Green v Eastleigh
Gateshead v Aldershot
Kidderminster v Chester
Lincoln v Southport
Macclesfield v Dover

Tranmere v Cheltenham
Welling v Wrexham

Tuesday, 23 February
Braintree v Halifax
Lincoln v Forest Green
Southport v Macclesfield
Wrexham v Kidderminster

Saturday, 27 February
Barrow v Forest Green
Cheltenham v Gateshead
Chester v Tranmere
Dover v Lincoln
Eastleigh v Woking
Halifax v Boreham Wood
Grimsby v Southport
Guiseley v Braintree
Kidderminster v Bromley
Macclesfield v Wrexham
Torquay v Altrincham
Welling v Aldershot

Tuesday, 1 March
Aldershot v Grimsby
Bromley v Welling
Eastleigh v Cheltenham

Saturday, 5 March
Altrincham v Macclesfield
Boreham Wood v Barrow
Braintree v Eastleigh
Chester v Bromley
Forest Green v Grimsby
Guiseley v Wrexham
Lincoln v Aldershot
Southport v Halifax
Torquay v Kidderminster
Tranmere v Gateshead
Welling v Cheltenham
Woking v Dover

Saturday, 12 March
Aldershot v Torquay
Barrow v Altrincham
Bromley v Guiseley
Cheltenham v Woking
Dover v Tranmere
Eastleigh v Chester
Gateshead v Forest Green
Grimsby v Braintree
Kidderminster v Halifax
Macclesfield v Lincoln
Southport v Welling
Wrexham v Boreham Wood

Saturday, 19 March
Altrincham v Aldershot
Barrow v Bromley

Boreham Wood v Macclesfield
Braintree v Cheltenham
Halifax v Eastleigh
Guiseley v Dover
Lincoln v Kidderminster
Torquay v Southport
Tranmere v Forest Green
Welling v Gateshead
Woking v Grimsby
Wrexham v Chester

Saturday, 26 March
Braintree v Bromley
Cheltenham v Boreham Wood
Chester v Barrow
Dover v Torquay
Eastleigh v Welling
Halifax v Altrincham
Forest Green v Aldershot
Gateshead v Macclesfield
Grimsby v Wrexham
Southport v Guiseley
Tranmere v Lincoln
Woking v Kidderminster

Monday, 28 March
Aldershot v Braintree
Altrincham v Southport
Barrow v Halifax
Boreham Wood v Dover
Bromley v Forest Green
Guiseley v Chester
Kidderminster v Tranmere
Lincoln v Gateshead
Macclesfield v Grimsby
Torquay v Eastleigh
Welling v Woking
Wrexham v Cheltenham

Saturday, 2 April
Aldershot v Barrow
Bromley v Lincoln
Cheltenham v Grimsby
Chester v Boreham Wood
Dover v Halifax
Eastleigh v Guiseley
Forest Green v Wrexham
Gateshead v Torquay
Kidderminster v Altrincham
Macclesfield v Braintree
Southport v Woking
Tranmere v Welling

Saturday, 9 April
Altrincham v Bromley
Barrow v Macclesfield
Boreham Wood v Southport
Braintree v Forest Green
Halifax v Aldershot
Grimsby v Eastleigh
Guiseley v Cheltenham
Lincoln v Chester
Torquay v Tranmere
Welling v Kidderminster
Woking v Gateshead
Wrexham v Dover

Saturday, 16 April
Aldershot v Boreham Wood
Bromley v Torquay
Cheltenham v Halifax
Chester v Welling
Dover v Grimsby
Eastleigh v Altrincham
Forest Green v Woking
Gateshead v Braintree
Kidderminster v Barrow
Macclesfield v Guiseley
Southport v Lincoln
Tranmere v Wrexham

Saturday, 23 April
Aldershot v Southport
Altrincham v Welling
Boreham Wood v Guiseley
Eastleigh v Tranmere
Forest Green v Halifax
Gateshead v Bromley
Grimsby v Chester
Kidderminster v Dover
Lincoln v Woking
Macclesfield v Cheltenham
Torquay v Barrow
Wrexham v Braintree

Saturday, 30 April
Barrow v Wrexham
Braintree v Altrincham
Bromley v Aldershot
Cheltenham v Lincoln
Chester v Gateshead
Dover v Forest Green
Halifax v Macclesfield
Guiseley v Torquay
Southport v Kidderminster
Tranmere v Grimsby
Welling v Boreham Wood
Woking v Eastleigh